SAINT THOMAS AQUINAS

SUMMA THEOLOGIAE
TERTIA PARS, 60-90

Translated by Fr. Laurence Shapcote, O.P.
Edited by John Mortensen and Enrique Alarcón

SUMMA THEOLOGIAE

Volume 20
Latin/English Edition of the Works of St. Thomas Aquinas

The Aquinas Institute for the Study of Sacred Doctrine
Lander, Wyoming
2012

This printing was funded in part by donations made in memory of:
Marcus Berquist, Rose Johanna Trumbull, John and Mary Deignan, and Thomas and Eleanor Sullivan.

The printing was also made possible by a donation from Patricia Lynch.

Published with the ecclesiastical approval of
The Most Reverend Paul D. Etienne, DD, STL
Bishop of Cheyenne
Given on November 10, 2012

PUBLISHER'S CATALOGING-IN-PUBLICATION DATA

Thomas Aquinas, St., 1225?-1274
 Summa Theologiae Tertia Pars, 60-90 / Saint Thomas Aquinas; edited by John Mortensen, Enrique Alarcón;
 translated by Fr. Laurence Shapcote, O.P.
 p. 448 cm.
 ISBN 978-1-62340-013-2

1. Thomas, Aquinas, Saint, 1225?-1274 -- Summa theologiae -- Tertia Pars -- 60-90.   2. Catholic Church -- Doctrines
-- Early works to 1800. 3. Theology, Doctrinal - -Early works to 1800.   I. Title. II. Series

BX1749.T512 2012
230'.2--dc23   2012953837

Notes on the Text

Latin Text of St. Thomas

The Latin text used in this volume is based on the Corpus Thomisticum text of the Fundación Tomás de Aquino <www.corpusthomisticum.org>. This text is based on the Leonine Edition, transcribed by Fr. Roberto Busa SJ, and revised by Dr. Enrique Alarcón and other editors and collaborators of this bilingual edition. © 2012 Fundación Tomás de Aquino, Pamplona. Used with permission.

English Translation of St. Thomas

The English translation of the *Summa Theologiae* was prepared by Fr. Laurence Shapcote, O.P. (1864-1947), of the English Dominican Province. It has been edited and revised by The Aquinas Institute and its collaborators.

The Aquinas Institute requests your assistance in the continued perfection of these texts.
If you discover any errors, please send a note to us by e-mail: admin@theaquinasinstitute.org.

DEDICATED WITH LOVE TO
OUR LADY OF MT. CARMEL

Contents

Summa Theologiae
Tertia Pars, 60-90

QUESTION 60

WHAT IS A SACRAMENT?

Post considerationem eorum quae pertinent ad mysteria verbi incarnati, considerandum est de Ecclesiae sacramentis, quae ab ipso verbo incarnato efficaciam habent. Et prima consideratio erit de sacramentis in communi; secunda de unoquoque sacramentorum in speciali.

Circa primum quinque consideranda sunt, primo, quid sit sacramentum; secundo, de necessitate sacramentorum; tertio, de effectibus sacramentorum; quarto, de causa eorum; quinto, de numero.

Circa primum quaeruntur octo.

Primo, utrum sacramentum sit in genere signi.

Secundo, utrum omne signum rei sacrae sit sacramentum.

Tertio, utrum sacramentum sit signum unius rei tantum, vel plurium.

Quarto, utrum sacramentum sit signum quod est res sensibilis.

Quinto, utrum ad sacramentum requiratur determinata res sensibilis.

Sexto, utrum ad sacramentum requiratur significatio quae est per verba.

Septimo, utrum requirantur determinata verba.

Octavo, utrum illis verbis possit aliquid addi vel subtrahi.

After considering those things that concern the mystery of the incarnate Word, we must consider the sacraments of the Church which derive their efficacy from the Word incarnate Himself. First we shall consider the sacraments in general; second, we shall consider specially each sacrament.

Concerning the first our consideration will be fivefold: (1) What is a sacrament? (2) Of the necessity of the sacraments; (3) of the effects of the sacraments; (4) Of their cause; (5) Of their number.

Under the first heading there are eight points of inquiry:

(1) Whether a sacrament is a kind of sign?

(2) Whether every sign of a sacred thing is a sacrament?

(3) Whether a sacrament is a sign of one thing only, or of several?

(4) Whether a sacrament is a sign that is something sensible?

(5) Whether some determinate sensible thing is required for a sacrament?

(6) Whether signification expressed by words is necessary for a sacrament?

(7) Whether determinate words are required?

(8) Whether anything may be added to or subtracted from these words?

Article 1

Whether a Sacrament Is a Kind of Sign?

AD PRIMUM SIC PROCEDITUR. Videtur quod sacramentum non sit in genere signi. Videtur enim sacramentum dici a sacrando, sicut medicamentum a medicando. Sed hoc magis videtur pertinere ad rationem causae quam ad rationem signi. Ergo sacramentum magis est in genere causae quam in genere signi.

PRAETEREA, sacramentum videtur occultum aliquid significare, secundum illud Tob. XII, *sacramentum regis abscondere bonum est*; et Ephes. III, *quae sit dispensatio sacramenti absconditi a saeculis in Deo*. Sed id quod est absconditum, videtur esse contra rationem signi, nam *signum est quod, praeter speciem quam sensibus ingerit, facit aliquid aliud in cognitionem venire*, ut patet per Augustinum, in II de Doct. Christ. Ergo videtur quod sacramentum non sit in genere signi.

OBJECTION 1: It seems that a sacrament is not a kind of sign. For sacrament appears to be derived from *sacrando* (sacring); just as medicament, from *medicando* (healing). But this seems to be of the nature of a cause rather than of a sign. Therefore a sacrament is a kind of cause rather than a kind of sign.

OBJ. 2: Further, sacrament seems to signify something hidden, according to Tob. 12:7: *It is good to hide the secret* (sacramentum) *of a king*; and Eph. 3:9: *What is the dispensation of the mystery* (sacramenti) *which hath been hidden from eternity in God*. But that which is hidden, seems foreign to the nature of a sign; for *a sign is that which conveys something else to the mind, besides the species which it impresses on the senses*, as Augustine explains (*De Doctr. Christ.* ii). Therefore it seems that a sacrament is not a kind of sign.

PRAETEREA, iuramentum quandoque sacramentum nominatur, dicitur enim in decretis, XXII Caus., qu. V, *parvuli qui sine aetate rationabili sunt, non cogantur iurare, et qui semel periuratus fuerit, nec testis sit post hoc, nec ad sacramentum,* idest ad iuramentum, *accedat.* Sed iuramentum non pertinet ad rationem signi. Ergo videtur quod sacramentum non sit in genere signi.

SED CONTRA est quod Augustinus dicit, in X de Civ. Dei, *sacrificium visibile invisibilis sacrificii sacramentum, idest sacrum signum, est.*

RESPONDEO dicendum quod omnia quae habent ordinem ad unum aliquid, licet diversimode, ab illo denominari possunt, sicut a sanitate quae est in animali, denominatur sanum non solum animal, quod est sanitatis subiectum, sed dicitur medicina sana inquantum est sanitatis effectiva, diaeta vero inquantum est conservativa eiusdem, et urina inquantum est significativa ipsius. Sic igitur sacramentum potest aliquid dici vel quia in se habet aliquam sanctitatem occultam, et secundum hoc sacramentum idem est quod sacrum secretum, vel quia habet aliquem ordinem ad hanc sanctitatem, vel causae vel signi vel secundum quamcumque aliam habitudinem. Specialiter autem nunc loquimur de sacramentis secundum quod important habitudinem signi. Et secundum hoc sacramentum ponitur in genere signi.

AD PRIMUM ergo dicendum quod, quia medicina se habet ut causa effectiva sanitatis, inde est quod omnia denominata a medicina dicuntur per ordinem ad unum primum agens, et per hoc, medicamentum importat causalitatem quandam. Sed sanctitas, a qua denominatur sacramentum, non significatur per modum causae efficientis, sed magis per modum causae formalis vel finalis. Et ideo non oportet quod sacramentum semper importet causalitatem.

AD SECUNDUM dicendum quod ratio illa procedit secundum quod sacramentum idem est quod sacrum secretum. Dicitur autem non solum Dei secretum, sed etiam regis, esse sacrum et sacramentum. Quia secundum antiquos sancta vel sacrosancta dicebantur quaecumque violari non licebat, sicut etiam muri civitatis, et personae in dignitatibus constitutae. Et ideo illa secreta, sive divina sive humana, quae non licet violari quibuslibet publicando, dicuntur sacra vel sacramenta.

AD TERTIUM dicendum quod etiam iuramentum habet quandam habitudinem ad res sacras, inquantum scilicet est quaedam contestatio facta per aliquod sacrum. Et secundum hoc dicitur esse sacramentum, non eadem ratione qua nunc loquimur de sacramentis; non tamen aequivoce sumpto nomine sacramenti, sed analogice, scilicet secundum diversam habitudinem ad aliquid unum, quod est res sacra.

OBJ. 3: Further, an oath is sometimes called a sacrament: for it is written in the *Decretals* (*Caus.* xxii, qu. 5): *Children who have not attained the use of reason must not be obliged to swear: and whoever has foresworn himself once, must no more be a witness, nor be allowed to take a sacrament,* i.e., an oath. But an oath is not a kind of sign, therefore it seems that a sacrament is not a kind of sign.

ON THE CONTRARY, Augustine says (*De Civ. Dei* x): *The visible sacrifice is the sacrament, i.e., the sacred sign, of the invisible sacrifice.*

I ANSWER THAT, All things that are ordained to one, even in different ways, can be denominated from it: thus, from health which is in an animal, not only is the animal said to be healthy through being the subject of health: but medicine also is said to be healthy through producing health; diet through preserving it; and urine, through being a sign of health. Consequently, a thing may be called a *sacrament*, either from having a certain hidden sanctity, and in this sense a sacrament is a *sacred secret*; or from having some relationship to this sanctity, which relationship may be that of a cause, or of a sign or of any other relation. But now we are speaking of sacraments in a special sense, as implying the habitude of sign: and in this way a sacrament is a kind of sign.

REPLY OBJ. 1: Because medicine is an efficient cause of health, consequently whatever things are denominated from medicine are to be referred to some first active cause: so that a medicament implies a certain causality. But sanctity from which a sacrament is denominated, is not there taken as an efficient cause, but rather as a formal or a final cause. Therefore it does not follow that a sacrament need always imply causality.

REPLY OBJ. 2: This argument considers sacrament in the sense of a *sacred secret*. Now not only God's but also the king's, secret, is said to be sacred and to be a sacrament: because according to the ancients, whatever it was unlawful to lay violent hands on was said to be holy or sacrosanct, such as the city walls, and persons of high rank. Consequently those secrets, whether Divine or human, which it is unlawful to violate by making them known to anybody whatever, are called *sacred secrets* or *sacraments*.

REPLY OBJ. 3: Even an oath has a certain relation to sacred things, in so far as it consists in calling a sacred thing to witness. And in this sense it is called a sacrament: not in the sense in which we speak of sacraments now; the word *sacrament* being thus used not equivocally but analogically, i.e., by reason of a different relation to the one thing, viz. something sacred.

Article 2

Whether Every Sign of a Holy Thing Is a Sacrament?

AD SECUNDUM SIC PROCEDITUR. Videtur quod non omne signum rei sacrae sit sacramentum. Omnes enim creaturae sensibiles sunt signa rerum sacrarum, secundum illud Rom. I, *invisibilia Dei per ea quae facta sunt intellecta conspiciuntur.* Nec tamen omnes res sensibiles possunt dici sacramenta. Non ergo omne signum rei sacrae est sacramentum.

PRAETEREA, omnia quae in veteri lege fiebant, Christum figurabant, qui est sanctus sanctorum, secundum illud I Cor. X, *omnia in figura contingebant illis,* et Coloss. II, *quae sunt umbra futurorum, corpus autem Christi.* Nec tamen omnia gesta patrum veteris testamenti, vel etiam omnes caeremoniae legis, sunt sacramenta, sed quaedam specialiter, sicut in secunda parte habitum est. Ergo videtur quod non omne signum sacrae rei sit sacramentum.

PRAETEREA, etiam in novo testamento multa geruntur in signum alicuius rei sacrae, quae tamen non dicuntur sacramenta, sicut aspersio aquae benedictae, consecratio altaris, et consimilia. Non ergo omne signum rei sacrae est sacramentum.

SED CONTRA est quod definitio convertitur cum definito. Sed quidam definiunt sacramentum per hoc quod est sacrae rei signum, et hoc etiam videtur ex auctoritate Augustini supra inducta. Ergo videtur quod omne signum rei sacrae sit sacramentum.

RESPONDEO dicendum quod signa dantur hominibus, quorum est per nota ad ignota pervenire. Et ideo proprie dicitur sacramentum quod est signum alicuius rei sacrae ad homines pertinentis, ut scilicet proprie dicatur sacramentum, secundum quod nunc de sacramentis loquimur, quod est signum rei sacrae inquantum est sanctificans homines.

AD PRIMUM ergo dicendum quod creaturae sensibiles significant aliquid sacrum, scilicet sapientiam et bonitatem divinam, inquantum sunt in seipsis sacra, non autem inquantum nos per ea sanctificamur. Et ideo non possunt dici sacramenta secundum quod nunc loquimur de sacramentis.

AD SECUNDUM dicendum quod quaedam ad vetus testamentum pertinentia significabant sanctitatem Christi secundum quod in se sanctus est. Quaedam vero significabant sanctitatem eius inquantum per eam nos sanctificamur, sicut immolatio agni paschalis significabat immolationem Christi, qua sanctificati sumus. Et talia dicuntur proprie veteris legis sacramenta.

AD TERTIUM dicendum quod res denominantur a fine et complemento. Dispositio autem non est finis, sed perfectio. Et ideo ea quae significant dispositionem ad

OBJECTION 1: It seems that not every sign of a sacred thing is a sacrament. For all sensible creatures are signs of sacred things; according to Rom. 1:20: *The invisible things of God are clearly seen being understood by the things that are made.* And yet all sensible things cannot be called sacraments. Therefore not every sign of a sacred thing is a sacrament.

OBJ. 2: Further, whatever was done under the Old Law was a figure of Christ Who is the *Holy of Holies* (Dan 9:24), according to 1 Cor. 10:11: *All (these) things happened to them in figure*; and Col. 2:17: *Which are a shadow of things to come, but the body is Christ's.* And yet not all that was done by the Fathers of the Old Testament, not even all the ceremonies of the Law, were sacraments, but only in certain special cases, as stated in the Second Part (I-II, Q. 101, A. 4). Therefore it seems that not every sign of a sacred thing is a sacrament.

OBJ. 3: Further, even in the New Testament many things are done in sign of some sacred thing; yet they are not called sacraments; such as sprinkling with holy water, the consecration of an altar, and such like. Therefore not every sign of a sacred thing is a sacrament.

ON THE CONTRARY, A definition is convertible with the thing defined. Now some define a sacrament as being *the sign of a sacred thing*; moreover, this is clear from the passage quoted above (A. 1) from Augustine. Therefore it seems that every sign of a sacred thing is a sacrament.

I ANSWER THAT, Signs are given to men, to whom it is proper to discover the unknown by means of the known. Consequently a sacrament properly so called is that which is the sign of some sacred thing pertaining to man; so that properly speaking a sacrament, as considered by us now, is defined as being the *sign of a holy thing so far as it makes men holy.*

REPLY OBJ. 1: Sensible creatures signify something holy, viz. Divine wisdom and goodness inasmuch as these are holy in themselves; but not inasmuch as we are made holy by them. Therefore they cannot be called sacraments as we understand sacraments now.

REPLY OBJ. 2: Some things pertaining to the Old Testament signified the holiness of Christ considered as holy in Himself. Others signified His holiness considered as the cause of our holiness; thus the sacrifice of the Paschal Lamb signified Christ's Sacrifice whereby we are made holy: and such like are properly styled sacraments of the Old Law.

REPLY OBJ. 3: Names are given to things considered in reference to their end and state of completeness. Now a disposition is not an end, whereas perfection is. Consequently

sanctitatem, non dicuntur sacramenta, de quibus procedit obiectio; sed solum ea quae significant perfectionem sanctitatis humanae.

things that signify disposition to holiness are not called sacraments, and with regard to these the objection is verified: only those are called sacraments which signify the perfection of holiness in man.

Article 3

Whether a Sacrament Is a Sign of One Thing Only?

Ad tertium sic proceditur. Videtur quod sacramentum non sit signum nisi unius rei. Id enim quo multa significantur, est signum ambiguum, et per consequens fallendi occasio, sicut patet de nominibus aequivocis. Sed omnis fallacia debet removeri a Christiana religione, secundum illud Coloss. II, *videte ne quis vos seducat per philosophiam et inanem fallaciam*. Ergo videtur quod sacramentum non sit signum plurium rerum.

Praeterea, sicut dictum est, sacramentum significat rem sacram inquantum est humanae sanctificationis causa. Sed una sola est causa sanctificationis humanae, scilicet sanguis Christi, secundum illud Heb. ult., *Iesus, ut sanctificaret per suum sanguinem populum, extra portam passus est*. Ergo videtur quod sacramentum non significet plura.

Praeterea, dictum est quod sacramentum proprie significat ipsum finem sanctificationis. Sed finis sanctificationis est vita aeterna, secundum illud Rom. VI, *habetis fructum vestrum in sanctificatione, finem vero vitam aeternam*. Ergo videtur quod sacramenta non significent nisi unam rem, scilicet vitam aeternam.

Sed contra est quod in sacramento altaris est duplex res significata, scilicet corpus Christi verum et mysticum, ut Augustinus dicit, in libro sententiarum prosperi.

Respondeo dicendum quod, sicut dictum est, sacramentum proprie dicitur quod ordinatur ad significandam nostram sanctificationem. In qua tria possunt considerari, videlicet ipsa causa sanctificationis nostrae, quae est passio Christi; et forma nostrae sanctificationis, quae consistit in gratia et virtutibus; et ultimus finis nostrae sanctificationis, qui est vita aeterna. Et haec omnia per sacramenta significantur. Unde sacramentum est et signum rememorativum eius quod praecessit, scilicet passionis Christi; et demonstrativum eius quod in nobis efficitur per Christi passionem, scilicet gratiae; et prognosticum, idest praenuntiativum, futurae gloriae.

Ad primum ergo dicendum quod tunc est signum ambiguum, praebens occasionem fallendi, quando significat multa quorum unum non ordinatur ad aliud. Sed quando significat multa secundum quod ex eis quodam ordine efficitur unum, tunc non est signum ambiguum, sed certum, sicut hoc nomen homo significat animam et

Objection 1: It seems that a sacrament is a sign of one thing only. For that which signifies many things is an ambiguous sign, and consequently occasions deception: this is clearly seen in equivocal words. But all deception should be removed from the Christian religion, according to Col. 2:8: *Beware lest any man cheat you by philosophy and vain deceit*. Therefore it seems that a sacrament is not a sign of several things.

Obj. 2: Further, as stated above (A. 2), a sacrament signifies a holy thing in so far as it makes man holy. But there is only one cause of man's holiness, viz. the blood of Christ; according to Heb. 13:12: *Jesus, that He might sanctify the people by His own blood, suffered without the gate*. Therefore it seems that a sacrament does not signify several things.

Obj. 3: Further, it has been said above (A. 2, ad 3) that a sacrament signifies properly the very end of sanctification. Now the end of sanctification is eternal life, according to Rom. 6:22: *You have your fruit unto sanctification, and the end life everlasting*. Therefore it seems that the sacraments signify one thing only, viz. eternal life.

On the contrary, In the Sacrament of the Altar, two things are signified, viz. Christ's true body, and Christ's mystical body; as Augustine says (*Liber Sent. Prosper.*).

I answer that, As stated above (A. 2) a sacrament properly speaking is that which is ordained to signify our sanctification. In which three things may be considered; viz. the very cause of our sanctification, which is Christ's passion; the form of our sanctification, which is grace and the virtues; and the ultimate end of our sanctification, which is eternal life. And all these are signified by the sacraments. Consequently a sacrament is a sign that is both a reminder of the past, i.e., the passion of Christ; and an indication of that which is effected in us by Christ's passion, i.e., grace; and a prognostic, that is, a foretelling of future glory.

Reply Obj. 1: Then is a sign ambiguous and the occasion of deception, when it signifies many things not ordained to one another. But when it signifies many things inasmuch as, through being mutually ordained, they form one thing, then the sign is not ambiguous but certain: thus this word *man* signifies the soul and body inasmuch as

corpus prout ex eis constituitur humana natura. Et hoc modo sacramentum significat tria praedicta secundum quod quodam ordine sunt unum.

AD SECUNDUM dicendum quod sacramentum, in hoc quod significat rem sanctificantem, oportet quod significet effectum, qui intelligitur in ipsa causa sanctificante prout est causa sanctificans.

AD TERTIUM dicendum quod sufficit ad rationem sacramenti quod significet perfectionem quae est forma, nec oportet quod solum significet perfectionem quae est finis.

together they form the human nature. In this way a sacrament signifies the three things aforesaid, inasmuch as by being in a certain order they are one thing.

REPLY OBJ. 2: Since a sacrament signifies that which sanctifies, it must needs signify the effect, which is implied in the sanctifying cause as such.

REPLY OBJ. 3: It is enough for a sacrament that it signify that perfection which consists in the form, nor is it necessary that it should signify only that perfection which is the end.

Article 4

Whether a Sacrament Is Always Something Sensible?

AD QUARTUM SIC PROCEDITUR. Videtur quod sacramentum non semper sit aliqua res sensibilis. Quia secundum philosophum, in libro priorum, omnis effectus suae causae signum est. Sed sicut sunt quidam effectus sensibiles, ita etiam sunt quidam effectus intelligibiles, sicut scientia est effectus demonstrationis. Ergo non omne signum est sensibile. Sufficit autem ad rationem sacramenti quod sit signum alicuius rei sacrae inquantum homo per eam sanctificatur, ut supra dictum est. Non ergo requiritur ad sacramentum quod sit aliqua res sensibilis.

PRAETEREA, sacramenta pertinent ad regnum Dei et cultum Dei. Sed res sensibiles non videntur pertinere ad cultum Dei, dicitur enim Ioan. IV, *spiritus est Deus, et eos qui adorant eum, in spiritu et veritate adorare oportet*; et Rom. XIV, *non est regnum Dei esca et potus*. Ergo res sensibiles non requiruntur ad sacramenta.

PRAETEREA, Augustinus dicit, in libro de Lib. Arbit., quod *res sensibiles sunt minima bona, sine quibus homo recte vivere potest*. Sed sacramenta sunt de necessitate salutis humanae, ut infra patebit, et ita sine eis homo recte vivere non potest. Non ergo res sensibiles requiruntur ad sacramenta.

SED CONTRA est quod Augustinus dicit, super Ioan., *accedit verbum ad elementum, et fit sacramentum*. Et loquitur ibi de elemento sensibili, quod est aqua. Ergo res sensibiles requiruntur ad sacramenta.

RESPONDEO dicendum quod divina sapientia unicuique rei providet secundum suum modum, et propter hoc dicitur, Sap. VIII, quod *suaviter disponit omnia*. Unde et Matth. XXV dicitur quod *dividit unicuique secundum propriam virtutem*. Est autem homini connaturale ut per sensibilia perveniat in cognitionem intelligibilium. Signum autem est per quod aliquis devenit

OBJECTION 1: It seems that a sacrament is not always something sensible. Because, according to the Philosopher (*Prior. Anal.* ii), every effect is a sign of its cause. But just as there are some sensible effects, so are there some intelligible effects; thus science is the effect of a demonstration. Therefore not every sign is sensible. Now all that is required for a sacrament is something that is a sign of some sacred thing, inasmuch as thereby man is sanctified, as stated above (A. 2). Therefore something sensible is not required for a sacrament.

OBJ. 2: Further, sacraments belong to the kingdom of God and the Divine worship. But sensible things do not seem to belong to the Divine worship: for we are told (John 4:24) that *God is a spirit; and they that adore Him, must adore Him in spirit and in truth*; and (Rom 14:17) that *the kingdom of God is not meat and drink*. Therefore sensible things are not required for the sacraments.

OBJ. 3: Further, Augustine says (*De Lib. Arb.* ii) that *sensible things are goods of least account, since without them man can live aright*. But the sacraments are necessary for man's salvation, as we shall show farther on (Q. 61, A. 1): so that man cannot live aright without them. Therefore sensible things are not required for the sacraments.

ON THE CONTRARY, Augustine says (*Tract. lxxx super Joan.*): *The word is added to the element and this becomes a sacrament*; and he is speaking there of water which is a sensible element. Therefore sensible things are required for the sacraments.

I ANSWER THAT, Divine wisdom provides for each thing according to its mode; hence it is written (Wis 8:1) that *she . . . ordereth all things sweetly*: wherefore also we are told (Matt 25:15) that she *gave to everyone according to his proper ability*. Now it is part of man's nature to acquire knowledge of the intelligible from the sensible. But a sign is that by means of which one attains to the knowledge

in cognitionem alterius. Unde, cum res sacrae quae per sacramenta significantur, sint quaedam spiritualia et intelligibilia bona quibus homo sanctificatur, consequens est ut per aliquas res sensibiles significatio sacramenti impleatur, sicut etiam per similitudinem sensibilium rerum in divina Scriptura res spirituales nobis describuntur. Et inde est quod ad sacramenta requiruntur res sensibiles, ut etiam Dionysius probat, in I cap. caelestis hierarchiae.

AD PRIMUM ergo dicendum quod unumquodque praecipue denominatur et definitur secundum illud quod convenit ei primo et per se, non autem per id quod convenit ei per aliud. Effectus autem sensibilis per se habet quod ducat in cognitionem alterius, quasi primo et per se homini innotescens, quia omnis nostra cognitio a sensu initium habet. Effectus autem intelligibiles non habent quod possint ducere in cognitionem alterius nisi inquantum sunt per aliud manifestati, idest per aliqua sensibilia. Et inde est quod primo et principaliter dicuntur signa quae sensibus offeruntur, sicut Augustinus dicit, in II de Doct. Christ., quod *signum est quod, praeter speciem quam ingerit sensibus, facit aliquid aliud in cognitionem venire*. Effectus autem intelligibiles non habent rationem signi nisi secundum quod sunt manifestati per aliqua signa. Et per hunc etiam modum quaedam quae non sunt sensibilia, dicuntur quodammodo sacramenta, inquantum sunt significata per aliqua sensibilia, de quibus infra agetur.

AD SECUNDUM dicendum, quod res sensibiles, prout in sua natura considerantur, non pertinent ad cultum vel regnum Dei, sed solum secundum quod sunt signa spiritualium rerum, in quibus regnum Dei consistit.

AD TERTIUM dicendum quod Augustinus ibi loquitur de rebus sensibilibus secundum quod in sua natura considerantur, non autem secundum quod assumuntur ad significandum spiritualia, quae sunt maxima bona.

of something else. Consequently, since the sacred things which are signified by the sacraments, are the spiritual and intelligible goods by means of which man is sanctified, it follows that the sacramental signs consist in sensible things: just as in the Divine Scriptures spiritual things are set before us under the guise of things sensible. And hence it is that sensible things are required for the sacraments; as Dionysius also proves in his book on the heavenly hierarchy (*Coel. Hier.* i).

REPLY OBJ. 1: The name and definition of a thing is taken principally from that which belongs to a thing primarily and essentially: and not from that which belongs to it through something else. Now a sensible effect being the primary and direct object of man's knowledge (since all our knowledge springs from the senses) by its very nature leads to the knowledge of something else: whereas intelligible effects are not such as to be able to lead us to the knowledge of something else, except in so far as they are manifested by some other thing, i.e., by certain sensibles. It is for this reason that the name sign is given primarily and principally to things which are offered to the senses; hence Augustine says (*De Doctr. Christ.* ii) that a sign *is that which conveys something else to the mind, besides the species which it impresses on the senses*. But intelligible effects do not partake of the nature of a sign except in so far as they are pointed out by certain signs. And in this way, too, certain things which are not sensible are termed sacraments as it were, in so far as they are signified by certain sensible things, of which we shall treat further on (Q. 63, A. 1, ad 2; A. 3, ad 2; Q. 73, A. 6; Q. 74, A. 1, ad 3).

REPLY OBJ. 2: Sensible things considered in their own nature do not belong to the worship or kingdom of God: but considered only as signs of spiritual things in which the kingdom of God consists.

REPLY OBJ. 3: Augustine speaks there of sensible things, considered in their nature; but not as employed to signify spiritual things, which are the highest goods.

Article 5

Whether Determinate Things Are Required for a Sacrament?

AD QUINTUM SIC PROCEDITUR. Videtur quod non requirantur determinatae res ad sacramenta. Res enim sensibiles requiruntur in sacramentis ad significandum, ut dictum est. Sed nihil prohibet diversis rebus sensibilibus idem significari, sicut in sacra Scriptura Deus aliquando metaphorice significatur per lapidem, quandoque per leonem, quandoque per solem, aut aliquid huiusmodi. Ergo videtur quod diversae res possint

OBJECTION 1: It seems that determinate things are not required for a sacrament. For sensible things are required in sacraments for the purpose of signification, as stated above (A. 4). But nothing hinders the same thing being signified by diverse sensible things: thus in Holy Scripture God is signified metaphorically, sometimes by a stone (2 Kgs 22:2; Zech. 3:9; 1 Cor. 10:4; Apoc. 4:3); sometimes by a lion (Isa 31:4; Apoc. 5:5); sometimes by the sun (Isa 60:19, 20; Mal. 4:2), or by something similar. Therefore it seems

congruere eidem sacramento. Non ergo determinatae res in sacramentis requiruntur.

PRAETEREA, magis necessaria est salus animae quam salus corporis. Sed in medicinis corporalibus, quae ad salutem corporis ordinantur, potest una res pro alia poni in eius defectu. Ergo multo magis in sacramentis, quae sunt medicinae spirituales ad salutem animae ordinatae, poterit una res assumi pro alia quando illa defuerit.

PRAETEREA, non est conveniens ut hominum salus arctetur per legem divinam, et praecipue per legem Christi, qui venit omnes salvare. Sed in statu legis naturae non requirebantur in sacramentis aliquae res determinatae, sed ex voto assumebantur, ut patet Gen. XXVIII, ubi se Iacob vovit Deo decimas et hostias pacificas oblaturum. Ergo videtur quod non debuit arctari homo, et praecipue in nova lege, ad alicuius rei determinatae usum in sacramentis.

SED CONTRA est quod dominus dicit, Ioan. III, *nisi quis renatus fuerit ex aqua et spiritu sancto, non potest introire in regnum Dei.*

RESPONDEO dicendum quod in usu sacramentorum duo possunt considerari, scilicet cultus divinus, et sanctificatio hominis, quorum primum pertinet ad hominem per comparationem ad Deum, secundum autem e converso pertinet ad Deum per comparationem ad hominem. Non autem pertinet ad aliquem determinare quod est in potestate alterius, sed solum illud quod est in sua potestate. Quia igitur sanctificatio hominis est in potestate Dei sanctificantis, non pertinet ad hominem suo iudicio assumere res quibus sanctificetur, sed hoc debet esse ex divina institutione determinatum. Et ideo in sacramentis novae legis, quibus homines sanctificantur, secundum illud I Cor. VI, *abluti estis, sanctificati estis,* oportet uti rebus ex divina institutione determinatis.

AD PRIMUM ergo dicendum quod, si idem possit per diversa signa significari, determinare tamen quo signo sit utendum ad significandum, pertinet ad significantem. Deus autem est qui nobis significat spiritualia per res sensibiles in sacramentis, et per verba similitudinaria in Scripturis. Et ideo, sicut iudicio spiritus sancti determinatum est quibus similitudinibus in certis Scripturae locis res spirituales significentur, ita etiam debet esse divina institutione determinatum quae res ad significandum assumantur in hoc vel in illo sacramento.

AD SECUNDUM dicendum quod res sensibiles habent naturaliter sibi inditas virtutes conferentes ad corporalem salutem, et ideo non refert, si duae earum eandem virtutem habeant, qua quis utatur. Sed ad sanctificationem non ordinantur ex aliqua virtute naturaliter indita, sed solum ex institutione divina. Et ideo oportuit divinitus determinari quibus rebus sensibilibus sit in sacramentis utendum.

that diverse things can be suitable to the same sacrament. Therefore determinate things are not required for the sacraments.

OBJ. 2: Further, the health of the soul is more necessary than that of the body. But in bodily medicines, which are ordained to the health of the body, one thing can be substituted for another which happens to be wanting. Therefore much more in the sacraments, which are spiritual remedies ordained to the health of the soul, can one thing be substituted for another when this happens to be lacking.

OBJ. 3: Further, it is not fitting that the salvation of men be restricted by the Divine Law: still less by the Law of Christ, Who came to save all. But in the state of the Law of nature determinate things were not required in the sacraments, but were put to that use through a vow, as appears from Gen. 28, where Jacob vowed that he would offer to God tithes and peace-offerings. Therefore it seems that man should not have been restricted, especially under the New Law, to the use of any determinate thing in the sacraments.

ON THE CONTRARY, our Lord said (John 3:5): *Unless a man be born again of water and the Holy Spirit, he cannot enter into the kingdom of God.*

I ANSWER THAT, In the use of the sacraments two things may be considered, namely, the worship of God, and the sanctification of man: the former of which pertains to man as referred to God, and the latter pertains to God in reference to man. Now it is not for anyone to determine that which is in the power of another, but only that which is in his own power. Since, therefore, the sanctification of man is in the power of God Who sanctifies, it is not for man to decide what things should be used for his sanctification, but this should be determined by Divine institution. Therefore in the sacraments of the New Law, by which man is sanctified according to 1 Cor. 6:11, *You are washed, you are sanctified*, we must use those things which are determined by Divine institution.

REPLY OBJ. 1: Though the same thing can be signified by diverse signs, yet to determine which sign must be used belongs to the signifier. Now it is God Who signifies spiritual things to us by means of the sensible things in the sacraments, and of similitudes in the Scriptures. And consequently, just as the Holy Spirit decides by what similitudes spiritual things are to be signified in certain passages of Scripture, so also must it be determined by Divine institution what things are to be employed for the purpose of signification in this or that sacrament.

REPLY OBJ. 2: Sensible things are endowed with natural powers conducive to the health of the body: and therefore if two of them have the same virtue, it matters not which we use. Yet they are ordained unto sanctification not through any power that they possess naturally, but only in virtue of the Divine institution. And therefore it was necessary that God should determine the sensible things to be employed in the sacraments.

AD TERTIUM dicendum quod, sicut Augustinus dicit, XIX contra Faust., diversa sacramenta diversis temporibus congruunt, sicut etiam diversis verbis significantur diversa tempora, scilicet praesens, praeteritum et futurum. Et ideo, sicut in statu legis naturae homines, nulla lege exterius data, solo interiori instinctu movebantur ad Deum colendum, ita etiam ex interiori instinctu determinabatur eis quibus rebus sensibilibus ad Dei cultum uterentur. Postmodum vero necesse fuit etiam exterius legem dari, tum propter obscurationem legis naturae ex peccatis hominum; tum etiam ad expressiorem significationem gratiae Christi, per quam humanum genus sanctificatur. Et ideo etiam necesse fuit res determinari quibus homines uterentur in sacramentis. Nec propter hoc arctatur via salutis, quia res quarum usus est necessarius in sacramentis, vel communiter habentur, vel parvo studio adhibito haberi possunt.

REPLY OBJ. 3: As Augustine says (*Contra Faust.* xix), diverse sacraments suit different times; just as different times are signified by different parts of the verb, viz. present, past, and future. Consequently, just as under the state of the Law of nature man was moved by inward instinct and without any outward law, to worship God, so also the sensible things to be employed in the worship of God were determined by inward instinct. But later on it became necessary for a law to be given (to man) from without: both because the Law of nature had become obscured by man's sins; and in order to signify more expressly the grace of Christ, by which the human race is sanctified. And hence the need for those things to be determinate, of which men have to make use in the sacraments. Nor is the way of salvation narrowed thereby: because the things which need to be used in the sacraments, are either in everyone's possession or can be had with little trouble.

Article 6

Whether Words Are Required for the Signification of the Sacraments?

AD SEXTUM SIC PROCEDITUR. Videtur quod in significatione sacramentorum non requirantur verba. Dicit enim Augustinus, contra Faustum, libro XIX, *quid sunt aliud quaeque corporalia sacramenta nisi quasi quaedam verba visibilia?* Et sic videtur quod addere verba rebus sensibilibus in sacramentis sit addere verba verbis. Sed hoc est superfluum. Non ergo requiruntur verba cum rebus sensibilibus in sacramentis.

PRAETEREA, sacramentum est aliquid unum. Ex his autem quae sunt diversorum generum, non videtur posse aliquid unum fieri. Cum igitur res sensibiles et verba sint diversorum generum, quia res sensibiles sunt a natura, verba autem a ratione; videtur quod in sacramentis non requirantur verba cum rebus sensibilibus.

PRAETEREA, sacramenta novae legis succedunt sacramentis veteris legis, quia, illis ablatis, ista sunt instituta, ut Augustinus dicit, XIX contra Faustum. Sed in sacramentis veteris legis non requirebatur aliqua forma verborum. Ergo nec in sacramentis novae legis.

SED CONTRA est quod apostolus dicit, Ephes. V, *Christus dilexit Ecclesiam, et tradidit semetipsum pro ea, ut illam sanctificaret, mundans eam lavacro aquae in verbo vitae.* Et Augustinus dicit, super Ioan., *accedit verbum ad elementum, et fit sacramentum.*

RESPONDEO dicendum quod sacramenta, sicut dictum est, adhibentur ad hominum sanctificationem sicut quaedam signa. Tripliciter ergo considerari possunt, et quolibet modo congruit eis quod verba rebus sensibilibus adiungantur. Primo enim possunt considerari ex

OBJECTION 1: It seems that words are not required for the signification of the sacraments. For Augustine says (*Contra Faust.* xix): *What else is a corporeal sacrament but a kind of visible word?* Wherefore to add words to the sensible things in the sacraments seems to be the same as to add words to words. But this is superfluous. Therefore words are not required besides the sensible things in the sacraments.

OBJ. 2: Further, a sacrament is some one thing, but it does not seem possible to make one thing of those that belong to different genera. Since, therefore, sensible things and words are of different genera, for sensible things are the product of nature, but words, of reason; it seems that in the sacraments, words are not required besides sensible things.

OBJ. 3: Further, the sacraments of the New Law succeed those of the Old Law: since *the former were instituted when the latter were abolished,* as Augustine says (*Contra Faust.* xix). But no form of words was required in the sacraments of the Old Law. Therefore neither is it required in those of the New Law.

ON THE CONTRARY, The Apostle says (Eph 5:25, 26): *Christ loved the Church, and delivered Himself up for it; that He might sanctify it, cleansing it by the laver of water in the word of life.* And Augustine says (*Tract. xxx in Joan.*): *The word is added to the element, and this becomes a sacrament.*

I ANSWER THAT, The sacraments, as stated above (AA. 2, 3), are employed as signs for man's sanctification. Consequently they can be considered in three ways: and in each way it is fitting for words to be added to the sensible signs. For in the first place they can be considered in regard

parte causae sanctificantis, quae est verbum incarnatum, cui sacramentum quodammodo conformatur in hoc quod rei sensibili verbum adhibetur, sicut in mysterio incarnationis carni sensibili est verbum Dei unitum.

Secundo possunt considerari sacramenta ex parte hominis qui sanctificatur, qui componitur ex anima et corpore, cui proportionatur sacramentalis medicina, quae per rem visibilem corpus tangit, et per verbum ab anima creditur. Unde Augustinus dicit, super illud Ioan. XV, *iam vos mundi estis propter sermonem etc., unde ista est tanta virtus aquae ut corpus tangat et cor abluat, nisi faciente verbo, non quia dicitur, sed quia creditur?*

Tertio potest considerari ex parte ipsius significationis sacramentalis. Dicit autem Augustinus, in II de Doct. Christ., quod *verba inter homines obtinuerunt principatum significandi,* quia verba diversimode formari possunt ad significandos diversos conceptus mentis, et propter hoc per verba magis distincte possumus exprimere quod mente concipimus. Et ideo ad perfectionem significationis sacramentalis necesse fuit ut significatio rerum sensibilium per aliqua verba determinaretur. Aqua enim significare potest et ablutionem propter, suam humiditatem, et refrigerium propter suam frigiditatem, sed cum dicitur, ego te baptizo, manifestatur quod aqua utimur in Baptismo ad significandam emundationem spiritualem.

AD PRIMUM ergo dicendum quod res visibiles sacramentorum dicuntur verba per similitudinem quandam, inquantum scilicet participant quandam vim significandi, quae principaliter est in ipsis verbis, ut dictum est. Et ideo non est superflua ingeminatio verborum cum in sacramentis rebus visibilibus verba adduntur, quia unum eorum determinatur per aliud, ut dictum est.

AD SECUNDUM dicendum quod, quamvis verba et aliae res sensibiles sint in diverso genere quantum pertinet ad naturam rei, conveniunt tamen ratione significandi. Quae perfectius est in verbis quam in aliis rebus. Et ideo ex verbis et rebus fit quodammodo unum in sacramentis sicut ex forma et materia, inquantum scilicet per verba perficitur significatio rerum, ut dictum est. Sub rebus autem comprehenduntur etiam ipsi actus sensibiles, puta ablutio et unctio et alia huiusmodi, quia in his est eadem ratio significandi et in rebus.

AD TERTIUM dicendum quod, sicut Augustinus dicit, contra Faustum, alia debent esse sacramenta rei praesentis, et alia rei futurae. Sacramenta autem veteris legis praenuntia erant Christi venturi. Et ideo non ita expresse significabant Christum sicut sacramenta novae legis, quae ab ipso Christo effluunt, et quandam similitudinem ipsius in se habent, ut dictum est. Utebantur tamen in veteri lege aliquibus verbis in his quae ad cultum Dei pertinent, tam sacerdotes, qui erant sacramentorum

to the cause of sanctification, which is the Word incarnate: to Whom the sacraments have a certain conformity, in that the word is joined to the sensible sign, just as in the mystery of the Incarnation the Word of God is united to sensible flesh.

Second, sacraments may be considered on the part of man who is sanctified, and who is composed of soul and body: to whom the sacramental remedy is adjusted, since it touches the body through the sensible element, and the soul through faith in the words. Hence Augustine says (*Tract. lxxx in Joan.*) on John 15:3, *Now you are clean by reason of the word*, etc.: *Whence hath water this so great virtue, to touch the body and wash the heart, but by the word doing it, not because it is spoken, but because it is believed?*

Third, a sacrament may be considered on the part of the sacramental signification. Now Augustine says (*De Doctr. Christ.* ii) that *words are the principal signs used by men*; because words can be formed in various ways for the purpose of signifying various mental concepts, so that we are able to express our thoughts with greater distinctness by means of words. And therefore in order to insure the perfection of sacramental signification it was necessary to determine the signification of the sensible things by means of certain words. For water may signify both a cleansing by reason of its humidity, and refreshment by reason of its being cool: but when we say, *I baptize thee*, it is clear that we use water in baptism in order to signify a spiritual cleansing.

REPLY OBJ. 1: The sensible elements of the sacraments are called words by way of a certain likeness, in so far as they partake of a certain significative power, which resides principally in the very words, as stated above. Consequently it is not a superfluous repetition to add words to the visible element in the sacraments; because one determines the other, as stated above.

REPLY OBJ. 2: Although words and other sensible things are not in the same genus, considered in their natures, yet have they something in common as to the thing signified by them: which is more perfectly done in words than in other things. Wherefore in the sacraments, words and things, like form and matter, combine in the formation of one thing, in so far as the signification of things is completed by means of words, as above stated. And under words are comprised also sensible actions, such as cleansing and anointing and such like: because they have a like signification with the things.

REPLY OBJ. 3: As Augustine says (*Contra Faust.* xix), the sacraments of things present should be different from sacraments of things to come. Now the sacraments of the Old Law foretold the coming of Christ. Consequently they did not signify Christ so clearly as the sacraments of the New Law, which flow from Christ Himself, and have a certain likeness to Him, as stated above. Nevertheless in the Old Law, certain words were used in things pertaining to the worship of God, both by the priests, who were the

illorum ministri, secundum illud Num. VI, *sic benedicetis filiis Israel, et dicetis eis, benedicat tibi dominus*, etc.; quam etiam illi qui illis sacramentis utebantur, secundum illud Deut. XXVI, *profiteor hodie coram domino Deo tuo*, et cetera.

ministers of those sacraments, according to Num. 6:23, 24: *Thus shall you bless the children of Israel, and you shall say to them: The Lord bless thee*, etc.; and by those who made use of those sacraments, according to Deut. 26:3: *I profess this day before the Lord thy God*, etc.

Article 7

Whether Determinate Words Are Required in the Sacraments?

AD SEPTIMUM SIC PROCEDITUR. Videtur quod non requirantur determinata verba in sacramentis. Ut enim philosophus dicit, *voces non sunt eaedem apud omnes*. Sed salus, quae per sacramentum quaeritur, est eadem apud omnes. Ergo non requiruntur aliqua determinata verba in sacramentis.

PRAETEREA, verba requiruntur in sacramentis inquantum sunt principaliter significativa, sicut supra dictum est. Sed contingit per diversa verba idem significari. Ergo non requiruntur determinata verba in sacramentis.

PRAETEREA, corruptio cuiuslibet rei variat eius speciem. Sed quidam corrupte verba proferunt, nec tamen propter hoc impediri creditur sacramentorum effectus, alioquin illiterati et balbi qui sacramenta conferunt, frequenter defectum in sacramentis inducerent. Ergo videtur quod non requirantur in sacramentis determinata verba.

SED CONTRA est quod dominus determinata verba protulit in consecratione sacramenti Eucharistiae, dicens, Matth. XXVI, *hoc est corpus meum*. Similiter etiam mandavit discipulis ut sub determinata forma verborum baptizarent, dicens, Matth. ult., *euntes, docete omnes gentes, baptizantes eos in nomine patris et filii et spiritus sancti*.

RESPONDEO dicendum quod, sicut dictum est, in sacramentis verba se habent per modum formae, res autem sensibiles per modum materiae. In omnibus autem compositis ex materia et forma principium determinationis est ex parte formae, quae est quodammodo finis et terminus materiae. Et ideo principalius requiritur ad esse rei determinata forma quam determinata materia, materia enim determinata quaeritur ut sit proportionata determinatae formae. Cum igitur in sacramentis requirantur determinatae res sensibiles, quae se habent in sacramentis sicut materia, multo magis requiritur in eis determinata forma verborum.

AD PRIMUM ergo dicendum quod, sicut Augustinus dicit, super Ioan., verbum operatur in sacramentis, non quia dicitur, idest, non secundum exteriorem sonum vocis, sed quia creditur, secundum sensum verborum qui fide tenetur. Et hic quidem sensus est idem apud omnes,

OBJECTION 1: It seems that determinate words are not required in the sacraments. For as the Philosopher says (*Peri Herm.* i), *words are not the same for all*. But salvation, which is sought through the sacraments, is the same for all. Therefore determinate words are not required in the sacraments.

OBJ. 2: Further, words are required in the sacraments forasmuch as they are the principal means of signification, as stated above (A. 6). But it happens that various words mean the same. Therefore determinate words are not required in the sacraments.

OBJ. 3: Further, corruption of anything changes its species. But some corrupt the pronunciation of words, and yet it is not credible that the sacramental effect is hindered thereby; else unlettered men and stammerers, in conferring sacraments, would frequently do so invalidly. Therefore it seems that determinate words are not required in the sacraments.

ON THE CONTRARY, our Lord used determinate words in consecrating the sacrament of the Eucharist, when He said (Matt 26:26): *This is My Body*. Likewise He commanded His disciples to baptize under a form of determinate words, saying (Matt 28:19): *Go ye and teach all nations, baptizing them in the name of the Father, and of the Son, and of the Holy Spirit*.

I ANSWER THAT, As stated above (A. 6, ad 2), in the sacraments the words are as the form, and sensible things are as the matter. Now in all things composed of matter and form, the determining principle is on the part of the form, which is as it were the end and terminus of the matter. Consequently for the being of a thing the need of a determinate form is prior to the need of determinate matter: for determinate matter is needed that it may be adapted to the determinate form. Since, therefore, in the sacraments determinate sensible things are required, which are as the sacramental matter, much more is there need in them of a determinate form of words.

REPLY OBJ. 1: As Augustine says (*Tract. lxxx super Joan.*), the word operates in the sacraments *not because it is spoken*, i.e., not by the outward sound of the voice, *but because it is believed* in accordance with the sense of the words which is held by faith. And this sense is indeed the

licet non eaedem voces quantum ad sonum. Et ideo, cuiuscumque linguae verbis proferatur talis sensus, perficitur sacramentum.

AD SECUNDUM dicendum quod, licet in qualibet lingua contingat diversis vocibus idem significari, semper tamen aliqua illarum vocum est qua principalius et communius homines illius linguae utuntur ad hoc significandum. Et talis vox assumi debet in significatione sacramenti. Sicut etiam inter res sensibiles illa assumitur ad significationem sacramenti cuius usus est communior ad actum per quem sacramenti effectus significatur, sicut aqua communius utuntur homines ad ablutionem corporalem, per quam spiritualis ablutio significatur; et ideo aqua assumitur ut materia in Baptismo.

AD TERTIUM dicendum quod ille qui corrupte profert verba sacramentalia, si hoc ex industria facit, non videtur intendere facere quod facit Ecclesia, et ita non videtur perfici sacramentum. Si autem hoc faciat ex errore vel lapsu linguae, si sit tanta corruptio quae omnino auferat sensum locutionis, non videtur perfici sacramentum. Et hoc praecipue contingit quando fit corruptio ex parte principii dictionis, puta si, loco eius quod est in nomine patris, dicat, in nomine matris. Si vero non totaliter auferatur sensus locutionis per huiusmodi corruptelam, nihilominus perficitur sacramentum. Et hoc praecipue contingit quando fit corruptio ex parte finis, puta si aliquis dicat patrias et filias. Quamvis enim huiusmodi verba corrupte prolata nihil significent ex virtute impositionis, accipiuntur tamen ut significantia ex accommodatione usus. Et ideo, licet mutetur sonus sensibilis, remanet tamen idem sensus.

Quod autem dictum est de differentia corruptionis circa principium vel finem dictionis, rationem habet quia apud nos variatio dictionis ex parte principii mutat significationem, variatio autem ex fine dictionis ut plurimum non mutat significationem. Quae tamen apud Graecos variatur etiam secundum principium dictionis in declinatione verborum.

Magis tamen videtur attendenda quantitas corruptionis ex parte dictionis. Quia ex utraque parte potest esse tam parva quod non aufert sensum verborum, et tam magna, quod aufert. Sed unum horum facilius accidit ex parte principii, aliud ex parte finis.

same for all, though the same words as to their sound be not used by all. Consequently no matter in what language this sense is expressed, the sacrament is complete.

REPLY OBJ. 2: Although it happens in every language that various words signify the same thing, yet one of those words is that which those who speak that language use principally and more commonly to signify that particular thing: and this is the word which should be used for the sacramental signification. So also among sensible things, that one is used for the sacramental signification which is most commonly employed for the action by which the sacramental effect is signified: thus water is most commonly used by men for bodily cleansing, by which the spiritual cleansing is signified: and therefore water is employed as the matter of baptism.

REPLY OBJ. 3: If he who corrupts the pronunciation of the sacramental words—does so on purpose, he does not seem to intend to do what the Church intends: and thus the sacrament seems to be defective. But if he do this through error or a slip of the tongue, and if he so far mispronounce the words as to deprive them of sense, the sacrament seems to be defective. This would be the case especially if the mispronunciation be in the beginning of a word, for instance, if one were to say *in nomine matris* instead of *in nomine Patris*. If, however, the sense of the words be not entirely lost by this mispronunciation, the sacrament is complete. This would be the case principally if the end of a word be mispronounced; for instance, if one were to say *patrias et filias*. For although the words thus mispronounced have no appointed meaning, yet we allow them an accommodated meaning corresponding to the usual forms of speech. And so, although the sensible sound is changed, yet the sense remains the same.

What has been said about the various mispronunciations of words, either at the beginning or at the end, holds forasmuch as with us a change at the beginning of a word changes the meaning, whereas a change at the end generally speaking does not effect such a change: whereas with the Greeks the sense is changed also in the beginning of words in the conjugation of verbs.

Nevertheless the principal point to observe is the extent of the corruption entailed by mispronunciation: for in either case it may be so little that it does not alter the sense of the words; or so great that it destroys it. But it is easier for the one to happen on the part of the beginning of the words, and the other at the end.

Article 8

Whether It Is Lawful to Add Anything to the Words in Which the Sacramental Form Consists?

AD OCTAVUM SIC PROCEDITUR. Videtur quod nihil liceat addere verbis in quibus consistit forma sacramentorum. Non enim minoris sunt necessitatis huiusmodi verba sacramentalia quam verba sacrae Scripturae. Sed verbis sacrae Scripturae nihil licet addere vel minuere, dicitur enim Deut. IV, *non addetis ad verbum quod vobis loquor, nec auferetis ab eo*; et Apoc. ult., *contestor omni audienti verba prophetiae libri huius, si quis apposuerit ad haec, apponet super eum Deus plagas scriptas in libro isto; et si quis diminuerit, auferet Deus partem eius de libro vitae.* Ergo videtur quod neque in formis sacramentorum liceat aliquid addere vel minuere.

PRAETEREA, verba se habent in sacramentis per modum formae, ut dictum est. Sed in formis quaelibet additio vel subtractio variat speciem, sicut et in numeris, ut dicitur in VIII Metaphys. Ergo videtur quod, si aliquid addatur vel subtrahatur a forma sacramenti, non erit idem sacramentum.

PRAETEREA, sicut ad formam sacramenti determinatus numerus dictionum requiritur, ita etiam requiritur determinatus ordo verborum, et etiam orationis continuitas. Si ergo additio vel subtractio non aufert sacramenti veritatem, videtur quod pari ratione nec transpositio verborum, aut etiam interpolatio pronuntiationis.

SED CONTRA est quod in formis sacramentorum quaedam apponuntur a quibusdam quae ab aliis non ponuntur, sicut Latini baptizant sub hac forma, ego te baptizo in nomine patris et filii et spiritus sancti; Graeci autem sub ista, baptizatur servus Christi n. in nomine patris, et cetera. Et tamen utrique verum conferunt sacramentum. Ergo in formis sacramentorum licet aliquid addere vel minuere.

RESPONDEO dicendum quod circa omnes istas mutationes quae possunt in formis sacramentorum contingere, duo videntur esse consideranda. Unum quidem ex parte eius qui profert verba, cuius intentio requiritur ad sacramentum, ut infra dicetur. Et ideo, si intendat per huiusmodi additionem vel diminutionem alium ritum inducere qui non sit ab Ecclesia receptus, non videtur perfici sacramentum, quia non videtur quod intendat facere id quod facit Ecclesia.

Aliud autem est considerandum ex parte significationis verborum. Cum enim verba operentur in sacramentis quantum ad sensum quem faciunt, ut supra dictum est, oportet considerare utrum per talem mutationem tollatur debitus sensus verborum, quia sic manifestum

OBJECTION 1: It seems that it is not lawful to add anything to the words in which the sacramental form consists. For these sacramental words are not of less importance than are the words of Holy Scripture. But it is not lawful to add anything to, or to take anything from, the words of Holy Scripture: for it is written (Deut 4:2): *You shall not add to the word that I speak to you, neither shall you take away from it*; and (Rev 22:18, 19): *I testify to everyone that heareth the words of the prophecy of this book: if any man shall add to these things, God shall add to him the plagues written in this book. And if any man shall take away . . . God shall take away his part out of the book of life.* Therefore it seems that neither is it lawful to add anything to, or to take anything from, the sacramental forms.

OBJ. 2: Further, in the sacraments words are by way of form, as stated above (A. 6, ad 2; A. 7). But any addition or subtraction in forms changes the species, as also in numbers (*Metaph.* viii). Therefore it seems that if anything be added to or subtracted from a sacramental form, it will not be the same sacrament.

OBJ. 3: Further, just as the sacramental form demands a certain number of words, so does it require that these words should be pronounced in a certain order and without interruption. If therefore, the sacrament is not rendered invalid by addition or subtraction of words, in like manner it seems that neither is it, if the words be pronounced in a different order or with interruptions.

ON THE CONTRARY, Certain words are inserted by some in the sacramental forms, which are not inserted by others: thus the Latins baptize under this form: *I baptize thee in the name of the Father, and of the Son, and of the Holy Spirit*; whereas the Greeks use the following form: *The servant of God, N . . . is baptized in the name of the Father*, etc. Yet both confer the sacrament validly. Therefore it is lawful to add something to, or to take something from, the sacramental forms.

I ANSWER THAT, With regard to all the variations that may occur in the sacramental forms, two points seem to call for our attention. One is on the part of the person who says the words, and whose intention is essential to the sacrament, as will be explained further on (Q. 64, A. 8). Wherefore if he intends by such addition or suppression to perform a rite other from that which is recognized by the Church, it seems that the sacrament is invalid: because he seems not to intend to do what the Church does.

The other point to be considered is the meaning of the words. For since in the sacraments, the words produce an effect according to the sense which they convey, as stated above (A. 7, ad 1), we must see whether the change of words destroys the essential sense of the words: because then the

est quod tollitur veritas sacramenti. Manifestum est autem quod, si diminuatur aliquid eorum quae sunt de substantia formae sacramentalis, tollitur debitus sensus verborum, et ideo non perficitur sacramentum. Unde Didymus dicit, in libro de spiritu sancto, *si quis ita baptizare conetur ut unum de praedictis nominibus praetermittat,* scilicet patris et filii et spiritus sancti, *sine perfectione baptizabit.* Si autem subtrahatur aliquid quod non sit de substantia formae, talis diminutio non tollit debitum sensum verborum, et per consequens nec sacramenti perfectionem. Sicut in forma Eucharistiae, quae est, hoc est enim corpus meum, ly enim sublatum non tollit debitum sensum verborum, et ideo non impedit perfectionem sacramenti, quamvis possit contingere quod ille qui praetermittit, peccet ex negligentia vel contemptu.

Circa additionem etiam contingit aliquid apponi quod est corruptivum debiti sensus, puta si aliquis dicat, *ego te baptizo in nomine patris maioris et filii minoris,* sicut Ariani baptizabant. Et ideo talis additio tollit veritatem sacramenti. Si vero sit talis additio quae non auferat debitum sensum, non tollitur sacramenti veritas. Nec refert utrum talis additio fiat in principio, medio vel fine. Ut, si aliquis dicat, ego te baptizo in nomine Dei patris omnipotentis, et filii eius unigeniti, et spiritus sancti Paracleti, erit verum Baptisma. Et similiter, si quis dicat, ego te baptizo in nomine patris et filii et spiritus sancti, et beata virgo te adiuvet, erit verum Baptisma.

Forte autem si diceret, ego te baptizo in nomine patris et filii et spiritus sancti et beatae virginis Mariae, non esset Baptismus, quia dicitur I Cor. I, *nunquid Paulus pro vobis crucifixus est? Aut in nomine Pauli baptizati estis?* Sed hoc verum est si sic intelligatur in nomine beatae virginis baptizari sicut in nomine Trinitatis, quo Baptismus consecratur, talis enim sensus esset contrarius verae fidei, et per consequens tolleret veritatem sacramenti. Si vero sic intelligatur quod additur, et in nomine beatae virginis, non quasi nomen beatae virginis aliquid operetur in Baptismo, sed ut eius intercessio prosit baptizato ad conservandam gratiam baptismalem, non tollitur perfectio sacramenti.

AD PRIMUM ergo dicendum quod verbis sacrae Scripturae non licet aliquid apponere quantum ad sensum, sed quantum ad expositionem sacrae Scripturae, multa verba eis a doctoribus apponuntur. Non tamen licet etiam verba sacrae Scripturae apponere ita quod dicantur esse de integritate sacrae Scripturae, quia hoc esset vitium falsitatis. Et similiter si quis diceret aliquid esse de necessitate formae quod non est.

AD SECUNDUM dicendum quod verba pertinent ad formam sacramenti ratione sensus significati. Et ideo,

sacrament is clearly rendered invalid. Now it is clear, if any substantial part of the sacramental form be suppressed, that the essential sense of the words is destroyed; and consequently the sacrament is invalid. Wherefore Didymus says (*De Spir. Sanct.* ii): *If anyone attempt to baptize in such a way as to omit one of the aforesaid names,* i.e., of the Father, Son, and Holy Spirit, *his baptism will be invalid.* But if that which is omitted be not a substantial part of the form, such an omission does not destroy the essential sense of the words, nor consequently the validity of the sacrament. Thus in the form of the Eucharist—*For this is My Body,* the omission of the word *for* does not destroy the essential sense of the words, nor consequently cause the sacrament to be invalid; although perhaps he who makes the omission may sin from negligence or contempt.

Again, it is possible to add something that destroys the essential sense of the words: for instance, if one were to say: *I baptize thee in the name of the Father Who is greater, and of the Son Who is less,* with which form the Arians baptized: and consequently such an addition makes the sacrament invalid. But if the addition be such as not to destroy the essential sense, the sacrament is not rendered invalid. Nor does it matter whether this addition be made at the beginning, in the middle, or at the end: For instance, if one were to say, *I baptize thee in the name of the Father Almighty, and of the only Begotten Son, and of the Holy Spirit, the Paraclete,* the baptism would be valid; and in like manner if one were to say, *I baptize thee in the name of the Father, and of the Son, and of the Holy Spirit; and may the Blessed Virgin succour thee,* the baptism would be valid.

Perhaps, however, if one were to say, *I baptize thee in the name of the Father, and of the Son, and of the Holy Spirit, and of the Blessed Virgin Mary,* the baptism would be void; because it is written (1 Cor 1:13): *Was Paul crucified for you or were you baptized in the name of Paul?* But this is true if the intention be to baptize in the name of the Blessed Virgin as in the name of the Trinity, by which baptism is consecrated: for such a sense would be contrary to faith, and would therefore render the sacrament invalid: whereas if the addition, *and in the name of the Blessed Virgin* be understood, not as if the name of the Blessed Virgin effected anything in baptism, but as intimating that her intercession may help the person baptized to preserve the baptismal grace, then the sacrament is not rendered void.

REPLY OBJ. 1: It is not lawful to add anything to the words of Holy Scripture as regards the sense; but many words are added by Doctors by way of explanation of the Holy Scriptures. Nevertheless, it is not lawful to add even words to Holy Scripture as though such words were a part thereof, for this would amount to forgery. It would amount to the same if anyone were to pretend that something is essential to a sacramental form, which is not so.

REPLY OBJ. 2: Words belong to a sacramental form by reason of the sense signified by them. Consequently any

quaecumque fiat additio vel subtractio vocum quae non addat aliquid aut subtrahat debito sensui, non tollitur species sacramenti.

AD TERTIUM dicendum quod, si sit tanta interruptio verborum quod intercipiatur intentio pronuntiantis, tollitur sensus sacramenti, et per consequens veritas eius. Non autem tollitur quando est parva interruptio proferentis, quae intentionem et intellectum non aufert.

Et idem etiam dicendum est de transpositione verborum. Quia, si tollit sensum locutionis, non perficitur sacramentum, sicut patet de negatione praeposita vel postposita signo. Si autem sit talis transpositio quae sensum locutionis non variat, non tollitur veritas sacramenti, secundum quod philosophus dicit quod *nomina et verba transposita idem significant.*

addition or suppression of words which does not add to or take from the essential sense, does not destroy the essence of the sacrament.

REPLY OBJ. 3: If the words are interrupted to such an extent that the intention of the speaker is interrupted, the sacramental sense is destroyed, and consequently, the validity of the sacrament. But this is not the case if the interruption of the speaker is so slight, that his intention and the sense of the words is not interrupted.

The same is to be said of a change in the order of the words. Because if this destroys the sense of the words, the sacrament is invalidated: as happens when a negation is made to precede or follow a word. But if the order is so changed that the sense of the words does not vary, the sacrament is not invalidated, according to the Philosopher's dictum: *Nouns and verbs mean the same though they be transposed* (*Peri Herm.* x).

QUESTION 61

THE NECESSITY OF THE SACRAMENTS

Deinde considerandum est de necessitate sacramentorum. Et circa hoc quaeruntur quatuor.

Primo, utrum sacramenta sint necessaria ad salutem humanam.

Secundo, utrum fuerint necessaria in statu ante peccatum.

Tertio, utrum fuerint necessaria in statu post peccatum ante Christum.

Quarto, utrum fuerint necessaria post Christi adventum.

We must now consider the necessity of the sacraments; concerning which there are four points of inquiry:

(1) Whether sacraments are necessary for man's salvation?

(2) Whether they were necessary in the state that preceded sin?

(3) Whether they were necessary in the state after sin and before Christ?

(4) Whether they were necessary after Christ's coming?

Article 1

Whether Sacraments Are Necessary for Man's Salvation?

AD PRIMUM SIC PROCEDITUR. Videtur quod sacramenta non fuerint necessaria ad humanam salutem. Dicit enim apostolus, I ad Tim. IV, *corporalis exercitatio ad modicum utilis est*. Sed usus sacramentorum pertinet ad corporalem exercitationem, eo quod sacramenta perficiuntur in significatione sensibilium rerum et verborum, ut dictum est. Ergo sacramenta non sunt necessaria ad humanam salutem.

PRAETEREA, II Cor. XII, apostolo dicitur, *sufficit tibi gratia mea*. Non autem sufficeret si sacramenta essent necessaria ad salutem. Non sunt ergo sacramenta saluti humanae necessaria.

PRAETEREA, posita causa sufficienti, nihil aliud videtur esse necessarium ad effectum. Sed passio Christi est sufficiens causa nostrae salutis, dicit enim apostolus, ad Rom. V, *si, cum inimici essemus, reconciliati sumus Deo per mortem filii eius, multo magis, reconciliati, salvi erimus in vita ipsius*. Non ergo requiruntur sacramenta ad salutem humanam.

SED CONTRA est quod Augustinus dicit, XIX contra Faust., *in nullum nomen religionis, seu verum seu falsum, coadunari homines possunt, nisi aliquo signaculorum vel sacramentorum visibilium consortio colligentur*. Sed necessarium est ad humanam salutem homines adunari in unum verae religionis nomen. Ergo sacramenta sunt necessaria ad humanam salutem.

RESPONDEO dicendum quod sacramenta sunt necessaria ad humanam salutem triplici ratione. Quarum prima sumenda est ex conditione humanae naturae, cuius proprium est ut per corporalia et sensibilia in spiritualia et intelligibilia deducatur. Pertinet autem ad

OBJECTION 1: It seems that sacraments are not necessary for man's salvation. For the Apostle says (1 Tim 4:8): *Bodily exercise is profitable to little*. But the use of sacraments pertains to bodily exercise; because sacraments are perfected in the signification of sensible things and words, as stated above (Q. 60, A. 6). Therefore sacraments are not necessary for the salvation of man.

OBJ. 2: Further, the Apostle was told (2 Cor 12:9): *My grace is sufficient for thee*. But it would not suffice if sacraments were necessary for salvation. Therefore sacraments are not necessary for man's salvation.

OBJ. 3: Further, given a sufficient cause, nothing more seems to be required for the effect. But Christ's Passion is the sufficient cause of our salvation; for the Apostle says (Rom 5:10): *If, when we were enemies, we were reconciled to God by the death of His Son: much more, being reconciled, shall we be saved by His life*. Therefore sacraments are not necessary for man's salvation.

ON THE CONTRARY, Augustine says (*Contra Faust.* xix): *It is impossible to keep men together in one religious denomination, whether true or false, except they be united by means of visible signs or sacraments*. But it is necessary for salvation that men be united together in the name of the one true religion. Therefore sacraments are necessary for man's salvation.

I ANSWER THAT, Sacraments are necessary unto man's salvation for three reasons. The first is taken from the condition of human nature which is such that it has to be led by things corporeal and sensible to things spiritual and intelligible. Now it belongs to Divine providence to provide for

divinam providentiam ut unicuique rei provideat secundum modum suae conditionis. Et ideo convenienter divina sapientia homini auxilia salutis confert sub quibusdam corporalibus et sensibilibus signis, quae sacramenta dicuntur.

Secunda ratio sumenda est ex statu hominis, qui peccando se subdidit per affectum corporalibus rebus. Ibi autem debet medicinale remedium homini adhiberi ubi patitur morbum. Et ideo conveniens fuit ut Deus per quaedam corporalia signa hominibus spiritualem medicinam adhiberet, nam, si spiritualia nuda ei proponerentur, eius animus applicari non posset, corporalibus deditus.

Tertia ratio sumenda est ex studio actionis humanae, quae praecipue circa corporalia versatur. Ne igitur esset homini durum si totaliter a corporalibus actibus abstraheretur, proposita sunt ei corporalia exercitia in sacramentis, quibus salubriter exerceretur, ad evitanda superstitiosa exercitia, quae consistunt in cultu Daemonum, vel qualitercumque noxia, quae consistunt in actibus peccatorum.

Sic igitur per sacramentorum institutionem homo convenienter suae naturae eruditur per sensibilia; humiliatur, se corporalibus subiectum recognoscens, dum sibi per corporalia subvenitur; praeservatur etiam a noxiis corporalibus per salubria exercitia sacramentorum.

AD PRIMUM ergo dicendum quod corporalis exercitatio, inquantum est corporalis, non multum utilis est. Sed exercitatio per usum sacramentorum non est pure corporalis, sed quodammodo est spiritualis, scilicet per significationem et causalitatem.

AD SECUNDUM dicendum quod gratia Dei est sufficiens causa humanae salutis. Sed Deus dat hominibus gratiam secundum modum eis convenientem. Et ideo necessaria sunt hominibus sacramenta ad gratiam consequendam.

AD TERTIUM dicendum quod passio Christi est causa sufficiens humanae salutis. Nec propter hoc sequitur quod sacramenta non sint necessaria ad humanam salutem, quia operantur in virtute passionis Christi, et passio Christi quodammodo applicatur hominibus per sacramenta, secundum illud apostoli, Rom. VI, *quicumque baptizati sumus in Christo Iesu, in morte ipsius baptizati sumus.*

each one according as its condition requires. Divine wisdom, therefore, fittingly provides man with means of salvation, in the shape of corporeal and sensible signs that are called sacraments.

The second reason is taken from the state of man who in sinning subjected himself by his affections to corporeal things. Now the healing remedy should be given to a man so as to reach the part affected by disease. Consequently it was fitting that God should provide man with a spiritual medicine by means of certain corporeal signs; for if man were offered spiritual things without a veil, his mind being taken up with the material world would be unable to apply itself to them.

The third reason is taken from the fact that man is prone to direct his activity chiefly towards material things. Lest, therefore, it should be too hard for man to be drawn away entirely from bodily actions, bodily exercise was offered to him in the sacraments, by which he might be trained to avoid superstitious practices, consisting in the worship of demons, and all manner of harmful action, consisting in sinful deeds.

It follows, therefore, that through the institution of the sacraments man, consistently with his nature, is instructed through sensible things; he is humbled, through confessing that he is subject to corporeal things, seeing that he receives assistance through them: and he is even preserved from bodily hurt, by the healthy exercise of the sacraments.

REPLY OBJ. 1: Bodily exercise, as such, is not very profitable: but exercise taken in the use of the sacraments is not merely bodily, but to a certain extent spiritual, viz. in its signification and in its causality.

REPLY OBJ. 2: God's grace is a sufficient cause of man's salvation. But God gives grace to man in a way which is suitable to him. Hence it is that man needs the sacraments that he may obtain grace.

REPLY OBJ. 3: Christ's Passion is a sufficient cause of man's salvation. But it does not follow that the sacraments are not also necessary for that purpose: because they obtain their effect through the power of Christ's Passion; and Christ's Passion is, so to say, applied to man through the sacraments according to the Apostle (Rom 6:3): *All we who are baptized in Christ Jesus, are baptized in His death.*

Article 2

Whether Before Sin Sacraments Were Necessary to Man?

AD SECUNDUM SIC PROCEDITUR. Videtur quod ante peccatum fuerint homini necessaria sacramenta. Quia, sicut dictum est, sacramenta sunt necessaria homini ad gratiam consequendam. Sed etiam in statu innocentiae homo indigebat gratia, sicut in prima parte habitum est. Ergo etiam in statu illo erant necessaria sacramenta.

PRAETEREA, sacramenta sunt convenientia homini secundum conditione humanae naturae, sicut dictum est. Sed eadem est natura hominis ante peccatum et post peccatum. Ergo videtur quod ante peccatum homo indiguerit sacramentis.

PRAETEREA, matrimonium est quoddam sacramentum, secundum illud Ephes. V, *sacramentum hoc magnum est, ego autem dico in Christo et Ecclesia.* Sed matrimonium fuit institutum ante peccatum, ut dicitur Gen. II. Ergo sacramenta erant necessaria homini ante peccatum.

SED CONTRA est quod medicina non est necessaria nisi aegroto, secundum illud Matth. IX, *non est opus sanis medicus.* Sed sacramenta sunt quaedam spirituales medicinae, quae adhibentur contra vulnera peccati. Ergo non fuerunt necessaria ante peccatum.

RESPONDEO dicendum quod in statu innocentiae sacramenta necessaria non fuerunt. Cuius ratio accipi potest ex rectitudine status illius, in quo superiora inferioribus dominabantur, et nullo modo dependebant ab eis, sicut enim mens suberat Deo, ita menti suberant inferiores animae vires, et ipsi animae corpus. Contra hunc autem ordinem esset si anima perficeretur, vel quantum ad scientiam vel quantum ad gratiam, per aliquid corporale, quod fit in sacramentis. Et ideo in statu innocentiae homo sacramentis non indigebat, non solum inquantum sacramenta ordinantur in remedium peccati, sed etiam inquantum ordinantur ad animae perfectionem.

AD PRIMUM ergo dicendum quod homo in statu innocentiae gratia indigebat, non tamen ut consequeretur gratiam per aliqua sensibilia signa, sed spiritualiter et invisibiliter.

AD SECUNDUM dicendum quod eadem est natura hominis ante peccatum et post peccatum, non tamen est idem naturae status. Nam post peccatum anima, etiam quantum ad superiorem partem, indiget accipere aliquid a corporalibus rebus ad sui perfectionem quod in illo statu homini necesse non erat.

AD TERTIUM dicendum quod matrimonium fuit institutum in statu innocentiae, non secundum quod est sacramentum, sed secundum quod est in officium naturae. Ex consequenti tamen aliquid significabat futurum circa Christum et Ecclesiam, sicut et omnia alia in figura Christi praecesserunt.

OBJECTION 1: It seems that before sin sacraments were necessary to man. For, as stated above (A. 1, ad 2) man needs sacraments that he may obtain grace. But man needed grace even in the state of innocence, as we stated in the First Part (Q. 95, A. 4; cf. I-II, Q. 109, A. 2; Q. 114, A. 2). Therefore sacraments were necessary in that state also.

OBJ. 2: Further, sacraments are suitable to man by reason of the conditions of human nature, as stated above (A. 1). But man's nature is the same before and after sin. Therefore it seems that before sin, man needed the sacraments.

OBJ. 3: Further, matrimony is a sacrament, according to Eph. 5:32: *This is a great sacrament; but I speak in Christ and in the Church.* But matrimony was instituted before sin, as may be seen in Gen. 2. Therefore sacraments were necessary to man before sin.

ON THE CONTRARY, None but the sick need remedies, according to Matt. 9:12: *They that are in health need not a physician.* Now the sacraments are spiritual remedies for the healing of wounds inflicted by sin. Therefore they were not necessary before sin.

I ANSWER THAT, Sacraments were not necessary in the state of innocence. This can be proved from the rectitude of that state, in which the higher (parts of man) ruled the lower, and nowise depended on them: for just as the mind was subject to God, so were the lower powers of the soul subject to the mind, and the body to the soul. And it would be contrary to this order if the soul were perfected either in knowledge or in grace, by anything corporeal; which happens in the sacraments. Therefore in the state of innocence man needed no sacraments, whether as remedies against sin or as means of perfecting the soul.

REPLY OBJ. 1: In the state of innocence man needed grace: not so that he needed to obtain grace by means of sensible signs, but in a spiritual and invisible manner.

REPLY OBJ. 2: Man's nature is the same before and after sin, but the state of his nature is not the same. Because after sin, the soul, even in its higher part, needs to receive something from corporeal things in order that it may be perfected: whereas man had no need of this in that state.

REPLY OBJ. 3: Matrimony was instituted in the state of innocence, not as a sacrament, but as a function of nature. Consequently, however, it foreshadowed something in relation to Christ and the Church: just as everything else foreshadowed Christ.

Article 3

Whether There Should Have Been Sacraments After Sin, Before Christ?

Ad tertium sic proceditur. Videtur quod post peccatum, ante Christum, sacramenta non debuerunt esse. Dictum est enim quod per sacramenta passio Christi hominibus applicatur, et sic passio Christi comparatur ad sacramenta sicut causa ad effectum. Sed effectus non praecedit causam. Ergo sacramenta non debuerunt esse ante Christi adventum.

Praeterea, sacramenta debent esse convenientia statui humani generis, ut patet per Augustinum, XIX contra Faustum. Sed status humani generis non fuit mutatus post peccatum usque ad reparationem factam per Christum. Ergo nec sacramenta debuerunt immutari, ut, praeter sacramenta legis naturae, alia statuerentur in lege Moysi.

Praeterea, quanto magis est aliquid propinquum perfecto, tanto magis debet ei assimilari. Sed perfectio salutis humanae per Christum facta est, cui propinquiora fuerunt sacramenta veteris legis quam ea quae fuerunt ante legem. Ergo debuerunt esse similiora sacramentis Christi. Cuius tamen contrarium apparet, ex eo quod sacerdotium Christi praedicitur esse futurum *secundum ordinem Melchisedech, et non secundum ordinem Aaron,* ut habetur Heb. VII. Non ergo convenienter fuerunt disposita ante Christum sacramenta.

Sed contra est quod Augustinus dicit, XIX contra Faust., quod *prima sacramenta, quae celebrabantur et observabantur ex lege, praenuntia erant Christi venturi.* Sed necessarium erat ad humanam salutem ut adventus Christi praenuntiaretur. Ergo necessarium erat ante Christum sacramenta quaedam disponi.

Respondeo dicendum quod sacramenta necessaria sunt ad humanam salutem inquantum sunt quaedam sensibilia signa invisibilium rerum quibus homo sanctificatur. Nullus autem sanctificari potest post peccatum nisi per Christum, *quem proposuit Deus propitiatorem per fidem in sanguine ipsius, ad ostensionem iustitiae suae, ut sit ipse iustus et iustificans eum qui ex fide est Iesu Christi.* Et ideo oportebat ante Christi adventum esse quaedam signa visibilia quibus homo fidem suam protestaretur de futuro salvatoris adventu. Et huiusmodi signa sacramenta dicuntur. Et sic patet quod ante Christi adventum necesse fuit quaedam sacramenta institui.

Ad primum ergo dicendum quod passio Christi est causa finalis veterum sacramentorum, quae scilicet ad ipsam significandam sunt instituta. Causa autem finalis non praecedit tempore, sed solum in intentione agentis. Et ideo non est inconveniens aliqua sacramenta ante Christi passionem fuisse.

Objection 1: It seems that there should have been no sacraments after sin, before Christ. For it has been stated that the Passion of Christ is applied to men through the sacraments: so that Christ's Passion is compared to the sacraments as cause to effect. But effect does not precede cause. Therefore there should have been no sacraments before Christ's coming.

Obj. 2: Further, sacraments should be suitable to the state of the human race, as Augustine declares (*Contra Faust.* xix). But the state of the human race underwent no change after sin until it was repaired by Christ. Neither, therefore, should the sacraments have been changed, so that besides the sacraments of the natural law, others should be instituted in the law of Moses.

Obj. 3: Further, the nearer a thing approaches to that which is perfect, the more like it should it be. Now the perfection of human salvation was accomplished by Christ; to Whom the sacraments of the Old Law were nearer than those that preceded the Law. Therefore they should have borne a greater likeness to the sacraments of Christ. And yet the contrary is the case, since it was foretold that the priesthood of Christ would be *according to the order of Melchisedech, and not . . . according to the order of Aaron* (Heb 7:11). Therefore sacraments were unsuitably instituted before Christ.

On the contrary, Augustine says (*Contra Faust.* xix) that *the first sacraments which the Law commanded to be solemnized and observed were announcements of Christ's future coming.* But it was necessary for man's salvation that Christ's coming should be announced beforehand. Therefore it was necessary that some sacraments should be instituted before Christ.

I answer that, Sacraments are necessary for man's salvation, in so far as they are sensible signs of invisible things whereby man is made holy. Now after sin no man can be made holy save through Christ, *Whom God hath proposed to be a propitiation, through faith in His blood, to the showing of His justice . . . that He Himself may be just, and the justifier of him who is of the faith of Jesus Christ* (Rom 3:25, 26). Therefore before Christ's coming there was need for some visible signs whereby man might testify to his faith in the future coming of a Savior. And these signs are called sacraments. It is therefore clear that some sacraments were necessary before Christ's coming.

Reply Obj. 1: Christ's Passion is the final cause of the old sacraments: for they were instituted in order to foreshadow it. Now the final cause precedes not in time, but in the intention of the agent. Consequently, there is no reason against the existence of sacraments before Christ's Passion.

Ad secundum dicendum quod status humani generis post peccatum et ante Christum dupliciter potest considerari. Uno modo, secundum fidei rationem. Et sic semper unus et idem permansit, quia scilicet iustificabantur homines per fidem futuri Christi adventus. Alio modo potest considerari secundum intensionem et remissionem peccati, et expressae cognitionis de Christo. Nam per incrementa temporum et peccatum coepit in homine magis dominari, in tantum quod, ratione hominis per peccatum obtenebrata, non sufficerent homini ad recte vivendum praecepta legis naturae, sed necesse fuit determinari praecepta in lege scripta; et cum his quaedam fidei sacramenta. Oportebat etiam ut per incrementa temporum magis explicaretur cognitio fidei, quia, ut Gregorius dicit, *per incrementa temporum crevit divinae cognitionis augmentum*. Et ideo etiam necesse fuit quod in veteri lege etiam quaedam sacramenta fidei quam habebant de Christo venturo, determinarentur quae quidem comparantur ad sacramenta quae fuerunt ante legem sicut determinatum ad indeterminatum; quia scilicet ante legem non fuit determinate praefixum homini quibus sacramentis uteretur, sicut fuit per legem. Quod erat necessarium et propter obtenebrationem legis naturalis; et ut esset determinatior fidei significatio.

Ad tertium dicendum quod sacramentum Melchisedech, quod fuit ante legem, magis assimilatur sacramento novae legis in materia, inquantum scilicet obtulit panem et vinum, ut habetur Gen. XIV, sicut etiam sacrificium novi testamenti oblatione panis et vini perficitur. Sacramenta tamen legis Mosaicae magis assimilantur rei significatae per sacramentum, scilicet passioni Christi, ut patet de agno paschali et aliis huiusmodi. Et hoc ideo ne, propter continuitatem temporis, si permaneret eadem sacramentorum species, videretur esse sacramenti eiusdem continuatio.

Reply Obj. 2: The state of the human race after sin and before Christ can be considered from two points of view. First, from that of faith: and thus it was always one and the same: since men were made righteous, through faith in the future coming of Christ. Second, according as sin was more or less intense, and knowledge concerning Christ more or less explicit. For as time went on sin gained a greater hold on man, so much so that it clouded man's reason, the consequence being that the precepts of the natural law were insufficient to make man live aright, and it became necessary to have a written code of fixed laws, and together with these certain sacraments of faith. For it was necessary, as time went on, that the knowledge of faith should be more and more unfolded, since, as Gregory says (*Hom. vi in Ezech.*): *With the advance of time there was an advance in the knowledge of Divine things.* Consequently in the old Law there was also a need for certain fixed sacraments significative of man's faith in the future coming of Christ: which sacraments are compared to those that preceded the Law, as something determinate to that which is indeterminate: inasmuch as before the Law it was not laid down precisely of what sacraments men were to make use: whereas this was prescribed by the Law; and this was necessary both on account of the overclouding of the natural law, and for the clearer signification of faith.

Reply Obj. 3: The sacrament of Melchisedech which preceded the Law is more like the Sacrament of the New Law in its matter: in so far as *he offered bread and wine* (Gen 14:18), just as bread and wine are offered in the sacrifice of the New Testament. Nevertheless the sacraments of the Mosaic Law are more like the thing signified by the sacrament, i.e., the Passion of Christ: as clearly appears in the Paschal Lamb and such like. The reason of this was lest, if the sacraments retained the same appearance, it might seem to be the continuation of one and the same sacrament, where there was no interruption of time.

Article 4

Whether There Was Need for Any Sacraments After Christ Came?

Ad quartum sic proceditur. Videtur quod post Christum non debuerint esse aliqua sacramenta. Veniente enim veritate, debet cessare figura. Sed *gratia et veritas per Iesum Christum facta est*, ut dicitur Ioan. I. Cum igitur sacramenta sint veritatis signa sive figurae, videtur quod post Christi passionem sacramenta esse non debuerint.

Praeterea, sacramenta in quibusdam elementis consistunt, ut ex supra dictis patet. Sed apostolus dicit, Galat. IV, quod, *cum essemus parvuli, sub elementis mundi eramus servientes*, nunc autem, temporis plenitudine

Objection 1: It seems that there was no need for any sacraments after Christ came. For the figure should cease with the advent of the truth. But *grace and truth came by Jesus Christ* (John 1:17). Since, therefore, the sacraments are signs or figures of the truth, it seems that there was no need for any sacraments after Christ's Passion.

Obj. 2: Further, the sacraments consist in certain elements, as stated above (Q. 60, A. 4). But the Apostle says (Gal 4:3, 4) that *when we were children we were serving under the elements of the world*: but that now *when the fullness*

veniente, iam non sumus parvuli. Ergo videtur quod non debeamus Deo servire sub elementis huius mundi, corporalibus sacramentis utendo.

PRAETEREA, *apud Deum non est transmutatio nec vicissitudinis obumbratio*, ut dicitur Iac. I. Sed hoc videtur ad quandam mutationem divinae voluntatis pertinere, quod alia sacramenta nunc exhibeat hominibus ad sanctificationem tempore gratiae, et alia ante Christum. Ergo videtur quod post Christum non debuerunt institui alia sacramenta.

SED CONTRA est quod Augustinus dicit, contra Faust. XIX, quod sacramenta veteris legis *sunt ablata, quia impleta, et alia sunt instituta virtute maiora, utilitate meliora, actu faciliora, numero pauciora.*

RESPONDEO dicendum quod, sicut antiqui patres salvati sunt per fidem Christi venturi, ita et nos salvamur per fidem Christi iam nati et passi. Sunt autem sacramenta quaedam signa protestantia fidem qua homo iustificatur. Oportet autem aliis signis significari futura, praeterita seu praesentia, ut enim Augustinus dicit, XIX contra Faust., *eadem res aliter annuntiatur facienda, aliter facta, sicut ipsa verba passurus et passus non similiter sonant.* Et ideo oportet quaedam alia sacramenta in nova lege esse, quibus significentur ea quae praecesserunt in Christo, praeter sacramenta veteris legis, quibus praenuntiabantur futura.

AD PRIMUM ergo dicendum quod, sicut Dionysius dicit, in V cap. Eccl. Hier., status novae legis medius est inter statum veteris legis, cuius figurae implentur in nova lege; et inter statum gloriae, in qua omnis nude et perfecte manifestabitur veritas. Et ideo tunc nulla erunt sacramenta. Nunc autem, quandiu per speculum in aenigmate cognoscimus, ut dicitur I Cor. XIII, oportet nos per aliqua sensibilia signa in spiritualia devenire. Quod pertinet ad rationem sacramentorum.

AD SECUNDUM dicendum quod sacramenta veteris legis apostolus vocat egena et infirma elementa, quia gratiam nec continebant, nec causabant. Et ideo utentes illis sacramentis dicit apostolus sub elementis mundi Deo servisse, quia scilicet nihil erant aliud quam elementa huius mundi. Nostra autem sacramenta gratiam continent et causant. Et ideo non est de eis similis ratio.

AD TERTIUM dicendum quod, sicut paterfamilias non ex hoc habere monstratur mutabilem voluntatem quod diversa praecepta familiae suae proponit pro temporum varietate, non eadem praecipiens hieme et aestate; ita non ostenditur aliqua mutatio esse circa Deum ex hoc quod alia sacramenta instituit post Christi adventum, et alia tempore legis; quia illa fuerunt congrua gratiae praefigurandae, haec autem sunt congrua gratiae praesentialiter demonstrandae.

of time has *come*, we are no longer children. Therefore it seems that we should not serve God under the elements of this world, by making use of corporeal sacraments.

OBJ. 3: Further, according to James 1:17 with God *there is no change, nor shadow of alteration*. But it seems to argue some change in the Divine will that God should give man certain sacraments for his sanctification now during the time of grace, and other sacraments before Christ's coming. Therefore it seems that other sacraments should not have been instituted after Christ.

ON THE CONTRARY, Augustine says (*Contra Faust.* xix) that the sacraments of the Old Law *were abolished because they were fulfilled; and others were instituted, fewer in number, but more efficacious, more profitable, and of easier accomplishment.*

I ANSWER THAT, As the ancient Fathers were saved through faith in Christ's future coming, so are we saved through faith in Christ's past birth and Passion. Now the sacraments are signs in protestation of the faith whereby man is justified; and signs should vary according as they signify the future, the past, or the present; for as Augustine says (*Contra Faust.* xix), *the same thing is variously pronounced as to be done and as having been done: for instance the word passurus (going to suffer) differs from passus (having suffered).* Therefore the sacraments of the New Law, that signify Christ in relation to the past, must needs differ from those of the Old Law, that foreshadowed the future.

REPLY OBJ. 1: As Dionysius says (*Eccl. Hier.* v), the state of the New Law is between the state of the Old Law, whose figures are fulfilled in the New, and the state of glory, in which all truth will be openly and perfectly revealed. Wherefore then there will be no sacraments. But now, so long as we know *through a glass in a dark manner,* (1 Cor 13:12) we need sensible signs in order to reach spiritual things: and this is the province of the sacraments.

REPLY OBJ. 2: The Apostle calls the sacraments of the Old Law *weak and needy elements* (Gal 4:9) because they neither contained nor caused grace. Hence the Apostle says that those who used these sacraments served God *under the elements of this world*: for the very reason that these sacraments were nothing else than the elements of this world. But our sacraments both contain and cause grace: consequently the comparison does not hold.

REPLY OBJ. 3: Just as the head of the house is not proved to have a changeable mind, through issuing various commands to his household at various seasons, ordering things differently in winter and summer; so it does not follow that there is any change in God, because He instituted sacraments of one kind after Christ's coming, and of another kind at the time of the Law. Because the latter were suitable as foreshadowing grace, the former as signifying the presence of grace.

QUESTION 62

THE SACRAMENTS' PRINCIPAL EFFECT, WHICH IS GRACE

Deinde considerandum est de effectu sacramentorum. Et primo, de effectu eius principali, qui est gratia; secundo de effectu secundario, qui est character. Circa primum quaeruntur sex.

Primo, utrum sacramenta novae legis sint causa gratiae.

Secundo, utrum gratia sacramentalis aliquid addat super gratiam virtutum et donorum.

Tertio, utrum sacramenta contineant gratiam.

Quarto, utrum sit in eis aliqua virtus ad causandum gratiam.

Quinto, utrum talis virtus in sacramentis derivetur a passione Christi.

Sexto, utrum sacramenta veteris legis gratiam causarent.

We have now to consider the effect of the sacraments. First of their principal effect, which is grace; second, of their secondary effect, which is a character. Concerning the first there are six points of inquiry:

(1) Whether the sacraments of the New Law are the cause of grace?

(2) Whether sacramental grace confers anything in addition to the grace of the virtues and gifts?

(3) Whether the sacraments contain grace?

(4) Whether there is any power in them for the causing of grace?

(5) Whether the sacraments derive this power from Christ's Passion?

(6) Whether the sacraments of the Old Law caused grace?

Article 1

Whether the Sacraments Are the Cause of Grace?

AD PRIMUM SIC PROCEDITUR. Videtur quod sacramenta non sint causa gratiae. Non enim idem videtur esse signum et causa, eo quod ratio signi videtur magis effectui competere. Sed sacramentum est signum gratiae. Non igitur est causa eius.

PRAETEREA, nullum corporale agere potest in rem spiritualem, eo quod agens est honorabilius patiente, ut Augustinus dicit, XII super Gen. ad Litt. Sed subiectum gratiae est mens hominis, quae est res spiritualis. Non ergo sacramenta possunt gratiam causare.

PRAETEREA, illud quod est proprium Dei, non debet alicui creaturae attribui. Sed causare gratiam est proprium Dei, secundum illud Psalmi, *gratiam et gloriam dabit dominus*. Cum ergo sacramenta consistant in quibusdam verbis et rebus creatis, non videtur quod possint gratiam causare.

SED CONTRA est quod Augustinus dicit, super Ioan., quod aqua baptismalis corpus tangit et cor abluit. Sed cor non abluitur nisi per gratiam. Ergo causat gratiam, et pari ratione alia Ecclesiae sacramenta.

RESPONDEO dicendum quod necesse est dicere sacramenta novae legis per aliquem modum gratiam causare. Manifestum est enim quod per sacramenta novae legis homo Christo incorporatur, sicut de Baptismo dicit apostolus, Galat. III, *quotquot in Christo baptizati estis,*

OBJECTION 1: It seems that the sacraments are not the cause of grace. For it seems that the same thing is not both sign and cause: since the nature of sign appears to be more in keeping with an effect. But a sacrament is a sign of grace. Therefore it is not its cause.

OBJ. 2: Further, nothing corporeal can act on a spiritual thing: since *the agent is more excellent than the patient*, as Augustine says (*Gen ad lit.* xii). But the subject of grace is the human mind, which is something spiritual. Therefore the sacraments cannot cause grace.

OBJ. 3: Further, what is proper to God should not be ascribed to a creature. But it is proper to God to cause grace, according to Ps. 83:12: *The Lord will give grace and glory*. Since, therefore, the sacraments consist in certain words and created things, it seems that they cannot cause grace.

ON THE CONTRARY, Augustine says (*Tract. lxxx in Joan.*) that the baptismal water *touches the body and cleanses the heart*. But the heart is not cleansed save through grace. Therefore it causes grace: and for like reason so do the other sacraments of the Church.

I ANSWER THAT, We must needs say that in some way the sacraments of the New Law cause grace. For it is evident that through the sacraments of the New Law man is incorporated with Christ: thus the Apostle says of Baptism (Gal 3:27): *As many of you as have been baptized in Christ*

Christum induistis. Non autem efficitur homo membrum Christi nisi per gratiam.

Quidam tamen dicunt quod non sunt causa gratiae aliquid operando, sed quia Deus, sacramentis adhibitis, in anima gratiam operatur. Et ponunt exemplum de illo qui, afferens denarium plumbeum, accipit centum libras ex regis ordinatione, non quod denarius ille aliquid operetur ad habendum praedictae pecuniae quantitatem; sed hoc operatur sola voluntas regis. Unde et Bernardus dicit, in quodam sermone in cena domini, *sicut investitur canonicus per librum, abbas per baculum, episcopus per anulum, sic divisiones gratiarum diversae sunt traditae sacramentis.* Sed si quis recte consideret, iste modus non transcendit rationem signi. Nam denarius plumbeus non est nisi quoddam signum regiae ordinationis de hoc quod pecunia recipiatur ab isto. Similiter liber est quoddam signum quo designatur traditio canonicatus. Secundum hoc igitur sacramenta novae legis nihil plus essent quam signa gratiae, cum tamen ex multis sanctorum auctoritatibus habeatur quod sacramenta novae legis non solum significant, sed causant gratiam.

Et ideo aliter dicendum, quod duplex est causa agens, principalis et instrumentalis. Principalis quidem operatur per virtutem suae formae, cui assimilatur effectus, sicut ignis suo calore calefacit. Et hoc modo non potest causare gratiam nisi Deus, quia gratia nihil est aliud quam quaedam participata similitudo divinae naturae, secundum illud II Pet. I, *magna nobis et pretiosa promissa donavit, ut divinae simus consortes naturae.* Causa vero instrumentalis non agit per virtutem suae formae, sed solum per motum quo movetur a principali agente. Unde effectus non assimilatur instrumento, sed principali agenti, sicut lectus non assimilatur securi, sed arti quae est in mente artificis. Et hoc modo sacramenta novae legis gratiam causant, adhibentur enim ex divina ordinatione ad gratiam in eis causandam. Unde Augustinus dicit, XIX contra Faust., haec omnia, scilicet sacramentalia, fiunt et transeunt, virtus tamen, scilicet Dei, quae per ista operatur, iugiter manet. Hoc autem proprie dicitur instrumentum, per quod aliquis operatur. Unde et Tit. III dicitur, *salvos nos fecit per lavacrum regenerationis.*

AD PRIMUM ergo dicendum quod causa principalis non proprie potest dici signum effectus, licet occulti, etiam si ipsa sit sensibilis et manifesta. Sed causa instrumentalis, si sit manifesta, potest dici signum effectus occulti, eo quod non solum est causa, sed quodammodo effectus, inquantum movetur a principali agente. Et secundum hoc, sacramenta novae legis simul sunt causa et signa. Et inde est quod, sicut communiter dicitur, efficiunt quod figurant. Ex quo etiam patet quod habent perfecte rationem sacramenti, inquantum ordinantur ad

have put on Christ. And man is made a member of Christ through grace alone.

Some, however, say that they are the cause of grace not by their own operation, but in so far as God causes grace in the soul when the sacraments are employed. And they give as an example a man who on presenting a leaden coin, receives, by the king's command, a hundred pounds: not as though the leaden coin, by any operation of its own, caused him to be given that sum of money; this being the effect of the mere will of the king. Hence Bernard says in a sermon on the Lord's Supper: *Just as a canon is invested by means of a book, an abbot by means of a crozier, a bishop by means of a ring, so by the various sacraments various kinds of grace are conferred.* But if we examine the question properly, we shall see that according to the above mode the sacraments are mere signs. For the leaden coin is nothing but a sign of the king's command that this man should receive money. In like manner the book is a sign of the conferring of a canonry. Hence, according to this opinion the sacraments of the New Law would be mere signs of grace; whereas we have it on the authority of many saints that the sacraments of the New Law not only signify, but also cause grace.

We must therefore say otherwise, that an efficient cause is twofold, principal and instrumental. The principal cause works by the power of its form, to which form the effect is likened; just as fire by its own heat makes something hot. In this way none but God can cause grace: since grace is nothing else than a participated likeness of the Divine Nature, according to 2 Pet. 1:4: *He hath given us most great and precious promises; that we may be partakers of the Divine Nature.* But the instrumental cause works not by the power of its form, but only by the motion whereby it is moved by the principal agent: so that the effect is not likened to the instrument but to the principal agent: for instance, the couch is not like the axe, but like the art which is in the craftsman's mind. And it is thus that the sacraments of the New Law cause grace: for they are instituted by God to be employed for the purpose of conferring grace. Hence Augustine says (*Contra Faust.* xix): *All these things,* viz. pertaining to the sacraments, *are done and pass away, but the power,* viz. of God, *which works by them, remains ever.* Now that is, properly speaking, an instrument by which someone works: wherefore it is written (Titus 3:5): *He saved us by the laver of regeneration.*

REPLY OBJ. 1: The principal cause cannot properly be called a sign of its effect, even though the latter be hidden and the cause itself sensible and manifest. But an instrumental cause, if manifest, can be called a sign of a hidden effect, for this reason, that it is not merely a cause but also in a measure an effect in so far as it is moved by the principal agent. And in this sense the sacraments of the New Law are both cause and signs. Hence, too, is it that, to use the common expression, *they effect what they signify.* From this it is clear that they perfectly fulfill the conditions of a

aliquid sacrum non solum per modum signi, sed etiam per modum causae.

AD SECUNDUM dicendum quod instrumentum habet duas actiones, unam instrumentalem, secundum quam operatur non in virtute propria, sed in virtute principalis agentis; aliam autem habet actionem propriam, quae competit sibi secundum propriam formam; sicut securi competit scindere ratione suae acuitatis, facere autem lectum inquantum est instrumentum artis. Non autem perficit actionem instrumentalem nisi exercendo actionem propriam; scindendo enim facit lectum. Et similiter sacramenta corporalia per propriam operationem quam exercent circa corpus, quod tangunt, efficiunt operationem instrumentalem ex virtute divina circa animam, sicut aqua Baptismi, abluendo corpus secundum propriam virtutem, abluit animam inquantum est instrumentum virtutis divinae; nam ex anima et corpore unum fit. Et hoc est quod Augustinus dicit, quod corpus tangit et cor abluit.

AD TERTIUM dicendum quod ratio illa procedit de eo quod est causa gratiae per modum principalis agentis, hoc enim est proprium Dei, ut dictum est.

sacrament; being ordained to something sacred, not only as a sign, but also as a cause.

REPLY OBJ. 2: An instrument has a twofold action; one is instrumental, in respect of which it works not by its own power but by the power of the principal agent: the other is its proper action, which belongs to it in respect of its proper form: thus it belongs to an axe to cut asunder by reason of its sharpness, but to make a couch, in so far as it is the instrument of an art. But it does not accomplish the instrumental action save by exercising its proper action: for it is by cutting that it makes a couch. In like manner the corporeal sacraments by their operation, which they exercise on the body that they touch, accomplish through the Divine institution an instrumental operation on the soul; for example, the water of baptism, in respect of its proper power, cleanses the body, and thereby, inasmuch as it is the instrument of the Divine power, cleanses the soul: since from soul and body one thing is made. And thus it is that Augustine says (*Gen ad lit.* xii) that it *touches the body and cleanses the heart.*

REPLY OBJ. 3: This argument considers that which causes grace as principal agent; for this belongs to God alone, as stated above.

Article 2

Whether Sacramental Grace Confers Anything in Addition to the Grace of the Virtues and Gifts?

AD SECUNDUM SIC PROCEDITUR. Videtur quod gratia sacramentalis non addat aliquid supra gratiam virtutum et donorum. Per gratiam enim virtutum et donorum perficitur anima sufficienter et quantum ad essentiam animae, et quantum ad eius potentias, ut patet ex his quae in secunda parte dicta sunt. Sed gratia ordinatur ad animae perfectionem. Ergo gratia sacramentalis non potest aliquid addere super gratiam virtutum et donorum.

PRAETEREA, defectus animae ex peccatis causantur. Sed omnia peccata sufficienter excluduntur per gratiam virtutum et donorum, quia nullum est peccatum quod non contrarietur alicui virtuti. Gratia ergo sacramentalis, cum ordinetur ad defectus animae tollendos, non potest aliquid addere super gratiam virtutum et donorum.

PRAETEREA, omnis additio vel subtractio in formis variat speciem, ut dicitur in VIII Metaphys. Si igitur gratia sacramentalis addat aliquid super gratiam virtutum et donorum, sequitur quod aequivoce dicatur gratia. Et sic nihil certum ostenditur ex hoc quod sacramenta dicuntur gratiam causare.

SED CONTRA est quod, si gratia sacramentalis non addit aliquid super gratiam donorum et virtutum, frustra sacramenta habentibus et dona et virtutes conferrentur.

OBJECTION 1: It seems that sacramental grace confers nothing in addition to the grace of the virtues and gifts. For the grace of the virtues and gifts perfects the soul sufficiently, both in its essence and in its powers; as is clear from what was said in the Second Part (I-II, Q. 110, AA. 3, 4). But grace is ordained to the perfecting of the soul. Therefore sacramental grace cannot confer anything in addition to the grace of the virtues and gifts.

OBJ. 2: Further, the soul's defects are caused by sin. But all sins are sufficiently removed by the grace of the virtues and gifts: because there is no sin that is not contrary to some virtue. Since, therefore, sacramental grace is ordained to the removal of the soul's defects, it cannot confer anything in addition to the grace of the virtues and gifts.

OBJ. 3: Further, every addition or subtraction of form varies the species (*Metaph.* viii). If, therefore, sacramental grace confers anything in addition to the grace of the virtues and gifts, it follows that it is called grace equivocally: and so we are none the wiser when it is said that the sacraments cause grace.

ON THE CONTRARY, If sacramental grace confers nothing in addition to the grace of the virtues and gifts, it is useless to confer the sacraments on those who have

In operibus autem Dei nihil est frustra. Ergo videtur quod gratia sacramentalis aliquid addat super gratiam virtutum et donorum.

RESPONDEO dicendum quod, sicut in secunda parte dictum est, gratia, secundum se considerata, perficit essentiam animae, inquantum participat quandam similitudinem divini esse. Et sicut ab essentia animae fluunt eius potentiae, ita a gratia fluunt quaedam perfectiones ad potentias animae, quae dicuntur virtutes et dona, quibus potentiae perficiuntur in ordine ad suos actus. Ordinantur autem sacramenta ad quosdam speciales effectus necessarios in vita Christiana, sicut Baptismus ordinatur ad quandam spiritualem regenerationem, qua homo moritur vitiis et fit membrum Christi; qui quidem effectus est aliquid speciale praeter actus potentiarum animae. Et eadem ratio est in aliis sacramentis. Sicut igitur virtutes et dona addunt super gratiam communiter dictam quandam perfectionem determinate ordinatam ad proprios actus potentiarum, ita gratia sacramentalis addit super gratiam communiter dictam, et super virtutes et dona, quoddam divinum auxilium ad consequendum sacramenti finem. Et per hunc modum gratia sacramentalis addit super gratiam virtutum et donorum.

AD PRIMUM ergo dicendum quod gratia virtutum et donorum sufficienter perficit essentiam et potentias animae quantum ad generalem ordinationem actuum. Sed quantum ad quosdam effectus speciales qui requiruntur in Christiana vita, requiritur sacramentalis gratia.

AD SECUNDUM dicendum quod per virtutes et dona sufficienter excluduntur vitia et peccata quantum ad praesens et futurum, inquantum scilicet impeditur homo per virtutes et dona a peccando. Sed quantum ad praeterita peccata, quae transeunt actu et permanent reatu, adhibetur homini remedium specialiter per sacramenta.

AD TERTIUM dicendum quod ratio sacramentalis gratiae se habet ad gratiam communiter dictam sicut ratio speciei ad genus. Unde, sicut non aequivoce dicitur animal communiter dictum et pro homine sumptum, ita non aequivoce dicitur gratia communiter sumpta et gratia sacramentalis.

the virtues and gifts. But there is nothing useless in God's works. Therefore it seems that sacramental grace confers something in addition to the grace of the virtues and gifts.

I ANSWER THAT, As stated in the Second Part (I-II, Q. 110, AA. 3, 4), grace, considered in itself, perfects the essence of the soul, in so far as it is a certain participated likeness of the Divine Nature. And just as the soul's powers flow from its essence, so from grace there flow certain perfections into the powers of the soul, which are called virtues and gifts, whereby the powers are perfected in reference to their actions. Now the sacraments are ordained unto certain special effects which are necessary in the Christian life: thus Baptism is ordained unto a certain spiritual regeneration, by which man dies to vice and becomes a member of Christ: which effect is something special in addition to the actions of the soul's powers: and the same holds true of the other sacraments. Consequently just as the virtues and gifts confer, in addition to grace commonly so called, a certain special perfection ordained to the powers' proper actions, so does sacramental grace confer, over and above grace commonly so called, and in addition to the virtues and gifts, a certain Divine assistance in obtaining the end of the sacrament. It is thus that sacramental grace confers something in addition to the grace of the virtues and gifts.

REPLY OBJ. 1: The grace of the virtues and gifts perfects the essence and powers of the soul sufficiently as regards ordinary conduct: but as regards certain special effects which are necessary in a Christian life, sacramental grace is needed.

REPLY OBJ. 2: Vices and sins are sufficiently removed by virtues and gifts, as to present and future time, in so far as they prevent man from sinning. But in regard to past sins, the acts of which are transitory whereas their guilt remains, man is provided with a special remedy in the sacraments.

REPLY OBJ. 3: Sacramental grace is compared to grace commonly so called, as species to genus. Wherefore just as it is not equivocal to use the term *animal* in its generic sense, and as applied to a man, so neither is it equivocal to speak of grace commonly so called and of sacramental grace.

Article 3

Whether the Sacraments of the New Law Contain Grace?

AD TERTIUM SIC PROCEDITUR. Videtur quod sacramenta novae legis non contineant gratiam. Contentum enim videtur esse in continente. Sed gratia non est in sacramento, neque sicut in subiecto, quia subiectum gratiae non est corpus sed spiritus; neque sicut in vase, quia

OBJECTION 1: It seems that the sacraments of the New Law do not contain grace. For it seems that what is contained is in the container. But grace is not in the sacraments; neither as in a subject, because the subject of grace is not a body but a spirit; nor as in a vessel, for according to

vas est locus mobilis, ut dicitur in IV Physic., esse autem in loco non convenit accidenti. Ergo videtur quod sacramenta novae legis non contineant gratiam.

Praeterea, sacramenta ordinantur ad hoc quod homines per ea gratiam consequantur. Sed gratia, cum sit accidens, non potest transire de subiecto in subiectum. Ergo pro nihilo esset gratia in sacramentis.

Praeterea, spirituale non continetur a corporali, etiam si in eo sit, non enim anima continetur a corpore, sed potius continet corpus. Ergo videtur quod gratia, cum sit quoddam spirituale, non contineatur in sacramento corporali.

Sed contra est quod Hugo de sancto Victore dicit, quod *sacramentum ex sanctificatione invisibilem gratiam continet*.

Respondeo dicendum quod multipliciter dicitur aliquid esse in alio, inter quos duplici modo gratia est in sacramentis. Uno modo, sicut in signis, nam sacramentum est signum gratiae. Alio modo, sicut in causa. Nam, sicut dictum est, sacramentum novae legis est instrumentalis gratiae causa. Unde gratia est in sacramento novae legis, non quidem secundum similitudinem speciei, sicut effectus est in causa univoca; neque etiam secundum aliquam formam propriam et permanentem proportionatam ad talem effectum, sicut sunt effectus in causis non univocis, puta res generatae in sole; sed secundum quandam instrumentalem virtutem, quae est fluens et incompleta in esse naturae, ut infra dicetur.

Ad primum ergo dicendum quod gratia non dicitur esse in sacramento sicut in subiecto; neque sicut in vase prout vas est locus quidam, sed prout vas dicitur instrumentum alicuius operis faciendi, secundum quod dicitur Ezech. IX, *unusquisque vas interfectionis habet in manu sua.*

Ad secundum dicendum quod, quamvis accidens non transeat a subiecto in subiectum, transit tamen a causa per instrumentum aliqualiter in subiectum, non ut eodem modo sit in eis, sed in unoquoque secundum propriam rationem.

Ad tertium dicendum quod spirituale existens perfecte in aliquo, continet ipsum, et non continetur ab eo. Sed gratia est in sacramento secundum esse fluens et incompletum. Et ideo non inconvenienter sacramentum dicitur gratiam continere.

Phys. iv, *a vessel is a movable place*, and an accident cannot be in a place. Therefore it seems that the sacraments of the New Law do not contain grace.

Obj. 2: Further, sacraments are instituted as means whereby men may obtain grace. But since grace is an accident it cannot pass from one subject to another. Therefore it would be of no account if grace were in the sacraments.

Obj. 3: Further, a spiritual thing is not contained by a corporeal, even if it be therein; for the soul is not contained by the body; rather does it contain the body. Since, therefore, grace is something spiritual, it seems that it cannot be contained in a corporeal sacrament.

On the contrary, Hugh of S. Victor says (*De Sacram.* i) that *a sacrament, through its being sanctified, contains an invisible grace.*

I answer that, A thing is said to be in another in various ways; in two of which grace is said to be in the sacraments. First, as in its sign; for a sacrament is a sign of grace. Second, as in its cause; for, as stated above (A. 1) a sacrament of the New Law is an instrumental cause of grace. Wherefore grace is in a sacrament of the New Law, not as to its specific likeness, as an effect in its univocal cause; nor as to some proper and permanent form proportioned to such an effect, as effects in non-univocal causes, for instance, as things generated are in the sun; but as to a certain instrumental power transient and incomplete in its natural being, as will be explained later on (A. 4).

Reply Obj. 1: Grace is said to be in a sacrament not as in its subject; nor as in a vessel considered as a place, but understood as the instrument of some work to be done, according to Ezech. 9:1: *Everyone hath a destroying vessel in his hand.*

Reply Obj. 2: Although an accident does not pass from one subject to another, nevertheless in a fashion it does pass from its cause into its subject through the instrument; not so that it be in each of these in the same way, but in each according to its respective nature.

Reply Obj. 3: If a spiritual thing exist perfectly in something, it contains it and is not contained by it. But, in a sacrament, grace has a passing and incomplete mode of being: and consequently it is not unfitting to say that the sacraments contain grace.

Article 4

Whether There Be in the Sacraments a Power of Causing Grace?

Ad quartum sic proceditur. Videtur quod in sacramentis non sit aliqua virtus gratiae causativa. Virtus enim gratiae causativa est virtus spiritualis. Sed in

Objection 1: It seems that there is not in the sacraments a power of causing grace. For the power of causing grace is a spiritual power. But a spiritual power cannot be

corpore non potest esse virtus spiritualis, neque ita quod sit propria ei, quia virtus fluit ab essentia rei, et ita non potest eam transcendere; neque ita quod recipiat eam ab alio, quia quod recipitur ab aliquo, est in eo per modum recipientis. Ergo in sacramentis non potest esse aliqua virtus gratiae causativa.

PRAETEREA, omne quod est, reducitur ad aliquod genus entis, et ad aliquem gradum boni. Sed non est dare in quo genere entis sit talis virtus, ut patet discurrenti per singula. Nec etiam potest reduci ad aliquem gradum bonorum, neque enim est inter minima bona, quia sacramenta sunt de necessitate salutis; neque etiam inter media bona, cuiusmodi sunt potentiae animae, quae sunt quaedam potentiae naturales; neque inter maxima bona, quia nec est gratia nec virtus mentis. Ergo videtur quod in sacramentis nulla sit virtus gratiae causativa.

PRAETEREA, si talis virtus est in sacramentis, non causatur in eis nisi per creationem a Deo. Sed inconveniens videtur quod tam nobilis creatura statim esse desinat sacramento perfecto. Ergo videtur quod nulla virtus sit in sacramentis ad gratiam causandam.

PRAETEREA, idem non potest esse in diversis. Sed ad sacramenta concurrunt diversa, scilicet verba et res, unius autem sacramenti non potest esse nisi una virtus. Ergo videtur quod in sacramentis nulla sit virtus.

SED CONTRA est quod Augustinus dicit, super Ioan., *quae tanta vis aquae ut corpus tangat et cor abluat?* Et Beda dicit quod *dominus tactu suae mundissimae carnis vim regenerativam contulit aquis.*

RESPONDEO dicendum quod illi qui ponunt quod sacramenta non causant gratiam nisi per quandam concomitantiam, ponunt quod in sacramento non sit aliqua virtus quae operetur ad sacramenti effectum, est tamen virtus divina sacramento coassistens, quae sacramentalem effectum operatur. Sed ponendo quod sacramentum est instrumentalis causa gratiae, necesse est simul ponere quod in sacramento sit quaedam virtus instrumentalis ad inducendum sacramentalem effectum. Et haec quidem virtus proportionatur instrumento. Unde comparatur ad virtutem absolutam et perfectam alicuius rei sicut comparatur instrumentum ad agens principale. Instrumentum enim, ut dictum est, non operatur nisi inquantum est motum a principali agente, quod per se operatur. Et ideo virtus principalis agentis habet permanens et completum esse in natura, virtus autem instrumentalis habet esse transiens ex uno in aliud, et incompletum; sicut et motus est actus imperfectus ab agente in patiens.

AD PRIMUM ergo dicendum quod virtus spiritualis non potest esse in re corporea per modum virtutis permanentis et completae, sicut ratio probat. Nihil tamen

in a body; neither as proper to it, because power flows from a thing's essence and consequently cannot transcend it; nor as derived from something else, because that which is received into anything follows the mode of the recipient. Therefore in the sacraments there is no power of causing grace.

OBJ. 2: Further, whatever exists is reducible to some kind of being and some degree of good. But there is no assignable kind of being to which such a power can belong; as anyone may see by running through them all. Nor is it reducible to some degree of good; for neither is it one of the goods of least account, since sacraments are necessary for salvation: nor is it an intermediate good, such as are the powers of the soul, which are natural powers; nor is it one of the greater goods, for it is neither grace nor a virtue of the mind. Therefore it seems that in the sacraments there is no power of causing grace.

OBJ. 3: Further, if there be such a power in the sacraments, its presence there must be due to nothing less than a creative act of God. But it seems unbecoming that so excellent a being created by God should cease to exist as soon as the sacrament is complete. Therefore it seems that in the sacraments there is no power for causing grace.

OBJ. 4: Further, the same thing cannot be in several. But several things concur in the completion of a sacrament, namely, words and things: while in one sacrament there can be but one power. Therefore it seems that there is no power of causing grace in the sacraments.

ON THE CONTRARY, Augustine says (*Tract. lxxx in Joan.*): *Whence hath water so great power, that it touches the body and cleanses the heart?* And Bede says that *Our Lord conferred a power of regeneration on the waters by the contact of His most pure body.*

I ANSWER THAT, Those who hold that the sacraments do not cause grace save by a certain coincidence, deny the sacraments any power that is itself productive of the sacramental effect, and hold that the Divine power assists the sacraments and produces their effect. But if we hold that a sacrament is an instrumental cause of grace, we must needs allow that there is in the sacraments a certain instrumental power of bringing about the sacramental effects. Now such power is proportionate to the instrument: and consequently it stands in comparison to the complete and perfect power of anything, as the instrument to the principal agent. For an instrument, as stated above (A. 1), does not work save as moved by the principal agent, which works of itself. And therefore the power of the principal agent exists in nature completely and perfectly: whereas the instrumental power has a being that passes from one thing into another, and is incomplete; just as motion is an imperfect act passing from agent to patient.

REPLY OBJ. 1: A spiritual power cannot be in a corporeal subject, after the manner of a permanent and complete power, as the argument proves. But there is nothing

prohibet in corpore esse virtutem spiritualem instrumentalem, inquantum scilicet corpus potest moveri ab aliqua substantia spirituali ad aliquem effectum spiritualem inducendum; sicut etiam in ipsa voce sensibili est quaedam vis spiritualis ad excitandum intellectum hominis, inquantum procedit a conceptione mentis. Et hoc modo vis spiritualis est in sacramentis, inquantum ordinantur a Deo ad effectum spiritualem.

AD SECUNDUM dicendum quod, sicut motus, eo quod est actus imperfectus, non proprie est in aliquo genere, sed reducitur ad genus actus perfecti, sicut alteratio ad qualitatem, ita virtus instrumentalis non est, proprie loquendo, in aliquo genere, sed reducitur ad genus et speciem virtutis perfectae.

AD TERTIUM dicendum quod, sicut virtus instrumentalis acquiritur instrumento ex hoc ipso quod movetur ab agente principali, ita et sacramentum consequitur spiritualem virtutem ex benedictione Christi et applicatione ministri ad usum sacramenti. Unde Augustinus dicit, in quodam sermone de Epiphania, *nec mirum quod aquam, hoc est substantiam corporalem, ad purificandam animam dicimus pervenire. Pervenit plane, et penetrat conscientiae universa latibula. Quamvis enim ipsa sit subtilis et tenuis, benedictione tamen Christi subtilior, occultas vitae causas ad secreta mentis subtili rore pertransit.*

AD QUARTUM dicendum quod, sicut eadem vis principalis agentis instrumentaliter invenitur in omnibus instrumentis ordinatis ad effectum, prout sunt quodam ordine unum; ita etiam eadem vis sacramentalis invenitur in verbis et rebus, prout ex verbis et rebus perficitur unum sacramentum.

to hinder an instrumental spiritual power from being in a body; in so far as a body can be moved by a particular spiritual substance so as to produce a particular spiritual effect; thus in the very voice which is perceived by the senses there is a certain spiritual power, inasmuch as it proceeds from a mental concept, of arousing the mind of the hearer. It is in this way that a spiritual power is in the sacraments, inasmuch as they are ordained by God unto the production of a spiritual effect.

REPLY OBJ. 2: Just as motion, through being an imperfect act, is not properly in a genus, but is reducible to a genus of perfect act, for instance, alteration to the genus of quality: so, instrumental power, properly speaking, is not in any genus, but is reducible to a genus and species of perfect act.

REPLY OBJ. 3: Just as an instrumental power accrues to an instrument through its being moved by the principal agent, so does a sacrament receive spiritual power from Christ's blessing and from the action of the minister in applying it to a sacramental use. Hence Augustine says in a sermon on the Epiphany (*St. Maximus of Turin*, Serm. xii): *Nor should you marvel, if we say that water, a corporeal substance, achieves the cleansing of the soul. It does indeed, and penetrates every secret hiding-place of the conscience. For subtle and clear as it is, the blessing of Christ makes it yet more subtle, so that it permeates into the very principles of life and searches the innermost recesses of the heart.*

REPLY OBJ. 4: Just as the one same power of the principal agent is instrumentally in all the instruments that are ordained unto the production of an effect, forasmuch as they are one as being so ordained: so also the one same sacramental power is in both words and things, forasmuch as words and things combine to form one sacrament.

Article 5

Whether the Sacraments of the New Law Derive Their Power from Christ's Passion?

AD QUINTUM SIC PROCEDITUR. Videtur quod sacramenta novae legis non habeant virtutem ex passione Christi. Virtus enim sacramentorum est ad gratiam causandam in anima, per quam spiritualiter vivit. Sed, sicut Augustinus dicit, super Ioan., *verbum prout erat in principio apud Deum, vivificat animas, secundum autem quod est caro factum, vivificat corpora.* Cum igitur passio Christi pertineat ad verbum secundum quod est caro factum, videtur quod non possit causare virtutem sacramentorum.

PRAETEREA, virtus sacramentorum videtur ex fide dependere, quia, sicut Augustinus dicit, super Ioan., verbum Dei perficit sacramentum, non quia dicitur, sed quia creditur. Sed fides nostra non solum respicit

OBJECTION 1: It seems that the sacraments of the New Law do not derive their power from Christ's Passion. For the power of the sacraments is in the causing of grace which is the principle of spiritual life in the soul. But as Augustine says (*Tract. xix in Joan.*): *The Word, as He was in the beginning with God, quickens souls; as He was made flesh, quickens bodies.* Since, therefore, Christ's Passion pertains to the Word as made flesh, it seems that it cannot cause the power of the sacraments.

OBJ. 2: Further, the power of the sacraments seems to depend on faith; for as Augustine says (*Tract. lxxx in Joan.*), the Divine Word perfects the sacrament *not because it is spoken, but because it is believed.* But our faith regards

passionem Christi, sed etiam alia mysteria humanitatis ipsius, et principalius etiam divinitatem eius. Ergo videtur quod sacramenta non habeant specialiter virtutem a passione Christi.

PRAETEREA, sacramenta ordinantur ad hominum iustificationem, secundum illud I Cor. VI, *abluti estis, et iustificati estis*. Sed iustificatio attribuitur resurrectioni, secundum illud Rom. IV, *resurrexit propter iustificationem nostram*. Ergo videtur quod sacramenta magis habeant virtutem a resurrectione Christi quam ab eius passione.

SED CONTRA est quod, super illud Rom. V, *in similitudinem praevaricationis Adae* etc., dicit Glossa, *ex latere Christi dormientis fluxerunt sacramenta, per quae salvata est Ecclesia*. Sic ergo videntur sacramenta virtutem habere ex passione Christi.

RESPONDEO dicendum quod, sicut dictum est, sacramentum operatur ad gratiam causandam per modum instrumenti. Est autem duplex instrumentum, unum quidem separatum, ut baculus; aliud autem coniunctum, ut manus. Per instrumentum autem coniunctum movetur instrumentum separatum, sicut baculus per manum. Principalis autem causa efficiens gratiae est ipse Deus, ad quem comparatur humanitas Christi sicut instrumentum coniunctum, sacramentum autem sicut instrumentum separatum. Et ideo oportet quod virtus salutifera derivetur a divinitate Christi per eius humanitatem in ipsa sacramenta.

Gratia autem sacramentalis ad duo praecipue ordinari videtur, videlicet ad tollendos defectus praeteritorum peccatorum, inquantum transeunt actu et remanent reatu; et iterum ad perficiendum animam in his quae pertinent ad cultum Dei secundum religionem Christianae vitae. Manifestum est autem ex his quae supra dicta sunt, quod Christus liberavit nos a peccatis nostris praecipue per suam passionem, non solum efficienter et meritorie, sed etiam satisfactorie. Similiter etiam per suam passionem initiavit ritum Christianae religionis, *offerens seipsum oblationem et hostiam Deo*, ut dicitur Ephes. V. Unde manifestum est quod sacramenta Ecclesiae specialiter habent virtutem ex passione Christi, cuius virtus quodammodo nobis copulatur per susceptionem sacramentorum. In cuius signum, de latere Christi pendentis in cruce fluxerunt aqua et sanguis, quorum unum pertinet ad Baptismum, aliud ad Eucharistiam, quae sunt potissima sacramenta.

AD PRIMUM ergo dicendum quod verbum prout erat in principio apud Deum, vivificat animas sicut agens principale, caro tamen eius, et mysteria in ea perpetrata, operantur instrumentaliter ad animae vitam. Ad vitam autem corporis non solum instrumentaliter, sed etiam per quandam exemplaritatem, ut supra dictum est.

not only Christ's Passion, but also the other mysteries of His humanity, and in a yet higher measure, His Godhead. Therefore it seems that the power of the sacraments is not due specially to Christ's Passion.

OBJ. 3: Further, the sacraments are ordained unto man's justification, according to 1 Cor. 6:11: *You are washed . . . you are justified*. Now justification is ascribed to the Resurrection, according to Rom. 4:25: *(Who) rose again for our justification*. Therefore it seems that the sacraments derive their power from Christ's Resurrection rather than from His Passion.

ON THE CONTRARY, on Rom. 5:14: *After the similitude of the transgression of Adam*, etc., the gloss says: *From the side of Christ asleep on the Cross flowed the sacraments which brought salvation to the Church*. Consequently, it seems that the sacraments derive their power from Christ's Passion.

I ANSWER THAT, As stated above (A. 1) a sacrament in causing grace works after the manner of an instrument. Now an instrument is twofold; the one, separate, as a stick, for instance; the other, united, as a hand. Moreover, the separate instrument is moved by means of the united instrument, as a stick by the hand. Now the principal efficient cause of grace is God Himself, in comparison with Whom Christ's humanity is as a united instrument, whereas the sacrament is as a separate instrument. Consequently, the saving power must needs be derived by the sacraments from Christ's Godhead through His humanity.

Now sacramental grace seems to be ordained principally to two things: namely, to take away the defects consequent on past sins, in so far as they are transitory in act, but endure in guilt; and, further, to perfect the soul in things pertaining to Divine Worship in regard to the Christian Religion. But it is manifest from what has been stated above (Q. 48, AA. 1, 2, 6; Q. 49, AA. 1, 3) that Christ delivered us from our sins principally through His Passion, not only by way of efficiency and merit, but also by way of satisfaction. Likewise by His Passion He inaugurated the Rites of the Christian Religion by offering *Himself—an oblation and a sacrifice to God* (Eph 5:2). Wherefore it is manifest that the sacraments of the Church derive their power specially from Christ's Passion, the virtue of which is in a manner united to us by our receiving the sacraments. It was in sign of this that from the side of Christ hanging on the Cross there flowed water and blood, the former of which belongs to Baptism, the latter to the Eucharist, which are the principal sacraments.

REPLY OBJ. 1: The Word, forasmuch as He was in the beginning with God, quickens souls as principal agent; but His flesh, and the mysteries accomplished therein, are as instrumental causes in the process of giving life to the soul: while in giving life to the body they act not only as instrumental causes, but also to a certain extent as exemplars, as we stated above (Q. 56, A. 1, ad 3).

AD SECUNDUM dicendum quod per fidem Christus habitat in nobis, ut dicitur Ephes. III. Et ideo virtus Christi copulatur nobis per fidem. Virtus autem remissiva peccatorum speciali quodam modo pertinet ad passionem ipsius. Et ideo per fidem passionis eius specialiter homines liberantur a peccatis, secundum illud Rom. III, *quem proposuit Deus propitiatorem per fidem in sanguine eius.* Et ideo virtus sacramentorum, quae ordinatur ad tollendum peccata, praecipue est ex fide passionis Christi.

AD TERTIUM dicendum quod iustificatio attribuitur resurrectioni ratione termini ad quem, qui est novitas vitae per gratiam. Attribuitur tamen passioni ratione termini a quo, scilicet quantum ad dimissionem culpae.

REPLY OBJ. 2: Christ dwells in us *by faith* (Eph 3:17). Consequently, by faith Christ's power is united to us. Now the power of blotting out sin belongs in a special way to His Passion. And therefore men are delivered from sin especially by faith in His Passion, according to Rom. 3:25: *Whom God hath proposed to be a propitiation through faith in His Blood.* Therefore the power of the sacraments which is ordained unto the remission of sins is derived principally from faith in Christ's Passion.

REPLY OBJ. 3: Justification is ascribed to the Resurrection by reason of the term *whither*, which is newness of life through grace. But it is ascribed to the Passion by reason of the term *whence*, i.e., in regard to the forgiveness of sin.

Article 6

Whether the Sacraments of the Old Law Caused Grace?

AD SEXTUM SIC PROCEDITUR. Videtur quod sacramenta veteris legis gratiam causarent. Quia sicut dictum est, sacramenta novae legis habent efficaciam ex fide passionis Christi. Sed fides passionis Christi fuit in veteri lege, sicut et in nova, *habemus enim eundem spiritum fidei,* ut habetur II Cor. IV. Sicut ergo sacramenta novae legis conferunt gratiam, ita etiam sacramenta veteris legis gratiam conferebant.

PRAETEREA, sanctificatio non fit nisi per gratiam. Sed per sacramenta veteris legis homines sanctificabantur, dicitur enim Levit. VIII, cumque sanctificasset eos, Moyses scilicet Aaron et filios eius, in vestitu suo, et cetera. Ergo videtur quod sacramenta veteris legis gratiam conferebant.

PRAETEREA, Beda dicit, in homilia circumcisionis, *idem salutiferae curationis auxilium circumcisio in lege contra originalis peccati vulnus agebat quod Baptismus agere revelatae tempore gratiae consuevit.* Sed Baptismus nunc confert gratiam. Ergo circumcisio gratiam conferebat. Et pari ratione alia sacramenta legalia, quia sicut Baptismus est ianua sacramentorum novae legis, ita circumcisio erat ianua sacramentorum veteris legis; propter quod apostolus dicit, Galat. V, *testificor omni circumcidenti se, quoniam debitor est universae legis faciendae.*

SED CONTRA est quod dicitur Galat. IV, *convertimini iterum ad infirma et egena elementa?* Glossa, *idest ad legem, quae dicitur infirma, quia perfecte non iustificat.* Sed gratia perfecte iustificat. Ergo sacramenta veteris legis gratiam non conferebant.

RESPONDEO dicendum quod non potest dici quod sacramenta veteris legis conferrent gratiam iustificantem per seipsa, idest propria virtute, quia sic non fuisset

OBJECTION 1: It seems that the sacraments of the Old Law caused grace. For, as stated above (A. 5, ad 2) the sacraments of the New Law derive their efficacy from faith in Christ's Passion. But there was faith in Christ's Passion under the Old Law, as well as under the New, since we have *the same spirit of faith* (2 Cor 4:13). Therefore just as the sacraments of the New Law confer grace, so did the sacraments of the Old Law.

OBJ. 2: Further, there is no sanctification save by grace. But men were sanctified by the sacraments of the Old Law: for it is written (Lev 8:31): *And when he,* i.e., Moses, *had sanctified them,* i.e., Aaron and his sons, *in their vestments,* etc. Therefore it seems that the sacraments of the Old Law conferred grace.

OBJ. 3: Further, Bede says in a homily on the Circumcision: *Under the Law circumcision provided the same health-giving balm against the wound of original sin, as baptism in the time of revealed grace.* But Baptism confers grace now. Therefore circumcision conferred grace; and in like manner, the other sacraments of the Law; for just as Baptism is the door of the sacraments of the New Law, so was circumcision the door of the sacraments of the Old Law: hence the Apostle says (Gal 5:3): *I testify to every man circumcising himself, that he is a debtor to the whole law.*

ON THE CONTRARY, It is written (Gal 4:9): *Turn you again to the weak and needy elements?* i.e., *to the Law,* says the gloss, *which is called weak, because it does not justify perfectly.* But grace justifies perfectly. Therefore the sacraments of the old Law did not confer grace.

I ANSWER THAT, It cannot be said that the sacraments of the Old Law conferred sanctifying grace of themselves, i.e., by their own power: since thus Christ's Passion would

necessaria passio Christi, secundum illud Galat. II, *si ex lege est iustitia, Christus gratis mortuus est.*

Sed nec potest dici quod ex passione Christi virtutem haberent conferendi gratiam iustificandi. Sicut enim ex praedictis patet, virtus passionis Christi copulatur nobis per fidem et sacramenta, differenter tamen, nam continuatio quae est per fidem, fit per actum animae; continuatio autem quae est per sacramenta, fit per usum exteriorum rerum. Nihil autem prohibet id quod est posterius tempore, antequam sit, movere, secundum quod praecedit in actu animae, sicut finis, qui est posterior tempore, movet agentem secundum quod est apprehensus et desideratus ab ipso. Sed illud quod nondum est in rerum natura, non movet secundum usum exteriorum rerum. Unde causa efficiens non potest esse posterior in esse, ordine durationis, sicut causa finalis. Sic igitur manifestum est quod a passione Christi, quae est causa humanae iustificationis, convenienter derivatur virtus iustificativa ad sacramenta novae legis, non autem ad sacramenta veteris legis.

Et tamen per fidem passionis Christi iustificabantur antiqui patres, sicut et nos. Sacramenta autem veteris legis erant quaedam illius fidei protestationes, inquantum significabant passionem Christi et effectus eius. Sic ergo patet quod sacramenta veteris legis non habebant in se aliquam virtutem qua operarentur ad conferendam gratiam iustificantem, sed solum significabant fidem, per quam iustificabantur.

AD PRIMUM ergo dicendum quod antiqui patres habebant fidem de passione Christi futura, quae, secundum quod erat in apprehensione animae, poterat iustificare. Sed nos habemus fidem de passione Christi praecedenti, quae potest iustificare etiam secundum realem usum sacramentalium rerum, ut dictum est.

AD SECUNDUM dicendum quod illa sanctificatio erat figuralis, per hoc enim sanctificari dicebantur quod applicabantur cultui divino secundum ritum veteris legis, qui totus ordinabatur ad figurandum passionem Christi.

AD TERTIUM dicendum quod de circumcisione multiplex fuit opinio. Quidam enim dixerunt quod per circumcisionem non conferebatur gratia, sed solum auferebatur peccatum. Sed hoc non potest esse, quia homo non iustificatur a peccato nisi per gratiam, secundum illud Rom. III, *iustificati gratis per gratiam ipsius.*

Et ideo alii dixerunt quod per circumcisionem conferebatur gratia quantum ad effectus remotivos culpae, sed non quantum ad effectus positivos. Sed hoc etiam videtur esse falsum. Quia per circumcisionem dabatur pueris facultas perveniendi ad gloriam, quae est ultimus effectus positivus gratiae. Et praeterea, secundum ordinem causae formalis, priores sunt naturaliter effectus

not have been necessary, according to Gal. 2:21: *If justice be by the Law, then Christ died in vain.*

But neither can it be said that they derived the power of conferring sanctifying grace from Christ's Passion. For as it was stated above (A. 5), the power of Christ's Passion is united to us by faith and the sacraments, but in different ways; because the link that comes from faith is produced by an act of the soul; whereas the link that comes from the sacraments, is produced by making use of exterior things. Now nothing hinders that which is subsequent in point of time, from causing movement, even before it exists in reality, in so far as it pre-exists in an act of the soul: thus the end, which is subsequent in point of time, moves the agent in so far as it is apprehended and desired by him. On the other hand, what does not yet actually exist, does not cause movement if we consider the use of exterior things. Consequently, the efficient cause cannot in point of time come into existence after causing movement, as does the final cause. It is therefore clear that the sacraments of the New Law do reasonably derive the power of justification from Christ's Passion, which is the cause of man's righteousness; whereas the sacraments of the Old Law did not.

Nevertheless the Fathers of old were justified by faith in Christ's Passion, just as we are. And the sacraments of the old Law were a kind of protestation of that faith, inasmuch as they signified Christ's Passion and its effects. It is therefore manifest that the sacraments of the Old Law were not endowed with any power by which they conduced to the bestowal of justifying grace: and they merely signified faith by which men were justified.

REPLY OBJ. 1: The Fathers of old had faith in the future Passion of Christ, which, inasmuch as it was apprehended by the mind, was able to justify them. But we have faith in the past Passion of Christ, which is able to justify, also by the real use of sacramental things as stated above.

REPLY OBJ. 2: That sanctification was but a figure: for they were said to be sanctified forasmuch as they gave themselves up to the Divine worship according to the rite of the Old Law, which was wholly ordained to the foreshadowing of Christ's Passion.

REPLY OBJ. 3: There have been many opinions about Circumcision. For, according to some, Circumcision conferred no grace, but only remitted sin. But this is impossible; because man is not justified from sin save by grace, according to Rom. 3:24: *Being justified freely by His grace.*

Wherefore others said that by Circumcision grace is conferred, as to the privative effects of sin, but not as to its positive effects. But this also appears to be false, because by Circumcision, children received the faculty of obtaining glory, which is the ultimate positive effect of grace. Moreover, as regards the order of the formal cause, positive effects are naturally prior to privative effects, though

positivi quam privativi, licet secundum ordinem causae materialis sit e converso, forma enim non excludit privationem nisi informando subiectum.

Et ideo alii dicunt quod circumcisio conferebat gratiam etiam quantum ad aliquem effectum positivum, qui est facere dignum vita aeterna, non tamen quantum ad hoc quod est reprimere concupiscentiam impellentem ad peccandum. Quod aliquando mihi visum est. Sed diligentius consideranti apparet hoc etiam non esse verum, quia minima gratia potest resistere cuilibet concupiscentiae et mereri vitam aeternam.

Et ideo melius dicendum videtur quod circumcisio erat signum fidei iustificantis, unde apostolus dicit, Rom. IV, quod *Abraham accepit signum circumcisionis, signaculum iustitiae fidei*. Et ideo in circumcisione conferebatur gratia inquantum erat signum passionis Christi futurae, ut infra patebit.

according to the order of the material cause, the reverse is the case: for a form does not exclude privation save by informing the subject.

Hence others say that Circumcision conferred grace also as regards a certain positive effect, i.e., by making man worthy of eternal life, but not so as to repress concupiscence which makes man prone to sin. And so at one time it seemed to me. But if the matter be considered carefully, this too appears to be untrue; because the very least grace is sufficient to resist any degree of concupiscence, and to merit eternal life.

And therefore it seems better to say that Circumcision was a sign of justifying faith: wherefore the Apostle says (Rom 4:11) that Abraham *received the sign of Circumcision, a seal of the justice of faith*. Consequently grace was conferred in Circumcision in so far as it was a sign of Christ's future Passion, as will be made clear further on (Q. 70, A. 4).

QUESTION 63

THE OTHER EFFECT OF THE SACRAMENTS, WHICH IS A CHARACTER

Deinde considerandum est de alio effectu sacramentorum, qui est character. Et circa hoc quaeruntur sex.

Primo, utrum ex sacramentis causetur character aliquis in anima.

Secundo, quid sit ille character.

Tertio, cuius sit character.

Quarto, in quo sit sicut in subiecto.

Quinto, utrum insit indelebiliter.

Sexto, utrum omnia sacramenta imprimant characterem.

We have now to consider the other effect of the sacraments, which is a character: and concerning this there are six points of inquiry:

(1) Whether by the sacraments a character is produced in the soul?

(2) What is this character?

(3) Of whom is this character?

(4) What is its subject?

(5) Is it indelible?

(6) Whether every sacrament imprints a character?

Article 1

Whether a Sacrament Imprints a Character on the Soul?

AD PRIMUM SIC PROCEDITUR. Videtur quod sacramentum non imprimat aliquem characterem in anima. Character enim significare videtur quoddam signum distinctivum. Sed distinctio membrorum Christi ab aliis fit per aeternam praedestinationem, quae non ponit aliquid in praedestinato, sed solum in Deo praedestinante, ut in prima parte habitum est, dicitur enim II ad Tim. II, *firmum fundamentum Dei stat, habens signaculum hoc, novit dominus qui sunt eius.* Ergo sacramenta non imprimunt characterem in anima.

PRAETEREA, character signum est distinctivum. Signum autem, ut Augustinus dicit, in II de Doct. Christ., *est quod, praeter speciem quam ingerit sensibus, facit aliquid aliud in cognitionem venire.* Nihil autem est in anima quod aliquam speciem sensibus ingerat. Ergo videtur quod in anima non imprimatur aliquis character per sacramenta.

PRAETEREA, sicut per sacramenta novae legis distinguitur fidelis ab infideli, ita etiam per sacramenta veteris legis. Sed sacramenta veteris legis non imprimebant aliquem characterem, unde et dicuntur iustitiae carnis, secundum apostolum, ad Heb. IX. Ergo videtur quod nec sacramenta novae legis.

SED CONTRA est quod apostolus dicit, II Cor. I, *qui unxit nos, Deus est, et qui signavit nos, et dedit pignus spiritus in cordibus nostris.* Sed nihil aliud importat character quam quandam signationem. Ergo videtur quod Deus per sacramenta nobis suum characterem imprimat.

OBJECTION 1: It seems that a sacrament does not imprint a character on the soul. For the word *character* seems to signify some kind of distinctive sign. But Christ's members are distinguished from others by eternal predestination, which does not imply anything in the predestined, but only in God predestinating, as we have stated in the First Part (Q. 23, A. 2). For it is written (2 Tim 2:19): *The sure foundation of God standeth firm, having this seal: The Lord knoweth who are His.* Therefore the sacraments do not imprint a character on the soul.

OBJ. 2: Further, a character is a distinctive sign. Now a sign, as Augustine says (*De Doctr. Christ.* ii) *is that which conveys something else to the mind, besides the species which it impresses on the senses.* But nothing in the soul can impress a species on the senses. Therefore it seems that no character is imprinted on the soul by the sacraments.

OBJ. 3: Further, just as the believer is distinguished from the unbeliever by the sacraments of the New Law, so was it under the Old Law. But the sacraments of the Old Law did not imprint a character; whence they are called *justices of the flesh* (Heb 9:10) by the Apostle. Therefore neither seemingly do the sacraments of the New Law.

ON THE CONTRARY, The Apostle says (2 Cor 1:21, 22): *He . . . that hath anointed us is God; Who also hath sealed us, and given the pledge of the spirit in our hearts.* But a character means nothing else than a kind of sealing. Therefore it seems that by the sacraments God imprints His character on us.

RESPONDEO dicendum quod, sicut ex praedictis patet, sacramenta novae legis ad duo ordinantur, videlicet ad remedium contra peccata; et ad perficiendum animam in his quae pertinent ad cultum Dei secundum ritum Christianae vitae. Quicumque autem ad aliquid certum deputatur, consuevit ad illud consignari, sicut milites qui adscribebantur ad militiam antiquitus solebant aliquibus characteribus corporalibus insigniri, eo quod deputabantur ad aliquid corporale. Et ideo, cum homines per sacramenta deputentur ad aliquid spirituale pertinens ad cultum Dei, consequens est quod per ea fideles aliquo spirituali charactere insigniantur. Unde Augustinus dicit, in II contra Parmenianum, *si militiae characterem in corpore suo non militans pavidus exhorruerit, et ad clementiam imperatoris confugerit, ac, prece fusa et venia impetrata, militare iam coeperit, nunquid, homine liberato atque correcto, character ille repetitur, ac non potius agnitus approbatur? An forte minus haerent sacramenta Christiana quam corporalis haec nota?*

AD PRIMUM ergo dicendum quod fideles Christi ad praemium quidem futurae gloriae deputantur signaculo praedestinationis divinae. Sed ad actus convenientes praesenti Ecclesiae deputantur quodam spirituali signaculo eis insignito, quod character nuncupatur.

AD SECUNDUM dicendum quod character animae impressus habet rationem signi inquantum per sensibile sacramentum imprimitur, per hoc enim scitur aliquis baptismali charactere insignitus, quod est ablutus aqua sensibili. Nihilominus tamen character, vel signaculum, dici potest per quandam similitudinem omne quod figurat alicui, vel distinguit ab alio, etiam si non sit sensibile, sicut Christus dicitur figura vel character paternae substantiae, secundum apostolum, Heb. I.

AD TERTIUM dicendum quod, sicut supra dictum est, sacramenta veteris legis non habebant in se spiritualem virtutem ad aliquem spiritualem effectum operantem. Et ideo in illis sacramentis non requirebatur aliquis spiritualis character, sed sufficiebat ibi corporalis circumcisio, quam apostolus signaculum nominat, Rom. IV.

I ANSWER THAT, As is clear from what has been already stated (Q. 62, A. 5) the sacraments of the New Law are ordained for a twofold purpose; namely, for a remedy against sins; and for the perfecting of the soul in things pertaining to the Divine worship according to the rite of the Christian life. Now whenever anyone is deputed to some definite purpose he is wont to receive some outward sign thereof; thus in olden times soldiers who enlisted in the ranks used to be marked with certain characters on the body, through being deputed to a bodily service. Since, therefore, by the sacraments men are deputed to a spiritual service pertaining to the worship of God, it follows that by their means the faithful receive a certain spiritual character. Wherefore Augustine says (*Contra Parmen.* ii): *If a deserter from the battle, through dread of the mark of enlistment on his body, throws himself on the emperor's clemency, and having besought and received mercy, return to the fight; is that character renewed, when the man has been set free and reprimanded? Is it not rather acknowledged and approved? Are the Christian sacraments, by any chance, of a nature less lasting than this bodily mark?*

REPLY OBJ. 1: The faithful of Christ are destined to the reward of the glory that is to come, by the seal of Divine Predestination. But they are deputed to acts becoming the Church that is now, by a certain spiritual seal that is set on them, and is called a character.

REPLY OBJ. 2: The character imprinted on the soul is a kind of sign in so far as it is imprinted by a sensible sacrament: since we know that a certain one has received the baptismal character, through his being cleansed by the sensible water. Nevertheless from a kind of likeness, anything that assimilates one thing to another, or discriminates one thing from another, even though it be not sensible, can be called a character or a seal; thus the Apostle calls Christ *the figure* or character *of the substance of the Father* (Heb 1:3).

REPLY OBJ. 3: As stated above (Q. 62, A. 6) the sacraments of the Old Law had not in themselves any spiritual power of producing a spiritual effect. Consequently in those sacraments there was no need of a spiritual character, and bodily circumcision sufficed, which the Apostle calls *a seal* (Rom 4:11).

Article 2

Whether a Character Is a Spiritual Power?

AD SECUNDUM SIC PROCEDITUR. Videtur quod character non sit spiritualis potestas. Character enim idem videtur esse quod figura, unde ad Heb. I, ubi dicitur, figura substantiae eius, in Graeco habetur loco figurae character. Sed figura est in quarta specie qualitatis, et

OBJECTION 1: It seems that a character is not a spiritual power. For *character* seems to be the same thing as *figure*; hence (Heb 1:3), where we read *figure of His substance*, for *figure* the Greek has charakter. Now *figure* is in the fourth species of quality, and thus differs from power which is in

ita differt a potestate, quae est in secunda specie qualitatis. Character ergo non est spiritualis potestas.

PRAETEREA, Dionysius dicit, II cap. Eccles. Hier., quod *divina beatitudo accedentem ad beatitudinem in sui participationem recipit, et proprio lumine, quasi quodam signo, ipsi tradit suam participationem.* Et sic videtur quod character sit quoddam lumen. Sed lumen pertinet magis ad tertiam speciem qualitatis. Non ergo character est potestas, quae videtur ad secundam speciem qualitatis pertinere.

PRAETEREA, a quibusdam character sic definitur, *character est signum sanctum communionis fidei et sanctae ordinationis, datum a hierarcha.* Signum autem est in genere relationis, non autem in genere potestatis. Non ergo character est spiritualis potestas.

PRAETEREA, potestas habet rationem causae et principii, ut patet in V Metaphys. Sed signum, quod ponitur in definitione characteris, magis pertinet ad rationem effectus. Character ergo non est spiritualis potestas.

SED CONTRA, philosophus dicit, in II Ethic., *tria sunt in anima, potentia, habitus et passio.* Sed character non est passio, quia passio cito transit, character autem indelebilis est, ut infra dicetur. Similiter etiam non est habitus. Quia nullus habitus est qui se possit ad bene et male habere. Character autem ad utrumque se habet, utuntur enim eo quidam bene, alii vero male. Quod in habitibus non contingit, nam habitu virtutis nullus utitur male, habitu malitiae nullus bene. Ergo relinquitur quod character sit potentia.

RESPONDEO dicendum quod, sicut dictum est, sacramenta novae legis characterem imprimunt inquantum per ea deputamur ad cultum Dei secundum ritum Christianae religionis. Unde Dionysius, in II cap. Eccles. Hier., cum dixisset quod Deus quodam signo tradit sui participationem accedenti, subiungit, perficiens eum divinum et communicatorem divinorum. Divinus autem cultus consistit vel in recipiendo aliqua divina, vel in tradendo aliis. Ad utrumque autem horum requiritur quaedam potentia, nam ad tradendum aliquid aliis, requiritur potentia activa; ad recipiendum autem requiritur potentia passiva. Et ideo character importat quandam potentiam spiritualem ordinatam ad ea quae sunt divini cultus.

Sciendum tamen quod haec spiritualis potentia est instrumentalis, sicut supra dictum est de virtute quae est in sacramentis. Habere enim sacramenti characterem competit ministris Dei, minister autem habet se per modum instrumenti, ut philosophus dicit, in I Polit. Et ideo, sicut virtus quae est in sacramentis, non est in genere per se, sed per reductionem, eo quod est quiddam fluens et incompletum; ita etiam character non proprie est in genere vel specie, sed reducitur ad secundam speciem qualitatis.

the second species. Therefore character is not a spiritual power.

OBJ. 2: Further, Dionysius says (*Eccl. Hier.* ii): *The Divine Beatitude admits him that seeks happiness to a share in Itself, and grants this share to him by conferring on him Its light as a kind of seal.* Consequently, it seems that a character is a kind of light. Now light belongs rather to the third species of quality. Therefore a character is not a power, since this seems to belong to the second species.

OBJ. 3: Further, character is defined by some thus: *A character is a holy sign of the communion of faith and of the holy ordination conferred by a hierarch.* Now a sign is in the genus of relation, not of power. Therefore a character is not a spiritual power.

OBJ. 4: Further, a power is in the nature of a cause and principle (*Metaph.* v). But a sign which is set down in the definition of a character is rather in the nature of an effect. Therefore a character is not a spiritual power.

ON THE CONTRARY, The Philosopher says (*Ethic.* ii): *There are three things in the soul, power, habit, and passion.* Now a character is not a passion: since a passion passes quickly, whereas a character is indelible, as will be made clear further on (A. 5). In like manner it is not a habit: because no habit is indifferent to acting well or ill: whereas a character is indifferent to either, since some use it well, some ill. Now this cannot occur with a habit: because no one abuses a habit of virtue, or uses well an evil habit. It remains, therefore, that a character is a power.

I ANSWER THAT, As stated above (A. 1), the sacraments of the New Law produce a character, in so far as by them we are deputed to the worship of God according to the rite of the Christian religion. Wherefore Dionysius (*Eccl. Hier.* ii), after saying that God *by a kind of sign grants a share of Himself to those that approach Him*, adds *by making them Godlike and communicators of Divine gifts.* Now the worship of God consists either in receiving Divine gifts, or in bestowing them on others. And for both these purposes some power is needed; for to bestow something on others, active power is necessary; and in order to receive, we need a passive power. Consequently, a character signifies a certain spiritual power ordained unto things pertaining to the Divine worship.

But it must be observed that this spiritual power is instrumental: as we have stated above (Q. 62, A. 4) of the virtue which is in the sacraments. For to have a sacramental character belongs to God's ministers: and a minister is a kind of instrument, as the Philosopher says (*Polit.* i). Consequently, just as the virtue which is in the sacraments is not of itself in a genus, but is reducible to a genus, for the reason that it is of a transitory and incomplete nature: so also a character is not properly in a genus or species, but is reducible to the second species of quality.

AD PRIMUM ergo dicendum quod figuratio est quaedam terminatio quantitatis. Unde, proprie loquendo, non est nisi in rebus corporeis, in spiritualibus autem dicitur metaphorice. Non autem ponitur aliquid in genere vel specie nisi per id quod de eo proprie praedicatur. Et ideo character non potest esse in quarta specie qualitatis, licet hoc quidam posuerint.

AD SECUNDUM dicendum quod in tertia specie qualitatis non sunt nisi sensibiles passiones, vel sensibiles qualitates. Character autem non est lumen sensibile. Et ita non est in tertia specie qualitatis, ut quidam dixerunt.

AD TERTIUM dicendum quod relatio quae importatur in nomine signi, oportet quod super aliquid fundetur. Non autem relatio huius signi quod est character, potest fundari immediate super essentiam animae, quia sic conveniret omni animae naturaliter. Et ideo oportet aliquid poni in anima super quod fundetur talis relatio. Et hoc est essentia characteris. Unde non oportebit quod sit in genere relationis, sicut quidam posuerunt.

AD QUARTUM dicendum quod character habet rationem signi per comparationem ad sacramentum sensibile a quo imprimitur. Sed secundum se consideratus, habet rationem principii, per modum iam dictum.

REPLY OBJ. 1: Configuration is a certain boundary of quantity. Wherefore, properly speaking, it is only in corporeal things; and of spiritual things is said metaphorically. Now that which decides the genus or species of a thing must needs be predicated of it properly. Consequently, a character cannot be in the fourth species of quality, although some have held this to be the case.

REPLY OBJ. 2: The third species of quality contains only sensible passions or sensible qualities. Now a character is not a sensible light. Consequently, it is not in the third species of quality as some have maintained.

REPLY OBJ. 3: The relation signified by the word *sign* must needs have some foundation. Now the relation signified by this sign which is a character, cannot be founded immediately on the essence of the soul: because then it would belong to every soul naturally. Consequently, there must be something in the soul on which such a relation is founded. And it is in this that a character essentially consists. Therefore it need not be in the genus *relation* as some have held.

REPLY OBJ. 4: A character is in the nature of a sign in comparison to the sensible sacrament by which it is imprinted. But considered in itself, it is in the nature of a principle, in the way already explained.

Article 3

Whether the Sacramental Character Is the Character of Christ?

AD TERTIUM SIC PROCEDITUR. Videtur quod character sacramentalis non sit character Christi. Dicitur enim Ephes. IV, *nolite contristare spiritum sanctum Dei, in quo signati estis.* Sed consignatio importatur in ratione characteris. Ergo character sacramentalis magis debet attribui spiritui sancto quam Christo.

PRAETEREA, character habet rationem signi. Est autem signum gratiae quae per sacramentum confertur. Gratia autem infunditur animae a tota Trinitate, unde dicitur in Psalmo, *gratiam et gloriam dabit dominus.* Ergo videtur quod character sacramentalis non debeat specialiter attribui Christo.

PRAETEREA, ad hoc aliquis characterem accipit ut eo a ceteris distinguatur. Sed distinctio sanctorum ab aliis fit per caritatem, quae *sola distinguit inter filios regni et filios perditionis,* ut Augustinus dicit, XV de Trin., unde et ipsi perditionis filii characterem bestiae habere dicuntur, ut patet Apoc. XIII. Caritas autem non attribuitur Christo, sed magis spiritui sancto, secundum illud Rom. V, *caritas Dei diffusa est in cordibus nostris per spiritum sanctum, qui datus est nobis*; vel etiam patri, secundum illud II Cor. ult., *gratia domini nostri Iesu*

OBJECTION 1: It seems that the sacramental character is not the character of Christ. For it is written (Eph 4:30): *Grieve not the Holy Spirit of God, whereby you are sealed.* But a character consists essentially in something that seals. Therefore the sacramental character should be attributed to the Holy Spirit rather than to Christ.

OBJ. 2: Further, a character has the nature of a sign. And it is a sign of the grace that is conferred by the sacrament. Now grace is poured forth into the soul by the whole Trinity; wherefore it is written (Ps 83:12): *The Lord will give grace and glory.* Therefore it seems that the sacramental character should not be attributed specially to Christ.

OBJ. 3: Further, a man is marked with a character that he may be distinguishable from others. But the saints are distinguishable from others by charity, which, as Augustine says (*De Trin.* xv), *alone separates the children of the Kingdom from the children of perdition*: wherefore also the children of perdition are said to have *the character of the beast* (Rev 13:16, 17). But charity is not attributed to Christ, but rather to the Holy Spirit according to Rom. 5:5: *The charity of God is poured forth in our hearts, by the Holy Spirit, Who is given to us*; or even to the Father, according to 2 Cor. 13:13: *The grace of our Lord Jesus Christ and the charity*

Christi et caritas Dei. Ergo videtur quod character sacramentalis non sit attribuendus Christo.

SED CONTRA est quod quidam sic definiunt characterem, *character est distinctio a charactere aeterno impressa animae rationali, secundum imaginem consignans Trinitatem creatam Trinitati creanti et recreanti, et distinguens a non configuratis, secundum statum fidei.* Sed character aeternus est ipse Christus, secundum illud Heb. I, *qui cum sit splendor gloriae et figura,* vel character, *substantiae eius.* Ergo videtur quod character proprie sit attribuendus Christo.

RESPONDEO dicendum quod, sicut ex supra dictis patet, character proprie est signaculum quoddam quo aliquid insignitur ut ordinandum in aliquem finem, sicut charactere insignitur denarius ad usum commutationum, et milites charactere insigniuntur quasi ad militiam deputati. Homo autem fidelis ad duo deputatur. Primo quidem, et principaliter, ad fruitionem gloriae. Et ad hoc insigniuntur signaculo gratiae, secundum illud Ezech. IX, *signa thau super frontes virorum gementium et dolentium*; et Apoc. VII, *nolite nocere terrae et mari neque arboribus, quoadusque signemus servos Dei nostri in frontibus eorum.*

Secundo autem deputatur quisque fidelis ad recipiendum vel tradendum aliis ea quae pertinent ad cultum Dei. Et ad hoc proprie deputatur character sacramentalis. Totus autem ritus Christianae religionis derivatur a sacerdotio Christi. Et ideo manifestum est quod character sacramentalis specialiter est character Christi, cuius sacerdotio configurantur fideles secundum sacramentales characteres, qui nihil aliud sunt quam quaedam participationes sacerdotii Christi, ab ipso Christo derivatae.

AD PRIMUM ergo dicendum quod apostolus ibi loquitur de configuratione secundum quam aliquis deputatur ad futuram gloriam, quae fit per gratiam. Quae spiritui sancto attribuitur, inquantum ex amore procedit quod Deus nobis aliquid gratis largiatur, quod ad rationem gratiae pertinet, spiritus autem sanctus amor est. Unde et I ad Cor. XII dicitur, *divisiones gratiarum sunt, idem autem spiritus.*

AD SECUNDUM dicendum quod character sacramentalis est res respectu sacramenti exterioris, et est sacramentum respectu ultimi effectus. Et ideo dupliciter potest aliquid characteri attribui. Uno modo, secundum rationem sacramenti. Et hoc modo est signum invisibilis gratiae, quae in sacramento confertur. Alio modo, secundum characteris rationem. Et hoc modo signum est configurativum alicui principali, apud quem residet auctoritas eius ad quod aliquis deputatur, sicut milites, qui deputantur ad pugnam, insigniuntur signo ducis, quo quodammodo ei configurantur. Et hoc modo illi qui deputantur ad cultum Christianum, cuius auctor est

of God. Therefore it seems that the sacramental character should not be attributed to Christ.

ON THE CONTRARY, Some define character thus: *A character is a distinctive mark printed in a man's rational soul by the eternal Character, whereby the created trinity is sealed with the likeness of the creating and re-creating Trinity, and distinguishing him from those who are not so enlikened, according to the state of faith.* But the eternal Character is Christ Himself, according to Heb. 1:3: *Who being the brightness of His glory and the figure,* or character, *of His substance.* It seems, therefore, that the character should properly be attributed to Christ.

I ANSWER THAT, As has been made clear above (A. 1), a character is properly a kind of seal, whereby something is marked, as being ordained to some particular end: thus a coin is marked for use in exchange of goods, and soldiers are marked with a character as being deputed to military service. Now the faithful are deputed to a twofold end. First and principally to the enjoyment of glory. And for this purpose they are marked with the seal of grace according to Ezech. 9:4: *Mark Thou upon the foreheads of the men that sigh and mourn*; and Apoc. 7:3: *Hurt not the earth, nor the sea, nor the trees, till we sign the servants of our God in their foreheads.*

Second, each of the faithful is deputed to receive, or to bestow on others, things pertaining to the worship of God. And this, properly speaking, is the purpose of the sacramental character. Now the whole rite of the Christian religion is derived from Christ's priesthood. Consequently, it is clear that the sacramental character is specially the character of Christ, to Whose character the faithful are likened by reason of the sacramental characters, which are nothing else than certain participations of Christ's Priesthood, flowing from Christ Himself.

REPLY OBJ. 1: The Apostle speaks there of that sealing by which a man is assigned to future glory, and which is effected by grace. Now grace is attributed to the Holy Spirit, inasmuch as it is through love that God gives us something gratis, which is the very nature of grace: while the Holy Spirit is love. Wherefore it is written (1 Cor 12:4): *There are diversities of graces, but the same Spirit.*

REPLY OBJ. 2: The sacramental character is a thing as regards the exterior sacrament, and a sacrament in regard to the ultimate effect. Consequently, something can be attributed to a character in two ways. First, if the character be considered as a sacrament: and thus it is a sign of the invisible grace which is conferred in the sacrament. Second, if it be considered as a character. And thus it is a sign conferring on a man a likeness to some principal person in whom is vested the authority over that to which he is assigned: thus soldiers who are assigned to military service, are marked with their leader's sign, by which they are, in a fashion, likened to him. And in this way those who are deputed to the

Christus, characterem accipiunt quo Christo configurantur. Unde proprie est character Christi.

AD TERTIUM dicendum quod charactere distinguitur aliquis ab alio per comparationem ad aliquem finem in quem ordinatur qui characterem accipit, sicut dictum est de charactere militari, quo in ordine ad pugnam distinguitur miles regis a milite hostis. Et similiter character fidelium est quo distinguuntur fideles Christi a servis Diaboli, vel in ordine ad vitam aeternam, vel in ordine ad cultum praesentis Ecclesiae. Quorum primum fit per caritatem et gratiam, ut obiectio procedit, secundum autem fit per characterem sacramentalem. Unde et character bestiae intelligi potest, per oppositum, vel obstinata malitia, qua aliqui deputantur ad poenam aeternam; vel professio illiciti cultus.

Christian worship, of which Christ is the author, receive a character by which they are likened to Christ. Consequently, properly speaking, this is Christ's character.

REPLY OBJ. 3: A character distinguishes one from another, in relation to some particular end, to which he, who receives the character is ordained: as has been stated concerning the military character (A. 1) by which a soldier of the king is distinguished from the enemy's soldier in relation to the battle. In like manner the character of the faithful is that by which the faithful of Christ are distinguished from the servants of the devil, either in relation to eternal life, or in relation to the worship of the Church that now is. Of these the former is the result of charity and grace, as the objection runs; while the latter results from the sacramental character. Wherefore the *character of the beast* may be understood by opposition, to mean either the obstinate malice for which some are assigned to eternal punishment, or the profession of an unlawful form of worship.

Article 4

Whether the Character Be Subjected in the Powers of the Soul?

AD QUARTUM SIC PROCEDITUR. Videtur quod character non sit in potentiis animae sicut in subiecto. Character enim dicitur esse dispositio ad gratiam. Sed gratia est in essentia animae sicut in subiecto, ut in secunda parte dictum est. Ergo videtur quod character sit in essentia animae, non autem in potentiis.

PRAETEREA, potentia animae non videtur esse subiectum alicuius nisi habitus vel dispositionis. Sed character, ut supra dictum est, non est habitus vel dispositio, sed magis potentia, cuius subiectum non est nisi essentia animae. Ergo videtur quod character non sit sicut in subiecto in potentia animae, sed magis in essentia ipsius.

PRAETEREA, potentiae animae rationalis distinguuntur per cognitivas et appetitivas. Sed non potest dici quod character sit tantum in potentia cognoscitiva, nec etiam tantum in potentia appetitiva, quia non ordinatur neque ad cognoscendum tantum, neque ad appetendum. Similiter etiam non potest dici quod sit in utraque, quia idem accidens non potest esse in diversis subiectis. Ergo videtur quod character non sit in potentia animae sicut in subiecto, sed magis in essentia.

SED CONTRA est quod, sicut in praemissa definitione characteris continetur, character imprimitur animae rationali secundum imaginem. Sed imago Trinitatis in anima attenditur secundum potentias. Ergo character in potentiis animae existit.

RESPONDEO dicendum quod, sicut dictum est, character est quoddam signaculum quo anima insignitur ad

OBJECTION 1: It seems that the character is not subjected in the powers of the soul. For a character is said to be a disposition to grace. But grace is subjected in the essence of the soul as we have stated in the Second Part (I-II, Q. 110, A. 4). Therefore it seems that the character is in the essence of the soul and not in the powers.

OBJ. 2: Further, a power of the soul does not seem to be the subject of anything save habit and disposition. But a character, as stated above (A. 2), is neither habit nor disposition, but rather a power: the subject of which is nothing else than the essence of the soul. Therefore it seems that the character is not subjected in a power of the soul, but rather in its essence.

OBJ. 3: Further, the powers of the soul are divided into those of knowledge and those of appetite. But it cannot be said that a character is only in a cognitive power, nor, again, only in an appetitive power: since it is neither ordained to knowledge only, nor to desire only. Likewise, neither can it be said to be in both, because the same accident cannot be in several subjects. Therefore it seems that a character is not subjected in a power of the soul, but rather in the essence.

ON THE CONTRARY, A character, according to its definition given above (A. 3), is imprinted in the rational soul *by way of an image*. But the image of the Trinity in the soul is seen in the powers. Therefore a character is in the powers of the soul.

I ANSWER THAT, As stated above (A. 3), a character is a kind of seal by which the soul is marked, so that it may

suscipiendum vel aliis tradendum ea quae sunt divini cultus. Divinus autem cultus in quibusdam actibus consistit. Ad actus autem proprie ordinantur potentiae animae, sicut essentia ordinatur ad esse. Et ideo character non est sicut in subiecto in essentia animae, sed in eius potentia.

AD PRIMUM ergo dicendum quod subiectum alicui accidenti attribuitur secundum rationem eius ad quod propinque disponit, non autem secundum rationem eius ad quod disponit remote vel indirecte. Character autem directe quidem et propinque disponit animam ad ea quae sunt divini cultus exequenda, et quia haec idonee non fiunt sine auxilio gratiae, quia, ut dicitur Ioan. IV, *eos qui adorant Deum, in spiritu et veritate adorare oportet*, ex consequenti divina largitas recipientibus characterem gratiam largitur, per quam digne impleant ea ad quae deputantur. Et ideo characteri magis est attribuendum subiectum secundum rationem actuum ad divinum cultum pertinentium, quam secundum rationem gratiae.

AD SECUNDUM dicendum quod essentia animae est subiectum potentiae naturalis, quae ex principiis essentiae procedit. Talis autem potentia non est character, sed est quaedam spiritualis potentia ab extrinseco adveniens. Unde, sicut essentia animae, per quam est naturalis vita hominis, perficitur per gratiam, qua anima spiritualiter vivit; ita potentia naturalis animae perficitur per spiritualem potentiam, quae est character. Habitus enim et dispositio pertinent ad potentiam animae, eo quod ordinantur ad actus, quorum potentiae sunt principia. Et eadem ratione omne quod ad actum ordinatur, est potentiae tribuendum.

AD TERTIUM dicendum quod, sicut dictum est, character ordinatur ad ea quae sunt divini cultus. Qui quidem est quaedam fidei protestatio per exteriora signa. Et ideo oportet quod character sit in cognitiva potentia animae, in qua est fides.

receive, or bestow on others, things pertaining to Divine worship. Now the Divine worship consists in certain actions: and the powers of the soul are properly ordained to actions, just as the essence is ordained to existence. Therefore a character is subjected not in the essence of the soul, but in its power.

REPLY OBJ. 1: The subject is ascribed to an accident in respect of that to which the accident disposes it proximately, but not in respect of that to which it disposes it remotely or indirectly. Now a character disposes the soul directly and proximately to the fulfilling of things pertaining to Divine worship: and because such cannot be accomplished suitably without the help of grace, since, according to John 4:24, *they that adore* God *must adore Him in spirit and in truth*, consequently, the Divine bounty bestows grace on those who receive the character, so that they may accomplish worthily the service to which they are deputed. Therefore the subject should be ascribed to a character in respect of those actions that pertain to the Divine worship, rather than in respect of grace.

REPLY OBJ. 2: The essence of the soul is the subject of the natural power, which flows from the principles of the essence. Now a character is not a power of this kind, but a spiritual power coming from without. Wherefore, just as the essence of the soul, from which man has his natural life, is perfected by grace from which the soul derives spiritual life; so the natural power of the soul is perfected by a spiritual power, which is a character. For habit and disposition belong to a power of the soul, since they are ordained to actions of which the powers are the principles. And in like manner whatever is ordained to action, should be attributed to a power.

REPLY OBJ. 3: As stated above, a character is ordained unto things pertaining to the Divine worship; which is a protestation of faith expressed by exterior signs. Consequently, a character needs to be in the soul's cognitive power, where also is faith.

Article 5

Whether a Character Can Be Blotted Out from the Soul?

AD QUINTUM SIC PROCEDITUR. Videtur quod character non insit animae indelebiliter. Quanto enim aliquod accidens est perfectius, tanto firmius inhaeret. Sed gratia est perfectior quam character, quia character ordinatur ad gratiam sicut ad ulteriorem finem. Gratia autem amittitur per peccatum. Ergo multo magis character.

PRAETEREA, per characterem aliquis deputatur divino cultui, sicut dictum est. Sed aliqui a cultu divino

OBJECTION 1: It seems that a character can be blotted out from the soul. Because the more perfect an accident is, the more firmly does it adhere to its subject. But grace is more perfect than a character; because a character is ordained unto grace as to a further end. Now grace is lost through sin. Much more, therefore, is a character so lost.

OBJ. 2: Further, by a character a man is deputed to the Divine worship, as stated above (AA. 3, 4). But some pass from the worship of God to a contrary worship by apostasy

transeunt ad contrarium cultum per apostasiam a fide. Ergo videtur quod tales amittant characterem sacramentalem.

Praeterea, cessante fine, cessare debet et id quod est ad finem, alioquin frustra remaneret, sicut post resurrectionem non erit matrimonium, quia cessabit generatio, ad quam matrimonium ordinatur cultus autem exterior, ad quem character ordinatur, non remanebit in patria, in qua nihil agetur in figura, sed totum in nuda veritate. Ergo character sacramentalis non remanet in perpetuum in anima. Et ita non inest indelebiliter.

Sed contra est quod Augustinus dicit, in II contra Parmenianum, non minus haerent sacramenta Christiana quam corporalis nota militiae. Sed character militaris non repetitur, sed agnitus approbatur, in eo qui veniam meretur ab imperatore post culpam. Ergo nec character sacramentalis deleri potest.

Respondeo dicendum quod, sicut dictum est, character sacramentalis est quaedam participatio sacerdotii Christi in fidelibus eius, ut scilicet, sicut Christus habet plenam spiritualis sacerdotii potestatem, ita fideles eius ei configurentur in hoc quod participant aliquam spiritualem potestatem respectu sacramentorum et eorum quae pertinent ad divinum cultum. Et propter hoc etiam Christo non competit habere characterem, sed potestas sacerdotii eius comparatur ad characterem sicut id quod est plenum et perfectum ad aliquam sui participationem. Sacerdotium autem Christi est aeternum, secundum illud Psalmi, *tu es sacerdos in aeternum secundum ordinem Melchisedech*. Et inde est quod omnis sanctificatio quae fit per sacerdotium eius, est perpetua, re consecrata manente. Quod patet etiam in rebus inanimatis, nam Ecclesiae vel altaris manet consecratio semper, nisi destruatur. Cum igitur anima sit subiectum characteris secundum intellectivam partem, in qua est fides, ut dictum est; manifestum est quod, sicut intellectus perpetuus est et incorruptibilis, ita character indelebiliter manet in anima.

Ad primum ergo dicendum quod aliter est in anima gratia, et aliter character. Nam gratia est in anima sicut quaedam forma habens esse completum in ea, character autem est in anima sicut quaedam virtus instrumentalis, ut supra dictum est. Forma autem completa est in subiecto secundum conditionem subiecti. Et quia anima est mutabilis secundum liberum arbitrium quandiu est in statu viae, consequens est quod insit animae mutabiliter. Sed virtus instrumentalis magis attenditur secundum conditionem principalis agentis. Et ideo character indelebiliter inest animae, non propter sui perfectionem, sed propter perfectionem sacerdotii Christi, a quo derivatur character sicut quaedam instrumentalis virtus.

Ad secundum dicendum quod, sicut ibidem Augustinus dicit, *nec ipsos apostatas videmus carere Baptismate, quibus per poenitentiam redeuntibus non restituitur, et*

from the faith. It seems, therefore, that such lose the sacramental character.

Obj. 3: Further, when the end ceases, the means to the end should cease also: thus after the resurrection there will be no marriage, because begetting will cease, which is the purpose of marriage. Now the exterior worship to which a character is ordained, will not endure in heaven, where there will be no shadows, but all will be truth without a veil. Therefore the sacramental character does not last in the soul for ever: and consequently it can be blotted out.

On the contrary, Augustine says (*Contra Parmen.* ii): *The Christian sacraments are not less lasting than the bodily mark* of military service. But the character of military service is not repeated, but is *recognized and approved* in the man who obtains the emperor's forgiveness after offending him. Therefore neither can the sacramental character be blotted out.

I answer that, As stated above (A. 3), in a sacramental character Christ's faithful have a share in His Priesthood; in the sense that as Christ has the full power of a spiritual priesthood, so His faithful are likened to Him by sharing a certain spiritual power with regard to the sacraments and to things pertaining to the Divine worship. For this reason it is unbecoming that Christ should have a character: but His Priesthood is compared to a character, as that which is complete and perfect is compared to some participation of itself. Now Christ's Priesthood is eternal, according to Ps. 109:4: *Thou art a priest for ever, according to the order of Melchisedech.* Consequently, every sanctification wrought by His Priesthood, is perpetual, enduring as long as the thing sanctified endures. This is clear even in inanimate things; for the consecration of a church or an altar lasts for ever unless they be destroyed. Since, therefore, the subject of a character is the soul as to its intellective part, where faith resides, as stated above (A. 4, ad 3); it is clear that, the intellect being perpetual and incorruptible, a character cannot be blotted out from the soul.

Reply Obj. 1: Both grace and character are in the soul, but in different ways. For grace is in the soul, as a form having complete existence therein: whereas a character is in the soul, as an instrumental power, as stated above (A. 2). Now a complete form is in its subject according to the condition of the subject. And since the soul as long as it is a wayfarer is changeable in respect of the free-will, it results that grace is in the soul in a changeable manner. But an instrumental power follows rather the condition of the principal agent: and consequently a character exists in the soul in an indelible manner, not from any perfection of its own, but from the perfection of Christ's Priesthood, from which the character flows like an instrumental power.

Reply Obj. 2: As Augustine says (*Contra Parmen.* ii), *even apostates are not deprived of their baptism, for when they repent and return to the fold they do not receive it again;*

ideo amitti non potuisse iudicatur. Et huius ratio est quia character est virtus instrumentalis, ut dictum est, ratio autem instrumenti consistit in hoc quod ab alio moveatur, non autem in hoc quod ipsum se moveat, quod pertinet ad voluntatem. Et ideo, quantumcumque voluntas moveatur in contrarium, character non removetur, propter immobilitatem principalis moventis.

Ad tertium dicendum quod, quamvis post hanc vitam non remaneat exterior cultus, remanet tamen finis illius cultus. Et ideo post hanc vitam remanet character, et in bonis ad eorum gloriam, et in malis ad eorum ignominiam, sicut etiam militaris character remanet in militibus post adeptam victoriam, et in his qui vicerunt ad gloriam, et in his qui sunt victi ad poenam.

whence we conclude that it cannot be lost. The reason of this is that a character is an instrumental power, as stated above (ad 1), and the nature of an instrument as such is to be moved by another, but not to move itself; this belongs to the will. Consequently, however much the will be moved in the contrary direction, the character is not removed, by reason of the immobility of the principal mover.

Reply Obj. 3: Although external worship does not last after this life, yet its end remains. Consequently, after this life the character remains, both in the good as adding to their glory, and in the wicked as increasing their shame: just as the character of the military service remains in the soldiers after the victory, as the boast of the conquerors, and the disgrace of the conquered.

Article 6

Whether a Character Is Imprinted by Each Sacrament of the New Law?

Ad sextum sic proceditur. Videtur quod per omnia sacramenta novae legis imprimatur character. Per omnia enim sacramenta novae legis fit aliquis particeps sacerdotii Christi. Sed character sacramentalis nihil est aliud quam participatio sacerdotii Christi, ut dictum est. Ergo videtur quod per omnia sacramenta novae legis imprimatur character.

Praeterea, character se habet ad animam in qua est, sicut consecratio ad res consecratas. Sed per quodlibet sacramentum novae legis homo recipit gratiam sanctificantem, ut supra dictum est. Ergo videtur quod per quodlibet sacramentum novae legis imprimatur character.

Praeterea, character est res et sacramentum. Sed in quolibet sacramento novae legis est aliquid quod est res tantum, et aliquid quod est sacramentum tantum, et aliquid quod est res et sacramentum. Ergo per quodlibet sacramentum novae legis imprimitur character.

Sed contra est quod sacramenta in quibus imprimitur character, non reiterantur, eo quod character est indelebilis, ut dictum est. Quaedam autem sacramenta iterantur, sicut patet de poenitentia et matrimonio. Ergo non omnia sacramenta imprimunt characterem.

Respondeo dicendum quod, sicut supra dictum est, sacramenta novae legis ad duo ordinantur, scilicet in remedium peccati, et ad cultum divinum. Est autem omnibus sacramentis commune quod per ea exhibetur aliquod remedium contra peccatum, per hoc quod gratiam conferunt. Non autem omnia sacramenta ordinantur directe ad divinum cultum, sicut patet de poenitentia, per quam homo liberatur a peccato, non autem

Objection 1: It seems that a character is imprinted by all the sacraments of the New Law: because each sacrament of the New Law makes man a participator in Christ's Priesthood. But the sacramental character is nothing but a participation in Christ's Priesthood, as already stated (AA. 3, 5). Therefore it seems that a character is imprinted by each sacrament of the New Law.

Obj. 2: Further, a character may be compared to the soul in which it is, as a consecration to that which is consecrated. But by each sacrament of the New Law man becomes the recipient of sanctifying grace, as stated above (Q. 62, A. 1). Therefore it seems that a character is imprinted by each sacrament of the New Law.

Obj. 3: Further, a character is both a reality and a sacrament. But in each sacrament of the New Law, there is something which is only a reality, and something which is only a sacrament, and something which is both reality and sacrament. Therefore a character is imprinted by each sacrament of the New Law.

On the contrary, Those sacraments in which a character is imprinted, are not reiterated, because a character is indelible, as stated above (A. 5): whereas some sacraments are reiterated, for instance, penance and matrimony. Therefore not all the sacraments imprint a character.

I answer that, As stated above (Q. 62, AA. 1, 5), the sacraments of the New Law are ordained for a twofold purpose, namely, as a remedy for sin, and for the Divine worship. Now all the sacraments, from the fact that they confer grace, have this in common, that they afford a remedy against sin: whereas not all the sacraments are directly ordained to the Divine worship. Thus it is clear that penance, whereby man is delivered from sin, does not afford

per hoc sacramentum exhibetur homini aliquid de novo pertinens ad divinum cultum, sed restituitur in statum pristinum.

Pertinet autem aliquod sacramentum ad divinum cultum tripliciter, uno modo, per modum ipsius actionis; alio modo, per modum agentis; tertio modo, per modum recipientis. Per modum quidem ipsius actionis pertinet ad divinum cultum Eucharistia, in qua principaliter divinus cultus consistit, inquantum est Ecclesiae sacrificium. Et per hoc idem sacramentum non imprimitur homini character, quia per hoc sacramentum non ordinatur homo ad aliquid aliud ulterius agendum vel recipiendum in sacramentis, cum potius sit *finis et consummatio omnium sacramentorum*, ut Dionysius dicit, III cap. Eccles. Hier. Continet tamen in seipso Christum, in quo non est character, sed tota sacerdotii plenitudo.

Sed ad agentes in sacramentis pertinet sacramentum ordinis, quia per hoc sacramentum deputantur homines ad sacramenta aliis tradenda. Sed ad recipientes pertinet sacramentum Baptismi, per quod homo accipit potestatem recipiendi alia Ecclesiae sacramenta, unde Baptismus dicitur esse ianua sacramentorum. Ad idem etiam ordinatur quodammodo confirmatio, ut infra suo loco dicetur. Et ideo per haec tria sacramenta character imprimitur, scilicet Baptismum, confirmationem et ordinem.

AD PRIMUM ergo dicendum quod per omnia sacramenta fit homo particeps sacerdotii Christi, utpote percipiens aliquem effectum eius, non tamen per omnia sacramenta aliquis deputatur ad agendum aliquid vel recipiendum quod pertineat ad cultum sacerdotii Christi. Quod quidem exigitur ad hoc quod sacramentum characterem imprimat.

AD SECUNDUM dicendum quod per omnia sacramenta sanctificatur homo, propter hoc quod sanctitas importat munditiam a peccato, quod fit per gratiam. Sed specialiter per quaedam sacramenta, quae characterem imprimunt, homo sanctificatur quadam consecratione, utpote deputatus ad divinum cultum, sicut etiam res inanimatae sanctificari dicuntur inquantum divino cultui deputantur.

AD TERTIUM dicendum quod, licet character sit res et sacramentum, non tamen oportet id quod est res et sacramentum, esse characterem. Quid autem sit res et sacramentum in aliis sacramentis, infra dicetur.

man any advance in the Divine worship, but restores him to his former state.

Now a sacrament may belong to the Divine worship in three ways: first in regard to the thing done; second, in regard to the agent; third, in regard to the recipient. In regard to the thing done, the Eucharist belongs to the Divine worship, for the Divine worship consists principally therein, so far as it is the sacrifice of the Church. And by this same sacrament a character is not imprinted on man; because it does not ordain man to any further sacramental action or benefit received, since rather is it *the end and consummation of all the sacraments*, as Dionysius says (*Eccl. Hier.* iii). But it contains within itself Christ, in Whom there is not the character, but the very plenitude of the Priesthood.

But it is the sacrament of order that pertains to the sacramental agents: for it is by this sacrament that men are deputed to confer sacraments on others: while the sacrament of Baptism pertains to the recipients, since it confers on man the power to receive the other sacraments of the Church; whence it is called the *door of the sacraments*. In a way Confirmation also is ordained for the same purpose, as we shall explain in its proper place (Q. 65, A. 3). Consequently, these three sacraments imprint a character, namely, Baptism, Confirmation, and order.

REPLY OBJ. 1: Every sacrament makes man a participator in Christ's Priesthood, from the fact that it confers on him some effect thereof. But every sacrament does not depute a man to do or receive something pertaining to the worship of the priesthood of Christ: while it is just this that is required for a sacrament to imprint a character.

REPLY OBJ. 2: Man is sanctified by each of the sacraments, since sanctity means immunity from sin, which is the effect of grace. But in a special way some sacraments, which imprint a character, bestow on man a certain consecration, thus deputing him to the Divine worship: just as inanimate things are said to be consecrated forasmuch as they are deputed to Divine worship.

REPLY OBJ. 3: Although a character is a reality and a sacrament, it does not follow that whatever is a reality and a sacrament, is also a character. With regard to the other sacraments we shall explain further on what is the reality and what is the sacrament.

QUESTION 64

THE CAUSES OF THE SACRAMENTS

Deinde considerandum est de causis sacramentorum, sive per auctoritatem sive per ministerium. Et circa hoc quaeruntur decem.

Primo, utrum solus Deus interius operetur in sacramentis.

Secundo, utrum institutio sacramentorum sit solum a Deo.

Tertio, de potestate quam Christus habuit in sacramentis.

Quarto, utrum illam potestatem potuerit aliis communicare.

Quinto, utrum potestas ministerii in sacramentis conveniat malis.

Sexto, utrum mali peccent dispensando sacramenta.

Septimo, utrum Angeli possint esse ministri sacramentorum.

Octavo, utrum intentio ministri requiratur in sacramentis.

Nono, utrum requiratur ibi recta fides; ita scilicet quod infidelis non possit tradere sacramentum.

Decimo, utrum requiratur ibi recta intentio.

In the next place we have to consider the causes of the sacraments, both as to authorship and as to ministration. Concerning which there are ten points of inquiry:

(1) Whether God alone works inwardly in the sacraments?

(2) Whether the institution of the sacraments is from God alone?

(3) Of the power which Christ exercised over the sacraments;

(4) Whether He could transmit that power to others?

(5) Whether the wicked can have the power of administering the sacraments?

(6) Whether the wicked sin in administering the sacraments?

(7) Whether the angels can be ministers of the sacraments?

(8) Whether the minister's intention is necessary in the sacraments?

(9) Whether right faith is required therein; so that it be impossible for an unbeliever to confer a sacrament?

(10) Whether a right intention is required therein?

Article 1

Whether God Alone, or the Minister Also, Works Inwardly Unto the Sacramental Effect?

AD PRIMUM SIC PROCEDITUR. Videtur quod non solus Deus, sed etiam minister, interius operetur ad effectum sacramenti. Interior enim effectus sacramenti est ut homo purgetur a peccatis, et illuminetur per gratiam. Sed ad ministros Ecclesiae pertinet purgare, illuminare et perficere, ut patet per Dionysium, in V cap. Coel. Hier. Ergo videtur quod non solus Deus, sed etiam ministri Ecclesiae operentur ad sacramenti effectum.

PRAETEREA, in collatione sacramentorum quaedam orationum suffragia proponuntur. Sed orationes iustorum sunt magis apud Deum exaudibiles quam quorumcumque, secundum illud Ioan. IX, *si quis Dei cultor est, et voluntatem Dei facit, hunc Deus exaudit.* Ergo videtur quod maiorem effectum sacramenti consequitur ille qui recipit illum a bono ministro. Sic ergo minister operatur aliquid ad interiorem effectum, et non solus Deus.

PRAETEREA, dignior est homo quam res inanimata. Sed res inanimata aliquid operatur ad effectum interiorem, *nam aqua corpus tangit et cor abluit*, ut Augustinus

OBJECTION 1: It seems that not God alone, but also the minister, works inwardly unto the sacramental effect. For the inward sacramental effect is to cleanse man from sin and enlighten him by grace. But it belongs to the ministers of the Church *to cleanse, enlighten and perfect*, as Dionysius explains (*Coel. Hier.* v). Therefore it seems that the sacramental effect is the work not only of God, but also of the ministers of the Church.

OBJ. 2: Further, certain prayers are offered up in conferring the sacraments. But the prayers of the righteous are more acceptable to God than those of any other, according to John 9:31: *If a man be a server of God, and doth His will, him He heareth.* Therefore it stems that a man obtains a greater sacramental effect if he receive it from a good minister. Consequently, the interior effect is partly the work of the minister and not of God alone.

OBJ. 3: Further, man is of greater account than an inanimate thing. But an inanimate thing contributes something to the interior effect: since *water touches the body and*

43

dicit, super Ioan. Ergo homo aliquid operatur ad interiorem effectum sacramenti, et non solus Deus.

SED CONTRA est quod dicitur Rom. VIII, *Deus qui iustificat.* Cum igitur interior effectus omnium sacramentorum sit iustificatio, videtur quod solus Deus operetur interiorem effectum sacramenti.

RESPONDEO dicendum quod operari aliquem effectum contingit dupliciter, uno modo, per modum principalis agentis; alio modo, per modum instrumenti. Primo igitur modo solus Deus operatur interiorem effectum sacramenti. Tum quia solus Deus illabitur animae, in qua sacramenti effectus consistit. Non autem potest aliquid immediate operari ubi non est. Tum quia gratia, quae est interior sacramenti effectus, est a solo Deo, ut in secunda parte habitum est. Character etiam, qui est interior quorundam sacramentorum effectus, est virtus instrumentalis, quae manat a principali agente, quod est Deus. Secundo autem modo homo potest operari ad interiorem effectum sacramenti, inquantum operatur per modum ministri. Nam eadem ratio est ministri et instrumenti, utriusque enim actio exterius adhibetur, sed sortitur effectum interiorem ex virtute principalis agentis, quod est Deus.

AD PRIMUM ergo dicendum quod purgatio, secundum quod attribuitur ministris Ecclesiae, non est a peccato, sed dicuntur diaconi purgare, inquantum vel immundos eiiciunt a coetu fidelium, vel eos sacris admonitionibus disponunt ad sacramentorum receptionem. Similiter etiam sacerdotes illuminare dicuntur sacrum populum, non quidem gratiam infundendo, sed sacramenta gratiae tradendo, ut patet per Dionysium ibidem.

AD SECUNDUM dicendum quod orationes quae dicuntur in sacramentorum collatione, proponuntur Deo non ex parte singularis personae, sed ex parte totius Ecclesiae, cuius preces sunt apud Deum exaudibiles, secundum illud Matth. XVIII, *si duo ex vobis consenserint super terram de omni re quamcumque petierint, fiet eis a patre meo.* Nihil tamen prohibet quin devotio viri iusti ad hoc aliquid operetur. Illud tamen quod est sacramenti effectus, non impetratur oratione Ecclesiae vel ministri, sed ex merito passionis Christi, cuius virtus operatur in sacramentis, ut dictum est. Unde effectus sacramenti non datur melior per meliorem ministrum. Aliquid tamen annexum impetrari potest recipienti sacramentum per devotionem ministri, nec tamen minister operatur illud, sed impetrat operandum a Deo.

AD TERTIUM dicendum quod res inanimatae non operantur ad interiorem effectum nisi instrumentaliter, ut dictum est. Et similiter homines non operantur ad sacramentorum effectum nisi per modum ministerii, ut dictum est.

cleanses the soul, as Augustine says (*Tract. lxxx in Joan.*). Therefore the interior sacramental effect is partly the work of man and not of God alone.

ON THE CONTRARY, It is written (Rom 8:33): *God that justifieth.* Since, then, the inward effect of all the sacraments is justification, it seems that God alone works the interior sacramental effect.

I ANSWER THAT, There are two ways of producing an effect; first, as a principal agent; second, as an instrument. In the former way the interior sacramental effect is the work of God alone: first, because God alone can enter the soul wherein the sacramental effect takes place; and no agent can operate immediately where it is not: second, because grace which is an interior sacramental effect is from God alone, as we have established in the Second Part (I-II, Q. 112, A. 1); while the character which is the interior effect of certain sacraments, is an instrumental power which flows from the principal agent, which is God. In the second way, however, the interior sacramental effect can be the work of man, in so far as he works as a minister. For a minister is of the nature of an instrument, since the action of both is applied to something extrinsic, while the interior effect is produced through the power of the principal agent, which is God.

REPLY OBJ. 1: Cleansing in so far as it is attributed to the ministers of the Church is not a washing from sin: deacons are said to *cleanse,* inasmuch as they remove the unclean from the body of the faithful, or prepare them by their pious admonitions for the reception of the sacraments. In like manner also priests are said to *enlighten* God's people, not indeed by giving them grace, but by conferring on them the sacraments of grace; as Dionysius explains (*Coel. Hier.* v).

REPLY OBJ. 2: The prayers which are said in giving the sacraments, are offered to God, not on the part of the individual, but on the part of the whole Church, whose prayers are acceptable to God, according to Matt. 18:19: *If two of you shall consent upon earth, concerning anything whatsoever they shall ask, it shall be done to them by My Father.* Nor is there any reason why the devotion of a just man should not contribute to this effect. But that which is the sacramental effect is not impetrated by the prayer of the Church or of the minister, but through the merit of Christ's Passion, the power of which operates in the sacraments, as stated above (Q. 62, A. 5). Wherefore the sacramental effect is made no better by a better minister. And yet something in addition may be impetrated for the receiver of the sacrament through the devotion of the minister: but this is not the work of the minister, but the work of God Who hears the minister's prayer.

REPLY OBJ. 3: Inanimate things do not produce the sacramental effect, except instrumentally, as stated above. In like manner neither do men produce the sacramental effect, except ministerially, as also stated above.

Article 2

Whether the Sacraments Are Instituted by God Alone?

AD SECUNDUM SIC PROCEDITUR. Videtur quod sacramenta non sint solum ex institutione divina. Ea enim quae sunt divinitus instituta, traduntur nobis in sacra Scriptura. Sed quaedam aguntur in sacramentis de quibus nulla fit mentio in sacra Scriptura, puta de chrismate quo homines confirmantur, et de oleo quo sacerdotes inunguntur, et de multis aliis, tam verbis quam factis, quibus utimur in sacramentis. Non ergo sacramenta sunt solum ex institutione divina.

PRAETEREA, sacramenta sunt quaedam signa. Res autem sensibiles naturaliter quaedam significant. Nec potest dici quod Deus quibusdam significationibus delectetur, et non aliis, quia ipse omnia quae fecit approbat. Hoc autem proprium videtur esse Daemonum, ut quibusdam signis ad aliquid alliciantur, dicit enim Augustinus, XXI de Civ. Dei, *illiciuntur Daemones per creaturas, quas non ipsi, sed Deus condidit, delectabilibus pro sua diversitate diversis, non ut animalia cibis, sed ut spiritus signis.* Non ergo videtur quod sacramenta indigeant esse ex institutione divina.

PRAETEREA, apostoli vicem Dei gesserunt in terris, unde apostolus dicit, II Cor. II, *nam et ego quod donavi, si quid donavi, propter vos in persona Christi,* idest, ac si ipse Christus donasset. Sic ergo videtur quod apostoli, et eorum successores, possint nova sacramenta instituere.

SED CONTRA est quod ille instituit aliquid qui dat ei robur et virtutem, sicut patet de institutoribus legum. Sed virtus sacramenti est a solo Deo, ut ex dictis patet. Ergo solus Deus potest instituere sacramentum.

RESPONDEO dicendum quod, sicut ex supra dictis patet, sacramenta instrumentaliter operantur ad spirituales effectus. Instrumentum autem habet virtutem a principali agente. Agens autem respectu sacramenti est duplex, scilicet instituens sacramentum; et utens sacramento instituto, applicando scilicet ipsum ad inducendum effectum. Virtus autem sacramenti non potest esse ab eo qui utitur sacramento, quia non operatur nisi per modum ministerii. Unde relinquitur quod virtus sacramenti sit ab eo qui instituit sacramentum. Cum igitur virtus sacramenti sit a solo Deo, consequens est quod solus Deus sit sacramentorum institutor.

AD PRIMUM ergo dicendum quod illa quae aguntur in sacramentis per homines instituta, non sunt de necessitate sacramenti, sed ad quandam solemnitatem, quae adhibetur sacramentis ad excitandam devotionem et reverentiam in his qui sacramenta suscipiunt. Ea vero

OBJECTION 1: It seems that the sacraments are not instituted by God alone. For those things which God has instituted are delivered to us in Holy Scripture. But in the sacraments certain things are done which are nowhere mentioned in Holy Scripture; for instance, the chrism with which men are confirmed, the oil with which priests are anointed, and many others, both words and actions, which we employ in the sacraments. Therefore the sacraments were not instituted by God alone.

OBJ. 2: Further, a sacrament is a kind of sign. Now sensible things have their own natural signification. Nor can it be said that God takes pleasure in certain significations and not in others; because He approves of all that He made. Moreover, it seems to be peculiar to the demons to be enticed to something by means of signs; for Augustine says (*De Civ. Dei* xxi): *The demons are enticed . . . by means of creatures, which were created not by them but by God, by various means of attraction according to their various natures, not as an animal is enticed by food, but as a spirit is drawn by a sign.* It seems, therefore, that there is no need for the sacraments to be instituted by God.

OBJ. 3: Further, the apostles were God's viceregents on earth: hence the Apostle says (2 Cor 2:10): *For what I have pardoned, if I have pardoned anything, for your sakes have I done it in the person of Christ,* i.e., as though Christ Himself had pardoned. Therefore it seems that the apostles and their successors can institute new sacraments.

ON THE CONTRARY, The institutor of anything is he who gives it strength and power: as in the case of those who institute laws. But the power of a sacrament is from God alone, as we have shown above (A. 1; Q. 62, A. 1). Therefore God alone can institute a sacrament.

I ANSWER THAT, As appears from what has been said above (A. 1; Q. 62, A. 1), the sacraments are instrumental causes of spiritual effects. Now an instrument has its power from the principal agent. But an agent in respect of a sacrament is twofold; viz. he who institutes the sacraments, and he who makes use of the sacrament instituted, by applying it for the production of the effect. Now the power of a sacrament cannot be from him who makes use of the sacrament: because he works but as a minister. Consequently, it follows that the power of the sacrament is from the institutor of the sacrament. Since, therefore, the power of the sacrament is from God alone, it follows that God alone can institute the sacraments.

REPLY OBJ. 1: Human institutions observed in the sacraments are not essential to the sacrament; but belong to the solemnity which is added to the sacraments in order to arouse devotion and reverence in the recipients. But those things that are essential to the sacrament, are instituted by

quae sunt de necessitate sacramenti, sunt ab ipso Christo instituta, qui est Deus et homo. Et licet non omnia sint tradita in Scripturis, habet tamen ea Ecclesia ex familiari apostolorum traditione, sicut apostolus dicit, I Cor. XI, *cetera cum venero disponam.*

AD SECUNDUM dicendum quod res sensibiles aptitudinem quandam habent ad significandum spirituales effectus ex sui natura, sed ista aptitudo determinatur ad specialem significationem ex institutione divina. Et hoc est quod Hugo de sancto Victore dicit, quod *sacramentum ex institutione significat.* Praeelegit tamen Deus quasdam res aliis ad significationes sacramentales, non quia ad eas contrahatur eius affectus, sed ut sit convenientior significatio.

AD TERTIUM dicendum quod apostoli, et eorum successores, sunt vicarii Dei quantum ad regimen Ecclesiae institutae per fidem et fidei sacramenta. Unde, sicut non licet eis constituere aliam Ecclesiam, ita non licet eis tradere aliam fidem, neque instituere alia sacramenta, sed per *sacramenta quae de latere Christi pendentis in cruce fluxerunt*, dicitur esse fabricata Ecclesia Christi.

Christ Himself, Who is God and man. And though they are not all handed down by the Scriptures, yet the Church holds them from the intimate tradition of the apostles, according to the saying of the Apostle (1 Cor 11:34): *The rest I will set in order when I come.*

REPLY OBJ. 2: From their very nature sensible things have a certain aptitude for the signifying of spiritual effects: but this aptitude is fixed by the Divine institution to some special signification. This is what Hugh of St. Victor means by saying (*De Sacram.* i) that *a sacrament owes its signification to its institution.* Yet God chooses certain things rather than others for sacramental signification, not as though His choice were restricted to them, but in order that their signification be more suitable to them.

REPLY OBJ. 3: The apostles and their successors are God's vicars in governing the Church which is built on faith and the sacraments of faith. Wherefore, just as they may not institute another Church, so neither may they deliver another faith, nor institute other sacraments: on the contrary, the Church is said to be built up with the sacraments *which flowed from the side of Christ while hanging on the Cross.*

Article 3

Whether Christ As Man Had the Power of Producing the Inward Sacramental Effect?

AD TERTIUM SIC PROCEDITUR. Videtur quod Christus, secundum quod homo, habuit potestatem operandi interiorem effectum sacramentorum dicit enim Ioannes Baptista, ut habetur Ioan. I, *qui me misit baptizare in aqua, ille mihi dixit, super quem videris spiritum descendentem et manentem super eum, hic est qui baptizat in spiritu sancto.* Sed baptizare in spiritu sancto est interius gratiam spiritus sancti conferre. Spiritus autem sanctus descendit super Christum inquantum homo, non inquantum Deus, quia sic ipse dat spiritum sanctum. Ergo videtur quod Christus, secundum quod homo, habuit potestatem interiorem effectum sacramentorum causandi.

PRAETEREA, Matth. IX dominus dicit, *sciatis quod filius hominis habet in terra potestatem dimittendi peccata.* Sed remissio peccatorum est interior effectus sacramenti. Ergo videtur quod Christus, secundum quod homo, interiorem effectum sacramentorum operatur.

PRAETEREA, institutio sacramentorum pertinet ad eum qui tanquam principale agens operatur ad interiorem sacramenti effectum. Manifestum est autem quod Christus sacramenta instituit. Ergo ipse est qui interius operatur sacramentorum effectum.

PRAETEREA, nullus potest sine sacramento effectum sacramenti conferre, nisi propria virtute sacramenti

OBJECTION 1: It seems that Christ as man had the power of producing the interior sacramental effect. For John the Baptist said (John 1:33): *He, Who sent me to baptize in water, said to me: He upon Whom thou shalt see the Spirit descending and remaining upon Him, He it is that baptizeth with the Holy Spirit.* But to baptize with the Holy Spirit is to confer inwardly the grace of the Holy Spirit. And the Holy Spirit descended upon Christ as man, not as God: for thus He Himself gives the Holy Spirit. Therefore it seems that Christ, as man, had the power of producing the inward sacramental effect.

OBJ. 2: Further, our Lord said (Matt 9:6): *That you may know that the Son of Man hath power on earth to forgive sins.* But forgiveness of sins is an inward sacramental effect. Therefore it seems that Christ as man produces the inward sacramental effect.

OBJ. 3: Further, the institution of the sacraments belongs to him who acts as principal agent in producing the inward sacramental effect. Now it is clear that Christ instituted the sacraments. Therefore it is He that produces the inward sacramental effect.

OBJ. 4: Further, no one can confer the sacramental effect without conferring the sacrament, except he produce

effectum operetur. Sed Christus sine sacramento contulit sacramenti effectum, ut patet in Magdalena, cui dixit, *dimittuntur tibi peccata.* Ergo videtur quod Christus, secundum quod homo, operetur interiorem sacramenti effectum.

PRAETEREA, illud in cuius virtute sacramentum operatur, est principale agens ad interiorem effectum. Sed sacramenta habent virtutem ex passione Christi et invocatione nominis eius, secundum illud I Cor. I, *nunquid Paulus pro vobis crucifixus est? Aut in nomine Pauli baptizati estis?* Ergo Christus, inquantum homo, operatur interiorem sacramenti effectum.

SED CONTRA est quod Augustinus dicit, *in sacramentis divina virtus secretius operatur salutem.* Divina autem virtus est Christi secundum quod est Deus, non autem secundum quod est homo. Ergo Christus non operatur interiorem sacramenti effectum secundum quod est homo, sed secundum quod est Deus.

RESPONDEO dicendum quod interiorem sacramentorum effectum operatur Christus et secundum quod est Deus, et secundum quod est homo, aliter tamen et aliter. Nam secundum quod est Deus, operatur in sacramentis per auctoritatem. Secundum autem quod est homo, operatur ad interiores effectus sacramentorum meritorie, et efficienter, sed instrumentaliter. Dictum est enim quod passio Christi, quae competit ei secundum humanam naturam, causa est nostrae iustificationis et meritorie, et effective, non quidem per modum principalis agentis, sive per auctoritatem, sed per modum instrumenti, inquantum humanitas est instrumentum divinitatis eius, ut supra dictum est.

Sed tamen, quia est instrumentum coniunctum divinitati in persona, habet quandam principalitatem et causalitatem respectu instrumentorum extrinsecorum, qui sunt ministri Ecclesiae et ipsa sacramenta, ut ex supra dictis patet. Et ideo, sicut Christus, inquantum Deus, habet potestatem auctoritatis in sacramentis, ita, inquantum homo, habet potestatem ministerii principalis, sive potestatem excellentiae. Quae quidem consistit in quatuor. Primo quidem, in hoc quod meritum et virtus passionis eius operatur in sacramentis, ut supra dictum est. Et quia virtus passionis copulatur nobis per fidem, secundum illud Rom. III, *quem proposuit Deus propitiatorem per fidem in sanguine eius,* quam fidem per invocationem nominis Christi protestamur, ideo, secundo, ad potestatem excellentiae quam Christus habet in sacramentis, pertinet quod in eius nomine sacramenta sanctificantur. Et quia ex institutione sacramenta virtutem obtinent, inde est quod, tertio, ad excellentiam potestatis Christi pertinet quod ipse, qui dedit virtutem sacramentis, potuit instituere sacramenta. Et quia causa non dependet ab effectu, sed potius e converso, quarto,

the sacramental effect by his own power. But Christ conferred the sacramental effect without conferring the sacrament; as in the case of Magdalen to whom He said: *Thy sins are forgiven Thee* (Luke 7:48). Therefore it seems that Christ, as man, produces the inward sacramental effect.

OBJ. 5: Further, the principal agent in causing the inward effect is that in virtue of which the sacrament operates. But the sacraments derive their power from Christ's Passion and through the invocation of His Name; according to 1 Cor. 1:13: *Was Paul then crucified for you? or were you baptized in the name of Paul?* Therefore Christ, as man, produces the inward sacramental effect.

ON THE CONTRARY, Augustine (Isidore, *Etym.* vi) says: *The Divine power in the sacraments works inwardly in producing their salutary effect.* Now the Divine power is Christ's as God, not as man. Therefore Christ produces the inward sacramental effect, not as man but as God.

I ANSWER THAT, Christ produces the inward sacramental effect, both as God and as man, but not in the same way. For, as God, He works in the sacraments by authority: but, as man, His operation conduces to the inward sacramental effects meritoriously and efficiently, but instrumentally. For it has been stated (Q. 48, AA. 1, 6; Q. 49, A. 1) that Christ's Passion which belongs to Him in respect of His human nature, is the cause of justification, both meritoriously and efficiently, not as the principal cause thereof, or by His own authority, but as an instrument, in so far as His humanity is the instrument of His Godhead, as stated above (Q. 13, AA. 2, 3; Q. 19, A. 1).

Nevertheless, since it is an instrument united to the Godhead in unity of Person, it has a certain headship and efficiency in regard to extrinsic instruments, which are the ministers of the Church and the sacraments themselves, as has been explained above (A. 1). Consequently, just as Christ, as God, has power of authority over the sacraments, so, as man, He has the power of ministry in chief, or power of excellence. And this consists in four things. First in this, that the merit and power of His Passion operates in the sacraments, as stated above (Q. 62, A. 5). And because the power of the Passion is communicated to us by faith, according to Rom. 3:25: *Whom God hath proposed to be a propitiation through faith in His blood,* which faith we proclaim by calling on the name of Christ: therefore, second, Christ's power of excellence over the sacraments consists in this, that they are sanctified by the invocation of His name. And because the sacraments derive their power from their institution, hence, third, the excellence of Christ's power consists in this, that He, Who gave them their power, could institute the sacraments. And since cause does not depend on effect, but rather conversely, fourth, it belongs to the

ad excellentiam potestatis Christi pertinet quod ipse potuit effectum sacramentorum sine exteriori sacramento conferre.

ET PER HOC patet responsio ad obiecta, utraque enim pars obiectionum vera est, ut dictum est, secundum aliquid.

excellence of Christ's power, that He could bestow the sacramental effect without conferring the exterior sacrament.

THUS it is clear how to solve the objections; for the arguments on either side are true to a certain extent, as explained above.

Article 4

Whether Christ Could Communicate to Ministers the Power Which He Had in the Sacraments?

AD QUARTUM SIC PROCEDITUR. Videtur quod Christus potestatem suam quam habuit in sacramentis, non potuerit ministris communicare. Ut enim argumentatur Augustinus, contra Maximinum, *si potuit et non voluit, invidus fuit.* Sed invidia longe fuit a Christo, in quo fuit summa plenitudo caritatis. Ergo, cum Christus non communicaverit suam potestatem ministris, videtur quod non potuerit communicare.

PRAETEREA, super illud Ioan. XIV, *maiora horum faciet*, dicit Augustinus, prorsus maius hoc esse dixerim, scilicet ut ex impio iustus fiat, quam creare caelum et terram. Sed Christus non potuit communicare suis discipulis quod crearent caelum et terram. Ergo neque quod iustificent impium. Cum igitur iustificatio impii fiat per potestatem Christi quam habet in sacramentis, videtur quod potestatem suam quam habet in sacramentis, non potuerit ministris communicare.

PRAETEREA, Christo inquantum est caput Ecclesiae, competit ut ab ipso gratia derivetur ad alios, secundum illud Ioan. I, *de plenitudine eius omnes accepimus.* Sed hoc non fuit aliis communicabile, quia sic Ecclesia esset monstruosa, multa capita habens. Ergo videtur quod Christus suam potestatem non potuerit ministris communicare.

SED CONTRA est quod, super illud Ioan. I, *ego nesciebam eum*, dicit Augustinus quod *non noverat potestatem Baptismi ipsum dominum habiturum et sibi retenturum.* Hoc autem non ignorasset Ioannes si talis potestas communicabilis non esset. Potuit ergo potestatem suam Christus ministris communicare.

RESPONDEO dicendum quod, sicut dictum est, Christus in sacramentis habuit duplicem potestatem. Unam auctoritatis, quae competit ei secundum quod Deus. Et talis potestas nulli creaturae potuit communicari, sicut nec divina essentia. Aliam potestatem habuit excellentiae, quae competit ei secundum quod homo. Et talem potestatem potuit ministris communicare, dando scilicet eis tantam gratiae plenitudinem ut eorum meritum operaretur ad sacramentorum effectus; ut ad invocationem nominum ipsorum sanctificarentur sacramenta; et

OBJECTION 1: It seems that Christ could not communicate to ministers the power which He had in the sacraments. For as Augustine argues against Maximin, *if He could, but would not, He was jealous of His power.* But jealousy was far from Christ Who had the fullness of charity. Since, therefore, Christ did not communicate His power to ministers, it seems that He could not.

OBJ. 2: Further, on John 14:12: *Greater than these shall he do*, Augustine says (*Tract. lxxii*): *I affirm this to be altogether greater*, namely, for a man from being ungodly to be made righteous, *than to create heaven and earth.* But Christ could not communicate to His disciples the power of creating heaven and earth: neither, therefore, could He give them the power of making the ungodly to be righteous. Since, therefore, the justification of the ungodly is effected by the power that Christ has in the sacraments, it seems that He could not communicate that power to ministers.

OBJ. 3: Further, it belongs to Christ as Head of the Church that grace should flow from Him to others, according to John 1:16: *Of His fullness we all have received.* But this could not be communicated to others; since then the Church would be deformed, having many heads. Therefore it seems that Christ could not communicate His power to ministers.

ON THE CONTRARY, on John 1:31: *I knew Him not*, Augustine says (*Tract. v*) that *he did not know that our Lord having the authority of baptizing . . . would keep it to Himself.* But John would not have been in ignorance of this, if such a power were incommunicable. Therefore Christ could communicate His power to ministers.

I ANSWER THAT, As stated above (A. 3), Christ had a twofold power in the sacraments. One was the power of authority, which belongs to Him as God: and this power He could not communicate to any creature; just as neither could He communicate the Divine Essence. The other was the power of excellence, which belongs to Him as man. This power He could communicate to ministers; namely, by giving them such a fullness of grace—that their merits would conduce to the sacramental effect—that by the invocation of their names, the sacraments would be sanctified—and

ut ipsi possent sacramenta instituere; et sine ritu sacramentorum effectum conferre solo imperio. Potest enim instrumentum coniunctum, quanto fuerit fortius, tanto magis virtutem suam instrumento separato tribuere, sicut manus baculo.

Ad primum ergo dicendum quod Christus non ex invidia praetermisit potestatem excellentiae ministris communicare, sed propter fidelium utilitatem, ne in homine spem ponerent, et essent diversa sacramenta, ex quibus divisio in Ecclesia oriretur; sicut apud illos qui dicebant, *ego sum Pauli, ego autem Apollo, ego vero Cephae*, ut dicitur I Cor. I.

Ad secundum dicendum quod obiectio illa procedit de potestate auctoritatis, quae convenit Christo secundum quod est Deus. Licet et potestas excellentiae possit auctoritas nominari per comparationem ad alios ministros. Unde super illud I Cor. I, *divisus est Christus?* Dicit Glossa quod *potuit eis dare auctoritatem Baptismi, quibus contulit ministerium.*

Ad tertium dicendum quod ad hoc inconveniens evitandum, ne scilicet multa capita in Ecclesia essent, Christus noluit potestatem suae excellentiae ministris communicare. Si tamen communicasset, ipse esset caput principaliter, alii vero secundario.

that they themselves might institute sacraments, and by their mere will confer the sacramental effect without observing the sacramental rite. For a united instrument, the more powerful it is, is all the more able to lend its power to the separated instrument; as the hand can to a stick.

Reply Obj. 1: It was not through jealousy that Christ refrained from communicating to ministers His power of excellence, but for the good of the faithful; lest they should put their trust in men, and lest there should be various kinds of sacraments, giving rise to division in the Church; as may be seen in those who said: *I am of Paul, I am of Apollo, and I of Cephas* (1 Cor 1:12).

Reply Obj. 2: This objection is true of the power of authority, which belongs to Christ as God. At the same time the power of excellence can be called authority in comparison to other ministers. Whence on 1 Cor. 1:13: *Is Christ divided?* the gloss says that *He could give power of authority in baptizing, to those to whom He gave the power of administering it.*

Reply Obj. 3: It was in order to avoid the incongruity of many heads in the Church, that Christ was unwilling to communicate to ministers His power of excellence. If, however, He had done so, He would have been Head in chief; the others in subjection to Him.

Article 5

Whether the Sacraments Can Be Conferred by Evil Ministers?

Ad quintum sic proceditur. Videtur quod per malos ministros sacramenta conferri non possint. Sacramenta enim novae legis ordinantur ad emundationem culpae et collationem gratiae. Sed mali, cum sint immundi, non possunt alios a peccato mundare, secundum illud Eccli. XXXIV, *ab immundo quis mundabitur?* Et etiam, cum gratiam non habeant, non videtur quod gratiam conferre possint, quia nullus dat quod non habet. Non ergo videtur quod per malos sacramenta conferri possint.

Praeterea, tota virtus sacramentorum derivatur a Christo, ut dictum est. Sed mali sunt praecisi a Christo, quia non habent caritatem, per quam membra capiti uniuntur, secundum illud I Ioan. IV, *qui manet in caritate, in Deo manet, et Deus in eo.* Ergo videtur quod per malos sacramenta conferri non possint.

Praeterea, si desit aliquid horum quae debitum est esse in sacramentis, non perficitur sacramentum, sicut si desit debita forma vel materia. Sed debitus minister sacramenti est ille qui caret macula peccati, secundum illud Levit. XXI, *homo de semine tuo per familias qui habuit maculam, non offeret panes Deo tuo, nec accedet ad*

Objection 1: It seems that the sacraments cannot be conferred by evil ministers. For the sacraments of the New Law are ordained for the purpose of cleansing from sin and for the bestowal of grace. Now evil men, being themselves unclean, cannot cleanse others from sin, according to Ecclus. 34:4: *Who can be made clean by the unclean?* Moreover, since they have not grace, it seems that they cannot give grace, for *no one gives what he has not*. It seems, therefore, that the sacraments cannot be conferred by wicked men.

Obj. 2: Further, all the power of the sacraments is derived from Christ, as stated above (A. 3; Q. 62, A. 5). But evil men are cut off from Christ: because they have not charity, by which the members are united to their Head, according to 1 John 4:16: *He that abideth in charity, abideth in God, and God in him*. Therefore it seems that the sacraments cannot be conferred by evil men.

Obj. 3: Further, if anything is wanting that is required for the sacraments, the sacrament is invalid; for instance, if the required matter or form be wanting. But the minister required for a sacrament is one who is without the stain of sin, according to Lev. 21:17, 18: *Whosoever of thy seed throughout their families, hath a blemish, he shall not offer*

ministerium eius. Ergo videtur quod, si minister sit malus, nihil efficiatur in sacramento.

SED CONTRA est quod Augustinus dicit, super illud Ioan. I, *super quem videris spiritum etc., quod non noverat Ioannes potestatem Baptismi ipsum dominum habiturum et sibi retenturum, sed ministerium plane transiturum in bonos et malos. Quid tibi facit malus minister, ubi bonus est dominus?*

RESPONDEO dicendum quod, sicut dictum est, ministri Ecclesiae instrumentaliter operantur in sacramentis, eo quod quodammodo eadem est ratio ministri et instrumenti. Sicut autem supra dictum est, instrumentum non agit secundum propriam formam, sed secundum virtutem eius a quo movetur. Et ideo accidit instrumento, inquantum est instrumentum, qualemcumque formam vel virtutem habeat, praeter id quod exigitur ad rationem instrumenti, sicut quod corpus medici, quod est instrumentum animae habentis artem, sit sanum vel infirmum; et sicut quod fistula per quam transit aqua, sit argentea vel plumbea. Unde ministri Ecclesiae possunt sacramenta conferre etiam si sint mali.

AD PRIMUM ergo dicendum quod ministri Ecclesiae neque a peccatis mundant homines ad sacramenta accedentes, neque gratiam conferunt, sua virtute, sed hoc facit Christus sua potestate per eos sicut per quaedam instrumenta. Et ideo effectus consequitur in suscipientibus sacramenta non secundum similitudinem ministrorum, sed secundum configurationem ad Christum.

AD SECUNDUM dicendum quod per caritatem membra Christi uniuntur suo capiti ut ab eo vitam recipiant, quia, ut dicitur I Ioan. III, *qui non diligit, manet in morte.* Potest autem aliquis operari per instrumentum carens vita, et a se separatum quantum ad corporis unionem, dummodo sit coniunctum per quandam motionem, aliter enim operatur artifex per manum, et aliter per securim. Sic igitur Christus operatur in sacramentis et per malos, tanquam per instrumenta carentia vita; et per bonos, tanquam per membra viventia.

AD TERTIUM dicendum quod aliquid est debitum esse in sacramento dupliciter. Uno modo, sicut existens de necessitate sacramenti. Quod quidem si desit, non perficitur sacramentum, sicut si desit debita forma vel debita materia. Alio modo est aliquid debitum esse in sacramento secundum quandam decentiam. Et hoc modo debitum est ut ministri sacramentorum sint boni.

bread to his God, neither shall he approach to minister to Him. Therefore it seems that if the minister be wicked, the sacrament has no effect.

ON THE CONTRARY, Augustine says on John 1:33: *He upon Whom thou shalt see the Spirit*, etc. (*Tract. v in Joan.*), that *John did not know that our Lord, having the authority of baptizing, would keep it to Himself, but that the ministry would certainly pass to both good and evil men . . . What is a bad minister to thee, where the Lord is good?*

I ANSWER THAT, As stated above (A. 1), the ministers of the Church work instrumentally in the sacraments, because, in a way, a minister is of the nature of an instrument. But, as stated above (Q. 62, AA. 1, 4), an instrument acts not by reason of its own form, but by the power of the one who moves it. Consequently, whatever form or power an instrument has in addition to that which it has as an instrument, is accidental to it: for instance, that a physician's body, which is the instrument of his soul, wherein is his medical art, be healthy or sickly; or that a pipe, through which water passes, be of silver or lead. Therefore the ministers of the Church can confer the sacraments, though they be wicked.

REPLY OBJ. 1: The ministers of the Church do not by their own power cleanse from sin those who approach the sacraments, nor do they confer grace on them: it is Christ Who does this by His own power while He employs them as instruments. Consequently, those who approach the sacraments receive an effect whereby they are enlikened not to the ministers but to Christ.

REPLY OBJ. 2: Christ's members are united to their Head by charity, so that they may receive life from Him; for as it is written (1 John 3:14): *He that loveth not abideth in death*. Now it is possible for a man to work with a lifeless instrument, and separated from him as to bodily union, provided it be united to him by some sort of motion: for a workman works in one way with his hand, in another with his axe. Consequently, it is thus that Christ works in the sacraments, both by wicked men as lifeless instruments, and by good men as living instruments.

REPLY OBJ. 3: A thing is required in a sacrament in two ways. First, as being essential to it: and if this be wanting, the sacrament is invalid; for instance, if the due form or matter be wanting. Second, a thing is required for a sacrament, by reason of a certain fitness. And in this way good ministers are required for a sacrament.

Article 6

Whether Wicked Men Sin in Administering the Sacraments?

AD SEXTUM SIC PROCEDITUR. Videtur quod mali ministrantes sacramenta non peccent. Sicut enim ministratur Deo in sacramentis, ita per opera caritatis, unde dicitur Heb. ult., *beneficentiae et communionis nolite oblivisci, talibus enim hostiis promeretur Deus.* Sed mali non peccant si ministrent Deo in operibus caritatis, quinimmo hoc est consulendum, secundum illud Dan. IV, *consilium meum regi placeat, peccata tua eleemosynis redime.* Ergo videtur quod mali non peccent in sacramentis ministrando.

PRAETEREA, quicumque communicat alicui in peccato, etiam ipse est reus peccati, secundum illud Rom. I, *dignus est morte non solum qui peccatum agit, sed etiam qui consentit facientibus.* Sed si mali ministri peccent sacramenta ministrando, illi qui ab eis sacramenta recipiunt, eis in peccato communicant. Ergo etiam ipsi peccarent. Quod videtur inconveniens.

PRAETEREA, nullus videtur esse perplexus, quia sic homo cogeretur desperare, quasi non posset peccatum evadere. Sed si mali peccarent sacramenta tradendo, essent perplexi, quia etiam quandoque peccarent si sacramenta non traderent, puta cum eis ex officio incumbit necessitas; dicitur enim I Cor. IX, *vae mihi est si non evangelizavero, necessitas enim mihi incumbit.* Quandoque etiam propter periculum, sicut si puer, in periculo mortis existens, offeratur alicui peccatori baptizandus. Ergo videtur quod mali non peccent sacramenta ministrando.

SED CONTRA est quod Dionysius dicit, I cap. Eccles. Hier., quod *malis non est fas neque tangere symbola,* idest sacramentalia signa. Et in epistola ad Demophilum dicit, *talis, scilicet peccator, audax videtur sacerdotalibus manum imponens; et non timet neque verecundatur, divina praeter dignitatem exequens, et Deum putans ignorare quod ipse in seipso cognovit; et decipere existimat falso nomine patrem ab ipso appellatum; et audet immundas infamias non dicam orationes, super divina signa Christiformiter enuntiare.*

RESPONDEO dicendum quod aliquis in agendo peccat ex hoc quod operatur non secundum quod oportet, ut patet per philosophum, in libro Ethicorum. Dictum est autem conveniens esse ut sacramentorum ministri sint iusti, quia ministri debent domino conformari, secundum illud Levit. XIX, *sancti eritis, quoniam ego sanctus sum;* et Eccli. X, *secundum iudicem populi, sic et ministri eius.* Et ideo non est dubium quin mali exhibentes se ministros Dei et Ecclesiae in dispensatione sacramentorum, peccent. Et quia hoc peccatum pertinet

OBJECTION 1: It seems that wicked men do not sin in administering the sacraments. For just as men serve God in the sacraments, so do they serve Him in works of charity; whence it is written (Heb 13:16): *Do not forget to do good and to impart, for by such sacrifices God's favor is obtained.* But the wicked do not sin in serving God by works of charity: indeed, they should be persuaded to do so, according to Dan. 4:24: *Let my counsel be acceptable* to the king; *Redeem thou thy sins with alms.* Therefore it seems that wicked men do not sin in administering the sacraments.

OBJ. 2: Further, whoever co-operates with another in his sin, is also guilty of sin, according to Rom. 1:32: *He is worthy of death; not only he that commits the sin, but also he who consents to them that do them.* But if wicked ministers sin in administering sacraments, those who receive sacraments from them, co-operate in their sin. Therefore they would sin also; which seems unreasonable.

OBJ. 3: Further, it seems that no one should act when in doubt, for thus man would be driven to despair, as being unable to avoid sin. But if the wicked were to sin in administering sacraments, they would be in a state of perplexity: since sometimes they would sin also if they did not administer sacraments; for instance, when by reason of their office it is their bounden duty to do so; for it is written (1 Cor 9:16): *For a necessity lieth upon me: Woe is unto me if I preach not the gospel.* Sometimes also on account of some danger; for instance, if a child in danger of death be brought to a sinner for baptism. Therefore it seems that the wicked do not sin in administering the sacraments.

ON THE CONTRARY, Dionysius says (*Eccl. Hier.* i) that *it is wrong for the wicked even to touch the symbols,* i.e., the sacramental signs. And he says in the epistle to Demophilus: *It seems presumptuous for such a man,* i.e., a sinner, *to lay hands on priestly things; he is neither afraid nor ashamed, all unworthy that he is, to take part in Divine things, with the thought that God does not see what he sees in himself: he thinks, by false pretenses, to cheat Him Whom he calls his Father; he dares to utter, in the person of Christ, words polluted by his infamy, I will not call them prayers, over the Divine symbols.*

I ANSWER THAT, A sinful action consists in this, that a man *fails to act as he ought to,* as the Philosopher explains (*Ethic.* ii). Now it has been said (A. 5, ad 3) that it is fitting for the ministers of sacraments to be righteous; because ministers should be like unto their Lord, according to Lev. 19:2: *Be ye holy, because I . . . am holy;* and Ecclus. 10:2: *As the judge of the people is himself, so also are his ministers.* Consequently, there can be no doubt that the wicked sin by exercising the ministry of God and the Church, by conferring the sacraments. And since this sin pertains to

ad irreverentiam Dei et contaminationem sanctorum, quantum est ex parte ipsius hominis peccatoris, licet sancta secundum seipsa incontaminabilia sint, consequens est quod tale peccatum ex genere suo est mortale.

AD PRIMUM ergo dicendum quod opera caritatis non sunt aliqua consecratione sanctificata, sed ipsa pertinent ad iustitiae sanctitatem sicut quaedam iustitiae partes. Et ideo homo qui se exhibet Deo ministrum in operibus caritatis, si sit iustus, amplius sanctificabitur, si vero sit peccator, per hoc ad sanctitatem disponitur. Sed sacramenta in seipsis sanctificationem quandam habent per mysticam consecrationem. Et ideo praeexigitur in ministro sanctitas iustitiae, ut congruat suo ministerio. Et ideo incongrue agit et peccat, si in peccato existens ad tale ministerium accedat.

AD SECUNDUM dicendum quod ille qui ad sacramenta accedit, suscipit quidem sacramentum a ministro Ecclesiae, non inquantum est talis persona, sed inquantum est Ecclesiae minister. Et ideo, quandiu ab Ecclesia toleratur in ministerio, ille qui ab eo suscipit sacramentum, non communicat peccato eius, sed communicat Ecclesiae, quae eum tanquam ministrum exhibet. Si vero ab Ecclesia non toleretur, puta cum degradatur vel excommunicatur vel suspenditur, peccat qui ab eo accipit sacramentum, quia communicat peccato ipsius.

AD TERTIUM dicendum quod ille qui est in peccato mortali, non est perplexus simpliciter, si ex officio ei incumbat sacramenta dispensare, quia potest poenitere de peccato et licite ministrare. Non est autem inconveniens quod sit perplexus supposito quodam, scilicet quod velit remanere in peccato.

In articulo tamen necessitatis non peccaret baptizando in casu in quo etiam posset laicus dispensare. Sic enim patet quod non exhibet se ministrum Ecclesiae, sed subvenit necessitatem patienti. Secus autem est in aliis sacramentis, quae non sunt tantae necessitatis sicut Baptismus, ut infra patebit.

irreverence towards God and the contamination of holy things, as far as the man who sins is concerned, although holy things in themselves cannot be contaminated; it follows that such a sin is mortal in its genus.

REPLY OBJ. 1: Works of charity are not made holy by some process of consecration, but they belong to the holiness of righteousness, as being in a way parts of righteousness. Consequently, when a man shows himself as a minister of God, by doing works of charity, if he be righteous, he will be made yet holier; but if he be a sinner, he is thereby disposed to holiness. On the other hand, the sacraments are holy in themselves owing to their mystical consecration. Wherefore the holiness of righteousness is required in the minister, that he may be suitable for his ministry: for which reason he acts unbecomingly and sins, if while in a state of sin he attempts to fulfill that ministry.

REPLY OBJ. 2: He who approaches a sacrament, receives it from a minister of the Church, not because he is such and such a man, but because he is a minister of the Church. Consequently, as long as the latter is tolerated in the ministry, he that receives a sacrament from him, does not communicate in his sin, but communicates with the Church from whom he has his ministry. But if the Church, by degrading, excommunicating, or suspending him, does not tolerate him in the ministry, he that receives a sacrament from him sins, because he communicates in his sin.

REPLY OBJ. 3: A man who is in mortal sin is not perplexed simply, if by reason of his office it be his bounden duty to minister sacraments; because he can repent of his sin and so minister lawfully. But there is nothing unreasonable in his being perplexed, if we suppose that he wishes to remain in sin.

However, in a case of necessity when even a lay person might baptize, he would not sin in baptizing. For it is clear that then he does not exercise the ministry of the Church, but comes to the aid of one who is in need of his services. It is not so with the other sacraments, which are not so necessary as baptism, as we shall show further on (Q. 65, AA. 3, 4; Q. 62, A. 3).

Article 7

Whether Angels Can Administer Sacraments?

AD SEPTIMUM SIC PROCEDITUR. Videtur quod Angeli possent sacramenta ministrare. Quidquid enim potest minister inferior, potest et superior, sicut quidquid potest diaconus, potest et sacerdos, sed non convertitur. Sed Angeli sunt superiores ministri in ordine

OBJECTION 1: It seems that angels can administer sacraments. Because a higher minister can do whatever the lower can; thus a priest can do whatever a deacon can: but not conversely. But angels are higher ministers in the hierarchical order than any men whatsoever, as Dionysius says

hierarchico quam etiam quicumque homines, ut patet per Dionysium, in libro Cael. Hier. Ergo, cum homines possint ministrare in sacramentis, videtur quod multo magis Angeli.

PRAETEREA, homines sancti assimilantur Angelis in caelo, ut dicitur Matth. XXII. Sed aliqui sancti in caelo existentes possunt ministrare in sacramentis, quia character sacramentalis est indelebilis, ut dictum est. Ergo videtur quod etiam Angeli in sacris possint ministrare.

PRAETEREA, sicut supra dictum est, Diabolus est caput malorum, et mali sunt membra eius. Sed per malos possunt dispensari sacramenta. Ergo videtur quod etiam per Daemones.

SED CONTRA est quod dicitur Heb. V, *omnis pontifex, ex hominibus assumptus, pro hominibus constituitur in his quae sunt ad Deum.* Sed Angeli boni vel mali non sunt ex hominibus. Ergo ipsi non constituuntur ministri in his quae sunt ad Deum, idest in sacramentis.

RESPONDEO dicendum quod, sicut supra dictum est, tota virtus sacramentorum a passione Christi derivatur, quae est Christi secundum quod homo. Cui in natura conformantur homines, non autem Angeli, sed potius secundum passionem dicitur modico ab Angelis minoratus, ut patet Heb. II. Et ideo ad homines pertinet dispensare sacramenta et in eis ministrare, non autem ad Angelos.

Sciendum tamen quod, sicut Deus virtutem suam non alligavit sacramentis quin possit sine sacramentis effectum sacramentorum conferre, ita etiam virtutem suam non alligavit Ecclesiae ministris, quin etiam Angelis possit virtutem tribuere ministrandi in sacramentis. Et quia boni Angeli sunt nuntii veritatis, si aliquod sacramentale ministerium a bonis Angelis perficeretur, esset ratum habendum, quia deberet constare hoc fieri voluntate divina, sicut quaedam templa dicuntur angelico ministerio consecrata. Si vero Daemones, qui sunt spiritus mendacii, aliquod sacramentale ministerium exhiberent, non esset ratum habendum.

AD PRIMUM ergo dicendum quod illud quod faciunt homines inferiori modo, scilicet per sacramenta sensibilia, quae sunt proportionata naturae ipsorum, faciunt Angeli, tanquam superiores ministri, superiori modo, scilicet invisibiliter purgando, illuminando et perficiendo.

AD SECUNDUM dicendum quod sancti qui sunt in caelo, sunt similes Angelis quantum ad participationem gloriae, non autem quantum ad conditionem naturae. Et per consequens neque quantum ad sacramenta.

AD TERTIUM dicendum quod mali homines non habent quod possint ministrare in sacramentis ex hoc quod per malitiam sunt membra Diaboli. Et ideo non

(*Coel. Hier.* ix). Therefore, since men can be ministers of sacraments, it seems that much more can angels be.

OBJ. 2: Further, in heaven holy men are likened to the angels (Matt 22:30). But some holy men, when in heaven, can be ministers of the sacraments; since the sacramental character is indelible, as stated above (Q. 63, A. 5). Therefore it seems that angels too can be ministers of sacraments.

OBJ. 3: Further, as stated above (Q. 8, A. 7), the devil is head of the wicked, and the wicked are his members. But sacraments can be administered by the wicked. Therefore it seems that they can be administered even by demons.

ON THE CONTRARY, It is written (Heb 5:1): *Every high priest taken from among men, is ordained for men in the things that appertain to God.* But angels whether good or bad are not taken from among men. Therefore they are not ordained ministers in the things that appertain to God, i.e., in the sacraments.

I ANSWER THAT, As stated above (A. 3; Q. 62, A. 5), the whole power of the sacraments flows from Christ's Passion, which belongs to Him as man. And Him in their very nature men, not angels, resemble; indeed, in respect of His Passion, He is described as being *a little lower than the angels* (Heb 2:9). Consequently, it belongs to men, but not to angels, to dispense the sacraments and to take part in their administration.

But it must be observed that as God did not bind His power to the sacraments, so as to be unable to bestow the sacramental effect without conferring the sacrament; so neither did He bind His power to the ministers of the Church so as to be unable to give angels power to administer the sacraments. And since good angels are messengers of truth; if any sacramental rite were performed by good angels, it should be considered valid, because it ought to be evident that this is being done by the will of God: for instance, certain churches are said to have been consecrated by the ministry of the angels. But if demons, who are *lying spirits*, were to perform a sacramental rite, it should be pronounced as invalid.

REPLY OBJ. 1: What men do in a less perfect manner, i.e., by sensible sacraments, which are proportionate to their nature, angels also do, as ministers of a higher degree, in a more perfect manner, i.e., invisibly—by cleansing, enlightening, and perfecting.

REPLY OBJ. 2: The saints in heaven resemble the angels as to their share of glory, but not as to the conditions of their nature: and consequently not in regard to the sacraments.

REPLY OBJ. 3: Wicked men do not owe their power of conferring sacraments to their being members of the devil.

sequitur quod Diabolus, qui est eorum caput, magis hoc possit.

Consequently, it does not follow that *a fortiori* the devil, their head, can do so.

Article 8

Whether the Minister's Intention Is Required for the Validity of a Sacrament?

AD OCTAVUM SIC PROCEDITUR. Videtur quod intentio ministri non requiratur ad perfectionem sacramenti. Minister enim in sacramento instrumentaliter operatur. Sed actio non perficitur secundum intentionem instrumenti, sed secundum intentionem principalis agentis. Ergo intentio ministri non requiritur ad perfectionem sacramenti.

PRAETEREA, non potest homini esse nota intentio alterius. Si igitur intentio ministri requiratur ad perfectionem sacramenti, non posset homini ad sacramentum accedenti esse notum quod sacramentum suscepisset. Et ita non posset habere certitudinem salutis, praecipue cum quaedam sacramenta sint de necessitate salutis, ut infra dicetur.

PRAETEREA, intentio hominis non potest esse ad id circa quod non est attentus. Sed aliquando illi qui in sacramentis ministrant, non attendunt ad ea quae dicunt vel faciunt, alia cogitantes. Ergo, secundum hoc, non perficitur sacramentum, propter intentionis defectum.

SED CONTRA est quod ea quae sunt praeter intentionem, sunt casualia. Quod non est dicendum de operatione sacramentorum. Ergo sacramenta requirunt intentionem ministri.

RESPONDEO dicendum quod, quando aliquid se habet ad multa, oportet quod per aliquid determinetur ad unum, si illud effici debeat. Ea vero quae in sacramentis aguntur, possunt diversimode agi, sicut ablutio aquae, quae fit in Baptismo, potest ordinari et ad munditiam corporalem, et ad sanitatem corporalem, et ad ludum et ad multa alia huiusmodi. Et ideo oportet quod determinetur ad unum, idest ad sacramentalem effectum, per intentionem abluentis. Et haec intentio exprimitur per verba quae in sacramentis dicuntur, puta cum dicit, ego te baptizo in nomine patris, et cetera.

AD PRIMUM ergo dicendum quod instrumentum inanimatum non habet aliquam intentionem respectu effectus, sed loco intentionis est motus quo movetur a principali agente. Sed instrumentum animatum, sicut est minister, non solum movetur, sed etiam quodammodo movet seipsum, inquantum sua voluntate movet membra ad operandum. Et ideo requiritur eius intentio, qua se subiiciat principali agenti, ut scilicet intendat facere quod facit Christus et Ecclesia.

OBJECTION 1: It seems that the minister's intention is not required for the validity of a sacrament. For the minister of a sacrament works instrumentally. But the perfection of an action does not depend on the intention of the instrument, but on that of the principal agent. Therefore the minister's intention is not necessary for the perfecting of a sacrament.

OBJ. 2: Further, one man's intention cannot be known to another. Therefore if the minister's intention were required for the validity of a sacrament, he who approaches a sacrament could not know whether he has received the sacrament. Consequently he could have no certainty in regard to salvation; the more that some sacraments are necessary for salvation, as we shall state further on (Q. 65, A. 4).

OBJ. 3: Further, a man's intention cannot bear on that to which he does not attend. But sometimes ministers of sacraments do not attend to what they say or do, through thinking of something else. Therefore in this respect the sacrament would be invalid through want of intention.

ON THE CONTRARY, What is unintentional happens by chance. But this cannot be said of the sacramental operation. Therefore the sacraments require the intention of the minister.

I ANSWER THAT, When a thing is indifferent to many uses, it must needs be determined to one, if that one has to be effected. Now those things which are done in the sacraments, can be done with various intent; for instance, washing with water, which is done in baptism, may be ordained to bodily cleanliness, to the health of the body, to amusement, and many other similar things. Consequently, it needs to be determined to one purpose, i.e., the sacramental effect, by the intention of him who washes. And this intention is expressed by the words which are pronounced in the sacraments; for instance the words, *I baptize thee in the name of the Father*, etc.

REPLY OBJ. 1: An inanimate instrument has no intention regarding the effect; but instead of the intention there is the motion whereby it is moved by the principal agent. But an animate instrument, such as a minister, is not only moved, but in a sense moves itself, in so far as by his will he moves his bodily members to act. Consequently, his intention is required, whereby he subjects himself to the principal agent; that is, it is necessary that he intend to do that which Christ and the Church do.

AD SECUNDUM dicendum quod circa hoc est duplex opinio. Quidam enim dicunt quod requiritur mentalis intentio in ministro, quae si desit, non perficitur sacramentum. Sed hunc defectum in pueris, qui non habent intentionem accedendi ad sacramentum, supplet Christus, qui interius baptizat. In adultis autem, quia intendunt sacramenta suscipere, supplet illum defectum fides et devotio.

Sed hoc satis posset dici quantum ad ultimum effectum, qui est iustificatio a peccatis, sed quantum ad effectum qui est res et sacramentum, scilicet quantum ad characterem, non videtur quod per devotionem accedentis possit suppleri; quia character nunquam imprimitur nisi per sacramentum.

Et ideo alii melius dicunt quod minister sacramenti agit in persona totius Ecclesiae, cuius est minister; in verbis autem quae proferuntur, exprimitur intentio Ecclesiae; quae sufficit ad perfectionem sacramenti, nisi contrarium exterius exprimatur ex parte ministri et recipientis sacramentum.

AD TERTIUM dicendum quod, licet ille qui aliud cogitat, non habeat actualem intentionem, habet tamen habitualem, quae sufficit ad perfectionem sacramenti, puta si, cum sacerdos accedit ad baptizandum, intendit facere circa baptizandum quod facit Ecclesia. Unde, si postea in ipso exercitio actus cogitatio eius ad alia rapiatur, ex virtute primae intentionis perficitur sacramentum. Quamvis studiose curare debeat sacramenti minister ut etiam actualem intentionem adhibeat. Sed hoc non totaliter est positum in hominis potestate, quia praeter intentionem, cum homo vult multum intendere, incipit alia cogitare; secundum illud Psalmi, *cor meum dereliquit me*.

REPLY OBJ. 2: On this point there are two opinions. For some hold that the mental intention of the minister is necessary; in the absence of which the sacrament is invalid: and that this defect in the case of children who have not the intention of approaching the sacrament, is made good by Christ, Who baptizes inwardly: whereas in adults, who have that intention, this defect is made good by their faith and devotion.

This might be true enough of the ultimate effect, i.e., justification from sins; but as to that effect which is both real and sacramental, viz. the character, it does not appear possible for it to be made good by the devotion of the recipient, since a character is never imprinted save by a sacrament.

Consequently, others with better reason hold that the minister of a sacrament acts in the person of the whole Church, whose minister he is; while in the words uttered by him, the intention of the Church is expressed; and that this suffices for the validity of the sacrament, except the contrary be expressed on the part either of the minister or of the recipient of the sacrament.

REPLY OBJ. 3: Although he who thinks of something else, has no actual intention, yet he has habitual intention, which suffices for the validity of the sacrament; for instance if, when a priest goes to baptize someone, he intends to do to him what the Church does. Wherefore if subsequently during the exercise of the act his mind be distracted by other matters, the sacrament is valid in virtue of his original intention. Nevertheless, the minister of a sacrament should take great care to have actual intention. But this is not entirely in man's power, because when a man wishes to be very intent on something, he begins unintentionally to think of other things, according to Ps. 39:18: *My heart hath forsaken me.*

Article 9

Whether Faith Is Required of Necessity in the Minister of a Sacrament?

AD NONUM SIC PROCEDITUR. Videtur quod fides ministri sit de necessitate sacramenti. Sicut enim dictum est, intentio ministri est necessaria ad sacramenti perfectionem. Sed fides intentionem dirigit, ut Augustinus dicit, contra Iulianum. Ergo, si desit vera fides in ministro, non perficitur sacramentum.

PRAETEREA, si minister Ecclesiae veram fidem non habet, videtur esse haereticus. Sed haeretici, ut videtur, non possunt sacramenta conferre. Dicit enim Cyprianus, in epistola contra haereticos, *omnia quaecumque faciunt haeretici, carnalia sunt et inania et falsa, ita ut nihil eorum quae illi gesserint, a nobis debeat probari.* Et

OBJECTION 1: It seems that faith is required of necessity in the minister of a sacrament. For, as stated above (A. 8), the intention of the minister is necessary for the validity of a sacrament. But *faith directs in intention* as Augustine says against Julian (In Psalm xxxi, cf. Contra Julian iv). Therefore, if the minister is without the true faith, the sacrament is invalid.

OBJ. 2: Further, if a minister of the Church has not the true faith, it seems that he is a heretic. But heretics, seemingly, cannot confer sacraments. For Cyprian says in an epistle against heretics (lxxiii): *Everything whatsoever heretics do, is carnal, void and counterfeit, so that nothing that they do should receive our approval.* And Pope Leo says in

Leo Papa dicit, in epistola ad Leonem Augustum, *manifestum est per crudelissimam et insanissimam vesaniam in Alexandrina sede omnium caelestium sacramentorum lumen extinctum. Intercepta est sacrificii oblatio, defecit chrismatis sanctificatio, et paricidalibus manibus impiorum omnia sese subtraxere mysteria.* Ergo vera fides ministri est de necessitate sacramenti.

PRAETEREA, illi qui non habent veram fidem, videntur esse per excommunicationem ab Ecclesia separati, dicitur enim in secunda canonica Ioannis, *si quis venit ad vos et hanc doctrinam non affert, nolite recipere eum in domum, nec ave dixeritis ei;* et Tit. III, *haereticum hominem, post primam et secundam correctionem, devita.* Sed excommunicatus non videtur conferre posse Ecclesiae sacramentum, cum sit ab Ecclesia separatus, ad cuius ministerium pertinet sacramentorum dispensatio. Ergo videtur quod vera fides ministri sit de necessitate sacramenti.

SED CONTRA est quod Augustinus dicit, contra Petilianum Donatistam, *mementote sacramentis Dei nihil obesse mores malorum hominum, quod illa vel non sint, vel minus sancta sint.*

RESPONDEO dicendum quod, sicut supra dictum est, quia minister in sacramentis instrumentaliter operatur, non agit in virtute propria, sed in virtute Christi. Sicut autem pertinet ad propriam virtutem hominis caritas, ita et fides. Unde, sicut non requiritur ad perfectionem sacramenti quod minister sit in caritate, sed possunt etiam peccatores sacramenta conferre, ut supra dictum est; ita non requiritur fides eius, sed infidelis potest verum sacramentum praebere, dummodo cetera adsint quae sunt de necessitate sacramenti.

AD PRIMUM ergo dicendum quod potest contingere quod aliquis patiatur defectum fidei circa aliquid aliud, et non circa veritatem sacramenti quod exhibet, puta si aliquis credat iuramentum esse in omni casu illicitum, et tamen credat Baptismum efficaciam habere ad salutem. Et sic talis infidelitas non impedit intentionem conferendi sacramentum. Si vero patiatur fidei defectum circa ipsum sacramentum quod exhibet, licet credat per id quod agitur exterius nullum sequi interiorem effectum, non tamen ignorat quod Ecclesia Catholica intendit per huiusmodi quae exterius aguntur, sacramentum praebere. Unde, non obstante infidelitate, potest intendere facere id quod facit Ecclesia, licet existimet id nihil esse. Et talis intentio sufficit ad sacramentum, quia, sicut supra dictum est, minister sacramenti agit in persona totius Ecclesiae, ex cuius fide suppletur id quod deest fidei ministro.

AD SECUNDUM dicendum quod haereticorum quidam in collatione sacramentorum formam Ecclesiae non servant. Et tales neque sacramentum conferunt, neque rem sacramenti. Quidam vero servant Ecclesiae

his epistle to Leo Augustus (clvi): *It is a matter of notoriety that the light of all the heavenly sacraments is extinguished in the see of Alexandria, by an act of dire and senseless cruelty. The sacrifice is no longer offered, the chrism is no longer consecrated, all the mysteries of religion have fled at the touch of the parricide hands of ungodly men.* Therefore a sacrament requires of necessity that the minister should have the true faith.

OBJ. 3: Further, those who have not the true faith seem to be separated from the Church by excommunication: for it is written in the second canonical epistle of John (10): *If any man come to you, and bring not this doctrine, receive him not into the house, nor say to him; God speed you:* and (Titus 3:10): *A man that is a heretic, after the first and second admonition avoid.* But it seems that an excommunicate cannot confer a sacrament of the Church: since he is separated from the Church, to whose ministry the dispensation of the sacraments belongs. Therefore a sacrament requires of necessity that the minister should have the true faith.

ON THE CONTRARY, Augustine says against the Donatist Petilian: *Remember that the evil lives of wicked men are not prejudicial to God's sacraments, by rendering them either invalid or less holy.*

I ANSWER THAT, As stated above (A. 5), since the minister works instrumentally in the sacraments, he acts not by his own but by Christ's power. Now just as charity belongs to a man's own power so also does faith. Wherefore, just as the validity of a sacrament does not require that the minister should have charity, and even sinners can confer sacraments, as stated above (A. 5); so neither is it necessary that he should have faith, and even an unbeliever can confer a true sacrament, provided that the other essentials be there.

REPLY OBJ. 1: It may happen that a man's faith is defective in regard to something else, and not in regard to the reality of the sacrament which he confers: for instance, he may believe that it is unlawful to swear in any case whatever, and yet he may believe that baptism is an efficient cause of salvation. And thus such unbelief does not hinder the intention of conferring the sacrament. But if his faith be defective in regard to the very sacrament that he confers, although he believe that no inward effect is caused by the thing done outwardly, yet he does know that the Catholic Church intends to confer a sacrament by that which is outwardly done. Wherefore, his unbelief notwithstanding, he can intend to do what the Church does, albeit he esteem it to be nothing. And such an intention suffices for a sacrament: because as stated above (A. 8, ad 2) the minister of a sacrament acts in the person of the Church by whose faith any defect in the minister's faith is made good.

REPLY OBJ. 2: Some heretics in conferring sacraments do not observe the form prescribed by the Church: and these confer neither the sacrament nor the reality of the sacrament. But some do observe the form prescribed by the

formam. Et tales conferunt quidem sacramentum, sed non conferunt rem sacramenti. Et hoc dico, si sunt manifeste ab Ecclesia praecisi. Quia ex hoc ipso quod aliquis accipit sacramenta ab eis, peccat, et per hoc impeditur ne effectum sacramenti consequatur. Unde Augustinus dicit, in libro de fide ad Petrum, *firmissime tene, et nullatenus dubites, extra Ecclesiam baptizatis, si ad Ecclesiam non redierint, Baptismo cumulari perniciem.* Et per hunc modum dicit Leo Papa *in sede Alexandrina sacramentorum lumen esse extinctum,* scilicet, quantum ad rem sacramenti, non autem quantum ad ipsum sacramentum.

Cyprianus autem nec sacramentum conferre haereticos credebat, sed in hoc eius sententia non tenetur. Unde Augustinus dicit, *martyrem Cyprianum, qui apud haereticos vel schismaticos datum Baptismum nolebat cognoscere, tanta merita, usque ad triumphum martyrii, secuta sunt, ut caritatis qua excellebat luce obumbratio illa fugaretur, et, si quid purgandum erat, passionis falce tolleretur.*

AD TERTIUM dicendum quod potestas ministrandi sacramenta pertinet ad spiritualem characterem, qui indelebilis est, ut ex supra dictis patet. Et ideo per hoc quod aliquis ab Ecclesia suspenditur vel excommunicatur, vel etiam degradatur, non amittit potestatem conferendi sacramentum, sed licentiam utendi hac potestate. Et ideo sacramentum quidem confert, sed tamen peccat conferendo. Et similiter ille qui ab eo accipit sacramentum, et sic non percipit rem sacramenti, nisi forte per ignorantiam excusetur.

Church: and these confer indeed the sacrament but not the reality. I say this in the supposition that they are outwardly cut off from the Church; because from the very fact that anyone receives the sacraments from them, he sins; and consequently is hindered from receiving the effect of the sacrament. Wherefore Augustine (Fulgentius, *De Fide ad Pet.*) says: *Be well assured and have no doubt whatever that those who are baptized outside the Church, unless they come back to the Church, will reap disaster from their Baptism.* In this sense Pope Leo says that *the light of the sacraments was extinguished in the Church of Alexandria;* viz. in regard to the reality of the sacrament, not as to the sacrament itself.

Cyprian, however, thought that heretics do not confer even the sacrament: but in this respect we do not follow his opinion. Hence Augustine says (*De unico Baptismo* xiii): *Though the martyr Cyprian refused to recognize Baptism conferred by heretics or schismatics, yet so great are his merits, culminating in the crown of martyrdom, that the light of his charity dispels the darkness of his fault, and if anything needed pruning, the sickle of his passion cut it off.*

REPLY OBJ. 3: The power of administering the sacraments belongs to the spiritual character which is indelible, as explained above (Q. 63, A. 3). Consequently, if a man be suspended by the Church, or excommunicated or degraded, he does not lose the power of conferring sacraments, but the permission to use this power. Wherefore he does indeed confer the sacrament, but he sins in so doing. He also sins that receives a sacrament from such a man: so that he does not receive the reality of the sacrament, unless ignorance excuses him.

Article 10

Whether the Validity of a Sacrament Requires a Good Intention in the Minister?

AD DECIMUM SIC PROCEDITUR. Videtur quod intentio recta ministri requiratur ad perfectionem sacramenti. Intentio enim ministri debet conformari intentioni Ecclesiae, ut ex dictis patet. Sed intentio Ecclesiae semper est recta. Ergo de necessitate ad sacramenti perfectionem requiritur intentio recta ministri.

PRAETEREA, perversa intentio deterior esse videtur quam intentio iocosa. Sed intentio iocosa tollit sacramentum, puta si aliquis non serio, sed ludo aliquem baptizaret. Ergo multo magis perversa intentio aufert sacramentum, puta si aliquis aliquem baptizaret ut postmodum eum occideret.

PRAETEREA, perversa intentio facit totum opus vitiosum, secundum illud Luc. XI, *si oculus tuus fuerit nequam, totum corpus tuum tenebrosum erit.* Sed sacramenta Christi non possunt inquinari per malos homines, sicut Augustinus dicit, contra Petilianum. Ergo

OBJECTION 1: It seems that the validity of a sacrament requires a good intention in the minister. For the minister's intention should be in conformity with the Church's intention, as explained above (A. 8, ad 1). But the intention of the Church is always good. Therefore the validity of a sacrament requires of necessity a good intention in the minister.

OBJ. 2: Further, a perverse intention seems worse than a playful one. But a playful intention destroys a sacrament: for instance, if someone were to baptize anybody not seriously but in fun. Much more, therefore, does a perverse intention destroy a sacrament: for instance, if somebody were to baptize a man in order to kill him afterwards.

OBJ. 3: Further, a perverse intention vitiates the whole work, according to Luke 11:34: *If thy eye be evil, thy whole body will be darksome.* But the sacraments of Christ cannot be contaminated by evil men; as Augustine says against

videtur quod, si sit perversa intentio ministri, non sit ibi verum sacramentum.

SED CONTRA est quod perversa intentio pertinet ad malitiam ministri. Sed malitia ministri non tollit sacramentum. Ergo nec perversa intentio.

RESPONDEO dicendum quod intentio ministri potest perverti dupliciter. Uno modo, respectu ipsius sacramenti, puta cum aliquis non intendit sacramentum conferre, sed delusorie aliquid agere. Et talis perversitas tollit veritatem sacramenti, praecipue quando suam intentionem exterius manifestat.

Alio modo potest perverti intentio ministri quantum ad id quod sequitur sacramentum, puta si sacerdos intendat aliquam feminam baptizare ut abutatur ea; vel si intendat conficere corpus Christi ut eo ad veneficia utatur. Et quia prius non dependet a posteriori, inde est quod talis intentionis perversitas veritatem sacramenti non tollit, sed ipse minister ex tali intentione graviter peccat.

AD PRIMUM ergo dicendum quod Ecclesiae intentio recta est et quantum ad sacramenti perfectionem, et quantum ad sacramenti usum, sed prima rectitudo perficit sacramentum, secunda operatur ad meritum. Et ideo minister qui conformat intentionem suam Ecclesiae quantum ad primam rectitudinem, non autem quantum ad secundam, perficit quidem sacramentum, sed non est sibi ad meritum.

AD SECUNDUM dicendum quod intentio ludicra vel iocosa excludit primam rectitudinem intentionis, per quam perficitur sacramentum. Et ideo non est similis ratio.

AD TERTIUM dicendum quod perversa intentio pervertit opus intendentis, non autem opus alterius. Et ideo ex perversa intentione ministri pervertitur id quod agit in sacramentis inquantum est opus eius, non inquantum est opus Christi, cuius est minister. Et est simile si minister alicuius hominis prava intentione deferret pauperibus eleemosynam, quam dominus recta intentione mandaret.

Petilian (*Cont. Litt. Petil* ii). Therefore it seems that, if the minister's intention is perverse, the sacrament is invalid.

ON THE CONTRARY, A perverse intention belongs to the wickedness of the minister. But the wickedness of the minister does not annul the sacrament: neither, therefore, does his perverse intention.

I ANSWER THAT, The minister's intention may be perverted in two ways. First in regard to the sacrament: for instance, when a man does not intend to confer a sacrament, but to make a mockery of it. Such a perverse intention takes away the truth of the sacrament, especially if it be manifested outwardly.

Second, the minister's intention may be perverted as to something that follows the sacrament: for instance, a priest may intend to baptize a woman so as to be able to abuse her; or to consecrate the Body of Christ, so as to use it for sorcery. And because that which comes first does not depend on that which follows, consequently such a perverse intention does not annul the sacrament; but the minister himself sins grievously in having such an intention.

REPLY OBJ. 1: The Church has a good intention both as to the validity of the sacrament and as to the use thereof: but it is the former intention that perfects the sacrament, while the latter conduces to the meritorious effect. Consequently, the minister who conforms his intention to the Church as to the former rectitude, but not as to the latter, perfects the sacrament indeed, but gains no merit for himself.

REPLY OBJ. 2: The intention of mimicry or fun excludes the first kind of right intention, necessary for the validity of a sacrament. Consequently, there is no comparison.

REPLY OBJ. 3: A perverse intention perverts the action of the one who has such an intention, not the action of another. Consequently, the perverse intention of the minister perverts the sacrament in so far as it is his action: not in so far as it is the action of Christ, Whose minister he is. It is just as if the servant of some man were to carry alms to the poor with a wicked intention, whereas his master had commanded him with a good intention to do so.

QUESTION 65

THE NUMBER OF THE SACRAMENTS

Deinde considerandum est de numero sacramentorum. Et circa hoc quaeruntur quatuor.

Primo, utrum sint septem sacramenta.

Secundo, de ordine eorum ad invicem.

Tertio, de comparatione eorum.

Quarto, utrum omnia sint de necessitate salutis.

We have now to consider the number of the sacraments: and concerning this there are four points of inquiry:

(1) Whether there are seven sacraments?

(2) The order of the sacraments among themselves;

(3) Their mutual comparison;

(4) Whether all the sacraments are necessary for salvation?

Article 1

Whether There Should Be Seven Sacraments?

AD PRIMUM SIC PROCEDITUR. Videtur quod non debeant esse septem sacramenta. Sacramenta enim efficaciam habent ex virtute divina, et ex virtute passionis Christi. Sed una est virtus divina, et una est Christi passio, *una enim oblatione consummavit sanctificatos in sempiternum*, ut dicitur Heb. X. Ergo non debuit esse nisi unum sacramentum.

PRAETEREA, sacramentum ordinatur contra defectum peccati. Hic autem est duplex, scilicet poena et culpa. Ergo sufficeret esse duo sacramenta.

PRAETEREA, sacramenta pertinent ad actiones ecclesiasticae hierarchiae, ut patet per Dionysium. Sed, sicut ipse dicit, tres sunt actiones hierarchicae, purgatio, illuminatio et perfectio. Ergo non debent esse nisi tria sacramenta.

PRAETEREA, Augustinus dicit, XIX contra Faustum, sacramenta novae legis sunt numero pauciora quam sacramenta veteris legis. Sed in veteri lege non erat aliquod sacramentum quod responderet confirmationi et extremae unctioni. Ergo neque debent numerari inter sacramenta novae legis.

PRAETEREA, luxuria non est gravius inter cetera peccata, ut patet ex his quae in secunda parte dicta sunt. Sed contra alia peccata non instituitur aliquod sacramentum. Ergo neque contra luxuriam debuit institui sacramentum matrimonii.

SED CONTRA, videtur quod sint plura sacramenta. Sacramenta enim dicuntur quaedam sacra signa. Sed multae aliae sanctificationes fiunt in Ecclesia secundum sensibilia signa, sicut aqua benedicta, consecratio altaris, et alia huiusmodi. Ergo sunt plura sacramenta quam septem.

PRAETEREA, Hugo de sancto Victore dicit quod sacramenta veteris legis fuerunt oblationes, decimae et

OBJECTION 1: It seems that there ought not to be seven sacraments. For the sacraments derive their efficacy from the Divine power, and the power of Christ's Passion. But the Divine power is one, and Christ's Passion is one; since *by one oblation He hath perfected for ever them that are sanctified* (Heb 10:14). Therefore there should be but one sacrament.

OBJ. 2: Further, a sacrament is intended as a remedy for the defect caused by sin. Now this is twofold, punishment and guilt. Therefore two sacraments would be enough.

OBJ. 3: Further, sacraments belong to the actions of the ecclesiastical hierarchy, as Dionysius explains (*Eccl. Hier.* v). But, as he says, there are three actions of the ecclesiastical hierarchy, namely, *to cleanse, to enlighten, to perfect*. Therefore there should be no more than three sacraments.

OBJ. 4: Further, Augustine says (*Contra Faust.* xix) that the *sacraments* of the New Law are *less numerous* than those of the Old Law. But in the Old Law there was no sacrament corresponding to Confirmation and Extreme Unction. Therefore these should not be counted among the sacraments of the New Law.

OBJ. 5: Further, lust is not more grievous than other sins, as we have made clear in the Second Part (I-II, Q. 74, A. 5; II-II, Q. 154, A. 3). But there is no sacrament instituted as a remedy for other sins. Therefore neither should matrimony be instituted as a remedy for lust.

OBJ. 6: On the other hand, It seems that there should be more than seven sacraments. For sacraments are a kind of sacred sign. But in the Church there are many sanctifications by sensible signs, such as Holy Water the Consecration of Altars, and such like. Therefore there are more than seven sacraments.

OBJ. 7: Further, Hugh of St. Victor (*De Sacram.* i) says that the sacraments of the Old Law were oblations, tithes

sacrificia. Sed sacrificium Ecclesiae est unum sacramentum, quod dicitur Eucharistia. Ergo etiam oblationes et decimae debent dici sacramenta.

PRAETEREA, tria sunt genera peccatorum, originale, mortale et veniale. Sed contra originale peccatum ordinatur Baptismus; contra mortale autem poenitentia. Ergo deberet esse aliud, praeter septem, quod ordinetur contra veniale.

RESPONDEO dicendum quod, sicut supra dictum est, ordinantur sacramenta Ecclesiae ad duo, scilicet, ad perficiendum hominem in his quae pertinent ad cultum Dei secundum religionem Christianae vitae; et etiam in remedium contra defectum peccati. Utroque autem modo convenienter ponuntur septem sacramenta.

Vita enim spiritualis conformitatem aliquam habet ad vitam corporalem, sicut et cetera corporalia similitudinem quandam spiritualium habent. In vita autem corporali dupliciter aliquis perficitur, uno modo, quantum ad personam propriam; alio modo, per respectum ad totam communitatem societatis in qua vivit, quia homo naturaliter est animal sociale. Respectu autem sui ipsius perficitur homo in vita corporali dupliciter, uno modo, per se, acquirendo scilicet aliquam vitae perfectionem; alio modo, per accidens, scilicet removendo impedimenta vitae, puta aegritudines, vel aliquid huiusmodi. Per se autem perficitur corporalis vita tripliciter. Primo quidem, per generationem, per quam homo incipit esse et vivere. Et loco huius in spirituali vita est Baptismus, qui est spiritualis regeneratio, secundum illud ad Tit. III, *per lavacrum regenerationis*, et cetera. Secundo, per augmentum, quo aliquis perducitur ad perfectam quantitatem et virtutem. Et loco huius in spirituali vita est confirmatio, in qua datur Spiritus Sanctus ad robur. Unde dicitur discipulis iam baptizatis, Luc. ult., *sedete in civitate quousque induamini virtute ex alto*. Tertio, per nutritionem, qua conservatur in homine vita et virtus. Et loco huius in spirituali vita est Eucharistia. Unde dicitur Ioan. VI, *nisi manducaveritis carnem filii hominis et biberitis eius sanguinem, non habebitis vitam in vobis*.

Et hoc quidem sufficeret homini si haberet et corporaliter et spiritualiter impassibilem vitam, sed quia homo incurrit interdum et corporalem infirmitatem et spiritualem, scilicet peccatum, ideo necessaria est homini curatio ab infirmitate. Quae quidem est duplex. Una quidem est sanatio, quae sanitatem restituit. Et loco huius in spirituali vita est poenitentia, secundum illud Psalmi, *sana animam meam, quia peccavi tibi*. Alia autem est restitutio valetudinis pristinae per convenientem diaetam et exercitium. Et loco huius in spirituali vita est extrema unctio, quae removet peccatorum reliquias, et hominem paratum reddit ad finalem gloriam. Unde dicitur Iac. V, *et si in peccatis sit, dimittetur ei*.

and sacrifices. But the Sacrifice of the Church is one sacrament, called the Eucharist. Therefore oblations also and tithes should be called sacraments.

OBJ. 8: Further, there are three kinds of sin, original, mortal and venial. Now Baptism is intended as a remedy against original sin, and Penance against mortal sin. Therefore besides the seven sacraments, there should be another against venial sin.

I ANSWER THAT, As stated above (Q. 62, A. 5; Q. 63, A. 1), the sacraments of the Church were instituted for a twofold purpose: namely, in order to perfect man in things pertaining to the worship of God according to the religion of Christian life, and to be a remedy against the defects caused by sin. And in either way it is becoming that there should be seven sacraments.

For spiritual life has a certain conformity with the life of the body: just as other corporeal things have a certain likeness to things spiritual. Now a man attains perfection in the corporeal life in two ways: first, in regard to his own person; second, in regard to the whole community of the society in which he lives, for man is by nature a social animal. With regard to himself man is perfected in the life of the body, in two ways; first, directly (*per se*), i.e., by acquiring some vital perfection; second, indirectly (*per accidens*), i.e., by the removal of hindrances to life, such as ailments, or the like. Now the life of the body is perfected directly, in three ways. First, by generation whereby a man begins to be and to live: and corresponding to this in the spiritual life there is Baptism, which is a spiritual regeneration, according to Titus 3:5: *By the laver of regeneration*, etc. Second, by growth whereby a man is brought to perfect size and strength: and corresponding to this in the spiritual life there is Confirmation, in which the Holy Spirit is given to strengthen us. Wherefore the disciples who were already baptized were bidden thus: *Stay you in the city till you be endued with power from on high* (Luke 24:49). Third, by nourishment, whereby life and strength are preserved to man; and corresponding to this in the spiritual life there is the Eucharist. Wherefore it is said (John 6:54): *Except you eat of the flesh of the Son of Man, and drink His blood, you shall not have life in you.*

And this would be enough for man if he had an impassible life, both corporally and spiritually; but since man is liable at times to both corporal and spiritual infirmity, i.e., sin, hence man needs a cure from his infirmity; which cure is twofold. One is the healing, that restores health: and corresponding to this in the spiritual life there is Penance, according to Ps. 40:5: *Heal my soul, for I have sinned against Thee.* The other is the restoration of former vigor by means of suitable diet and exercise: and corresponding to this in the spiritual life there is Extreme Unction, which removes the remainder of sin, and prepares man for final glory. Wherefore it is written (Jas 5:15): *And if he be in sins they shall be forgiven him.*

Perficitur autem homo in ordine ad totam communitatem dupliciter. Uno modo, per hoc quod accipit potestatem regendi multitudinem, et exercendi actus publicos. Et loco huius in spirituali vita est sacramentum ordinis, secundum illud Heb. VII, quod sacerdotes hostias offerunt non solum pro se, sed etiam pro populo. Secundo, quantum ad naturalem propagationem. Quod fit per matrimonium, tam in corporali quam in spirituali vita, eo quod est non solum sacramentum, sed naturae officium.

Ex his etiam patet sacramentorum numerus secundum quod ordinantur contra defectum peccati. Nam Baptismus ordinatur contra carentiam vitae spiritualis; confirmatio contra infirmitatem animi quae in nuper natis invenitur; Eucharistia contra labilitatem animi ad peccandum; poenitentia contra actuale peccatum post Baptismum commissum; extrema unctio contra reliquias peccatorum, quae scilicet non sunt sufficienter per poenitentiam sublatae, aut ex negligentia aut ex ignorantia; ordo contra dissolutionem multitudinis; matrimonium in remedium contra concupiscentiam personalem, et contra defectum multitudinis qui per mortem accidit.

Quidam vero accipiunt numerum sacramentorum per quandam adaptationem ad virtutes, et ad defectus culparum et poenalitatum, dicentes quod fidei respondet Baptismus, et ordinatur contra culpam originalem; spei extrema unctio, et ordinatur contra culpam venialem; caritati Eucharistia, et ordinatur contra poenalitatem malitiae; prudentiae ordo, et ordinatur contra ignorantiam; iustitiae poenitentia, et ordinatur contra peccatum mortale; temperantiae matrimonium, et ordinatur contra concupiscentiam; fortitudini confirmatio, et ordinatur contra infirmitatem.

AD PRIMUM ergo dicendum quod idem agens principale utitur diversis instrumentis ad diversos effectus, secundum congruentiam operum. Et similiter virtus divina et passio Christi operatur in nobis per diversa sacramenta quasi per diversa instrumenta.

AD SECUNDUM dicendum quod culpa et poena diversitatem habent et secundum speciem, inquantum sunt diversae species culparum et poenarum; et secundum diversos hominum status et habitudines. Et secundum hoc oportuit multiplicari sacramenta, ut ex dictis patet.

AD TERTIUM dicendum quod in actionibus hierarchicis considerantur et agentes, et recipientes, et actiones. Agentes autem sunt ministri Ecclesiae. Ad quos pertinet ordinis sacramentum. Recipientes autem sunt illi qui ad sacramenta accedunt. Qui producuntur per matrimonium. Actiones autem sunt purgatio, illuminatio et perfectio. Sed sola purgatio non potest esse sacramentum novae legis, quod gratiam confert, sed pertinet ad quaedam sacramentalia, quae sunt catechismus et

In regard to the whole community, man is perfected in two ways. First, by receiving power to rule the community and to exercise public acts: and corresponding to this in the spiritual life there is the sacrament of order, according to the saying of Heb. 7:27, that priests offer sacrifices not for themselves only, but also for the people. Second in regard to natural propagation. This is accomplished by Matrimony both in the corporal and in the spiritual life: since it is not only a sacrament but also a function of nature.

We may likewise gather the number of the sacraments from their being instituted as a remedy against the defect caused by sin. For Baptism is intended as a remedy against the absence of spiritual life; Confirmation, against the infirmity of soul found in those of recent birth; the Eucharist, against the soul's proneness to sin; Penance, against actual sin committed after baptism; Extreme Unction, against the remainders of sins—of those sins, namely, which are not sufficiently removed by Penance, whether through negligence or through ignorance; order, against divisions in the community; Matrimony, as a remedy against concupiscence in the individual, and against the decrease in numbers that results from death.

Some, again, gather the number of sacraments from a certain adaptation to the virtues and to the defects and penal effects resulting from sin. They say that Baptism corresponds to Faith, and is ordained as a remedy against original sin; Extreme Unction, to Hope, being ordained against venial sin; the Eucharist, to Charity, being ordained against the penal effect which is malice; Order, to Prudence, being ordained against ignorance; Penance to Justice, being ordained against mortal sin; Matrimony, to Temperance, being ordained against concupiscence; Confirmation, to Fortitude, being ordained against infirmity.

REPLY OBJ. 1: The same principal agent uses various instruments unto various effects, in accordance with the thing to be done. In the same way the Divine power and the Passion of Christ work in us through the various sacraments as through various instruments.

REPLY OBJ. 2: Guilt and punishment are diversified both according to species, inasmuch as there are various species of guilt and punishment, and according to men's various states and habitudes. And in this respect it was necessary to have a number of sacraments, as explained above.

REPLY OBJ. 3: In hierarchical actions we must consider the agents, the recipients and the actions. The agents are the ministers of the Church; and to these the sacrament of order belongs. The recipients are those who approach the sacraments: and these are brought into being by Matrimony. The actions are *cleansing*, *enlightening*, and *perfecting*. Mere cleansing, however, cannot be a sacrament of the New Law, which confers grace: yet it belongs to certain sacramentals, i.e., catechism and exorcism. But cleansing coupled with

exorcismus. Purgatio autem et illuminatio simul, secundum Dionysium, pertinet ad Baptismum, et, propter recidivum, secundario pertinet ad poenitentiam et extremam unctionem. Perfectio autem, quantum ad virtutem quidem, quae est quasi perfectio formalis, pertinet ad confirmationem, quantum autem ad consecutionem finis, pertinet ad Eucharistiam.

AD QUARTUM dicendum quod in sacramento confirmationis datur plenitudo spiritus sancti ad robur; in extrema autem unctione praeparatur homo ut recipiat immediate gloriam; quorum neutrum competit veteri testamento. Et ideo nihil potuit his sacramentis in veteri lege respondere. Nihilominus tamen sacramenta veteris legis fuerunt plura numero, propter diversitatem sacrificiorum et caeremoniarum.

AD QUINTUM dicendum quod contra concupiscentiam venereorum oportuit specialiter remedium adhiberi per aliquod sacramentum, primo quidem, quia per huiusmodi concupiscentiam non solum vitiatur persona, sed etiam natura; secundo, propter vehementiam eius, qua rationem absorbet.

AD SEXTUM dicendum quod aqua benedicta et aliae consecrationes non dicuntur sacramenta, quia non perducunt ad sacramenti effectum, qui est gratiae consecutio. Sed sunt dispositiones quaedam ad sacramenta, vel removendo prohibens, sicut aqua benedicta ordinatur contra insidias Daemonum, et contra peccata venialia; vel idoneitatem quandam faciendo ad sacramenti perceptionem, sicut consecratur altare et vasa propter reverentiam Eucharistiae.

AD SEPTIMUM dicendum quod oblationes et decimae erant, tam in lege naturae quam in lege Moysi, ordinatae non solum in subsidium ministrorum et pauperum, sed etiam in figuram, et ideo erant sacramenta. Nunc autem non remanserunt inquantum sunt figuralia, et ideo non sunt sacramenta.

AD OCTAVUM dicendum quod ad deletionem venialis peccati non requiritur infusio gratiae. Unde, cum in quolibet sacramento novae legis gratia infundatur, nullum sacramentum novae legis instituitur directe contra veniale; quod tollitur per quaedam sacramentalia, puta per aquam benedictam, et alia huiusmodi. Quidam tamen dicunt extremam unctionem contra veniale peccatum ordinari. Sed de hoc suo loco dicetur.

enlightening, according to Dionysius, belongs to Baptism; and, for him who falls back into sin, they belong secondarily to Penance and Extreme Unction. And perfecting, as regards power, which is, as it were, a formal perfection, belongs to Confirmation: while, as regards the attainment of the end, it belongs to the Eucharist.

REPLY OBJ. 4: In the sacrament of Confirmation we receive the fullness of the Holy Spirit in order to be strengthened; while in Extreme Unction man is prepared for the immediate attainment of glory; and neither of these two purposes was becoming to the Old Testament. Consequently, nothing in the Old Law could correspond to these sacraments. Nevertheless, the sacraments of the Old Law were more numerous, on account of the various kinds of sacrifices and ceremonies.

REPLY OBJ. 5: There was need for a special sacrament to be applied as a remedy against venereal concupiscence: first because by this concupiscence, not only the person but also the nature is defiled: second, by reason of its vehemence whereby it clouds the reason.

REPLY OBJ. 6: Holy Water and other consecrated things are not called sacraments, because they do not produce the sacramental effect, which is the receiving of grace. They are, however, a kind of disposition to the sacraments: either by removing obstacles, thus holy water is ordained against the snares of the demons, and against venial sins: or by making things suitable for the conferring of a sacrament; thus the altar and vessels are consecrated through reverence for the Eucharist.

REPLY OBJ. 7: Oblations and tithes, both the Law of nature and in the Law of Moses, are ordained not only for the sustenance of the ministers and the poor, but also figuratively; and consequently they were sacraments. But now they remain no longer as figures, and therefore they are not sacraments.

REPLY OBJ. 8: The infusion of grace is not necessary for the blotting out of venial sin. Wherefore, since grace is infused in each of the sacraments of the New Law, none of them was instituted directly against venial sin. This is taken away by certain sacramentals, for instance, Holy Water and such like. Some, however, hold that Extreme Unction is ordained against venial sin. But of this we shall speak in its proper place (Suppl., Q. 30, A. 1).

Article 2

Whether the Order of the Sacraments, As Given Above, Is Becoming?

AD SECUNDUM SIC PROCEDITUR. Videtur quod inconvenienter sacramenta ordinentur secundum modum praedictum. Ut enim apostolus dicit, I Cor. XV, *prius est quod est animale, deinde quod spirituale.* Sed per matrimonium generatur homo prima generatione, quae est animalis, per Baptismum autem regeneratur homo secunda generatione quae est spiritualis. Ergo matrimonium debet praecedere Baptismum.

PRAETEREA, per sacramentum ordinis aliquis accipit potestatem agendi actiones sacramentales. Sed agens est prior sua actione. Ergo ordo debet praecedere Baptismum et alia sacramenta.

PRAETEREA, Eucharistia est spirituale nutrimentum, confirmatio autem comparatur augmento. Nutrimentum autem est causa augmenti, et per consequens prius. Ergo Eucharistia est prior confirmatione.

PRAETEREA, poenitentia praeparat hominem ad Eucharistiam. Sed dispositio praecedit perfectionem. Ergo poenitentia debet praecedere Eucharistiam.

PRAETEREA, quod est propinquius fini ultimo, est posterius. Sed extrema unctio, inter omnia sacramenta, propinquior est ultimo fini beatitudinis. Ergo debet habere ultimum locum inter sacramenta.

IN CONTRARIUM est quod communiter ordinantur ab omnibus sacramenta sicut dictum est.

RESPONDEO dicendum quod ratio ordinis sacramentorum apparet ex his quae supra dicta sunt. Nam sicut unum est prius quam multitudo, ita sacramenta quae ordinantur ad perfectionem unius personae, naturaliter praecedunt ea quae ordinantur ad perfectionem multitudinis. Et ideo ultimo inter sacramenta ponuntur ordo et matrimonium, quae ordinantur ad multitudinis perfectionem, matrimonium tamen post ordinem, eo quod minus participat de ratione spiritualis vitae, ad quam ordinantur sacramenta. Inter ea vero quae ordinantur ad perfectionem unius personae, naturaliter sunt priora illa quae per se ordinantur ad perfectionem spiritualis vitae, quam illa quae ordinantur per accidens, scilicet ad removendum nocivum accidens superveniens, cuiusmodi sunt poenitentia et extrema unctio. Posterior tamen est naturaliter extrema unctio, quae conservat sanationem quam poenitentia inchoat.

Inter alia vero tria, manifestum est quod Baptismus, qui est spiritualis regeneratio, est primum; et deinde confirmatio, quae ordinatur ad formalem perfectionem virtutis; et postmodum Eucharistia, quae ordinatur ad perfectionem finis.

AD PRIMUM ergo dicendum quod matrimonium, secundum quod ordinatur ad animalem vitam, est naturae

OBJECTION 1: It seems that the order of the sacraments as given above is unbecoming. For according to the Apostle (1 Cor 15:46), *that was . . . first . . . which is natural, afterwards that which is spiritual.* But man is begotten through Matrimony by a first and natural generation; while in Baptism he is regenerated as by a second and spiritual generation. Therefore Matrimony should precede Baptism.

OBJ. 2: Further, through the sacrament of order man receives the power of agent in sacramental actions. But the agent precedes his action. Therefore order should precede Baptism and the other sacraments.

OBJ. 3: Further, the Eucharist is a spiritual food; while Confirmation is compared to growth. But food causes, and consequently precedes, growth. Therefore the Eucharist precedes Confirmation.

OBJ. 4: Further, Penance prepares man for the Eucharist. But a disposition precedes perfection. Therefore Penance should precede the Eucharist.

OBJ. 5: Further, that which is nearer the last end comes after other things. But, of all the sacraments, Extreme Unction is nearest to the last end which is Happiness. Therefore it should be placed last among the sacraments.

ON THE CONTRARY, The order of the sacraments, as given above, is commonly adopted by all.

I ANSWER THAT, The reason of the order among the sacraments appears from what has been said above (A. 1). For just as unity precedes multitude, so those sacraments which are intended for the perfection of the individual, naturally precede those which are intended for the perfection of the multitude; and consequently the last place among the sacraments is given to order and Matrimony, which are intended for the perfection of the multitude: while Matrimony is placed after order, because it has less participation in the nature of the spiritual life, to which the sacraments are ordained. Moreover, among things ordained to the perfection of the individual, those naturally come first which are ordained directly to the perfection of the spiritual life, and afterwards, those which are ordained thereto indirectly, viz. by removing some supervening accidental cause of harm; such are Penance and Extreme Unction: while, of these, Extreme Unction is naturally placed last, for it preserves the healing which was begun by Penance.

Of the remaining three, it is clear that Baptism which is a spiritual regeneration, comes first; then Confirmation, which is ordained to the formal perfection of power; and after these the Eucharist which is ordained to final perfection.

REPLY OBJ. 1: Matrimony as ordained to natural life is a function of nature. But in so far as it has something

officium. Sed secundum quod habet aliquid spiritualitatis, est sacramentum. Et quia minimum habet de spiritualitate, ultimo ponitur inter sacramenta.

AD SECUNDUM dicendum quod, ad hoc quod aliquid sit agens, praesupponitur quod sit in se perfectum. Et ideo priora sunt sacramenta quibus aliquis in seipso perficitur, quam sacramentum ordinis, in quo aliquis constituitur perfector aliorum.

AD TERTIUM dicendum quod nutrimentum et praecedit augmentum, sicut causa eius; et subsequitur augmentum, sicut conservans hominem in perfecta quantitate et virtute. Et ideo potest Eucharistia praemitti confirmationi, ut Dionysius facit, in libro Eccl. Hier., et potest postponi, sicut Magister facit, in IV sententiarum.

AD QUARTUM dicendum quod ratio illa recte procederet si poenitentia ex necessitate requireretur ut praeparatoria ad Eucharistiam. Sed hoc non est verum, nam si aliquis esset sine peccato mortali, non indigeret poenitentia ad sumptionem Eucharistiae. Et sic patet quod per accidens poenitentia praeparat ad Eucharistiam, scilicet, supposito peccato. Unde dicitur II Paral. ult., *tu, domine iustorum, non posuisti poenitentiam iustis.*

AD QUINTUM dicendum quod extrema unctio, propter rationem inductam, est ultimum inter sacramenta quae ordinantur ad perfectionem unius personae.

spiritual it is a sacrament. And because it has the least amount of spirituality it is placed last.

REPLY OBJ. 2: For a thing to be an agent it must first of all be perfect in itself. Wherefore those sacraments by which a man is perfected in himself, are placed before the sacrament of order, in which a man is made a perfecter of others.

REPLY OBJ. 3: Nourishment both precedes growth, as its cause; and follows it, as maintaining the perfection of size and power in man. Consequently, the Eucharist can be placed before Confirmation, as Dionysius places it (*Eccl. Hier.* iii, iv), and can be placed after it, as the Master does (iv, 2, 8).

REPLY OBJ. 4: This argument would hold if Penance were required of necessity as a preparation to the Eucharist. But this is not true: for if anyone be without mortal sin, he does not need Penance in order to receive the Eucharist. Thus it is clear that Penance is an accidental preparation to the Eucharist, that is to say, sin being supposed. Wherefore it is written in the last chapter of the second Book of Paralipomenon (cf. 2 Paral 33:18): *Thou, O Lord of the righteous, didst not impose penance on righteous men.*

REPLY OBJ. 5: Extreme Unction, for this very reason, is given the last place among those sacraments which are ordained to the perfection of the individual.

Article 3

Whether the Eucharist Is the Greatest of the Sacraments?

AD TERTIUM SIC PROCEDITUR. Videtur quod sacramentum Eucharistiae non sit potissimum inter sacramenta. Bonum enim commune potius est quam bonum unius, ut dicitur I Ethic. Sed matrimonium ordinatur ad bonum commune speciei humanae per viam generationis, sacramentum autem Eucharistiae ordinatur ad bonum proprium sumentis. Ergo non est potissimum sacramentorum.

PRAETEREA, digniora sacramenta esse videntur quae per maiorem ministrum conferuntur. Sed sacramentum confirmationis et sacramentum ordinis non conferuntur nisi per episcopum, qui est maior minister quam simplex minister, qui est sacerdos, per quem confertur Eucharistiae sacramentum. Ergo illa sacramenta sunt potiora.

PRAETEREA, sacramenta tanto sunt potiora quanto maiorem virtutem habent. Sed quaedam sacramenta imprimunt characterem, scilicet Baptismus, confirmatio et ordo, quod non facit Eucharistia. Ergo illa sacramenta sunt potiora.

OBJECTION 1: It seems that the Eucharist is not the principal of the sacraments. For the common good is of more account than the good of the individual (*I Ethic.* ii). But Matrimony is ordained to the common good of the human race by means of generation: whereas the sacrament of the Eucharist is ordained to the private good of the recipient. Therefore it is not the greatest of the sacraments.

OBJ. 2: Further, those sacraments, seemingly, are greater, which are conferred by a greater minister. But the sacraments of Confirmation and order are conferred by a bishop only, who is a greater minister than a mere minister such as a priest, by whom the sacraments of the Eucharist is conferred. Therefore those sacraments are greater.

OBJ. 3: Further, those sacraments are greater that have the greater power. But some of the sacraments imprint a character, viz. Baptism, Confirmation and order; whereas the Eucharist does not. Therefore those sacraments are greater.

PRAETEREA, illud videtur esse potius ex quo alia dependent et non e converso. Sed ex Baptismo dependet Eucharistia, non enim potest aliquis Eucharistiam accipere nisi fuerit baptizatus. Ergo Baptismus est potior Eucharistia.

SED CONTRA est quod Dionysius dicit, III cap. Eccles. Hier., quod *non contingit aliquem perfici perfectione hierarchica nisi per divinissimam Eucharistiam*. Ergo hoc sacramentum potissimum et perfectivum est omnium aliorum.

RESPONDEO dicendum quod, simpliciter loquendo, sacramentum Eucharistiae est potissimum inter alia sacramenta. Quod quidem tripliciter apparet. Primo quidem, ex eo quod in eo continetur ipse Christus substantialiter, in aliis autem sacramentis continetur quaedam virtus instrumentalis participata a Christo, ut ex supra dictis patet. Semper autem quod est per essentiam, potius est eo quod est per participationem.

Secundo hoc apparet ex ordine sacramentorum ad invicem, nam omnia alia sacramenta ordinari videntur ad hoc sacramentum sicut ad finem. Manifestum est enim quod sacramentum ordinis ordinatur ad Eucharistiae consecrationem. Sacramentum vero Baptismi ordinatur ad Eucharistiae receptionem. In quo etiam perficitur aliquis per confirmationem, ut non vereatur se subtrahere a tali sacramento. Per poenitentiam etiam et extremam unctionem praeparatur homo ad digne sumendum corpus Christi. Matrimonium autem saltem sua significatione attingit hoc sacramentum, inquantum significat coniunctionem Christi et Ecclesiae, cuius unitas per sacramentum Eucharistiae figuratur, unde et apostolus dicit, Ephes. V, *sacramentum hoc magnum est, ego autem dico in Christo et in Ecclesia.*

Tertio hoc apparet ex ritu sacramentorum. Nam fere omnia sacramenta in Eucharistia consummantur, ut dicit Dionysius, III cap. Eccles. Hier., sicut patet quod ordinati communicant, et etiam baptizati si sint adulti.

Aliorum autem sacramentorum comparatio ad invicem potest esse multipliciter. Nam in via necessitatis, Baptismus est potissimum sacramentorum; in via autem perfectionis, sacramentum ordinis; medio autem modo se habet sacramentum confirmationis. Sacramentum vero poenitentiae et extremae unctionis sunt inferioris gradus a praedictis sacramentis, quia, sicut dictum est, ordinantur ad vitam Christianam non per se, sed quasi per accidens, scilicet in remedium supervenientis defectus. Inter quae tamen extrema unctio comparatur ad poenitentiam sicut confirmatio ad Baptismum, ita scilicet quod poenitentia est maioris necessitatis, sed extrema unctio est maioris perfectionis.

AD PRIMUM ergo dicendum quod matrimonium ordinatur ad bonum commune corporaliter. Sed bonum

OBJ. 4: Further, that seems to be greater, on which others depend without its depending on them. But the Eucharist depends on Baptism: since no one can receive the Eucharist except he has been baptized. Therefore Baptism is greater than the Eucharist.

ON THE CONTRARY, Dionysius says (*Eccl. Hier.* iii) that *No one receives hierarchical perfection save by the most Godlike Eucharist.* Therefore this sacrament is greater than all the others and perfects them.

I ANSWER THAT, Absolutely speaking, the sacrament of the Eucharist is the greatest of all the sacraments: and this may be shown in three ways. First of all because it contains Christ Himself substantially: whereas the other sacraments contain a certain instrumental power which is a share of Christ's power, as we have shown above (Q. 62, A. 4, ad 3, A. 5). Now that which is essentially such is always of more account than that which is such by participation.

Second, this is made clear by considering the relation of the sacraments to one another. For all the other sacraments seem to be ordained to this one as to their end. For it is manifest that the sacrament of order is ordained to the consecration of the Eucharist: and the sacrament of Baptism to the reception of the Eucharist: while a man is perfected by Confirmation, so as not to fear to abstain from this sacrament. By Penance and Extreme Unction man is prepared to receive the Body of Christ worthily. And Matrimony at least in its signification, touches this sacrament; in so far as it signifies the union of Christ with the Church, of which union the Eucharist is a figure: hence the Apostle says (Eph 5:32): *This is a great sacrament: but I speak in Christ and in the Church.*

Third, this is made clear by considering the rites of the sacraments. For nearly all the sacraments terminate in the Eucharist, as Dionysius says (*Eccl. Hier.* iii): thus those who have been ordained receive Holy Communion, as also do those who have been baptized, if they be adults.

The remaining sacraments may be compared to one another in several ways. For on the ground of necessity, Baptism is the greatest of the sacraments; while from the point of view of perfection, order comes first; while Confirmation holds a middle place. The sacraments of Penance and Extreme Unction are on a degree inferior to those mentioned above; because, as stated above (A. 2), they are ordained to the Christian life, not directly, but accidentally, as it were, that is to say, as remedies against supervening defects. And among these, Extreme Unction is compared to Penance, as Confirmation to Baptism; in such a way, that Penance is more necessary, whereas Extreme Unction is more perfect.

REPLY OBJ. 1: Matrimony is ordained to the common good as regards the body. But the common spiritual good

commune spirituale totius Ecclesiae continetur substantialiter in ipso Eucharistiae sacramento.

AD SECUNDUM dicendum quod per ordinem et confirmationem deputantur fideles Christi ad aliqua specialia officia, quod pertinet ad officium principis. Et ideo tradere huiusmodi sacramenta pertinet ad solum episcopum, qui est quasi princeps in Ecclesia. Per sacramentum vero Eucharistiae non deputatur homo ad aliquod officium, sed magis hoc sacramentum est finis omnium officiorum, ut dictum est.

AD TERTIUM dicendum quod character sacramentalis, sicut supra dictum est, quaedam participatio est sacerdotii Christi. Unde sacramentum quod ipsum Christum coniungit homini, est dignius sacramento quod imprimit Christi characterem.

AD QUARTUM dicendum quod ratio illa procedit ex parte necessitatis. Sic enim Baptismus, cum sit maximae necessitatis, est potissimum sacramentorum. Sicut ordo et confirmatio habent quandam excellentiam ratione ministerii; et matrimonium ratione significationis. Nihil enim prohibet aliquid esse secundum quid dignius, quod tamen non est dignius simpliciter.

of the whole Church is contained substantially in the sacrament itself of the Eucharist.

REPLY OBJ. 2: By order and Confirmation the faithful of Christ are deputed to certain special duties; and this can be done by the prince alone. Consequently the conferring of these sacraments belongs exclusively to a bishop, who is, as it were, a prince in the Church. But a man is not deputed to any duty by the sacrament of the Eucharist, rather is this sacrament the end of all duties, as stated above.

REPLY OBJ. 3: The sacramental character, as stated above (Q. 63, A. 3), is a kind of participation in Christ's priesthood. Wherefore the sacrament that unites man to Christ Himself, is greater than a sacrament that imprints Christ's character.

REPLY OBJ. 4: This argument proceeds on the ground of necessity. For thus Baptism, being of the greatest necessity, is the greatest of the sacraments, just as order and Confirmation have a certain excellence considered in their administration; and Matrimony by reason of its signification. For there is no reason why a thing should not be greater from a certain point of view which is not greater absolutely speaking.

Article 4

Whether All the Sacraments Are Necessary for Salvation?

AD QUARTUM SIC PROCEDITUR. Videtur quod omnia sacramenta sunt de necessitate salutis. Id enim quod non est necessarium, videtur esse superfluum. Sed nullum sacramentum est superfluum, quia Deus nihil facit frustra. Ergo omnia sacramenta sunt de necessitate salutis.

PRAETEREA, sicut de Baptismo dicitur, *nisi quis renatus fuerit ex aqua et spiritu sancto, non potest introire in regnum Dei*, ita de Eucharistia dicitur, Ioan. VI, *nisi manducaveritis carnem filii hominis et biberitis eius sanguinem, non habebitis vitam in vobis*. Ergo, sicut Baptismus est sacramentum necessitatis, ita et Eucharistia.

PRAETEREA, sine sacramento Baptismi potest aliquis salvus fieri, dummodo non contemptus religionis, sed necessitas sacramentum excludat, ut infra dicetur. Sed in quolibet sacramento contemptus religionis impedit hominis salutem. Ergo, pari ratione, omnia sacramenta sunt de necessitate salutis.

SED CONTRA est quod pueri salvantur per solum Baptismum, sine aliis sacramentis.

RESPONDEO dicendum quod necessarium respectu finis, de quo nunc loquimur, dicitur aliquid dupliciter.

OBJECTION 1: It seems that all the sacraments are necessary for salvation. For what is not necessary seems to be superfluous. But no sacrament is superfluous, because *God does nothing without a purpose* (De Coelo et Mundo i). Therefore all the sacraments are necessary for salvation.

OBJ. 2: Further, just as it is said of Baptism (John 3:5): *Unless a man be born again of water and the Holy Spirit, he cannot enter in to the kingdom of God*, so of the Eucharist is it said (John 6:54): *Except you eat of the flesh of the Son of Man, and drink of His blood, you shall not have life in you.* Therefore, just as Baptism is a necessary sacrament, so is the Eucharist.

OBJ. 3: Further, a man can be saved without the sacrament of Baptism, provided that some unavoidable obstacle, and not his contempt for religion, debar him from the sacrament, as we shall state further on (Q. 68, A. 2). But contempt of religion in any sacrament is a hindrance to salvation. Therefore, in like manner, all the sacraments are necessary for salvation.

ON THE CONTRARY, Children are saved by Baptism alone without the other sacraments.

I ANSWER THAT, Necessity of end, of which we speak now, is twofold. First, a thing may be necessary so that

Uno modo, sine quo non potest esse finis, sicut cibus est necessarius vitae humanae. Et hoc est simpliciter necessarium ad finem. Alio modo dicitur esse necessarium id sine quo non habetur finis ita convenienter, sicut equus necessarius est ad iter. Hoc autem non est simpliciter necessarium ad finem.

Primo igitur modo necessitatis sunt tria sacramenta necessaria. Duo quidem personae singulari, Baptismus quidem simpliciter et absolute; poenitentia autem, supposito peccato mortali post Baptismum. Sacramentum autem ordinis est necessarium Ecclesiae, quia, *ubi non est gubernator, populus corruet*, ut dicitur Proverb. XI.

Sed secundo modo sunt necessaria alia sacramenta. Nam confirmatio perficit Baptismum quodammodo; extrema unctio poenitentiam; matrimonium vero Ecclesiae multitudinem per propagationem conservat.

AD PRIMUM ergo dicendum quod ad hoc quod aliquid non sit superfluum, sufficit necessarium primo vel secundo modo. Et sic sunt necessaria sacramenta, ut dictum est.

AD SECUNDUM dicendum quod illud verbum domini est intelligendum de spirituali manducatione, et non de sola sacramentali, ut Augustinus exponit, super Ioannem.

AD TERTIUM dicendum quod, licet omnium sacramentorum contemptus sit saluti contrarius, non tamen est contemptus sacramenti ex hoc quod aliquis non curat accipere sacramentum quod non est de necessitate salutis. Alioquin qui non accipiunt ordinem, et qui non contrahunt matrimonium, contemnerent huiusmodi sacramenta.

without it the end cannot be attained; thus food is necessary for human life. And this is simple necessity of end. Second, a thing is said to be necessary, if, without it, the end cannot be attained so becomingly: thus a horse is necessary for a journey. But this is not simple necessity of end.

In the first way, three sacraments are necessary for salvation. Two of them are necessary to the individual; Baptism, simply and absolutely; Penance, in the case of mortal sin committed after Baptism; while the sacrament of order is necessary to the Church, since *where there is no governor the people shall fall* (Prov 11:14).

But in the second way the other sacraments are necessary. For in a sense Confirmation perfects Baptism; Extreme Unction perfects Penance; while Matrimony, by multiplying them, preserves the numbers in the Church.

REPLY OBJ. 1: For a thing not to be superfluous it is enough if it be necessary either in the first or the second way. It is thus that the sacraments are necessary, as stated above.

REPLY OBJ. 2: These words of our Lord are to be understood of spiritual, and not of merely sacramental, eating, as Augustine explains (*Tract. xxvi super Joan.*).

REPLY OBJ. 3: Although contempt of any of the sacraments is a hindrance to salvation, yet it does not amount to contempt of the sacrament, if anyone does not trouble to receive a sacrament that is not necessary for salvation. Else those who do not receive orders, and those who do not contract Matrimony, would be guilty of contempt of those sacraments.

QUESTION 66

THE SACRAMENT OF BAPTISM

Deinde considerandum est de singulis sacramentis in speciali. Et primo, de Baptismo; secundo, de confirmatione; tertio, de Eucharistia; quarto, de poenitentia; quinto, de extrema unctione; sexto, de ordine; septimo, de matrimonio.

Circa primum occurrit duplex consideratio, prima, de ipso Baptismo; secunda, de praeparatoriis Baptismi.

Circa primum quatuor consideranda occurrunt, primo, de his quae pertinent ad sacramentum Baptismi; secundo, de ministro huius sacramenti; tertio, de recipientibus hoc sacramentum; quarto, de effectu huius sacramenti.

Circa primum quaeruntur duodecim.

Primo, quid sit Baptismus, utrum sit ablutio.

Secundo, de institutione huius sacramenti.

Tertio, utrum aqua sit propria materia huius sacramenti.

Quarto, utrum requiratur aqua simplex.

Quinto, utrum haec sit conveniens forma huius sacramenti, ego te baptizo in nomine patris et filii et spiritus sancti.

Sexto, utrum sub hac forma possit aliquis baptizari, ego te baptizo in nomine Christi.

Septimo, utrum immersio sit de necessitate Baptismi.

Octavo, utrum requiratur trina immersio.

Nono, utrum Baptismus possit iterari.

Decimo, de ritu Baptismi.

Undecimo, de distinctione Baptismatum.

Duodecimo, de comparatione Baptismatum.

We have now to consider each sacrament specially: (1) Baptism; (2) Confirmation; (3) the Eucharist; (4) Penance; (5) Extreme Unction; (6) Order; (7) Matrimony.

Concerning the first, our consideration will be twofold: (1) of Baptism itself; (2) of things preparatory to Baptism.

Concerning the first, four points arise for our consideration: (1) Things pertaining to the sacrament of Baptism; (2) The minister of this sacrament; (3) The recipients of this sacrament; (4) The effect of this sacrament.

Concerning the first there are twelve points of inquiry:

(1) What is Baptism? Is it a washing?

(2) Of the institution of this sacrament;

(3) Whether water be the proper matter of this sacrament?

(4) Whether plain water be required?

(5) Whether this be a suitable form of this sacrament: *I baptize thee in the name of the Father, and of the Son, and of the Holy Spirit*?

(6) Whether one could baptize with this form: *I baptize thee in the name of Christ?*

(7) Whether immersion is necessary for Baptism?

(8) Whether trine immersion is necessary?

(9) Whether Baptism can be reiterated?

(10) Of the Baptismal rite;

(11) Of the various kinds of Baptism;

(12) Of the comparison between various Baptisms.

Article 1

Whether Baptism Is the Mere Washing?

AD PRIMUM SIC PROCEDITUR. Videtur quod Baptismus non sit ipsa ablutio. Ablutio enim corporalis transit. Baptismus autem permanet. Ergo Baptismus non est ipsa ablutio, sed potius *regeneratio et sigillum et custodia et illuminatio*, ut Damascenus dicit, in IV libro.

PRAETEREA, Hugo de sancto Victore dicit quod *Baptismus est aqua diluendis criminibus sanctificata per verbum Dei*. Aqua autem non est ipsa ablutio, sed ablutio est quidam usus aquae.

OBJECTION 1: It seems that Baptism is not the mere washing. For the washing of the body is something transitory: but Baptism is something permanent. Therefore Baptism is not the mere washing; but rather is it *the regeneration, the seal, the safeguarding, the enlightenment*, as Damascene says (*De Fide Orth.* iv).

OBJ. 2: Further, Hugh of St. Victor says (*De Sacram.* ii) that *Baptism is water sanctified by God's word for the blotting out of sins*. But the washing itself is not water, but a certain use of water.

Praeterea, Augustinus dicit, super Ioan., *accedit verbum ad elementum et fit sacramentum*. Elementum autem est ipsa aqua. Ergo Baptismus est ipsa aqua, non autem ablutio.

Sed contra est quod dicitur Eccli. XXXIV, *qui baptizatur a mortuo et iterum tangit mortuum, quid proficit lotio eius?* Videtur ergo quod Baptismus sit ipsa ablutio, sive lotio.

Respondeo dicendum quod in sacramento Baptismi est tria considerare, aliquid scilicet quod est sacramentum tantum; aliquid autem quod est res et sacramentum; aliquid autem quod est res tantum. Sacramentum autem tantum est aliquid visibile exterius existens, quod scilicet est signum interioris effectus, hoc enim pertinet ad rationem sacramenti. Exterius autem suppositum sensui est et ipsa aqua, et usus eius, qui est ablutio. Quidam ergo existimaverunt quod ipsa aqua sit sacramentum. Quod quidem sonare videntur verba Hugonis de sancto Victore. Nam ipse in communi definitione sacramenti dicit quod est materiale elementum, et in definitione Baptismi dicit quod est aqua.

Sed hoc non est verum. Cum enim sacramenta novae legis sanctificationem quandam operentur, ibi perficitur sacramentum ubi perficitur sanctificatio. In aqua autem non perficitur sanctificatio, sed est ibi quaedam sanctificationis virtus instrumentalis, non permanens, sed fluens in hominem, qui est verae sanctificationis subiectum. Et ideo sacramentum non perficitur in ipsa aqua, sed in applicatione aquae ad hominem, quae est ablutio. Et ideo Magister, in III dist. IV Sent., dicit quod *Baptismus est ablutio corporis exterior facta sub forma praescripta verborum*.

Res autem et sacramentum est character baptismalis, qui est res significata per exteriorem ablutionem, et est signum sacramentale interioris iustificationis. Quae est res tantum huius sacramenti, scilicet, significata et non significans.

Ad primum ergo dicendum quod id quod est sacramentum et res, scilicet character, et id quod est res tantum, scilicet interior iustificatio, permanent, sed character permanet indelebiliter, ut supra dictum est; iustificatio autem permanet, sed amissibiliter. Damascenus ergo Baptismum definivit, non quantum ad id quod exterius agitur, quod est sacramentum tantum, sed quantum ad id quod est interius. Unde posuit duo pertinentia ad characterem, scilicet sigillum et custodiam, inquantum ipse character, qui sigillum dicitur, quantum est de se, custodit animam in bono. Duo etiam ponit pertinentia ad ultimam rem sacramenti, scilicet regenerationem, quae ad hoc pertinet quod per Baptismum homo inchoat novam vitam iustitiae; et illuminationem, quae pertinet specialiter ad fidem, per quam homo spiritualem vitam accipit, secundum illud Habacuc II, *iustus autem ex fide vivit*; Baptismus autem est quaedam fidei

Obj. 3: Further, Augustine says (*Tract. lxxx super Joan.*): *The word is added to the element, and this becomes a sacrament.* Now, the element is the water. Therefore Baptism is the water and not the washing.

On the contrary, It is written (Sir 34:30): *He that washeth himself (baptizatur) after touching the dead, if he touch him again, what does his washing avail?* It seems, therefore, that Baptism is the washing or bathing.

I answer that, In the sacrament of Baptism, three things may be considered: namely, that which is sacrament only; that which is reality and sacrament; and that which is reality only. That which is sacrament only, is something visible and outward; the sign, namely, of the inward effect: for such is the very nature of a sacrament. And this outward something that can be perceived by the sense is both the water itself and its use, which is the washing. Hence some have thought that the water itself is the sacrament: which seems to be the meaning of the passage quoted from Hugh of St. Victor. For in the general definition of a sacrament he says that it is *a material element*: and in defining Baptism he says it is *water*.

But this is not true. For since the sacraments of the New Law effect a certain sanctification, there the sacrament is completed where the sanctification is completed. Now, the sanctification is not completed in water; but a certain sanctifying instrumental virtue, not permanent but transient, passes from the water, in which it is, into man who is the subject of true sanctification. Consequently the sacrament is not completed in the very water, but in applying the water to man, i.e., in the washing. Hence the Master (iv, 3) says that *Baptism is the outward washing of the body done together with the prescribed form of words*.

The Baptismal character is both reality and sacrament: because it is something real signified by the outward washing; and a sacramental sign of the inward justification: and this last is the reality only, in this sacrament—namely, the reality signified and not signifying.

Reply Obj. 1: That which is both sacrament and reality—i.e., the character—and that which is reality only—i.e., the inward justification—remain: the character remains and is indelible, as stated above (Q. 63, A. 5); the justification remains, but can be lost. Consequently Damascene defined Baptism, not as to that which is done outwardly, and is the sacrament only; but as to that which is inward. Hence he sets down two things as pertaining to the character—namely, *seal* and *safeguarding*; inasmuch as the character which is called a seal, so far as itself is concerned, safeguards the soul in good. He also sets down two things as pertaining to the ultimate reality of the sacrament—namely, *regeneration* which refers to the fact that man by being baptized begins the new life of righteousness; and *enlightenment*, which refers especially to faith, by which man receives spiritual life, according to Hab. 2 (Heb 10:38; cf. Hab 2:4): *But (My) just man liveth by faith*; and Baptism is

protestatio. Unde dicitur fidei sacramentum. Et similiter Dionysius Baptismum definivit per ordinem ad alia sacramenta, dicens, II cap. Eccles. Hier., quod *est quoddam principium sanctissimorum mandatorum sacrae actionis, ad eorum susceptivam opportunitatem formans nostros animales habitus.* Et iterum in ordine ad caelestem gloriam, quae est universalis finis sacramentorum, cum subdit, ad supercaelestis quietis anagogen nostrum iter faciens. Et iterum quantum ad principium spiritualis vitae, per hoc quod subdit, sacrae et divinissimae nostrae regenerationis traditio.

AD SECUNDUM dicendum quod, sicut dictum est, opinionem Hugonis de sancto Victore in hac parte sequi non oportet. Potest tamen verificari ut Baptismus dicatur aqua esse, quia aqua est materiale Baptismi principium. Et sic erit praedicatio per causam.

AD TERTIUM dicendum quod, accedente verbo ad elementum fit sacramentum, non quidem in ipso elemento, sed in homine, cui adhibetur elementum per usum ablutionis. Et hoc etiam significat ipsum verbum quod accedit ad elementum, cum dicitur, ego te baptizo, et cetera.

a sort of protestation of faith; whence it is called the *Sacrament of Faith*. Likewise Dionysius defined Baptism by its relation to the other sacraments, saying (*Eccl. Hier.* ii) that it is *the principle that forms the habits of the soul for the reception of those most holy words and sacraments*; and again by its relation to heavenly glory, which is the universal end of all the sacraments, when he adds, *preparing the way for us, whereby we mount to the repose of the heavenly kingdom*; and again as to the beginning of spiritual life, when he adds, *the conferring of our most sacred and Godlike regeneration.*

REPLY OBJ. 2: As already stated, the opinion of Hugh of St. Victor on this question is not to be followed. Nevertheless the saying that *Baptism is water* may be verified in so far as water is the material principle of Baptism: and thus there would be *causal predication.*

REPLY OBJ. 3: When the words are added, the element becomes a sacrament, not in the element itself, but in man, to whom the element is applied, by being used in washing him. Indeed, this is signified by those very words which are added to the element, when we say: *I baptize thee*, etc.

Article 2

Whether Baptism Was Instituted After Christ's Passion?

AD SECUNDUM SIC PROCEDITUR. Videtur quod Baptismus fuerit institutus post Christi passionem. Causa enim praecedit effectum. Sed passio Christi operatur in sacramentis novae legis. Ergo passio Christi praecedit institutionem sacramentorum novae legis. Et praecipue institutionem Baptismi, cum apostolus dicat, Rom. VI, *quicumque baptizati sumus in Christo Iesu, in morte ipsius baptizati sumus*, et cetera.

PRAETEREA, sacramenta novae legis efficaciam habent ex mandato Christi. Sed Christus mandatum baptizandi dedit discipulis post passionem et resurrectionem suam, *dicens, euntes, docete omnes gentes, baptizantes eos in nomine patris*, etc., ut habetur Matth. ult. Ergo videtur quod post passionem Christi Baptismus fuerit institutus.

PRAETEREA, Baptismus est sacramentum necessitatis, ut supra dictum est, et ita videtur quod ex quo Baptismus institutus fuit, homines obligarentur ad Baptismum. Sed ante passionem Christi homines non obligabantur ad Baptismum, quia adhuc circumcisio suam virtutem habebat, in cuius loco successit Baptismus. Ergo videtur quod Baptismus non fuerit institutus ante passionem Christi.

SED CONTRA est quod Augustinus dicit, in quodam sermone Epiphaniae, *ex quo Christus in aquis*

OBJECTION 1: It seems that Baptism was instituted after Christ's Passion. For the cause precedes the effect. Now Christ's Passion operates in the sacraments of the New Law. Therefore Christ's Passion precedes the institution of the sacraments of the New Law: especially the sacrament of Baptism since the Apostle says (Rom 6:3): *All we, who are baptized in Christ Jesus, are baptized in His death*, etc.

OBJ. 2: Further, the sacraments of the New Law derive their efficacy from the mandate of Christ. But Christ gave the disciples the mandate of Baptism after His Passion and Resurrection, when He said: *Going, teach ye all nations, baptizing them in the name of the Father*, etc. (Matt 28:19). Therefore it seems that Baptism was instituted after Christ's Passion.

OBJ. 3: Further, Baptism is a necessary sacrament, as stated above (Q. 65, A. 4): wherefore, seemingly, it must have been binding on man as soon as it was instituted. But before Christ's Passion men were not bound to be baptized: for Circumcision was still in force, which was supplanted by Baptism. Therefore it seems that Baptism was not instituted before Christ's Passion.

ON THE CONTRARY, Augustine says in a sermon on the Epiphany (*Append. Serm., clxxxv*): *As soon as Christ was*

immergitur, ex eo omnium peccata abluit aqua. Sed hoc fuit ante Christi passionem. Ergo Baptismus ante Christi passionem fuit institutus.

RESPONDEO dicendum quod, sicut dictum est supra, sacramenta ex sui institutione habent quod conferant gratiam. Unde tunc videtur aliquod sacramentum institui, quando accipit virtutem producendi suum effectum. Hanc autem virtutem accepit Baptismus quando Christus est baptizatus. Unde tunc vere Baptismus institutus fuit, quantum ad ipsum sacramentum. Sed necessitas utendi hoc sacramento indicta fuit hominibus post passionem et resurrectionem. Tum quia in passione Christi terminata sunt figuralia sacramenta, quibus succedit Baptismus et alia sacramenta novae legis. Tum etiam quia per Baptismum configuratur homo passioni et resurrectioni Christi, inquantum moritur peccato et incipit novam iustitiae vitam. Et ideo oportuit Christum pati prius et resurgere quam hominibus indiceretur necessitas se configurandi morti et resurrectioni eius.

AD PRIMUM ergo dicendum quod etiam ante passionem Christi Baptismus habebat efficaciam a Christi passione, inquantum eam praefigurabat, aliter tamen quam sacramenta veteris legis. Nam illa erant figurae tantum, Baptismus autem ab ipso Christo virtutem habebat iustificandi, per cuius virtutem etiam ipsa passio salutifera fuit.

AD SECUNDUM dicendum quod homines non debebant multiplicibus figuris arctari per Christum, qui venerat sua veritate figuras impletas auferre. Et ideo ante passionem suam Baptismum institutum non posuit sub praecepto, sed voluit ad eius exercitium homines assuefieri; et praecipue in populo Iudaeorum, apud quem omnia facta figuralia erant, ut Augustinus dicit, contra Faustum. Post passionem vero et resurrectionem, non solum Iudaeis, sed etiam gentilibus suo praecepto necessitatem Baptismi imposuit, dicens, *euntes, docete omnes gentes.*

AD TERTIUM dicendum quod sacramenta non sunt obligatoria nisi quando sub praecepto ponuntur. Quod quidem non fuit ante passionem, ut dictum est. Quod enim dominus ante passionem Nicodemo dixit, Ioan. III, *nisi quis renatus fuerit ex aqua et spiritu sancto, non potest introire in regnum Dei*, magis videtur ad futurum respicere quam ad praesens tempus.

plunged into the waters, the waters washed away the sins of all. But this was before Christ's Passion. Therefore Baptism was instituted before Christ's Passion.

I ANSWER THAT, As stated above (Q. 62, A. 1), sacraments derive from their institution the power of conferring grace. Wherefore it seems that a sacrament is then instituted, when it receives the power of producing its effect. Now Baptism received this power when Christ was baptized. Consequently Baptism was truly instituted then, if we consider it as a sacrament. But the obligation of receiving this sacrament was proclaimed to mankind after the Passion and Resurrection. First, because Christ's Passion put an end to the figurative sacraments, which were supplanted by Baptism and the other sacraments of the New Law. Second, because by Baptism man is *made conformable* to Christ's Passion and Resurrection, in so far as he dies to sin and begins to live anew unto righteousness. Consequently it behooved Christ to suffer and to rise again, before proclaiming to man his obligation of conforming himself to Christ's Death and Resurrection.

REPLY OBJ. 1: Even before Christ's Passion, Baptism, inasmuch as it foreshadowed it, derived its efficacy therefrom; but not in the same way as the sacraments of the Old Law. For these were mere figures: whereas Baptism derived the power of justifying from Christ Himself, to Whose power the Passion itself owed its saving virtue.

REPLY OBJ. 2: It was not meet that men should be restricted to a number of figures by Christ, Who came to fulfill and replace the figure by His reality. Therefore before His Passion He did not make Baptism obligatory as soon as it was instituted; but wished men to become accustomed to its use; especially in regard to the Jews, to whom all things were figurative, as Augustine says (*Contra Faust.* iv). But after His Passion and Resurrection He made Baptism obligatory, not only on the Jews, but also on the Gentiles, when He gave the commandment: *Going, teach ye all nations.*

REPLY OBJ. 3: Sacraments are not obligatory except when we are commanded to receive them. And this was not before the Passion, as stated above. For our Lord's words to Nicodemus (John 3:5), *Unless a man be born again of water and the Holy Spirit, he cannot enter into the kingdom of God*, seem to refer to the future rather than to the present.

Article 3

Whether Water Is the Proper Matter of Baptism?

AD TERTIUM SIC PROCEDITUR. Videtur quod aqua non sit propria materia Baptismi. Baptismus enim, secundum Dionysium et Damascenum, habet vim illuminativam. Sed illuminatio maxime competit igni. Ergo Baptismus magis debet fieri in igne quam in aqua, praesertim cum Ioannes Baptista, praenuntians Christi Baptismum, dicat, *ille vos baptizabit in spiritu sancto et igni.*

PRAETEREA, in Baptismo significatur ablutio peccatorum. Sed multa alia sunt ablutiva quam aqua, sicut vinum et oleum et alia huiusmodi. Ergo etiam in his potest fieri Baptismus. Non ergo aqua est propria materia Baptismi.

PRAETEREA, sacramenta Ecclesiae fluxerunt de latere Christi pendentis in cruce, ut supra dictum est. Sed inde fluxit non solum aqua, sed etiam sanguis. Ergo videtur quod etiam in sanguine possit fieri Baptismus. Quod etiam magis videtur convenire cum effectu Baptismi, quia dicitur Apoc. I, *lavit nos a peccatis nostris in sanguine suo.*

PRAETEREA, sicut Augustinus et Beda dicunt, *Christus tactu suae mundissimae carnis vim regenerativam et purgativam contulit aquis.* Sed non omnis aqua continuatur cum aqua Iordanis, quam Christus tetigit sua carne. Ergo videtur quod non in omni aqua possit fieri Baptismus. Et ita aqua, inquantum huiusmodi, non est propria materia Baptismi.

PRAETEREA, si aqua secundum se esset propria Baptismi materia, non oporteret aliquid aliud fieri circa aquam, ad hoc quod in ea Baptismus fieret. Sed in solemni Baptismo aqua in qua debet celebrari Baptismus, exorcizatur et benedicitur. Ergo videtur quod aqua secundum se non sit propria materia Baptismi.

SED CONTRA est quod dominus dicit, Ioan. III, *nisi quis renatus fuerit ex aqua et spiritu sancto, non potest introire in regnum Dei.*

RESPONDEO dicendum quod ex institutione divina aqua est propria materia Baptismi. Et hoc convenienter. Primo quidem, quantum ad ipsam rationem Baptismi, qui est regeneratio in spiritualem vitam, quod maxime congruit aquae. Unde et semina, ex quibus generantur omnia viventia, scilicet plantae et animalia, humida sunt, et ad aquam pertinent. Propter quod quidam philosophi posuerunt aquam omnium rerum principium.

Secundo, quantum ad effectus Baptismi, quibus competunt aquae proprietates. Quae sua humiditate lavat, ex quo conveniens est ad significandum et causandum ablutionem peccatorum. Sua frigiditate etiam temperat superfluitatem caloris, et ex hoc competit ad

OBJECTION 1: It seems that water is not the proper matter of Baptism. For Baptism, according to Dionysius (*Eccl. Hier.* v) and Damascene (*De Fide Orth.* iv), has a power of enlightening. But enlightenment is a special characteristic of fire. Therefore Baptism should be conferred with fire rather than with water: and all the more since John the Baptist said when foretelling Christ's Baptism (Matt 3:11): *He shall baptize you in the Holy Spirit and fire.*

OBJ. 2: Further, the washing away of sins is signified in Baptism. But many other things besides water are employed in washing, such as wine, oil, and such like. Therefore Baptism can be conferred with these also; and consequently water is not the proper matter of Baptism.

OBJ. 3: Further, the sacraments of the Church flowed from the side of Christ hanging on the cross, as stated above (Q. 62, A. 5). But not only water flowed therefrom, but also blood. Therefore it seems that Baptism can also be conferred with blood. And this seems to be more in keeping with the effect of Baptism, because it is written (Rev 1:5): *(Who) washed us from our sins in His own blood.*

OBJ. 4: Further, as Augustine (cf. Master of the *Sentences*, iv, 3) and Bede (*Exposit. in Luc.* iii, 21) say, Christ, by *the touch of His most pure flesh, endowed the waters with a regenerating and cleansing virtue.* But all waters are not connected with the waters of the Jordan which Christ touched with His flesh. Consequently it seems that Baptism cannot be conferred with any water; and therefore water, as such, is not the proper matter of Baptism.

OBJ. 5: Further, if water, as such, were the proper matter of Baptism, there would be no need to do anything to the water before using it for Baptism. But in solemn Baptism the water which is used for baptizing, is exorcized and blessed. Therefore it seems that water, as such, is not the proper matter of Baptism.

ON THE CONTRARY, our Lord said (John 3:5): *Unless a man be born again of water and the Holy Spirit, he cannot enter into the kingdom of God.*

I ANSWER THAT, By Divine institution water is the proper matter of Baptism; and with reason. First, by reason of the very nature of Baptism, which is a regeneration unto spiritual life. And this answers to the nature of water in a special degree; wherefore seeds, from which all living things, viz. plants and animals are generated, are moist and akin to water. For this reason certain philosophers held that water is the first principle of all things.

Second, in regard to the effects of Baptism, to which the properties of water correspond. For by reason of its moistness it cleanses; and hence it fittingly signifies and causes the cleansing from sins. By reason of its coolness it tempers superfluous heat: wherefore it fittingly mitigates the

mitigandum concupiscentiam fomitis. Sua diaphanitate est luminis susceptiva, unde competit Baptismo inquantum est fidei sacramentum.

Tertio, quia convenit ad repraesentandum mysteria Christi, quibus iustificamur. Ut enim dicit Chrysostomus, super illud Ioan., *nisi quis renatus fuerit etc., sicut in quodam sepulcro, in aqua, submergentibus nobis capita, vetus homo sepelitur, et submersus deorsum occultatur, et deinde novus rursus ascendit.*

Quarto, quia ratione suae communitatis et abundantiae est conveniens materia necessitati huius sacramenti, potest enim ubique de facili haberi.

AD PRIMUM ergo dicendum quod illuminatio pertinet ad ignem active. Ille autem qui baptizatur, non efficitur illuminans, sed illuminatus per fidem, quae est ex auditu, ut dicitur Rom. X. Et ideo magis competit aqua Baptismo quam ignis.

Quod autem dicitur, baptizabit vos in spiritu sancto et igni, potest per ignem, ut Hieronymus dicit, intelligi Spiritus Sanctus, qui super discipulos in igneis linguis apparuit, ut dicitur Act. II. Vel per ignem potest intelligi tribulatio, ut Chrysostomus dicit, super Matth., quia tribulatio peccata purgat, et concupiscentiam diminuit. Vel quia, ut Hilarius dicit, super Matth., *baptizatis in spiritu sancto reliquum est consummari igne iudicii.*

AD SECUNDUM dicendum quod vinum et oleum communiter non sumuntur ad usum ablutionis, sicut aqua. Nec etiam ita perfecte abluunt, quia ex illorum ablutione remanet aliqua infectio quantum ad odorem, quod non contingit de aqua. Illa etiam non ita communiter et abundanter habentur sicut aqua.

AD TERTIUM dicendum quod ex latere Christi fluxit aqua ad abluendum, sanguis autem ad redimendum. Et ideo sanguis competit sacramento Eucharistiae, aqua autem sacramento Baptismi. Qui tamen habet vim ablutivam ex virtute sanguinis Christi.

AD QUARTUM dicendum quod virtus Christi derivata est ad omnem aquam, non propter continuitatem loci, sed propter similitudinem speciei, ut dicit Augustinus, in quodam sermone Epiphaniae, *quae de salvatoris Baptismate benedictio fluxit, tanquam fluvius spiritalis, omnium gurgitum tractus, universorum fontium venas implevit.*

AD QUINTUM dicendum quod illa benedictio quae adhibetur aquae, non est de necessitate Baptismi, sed pertinet ad quandam solemnitatem, per quam excitatur devotio fidelium, et impeditur astutia Daemonis, ne impediat Baptismi effectum.

concupiscence of the fomes. By reason of its transparency, it is susceptive of light; hence its adaptability to Baptism as the *sacrament of Faith.*

Third, because it is suitable for the signification of the mysteries of Christ, by which we are justified. For, as Chrysostom says (*Hom. xxv in Joan.*) on John 3:5, *Unless a man be born again,* etc., *When we dip our heads under the water as in a kind of tomb our old man is buried, and being submerged is hidden below, and thence he rises again renewed.*

Fourth, because by being so universal and abundant, it is a matter suitable to our need of this sacrament: for it can easily be obtained everywhere.

REPLY OBJ. 1: Fire enlightens actively. But he who is baptized does not become an enlightener, but is enlightened by faith, which *cometh by hearing* (Rom 10:17). Consequently water is more suitable, than fire, for Baptism.

But when we find it said: *He shall baptize you in the Holy Spirit and fire,* we may understand fire, as Jerome says (*In Matth.* ii), to mean the Holy Spirit, Who appeared above the disciples under the form of fiery tongues (Acts 2:3). Or we may understand it to mean tribulation, as Chrysostom says (*Hom. iii in Matth.*): because tribulation washes away sin, and tempers concupiscence. Or again, as Hilary says (*Super Matth.* ii) that *when we have been baptized in the Holy Spirit,* we still have to be *perfected by the fire of the judgment.*

REPLY OBJ. 2: Wine and oil are not so commonly used for washing, as water. Neither do they wash so efficiently: for whatever is washed with them, contracts a certain smell therefrom; which is not the case if water be used. Moreover, they are not so universal or so abundant as water.

REPLY OBJ. 3: Water flowed from Christ's side to wash us; blood, to redeem us. Wherefore blood belongs to the sacrament of the Eucharist, while water belongs to the sacrament of Baptism. Yet this latter sacrament derives its cleansing virtue from the power of Christ's blood.

REPLY OBJ. 4: Christ's power flowed into all waters, by reason of, not connection of place, but likeness of species, as Augustine says in a sermon on the Epiphany (*Append. Serm. cxxxv*): *The blessing that flowed from the Savior's Baptism, like a mystic river, swelled the course of every stream, and filled the channels of every spring.*

REPLY OBJ. 5: The blessing of the water is not essential to Baptism, but belongs to a certain solemnity, whereby the devotion of the faithful is aroused, and the cunning of the devil hindered from impeding the baptismal effect.

Article 4

Whether Plain Water Is Necessary for Baptism?

AD QUARTUM SIC PROCEDITUR. Videtur quod ad Baptismum non requiratur aqua simplex. Aqua enim quae apud nos est, non est aqua pura, quod praecipue apparet de aqua maris, in qua plurimum admiscetur de terrestri, ut patet per philosophum, in libro Meteorol. Et tamen in tali aqua potest fieri Baptismus. Ergo non requiritur aqua simplex et pura ad Baptismum.

PRAETEREA, in solemni celebratione Baptismi aquae infunditur chrisma. Sed hoc videtur impedire puritatem et simplicitatem aquae. Ergo aqua pura et simplex non requiritur ad Baptismum.

PRAETEREA, aqua fluens de latere Christi pendentis in cruce fuit significativa Baptismi, ut dictum est. Sed aqua illa non videtur fuisse aqua pura, eo quod in corpore mixto, cuiusmodi fuit corpus Christi, non sunt elementa in actu. Ergo videtur quod non requiratur aqua pura vel simplex ad Baptismum.

PRAETEREA, lixivium non videtur esse aqua pura, habet enim contrarias proprietates aquae, scilicet calefaciendi et desiccandi. Et tamen in lixivio videtur posse fieri Baptismus, sicut et in aquis balneorum, quae transeunt per venas sulphureas, sicut et lixivium colatur per cineres. Ergo videtur quod aqua simplex non requiratur ad Baptismum.

PRAETEREA, aqua rosacea generatur per sublimationem a rosis, sicut etiam aquae alchimicae generantur per sublimationem ab aliquibus corporibus. Sed in his aquis, ut videtur, potest fieri Baptismus, sicut et in aquis pluvialibus, quae per sublimationem vaporum generantur. Cum igitur huiusmodi aquae non sint purae et simplices, videtur quod aqua pura et simplex non requiratur ad Baptismum.

SED CONTRA est quod propria materia Baptismi est aqua, ut dictum est. Sed speciem aquae non habet nisi aqua simplex. Ergo aqua pura et simplex ex necessitate requiritur ad Baptismum.

RESPONDEO dicendum quod aqua suam puritatem et simplicitatem potest amittere dupliciter, uno modo, per mixtionem alterius corporis; alio modo, per alterationem. Utrumque autem horum contingit fieri dupliciter, scilicet per artem, et per naturam. Ars autem deficit ab operatione naturae, quia natura dat formam substantialem, quod ars facere non potest, sed omnes formae artificiales sunt accidentales; nisi forte apponendo proprium agens ad propriam materiam, sicut ignem combustibili, per quem modum a quibusdam quaedam animalia per putrefactionem generantur.

Quaecumque igitur transmutatio circa aquam facta est per artem, sive commiscendo sive alterando, non transmutatur species aquae. Unde in tali aqua potest fieri

OBJECTION 1: It seems that plain water is not necessary for Baptism. For the water which we have is not plain water; as appears especially in sea-water, in which there is a considerable proportion of the earthly element, as the Philosopher shows (*Meteor.* ii). Yet this water may be used for Baptism. Therefore plain and pure water is not necessary for Baptism.

OBJ. 2: Further, in the solemn celebration of Baptism, chrism is poured into the water. But this seems to take away the purity and plainness of the water. Therefore pure and plain water is not necessary for Baptism.

OBJ. 3: Further, the water that flowed from the side of Christ hanging on the cross was a figure of Baptism, as stated above (A. 3, ad 3). But that water, seemingly, was not pure, because the elements do not exist actually in a mixed body, such as Christ's. Therefore it seems that pure or plain water is not necessary for Baptism.

OBJ. 4: Further, lye does not seem to be pure water, for it has the properties of heating and drying, which are contrary to those of water. Nevertheless it seems that lye can be used for Baptism; for the water of the Baths can be so used, which has filtered through a sulphurous vein, just as lye percolates through ashes. Therefore it seems that plain water is not necessary for Baptism.

OBJ. 5: Further, rose-water is distilled from roses, just as chemical waters are distilled from certain bodies. But seemingly, such like waters may be used in Baptism; just as rain-water, which is distilled from vapors. Since, therefore, such waters are not pure and plain water, it seems that pure and plain water is not necessary for Baptism.

ON THE CONTRARY, The proper matter of Baptism is water, as stated above (A. 3). But plain water alone has the nature of water. Therefore pure plain water is necessary for Baptism.

I ANSWER THAT, Water may cease to be pure or plain water in two ways: first, by being mixed with another body; second, by alteration. And each of these may happen in a twofold manner; artificially and naturally. Now art fails in the operation of nature: because nature gives the substantial form, which art cannot give; for whatever form is given by art is accidental; except perchance when art applies a proper agent to its proper matter, as fire to a combustible; in which manner animals are produced from certain things by way of putrefaction.

Whatever artificial change, then, takes place in the water, whether by mixture or by alteration, the water's nature is not changed. Consequently such water can be used for

Baptismus, nisi forte aqua admisceatur per artem in tam parva quantitate alicui corpori quod compositum magis sit aliud quam aqua; sicut lutum magis est terra quam aqua, et vinum lymphatum magis est vinum quam aqua.

Sed transmutatio quae fit a natura, quandoque quidem speciem aquae solvit, et hoc fit quando aqua efficitur per naturam de substantia alicuius corporis mixti; sicut aqua conversa in liquorem uvae est vinum, unde non habet speciem aquae. Aliquando autem fit per naturam transmutatio aquae sine solutione speciei, et hoc tam per alterationem, sicut patet de aqua calefacta a sole; quam etiam per mixtionem, sicut patet de aqua fluminis turbida ex permixtione terrestrium partium.

Sic igitur dicendum est quod in qualibet aqua, qualitercumque transmutata, dummodo non solvatur species aquae, potest fieri Baptismus. Si autem solvatur species aquae, non potest fieri Baptismus.

AD PRIMUM ergo dicendum quod transmutatio facta in aqua maris, et in aliis aquis quae penes nos sunt, non est tanta quae solvat speciem aquae. Et ideo in huiusmodi aquis potest fieri Baptismus.

AD SECUNDUM dicendum quod admixtio chrismatis non solvit speciem aquae. Sicut nec etiam aqua decoctionis carnium, aut aliorum huiusmodi, nisi forte sit facta tanta resolutio corporum lixatorum in aqua quod liquor plus habeat de aliena substantia quam de aqua; quod ex spissitudine perspici potest. Si tamen ex liquore sic inspissato exprimatur aqua subtilis, potest in ea fieri Baptismus, sicut et in aqua quae exprimitur ex luto, licet in luto Baptismus fieri non possit.

AD TERTIUM dicendum quod aqua fluens de latere Christi pendentis in cruce non fuit humor phlegmaticus, ut quidam dixerunt. In tali enim humore non posset fieri Baptismus, sicut nec in sanguine animalis, aut in vino, aut in quocumque liquore alicuius plantae. Fuit autem aqua pura miraculose egrediens a corpore mortuo, sicut et sanguis, ad comprobandam veritatem dominici corporis, contra Manichaeorum errorem, ut scilicet per aquam, quae est unum quatuor elementorum, ostenderetur corpus Christi vere fuisse compositum ex quatuor elementis; per sanguinem vero ostenderetur esse compositum ex quatuor humoribus.

AD QUARTUM dicendum quod in lixivio, et in aquis sulphureorum balneorum, potest fieri Baptismus, quia tales aquae non incorporantur per artem vel naturam aliquibus corporibus mixtis, sed solum alterationem quandam recipiunt ex hoc quod transeunt per aliqua corpora.

AD QUINTUM dicendum quod aqua rosacea est liquor rosae resolutus. Unde in ea non potest fieri Baptismus. Et, eadem ratione, nec in aquis alchimicis, sicut in vino. Nec est eadem ratio de aquis pluvialibus, quae

Baptism: unless perhaps such a small quantity of water be mixed artificially with a body that the compound is something other than water; thus mud is earth rather than water, and diluted wine is wine rather than water.

But if the change be natural, sometimes it destroys the nature of the water; and this is when by a natural process water enters into the substance of a mixed body: thus water changed into the juice of the grape is wine, wherefore it has not the nature of water. Sometimes, however, there may be a natural change of the water, without destruction of species: and this, both by alteration, as we may see in the case of water heated by the sun; and by mixture, as when the water of a river has become muddy by being mixed with particles of earth.

We must therefore say that any water may be used for Baptism, no matter how much it may be changed, as long as the species of water is not destroyed; but if the species of water be destroyed, it cannot be used for Baptism.

REPLY OBJ. 1: The change in sea-water and in other waters which we have to hand, is not so great as to destroy the species of water. And therefore such waters may be used for Baptism.

REPLY OBJ. 2: Chrism does not destroy the nature of the water by being mixed with it: just as neither is water changed wherein meat and the like are boiled: except the substance boiled be so dissolved that the liquor be of a nature foreign to water; in this we may be guided by the specific gravity (spissitudine). If, however, from the liquor thus thickened plain water be strained, it can be used for Baptism: just as water strained from mud, although mud cannot be used for baptizing.

REPLY OBJ. 3: The water which flowed from the side of Christ hanging on the cross, was not the phlegmatic humor, as some have supposed. For a liquid of this kind cannot be used for Baptism, as neither can the blood of an animal, or wine, or any liquid extracted from plants. It was pure water gushing forth miraculously like the blood from a dead body, to prove the reality of our Lord's body, and confute the error of the Manichees: water, which is one of the four elements, showing Christ's body to be composed of the four elements; blood, proving that it was composed of the four humors.

REPLY OBJ. 4: Baptism may be conferred with lye and the waters of Sulphur Baths: because such like waters are not incorporated, artificially or naturally, with certain mixed bodies, and suffer only a certain alteration by passing through certain bodies.

REPLY OBJ. 5: Rose-water is a liquid distilled from roses: consequently it cannot be used for Baptism. For the same reason chemical waters cannot be used, as neither can wine. Nor does the comparison hold with rain-water, which

generantur ex maiori parte ex subtiliatione vaporum resolutorum ex aquis, minimum autem ibi est de liquoribus corporum mixtorum, qui tamen per huiusmodi sublimationem, virtute naturae, quae est fortior arte, resolvuntur in veram aquam, quod ars facere non potest. Unde aqua pluvialis nullam proprietatem retinet alicuius corporis mixti, quod de aquis rosaceis et de aquis alchimicis dici non potest.

for the most part is formed by the condensing of vapors, themselves formed from water, and contains a minimum of the liquid matter from mixed bodies; which liquid matter by the force of nature, which is stronger than art, is transformed in this process of condensation into real water, a result which cannot be produced artificially. Consequently rain-water retains no properties of any mixed body; which cannot be said of rose-water or chemical waters.

Article 5

Whether This Be a Suitable Form of Baptism: I Baptize Thee in the Name of the Father, and of the Son, and of the Holy Spirit?

AD QUINTUM SIC PROCEDITUR. Videtur quod haec non sit conveniens forma Baptismi, *ego te baptizo in nomine patris et filii et spiritus sancti.* Actus enim magis debet attribui principali agenti quam ministro. Sed in sacramento minister agit ut instrumentum, ut supra dictum est, principale autem agens in Baptismo est Christus, secundum illud Ioan. I, *super quem videris spiritum descendentem et manentem, hic est qui baptizat.* Inconvenienter ergo minister dicit, ego te baptizo, praesertim quia in hoc quod dicitur baptizo, intelligitur ego, et sic videtur superflue apponi.

PRAETEREA, non oportet quod ille qui aliquem actum exercet, de actu exercito faciat mentionem, sicut ille qui docet, non oportet quod dicat, ego vos doceo. Dominus autem simul tradidit praeceptum baptizandi et docendi, dicens, *euntes, docete omnes gentes,* et cetera. Ergo non oportet quod in forma Baptismi fiat mentio de actu Baptismi.

PRAETEREA, ille qui baptizatur, quandoque non intelligit verba, puta si sit surdus aut puer. Frustra autem ad talem sermo dirigitur, secundum illud Eccli., *ubi non est auditus, non effundas sermonem.* Ergo inconvenienter dicitur, ego te baptizo, sermone directo ad eum qui baptizatur.

PRAETEREA, contingit simul plures baptizari a pluribus, sicut apostoli baptizaverunt una die tria millia, et alia die quinque millia, ut dicitur Act. II et IV. Non ergo debet forma Baptismi determinari in singulari numero, ut dicatur, ego te baptizo, sed potest dici, nos vos baptizamus.

PRAETEREA, Baptismus virtutem habet a passione Christi. Sed per formam Baptismus sanctificatur. Ergo videtur quod in forma Baptismi debeat fieri mentio de passione Christi.

PRAETEREA, nomen designat proprietatem rei. Sed tres sunt proprietates personales divinarum personarum, ut in prima parte dictum est. Non ergo debet dici,

OBJECTION 1: It seems that this is not a suitable form of Baptism: *I baptize thee in the name of the Father, and of the Son, and of the Holy Spirit.* For action should be ascribed to the principal agent rather than to the minister. Now the minister of a sacrament acts as an instrument, as stated above (Q. 64, A. 1); while the principal agent in Baptism is Christ, according to John 1:33, *He upon Whom thou shalt see the Spirit descending and remaining upon Him, He it is that baptizeth.* It is therefore unbecoming for the minister to say, *I baptize thee*: the more so that *Ego* (I) is understood in the word *baptizo* (I baptize), so that it seems redundant.

OBJ. 2: Further, there is no need for a man who does an action, to make mention of the action done; thus he who teaches, need not say, *I teach you.* Now our Lord gave at the same time the precepts both of baptizing and of teaching, when He said (Matt 28:19): *Going, teach ye all nations,* etc. Therefore there is no need in the form of Baptism to mention the action of baptizing.

OBJ. 3: Further, the person baptized sometimes does not understand the words; for instance, if he be deaf, or a child. But it is useless to address such a one; according to Ecclus. 32:6: *Where there is no hearing, pour not out words.* Therefore it is unfitting to address the person baptized with these words: *I baptize thee.*

OBJ. 4: Further, it may happen that several are baptized by several at the same time; thus the apostles on one day baptized three thousand, and on another, five thousand (Acts 2, 4). Therefore the form of Baptism should not be limited to the singular number in the words, *I baptize thee*: but one should be able to say, *We baptize you.*

OBJ. 5: Further, Baptism derives its power from Christ's Passion. But Baptism is sanctified by the form. Therefore it seems that Christ's Passion should be mentioned in the form of Baptism.

OBJ. 6: Further, a name signifies a thing's property. But there are three Personal Properties of the Divine Persons, as stated in the First Part (Q. 32, A. 3). Therefore we should

in nomine patris et filii et spiritus sancti, sed, in nominibus.

PRAETEREA, persona patris non solum significatur nomine patris, sed etiam nomine innascibilis et genitoris; filius etiam significatur nomine verbi et imaginis et geniti; spiritus etiam sanctus potest significari nomine doni et amoris, et nomine procedentis. Ergo videtur quod etiam his nominibus utendo perficitur Baptismus.

SED CONTRA est quod dominus dicit, Matth. ult., *euntes, docete omnes gentes, baptizantes eos in nomine patris et filii et spiritus sancti.*

RESPONDEO dicendum quod Baptismus per suam formam consecratur, secundum illud Ephes. V, *mundans eam lavacro aquae in verbo vitae*, et Augustinus dicit, in libro de unico Baptismo, quod *Baptismus verbis evangelicis consecratur*. Et ideo oportet quod in forma Baptismi exprimatur causa Baptismi. Est autem eius duplex causa, una quidem principalis, a qua virtutem habet, quae est sancta Trinitas; alia autem est instrumentalis, scilicet minister, qui tradit exterius sacramentum. Et ideo debet in forma Baptismi de utraque fieri mentio. Minister autem tangitur cum dicitur, ego te baptizo, causa autem principalis, cum dicitur, in nomine patris et filii et spiritus sancti. Unde haec est conveniens forma Baptismi, *ego te baptizo in nomine patris et filii et spiritus sancti.*

AD PRIMUM ergo dicendum quod actio attribuitur instrumento sicut immediate agenti, attribuitur autem principali agenti sicut in cuius virtute instrumentum agit. Et ideo in forma Baptismi convenienter significatur minister ut exercens actum Baptismi, per hoc quod dicitur, ego te baptizo, et ipse dominus baptizandi actum attribuit ministris, dicens, baptizantes eos, et cetera. Causa autem principalis significatur ut in cuius virtute sacramentum agitur, per hoc quod dicitur, *in nomine patris et filii et spiritus sancti*, non enim Christus baptizat sine patre et spiritu sancto.

Graeci autem non attribuunt actum Baptismi ministris, ad evitandum antiquorum errorem, qui virtutem Baptismi Baptistis attribuebant, dicentes, *ego sum Pauli, et ego Cephae*. Et ideo dicunt, *baptizetur servus Christi talis in nomine patris*, et cetera. Et quia exprimitur actus exercitus per ministrum cum invocatione Trinitatis, verum perficitur sacramentum. Quod autem additur ego in forma nostra, non est de substantia formae, sed ponitur ad maiorem expressionem intentionis.

AD SECUNDUM dicendum quod, quia ablutio hominis in aqua propter multa fieri potest, oportet quod determinetur in verbis formae ad quid fiat. Quod quidem non fit per hoc quod dicitur, *in nomine patris et filii et spiritus sancti*, quia omnia in tali nomine facere debemus, ut habetur Coloss. III. Et ideo, si non exprimatur actus Baptismi, vel per modum nostrum vel per modum

not say, *in the name*, but *in the names of the Father, and of the Son, and of the Holy Spirit*.

OBJ. 7: Further, the Person of the Father is designated not only by the name Father, but also by that of *Unbegotten and Begetter*; and the Son by those of *Word, Image*, and *Begotten*; and the Holy Spirit by those of *Gift, Love*, and the *Proceeding One*. Therefore it seems that Baptism is valid if conferred in these names.

ON THE CONTRARY, our Lord said (Matt 28:19): *Going . . . teach ye all nations, baptizing them in the name of the Father, and of the Son, and of the Holy Spirit.*

I ANSWER THAT, Baptism receives its consecration from its form, according to Eph. 5:26: *Cleansing it by the laver of water in the word of life*. And Augustine says (*De Unico Baptismo* iv) that *Baptism is consecrated by the words of the Gospel*. Consequently the cause of Baptism needs to be expressed in the baptismal form. Now this cause is twofold; the principal cause from which it derives its virtue, and this is the Blessed Trinity; and the instrumental cause, viz. the minister who confers the sacrament outwardly. Wherefore both causes should be expressed in the form of Baptism. Now the minister is designated by the words, *I baptize thee*; and the principal cause in the words, *in the name of the Father, and of the Son, and of the Holy Spirit*. Therefore this is the suitable form of Baptism: *I baptize thee in the name of the Father, and of the Son, and of the Holy Spirit.*

REPLY OBJ. 1: Action is attributed to an instrument as to the immediate agent; but to the principal agent inasmuch as the instrument acts in virtue thereof. Consequently it is fitting that in the baptismal form the minister should be mentioned as performing the act of baptizing, in the words, *I baptize thee*; indeed, our Lord attributed to the ministers the act of baptizing, when He said: *Baptizing them*, etc. But the principal cause is indicated as conferring the sacrament by His own power, in the words, *in the name of the Father, and of the Son, and of the Holy Spirit*: for Christ does not baptize without the Father and the Holy Spirit.

The Greeks, however, do not attribute the act of baptizing to the minister, in order to avoid the error of those who in the past ascribed the baptismal power to the baptizers, saying (1 Cor 1:12): *I am of Paul . . . and I of Cephas*. Wherefore they use the form: *May the servant of Christ, N . . ., be baptized, in the name of the Father*, etc. And since the action performed by the minister is expressed with the invocation of the Trinity, the sacrament is validly conferred. As to the addition of *Ego* in our form, it is not essential; but it is added in order to lay greater stress on the intention.

REPLY OBJ. 2: Since a man may be washed with water for several reasons, the purpose for which it is done must be expressed by the words of the form. And this is not done by saying: *In the name of the Father, and of the Son, and of the Holy Spirit*; because we are bound to do all things in that Name (Col 3:17). Wherefore unless the act of baptizing be expressed, either as we do, or as the Greeks do, the

Graecorum, non perficitur sacramentum, secundum illam decretalem Alexandri III, *si quis puerum ter in aquam merserit in nomine patris et filii et spiritus sancti amen, et non dixerit, ego te baptizo in nomine patris et filii et spiritus sancti amen, non est puer baptizatus.*

AD TERTIUM dicendum quod verba quae proferuntur in formis sacramentorum, non pronuntiantur solum causa significandi, sed etiam causa efficiendi, inquantum habent efficaciam ab illo verbo per quod facta sunt omnia. Et ideo convenienter diriguntur non solum ad homines, sed etiam ad creaturas insensibiles, ut cum dicitur, *exorcizo te, creatura salis.*

AD QUARTUM dicendum quod plures simul non possunt unum baptizare, quia actus multiplicatur secundum multiplicationem agentium, si perfecte ab unoquoque agatur. Et sic, si convenirent duo quorum unus esset mutus, qui non posset proferre verba, et alius carens manibus, qui non posset exercere actum, non possent ambo simul baptizare, uno dicente verba et alio exercente actum.

Possunt autem, si necessitas exigit, plures simul baptizari, quia nullus eorum recipiet nisi unum Baptismum. Sed tunc oportebit dicere, ego baptizo vos. Nec erit mutatio formae, quia vos nihil aliud est quam te et te. Quod autem dicitur nos, non est idem quod ego et ego, sed, ego et tu, et sic iam mutaretur forma.

Similiter autem mutaretur forma si diceretur, ego baptizo me. Et ideo nullus potest baptizare seipsum. Propter quod etiam Christus a Ioanne voluit baptizari, ut dicitur extra, de Baptismo et eius effectu, cap. debitum.

AD QUINTUM dicendum quod passio Christi, etsi sit principalis causa respectu ministri, est tamen causa instrumentalis respectu sanctae Trinitatis. Et ideo potius commemoratur Trinitas quam passio Christi.

AD SEXTUM dicendum quod, etsi sint tria nomina personalia trium personarum, est tamen unum nomen essentiale. Virtus autem divina, quae operatur in Baptismo, ad essentiam pertinet. Et ideo dicitur in nomine, et non in nominibus.

AD SEPTIMUM dicendum quod, sicut aqua sumitur ad Baptismum quia eius usus est communior ad abluendum, ita ad significandum tres personas in forma Baptismi assumuntur illa nomina quibus communius consueverunt nominari personae in illa lingua. Nec in aliis nominibus perficitur sacramentum.

sacrament is not valid; according to the *Decretal* of Alexander III: *If anyone dip a child thrice in the water in the name of the Father, and of the Son, and of the Holy Spirit, Amen, without saying, I baptize thee in the name of the Father, and of the Son, and of the Holy Spirit, Amen, the child is not baptized.*

REPLY OBJ. 3: The words which are uttered in the sacramental forms, are said not merely for the purpose of signification, but also for the purpose of efficiency, inasmuch as they derive efficacy from that Word, by Whom *all things were made.* Consequently they are becomingly addressed not only to men, but also to insensible creatures; for instance, when we say: *I exorcize thee, creature of salt* (*Roman Ritual*).

REPLY OBJ. 4: Several cannot baptize one at the same time: because an action is multiplied according to the number of the agents, if it be done perfectly by each. So that if two were to combine, of whom one were mute, and unable to utter the words, and the other were without hands, and unable to perform the action, they could not both baptize at the same time, one saying the words and the other performing the action.

On the other hand, in a case of necessity, several could be baptized at the same time; for no single one of them would receive more than one baptism. But it would be necessary, in that case, to say: *I baptize ye.* Nor would this be a change of form, because *ye* is the same as *thee and thee.* Whereas *we* does not mean *I and I*, but *I and thou*; so that this would be a change of form.

Likewise it would be a change of form to say, *I baptize myself*: consequently no one can baptize himself. For this reason did Christ choose to be baptized by John (Extra, *De Baptismo et ejus effectu*, cap. *Debitum*).

REPLY OBJ. 5: Although Christ's Passion is the principal cause as compared to the minister, yet it is an instrumental cause as compared to the Blessed Trinity. For this reason the Trinity is mentioned rather than Christ's Passion.

REPLY OBJ. 6: Although there are three personal names of the three Persons, there is but one essential name. Now the Divine power which works in Baptism, pertains to the Essence; and therefore we say, *in the name*, and not, *in the names.*

REPLY OBJ. 7: Just as water is used in Baptism, because it is more commonly employed in washing, so for the purpose of designating the three Persons, in the form of Baptism, those names are chosen, which are generally used, in a particular language, to signify the Persons. Nor is the sacrament valid if conferred in any other names.

Article 6

Whether Baptism Can Be Conferred in the Name of Christ?

AD SEXTUM SIC PROCEDITUR. Videtur quod in nomine Christi possit dari Baptismus. Sicut enim *una est fides, et unum Baptisma*, ut dicitur Ephes. IV. Sed Act. VIII dicitur quod *in nomine Iesu Christi baptizabantur viri et mulieres*. Ergo etiam nunc potest dari Baptismus in nomine Christi.

PRAETEREA, Ambrosius dicit, *si Christum dicas, et patrem, a quo unctus est, et ipsum qui unctus est, filium, et spiritum, quo unctus est, designasti.* Sed in nomine Trinitatis potest fieri Baptismus. Ergo et in nomine Christi.

PRAETEREA, Nicolaus Papa, ad consulta Bulgarorum respondens, dicit, *qui in nomine sanctae Trinitatis, vel tantum in nomine Christi, sicut in actibus apostolorum legitur, baptizati sunt, unum quippe idemque est, ut sanctus ait Ambrosius, rebaptizari non debent.* Rebaptizarentur autem si in hac forma baptizati sacramentum Baptismi non reciperent. Ergo potest consecrari Baptismus in nomine Christi sub hac forma, ego te baptizo in nomine Christi.

SED CONTRA est quod Pelagius Papa scribit Gaudentio episcopo, *si hi qui in locis dilectionis tuae vicinis commorari dicuntur, se solummodo in nomine domini baptizatos fuisse confitentur, sine cuiusquam dubitationis ambiguo, eos ad fidem Catholicam venientes in sanctae Trinitatis nomine baptizabis.* Didymus etiam dicit, in libro de spiritu sancto, *licet quis possit existere mentis alienae qui ita baptizaret ut unum de praedictis nominibus, scilicet trium personarum, praetermittat, sine perfectione baptizabit.*

RESPONDEO dicendum quod, sicut supra dictum est, sacramenta habent efficaciam ab institutione Christi. Et ideo, si praetermittatur aliquid eorum quae Christus instituit circa aliquod sacramentum, efficacia caret, nisi ex speciali dispensatione eius, qui virtutem suam sacramentis non alligavit. Christus autem instituit sacramentum Baptismi dari cum invocatione Trinitatis. Et ideo quidquid desit ad invocationem plenam Trinitatis, tollit integritatem Baptismi.

Nec obstat quod in nomine unius personae intelligitur alia, sicut in nomine patris intelligitur filius; aut quod ille qui nominat unam solam personam, potest habere rectam fidem de tribus. Quia ad sacramentum, sicut requiritur materia sensibilis, ita et forma sensibilis. Unde non sufficit intellectus vel fides Trinitatis ad perfectionem sacramenti, nisi sensibilibus verbis Trinitas exprimatur. Unde et in Baptismo Christi, ubi fuit origo sanctificationis nostri Baptismi, affuit Trinitas sensibilibus,

OBJECTION 1: It seems that Baptism can be conferred in the name of Christ. For just as there is *one Faith*, so is there *one Baptism* (Eph 4:5). But it is related (Acts 8:12) that *in the name of Jesus Christ they were baptized, both men and women.* Therefore now also can Baptism be conferred in the name of Christ.

OBJ. 2: Further, Ambrose says (*De Spir. Sanct.* i): *If you mention Christ, you designate both the Father by Whom He was anointed, and the Son Himself, Who was anointed, and the Holy Spirit with Whom He was anointed.* But Baptism can be conferred in the name of the Trinity: therefore also in the name of Christ.

OBJ. 3: Further, Pope Nicholas I, answering questions put to him by the Bulgars, said: *Those who have been baptized in the name of the Trinity, or only in the name of Christ, as we read in the Acts of the Apostles (it is all the same, as Blessed Ambrose saith), must not be rebaptized.* But they would be baptized again if they had not been validly baptized with that form. Therefore Baptism can be celebrated in the name of Christ by using this form: *I baptize thee in the name of Christ.*

ON THE CONTRARY, Pope Pelagius II wrote to the Bishop Gaudentius: *If any people living in your Worship's neighborhood, avow that they have been baptized in the name of the Lord only, without any hesitation baptize them again in the name of the Blessed Trinity, when they come in quest of the Catholic Faith.* Didymus, too, says (*De Spir. Sanct.*): *If indeed there be such a one with a mind so foreign to faith as to baptize while omitting one of the aforesaid names,* viz. of the three Persons, *he baptizes invalidly.*

I ANSWER THAT, As stated above (Q. 64, A. 3), the sacraments derive their efficacy from Christ's institution. Consequently, if any of those things be omitted which Christ instituted in regard to a sacrament, it is invalid; save by special dispensation of Him Who did not bind His power to the sacraments. Now Christ commanded the sacrament of Baptism to be given with the invocation of the Trinity. And consequently whatever is lacking to the full invocation of the Trinity, destroys the integrity of Baptism.

Nor does it matter that in the name of one Person another is implied, as the name of the Son is implied in that of the Father, or that he who mentions the name of only one Person may believe aright in the Three; because just as a sacrament requires sensible matter, so does it require a sensible form. Hence, for the validity of the sacrament it is not enough to imply or to believe in the Trinity, unless the Trinity be expressed in sensible words. For this reason at Christ's Baptism, wherein was the source of the sanctification of our Baptism, the Trinity was present in sensible

scilicet pater in voce, filius in humana natura, Spiritus Sanctus in columba.

AD PRIMUM ergo dicendum quod ex speciali Christi revelatione apostoli in primitiva Ecclesia in nomine Christi baptizabant, ut nomen Christi, quod erat odiosum Iudaeis et gentibus, honorabile redderetur, per hoc quod ad eius invocationem Spiritus Sanctus dabatur in Baptismo.

AD SECUNDUM dicendum quod Ambrosius assignat rationem quare convenienter talis dispensatio fieri potuit in primitiva Ecclesia, quia scilicet in nomine Christi tota Trinitas intelligitur; et ideo servabatur ad minus integritate intelligibili forma quam Christus tradidit in Evangelio.

AD TERTIUM dicendum quod Nicolaus Papa dictum suum confirmat ex duobus praemissis. Et ideo eius responsio patet ex primis duabus solutionibus.

signs: viz. the Father in the voice, the Son in the human nature, the Holy Spirit in the dove.

REPLY OBJ. 1: It was by a special revelation from Christ that in the primitive Church the apostles baptized in the name of Christ; in order that the name of Christ, which was hateful to Jews and Gentiles, might become an object of veneration, in that the Holy Spirit was given in Baptism at the invocation of that Name.

REPLY OBJ. 2: Ambrose here gives this reason why exception could, without inconsistency, be allowed in the primitive Church; namely, because the whole Trinity is implied in the name of Christ, and therefore the form prescribed by Christ in the Gospel was observed in its integrity, at least implicitly.

REPLY OBJ. 3: Pope Nicolas confirms his words by quoting the two authorities given in the preceding objections: wherefore the answer to this is clear from the two solutions given above.

Article 7

Whether Immersion in Water Is Necessary for Baptism?

AD SEPTIMUM SIC PROCEDITUR. Videtur quod immersio in aqua sit de necessitate Baptismi. Ut enim dicitur Ephes. IV, *una fides, unum Baptisma.* Sed apud multos communis modus baptizandi est per immersionem. Ergo videtur quod non possit esse Baptismus sine immersione.

PRAETEREA, apostolus dicit, Rom. VI, *quicumque baptizati sumus in Christo Iesu, in morte ipsius baptizati sumus, consepulti enim sumus cum illo per Baptismum in morte.* Sed hoc fit per immersionem, dicit enim Chrysostomus, super illud Ioan. III, *nisi quis renatus fuerit ex aqua et spiritu sancto, etc., sicut in quodam sepulcro, in aqua, submergentibus nobis capita, vetus homo sepelitur, et submersus deorsum occultatur, deinde novus rursus ascendit.* Ergo videtur quod immersio sit de necessitate Baptismi.

PRAETEREA, si sine immersione totius corporis posset fieri Baptismus, sequeretur quod pari ratione sufficeret quamlibet partem aqua perfundi. Sed hoc videtur inconveniens, quia originale peccatum, contra quod praecipue datur Baptismus, non est in una tantum corporis parte. Ergo videtur quod requiratur immersio ad Baptismum, et non sufficiat sola aspersio.

SED CONTRA est quod Heb. X dicitur, *accedamus ad eum vero corde in plenitudine fidei, aspersi corda a conscientia mala, et abluti corpus aqua munda.*

RESPONDEO dicendum quod aqua assumitur in sacramento Baptismi ad usum ablutionis corporalis, per

OBJECTION 1: It seems that immersion in water is necessary for Baptism. Because it is written (Eph 4:5): *One faith, one baptism.* But in many parts of the world the ordinary way of baptizing is by immersion. Therefore it seems that there can be no Baptism without immersion.

OBJ. 2: Further, the Apostle says (Rom 6:3, 4): *All we who are baptized in Christ Jesus, are baptized in His death: for we are buried together with Him, by Baptism into death.* But this is done by immersion: for Chrysostom says on John 3:5: *Unless a man be born again of water and the Holy Spirit*, etc.: *When we dip our heads under the water as in a kind of tomb, our old man is buried, and being submerged, is hidden below, and thence he rises again renewed.* Therefore it seems that immersion is essential to Baptism.

OBJ. 3: Further, if Baptism is valid without total immersion of the body, it would follow that it would be equally sufficient to pour water over any part of the body. But this seems unreasonable; since original sin, to remedy which is the principal purpose of Baptism, is not in only one part of the body. Therefore it seems that immersion is necessary for Baptism, and that mere sprinkling is not enough.

ON THE CONTRARY, It is written (Heb 10:22): *Let us draw near with a true heart in fullness of faith, having our hearts sprinkled from an evil conscience, and our bodies washed with clean water.*

I ANSWER THAT, In the sacrament of Baptism water is put to the use of a washing of the body, whereby to signify

quam significatur interior ablutio peccatorum. Ablutio autem fieri potest per aquam non solum per modum immersionis, sed etiam per modum aspersionis vel effusionis. Et ideo, quamvis tutius sit baptizare per modum immersionis, quia hoc habet communior usus; potest tamen fieri Baptismus per modum aspersionis; vel etiam per modum effusionis, secundum illud Ezech. XXXVI, *effundam super vos aquam mundam*, sicut et beatus Laurentius legitur baptizasse. Et hoc praecipue propter necessitatem. Vel quia est magna multitudo baptizandorum, sicut patet Act. II et IV, ubi dicitur quod crediderunt una die tria millia, et alia quinque millia. Quandoque autem potest imminere necessitas propter paucitatem aquae; vel propter debilitatem ministri, qui non potest sustentare baptizandum; vel propter debilitatem baptizandi, cui posset imminere periculum mortis ex immersione. Et ideo dicendum est quod immersio non est de necessitate Baptismi.

AD PRIMUM ergo dicendum quod ea quae sunt per accidens, non variant substantiam rei. Per se autem requiritur ad Baptismum corporalis ablutio per aquam, unde et Baptismus lavacrum nominatur, secundum illud Ephes. V, *mundans eam lavacro aquae in verbo vitae.* Sed quod fiat ablutio hoc vel illo modo, accidit Baptismo. Et ideo talis diversitas non tollit unitatem Baptismi.

AD SECUNDUM dicendum quod in immersione expressius repraesentatur figura sepulturae Christi, et ideo hic modus baptizandi est communior et laudabilior. Sed in aliis modis baptizandi repraesentatur aliquo modo, licet non ita expresse, nam, quocumque modo fiat ablutio, corpus hominis, vel aliqua pars eius, aquae supponitur, sicut corpus Christi fuit positum sub terra.

AD TERTIUM dicendum quod principalis pars corporis, praecipue quantum ad exteriora membra, est caput, in quo vigent omnes sensus et interiores et exteriores. Et ideo, si totum corpus aqua non possit perfundi, propter aquae paucitatem vel propter aliquam aliam causam, oportet caput perfundere, in quo manifestatur principium animalis vitae.

Et licet per membra quae generationi deserviunt peccatum originale traducatur, non tamen sunt membra illa potius aspergenda quam caput, quia per Baptismum non tollitur transmissio originalis in prolem per actum generationis, sed liberatur anima a macula et reatu peccati quod incurrit. Et ideo debet praecipue lavari illa pars corporis in qua manifestantur opera animae.

In veteri tamen lege remedium contra originale peccatum institutum erat in membro generationis, quia adhuc ille per quem originale erat amovendum, nasciturus erat ex semine Abrahae, cuius fidem circumcisio significabat, ut dicitur Rom. IV.

---

the inward washing away of sins. Now washing may be done with water not only by immersion, but also by sprinkling or pouring. And, therefore, although it is safer to baptize by immersion, because this is the more ordinary fashion, yet Baptism can be conferred by sprinkling or also by pouring, according to Ezech. 36:25: *I will pour upon you clean water*, as also the Blessed Lawrence is related to have baptized. And this especially in cases of urgency: either because there is a great number to be baptized, as was clearly the case in Acts 2 and 4, where we read that on one day three thousand believed, and on another five thousand: or through there being but a small supply of water, or through feebleness of the minister, who cannot hold up the candidate for Baptism; or through feebleness of the candidate, whose life might be endangered by immersion. We must therefore conclude that immersion is not necessary for Baptism.

REPLY OBJ. 1: What is accidental to a thing does not diversify its essence. Now bodily washing with water is essential to Baptism: wherefore Baptism is called a *laver*, according to Eph. 5:26: *Cleansing it by the laver of water in the word of life.* But that the washing be done this or that way, is accidental to Baptism. And consequently such diversity does not destroy the oneness of Baptism.

REPLY OBJ. 2: Christ's burial is more clearly represented by immersion: wherefore this manner of baptizing is more frequently in use and more commendable. Yet in the other ways of baptizing it is represented after a fashion, albeit not so clearly; for no matter how the washing is done, the body of a man, or some part thereof, is put under water, just as Christ's body was put under the earth.

REPLY OBJ. 3: The principal part of the body, especially in relation to the exterior members, is the head, wherein all the senses, both interior and exterior, flourish. And therefore, if the whole body cannot be covered with water, because of the scarcity of water, or because of some other reason, it is necessary to pour water over the head, in which the principle of animal life is made manifest.

And although original sin is transmitted through the members that serve for procreation, yet those members are not to be sprinkled in preference to the head, because by Baptism the transmission of original sin to the offspring by the act of procreation is not deleted, but the soul is freed from the stain and debt of sin which it has contracted. Consequently that part of the body should be washed in preference, in which the works of the soul are made manifest.

Nevertheless in the Old Law the remedy against original sin was affixed to the member of procreation; because He through Whom original sin was to be removed, was yet to be born of the seed of Abraham, whose faith was signified by circumcision according to Rom. 4:11.

Article 8

Whether Trine Immersion Is Essential to Baptism?

AD OCTAVUM SIC PROCEDITUR. Videtur quod trina immersio sit de necessitate Baptismi. Dicit enim Augustinus, in quodam sermone de symbolo ad baptizatos, *recte tertio mersi estis, quia accepistis Baptismum in nomine Trinitatis. Recte tertio mersi estis, quia accepistis Baptismum in nomine Iesu Christi, qui tertia die resurrexit a mortuis. Illa enim tertio repetita immersio typum dominicae exprimit sepulturae, per quam Christo consepulti estis in Baptismo.* Sed utrumque videtur ad necessitatem Baptismi pertinere, scilicet et quod significetur in Baptismo Trinitas personarum; et quod fiat configuratio ad sepulturam Christi. Ergo videtur quod trina immersio sit de necessitate Baptismi.

PRAETEREA, sacramenta ex mandato Christi efficaciam habent. Sed trina immersio est ex mandato Christi, scripsit enim Pelagius Papa Gaudentio episcopo, *evangelicum praeceptum, ipso domino Deo et salvatore nostro Iesu Christo tradente, nos admonet in nomine Trinitatis, trina etiam immersione, sanctum Baptismum unicuique tribuere.* Ergo, sicut baptizare in nomine Trinitatis est de necessitate Baptismi, ita baptizare trina immersione videtur esse de necessitate Baptismi.

PRAETEREA, si trina immersio non sit de necessitate Baptismi, ergo ad primam immersionem aliquis Baptismi consequitur sacramentum. Si vero addatur secunda et tertia, videtur quod secundo vel tertio baptizetur, quod est inconveniens. Non ergo una immersio sufficit ad sacramentum Baptismi, sed trina videtur esse de necessitate ipsius.

SED CONTRA est quod Gregorius scribit Leandro episcopo, *reprehensibile esse nullatenus potest infantem in Baptismate vel tertio vel semel immergere, quoniam et in tribus immersionibus personarum Trinitas, et una potest divinitatis singularitas designari.*

RESPONDEO dicendum quod, sicut prius dictum est, ad Baptismum per se requiritur ablutio aquae, quae est de necessitate sacramenti, modus autem ablutionis per accidens se habet ad sacramentum. Et ideo, sicut ex praedicta auctoritate Gregorii patet, quantum est de se, utrumque licite fieri potest, scilicet et semel et ter immergere, quia unica immersione significatur unitas mortis Christi, et unitas deitatis; per trinam autem immersionem significatur triduum sepulturae Christi, et etiam Trinitas personarum.

Sed diversis ex causis, secundum ordinationem Ecclesiae, quandoque institutus est unus modus, quandoque alius. Quia enim a principio nascentis Ecclesiae quidam de Trinitate male sentiebant, Christum purum hominem aestimantes, nec dici filium Dei et Deum nisi per meritum eius, quod praecipue fuit in morte, ideo

OBJECTION 1: It seems that trine immersion is essential to Baptism. For Augustine says in a sermon on the Symbol, addressed to the Neophytes: *Rightly were you dipped three times, since you were baptized in the name of the Trinity. Rightly were you dipped three times, because you were baptized in the name of Jesus Christ, Who on the third day rose again from the dead. For that thrice repeated immersion reproduces the burial of the Lord by which you were buried with Christ in Baptism.* Now both seem to be essential to Baptism, namely, that in Baptism the Trinity of Persons should be signified, and that we should be conformed to Christ's burial. Therefore it seems that trine immersion is essential to Baptism.

OBJ. 2: Further, the sacraments derive their efficacy from Christ's mandate. But trine immersion was commanded by Christ: for Pope Pelagius II wrote to Bishop Gaudentius: *The Gospel precept given by our Lord God Himself, our Savior Jesus Christ, admonishes us to confer the sacrament of Baptism to each one in the name of the Trinity and also with trine immersion.* Therefore, just as it is essential to Baptism to call on the name of the Trinity, so is it essential to baptize by trine immersion.

OBJ. 3: Further, if trine immersion be not essential to Baptism, it follows that the sacrament of Baptism is conferred at the first immersion; so that if a second or third immersion be added, it seems that Baptism is conferred a second or third time, which is absurd. Therefore one immersion does not suffice for the sacrament of Baptism, and trine immersion is essential thereto.

ON THE CONTRARY, Gregory wrote to the Bishop Leander: *It cannot be in any way reprehensible to baptize an infant with either a trine or a single immersion: since the Trinity can be represented in the three immersions, and the unity of the Godhead in one immersion.*

I ANSWER THAT As stated above (A. 7, ad 1), washing with water is of itself required for Baptism, being essential to the sacrament: whereas the mode of washing is accidental to the sacrament. Consequently, as Gregory in the words above quoted explains, both single and trine immersion are lawful considered in themselves; since one immersion signifies the oneness of Christ's death and of the Godhead; while trine immersion signifies the three days of Christ's burial, and also the Trinity of Persons.

But for various reasons, according as the Church has ordained, one mode has been in practice, at one time, the other at another time. For since from the very earliest days of the Church some have had false notions concerning the Trinity, holding that Christ is a mere man, and that He is not called the *Son of God* or *God* except by reason of His

non baptizabant in nomine Trinitatis, sed in commemorationem mortis Christi, et una immersione. Quod reprobatum fuit in primitiva Ecclesia. Unde in canonibus apostolorum legitur, *si quis presbyter aut episcopus non trinam immersionem unius ministerii, sed semel mergat in Baptismate, quod dari a quibusdam dicitur in morte domini, deponatur, non enim nobis dixit dominus, in morte mea baptizate, sed, in nomine patris et filii et spiritus sancti.*

Postmodum vero inolevit quorundam schismaticorum et haereticorum error homines rebaptizantium, sicut de Donatistis Augustinus narrat, super Ioan. Et ideo, in detestationem erroris eorum, fuit statutum in Concilio Toletano quod fieret una sola immersio, ubi sic legitur, *propter vitandum schismatis scandalum, vel haeretici dogmatis usum, simplam teneamus Baptismi immersionem.*

Sed, cessante tali causa, communiter observatur in Baptismo trina immersio. Et ideo graviter peccaret aliter baptizans, quasi ritum Ecclesiae non observans. Nihilominus tamen esset Baptismus.

Ad primum ergo dicendum quod Trinitas est sicut agens principale in Baptismo. Similitudo autem agentis pervenit ad effectum secundum formam, et non secundum materiam. Et ideo significatio Trinitatis fit in Baptismo per verba formae. Nec est de necessitate quod significetur Trinitas per usum materiae, sed hoc fit ad maiorem expressionem.

Similiter etiam mors Christi figuratur sufficienter in unica immersione. Triduum autem sepulturae non est de necessitate nostrae salutis, quia etiam si una die fuisset sepultus vel mortuus, suffecisset ad perficiendam nostram redemptionem; sed triduum illud ordinatur ad manifestandam veritatem mortis, ut supra dictum est. Et ideo patet quod trina immersio nec ex parte Trinitatis, nec ex parte passionis Christi, est de necessitate sacramenti.

Ad secundum dicendum quod Pelagius Papa intelligit trinam immersionem esse ex mandato Christi in suo simili, in hoc scilicet quod Christus praecepit baptizari *in nomine patris et filii et spiritus sancti.* Non tamen est similis ratio de forma et de usu materiae, ut dictum est.

Ad tertium dicendum quod, sicut supra dictum est, intentio requiritur ad Baptismum. Et ideo ex intentione ministri Ecclesiae, qui intendit unum Baptismum dare trina immersione, efficitur unum Baptisma. Unde Hieronymus dicit, super epistolam ad Philipp., *licet ter baptizetur, idest immergatur, propter mysterium Trinitatis, tamen unum Baptisma reputatur.*

merit, which was chiefly in His death; for this reason they did not baptize in the name of the Trinity, but in memory of Christ's death, and with one immersion. And this was condemned in the early Church. Wherefore in the Apostolic Canons (xlix) we read: *If any priest or bishop confer baptism not with the trine immersion in the one administration, but with one immersion, which baptism is said to be conferred by some in the death of the Lord, let him be deposed:* for our Lord did not say, *Baptize ye in My death,* but *In the name of the Father and of the Son, and of the Holy Spirit.*

Later on, however, there arose the error of certain schismatics and heretics who rebaptized: as Augustine (*Super. Joan.,* cf. *De Haeres.* lxix) relates of the Donatists. Wherefore, in detestation of their error, only one immersion was ordered to be made, by the (fourth) council of Toledo, in the acts of which we read: *In order to avoid the scandal of schism or the practice of heretical teaching let us hold to the single baptismal immersion.*

But now that this motive has ceased, trine immersion is universally observed in Baptism: and consequently anyone baptizing otherwise would sin gravely, through not following the ritual of the Church. It would, however, be valid Baptism.

Reply Obj. 1: The Trinity acts as principal agent in Baptism. Now the likeness of the agent enters into the effect, in regard to the form and not in regard to the matter. Wherefore the Trinity is signified in Baptism by the words of the form. Nor is it essential for the Trinity to be signified by the manner in which the matter is used; although this is done to make the signification clearer.

In like manner Christ's death is sufficiently represented in the one immersion. And the three days of His burial were not necessary for our salvation, because even if He had been buried or dead for one day, this would have been enough to consummate our redemption: yet those three days were ordained unto the manifestation of the reality of His death, as stated above (Q. 53, A. 2). It is therefore clear that neither on the part of the Trinity, nor on the part of Christ's Passion, is the trine immersion essential to the sacrament.

Reply Obj. 2: Pope Pelagius understood the trine immersion to be ordained by Christ in its equivalent; in the sense that Christ commanded Baptism to be conferred *in the name of the Father, and of the Son, and of the Holy Spirit.* Nor can we argue from the form to the use of the matter, as stated above (ad 1).

Reply Obj. 3: As stated above (Q. 64, A. 8), the intention is essential to Baptism. Consequently, one Baptism results from the intention of the Church's minister, who intends to confer one Baptism by a trine immersion. Wherefore Jerome says on Eph. 4:5, 6: *Though the Baptism,* i.e., the immersion, *be thrice repeated, on account of the mystery of the Trinity, yet it is reputed as one Baptism.*

Si vero intenderet ad unamquamque immersionem unum Baptisma dare, ad singulas immersiones repetens verba formae, peccaret, quantum in se est, pluries baptizans.

If, however, the intention were to confer one Baptism at each immersion together with the repetition of the words of the form, it would be a sin, in itself, because it would be a repetition of Baptism.

Article 9

Whether Baptism May Be Reiterated?

AD NONUM SIC PROCEDITUR. Videtur quod Baptismus possit iterari. Baptismus enim videtur institutus ad ablutionem peccatorum. Sed peccata iterantur. Ergo multo magis Baptismus debet iterari, quia misericordia Christi transcendit hominis culpam.

PRAETEREA, Ioannes Baptista praecipue fuit a Christo commendatus, cum de eo dictum sit, Matth. XI, *inter natos mulierum non surrexit maior Ioanne Baptista.* Sed baptizati a Ioanne iterum rebaptizantur, ut habetur Act. XIX, ubi dicitur quod Paulus baptizavit eos qui erant baptizati Baptismo Ioannis. Ergo multo fortius illi qui sunt baptizati ab haereticis vel peccatoribus, sunt rebaptizandi.

PRAETEREA, in Nicaeno Concilio statutum est, *si quis confugeret ad Ecclesiam Catholicam de Paulianistis et Cataphrygis, baptizari eos debere.* Videtur autem esse eadem ratio de haereticis aliis. Ergo baptizati ab haereticis debent esse rebaptizati.

PRAETEREA, Baptismus est necessarius ad salutem. Sed de quibusdam baptizatis aliquando dubitatur an sint baptizati. Ergo videtur quod debeant iterum rebaptizari.

PRAETEREA, Eucharistia est perfectius sacramentum quam Baptismus, ut supra dictum est. Sed sacramentum Eucharistiae iteratur. Ergo multo magis Baptismus potest iterari.

SED CONTRA est quod dicitur Ephes. IV, *una fides, unum Baptisma.*

RESPONDEO dicendum quod Baptismus iterari non potest.

Primo quidem, quia Baptismus est quaedam spiritualis regeneratio, prout scilicet aliquis moritur veteri vitae, et incipit novam vitam agere. Unde dicitur Ioan. III, *nisi quis renatus fuerit ex aqua et spiritu sancto, non potest videre regnum Dei.* Unius autem non est nisi una generatio. Et ideo non potest Baptismus iterari, sicut nec carnalis generatio. Unde Augustinus dicit, super illud Ioan. III, *nunquid potest in ventrem matris suae iterato introire et renasci, sic tu,* inquit, *intellige nativitatem spiritus, quo modo intellexit Nicodemus nativitatem carnis. Quo modo enim uterus non potest repeti, sic nec Baptismus.*

OBJECTION 1: It seems that Baptism may be reiterated. For Baptism was instituted, seemingly, in order to wash away sins. But sins are reiterated. Therefore much more should Baptism be reiterated: because Christ's mercy surpasses man's guilt.

OBJ. 2: Further, John the Baptist received special commendation from Christ, Who said of him (Matt 11:11): *There hath not risen among them that are born of women, a greater than John the Baptist.* But those whom John had baptized were baptized again, according to Acts 19:1–7, where it is stated that Paul rebaptized those who had received the Baptism of John. Much more, therefore, should those be rebaptized, who have been baptized by heretics or sinners.

OBJ. 3: Further, it was decreed in the Council of Nicaea (Can. xix) that if *any of the Paulianists or Cataphrygians should be converted to the Catholic Church, they were to be baptized*: and this seemingly should be said in regard to other heretics. Therefore those whom the heretics have baptized, should be baptized again.

OBJ. 4: Further, Baptism is necessary for salvation. But sometimes there is a doubt about the baptism of those who really have been baptized. Therefore it seems that they should be baptized again.

OBJ. 5: Further, the Eucharist is a more perfect sacrament than Baptism, as stated above (Q. 65, A. 3). But the sacrament of the Eucharist is reiterated. Much more reason, therefore, is there for Baptism to be reiterated.

ON THE CONTRARY, It is written, (Eph 4:5): *One faith, one Baptism.*

I ANSWER THAT, Baptism cannot be reiterated.

First, because Baptism is a spiritual regeneration; inasmuch as a man dies to the old life, and begins to lead the new life. Whence it is written (John 3:5): *Unless a man be born again of water and the Holy Spirit, He cannot see the kingdom of God.* Now one man can be begotten but once. Wherefore Baptism cannot be reiterated, just as neither can carnal generation. Hence Augustine says on John 3:4: '*Can he enter a second time into his mother's womb and be born again*': *So thou*, says he, *must understand the birth of the Spirit, as Nicodemus understood the birth of the flesh . . . . As there is no return to the womb, so neither is there to Baptism.*

Secundo, quia in morte Christi baptizamur, per quam morimur peccato et resurgimus in novitatem vitae. Christus autem semel tantum mortuus est. Et ideo nec Baptismus iterari debet. Propter quod, Heb. VI, contra quosdam rebaptizari volentes dicitur, *rursus crucifigentes sibimetipsis filium Dei*, ubi Glossa dicit, *una Christi mors unum Baptisma consecravit*.

Tertio, quia Baptismus imprimit characterem, qui est indelebilis, et cum quadam consecratione datur. Unde, sicut aliae consecrationes non iterantur in Ecclesia, ita nec Baptismus. Et hoc est quod Augustinus dicit, in II contra epistolam Parmeniani, quod *character militaris non repetitur; et quod non minus haeret sacramentum Christi quam corporalis haec nota, cum videamus nec apostatas carere Baptismate, quibus utique per poenitentiam redeuntibus non restituitur.*

Quarto, quia Baptismus principaliter datur contra originale peccatum. Et ideo, sicut originale peccatum non iteratur, ita etiam nec Baptismus iteratur, quia, ut dicitur Rom. V, *sicut per unius delictum in omnes homines in condemnationem, sic per unius iustitiam in omnes homines in iustificationem vitae.*

AD PRIMUM ergo dicendum quod Baptismus operatur in virtute passionis Christi, sicut supra dictum est. Et ideo, sicut peccata sequentia virtutem passionis Christi non auferunt, ita etiam non auferunt Baptismum, ut necesse sit ipsum iterari, sed, poenitentia superveniente, tollitur peccatum, quod impediebat effectum Baptismi.

AD SECUNDUM dicendum quod, sicut Augustinus dicit, super illud Ioan. I, *sed ego nesciebam eum, ecce, post Ioannem baptizatum est, post homicidam non est baptizatum, quia Ioannes dedit Baptismum suum, homicida dedit Baptismum Christi; quia sacramentum tam sanctum est ut nec homicida ministrante polluatur.*

AD TERTIUM dicendum quod Pauliani et Cataphrygae non baptizabant in nomine Trinitatis. Unde Gregorius dicit, scribens Quirico episcopo, *hi haeretici qui in Trinitatis nomine minime baptizantur, sicut sunt Bonosiani et Cataphrygae*, qui scilicet idem sentiebant cum Paulianis, *quia et isti Christum Deum non credunt*, existimantes scilicet ipsum esse purum hominem, *et isti, scilicet Cataphrygae, spiritum sanctum perverso sensu esse purum hominem, Montanum scilicet, credunt, qui cum ad sanctam Ecclesiam veniunt, baptizantur, quia Baptisma non fuit quod, in errore positi, sanctae Trinitatis nomine minime perceperunt.* Sed, sicut in regulis ecclesiasticis dicitur, *si qui apud illos haereticos baptizati sunt qui in sanctae Trinitatis confessione baptizant, et veniunt ad Catholicam fidem, recipiantur ut baptizati.*

AD QUARTUM dicendum quod, sicut dicit decretalis Alexandri III, *de quibus dubium est an baptizati fuerint, baptizentur his verbis praemissis, si baptizatus es, non te*

Second, because *we are baptized in Christ's death*, by which we die unto sin and rise again unto *newness of life* (cf. Rom. 6:3, 4). Now *Christ died* but *once* (Rom 6:10). Wherefore neither should Baptism be reiterated. For this reason (Heb 6:6) is it said against some who wished to be baptized again: *Crucifying again to themselves the Son of God*; on which the gloss observes: *Christ's one death hallowed the one Baptism.*

Third, because Baptism imprints a character, which is indelible, and is conferred with a certain consecration. Wherefore, just as other consecrations are not reiterated in the Church, so neither is Baptism. This is the view expressed by Augustine, who says (*Contra Epist. Parmen.* ii) that *the military character is not renewed*: and that *the sacrament of Christ is not less enduring than this bodily mark, since we see that not even apostates are deprived of Baptism, since when they repent and return they are not baptized anew.*

Fourth, because Baptism is conferred principally as a remedy against original sin. Wherefore, just as original sin is not renewed, so neither is Baptism reiterated, for as it is written (Rom 5:18), *as by the offense of one, unto all men to condemnation, so also by the justice of one, unto all men to justification of life.*

REPLY OBJ. 1: Baptism derives its efficacy from Christ's Passion, as stated above (A. 2, ad 1). Wherefore, just as subsequent sins do not cancel the virtue of Christ's Passion, so neither do they cancel Baptism, so as to call for its repetition. On the other hand the sin which hindered the effect of Baptism is blotted out on being submitted to Penance.

REPLY OBJ. 2: As Augustine says on John 1:33: *'And I knew Him not'*: Behold; after John had baptized, Baptism was administered; after a murderer has baptized, it is not administered: because John gave his own Baptism; the murderer, Christ's; for that sacrament is so sacred, that not even a murderer's administration contaminates it.

REPLY OBJ. 3: The Paulianists and Cataphrygians used not to baptize in the name of the Trinity. Wherefore Gregory, writing to the Bishop Quiricus, says: *Those heretics who are not baptized in the name of the Trinity, such as the Bonosians and Cataphrygians* (who were of the same mind as the Paulianists), *since the former believe not that Christ is God* (holding Him to be a mere man), *while the latter*, i.e., the Cataphrygians, *are so perverse as to deem a mere man*, viz. Montanus, *to be the Holy Spirit: all these are baptized when they come to holy Church, for the baptism which they received while in that state of error was no Baptism at all*, not being conferred in the name of the Trinity. On the other hand, as set down in *De Eccles. Dogm.* xxii: *Those heretics who have been baptized in the confession of the name of the Trinity are to be received as already baptized when they come to the Catholic Faith.*

REPLY OBJ. 4: According to the *Decretal* of Alexander III: *Those about whose Baptism there is a doubt are to be baptized with these words prefixed to the form: 'If thou art*

rebaptizo, sed si non baptizatus es, ego te baptizo, et cetera. Non enim videtur iterari quod nescitur esse factum.

AD QUINTUM dicendum quod utrumque sacramentum, scilicet Baptismi et Eucharistiae, est repraesentativum dominicae mortis et passionis, aliter tamen et aliter. Nam in Baptismo commemoratur mors Christi inquantum homo Christo commoritur ut in novam vitam regeneretur. Sed in sacramento Eucharistiae commemoratur mors Christi inquantum ipse Christus passus exhibetur nobis quasi paschale convivium, secundum illud I Cor. V, *Pascha nostrum immolatus est Christus, itaque epulemur.* Et quia homo semel nascitur, multoties autem cibatur, semel tantum datur Baptismus, multoties autem Eucharistia.

baptized, I do not rebaptize thee; but if thou art not baptized, I baptize thee,' etc.: for that does not appear to be repeated, which is not known to have been done.

REPLY OBJ. 5: Both sacraments, viz. Baptism and the Eucharist, are a representation of our Lord's death and Passion, but not in the same way. For Baptism is a commemoration of Christ's death in so far as man dies with Christ, that he may be born again into a new life. But the Eucharist is a commemoration of Christ's death, in so far as the suffering Christ Himself is offered to us as the Paschal banquet, according to 1 Cor. 5:7, 8: *Christ our pasch is sacrificed; therefore let us feast.* And forasmuch as man is born once, whereas he eats many times, so is Baptism given once, but the Eucharist frequently.

Article 10

Whether the Church Observes a Suitable Rite in Baptizing?

AD DECIMUM SIC PROCEDITUR. Videtur quod non sit conveniens ritus quo Ecclesia utitur in baptizando. Ut enim dicit Chrysostomus, *nunquam aquae Baptismi purgare peccata credentium possent, nisi tactu dominici corporis sanctificatae fuissent.* Hoc autem factum fuit in Baptismo Christi, qui celebratur in festo Epiphaniae. Ergo magis deberet celebrari solemnis Baptismus in festo Epiphaniae quam in vigilia Paschae et in vigilia Pentecostes.

PRAETEREA, ad idem sacramentum non videtur pertinere diversarum materierum usus. Sed ab Baptismum pertinet ablutio aquae. Inconvenienter igitur ille qui baptizatur bis inungitur oleo sancto, primum in pectore, deinde inter scapulas, tertio, chrismate in vertice.

PREATEREA, *in Christo Iesu non est masculus neque femina, barbarus et Scytha,* et eadem ratione nec aliquae aliae huiusmodi differentiae. Multo igitur minus diversitas vestium aliquid operatur in fide Christi. Inconvenienter ergo baptizatis traditur candida vestis.

PRAETEREA, sine huiusmodi observantiis potest Baptismus celebrari. Haec igitur quae dicta sunt, videntur esse superflua, et ita inconvenienter ab Ecclesia instituta esse in ritu Baptismi.

SED CONTRA est quod Ecclesia regitur spiritu sancto, qui nihil inordinatum operatur.

RESPONDEO dicendum quod in sacramento Baptismi aliquid agitur quod est de necessitate sacramenti, et aliquid est quod ad quandam solemnitatem sacramenti pertinet. De necessitate quidem sacramenti est et forma,

OBJECTION 1: It seems that the Church observes an unsuitable rite in baptizing. For as Chrysostom (*Chromatius, in Matth.* 3:15) says: *The waters of Baptism would never avail to purge the sins of them that believe, had they not been hallowed by the touch of our Lord's body.* Now this took place at Christ's Baptism, which is commemorated in the Feast of the Epiphany. Therefore solemn Baptism should be celebrated at the Feast of the Epiphany rather than on the eves of Easter and Whitsunday.

OBJ. 2: Further, it seems that several matters should not be used in the same sacrament. But water is used for washing in Baptism. Therefore it is unfitting that the person baptized should be anointed thrice with holy oil first on the breast, and then between the shoulders, and a third time with chrism on the top of the head.

OBJ. 3: Further, *in Christ Jesus . . . there is neither male nor female* (Gal 3:23) . . . *neither Barbarian nor Scythian* (Col 3:11), nor, in like manner, any other such like distinctions. Much less, therefore can a difference of clothing have any efficacy in the Faith of Christ. It is consequently unfitting to bestow a white garment on those who have been baptized.

OBJ. 4: Further, Baptism can be celebrated without such like ceremonies. Therefore it seems that those mentioned above are superfluous; and consequently that they are unsuitably inserted by the Church in the baptismal rite.

ON THE CONTRARY, The Church is ruled by the Holy Spirit, Who does nothing inordinate.

I ANSWER THAT, In the sacrament of Baptism something is done which is essential to the sacrament, and something which belongs to a certain solemnity of the sacrament. Essential indeed, to the sacrament are both the

quae designat principalem causam sacramenti; et minister, qui est causa instrumentalis; et usus materiae, scilicet ablutio in aqua, quae designat principalem sacramenti effectum. Cetera vero omnia quae in ritu baptizandi observat Ecclesia, magis pertinent ad quandam solemnitatem sacramenti.

Quae quidem adhibentur sacramento propter tria. Primo quidem, ad excitandam devotionem fidelium, et reverentiam ad sacramentum. Si enim simpliciter fieret ablutio in aqua, absque solemnitate, de facili ab aliquibus aestimaretur quasi quaedam communis ablutio.

Secundo, ad fidelium instructionem. Simplices enim, qui litteris non erudiuntur, oportet erudire per aliqua sensibilia signa, puta per picturas, et aliqua huiusmodi. Et per hunc modum per ea quae in sacramentis aguntur, vel instruuntur, vel sollicitantur ad quaerendum de his quae per huiusmodi sensibilia signa significantur. Et ideo, quia, praeter principalem sacramenti effectum, oportet quaedam alia scire circa Baptismum, conveniens fuit ut etiam quibusdam exterioribus signis repraesentarentur.

Tertio, quia per orationes et benedictiones et alia huiusmodi cohibetur vis Daemonis ab impedimento sacramentalis effectus.

Ad primum ergo dicendum quod Christus in Epiphania baptizatus est Baptismo Ioannis, ut supra dictum est, quo quidem Baptismo non baptizantur fideles, sed potius Baptismo Christi. Qui quidem habet efficaciam ex passione Christi, secundum illud Rom. VI, *quicumque baptizati sumus in Christo Iesu, in morte ipsius baptizati sumus; et ex spiritu sancto*, secundum illud Ioan. III, *nisi quis renatus fuerit ex aqua et spiritu sancto*. Et ideo solemnis Baptismus agitur in Ecclesia et in vigilia Paschae, quando fit commemoratio dominicae sepulturae, et resurrectionis eiusdem; propter quod et dominus post resurrectionem praeceptum de Baptismo discipulis dedit, ut habetur Matth. ult., et in vigilia Pentecostes, quando incipit celebrari solemnitas spiritus sancti; unde et apostoli leguntur ipso die Pentecostes, quo spiritum sanctum receperant, tria millia baptizasse.

Ad secundum dicendum quod usus aquae adhibetur in Baptismo quasi pertinens ad substantiam sacramenti, sed usus olei vel chrismatis adhibetur ad quandam solemnitatem. Nam primo, baptizandus inungitur oleo sancto et in pectore et in scapulis, quasi athleta Dei, ut Ambrosius dicit, in libro de sacramentis, sicut pugiles inungi consueverunt. Vel, sicut Innocentius dicit, in quadam decretali de sacra unctione, *baptizandus in pectore inungitur, ut spiritus sancti donum recipiat, errorem abiiciat et ignorantiam, et fidem rectam suscipiat, quia iustus ex fide vivit; inter scapulas autem inungitur, ut spiritus sancti gratiam induat, exuat negligentiam et torporem, et bonam operationem exerceat; ut per fidei sacramentum sit*

form which designates the principal cause of the sacrament; and the minister who is the instrumental cause; and the use of the matter, namely, washing with water, which designates the principal sacramental effect. But all the other things which the Church observes in the baptismal rite, belong rather to a certain solemnity of the sacrament.

And these, indeed, are used in conjunction with the sacrament for three reasons. First, in order to arouse the devotion of the faithful, and their reverence for the sacrament. For if there were nothing done but a mere washing with water, without any solemnity, some might easily think it to be an ordinary washing.

Second, for the instruction of the faithful. Because simple and unlettered folk need to be taught by some sensible signs, for instance, pictures and the like. And in this way by means of the sacramental ceremonies they are either instructed, or urged to seek the signification of such like sensible signs. And consequently, since, besides the principal sacramental effect, other things should be known about Baptism, it was fitting that these also should be represented by some outward signs.

Third, because the power of the devil is restrained, by prayers, blessings, and the like, from hindering the sacramental effect.

Reply Obj. 1: Christ was baptized on the Epiphany with the Baptism of John, as stated above (Q. 39, A. 2), with which baptism, indeed, the faithful are not baptized, rather are they baptized with Christ's Baptism. This has its efficacy from the Passion of Christ, according to Rom. 6:3: *We who are baptized in Christ Jesus, are baptized in His death*; and in the Holy Spirit, according to John 3:5: *Unless a man be born again of water and the Holy Spirit*. Therefore it is that solemn Baptism is held in the Church, both on Easter Eve, when we commemorate our Lord's burial and resurrection; for which reason our Lord gave His disciples the commandment concerning Baptism as related by Matthew (28:19): and on Whitsun-eve, when the celebration of the Feast of the Holy Spirit begins; for which reason the apostles are said to have baptized three thousand on the very day of Pentecost when they had received the Holy Spirit.

Reply Obj. 2: The use of water in Baptism is part of the substance of the sacrament; but the use of oil or chrism is part of the solemnity. For the candidate is first of all anointed with Holy oil on the breast and between the shoulders, as *one who wrestles for God*, to use Ambrose's expression (*De Sacram.* i): thus are prize-fighters wont to besmear themselves with oil. Or, as Innocent III says in a *Decretal* on the Holy Unction: *The candidate is anointed on the breast, in order to receive the gift of the Holy Spirit, to cast off error and ignorance, and to acknowledge the true faith, since 'the just man liveth by faith'; while he is anointed between the shoulders, that he may be clothed with the grace of the Holy Spirit, lay aside indifference and sloth, and become*

munditia cogitationum in pectore, et fortitudo laborum in scapulis. Post Baptismum vero, ut Rabanus dicit, *statim signatur in cerebro a presbytero cum sacro chrismate, sequente simul et oratione, ut Christi regni particeps fiat, et a Christo Christianus possit vocari.* Vel, sicut Ambrosius dicit, unguentum super caput effunditur, quia *sapientis sensus in capite eius,* ut scilicet sit paratus omni petenti de fide reddere rationem.

AD TERTIUM dicendum quod vestis illa candida traditur baptizato, non quidem ea ratione quod non liceat ei aliis vestibus uti, sed in signum gloriosae resurrectionis, ad quam homines per Baptismum regenerantur; et ad designandam puritatem vitae, quam debent post Baptismum observare, secundum illud Rom. VI, *in novitate vitae ambulemus.*

AD QUARTUM dicendum quod ea quae pertinent ad solemnitatem sacramenti, etsi non sint de necessitate sacramenti, non tamen sunt superflua, quia sunt ad bene esse sacramenti, ut supra dictum est.

active in good works; so that the sacrament of faith may purify the thoughts of his heart, and strengthen his shoulders for the burden of labor. But after Baptism, as Rabanus says (*De Sacram.* iii), *he is forthwith anointed on the head by the priest with Holy Chrism, who proceeds at once to offer up a prayer that the neophyte may have a share in Christ's kingdom, and be called a Christian after Christ.* Or, as Ambrose says (*De Sacram.* iii), his head is anointed, because *the senses of a wise man are in his head* (Eccl 2:14): to wit, that he may *be ready to satisfy everyone that asketh* him to give *a reason of his faith* (cf. 1 Pet. 3:15; Innocent III, *Decretal* on Holy Unction).

REPLY OBJ. 3: This white garment is given, not as though it were unlawful for the neophyte to use others: but as a sign of the glorious resurrection, unto which men are born again by Baptism; and in order to designate the purity of life, to which he will be bound after being baptized, according to Rom. 6:4: *That we may walk in newness of life.*

REPLY OBJ. 4: Although those things that belong to the solemnity of a sacrament are not essential to it, yet are they not superfluous, since they pertain to the sacrament's well-being, as stated above.

Article 11

Whether Three Kinds of Baptism Are Fittingly Described—viz. Baptism of Water, of Blood, and of the Spirit?

AD UNDECIMUM SIC PROCEDITUR. Videtur quod inconvenienter describantur tria Baptismata, scilicet aquae, sanguinis et flaminis, scilicet spiritus sancti. Quia apostolus dicit, Ephes. IV, *una fides, unum Baptisma.* Sed non est nisi una fides. Ergo non debent tria Baptismata esse.

PRAETEREA, Baptismus est quoddam sacramentum, ut ex supra dictis patet. Sed solum Baptismus aquae est sacramentum. Ergo non debent poni alii duo Baptismi.

PRAETEREA, Damascenus, in IV libro, determinat plura alia genera Baptismatum. Non ergo solum debent poni tria Baptismata.

SED CONTRA est quod, super illud Heb. VI, Baptismatum doctrinae, dicit Glossa, *pluraliter dicit, quia est Baptismus aquae, poenitentiae, et sanguinis.*

RESPONDEO dicendum quod, sicut supra dictum est, Baptismus aquae efficaciam habet a passione Christi, cui aliquis configuratur per Baptismum; et ulterius, sicut a prima causa, a spiritu sancto. Licet autem effectus dependeat a prima causa, causa tamen superexcedit effectum, nec dependet ab effectu. Et ideo, praeter Baptismum aquae, potest aliquis consequi sacramenti effectum ex passione Christi, inquantum quis ei conformatur

OBJECTION 1: It seems that the three kinds of Baptism are not fittingly described as Baptism of Water, of Blood, and of the Spirit, i.e., of the Holy Spirit. Because the Apostle says (Eph 4:5): *One Faith, one Baptism.* Now there is but one Faith. Therefore there should not be three Baptisms.

OBJ. 2: Further, Baptism is a sacrament, as we have made clear above (Q. 65, A. 1). Now none but Baptism of Water is a sacrament. Therefore we should not reckon two other Baptisms.

OBJ. 3: Further, Damascene (*De Fide Orth.* iv) distinguishes several other kinds of Baptism. Therefore we should admit more than three Baptisms.

ON THE CONTRARY, on Heb. 6:2, *Of the doctrine of Baptisms,* the gloss says: *He uses the plural, because there is Baptism of Water, of Repentance, and of Blood.*

I ANSWER THAT, As stated above (Q. 62, A. 5), Baptism of Water has its efficacy from Christ's Passion, to which a man is conformed by Baptism, and also from the Holy Spirit, as first cause. Now although the effect depends on the first cause, the cause far surpasses the effect, nor does it depend on it. Consequently, a man may, without Baptism of Water, receive the sacramental effect from Christ's Passion, in so far as he is conformed to Christ by suffering for

pro Christo patiendo. Unde dicitur Apoc. VII, *hi sunt qui venerunt ex tribulatione magna, et laverunt stolas suas et dealbaverunt eas in sanguine agni.* Eadem etiam ratione aliquis per virtutem spiritus sancti consequitur effectum Baptismi, non solum sine Baptismo aquae, sed etiam sine Baptismo sanguinis, inquantum scilicet alicuius cor per spiritum sanctum movetur ad credendum et diligendum Deum, et poenitendum de peccatis; unde etiam dicitur Baptismus poenitentiae. Et de hoc dicitur Isaiae IV, *si abluerit dominus sordes filiarum Sion, et sanguinem Ierusalem laverit de medio eius, in spiritu iudicii et spiritu ardoris.* Sic igitur utrumque aliorum Baptismatum nominatur Baptismus, inquantum supplet vicem Baptismi. Unde dicit Augustinus, in IV libro de unico Baptismo parvulorum, *Baptismi vicem aliquando implere passionem, de latrone illo cui non baptizato dictum est, hodie mecum eris in Paradiso, beatus Cyprianus non leve documentum assumit. Quod etiam atque etiam considerans, invenio non tantum passionem pro nomine Christi id quod ex Baptismo deerat posse supplere, sed etiam fidem conversionemque cordis, si forte ad celebrandum mysterium Baptismi in angustiis temporum succurri non potest.*

AD PRIMUM ergo dicendum quod alia duo Baptismata includuntur in Baptismo aquae, qui efficaciam habet et ex passione Christi et ex spiritu sancto. Et ideo per hoc non tollitur unitas Baptismatis.

AD SECUNDUM dicendum quod, sicut supra dictum est, sacramentum habet rationem signi. Alia vero duo conveniunt cum Baptismo aquae, non quidem quantum ad rationem signi, sed quantum ad effectum Baptismatis. Et ideo non sunt sacramenta.

AD TERTIUM dicendum quod Damascenus ponit quaedam Baptismata figuralia. Sicut diluvium, quod fuit signum nostri Baptismi quantum ad salvationem fidelium in Ecclesia, sicut *tunc paucae animae salvae factae sunt in arca,* ut dicitur I Petr. III. Ponit etiam transitum maris rubri, qui significat nostrum Baptisma quantum ad liberationem a servitute peccati; unde apostolus dicit, I Cor. X, quod *omnes baptizati sunt in nube et in mari.* Ponit etiam ablutiones diversas quae fiebant in veteri lege, praefigurantes nostrum Baptisma quantum ad purgationem peccatorum. Ponit etiam Baptismum Ioannis, qui fuit praeparatorius ad nostrum Baptisma.

Him. Hence it is written (Rev 7:14): *These are they who are come out of great tribulation, and have washed their robes and have made them white in the blood of the Lamb.* In like manner a man receives the effect of Baptism by the power of the Holy Spirit, not only without Baptism of Water, but also without Baptism of Blood: forasmuch as his heart is moved by the Holy Spirit to believe in and love God and to repent of his sins: wherefore this is also called Baptism of Repentance. Of this it is written (Isa 4:4): *If the Lord shall wash away the filth of the daughters of Zion, and shall wash away the blood of Jerusalem out of the midst thereof, by the spirit of judgment, and by the spirit of burning.* Thus, therefore, each of these other Baptisms is called Baptism, forasmuch as it takes the place of Baptism. Wherefore Augustine says (*De Unico Baptismo Parvulorum* iv): *The Blessed Cyprian argues with considerable reason from the thief to whom, though not baptized, it was said: 'Today shalt thou be with Me in Paradise' that suffering can take the place of Baptism. Having weighed this in my mind again and again, I perceive that not only can suffering for the name of Christ supply for what was lacking in Baptism, but even faith and conversion of heart, if perchance on account of the stress of the times the celebration of the mystery of Baptism is not practicable.*

REPLY OBJ. 1: The other two Baptisms are included in the Baptism of Water, which derives its efficacy, both from Christ's Passion and from the Holy Spirit. Consequently for this reason the unity of Baptism is not destroyed.

REPLY OBJ. 2: As stated above (Q. 60, A. 1), a sacrament is a kind of sign. The other two, however, are like the Baptism of Water, not, indeed, in the nature of sign, but in the baptismal effect. Consequently they are not sacraments.

REPLY OBJ. 3: Damascene enumerates certain figurative Baptisms. For instance, *the Deluge* was a figure of our Baptism, in respect of the salvation of the faithful in the Church; since then *a few . . . souls were saved in the ark,* according to 1 Pet. 3:20. He also mentions *the crossing of the Red Sea*: which was a figure of our Baptism, in respect of our delivery from the bondage of sin; hence the Apostle says (1 Cor 10:2) that *all . . . were baptized in the cloud and in the sea.* And again he mentions *the various washings which were customary under the Old Law,* which were figures of our Baptism, as to the cleansing from sins: also *the Baptism of John,* which prepared the way for our Baptism.

Article 12

Whether the Baptism of Blood Is the Most Excellent of These?

AD DUODECIMUM SIC PROCEDITUR. Videtur quod Baptismus sanguinis non sit potissimus inter tria Baptismata. Baptismus enim aquae imprimit characterem.

OBJECTION 1: It seems that the Baptism of Blood is not the most excellent of these three. For the Baptism of Water impresses a character; which the Baptism of Blood cannot

Quod quidem Baptismus sanguinis non facit. Ergo Baptismus sanguinis non est potior quam Baptismus aquae.

PRAETEREA, Baptismus sanguinis non valet sine Baptismo flaminis, qui est per caritatem, dicitur enim I Cor. XIII, *si tradidero corpus meum ita ut ardeam, caritatem autem non habuero, nihil mihi prodest.* Sed Baptismus flaminis valet sine Baptismo sanguinis, non enim soli martyres salvantur. Ergo Baptismus sanguinis non est potissimus.

PRAETEREA, sicut Baptismus aquae habet efficaciam a passione Christi, cui, secundum praedicta, respondet Baptismus sanguinis, ita passio Christi efficaciam habet a spiritu sancto, secundum illud Heb. IX, *sanguis Christi, qui per spiritum sanctum obtulit semetipsum pro nobis, emundabit conscientias nostras ab operibus mortuis, et cetera.* Ergo Baptismus flaminis potior est quam Baptismus sanguinis. Non ergo Baptismus sanguinis est potissimus.

SED CONTRA est quod Augustinus, ad Fortunatum, loquens de comparatione Baptismatum, dicit, *baptizatus confitetur fidem suam coram sacerdote, martyr coram persecutore. Ille post confessionem suam aspergitur aqua, hic sanguine. Ille per impositionem manus pontificis recipit spiritum sanctum, hic templum efficitur spiritus sancti.*

RESPONDEO dicendum quod, sicut dictum est, effusio sanguinis pro Christo, et operatio interior spiritus sancti, dicuntur Baptismata inquantum efficiunt effectum Baptismi aquae. Baptismus autem aquae efficaciam habet a passione Christi et a spiritu sancto, ut dictum est. Quae quidem duae causae operantur in quolibet horum trium Baptismatum, excellentissime autem in Baptismo sanguinis. Nam passio Christi operatur quidem in Baptismo aquae per quandam figuralem repraesentationem; in Baptismo autem flaminis vel poenitentiae per quandam affectionem; sed in Baptismo sanguinis per imitationem operis. Similiter etiam virtus spiritus sancti operatur in Baptismo aquae per quandam virtutem latentem; in Baptismo autem poenitentiae per cordis commotionem; sed in Baptismo sanguinis per potissimum dilectionis et affectionis fervorem, secundum illud Ioan. XV, *maiorem hac dilectionem nemo habet, ut animam suam ponat quis pro amicis suis.*

AD PRIMUM ergo dicendum quod character est res et sacramentum. Non autem dicimus quod Baptismus sanguinis praeeminentiam habeat secundum rationem sacramenti, sed quantum ad sacramenti effectum.

AD SECUNDUM dicendum quod effusio sanguinis non habet rationem Baptismi si sit sine caritate. Ex quo patet quod Baptismus sanguinis includit Baptismum flaminis, et non e converso. Unde ex hoc probatur perfectior.

do. Therefore the Baptism of Blood is not more excellent than the Baptism of Water.

OBJ. 2: Further, the Baptism of Blood is of no avail without the Baptism of the Spirit, which is by charity; for it is written (1 Cor 13:3): *If I should deliver my body to be burned, and have not charity, it profiteth me nothing.* But the Baptism of the Spirit avails without the Baptism of Blood; for not only the martyrs are saved. Therefore the Baptism of Blood is not the most excellent.

OBJ. 3: Further, just as the Baptism of Water derives its efficacy from Christ's Passion, to which, as stated above (A. 11), the Baptism of Blood corresponds, so Christ's Passion derives its efficacy from the Holy Spirit, according to Heb. 9:14: *The Blood of Christ, Who by the Holy Spirit offered Himself unspotted unto God, shall cleanse our conscience from dead works*, etc. Therefore the Baptism of the Spirit is more excellent than the Baptism of Blood. Therefore the Baptism of Blood is not the most excellent.

ON THE CONTRARY, Augustine (*Ad Fortunatum*) speaking of the comparison between Baptisms says: *The newly baptized confesses his faith in the presence of the priest: the martyr in the presence of the persecutor. The former is sprinkled with water, after he has confessed; the latter with his blood. The former receives the Holy Spirit by the imposition of the bishop's hands; the latter is made the temple of the Holy Spirit.*

I ANSWER THAT, As stated above (A. 11), the shedding of blood for Christ's sake, and the inward operation of the Holy Spirit, are called baptisms, in so far as they produce the effect of the Baptism of Water. Now the Baptism of Water derives its efficacy from Christ's Passion and from the Holy Spirit, as already stated (A. 11). These two causes act in each of these three Baptisms; most excellently, however, in the Baptism of Blood. For Christ's Passion acts in the Baptism of Water by way of a figurative representation; in the Baptism of the Spirit or of Repentance, by way of desire; but in the Baptism of Blood, by way of imitating the (Divine) act. In like manner, too, the power of the Holy Spirit acts in the Baptism of Water through a certain hidden power; in the Baptism of Repentance by moving the heart; but in the Baptism of Blood by the highest degree of fervor of dilection and love, according to John 15:13: *Greater love than this no man hath that a man lay down his life for his friends.*

REPLY OBJ. 1: A character is both reality and a sacrament. And we do not say that the Baptism of Blood is more excellent, considering the nature of a sacrament; but considering the sacramental effect.

REPLY OBJ. 2: The shedding of blood is not in the nature of a Baptism if it be without charity. Hence it is clear that the Baptism of Blood includes the Baptism of the Spirit, but not conversely. And from this it is proved to be more perfect.

AD TERTIUM dicendum quod Baptismus sanguinis praeeminentiam habet non solum ex parte passionis Christi, sed etiam ex parte spiritus sancti, ut dictum est.

REPLY OBJ. 3: The Baptism owes its pre-eminence not only to Christ's Passion, but also to the Holy Spirit, as stated above.

QUESTION 67

THE MINISTERS OF THE SACRAMENT OF BAPTISM

Deinde considerandum est de ministris per quos traditur sacramentum Baptismi. Et circa hoc quaeruntur octo.

Primo, utrum ad diaconum pertineat baptizare.

Secundo, utrum pertineat ad presbyterum, vel solum ad episcopum.

Tertio, utrum laicus possit sacramentum Baptismi conferre.

Quarto, utrum hoc possit facere mulier.

Quinto, utrum non baptizatus possit baptizare.

Sexto, utrum plures possint simul baptizare unum et eundem.

Septimo, utrum necesse sit esse aliquem qui baptizatum de sacro fonte recipiat.

Octavo, utrum suscipiens aliquem de sacro fonte obligetur ad eius instructionem.

We have now to consider the ministers by whom the sacrament of Baptism is conferred. And concerning this there are eight points of inquiry:

(1) Whether it belongs to a deacon to baptize?

(2) Whether this belongs to a priest, or to a bishop only?

(3) Whether a layman can confer the sacrament of Baptism?

(4) Whether a woman can do this?

(5) Whether an unbaptized person can baptize?

(6) Whether several can at the same time baptize one and the same person?

(7) Whether it is essential that someone should raise the person baptized from the sacred font?

(8) Whether he who raises someone from the sacred font is bound to instruct him?

Article 1

Whether It Is Part of a Deacon's Duty to Baptize?

AD PRIMUM SIC PROCEDITUR. Videtur quod ad officium diaconi pertineat baptizare. Simul enim iniungitur a domino officium praedicandi et baptizandi, secundum illud Matth. ult., *euntes, docete omnes gentes, baptizantes eos,* et cetera. Sed ad officium diaconi pertinet evangelizare. Ergo videtur quod etiam ad officium diaconi pertineat baptizare.

PRAETEREA, secundum Dionysium, V cap. Eccl. Hier., purgare pertinet ad officium diaconi. Sed purgatio a peccatis maxime fit per Baptismum, secundum illud Ephes. V, *mundans eam lavacro aquae in verbo vitae.* Ergo videtur quod baptizare pertineat ad diaconem.

PRAETEREA, de beato Laurentio legitur quod, cum ipse esset diaconus, plurimos baptizabat. Ergo videtur quod ad diacones pertinet baptizare.

SED CONTRA est quod Gelasius Papa dicit, et habetur in decretis, XCIII dist., *diacones propriam constituimus observare mensuram.* Et infra, *absque episcopo vel presbytero baptizare non audeant, nisi, praedictis ordinibus longius constitutis, necessitas extrema compellat.*

RESPONDEO dicendum quod, sicut caelestium ordinum proprietates et eorum officia ex eorum nominibus accipiuntur, ut dicit Dionysius, VII cap. Cael. Hier.; ita etiam ex nominibus ecclesiasticorum ordinum accipi potest quid ad unumquemque pertineat ordinem.

OBJECTION 1: It seems that it is part of a deacon's duty to baptize. Because the duties of preaching and of baptizing were enjoined by our Lord at the same time, according to Matt. 28:19: *Going . . . teach ye all nations, baptizing them,* etc. But it is part of a deacon's duty to preach the gospel. Therefore it seems that it is also part of a deacon's duty to baptize.

OBJ. 2: Further, according to Dionysius (*Eccl. Hier.* v) to *cleanse* is part of the deacon's duty. But cleansing from sins is effected specially by Baptism, according to Eph. 5:26: *Cleansing it by the laver of water in the word of life.* Therefore it seems that it belongs to a deacon to baptize.

OBJ. 3: Further, it is told of Blessed Laurence, who was a deacon, that he baptized many. Therefore it seems that it belongs to deacons to baptize.

ON THE CONTRARY, Pope Gelasius I says (the passage is to be found in the *Decrees*, dist. 93): *We order the deacons to keep within their own province*; and further on: *Without bishop or priest they must not dare to baptize, except in cases of extreme urgency, when the aforesaid are a long way off.*

I ANSWER THAT, Just as the properties and duties of the heavenly orders are gathered from their names, as Dionysius says (*Coel. Hier.* vi), so can we gather, from the names of the ecclesiastical orders, what belongs to each order. Now *deacons* are so called from being *ministers*; because,

Dicuntur autem diacones quasi ministri, quia videlicet ad diacones non pertinet aliquod sacramentum principaliter et quasi ex proprio officio praebere, sed ministerium adhibere aliis maioribus in sacramentorum exhibitione. Et sic ad diaconem non pertinet quasi ex proprio officio tradere sacramentum Baptismi, sed in collatione huius sacramenti et aliorum assistere et ministrare maioribus. Unde Isidorus dicit, *ad diaconum pertinet assistere et ministrare sacerdotibus in omnibus quae aguntur in sacramentis Christi, in Baptismo scilicet, in chrismate, in patena et calice.*

AD PRIMUM ergo dicendum quod ad diaconum pertinet recitare Evangelium in Ecclesia, et praedicare ipsum per modum catechizantis, unde et Dionysius dicit quod diaconi habent officium super immundos, inter quos ponit catechumenos. Sed docere, id est exponere Evangelium, pertinet proprie ad episcopum, cuius actus est perficere, secundum Dionysium, V cap. Eccl. Hier.; perficere autem idem est quod docere. Unde non sequitur quod ad diacones pertineat officium baptizandi.

AD SECUNDUM dicendum quod, sicut Dionysius dicit, II cap. Eccl. Hier., Baptismus non solum habet vim purgativam, sed etiam illuminativam virtutem. Et ideo excedit officium diaconi, ad quem pertinet solum purgare, scilicet vel repellendo immundos, vel disponendo eos ad sacramenti susceptionem.

AD TERTIUM dicendum quod, quia Baptismus est sacramentum necessitatis, permittitur diaconibus, necessitate urgente in absentia maiorum, baptizare, sicut patet ex auctoritate Gelasii super inducta. Et hoc modo beatus Laurentius, diaconus existens, baptizavit.

to wit, it is not in the deacon's province to be the chief and official celebrant in conferring a sacrament, but to minister to others, his elders, in the sacramental dispensations. And so it does not belong to a deacon to confer the sacrament of Baptism officially as it were; but to assist and serve his elders in the bestowal of this and other sacraments. Hence Isidore says (*Epist. ad Ludifred.*): *It is a deacon's duty to assist and serve the priests, in all the rites of Christ's sacraments, viz. those of Baptism, of the Chrism, of the Paten and Chalice.*

REPLY OBJ. 1: It is the deacon's duty to read the Gospel in church, and to preach it as one catechizing; hence Dionysius says (*Eccl. Hier.* v) that a deacon's office involves power over the unclean among whom he includes the catechumens. But to teach, i.e., to expound the Gospel, is the proper office of a bishop, whose action is *to perfect*, as Dionysius teaches (*Eccl. Hier.* v); and *to perfect* is the same as *to teach*. Consequently, it does not follow that the office of baptizing belongs to deacons.

REPLY OBJ. 2: As Dionysius says (*Eccl. Hier.* ii), Baptism has a power not only of *cleansing* but also of *enlightening*. Consequently, it is outside the province of the deacon whose duty it is to cleanse only: viz. either by driving away the unclean, or by preparing them for the reception of a sacrament.

REPLY OBJ. 3: Because Baptism is a necessary sacrament, deacons are allowed to baptize in cases of urgency when their elders are not at hand; as appears from the authority of Gelasius quoted above. And it was thus that Blessed Laurence, being but a deacon, baptized.

Article 2

Whether to Baptize Is Part of the Priestly Office, or Proper to That of Bishops?

AD SECUNDUM SIC PROCEDITUR. Videtur quod baptizare non pertineat ad officium presbyterorum, sed solum episcoporum. Quia, sicut dictum est, sub eodem praecepto iniungitur, Matth. ult., officium docendi et baptizandi. Sed docere, quod est perficere, pertinet ad officium episcopi, ut patet per Dionysium, V et VI cap. Eccl. Hier. Ergo et baptizare pertinet tantum ad officium episcopi.

PRAETEREA, per Baptismum annumeratur aliquis populo Christiano, quod quidem videtur ad officium solius principis pertinere. Sed principatum in Ecclesia tenent episcopi, ut dicitur in Glossa Luc. X, qui etiam tenent locum apostolorum, de quibus dicitur in Psalmo, *constitues eos principes super omnem terram.* Ergo videtur quod baptizare pertineat solum ad officium episcopi.

OBJECTION 1: It seems that to baptize is not part of the priestly office, but proper to that of bishops. Because, as stated above (A. 1, Obj. 1), the duties of teaching and baptizing are enjoined in the same precept (Matt 28:19). But to teach, which is *to perfect*, belongs to the office of bishop, as Dionysius declares (*Eccl. Hier.* v, vi). Therefore to baptize also belongs to the episcopal office.

OBJ. 2: Further, by Baptism a man is admitted to the body of the Christian people: and to do this seems consistent with no other than the princely office. Now the bishops hold the position of princes in the Church, as the gloss observes on Luke 10:1: indeed, they even take the place of the apostles, of whom it is written (Ps 44:17): *Thou shalt make them princes over all the earth.* Therefore it seems that to baptize belongs exclusively to the office of bishops.

PRAETEREA, Isidorus dicit quod *ad episcopum pertinet basilicarum consecratio, unctio altaris, et confectio chrismatis, ipse ordines ecclesiasticos distribuit, et sacras virgines benedicit.* Sed his omnibus maius est sacramentum Baptismi. Ergo videtur quod multo magis ad officium solius episcopi pertinet baptizare.

SED CONTRA est quod Isidorus dicit, in libro de officiis, *constat Baptisma solis sacerdotibus esse traditum.*

RESPONDEO dicendum quod sacerdotes ad hoc consecrantur ut sacramentum corporis Christi conficiant, sicut supra dictum est. Illud autem est sacramentum ecclesiasticae unitatis, secundum illud apostoli, I Cor. X, *unus panis et unum corpus multi sumus, omnes qui de uno pane et de uno calice participamus.* Per Baptismum autem aliquis fit particeps ecclesiasticae unitatis, unde et accipit ius accedendi ad mensam domini. Et ideo, sicut ad sacerdotem pertinet consecrare Eucharistiam, ad quod principaliter ordinatur sacerdotium, ita ad proprium officium sacerdotis pertinet baptizare, eiusdem enim videtur esse operari totum, et partem in toto disponere.

AD PRIMUM ergo dicendum quod utrumque officium, scilicet docendi et baptizandi, dominus apostolis iniunxit, quorum vicem gerunt episcopi, aliter tamen et aliter. Nam officium docendi commisit eis Christus ut ipsi per se illud exercerent, tanquam principalissimum, unde et ipsi apostoli dixerunt, Act. VI, *non est aequum nos relinquere verbum Dei et ministrare mensis.* Officium autem baptizandi commisit apostolis ut per alios exercendum, unde et apostolus dicit, I Cor. I, *non misit me Christus baptizare, sed evangelizare.* Et hoc ideo quia in baptizando nihil operatur meritum et sapientia ministri, sicut in docendo, ut patet ex supra dictis. In cuius etiam signum, nec ipse dominus baptizavit, sed discipuli eius, ut dicitur Ioan. IV. Nec tamen per hoc excluditur quin episcopi possint baptizare, quia quod potest potestas inferior, potest et superior. Unde et apostolus ibidem dicit se quosdam baptizasse.

AD SECUNDUM dicendum quod in qualibet republica ea quae sunt minora, pertinent ad minora officia, maiora vero maioribus reservantur, secundum illud Exod. XVIII, *quidquid maius fuerit, referent ad te, et ipsi tantummodo minora iudicent.* Et ideo ad minores principes civitatis pertinet disponere de infimo populo, ad summos autem pertinet disponere ea quae pertinent ad maiores civitatis. Per Baptismum autem non adipiscitur aliquis nisi infimum gradum in populo Christiano. Et ideo baptizare pertinet ad minores principes Ecclesiae,

OBJ. 3: Further, Isidore says (*Epist. ad Ludifred.*) that *it belongs to the bishop to consecrate churches, to anoint altars, to consecrate* (conficere) *the chrism; he it is that confers the ecclesiastical orders, and blesses the consecrated virgins.* But the sacrament of Baptism is greater than all these. Therefore much more reason is there why to baptize should belong exclusively to the episcopal office.

ON THE CONTRARY, Isidore says (*De Officiis.* ii): *It is certain that Baptism was entrusted to priests alone.*

I ANSWER THAT, Priests are consecrated for the purpose of celebrating the sacrament of Christ's Body, as stated above (Q. 65, A. 3). Now that is the sacrament of ecclesiastical unity, according to the Apostle (1 Cor 10:17): *We, being many, are one bread, one body, all that partake of one bread and one chalice.* Moreover, by Baptism a man becomes a participator in ecclesiastical unity, wherefore also he receives the right to approach our Lord's Table. Consequently, just as it belongs to a priest to consecrate the Eucharist, which is the principal purpose of the priesthood, so it is the proper office of a priest to baptize: since it seems to belong to one and the same, to produce the whole and to dispose the part in the whole.

REPLY OBJ. 1: Our Lord enjoined on the apostles, whose place is taken by the bishops, both duties, namely, of teaching and of baptizing, but in different ways. Because Christ committed to them the duty of teaching, that they might exercise it themselves as being the most important duty of all: wherefore the apostles themselves said (Acts 6:2): *It is not reason that we should leave the word of God and serve tables.* On the other hand, He entrusted the apostles with the office of baptizing, to be exercised vicariously; wherefore the Apostle says (1 Cor 1:17): *Christ sent me not to baptize, but to preach the Gospel.* And the reason for this was that the merit and wisdom of the minister have no bearing on the baptismal effect, as they have in teaching, as may be seen from what we have stated above (Q. 64, A. 1, ad 2; AA. 5, 9). A proof of this is found also in the fact that our Lord Himself did not baptize, but His disciples, as John relates (4:2). Nor does it follow from this that bishops cannot baptize; since what a lower power can do, that can also a higher power. Wherefore also the Apostle says (1 Cor 1:14, 16) that he had baptized some.

REPLY OBJ. 2: In every commonwealth minor affairs are entrusted to lower officials, while greater affairs are restricted to higher officials; according to Ex. 18:22: *When any great matter soever shall fall out, let them refer it to thee, and let them judge the lesser matters only.* Consequently it belongs to the lower officials of the state to decide matters concerning the lower orders; while to the highest it belongs to set in order those matters that regard the higher orders of the state. Now by Baptism a man attains only to the lowest rank among the Christian people: and consequently

idest presbyteros, qui tenent locum septuaginta duorum discipulorum Christi, ut dicit Glossa Luc. X.

it belongs to the lesser officials of the Church to baptize, namely, the priests, who hold the place of the seventy-two disciples of Christ, as the gloss says in the passage quoted from Luke 10.

AD TERTIUM dicendum quod, sicut supra dictum est, sacramentum Baptismi est potissimum necessitate, sed quantum ad perfectionem, sunt quaedam alia potiora, quae episcopis reservantur.

REPLY OBJ. 3: As stated above (Q. 65, A. 3), the sacrament of Baptism holds the first place in the order of necessity; but in the order of perfection there are other greater sacraments which are reserved to bishops.

Article 3

Whether a Layman Can Baptize?

AD TERTIUM SIC PROCEDITUR. Videtur quod laicus baptizare non possit. Baptizare enim, sicut dictum est, proprie pertinet ad ordinem sacerdotalem. Sed ea quae sunt ordinis, non possunt committi non habenti ordinem. Ergo videtur quod laicus, qui non habet ordinem, baptizare non possit.

PRAETEREA, maius est baptizare quam alia sacramentalia Baptismi perficere, sicut catechizare et exorcizare et aquam baptismalem benedicere. Sed haec non possunt fieri a laicis, sed solum a sacerdotibus. Ergo videtur quod multo minus laici possint baptizare.

PRAETEREA, sicut Baptismus est sacramentum necessitatis, ita et poenitentia. Sed laicus non potest absolvere in foro poenitentiali. Ergo neque potest baptizare.

SED CONTRA est quod Gelasius Papa et Isidorus dicunt, quod *baptizare, necessitate imminente, laicis Christianis plerumque conceditur.*

RESPONDEO dicendum quod ad misericordiam eius qui *vult omnes homines salvos fieri*, pertinet ut in his quae sunt de necessitate salutis, homo de facili remedium inveniat. Inter omnia autem alia sacramenta maximae necessitatis est Baptismus, qui est regeneratio hominis in vitam spiritualem, quia pueris aliter subveniri non potest; et adulti non possunt aliter quam per Baptismum plenam remissionem consequi et quantum ad culpam et quantum ad poenam. Et ideo, ut homo circa remedium tam necessarium defectum pati non possit, institutum est ut et materia Baptismi sit communis, scilicet aqua, quae a quolibet haberi potest; et minister Baptismi etiam sit quicumque, etiam non ordinatus; ne propter defectum Baptismi homo salutis suae dispendium patiatur.

AD PRIMUM ergo dicendum quod baptizare pertinet ad ordinem sacerdotalem secundum quandam convenientiam et solemnitatem, non autem hoc est de necessitate sacramenti. Unde etiam si extra necessitatis articulum laicus baptizet, peccat quidem, tamen sacramentum Baptismi confert, nec est rebaptizandus ille qui sic est baptizatus.

OBJECTION 1: It seems that a layman cannot baptize. Because, as stated above (A. 2), to baptize belongs properly to the priestly order. But those things which belong to an order cannot be entrusted to one that is not ordained. Therefore it seems that a layman, who has no orders, cannot baptize.

OBJ. 2: Further, it is a greater thing to baptize, than to perform the other sacramental rites of Baptism, such as to catechize, to exorcize, and to bless the baptismal water. But these things cannot be done by laymen, but only by priests. Therefore it seems that much less can laymen baptize.

OBJ. 3: Further, just as Baptism is a necessary sacrament, so is Penance. But a layman cannot absolve in the tribunal of Penance. Neither, therefore, can he baptize.

ON THE CONTRARY, Pope Gelasius I and Isidore say that *it is often permissible for Christian laymen to baptize, in cases of urgent necessity.*

I ANSWER THAT, It is due to the mercy of Him *Who will have all men to be saved* (1 Tim 2:4) that in those things which are necessary for salvation, man can easily find the remedy. Now the most necessary among all the sacraments is Baptism, which is man's regeneration unto spiritual life: since for children there is no substitute, while adults cannot otherwise than by Baptism receive a full remission both of guilt and of its punishment. Consequently, lest man should have to go without so necessary a remedy, it was ordained, both that the matter of Baptism should be something common that is easily obtainable by all, i.e., water; and that the minister of Baptism should be anyone, even not in orders, lest from lack of being baptized, man should suffer loss of his salvation.

REPLY OBJ. 1: To baptize belongs to the priestly order by reason of a certain appropriateness and solemnity; but this is not essential to the sacrament. Consequently, if a layman were to baptize even outside a case of urgency; he would sin, yet he would confer the sacrament; nor would the person thus baptized have to be baptized again.

AD SECUNDUM dicendum quod illa sacramentalia Baptismi pertinent ad solemnitatem, non autem ad necessitatem Baptismi. Et ideo fieri non debent nec possunt a laico, sed solum a sacerdote, cuius est solemniter baptizare.

AD TERTIUM dicendum quod, sicut supra dictum est, poenitentia non est tantae necessitatis sicut Baptismus, potest enim per contritionem suppleri defectus sacerdotalis absolutionis quae non liberat a tota poena, nec etiam pueris adhibetur. Et ideo non est simile de Baptismo, cuius effectus per nihil aliud suppleri potest.

REPLY OBJ. 2: These sacramental rites of Baptism belong to the solemnity of, and are not essential to, Baptism. And therefore they neither should nor can be done by a layman, but only by a priest, whose office it is to baptize solemnly.

REPLY OBJ. 3: As stated above (Q. 65, AA. 3, 4), Penance is not so necessary as Baptism; since contrition can supply the defect of the priestly absolution which does not free from the whole punishment, nor again is it given to children. Therefore the comparison with Baptism does not stand, because its effect cannot be supplied by anything else.

Article 4

Whether a Woman Can Baptize?

AD QUARTUM SIC PROCEDITUR. Videtur quod mulier non possit baptizare. Legitur enim in Carthaginensi Concilio, *mulier, quamvis docta et sancta, viros in conventu docere, vel alios baptizare non praesumat.* Sed nullo modo licet mulieri docere in conventu, secundum illud I Cor. XIV, *turpe est mulieri in Ecclesia loqui.* Ergo videtur quod nec etiam aliquo modo liceat mulieri baptizare.

PRAETEREA, baptizare pertinet ad officium praelationis, unde a sacerdotibus habentibus curam animarum debet accipi Baptismus. Sed hoc non potest competere feminae, secundum illud I Tim. II, *docere mulieri non permitto, nec dominari in viros, sed subditam esse.* Ergo mulier baptizare non potest.

PRAETEREA, in spirituali regeneratione videtur aqua habere locum materni uteri, ut Augustinus dicit, super illud Ioan. III, *nunquid homo potest in ventrem matris suae iterato introire et renasci?* Ille autem qui baptizat, videtur magis habere patris officium. Sed hoc non competit mulieri. Ergo mulier baptizare non potest.

SED CONTRA est quod Urbanus Papa dicit, et habetur in decretis, XXX, qu. III, *super quibus consuluit nos tua dilectio, hoc videtur nobis hac sententia respondendum, ut Baptismus sit si, necessitate instante, femina puerum in nomine Trinitatis baptizaverit.*

RESPONDEO dicendum quod Christus est qui principaliter baptizat, secundum illud Ioan. I, *super quem videris spiritum descendentem et manentem, hic est qui baptizat.* Dicitur autem Coloss. III quod *in Christo non est masculus neque femina.* Et ideo, sicut masculus laicus potest baptizare, quasi minister Christi, ita etiam et femina.

Quia tamen *caput mulieris est vir, et caput viri Christus*, ut dicitur I Cor. XI; non debet mulier baptizare si adsit copia viri. Sicut nec laicus praesente clerico, nec clericus praesente sacerdote. Qui tamen potest baptizare

OBJECTION 1: It seems that a woman cannot baptize. For we read in the acts of the Council of Carthage (iv): *However learned and holy a woman may be, she must not presume to teach men in the church, or to baptize.* But in no case is a woman allowed to teach in church, according to 1 Cor. 14:35: *It is a shame for a woman to speak in the church.* Therefore it seems that neither is a woman in any circumstances permitted to baptize.

OBJ. 2: Further, to baptize belongs to those having authority. wherefore baptism should be conferred by priests having charge of souls. But women are not qualified for this; according to 1 Tim. 2:12: *I suffer not a woman to teach, nor to use authority over man, but to be subject to him.* Therefore a woman cannot baptize.

OBJ. 3: Further, in the spiritual regeneration water seems to hold the place of the mother's womb, as Augustine says on John 3:4, *Can a man enter a second time into his mother's womb, and be born again?* While he who baptizes seems to hold rather the position of father. But this is unfitting for a woman. Therefore a woman cannot baptize.

ON THE CONTRARY, Pope Urban II says (*Decreta* xxx): *In reply to the questions asked by your beatitude, we consider that the following answer should be given: that the baptism is valid when, in cases of necessity, a woman baptizes a child in the name of the Trinity.*

I ANSWER THAT, Christ is the chief Baptizer, according to John 1:33: *He upon Whom thou shalt see the Spirit descending and remaining upon Him, He it is that baptizeth.* For it is written in Col. 3 (cf. Gal. 3:28), that in Christ there is neither male nor female. Consequently, just as a layman can baptize, as Christ's minister, so can a woman.

But since *the head of the woman is the man*, and *the head of . . . man, is Christ* (1 Cor 11:3), a woman should not baptize if a man be available for the purpose; just as neither should a layman in the presence of a cleric, nor a cleric in

praesente episcopo, eo quod hoc pertinet ad officium sacerdotis.

Ad primum ergo dicendum quod, sicut mulieri non permittitur publice docere, potest tamen privata doctrina vel monitione aliquem instruere; ita non permittitur publice et solemniter baptizare, sed tamen potest baptizare in necessitatis articulo.

Ad secundum dicendum quod, quando Baptismus solemniter et ordinate celebratur, debet aliquis sacramentum Baptismi suscipere a presbytero curam animarum habente, vel ab aliquo vice eius. Hoc tamen non requiritur in articulo necessitatis, in quo potest mulier baptizare.

Ad tertium dicendum quod in generatione carnali masculus et femina operantur secundum virtutem propriae naturae, et ideo femina non potest esse principium generationis activum, sed passivum tantum. Sed in generatione spirituali neuter operatur virtute propria, sed instrumentaliter tantum per virtutem Christi. Et ideo eodem modo potest et vir et mulier in casu necessitatis baptizare.

Si tamen mulier extra casum necessitatis baptizaret, non esset rebaptizandus, sicut et de laico dictum est. Peccaret tamen ipsa baptizans, et alii qui ad hoc cooperarentur, vel Baptismum ab ea suscipiendo, vel ei baptizandum aliquem offerendo.

the presence of a priest. The last, however, can baptize in the presence of a bishop, because it is part of the priestly office.

Reply Obj. 1: Just as a woman is not suffered to teach in public, but is allowed to instruct and admonish privately; so she is not permitted to baptize publicly and solemnly, and yet she can baptize in a case of urgency.

Reply Obj. 2: When Baptism is celebrated solemnly and with due form, it should be conferred by a priest having charge of souls, or by one representing him. But this is not required in cases of urgency, when a woman may baptize.

Reply Obj. 3: In carnal generation male and female co-operate according to the power of their proper nature; wherefore the female cannot be the active, but only the passive, principle of generation. But in spiritual generation they do not act, either of them, by their proper power, but only instrumentally by the power of Christ. Consequently, on the same grounds either man or woman can baptize in a case of urgency.

If, however, a woman were to baptize without any urgency for so doing, there would be no need of rebaptism: as we have said in regard to laymen (A. 3, ad 1). But the baptizer herself would sin, as also those who took part with her therein, either by receiving Baptism from her, or by bringing someone to her to be baptized.

Article 5

Whether One That Is Not Baptized Can Confer the Sacrament of Baptism?

Ad quintum sic proceditur. Videtur quod ille qui non est baptizatus, non possit sacramentum Baptismi conferre. Nullus enim dat quod non habet. Sed nonbaptizatus non habet sacramentum Baptismi. Ergo non potest ipsum conferre.

Praeterea, sacramentum Baptismi confert aliquis inquantum est minister Ecclesiae. Sed ille qui non est baptizatus, nullo modo pertinet ad Ecclesiam, scilicet nec re nec sacramento. Ergo non potest sacramentum Baptismi conferre.

Praeterea, maius est sacramentum conferre quam suscipere. Sed nonbaptizatus non potest alia sacramenta suscipere. Ergo multo minus potest aliquod sacramentum conferre.

Sed contra est quod Isidorus dicit, *Romanus pontifex non hominem iudicat qui baptizat, sed spiritum Dei subministrare gratiam Baptismi, licet Paganus sit qui baptizat.* Sed ille qui est baptizatus, non dicitur Paganus.

Objection 1: It seems that one that is not baptized cannot confer the sacrament of Baptism. For *none gives what he has not.* But a non-baptized person has not the sacrament of Baptism. Therefore he cannot give it.

Obj. 2: Further, a man confers the sacrament of Baptism inasmuch as he is a minister of the Church. But one that is not baptized, belongs nowise to the Church, i.e., neither really nor sacramentally. Therefore he cannot confer the sacrament of Baptism.

Obj. 3: Further, it is more to confer a sacrament than to receive it. But one that is not baptized, cannot receive the other sacraments. Much less, therefore, can he confer any sacrament.

On the contrary, Isidore says: *The Roman Pontiff does not consider it to be the man who baptizes, but that the Holy Spirit confers the grace of Baptism, though he that baptizes be a pagan.* But he who is baptized, is not called

Ergo non baptizatus potest conferre sacramentum Baptismi.

RESPONDEO dicendum quod hanc quaestionem Augustinus indeterminatam reliquit. Dicit enim, in II contra epistolam Parmeniani, *haec quidem alia quaestio est, utrum et ab his qui nunquam fuerunt Christiani, possit Baptismus dari, nec aliquid hinc temere affirmandum est, sine auctoritate tanti sacri Concilii quantum tantae rei sufficit.* Postmodum vero per Ecclesiam determinatum est quod nonbaptizati, sive sint Iudaei sive Pagani, possunt sacramentum Baptismi conferre, dummodo in forma Ecclesiae baptizent. Unde Nicolaus Papa respondet ad consulta Bulgarorum, *a quodam nescitis Christiano an Pagano, multos in patria vestra baptizatos asseritis. Hi si in nomine Trinitatis baptizati sunt, rebaptizari non debent.* Si autem forma Ecclesiae non fuerit observata, sacramentum Baptismi non confertur. Et sic intelligendum est quod Gregorius II scribit Bonifacio episcopo, *quos a Paganis baptizatos asseruisti,* scilicet Ecclesiae forma non servata, *ut de novo baptizes in nomine Trinitatis, mandamus.* Et huius ratio est quia, sicut ex parte materiae, quantum ad necessitatem sacramenti, sufficit quaecumque aqua, ita etiam sufficit ex parte ministri quicumque homo. Et ideo etiam nonbaptizatus in articulo necessitatis baptizare potest. Ut sic duo nonbaptizati se invicem baptizent, dum prius unus baptizaret alium, et postea baptizaretur ab eodem, et consequeretur uterque non solum sacramentum, sed etiam rem sacramenti. Si vero extra articulum necessitatis hoc fieret, uterque graviter peccaret, scilicet baptizans et baptizatus, et per hoc impediretur Baptismi effectus, licet non tolleretur ipsum sacramentum.

AD PRIMUM ergo dicendum quod homo baptizans adhibet tantum exterius ministerium, sed Christus est qui interius baptizat, qui potest uti omnibus hominibus ad quodcumque voluerit. Et ideo nonbaptizati possunt baptizare, quia, ut Nicolaus Papa dicit, Baptismus non est illorum, scilicet baptizantium, sed eius, scilicet Christi.

AD SECUNDUM dicendum quod ille qui non est baptizatus, quamvis non pertineat ad Ecclesiam re vel sacramento, potest tamen ad eam pertinere intentione et similitudine actus, inquantum scilicet intendit facere quod facit Ecclesia, et formam Ecclesiae servat in baptizando, et sic operatur ut minister Christi, qui virtutem suam non alligavit baptizatis, sicut nec etiam sacramentis.

AD TERTIUM dicendum quod alia sacramenta non sunt tantae necessitatis sicut Baptismus. Et ideo magis conceditur quod nonbaptizatus possit baptizare, quam quod possit alia sacramenta suscipere.

a pagan. Therefore he who is not baptized can confer the sacrament of Baptism.

I ANSWER THAT, Augustine left this question without deciding it. For he says (*Contra Ep. Parmen.* ii): *This is indeed another question, whether even those can baptize who were never Christians; nor should anything be rashly asserted hereupon, without the authority of a sacred council such as suffices for so great a matter.* But afterwards it was decided by the Church that the unbaptized, whether Jews or pagans, can confer the sacrament of Baptism, provided they baptize in the form of the Church. Wherefore Pope Nicolas I replies to the questions propounded by the Bulgars: *You say that many in your country have been baptized by someone, whether Christian or pagan you know not. If these were baptized in the name of the Trinity, they must not be rebaptized.* But if the form of the Church be not observed, the sacrament of Baptism is not conferred. And thus is to be explained what Gregory II writes to Bishop Boniface: *Those whom you assert to have been baptized by pagans,* namely, with a form not recognized by the Church, *we command you to rebaptize in the name of the Trinity.* And the reason of this is that, just as on the part of the matter, as far as the essentials of the sacrament are concerned, any water will suffice, so, on the part of the minister, any man is competent. Consequently, an unbaptized person can baptize in a case of urgency. So that two unbaptized persons may baptize one another, one baptizing the other and being afterwards baptized by him: and each would receive not only the sacrament but also the reality of the sacrament. But if this were done outside a case of urgency, each would sin grievously, both the baptizer and the baptized, and thus the baptismal effect would be frustrated, although the sacrament itself would not be invalidated.

REPLY OBJ. 1: The man who baptizes offers but his outward ministration; whereas Christ it is Who baptizes inwardly, Who can use all men to whatever purpose He wills. Consequently, the unbaptized can baptize: because, as Pope Nicolas I says, *the Baptism is not theirs,* i.e., the baptizers', *but His,* i.e., Christ's.

REPLY OBJ. 2: He who is not baptized, though he belongs not to the Church either in reality or sacramentally, can nevertheless belong to her in intention and by similarity of action, namely, in so far as he intends to do what the Church does, and in baptizing observes the Church's form, and thus acts as the minister of Christ, Who did not confine His power to those that are baptized, as neither did He to the sacraments.

REPLY OBJ. 3: The other sacraments are not so necessary as Baptism. And therefore it is allowable that an unbaptized person should baptize rather than that he should receive other sacraments.

Article 6

Whether Several Can Baptize at the Same Time?

Ad sextum sic proceditur. Videtur quod plures possint simul baptizare. In multitudine enim continetur unum, sed non convertitur. Unde videtur quod quidquid potest facere unus, possint facere multi, et non e converso, sicut multi trahunt navem quam unus trahere non posset. Sed unus homo potest baptizare. Ergo et plures possunt simul unum baptizare.

Praeterea, difficilius est quod unum agens agat in plura quam quod plures agentes agant simul in unum. Sed unus homo potest simul baptizare plures. Ergo multo magis plures possunt simul unum baptizare.

Praeterea, Baptismus est sacramentum maximae necessitatis. Sed in aliquo casu videtur esse necessarium quod plures simul unum baptizarent, puta si aliquis parvulus esset in articulo mortis, et adessent duo quorum alter esset mutus, et alter manibus et brachiis careret; tunc enim oporteret quod mutilatus verba proferret, et mutus Baptismum exerceret. Ergo videtur quod plures possint simul unum baptizare.

Sed contra est quod unius agentis una est actio. Si ergo plures unum baptizarent, videretur sequi quod essent plures Baptismi. Quod est contra id quod dicitur Ephes. IV, *una fides, unum Baptisma.*

Respondeo dicendum quod sacramentum Baptismi praecipue habet virtutem ex forma, quam apostolus nominat verbum vitae, Ephes. V. Et ideo considerare oportet, si plures unum simul baptizarent, qua forma uterentur. Si enim dicerent, nos te baptizamus in nomine patris et filii et spiritus sancti, dicunt quidam quod non conferretur sacramentum Baptismi eo quod non servaretur forma Ecclesiae, quae sic habet, *ego te baptizo in nomine patris et filii et spiritus sancti.* Sed hoc excluditur per formam baptizandi qua utitur Ecclesia Graecorum. Possent enim dicere, *baptizatur servus Christi n. in nomine patris et filii et spiritus sancti,* sub qua forma Graeci Baptismum suscipiunt, quae tamen forma multo magis dissimilis est formae qua nos utimur, quam si diceretur, nos te baptizamus.

Sed considerandum est quod ex tali forma, nos te baptizamus, exprimitur talis intentio quod plures conveniunt ad unum Baptismum conferendum. Quod quidem videtur esse contra rationem ministerii, homo enim non baptizat nisi ut minister Christi et vicem eius gerens; unde, sicut unus est Christus, ita oportet esse unum ministrum qui Christum repraesentet. Propter quod signanter apostolus dicit, Ephes. IV, *unus dominus, una*

Objection 1: It seems that several can baptize at the same time. For unity is contained in multitude, but not vice versa. Wherefore it seems that many can do whatever one can but not vice versa: thus many draw a ship which one could draw. But one man can baptize. Therefore several, too, can baptize one at the same time.

Obj. 2: Further, it is more difficult for one agent to act on many things, than for many to act at the same time on one. But one man can baptize several at the same time. Much more, therefore, can many baptize one at the same time.

Obj. 3: Further, Baptism is a sacrament of the greatest necessity. Now in certain cases it seems necessary for several to baptize one at the same time; for instance, suppose a child to be in danger of death, and two persons present, one of whom is dumb, and the other without hands or arms; for then the mutilated person would have to pronounce the words, and the dumb person would have to perform the act of baptizing. Therefore it seems that several can baptize one at the same time.

On the contrary, Where there is one agent there is one action. If, therefore, several were to baptize one, it seems to follow that there would be several baptisms: and this is contrary to Eph. 4:5: *one Faith, one Baptism.*

I answer that, The Sacrament of Baptism derives its power principally from its form, which the Apostle calls *the word of life* (Eph 5:26). Consequently, if several were to baptize one at the same time, we must consider what form they would use. For were they to say: *We baptize thee in the name of the Father and of the Son and of the Holy Spirit,* some maintain that the sacrament of Baptism would not be conferred, because the form of the Church would not be observed, i.e., *I baptize thee in the name of the Father and of the Son and of the Holy Spirit.* But this reasoning is disproved by the form observed in the Greek Church. For they might say: *The servant of God, N . . ., is baptized in the name of the Father and of the Son and of the Holy Spirit,* under which form the Greeks receive the sacrament of Baptism: and yet this form differs far more from the form that we use, than does this: *We baptize thee.*

The point to be observed, however, is this, that by this form, *We baptize thee,* the intention expressed is that several concur in conferring one Baptism: and this seems contrary to the notion of a minister; for a man does not baptize save as a minister of Christ, and as standing in His place; wherefore just as there is one Christ, so should there be one minister to represent Christ. Hence the Apostle says pointedly (Eph 4:5): *one Lord, one Faith, one Baptism.* Consequently,

fides, unum Baptisma. Et ideo contraria intentio videtur excludere Baptismi sacramentum.

Si vero uterque diceret, *ego te baptizo in nomine patris et filii et spiritus sancti,* uterque exprimeret suam intentionem quasi ipse singulariter Baptismum conferret. Quod posset contingere in eo casu in quo contentiose uterque aliquem baptizare conaretur. Et tunc manifestum est quod ille qui prius verba proferret, daret Baptismi sacramentum. Alius vero, quantumcumque ius baptizandi haberet, etsi verba pronuntiare praesumeret, esset puniendus tanquam rebaptizator. Si autem omnino simul verba proferrent et hominem immergerent aut aspergerent, essent puniendi de inordinato modo baptizandi, et non de iteratione Baptismi, quia uterque intenderet nonbaptizatum baptizare, et uterque, quantum est in se, baptizaret. Nec traderent aliud et aliud sacramentum, sed Christus, qui est unus interius baptizans, unum sacramentum per utrumque conferret.

AD PRIMUM ergo dicendum quod ratio illa locum habet in his quae agunt propria virtute. Sed homines non baptizant propria virtute, sed virtute Christi, qui, cum sit unus, per unum ministrum perficit suum opus.

AD SECUNDUM dicendum quod in casu necessitatis unus posset simul plures baptizare sub hac forma, ego vos baptizo, puta si immineret ruina aut gladius aut aliquid huiusmodi, quod moram omnino non pateretur, si singillatim omnes baptizarentur. Nec per hoc diversificaretur forma Ecclesiae, quia plurale non est nisi singulare geminatum, praesertim cum pluraliter dicatur, Matth. ult., baptizantes eos, et cetera. Nec est simile de baptizante et baptizato. Quia Christus, qui principaliter baptizat, est unus, sed multi per Baptismum efficiuntur unum in Christo.

AD TERTIUM dicendum quod, sicut supra dictum est, integritas Baptismi consistit in forma verborum et in usu materiae. Et ideo neque ille qui tantum verba profert baptizat, neque ille qui immergit. Et ideo, si unus verba proferat et alius immergit, nulla forma verborum poterit esse conveniens. Neque enim poterit dici, ego te baptizo, cum ipse non immergat, et per consequens non baptizet. Neque etiam poterit dicere, nos te baptizamus, cum neuter baptizet. Si enim duo sint quorum unus unam partem libri scribat et alius aliam, non est propria locutio, nos scripsimus librum istum, sed synecdochica, inquantum totum ponitur pro parte.

an intention which is in opposition to this seems to annul the sacrament of Baptism.

On the other hand, if each were to say: *I baptize thee in the name of the Father and of the Son and of the Holy Spirit,* each would signify his intention as though he were conferring Baptism independently of the other. This might occur in the case where both were striving to baptize someone; and then it is clear that whichever pronounced the words first would confer the sacrament of Baptism; while the other, however great his right to baptize, if he presume to utter the words, would be liable to be punished as a rebaptizer. If, however, they were to pronounce the words absolutely at the same time, and dipped or sprinkled the man together, they should be punished for baptizing in an improper manner, but not for rebaptizing: because each would intend to baptize an unbaptized person, and each, so far as he is concerned, would baptize. Nor would they confer several sacraments: but the one Christ baptizing inwardly would confer one sacrament by means of both together.

REPLY OBJ. 1: This argument avails in those agents that act by their own power. But men do not baptize by their own, but by Christ's power, Who, since He is one, perfects His work by means of one minister.

REPLY OBJ. 2: In a case of necessity one could baptize several at the same time under this form: *I baptize ye*: for instance, if they were threatened by a falling house, or by the sword or something of the kind, so as not to allow of the delay involved by baptizing them singly. Nor would this cause a change in the Church's form, since the plural is nothing but the singular doubled: especially as we find the plural expressed in Matt. 28:19: *Baptizing them,* etc. Nor is there parity between the baptizer and the baptized; since Christ, the baptizer in chief, is one: while many are made one in Christ by Baptism.

REPLY OBJ. 3: As stated above (Q. 66, A. 1), the integrity of Baptism consists in the form of words and the use of the matter. Consequently, neither he who only pronounces the words, baptizes, nor he who dips. Wherefore if one pronounces the words and the other dips, no form of words can be fitting. For neither could he say: *I baptize thee*: since he dips not, and therefore baptizes not. Nor could they say: *We baptize thee*: since neither baptizes. For if of two men, one write one part of a book, and the other write the other, it would not be a proper form of speech to say: *We wrote this book*, but the figure of synecdoche in which the whole is put for the part.

Article 7

Whether in Baptism It Is Necessary for Someone to Raise the Baptized from the Sacred Font?

AD SEPTIMUM SIC PROCEDITUR. Videtur quod in Baptismo non requiratur aliquis qui baptizatum de sacro fonte levet. Baptismus enim noster per Baptismum Christi consecratur, et ei conformatur. Sed Christus baptizatus non est ab aliquo de fonte susceptus, sed, sicut dicitur Matth. III, *baptizatus Iesus confestim ascendit de aqua.* Ergo videtur quod nec in aliorum Baptismo requiratur aliquis qui baptizatum de sacro fonte suscipiat.

PRAETEREA, Baptismus est spiritualis regeneratio, ut supra dictum est. Sed in carnali generatione non requiritur nisi principium activum, quod est pater, et principium passivum, quod est mater. Cum igitur in Baptismo locum patris obtineat ille qui baptizat, locum autem matris ipsa aqua Baptismi, ut Augustinus dicit, in quodam sermone Epiphaniae; videtur quod non requiratur aliquis alius qui baptizatum de sacro fonte levet.

PRAETEREA, in sacramentis Ecclesiae nihil derisorium fieri debet. Sed hoc derisorium videtur, quod adulti baptizati, qui seipsos sustentare possunt et de sacro fonte exire, ab alio suscipiantur. Ergo videtur quod non requiratur aliquis, praecipue in Baptismo adultorum, qui baptizatum de sacro fonte levet.

SED CONTRA est quod Dionysius dicit, II cap. Eccl. Hier., quod *sacerdotes, assumentes baptizatum, tradunt adductionis susceptori et duci.*

RESPONDEO dicendum quod spiritualis regeneratio, quae fit per Baptismum, assimilatur quodammodo generationi carnali, unde dicitur I Pet. II, *sicut modo geniti infantes rationabiles sine dolo lac concupiscite.* In generatione autem carnali parvulus nuper natus indiget nutrice et paedagogo. Unde et in spirituali generatione Baptismi requiritur aliquis qui fungatur vice nutricis et paedagogi, informando et instruendo eum qui est novitius in fide, de his quae pertinent ad fidem et ad vitam Christianam, ad quod praelati Ecclesiae vacare non possunt, circa communem curam populi occupati, parvuli enim et novitii indigent speciali cura praeter communem. Et ideo requiritur quod aliquis suscipiat baptizatum de sacro fonte quasi in suam instructionem et tutelam. Et hoc est quod Dionysius dicit, ult. cap. Eccl. Hier., *divinis nostris ducibus, idest apostolis, ad mentem venit et visum est suscipere infantes secundum istum modum quod parentes pueri traderent puerum cuidam docto in divinis paedagogo, et reliquum sub ipso puer ageret, sicut sub divino patre et salvationis sanctae susceptore.*

OBJECTION 1: It seems that in Baptism it is not necessary for someone to raise the baptized from the sacred font. For our Baptism is consecrated by Christ's Baptism and is conformed thereto. But Christ when baptized was not raised by anyone from the font, but according to Matt. 3:16, *Jesus being baptized, forthwith came out of the water.* Therefore it seems that neither when others are baptized should anyone raise the baptized from the sacred font.

OBJ. 2: Further, Baptism is a spiritual regeneration, as stated above (A. 3). But in carnal generation nothing else is required but the active principle, i.e., the father, and the passive principle, i.e., the mother. Since, then, in Baptism he that baptizes takes the place of the father, while the very water of Baptism takes the place of the mother, as Augustine says in a sermon on the Epiphany (cxxxv); it seems that there is no further need for someone to raise the baptized from the sacred font.

OBJ. 3: Further, nothing ridiculous should be observed in the sacraments of the Church. But it seems ridiculous that after being baptized, adults who can stand up of themselves and leave the sacred font, should be held up by another. Therefore there seems no need for anyone, especially in the Baptism of adults, to raise the baptized from the sacred font.

ON THE CONTRARY, Dionysius says (*Eccl. Hier.* ii) that *the priests taking the baptized hand him over to his sponsor and guide.*

I ANSWER THAT, The spiritual regeneration, which takes place in Baptism, is in a certain manner likened to carnal generation: wherefore it is written (1 Pet 2:2): *As new-born babes, endowed with reason desire milk without guile.* Now, in carnal generation the new-born child needs nourishment and guidance: wherefore, in spiritual generation also, someone is needed to undertake the office of nurse and tutor by forming and instructing one who is yet a novice in the Faith, concerning things pertaining to Christian faith and mode of life, which the clergy have not the leisure to do through being busy with watching over the people generally: because little children and novices need more than ordinary care. Consequently someone is needed to receive the baptized from the sacred font as though for the purpose of instructing and guiding them. It is to this that Dionysius refers (*Eccl. Hier.* xi) saying: *It occurred to our heavenly guides,* i.e., the Apostles, *and they decided, that infants should be taken charge of thus: that the parents of the child should hand it over to some instructor versed in holy things, who would thenceforth take charge of the child, and be to it a spiritual father and a guide in the road of salvation.*

AD PRIMUM ergo dicendum quod Christus non est baptizatus ut ipse regeneraretur, sed ut alios regeneraret. Et ideo ipse post Baptismum non indiguit paedagogo tanquam parvulus.

AD SECUNDUM dicendum quod in generatione carnali non requiritur ex necessitate nisi pater et mater, sed ad facilem partum, et educationem pueri convenientem, requiritur obstetrix et nutrix et paedagogus. Quorum vicem implet in Baptismo ille qui puerum de sacro fonte levat. Unde non est de necessitate sacramenti, sed unus solus potest in aqua baptizare, necessitate imminente.

AD TERTIUM dicendum quod baptizatus non suscipitur a patrino de sacro fonte propter imbecillitatem corporalem, sed propter imbecillitatem spiritualem, ut dictum est.

REPLY OBJ. 1: Christ was baptized not that He might be regenerated, but that He might regenerate others: wherefore after His Baptism He needed no tutor like other children.

REPLY OBJ. 2: In carnal generation nothing is essential besides a father and a mother: yet to ease the latter in her travail, there is need for a midwife; and for the child to be suitably brought up there is need for a nurse and a tutor: while their place is taken in Baptism by him who raises the child from the sacred font. Consequently this is not essential to the sacrament, and in a case of necessity one alone can baptize with water.

REPLY OBJ. 3: It is not on account of bodily weakness that the baptized is raised from the sacred font by the godparent, but on account of spiritual weakness, as stated above.

Article 8

Whether He Who Raises Anyone from the Sacred Font Is Bound to Instruct Him?

AD OCTAVUM SIC PROCEDITUR. Videtur quod ille qui suscipit aliquem de sacro fonte, non obligetur ad eius instructionem. Quia nullus potest instruere nisi instructus. Sed etiam quidam non instructi sed simplices admittuntur ad aliquem de sacro fonte suscipiendum. Ergo ille qui suscipit baptizatum, non obligatur ad eius instructionem.

PRAETEREA, filius magis a patre instruitur quam ab alio extraneo, nam filius habet a patre, esse et nutrimentum et disciplinam, ut philosophus dicit, VIII Ethic. Si ergo ille qui suscipit baptizatum, tenetur eum instruere, magis esset conveniens quod pater carnalis filium suum de Baptismo suscipiat quam alius. Quod tamen videtur esse prohibitum, ut habetur in decretis, XXX, qu. I, cap. pervenit et dictum est.

PRAETEREA, plures magis possunt instruere quam unus solus. Si ergo ille qui suscipit aliquem baptizatum, teneretur eum instruere, magis deberent plures suscipere quam unus solus. Cuius contrarium habetur in decreto Leonis Papae, *non plures, inquit, ad suscipiendum de Baptismo infantem quam unus accedant, sive vir sive mulier.*

SED CONTRA est quod Augustinus dicit, in quodam sermone paschali, *vos ante omnia, tam viros quam mulieres, qui filios in Baptismate suscepistis, moneo ut vos cognoscatis fideiussores apud Deum exstitisse pro illis quos visi estis de sacro fonte suscipere.*

RESPONDEO dicendum quod unusquisque obligatur ad exequendum officium quod accipit. Dictum est autem quod ille qui suscipit aliquem de sacro fonte, assumit sibi officium paedagogi. Et ideo obligatur ad habendam

OBJECTION 1: It seems that he who raises anyone from the sacred font is not bound to instruct him. For none but those who are themselves instructed can give instruction. But even the uneducated and ill-instructed are allowed to raise people from the sacred font. Therefore he who raises a baptized person from the font is not bound to instruct him.

OBJ. 2: Further, a son is instructed by his father better than by a stranger: for, as the Philosopher says (*Ethic.* viii), a son receives from his father, *being, food, and education.* If, therefore, godparents are bound to instruct their godchildren, it would be fitting for the carnal father, rather than another, to be the godparent of his own child. And yet this seems to be forbidden, as may be seen in the *Decretals* (xxx, qu. 1, Cap. *Pervenit and Dictum est*).

OBJ. 3: Further, it is better for several to instruct than for one only. If, therefore, godparents are bound to instruct their godchildren, it would be better to have several godparents than only one. Yet this is forbidden in a decree of Pope Leo, who says: *A child should not have more than one godparent, be this a man or a woman.*

ON THE CONTRARY, Augustine says in a sermon for Easter (clxviii): *In the first place I admonish you, both men and women, who have raised children in Baptism, that ye stand before God as sureties for those whom you have been seen to raise from the sacred font.*

I ANSWER THAT, Every man is bound to fulfill those duties which he has undertaken to perform. Now it has been stated above (A. 7) that godparents take upon themselves the duties of a tutor. Consequently they are bound to

curam de ipso, si necessitas immineret, sicut eo tempore et loco in quo baptizati inter infideles nutriuntur. Sed ubi nutriuntur inter Catholicos Christianos, satis possunt ab hac cura excusari, praesumendo quod a suis parentibus diligenter instruantur. Si tamen quocumque modo sentirent contrarium, tenerentur secundum suum modum saluti spiritualium filiorum curam impendere.

AD PRIMUM ergo dicendum quod, ubi immineret periculum, oporteret esse aliquem doctum in divinis, sicut Dionysius dicit, qui baptizandum de sacro fonte susciperet. Sed ubi hoc periculum non imminet, propter hoc quod pueri nutriuntur inter Catholicos, admittuntur quicumque ad hoc officium, quia ea quae pertinent ad Christianam vitam et fidem, publice omnibus nota sunt. Et tamen ille qui non est baptizatus non potest suscipere baptizatum, ut est declaratum in Concilio Maguntino, licet nonbaptizatus possit baptizare, quia persona baptizantis est de necessitate sacramenti, non autem persona suscipientis, sicut dictum est.

AD SECUNDUM dicendum quod, sicut est alia generatio spiritualis a carnali, ita etiam debet esse alia disciplina, secundum illud Heb. XII, *patres quidem carnis nostrae habuimus eruditores, et reverebamur eos. Non multo magis obtemperabimus patri spirituum, et vivemus?* Et ideo alius debet esse pater spiritualis a patre carnali, nisi necessitas contrarium exigat.

AD TERTIUM dicendum quod confusio disciplinae esset nisi esset unus principalis instructor. Et ideo in Baptismo unus debet esse principalis susceptor. Alii tamen possunt admitti quasi coadiutores.

watch over their godchildren when there is need for them to do so: for instance when and where children are brought up among unbelievers. But if they are brought up among Catholic Christians, the godparents may well be excused from this responsibility, since it may be presumed that the children will be carefully instructed by their parents. If, however, they perceive in any way that the contrary is the case, they would be bound, as far as they are able, to see to the spiritual welfare of their godchildren.

REPLY OBJ. 1: Where the danger is imminent, the godparent, as Dionysius says (*Eccl. Hier.* vii), should be someone *versed in holy things*. But where the danger is not imminent, by reason of the children being brought up among Catholics, anyone is admitted to this position, because the things pertaining to the Christian rule of life and faith are known openly by all. Nevertheless an unbaptized person cannot be a godparent, as was decreed in the Council of Mainz, although an unbaptized person: because the person baptizing is essential to the sacrament, wherefore as the godparent is not, as stated above (A. 7, ad 2).

REPLY OBJ. 2: Just as spiritual generation is distinct from carnal generation, so is spiritual education distinct from that of the body; according to Heb. 12:9: *Moreover we have had fathers of our flesh for instructors, and we reverenced them: shall we not much more obey the Father of Spirits, and live?* Therefore the spiritual father should be distinct from the carnal father, unless necessity demanded otherwise.

REPLY OBJ. 3: Education would be full of confusion if there were more than one head instructor. Wherefore there should be one principal sponsor in Baptism: but others can be allowed as assistants.

QUESTION 68

THOSE WHO RECEIVE BAPTISM

Deinde considerandum est de suscipientibus Baptismum. Et circa hoc quaeruntur duodecim.

Primo, utrum omnes teneantur ad suscipiendum Baptismum.

Secundo, utrum aliquis possit salvari sine Baptismo.

Tertio, utrum Baptismus sit differendus.

Quarto, utrum peccatores sint baptizandi.

Quinto, utrum peccatoribus baptizatis sint imponenda opera satisfactoria.

Sexto, utrum requiratur confessio peccatorum.

Septimo, utrum requiratur intentio ex parte baptizati.

Octavo, utrum requiratur fides.

Nono, utrum pueri sint baptizandi.

Decimo, utrum pueri Iudaeorum sint baptizandi invitis parentibus.

Undecimo, utrum aliqui sint baptizandi in maternis uteris existentes.

Duodecimo, utrum furiosi et amentes sint baptizandi.

We have now to consider those who receive Baptism; concerning which there are twelve points of inquiry:

(1) Whether all are bound to receive Baptism?

(2) Whether a man can be saved without Baptism?

(3) Whether Baptism should be deferred?

(4) Whether sinners should be baptized?

(5) Whether works of satisfaction should be enjoined on sinners that have been baptized?

(6) Whether Confession of sins is necessary?

(7) Whether an intention is required on the part of the one baptized?

(8) Whether faith is necessary?

(9) Whether infants should be baptized?

(10) Whether the children of Jews should be baptized against the will of their parents?

(11) Whether anyone should be baptized in the mother's womb?

(12) Whether madmen and imbeciles should be baptized?

Article 1

Whether All Are Bound to Receive Baptism?

AD PRIMUM SIC PROCEDITUR. Videtur quod non teneantur omnes ad susceptionem Baptismi. Per Christum enim non est hominibus arctata via salutis. Sed ante Christi adventum poterant homines salvari sine Baptismo. Ergo etiam post Christi adventum.

PRAETEREA, Baptismus maxime videtur esse institutus in remedium peccati originalis. Sed ille qui est baptizatus, cum non habeat originale peccatum, non videtur quod possit transfundere in prolem. Ergo filii baptizatorum non videntur esse baptizandi.

PRAETEREA, Baptismus datur ad hoc quod aliquis per gratiam a peccato mundetur. Sed hoc consequuntur illi qui sunt sanctificati in utero, sine Baptismo. Ergo non tenentur ad suscipiendum Baptismum.

SED CONTRA est quod dicitur Ioan. III, *nisi quis renatus fuerit ex aqua et spiritu sancto, non potest introire in regnum Dei*. Et in libro de ecclesiasticis dogmatibus dicitur, *baptizatis tantum iter salutis esse credimus*.

OBJECTION 1: It seems that not all are bound to receive Baptism. For Christ did not narrow man's road to salvation. But before Christ's coming men could be saved without Baptism: therefore also after Christ's coming.

OBJ. 2: Further, Baptism seems to have been instituted principally as a remedy for original sin. Now, since a man who is baptized is without original sin, it seems that he cannot transmit it to his children. Therefore it seems that the children of those who have been baptized, should not themselves be baptized.

OBJ. 3: Further, Baptism is given in order that a man may, through grace, be cleansed from sin. But those who are sanctified in the womb, obtain this without Baptism. Therefore they are not bound to receive Baptism.

ON THE CONTRARY, It is written (John 3:5): *Unless a man be born again of water and the Holy Spirit, he cannot enter into the kingdom of God*. Again it is stated in *De Eccl. Dogm.* xli, that *we believe the way of salvation to be open to those only who are baptized*.

RESPONDEO dicendum quod ad illud homines tenentur sine quo salutem consequi non possunt. Manifestum est autem quod nullus salutem potest consequi nisi per Christum, unde et apostolus dicit, Rom. V, *sicut per unius delictum in omnes homines in condemnationem, sic et per unius iustitiam in omnes homines in iustificationem vitae.* Ad hoc autem datur Baptismus ut aliquis, per ipsum regeneratus, incorporetur Christo, factus membrum ipsius, unde dicitur Gal. III, *quicumque in Christo baptizati estis, Christum induistis.* Unde manifestum est quod omnes ad Baptismum tenentur; et sine eo non potest esse salus hominibus.

AD PRIMUM ergo dicendum quod nunquam homines potuerunt salvari, etiam ante Christi adventum, nisi fierent membra Christi, quia, ut dicitur Act. IV, *non est aliud nomen datum hominibus in quo oporteat nos salvos fieri.* Sed ante adventum Christi, homines Christo incorporabantur per fidem futuri adventus, cuius fidei signaculum erat circumcisio, ut apostolus dicit, Rom. IV. Ante vero quam circumcisio institueretur, sola fide, ut Gregorius dicit, cum sacrificiorum oblatione, quibus suam fidem antiqui patres profitebantur, homines Christo incorporabantur. Post adventum etiam Christi, homines per fidem Christo incorporantur, secundum illud Ephes. III *habitare Christum per fidem in cordibus vestris.* Sed alio signo manifestatur fides rei iam praesentis quam demonstrabatur quando erat futura, sicut aliis verbis significatur praesens, praeteritum et futurum. Et ideo, licet ipsum sacramentum Baptismi non semper fuerit necessarium ad salutem, fides tamen, cuius Baptismus sacramentum est, semper necessaria fuit.

AD SECUNDUM dicendum quod, sicut in secunda parte dictum est, illi qui baptizantur, renovantur per Baptismum secundum spiritum, corpus tamen remanet subiectum vetustati peccati, secundum illud Rom. VIII, *corpus quidem mortuum est propter peccatum, spiritus vero vivit propter iustificationem.* Unde Augustinus probat, in libro contra Iulianum, quod *non baptizatur in homine quidquid in eo est.* Manifestum est autem quod homo non generat generatione carnali secundum spiritum, sed secundum carnem. Et ideo filii baptizatorum cum peccato originali nascuntur. Unde indigent baptizari.

AD TERTIUM dicendum quod illi qui sunt sanctificati in utero, consequuntur quidem gratiam emundantem a peccato originali, non tamen ex hoc ipso consequuntur characterem, quo Christo configurentur. Et propter hoc, si aliqui nunc sanctificarentur in utero, necesse esset eos baptizari, ut per susceptionem characteris aliis membris Christi conformarentur.

I ANSWER THAT, Men are bound to that without which they cannot obtain salvation. Now it is manifest that no one can obtain salvation but through Christ; wherefore the Apostle says (Rom 5:18): *As by the offense of one unto all men unto condemnation; so also by the justice of one, unto all men unto justification of life.* But for this end is Baptism conferred on a man, that being regenerated thereby, he may be incorporated in Christ, by becoming His member: wherefore it is written (Gal 3:27): *As many of you as have been baptized in Christ, have put on Christ.* Consequently it is manifest that all are bound to be baptized: and that without Baptism there is no salvation for men.

REPLY OBJ. 1: At no time, not even before the coming of Christ, could men be saved unless they became members of Christ: because, as it is written (Acts 4:12), *there is no other name under heaven given to men, whereby we must be saved.* But before Christ's coming, men were incorporated in Christ by faith in His future coming: of which faith circumcision was the *seal*, as the Apostle calls it (Rom 4:11): whereas before circumcision was instituted, men were incorporated in Christ by *faith alone*, as Gregory says (*Moral.* iv), together with the offering of sacrifices, by means of which the Fathers of old made profession of their faith. Again, since Christ's coming, men are incorporated in Christ by faith; according to Eph. 3:17: *That Christ may dwell by faith in your hearts.* But faith in a thing already present is manifested by a sign different from that by which it was manifested when that thing was yet in the future: just as we use other parts of the verb, to signify the present, the past, and the future. Consequently although the sacrament itself of Baptism was not always necessary for salvation, yet faith, of which Baptism is the sacrament, was always necessary.

REPLY OBJ. 2: As we have stated in the I-II, Q. 81, A. 3, ad 2, those who are baptized are renewed in spirit by Baptism, while their body remains subject to the oldness of sin, according to Rom. 8:10: *The body, indeed, is dead because of sin, but the spirit liveth because of justification.* Wherefore Augustine (*Contra Julian.* vi) proves that *not everything that is in man is baptized.* Now it is manifest that in carnal generation man does not beget in respect of his soul, but in respect of his body. Consequently the children of those who are baptized are born with original sin; wherefore they need to be baptized.

REPLY OBJ. 3: Those who are sanctified in the womb, receive indeed grace which cleanses them from original sin, but they do not therefore receive the character, by which they are conformed to Christ. Consequently, if any were to be sanctified in the womb now, they would need to be baptized, in order to be conformed to Christ's other members by receiving the character.

Article 2

Whether a Man Can Be Saved Without Baptism?

AD SECUNDUM SIC PROCEDITUR. Videtur quod sine Baptismo nullus possit salvari. Dicit enim dominus, Ioan. III, *nisi quis renatus fuerit ex aqua et spiritu sancto, non potest introire in regnum Dei.* Sed illi soli salvantur qui regnum Dei intrant. Ergo nullus potest salvari sine Baptismo, quo aliquis regeneratur ex aqua et spiritu sancto.

PRAETEREA, in libro de ecclesiasticis dogmatibus dicitur, *nullum catechumenum, quamvis in bonis operibus defunctum, aeternam vitam habere credimus, excepto martyrio, ubi tota sacramenta Baptismi complentur.* Sed si aliquis sine Baptismo possit salvari, maxime hoc haberet locum in catechumenis bona opera habentibus, qui videntur habere fidem per dilectionem operantem. Videtur ergo quod sine Baptismo nullus possit salvari.

PRAETEREA, sicut supra dictum est, Baptismi sacramentum est de necessitate salutis. Necessarium autem est sine quo non potest aliquid esse, ut dicitur in V Metaphys. Ergo videtur quod sine Baptismo nullus possit consequi salutem.

SED CONTRA est quod Augustinus dicit, super Levit., *invisibilem sanctificationem quibusdam affuisse et profuisse sine visibilibus sacramentis, visibilem vero sanctificationem, quae fit sacramento visibili, sine invisibili posse adesse, sed non prodesse.* Cum ergo sacramentum Baptismi ad visibilem sanctificationem pertineat, videtur quod sine sacramento Baptismi aliquis possit salutem consequi per invisibilem sanctificationem.

RESPONDEO dicendum quod sacramentum Baptismi dupliciter potest alicui deesse. Uno modo, et re et voto, quod contingit in illis qui nec baptizantur nec baptizari volunt. Quod manifeste ad contemptum sacramenti pertinet, quantum ad illos qui habent usum liberi arbitrii. Et ideo hi quibus hoc modo deest Baptismus, salutem consequi non possunt, quia nec sacramentaliter nec mentaliter Christo incorporantur, per quem solum est salus.

Alio modo potest sacramentum Baptismi alicui deesse re, sed non voto, sicut cum aliquis baptizari desiderat, sed aliquo casu praevenitur morte antequam Baptismum suscipiat. Talis autem sine Baptismo actuali salutem consequi potest, propter desiderium Baptismi, quod procedit ex fide per dilectionem operante, per quam Deus interius hominem sanctificat, cuius potentia sacramentis visibilibus non alligatur. Unde Ambrosius dicit de Valentiniano, qui catechumenus mortuus fuit, *quem regeneraturus eram, amisi, veruntamen ille gratiam quam poposcit, non amisit.*

OBJECTION 1: It seems that no man can be saved without Baptism. For our Lord said (John 3:5): *Unless a man be born again of water and the Holy Spirit, he cannot enter the kingdom of God.* But those alone are saved who enter God's kingdom. Therefore none can be saved without Baptism, by which a man is born again of water and the Holy Spirit.

OBJ. 2: Further, in the book *De Eccl. Dogm.* xli, it is written: *We believe that no catechumen, though he die in his good works, will have eternal life, except he suffer martyrdom, which contains all the sacramental virtue of Baptism.* But if it were possible for anyone to be saved without Baptism, this would be the case specially with catechumens who are credited with good works, for they seem to have the *faith that worketh by charity* (Gal 5:6). Therefore it seems that none can be saved without Baptism.

OBJ. 3: Further, as stated above (A. 1; Q. 65, A. 4), the sacrament of Baptism is necessary for salvation. Now that is necessary *without which something cannot be* (Metaph. v). Therefore it seems that none can obtain salvation without Baptism.

ON THE CONTRARY, Augustine says (*Super Levit.* lxxxiv) that *some have received the invisible sanctification without visible sacraments, and to their profit; but though it is possible to have the visible sanctification, consisting in a visible sacrament, without the invisible sanctification, it will be to no profit.* Since, therefore, the sacrament of Baptism pertains to the visible sanctification, it seems that a man can obtain salvation without the sacrament of Baptism, by means of the invisible sanctification.

I ANSWER THAT, The sacrament of Baptism may be wanting to someone in two ways. First, both in reality and in desire; as is the case with those who neither are baptized, nor wished to be baptized: which clearly indicates contempt of the sacrament, in regard to those who have the use of the free-will. Consequently those to whom Baptism is wanting thus, cannot obtain salvation: since neither sacramentally nor mentally are they incorporated in Christ, through Whom alone can salvation be obtained.

Second, the sacrament of Baptism may be wanting to anyone in reality but not in desire: for instance, when a man wishes to be baptized, but by some ill-chance he is forestalled by death before receiving Baptism. And such a man can obtain salvation without being actually baptized, on account of his desire for Baptism, which desire is the outcome of *faith that worketh by charity*, whereby God, Whose power is not tied to visible sacraments, sanctifies man inwardly. Hence Ambrose says of Valentinian, who died while yet a catechumen: *I lost him whom I was to regenerate: but he did not lose the grace he prayed for.*

Ad primum ergo dicendum quod, sicut dicitur I Reg. XVI, *homines vident ea quae parent, dominus autem intuetur cor.* Ille autem qui desiderat per Baptismum regenerari ex aqua et spiritu sancto, corde quidem regeneratus est, licet non corpore, sicut et apostolus dicit, Rom. II, quod *circumcisio cordis est in spiritu, non in littera; cuius laus non ex hominibus, sed ex Deo est.*

Ad secundum dicendum quod nullus pervenit ad vitam aeternam nisi absolutus ab omni culpa et reatu poenae. Quae quidem universalis absolutio fit in perceptione Baptismi, et in martyrio, propter quod dicitur quod in martyrio omnia sacramenta Baptismi complentur, scilicet quantum ad plenam liberationem a culpa et poena. Si quis ergo catechumenus sit habens desiderium Baptismi (quia aliter in bonis operibus non moreretur, quae non possunt esse sine fide per dilectionem operante), talis decedens non statim pervenit ad vitam aeternam, sed patietur poenam pro peccatis praeteritis, *ipse tamen salvus erit sic quasi per ignem*, ut dicitur I Cor. III.

Ad tertium dicendum quod pro tanto dicitur sacramentum Baptismi esse de necessitate salutis, quia non potest esse hominis salus nisi saltem in voluntate habeatur, quae apud Deum reputatur pro facto.

Reply Obj. 1: As it is written (1 Kgs 16:7), *man seeth those things that appear, but the Lord beholdeth the heart.* Now a man who desires to be *born again of water and the Holy Spirit* by Baptism, is regenerated in heart though not in body. Thus the Apostle says (Rom 2:29) that *the circumcision is that of the heart, in the spirit, not in the letter; whose praise is not of men but of God.*

Reply Obj. 2: No man obtains eternal life unless he be free from all guilt and debt of punishment. Now this plenary absolution is given when a man receives Baptism, or suffers martyrdom: for which reason is it stated that martyrdom *contains all the sacramental virtue of Baptism*, i.e., as to the full deliverance from guilt and punishment. Suppose, therefore, a catechumen to have the desire for Baptism (else he could not be said to die in his good works, which cannot be without *faith that worketh by charity*), such a one, were he to die, would not forthwith come to eternal life, but would suffer punishment for his past sins, *but he himself shall be saved, yet so as by fire* as is stated 1 Cor. 3:15.

Reply Obj. 3: The sacrament of Baptism is said to be necessary for salvation in so far as man cannot be saved without, at least, Baptism of desire; *which, with God, counts for the deed* (Augustine, *Enarr.* in Ps. 57).

Article 3

Whether Baptism Should Be Deferred?

Ad tertium sic proceditur. Videtur quod Baptismus sit differendus. Dicit enim Leo Papa, *duo tempora, idest Pascha et Pentecoste, ad baptizandum a Romano pontifice legitima praefixa sunt. Unde dilectionem vestram monemus ut nullos alios dies huic observationi misceatis.* Videtur ergo quod oporteat non statim aliquos baptizari, sed usque ad praedicta tempora Baptismum differri.

Praeterea, in Concilio Agathensi legitur, *Iudaei, quorum perfidia frequenter ad vomitum redit, si ad leges Catholicas venire voluerint, octo menses inter catechumenos Ecclesiae limen introeant, et, si pura fide venire noscantur, tunc demum Baptismi gratiam mereantur.* Non ergo statim sunt homines baptizandi, sed usque ad certum tempus est differendum Baptisma.

Praeterea, sicut dicitur Isaiae XXVII, *iste est omnis fructus, ut auferatur peccatum.* Sed magis videtur auferri peccatum, vel etiam diminui, si Baptismus differatur. Primo quidem, quia peccantes post Baptismum gravius peccant, secundum illud Heb. X, *quanto magis putatis deteriora mereri supplicia qui sanguinem testamenti pollutum duxerit, in quo sanctificatus est*, scilicet per Baptismum? Secundo, quia Baptismus tollit peccata praeterita, non autem futura, unde, quanto Baptismus

Objection 1: It seems that Baptism should be deferred. For Pope Leo says (*Epist. xvi*): *Two seasons*, i.e., Easter and Whitsuntide, *are fixed by the Roman Pontiff for the celebration of Baptism. Wherefore we admonish your Beatitude not to add any other days to this custom.* Therefore it seems that Baptism should be conferred not at once, but delayed until the aforesaid seasons.

Obj. 2: Further, we read in the decrees of the Council of Agde (Can. xxxiv): *If Jews whose bad faith often 'returns to the vomit,' wish to submit to the Law of the Catholic Church, let them for eight months enter the porch of the church with the catechumens; and if they are found to come in good faith then at last they may deserve the grace of Baptism.* Therefore men should not be baptized at once, and Baptism should be deferred for a certain fixed time.

Obj. 3: Further, as we read in Isa. 27:9, *this is all the fruit, that the sin . . . should be taken away.* Now sin seems to be taken away, or at any rate lessened, if Baptism be deferred. First, because those who sin after Baptism, sin more grievously, according to Heb. 10:29: *How much more, do you think, he deserveth worse punishments, who hath . . . esteemed the blood of the testament*, i.e., Baptism, *unclean, by which he was sanctified?* Second, because Baptism takes away past, but not future, sins: wherefore the more it is

magis differtur, tanto plura peccata tollet. Videtur ergo quod Baptismus debeat diu differri.

SED CONTRA est quod dicitur Eccli. V, *ne tardes converti ad dominum, et ne differas de die in diem.* Sed perfecta conversio ad Deum est eorum qui regenerantur in Christo per Baptismum. Non ergo Baptismus debet differri de die in diem.

RESPONDEO dicendum quod circa hoc distinguendum est utrum sint baptizandi pueri vel adulti. Si enim pueri sint baptizandi, non est differendum Baptisma. Primo quidem, quia non expectatur in eis maior instructio, aut etiam plenior conversio. Secundo, propter periculum mortis, quia non potest alio remedio subveniri nisi per sacramentum Baptismi.

Adultis vero subveniri potest per solum Baptismi desiderium, ut supra dictum est. Et ideo adultis non statim cum convertuntur, est sacramentum Baptismi conferendum, sed oportet differre usque ad aliquod certum tempus. Primo quidem, propter cautelam Ecclesiae, ne decipiatur, ficte accedentibus conferens, secundum illud I Ioan. IV, *nolite omni spiritui credere, sed probate spiritus si ex Deo sunt.* Quae quidem probatio sumitur de accedentibus ad Baptismum, quando per aliquod spatium eorum fides et mores examinantur. Secundo, hoc est necessarium ad utilitatem eorum qui baptizantur, quia aliquo temporis spatio indigent ad hoc quod plene instruantur de fide, et exercitentur in his quae pertinent ad vitam Christianam. Tertio, hoc est necessarium ad quandam reverentiam sacramenti, dum in solemnitatibus praecipuis, scilicet Paschae et Pentecostes, homines ad Baptismum admittuntur, et ita devotius sacramentum suscipiunt.

Haec tamen dilatio est praetermittenda duplici ratione. Primo quidem, quando illi qui sunt baptizandi, apparent perfecte instructi in fide et ad Baptismum idonei, sicut Philippus statim baptizavit eunuchum, ut habetur Act. VIII; et Petrus Cornelium et eos qui cum ipso erant, ut habetur Act. X. Secundo, propter infirmitatem, aut aliquod periculum mortis. Unde Leo Papa dicit, *hi qui necessitate mortis, aegritudinis, obsidionis et persecutionis et naufragii, urgentur, omni tempore debent baptizari.* Si tamen aliquis praeveniatur morte, articulo necessitatis sacramentum excludente, dum expectat tempus ab Ecclesia institutum, salvatur, licet per ignem, ut supra dictum est. Peccat autem si ultra tempus ab Ecclesia statutum differret accipere Baptismum, nisi ex causa necessaria et licentia praelatorum Ecclesiae. Sed tamen et hoc peccatum cum aliis deleri potest per succedentem contritionem, quae supplet vicem Baptismi, ut supra dictum est.

AD PRIMUM ergo dicendum quod illud mandatum Leonis Papae de observandis duobus temporibus in Baptismo, intelligendum est, excepto tamen periculo mortis (quod semper in pueris est timendum), ut dictum est.

deferred, the more sins it takes away. Therefore it seems that Baptism should be deferred for a long time.

ON THE CONTRARY, It is written (Sir 5:8): *Delay not to be converted to the Lord, and defer it not from day to day.* But the perfect conversion to God is of those who are regenerated in Christ by Baptism. Therefore Baptism should not be deferred from day to day.

I ANSWER THAT, In this matter we must make a distinction and see whether those who are to be baptized are children or adults. For if they be children, Baptism should not be deferred. First, because in them we do not look for better instruction or fuller conversion. Second, because of the danger of death, for no other remedy is available for them besides the sacrament of Baptism.

On the other hand, adults have a remedy in the mere desire for Baptism, as stated above (A. 2). And therefore Baptism should not be conferred on adults as soon as they are converted, but it should be deferred until some fixed time. First, as a safeguard to the Church, lest she be deceived through baptizing those who come to her under false pretenses, according to 1 John 4:1: *Believe not every spirit, but try the spirits, if they be of God.* And those who approach Baptism are put to this test, when their faith and morals are subjected to proof for a space of time. Second, this is needful as being useful for those who are baptized; for they require a certain space of time in order to be fully instructed in the faith, and to be drilled in those things that pertain to the Christian mode of life. Third, a certain reverence for the sacrament demands a delay whereby men are admitted to Baptism at the principal festivities, viz. of Easter and Pentecost, the result being that they receive the sacrament with greater devotion.

There are, however, two reasons for forgoing this delay. First, when those who are to be baptized appear to be perfectly instructed in the faith and ready for Baptism; thus, Philip baptized the Eunuch at once (Acts 8); and Peter, Cornelius and those who were with him (Acts 10). Second, by reason of sickness or some kind of danger of death. Wherefore Pope Leo says (*Epist. xvi*): *Those who are threatened by death, sickness, siege, persecution, or shipwreck, should be baptized at any time.* Yet if a man is forestalled by death, so as to have no time to receive the sacrament, while he awaits the season appointed by the Church, he is saved, yet *so as by fire*, as stated above (A. 2, ad 2). Nevertheless he sins if he defer being baptized beyond the time appointed by the Church, except this be for an unavoidable cause and with the permission of the authorities of the Church. But even this sin, with his other sins, can be washed away by his subsequent contrition, which takes the place of Baptism, as stated above (Q. 66, A. 11).

REPLY OBJ. 1: This decree of Pope Leo, concerning the celebration of Baptism at two seasons, is to be understood *with the exception of the danger of death* (which is always to be feared in children) as stated above.

AD SECUNDUM dicendum quod illud de Iudaeis est statutum ad Ecclesiae cautelam, ne simplicium fidem corrumpant, si non fuerint plene conversi. Et tamen, ut ibidem subditur, *si infra tempus praescriptum aliquod periculum infirmitatis incurrerint, debent baptizari.*

AD TERTIUM dicendum quod Baptismus per gratiam quam confert non solum removet peccata praeterita, sed etiam impedit peccata futura ne fiant. Hoc autem considerandum est, ut homines non peccent, secundarium est ut levius peccent, vel etiam ut eorum peccata mundentur; secundum illud I Ioan. II, *filioli mei, haec scribo vobis ut non peccetis. Sed et si quis peccaverit, advocatum habemus apud patrem Iesum Christum iustum, et ipse est propitiatio pro peccatis nostris.*

REPLY OBJ. 2: This decree concerning the Jews was for a safeguard to the Church, lest they corrupt the faith of simple people, if they be not fully converted. Nevertheless, as the same passage reads further on, *if within the appointed time they are threatened with danger of sickness, they should be baptized.*

REPLY OBJ. 3: Baptism, by the grace which it bestows, removes not only past sins, but hinders the commission of future sins. Now this is the point to be considered—that men may not sin: it is a secondary consideration that their sins be less grievous, or that their sins be washed away, according to 1 John 2:1, 2: *My little children, these things I write to you, that you may not sin. But if any man sin, we have an advocate with the Father, Jesus Christ the just; and He is the propitiation for our sins.*

Article 4

Whether Sinners Should Be Baptized?

AD QUARTUM SIC PROCEDITUR. Videtur quod peccatores sint baptizandi. Dicitur enim Zach. XIII, *in die illa erit fons patens domui David et habitantibus Ierusalem in ablutionem peccatoris et menstruatae*, quod quidem intelligitur de fonte baptismali. Ergo videtur quod sacramentum Baptismi sit etiam peccatoribus exhibendum.

PRAETEREA, dominus dicit, Matth. IX, *non est opus valentibus medicus, sed male habentibus.* Male autem habentes sunt peccatores. Cum igitur spiritualis medici, scilicet Christi, medicina sit Baptismus, videtur quod peccatoribus sacramentum Baptismi sit exhibendum.

PRAETEREA, nullum subsidium peccatoribus debet subtrahi. Sed peccatores baptizati ex ipso charactere baptismali spiritualiter adiuvantur, cum sit quaedam dispositio ad gratiam. Ergo videtur quod sacramentum Baptismi sit peccatoribus exhibendum.

SED CONTRA est quod Augustinus dicit, *qui creavit te sine te, non iustificabit te sine te.* Sed peccator, cum habeat voluntatem non dispositam, non cooperatur Deo. Ergo frustra adhibetur sibi Baptismus ad iustificationem.

RESPONDEO dicendum quod aliquis potest dici peccator dupliciter. Uno modo, propter maculam et reatum praeteritum. Et sic peccatoribus est sacramentum Baptismi conferendum, quia est ad hoc specialiter institutum ut per ipsum peccatorum sordes mundentur, secundum illud Ephes. V, *mundans eam, scilicet Ecclesiam, lavacro aquae in verbo vitae.*

Alio modo potest dici aliquis peccator ex voluntate peccandi et proposito persistendi in peccato. Et sic peccatoribus non est sacramentum Baptismi conferendum.

OBJECTION 1: It seems that sinners should be baptized. For it is written (Zech 13:1): *In that day there shall be a fountain open to the House of David, and to the inhabitants of Jerusalem: for the washing of the sinner and of the unclean woman*: and this is to be understood of the fountain of Baptism. Therefore it seems that the sacrament of Baptism should be offered even to sinners.

OBJ. 2: Further, our Lord said (Matt 9:12): *They that are in health need not a physician, but they that are ill.* But they that are ill are sinners. Therefore since Baptism is the remedy of Christ the physician of our souls, it seems that this sacrament should be offered to sinners.

OBJ. 3: Further, no assistance should be withdrawn from sinners. But sinners who have been baptized derive spiritual assistance from the very character of Baptism, since it is a disposition to grace. Therefore it seems that the sacrament of Baptism should be offered to sinners.

ON THE CONTRARY, Augustine says (*Serm. clxix*): *He Who created thee without thee, will not justify thee without thee.* But since a sinner's will is ill-disposed, he does not cooperate with God. Therefore it is useless to employ Baptism as a means of justification.

I ANSWER THAT, A man may be said to be a sinner in two ways. First, on account of the stain and the debt of punishment incurred in the past: and on sinners in this sense the sacrament of Baptism should be conferred, since it is instituted specially for this purpose, that by it the uncleanness of sin may be washed away, according to Eph. 5:26: *Cleansing it by the laver of water in the word of life.*

Second, a man may be called a sinner because he wills to sin and purposes to remain in sin: and on sinners in this sense the sacrament of Baptism should not be conferred.

Primo quidem, quia per Baptismum homines Christo incorporantur, secundum illud Galat. III, *quicumque in Christo baptizati estis, Christum induistis.* Quandiu autem aliquis habet voluntatem peccandi, non potest esse Christo coniunctus, secundum illud II Cor. VI, *quae participatio iustitiae cum iniquitate?* Unde et Augustinus dicit, in libro de poenitentia, quod *nullus suae voluntatis arbiter constitutus potest novam vitam inchoare, nisi eum veteris vitae poeniteat.* Secundo, quia in operibus Christi et Ecclesiae nihil debet fieri frustra. Frustra autem est quod non pertingit ad finem ad quem est ordinatum. Nullus autem habens voluntatem peccandi simul potest a peccato mundari, ad quod ordinatur Baptismus, quia hoc esset ponere contradictoria esse simul. Tertio, quia in sacramentalibus signis non debet esse aliqua falsitas. Est autem signum falsum cui res significata non respondet. Ex hoc autem quod aliquis lavandum se praebet per Baptismum, significatur quod se disponat ad interiorem ablutionem. Quod non contingit de eo qui habet propositum persistendi in peccato. Unde manifestum est quod talibus sacramentum Baptismi non est conferendum.

AD PRIMUM ergo dicendum quod illud verbum est intelligendum de peccatoribus qui habent voluntatem recedendi a peccato.

AD SECUNDUM dicendum quod spiritualis medicus, scilicet Christus, dupliciter operatur. Uno modo, interius per seipsum, et sic praeparat voluntatem hominis ut bonum velit et malum odiat. Alio modo operatur per ministros, exterius adhibendo sacramenta, et sic operatur perficiendo id quod est exterius inchoatum. Et ideo sacramentum Baptismi non est exhibendum nisi ei in quo interioris conversionis aliquod signum apparet, sicut nec medicina corporalis adhibetur infirmo nisi in eo aliquis motus vitalis appareat.

AD TERTIUM dicendum quod Baptismus est fidei sacramentum. Fides autem informis non sufficit ad salutem, nec ipsa est fundamentum, sed sola fides formata, quae per dilectionem operatur, ut Augustinus dicit, in libro de fide et operibus. Unde nec sacramentum Baptismi salutem conferre potest cum voluntate peccandi, quae fidei formam excludit. Non autem est per impressionem characteris baptismalis aliquis disponendus ad gratiam, quandiu apparet in eo voluntas peccandi, quia, Deus neminem ad virtutem compellit, sicut Damascenus dicit.

First, indeed, because by Baptism men are incorporated in Christ, according to Gal. 3:27: *As many of you as have been baptized in Christ, have put on Christ.* Now so long as a man wills to sin, he cannot be united to Christ, according to 2 Cor. 6:14: *What participation hath justice with injustice?* Wherefore Augustine says in his book on Penance (*Serm. cccli*) that *no man who has the use of free-will can begin the new life, except he repent of his former life.* Second, because there should be nothing useless in the works of Christ and of the Church. Now that is useless which does not reach the end to which it is ordained; and, on the other hand, no one having the will to sin can, at the same time, be cleansed from sin, which is the purpose of Baptism; for this would be to combine two contradictory things. Third, because there should be no falsehood in the sacramental signs. Now a sign is false if it does not correspond with the thing signified. But the very fact that a man presents himself to be cleansed by Baptism, signifies that he prepares himself for the inward cleansing: while this cannot be the case with one who purposes to remain in sin. Therefore it is manifest that on such a man the sacrament of Baptism is not to be conferred.

REPLY OBJ. 1: The words quoted are to be understood of those sinners whose will is set on renouncing sin.

REPLY OBJ. 2: The physician of souls, i.e., Christ, works in two ways. First, inwardly, by Himself: and thus He prepares man's will so that it wills good and hates evil. Second, He works through ministers, by the outward application of the sacraments: and in this way His work consists in perfecting what was begun outwardly. Therefore the sacrament of Baptism is not to be conferred save on those in whom there appears some sign of their interior conversion: just as neither is bodily medicine given to a sick man, unless he show some sign of life.

REPLY OBJ. 3: Baptism is the sacrament of faith. Now dead faith does not suffice for salvation; nor is it the foundation, but living faith alone, *that worketh by charity* (Gal 5:6), as Augustine says (*De Fide et oper.*). Neither, therefore, can the sacrament of Baptism give salvation to a man whose will is set on sinning, and hence expels the form of faith. Moreover, the impression of the baptismal character cannot dispose a man for grace as long as he retains the will to sin; for *God compels no man to be virtuous*, as Damascene says (*De Fide Orth.* ii).

Article 5

Whether Works of Satisfaction Should Be Enjoined on Sinners That Have Been Baptized?

AD QUINTUM SIC PROCEDITUR. Videtur quod peccatoribus baptizatis sint opera satisfactoria imponenda. Hoc enim ad iustitiam Dei pertinere videtur, ut pro quolibet peccato aliquis puniatur, secundum illud Eccle. ult., *cuncta quae fiunt adducet Deus in iudicium.* Sed opera satisfactoria imponuntur peccatoribus in poenam praeteritorum peccatorum. Ergo videtur quod peccatoribus baptizatis sint opera satisfactoria imponenda.

PRAETEREA, per opera satisfactoria exercitantur peccatores de novo conversi ad iustitiam, et subtrahuntur occasiones peccandi, nam *satisfacere est peccatorum causas excidere et peccatis aditum non indulgere.* Sed hoc maxime necessarium est nuper baptizatis. Ergo videtur quod opera satisfactoria sint baptizatis iniungenda.

PRAETEREA, non minus debitum est ut homo Deo satisfaciat quam proximo. Sed nuper baptizatis iniungendum est quod satisfaciant proximis, si eos laeserunt. Ergo etiam est eis iniungendum ut Deo satisfaciant per opera poenitentiae.

SED CONTRA est quod Ambrosius, super Rom. XI, *sine poenitentia sunt dona Dei et vocatio,* dicit, *gratia Dei in Baptismo non requirit gemitum neque planctum, vel etiam opus aliquod, sed solam fidem, et omnia gratis condonat.*

RESPONDEO dicendum quod, sicut apostolus dicit, Rom. VI, *quicumque baptizati sumus in Christo Iesu, in morte ipsius baptizati sumus, consepulti enim sumus ei per Baptismum in mortem,* ita scilicet quod homo per Baptismum incorporatur ipsi morti Christi. Manifestum est autem ex supra dictis quod mors Christi satisfactoria fuit sufficienter pro peccatis, *non solum nostris, sed etiam totius mundi,* ut dicitur I Ioan. II. Et ideo ei qui baptizatur pro quibuscumque peccatis non est aliqua satisfactio iniungenda, hoc autem esset iniuriam facere passioni et morti Christi, quasi ipsa non esset sufficiens ad plenariam satisfactionem pro peccatis baptizandorum.

AD PRIMUM ergo dicendum quod, sicut Augustinus dicit, in libro de Baptismo parvulorum, *ad hoc Baptismus valet ut baptizati Christo incorporentur ut membra eius.* Unde ipsa poena Christi fuit satisfactoria pro peccatis baptizandorum, sicut et poena unius membri potest esse satisfactoria pro peccato alterius membri. Unde Isaiae LIII dicitur, *vere languores nostros ipse tulit, et dolores nostros ipse portavit.*

AD SECUNDUM dicendum quod nuper baptizati exercitandi sunt ad iustitiam, non per opera poenalia, sed per opera facilia, *ut quasi quodam lacte facilis*

OBJECTION 1: It seems that works of satisfaction should be enjoined on sinners that have been baptized. For God's justice seems to demand that a man should be punished for every sin of his, according to Eccles. 12:14: *All things that are done, God will bring into judgment.* But works of satisfaction are enjoined on sinners in punishment of past sins. Therefore it seems that works of satisfaction should be enjoined on sinners that have been baptized.

OBJ. 2: Further, by means of works of satisfaction sinners recently converted are drilled into righteousness, and are made to avoid the occasions of sin: *for satisfaction consists in extirpating the causes of vice, and closing the doors to sin* (De Eccl. Dogm. iv). But this is most necessary in the case of those who have been baptized recently. Therefore it seems that works of satisfaction should be enjoined on sinners.

OBJ. 3: Further, man owes satisfaction to God not less than to his neighbor. But if those who were recently baptized have injured their neighbor, they should be told to make reparation to God by works of penance.

ON THE CONTRARY, Ambrose commenting on Rom. 11:29: *The gifts and the calling of God are without repentance,* says: *The grace of God requires neither sighs nor groans in Baptism, nor indeed any work at all, but faith alone; and remits all, gratis.*

I ANSWER THAT, As the Apostle says (Rom 6:3, 4), *all we who are baptized in Christ Jesus, are baptized in His death: for we are buried together with Him, by Baptism unto death;* which is to say that by Baptism man is incorporated in the very death of Christ. Now it is manifest from what has been said above (Q. 48, AA. 2, 4; Q. 49, A. 3) that Christ's death satisfied sufficiently for sins, *not for ours only, but also for those of the whole world,* according to 1 John 2:2. Consequently no kind of satisfaction should be enjoined on one who is being baptized, for any sins whatever: and this would be to dishonor the Passion and death of Christ, as being insufficient for the plenary satisfaction for the sins of those who were to be baptized.

REPLY OBJ. 1: As Augustine says in his book on Infant Baptism (De Pecc. Merit. et Remiss. i), *the effect of Baptism is to make those, who are baptized, to be incorporated in Christ as His members.* Wherefore the very pains of Christ were satisfactory for the sins of those who were to be baptized; just as the pain of one member can be satisfactory for the sin of another member. Hence it is written (Isa 53:4): *Surely He hath borne our infirmities and carried our sorrows.*

REPLY OBJ. 2: Those who have been lately baptized should be drilled into righteousness, not by penal, but by *easy works, so as to advance to perfection by taking exercise,*

exercitii promoveantur ad perfectiora, ut Glossa dicit, super illud Psalmi, *sicut ablactatus super matre sua.* Unde et dominus discipulos suos de novo conversos a ieiunio excusavit, ut patet Matth. IX. Et hoc est quod dicitur I Pet. II, *sicut modo geniti infantes lac concupiscite, ut in eo crescatis in salutem.*

AD TERTIUM dicendum quod restituere male ablata proximis, et satisfacere de iniuriis illatis, est cessare a peccando, quia hoc ipsum quod est detinere aliena et proximum non placare, est peccatum. Et ideo peccatoribus baptizatis iniungendum est quod satisfaciant proximis, sicut et quod desistant a peccato. Non est autem eis iniungendum quod pro peccatis praeteritis aliquam poenam patiantur.

as infants by taking milk, as a gloss says on Ps. 130:2: *As a child that is weaned is towards his mother.* For this reason did our Lord excuse His disciples from fasting when they were recently converted, as we read in Matt. 9:14, 15: and the same is written 1 Pet. 2:2: *As new-born babes desire . . . milk . . . that thereby you may grow unto salvation.*

REPLY OBJ. 3: To restore what has been ill taken from one's neighbor, and to make satisfaction for wrong done to him, is to cease from sin: for the very fact of retaining what belongs to another and of not being reconciled to one's neighbor, is a sin. Wherefore those who are baptized should be enjoined to make satisfaction to their neighbor, as also to desist from sin. But they are not to be enjoined to suffer any punishment for past sins.

Article 6

Whether Sinners Who Are Going to Be Baptized Are Bound to Confess Their Sins?

AD SEXTUM SIC PROCEDITUR. Videtur quod peccatores ad Baptismum accedentes teneantur sua peccata confiteri. Dicitur enim Matth. III quod *baptizabantur multi a Ioanne in Iordane, confitentes peccata sua.* Sed Baptismus Christi est perfectior quam Baptismus Ioannis. Ergo videtur quod multo magis illi qui sunt baptizandi Baptismo Christo, debeant sua peccata confiteri.

PRAETEREA, Prov. XXVIII dicitur, *qui abscondit scelera sua, non dirigetur, qui autem confessus fuerit et reliquerit ea, misericordiam consequetur.* Sed ad hoc aliqui baptizantur ut de peccatis suis misericordiam consequantur. Ergo baptizandi debent sua peccata confiteri.

PRAETEREA, poenitentia requiritur ante Baptismum, secundum illud Act. II, *agite poenitentiam, et baptizetur unusquisque vestrum.* Sed confessio est pars poenitentiae. Ergo videtur quod confessio peccatorum requiratur ante Baptismum.

SED CONTRA est quod confessio peccatorum debet esse cum fletu, ut dicit Augustinus, in libro de poenitentia, *omnis ista varietas consideranda est et deflenda.* Sed, sicut Ambrosius dicit, *gratia Dei in Baptismo non requirit gemitum neque planctum.* Ergo a baptizandis non est requirenda confessio peccatorum.

RESPONDEO dicendum quod duplex est peccatorum confessio. Una quidem interior, quae fit Deo. Et talis confessio peccatorum requiritur ante Baptismum, ut scilicet homo, peccata sua recogitans, de eis doleat, *non enim potest inchoare novam vitam, nisi poeniteat eum veteris vitae,* ut Augustinus dicit, in libro de poenitentia. Alia vero est confessio peccatorum exterior, quae fit sacerdoti. Et talis confessio non requiritur ante Baptismum. Primo quidem, quia talis confessio, cum respiciat personam

OBJECTION 1: It seems that sinners who are going to be baptized are bound to confess their sins. For it is written (Matt 3:6) that many *were baptized* by John *in the Jordan confessing their sins.* But Christ's Baptism is more perfect than John's. Therefore it seems that there is yet greater reason why they who are about to receive Christ's Baptism should confess their sins.

OBJ. 2: Further, it is written (Prov 28:13): *He that hideth his sins, shall not prosper; but he that shall confess and forsake them, shall obtain mercy.* Now for this is a man baptized, that he may obtain mercy for his sins. Therefore those who are going to be baptized should confess their sins.

OBJ. 3: Further, Penance is required before Baptism, according to Acts 2:38: *Do penance and be baptized every one of you.* But confession is a part of Penance. Therefore it seems that confession of sins should take place before Baptism.

ON THE CONTRARY, Confession of sins should be sorrowful: thus Augustine says (*De Vera et Falsa Poenit.* xiv): *All these circumstances should be taken into account and deplored.* Now, as Ambrose says on Rom. 11:29, *the grace of God requires neither sighs nor groans in Baptism.* Therefore confession of sins should not be required of those who are going to be baptized.

I ANSWER THAT, Confession of sins is twofold. One is made inwardly to God: and such confession of sins is required before Baptism: in other words, man should call his sins to mind and sorrow for them; since *he cannot begin the new life, except he repent of his former life*, as Augustine says in his book on Penance (*Serm. ccli*). The other is the outward confession of sins, which is made to a priest; and such confession is not required before Baptism. First, because this confession, since it is directed to the person of

ministri, pertinet ad poenitentiae sacramentum, quod non requiritur ante Baptismum, qui est ianua omnium sacramentorum. Secundo, quia confessio exterior, quae fit sacerdoti, ordinatur ad hoc quod sacerdos confitentem absolvat a peccatis, et liget ad opera satisfactoria, quae baptizatis non sunt imponenda, ut supra dictum est. Nec etiam baptizati indigent remissione peccatorum per claves Ecclesiae, quibus omnia remittuntur per Baptismum. Tertio, quia ipsa particularis confessio homini facta est poenosa, propter verecundiam confitentis. Baptizato autem nulla exterior poena imponitur.

Et ideo a baptizatis non requiritur specialis confessio peccatorum, sed sufficit generalis, quam faciunt cum, secundum ritum Ecclesiae, abrenuntiant Satanae et omnibus operibus eius. Et hoc modo dicit quaedam Glossa Matth. III, quod *in Baptismo Ioannis exemplum datur baptizandis confitendi peccata et promittendi meliora.*

Si qui tamen baptizandi ex devotione sua peccata confiteri vellent, esset eorum confessio audienda, non ad hoc quod satisfactio eis imponeretur; sed ad hoc quod contra peccata consueta eis spiritualis vitae informatio tradatur.

AD PRIMUM ergo dicendum quod in Baptismo Ioannis non remittebantur peccata, sed erat Baptismus poenitentiae. Et ideo accedentes ad illud Baptisma convenienter confitebantur peccata, ut secundum qualitatem peccatorum eis poenitentia determinaretur. Sed Baptismus Christi est sine exteriori poenitentia, ut Ambrosius dicit. Unde non est similis ratio.

AD SECUNDUM dicendum quod baptizatis sufficit confessio interior Deo facta, et etiam exterior generalis, ad hoc quod dirigantur et misericordiam consequantur, nec requiritur confessio specialis exterior, ut dictum est.

AD TERTIUM dicendum quod confessio est pars poenitentiae sacramentalis, quae non requiritur ante Baptismum, ut dictum est, sed requiritur interioris poenitentiae virtus.

the minister, belongs to the sacrament of Penance, which is not required before Baptism, which is the door of all the sacraments. Second, because the reason why a man makes outward confession to a priest, is that the priest may absolve him from his sins, and bind him to works of satisfaction, which should not be enjoined on the baptized, as stated above (A. 5). Moreover those who are being baptized do not need to be released from their sins by the keys of the Church, since all are forgiven them in Baptism. Third, because the very act of confession made to a man is penal, by reason of the shame it inflicts on the one confessing: whereas no exterior punishment is enjoined on a man who is being baptized.

Therefore no special confession of sins is required of those who are being baptized; but that general confession suffices which they make when in accordance with the Church's ritual they *renounce Satan and all his works.* And in this sense a gloss explains Matt. 3:6, saying that in John's Baptism *those who are going to be baptized learn that they should confess their sins and promise to amend their life.*

If, however, any persons about to be baptized, wish, out of devotion, to confess their sins, their confession should be heard; not for the purpose of enjoining them to do satisfaction, but in order to instruct them in the spiritual life as a remedy against their vicious habits.

REPLY OBJ. 1: Sins were not forgiven in John's Baptism, which, however, was the Baptism of Penance. Consequently it was fitting that those who went to receive that Baptism, should confess their sins, so that they should receive a penance in proportion to their sins. But Christ's Baptism is without outward penance, as Ambrose says (on Rom 11:29); and therefore there is no comparison.

REPLY OBJ. 2: It is enough that the baptized make inward confession to God, and also an outward general confession, for them to *prosper and obtain mercy*: and they need no special outward confession, as stated above.

REPLY OBJ. 3: Confession is a part of sacramental Penance, which is not required before Baptism, as stated above: but the inward virtue of Penance is required.

Article 7

Whether the Intention of Receiving the Sacrament of Baptism Is Required on the Part of the One Baptized?

AD SEPTIMUM SIC PROCEDITUR. Videtur quod ex parte baptizati non requiratur intentio suscipiendi sacramentum Baptismi. Baptizatus enim se habet sicut patiens in sacramento. Intentio autem non requiritur ex parte patientis, sed ex parte agentis. Ergo videtur quod ex parte baptizati non requiratur intentio suscipiendi Baptismum.

OBJECTION 1: It seems that the intention of receiving the sacrament of Baptism is not required on the part of the one baptized. For the one baptized is, as it were, *patient* in the sacrament. But an intention is required not on the part of the patient but on the part of the agent. Therefore it seems that the intention of receiving Baptism is not required on the part of the one baptized.

PRAETEREA, si praetermittatur id quod requiritur ad Baptismum, homo est denuo baptizandus, sicut cum praetermittitur invocatio Trinitatis, sicut supra dictum est. Sed ex hoc non videtur aliquis denuo baptizandus quod intentionem non habebat suscipiendi Baptismum, alioquin, cum de intentione baptizati non constet, quilibet posset petere se denuo baptizari propter intentionis defectum. Non videtur ergo quod intentio requiratur ex parte baptizati ut suscipiat sacramentum.

PRAETEREA, Baptismus contra peccatum originale datur. Sed originale peccatum contrahitur sine intentione nascentis. Ergo Baptismus, ut videtur, intentionem non requirit ex parte baptizati.

SED CONTRA est quod, secundum ritum Ecclesiae, baptizandi profitentur se petere ab Ecclesia Baptismum. Per quod profitentur suam intentionem de susceptione sacramenti.

RESPONDEO dicendum quod per Baptismum aliquis moritur veteri vitae peccati, et incipit quandam vitae novitatem, secundum illud Rom. VI, *consepulti sumus Christo per Baptismum in mortem, ut, quomodo Christus resurrexit a mortuis, ita et nos in novitate vitae ambulemus.* Et ideo, sicut ad hoc quod homo moriatur veteri vitae, requiritur, secundum Augustinum, in habente usum liberi arbitrii, voluntas qua eum veteris vitae poeniteat; ita requiritur voluntas qua intendat vitae novitatem, cuius principium est ipsa susceptio sacramenti. Et ideo ex parte baptizati requiritur voluntas, sive intentio, suscipiendi sacramentum.

AD PRIMUM ergo dicendum quod in iustificatione, quae fit per Baptismum, non est passio coacta, sed voluntaria. Et ideo requiritur intentio recipiendi id quod ei datur.

AD SECUNDUM dicendum quod, si in adulto deesset intentio suscipiendi sacramentum, esset rebaptizandus. Si tamen hoc non constaret, esset dicendum, si non es baptizatus, ego te baptizo.

AD TERTIUM dicendum quod Baptismus ordinatur non solum contra originale peccatum, sed etiam contra actualia, quae per voluntatem et intentionem causantur.

OBJ. 2: Further, if what is necessary for Baptism be omitted, the Baptism must be repeated; for instance, if the invocation of the Trinity be omitted, as stated above (Q. 66, A. 9, ad 3). But it does not seem that a man should be rebaptized through not having had the intention of receiving Baptism: else, since his intention cannot be proved, anyone might ask to be baptized again on account of his lack of intention. Therefore it seems that no intention is required on the part of the one baptized, in order that he receive the sacrament.

OBJ. 3: Further, Baptism is given as a remedy for original sin. But original sin is contracted without the intention of the person born. Therefore, seemingly, Baptism requires no intention on the part of the person baptized.

ON THE CONTRARY, According to the Church's ritual, those who are to be baptized ask of the Church that they may receive Baptism: and thus they express their intention of receiving the sacrament.

I ANSWER THAT, By Baptism a man dies to the old life of sin, and begins a certain newness of life, according to Rom. 6:4: *We are buried together with* Christ *by Baptism into death; that, as Christ is risen from the dead . . . so we also may walk in newness of life.* Consequently, just as, according to Augustine (*Serm. cccli*), he who has the use of free-will, must, in order to die to the old life, *will to repent of his former life*; so must he, of his own will, intend to lead a new life, the beginning of which is precisely the receiving of the sacrament. Therefore on the part of the one baptized, it is necessary for him to have the will or intention of receiving the sacrament.

REPLY OBJ. 1: When a man is justified by Baptism, his passiveness is not violent but voluntary: wherefore it is necessary for him to intend to receive that which is given him.

REPLY OBJ. 2: If an adult lack the intention of receiving the sacrament, he must be rebaptized. But if there be doubt about this, the form to be used should be: *If thou art not baptized, I baptize thee.*

REPLY OBJ. 3: Baptism is a remedy not only against original, but also against actual sins, which are caused by our will and intention.

Article 8

Whether Faith Is Required on the Part of the One Baptized?

AD OCTAVUM SIC PROCEDITUR. Videtur quod fides requiratur ex parte baptizati. Sacramentum enim Baptismi a Christo est institutum. Sed Christus, formam Baptismi tradens, fidem Baptismo praemittit, dicens, Marc.

OBJECTION 1: It seems that faith is required on the part of the one baptized. For the sacrament of Baptism was instituted by Christ. But Christ, in giving the form of Baptism, makes faith to precede Baptism (Mark 16:16): *He that*

ult., *qui crediderit et baptizatus fuerit, salvus erit.* Ergo videtur quod, nisi sit fides, non possit esse sacramentum Baptismi.

PRAETEREA, nihil frustra in sacramentis Ecclesiae agitur. Sed secundum ritum Ecclesiae, qui accedit ad Baptismum de fide interrogatur, cum dicitur, *credis in Deum patrem omnipotentem?* Ergo videtur quod fides ad Baptismum requiratur.

PRAETEREA, ad Baptismum requiritur intentio suscipiendi sacramentum. Sed hoc non potest esse sine recta fide, cum Baptismus sit rectae fidei sacramentum, per eum enim incorporantur homines Christo, ut Augustinus dicit, in libro de Baptismo parvulorum; hoc autem esse non potest sine recta fide, secundum illud Ephes. III, *habitare Christum per fidem in cordibus vestris.* Ergo videtur quod ille qui non habet rectam fidem, non possit suscipere sacramentum Baptismi.

PRAETEREA, infidelitas est gravissimum peccatum, ut in secunda parte habitum est. Sed permanentes in peccato non sunt baptizandi. Ergo nec etiam permanentes in infidelitate.

SED CONTRA est quod Gregorius, scribens Quirico episcopo, dicit, *ab antiqua patrum institutione didicimus ut qui apud haeresim in Trinitatis nomine baptizantur, cum ad sanctam Ecclesiam redeunt, aut unctione chrismatis, aut impositione manus, aut sola professione fidei, ad sinum matris Ecclesiae revocentur.* Hoc autem non esset, si fides ex necessitate requireretur ad susceptionem Baptismi.

RESPONDEO dicendum quod, sicut ex dictis patet, duo efficiuntur in anima per Baptismum, scilicet character et gratia. Dupliciter ergo aliquid ex necessitate requiritur ad Baptismum. Uno modo, sine quo gratia haberi non potest, quae est ultimus effectus sacramenti. Et hoc modo recta fides ex necessitate requiritur ad Baptismum, quia, sicut dicitur Rom. III, *iustitia Dei est per fidem Iesu Christi.*

Alio modo requiritur aliquid ex necessitate ad Baptismum, sine quo character Baptismi imprimi non potest. Et sic recta fides baptizati non requiritur ex necessitate ad Baptismum, sicut nec recta fides baptizantis, dummodo adsint cetera quae sunt de necessitate sacramenti. Non enim sacramentum perficitur per iustitiam hominis dantis vel suscipientis Baptismum, sed per virtutem Dei.

AD PRIMUM ergo dicendum quod dominus loquitur ibi de Baptismo secundum quod perducit homines ad salutem secundum gratiam iustificantem, quod quidem sine recta fide esse non potest. Et ideo signanter dicit, *qui crediderit et baptizatus fuerit, salvus erit.*

AD SECUNDUM dicendum quod Ecclesia intendit homines baptizare ut emundentur a peccato, secundum illud Isaiae XXVII, *hic est omnis fructus, ut auferatur*

believeth and is baptized, shall be saved. Therefore it seems that without faith there can be no sacrament of Baptism.

OBJ. 2: Further, nothing useless is done in the sacraments of the Church. But according to the Church's ritual, the man who comes to be baptized is asked concerning his faith: *Dost thou believe in God the Father Almighty?* Therefore it seems that faith is required for Baptism.

OBJ. 3: Further, the intention of receiving the sacrament is required for Baptism. But this cannot be without right faith, since Baptism is the sacrament of right faith: for thereby men *are incorporated in Christ,* as Augustine says in his book on Infant Baptism (*De Pecc. Merit. et Remiss.* i); and this cannot be without right faith, according to Eph. 3:17: *That Christ may dwell by faith in your hearts.* Therefore it seems that a man who has not right faith cannot receive the sacrament of Baptism.

OBJ. 4: Further, unbelief is a most grievous sin, as we have shown in the Second Part (II-II, Q. 10, A. 3). But those who remain in sin should not be baptized: therefore neither should those who remain in unbelief.

ON THE CONTRARY, Gregory writing to the bishop Quiricus says: *We have learned from the ancient tradition of the Fathers that when heretics, baptized in the name of the Trinity, come back to Holy Church, they are to be welcomed to her bosom, either with the anointing of chrism, or the imposition of hands, or the mere profession of faith.* But such would not be the case if faith were necessary for a man to receive Baptism.

I ANSWER THAT, As appears from what has been said above (Q. 63, A. 6; Q. 66, A. 9) Baptism produces a twofold effect in the soul, viz. the character and grace. Therefore in two ways may a thing be necessary for Baptism. First, as something without which grace, which is the ultimate effect of the sacrament, cannot be had. And thus right faith is necessary for Baptism, because, as it appears from Rom. 3:22, the justice of God is by faith of Jesus Christ.

Second, something is required of necessity for Baptism, because without it the baptismal character cannot be imprinted. And thus right faith is not necessary in the one baptized any more than in the one who baptizes: provided the other conditions are fulfilled which are essential to the sacrament. For the sacrament is not perfected by the righteousness of the minister or of the recipient of Baptism, but by the power of God.

REPLY OBJ. 1: Our Lord is speaking there of Baptism as bringing us to salvation by giving us sanctifying grace: which of course cannot be without right faith: wherefore He says pointedly: *He that believeth and is baptized, shall be saved.*

REPLY OBJ. 2: The Church's intention in baptizing men is that they may be cleansed from sin, according to Isa. 27:9: *This is all the fruit, that the sin . . . should be taken*

peccatum. Et ideo, quantum est de se, non intendit dare Baptismum nisi habentibus rectam fidem, sine qua non est remissio peccatorum. Et propter hoc interrogat ad Baptismum accedentes, an credant. Si tamen sine recta fide aliquis Baptismum suscipiat extra Ecclesiam, non percipit illud ad suam salutem. Unde Augustinus dicit, *Ecclesia Paradiso comparata indicat nobis posse quidem Baptismum eius homines etiam foris accipere, sed salutem beatitudinis extra eam neminem percipere vel tenere.*

AD TERTIUM dicendum quod etiam non habens rectam fidem circa alios articulos, potest habere rectam fidem circa sacramentum Baptismi, et ita non impeditur quin possit habere intentionem suscipiendi sacramentum Baptismi. Si tamen etiam circa hoc sacramentum non recte sentiat, sufficit ad perceptionem sacramenti generalis intentio qua intendit suscipere Baptismum sicut Christus instituit, et sicut Ecclesia tradit.

AD QUARTUM dicendum quod, sicut sacramentum Baptismi non est conferendum ei qui non vult ab aliis peccatis recedere, ita nec etiam ei qui non vult infidelitatem deserere. Uterque tamen suscipit sacramentum si ei conferatur, licet non ad salutem.

away. And therefore, as far as she is concerned, she does not intend to give Baptism save to those who have right faith, without which there is no remission of sins. And for this reason she asks those who come to be baptized whether they believe. If, on the contrary, anyone, without right faith, receive Baptism outside the Church, he does not receive it unto salvation. Hence Augustine says (*De Baptism. contr. Donat.* iv): *From the Church being compared to Paradise we learn that men can receive her Baptism even outside her fold, but that elsewhere none can receive or keep the salvation of the blessed.*

REPLY OBJ. 3: Even he who has not right faith on other points, can have right faith about the sacrament of Baptism: and so he is not hindered from having the intention of receiving that sacrament. Yet even if he think not aright concerning this sacrament, it is enough, for the receiving of the sacrament, that he should have a general intention of receiving Baptism, according as Christ instituted, and as the Church bestows it.

REPLY OBJ. 4: Just as the sacrament of Baptism is not to be conferred on a man who is unwilling to give up his other sins, so neither should it be given to one who is unwilling to renounce his unbelief. Yet each receives the sacrament if it be conferred on him, though not unto salvation.

Article 9

Whether Children Should Be Baptized?

AD NONUM SIC PROCEDITUR. Videtur quod pueri non sint baptizandi. In eo enim qui baptizatur requiritur intentio suscipiendi sacramentum, ut supra dictum est. Huiusmodi autem intentionem non possunt pueri habere, cum non habeant usum liberi arbitrii. Ergo videtur quod non possint suscipere sacramentum Baptismi.

PRAETEREA, Baptismus est fidei sacramentum, ut supra dictum est. Sed pueri non habent fidem, quae consistit in credentium voluntate, ut Augustinus dicit, super Ioan. Nec etiam potest dici quod salventur in fide parentum, quia quandoque parentes sunt infideles, et sic magis per eorum infidelitatem damnarentur. Ergo videtur quod pueri non possint baptizari.

PRAETEREA, I Pet. III dicitur quod *homines salvos facit Baptisma, non carnis depositio sordium, sed conscientiae bonae interrogatio in Deum.* Sed pueri neque conscientiam habent bonam vel malam, cum non habeant usum rationis, neque etiam convenienter ipsi interrogantur cum non intelligant. Ergo non debent pueri baptizari.

OBJECTION 1: It seems that children should not be baptized. For the intention to receive the sacrament is required in one who is being baptized, as stated above (A. 7). But children cannot have such an intention, since they have not the use of free-will. Therefore it seems that they cannot receive the sacrament of Baptism.

OBJ. 2: Further, Baptism is the sacrament of faith, as stated above (Q. 39, A. 5; Q. 66, A. 1, ad 1). But children have not faith, which demands an act of the will on the part of the believer, as Augustine says (*Super Joan. xxvi*). Nor can it be said that their salvation is implied in the faith of their parents; since the latter are sometimes unbelievers, and their unbelief would conduce rather to the damnation of their children. Therefore it seems that children cannot be baptized.

OBJ. 3: Further, it is written (1 Pet 3:21) that *Baptism saveth* men; *not the putting away of the filth of the flesh, but the examination of a good conscience towards God.* But children have no conscience, either good or bad, since they have not the use of reason: nor can they be fittingly examined, since they understand not. Therefore children should not be baptized.

SED CONTRA est quod Dionysius dicit, ult. cap. Eccl. Hier., *divini nostri duces, scilicet apostoli, probaverunt infantes recipi ad Baptismum.*

RESPONDEO dicendum quod, sicut apostolus dicit, Rom. V, *si unius delicto mors regnavit per unum, scilicet per Adam, multo magis abundantiam gratiae et donationis et iustitiae accipientes in vita regnabunt per unum, Iesum Christum.* Pueri autem ex peccato Adae peccatum originale contrahunt, quod patet ex hoc quod sunt mortalitati subiecti, quae per peccatum primi hominis in omnes pertransiit, ut ibidem apostolus dicit. Unde multo magis pueri possunt per Christum gratiam suscipere, ut regnent in vita aeterna. Ipse autem dominus dicit, Ioan. III, *nisi quis renatus fuerit ex aqua et spiritu sancto, non potest introire in regnum Dei.* Unde necessarium fuit pueros baptizare, ut, sicut per Adam damnationem incurrerunt nascendo, ita per Christum salutem consequantur renascendo. Fuit etiam conveniens pueros baptizari ut a pueritia nutriti in his quae sunt Christianae vitae, firmius in ea perseverent, iuxta illud Prov. XXII, *adolescens iuxta viam suam, etiam cum senuerit, non recedet ab ea.* Et hanc rationem assignat Dionysius, ult. cap. Eccl. Hier.

AD PRIMUM ergo dicendum quod regeneratio spiritualis, quae fit per Baptismum, quodammodo similis est nativitati carnali, quantum ad hoc quod, sicut pueri in maternis uteris constituti non per seipsos nutrimentum accipiunt, sed ex nutrimento matris sustentantur, ita etiam pueri non habentes usum rationis, quasi in utero matris Ecclesiae constituti, non per seipsos, sed per actum Ecclesiae salutem suscipiunt. Unde Augustinus dicit, in libro de peccatorum meritis et Remiss., *mater Ecclesia os maternum parvulis praebet, ut sacris mysteriis imbuantur, quia nondum possunt corde proprio credere ad iustitiam, nec ore proprio confiteri ad salutem. Si autem propterea recte fideles vocantur quoniam fidem per verba gestantium quodammodo profitentur, cur etiam non poenitentes habeantur, cum per eorundem verba gestantium Diabolo et huic saeculo abrenuntiare monstrentur?* Et eadem ratione possunt dici intendentes, non per actum propriae intentionis, cum ipsi quandoque contranitantur et plorent, sed per actum eorum a quibus offeruntur.

AD SECUNDUM dicendum quod, sicut Augustinus, scribens Bonifacio, dicit, *in Ecclesia salvatoris parvuli per alios credunt, sicut ex aliis quae in Baptismo remittuntur peccata traxerunt.* Nec impeditur eorum salus si parentes sint infideles, quia, sicut Augustinus dicit, eidem Bonifacio scribens, *offeruntur parvuli ad percipiendam spiritualem gratiam, non tam ab eis quorum gestantur manibus (quamvis et ab ipsis, si et ipsi boni fideles sunt), quam ab universa societate sanctorum atque fidelium. Ab*

ON THE CONTRARY, Dionysius says (*Eccl. Hier.* iii): *Our heavenly guides, i.e., the Apostles, approved of infants being admitted to Baptism.*

I ANSWER THAT, As the Apostle says (Rom 5:17), *if by one man's offense death reigned through one,* namely Adam, *much more they who receive abundance of grace, and of the gift, and of justice, shall reign in life through one, Jesus Christ.* Now children contract original sin from the sin of Adam; which is made clear by the fact that they are under the ban of death, which *passed upon all* on account of the sin of the first man, as the Apostle says in the same passage (Rom 5:12). Much more, therefore, can children receive grace through Christ, so as to reign in eternal life. But our Lord Himself said (John 3:5): *Unless a man be born again of water and the Holy Spirit, he cannot enter into the kingdom of God.* Consequently it became necessary to baptize children, that, as in birth they incurred damnation through Adam so in a second birth they might obtain salvation through Christ. Moreover it was fitting that children should receive Baptism, in order that being reared from childhood in things pertaining to the Christian mode of life, they may the more easily persevere therein; according to Prov. 22:5: *A young man according to his way, even when he is old, he will not depart from it.* This reason is also given by Dionysius (*Eccl. Hier.* iii).

REPLY OBJ. 1: The spiritual regeneration effected by Baptism is somewhat like carnal birth, in this respect, that as the child while in the mother's womb receives nourishment not independently, but through the nourishment of its mother, so also children before the use of reason, being as it were in the womb of their mother the Church, receive salvation not by their own act, but by the act of the Church. Hence Augustine says (*De Pecc. Merit. et Remiss.* i): *The Church, our mother, offers her maternal mouth for her children, that they may imbibe the sacred mysteries: for they cannot as yet with their own hearts believe unto justice, nor with their own mouths confess unto salvation . . . And if they are rightly said to believe, because in a certain fashion they make profession of faith by the words of their sponsors, why should they not also be said to repent, since by the words of those same sponsors they evidence their renunciation of the devil and this world?* For the same reason they can be said to intend, not by their own act of intention, since at times they struggle and cry; but by the act of those who bring them to be baptized.

REPLY OBJ. 2: As Augustine says, writing to Boniface (*Cont. duas Ep. Pelag.* i), *in the Church of our Savior little children believe through others, just as they contracted from others those sins which are remitted in Baptism.* Nor is it a hindrance to their salvation if their parents be unbelievers, because, as Augustine says, writing to the same Boniface (*Ep.* xcviii), *little children are offered that they may receive grace in their souls, not so much from the hands of those that carry them (yet from these too, if they be good and faithful)*

omnibus namque offerri recte intelliguntur, quibus placet quod offeruntur, et quorum caritate ad communionem sancti spiritus adiunguntur. Infidelitas autem propriorum parentum, etiam si eos post Baptismum Daemoniorum sacrificiis imbuere conentur, pueris non nocet. Quia, ut ibidem Augustinus dicit, *puer semel generatus per aliorum voluntatem, deinceps non potest vinculo alienae iniquitatis obstringi, ubi nulla sua voluntate consentit, secundum illud, Ezech. XVIII, sicut anima patris mea est, et anima filii, anima quae peccaverit, ipsa morietur. Sed ideo ex Adam traxit quod sacramenti illius gratia solveretur, quia nondum erat anima separata vivens.* Fides autem unius, immo totius Ecclesiae, parvulo prodest per operationem spiritus sancti, qui unit Ecclesiam et bona unius alteri communicat.

AD TERTIUM dicendum quod, sicut puer, cum baptizatur, non per seipsum, sed per alios credit; ita non per seipsum, sed per alios interrogatur, et interrogati confitentur fidem Ecclesiae in persona pueri, qui huic fidei aggregatur per fidei sacramentum. Conscientiam autem bonam consequitur puer etiam in seipso, non quidem actu, sed habitu, per gratiam iustificantem.

as from the whole company of the saints and the faithful. For they are rightly considered to be offered by those who are pleased at their being offered, and by whose charity they are united in communion with the Holy Spirit. And the unbelief of their own parents, even if after Baptism these strive to infect them with the worship of demons, hurts not the children. For as Augustine says (*Cont. duas Ep. Pelag.* i) *when once the child has been begotten by the will of others, he cannot subsequently be held by the bonds of another's sin so long as he consent not with his will, according to Ezech. 18:4: 'As the soul of the Father, so also the soul of the son is mine; the soul that sinneth, the same shall die.' Yet he contracted from Adam that which was loosed by the grace of this sacrament, because as yet he was not endowed with a separate existence.* But the faith of one, indeed of the whole Church, profits the child through the operation of the Holy Spirit, Who unites the Church together, and communicates the goods of one member to another.

REPLY OBJ. 3: Just as a child, when he is being baptized, believes not by himself but by others, so is he examined not by himself but through others, and these in answer confess the Church's faith in the child's stead, who is aggregated to this faith by the sacrament of faith. And the child acquires a good conscience in himself, not indeed as to the act, but as to the habit, by sanctifying grace.

Article 10

Whether Children of Jews or Other Unbelievers Should Be Baptized Against the Will of Their Parents?

AD DECIMUM SIC PROCEDITUR. Videtur quod pueri Iudaeorum vel aliorum infidelium sint baptizandi, etiam invitis parentibus. Magis enim debet homini subveniri contra periculum mortis aeternae quam contra periculum mortis temporalis. Sed puero in periculo mortis temporalis existenti est subveniendum, etiam si parentes per malitiam contraniterentur. Ergo multo magis est subveniendum pueris infidelium filiis contra periculum mortis aeternae, etiam invitis parentibus.

PRAETEREA, filii servorum sunt servi, et in potestate dominorum. Sed Iudaei sunt servi regum et principum, et quicumque etiam alii infideles. Ergo absque omni iniuria possunt principes Iudaeorum filios, vel aliorum servorum infidelium, facere baptizari.

PRAETEREA, quilibet homo est magis Dei, a quo habet animam, quam patris carnalis, a quo habet corpus. Non est ergo iniustum si pueri infidelium filii parentibus carnalibus auferantur, et Deo per Baptismum consecrentur.

SED CONTRA est quod in decretis, dist. XLV, ex Concilio Toletano, sic dicitur, *de Iudaeis praecepit sancta*

OBJECTION 1: It seems that children of Jews or other unbelievers should be baptized against the will of their parents. For it is a matter of greater urgency to rescue a man from the danger of eternal death than from the danger of temporal death. But one ought to rescue a child that is threatened by the danger of temporal death, even if its parents through malice try to prevent its being rescued. Therefore much more reason is there for rescuing the children of unbelievers from the danger of eternal death, even against their parents' will.

OBJ. 2: The children of slaves are themselves slaves, and in the power of their masters. But Jews and all other unbelievers are the slaves of kings and rulers. Therefore without any injustice rulers can have the children of Jews baptized, as well as those of other slaves who are unbelievers.

OBJ. 3: Further, every man belongs more to God, from Whom he has his soul, than to his carnal father, from whom he has his body. Therefore it is not unjust if the children of unbelievers are taken away from their carnal parents, and consecrated to God by Baptism.

ON THE CONTRARY, It is written in the *Decretals* (Dist. xlv), quoting the council of Toledo: *In regard to the*

synodus nemini deinceps ad credendum vim inferre, non enim tales inviti salvandi sunt, sed volentes, ut integra sit forma iustitiae.

RESPONDEO dicendum quod pueri infidelium filii aut habent usum rationis, aut non habent. Si autem habent, iam, quantum ad ea quae sunt iuris divini vel naturalis, incipiunt suae potestatis esse. Et ideo propria voluntate, invitis parentibus, possunt Baptismum suscipere, sicut et matrimonium contrahere. Et ideo tales licite moneri possunt et induci ad suscipiendum Baptismum.

Si vero nondum habent usum liberi arbitrii, secundum ius naturale sunt sub cura parentum, quandiu ipsi sibi providere non possunt. Unde etiam et de pueris antiquorum dicitur quod salvabantur in fide parentum. Et ideo contra iustitiam naturalem esset si tales pueri, invitis parentibus, baptizarentur, sicut etiam si aliquis habens usum rationis baptizaretur invitus. Esset etiam periculosum taliter filios infidelium baptizare, quia de facili ad infidelitatem redirent, propter naturalem affectum ad parentes. Et ideo non habet hoc Ecclesiae consuetudo, quod filii infidelium, invitis parentibus, baptizentur.

AD PRIMUM ergo dicendum quod a morte corporali non est aliquis eripiendus contra ordinem iuris civilis, puta, si aliquis a suo iudice condemnetur ad mortem, nullus debet eum violenter a morte eripere. Unde nec aliquis debet irrumpere ordinem iuris naturae, quo filius est sub cura patris, ut eum liberet a periculo mortis aeternae.

AD SECUNDUM dicendum quod Iudaei sunt servi principum servitute civili, quae non excludit ordinem iuris naturalis vel divini.

AD TERTIUM dicendum quod homo ordinatur ad Deum per rationem, per quam Deum cognoscere potest. Unde puer, antequam usum rationis habeat, naturali ordine ordinatur in Deum per rationem parentum, quorum curae naturaliter subiacet, et secundum eorum dispositionem sunt circa ipsum divina agenda.

Jews the holy synod commands that henceforward none of them be forced to believe: for such are not to be saved against their will, but willingly, that their righteousness may be without flaw.

I ANSWER THAT, The children of unbelievers either have the use of reason or they have not. If they have, then they already begin to control their own actions, in things that are of Divine or natural law. And therefore of their own accord, and against the will of their parents, they can receive Baptism, just as they can contract marriage. Consequently such can lawfully be advised and persuaded to be baptized.

If, however, they have not yet the use of free-will, according to the natural law they are under the care of their parents as long as they cannot look after themselves. For which reason we say that even the children of the ancients *were saved through the faith of their parents.* Wherefore it would be contrary to natural justice if such children were baptized against their parents' will; just as it would be if one having the use of reason were baptized against his will. Moreover under the circumstances it would be dangerous to baptize the children of unbelievers; for they would be liable to lapse into unbelief, by reason of their natural affection for their parents. Therefore it is not the custom of the Church to baptize the children of unbelievers against their parents' will.

REPLY OBJ. 1: It is not right to rescue a man from death of the body against the order of civil law: for instance, if a man be condemned to death by the judge who has tried him, none should use force in order to rescue him from death. Consequently, neither should anyone infringe the order of the natural law, in virtue of which a child is under the care of its father, in order to rescue it from the danger of eternal death.

REPLY OBJ. 2: Jews are slaves of rulers by civil slavery, which does not exclude the order of the natural and Divine law.

REPLY OBJ. 3: Man is ordained unto God through his reason, by which he can know God. Wherefore a child, before it has the use of reason, is ordained to God, by a natural order, through the reason of its parents, under whose care it naturally lies, and it is according to their ordering that things pertaining to God are to be done in respect of the child.

Article 11

Whether a Child Can Be Baptized While Yet in Its Mother's Womb?

AD UNDECIMUM SIC PROCEDITUR. Videtur quod in maternis uteris existentes possint baptizari. Efficacius est enim donum Christi ad salutem quam peccatum Adae

OBJECTION 1: It seems that a child can be baptized while yet in its mother's womb. For the gift of Christ is more efficacious unto salvation than Adam's sin unto

ad damnationem, ut apostolus dicit, Rom. V. Sed pueri in maternis uteris existentes damnantur propter peccatum Adae. Ergo multo magis salvari possunt per donum Christi. Quod quidem fit per Baptismum. Ergo pueri in maternis uteris existentes possunt baptizari.

PRAETEREA, puer in utero matris existens aliquid matris esse videtur. Sed, baptizata matre, baptizatur quidquid est eius intra ipsam existens. Ergo videtur quod, baptizata matre, baptizetur puer in utero eius existens.

PRAETEREA, mors aeterna peior est quam mors corporalis. Sed de duobus malis minus malum eligendum est. Si ergo puer in utero matris existens baptizari non potest, melius esset quod mater aperiretur et puer vi eductus baptizaretur, quam quod puer aeternaliter damnaretur, absque Baptismo decedens.

PRAETEREA, contingit quandoque quod aliqua pars pueri prius egreditur, sicut legitur Gen. XXXVIII quod, pariente Thamar, *in ipsa effusione infantium, unus protulit manum, in qua obstetrix ligavit coccinum, dicens, iste egredietur prior. Illo vero manum retrahente, egressus est alter.* Quandoque autem in tali casu imminet periculum mortis. Ergo videtur quod illa pars debeat baptizari, puero adhuc in materno utero existente.

SED CONTRA est quod Augustinus, in epistola ad Dardanum, dicit, *nemo renascitur nisi primo nascatur.* Sed Baptismus est quaedam spiritualis regeneratio. Non ergo debet aliquis baptizari priusquam ex utero nascatur.

RESPONDEO dicendum quod de necessitate Baptismi est quod corpus baptizandi aliquo modo aqua abluatur, cum Baptismus sit quaedam ablutio, ut supra dictum est. Corpus autem infantis, antequam nascatur ex utero, non potest aliquo modo ablui aqua, nisi forte dicatur quod ablutio baptismalis qua corpus matris lavatur, ad filium in ventre existentem perveniat. Sed hoc non potest esse, tum quia anima pueri, ad cuius sanctificationem ordinatur Baptismus, distincta est ab anima matris; tum quia corpus puerperii animati iam est formatum, et per consequens a corpore matris distinctum. Et ideo Baptismus quo mater baptizatur, non redundat in prolem in utero existentem. Unde Augustinus dicit, contra Iulianum, *si ad matris corpus id quod in ea concipitur pertinet, ita ut eius pars imputetur, non baptizaretur infans cuius mater baptizata est, aliquo mortis urgente periculo, cum gestaret in utero. Nunc vero, cum etiam ipse, scilicet infans, baptizetur, non utique ad maternum corpus, cum esset in utero, pertinebat.* Et ita relinquitur quod nullo modo existentes in maternis uteris baptizari possunt.

AD PRIMUM ergo dicendum quod pueri in maternis uteris existentes nondum prodierunt in lucem, ut cum

condemnation, as the Apostle says (Rom 5:15). But a child while yet in its mother's womb is under sentence of condemnation on account of Adam's sin. For much more reason, therefore, can it be saved through the gift of Christ, which is bestowed by means of Baptism. Therefore a child can be baptized while yet in its mother's womb.

OBJ. 2: Further, a child, while yet in its mother's womb, seems to be part of its mother. Now, when the mother is baptized, whatever is in her and part of her, is baptized. Therefore it seems that when the mother is baptized, the child in her womb is baptized.

OBJ. 3: Further, eternal death is a greater evil than death of the body. But of two evils the less should be chosen. If, therefore, the child in the mother's womb cannot be baptized, it would be better for the mother to be opened, and the child to be taken out by force and baptized, than that the child should be eternally damned through dying without Baptism.

OBJ. 4: Further, it happens at times that some part of the child comes forth first, as we read in Gen. 38:27: *In the very delivery of the infants, one put forth a hand, whereon the midwife tied a scarlet thread, saying: This shall come forth the first. But he drawing back his hand, the other came forth.* Now sometimes in such cases there is danger of death. Therefore it seems that that part should be baptized, while the child is yet in its mother's womb.

ON THE CONTRARY, Augustine says (*Ep. ad Dardan.*): *No one can be born a second time unless he be born first.* But Baptism is a spiritual regeneration. Therefore no one should be baptized before he is born from the womb.

I ANSWER THAT, It is essential to Baptism that some part of the body of the person baptized be in some way washed with water, since Baptism is a kind of washing, as stated above (Q. 66, A. 1). But an infant's body, before being born from the womb, can nowise be washed with water; unless perchance it be said that the baptismal water, with which the mother's body is washed, reaches the child while yet in its mother's womb. But this is impossible: both because the child's soul, to the sanctification of which Baptism is ordained, is distinct from the soul of the mother; and because the body of the animated infant is already formed, and consequently distinct from the body of the mother. Therefore the Baptism which the mother receives does not overflow on to the child which is in her womb. Hence Augustine says (*Cont. Julian.* vi): *If what is conceived within a mother belonged to her body, so as to be considered a part thereof, we should not baptize an infant whose mother, through danger of death, was baptized while she bore it in her womb. Since, then, it,* i.e., the infant, *is baptized, it certainly did not belong to the mother's body while it was in the womb.* It follows, therefore, that a child can nowise be baptized while in its mother's womb.

REPLY OBJ. 1: Children while in the mother's womb have not yet come forth into the world to live among other

aliis hominibus vitam ducant. Unde non possunt subiici actioni humanae, ut per eorum ministerium sacramenta recipiant ad salutem. Possunt tamen subiici operationi Dei, apud quem vivunt, ut quodam privilegio gratiae sanctificationem consequantur, sicut patet de sanctificatis in utero.

Ad secundum dicendum quod membrum interius matris est aliquid eius per continuationem et unionem materialis partis ad totum. Puer autem in utero matris existens est aliquid eius per quandam colligationem corporum distinctorum. Unde non est similis ratio.

Ad tertium dicendum quod *non sunt facienda mala ut veniant bona*, ut dicitur Rom. III. Et ideo non debet homo occidere matrem ut baptizet puerum. Si tamen mater mortua fuerit vivente puero in utero, aperiri debet, ut puer baptizetur.

Ad quartum dicendum quod expectanda est totalis egressio pueri ex utero ad Baptismum, nisi mors immineat. Si tamen primo caput egrediatur, in quo fundatur sensus, debet baptizari, periculo imminente, et non est postea rebaptizandus, si eum perfecte nasci contigerit. Et videtur idem faciendum quaecumque alia pars egrediatur, periculo imminente. Quia tamen in nulla partium exteriorum integritas ita consistit sicut in capite, videtur quibusdam quod, propter dubium, quacumque alia parte corporis abluta, puer post perfectam nativitatem sit baptizandus sub hac forma, si non es baptizatus, ego te baptizo, et cetera.

men. Consequently they cannot be subject to the action of man, so as to receive the sacrament, at the hands of man, unto salvation. They can, however, be subject to the action of God, in Whose sight they live, so as, by a kind of privilege, to receive the grace of sanctification; as was the case with those who were sanctified in the womb.

Reply Obj. 2: An internal member of the mother is something of hers by continuity and material union of the part with the whole: whereas a child while in its mother's womb is something of hers through being joined with, and yet distinct from her. Wherefore there is no comparison.

Reply Obj. 3: We should *not do evil that there may come good* (Rom 3:8). Therefore it is wrong to kill a mother that her child may be baptized. If, however, the mother die while the child lives yet in her womb, she should be opened that the child may be baptized.

Reply Obj. 4: Unless death be imminent, we should wait until the child has entirely come forth from the womb before baptizing it. If, however, the head, wherein the senses are rooted, appear first, it should be baptized, in cases of danger: nor should it be baptized again, if perfect birth should ensue. And seemingly the same should be done in cases of danger no matter what part of the body appear first. But as none of the exterior parts of the body belong to its integrity in the same degree as the head, some hold that since the matter is doubtful, whenever any other part of the body has been baptized, the child, when perfect birth has taken place, should be baptized with the form: *If thou art not baptized, I baptize thee*, etc.

Article 12

Whether Madmen and Imbeciles Should Be Baptized?

Ad duodecimum sic proceditur. Videtur quod furiosi et amentes non debeant baptizari. Ad susceptionem enim Baptismi requiritur intentio in eo qui baptizatur, ut supra dictum est. Sed furiosi et amentes, cum careant usu rationis, non possunt habere nisi inordinatam intentionem. Ergo non debent baptizari.

Praeterea, homo bruta animalia superexcedit in hoc quod habet rationem. Sed furiosi et amentes non habent usum rationis, et quandoque etiam in eis non expectatur, sicut expectatur in pueris. Ergo videtur quod, sicut bruta animalia non baptizantur, ita etiam nec tales furiosi et amentes debeant baptizari.

Praeterea, magis ligatus est usus rationis in furiosis vel amentibus quam in dormientibus. Sed Baptismus non consuevit dari dormientibus. Ergo non debet dari amentibus et furiosis.

Sed contra est quod Augustinus dicit, IV Confess., de amico suo, qui, cum desperaretur, baptizatus est. Et

Objection 1: It seems that madmen and imbeciles should not be baptized. For in order to receive Baptism, the person baptized must have the intention, as stated above (A. 7). But since madmen and imbeciles lack the use of reason, they can have but a disorderly intention. Therefore they should not be baptized.

Obj. 2: Further, man excels irrational animals in that he has reason. But madmen and imbeciles lack the use of reason, indeed in some cases we do not expect them ever to have it, as we do in the case of children. It seems, therefore, that just as irrational animals are not baptized, so neither should madmen and imbeciles in those cases be baptized.

Obj. 3: Further, the use of reason is suspended in madmen and imbeciles more than it is in one who sleeps. But it is not customary to baptize people while they sleep. Therefore it should not be given to madmen and imbeciles.

On the contrary, Augustine says (*Confess.* iv) of his friend that *he was baptized when his recovery was despaired*

tamen in ipso Baptismus efficaciam habuit. Unde et carentibus usu rationis aliquando Baptismus dari debet.

Respondeo dicendum quod circa amentes et furiosos est distinguendum. Quidam enim sunt a nativitate tales, nulla habentes lucida intervalla, in quibus etiam nullus usus rationis apparet. Et de talibus, quantum ad Baptismi susceptionem, videtur esse idem iudicium et de pueris, qui baptizantur in fide Ecclesiae, ut supra dictum est.

Alii vero sunt amentes qui ex sana mente quam habuerunt prius, in amentiam inciderunt. Et tales sunt iudicandi secundum voluntatem quam habuerunt dum sanae mentis existerent. Et ideo, si tunc apparuit in eis voluntas suscipiendi Baptismum, debet exhiberi eis in furia vel amentia constitutis, etiam si tunc contradicant. Alioquin, si nulla voluntas suscipiendi Baptismum in eis apparuit dum sanae mentis essent, non sunt baptizandi.

Quidam vero sunt qui, etsi a nativitate fuerint furiosi et amentes, habent tamen aliqua lucida intervalla, in quibus recta ratione uti possunt. Unde, si tunc baptizari voluerint, baptizari possunt etiam in amentia constituti. Et debet eis sacramentum tunc conferri si periculum timeatur, alioquin melius est ut tempus expectetur in quo sint sanae mentis ad hoc quod devotius suscipiant sacramentum. Si autem tempore lucidi intervalli non appareat in eis voluntas Baptismum suscipiendi, baptizari non debent in amentia constituti.

Quidam vero sunt qui, etsi non omnino sanae mentis existant, in tantum tamen ratione utuntur quod possunt de sua salute cogitare, et intelligere sacramenti virtutem. Et de talibus idem est iudicium sicut de his qui sanae mentis existunt, qui baptizantur volentes, non inviti.

Ad primum ergo dicendum quod amentes qui nunquam habuerunt nec habent usum rationis, baptizantur ex intentione Ecclesiae, sicut ex ritu Ecclesiae credunt et poenitent, sicut supra de pueris dictum est. Illi vero qui aliquo tempore habuerunt vel habent usum rationis, secundum propriam intentionem baptizantur, quam habent vel habuerunt tempore sanae mentis.

Ad secundum dicendum quod furiosi vel amentes carent usu rationis per accidens, scilicet propter aliquod impedimentum organi corporalis, non autem propter defectum animae rationalis, sicut bruta animalia. Unde non est de eis similis ratio.

Ad tertium dicendum quod dormientes non sunt baptizandi nisi periculum mortis immineat. In quo casu baptizari debent si prius voluntas apparuit in eis suscipiendi Baptismum, sicut et de amentibus dictum est, sicut Augustinus narrat, in IV libro Confess., de amico

of: and yet Baptism was efficacious with him. Therefore Baptism should sometimes be given to those who lack the use of reason.

I answer that, In the matter of madmen and imbeciles a distinction is to be made. For some are so from birth, and have no lucid intervals, and show no signs of the use of reason. And with regard to these it seems that we should come to the same decision as with regard to children who are baptized in the Faith of the Church, as stated above (A. 9, ad 2).

But there are others who have fallen from a state of sanity into a state of insanity. And with regard to these we must be guided by their wishes as expressed by them when sane: so that, if then they manifested a desire to receive Baptism, it should be given to them when in a state of madness or imbecility, even though then they refuse. If, on the other hand, while sane they showed no desire to receive Baptism, they must not be baptized.

Again, there are some who, though mad or imbecile from birth, have, nevertheless, lucid intervals, in which they can make right use of reason. Wherefore, if then they express a desire for Baptism, they can be baptized though they be actually in a state of madness. And in this case the sacrament should be bestowed on them if there be fear of danger otherwise it is better to wait until the time when they are sane, so that they may receive the sacrament more devoutly. But if during the interval of lucidity they manifest no desire to receive Baptism, they should not be baptized while in a state of insanity.

Lastly there are others who, though not altogether sane, yet can use their reason so far as to think about their salvation, and understand the power of the sacrament. And these are to be treated the same as those who are sane, and who are baptized if they be willing, but not against their will.

Reply Obj. 1: Imbeciles who never had, and have not now, the use of reason, are baptized, according to the Church's intention, just as according to the Church's ritual, they believe and repent; as we have stated above of children (A. 9, ad Obj.). But those who have had the use of reason at some time, or have now, are baptized according to their own intention, which they have now, or had when they were sane.

Reply Obj. 2: Madmen and imbeciles lack the use of reason accidentally, i.e., through some impediment in a bodily organ; but not like irrational animals through want of a rational soul. Consequently the comparison does not hold.

Reply Obj. 3: A person should not be baptized while asleep, except he be threatened with the danger of death. In which case he should be baptized, if previously he has manifested a desire to receive Baptism, as we have stated in reference to imbeciles: thus Augustine relates of his friend

suo, qui baptizatus est nesciens, propter periculum mortis.

that *he was baptized while unconscious*, because he was in danger of death (*Confess.* iv).

Question 69

The Effects of Baptism

Deinde considerandum est de effectibus Baptismi. Et circa hoc quaeruntur decem.

Primo, utrum per Baptismum auferantur omnia peccata.

Secundo, utrum per Baptismum liberetur homo ab omni poena.

Tertio, utrum Baptismus auferat poenalitatem huius vitae.

Quarto, utrum per Baptismum conferantur homini gratiae et virtutes

Quinto, de effectibus virtutum qui per Baptismum conferuntur.

Sexto, utrum etiam parvuli in Baptismo gratias et virtutes accipiant.

Septimo, utrum per Baptismum aperiatur baptizatis ianua regni caelestis.

Octavo, utrum Baptismus aequalem effectum habeat in omnibus baptizatis.

Nono, utrum fictio impediat effectum Baptismi.

Decimo, utrum, recedente fictione, Baptismus obtineat suum effectum.

We must now consider the effects of Baptism, concerning which there are ten points of inquiry:

(1) Whether all sins are taken away by Baptism?

(2) Whether man is freed from all punishment by Baptism?

(3) Whether Baptism takes away the penalties of sin that belong to this life?

(4) Whether grace and virtues are bestowed on man by Baptism?

(5) Of the effects of virtue which are conferred by Baptism?

(6) Whether even children receive grace and virtues in Baptism?

(7) Whether Baptism opens the gates of the heavenly kingdom to those who are baptized?

(8) Whether Baptism produces an equal effect in all who are baptized?

(9) Whether insincerity hinders the effect of Baptism?

(10) Whether Baptism takes effect when the insincerity ceases?

Article 1

Whether All Sins Are Taken Away by Baptism?

Ad primum sic proceditur. Videtur quod per Baptismum non tollantur omnia peccata. Baptismus enim est quaedam spiritualis regeneratio, quae contraponitur generationi carnali. Sed per generationem carnalem homo contrahit solum originale peccatum. Ergo per Baptismum solvitur solum originale peccatum.

Praeterea, poenitentia est sufficiens causa remissionis actualium peccatorum. Sed ante Baptismum in adultis requiritur poenitentia, secundum illud Act. II, *poenitentiam agite, et baptizetur unusquisque vestrum.* Ergo Baptismus nihil operatur circa remissionem peccatorum actualium.

Praeterea, diversorum morborum diversae sunt medicinae, quia, sicut Hieronymus dicit, *non sanat oculum quod sanat calcaneum.* Sed peccatum originale, quod per Baptismum tollitur, est aliud genus peccati a peccato actuali. Ergo non omnia peccata remittuntur per Baptismum.

Objection 1: It seems that not all sins are taken away by Baptism. For Baptism is a spiritual regeneration, which corresponds to carnal generation. But by carnal generation man contracts none but original sin. Therefore none but original sin is taken away by Baptism.

Obj. 2: Further, Penance is a sufficient cause of the remission of actual sins. But penance is required in adults before Baptism, according to Acts 2:38: *Do penance and be baptized every one of you.* Therefore Baptism has nothing to do with the remission of actual sins.

Obj. 3: Further, various diseases demand various remedies: because as Jerome says on Mk. 9:27, 28: *What is a cure for the heel is no cure for the eye.* But original sin, which is taken away by Baptism, is generically distinct from actual sin. Therefore not all sins are taken away by Baptism.

Sed contra est quod dicitur Ezech. XXXVI, *effundam super vos aquam mundam, et mundabimini ab omnibus inquinamentis vestris.*

Respondeo dicendum quod, sicut apostolus dicit, Rom. VI, *quicumque baptizati sumus in Christo Iesu, in morte ipsius baptizati sumus.* Et postea concludit, *ita et vos existimate mortuos quidem esse peccato, viventes autem Deo in Christo Iesu domino nostro.* Ex quo patet quod per Baptismum homo moritur vetustati peccati, et incipit vivere novitati gratiae. Omne autem peccatum pertinet ad pristinam vetustatem. Unde consequens est quod omne peccatum per Baptismum tollatur.

Ad primum ergo dicendum quod, sicut apostolus dicit, Rom. V, peccatum Adae non tantum potest quantum donum Christi, quod in Baptismo percipitur, *nam iudicium ex uno in condemnationem, gratia autem ex multis delictis in iustificationem.* Unde et Augustinus dicit, in libro de Baptismo parvulorum, quod, *generante carne, tantummodo trahitur peccatum originale, regenerante autem spiritu, non solum originalis, sed etiam voluntariorum fit remissio peccatorum.*

Ad secundum dicendum quod nullius peccati remissio fieri potest nisi per virtutem passionis Christi, unde et apostolus dicit, Heb. IX, quod *sine sanguinis effusione non fit remissio.* Unde motus voluntatis humanae non sufficeret ad remissionem culpae, nisi adesset fides passionis Christi et propositum participandi ipsam, vel suscipiendo Baptismum, vel subiiciendo se clavibus Ecclesiae. Et ideo, quando aliquis adultus poenitens ad Baptismum accedit, consequitur quidem remissionem omnium peccatorum ex proposito Baptismi, perfectius autem ex reali susceptione Baptismi.

Ad tertium dicendum quod ratio illa procedit de particularibus medicinis. Baptismus autem operatur in virtute passionis Christi, quae est universalis medicina omnium peccatorum, et per Baptismum omnia peccata solvuntur.

On the contrary, It is written (Ezek 36:25): *I will pour upon you clean water, and you shall be cleansed from all your filthiness.*

I answer that, As the Apostle says (Rom 6:3), *all we, who are baptized in Christ Jesus, are baptized in His death.* And further on he concludes (Rom 6:11): *So do you also reckon that you are dead to sin, but alive unto God in Christ Jesus our Lord.* Hence it is clear that by Baptism man dies unto the oldness of sin, and begins to live unto the newness of grace. But every sin belongs to the primitive oldness. Consequently every sin is taken away by Baptism.

Reply Obj. 1: As the Apostle says (Rom 5:15, 16), the sin of Adam was not so far-reaching as the gift of Christ, which is bestowed in Baptism: *for judgment was by one unto condemnation; but grace is of many offenses, unto justification.* Wherefore Augustine says in his book on Infant Baptism (*De Pecc. Merit. et Remiss.* i), that *in carnal generation, original sin alone is contracted; but when we are born again of the Spirit, not only original sin but also wilfull sin is forgiven.*

Reply Obj. 2: No sin can be forgiven save by the power of Christ's Passion: hence the Apostle says (Heb 9:22) that *without shedding of blood there is no remission.* Consequently no movement of the human will suffices for the remission of sin, unless there be faith in Christ's Passion, and the purpose of participating in it, either by receiving Baptism, or by submitting to the keys of the Church. Therefore when an adult approaches Baptism, he does indeed receive the forgiveness of all his sins through his purpose of being baptized, but more perfectly through the actual reception of Baptism.

Reply Obj. 3: This argument is true of special remedies. But Baptism operates by the power of Christ's Passion, which is the universal remedy for all sins; and so by Baptism all sins are loosed.

Article 2

Whether Man Is Freed by Baptism from All Debt of Punishment Due to Sin?

Ad secundum sic proceditur. Videtur quod per Baptismum non liberetur homo ab omni reatu peccati. Dicit enim apostolus, Rom. XIII, *quae a Deo sunt, ordinata sunt.* Sed culpa non ordinatur nisi per poenam, ut Augustinus dicit. Ergo per Baptismum non tollitur reatus poenae praecedentium peccatorum.

Praeterea, effectus sacramenti aliquam similitudinem habet cum ipso sacramento, quia sacramenta novae legis efficiunt quod figurant, ut supra dictum est. Sed ablutio baptismalis habet quidem aliquam

Objection 1: It seems that man is not freed by Baptism from all debt of punishment due to sin. For the Apostle says (Rom 13:1): *Those things that are of God are well ordered.* But guilt is not set in order save by punishment, as Augustine says (*Ep. cxl*). Therefore Baptism does not take away the debt of punishment due to sins already committed.

Obj. 2: Further, the effect of a sacrament has a certain likeness to the sacrament itself; since the sacraments of the New Law *effect what they signify*, as stated above (Q. 62, A. 1, ad 1). But the washing of Baptism has indeed a certain

similitudinem cum ablutione maculae, nullam autem similitudinem habere videtur cum subtractione reatus poenae. Non ergo per Baptismum tollitur reatus poenae.

PRAETEREA, sublato reatu poenae, aliquis non remanet dignus poena, et ita iniustum esset eum puniri. Si igitur per Baptismum tollitur reatus poenae, iniustum esset post Baptismum suspendere latronem, qui antea homicidium commisit. Et ita per Baptismum tolleretur rigor humanae disciplinae, quod est inconveniens. Non ergo per Baptismum tollitur reatus poenae.

SED CONTRA est quod Ambrosius dicit, super illud Rom. XI, *sine poenitentia sunt dona Dei et vocatio*, gratia, inquit, Dei in Baptismo omnia gratis condonat.

RESPONDEO dicendum quod, sicut supra dictum est, per Baptismum aliquis incorporatur passioni et morti Christi, secundum illud Rom. VI, *si mortui sumus cum Christo, credimus quia etiam simul vivemus cum Christo.* Ex quo patet quod omni baptizato communicatur passio Christi ad remedium ac si ipse passus et mortuus esset. Passio autem Christi, sicut supra dictum est, est sufficiens satisfactio pro omnibus peccatis omnium hominum. Et ideo ille qui baptizatur liberatur a reatu omnis poenae sibi debitae pro peccatis, ac si ipse sufficienter satisfecisset pro omnibus peccatis suis.

AD PRIMUM ergo dicendum quod, quia poena passionis Christi communicatur baptizato, inquantum fit membrum Christi, ac si ipse poenam illam sustinuisset, eius peccata remanent ordinata per poenam passionis Christi.

AD SECUNDUM dicendum quod aqua non solum abluit, sed etiam refrigerat. Et ita suo refrigerio significat subtractionem reatus poenae, sicut sua ablutione significat emundationem a culpa.

AD TERTIUM dicendum quod in poenis quae iudicio humano inferuntur, non solum attenditur qua poena sit homo dignus quoad Deum, sed etiam in quo sit obligatus quoad homines, qui sunt laesi et scandalizati per peccatum alicuius. Et ideo, licet homicida per Baptismum liberetur a reatu poenae quoad Deum, remanet tamen adhuc obligatus quoad homines, quos iustum est aedificari de poena, sicut sunt scandalizati de culpa. Pie tamen talibus princeps posset poenam indulgere.

likeness with the cleansing from the stain of sin, but none, seemingly, with the remission of the debt of punishment. Therefore the debt of punishment is not taken away by Baptism.

OBJ. 3: Further, when the debt of punishment has been remitted, a man no longer deserves to be punished, and so it would be unjust to punish him. If, therefore, the debt of punishment be remitted by Baptism, it would be unjust, after Baptism, to hang a thief who had committed murder before. Consequently the severity of human legislation would be relaxed on account of Baptism; which is undesirable. Therefore Baptism does not remit the debt of punishment.

ON THE CONTRARY, Ambrose, commenting on Rom. 11:29, *The gifts and the calling of God are without repentance*, says: *The grace of God in Baptism remits all, gratis.*

I ANSWER THAT, As stated above (Q. 49, A. 3, ad 2; Q. 68, AA. 1, 4, 5) by Baptism a man is incorporated in the Passion and death of Christ, according to Rom. 6:8: *If we be dead with Christ, we believe that we shall live also together with Christ.* Hence it is clear that the Passion of Christ is communicated to every baptized person, so that he is healed just as if he himself had suffered and died. Now Christ's Passion, as stated above (Q. 68, A. 5), is a sufficient satisfaction for all the sins of all men. Consequently he who is baptized, is freed from the debt of all punishment due to him for his sins, just as if he himself had offered sufficient satisfaction for all his sins.

REPLY OBJ. 1: Since the pains of Christ's Passion are communicated to the person baptized, inasmuch as he is made a member of Christ, just as if he himself had borne those pains, his sins are set in order by the pains of Christ's Passion.

REPLY OBJ. 2: Water not only cleanses but also refreshes. And thus by refreshing it signifies the remission of the debt of punishment, just as by cleansing it signifies the washing away of guilt.

REPLY OBJ. 3: In punishments inflicted by a human tribunal, we have to consider not only what punishment a man deserves in respect of God, but also to what extent he is indebted to men who are hurt and scandalized by another's sin. Consequently, although a murderer is freed by Baptism from his debt of punishment in respect of God, he remains, nevertheless, in debt to men; and it is right that they should be edified at his punishment, since they were scandalized at his sin. But the sovereign may remit the penalty to such like out of kindness.

Article 3

Whether Baptism Should Take Away the Penalties of Sin That Belong to This Life?

Ad tertium sic proceditur. Videtur quod per Baptismum debeant auferri poenalitates praesentis vitae. Ut enim apostolus dicit, Rom. V, donum Christi potentius est quam peccatum Adae. Sed per peccatum Adae, ut ibidem apostolus dicit, *mors in hunc mundum intravit*, et per consequens omnes aliae poenalitates praesentis vitae. Ergo multo magis per donum Christi, quod in Baptismo percipitur, homo a poenalitatibus praesentis vitae debet liberari.

Praeterea, Baptismus aufert et culpam originalem et actualem, sicut supra dictum est. Sic autem aufert actualem culpam quod liberat ab omni reatu poenae consequentis actualem culpam. Ergo etiam liberat a poenalitatibus praesentis vitae, quae sunt poena originalis peccati.

Praeterea, remota causa, removetur effectus. Sed causa harum poenalitatum est peccatum originale, quod tollitur per Baptismum. Ergo non debent huiusmodi poenalitates remanere.

Sed contra est quod, super illud Rom. VI, *destruatur corpus peccati*, dicit Glossa, *per Baptismum id agitur ut vetus homo crucifigatur et corpus peccati destruatur, non ita ut in ipsa vivente carne concupiscentia respersa et innata repente absumatur et non sit, sed ne obsit mortuo quae inerat nato*. Ergo pari ratione nec aliae poenalitates per Baptismum tolluntur.

Respondeo dicendum quod Baptismus habet virtutem auferendi poenalitates praesentis vitae, non tamen eas aufert in praesenti vita, sed eius virtute auferentur a iustis in resurrectione, *quando mortale hoc induet immortalitatem*, ut dicitur I Cor. XV. Et hoc rationabiliter. Primo quidem, quia per Baptismum homo incorporatur Christo et efficitur membrum eius, ut supra dictum est. Et ideo conveniens est ut id agatur in membro incorporato quod est actum in capite. Christus autem a principio suae conceptionis fuit plenus gratia et veritate, habuit tamen corpus passibile, quod per passionem et mortem est ad vitam gloriosam resuscitatum. Unde et Christianus in Baptismo gratiam consequitur quantum ad animam, habet tamen corpus passibile, in quo pro Christo possit pati; sed tandem resuscitabitur ad impassibilem vitam. Unde apostolus dicit, Rom. VIII, *qui suscitavit Iesum Christum a mortuis, vivificabit et mortalia corpora nostra, propter inhabitantem spiritum eius in nobis*. Et infra eodem, *heredes quidem Dei, coheredes autem Christi, si tamen compatimur, ut et simul glorificemur*.

Objection 1: It seems that Baptism should take away the penalties of sin that belong to this life. For as the Apostle says (Rom 5:15), the gift of Christ is farther-reaching than the sin of Adam. But through Adam's sin, as the Apostle says (Rom 5:12), *death entered into this world*, and, consequently, all the other penalties of the present life. Much more, therefore, should man be freed from the penalties of the present life, by the gift of Christ which is received in Baptism.

Obj. 2: Further, Baptism takes away the guilt of both original and actual sin. Now it takes away the guilt of actual sin in such a way as to free man from all debt of punishment resulting therefrom. Therefore it also frees man from the penalties of the present life, which are a punishment of original sin.

Obj. 3: Further, if the cause be removed, the effect is removed. But the cause of these penalties is original sin, which is taken away by Baptism. Therefore such like penalties should not remain.

On the contrary, on Rom. 6:6, *that the body of sin may be destroyed*, a gloss says: *The effect of Baptism is that the old man is crucified, and the body of sin destroyed, not as though the living flesh of man were delivered by the destruction of that concupiscence with which it has been bespattered from its birth; but that it may not hurt him, when dead, though it was in him when he was born*. Therefore for the same reason neither are the other penalties taken away by Baptism.

I answer that, Baptism has the power to take away the penalties of the present life yet it does not take them away during the present life, but by its power they will be taken away from the just in the resurrection when *this mortal hath put on immortality* (1 Cor 15:54). And this is reasonable. First, because, by Baptism, man is incorporated in Christ, and is made His member, as stated above (A. 3; Q. 68, A. 5). Consequently it is fitting that what takes place in the Head should take place also in the member incorporated. Now, from the very beginning of His conception Christ was *full of grace and truth*, yet He had a passible body, which through His Passion and death was raised up to a life of glory. Wherefore a Christian receives grace in Baptism, as to his soul; but he retains a passible body, so that he may suffer for Christ therein: yet at length he will be raised up to a life of impassibility. Hence the Apostle says (Rom 8:11): *He that raised up Jesus Christ from the dead, shall quicken also our mortal bodies, because of His Spirit that dwelleth in us*: and further on in the same chapter (Rom 8:17): *Heirs indeed of God, and joint heirs with Christ: yet so, if we suffer with Him, that we may be also glorified with Him*.

Secundo, hoc est conveniens propter spirituale exercitium, ut videlicet contra concupiscentiam et alias passibilitates pugnans homo victoriae coronam acciperet. Unde super illud Rom. VI, *ut destruatur corpus peccati,* dicit Glossa, *si post Baptismum vixerit homo in carne, habet concupiscentiam cum qua pugnet, eamque, adiuvante Deo, superet.* In cuius figura dicitur Iudic. III, *hae sunt gentes quas dominus dereliquit ut erudiret in eis Israelem, et postea discerent filii eorum certare cum hostibus, et habere consuetudinem praeliandi.*

Tertio, hoc fuit conveniens ne homines ad Baptismum accederent propter impassibilitatem praesentis vitae, et non propter gloriam vitae aeternae. Unde et apostolus dicit, I Cor. XV, *si in hac vita tantum sperantes sumus in Christo, miserabiliores sumus omnibus hominibus.*

AD PRIMUM ergo dicendum quod, sicut Glossa dicit, Rom. VI, super illud, *ut ultra non serviamus peccato, sicut aliquis capiens hostem atrocissimum non statim interficit eum, sed patitur eum cum dedecore et dolore aliquantulum vivere; ita et Christus prius poenam alligavit, in futuro autem perimet.*

AD SECUNDUM dicendum quod, sicut ibidem dicit Glossa, *duplex est poena peccati, gehennalis et temporalis. Gehennalem prorsus delevit Christus, ut eam non sentiant baptizati et vere poenitentes. Temporalem vero nondum penitus tulit, manet enim fames sitis et mors. Sed regnum et dominium eius deiecit,* ut scilicet haec homo non timeat, et tandem in novissimo eam penitus exterminabit.

AD TERTIUM dicendum quod, sicut in secunda parte dictum est, peccatum originale hoc modo processit quod primo persona infecit naturam, postmodum vero natura infecit personam. Christus vero converso ordine prius reparat id quod personae est, postmodum simul in omnibus reparabit id quod naturae est. Et ideo culpam originalis peccati, et etiam poenam carentiae visionis divinae, quae respiciunt personam, statim per Baptismum tollit ab homine. Sed poenalitates praesentis vitae, sicut mors, fames, sitis et alia huiusmodi, respiciunt naturam, ex cuius principiis causantur, prout est destituta originali iustitia. Et ideo isti defectus non tollentur nisi in ultima reparatione naturae per resurrectionem gloriosam.

Second, this is suitable for our spiritual training: namely, in order that, by fighting against concupiscence and other defects to which he is subject, man may receive the crown of victory. Wherefore on Rom. 6:6, *that the body of sin may be destroyed,* a gloss says: *If a man after Baptism live in the flesh, he has concupiscence to fight against, and to conquer by God's help.* In sign of which it is written (Judg 3:1, 2): *These are the nations which the Lord left, that by them He might instruct Israel . . . that afterwards their children might learn to fight with their enemies, and to be trained up to war.*

Third, this was suitable, lest men might seek to be baptized for the sake of impassibility in the present life, and not for the sake of the glory of life eternal. Wherefore the Apostle says (1 Cor 15:19): *If in this life only we have hope in Christ, we are of all men most miserable.*

REPLY OBJ. 1: As a gloss says on Rom. 6:6, *that we may serve sin no longer—Like a man who, having captured a redoubtable enemy, slays him not forthwith, but suffers him to live for a little time in shame and suffering; so did Christ first of all fetter our punishment, but at a future time He will destroy it.*

REPLY OBJ. 2: As the gloss says on the same passage (cf. ad 1), *the punishment of sin is twofold, the punishment of hell, and temporal punishment. Christ entirely abolished the punishment of hell, so that those who are baptized and truly repent, should not be subject to it. He did not, however, altogether abolish temporal punishment yet awhile; for hunger, thirst, and death still remain. But He overthrew its kingdom and power* in the sense that man should no longer be in fear of them: *and at length He will altogether exterminate it at the last day.*

REPLY OBJ. 3: As we stated in the Second Part (I-II, Q. 81, A. 1; Q. 82, A. 1, ad 2), original sin spread in this way, that at first the person infected the nature, and afterwards the nature infected the person. Whereas Christ in reverse order at first repairs what regards the person, and afterwards will simultaneously repair what pertains to the nature in all men. Consequently by Baptism He takes away from man forthwith the guilt of original sin and the punishment of being deprived of the heavenly vision. But the penalties of the present life, such as death, hunger, thirst, and the like, pertain to the nature, from the principles of which they arise, inasmuch as it is deprived of original justice. Therefore these defects will not be taken away until the ultimate restoration of nature through the glorious resurrection.

Article 4

Whether Grace and Virtues Are Bestowed on Man by Baptism?

AD QUARTUM SIC PROCEDITUR. Videtur quod per Baptismum non conferantur homini gratia et virtutes. Quia, sicut supra dictum est, sacramenta novae legis efficiunt quod figurant. Sed per ablutionem Baptismi significatur emundatio animae a culpa, non autem informatio animae per gratiam et virtutes. Videtur igitur quod per Baptismum non conferantur homini gratia et virtutes.

PRAETEREA, illud quod iam aliquis adeptus est, non indiget iterum suscipere. Sed aliqui accedunt ad Baptismum iam habentes gratiam et virtutes; sicut Act. X legitur, *vir quidam erat in Caesarea, nomine Cornelius, centurio cohortis quae dicitur Italica, religiosus et timens Deum*; qui tamen postea a Petro baptizatus est. Non ergo per Baptismum conferuntur gratia et virtutes.

PRAETEREA, virtus est habitus, ad cuius rationem pertinet quod sit qualitas difficile mobilis, per quam aliquis faciliter et delectabiliter operetur. Sed post Baptismum remanet in hominibus pronitas ad malum, per quod tollitur virtus; et consequitur difficultatem quis ad bonum, quod est actus virtutis. Ergo per Baptismum non consequitur homo gratiam et virtutes.

SED CONTRA est quod, ad Tit. III, dicit apostolus, *salvos nos fecit per lavacrum regenerationis, idest per Baptismum, et renovationis spiritus sancti, quem effudit in nos abunde, idest ad remissionem peccatorum et copiam virtutum*, ut Glossa ibidem exponit. Sic ergo in Baptismo datur gratia spiritus sancti et copia virtutum.

RESPONDEO dicendum quod, sicut Augustinus dicit, in libro de Baptismo parvulorum, *ad hoc Baptismus valet, ut baptizati Christo incorporentur ut membra eius.* A capite autem Christo in omnia membra eius gratiae et virtutis plenitudo derivatur, secundum illud Ioan. I, *de plenitudine eius nos omnes accepimus.* Unde manifestum est quod per Baptismum aliquis consequitur gratiam et virtutes.

AD PRIMUM ergo dicendum quod, sicut aqua Baptismi per suam ablutionem significat emundationem culpae, et per suum refrigerium significat liberationem a poena, ita per naturalem claritatem significat splendorem gratiae et virtutum.

AD SECUNDUM dicendum quod, sicut dictum est, remissionem peccatorum aliquis consequitur ante Baptismum secundum quod habet Baptismum in voto, vel explicite vel implicite et tamen, cum realiter suscipit Baptismum, fit plenior remissio, quantum ad liberationem a tota poena. Ita etiam ante Baptismum Cornelius et alii similes consequuntur gratiam et virtutes per fidem

OBJECTION 1: It seems that grace and virtues are not bestowed on man by Baptism. Because, as stated above (Q. 62, A. 1, ad 1), the sacraments of the New Law *effect what they signify.* But the baptismal cleansing signifies the cleansing of the soul from guilt, and not the fashioning of the soul with grace and virtues. Therefore it seems that grace and virtues are not bestowed on man by Baptism.

OBJ. 2: Further, one does not need to receive what one has already acquired. But some approach Baptism who have already grace and virtues: thus we read (Acts 10:1, 2): *There was a certain man in Cesarea, named Cornelius, a centurion of that which is called the Italian band, a religious man and fearing God*; who, nevertheless, was afterwards baptized by Peter. Therefore grace and virtues are not bestowed by Baptism.

OBJ. 3: Further, virtue is a habit: which is defined as a *quality not easily removed, by which one may act easily and pleasurably.* But after Baptism man retains proneness to evil which removes virtue; and experiences difficulty in doing good, in which the act of virtue consists. Therefore man does not acquire grace and virtue in Baptism.

ON THE CONTRARY, The Apostle says (Titus 3:5, 6): *He saved us by the laver of regeneration,* i.e., by Baptism, *and renovation of the Holy Spirit, Whom He hath poured forth upon us abundantly,* i.e., unto the remission of sins and the fullness of virtues, as a gloss expounds. Therefore the grace of the Holy Spirit and the fullness of virtues are given in Baptism.

I ANSWER THAT, As Augustine says in the book on Infant Baptism (*De Pecc. Merit. et Remiss. i*) *the effect of Baptism is that the baptized are incorporated in Christ as His members.* Now the fullness of grace and virtues flows from Christ the Head to all His members, according to John 1:16: *Of His fullness we all have received.* Hence it is clear that man receives grace and virtues in Baptism.

REPLY OBJ. 1: As the baptismal water by its cleansing signifies the washing away of guilt, and by its refreshment the remission of punishment, so by its natural clearness it signifies the splendor of grace and virtues.

REPLY OBJ. 2: As stated above (A. 1, ad 2; Q. 68, A. 2) man receives the forgiveness of sins before Baptism in so far as he has Baptism of desire, explicitly or implicitly; and yet when he actually receives Baptism, he receives a fuller remission, as to the remission of the entire punishment. So also before Baptism Cornelius and others like him receive grace and virtues through their faith in Christ and

Christi et desiderium Baptismi, implicite vel explicite, postmodum tamen in Baptismo maiorem copiam gratiae et virtutum consequuntur. Unde super illud Psalmi, *super aquam refectionis educavit me*, dicit Glossa, *per augmentum virtutis et bonae operationis educavit in Baptismo.*

AD TERTIUM dicendum quod difficultas ad bonum et pronitas ad malum inveniuntur in baptizatis, non propter defectum habitus virtutum, sed propter concupiscentiam, quae non tollitur in Baptismo. Sicut tamen per Baptismum diminuitur concupiscentia, ut non dominetur, ita etiam diminuitur utrumque istorum, ne homo ab his superetur.

their desire for Baptism, implicit or explicit: but afterwards when baptized, they receive a yet greater fullness of grace and virtues. Hence in Ps. 22:2, *He hath brought me up on the water of refreshment*, a gloss says: *He has brought us up by an increase of virtue and good deeds in Baptism.*

REPLY OBJ. 3: Difficulty in doing good and proneness to evil are in the baptized, not through their lacking the habits of the virtues, but through concupiscence which is not taken away in Baptism. But just as concupiscence is diminished by Baptism, so as not to enslave us, so also are both the aforesaid defects diminished, so that man be not overcome by them.

Article 5

Whether Certain Acts of the Virtues Are Fittingly Set Down As Effects of Baptism,
to Wit—Incorporation in Christ, Enlightenment, and Fruitfulness?

AD QUINTUM SIC PROCEDITUR. Videtur quod inconvenienter attribuantur Baptismo pro effectibus quidam actus virtutum, scilicet, incorporatio ad Christum, illuminatio, fecundatio. Non enim Baptismus datur adulto nisi fideli, secundum illud Marc. ult., *qui crediderit et baptizatus fuerit, salvus erit*. Sed per fidem aliquis incorporatur Christo, secundum illud Ephes. III, *habitare Christum per fidem in cordibus vestris*. Ergo nullus baptizatur nisi iam Christo incorporatus. Non ergo est effectus Baptismi incorporari Christo.

PRAETEREA, illuminatio fit per doctrinam, secundum illud Ephes. III *mihi omnium minimo data est gratia haec, illuminare omnes*, et cetera. Sed doctrina praecedit Baptismum in catechismo. Non ergo est effectus Baptismi.

PRAETEREA, fecunditas pertinet ad generationem activam. Sed per Baptismum aliquis regeneratur spiritualiter. Ergo fecunditas non est effectus Baptismi.

SED CONTRA est quod Augustinus dicit, in libro de Baptismo parvulorum, quod *ad hoc valet Baptismus ut baptizati Christo incorporentur*. Dionysius etiam, II cap. Eccl. Hier., illuminationem attribuit Baptismo. Et super illud Psalmi, *super aquam refectionis educavit*, dicit Glossa quod *anima peccatorum, ariditate sterilis, fecundatur per Baptismum.*

RESPONDEO dicendum quod per Baptismum aliquis regeneratur in spiritualem vitam, quae est propria fidelium Christi, sicut apostolus dicit, Galat. II, *quod autem nunc vivo in carne, in fide vivo filii Dei*. Vita autem non est nisi membrorum capiti unitorum, a quo sensum et motum suscipiunt. Et ideo necesse est quod per Baptismum aliquis incorporetur Christo quasi membrum ipsius. Sicut autem a capite naturali derivatur ad membra

OBJECTION 1: It seems that certain acts of the virtues are unfittingly set down as effects of Baptism, to wit—*incorporation in Christ, enlightenment, and fruitfulness*. For Baptism is not given to an adult, except he believe; according to Mk. 16:16: *He that believeth and is baptized, shall be saved*. But it is by faith that man is incorporated in Christ, according to Eph. 3:17: *That Christ may dwell by faith in your hearts*. Therefore no one is baptized except he be already incorporated in Christ. Therefore incorporation with Christ is not the effect of Baptism.

OBJ. 2: Further, enlightenment is caused by teaching, according to Eph. 3:8, 9: *To me the least of all the saints, is given this grace . . . to enlighten all men*, etc. But teaching by the catechism precedes Baptism. Therefore it is not the effect of Baptism.

OBJ. 3: Further, fruitfulness pertains to active generation. But a man is regenerated spiritually by Baptism. Therefore fruitfulness is not an effect of Baptism.

ON THE CONTRARY, Augustine says in the book on Infant Baptism (*De Pecc. Merit. et Remiss.* i) that *the effect of Baptism is that the baptized are incorporated in Christ*. And Dionysius (*Eccl. Hier.* ii) ascribes enlightenment to Baptism. And on Ps. 22:2, *He hath brought me up on the water of refreshment*, a gloss says that *the sinner's soul, sterilized by drought, is made fruitful by Baptism.*

I ANSWER THAT, By Baptism man is born again unto the spiritual life, which is proper to the faithful of Christ, as the Apostle says (Gal 2:20): *And that I live now in the flesh; I live in the faith of the Son of God*. Now life is only in those members that are united to the head, from which they derive sense and movement. And therefore it follows of necessity that by Baptism man is incorporated in Christ, as one of His members. Again, just as the members derive

sensus et motus, ita a capite spirituali, quod est Christus, derivatur ad membra eius sensus spiritualis, qui consistit in cognitione veritatis, et motus spiritualis, qui est per gratiae instinctum. Unde Ioan. I dicitur, *vidimus eum plenum gratiae et veritatis, et de plenitudine eius omnes accepimus.* Et ideo consequens est quod baptizati illuminentur a Christo circa cognitionem veritatis, et fecundentur ab eo fecunditate bonorum operum per gratiae infusionem.

AD PRIMUM ergo dicendum quod adulti prius credentes in Christum sunt ei incorporati mentaliter. Sed postmodum, cum baptizantur, incorporantur ei quodammodo corporaliter, scilicet per visibile sacramentum, sine cuius proposito nec mentaliter incorporari potuissent.

AD SECUNDUM dicendum quod doctor illuminat exterius per ministerium catechizando, sed Deus illuminat interius baptizatos, praeparans corda eorum ad recipiendam doctrinam veritatis, secundum illud Ioan. VI, *scriptum est in prophetis, erunt omnes docibiles Dei.*

AD TERTIUM dicendum quod effectus Baptismi ponitur fecunditas qua aliquis producit bona opera, non autem fecunditas qua aliquis generat alios in Christo, sicut apostolus dicit, I Cor. IV, *in Christo Iesu per Evangelium ego vos genui.*

sense and movement from the material head, so from their spiritual Head, i.e., Christ, do His members derive spiritual sense consisting in the knowledge of truth, and spiritual movement which results from the instinct of grace. Hence it is written (John 1:14, 16): *We have seen Him . . . full of grace and truth; and of His fullness we all have received.* And it follows from this that the baptized are enlightened by Christ as to the knowledge of truth, and made fruitful by Him with the fruitfulness of good works by the infusion of grace.

REPLY OBJ. 1: Adults who already believe in Christ are incorporated in Him mentally. But afterwards, when they are baptized, they are incorporated in Him, corporally, as it were, i.e., by the visible sacrament; without the desire of which they could not have been incorporated in Him even mentally.

REPLY OBJ. 2: The teacher enlightens outwardly and ministerially by catechizing: but God enlightens the baptized inwardly, by preparing their hearts for the reception of the doctrines of truth, according to John 6:45: *It is written in the prophets . . . They shall all be taught of God.*

REPLY OBJ. 3: The fruitfulness which I ascribed as an effect of Baptism is that by which man brings forth good works; not that by which he begets others in Christ, as the Apostle says (1 Cor 4:15): *In Christ Jesus by the Gospel I have begotten you.*

Article 6

Whether Children Receive Grace and Virtue in Baptism?

AD SEXTUM SIC PROCEDITUR. Videtur quod pueri in Baptismo non consequantur gratiam et virtutes. Gratia enim et virtutes non habentur sine fide et caritate. Sed *fides*, ut Augustinus dicit, *consistit in credentium voluntate*, et similiter etiam caritas consistit in diligentium voluntate, cuius usum pueri non habent, et sic non habent fidem et caritatem. Ergo pueri in Baptismo non recipiunt gratiam et virtutes.

PRAETEREA, super illud Ioan. XIV, *maiora horum faciet*, dicit Augustinus quod ut ex impio iustus fiat, *in illo, sed non sine illo Christus operatur.* Sed puer, cum non habeat usum liberi arbitrii, non cooperatur Christo ad suam iustificationem, immo quandoque pro posse renititur. Ergo non iustificatur per gratiam et virtutes.

PRAETEREA, Rom. IV dicitur, *ei qui non operatur, credenti autem in eum qui iustificat impium, reputabitur fides eius ad iustitiam, secundum propositum gratiae Dei.* Sed puer non est credens in eum qui iustificat impium. Ergo non consequitur gratiam iustificantem neque virtutes.

OBJECTION 1: It seems that children do not receive grace and virtues in Baptism. For grace and virtues are not possessed without faith and charity. But faith, as Augustine says (*Ep. xcviii*), *depends on the will of the believer*: and in like manner charity depends on the will of the lover. Now children have not the use of the will, and consequently they have neither faith nor charity. Therefore children do not receive grace and virtues in Baptism.

OBJ. 2: Further, on John 14:12, *Greater than these shall he do*, Augustine says that in order for the ungodly to be made righteous *Christ worketh in him, but not without him.* But a child, through not having the use of free-will, does not co-operate with Christ unto its justification: indeed at times it does its best to resist. Therefore it is not justified by grace and virtues.

OBJ. 3: Further, it is written (Rom 4:5): *To him that worketh not, yet believing in Him that justifieth the ungodly, his faith is reputed to justice according to the purpose of the grace of God.* But a child believeth not *in Him that justifieth the ungodly.* Therefore a child receives neither sanctifying grace nor virtues.

PRAETEREA, quod ex carnali intentione agitur, non videtur habere spiritualem effectum. Sed quandoque pueri ad Baptismum deferuntur carnali intentione, ut scilicet corporaliter sanentur. Non ergo consequuntur spiritualem effectum gratiae et virtutum.

SED CONTRA est quod Augustinus dicit, in Enchirid., *parvuli renascendo moriuntur illi peccato quod nascendo contraxerunt, et per hoc ad illos etiam pertinet quod dicitur, consepulti sumus cum illo per Baptismum in mortem,* (subditur autem) *ut, quomodo resurrexit Christus a mortuis per gloriam patris ita et nos in novitate vitae ambulemus.* Sed novitas vitae est per gratiam et virtutes. Ergo pueri consequuntur in Baptismo gratiam et virtutes.

RESPONDEO dicendum quod quidam antiqui posuerunt quod pueris in Baptismo non dantur gratia et virtutes, sed imprimitur eis character Christi, cuius virtute, cum ad perfectam aetatem venerint, consequuntur gratiam et virtutes. Sed hoc patet esse falsum dupliciter. Primo quidem, quia pueri, sicut et adulti, in Baptismo efficiuntur membra Christi. Unde necesse est quod a capite recipiant influxum gratiae et virtutis. Secundo, quia secundum hoc pueri decedentes post Baptismum non pervenirent ad vitam aeternam, quia, ut dicitur Rom. VI, *gratia Dei est vita aeterna.* Et ita nihil profuisset eis ad salutem baptizatos fuisse.

Causa autem erroris fuit quia nescierunt distinguere inter habitum et actum. Et sic, videntes pueros inhabiles ad actus virtutum, crediderunt eos post Baptismum nullatenus virtutem habere. Sed ista impotentia operandi non accidit pueris ex defectu habituum, sed ex impedimento corporali, sicut etiam dormientes, quamvis habeant habitus virtutum, impediuntur tamen ab actibus propter somnum.

AD PRIMUM ergo dicendum quod fides et caritas consistunt in voluntate hominum, ita tamen quod habitus harum et aliarum virtutum requirunt potentiam voluntatis, quae est in pueris; sed actus virtutum requirunt actum voluntatis, qui non est in pueris. Et hoc modo Augustinus dicit, in libro de Baptismo parvulorum, quod *parvulum, etsi nondum illa fides quae in credentium voluntate consistit, iam tamen ipsius fidei sacramentum,* quod scilicet causat habitum fidei, *fidelem facit.*

AD SECUNDUM dicendum quod, sicut Augustinus dicit, in libro de caritate, *nemo ex aqua et spiritu sancto renascitur nisi volens.* Quod non de parvulis, sed de adultis intelligendum est. Et similiter de adultis intelligendum est quod homo a Christo sine ipso non iustificatur. Quod autem parvuli baptizandi, prout viribus possunt, reluctantur, non eis imputatur, *quia in tantum nesciunt quid faciunt, ut nec facere videantur,* ut Augustinus dicit, in libro de praesentia Dei ad Dardanum.

OBJ. 4: Further, what is done with a carnal intention does not seem to have a spiritual effect. But sometimes children are taken to Baptism with a carnal intention, to wit, that their bodies may be healed. Therefore they do not receive the spiritual effect consisting in grace and virtue.

ON THE CONTRARY, Augustine says (*Enchiridion* lii): *When little children are baptized, they die to that sin which they contracted in birth: so that to them also may be applied the words: 'We are buried together with Him by Baptism unto death':* (and he continues thus) *'that as Christ is risen from the dead by the glory of the Father, so we also may walk in newness of life.'* Now newness of life is through grace and virtues. Therefore children receive grace and virtues in Baptism.

I ANSWER THAT, Some of the early writers held that children do not receive grace and virtues in Baptism, but that they receive the imprint of the character of Christ, by the power of which they receive grace and virtue when they arrive at the perfect age. But this is evidently false, for two reasons. First, because children, like adults, are made members of Christ in Baptism; hence they must, of necessity, receive an influx of grace and virtues from the Head. Second, because, if this were true, children that die after Baptism, would not come to eternal life; since according to Rom. 6:23, *the grace of God is life everlasting.* And consequently Baptism would not have profited them unto salvation.

Now the source of their error was that they did not recognize the distinction between habit and act. And so, seeing children to be incapable of acts of virtue, they thought that they had no virtues at all after Baptism. But this inability of children to act is not due to the absence of habits, but to an impediment on the part of the body: thus also when a man is asleep, though he may have the habits of virtue, yet is he hindered from virtuous acts through being asleep.

REPLY OBJ. 1: Faith and charity depend on man's will, yet so that the habits of these and other virtues require the power of the will which is in children; whereas acts of virtue require an act of the will, which is not in children. In this sense Augustine says in the book on Infant Baptism (*Ep. xcviii*): *The little child is made a believer, not as yet by that faith which depends on the will of the believer, but by the sacrament of faith itself,* which causes the habit of faith.

REPLY OBJ. 2: As Augustine says in his book on Charity (*Ep. Joan. ad Parth. iii*), *no man is born of water and the Holy Spirit unwillingly* which is to be understood not of little children but of adults. In like manner we are to understand as applying to adults, that man *without himself is not justified by Christ.* Moreover, if little children who are about to be baptized resist as much as they can, *this is not imputed to them, since so little do they know what they do, that they seem not to do it at all*: as Augustine says in a book on the Presence of God, addressed to Dardanus (*Ep. clxxxvii*).

AD TERTIUM dicendum quod, sicut Augustinus dicit, *parvulis mater Ecclesia aliorum pedes accommodat ut veniant, aliorum cor ut credant, aliorum linguam ut fateantur.* Et ita pueri credunt, non per actum proprium, sed per fidem Ecclesiae, quae eis communicatur. Et huius fidei virtute conferuntur eis gratia et virtutes.

AD QUARTUM dicendum quod carnalis intentio deferentium pueros ad Baptismum nihil eis nocet, sicut nec culpa unius nocet alteri, nisi consentiat. Unde Augustinus dicit, in epistola ad Bonifacium, *non illud te moveat quod quidam non ea fide ad Baptismum percipiendum parvulos ferunt ut gratia spirituali ad vitam regenerentur aeternam, sed hoc eos putant remedio corporalem retinere vel recipere sanitatem. Non enim propterea illi non regenerantur, quia non ab istis hac intentione offeruntur.*

REPLY OBJ. 3: As Augustine says (*Serm. clxxvi*): *Mother Church lends other feet to the little children that they may come; another heart that they may believe; another tongue that they may confess.* So that children believe, not by their own act, but by the faith of the Church, which is applied to them: by the power of which faith, grace and virtues are bestowed on them.

REPLY OBJ. 4: The carnal intention of those who take children to be baptized does not hurt the latter, as neither does one's sin hurt another, unless he consent. Hence Augustine says in his letter to Boniface (*Ep. xcviii*): *Be not disturbed because some bring children to be baptized, not in the hope that they may be born again to eternal life by the spiritual grace, but because they think it to be a remedy whereby they may preserve or recover health. For they are not deprived of regeneration, through not being brought for this intention.*

Article 7

Whether the Effect of Baptism Is to Open the Gates of the Heavenly Kingdom?

AD SEPTIMUM SIC PROCEDITUR. Videtur quod effectus Baptismi non sit apertio ianuae regni caelestis. Illud enim quod est apertum, non indiget apertione. Sed ianua regni caelestis est aperta per passionem Christi, unde Apoc. IV dicitur, *post haec vidi ostium magnum apertum in caelo.* Non est ergo effectus Baptismi apertio ianuae regni caelestis.

PRAETEREA, Baptismus omni tempore ex quo institutus fuit, habet suum effectum. Sed quidam baptizati sunt Baptismo Christi ante eius passionem, ut habetur Ioan. III, quibus, si tunc decessissent, introitus regni caelestis non patebat, in quod nullus ante Christum introivit, secundum illud Mich. II, *ascendit pandens iter ante eos.* Non est ergo effectus Baptismi apertio ianuae regni caelestis.

PRAETEREA, baptizati adhuc sunt obnoxii morti et aliis poenalitatibus vitae praesentis, ut supra dictum est. Sed nulli est apertus aditus regni caelestis quandiu est obnoxius poenae, sicut patet de illis qui sunt in Purgatorio. Non ergo est effectus Baptismi apertio ianuae regni caelestis.

SED CONTRA est quod super illud Luc. III, *apertum est caelum,* dicit Glossa Bedae, *virtus hic Baptismatis ostenditur, de quo quisque cum egreditur, ei regni caelestis ianua aperitur.*

RESPONDEO dicendum quod aperire ianuam regni caelestis est amovere impedimentum quo aliquis impeditur regnum caeleste intrare. Hoc autem impedimentum

OBJECTION 1: It seems that it is not the effect of Baptism, to open the gates of the heavenly kingdom. For what is already opened needs no opening. But the gates of the heavenly kingdom were opened by Christ's Passion: hence it is written (Rev 4:1): *After these things I looked and behold (a great) door was opened in heaven.* Therefore it is not the effect of Baptism, to open the gates of the heavenly kingdom.

OBJ. 2: Further, Baptism has had its effects ever since it was instituted. But some were baptized with Christ's Baptism, before His Passion, according to John 3:22, 26: and if they had died then, the gates of the heavenly kingdom would not have been opened to them, since none entered therein before Christ, according to Mic. 2:13: *He went up that shall open the way before them.* Therefore it is not the effect of Baptism, to open the gates of the heavenly kingdom.

OBJ. 3: Further, the baptized are still subject to death and the other penalties of the present life, as stated above (A. 3). But entrance to the heavenly kingdom is opened to none that are subject to punishment: as is clear in regard to those who are in purgatory. Therefore it is not the effect of Baptism, to open the gates of the heavenly kingdom.

ON THE CONTRARY, on Luke 3:21, *Heaven was opened,* the gloss of Bede says: *We see here the power of Baptism; from which when a man comes forth, the gates of the heavenly kingdom are opened unto him.*

I ANSWER THAT, To open the gates of the heavenly kingdom is to remove the obstacle that prevents one from entering therein. Now this obstacle is guilt and the debt of

est culpa et reatus poenae. Ostensum est autem supra quod per Baptismum totaliter omnis culpa et etiam omnis reatus poenae tollitur. Unde consequens est quod effectus Baptismi sit apertio regni caelestis.

AD PRIMUM ergo dicendum quod Baptismus intantum aperit baptizato ianuam regni caelestis, inquantum incorporat eum passioni Christi, virtutem eius homini applicando.

AD SECUNDUM dicendum quod, quando passio Christi nondum erat realiter perfecta sed solum in fide credentium, Baptismus proportionaliter causabat ianuae apertionem, non quidem in re, sed in spe. Baptizati enim tunc decedentes ex certa spe introitum regni caelestis expectabant.

AD TERTIUM dicendum quod baptizatus non est obnoxius morti et poenalitatibus vitae praesentis propter reatum personae, sed propter statum naturae. Et ideo propter hoc non impeditur ab introitu regni caelestis, quando anima separatur a corpore per mortem, quasi iam persoluto eo quod naturae debebatur.

punishment. But it has been shown above (AA. 1, 2) that all guilt and also all debt of punishment are taken away by Baptism. It follows, therefore, that the effect of Baptism is to open the gates of the heavenly kingdom.

REPLY OBJ. 1: Baptism opens the gates of the heavenly kingdom to the baptized in so far as it incorporates them in the Passion of Christ, by applying its power to man.

REPLY OBJ. 2: When Christ's Passion was not as yet consummated actually but only in the faith of believers, Baptism proportionately caused the gates to be opened, not in fact but in hope. For the baptized who died then looked forward, with a sure hope, to enter the heavenly kingdom.

REPLY OBJ. 3: The baptized are subject to death and the penalties of the present life, not by reason of a personal debt of punishment but by reason of the state of their nature. And therefore this is no bar to their entrance to the heavenly kingdom, when death severs the soul from the body; since they have paid, as it were, the debt of nature.

Article 8

Whether Baptism Has an Equal Effect in All?

AD OCTAVUM SIC PROCEDITUR. Videtur quod Baptismus non habeat in omnibus aequalem effectum. Effectus enim Baptismi est remotio culpae. Sed in quibusdam plura peccata tollit quam in aliis, nam in pueris tollit solum peccatum originale; in adultis autem etiam actualia, in quibusdam plura, in quibusdam vero pauciora. Non ergo aequalem effectum habet Baptismus in omnibus.

PRAETEREA, per Baptismum conferuntur homini gratia et virtutes. Sed quidam post Baptismum videntur habere maiorem gratiam et perfectiorem virtutem quam alii baptizati. Non ergo Baptismus habet aequalem effectum in omnibus.

PRAETEREA, natura perficitur per gratiam sicut materia per formam. Sed forma recipitur in materia secundum eius capacitatem. Cum ergo in quibusdam baptizatis, etiam pueris, sit maior capacitas naturalium quam in aliis, videtur quod quidam maiorem gratiam consequantur quam alii.

PRAETEREA, quidam in Baptismo consequuntur non solum spiritualem salutem, sed etiam corporalem, sicut patet de Constantino, qui in Baptismo mundatus est a lepra. Non autem omnes infirmi corporalem salutem consequuntur in Baptismo. Ergo non habet aequalem effectum in omnibus.

OBJECTION 1: It seems that Baptism has not an equal effect in all. For the effect of Baptism is to remove guilt. But in some it takes away more sins than in others; for in children it takes away only original sins, whereas in adults it takes away actual sins, in some many, in others few. Therefore Baptism has not an equal effect in all.

OBJ. 2: Further, grace and virtues are bestowed on man by Baptism. But some, after Baptism, seem to have more grace and more perfect virtue than others who have been baptized. Therefore Baptism has not an equal effect in all.

OBJ. 3: Further, nature is perfected by grace, as matter by form. But a form is received into matter according to its capacity. Therefore, since some of the baptized, even children, have greater capacity for natural gifts than others have, it seems that some receive greater grace than others.

OBJ. 4: Further, in Baptism some receive not only spiritual, but also bodily health; thus Constantine was cleansed in Baptism from leprosy. But all the infirm do not receive bodily health in Baptism. Therefore it has not an equal effect in all.

Sed contra est quod dicitur Ephes. IV, *una fides, unum Baptisma*. Uniformis autem causae est uniformis effectus. Ergo Baptismus habet aequalem effectum in omnibus.

Respondeo dicendum quod duplex est effectus Baptismi, unus per se, et alius per accidens. Per se quidem effectus Baptismi est id ad quod Baptismus est institutus, scilicet ad generandum homines in spiritualem vitam. Unde, quia omnes pueri aequaliter se habent ad Baptismum, quia non in fide propria, sed in fide Ecclesiae baptizantur, omnes aequalem effectum percipiunt in Baptismo. Adulti vero, qui per propriam fidem ad Baptismum accedunt, non aequaliter se habent ad Baptismum, quidam enim cum maiori, quidam cum minori devotione ad Baptismum accedunt. Et ideo quidam plus, quidam minus de gratia novitatis accipiunt, sicut etiam ab eodem igne accipit plus caloris qui plus ei appropinquat, licet ignis, quantum est de se, aequaliter ad omnes suum calorem effundat.

Effectus autem Baptismi per accidens est ad quem Baptismus non est ordinatus, sed divina virtus hoc in Baptismo miraculose operatur, sicut super illud Rom. VI, *ut ultra non serviamus peccato*, dicit Glossa, *non hoc praestatur in Baptismo, nisi forte miraculo ineffabili creatoris, ut lex peccati, quae est in membris, prorsus extinguatur*. Et tales effectus non aequaliter suscipiuntur ab omnibus baptizatis, etiam si cum aequali devotione accedant, sed dispensantur huiusmodi effectus secundum ordinem providentiae divinae.

Ad primum ergo dicendum quod minima gratia baptismalis sufficiens est ad delendum cuncta peccata. Unde hoc non est propter maiorem efficaciam Baptismi quod in quibusdam plura, in quibusdam pauciora peccata solvit, sed propter conditionem subiecti, quia in quolibet solvit quodcumque invenerit.

Ad secundum dicendum quod hoc quod in baptizatis maior vel minor gratia apparet, potest dupliciter contingere. Uno modo, quia unus in Baptismo percipit maiorem gratiam quam alius propter maiorem devotionem, ut dictum est. Alio modo quia, etiam si aequalem gratiam percipiant, non aequaliter ea utuntur, sed unus studiosius in ea proficit, alius per negligentiam gratiae Dei deest.

Ad tertium dicendum quod diversa capacitas in hominibus non est ex diversitate mentis, quae per Baptismum renovatur, cum omnes homines, eiusdem speciei existentes, in forma conveniant, sed ex diversa dispositione corporum. Secus autem est in Angelis, qui differunt specie. Et ideo Angelis dantur dona gratuita secundum diversam capacitatem naturalium, non autem hominibus.

On the contrary, It is written (Eph 4:5): *One Faith, one Baptism*. But a uniform cause has a uniform effect. Therefore Baptism has an equal effect in all.

I answer that, The effect of Baptism is twofold, the essential effect, and the accidental. The essential effect of Baptism is that for which Baptism was instituted, namely, the begetting of men unto spiritual life. Therefore, since all children are equally disposed to Baptism, because they are baptized not in their own faith, but in that of the Church, they all receive an equal effect in Baptism. Whereas adults, who approach Baptism in their own faith, are not equally disposed to Baptism; for some approach thereto with greater, some with less, devotion. And therefore some receive a greater, some a smaller share of the grace of newness; just as from the same fire, he receives more heat who approaches nearest to it, although the fire, as far as it is concerned, sends forth its heat equally to all.

But the accidental effect of Baptism, is that to which Baptism is not ordained, but which the Divine power produces miraculously in Baptism: thus on Rom. 6:6, *that we may serve sin no longer*, a gloss says: *this is not bestowed in Baptism, save by an ineffable miracle of the Creator, so that the law of sin, which is in our members, be absolutely destroyed*. And such like effects are not equally received by all the baptized, even if they approach with equal devotion: but they are bestowed according to the ordering of Divine providence.

Reply Obj. 1: The least baptismal grace suffices to blot out all sins. Wherefore that in some more sins are loosed than in others is not due to the greater efficacy of Baptism, but to the condition of the recipient: for in each one it looses whatever it finds.

Reply Obj. 2: That greater or lesser grace appears in the baptized, may occur in two ways. First, because one receives greater grace in Baptism than another, on account of his greater devotion, as stated above. Second, because, though they receive equal grace, they do not make an equal use of it, but one applies himself more to advance therein, while another by his negligence baffles grace.

Reply Obj. 3: The various degrees of capacity in men arise, not from a variety in the mind which is renewed by Baptism (since all men, being of one species, are of one form), but from the diversity of bodies. But it is otherwise with the angels, who differ in species. And therefore gratuitous gifts are bestowed on the angels according to their diverse capacity for natural gifts, but not on men.

AD QUARTUM dicendum quod sanitas corporalis non est per se effectus Baptismi, sed est quoddam miraculosum opus providentiae divinae.

REPLY OBJ. 4: Bodily health is not the essential effect of Baptism, but a miraculous work of Divine providence.

Article 9

Whether Insincerity Hinders the Effect of Baptism?

AD NONUM SIC PROCEDITUR. Videtur quod fictio non impediat effectum Baptismi. Dicit enim apostolus, Galat. III, *quicumque in Christo baptizati estis, Christum induistis.* Sed omnes qui Baptismum Christi suscipiunt, baptizantur in Christo. Ergo omnes induunt Christum. Quod est percipere Baptismi effectum. Et ita fictio non impedit Baptismi effectum.

PRAETEREA, in Baptismo operatur virtus divina, quae potest voluntatem hominis mutare in bonum. Sed effectus causae agentis non potest impediri per id quod ab illa causa potest auferri. Ergo fictio non potest impedire Baptismi effectum.

PRAETEREA, Baptismi effectus est gratia, cui peccatum opponitur. Sed multa sunt alia peccata graviora quam fictio, de quibus non dicitur quod effectum Baptismi impediant. Ergo neque fictio impedit effectum Baptismi.

SED CONTRA est quod dicitur Sap. I, *Spiritus Sanctus disciplinae effugiet fictum.* Sed effectus Baptismi est a spiritu sancto. Ergo fictio impedit effectum Baptismi.

RESPONDEO dicendum quod, sicut Damascenus dicit, *Deus non cogit hominem ad iustitiam.* Et ideo ad hoc quod aliquis iustificetur per Baptismum, requiritur quod voluntas hominis amplectatur et Baptismum et Baptismi effectum. Dicitur autem aliquis fictus per hoc quod voluntas eius contradicit vel Baptismo, vel eius effectui. Nam secundum Augustinum, quatuor modis dicitur aliquis fictus, uno modo, ille qui non credit, cum tamen Baptismus sit fidei sacramentum; alio modo, per hoc quod contemnit ipsum sacramentum; tertio modo, per hoc quod aliter celebrat sacramentum, non servans ritum Ecclesiae; quarto, per hoc quod aliquis indevote accedit. Unde manifestum est quod fictio impedit effectum Baptismi.

AD PRIMUM ergo dicendum quod baptizari in Christo potest intelligi dupliciter. Uno modo, in Christo, idest, in Christi conformitate. Et sic quicumque baptizantur in Christo conformati ei per fidem et caritatem, induunt Christum per gratiam. Alio modo dicuntur aliqui baptizari in Christo, inquantum accipiunt Christi sacramentum. Et sic omnes induunt Christum per configurationem characteris, non autem per conformitatem gratiae.

OBJECTION 1: It seems that insincerity does not hinder the effect of Baptism. For the Apostle says (Gal 3:27): *As many of you as have been baptized in Christ Jesus, have put on Christ.* But all that receive the Baptism of Christ, are baptized in Christ. Therefore they all put on Christ: and this is to receive the effect of Baptism. Consequently insincerity does not hinder the effect of Baptism.

OBJ. 2: Further, the Divine power which can change man's will to that which is better, works in Baptism. But the effect of the efficient cause cannot be hindered by that which can be removed by that cause. Therefore insincerity cannot hinder the effect of Baptism.

OBJ. 3: Further, the effect of Baptism is grace, to which sin is in opposition. But many other sins are more grievous than insincerity, which are not said to hinder the effect of Baptism. Therefore neither does insincerity.

ON THE CONTRARY, It is written (Wis 1:5): *The Holy Spirit of discipline will flee from the deceitful.* But the effect of Baptism is from the Holy Spirit. Therefore insincerity hinders the effect of Baptism.

I ANSWER THAT, As Damascene says (*De Fide Orth.* ii), *God does not compel man to be righteous.* Consequently in order that a man be justified by Baptism, his will must needs embrace both Baptism and the baptismal effect. Now, a man is said to be insincere by reason of his will being in contradiction with either Baptism or its effect. For, according to Augustine (*De Bapt. cont. Donat.* vii), a man is said to be insincere, in four ways: first, because he does not believe, whereas Baptism is the sacrament of Faith; second, through scorning the sacrament itself; third, through observing a rite which differs from that prescribed by the Church in conferring the sacrament; fourth, through approaching the sacrament without devotion. Wherefore it is manifest that insincerity hinders the effect of Baptism.

REPLY OBJ. 1: *To be baptized in Christ*, may be taken in two ways. First, *in Christ*, i.e., *in conformity with Christ.* And thus whoever is baptized in Christ so as to be conformed to Him by Faith and Charity, puts on Christ by grace. Second, a man is said to be baptized in Christ, in so far as he receives Christ's sacrament. And thus all put on Christ, through being configured to Him by the character, but not through being conformed to Him by grace.

AD SECUNDUM dicendum quod, quando Deus voluntatem hominis de malo in bonum mutat, tunc homo non accedit fictus. Sed non semper hoc Deus facit. Nec ad hoc sacramentum ordinatur, ut de ficto fiat aliquis non fictus, sed ut non fictus aliquis accedens iustificetur.

AD TERTIUM dicendum quod fictus dicitur aliquis ex eo quod demonstrat se aliquid velle quod non vult. Quicumque autem accedit ad Baptismum, ex hoc ipso ostendit se rectam fidem Christi habere, et hoc sacramentum venerari, et velle se Ecclesiae conformare, et velle a peccato recedere. Unde cuicumque peccato vult homo inhaerere, si ad Baptismum accedit, fictus accedit, quod est indevote accedere. Sed hoc intelligendum est de peccato mortali, quod gratiae contrariatur, non autem de peccato veniali. Unde fictio hic quodammodo includit omne peccatum.

REPLY OBJ. 2: When God changes man's will from evil to good, man does not approach with insincerity. But God does not always do this. Nor is this the purpose of the sacrament, that an insincere man be made sincere; but that he who comes in sincerity, be justified.

REPLY OBJ. 3: A man is said to be insincere who makes a show of willing what he wills not. Now whoever approaches Baptism, by that very fact makes a show of having right faith in Christ, of veneration for this sacrament, and of wishing to conform to the Church, and to renounce sin. Consequently, to whatever sin a man wishes to cleave, if he approach Baptism, he approaches insincerely, which is the same as to approach without devotion. But this must be understood of mortal sin, which is in opposition to grace: but not of venial sin. Consequently, here insincerity includes, in a way, every sin.

Article 10

Whether Baptism Produces Its Effect When the Insincerity Ceases?

AD DECIMUM SIC PROCEDITUR. Videtur quod, fictione recedente, Baptismus suum effectum non consequatur. Opus enim mortuum, quod est sine caritate, non potest unquam vivificari. Sed ille qui fictus accedit ad Baptismum, recipit sacramentum sine caritate. Ergo nunquam potest vivificari hoc modo ut gratiam conferat.

PRAETEREA, fictio videtur esse fortior quam Baptismus, cum impediat eius effectum. Sed fortius non tollitur a debiliori. Ergo peccatum fictionis non potest tolli per Baptismum fictione impeditum. Et sic Baptismus non consequetur suum effectum, qui est remissio omnium peccatorum.

PRAETEREA, contingit quod aliquis ficte accedit ad Baptismum, et post Baptismum multa peccata committit. Quae tamen per Baptismum non tollentur, quia Baptismus tollit peccata praeterita, non futura. Ergo Baptismus talis nunquam consequetur suum effectum, qui est remissio omnium peccatorum.

SED CONTRA est quod Augustinus dicit, in libro de Baptismo, *tunc valere incipit ad salutem Baptismus, cum illa fictio veraci confessione recesserit, quae, corde in malitia vel sacrilegio perseverante, peccatorum ablutionem non sinebat fieri.*

RESPONDEO dicendum quod, sicut supra dictum est, Baptismus est quaedam spiritualis regeneratio. Cum autem aliquid generatur, simul cum forma recipit effectum formae, nisi sit aliquid impediens; quo remoto, forma rei generatae perficit suum effectum, sicut simul cum corpus grave generatur, movetur deorsum, nisi sit aliquid prohibens; quo remoto, statim incipit moveri deorsum.

OBJECTION 1: It seems that Baptism does not produce its effect, when the insincerity ceases. For a dead work, which is void of charity, can never come to life. But he who approaches Baptism insincerely, receives the sacrament without charity. Therefore it can never come to life so as to bestow grace.

OBJ. 2: Further, insincerity seems to be stronger than Baptism, because it hinders its effect. But the stronger is not removed by the weaker. Therefore the sin of insincerity cannot be taken away by Baptism which has been hindered by insincerity. And thus Baptism will not receive its full effect, which is the remission of all sins.

OBJ. 3: Further, it may happen that a man approach Baptism insincerely, and afterwards commit a number of sins. And yet these sins will not be taken away by Baptism; because Baptism washes away past, not future, sins. Such a Baptism, therefore, will never have its effect, which is the remission of all sins.

ON THE CONTRARY, Augustine says (*De Bapt. cont. Donat.* i): *Then does Baptism begin to have its salutary effect, when truthful confession takes the place of that insincerity which hindered sins from being washed away, so long as the heart persisted in malice and sacrilege.*

I ANSWER THAT, As stated above (Q. 66, A. 9), Baptism is a spiritual regeneration. Now when a thing is generated, it receives together with the form, the form's effect, unless there be an obstacle; and when this is removed, the form of the thing generated produces its effect: thus at the same time as a weighty body is generated, it has a downward movement, unless something prevent this; and when

Et similiter quando aliquis baptizatur, accipit characterem, quasi formam, et consequitur proprium effectum, qui est gratia remittens omnia peccata. Impeditur autem quandoque per fictionem. Unde oportet quod, ea remota per poenitentiam, Baptismus statim consequatur suum effectum.

AD PRIMUM ergo dicendum quod sacramentum Baptismi est opus Dei, et non hominis. Et ideo non est mortuum in ficto, qui sine caritate baptizatur.

AD SECUNDUM dicendum quod fictio non removetur per Baptismum, sed per poenitentiam, qua remota, Baptismus aufert omnem culpam et reatum omnium peccatorum praecedentium Baptismum, et etiam simul existentium cum Baptismo. Unde Augustinus dicit, in libro de Baptismo, *solvitur hesternus dies, et quidquid superest solvitur, et ipsa hora momentumque ante Baptismum et in Baptismo. Deinceps autem continuo reus esse incipit.* Et sic ad effectum Baptismi consequendum concurrit Baptismus et poenitentia, sed Baptismus sicut causa per se agens; poenitentia sicut causa per accidens, idest removens prohibens.

AD TERTIUM dicendum quod effectus Baptismi non est tollere peccata futura, sed praesentia vel praeterita. Et ideo, recedente fictione, peccata sequentia remittuntur quidem, sed per poenitentiam, non per Baptismum. Unde non remittuntur quantum ad totum reatum, sicut peccata praecedentia Baptismum.

the obstacle is removed, it begins forthwith to move downwards. In like manner when a man is baptized, he receives the character, which is like a form; and he receives in consequence its proper effect, which is grace whereby all his sins are remitted. But this effect is sometimes hindered by insincerity. Wherefore, when this obstacle is removed by Penance, Baptism forthwith produces its effect.

REPLY OBJ. 1: The sacrament of Baptism is the work of God, not of man. Consequently, it is not dead in the man, who being insincere, is baptized without charity.

REPLY OBJ. 2: Insincerity is not removed by Baptism but by Penance: and when it is removed, Baptism takes away all guilt, and all debt of punishment due to sins, whether committed before Baptism, or even co-existent with Baptism. Hence Augustine says (*De Bapt. cont. Donat.* i): *Yesterday is blotted out, and whatever remains over and above, even the very last hour and moment preceding Baptism, the very moment of Baptism. But from that moment forward he is bound by his obligations.* And so both Baptism and Penance concur in producing the effect of Baptism, but Baptism as the direct efficient cause, Penance as the indirect cause, i.e., as removing the obstacle.

REPLY OBJ. 3: The effect of Baptism is to take away not future, but present and past sins. And consequently, when the insincerity passes away, subsequent sins are indeed remitted, but by Penance, not by Baptism. Wherefore they are not remitted, like the sins which preceded Baptism, as to the whole debt of punishment.

QUESTION 70

CIRCUMCISION

Deinde considerandum est de praeparatoriis ab Baptismum. Et primo quidem, de praeparatorio quod praecessit Baptismum, scilicet de circumcisione; secundo, de praeparatoriis quae currunt simul cum Baptismo, scilicet de catechismo et exorcismo.

Circa primum quaeruntur quatuor.

Primo, utrum circumcisio fuerit praeparatoria et figurativa Baptismi.

Secundo, de institutione ipsius.

Tertio, de ritu eius.

Quarto, de effectu ipsius.

We have now to consider things that are preparatory to Baptism: and (1) that which preceded Baptism, viz. Circumcision, (2) those which accompany Baptism, viz. Catechism and Exorcism.

Concerning the first there are four points of inquiry:
(1) Whether circumcision was a preparation for, and a figure of, Baptism?
(2) Its institution;
(3) Its rite;
(4) Its effect.

Article 1

Whether Circumcision Was a Preparation For, and a Figure of Baptism?

AD PRIMUM SIC PROCEDITUR. Videtur quod circumcisio non fuerit praeparatoria et figurativa Baptismi. Omnis enim figura habet aliquam similitudinem cum suo figurato. Sed circumcisio nullam habet similitudinem cum Baptismo. Ergo videtur quod non fuerit praeparativa et figurativa Baptismi.

PRAETEREA, apostolus dicit, I Cor. X, de antiquis patribus loquens, *quod omnes in nube et in mari baptizati sunt*, non autem dicit quod in circumcisione baptizati sint. Ergo protectio columnae nubis, et transitus maris rubri, magis fuerunt praeparatoria ad Baptismum et figurativa ipsius quam circumcisio.

PRAETEREA, supra dictum est quod Baptismus Ioannis fuit praeparatorius ad Baptismum Christi. Si ergo circumcisio fuit praeparatoria et figurativa Baptismi Christi, videtur quod Baptismus Ioannis fuit superfluus. Quod est inconveniens. Non ergo circumcisio fuit praeparatoria et figurativa Baptismi.

SED CONTRA est quod apostolus dicit, Coloss. II, *circumcisi estis circumcisione non manu facta in exspoliatione corporis carnis, sed circumcisione Iesu Christi, consepulti ei in Baptismo.*

RESPONDEO dicendum quod Baptismus dicitur sacramentum fidei, inquantum scilicet in Baptismo fit quaedam fidei professio, et per Baptismum aggregatur homo congregationi fidelium. Eadem autem est fides nostra et antiquorum patrum, secundum illud apostoli, II Cor. IV, *habentes eundem spiritum fidei credimus.* Circumcisio autem erat quaedam protestatio fidei, unde et per circumcisionem antiqui congregabantur collegio

OBJECTION 1: It seems that circumcision was not a preparation for, and a figure of Baptism. For every figure has some likeness to that which it foreshadows. But circumcision has no likeness to Baptism. Therefore it seems that it was not a preparation for, and a figure of Baptism.

OBJ. 2: Further, the Apostle, speaking of the Fathers of old, says (1 Cor 10:2), that *all were baptized in the cloud, and in the sea*: but not that they were baptized in circumcision. Therefore the protecting pillar of a cloud, and the crossing of the Red Sea, rather than circumcision, were a preparation for, and a figure of Baptism.

OBJ. 3: Further, it was stated above (Q. 38, AA. 1, 3) that the baptism of John was a preparation for Christ's. Consequently, if circumcision was a preparation for, and a figure of Christ's Baptism, it seems that John's baptism was superfluous: which is unseemly. Therefore circumcision was not a preparation for, and a figure of Baptism.

ON THE CONTRARY, The Apostle says (Col 2:11, 12): *You are circumcised with circumcision, not made by hand in despoiling the body of the flesh, but in the circumcision of Christ, buried with Him in Baptism.*

I ANSWER THAT, Baptism is called the Sacrament of Faith; in so far, to wit, as in Baptism man makes a profession of faith, and by Baptism is aggregated to the congregation of the faithful. Now our faith is the same as that of the Fathers of old, according to the Apostle (2 Cor 4:13): *Having the same spirit of faith . . . we . . . believe.* But circumcision was a protestation of faith; wherefore by circumcision also men of old were aggregated to the body of the faithful.

fidelium. Unde manifestum est quod circumcisio fuerit praeparatoria ad Baptismum et praefigurativa ipsius, secundum quod antiquis patribus omnia in figura futuri contingebant, ut dicitur I Cor. X, sicut et fides eorum erat de futuro.

Ad primum ergo dicendum quod circumcisio habebat similitudinem cum Baptismo quantum ad spiritualem effectum Baptismi. Nam sicut per circumcisionem auferebatur quaedam carnalis pellicula, ita per Baptismum homo exspoliatur a carnali conversatione.

Ad secundum dicendum quod protectio columnae nubis, et transitus maris rubri, fuerunt quidem figurae nostri Baptismi, quo renascimur ex aqua, significata per mare rubrum, et spiritu sancto, significato per columnam nubis, non tamen per haec fiebat aliqua professio fidei, sicut per circumcisionem. Et ideo praedicta duo erant tantum figurae, et non sacramenta. Circumcisio autem erat sacramentum, et praeparatorium ad Baptismum, minus tamen expresse figurans Baptismum, quantum ad exteriora, quam praedicta. Et ideo apostolus potius fecit mentionem de praedictis quam de circumcisione.

Ad tertium dicendum quod Baptismus Ioannis fuit praeparatorius ad Baptismum Christi quantum ad exercitium actus. Sed circumcisio quantum ad professionem fidei, quae requiritur in Baptismo, sicut dictum est.

Consequently, it is manifest that circumcision was a preparation for Baptism and a figure thereof, forasmuch as *all things happened* to the Fathers of old *in figure* (1 Cor 10:11); just as their faith regarded things to come.

Reply Obj. 1: Circumcision was like Baptism as to the spiritual effect of the latter. For just as circumcision removed a carnal pellicule, so Baptism despoils man of carnal behavior.

Reply Obj. 2: The protecting pillar of cloud and the crossing of the Red Sea were indeed figures of our Baptism, whereby we are born again of water, signified by the Red Sea; and of the Holy Spirit, signified by the pillar of cloud: yet man did not make, by means of these, a profession of faith, as by circumcision; so that these two things were figures but not sacraments. But circumcision was a sacrament, and a preparation for Baptism; although less clearly figurative of Baptism, as to externals, than the aforesaid. And for this reason the Apostle mentions them rather than circumcision.

Reply Obj. 3: John's baptism was a preparation for Christ's as to the act done: but circumcision, as to the profession of faith, which is required in Baptism, as stated above.

Article 2

Whether Circumcision Was Instituted in a Fitting Manner?

Ad secundum sic proceditur. Videtur quod circumcisio fuerit inconvenienter instituta. Sicut enim dictum est, in circumcisione fiebat quaedam professio fidei. Sed a peccato primi hominis nullus unquam salvari potuit nisi per fidem passionis Christi, secundum illud Rom. III, *quem proposuit Deus propitiatorem per fidem in sanguine ipsius.* Ergo statim post peccatum primi hominis circumcisio institui debuit, et non tempore Abrahae.

Praeterea, in circumcisione profitebatur homo observantiam veteris legis, sicut in Baptismo profitetur observantiam novae legis, unde apostolus dicit, Galat. V, *testificor omni homini circumcidenti se quoniam debitor est universae legis faciendae.* Sed legalis observantia non est tradita tempore Abrahae, sed magis tempore Moysi. Ergo inconvenienter instituta est circumcisio tempore Abrahae.

Praeterea, circumcisio fuit figurativa et praeparativa Baptismi. Sed Baptismus exhibetur omnibus populis, secundum illud Matth. ult., *euntes, docete omnes gentes, baptizantes eos.* Ergo circumcisio non debuit institui

Objection 1: It seems that circumcision was instituted in an unfitting manner. For as stated above (A. 1) a profession of faith was made in circumcision. But none could ever be delivered from the first man's sin, except by faith in Christ's Passion, according to Rom. 3:25: *Whom God hath proposed to be a propitiation, through faith in His blood.* Therefore circumcision should have been instituted forthwith after the first man's sin, and not at the time of Abraham.

Obj. 2: Further, in circumcision man made profession of keeping the Old Law, just as in Baptism he makes profession of keeping the New Law; wherefore the Apostle says (Gal 5:3): *I testify . . . to every man circumcising himself, that he is a debtor to do the whole Law.* But the observance of the Law was not promulgated at the time of Abraham, but rather at the time of Moses. Therefore it was unfitting for circumcision to be instituted at the time of Abraham.

Obj. 3: Further, circumcision was a figure of, and a preparation for, Baptism. But Baptism is offered to all nations, according to Matt. 28:19: *Going . . . teach ye all nations, baptizing them.* Therefore circumcision should have

ut observanda tantum ab uno populo Iudaeorum, sed ab omnibus populis.

PRAETEREA, carnalis circumcisio debet respondere spirituali sicut figura figurato. Sed spiritualis circumcisio, quae fit per Christum, indifferenter convenit utrique sexui, quia *in Christo Iesu non est masculus neque femina*, ut dicitur Coloss. III. Ergo inconvenienter est circumcisio instituta, quae competit solum maribus.

SED CONTRA est quod, sicut legitur Gen. XVII, circumcisio est instituta a Deo, cuius perfecta sunt opera.

RESPONDEO dicendum quod, sicut dictum est, circumcisio erat praeparatoria ad Baptismum inquantum erat quaedam professio fidei Christi, quam et nos in Baptismo profitemur. Inter antiquos autem patres, primus Abraham promissionem accepit de Christo nascituro, cum dictum est ei, Gen. XXII, *in semine tuo benedicentur omnes gentes terrae*. Et ipse etiam primus se a societate infidelium segregavit, secundum mandatum domini dicentis sibi, *egredere de terra tua et de cognatione tua*. Et ideo convenienter circumcisio fuit instituta in Abraham.

AD PRIMUM ergo dicendum quod immediate post peccatum primi parentis, propter doctrinam ipsius Adae, qui plene instructus fuerat de divinis, adhuc fides et ratio naturalis vigebat in homine in tantum quod non oportebat determinari hominibus aliqua signa fidei et salutis, sed unusquisque pro suo libitu fidem suam profitentibus signis protestabatur. Sed circa tempus Abrahae diminuta erat fides, plurimis ad idololatriam declinantibus. Obscurata etiam erat ratio naturalis per augmentum carnalis concupiscentiae usque ad peccata contra naturam. Et ideo convenienter tunc, et non ante, fuit instituta circumcisio, ad profitendum fidem et minuendum carnalem concupiscentiam.

AD SECUNDUM dicendum quod legalis observantia tradi non debuit nisi populo iam congregato, quia lex ordinatur ad bonum publicum, ut in secunda parte dictum est. Populus autem fidelium congregandus erat aliquo signo sensibili, quod est necessarium ad hoc quod homines in quacumque religione adunentur, sicut Augustinus dicit, contra Faustum. Et ideo oportuit prius institui circumcisionem quam lex daretur. Illi autem patres qui fuerunt ante legem, familias suas instruxerunt de rebus divinis per modum paternae admonitionis. Unde et dominus dicit de Abraham, *scio quod praecepturus sit filiis suis et domui suae post se ut custodiant viam domini*.

AD TERTIUM dicendum quod Baptismus in se continet perfectionem salutis, ad quam Deus omnes homines vocat, secundum illud I Tim. II *qui vult omnes homines*

been instituted as binding, not the Jews only, but also all nations.

OBJ. 4: Further, carnal circumcision should correspond to spiritual circumcision, as the shadow to the reality. But spiritual circumcision which is of Christ, regards indifferently both sexes, since *in Christ Jesus there is neither male nor female*, as is written Col. 3. Therefore the institution of circumcision which concerns only males, was unfitting.

ON THE CONTRARY, We read (Gen 17) that circumcision was instituted by God, Whose *works are perfect* (Deut 32:4).

I ANSWER THAT, As stated above (A. 1) circumcision was a preparation for Baptism, inasmuch as it was a profession of faith in Christ, which we also profess in Baptism. Now among the Fathers of old, Abraham was the first to receive the promise of the future birth of Christ, when it was said to him: *In thy seed shall all the nations of the earth be blessed* (Gen 22:18). Moreover, he was the first to cut himself off from the society of unbelievers, in accordance with the commandment of the Lord, Who said to him (Gen 13:1): *Go forth out of thy country and from thy kindred*. Therefore circumcision was fittingly instituted in the person of Abraham.

REPLY OBJ. 1: Immediately after the sin of our first parent, on account of the knowledge possessed by Adam, who was fully instructed about Divine things, both faith and natural reason flourished in man to such an extent, that there was no need for any signs of faith and salvation to be prescribed to him, but each one was wont to make protestation of his faith, by outward signs of his profession, according as he thought best. But about the time of Abraham faith was on the wane, many being given over to idolatry. Moreover, by the growth of carnal concupiscence natural reason was clouded even in regard to sins against nature. And therefore it was fitting that then, and not before, circumcision should be instituted, as a profession of faith and a remedy against carnal concupiscence.

REPLY OBJ. 2: The observance of the Law was not to be promulgated until the people were already gathered together: because the law is ordained to the public good, as we have stated in the Second Part (I-II, Q. 90, A. 2). Now it behooved the body of the faithful to be gathered together by a sensible sign, which is necessary in order that men be united together in any religion, as Augustine says (*Contra Faust.* xix). Consequently, it was necessary for circumcision to be instituted before the giving of the Law. Those Fathers, however, who lived before the Law, taught their families concerning Divine things by way of paternal admonition. Hence the Lord said of Abraham (Gen 18:19): *I know that he will command his children, and his household after him to keep the way of the Lord*.

REPLY OBJ. 3: Baptism contains in itself the perfection of salvation, to which God calls all men, according to 1 Tim. 2:4: *Who will have all men to be saved*. Wherefore

salvos fieri. Et ideo Baptismus omnibus populis proponitur. Circumcisio autem non continebat perfectionem salutis, sed significabat ipsam ut fiendam per Christum, qui erat ex Iudaeorum populo nasciturus. Et ideo illi soli populo data est circumcisio.

Ad quartum dicendum quod circumcisionis institutio est ut signum fidei Abrahae, qui credidit se patrem futurum Christi sibi repromissi, et ideo convenienter solis maribus competebat. Peccatum etiam originale, contra quod specialiter circumcisio ordinabatur, a patre trahitur, non a matre, ut in secunda parte dictum est. Sed Baptismus continet virtutem Christi, qui est universalis salutis causa omnium, et remissio omnium peccatorum.

Baptism is offered to all nations. On the other hand circumcision did not contain the perfection of salvation, but signified it as to be achieved by Christ, Who was to be born of the Jewish nation. For this reason circumcision was given to that nation alone.

Reply Obj. 4: The institution of circumcision is as a sign of Abraham's faith, who believed that he himself would be the father of Christ Who was promised to him: and for this reason it was suitable that it should be for males only. Again, original sin, against which circumcision was specially ordained, is contracted from the father, not from the mother, as was stated in the Second Part (I-II, Q. 81, A. 5). But Baptism contains the power of Christ, Who is the universal cause of salvation for all, and is *The Remission of all sins* (Post-Communion, Tuesday in Whitweek).

Article 3

Whether the Rite of Circumcision Was Fitting?

Ad tertium sic proceditur. Videtur quod ritus circumcisionis non fuerit conveniens. Circumcisio enim, ut dictum est, fidei quaedam professio est. Sed fides in vi apprehensiva existit, cuius operationes maxime apparent in capite. Ergo magis debuit signum circumcisionis dari in capite quam in membro generationis.

Praeterea, ad usum sacramentorum sumimus ea quorum est communior usus, sicut aqua ad abluendum, et panem ad reficiendum. Sed ad incidendum communius utimur cultello ferreo quam petrino. Ergo circumcisio non debuit fieri cultello petrino.

Praeterea, sicut Baptismus instituitur in remedium originalis peccati, ita et circumcisio, sicut Beda dicit. Sed nunc Baptismus non differtur usque ad octavum diem, ne pueris periculum damnationis immineat propter originale peccatum, si non baptizati decedant. Quandoque etiam tardatur Baptismus post octavum diem. Ergo etiam circumcisioni non debuit determinari octavus dies, sed debebat quandoque praeveniri, sicut etiam quandoque tardabatur.

Sed contra est quod Rom. IV, super illud, *et signum accepit circumcisionis*, determinatur in Glossa praedictus circumcisionis ritus.

Respondeo dicendum quod, sicut dictum est, circumcisio quoddam signum fidei est institutum a Deo, *cuius sapientiae non est numerus.* Determinare autem convenientia signa est sapientiae opus. Et ideo concedendum est quod ritus circumcisionis fuit conveniens.

Ad primum ergo dicendum quod circumcisio convenienter fiebat in membro generationis. Primo quidem, quia erat signum fidei qua Abraham credidit Christum

Objection 1: It seems that the rite of circumcision was unfitting. For circumcision, as stated above (AA. 1, 2), was a profession of faith. But faith is in the apprehensive power, whose operations appear mostly in the head. Therefore the sign of circumcision should have been conferred on the head rather than on the virile member.

Obj. 2: Further, in the sacraments we make use of such things as are in more frequent use; for instance, water, which is used for washing, and bread, which we use for nourishment. But, in cutting, we use an iron knife more commonly than a stone knife. Therefore circumcision should not have been performed with a stone knife.

Obj. 3: Further, just as Baptism was instituted as a remedy against original sin, so also was circumcision, as Bede says (*Hom. in Circum.*). But now Baptism is not put off until the eighth day, lest children should be in danger of loss on account of original sin, if they should die before being baptized. On the other hand, sometimes Baptism is put off until after the eighth day. Therefore the eighth day should not have been fixed for circumcision, but this day should have been anticipated, just as sometimes it was deferred.

On the contrary, The aforesaid rite of circumcision is fixed by a gloss on Rom. 4:11: *And he received the sign of circumcision.*

I answer that, As stated above (A. 2), circumcision was established, as a sign of faith, by God *of* Whose *wisdom there is no number* (Ps 146:5). Now to determine suitable signs is a work of wisdom. Consequently, it must be allowed that the rite of circumcision was fitting.

Reply Obj. 1: It was fitting for circumcision to be performed on the virile member. First, because it was a sign of that faith whereby Abraham believed that Christ would

ex suo semine nasciturum. Secundo, quia erat in remedium peccati originalis, quod per actum generationis traducitur. Tertio, quia ordinabatur ad diminutionem carnalis concupiscentiae, quae praecipue in membris illis viget, propter abundantiam delectationis venereorum.

AD SECUNDUM dicendum quod cultellus lapideus non erat de necessitate circumcisionis. Unde non invenitur tale instrumentum praecepto divino determinatum; neque communiter tali instrumento Iudaei utebantur ad circumcidendum; sed neque modo utuntur. Leguntur tamen aliquae circumcisiones famosae cultello lapideo factae, sicut legitur Exod. IV, quod *tulit Sephora acutissimam petram et circumcidit praeputium filii sui*; et Iosue V dicitur, *fac tibi cultros lapideos, et circumcide secundo filios Israel*. Per quod figurabatur circumcisionem spiritualem esse faciendam per Christum, de quo dicitur, I Cor. X, *petra autem erat Christus*.

AD TERTIUM dicendum quod octavus dies determinatus erat circumcisioni, tum propter mysterium, quia in octava aetate, quae est aetas resurgentium, quasi in octavo die, perficietur per Christum spiritualis circumcisio, quando auferet ab electis non solum culpam, sed etiam omnem poenalitatem. Tum etiam propter teneritudinem infantis ante octavum diem. Unde etiam de aliis animalibus Levit. XXII praecipitur, *bos, ovis et capra, cum generata fuerint, septem diebus erunt sub ubere matris suae, die autem octavo et deinceps offerri poterunt domino*.

Erat autem octavus dies de necessitate praecepti, ita scilicet quod octavum diem praetermittentes peccabant, etiam si esset sabbatum; secundum illud Ioan. VII, *circumcisionem accipit homo in sabbato, ut non solvatur lex Moysi*. Non tamen erat de necessitate sacramenti, quia, si aliqui essent omittentes octavum diem, postea poterant circumcidi.

Quidam etiam dicunt quod, propter periculum imminentis mortis, poterat octavus dies praeveniri. Sed hoc nec ex auctoritate Scripturae, nec ex consuetudine Iudaeorum haberi potest. Unde melius est dicendum, sicut etiam Hugo de sancto Victore dicit, quod octavus dies nulla necessitate praeveniebatur. Unde super illud Prov. IV, *unigenitus eram coram matre mea*, dicit Glossa quod alius Bersabee parvulus non computabatur, quia, ante octavum diem mortuus, nominatus non fuit; et per consequens nec circumcisus.

be born of his seed. Second, because it was to be a remedy against original sin, which is contracted through the act of generation. Third, because it was ordained as a remedy for carnal concupiscence, which thrives principally in those members, by reason of the abundance of venereal pleasure.

REPLY OBJ. 2: A stone knife was not essential to circumcision. Wherefore we do not find that an instrument of this description is required by any divine precept; nor did the Jews, as a rule, make use of such a knife for circumcision; indeed, neither do they now. Nevertheless, certain well-known circumcisions are related as having been performed with a stone knife, thus (Exod 4:25) we read that *Sephora took a very sharp stone and circumcised the foreskin of her son*, and (Josh 5:2): *Make thee knives of stone, and circumcise the second time the children of Israel*. Which signified that spiritual circumcision would be done by Christ, of Whom it is written (1 Cor 10:4): *Now the rock was Christ*.

REPLY OBJ. 3: The eighth day was fixed for circumcision: first, because of the mystery; since, Christ, by taking away from the elect, not only guilt but also all penalties, will perfect the spiritual circumcision, in the eighth age (which is the age of those that rise again), as it were, on the eighth day. Second, on account of the tenderness of the infant before the eighth day. Wherefore even in regard to other animals it is prescribed (Lev 22:27): *When a bullock, or a sheep, or a goat, is brought forth, they shall be seven days under the udder of their dam: but the eighth day and thenceforth, they may be offered to the Lord*.

Moreover, the eighth day was necessary for the fulfilment of the precept; so that, to wit, those who delayed beyond the eighth day, sinned, even though it were the sabbath, according to John 7:23: *(If) a man receives circumcision on the sabbath-day, that the Law of Moses may not be broken*. But it was not necessary for the validity of the sacrament: because if anyone delayed beyond the eighth day, they could be circumcised afterwards.

Some also say that in imminent danger of death, it was allowable to anticipate the eighth day. But this cannot be proved either from the authority of Scripture or from the custom of the Jews. Wherefore it is better to say with Hugh of St. Victor (*De Sacram.* i) that the eighth day was never anticipated for any motive, however urgent. Hence on Prov. 4:3: *I was . . . an only son in the sight of my mother*, a gloss says, that Bersabee's other baby boy did not count because through dying before the eighth day it received no name; and consequently neither was it circumcised.

Article 4

Whether Circumcision Bestowed Sanctifying Grace?

AD QUARTUM SIC PROCEDITUR. Videtur quod circumcisio non conferebat gratiam iustificantem. Dicit enim apostolus, Galat. II, *si ex lege est iustitia, Christus gratis mortuus est*, idest sine causa. Sed circumcisio erat quaedam obligatio legis implendae, secundum illud Galat. V, *testificor omni homini circumcidenti se quoniam debitor est universae legis faciendae.* Ergo, si ex circumcisione est iustitia, Christus gratis, idest sine causa, mortuus est. Sed hoc est inconveniens. Non ergo ex circumcisione erat gratia iustificans a peccato.

PRAETEREA, ante institutionem circumcisionis sola fides ad iustificationem sufficiebat, dicit enim Gregorius, in Moral., *quod apud nos valet aqua Baptismatis, hoc egit apud veteres pro parvulis sola fides.* Sed virtus fidei non est imminuta propter mandatum circumcisionis. Ergo sola fides parvulos iustificabat, et non circumcisio.

PRAETEREA, Iosue V legitur quod *populus qui natus est in deserto per quadraginta annos, incircumcisus fuit.* Si ergo per circumcisionem auferebatur peccatum originale, videtur quod omnes qui in deserto mortui sunt, tam parvuli quam adulti, fuerint damnati. Et eadem obiectio est de pueris qui moriebantur ante octavum diem circumcisionis, qui praeveniri non debebat, sicut dictum est.

PRAETEREA, nihil impedit introitum regni caelestis nisi peccatum. Sed circumcisi ante passionem impediebantur ab introitu regni caelestis. Non ergo per circumcisionem homines iustificabantur a peccato.

PRAETEREA, peccatum originale non dimittitur sine actuali, quia *impium est a Deo dimidiam sperare veniam*, ut Augustinus dicit. Sed nunquam legitur quod per circumcisionem remitteretur actuale peccatum. Ergo neque etiam originale per eam dimittebatur.

SED CONTRA est quod Augustinus dicit, ad Valerium contra Iulianum, *ex quo instituta est circumcisio in populo Dei, quod erat signaculum iustitiae fidei, ad sanctificationem purgationis valebat parvulis originalis veterisque peccati, sicut etiam Baptismus ex illo coepit valere tempore ad innovationem hominis, ex quo institutus est.*

RESPONDEO dicendum quod ab omnibus communiter ponitur quod in circumcisione originale peccatum remittebatur. Quidam tamen dicebant quod non conferebatur gratia, sed solum remittebatur peccatum. Quod Magister ponit in I dist. IV Sent., et Rom. IV in Glossa. Sed hoc non potest esse, quia culpa non remittitur nisi per gratiam, secundum illud Rom. III, *iustificati gratis per gratiam ipsius*, et cetera.

OBJECTION 1: It seems that circumcision did not bestow sanctifying grace. For the Apostle says (Gal 2:21): *If justice be by the Law, then Christ died in vain*, i.e., without cause. But circumcision was an obligation imposed by the Law, according to Gal. 5:3: *I testify . . . to every man circumcising himself, that he is a debtor to do the whole law.* Therefore, if justice be by circumcision, *Christ died in vain*, i.e., without cause. But this cannot be allowed. Therefore circumcision did not confer grace whereby the sinner is made righteous.

OBJ. 2: Further, before the institution of circumcision faith alone sufficed for justification; hence Gregory says (*Moral.* iv): *Faith alone did of old in behalf of infants that for which the water of Baptism avails with us.* But faith has lost nothing of its strength through the commandment of circumcision. Therefore faith alone justified little ones, and not circumcision.

OBJ. 3: Further, we read (Josh 5:5, 6) that *the people that were born in the desert, during the forty years . . . were uncircumcised.* If, therefore, original sin was taken away by circumcision, it seems that all who died in the desert, both little children and adults, were lost. And the same argument avails in regard to those who died before the eighth day, which was that of circumcision, which day could not be anticipated, as stated above (A. 3, ad 3).

OBJ. 4: Further, nothing but sin closes the entrance to the heavenly kingdom. But before the Passion the entrance to the heavenly kingdom was closed to the circumcised. Therefore men were not justified from sin by circumcision.

OBJ. 5: Further, original sin is not remitted without actual sin being remitted also: because *it is wicked to hope for half forgiveness from God*, as Augustine says (*De Vera et Falsa Poenit.* ix). But we read nowhere of circumcision as remitting actual sin. Therefore neither did it remit original sin.

ON THE CONTRARY, Augustine says, writing to Valerius in answer to Julian (*De Nup. et Concup.* ii): *From the time that circumcision was instituted among God's people, as 'a seal of the justice of the faith,' it availed little children unto sanctification by cleansing them from the original and bygone sin; just as Baptism also from the time of its institution began to avail unto the renewal of man.*

I ANSWER THAT, All are agreed in saying that original sin was remitted in circumcision. But some said that no grace was conferred, and that the only effect was to remit sin. The Master holds this opinion (*Sent.* iv, D, 1), and in a gloss on Rom. 4:11. But this is impossible, since guilt is not remitted except by grace, according to Rom. 3:2: *Being justified freely by His grace*, etc.

Et ideo alii dixerunt quod per circumcisionem conferebatur gratia quantum ad effectus remissionis culpae, sed non quantum ad effectus positivos, ne dicere cogerentur quod gratia in circumcisione collata sufficiebat ad implendum mandata legis, et ita superfluus fuit adventus Christi. Sed etiam haec positio stare non potest. Primo quidem, quia per circumcisionem dabatur pueris facultas suo tempore perveniendi ad gloriam, quae est ultimus effectus positivus gratiae. Secundo, quia priores sunt naturaliter, secundum ordinem causae formalis, effectus positivi quam privativi, licet secundum ordinem causae materialis sit e converso, forma enim non excludit privationem nisi informando subiectum.

Et ideo alii dixerunt quod in circumcisione conferebatur gratia etiam quantum ad aliquem effectum positivum, qui est facere dignum vita aeterna, sed non quantum ad omnes effectus, quia non sufficiebat reprimere concupiscentiam fomitis, nec etiam ad implendum mandata legis. Quod etiam aliquando mihi visum est. Sed diligenter consideranti apparet quod non est verum. Quia minima gratia potest resistere cuilibet concupiscentiae, et vitare omne peccatum mortale, quod committitur in transgressione mandatorum legis, minima enim caritas plus diligit Deum quam cupiditas millia auri et argenti.

Et ideo dicendum quod in circumcisione conferebatur gratia quantum ad omnes gratiae effectus, aliter tamen quam in Baptismo. Nam in Baptismo confertur gratia ex virtute ipsius Baptismi, quam habet inquantum est instrumentum passionis Christi iam perfectae. Circumcisio autem conferebat gratiam inquantum erat signum fidei passionis Christi futurae, ita scilicet quod homo qui accipiebat circumcisionem, profitebatur se suscipere talem fidem; vel adultus pro se, vel alius pro parvulis. Unde et apostolus dicit, Rom. IV, quod *Abraham accepit signum circumcisionis, signaculum iustitiae fidei*, quia scilicet iustitia ex fide erat significata, non ex circumcisione significante. Et quia Baptismus operatur instrumentaliter in virtute passionis Christi, non autem circumcisio, ideo Baptismus imprimit characterem incorporantem hominem Christo, et copiosiorem gratiam confert quam circumcisio, maior enim est effectus rei iam praesentis quam spei.

AD PRIMUM ergo dicendum quod ratio illa procederet si ex circumcisione esset iustitia aliter quam per fidem passionis Christi.

AD SECUNDUM dicendum quod, sicut ante institutionem circumcisionis fides Christi futuri iustificabat tam pueros quam adultos, ita et circumcisione data. Sed antea non requirebatur aliquod signum protestativum huius fidei, quia nondum homines fideles seorsum ab

Wherefore others said that grace was bestowed by circumcision, as to that effect which is the remission of guilt, but not as to its positive effects; lest they should be compelled to say that the grace bestowed in circumcision sufficed for the fulfilling of the precepts of the Law, and that, consequently, the coming of Christ was unnecessary. But neither can this opinion stand. First, because by circumcision children received the power of obtaining glory at the allotted time, which is the last positive effect of grace. Second, because, in the order of the formal cause, positive effects naturally precede those that denote privation, although it is the reverse in the order of the material cause: since a form does not remove a privation save by informing the subject.

Consequently, others said that grace was conferred in circumcision, also as a particular positive effect consisting in being made worthy of eternal life; but not as to all its effects, for it did not suffice for the repression of the concupiscence of the fomes, nor again for the fulfilment of the precepts of the Law. And this was my opinion at one time (*Sent.* iv, D, 1; Q. 2, A. 4). But if one consider the matter carefully, it is clear that this is not true. Because the least grace can resist any degree of concupiscence, and avoid every mortal sin, that is committed in transgressing the precepts of the Law; for the smallest degree of charity loves God more than cupidity loves *thousands of gold and silver* (Ps 118:72).

We must say, therefore, that grace was bestowed in circumcision as to all the effects of grace, but not as in Baptism. Because in Baptism grace is bestowed by the very power of Baptism itself, which power Baptism has as the instrument of Christ's Passion already consummated. Whereas circumcision bestowed grace, inasmuch as it was a sign of faith in Christ's future Passion: so that the man who was circumcised, professed to embrace that faith; whether, being an adult, he made profession for himself, or, being a child, someone else made profession for him. Hence, too, the Apostle says (Rom 4:11), that Abraham *received the sign of circumcision, a seal of the justice of the faith*: because, to wit, justice was of faith signified: not of circumcision signifying. And since Baptism operates instrumentally by the power of Christ's Passion, whereas circumcision does not, therefore Baptism imprints a character that incorporates man in Christ, and bestows grace more copiously than does circumcision; since greater is the effect of a thing already present, than of the hope thereof.

REPLY OBJ. 1: This argument would prove if justice were of circumcision otherwise than through faith in Christ's Passion.

REPLY OBJ. 2: Just as before the institution of circumcision, faith in Christ to come justified both children and adults, so, too, after its institution. But before, there was no need of a sign expressive of this faith; because as yet believers had not begun to be united together apart from

infidelibus coeperant adunari ad cultum unius Dei. Probabile tamen est quod parentes fideles pro parvulis natis, et maxime in periculo existentibus, aliquas preces Deo funderent, vel aliquam benedictionem eis adhiberent, quod erat quoddam signaculum fidei, sicut adulti pro seipsis preces et sacrificia offerebant.

AD TERTIUM dicendum quod populus in deserto praetermittens mandatum circumcisionis excusabatur, tum quia nesciebant quando castra movebantur; tum quia, ut Damascenus dicit, non necesse erat eos aliquod signum distinctionis habere quando seorsum ab aliis populis habitabant. Et tamen, ut Augustinus dicit, inobedientiam incurrebant qui ex contemptu praetermittebant.

Videtur tamen quod nulli incircumcisi mortui fuerint in deserto, quia in Psalmo dicitur, *non erat in tribubus eorum infirmus*, sed illi soli videntur mortui in deserto qui fuerant in Aegypto circumcisi. Si tamen aliqui ibi incircumcisi mortui sunt, eadem ratio est de his et de his qui moriebantur ante circumcisionis institutionem. Quod etiam intelligendum est de pueris qui moriebantur ante octavum diem tempore legis.

AD QUARTUM dicendum quod in circumcisione auferebatur originale peccatum ex parte personae, remanebat tamen impedimentum intrandi in regnum caelorum ex parte totius naturae, quod fuit sublatum per passionem Christi. Et ideo etiam Baptismus ante passionem Christi non introducebat in regnum. Sed circumcisio, si haberet locum post passionem Christi, introduceret in regnum.

AD QUINTUM dicendum quod adulti, quando circumcidebantur, consequebantur remissionem non solum originalis, sed etiam actualium peccatorum, non tamen ita quod liberarentur ab omni reatu poenae, sicut in Baptismo, in quo confertur copiosior gratia.

unbelievers for the worship of one God. It is probable, however, that parents who were believers offered up some prayers to God for their children, especially if these were in any danger. Or bestowed some blessing on them, as a *seal of faith*; just as the adults offered prayers and sacrifices for themselves.

REPLY OBJ. 3: There was an excuse for the people in the desert failing to fulfill the precept of circumcision, both because they knew not when the camp was removed, and because, as Damascene says (*De Fide Orth*. iv) they needed no distinctive sign while they dwelt apart from other nations. Nevertheless, as Augustine says (*QQ. in Josue* vi), those were guilty of disobedience who failed to obey through contempt.

It seems, however, that none of the uncircumcised died in the desert, for it is written (Ps 104:37): *There was not among their tribes one that was feeble*: and that those alone died in the desert, who had been circumcised in Egypt. If, however, some of the uncircumcised did die there, the same applies to them as to those who died before the institution of circumcision. And this applies also to those children who, at the time of the Law, died before the eighth day.

REPLY OBJ. 4: Original sin was taken away in circumcision, in regard to the person; but on the part of the entire nature, there remained the obstacle to the entrance of the kingdom of heaven, which obstacle was removed by Christ's Passion. Consequently, before Christ's Passion not even Baptism gave entrance to the kingdom. But were circumcision to avail after Christ's Passion, it would give entrance to the kingdom.

REPLY OBJ. 5: When adults were circumcised, they received remission not only of original, but also of actual sin: yet not so as to be delivered from all debt of punishment, as in Baptism, in which grace is conferred more copiously.

QUESTION 71

The Preparations That Accompany Baptism

Deinde considerandum est de praeparatoriis quae simul currunt cum Baptismo. Et circa hoc quaeruntur quatuor.

Primo, utrum catechismus debeat praecedere Baptismum.

Secundo, utrum Baptismum debeat praecedere exorcismus.

Tertio, utrum ea quae aguntur in catechismo et exorcismo aliquid efficiant, vel solum significent.

Quarto, utrum baptizandi debeant catechizari vel exorcizari per sacerdotes.

We have now to consider the preparations that accompany Baptism: concerning which there are four points of inquiry:

(1) Whether catechism should precede Baptism?

(2) Whether exorcism should precede Baptism?

(3) Whether what is done in catechizing and exorcizing, effects anything, or is a mere sign?

(4) Whether those who are to be baptized should be catechized or exorcized by priests?

Article 1

Whether Catechism Should Precede Baptism?

Ad primum sic proceditur. Videtur quod catechismus non debeat praecedere Baptismum. Per Baptismum enim regenerantur homines ad vitam spiritualem. Sed prius accipit homo vitam quam doctrinam. Non ergo prius debet homo catechizari, idest doceri, quam baptizari.

Praeterea, Baptismus exhibetur non solum adultis, sed etiam pueris, qui non sunt doctrinae perceptibiles, eo quod non habent usum rationis. Ergo ridiculum est eos catechizari.

Praeterea, in catechismo confitetur catechizatus suam fidem. Confiteri autem fidem suam non potest puer, neque per seipsum, neque etiam aliquis alius pro eo, tum quia nullus potest alium ad aliquid obligare; tum quia non potest aliquis scire utrum puer, cum ad legitimam aetatem pervenerit, assentiat fidei. Non ergo debet catechismus praecedere Baptismum.

Sed contra est quod Rabanus, de institutione clericorum, dicit, *ante Baptismum, catechizandi debet hominem praevenire officium, ut fidei primum catechumenus accipiat rudimentum.*

Respondeo dicendum quod, sicut supra dictum est, Baptismus est fidei sacramentum, cum sit quaedam professio fidei Christianae. Ad hoc autem quod aliquis fidem accipiat, requiritur quod de fide instruatur, secundum illud Rom. X, *quomodo credent quem non audierunt? Quomodo autem audient sine praedicante?* Et ideo ante Baptismum convenienter praecedit catechismus. Unde et dominus, praeceptum baptizandi discipulis

Objection 1: It seems that catechism should not precede Baptism. For by Baptism men are regenerated unto the spiritual life. But man begins to live before being taught. Therefore man should not be catechized, i.e., taught, before being baptized.

Obj. 2: Further, Baptism is given not only to adults, but also to children, who are not capable of being taught, since they have not the use of reason. Therefore it is absurd to catechize them.

Obj. 3: Further, a man, when catechized, confesses his faith. Now a child cannot confess its faith by itself, nor can anyone else in its stead; both because no one can bind another to do anything; and because one cannot know whether the child, having come to the right age, will give its assent to faith. Therefore catechism should not precede Baptism.

On the contrary, Rabanus says (*De Instit. Cleric.* i): *Before Baptism man should be prepared by catechism, in order that the catechumen may receive the rudiments of faith.*

I answer that, As stated above (Q. 70, A. 1), Baptism is the Sacrament of Faith: since it is a profession of the Christian faith. Now in order that a man receive the faith, he must be instructed therein, according to Rom. 10:14: *How shall they believe Him, of Whom they have not heard? And how shall they hear without a preacher?* And therefore it is fitting that catechism should precede Baptism. Hence when our Lord bade His disciples to baptize, He made

tradens, praemittit doctrinam Baptismo, dicens, *euntes, docete omnes gentes, baptizantes eos*, et cetera.

AD PRIMUM ergo dicendum quod vita gratiae, in qua regeneratur aliquis, praesupponit vitam naturae rationalis, in qua potest homo particeps esse doctrinae.

AD SECUNDUM dicendum quod, sicut mater Ecclesia, ut supra dictum est, accommodat pueris baptizandis *aliorum pedes ut veniant, et aliorum cor ut credant*, ita etiam accommodat eis aliorum aures ut audiant, et intellectum ut per alios instruantur. Et ideo eadem ratione sunt catechizandi qua sunt baptizandi.

AD TERTIUM dicendum quod ille qui pro puero baptizato respondet, credo, non praedicit puerum crediturum cum ad legitimos annos pervenerit, alioquin diceret, credet, sed profitetur fidem Ecclesiae in persona pueri, cui communicatur, cuius sacramentum ei attribuitur, et ad quam obligatur per alium. Non est enim inconveniens quod aliquis obligetur per alium in his quae sunt de necessitate salutis. Similiter etiam patrinus pro puero respondens promittit se operam daturum ad hoc quod puer credat. Quod tamen non sufficeret in adultis usum rationis habentibus.

teaching to precede Baptism, saying: *Go ye . . . and teach all nations, baptizing them*, etc.

REPLY OBJ. 1: The life of grace unto which a man is regenerated, presupposes the life of the rational nature, in which man is capable of receiving instruction.

REPLY OBJ. 2: Just as Mother Church, as stated above (Q. 69, A. 6, ad 3), lends children another's feet that they may come, and another's heart that they may believe, so, too, she lends them another's ears, that they may hear, and another's mind, that through others they may be taught. And therefore, as they are to be baptized, on the same grounds they are to be instructed.

REPLY OBJ. 3: He who answers in the child's stead: *I do believe*, does not foretell that the child will believe when it comes to the right age, else he would say: *He will believe*; but in the child's stead he professes the Church's faith which is communicated to that child, the sacrament of which faith is bestowed on it, and to which faith he is bound by another. For there is nothing unfitting in a person being bound by another in things necessary for salvation. In like manner the sponsor, in answering for the child, promises to use his endeavors that the child may believe. This, however, would not be sufficient in the case of adults having the use of reason.

Article 2

Whether Exorcism Should Precede Baptism?

AD SECUNDUM SIC PROCEDITUR. Videtur quod exorcismus non debeat praecedere Baptismum. Exorcismus enim est contra energumenos, idest arreptitios, ordinatus. Sed non omnes sunt tales. Ergo exorcismus non debet praecedere Baptismum.

PRAETEREA, quandiu homo subiacet peccato, Diabolus in eo potestatem habet, ut dicitur Ioan. VIII, *qui facit peccatum, servus est peccati*. Sed peccatum tollitur per Baptismum. Non ergo ante Baptismum sunt homines exorcizandi.

PRAETEREA, ad arcendum Daemonum potestatem est introducta aqua benedicta. Non ergo ad hoc oportebat aliud remedium adhiberi per exorcismos.

SED CONTRA est quod Caelestinus Papa dicit, *sive parvuli sive iuvenes ad regenerationis veniant sacramentum, non prius fontem vitae adeant quam exorcismis et exsufflationibus clericorum spiritus immundus ab eis abiiciatur.*

RESPONDEO dicendum quod quicumque opus aliquod sapienter facere proponit, prius removet impedimenta sui operis, unde dicitur Ierem. IV, *novate vobis novale, et nolite serere super spinas*. Diabolus autem hostis est humanae salutis, quae homini per Baptismum

OBJECTION 1: It seems that exorcism should not precede Baptism. For exorcism is ordained against energumens or those who are possessed. But not all are such like. Therefore exorcism should not precede Baptism.

OBJ. 2: Further, so long as man is a subject of sin, the devil has power over him, according to John 8:34: *Whosoever committeth sin is the servant of sin*. But sin is taken away by Baptism. Therefore men should not be exorcized before Baptism.

OBJ. 3: Further, Holy water was introduced in order to ward off the power of the demons. Therefore exorcism was not needed as a further remedy.

ON THE CONTRARY, Pope Celestine says (*Epist. ad Episcop. Galliae*): *Whether children or young people approach the sacrament of regeneration, they should not come to the fount of life before the unclean spirit has been expelled from them by the exorcisms and breathings of the clerics.*

I ANSWER THAT, Whoever purposes to do a work wisely, first removes the obstacles to his work; hence it is written (Jer 4:3): *Break up anew your fallow ground and sow not upon thorns*. Now the devil is the enemy of man's salvation, which man acquires by Baptism; and he has a certain

acquiritur; et habet potestatem aliquam in homine ex hoc ipso quod subditur originali peccato, vel etiam actuali. Unde etiam convenienter ante Baptismum expelluntur Daemones per exorcismos, ne salutem hominis impediant. Quam quidem expulsionem significat exsufflatio. Benedictio autem, cum manus impositione, praecludit expulso viam ne redire possit. Sal autem in os missum, et narium et aurium sputo linitio, significat receptionem doctrinae fidei quantum ad aures, et approbationem quantum ad nares, et confessionem quantum ad os. Olei vero inunctio significat aptitudinem hominis ad pugnandum contra Daemones.

Ad primum ergo dicendum quod energumeni dicuntur quasi interius laborantes extrinseca operatione Diaboli. Et quamvis non omnes accedentes ad Baptismum corporaliter ab eo vexentur, omnes tamen non baptizati potestati Daemonum subiiciuntur, saltem propter reatum originalis peccati.

Ad secundum dicendum quod in Baptismo per ablutionem excluditur potestas Daemonis ab homine quantum ad hoc quod impedit eum a perceptione gloriae. Sed exorcismi excludunt potestatem Daemonis inquantum impedit hominem a perceptione sacramenti.

Ad tertium dicendum quod aqua benedicta datur contra impugnationes Daemonum quae sunt ab exteriori. Sed exorcismus ordinatur contra impugnationes Daemonum quae sunt ab interiori, unde, energumeni dicuntur, quasi interius laborantes, illi qui exorcizantur.

Vel dicendum quod, sicut remedium contra peccatum secundo datur poenitentia, quia Baptismus non iteratur; ita in remedium contra impugnationes Daemonum secundo datur aqua benedicta, quia exorcismi baptismales non iterantur.

power over man from the very fact that the latter is subject to original, or even actual, sin. Consequently it is fitting that before Baptism the demons should be cast out by exorcisms, lest they impede man's salvation. Which expulsion is signified by the breathing; while the blessing, with the imposition of hands, bars the way against the return of him who was cast out. Then the salt which is put in the mouth, and the anointing of the nose and ears with spittle, signify the receiving of doctrine, as to the ears; consent thereto as to the nose; and confession thereof, as to the mouth. And the anointing with oil signifies man's ability to fight against the demons.

Reply Obj. 1: The energumens are so-called from *laboring inwardly* under the outward operation of the devil. And though not all that approach Baptism are troubled by him in their bodies, yet all who are not baptized are subject to the power of the demons, at least on account of the guilt of original sin.

Reply Obj. 2: The power of the devil in so far as he hinders man from obtaining glory, is expelled from man by the baptismal ablution; but in so far as he hinders man from receiving the sacrament, his power is cast out by the exorcisms.

Reply Obj. 3: Holy water is used against the assaults of demons from without. But exorcisms are directed against those assaults of the demons which are from within. Hence those who are exorcized are called energumens, as it were *laboring inwardly.*

Or we may say that just as Penance is given as a further remedy against sin, because Baptism is not repeated; so Holy Water is given as a further remedy against the assaults of demons, because the baptismal exorcisms are not given a second time.

Article 3

Whether What Is Done in the Exorcism Effects Anything, or Is a Mere Sign?

Ad tertium sic proceditur. Videtur quod ea quae aguntur in exorcismo non efficiant aliquid, sed solum significent. Si enim puer post exorcismos moriatur ante Baptismum, salutem non consequitur. Sed ad hoc ordinatur effectus eorum quae in sacramentis aguntur, ut homo consequatur salutem, unde et Marc. ult. dicitur, *qui crediderit et baptizatus fuerit, salvus erit.* Ergo ea quae aguntur in exorcismo nihil efficiunt, sed solum significant.

Praeterea, hoc solum requiritur ad sacramentum novae legis ut sit signum et causa, sicut supra dictum est. Si ergo ea quae aguntur in exorcismo aliquid efficiant, videtur quod singula sint quaedam sacramenta.

Objection 1: It seems that what is done in the exorcism does not effect anything, but is a mere sign. For if a child die after the exorcisms, before being baptized, it is not saved. But the effects of what is done in the sacraments are ordained to the salvation of man; hence it is written (Mark 16:16): *He that believeth and is baptized shall be saved.* Therefore what is done in the exorcism effects nothing, but is a mere sign.

Obj. 2: Further, nothing is required for a sacrament of the New Law, but that it should be a sign and a cause, as stated above (Q. 62, A. 1). If, therefore, the things done in the exorcism effect anything, it seems that each of them is a sacrament.

Praeterea, sicut exorcismus ordinatur ad Baptismum, ita, si aliquid in exorcismo efficitur, ordinatur ad effectum Baptismi. Sed dispositio ex necessitate praecedit formam perfectam, quia forma non recipitur nisi in materia disposita. Sequeretur ergo quod nullus posset consequi effectum Baptismi nisi prius exorcizatus, quod patet esse falsum. Non ergo ea quae aguntur in exorcismis aliquem effectum habent.

Praeterea, sicut quaedam aguntur in exorcismo ante Baptismum, ita etiam quaedam aguntur post Baptismum, sicut quod sacerdos baptizatum ungit in vertice. Sed ea quae post Baptismum aguntur non videntur aliquid efficere, quia secundum hoc, effectus Baptismi esset imperfectus. Ergo nec ea quae ante Baptismum aguntur in exorcismo.

Sed contra est quod Augustinus dicit, in libro de symbolo, *parvuli exsufflantur et exorcizantur, ut pellatur ab eis Diaboli potestas inimica, quae decepit hominem.* Nihil autem agitur frustra per Ecclesiam. Ergo per huiusmodi exsufflationes hoc agitur ut Daemonum potestas expellatur.

Respondeo dicendum quod quidam dicunt ea quae in exorcismo aguntur nihil efficere, sed solum significare. Sed hoc patet esse falsum, per hoc quod Ecclesia in exorcismis imperativis verbis utitur ad expellendum Daemonis potestatem, puta cum dicit, *ergo, maledicte Diabole, exi ab eo*, et cetera.

Et ideo dicendum est quod aliquem effectum habent, differenter tamen ab ipso Baptismo. Nam per Baptismum datur homini gratia ad plenam remissionem culparum. Per ea vero quae in exorcismo aguntur, excluditur duplex impedimentum gratiae salutaris percipiendae. Quorum unum est impedimentum extrinsecum, prout Daemones salutem hominis impedire conantur. Et hoc impedimentum excluditur per exsufflationes, quibus potestas Daemonis repellitur, ut patet ex inducta auctoritate Augustini, quantum scilicet ad hoc quod non praestet impedimentum sacramento suscipiendo. Manet tamen potestas Daemonis in homine quantum ad maculam peccati et reatum poenae, quousque peccatum per Baptismum tollatur. Et secundum hoc Cyprianus dicit, *scias Diaboli nequitiam posse remanere usque ad aquam salutarem, in Baptismo autem omnem nequitiam amittere.*

Aliud autem impedimentum est intrinsecum, prout scilicet homo ex infectione originalis peccati habet sensus praeclusos ad percipienda salutis mysteria. Unde Rabanus, de institutione clericorum, dicit quod *per salivam typicam et sacerdotis tactum sapientia et virtus divina salutem catechumenis operatur, ut aperiantur eis nares ad recipiendum odorem notitiae Dei, ut aperiantur aures ad audiendum mandata Dei, ut aperiantur illis sensus in intimo corde ad respondendum.*

Ad primum ergo dicendum quod per ea quae aguntur in exorcismo non tollitur culpa, propter quam homo

Obj. 3: Further, just as the exorcism is ordained to Baptism, so if anything be effected in the exorcism, it is ordained to the effect of Baptism. But disposition must needs precede the perfect form: because form is not received save into matter already disposed. It would follow, therefore, that none could obtain the effect of Baptism unless he were previously exorcized; which is clearly false. Therefore what is done in the exorcisms has no effect.

Obj. 4: Further, just as some things are done in the exorcism before Baptism, so are some things done after Baptism; for instance, the priest anoints the baptized on the top of the head. But what is done after Baptism seems to have no effect; for, if it had, the effect of Baptism would be imperfect. Therefore neither have those things an effect, which are done in exorcism before Baptism.

On the contrary, Augustine says (*De Symbolo* I): *Little children are breathed upon and exorcized, in order to expel from them the devil's hostile power, which deceived man.* But the Church does nothing in vain. Therefore the effect of these breathings is that the power of the devils is expelled.

I answer that, Some say that the things done in the exorcism have no effect, but are mere signs. But this is clearly false; since in exorcizing, the Church uses words of command to cast out the devil's power, for instance, when she says: *Therefore, accursed devil, go out from him*, etc.

Therefore we must say that they have some effect, but, other than that of Baptism. For Baptism gives man grace unto the full remission of sins. But those things that are done in the exorcism remove the twofold impediment against the reception of saving grace. Of these, one is the outward impediment, so far as the demons strive to hinder man's salvation. And this impediment is removed by the breathings, whereby the demon's power is cast out, as appears from the passage quoted from Augustine, i.e., as to the devil not placing obstacles against the reception of the sacrament. Nevertheless, the demon's power over man remains as to the stain of sin, and the debt of punishment, until sin be washed away by Baptism. And in this sense Cyprian says (*Epist. lxxvi*): *Know that the devil's evil power remains until the pouring of the saving water: but in Baptism he loses it all.*

The other impediment is within, forasmuch as, from having contracted original sin, man's sense is closed to the perception of the mysteries of salvation. Hence Rabanus says (*De Instit. Cleric.* i) that *by means of the typifying spittle and the touch of the priest, the Divine wisdom and power brings salvation to the catechumen, that his nostrils being opened he may perceive the odor of the knowledge of God, that his ears be opened to hear the commandments of God, that his senses be opened in his inmost heart to respond.*

Reply Obj. 1: What is done in the exorcism does not take away the sin for which man is punished after death;

punitur post mortem, sed solum tolluntur impedimenta recipiendi remissionem culpae per sacramentum. Unde post mortem exorcismus non valet sine Baptismo.

Praepositinus autem dicit quod pueri exorcizati, si moriantur ante Baptismum, minores tenebras patientur. Sed hoc non videtur verum, quia tenebrae illae sunt carentia divinae visionis, quae non recipit magis et minus.

AD SECUNDUM dicendum quod de ratione sacramenti est quod perficiat principalem effectum, qui est gratia remittens culpam, vel supplens aliquem hominis defectum. Quod quidem non fit per ea quae aguntur in exorcismo, sed solum huiusmodi impedimenta tolluntur. Et ideo non sunt sacramenta, sed sacramentalia quaedam.

AD TERTIUM dicendum quod dispositio sufficiens ad suscipiendam gratiam baptismalem est fides et intentio, vel propria eius qui baptizatur, si sit adultus, vel Ecclesiae, si sit parvulus. Ea vero quae aguntur in exorcismo, ordinantur ad removendum impedimenta. Et ideo sine eis potest aliquis consequi effectum Baptismi.

Non tamen sunt huiusmodi praetermittenda, nisi in necessitatis articulo. Et tunc, cessante periculo, debent suppleri, ut servetur uniformitas in Baptismo. Nec frustra supplentur post Baptismum, quia, sicut impeditur effectus Baptismi antequam percipiatur, ita potest impediri postquam fuerit perceptus.

AD QUARTUM dicendum quod eorum quae aguntur post Baptismum circa baptizatum, aliquid est quod non solum significat, sed efficit, puta inunctio quae fit in vertice, quae operatur conservationem gratiae baptismalis. Aliquid autem est quod nihil efficit, sed solum significat, sicut quod datur eis vestis candida, ad significandam novitatem vitae.

but only the impediments against his receiving the remission of sin through the sacrament. Wherefore exorcism avails a man nothing after death if he has not been baptized.

Praepositivus, however, says that children who die after being exorcized but before being baptized are subjected to lesser darkness. But this does not seem to be true: because that darkness consists in privation of the vision of God, which cannot be greater or lesser.

REPLY OBJ. 2: It is essential to a sacrament to produce its principal effect, which is grace that remits sin, or supplies some defect in man. But those things that are done in the exorcism do not effect this; they merely remove these impediments. Consequently, they are not sacraments but sacramentals.

REPLY OBJ. 3: The disposition that suffices for receiving the baptismal grace is the faith and intention, either of the one baptized, if it be an adult, or of the Church, if it be a child. But these things that are done in the exorcism, are directed to the removal of the impediments. And therefore one may receive the effect of Baptism without them.

Yet they are not to be omitted save in a case of necessity. And then, if the danger pass, they should be supplied, that uniformity in Baptism may be observed. Nor are they supplied to no purpose after Baptism: because, just as the effect of Baptism may be hindered before it is received, so can it be hindered after it has been received.

REPLY OBJ. 4: Of those things that are done after Baptism in respect of the person baptized, something is done which is not a mere sign, but produces an effect, for instance, the anointing on the top of the head, the effect of which is the preservation of baptismal grace. And there is something which has no effect, but is a mere sign, for instance, the baptized are given a white garment to signify the newness of life.

Article 4

Whether It Belongs to a Priest to Catechize and Exorcize the Person to Be Baptized?

AD QUARTUM SIC PROCEDITUR. Videtur quod non sit sacerdotis catechizare et exorcizare baptizandum. Ad officium enim ministrorum pertinet habere operationem super immundos, ut Dionysius, V cap. Eccl. Hier., dicit. Sed catechumeni, qui instruuntur in catechismo, et energumeni, qui purgantur in exorcismo, computantur inter immundos, ut Dionysius ibidem dicit. Ergo catechizare et exorcizare non pertinet ad officium sacerdotis, sed potius ministrorum.

PRAETEREA, catechumeni instruuntur de fide per sacram Scripturam, quae in Ecclesia per ministros recitatur, sicut enim per lectores in Ecclesia legitur vetus

OBJECTION 1: It seems that it does not belong to a priest to catechize and exorcize the person to be baptized. For it belongs to the office of ministers to operate on the unclean, as Dionysius says (*Eccl. Hier.* v). But catechumens who are instructed by catechism, and *energumens* who are cleansed by exorcism, are counted among the unclean, as Dionysius says in the same place. Therefore to catechize and to exorcize do not belong to the office of the priests, but rather to that of the ministers.

OBJ. 2: Further, catechumens are instructed in the Faith by the Holy Scripture which is read in the church by ministers: for just as the Old Testament is recited by the Readers,

testamentum, ita etiam per diacones et subdiacones legitur novum. Et sic ad ministros pertinet catechizare. Similiter etiam et exorcizare, ut videtur, ad ministros pertinet. Dicit enim Isidorus, in quadam epistola, *ad exorcistam pertinet exorcismos memoriter retinere, manusque super energumenos et catechumenos in exorcismo imponere.* Non ergo pertinet ad officium sacerdotis catechizare et exorcizare.

Praeterea, catechizare idem est quod docere, et hoc idem est quod perficere. Quod ad officium episcoporum pertinet, ut dicit Dionysius, V cap. Eccl. Hier. Non ergo pertinet ad officium sacerdotis.

Sed contra est quod Nicolaus Papa dicit, *catechismi baptizandorum a sacerdotibus uniuscuiusque Ecclesiae fieri possunt.* Gregorius etiam, super Ezech., dicit, *sacerdotes, cum per exorcismi gratiam manum credentibus imponunt, quid aliud faciunt nisi quod Daemonia eiiciuntur.*

Respondeo dicendum quod minister comparatur ad sacerdotem sicut secundarium et instrumentale agens ad principale, ut indicat ipsum nomen ministri. Agens autem secundarium non agit sine principali agente in operando. Quanto autem operatio est potior, tanto principale agens indiget potioribus instrumentis. Potior autem est operatio sacerdotis inquantum confert ipsum sacramentum, quam in praeparatoriis ad sacramentum. Et ideo supremi ministri, qui dicuntur diacones, cooperantur sacerdoti in ipsa collatione sacramentorum, dicit enim Isidorus quod *ad diaconum pertinet assistere sacerdotibus et ministrare in omnibus quae aguntur in sacramentis Christi, in Baptismo scilicet, in chrismate, patena et calice.* Inferiores autem ministri cooperantur sacerdoti in his quae sunt praeparatoria ad sacramenta, sicut lectores in catechismo, exorcistae in exorcismo.

Ad primum ergo dicendum quod super immundos ministri habent operationem ministerialem et quasi instrumentalem, sed sacerdos principalem.

Ad secundum dicendum quod lectores et exorcistae habent officium catechizandi et exorcizandi, non quidem principaliter, sed sicut in his sacerdoti ministrantes.

Ad tertium dicendum quod multiplex est instructio. Una conversiva ad fidem. Quam Dionysius attribuit episcopo, in II cap. Eccl. Hier., et potest competere cuilibet praedicatori, vel etiam cuilibet fideli. Secunda est instructio qua quis eruditur de fidei rudimentis, et qualiter se debeat habere in susceptione sacramentorum. Et haec pertinet secundario quidem ad ministros, principaliter autem ad sacerdotes. Tertia est instructio de conversatione Christianae vitae. Et haec pertinet ad patrinos. Quarta est instructio de profundis mysteriis fidei, et perfectione Christianae vitae. Et haec ex officio pertinet ad episcopos.

so the New Testament is read by the Deacons and Subdeacons. And thus it belongs to the ministers to catechize. In like manner it belongs, seemingly, to the ministers to exorcize. For Isidore says (*Epist. ad Ludifred.*): *The exorcist should know the exorcisms by heart, and impose his hands on the energumens and catechumens during the exorcism.* Therefore it belongs not to the priestly office to catechize and exorcize.

Obj. 3: Further, *to catechize* is the same as *to teach*, and this is the same as *to perfect*. Now this belongs to the office of a bishop, as Dionysius says (*Eccl. Hier.* v). Therefore it does not belong to the priestly office.

On the contrary, Pope Nicolas I says: *The catechizing of those who are to be baptized can be undertaken by the priests attached to each church.* And Gregory says (*Hom. xxix super Ezech.*): *When priests place their hands on believers for the grace of exorcism, what else do they but cast out the devils?*

I answer that, The minister compared to the priest, is as a secondary and instrumental agent to the principal agent: as is implied in the very word *minister*. Now the secondary agent does nothing without the principal agent in operating. And the more mighty the operation, so much the mightier instruments does the principal agent require. But the operation of the priest in conferring the sacrament itself is mightier than in those things that are preparatory to the sacrament. And so the highest ministers who are called deacons co-operate with the priest in bestowing the sacraments themselves: for Isidore says (*Epist. ad Ludifred.*) that *it belongs to the deacons to assist the priests in all things that are done in Christ's sacraments, in Baptism, to wit, in the Chrism, in the Paten and Chalice*; while the inferior ministers assist the priest in those things which are preparatory to the sacraments: the readers, for instance, in catechizing; the exorcists in exorcizing.

Reply Obj. 1: The minister's operation in regard to the unclean is ministerial and, as it were, instrumental, but the priest's is principal.

Reply Obj. 2: To readers and exorcists belongs the duty of catechizing and exorcizing, not, indeed, principally, but as ministers of the priest in these things.

Reply Obj. 3: Instruction is manifold. One leads to the embracing of the Faith; and is ascribed by Dionysius to bishops (*Eccl. Hier.* ii) and can be undertaken by any preacher, or even by any believer. Another is that by which a man is taught the rudiments of faith, and how to comport himself in receiving the sacraments: this belongs secondarily to the ministers, primarily to the priests. A third is instruction in the mode of Christian life: and this belongs to the sponsors. A fourth is the instruction in the profound mysteries of faith, and on the perfection of Christian life: this belongs to bishops ex officio, in virtue of their office.

QUESTION 72

THE SACRAMENT OF CONFIRMATION

Consequenter considerandum est de sacramento confirmationis. Et circa hoc quaeruntur duodecim.

Primo, utrum confirmatio sit sacramentum.

Secundo, de materia eius.

Tertio, utrum sit de necessitate sacramenti quod chrisma fuerit prius per episcopum consecratum.

Quarto, de forma ipsius.

Quinto, utrum imprimat characterem.

Sexto, utrum character confirmationis praesupponat characterem baptismalem.

Septimo, utrum conferat gratiam.

Octavo, cui competat recipere hoc sacramentum.

Nono, in qua parte.

Decimo, utrum requiratur aliquis qui teneat confirmandum.

Undecimo, utrum hoc sacramentum per solos episcopos detur.

Duodecimo, de ritu eius.

We have now to consider the Sacrament of Confirmation. Concerning this there are twelve points of inquiry:

(1) Whether Confirmation is a sacrament?

(2) Its matter;

(3) Whether it is essential to the sacrament that the chrism should have been previously consecrated by a bishop?

(4) Its form;

(5) Whether it imprints a character?

(6) Whether the character of Confirmation presupposes the character of Baptism?

(7) Whether it bestows grace?

(8) Who is competent to receive this sacrament?

(9) In what part of the body?

(10) Whether someone is required to stand for the person to be confirmed?

(11) Whether this sacrament is given by bishops only?

(12) Of its rite.

Article 1

Whether Confirmation Is a Sacrament?

AD PRIMUM SIC PROCEDITUR. Videtur quod confirmatio non sit sacramentum. Sacramenta enim ex divina institutione efficaciam habent, sicut supra dictum est. Sed confirmatio non legitur a Christo instituta. Ergo non est sacramentum.

PRAETEREA, sacramenta novae legis in veteri praefigurata fuerunt, ut apostolus dicit, I Cor. X, quod *omnes in Moyse baptizati sunt in nube et in mari, et omnes eandem spiritualem escam manducaverunt, et omnes eundem potum spiritualem biberunt.* Sed confirmatio non fuit praefigurata in veteri testamento. Ergo non est sacramentum.

PRAETEREA, sacramenta ordinantur ad hominum salutem. Sed sine confirmatione potest esse salus, nam pueri baptizati sine confirmatione decedentes salvantur. Ergo confirmatio non est sacramentum.

PRAETEREA, per omnia sacramenta Ecclesiae homo Christo conformatur, qui est sacramentorum auctor. Sed per confirmationem homo Christo conformari non potest, qui non legitur esse confirmatus.

OBJECTION 1: It seems that Confirmation is not a sacrament. For sacraments derive their efficacy from the Divine institution, as stated above (Q. 64, A. 2). But we read nowhere of Confirmation being instituted by Christ. Therefore it is not a sacrament.

OBJ. 2: Further, the sacraments of the New Law were foreshadowed in the Old Law; thus the Apostle says (1 Cor 10:2–4), that *all in Moses were baptized, in the cloud and in the sea; and did all eat the same spiritual food, and all drank the same spiritual drink.* But Confirmation was not foreshadowed in the Old Testament. Therefore it is not a sacrament.

OBJ. 3: Further, the sacraments are ordained unto man's salvation. But man can be saved without Confirmation: since children that are baptized, who die before being confirmed, are saved. Therefore Confirmation is not a sacrament.

OBJ. 4: Further, by all the sacraments of the Church, man is conformed to Christ, Who is the Author of the sacraments. But man cannot be conformed to Christ by Confirmation, since we read nowhere of Christ being confirmed.

SED CONTRA est quod Melchiades Papa scribit Hispaniarum episcopis, *de his super quibus rogastis nos vos informari, idest, utrum maius sit sacramentum manus impositio episcoporum an Baptismus, scitote utrumque magnum esse sacramentum.*

RESPONDEO dicendum quod sacramenta novae legis ordinantur ad speciales gratiae effectus, et ideo, ubi occurrit aliquis specialis effectus gratiae, ibi ordinatur speciale sacramentum. Quia vero sensibilia et corporalia gerunt spiritualium et intelligibilium similitudinem, ex his quae in vita corporali aguntur, percipere possumus quid in spirituali vita speciale existat. Manifestum est autem quod in vita corporali specialis quaedam perfectio est quod homo ad perfectam aetatem perveniat, et perfectas actiones hominis agere possit, unde et apostolus dicit, I Cor. XIII, *cum autem factus sum vir, evacuavi quae erant parvuli.* Et inde etiam est quod, praeter motum generationis, quo aliquis accipit vitam corporalem, est motus augmenti, quo aliquis perducitur ad perfectam aetatem. Sic igitur et vitam spiritualem homo accipit per Baptismum, qui est spiritualis regeneratio. In confirmatione autem homo accipit quasi quandam aetatem perfectam spiritualis vitae. Unde Melchiades Papa dicit, *Spiritus Sanctus, qui super aquas Baptismi salutifero descendit lapsu, in fonte plenitudinem tribuit ad innocentiam, in confirmatione augmentum praestat ad gratiam. In Baptismo regeneramur ad vitam, post Baptismum roboramur.* Et ideo manifestum est quod confirmatio est speciale sacramentum.

AD PRIMUM ergo dicendum quod circa institutionem huius sacramenti est triplex opinio. Quidam enim dixerunt quod hoc sacramentum non fuit institutum nec a Christo nec ab apostolis, sed postea processu temporis in quodam Concilio. Alii vero dixerunt quod fuit institutum ab apostolis. Sed hoc non potest esse, quia instituere novum sacramentum pertinet ad potestatem excellentiae, quae competit soli Christo.

Et ideo dicendum quod Christus instituit hoc sacramentum, non exhibendo, sed promittendo, secundum illud Ioan. XVI, *nisi ego abiero, Paraclitus non veniet ad vos, si autem abiero, mittam eum ad vos.* Et hoc ideo quia in hoc sacramento datur plenitudo spiritus sancti, quae non erat danda ante Christi resurrectionem et ascensionem, secundum illud Ioan. VII, *nondum erat spiritus datus, quia Iesus nondum erat glorificatus.*

AD SECUNDUM dicendum quod confirmatio est sacramentum plenitudinis gratiae, et ideo non potuit habere aliquid respondens in veteri lege, quia *nihil ad perfectum adduxit lex,* ut dicitur Heb. VII.

AD TERTIUM dicendum quod, sicut supra dictum est, omnia sacramenta sunt aliqualiter necessaria ad salutem, sed quaedam sine quibus non est salus, quaedam

ON THE CONTRARY, Pope Melchiades wrote to the bishops of Spain: *Concerning the point on which you sought to be informed, i.e., whether the imposition of the bishop's hand were a greater sacrament than Baptism, know that each is a great sacrament.*

I ANSWER THAT, The sacraments of the New Law are ordained unto special effects of grace: and therefore where there is a special effect of grace, there we find a special sacrament ordained for the purpose. But since sensible and material things bear a likeness to things spiritual and intelligible, from what occurs in the life of the body, we can perceive that which is special to the spiritual life. Now it is evident that in the life of the body a certain special perfection consists in man's attaining to the perfect age, and being able to perform the perfect actions of a man: hence the Apostle says (1 Cor 13:11): *When I became a man, I put away the things of a child.* And thence it is that besides the movement of generation whereby man receives life of the body, there is the movement of growth, whereby man is brought to the perfect age. So therefore does man receive spiritual life in Baptism, which is a spiritual regeneration: while in Confirmation man arrives at the perfect age, as it were, of the spiritual life. Hence Pope Melchiades says: *The Holy Spirit, Who comes down on the waters of Baptism bearing salvation in His flight, bestows at the font, the fullness of innocence; but in Confirmation He confers an increase of grace. In Baptism we are born again unto life; after Baptism we are strengthened.* And therefore it is evident that Confirmation is a special sacrament.

REPLY OBJ. 1: Concerning the institution of this sacrament there are three opinions. Some (Alexander of Hales, *Summa Theol.* P. IV, Q. IX; St. Bonaventure, *Sent.* iv, D, 7) have maintained that this sacrament was instituted neither by Christ, nor by the apostles; but later in the course of time by one of the councils. Others (Pierre de Tarentaise, *Sent.* iv, D, 7) held that it was instituted by the apostles. But this cannot be admitted; since the institution of a new sacrament belongs to the power of excellence, which belongs to Christ alone.

And therefore we must say that Christ instituted this sacrament not by bestowing, but by promising it, according to John 16:7: *If I go not, the Paraclete will not come to you, but if I go, I will send Him to you.* And this was because in this sacrament the fullness of the Holy Spirit is bestowed, which was not to be given before Christ's Resurrection and Ascension; according to John 7:39: *As yet the Spirit was not given, because Jesus was not yet glorified.*

REPLY OBJ. 2: Confirmation is the sacrament of the fullness of grace: wherefore there could be nothing corresponding to it in the Old Law, since *the Law brought nothing to perfection* (Heb 7:19).

REPLY OBJ. 3: As stated above (Q. 65, A. 4), all the sacraments are in some way necessary for salvation: but some, so that there is no salvation without them; some as

vero sicut quae operantur ad perfectionem salutis. Et hoc modo confirmatio est de necessitate salutis, quamvis sine ea possit esse salus, dummodo non praetermittatur ex contemptu sacramenti.

AD QUARTUM dicendum quod illi qui confirmationem accipiunt, quae est sacramentum plenitudinis gratiae, Christo conformantur inquantum ipse a primo instanti suae conceptionis fuit *plenus gratiae et veritatis*, ut dicitur Ioan. I. Quae quidem plenitudo declarata est in Baptismo, quando *Spiritus Sanctus descendit corporali specie super eum*. Unde et Luc. IV dicitur quod *Iesus plenus spiritu sancto regressus est a Iordane*. Non autem conveniebat dignitati Christi, qui est sacramentorum auctor, ut a sacramento plenitudinem gratiae acciperet.

conducing to the perfection of salvation; and thus it is that Confirmation is necessary for salvation: although salvation is possible without it, provided it be not omitted out of contempt.

REPLY OBJ. 4: Those who receive Confirmation, which is the sacrament of the fullness of grace, are conformed to Christ, inasmuch as from the very first instant of His conception He was *full of grace and truth* (John 1:14). This fullness was made known at His Baptism, when *the Holy Spirit descended in a bodily shape . . . upon Him* (Luke 3:22). Hence (Luke 4:1) it is written that *Jesus being full of the Holy Spirit, returned from the Jordan*. Nor was it fitting to Christ's dignity, that He, Who is the Author of the sacraments, should receive the fullness of grace from a sacrament.

Article 2

Whether Chrism Is a Fitting Matter for This Sacrament?

AD SECUNDUM SIC PROCEDITUR. Videtur quod chrisma non sit conveniens materia huius sacramenti. Hoc enim sacramentum, ut dictum est, institutum est a Christo promittente discipulis spiritum sanctum. Sed ipse misit eis spiritum sanctum absque chrismatis unctione. Ipsi etiam apostoli hoc sacramentum conferebant per solam manus impositionem, absque chrismate, dicitur enim Act. VIII quod *apostoli imponebant manus super baptizatos, et accipiebant spiritum sanctum*. Ergo chrisma non est materia huius sacramenti, quia materia est de necessitate sacramenti.

PRAETEREA, confirmatio quodammodo perficit sacramentum Baptismi, sicut supra dictum est, et ita debet ei conformari sicut perfectio perfectibili. Sed in Baptismo est materia simplex elementum, scilicet aqua. Ergo huius sacramenti non est conveniens materia chrisma, quod conficitur ex oleo et balsamo.

PRAETEREA, oleum assumitur in materia huius sacramenti ad inungendum. Sed quolibet oleo potest fieri inunctio, puta oleo quod fit ex nucibus, et ex quibuscumque aliis rebus. Non ergo solum oleum olivarum debet assumi ad huiusmodi sacramentum.

PRAETEREA, supra dictum est quod aqua assumitur ut materia ad baptizandum quia ubique de facili invenitur. Sed oleum olivarum non ubique invenitur, et multo minus balsamum. Non ergo chrisma, quod ex his conficitur, est conveniens materia huius sacramenti.

SED CONTRA est quod Gregorius dicit, in registro, *presbyteri baptizatos infantes signare in frontibus sacro chrismate non praesumant*. Ergo chrisma est materia huius sacramenti.

OBJECTION 1: It seems that chrism is not a fitting matter for this sacrament. For this sacrament, as stated above (A. 1, ad 1), was instituted by Christ when He promised His disciples the Holy Spirit. But He sent them the Holy Spirit without their being anointed with chrism. Moreover, the apostles themselves bestowed this sacrament without chrism, by the mere imposition of hands: for it is written (Acts 8:17) that the apostles *laid their hands upon* those who were baptized, *and they received the Holy Spirit*. Therefore chrism is not the matter of this sacrament: since the matter is essential to the sacrament.

OBJ. 2: Further, Confirmation perfects, in a way, the sacrament of Baptism, as stated above (Q. 65, AA. 3, 4): and so it ought to be conformed to it as perfection to the thing perfected. But the matter, in Baptism, is a simple element, viz. water. Therefore chrism, which is made of oil and balm, is not a fitting matter for this sacrament.

OBJ. 3: Further, oil is used as the matter of this sacrament for the purpose of anointing. But any oil will do for anointing: for instance, oil made from nuts, and from anything else. Therefore not only olive oil should be used for this sacrament.

OBJ. 4: Further, it has been stated above (Q. 66, A. 3) that water is used as the matter of Baptism, because it is easily procured everywhere. But olive oil is not to be procured everywhere; and much less is balm. Therefore chrism, which is made of these, is not a fitting matter for this sacrament.

ON THE CONTRARY, Gregory says (*Registr.* iv): *Let no priest dare to sign the baptized infants on the brow with the sacred chrism*. Therefore chrism is the matter of this sacrament.

RESPONDEO dicendum quod chrisma est conveniens materia huius sacramenti. Sicut enim dictum est, in hoc sacramento datur plenitudo spiritus sancti ad robur spirituale, quod competit perfectae aetati. Homo autem, cum ad perfectam aetatem pervenerit, incipit iam communicare actiones suas ad alios, antea vero quasi singulariter sibi ipsi vivit. Gratia vero spiritus sancti in oleo designatur, unde Christus dicitur esse, unctus oleo laetitiae, propter plenitudinem spiritus sancti quam habuit. Et ideo oleum competit materiae huius sacramenti. Admiscetur autem balsamum propter fragrantiam odoris, quae redundat ad alios, unde et apostolus dicit, II Cor. II, *Christi bonus odor sumus*, et cetera. Et licet multa alia sint odorifera, tamen praecipue accipitur balsamum, propter hoc quod habet praecipuum odorem, et quia etiam incorruptionem praestat, unde Eccli. XXIV dicitur, *quasi balsamum non mixtum odor meus*.

AD PRIMUM ergo dicendum quod Christus ex potestate quam habet in sacramentis, contulit apostolis rem huius sacramenti, idest plenitudinem spiritus sancti, sine sacramento, eo quod ipsi *primitias spiritus sancti acceperunt*, sicut dicitur Rom. VIII. Nihilominus tamen aliquid conforme materiae huius sacramenti exhibitum fuit apostolis sensibiliter in collatione spiritus sancti. Quod enim Spiritus Sanctus sensibiliter super eos descendit in specie ignis, ad eandem significationem refertur ad quam refertur oleum, nisi quod ignis habet vim activam, oleum autem vim passivam, inquantum est materia et fomentum ignis. Et hoc satis competebat, nam per apostolos gratia spiritus sancti erat ad alios derivanda. Super apostolos etiam Spiritus Sanctus descendit in figura linguae. Quod ad idem refertur significandum quod significat balsamum, nisi quod lingua per locutionem est communicativa ad alterum, balsamum vero per odorem; quia scilicet apostoli replebantur spiritu sancto ut fidei doctores, alii vero fideles ut operatores eorum quae pertinent ad aedificationem fidelium.

Similiter etiam ad impositionem manus apostolorum, et etiam ad eorum praedicationem, descendebat plenitudo spiritus sancti super fideles sub visibilibus signis, sicut a principio descenderat super apostolos, unde Petrus dicit, Act. XI, *cum coepissem loqui, cecidit Spiritus Sanctus super eos, sicut et in nos in initio*. Et ideo non erat necessaria sensibilis materia sacramentalis, ubi sensibilia signa miraculose exhibebantur divinitus.

Utebantur tamen apostoli communiter chrismate in exhibitione sacramenti, quando huiusmodi visibilia signa non exhibebantur. Dicit enim Dionysius, IV cap. Eccl. Hier., *est quaedam perfectiva operatio, quam duces nostri, idest apostoli, chrismatis hostiam nominant*.

AD SECUNDUM dicendum quod Baptismus datur ad spiritualem vitam simpliciter consequendam, et ideo competit illi sacramento materia simplex. Sed hoc sacramentum datur ad plenitudinem consequendam spiritus

I ANSWER THAT, Chrism is the fitting matter of this sacrament. For, as stated above (A. 1), in this sacrament the fullness of the Holy Spirit is given for the spiritual strength which belongs to the perfect age. Now when man comes to perfect age he begins at once to have intercourse with others; whereas until then he lives an individual life, as it were, confined to himself. Now the grace of the Holy Spirit is signified by oil; hence Christ is said to be *anointed with the oil of gladness* (Ps 44:8), by reason of His being gifted with the fullness of the Holy Spirit. Consequently oil is a suitable matter of this sacrament. And balm is mixed with the oil, by reason of its fragrant odor, which spreads about: hence the Apostle says (2 Cor 2:15): *We are the good odor of Christ*, etc. And though many other things be fragrant, yet preference is given to balm, because it has a special odor of its own, and because it confers incorruptibility: hence it is written (Sir 24:21): *My odor is as the purest balm*.

REPLY OBJ. 1: Christ, by the power which He exercises in the sacraments, bestowed on the apostles the reality of this sacrament, i.e., the fullness of the Holy Spirit, without the sacrament itself, because they had received *the first fruits of the Spirit* (Rom 8:23). Nevertheless, something of keeping with the matter of this sacrament was displayed to the apostles in a sensible manner when they received the Holy Spirit. For that the Holy Spirit came down upon them in a sensible manner under the form of fire, refers to the same signification as oil: except in so far as fire has an active power, while oil has a passive power, as being the matter and incentive of fire. And this was quite fitting: for it was through the apostles that the grace of the Holy Spirit was to flow forth to others. Again, the Holy Spirit came down on the apostles in the shape of a tongue. Which refers to the same signification as balm: except in so far as the tongue communicates with others by speech, but balm, by its odor; because, to wit, the apostles were filled with the Holy Spirit, as teachers of the Faith; but the rest of the believers, as doing that which gives edification to the faithful.

In like manner, too, when the apostles imposed their hands, and when they preached, the fullness of the Holy Spirit came down under visible signs on the faithful, just as, at the beginning, He came down on the apostles: hence Peter said (Acts 11:15): *When I had begun to speak, the Holy Spirit fell upon them, as upon us also in the beginning*. Consequently there was no need for sacramental sensible matter, where God sent sensible signs miraculously.

However, the apostles commonly made use of chrism in bestowing the sacrament, when such like visible signs were lacking. For Dionysius says (*Eccl. Hier.* iv): *There is a certain perfecting operation which our guides*, i.e., the apostles, *call the sacrifice of Chrism*.

REPLY OBJ. 2: Baptism is bestowed that spiritual life may be received simply; wherefore simple matter is fitting to it. But this sacrament is given that we may receive the fullness of the Holy Spirit, Whose operations are manifold,

sancti, cuius est multiformis operatio, secundum illud Sap. VII, *est autem in illa Spiritus Sanctus, unicus, multiplex*, et I Cor. XII dicitur, *divisiones gratiarum sunt, idem autem spiritus*. Et ideo convenienter huius sacramenti est materia composita.

AD TERTIUM dicendum quod proprietates olei quibus significatur Spiritus Sanctus, magis inveniuntur in oleo olivarum quam in quocumque alio oleo. Unde et ipsa oliva, semper frondibus virens, virorem et misericordiam spiritus sancti significat.

Hoc etiam oleum proprie dicitur oleum, et maxime habetur in usu ubi haberi potest. Quilibet autem alius liquor ex similitudine huius oleum nominatur, nec est in usu communi, nisi in supplementum apud eos quibus deest oleum olivarum. Et ideo hoc oleum solum assumitur in usum huius et quorundam aliorum sacramentorum.

AD QUARTUM dicendum quod Baptismus est sacramentum absolutae necessitatis, et ideo eius materia debet ubique inveniri. Sufficit autem quod materia huius sacramenti, quod non est tantae necessitatis, possit de facili ad omnia loca terrarum deferri.

according to Wis. 7:22, *In her is the* Holy *Spirit . . . one, manifold*; and 1 Cor. 12:4, *There are diversities of graces, but the same Spirit*. Consequently a compound matter is appropriate to this sacrament.

REPLY OBJ. 3: These properties of oil, by reason of which it symbolizes the Holy Spirit, are to be found in olive oil rather than in any other oil. In fact, the olive-tree itself, through being an evergreen, signifies the refreshing and merciful operation of the Holy Spirit.

Moreover, this oil is called oil properly, and is very much in use, wherever it is to be had. And whatever other liquid is so called, derives its name from its likeness to this oil: nor are the latter commonly used, unless it be to supply the want of olive oil. Therefore it is that this oil alone is used for this and certain other sacraments.

REPLY OBJ. 4: Baptism is the sacrament of absolute necessity; and so its matter should be at hand everywhere. But it is enough that the matter of this sacrament, which is not of such great necessity, be easily sent to all parts of the world.

Article 3

Whether It Is Essential to This Sacrament That the Chrism Which Is Its Matter Be Previously Consecrated by a Bishop?

AD TERTIUM SIC PROCEDITUR. Videtur quod non sit de necessitate huius sacramenti quod chrisma, quod est materia huius sacramenti, fuerit prius per episcopum consecratum. Baptismus enim, in quo fit plena remissio peccatorum, non est minoris efficaciae quam hoc sacramentum. Sed, licet quaedam sanctificatio adhibeatur aquae baptismali ante Baptismum, non tamen est de necessitate sacramenti, quia in articulo necessitatis praeteriri potest. Ergo nec est de necessitate huius sacramenti quod chrisma fuerit per episcopum consecratum.

PRAETEREA, idem non debet bis consecrari. Sed materia sacramenti sanctificatur in ipsa collatione sacramenti per formam verborum qua confertur sacramentum, unde et Augustinus dicit, super Ioan., *accedit verbum ad elementum et fit sacramentum*. Non ergo debet prius chrisma consecrari quam hoc sacramentum tradatur.

PRAETEREA, omnis consecratio quae fit in sacramentis, ad consecutionem gratiae ordinatur. Sed materia sensibilis confecta ex oleo et balsamo non est capax gratiae. Ergo non debet ei aliqua consecratio adhiberi.

SED CONTRA est quod Innocentius Papa dicit, *presbyteris, cum baptizant, ungere baptizatos chrismate liceat, quod ab episcopo fuerat consecratum, non tamen frontem*

OBJECTION 1: It seems that it is not essential to this sacrament, that the chrism, which is its matter, be previously consecrated by a bishop. For Baptism which bestows full remission of sins is not less efficacious than this sacrament. But, though the baptismal water receives a kind of blessing before being used for Baptism; yet this is not essential to the sacrament: since in a case of necessity it can be dispensed with. Therefore neither is it essential to this sacrament that the chrism should be previously consecrated by a bishop.

OBJ. 2: Further, the same should not be consecrated twice. But the sacramental matter is sanctified, in the very conferring of the sacrament, by the form of words wherein the sacrament is bestowed; hence Augustine says (*Tract. lxxx in Joan.*): *The word is added to the element, and this becomes a sacrament*. Therefore the chrism should not be consecrated before this sacrament is given.

OBJ. 3: Further, every consecration employed in the sacraments is ordained to the bestowal of grace. But the sensible matter composed of oil and balm is not receptive of grace. Therefore it should not be consecrated.

ON THE CONTRARY, Pope Innocent I says (*Ep. ad Decent.*): *Priests, when baptizing, may anoint the baptized with chrism, previously consecrated by a bishop:*

ex eodem oleo signare, quod solis debetur episcopis, cum tradunt Paraclitum; quod quidem fit in hoc sacramento. Ergo ad hoc sacramentum requiritur quod materia huius sacramenti prius per episcopum consecretur.

RESPONDEO dicendum quod tota sacramentorum sanctificatio a Christo derivatur, ut supra dictum est. Est autem considerandum quod quibusdam sacramentis habentibus materiam corpoream Christus est usus, scilicet Baptismo et etiam Eucharistia. Et ideo ex ipso usu Christi materiae horum sacramentorum aptitudinem acceperunt ad perfectionem sacramenti. Unde Chrysostomus dicit quod *nunquam aquae Baptismi purgare peccata credentium possent, nisi tactu dominici corporis sanctificatae fuissent*. Et ipse similiter dominus, accipiens panem, benedixit, similiter autem et calicem, ut habetur Matth. XXVI et Luc. XXII. Et propter hoc non est de necessitate horum sacramentorum quod materia prius benedicatur, quia sufficit benedictio Christi. Si qua vero benedictio adhibeatur, pertinet ad solemnitatem sacramenti, non autem ad necessitatem. Unctionibus autem visibilibus Christus non est usus, ne fieret iniuria invisibili unctioni qua est unctus prae consortibus suis. Et ideo tam chrisma quam oleum sanctum et oleum infirmorum prius benedicuntur quam adhibeantur ad usum sacramenti.

AD PRIMUM ergo patet responsio ex dictis.

AD SECUNDUM dicendum quod utraque consecratio chrismatis non refertur ad idem. Sicut enim instrumentum virtutem instrumentalem acquirit dupliciter, scilicet quando accipit formam instrumenti, et quando movetur a principali agente ita etiam materia sacramenti duplici sanctificatione indiget, per quarum unam fit propria materia sacramenti, per aliam vero applicatur ad effectum.

AD TERTIUM dicendum quod materia corporalis non est capax gratiae quasi gratiae subiectum, sed solum sicut gratiae instrumentum, ut supra dictum est. Et ad hoc materia sacramenti consecratur, vel ab ipso Christo, vel ab episcopo, qui gerit in Ecclesia personam Christi.

but they must not sign the brow with the same oil; this belongs to the bishop alone, when he gives the Paraclete. Now this is done in this sacrament. Therefore it is necessary for this sacrament that its matter be previously consecrated by a bishop.

I ANSWER THAT, The entire sanctification of the sacraments is derived from Christ, as stated above (Q. 64, A. 3). But it must be observed that Christ did use certain sacraments having a corporeal matter, viz. Baptism, and also the Eucharist. And consequently, from Christ's very act in using them, the matter of these sacraments received a certain aptitude to the perfection of the sacrament. Hence Chrysostom (Chromatius, *In Matth.* 3:15) says that *the waters of Baptism could never wash away the sins of believers, had they not been sanctified by contact with our Lord's body.* And again, our Lord Himself *taking bread . . . blessed . . . and in like manner the chalice* (Matt 26:26, 27; Luke 22:19, 20). For this reason there is no need for the matter of these sacraments to be blessed previously, since Christ's blessing is enough. And if any blessing be used, it belongs to the solemnity of the sacrament, not to its essence. But Christ did not make use of visible anointings, so as not to slight the invisible unction whereby He was *anointed above* His *fellows* (Ps 44:8). And hence both chrism, and the holy oil, and the oil of the sick are blessed before being put to sacramental use.

THIS SUFFICES for the reply to the First Objection.

REPLY OBJ. 2: Each consecration of the chrism has not the same object. For just as an instrument derives instrumental power in two ways, viz. when it receives the form of an instrument, and when it is moved by the principal agent; so too the sacramental matter needs a twofold sanctification, by one of which it becomes fit matter for the sacrament, while by the other it is applied to the production of the effect.

REPLY OBJ. 3: Corporeal matter is receptive of grace, not so as to be the subject of grace, but only as the instrument of grace, as explained above (Q. 62, A. 3). And this sacramental matter is consecrated, either by Christ, or by a bishop, who, in the Church, impersonates Christ.

Article 4

Whether the Proper Form of This Sacrament Is: I Sign Thee with the Sign of the Cross, Etc.?

AD QUARTUM SIC PROCEDITUR. Videtur quod haec non sit conveniens forma huius sacramenti, *consigno te signo crucis, confirmo te chrismate salutis, in nomine patris et filii et spiritus sancti, amen.* Usus enim sacramentorum a Christo et ab apostolis derivatur. Sed neque Christus hanc formam instituit, nec apostoli ea usi

OBJECTION 1: It seems that the proper form of this sacrament is not: *I sign thee with the sign of the cross, I confirm thee with the chrism of salvation, in the name of the Father and of the Son and of the Holy Spirit. Amen.* For the use of the sacraments is derived from Christ and the apostles. But neither did Christ institute this form, nor do we read of

leguntur. Ergo haec non est conveniens forma huius sacramenti.

Praeterea, sicut sacramentum est idem apud omnes, ita et forma debet esse eadem, quia quaelibet res habet unitatem, sicut et esse, a sua forma. Sed hac forma non omnes utuntur, quidam enim dicunt, *confirmo te chrismate sanctificationis.* Ergo haec non est conveniens forma huius sacramenti.

Praeterea, sacramentum hoc debet conformari Baptismo sicut perfectio perfectibili, ut supra dictum est. Sed in forma Baptismi non fit mentio de consignatione characteris; nec etiam de cruce Christi, cum tamen per Baptismum homo Christo commoriatur, ut apostolus dicit, Rom. VI; nec etiam fit mentio de effectu salutis, cum tamen Baptismus sit de necessitate salutis. In forma etiam Baptismi ponitur unus actus tantum; et exprimitur persona baptizantis, cum dicitur, ego te baptizo; cuius contrarium apparet in forma praedicta. Non ergo est conveniens forma huius sacramenti.

Sed contra est auctoritas Ecclesiae, quae hac forma communiter utitur.

Respondeo dicendum quod praedicta forma est conveniens huic sacramento. Sicut enim forma rei naturalis dat ei speciem, ita forma sacramenti continere debet quidquid pertinet ad speciem sacramenti. Sicut autem ex supra dictis patet, in hoc sacramento datur Spiritus Sanctus ad robur spiritualis pugnae. Et ideo in hoc sacramento tria sunt necessaria, quae continentur in forma praedicta. Quorum primum est causa conferens plenitudinem roboris spiritualis, quae est sancta Trinitas. Quae exprimitur cum dicitur, in nomine patris et cetera. Secundum est ipsum robur spirituale, quod homini confertur per sacramentum materiae visibilis ad salutem. Quod quidem tangitur cum dicitur, confirmo te chrismate salutis. Tertium est signum quod pugnatori datur, sicut et in pugna corporali, sicut milites signis ducum insigniuntur. Et quantum ad hoc dicitur, consigno te signo crucis, in quo scilicet *rex noster triumphavit*, ut dicitur Coloss. II.

Ad primum ergo dicendum quod, sicut supra dictum est, per ministerium apostolorum quandoque dabatur effectus huius sacramenti, scilicet plenitudo spiritus sancti, quibusdam visibilibus signis miraculose a Deo confectis, qui potest effectum sacramenti sine sacramento conferre. Et tunc non erat necessaria nec materia nec forma huius sacramenti. Quandoque autem tanquam ministri sacramentorum hoc sacramentum praebebant. Et tunc, sicut materia, ita et forma ex mandato Christi utebantur. Multa enim servabant apostoli in sacramentorum collatione quae in Scripturis communiter propositis non sunt tradita. Unde Dionysius dicit, in fine Eccl. Hier., *consummativas invocationes*, idest verba quibus

the apostles making use of it. Therefore it is not the proper form of this sacrament.

Obj. 2: Further, just as the sacrament is the same everywhere, so should the form be the same: because everything has unity, just as it has being, from its form. But this form is not used by all: for some say: *I confirm thee with the chrism of sanctification.* Therefore the above is not the proper form of this sacrament.

Obj. 3: Further, this sacrament should be conformed to Baptism, as the perfect to the thing perfected, as stated above (A. 2, Obj. 2). But in the form of Baptism no mention is made of signing the character; nor again of the cross of Christ, though in Baptism man dies with Christ, as the Apostle says (Rom 6:3–8); nor of the effect which is salvation, though Baptism is necessary for salvation. Again, in the baptismal form, only one action is included; and the person of the baptizer is expressed in the words: *I baptize thee*, whereas the contrary is to be observed in the above form. Therefore this is not the proper form of this sacrament.

On the contrary, Is the authority of the Church, who always uses this form.

I answer that, The above form is appropriate to this sacrament. For just as the form of a natural thing gives it its species, so a sacramental form should contain whatever belongs to the species of the sacrament. Now as is evident from what has been already said (AA. 1, 2), in this sacrament the Holy Spirit is given for strength in the spiritual combat. Wherefore in this sacrament three things are necessary; and they are contained in the above form. The first of these is the cause conferring fullness of spiritual strength which cause is the Blessed Trinity: and this is expressed in the words, *In the name of the Father*, etc. The second is the spiritual strength itself bestowed on man unto salvation by the sacrament of visible matter; and this is referred to in the words, *I confirm thee with the chrism of salvation.* The third is the sign which is given to the combatant, as in a bodily combat: thus are soldiers marked with the sign of their leaders. And to this refer the words, *I sign thee with the sign of the cross*, in which sign, to wit, our King triumphed (cf. Col. 2:15).

Reply Obj. 1: As stated above (A. 2, ad 1), sometimes the effect of this sacrament, i.e., the fullness of the Holy Spirit, was given through the ministry of the apostles, under certain visible signs, wrought miraculously by God, Who can bestow the sacramental effect, independently of the sacrament. In these cases there was no need for either the matter or the form of this sacrament. On the other hand, sometimes they bestowed this sacrament as ministers of the sacraments. And then, they used both matter and form according to Christ's command. For the apostles, in conferring the sacraments, observed many things which are not handed down in those Scriptures that are in general use. Hence Dionysius says at the end of his treatise on

perficiuntur sacramenta, *non est iustum Scripturas interpretantibus, neque mysticum earum, aut in ipsis operatas ex Deo virtutes, ex occulto ad commune adducere, sed nostra sacra traditio sine pompa, idest occulte, edocet eas.* Unde et apostolus dicit, loquens de celebratione Eucharistiae, I Cor. XI, *cetera cum venero disponam.*

AD SECUNDUM dicendum quod sanctitas est salutis causa. Et ideo in idem redit quod dicitur chrismate salutis, et sanctificationis.

AD TERTIUM dicendum quod Baptismus est regeneratio in spiritualem vitam, qua homo vivit in seipso. Et ideo non ponitur in forma Baptismi nisi ipse actus ad ipsum hominem pertinens sanctificandum. Sed hoc sacramentum non solum ordinatur ad hoc quod homo sanctificetur in seipso, sed exponitur cuidam pugnae exteriori. Et ideo non solum fit mentio de interiori sanctificatione, cum dicitur, confirmo te chrismate salutis, sed etiam consignatur homo exterius, quasi vexillo crucis, ad pugnam exteriorem spiritualem, quod significatur cum dicitur, consigno te signo crucis.

In ipso autem verbo baptizandi, quod ablutionem significat, potest intelligi et materia, quae est aqua abluens, et effectus salutis. Quae non intelliguntur in verbo confirmandi, et ideo oportuit haec ponere.

Dictum est autem supra quod hoc quod dicitur, ego, non est de necessitate formae baptismalis, quia intelligitur in verbo primae personae. Apponitur tamen ad exprimendam intentionem. Quod non est ita necessarium in confirmatione, quae non exhibetur nisi ab excellenti ministro, ut infra dicetur.

the *Ecclesiastical Hierarchy* (chap. vii): *It is not allowed to explain in writing the prayers which are used in the sacraments, and to publish their mystical meaning, or the power which, coming from God, gives them their efficacy; we learn these things by holy tradition without any display,* i.e., secretly. Hence the Apostle, speaking of the celebration of the Eucharist, writes (1 Cor 11:34): *The rest I will set in order, when I come.*

REPLY OBJ. 2: Holiness is the cause of salvation. Therefore it comes to the same whether we say *chrism of salvation* or *of sanctification.*

REPLY OBJ. 3: Baptism is the regeneration unto the spiritual life, whereby man lives in himself. And therefore in the baptismal form that action alone is expressed which refers to the man to be sanctified. But this sacrament is ordained not only to the sanctification of man in himself, but also to strengthen him in his outward combat. Consequently not only is mention made of interior sanctification, in the words, *I confirm thee with the chrism of salvation*: but furthermore man is signed outwardly, as it were with the standard of the cross, unto the outward spiritual combat; and this is signified by the words, *I sign thee with the sign of the cross.*

But in the very word *baptize*, which signifies *to cleanse*, we can understand both the matter, which is the cleansing water, and the effect, which is salvation. Whereas these are not understood by the word *confirm*; and consequently they had to be expressed.

Again, it has been said above (Q. 66, A. 5, ad 1) that the pronoun *I* is not necessary to the Baptismal form, because it is included in the first person of the verb. It is, however, included in order to express the intention. But this does not seem so necessary in Confirmation, which is conferred only by a minister of excellence, as we shall state later on (A. 11).

Article 5

Whether the Sacrament of Confirmation Imprints a Character?

AD QUINTUM SIC PROCEDITUR. Videtur quod sacramentum confirmationis non imprimat characterem. Character enim importat quoddam signum distinctivum. Sed per sacramentum confirmationis non distinguitur homo ab infidelibus, hoc enim fit per Baptismum, nec etiam ab aliis fidelibus, quia hoc sacramentum ordinatur ad pugnam spiritualem, quae omnibus fidelibus indicitur. Non ergo in hoc sacramento imprimitur aliquis character.

PRAETEREA, supra dictum est quod character est quaedam potentia spiritualis. Potentia autem non est nisi activa vel passiva. Potentia autem activa in sacramentis

OBJECTION 1: It seems that the sacrament of Confirmation does not imprint a character. For a character means a distinctive sign. But a man is not distinguished from unbelievers by the sacrament of Confirmation, for this is the effect of Baptism; nor from the rest of the faithful, because this sacrament is ordained to the spiritual combat, which is enjoined to all the faithful. Therefore a character is not imprinted in this sacrament.

OBJ. 2: Further, it was stated above (Q. 63, A. 2) that a character is a spiritual power. Now a power must be either active or passive. But the active power in the sacraments is

confertur per sacramentum ordinis, potentia autem passiva, sive receptiva, per sacramentum Baptismi. Ergo per sacramentum confirmationis nullus character imprimitur.

Praeterea, in circumcisione, quae est character corporalis, non imprimitur aliquis spiritualis character. Sed in hoc sacramento imprimitur quidam character corporalis, dum scilicet homo chrismate signatur signo crucis in fronte. Non ergo imprimitur in hoc sacramento character spiritualis.

Sed contra, in omni sacramento quod non iteratur, imprimitur character. Sed hoc sacramentum non iteratur, dicit enim Gregorius, *de homine qui a pontifice confirmatus fuerit denuo, talis iteratio prohibenda est.* Ergo in confirmatione imprimitur character.

Respondeo dicendum quod, sicut supra dictum est, character est quaedam spiritualis potestas ad aliquas sacras actiones ordinata. Dictum est autem supra quod, sicut Baptismus est quaedam spiritualis generatio in vitam Christianam, ita etiam confirmatio est quoddam spirituale augmentum promovens hominem in spiritualem aetatem perfectam. Manifestum est autem ex similitudine corporalis vitae quod alia est actio hominis statim nati, et alia actio competit ei cum ad perfectam aetatem pervenerit. Et ideo per sacramentum confirmationis datur homini potestas spiritualis ad quasdam actiones alias sacras, praeter illas ad quas datur ei potestas in Baptismo. Nam in Baptismo accipit potestatem ad ea agenda quae ad propriam pertinent salutem, prout secundum seipsum vivit, sed in confirmatione accipit potestatem ad agendum ea quae pertinent ad pugnam spiritualem contra hostes fidei. Sicut patet exemplo apostolorum, qui, antequam plenitudinem spiritus sancti acciperent, erant in cenaculo perseverantes in oratione; postmodum autem egressi non verebantur fidem publice fateri, etiam coram inimicis fidei Christianae. Et ideo manifestum est quod in sacramento confirmationis imprimitur character.

Ad primum ergo dicendum quod pugna spiritualis contra hostes invisibiles omnibus competit. Sed contra hostes visibiles, idest contra persecutores fidei pugnare, nomen Christi confitendo, est confirmatorum, qui iam sunt perducti spiritualiter ad virilem aetatem, secundum quod dicitur I Ioan. II, *scribo vobis, iuvenes, quoniam fortes estis, et verbum Dei in vobis manet, et vicistis malignum.* Et ideo character confirmationis est signum distinctivum, non infidelium a fidelibus, sed spiritualiter provectorum ab his quibus dicitur, *sicut modo geniti infantes.*

Ad secundum dicendum quod omnia sacramenta sunt quaedam fidei protestationes. Sicut igitur baptizatus accipit potestatem spiritualem ad protestandum

conferred by the sacrament of order: while the passive or receptive power is conferred by the sacrament of Baptism. Therefore no character is imprinted by the sacrament of Confirmation.

Obj. 3: Further, in circumcision, which is a character of the body, no spiritual character is imprinted. But in this sacrament a character is imprinted on the body, when the sign of the cross is signed with chrism on man's brow. Therefore a spiritual character is not imprinted by this sacrament.

On the contrary, A character is imprinted in every sacrament that is not repeated. But this sacrament is not repeated: for Gregory II says (*Ep. iv ad Bonifac.*): *As to the man who was confirmed a second time by a bishop, such a repetition must be forbidden.* Therefore a character is imprinted in Confirmation.

I answer that, As stated above (Q. 63, A. 2), a character is a spiritual power ordained to certain sacred actions. Now it has been said above (A. 1; Q. 65, A. 1) that, just as Baptism is a spiritual regeneration unto Christian life, so also is Confirmation a certain spiritual growth bringing man to perfect spiritual age. But it is evident, from a comparison with the life of the body, that the action which is proper to man immediately after birth, is different from the action which is proper to him when he has come to perfect age. And therefore by the sacrament of Confirmation man is given a spiritual power in respect of sacred actions other than those in respect of which he receives power in Baptism. For in Baptism he receives power to do those things which pertain to his own salvation, forasmuch as he lives to himself: whereas in Confirmation he receives power to do those things which pertain to the spiritual combat with the enemies of the Faith. This is evident from the example of the apostles, who, before they received the fullness of the Holy Spirit, were in the *upper room . . . persevering . . . in prayer* (Acts 1:13, 14); whereas afterwards they went out and feared not to confess their faith in public, even in the face of the enemies of the Christian Faith. And therefore it is evident that a character is imprinted in the sacrament of Confirmation.

Reply Obj. 1: All have to wage the spiritual combat with our invisible enemies. But to fight against visible foes, viz. against the persecutors of the Faith, by confessing Christ's name, belongs to the confirmed, who have already come spiritually to the age of virility, according to 1 John 2:14: *I write unto you, young men, because you are strong, and the word of God abideth in you, and you have overcome the wicked one.* And therefore the character of Confirmation is a distinctive sign, not between unbelievers and believers, but between those who are grown up spiritually and those of whom it is written: *As new-born babes* (1 Pet 2:2).

Reply Obj. 2: All the sacraments are protestations of faith. Therefore just as he who is baptized receives the power of testifying to his faith by receiving the other sacraments;

fidem per susceptionem aliorum sacramentorum; ita confirmatus accipit potestatem publice fidem Christi verbis profitendi, quasi ex officio.

Ad tertium dicendum quod sacramenta veteris legis dicuntur iustitia carnis, ut patet Heb. IX, quia scilicet interius nihil efficiebant. Et ideo in circumcisione imprimebatur character solum in corpore, non autem in anima. Sed in confirmatione cum charactere corporali imprimitur simul character spiritualis, eo quod est sacramentum novae legis.

so he who is confirmed receives the power of publicly confessing his faith by words, as it were *ex officio*.

Reply Obj. 3: The sacraments of the Old Law are called *justice of the flesh* (Heb 9:10) because, to wit, they wrought nothing inwardly. Consequently in circumcision a character was imprinted in the body only, but not in the soul. But in Confirmation, since it is a sacrament of the New Law, a spiritual character is imprinted at the same time, together with the bodily character.

Article 6

Whether the Character of Confirmation Presupposes of Necessity, the Baptismal Character?

Ad sextum sic proceditur. Videtur quod character confirmationis non praesupponat ex necessitate characterem baptismalem. Sacramentum enim confirmationis ordinatur ad confitendum publice fidem Christi. Sed multi etiam ante Baptismum sunt fidem Christi publice confessi, sanguinem fundentes pro fide. Ergo character confirmationis non praesupponit characterem baptismalem.

Praeterea, de apostolis non legitur quod fuerint baptizati, praesertim cum dicatur, Ioan. IV, quod *ipse Christus non baptizabat, sed discipuli eius*. Et tamen postea fuerunt confirmati per adventum spiritus sancti. Ergo similiter alii possunt confirmari antequam baptizentur.

Praeterea, Act. X dicitur quod, *adhuc loquente Petro, cecidit Spiritus Sanctus super omnes qui audiebant verbum, et audiebant eos loquentes linguis*, et postea iussit eos baptizari. Ergo pari ratione possunt alii prius confirmari quam baptizentur.

Sed contra est quod Rabanus dicit, de Institut. Cleric., *novissime a summo sacerdote per impositionem manus Paraclitus traditur baptizato, ut roboretur per spiritum sanctum ad praedicandum.*

Respondeo dicendum quod character confirmationis ex necessitate praesupponit characterem baptismalem, ita scilicet quod, si aliquis non baptizatus confirmaretur, nihil reciperet, sed oporteret ipsum iterato confirmari post Baptismum. Cuius ratio est quia sic se habet confirmatio ad Baptismum sicut augmentum ad generationem, ut ex supra dictis patet. Manifestum est autem quod nullus potest promoveri in aetatem perfectam nisi primo fuerit natus. Et similiter, nisi aliquis primo fuerit baptizatus, non potest sacramentum confirmationis accipere.

Ad primum ergo dicendum quod virtus divina non est alligata sacramentis. Unde potest conferri homini

Objection 1: It seems that the character of Confirmation does not presuppose, of necessity, the baptismal character. For the sacrament of Confirmation is ordained to the public confession of the Faith of Christ. But many, even before Baptism, have publicly confessed the Faith of Christ by shedding their blood for the Faith. Therefore the character of Confirmation does not presuppose the baptismal character.

Obj. 2: Further, it is not related of the apostles that they were baptized; especially since it is written (John 4:2) that Christ *Himself did not baptize, but His disciples*. Yet afterwards they were confirmed by the coming of the Holy Spirit. Therefore, in like manner, others can be confirmed before being baptized.

Obj. 3: Further, it is written (Acts 10:44–48) that *while Peter was yet speaking . . . the Holy Spirit fell on all them that heard the word . . . and they heard them speaking with tongues*: and afterwards *he commanded them to be baptized.* Therefore others with equal reason can be confirmed before being baptized.

On the contrary, Rabanus says (*De Instit. Cleric.* i): *Lastly the Paraclete is given to the baptized by the imposition of the high priest's hands, in order that the baptized may be strengthened by the Holy Spirit so as to publish his faith.*

I answer that, The character of Confirmation, of necessity supposes the baptismal character: so that, in effect, if one who is not baptized were to be confirmed, he would receive nothing, but would have to be confirmed again after receiving Baptism. The reason of this is that, Confirmation is to Baptism as growth to birth, as is evident from what has been said above (A. 1; Q. 65, A. 1). Now it is clear that no one can be brought to perfect age unless he be first born: and in like manner, unless a man be first baptized, he cannot receive the sacrament of Confirmation.

Reply Obj. 1: The Divine power is not confined to the sacraments. Hence man can receive spiritual strength to

spirituale robur ad confitendum publice fidem Christi absque sacramento confirmationis, sicut etiam potest consequi remissionem peccatorum sine Baptismo. Tamen, sicut nullus consequitur effectum Baptismi sine voto Baptismi, ita nullus consequitur effectum confirmationis sine voto ipsius. Quod potest haberi etiam ante susceptionem Baptismi.

Ad secundum dicendum quod, sicut Augustinus dicit, ex hoc quod dominus dicit, Ioan. XIII, *qui lotus est, non indiget nisi ut pedes lavet, intelligimus Petrum et alios Christi discipulos fuisse baptizatos, sive Baptismo Ioannis, sicut nonnulli arbitrantur; sive, quod magis credibile est, Baptismo Christi. Neque enim renuit ministerium baptizandi, ut haberet servos per quos ceteros baptizaret.*

Ad tertium dicendum quod audientes praedicationem Petri acceperunt effectum confirmationis miraculose, non tamen sacramentum confirmationis. Dictum est autem quod effectus confirmationis potest alicui conferri ante Baptismum, non autem sacramentum confirmationis. Sicut enim effectus confirmationis, qui est robur spirituale, praesupponit effectum Baptismi, qui est iustificatio, ita sacramentum confirmationis praesupponit sacramentum Baptismi.

confess the Faith of Christ publicly, without receiving the sacrament of Confirmation: just as he can also receive remission of sins without Baptism. Yet, just as none receive the effect of Baptism without the desire of Baptism; so none receive the effect of Confirmation, without the desire of Confirmation. And man can have this even before receiving Baptism.

Reply Obj. 2: As Augustine says (*Ep. cclxv*), from our Lord's words, *'He that is washed, needeth not but to wash his feet' (John 13:10), we gather that Peter and Christ's other disciples had been baptized, either with John's Baptism, as some think; or with Christ's, which is more credible. For He did not refuse to administer Baptism, so as to have servants by whom to baptize others.*

Reply Obj. 3: Those who heard the preaching of Peter received the effect of Confirmation miraculously: but not the sacrament of Confirmation. Now it has been stated (ad 1) that the effect of Confirmation can be bestowed on man before Baptism, whereas the sacrament cannot. For just as the effect of Confirmation, which is spiritual strength, presupposes the effect of Baptism, which is justification, so the sacrament of Confirmation presupposes the sacrament of Baptism.

Article 7

Whether Sanctifying Grace Is Bestowed in This Sacrament?

Ad septimum sic proceditur. Videtur quod per hoc sacramentum gratia gratum faciens non conferatur. Gratia enim gratum faciens ordinatur contra culpam. Sed hoc sacramentum, sicut dictum est, non exhibetur nisi baptizatis, qui sunt a culpa mundati. Ergo per hoc sacramentum gratia gratum faciens non confertur.

Praeterea, peccatores maxime indigent gratia gratum faciente, per quam solam iustificari possunt. Si ergo per hoc sacramentum gratia gratum faciens confertur, videtur quod deberet dari hominibus in peccato existentibus. Quod tamen non est verum.

Praeterea, gratia gratum faciens specie non differt, cum ad unum effectum ordinetur. Sed duae formae eiusdem speciei non possunt esse in eodem subiecto. Cum ergo gratia gratum faciens conferatur homini per Baptismum, videtur quod per sacramentum confirmationis, quod non exhibetur nisi baptizato, gratia gratum faciens non conferatur.

Sed contra est quod Melchiades Papa dicit, *Spiritus Sanctus in fonte Baptismi plenitudinem tribuit ad innocentiam, in confirmatione augmentum praestat ad gratiam.*

Respondeo dicendum quod in hoc sacramento, sicut dictum est, datur baptizato Spiritus Sanctus ad robur,

Objection 1: It seems that sanctifying grace is not bestowed in this sacrament. For sanctifying grace is ordained against sin. But this sacrament, as stated above (A. 6) is given only to the baptized, who are cleansed from sin. Therefore sanctifying grace is not bestowed in this sacrament.

Obj. 2: Further, sinners especially need sanctifying grace, by which alone can they be justified. If, therefore, sanctifying grace is bestowed in this sacrament, it seems that it should be given to those who are in sin. And yet this is not true.

Obj. 3: Further, there can only be one species of sanctifying grace, since it is ordained to one effect. But two forms of the same species cannot be in the same subject. Since, therefore, man receives sanctifying grace in Baptism, it seems that sanctifying grace is not bestowed in Confirmation, which is given to none but the baptized.

On the contrary, Pope Melchiades says (*Ep. ad Episc. Hispan.*): *The Holy Spirit bestows at the font the fullness of innocence; but in Confirmation He confers an increase of grace.*

I answer that, In this sacrament, as stated above (AA. 1, 4), the Holy Spirit is given to the baptized for

sicut apostolis datus est in die Pentecostes, ut legitur Act. II; et sicut dabatur baptizatis per impositionem manus apostolorum, ut dicitur Act. VIII. Ostensum est autem in prima parte quod missio seu datio spiritus sancti non est nisi cum gratia gratum faciente. Unde manifestum est quod gratia gratum faciens confertur in hoc sacramento.

Ad primum ergo dicendum quod gratiae gratum facientis est remissio culpae, habet tamen et alios effectus, quia sufficit ad hoc quod promoveat hominem per omnes gradus usque in vitam aeternam. Unde et Paulo dictum est, II Cor. XII, *sufficit tibi gratia mea*, et ipse de se dicit, I Cor. XV, *gratia Dei sum id quod sum*. Et ideo gratia gratum faciens non solum datur ad remissionem culpae, sed etiam ad augmentum et firmitatem iustitiae. Et sic confertur in hoc sacramento.

Ad secundum dicendum quod, sicut ex ipso nomine apparet, hoc sacramentum datur ad confirmandum quod prius invenerit. Et ideo non debet dari his qui non habent gratiam. Et propter hoc, sicut non datur non baptizatis, ita non debet dari adultis peccatoribus, nisi per poenitentiam reparatis. Unde dicitur in Aurelianensi Concilio, *ut ieiuni ad confirmationem veniant, ut moneantur confessionem facere prius, ut mundi donum spiritus sancti valeant accipere*. Et tunc per hoc sacramentum perficitur poenitentiae effectus, sicut et Baptismi, quia per gratiam collatam in hoc sacramento consequetur poenitens pleniorem remissionem peccati. Et si aliquis adultus in peccato existens cuius conscientiam non habet, vel si etiam non perfecte contritus accedat, per gratiam collatam in hoc sacramento consequetur remissionem peccatorum.

Ad tertium dicendum quod, sicut dictum est, gratia sacramentalis addit super gratiam gratum facientem communiter sumptam aliquid effectivum specialis effectus, ad quod ordinatur sacramentum. Si ergo consideretur gratia in hoc sacramento collata quantum ad id quod est commune, sic per hoc sacramentum non confertur aliqua alia gratia quam per Baptismum, sed quae prius inerat, augetur. Si autem consideretur quantum ad illud speciale quod superadditur, sic non est eiusdem speciei cum ipsa.

strength: just as He was given to the apostles on the day of Pentecost, as we read in Acts 2; and just as He was given to the baptized by the imposition of the apostles' hands, as related in Acts 8:17. Now it has been proved in the First Part (Q. 43, A. 3) that the Holy Spirit is not sent or given except with sanctifying grace. Consequently it is evident that sanctifying grace is bestowed in this sacrament.

Reply Obj. 1: Sanctifying grace does indeed take away sin; but it has other effects also, because it suffices to carry man through every step as far as eternal life. Hence to Paul was it said (2 Cor 12:9): *My grace is sufficient for thee*: and he says of himself (1 Cor 15:10): *By the grace of God I am what I am*. Therefore sanctifying grace is given not only for the remission of sin, but also for growth and stability in righteousness. And thus is it bestowed in this sacrament.

Reply Obj. 2: Further, as appears from its very name, this sacrament is given in order *to confirm* what it finds already there. And consequently it should not be given to those who are not in a state of grace. For this reason, just as it is not given to the unbaptized, so neither should it be given to the adult sinners, except they be restored by Penance. Wherefore was it decreed in the Council of Orleans (Can. iii) that *men should come to Confirmation fasting; and should be admonished to confess their sins first, so that being cleansed they may be able to receive the gift of the Holy Spirit*. And then this sacrament perfects the effects of Penance, as of Baptism: because by the grace which he has received in this sacrament, the penitent will obtain fuller remission of his sin. And if any adult approach, being in a state of sin of which he is not conscious or for which he is not perfectly contrite, he will receive the remission of his sins through the grace bestowed in this sacrament.

Reply Obj. 3: As stated above (Q. 62, A. 2), the sacramental grace adds to the sanctifying grace taken in its wide sense, something that produces a special effect, and to which the sacrament is ordained. If, then, we consider, in its wide sense, the grace bestowed in this sacrament, it does not differ from that bestowed in Baptism, but increases what was already there. On the other hand, if we consider it as to that which is added over and above, then one differs in species from the other.

Article 8

Whether This Sacrament Should Be Given to All?

Ad octavum sic proceditur. Videtur quod hoc sacramentum non sit omnibus exhibendum. Hoc enim sacramentum ad quandam excellentiam datur, ut dictum est. Sed id quod ad excellentiam pertinet, non

Objection 1: It seems that this sacrament should not be given to all. For this sacrament is given in order to confer a certain excellence, as stated above (A. 11, ad 2). But all are

competit omnibus. Ergo hoc sacramentum non debet omnibus dari.

PRAETEREA, per hoc sacramentum augetur aliquis spiritualiter in perfectam aetatem. Sed perfecta aetas repugnat aetati puerili. Ergo ad minus pueris dari non debet.

PRAETEREA, sicut Melchiades Papa dicit, *post Baptismum confirmamur ad pugnam*. Sed pugnare non competit mulieribus, propter fragilitatem sexus. Ergo nec mulieribus hoc sacramentum debet dari.

PRAETEREA, Melchiades Papa dicit, *quamvis continuo transituris sufficiant regenerationis beneficia, victuris tamen confirmationis beneficia necessaria sunt. Confirmatio armat et instruit ad agones mundi huius et praelia reservandos. Qui autem post Baptismum cum acquisita innocentia immaculatus pervenerit ad mortem, confirmatur morte, quia iam non potest peccare post mortem.* Ergo statim morituris non debet hoc sacramentum conferri. Et sic non debet omnibus dari.

SED CONTRA est quod dicitur Act. II, quod Spiritus Sanctus veniens replevit totam domum, per quam significatur Ecclesia, et postea subditur quod repleti sunt omnes spiritu sancto. Sed ad illam plenitudinem consequendam hoc sacramentum datur. Ergo est omnibus qui sunt in Ecclesia exhibendum.

RESPONDEO dicendum quod, sicut dictum est, per hoc sacramentum promovetur homo spiritualiter in aetatem perfectam. Hoc autem est de intentione naturae, ut omnis qui corporaliter nascitur, ad perfectam aetatem perveniat, sed hoc quandoque impeditur propter corruptibilitatem corporis, quod morte praevenitur. Multo autem magis de intentione Dei est omnia ad perfectionem perducere, ex cuius imitatione hoc natura participat, unde et Deut. XXXII dicitur, *Dei perfecta sunt opera*. Anima autem, ad quam pertinet spiritualis nativitas et spiritualis aetatis perfectio, immortalis est, et potest, sicut tempore senectutis spiritualem nativitatem consequi, ita tempore iuventutis et pueritiae consequi perfectam aetatem; quia huiusmodi corporales aetates animae non praeiudicant. Et ideo hoc sacramentum debet omnibus exhiberi.

AD PRIMUM ergo dicendum quod hoc sacramentum datur ad quandam excellentiam, non quidem unius hominis ad alium, sicut sacramentum ordinis, sed hominis ad seipsum, sicut idem, perfectus vir existens, habet excellentiam ad se puerum.

AD SECUNDUM dicendum quod, sicut dictum est, corporalis aetas non praeiudicat animae. Unde etiam in puerili aetate homo potest consequi perfectionem spiritualis aetatis, de qua dicitur Sap. IV, *senectus venerabilis*

not suited for that which belongs to excellence. Therefore this sacrament should not be given to all.

OBJ. 2: Further, by this sacrament man advances spiritually to perfect age. But perfect age is inconsistent with childhood. Therefore at least it should not be given to children.

OBJ. 3: Further, as Pope Melchiades says (*Ep. ad Episc. Hispan.*) *after Baptism we are strengthened for the combat*. But women are incompetent to combat, by reason of the frailty of their sex. Therefore neither should women receive this sacrament.

OBJ. 4: Further, Pope Melchiades says (*Ep. ad Episc. Hispan.*): *Although the benefit of Regeneration suffices for those who are on the point of death, yet the graces of Confirmation are necessary for those who are to conquer. Confirmation arms and strengthens those to whom the struggles and combats of this world are reserved. And he who comes to die, having kept unsullied the innocence he acquired in Baptism, is confirmed by death; for after death he can sin no more.* Therefore this sacrament should not be given to those who are on the point of death: and so it should not be given to all.

ON THE CONTRARY, It is written (Acts 2:2) that the Holy Spirit in coming, *filled the whole house*, whereby the Church is signified; and afterwards it is added that *they were all filled with the Holy Spirit*. But this sacrament is given that we may receive that fullness. Therefore it should be given to all who belong to the Church.

I ANSWER THAT, As stated above (A. 1), man is spiritually advanced by this sacrament to perfect age. Now the intention of nature is that everyone born corporally, should come to perfect age: yet this is sometimes hindered by reason of the corruptibility of the body, which is forestalled by death. But much more is it God's intention to bring all things to perfection, since nature shares in this intention inasmuch as it reflects Him: hence it is written (Deut 32:4): *The works of God are perfect*. Now the soul, to which spiritual birth and perfect spiritual age belong, is immortal; and just as it can in old age attain to spiritual birth, so can it attain to perfect (spiritual) age in youth or childhood; because the various ages of the body do not affect the soul. Therefore this sacrament should be given to all.

REPLY OBJ. 1: This sacrament is given in order to confer a certain excellence, not indeed, like the sacrament of order, of one man over another, but of man in regard to himself: thus the same man, when arrived at maturity, excels himself as he was when a boy.

REPLY OBJ. 2: As stated above, the age of the body does not affect the soul. Consequently even in childhood man can attain to the perfection of spiritual age, of which it is written (Wis 4:8): *Venerable old age is not that of long time,*

est non diuturna, neque numero annorum computata. Et inde est quod multi in puerili aetate, propter robur spiritus sancti perceptum, usque ad sanguinem fortiter certaverunt pro Christo.

AD TERTIUM dicendum quod, sicut Chrysostomus dicit, in homilia de Machabaeis, *in mundanis agonibus aetatis et formae generisque dignitas requiritur, et ideo servis ac mulieribus, senibus ac pueris, ad eos aditus denegatur. In caelestibus autem omni personae et aetati et sexui indiscreta facultate stadium patet.* Et in homilia de militia spirituali dicit, *apud Deum femineus etiam militat sexus, multae namque feminae animo virili spiritualem militiam gesserunt. Quaedam enim interioris hominis virtute viros aequaverunt in agonibus martyrum, quaedam etiam fortiores viris exstiterunt.* Et ideo mulieribus hoc sacramentum conferendum est.

AD QUARTUM dicendum quod, sicut dictum est, anima, ad quam pertinet spiritualis aetas, immortalis est. Et ideo morituris hoc sacramentum dandum est, ut in resurrectione perfecti appareant, secundum illud Ephes. IV, *donec occurramus in virum perfectum, in mensuram aetatis plenitudinis Christi.* Et ideo Hugo de sancto Victore dicit, *omnino periculosum esset, si ab hac vita sine confirmatione migrare contingeret,* non quia damnaretur, nisi forte per contemptum; sed quia detrimentum perfectionis pateretur. Unde etiam pueri confirmati decedentes maiorem gloriam consequuntur, sicut et hic maiorem obtinent gratiam. Auctoritas autem illa intelligitur quantum ad hoc, quod morituris non est necessarium hoc sacramentum propter periculum pugnae praesentis.

nor counted by the number of years. And hence it is that many children, by reason of the strength of the Holy Spirit which they had received, fought bravely for Christ even to the shedding of their blood.

REPLY OBJ. 3: As Chrysostom says (*Hom. i De Machab.*), in earthly contests fitness of age, physique and rank are required; and consequently slaves, women, old men, and boys are debarred from taking part therein. But in the heavenly combats, the Stadium is open equally to all, to every age, and to either sex. Again, he says (*Hom. de Militia Spirit.*): In God's eyes even women fight, for many a woman has waged the spiritual warfare with the courage of a man. For some have rivaled men in the courage with which they have suffered martyrdom; and some indeed have shown themselves stronger than men. Therefore this sacrament should be given to women.

REPLY OBJ. 4: As we have already observed, the soul, to which spiritual age belongs, is immortal. Wherefore this sacrament should be given to those on the point of death, that they may be seen to be perfect at the resurrection, according to Eph. 4:13: *Until we all meet into the unity of faith . . . unto the measure of the age of the fullness of Christ.* And hence Hugh of St. Victor says (*De Sacram. ii*), *It would be altogether hazardous, if anyone happened to go forth from this life without being confirmed*: not that such a one would be lost, except perhaps through contempt; but that this would be detrimental to his perfection. And therefore even children dying after Confirmation obtain greater glory, just as here below they receive more grace. The passage quoted is to be taken in the sense that, with regard to the dangers of the present combat, those who are on the point of death do not need this sacrament.

Article 9

Whether This Sacrament Should Be Given to Man on the Forehead?

AD NONUM SIC PROCEDITUR. Videtur quod hoc sacramentum non sit conferendum homini in fronte. Hoc enim sacramentum est perfectivum Baptismi, ut supra dictum est. Sed sacramentum Baptismi confertur homini in toto corpore. Ergo hoc sacramentum non debet conferri solum in fronte.

PRAETEREA, hoc sacramentum datur ad robur spirituale, ut supra dictum est. Sed spirituale robur maxime consistit in corde. Ergo hoc sacramentum magis debet conferri supra cor quam in fronte.

PRAETEREA, hoc sacramentum datur homini ad hoc quod libere fidem Christi confiteatur. Sed *ore fit confessio ad salutem,* ut dicitur Rom. X. Ergo hoc sacramentum magis debet conferri circa os quam in fronte.

OBJECTION 1: It seems that this sacrament should not be given to man on the forehead. For this sacrament perfects Baptism, as stated above (Q. 65, AA. 3, 4). But the sacrament of Baptism is given to man over his whole body. Therefore this sacrament should not be given on the forehead only.

OBJ. 2: Further, this sacrament is given for spiritual strength, as stated above (AA. 1, 2, 4). But spiritual strength is situated principally in the heart. Therefore this sacrament should be given over the heart rather than on the forehead.

OBJ. 3: Further, this sacrament is given to man that he may freely confess the faith of Christ. But *with the mouth, confession is made unto salvation,* according to Rom. 10:10. Therefore this sacrament should be given about the mouth rather than on the forehead.

SED CONTRA est quod Rabanus dicit, in libro de Institut. Cleric., *signatur baptizatus chrismate in summitate capitis per sacerdotem, per pontificem vero in fronte.*

RESPONDEO dicendum quod, sicut supra dictum est, in hoc sacramento homo accipit spiritum sanctum ad robur spiritualis pugnae, ut fortiter etiam inter adversarios fidei fidem Christi confiteatur. Unde convenienter signatur chrismate signo crucis in fronte, propter duo. Primo quidem, quia insignitur signo crucis sicut miles signo ducis, quod quidem debet esse evidens et manifestum. Inter omnia autem loca corporis humani maxime manifestus est frons, qui quasi nunquam obtegitur. Et ideo linitur confirmatus chrismate in fronte, ut in manifesto demonstraret se esse Christianum, sicut et apostoli post receptum spiritum sanctum se manifestaverunt, qui prius in cenaculo latebant.

Secundo, quia aliquis impeditur a libera confessione nominis Christi propter duo, scilicet propter timorem, et propter verecundiam. Utriusque autem horum signum maxime manifestatur in fronte, propter propinquitatem imaginationis, et propter hoc quod spiritus a corde directe ad frontem ascendunt, unde *verecundati erubescunt, timentes autem pallescunt,* ut dicitur in IV Ethic. Et ideo in fronte signatur chrismate, ut neque propter timorem neque propter erubescentiam nomen Christi confiteri praetermittat.

AD PRIMUM ergo dicendum quod per Baptismum regeneramur ad vitam spiritualem, quae ad totum hominem pertinet. Sed in confirmatione roboramur ad pugnam, cuius signum ferendum est in fronte, quasi in evidenti loco.

AD SECUNDUM dicendum quod principium fortitudinis est in corde, sed signum apparet in fronte, unde dicitur Ezech. III, *ecce, dedi frontem tuam duriorem frontibus eorum.* Et ideo sacramentum Eucharistiae, quo homo in seipso confirmatur, pertinet ad cor, secundum illud Psalmi, *panis cor hominis confirmet.* Sed sacramentum confirmationis requiritur in signum fortitudinis ad alios. Et ideo exhibetur in fronte.

AD TERTIUM dicendum quod hoc sacramentum datur ad libere confitendum, non autem ad confitendum simpliciter, quia hoc fit etiam in Baptismo. Et ideo non debet dari in ore, sed in fronte, ubi apparent signa passionum quibus libera confessio impeditur.

ON THE CONTRARY, Rabanus says (*De Instit. Cleric.* i): *The baptized is signed by the priest with chrism on the top of the head, but by the bishop on the forehead.*

I ANSWER THAT, As stated above (AA. 1, 4), in this sacrament man receives the Holy Spirit for strength in the spiritual combat, that he may bravely confess the Faith of Christ even in face of the enemies of that Faith. Wherefore he is fittingly signed with the sign of the cross on the forehead, with chrism, for two reasons. First, because he is signed with the sign of the cross, as a soldier with the sign of his leader, which should be evident and manifest. Now, the forehead, which is hardly ever covered, is the most conspicuous part of the human body. Wherefore the confirmed is anointed with chrism on the forehead, that he may show publicly that he is a Christian: thus too the apostles after receiving the Holy Spirit showed themselves in public, whereas before they remained hidden in the upper room.

Second, because man is hindered from freely confessing Christ's name, by two things—by fear and by shame. Now both these things betray themselves principally on the forehead on account of the proximity of the imagination, and because the (vital) spirits mount directly from the heart to the forehead: hence *those who are ashamed, blush, and those who are afraid, pale (Ethic.* iv). And therefore man is signed with chrism, that neither fear nor shame may hinder him from confessing the name of Christ.

REPLY OBJ. 1: By baptism we are regenerated unto spiritual life, which belongs to the whole man. But in Confirmation we are strengthened for the combat; the sign of which should be borne on the forehead, as in a conspicuous place.

REPLY OBJ. 2: The principle of fortitude is in the heart, but its sign appears on the forehead: wherefore it is written (Ezek 3:8): *Behold I have made . . . thy forehead harder than their foreheads.* Hence the sacrament of the Eucharist, whereby man is confirmed in himself, belongs to the heart, according to Ps. 103:15: *That bread may strengthen man's heart.* But the sacrament of Confirmation is required as a sign of fortitude against others; and for this reason it is given on the forehead.

REPLY OBJ. 3: This sacrament is given that we may confess freely: but not that we may confess simply, for this is also the effect of Baptism. And therefore it should not be given on the mouth, but on the forehead, where appear the signs of those passions which hinder free confession.

Article 10

Whether He Who Is Confirmed Needs One to Stand for Him?

AD DECIMUM SIC PROCEDITUR. Videtur quod ille qui confirmatur non debet ab alio teneri ad confirmationem. Hoc enim sacramentum non solum pueris, sed etiam adultis exhibetur. Adulti autem per seipsos stare possunt. Ergo ridiculum est quod ab alio teneantur.

PRAETEREA, ille qui iam est de Ecclesia, liberum habet accessum ad Ecclesiae principem, qui est episcopus. Sed hoc sacramentum, sicut dictum est, non exhibetur nisi baptizato, qui iam est membrum Ecclesiae. Ergo videtur quod non debeat per alium exhiberi episcopo ad hoc sacramentum recipiendum.

PRAETEREA, hoc sacramentum datur ad robur spirituale. Quod magis viget in viris quam in mulieribus, secundum illud Prov. ult., *mulierem fortem quis inveniet?* Ergo ad minus mulier non debet tenere virum ad confirmationem.

SED CONTRA est quod Innocentius Papa dicit, et habetur in decretis, XXX, qu. IV, *si quis ex coniugio filium aut filiam alterius de sacro fonte susceperit, aut ad chrisma tenuerit*, et cetera. Ergo, sicut requiritur quod aliquis baptizatum de sacro fonte levet, ita debet aliquis teneri ad sacramentum confirmationis accipiendum.

RESPONDEO dicendum quod, sicut dictum est, hoc sacramentum exhibetur homini ad robur pugnae spiritualis. Sicut autem aliquis de novo natus indiget instructore in his quae pertinent ad conversationem vitae, secundum illud Heb. XII, *patres quidem carnis nostrae habuimus eruditores, et obtemperabamus eis*; ita illi qui assumuntur ad pugnam, indigent eruditoribus a quibus instruantur de his quae pertinent ad modum certaminis; et ideo in bellis materialibus constituuntur duces et centuriones, per quos alii gubernentur. Et propter hoc etiam ille qui accipit hoc sacramentum, ab alio tenetur, quasi per alium in pugna erudiendus.

Similiter etiam, quia per hoc sacramentum confertur homini perfectio spiritualis aetatis, sicut dictum est; ideo ille qui ad hoc sacramentum accedit, sustentatur, quasi adhuc spiritualiter imbecillis et puer.

AD PRIMUM ergo dicendum quod, licet ille qui confirmatur sit adultus corporaliter, nondum tamen est adultus spiritualiter.

AD SECUNDUM dicendum quod, licet baptizatus sit effectus membrum Ecclesiae, nondum tamen est adscriptus militiae Christianae. Et ideo episcopo, tanquam duci exercitus, per alium exhibetur iam militiae Christianae adscriptum. Non enim debet alium ad confirmationem tenere qui nondum est confirmatus.

AD TERTIUM dicendum quod, sicut dicitur Coloss. III, *in Christo Iesu non est masculus neque femina*. Et

OBJECTION 1: It seems that he who is confirmed needs no one to stand for him. For this sacrament is given not only to children but also to adults. But adults can stand for themselves. Therefore it is absurd that someone else should stand for them.

OBJ. 2: Further, he that belongs already to the Church, has free access to the prince of the Church, i.e., the bishop. But this sacrament, as stated above (A. 6), is given only to one that is baptized, who is already a member of the Church. Therefore it seems that he should not be brought by another to the bishop in order to receive this sacrament.

OBJ. 3: Further, this sacrament is given for spiritual strength, which has more vigor in men than in women, according to Prov. 31:10: *Who shall find a valiant woman?* Therefore at least a woman should not stand for a man in confirmation.

ON THE CONTRARY, Are the following words of Pope Innocent, which are to be found in the *Decretals* (XXX, Q. 4): *If anyone raise the children of another's marriage from the sacred font, or stand for them in Confirmation*, etc. Therefore, just as someone is required as sponsor of one who is baptized, so is someone required to stand for him who is to be confirmed.

I ANSWER THAT, As stated above (AA. 1, 4, 9), this sacrament is given to man for strength in the spiritual combat. Now, just as one newly born requires someone to teach him things pertaining to ordinary conduct, according to Heb. 12:9: *We have had fathers of our flesh, for instructors, and we obeyed them*; so they who are chosen for the fight need instructors by whom they are informed of things concerning the conduct of the battle, and hence in earthly wars, generals and captains are appointed to the command of the others. For this reason he also who receives this sacrament, has someone to stand for him, who, as it were, has to instruct him concerning the fight.

Likewise, since this sacrament bestows on man the perfection of spiritual age, as stated above (AA. 2, 5), therefore he who approaches this sacrament is upheld by another, as being spiritually a weakling and a child.

REPLY OBJ. 1: Although he who is confirmed, be adult in body, nevertheless he is not yet spiritually adult.

REPLY OBJ. 2: Though he who is baptized is made a member of the Church, nevertheless he is not yet enrolled as a Christian soldier. And therefore he is brought to the bishop, as to the commander of the army, by one who is already enrolled as a Christian soldier. For one who is not yet confirmed should not stand for another in Confirmation.

REPLY OBJ. 3: According to Col. 3, *in Christ Jesus there is neither male nor female*. Consequently it matters not

ideo non differt utrum masculus vel femina teneat aliquem in confirmatione.

whether a man or a woman stand for one who is to be confirmed.

Article 11

Whether Only a Bishop Can Confer This Sacrament?

AD UNDECIMUM SIC PROCEDITUR. Videtur quod non solus episcopus hoc sacramentum conferre possit. Gregorius enim, scribens Ianuario episcopo, dicit, *pervenit ad nos quosdam scandalizatos fuisse quod presbyteros chrismate tangere eos qui baptizati sunt, prohibuimus. Et nos quidem secundum veterem usum nostrae Ecclesiae fecimus, sed si omnino hac de re aliqui contristantur, ubi episcopi desunt, ut presbyteri etiam in frontibus baptizatos chrismate tangere debeant, concedimus.* Sed illud quod pertinet ad necessitatem sacramentorum, non est propter vitandum scandalum immutandum. Ergo videtur quod non sit de necessitate huius sacramenti quod ab episcopo conferatur.

PRAETEREA, sacramentum Baptismi videtur esse maioris efficaciae quam sacramentum confirmationis, quia per Baptismum fit plena remissio peccatorum et quantum ad culpam et quantum ad poenam, quod non fit in hoc sacramento. Sed simplex sacerdos ex suo officio potest tradere sacramentum Baptismi, et in necessitate quilibet, etiam non ordinatus, potest baptizare. Ergo non est de necessitate huius sacramenti quod ab episcopo conferatur.

PRAETEREA, summitas capitis, ubi secundum medicos est locus rationis (scilicet particularis, quae dicitur virtus cogitativa), est nobilior fronte, ubi est locus imaginativae virtutis. Sed simplex sacerdos potest baptizatos chrismate ungere in vertice. Ergo multo magis potest eos chrismate signare in fronte, quod pertinet ad hoc sacramentum.

SED CONTRA est quod Eusebius Papa dicit, *manus impositionis sacramentum magna veneratione tenendum est, quod ab aliis perfici non potest nisi a summis sacerdotibus. Nec tempore apostolorum ab aliis quam ab ipsis apostolis legitur aut scitur peractum esse, nec ab aliis quam qui eorum locum tenent, unquam perfici potest, aut fieri debet. Nam si aliter praesumptum fuerit, irritum habeatur et vacuum, nec inter ecclesiastica unquam reputabitur sacramenta.* Est igitur de necessitate huius sacramenti, quod dicitur sacramentum manus impositionis, quod ab episcopo tradatur.

RESPONDEO dicendum quod in quolibet opere ultima consummatio supremae arti aut virtuti reservatur, sicut praeparatio materiae pertinet ad inferiores

OBJECTION 1: It seems that not only a bishop can confer this sacrament. For Gregory (*Regist.* iv), writing to Bishop Januarius, says: *We hear that some were scandalized because we forbade priests to anoint with chrism those who have been baptized. Yet in doing this we followed the ancient custom of our Church: but if this trouble some so very much we permit priests, where no bishop is to be had, to anoint the baptized on the forehead with chrism.* But that which is essential to the sacraments should not be changed for the purpose of avoiding scandal. Therefore it seems that it is not essential to this sacrament that it be conferred by a bishop.

OBJ. 2: Further, the sacrament of Baptism seems to be more efficacious than the sacrament of Confirmation: since it bestows full remission of sins, both as to guilt and as to punishment, whereas this sacrament does not. But a simple priest, in virtue of his office, can give the sacrament of Baptism: and in a case of necessity anyone, even without orders, can baptize. Therefore it is not essential to this sacrament that it be conferred by a bishop.

OBJ. 3: Further, the top of the head, where according to medical men the reason is situated (i.e., the *particular reason*, which is called the *cogitative faculty*), is more noble than the forehead, which is the site of the imagination. But a simple priest can anoint the baptized with chrism on the top of the head. Therefore much more can he anoint them with chrism on the forehead, which belongs to this sacrament.

ON THE CONTRARY, Pope Eusebius (*Ep. iii ad Ep. Tusc.*) says: *The sacrament of the imposition of the hand should be held in great veneration, and can be given by none but the high priests. Nor is it related or known to have been conferred in apostolic times by others than the apostles themselves; nor can it ever be either licitly or validly performed by others than those who stand in their place. And if anyone presume to do otherwise, it must be considered null and void; nor will such a thing ever be counted among the sacraments of the Church.* Therefore it is essential to this sacrament, which is called *the sacrament of the imposition of the hand*, that it be given by a bishop.

I ANSWER THAT, In every work the final completion is reserved to the supreme act or power; thus the preparation of the matter belongs to the lower craftsmen, the higher

artifices, superior autem dat formam, supremus autem est ad quem pertinet usus, qui est finis artificiatorum; et epistola quae a notario scribitur, a domino signatur. Fideles autem Christi sunt quoddam divinum opus, secundum illud I Cor. III, *Dei aedificatio estis*, sunt etiam quasi quaedam epistola spiritu Dei scripta, sicut dicitur II Cor. III. Hoc autem confirmationis sacramentum est quasi ultima consummatio sacramenti Baptismi, ita scilicet quod per Baptismum aedificatur homo in domum spiritualem, et conscribitur quasi quaedam spiritualis epistola; sed per sacramentum confirmationis, quasi domus aedificata, dedicatur in templum spiritus sancti; et quasi epistola conscripta, signatur signo crucis. Et ideo collatio huius sacramenti episcopis reservatur, qui obtinent summam potestatem in Ecclesia, sicut in primitiva Ecclesia per impositionem manus apostolorum, quorum vicem gerunt episcopi, plenitudo spiritus sancti dabatur, ut habetur Act. VIII. Unde Urbanus Papa dicit, *omnes fideles per manus impositionem episcoporum spiritum sanctum post Baptismum accipere debent, ut pleni Christiani inveniantur.*

Ad primum ergo dicendum quod Papa in Ecclesia habet plenitudinem potestatis, ex qua potest quaedam quae sunt superiorum ordinum, committere inferioribus quibusdam, sicut presbyteris concedit conferre minores ordines, quod pertinet ad potestatem episcopalem. Et ex hac plenitudine potestatis concessit beatus Gregorius Papa quod simplices sacerdotes conferrent hoc sacramentum, quandiu scandalum tolleretur.

Ad secundum dicendum quod sacramentum Baptismi est efficacius quam hoc sacramentum quantum ad remotionem mali, eo quod est spiritualis generatio, quae est mutatio de non esse in esse. Hoc autem sacramentum est efficacius ad proficiendum in bono, quia est quoddam spirituale augmentum de esse imperfecto ad esse perfectum. Et ideo hoc sacramentum digniori ministro committitur.

Ad tertium dicendum quod, sicut Rabanus dicit, in libro de Institut. Cleric., *signatur baptizatus chrismate in summitate capitis per sacerdotem, per pontificem vero in fronte, ut priori unctione significetur super ipsum spiritus sancti descensio ad habitationem Deo consecrandam, in secunda quoque ut eiusdem spiritus sancti septiformis gratia, cum omni plenitudine sanctitatis et scientiae et virtutis, venire in hominem declaretur.* Non ergo propter digniorem partem, sed propter potiorem effectum, haec unctio episcopis reservatur.

gives the form, but the highest of all is he to whom pertains the use, which is the end of things made by art; thus also the letter which is written by the clerk, is signed by his employer. Now the faithful of Christ are a Divine work, according to 1 Cor. 3:9: *You are God's building*; and they are also *an epistle*, as it were, *written with the Spirit of God*, according to 2 Cor. 3:2, 3. And this sacrament of Confirmation is, as it were, the final completion of the sacrament of Baptism; in the sense that by Baptism man is built up into a spiritual dwelling, and is written like a spiritual letter; whereas by the sacrament of Confirmation, like a house already built, he is consecrated as a temple of the Holy Spirit, and as a letter already written, is signed with the sign of the cross. Therefore the conferring of this sacrament is reserved to bishops, who possess supreme power in the Church: just as in the primitive Church, the fullness of the Holy Spirit was given by the apostles, in whose place the bishops stand (Acts 8). Hence Pope Urban I says: *All the faithful should, after Baptism, receive the Holy Spirit by the imposition of the bishop's hand, that they may become perfect Christians.*

Reply Obj. 1: The Pope has the plenitude of power in the Church, in virtue of which he can commit to certain lower orders things that belong to the higher orders: thus he allows priests to confer minor orders, which belong to the episcopal power. And in virtue of this fullness of power the Pope, Blessed Gregory, allowed simple priests to confer this sacrament, so long as the scandal was ended.

Reply Obj. 2: The sacrament of Baptism is more efficacious than this sacrament as to the removal of evil, since it is a spiritual birth, that consists in change from non-being to being. But this sacrament is more efficacious for progress in good; since it is a spiritual growth from imperfect being to perfect being. And hence this sacrament is committed to a more worthy minister.

Reply Obj. 3: As Rabanus says (*De Instit. Cleric.* i), *the baptized is signed by the priest with chrism on the top of the head, but by the bishop on the forehead; that the former unction may symbolize the descent of the Holy Spirit on him, in order to consecrate a dwelling to God: and that the second also may teach us that the sevenfold grace of the same Holy Spirit descends on man with all fullness of sanctity, knowledge and virtue.* Hence this unction is reserved to bishops, not on account of its being applied to a more worthy part of the body, but by reason of its having a more powerful effect.

Article 12

Whether the Rite of This Sacrament Is Appropriate?

AD DUODECIMUM SIC PROCEDITUR. Videtur quod ritus huius sacramenti non sit conveniens. Sacramentum enim Baptismi est maioris necessitatis quam hoc sacramentum, ut supra dictum est. Sed Baptismo deputantur certa tempora, scilicet Pascha et Pentecoste. Ergo etiam huic sacramento aliquod certum tempus debet praefigi.

PRAETEREA, sicut hoc sacramentum requirit devotionem et dantis et recipientis, ita etiam et sacramentum Baptismi. Sed in sacramento Baptismi non requiritur quod a ieiunis sumatur vel conferatur. Ergo videtur inconvenienter statutum in Aureliansi Concilio, *ut ieiuni ad confirmationem veniant*; et in Concilio Meldensi *ut episcopi non nisi ieiuni per impositionem manus spiritum sanctum tradant.*

PRAETEREA, chrisma est quoddam signum plenitudinis spiritus sancti, ut supra dictum est. Sed plenitudo spiritus sancti data est fidelibus Christi in die Pentecostes, ut habetur Act. II. Magis ergo deberet chrisma confici et benedici in festo Pentecostes quam in cena domini.

SED CONTRA est usus Ecclesiae, quae a spiritu sancto gubernatur.

RESPONDEO dicendum quod dominus, Matth. XVIII, fidelibus suis promisit dicens, *ubi fuerint duo vel tres congregati in nomine meo, ibi sum in medio eorum.* Et ideo firmiter tenendum est quod ordinationes Ecclesiae dirigantur secundum sapientiam Christi. Et propter hoc certum esse debet ritus quos Ecclesia observat in hoc et in aliis sacramentis, esse convenientes.

AD PRIMUM ergo dicendum quod, sicut Melchiades Papa dicit, *ita coniuncta sunt haec duo sacramenta, scilicet Baptismi et confirmationis, ut ab invicem nisi morte praeveniente nullatenus possint segregari, et unum sine altero rite perfici non possit.* Et ideo eadem tempora sunt praefixa Baptismo solemniter celebrando et huic sacramento. Sed quia hoc sacramentum a solis episcopis datur, qui non sunt semper praesentes ubi presbyteri baptizant, oportuit, quantum ad communem usum, sacramentum confirmationis etiam in alia tempora differri.

AD SECUNDUM dicendum quod ab illa prohibitione excipiuntur infirmi et morte periclitantes, sicut in statuto Meldensis Concilii legitur. Et ideo, propter multitudinem fidelium, et propter pericula imminentia, sustinetur ut hoc sacramentum, quod non nisi ab episcopis dari potest, etiam a non ieiunis detur vel accipiatur, quia unus episcopus, praecipue in magna dioecesi, non sufficeret ad omnes confirmandos, si ei tempus arctaretur. Ubi tamen congrue observari potest, convenientius est ut a ieiunis detur et accipiatur.

OBJECTION 1: It seems that the rite of this sacrament is not appropriate. For the sacrament of Baptism is of greater necessity than this, as stated above (A. 2, ad 4; Q. 65, AA. 3, 4). But certain seasons are fixed for Baptism, viz. Easter and Pentecost. Therefore some fixed time of the year should be chosen for this sacrament.

OBJ. 2: Further, just as this sacrament requires devotion both in the giver and in the receiver, so also does the sacrament of Baptism. But in the sacrament of Baptism it is not necessary that it should be received or given fasting. Therefore it seems unfitting for the Council of Orleans to declare that *those who come to Confirmation should be fasting*; and the Council of Meaux, *that bishops should not give the Holy Spirit with imposition of the hand except they be fasting.*

OBJ. 3: Further, chrism is a sign of the fullness of the Holy Spirit, as stated above (A. 2). But the fullness of the Holy Spirit was given to Christ's faithful on the day of Pentecost, as related in Acts 2:1. Therefore the chrism should be mixed and blessed on the day of Pentecost rather than on Maundy Thursday.

ON THE CONTRARY, Is the use of the Church, who is governed by the Holy Spirit.

I ANSWER THAT, Our Lord promised His faithful (Matt 18:20) saying: *Where there are two or three gathered together in My name, there am I in the midst of them.* And therefore we must hold firmly that the Church's ordinations are directed by the wisdom of Christ. And for this reason we must look upon it as certain that the rite observed by the Church, in this and the other sacraments, is appropriate.

REPLY OBJ. 1: As Pope Melchiades says (*Ep. ad Epis. Hispan.*), *these two sacraments*, viz. Baptism and Confirmation, *are so closely connected that they can nowise be separated save by death intervening, nor can one be duly celebrated without the other.* Consequently the same seasons are fixed for the solemn celebration of Baptism and of this sacrament. But since this sacrament is given only by bishops, who are not always present where priests are baptizing, it was necessary, as regards the common use, to defer the sacrament of Confirmation to other seasons also.

REPLY OBJ. 2: The sick and those in danger of death are exempt from this prohibition, as we read in the decree of the Council of Meaux. And therefore, on account of the multitude of the faithful, and on account of imminent dangers, it is allowed for this sacrament, which can be given by none but a bishop, to be given or received even by those who are not fasting: since one bishop, especially in a large diocese, would not suffice to confirm all, if he were confined to certain times. But where it can be done conveniently, it is more becoming that both giver and receiver should be fasting.

AD TERTIUM dicendum quod, sicut ex Concilio Martini Papae habetur, *omni tempore licebat chrisma conficere.* Sed quia solemnis Baptismus, ad quem requiritur usus chrismatis, in vigilia Paschae celebratur, congrue ordinatum est ut per biduum ante ab episcopo chrisma benedicatur, ut possit per dioecesim destinari. Dies etiam ille satis congruit ad materias sacramentorum benedicendas, in quo fuit Eucharistiae sacramentum institutum, ad quod omnia alia sacramenta quodammodo ordinantur, sicut dictum est.

REPLY OBJ. 3: According to the acts of the Council of Pope Martin, *it was lawful at all times to prepare the chrism.* But since solemn Baptism, for which chrism has to be used, is celebrated on Easter Eve, it was rightly decreed, that chrism should be consecrated by the bishop two days beforehand, that it may be sent to the various parts of the diocese. Moreover, this day is sufficiently appropriate to the blessing of sacramental matter, since thereon was the Eucharist instituted, to which, in a certain way, all the other sacraments are ordained, as stated above (Q. 65, A. 3).

QUESTION 73

THE SACRAMENT OF THE EUCHARIST

Consequenter considerandum est de sacramento Eucharistiae. Et primo, de ipso sacramento; secundo, de materia; tertio, de forma; quarto, de effectu; quinto, de recipientibus hoc sacramentum; sexto, de ministro; septimo, de ritu.

Circa primum quaeruntur sex.

Primo, utrum Eucharistia sit sacramentum.

Secundo, utrum sit unum vel plura.

Tertio, utrum sit de necessitate salutis.

Quarto, de nominibus eius.

Quinto, de institutione ipsius.

Sexto, de figuris eius.

We have now to consider the sacrament of the Eucharist; and first of all we treat of the sacrament itself; second, of its matter; third, of its form; fourth, of its effects; fifth, of the recipients of this sacrament; sixth, of the minister; seventh, of the rite.

Under the first heading there are six points of inquiry:

(1) Whether the Eucharist is a sacrament?

(2) Whether it is one or several sacraments?

(3) Whether it is necessary for salvation?

(4) Its names;

(5) Its institution;

(6) Its figures.

Article 1

Whether the Eucharist Is a Sacrament?

AD PRIMUM SIC PROCEDITUR. Videtur quod Eucharistia non sit sacramentum. Ad idem enim non debent ordinari duo sacramenta, quia unumquodque sacramentum efficax est ad suum effectum producendum. Cum ergo ad perfectionem ordinetur confirmatio et Eucharistia, ut Dionysius dicit, IV cap. Eccl. Hier., videtur Eucharistia non esse sacramentum, cum confirmatio sit sacramentum, ut prius habitum est.

PRAETEREA, in quolibet sacramento novae legis id quod visibiliter subiicitur sensui, efficit invisibilem effectum sacramenti, sicut ablutio aquae causat et characterem baptismalem et ablutionem spiritualem, ut supra dictum est. Sed species panis et vini, quae subiiciuntur sensui in hoc sacramento, non efficiunt neque ipsum corpus Christi verum, quod est res et sacramentum, neque corpus mysticum, quod est res tantum in Eucharistia. Ergo videtur quod Eucharistia non sit sacramentum novae legis.

PRAETEREA, sacramenta novae legis habentia materiam in usu materiae perficiuntur, sicut Baptismus in ablutione, et confirmatio in chrismatis consignatione. Si ergo Eucharistia sit sacramentum, perficeretur in usu materiae, non in consecratione ipsius materiae. Quod patet esse falsum, quia forma huius sacramenti sunt verba quae in consecratione materiae dicuntur, ut infra patebit. Ergo Eucharistia non est sacramentum.

SED CONTRA est quod in collecta dicitur, *hoc tuum sacramentum non sit nobis reatus ad poenam.*

OBJECTION 1: It seems that the Eucharist is not a sacrament. For two sacraments ought not to be ordained for the same end, because every sacrament is efficacious in producing its effect. Therefore, since both Confirmation and the Eucharist are ordained for perfection, as Dionysius says (*Eccl. Hier.* iv), it seems that the Eucharist is not a sacrament, since Confirmation is one, as stated above (Q. 65, A. 1; Q. 72, A. 1).

OBJ. 2: Further, in every sacrament of the New Law, that which comes visibly under our senses causes the invisible effect of the sacrament, just as cleansing with water causes the baptismal character and spiritual cleansing, as stated above (Q. 63, A. 6; Q. 66, AA. 1, 3, 7). But the species of bread and wine, which are the objects of our senses in this sacrament, neither produce Christ's true body, which is both reality and sacrament, nor His mystical body, which is the reality only in the Eucharist. Therefore, it seems that the Eucharist is not a sacrament of the New Law.

OBJ. 3: Further, sacraments of the New Law, as having matter, are perfected by the use of the matter, as Baptism is by ablution, and Confirmation by signing with chrism. If, then, the Eucharist be a sacrament, it would be perfected by the use of the matter, and not by its consecration. But this is manifestly false, because the words spoken in the consecration of the matter are the form of this sacrament, as will be shown later on (Q. 78, A. 1). Therefore the Eucharist is not a sacrament.

ON THE CONTRARY, It is said in the Collect: *May this Thy Sacrament not make us deserving of punishment.*

175

RESPONDEO dicendum quod sacramenta Ecclesiae ordinantur ad subveniendum homini in vita spirituali. Vita autem spiritualis vitae corporali conformatur, eo quod corporalia spiritualium similitudinem gerunt. Manifestum est autem quod, sicut ad vitam corporalem requiritur generatio, per quam homo vitam accipit, et augmentum, quo homo perducitur ad perfectionem vitae; ita etiam requiritur alimentum, quo homo conservatur in vita. Et ideo, sicut ad vitam spiritualem oportuit esse Baptismum, qui est spiritualis generatio, et confirmationem, quae est spirituale augmentum; ita oportuit esse sacramentum Eucharistiae, quod est spirituale alimentum.

AD PRIMUM ergo dicendum quod duplex est perfectio. Una quae est in ipso homine, ad quam perducitur per augmentum. Et talis perfectio competit confirmationi. Alia autem est perfectio quam homo consequitur ex adiunctione cibi vel indumenti, vel alicuius huiusmodi. Et talis perfectio competit Eucharistiae, quae est spiritualis refectio.

AD SECUNDUM dicendum quod aqua Baptismi non causat aliquem spiritualem effectum propter ipsam aquam, sed propter virtutem spiritus sancti in aqua existentem, unde Chrysostomus dicit, super illud Ioan. V, *Angelus domini secundum tempus etc., in baptizatis non simpliciter aqua operatur, sed, cum spiritus sancti susceperit gratiam, tunc omnia solvit peccata.* Sicut autem se habet virtus spiritus sancti ad aquam Baptismi, ita se habet corpus Christi verum ad species panis et vini. Unde species panis et vini non efficiunt aliquid nisi virtute corporis Christi veri.

AD TERTIUM dicendum quod sacramentum dicitur ex eo quod continet aliquid sacrum. Potest autem aliquid esse sacrum dupliciter, scilicet absolute, et in ordine ad aliud. Haec est autem differentia inter Eucharistiam et alia sacramenta habentia materiam sensibilem, quod Eucharistia continet aliquid sacrum absolute, scilicet ipsum Christum, aqua vero Baptismi continet aliquid sacrum in ordine ad aliud, scilicet virtutem ad sanctificandum, et eadem ratio est de chrismate et similibus. Et ideo sacramentum Eucharistiae perficitur in ipsa consecratione materiae, alia vero sacramenta perficiuntur in applicatione materiae ad hominem sanctificandum. Et ex hoc etiam consequitur alia differentia. Nam in sacramento Eucharistiae id quod est res et sacramentum, est in ipsa materia; id autem quod est res tantum, est in suscipiente, scilicet gratia quae confertur. In Baptismo autem utrumque est in suscipiente, et character, qui est res et sacramentum; et gratia remissionis peccatorum, quae est res tantum. Et eadem ratio est de aliis sacramentis.

I ANSWER THAT, The Church's sacraments are ordained for helping man in the spiritual life. But the spiritual life is analogous to the corporeal, since corporeal things bear a resemblance to spiritual. Now it is clear that just as generation is required for corporeal life, since thereby man receives life; and growth, whereby man is brought to maturity: so likewise food is required for the preservation of life. Consequently, just as for the spiritual life there had to be Baptism, which is spiritual generation; and Confirmation, which is spiritual growth: so there needed to be the sacrament of the Eucharist, which is spiritual food.

REPLY OBJ. 1: Perfection is twofold. The first lies within man himself; and he attains it by growth: such perfection belongs to Confirmation. The other is the perfection which comes to man from the addition of food, or clothing, or something of the kind; and such is the perfection befitting the Eucharist, which is the spiritual refreshment.

REPLY OBJ. 2: The water of Baptism does not cause any spiritual effect by reason of the water, but by reason of the power of the Holy Spirit, which power is in the water. Hence on John 5:4, *An angel of the Lord at certain times*, etc., Chrysostom observes: *The water does not act simply as such upon the baptized, but when it receives the grace of the Holy Spirit, then it looses all sins.* But the true body of Christ bears the same relation to the species of the bread and wine, as the power of the Holy Spirit does to the water of Baptism: hence the species of the bread and wine produce no effect except from the virtue of Christ's true body.

REPLY OBJ. 3: A sacrament is so termed because it contains something sacred. Now a thing can be styled sacred from two causes; either absolutely, or in relation to something else. The difference between the Eucharist and other sacraments having sensible matter is that whereas the Eucharist contains something which is sacred absolutely, namely, Christ's own body; the baptismal water contains something which is sacred in relation to something else, namely, the sanctifying power: and the same holds good of chrism and such like. Consequently, the sacrament of the Eucharist is completed in the very consecration of the matter, whereas the other sacraments are completed in the application of the matter for the sanctifying of the individual. And from this follows another difference. For, in the sacrament of the Eucharist, what is both reality and sacrament is in the matter itself, but what is reality only, namely, the grace bestowed, is in the recipient; whereas in Baptism both are in the recipient, namely, the character, which is both reality and sacrament, and the grace of pardon of sins, which is reality only. And the same holds good of the other sacraments.

Article 2

Whether the Eucharist Is One Sacrament or Several?

AD SECUNDUM SIC PROCEDITUR. Videtur quod Eucharistia non sit unum sacramentum, sed plura. Dicitur enim in collecta, *purificent nos, quaesumus, domine, sacramenta quae sumpsimus*, quod quidem dicitur propter Eucharistiae sumptionem. Ergo Eucharistia non est unum sacramentum, sed plura.

PRAETEREA, impossibile est, multiplicato genere, non multiplicari speciem, sicut quod unus homo sit plura animalia. Sed signum est genus sacramenti, ut supra dictum est. Cum igitur in Eucharistia sint plura signa, scilicet panis et vini, videtur consequens esse quod sint plura sacramenta.

PRAETEREA, hoc sacramentum perficitur in consecratione materiae, sicut dictum est. Sed in hoc sacramento est duplex materiae consecratio. Ergo est duplex sacramentum.

SED CONTRA est quod apostolus dicit, I Cor. X, *unus panis et unum corpus multi sumus, omnes qui de uno pane et uno calice participamus.* Ex quo patet quod Eucharistia sit sacramentum ecclesiasticae unitatis. Sed sacramentum similitudinem gerit rei cuius est sacramentum. Ergo Eucharistia est unum sacramentum.

RESPONDEO dicendum quod, sicut dicitur V Metaphys., unum dicitur non solum quod est indivisibile vel quod est continuum, sed etiam quod est perfectum, sicut cum dicitur una domus, et unus homo. Est autem unum perfectione ad cuius integritatem concurrunt omnia quae requiruntur ad finem eiusdem, sicut homo integratur ex omnibus membris necessariis operationi animae, et domus ex partibus quae sunt necessariae ad inhabitandum. Et sic hoc sacramentum dicitur unum. Ordinatur enim ad spiritualem refectionem, quae corporali conformatur. Ad corporalem autem refectionem duo requiruntur, scilicet cibus, qui est alimentum siccum; et potus, qui est alimentum humidum. Et ideo etiam ad integritatem huius sacramenti duo concurrunt, scilicet spiritualis cibus et spiritualis potus, secundum illud Ioan. VI, *caro mea vere est cibus, et sanguis meus vere est potus.* Ergo hoc sacramentum multa quidem materialiter est, sed unum formaliter et perfective.

AD PRIMUM ergo dicendum quod in collecta eadem et pluraliter dicitur primo, *purificent nos sacramenta quae sumpsimus*; et postea singulariter subditur, *hoc tuum sacramentum non sit nobis reatus ad poenam*, ad ostendendum quod hoc sacramentum quodammodo est multa, simpliciter autem unum.

AD SECUNDUM dicendum quod panis et vinum materialiter quidem sunt plura signa, formaliter vero et perfective unum, inquantum ex eis perficitur una refectio.

OBJECTION 1: It seems that the Eucharist is not one sacrament but several, because it is said in the Collect: *May the sacraments which we have received purify us, O Lord*: and this is said on account of our receiving the Eucharist. Consequently the Eucharist is not one sacrament but several.

OBJ. 2: Further, it is impossible for genera to be multiplied without the species being multiplied: thus it is impossible for one man to be many animals. But, as stated above (Q. 60, A. 1), sign is the genus of sacrament. Since, then, there are more signs than one, to wit, bread and wine, it seems to follow that here must be more sacraments than one.

OBJ. 3: Further, this sacrament is perfected in the consecration of the matter, as stated above (A. 1, ad 3). But in this sacrament there is a double consecration of the matter. Therefore, it is a twofold sacrament.

ON THE CONTRARY, The Apostle says (1 Cor 10:17): *For we, being many, are one bread, one body, all that partake of one bread*: from which it is clear that the Eucharist is the sacrament of the Church's unity. But a sacrament bears the likeness of the reality whereof it is the sacrament. Therefore the Eucharist is one sacrament.

I ANSWER THAT, As stated in *Metaph.* v, a thing is said to be one, not only from being indivisible, or continuous, but also when it is complete; thus we speak of one house, and one man. A thing is one in perfection, when it is complete through the presence of all that is needed for its end; as a man is complete by having all the members required for the operation of his soul, and a house by having all the parts needful for dwelling therein. And so this sacrament is said to be one. Because it is ordained for spiritual refreshment, which is conformed to corporeal refreshment. Now there are two things required for corporeal refreshment, namely, food, which is dry sustenance, and drink, which is wet sustenance. Consequently, two things concur for the integrity of this sacrament, to wit, spiritual food and spiritual drink, according to John: *My flesh is meat indeed, and My blood is drink indeed.* Therefore, this sacrament is materially many, but formally and perfectively one.

REPLY OBJ. 1: The same Collect at first employs the plural: *May the sacraments which we have received purify us*; and afterwards the singular number: *May this sacrament of Thine not make us worthy of punishment*: so as to show that this sacrament is in a measure several, yet simply one.

REPLY OBJ. 2: The bread and wine are materially several signs, yet formally and perfectively one, inasmuch as one refreshment is prepared therefrom.

AD TERTIUM dicendum quod ex hoc quod est duplex consecratio huius sacramenti, non potest plus haberi nisi quod hoc sacramentum materialiter est multa, ut dictum est.

REPLY OBJ. 3: From the double consecration of the matter no more can be gathered than that the sacrament is several materially, as stated above.

Article 3

Whether the Eucharist Is Necessary for Salvation?

AD TERTIUM SIC PROCEDITUR. Videtur quod hoc sacramentum sit de necessitate salutis. Dicit enim dominus, Ioan. VI, *nisi manducaveritis carnem filii hominis et biberitis eius sanguinem, non habebitis vitam in vobis.* Sed in hoc sacramento manducatur caro Christi et bibitur sanguis eius. Ergo sine hoc sacramento non potest homo habere salutem spiritualis vitae.

PRAETEREA, hoc sacramentum est quoddam spirituale alimentum. Sed alimentum corporale est de necessitate corporalis salutis. Ergo etiam hoc sacramentum est de necessitate salutis spiritualis.

PRAETEREA, sicut Baptismus est sacramentum dominicae passionis, sine qua non est salus, ita et Eucharistia, dicit enim apostolus, I Cor. XI, *quotiescumque manducaveritis panem hunc et calicem biberitis, mortem domini annuntiabitis, donec veniat.* Ergo, sicut Baptismus est de necessitate salutis, ita hoc sacramentum.

SED CONTRA est quod scribit Augustinus Bonifacio, contra Pelagianos, *nec id cogitetis, parvulos vitam habere non posse, qui sunt expertes corporis et sanguinis Christi.*

RESPONDEO dicendum quod in hoc sacramento duo est considerare, scilicet ipsum sacramentum, et rem sacramenti. Dictum est autem quod res sacramenti est unitas corporis mystici, sine qua non potest esse salus, nulli enim patet aditus salutis extra Ecclesiam, sicut nec in diluvio absque arca Noe, quae significat Ecclesiam, ut habetur I Petr. III. Dictum est autem supra quod res alicuius sacramenti haberi potest ante perceptionem sacramenti, ex ipso voto sacramenti percipiendi. Unde ante perceptionem huius sacramenti, potest homo habere salutem ex voto percipiendi hoc sacramentum, sicut et ante Baptismum ex voto Baptismi, ut supra dictum est. Tamen est differentia quantum ad duo. Primo quidem, quia Baptismus est principium spiritualis vitae, et ianua sacramentorum. Eucharistia vero est quasi consummatio spiritualis vitae, et omnium sacramentorum finis, ut supra dictum est, per sanctificationes enim omnium sacramentorum fit praeparatio ad suscipiendam vel consecrandam Eucharistiam. Et ideo perceptio Baptismi est necessaria ad inchoandam spiritualem vitam, perceptio autem Eucharistiae est necessaria ad consummandam ipsam, non ad hoc quod simpliciter habeatur, sed sufficit

OBJECTION 1: It seems that this sacrament is necessary for salvation. For our Lord said (John 6:54): *Except you eat the flesh of the Son of Man, and drink His blood, you shall not have life in you.* But Christ's flesh is eaten and His blood drunk in this sacrament. Therefore, without this sacrament man cannot have the health of spiritual life.

OBJ. 2: Further, this sacrament is a kind of spiritual food. But bodily food is requisite for bodily health. Therefore, also is this sacrament, for spiritual health.

OBJ. 3: Further, as Baptism is the sacrament of our Lord's Passion, without which there is no salvation, so also is the Eucharist. For the Apostle says (1 Cor 11:26): *For as often as you shall eat this bread, and drink the chalice, you shall show the death of the Lord, until He come.* Consequently, as Baptism is necessary for salvation, so also is this sacrament.

ON THE CONTRARY, Augustine writes (*Ad Bonifac. contra Pelag.* I): *Nor are you to suppose that children cannot possess life, who are deprived of the body and blood of Christ.*

I ANSWER THAT, Two things have to be considered in this sacrament, namely, the sacrament itself, and what is contained in it. Now it was stated above (A. 1, Obj. 2) that the reality of the sacrament is the unity of the mystical body, without which there can be no salvation; for there is no entering into salvation outside the Church, just as in the time of the deluge there was none outside the Ark, which denotes the Church, according to 1 Pet. 3:20, 21. And it has been said above (Q. 68, A. 2), that before receiving a sacrament, the reality of the sacrament can be had through the very desire of receiving the sacrament. Accordingly, before actual reception of this sacrament, a man can obtain salvation through the desire of receiving it, just as he can before Baptism through the desire of Baptism, as stated above (Q. 68, A. 2). Yet there is a difference in two respects. First of all, because Baptism is the beginning of the spiritual life, and the door of the sacraments; whereas the Eucharist is, as it were, the consummation of the spiritual life, and the end of all the sacraments, as was observed above (Q. 63, A. 6): for by the hallowings of all the sacraments preparation is made for receiving or consecrating the Eucharist. Consequently, the reception of Baptism is necessary for starting

eam habere in voto, sicut et finis habetur in desiderio et intentione. Alia differentia est, quia per Baptismum ordinatur homo ad Eucharistiam. Et ideo ex hoc ipso quod pueri baptizantur, ordinantur per Ecclesiam ad Eucharistiam. Et sic, sicut ex fide Ecclesiae credunt, sic ex intentione Ecclesiae desiderant Eucharistiam, et per consequens recipiunt rem ipsius. Sed ad Baptismum non ordinantur per aliud praecedens sacramentum. Et ideo, ante susceptionem Baptismi, non habent pueri aliquo modo Baptismum in voto, sed soli adulti. Unde rem sacramenti percipere non possunt sine perceptione sacramenti. Et ideo hoc sacramentum non hoc modo est de necessitate salutis sicut Baptismus.

AD PRIMUM ergo dicendum quod, sicut Augustinus dicit, exponens illud verbum Ioannis, hunc cibum et potum, scilicet carnis suae et sanguinis, *societatem vult intelligi corporis et membrorum suorum, quod est Ecclesia, in praedestinatis et vocatis et iustificatis et glorificatis sanctis et fidelibus eius.* Unde, sicut ipse dicit, in epistola ad Bonifacium, *nulli est aliquatenus ambigendum tunc unumquemque fidelium corporis sanguinisque domini participem fieri, quando in Baptismate membrum corporis Christi efficitur, nec alienari ab illius panis calicisque consortio, etiam si, antequam panem illum comedat et calicem bibat, de hoc saeculo in unitate corporis Christi constitutus abscedat.*

AD SECUNDUM dicendum quod haec est differentia inter alimentum corporale et spirituale, quod alimentum corporale convertitur in substantiam eius qui nutritur, et ideo non potest homini valere ad vitae conservationem alimentum corporale nisi realiter sumatur. Sed alimentum spirituale convertit hominem in seipsum, secundum illud quod Augustinus dicit, in libro Confess., quod *quasi audivit vocem Christi dicentis, nec tu me mutabis in te, sicut cibum carnis tuae, sed tu mutaberis in me.* Potest autem aliquis in Christum mutari et ei incorporari voto mentis, etiam sine huius sacramenti perceptione. Et ideo non est simile.

AD TERTIUM dicendum quod Baptismus est sacramentum mortis et passionis Christi prout homo regeneratur in Christo virtute passionis eius. Sed Eucharistia est sacramentum passionis Christi prout homo perficitur in unione ad Christum passum. Unde, sicut Baptismus dicitur sacramentum fidei, quae est fundamentum spiritualis vitae; ita Eucharistia dicitur sacramentum caritatis, quae est vinculum perfectionis, ut dicitur Coloss. III.

the spiritual life, while the receiving of the Eucharist is requisite for its consummation; by partaking not indeed actually, but in desire, as an end is possessed in desire and intention. Another difference is because by Baptism a man is ordained to the Eucharist, and therefore from the fact of children being baptized, they are destined by the Church to the Eucharist; and just as they believe through the Church's faith, so they desire the Eucharist through the Church's intention, and, as a result, receive its reality. But they are not disposed for Baptism by any previous sacrament, and consequently before receiving Baptism, in no way have they Baptism in desire; but adults alone have: consequently, they cannot have the reality of the sacrament without receiving the sacrament itself. Therefore this sacrament is not necessary for salvation in the same way as Baptism is.

REPLY OBJ. 1: As Augustine says, explaining John 6:54, *This food and this drink*, namely, of His flesh and blood: *He would have us understand the fellowship of His body and members, which is the Church in His predestined, and called, and justified, and glorified, His holy and believing ones.* Hence, as he says in his Epistle to Boniface (Pseudo-Beda, *in 1 Cor.* 10:17): *No one should entertain the slightest doubt, that then every one of the faithful becomes a partaker of the body and blood of Christ, when in Baptism he is made a member of Christ's body; nor is he deprived of his share in that body and chalice even though he depart from this world in the unity of Christ's body, before he eats that bread and drinks of that chalice.*

REPLY OBJ. 2: The difference between corporeal and spiritual food lies in this, that the former is changed into the substance of the person nourished, and consequently it cannot avail for supporting life except it be partaken of; but spiritual food changes man into itself, according to that saying of Augustine (*Confess.* vii), that he heard the voice of Christ as it were saying to him: *Nor shalt thou change Me into thyself, as food of thy flesh, but thou shalt be changed into Me.* But one can be changed into Christ, and be incorporated in Him by mental desire, even without receiving this sacrament. And consequently the comparison does not hold.

REPLY OBJ. 3: Baptism is the sacrament of Christ's death and Passion, according as a man is born anew in Christ in virtue of His Passion; but the Eucharist is the sacrament of Christ's Passion according as a man is made perfect in union with Christ Who suffered. Hence, as Baptism is called the sacrament of Faith, which is the foundation of the spiritual life, so the Eucharist is termed the sacrament of Charity, which is *the bond of perfection* (Col 3:14).

Article 4

Whether This Sacrament Is Suitably Called by Various Names?

AD QUARTUM SIC PROCEDITUR. Videtur quod inconvenienter hoc sacramentum pluribus nominibus nominetur. Nomina enim debent respondere rebus. Sed hoc sacramentum est unum, ut dictum est. Ergo non debet pluribus nominibus nominari.

PRAETEREA, species non notificatur convenienter per id quod est commune toti generi. Sed Eucharistia est sacramentum novae legis. Omnibus autem sacramentis commune est quod in eis confertur gratia, quod significat nomen Eucharistiae, quod est idem quod bona gratia. Omnia etiam sacramenta remedium nobis afferunt in via praesentis vitae, quod pertinet ad rationem viatici. In omnibus etiam sacramentis fit aliquid sacrum, quod pertinet ad rationem sacrificii. Et per omnia sacramenta sibi invicem fideles communicant, quod significat hoc nomen synaxis in Graeco, vel communio in Latino. Ergo haec nomina non convenienter adaptantur huic sacramento.

PRAETEREA, hostia videtur idem esse quod sacrificium. Sicut ergo non proprie dicitur sacrificium, ita nec proprie dicitur hostia.

SED CONTRA est quod usus fidelium habet.

RESPONDEO dicendum quod hoc sacramentum habet triplicem significationem. Unam quidem respectu praeteriti, inquantum scilicet est commemorativum dominicae passionis, quae fuit verum sacrificium, ut supra dictum est. Et secundum hoc nominatur sacrificium.

Aliam autem significationem habet respectu rei praesentis, scilicet ecclesiasticae unitatis, cui homines congregantur per hoc sacramentum. Et secundum hoc nominatur communio vel synaxis, dicit enim Damascenus, IV libro, quod *dicitur communio, quia communicamus per ipsam Christo; et quia participamus eius carne et deitate; et quia communicamus et unimur ad invicem per ipsam.*

Tertiam significationem habet respectu futuri, inquantum scilicet hoc sacramentum est praefigurativum fruitionis Dei, quae erit in patria. Et secundum hoc dicitur viaticum, quia hoc praebet nobis viam illuc perveniendi. Et secundum hoc etiam dicitur Eucharistia, idest bona gratia, quia *gratia Dei est vita aeterna*, ut dicitur Rom. VI; vel quia realiter continet Christum, qui est plenus gratia.

Dicitur etiam in Graeco metalepsis, idest assumptio, quia, ut Damascenus dicit, *per hoc filii deitatem assumimus.*

OBJECTION 1: It seems that this sacrament is not suitably called by various names. For names should correspond with things. But this sacrament is one, as stated above (A. 2). Therefore, it ought not to be called by various names.

OBJ. 2: Further, a species is not properly denominated by what is common to the whole genus. But the Eucharist is a sacrament of the New Law; and it is common to all the sacraments for grace to be conferred by them, which the name *Eucharist* denotes, for it is the same thing as *good grace*. Furthermore, all the sacraments bring us help on our journey through this present life, which is the notion conveyed by *Viaticum*. Again something sacred is done in all the sacraments, which belongs to the notion of *Sacrifice*; and the faithful intercommunicate through all the sacraments, which this Greek word *Synaxis* and the Latin *Communio* express. Therefore, these names are not suitably adapted to this sacrament.

OBJ. 3: Further, a host seems to be the same as a sacrifice. Therefore, as it is not properly called a sacrifice, so neither is it properly termed a *Host*.

ON THE CONTRARY, is the use of these expressions by the faithful.

I ANSWER THAT, This sacrament has a threefold significance. One with regard to the past, inasmuch as it is commemorative of our Lord's Passion, which was a true sacrifice, as stated above (Q. 48, A. 3), and in this respect it is called a *Sacrifice*.

With regard to the present it has another meaning, namely, that of Ecclesiastical unity, in which men are aggregated through this Sacrament; and in this respect it is called *Communion* or *Synaxis*. For Damascene says (*De Fide Orth.* iv) that *it is called Communion because we communicate with Christ through it, both because we partake of His flesh and Godhead, and because we communicate with and are united to one another through it.*

With regard to the future it has a third meaning, inasmuch as this sacrament foreshadows the Divine fruition, which shall come to pass in heaven; and according to this it is called *Viaticum*, because it supplies the way of winning thither. And in this respect it is also called the *Eucharist*, that is, *good grace*, because *the grace of God is life everlasting* (Rom 6:23); or because it really contains Christ, Who is *full of grace*.

In Greek, moreover, it is called *Metalepsis*, i.e., *Assumption*, because, as Damascene says (*De Fide Orth.* iv), *we thereby assume the Godhead of the Son.*

Ad primum ergo dicendum quod nihil prohibet idem pluribus nominibus nominari secundum diversas proprietates vel effectus.

Ad secundum dicendum quod id quod est commune omnibus sacramentis, attribuitur antonomastice ei, propter eius excellentiam.

Ad tertium dicendum quod hoc sacramentum dicitur sacrificium, inquantum repraesentat ipsam passionem Christi. Dicitur autem hostia, inquantum continet ipsum Christum, qui est hostia suavitatis, ut dicitur Ephes. V.

Reply Obj. 1: There is nothing to hinder the same thing from being called by several names, according to its various properties or effects.

Reply Obj. 2: What is common to all the sacraments is attributed antonomastically to this one on account of its excellence.

Reply Obj. 3: This sacrament is called a *Sacrifice* inasmuch as it represents the Passion of Christ; but it is termed a *Host* inasmuch as it contains Christ, Who is *a host (sacrifice) . . . of sweetness* (Eph 5:2).

Article 5

Whether the Institution of This Sacrament Was Appropriate?

Ad quintum sic proceditur. Videtur quod non fuerit conveniens institutio istius sacramenti. Ut enim philosophus dicit, in II de Generat., *ex eisdem nutrimur ex quibus sumus*. Sed per Baptismum, qui est spiritualis regeneratio, accipimus esse spirituale, ut Dionysius dicit, II cap. Eccles. Hier. Ergo per Baptismum etiam nutrimur. Non ergo fuit necessarium instituere hoc sacramentum quasi spirituale nutrimentum.

Praeterea, per hoc sacramentum homines Christo uniuntur sicut membra capiti. Sed Christus est caput omnium hominum, etiam qui fuerunt ab initio mundi, ut supra dictum est. Ergo non debuit institutio huius sacramenti differri usque ad cenam domini.

Praeterea, hoc sacramentum dicitur esse memoriale dominicae passionis, secundum illud Matth. XXVI, *hoc facite in meam commemorationem*. Sed memoria est praeteritorum. Ergo hoc sacramentum non debuit institui ante Christi passionem.

Praeterea, per Baptismum aliquis ordinatur ad Eucharistiam, quae non nisi baptizatis dari debet. Sed Baptismus institutus fuit post Christi passionem et resurrectionem, ut patet Matth. ult. Ergo inconvenienter hoc sacramentum fuit ante passionem Christi institutum.

Sed contra est quod hoc sacramentum institutum est a Christo, de quo dicitur Marc. VII, *bene omnia fecit*.

Respondeo dicendum quod convenienter hoc sacramentum institutum fuit in cena, in qua scilicet Christus ultimo cum discipulis suis fuit conversatus. Primo quidem, ratione continentiae huius sacramenti. Continetur enim ipse Christus in Eucharistia sicut in sacramento. Et ideo, quando ipse Christus in propria specie a discipulis discessurus erat, in sacramentali specie seipsum eis reliquit, sicut in absentia imperatoris exhibetur

Objection 1: It seems that the institution of this sacrament was not appropriate, because as the Philosopher says (*De Gener.* ii): *We are nourished by the things from whence we spring*. But by Baptism, which is spiritual regeneration, we receive our spiritual being, as Dionysius says (*Eccl. Hier.* ii). Therefore we are also nourished by Baptism. Consequently there was no need to institute this sacrament as spiritual nourishment.

Obj. 2: Further, men are united with Christ through this sacrament as the members with the head. But Christ is the Head of all men, even of those who have existed from the beginning of the world, as stated above (Q. 8, AA. 3, 6). Therefore the institution of this sacrament should not have been postponed till the Lord's supper.

Obj. 3: Further, this sacrament is called the memorial of our Lord's Passion, according to Matt. 26 (Luke 22:19): *Do this for a commemoration of Me*. But a commemoration is of things past. Therefore, this sacrament should not have been instituted before Christ's Passion.

Obj. 4: Further, a man is prepared by Baptism for the Eucharist, which ought to be given only to the baptized. But Baptism was instituted by Christ after His Passion and Resurrection, as is evident from Matt. 28:19. Therefore, this sacrament was not suitably instituted before Christ's Passion.

On the contrary, This sacrament was instituted by Christ, of Whom it is said (Mark 7:37) that *He did all things well*.

I answer that, This sacrament was appropriately instituted at the supper, when Christ conversed with His disciples for the last time. First of all, because of what is contained in the sacrament: for Christ is Himself contained in the Eucharist sacramentally. Consequently, when Christ was going to leave His disciples in His proper species, He left Himself with them under the sacramental species; as the Emperor's image is set up to be reverenced in his absence.

veneranda eius imago. Unde Eusebius dicit, *quia corpus assumptum ablaturus erat ab oculis et illaturus sideribus, necesse erat ut die cenae sacramentum corporis et sanguinis sui consecraret nobis, ut coleretur iugiter per mysterium quod semel offerebatur in pretium.*

Secundo, quia sine fide passionis Christi nunquam potuit esse salus, secundum illud Rom. III, *quem proposuit Deus propitiatorem per fidem in sanguine ipsius.* Et ideo oportuit omni tempore apud homines esse aliquod repraesentativum dominicae passionis. Cuius in veteri quidem testamento praecipuum sacramentum erat agnus paschalis, unde et apostolus dicit, I Cor. V, *Pascha nostrum immolatus est Christus.* Successit autem ei in novo testamento Eucharistiae sacramentum, quod est rememorativum praeteritae passionis, sicut et illud fuit praefigurativum futurae. Et ideo conveniens fuit, imminente passione, celebrato priori sacramento, novum sacramentum instituere, ut Leo Papa dicit.

Tertio, quia ea quae ultimo dicuntur, maxime ab amicis recedentibus, magis memoriae commendantur, praesertim quia tunc magis inflammatur affectus ad amicos, ea vero ad quae magis afficimur, profundius animo imprimuntur. Quia igitur, ut beatus Alexander Papa dicit, *nihil in sacrificiis maius esse potest quam corpus et sanguis Christi, nec ulla oblatio hac potior est,* ideo, ut in maiori veneratione haberetur, dominus in ultimo discessu suo a discipulis hoc sacramentum instituit. Et hoc est quod Augustinus dicit, in libro responsionum ad Ianuarium, *salvator, quo vehementius commendaret mysterii illius altitudinem, ultimum hoc voluit infigere cordibus et memoriae discipulorum, a quibus ad passionem discessurus erat.*

AD PRIMUM ergo dicendum quod ex eisdem nutrimur ex quibus sumus, non tamen eodem modo nobis advenientibus. Nam ea ex quibus sumus, nobis adveniunt per generationem, eadem autem, inquantum ex eis nutrimur, nobis adveniunt per manducationem. Unde et, sicut per Baptismum regeneramur in Christo, ita per Eucharistiam manducamus Christum.

AD SECUNDUM dicendum quod Eucharistia est sacramentum perfectum dominicae passionis, tanquam continens ipsum Christum passum. Et ideo non potuit institui ante incarnationem, sed tunc habebant locum sacramenta quae erant tantum praefigurativa dominicae passionis.

AD TERTIUM dicendum quod sacramentum illud fuit institutum in cena ut in futurum esset memoriale dominicae passionis, ea perfecta. Unde signanter dicit, *haec quotiescumque feceritis,* de futuro loquens.

AD QUARTUM dicendum quod institutio respondet ordini intentionis. Sacramentum autem Eucharistiae, quamvis sit posterius Baptismo in perceptione, est

Hence Eusebius says: *Since He was going to withdraw His assumed body from their eyes, and bear it away to the stars, it was needful that on the day of the supper He should consecrate the sacrament of His body and blood for our sakes, in order that what was once offered up for our ransom should be fittingly worshiped in a mystery.*

Second, because without faith in the Passion there could never be any salvation, according to Rom. 3:25: *Whom God hath proposed to be a propitiation, through faith in His blood.* It was necessary accordingly that there should be at all times among men something to show forth our Lord's Passion; the chief sacrament of which in the old Law was the Paschal Lamb. Hence the Apostle says (1 Cor 5:7): *Christ our Pasch is sacrificed.* But its successor under the New Testament is the sacrament of the Eucharist, which is a remembrance of the Passion now past, just as the other was figurative of the Passion to come. And so it was fitting that when the hour of the Passion was come, Christ should institute a new Sacrament after celebrating the old, as Pope Leo I says (*Serm. lviii*).

Third, because last words, chiefly such as are spoken by departing friends, are committed most deeply to memory; since then especially affection for friends is more enkindled, and the things which affect us most are impressed the deepest in the soul. Consequently, since, as Pope Alexander I says, *among sacrifices there can be none greater than the body and blood of Christ, nor any more powerful oblation;* our Lord instituted this sacrament at His last parting with His disciples, in order that it might be held in the greater veneration. And this is what Augustine says (*Respons. ad Januar. i*): *In order to commend more earnestly the death of this mystery, our Savior willed this last act to be fixed in the hearts and memories of the disciples whom He was about to quit for the Passion.*

REPLY OBJ. 1: We are nourished from the same things of which we are made, but they do not come to us in the same way; for those out of which we are made come to us through generation, while the same, as nourishing us, come to us through being eaten. Hence, as we are new-born in Christ through Baptism, so through the Eucharist we eat Christ.

REPLY OBJ. 2: The Eucharist is the perfect sacrament of our Lord's Passion, as containing Christ crucified; consequently it could not be instituted before the Incarnation; but then there was room for only such sacraments as were prefigurative of the Lord's Passion.

REPLY OBJ. 3: This sacrament was instituted during the supper, so as in the future to be a memorial of our Lord's Passion as accomplished. Hence He said expressively: *As often as ye shall do these things,* speaking of the future.

REPLY OBJ. 4: The institution responds to the order of intention. But the sacrament of the Eucharist, although after Baptism in the receiving, is yet previous to it in intention;

tamen prius in intentione. Et ideo debuit prius institui. Vel potest dici quod Baptismus iam erat institutus in ipso Christi Baptismo. Unde et iam aliqui ipso Christi Baptismo erant baptizati, ut legitur Ioan. III.

and therefore it behooved to be instituted first. Or else it can be said that Baptism was already instituted in Christ's Baptism; hence some were already baptized with Christ's Baptism, as we read in John 3:22.

Article 6

Whether the Paschal Lamb Was the Chief Figure of This Sacrament?

AD SEXTUM SIC PROCEDITUR. Videtur quod agnus paschalis non fuerit praecipua figura huius sacramenti. Christus enim dicitur sacerdos secundum ordinem Melchisedech, propter hoc quod Melchisedech gessit figuram sacrificii Christi, offerens panem et vinum. Sed expressio similitudinis facit quod unum ab alio denominetur. Ergo videtur quod oblatio Melchisedech fuerit potissima figura huius sacramenti.

PRAETEREA, transitus maris rubri fuit figura Baptismi, secundum illud I Cor. X, *omnes baptizati sunt in nube et in mari*. Sed immolatio agni paschalis praecessit transitum maris rubri, quem subsecutum est manna, sicut Eucharistia sequitur Baptismum. Ergo manna est expressior figura huius sacramenti quam agnus paschalis.

PRAETEREA, potissima virtus huius sacramenti est quod introducit nos in regnum caelorum, sicut quoddam viaticum. Sed hoc maxime figuratum fuit in sacramento expiationis, quando *pontifex intrabat semel in anno cum sanguine in sancta sanctorum*, sicut apostolus probat, Heb. IX. Ergo videtur quod illud sacrificium fuerit expressior figura huius sacramenti quam agnus paschalis.

SED CONTRA est quod apostolus dicit, I Cor. V, *Pascha nostrum immolatus est Christus. Itaque epulemur in azymis sinceritatis et veritatis.*

RESPONDEO dicendum quod in hoc sacramento tria considerare possumus, scilicet id quod est sacramentum tantum, scilicet panis et vinum; et id quod est res et sacramentum, scilicet corpus Christi verum; et id quod est res tantum, scilicet effectus huius sacramenti. Quantum igitur ad id quod est sacramentum tantum potissima figura fuit huius sacramenti oblatio Melchisedech, qui obtulit panem et vinum. Quantum autem ad ipsum Christum passum, qui continetur in hoc sacramento, figurae eius fuerunt omnia sacrificia veteris testamenti; et praecipue sacrificium expiationis, quod erat solemnissimum. Quantum autem ad effectum, fuit praecipua eius figura manna, quod *habebat in se omnis saporis suavitatem*, ut dicitur Sap. XVI, sicut et gratia huius sacramenti quantum ad omnia reficit mentem.

Sed agnus paschalis quantum ad haec tria praefigurabat hoc sacramentum. Quantum enim ad primum, quia

OBJECTION 1: It seems that the Paschal Lamb was not the chief figure of this sacrament, because (Ps 109:4) Christ is called *a priest according to the order of Melchisedech*, since Melchisedech bore the figure of Christ's sacrifice, in offering bread and wine. But the expression of likeness causes one thing to be named from another. Therefore, it seems that Melchisedech's offering was the principal figure of this sacrament.

OBJ. 2: Further, the passage of the Red Sea was a figure of Baptism, according to 1 Cor. 10:2: *All . . . were baptized in the cloud and in the sea*. But the immolation of the Paschal Lamb was previous to the passage of the Red Sea, and the Manna came after it, just as the Eucharist follows Baptism. Therefore the Manna is a more expressive figure of this sacrament than the Paschal Lamb.

OBJ. 3: Further, the principal power of this sacrament is that it brings us into the kingdom of heaven, being a kind of *viaticum*. But this was chiefly prefigured in the sacrament of expiation when the *high-priest entered once a year into the Holy of Holies with blood*, as the Apostle proves in Heb. 9. Consequently, it seems that that sacrifice was a more significant figure of this sacrament than was the Paschal Lamb.

ON THE CONTRARY, The Apostle says (1 Cor 5:7, 8): *Christ our Pasch is sacrificed; therefore let us feast . . . with the unleavened bread of sincerity and truth.*

I ANSWER THAT, We can consider three things in this sacrament: namely, that which is sacrament only, and this is the bread and wine; that which is both reality and sacrament, to wit, Christ's true body; and lastly that which is reality only, namely, the effect of this sacrament. Consequently, in relation to what is sacrament only, the chief figure of this sacrament was the oblation of Melchisedech, who offered up bread and wine. In relation to Christ crucified, Who is contained in this sacrament, its figures were all the sacrifices of the Old Testament, especially the sacrifice of expiation, which was the most solemn of all. While with regard to its effect, the chief figure was the Manna, *having in it the sweetness of every taste* (Wis 16:20), just as the grace of this sacrament refreshes the soul in all respects.

The Paschal Lamb foreshadowed this sacrament in these three ways. First of all, because it was eaten with

manducabatur cum panibus azymis, secundum illud Exod. XII, *edent carnes et azymos panes.* Quantum vero ad secundum, quia immolabatur ab omni multitudine filiorum Israel quartadecima luna, quod fuit figura passionis Christi, qui propter innocentiam dicitur agnus. Quantum vero ad effectum, quia per sanguinem agni paschalis protecti sunt filii Israel a devastante Angelo, et educti de Aegyptiaca servitute. Et quantum ad hoc, ponitur figura huius sacramenti praecipua agnus paschalis, quia secundum omnia eam repraesentat.

ET PER HOC patet responsio ad obiecta.

unleavened loaves, according to Ex. 12:8: *They shall eat flesh . . . and unleavened bread.* As to the second because it was immolated by the entire multitude of the children of Israel on the fourteenth day of the moon; and this was a figure of the Passion of Christ, Who is called the Lamb on account of His innocence. As to the effect, because by the blood of the Paschal Lamb the children of Israel were preserved from the destroying Angel, and brought from the Egyptian captivity; and in this respect the Paschal Lamb is the chief figure of this sacrament, because it represents it in every respect.

FROM THIS the answer to the Objections is manifest.

Question 74

The Matter of The Eucharist

Deinde considerandum est de materia huius sacramenti. Et primo, de specie materiae; secundo, de conversione panis et vini in corpus Christi; tertio, de modo existendi corporis Christi in hoc sacramento; quarto, de accidentibus panis et vini quae in hoc sacramento remanent.

Circa primum quaeruntur octo.

Primo, utrum panis et vinum sint materia huius sacramenti.

Secundo, utrum ad materiam huius sacramenti requiratur determinata quantitas.

Tertio, utrum materia huius sacramenti sit panis triticeus.

Quarto, utrum sit panis azymus, vel fermentatus.

Quinto, utrum materia huius sacramenti sit vinum de vite.

Sexto, utrum sit admiscenda aqua.

Septimo, utrum aqua sit de necessitate huius sacramenti.

Octavo, de quantitate aquae quae apponitur.

We have now to consider the matter of this sacrament: and first of all as to its species; second, the change of the bread and wine into the body of Christ; third, the manner in which Christ's body exists in this sacrament; fourth, the accidents of bread and wine which continue in this sacrament.

Under the first heading there are eight points for inquiry:

(1) Whether bread and wine are the matter of this sacrament?

(2) Whether a determinate quantity of the same is required for the matter of this sacrament?

(3) Whether the matter of this sacrament is wheaten bread?

(4) Whether it is unleavened or fermented bread?

(5) Whether the matter of this sacrament is wine from the grape?

(6) Whether water should be mixed with it?

(7) Whether water is of necessity for this sacrament?

(8) Of the quantity of the water added.

Article 1

Whether the Matter of This Sacrament Is Bread and Wine?

Ad primum sic proceditur. Videtur quod materia huius sacramenti non sit panis et vinum. Hoc enim sacramentum perfectius debet repraesentare passionem Christi quam sacramenta veteris legis. Sed carnes animalium, quae erant materia sacramentorum veteris legis, expressius repraesentant passionem Christi quam panis et vinum. Ergo materia huius sacramenti magis debent esse carnes animalium quam panis et vinum.

Praeterea, hoc sacramentum est ubique celebrandum. Sed in multis terris non invenitur panis, et in multis non invenitur vinum. Ergo panis et vinum non est conveniens materia huius sacramenti.

Praeterea, hoc sacramentum competit sanis et infirmis. Sed vinum nocet quibusdam infirmis. Ergo videtur quod vinum non debeat esse materia huius sacramenti.

Sed contra est quod Alexander Papa dicit, *in sacramentorum oblationibus panis tantum et vinum aqua permixtum in sacrificium offerantur.*

Objection 1: It seems that the matter of this sacrament is not bread and wine. Because this sacrament ought to represent Christ's Passion more fully than did the sacraments of the Old Law. But the flesh of animals, which was the matter of the sacraments under the Old Law, shows forth Christ's Passion more fully than bread and wine. Therefore the matter of this sacrament ought rather to be the flesh of animals than bread and wine.

Obj. 2: Further, this sacrament is to be celebrated in every place. But in many lands bread is not to be found, and in many places wine is not to be found. Therefore bread and wine are not a suitable matter for this sacrament.

Obj. 3: Further, this sacrament is for both hale and weak. But to some weak persons wine is hurtful. Therefore it seems that wine ought not to be the matter of this sacrament.

On the contrary, Pope Alexander I says (*Ep. ad omnes orth.* i): *In oblations of the sacraments only bread and wine mixed with water are to be offered.*

Respondeo dicendum quod circa materiam huius sacramenti aliqui multipliciter erraverunt. Quidam enim, qui dicuntur Artotyritae, ut Augustinus dicit, in libro de haeresibus, *offerunt panem et caseum in hoc sacramento, dicentes a primis hominibus oblationes de fructibus terrae et ovium fuisse celebratas.* Alii vero, scilicet Cataphrygae et Pepuziani, *de infantis sanguine, quem de toto eius corpore minutis punctionum vulneribus extorquent, quasi Eucharistiam suam conficere perhibentur, miscendo eum farinae, panem inde facientes.* Quidam vero, qui dicuntur aquarii, aquam solam, sub specie sobrietatis, in hoc sacramento offerunt.

Omnes autem hi errores, et similes, excluduntur per hoc quod Christus hoc sacramentum sub specie panis et vini instituit, sicut patet Matth. XXVI. Unde panis et vinum sunt materia conveniens huius sacramenti. Et hoc rationabiliter. Primo quidem, quantum ad usum huius sacramenti, qui est manducatio. Sicut enim aqua assumitur in sacramento Baptismi ad usum spiritualis ablutionis quia corporalis ablutio communiter fit in aqua, ita panis et vinum, quibus communius homines reficiuntur, assumuntur in hoc sacramento ad usum spiritualis manducationis.

Secundo, quantum ad passionem Christi, in qua sanguis a corpore est separatus. Et ideo in hoc sacramento, quod est memoriale dominicae passionis, seorsum sumitur panis ut sacramentum corporis, et vinum ut sacramentum sanguinis.

Tertio, quantum ad effectum consideratum in unoquoque sumentium. Quia, ut Ambrosius dicit, super epistolam ad Corinthios, hoc sacramentum valet ad tuitionem corporis et animae, et ideo caro Christi sub specie panis pro salute corporis, sanguis vero sub specie vini pro salute animae offertur, sicut dicitur Levit. XVII, quod animalis anima in sanguine est.

Quarto, quantum ad effectum respectu totius Ecclesiae, quae constituitur ex diversis fidelibus, sicut *panis conficitur ex diversis granis, et vinum fluit ex diversis uvis,* ut dicit Glossa super illud I Cor. X, *multi unum corpus sumus,* et cetera.

Ad primum ergo dicendum quod, licet carnes animalium occisorum expresse repraesentent Christi passionem, tamen minus competunt ad communem usum huius sacramenti, et ad ecclesiasticam unitatem significandam.

Ad secundum dicendum quod, licet non in omnibus terris nascatur triticum et vinum, tamen de facili ad omnes terras deferri potest quantum sufficit ad usum huius sacramenti. Nec propter defectum alterius, est unum tantum sine altero consecrandum, quia non esset perfectum sacrificium.

Ad tertium dicendum quod vinum in modica quantitate sumptum non potest aegrotanti multum

I **answer that**, Some have fallen into various errors about the matter of this sacrament. Some, known as the Artotyrytae, as Augustine says (*De Haeres.* xxviii), *offer bread and cheese in this sacrament, contending that oblations were celebrated by men in the first ages, from fruits of the earth and sheep.* Others, called Cataphrygae and Pepuziani, *are reputed to have made their Eucharistic bread with infants' blood drawn from tiny punctures over the entire body, and mixed with flour.* Others, styled Aquarii, under guise of sobriety, offer nothing but water in this sacrament.

Now all these and similar errors are excluded by the fact that Christ instituted this sacrament under the species of bread and wine, as is evident from Matt. 26. Consequently, bread and wine are the proper matter of this sacrament. And the reasonableness of this is seen first, in the use of this sacrament, which is eating: for, as water is used in the sacrament of Baptism for the purpose of spiritual cleansing, since bodily cleansing is commonly done with water; so bread and wine, wherewith men are commonly fed, are employed in this sacrament for the use of spiritual eating.

Second, in relation to Christ's Passion, in which the blood was separated from the body. And therefore in this sacrament, which is the memorial of our Lord's Passion, the bread is received apart as the sacrament of the body, and the wine as the sacrament of the blood.

Third, as to the effect, considered in each of the partakers. For, as Ambrose (*Mag. Sent.* iv, D, xi) says on 1 Cor. 11:20, this sacrament *avails for the defense of soul and body*; and therefore *Christ's body is offered* under the species of bread *for the health of the body, and the blood* under the species of wine *for the health of the soul,* according to Lev. 17:14: *The life of the animal is in the blood.*

Fourth, as to the effect with regard to the whole Church, which is made up of many believers, just *as bread is composed of many grains, and wine flows from many grapes,* as the gloss observes on 1 Cor. 10:17: *We being many are . . . one body,* etc.

Reply Obj. 1: Although the flesh of slaughtered animals represents the Passion more forcibly, nevertheless it is less suitable for the common use of this sacrament, and for denoting the unity of the Church.

Reply Obj. 2: Although wheat and wine are not produced in every country, yet they can easily be conveyed to every land, that is, as much as is needful for the use of this sacrament: at the same time one is not to be consecrated when the other is lacking, because it would not be a complete sacrament.

Reply Obj. 3: Wine taken in small quantity cannot do the sick much harm: yet if there be fear of harm, it is not

nocere. Et tamen, si nocumentum timeatur, non est necesse quod omnes accipientes corpus Christi, etiam sanguinem accipiant, ut infra dicetur.

necessary for all who take Christ's body to partake also of His blood, as will be stated later (Q. 80, A. 12).

Article 2

Whether a Determinate Quantity of Bread and Wine Is Required for the Matter of This Sacrament?

AD SECUNDUM SIC PROCEDITUR. Videtur quod requiratur determinata quantitas panis et vini ad materiam huius sacramenti. Effectus enim gratiae non sunt minus ordinati quam effectus naturae. Sed, sicut dicitur in II de anima, *omnium natura constantium positus est terminus et ratio magnitudinis et augmenti.* Ergo multo magis in hoc sacramento, quod dicitur Eucharistia, idest bona gratia, requiritur determinata quantitas panis et vini.

PRAETEREA, ministris Ecclesiae non est a Christo data potestas ad ea quae pertinent ad irrisionem fidei et sacramentorum eius, secundum illud II Cor. X, *secundum potestatem quam dedit mihi Deus in aedificationem, et non in destructionem.* Sed hoc esset ad irrisionem sacramenti, si sacerdos vellet consecrare totum panem qui venditur in foro, et totum vinum quod est in cellario. Ergo hoc facere non potest.

PRAETEREA, si aliquis baptizetur in mari, non tota aqua maris sanctificatur per formam Baptismi, sed sola illa aqua qua corpus baptizati abluitur. Ergo nec in hoc sacramento superflua quantitas panis consecrari potest.

SED CONTRA est quod multum opponitur pauco, et magnum parvo. Sed nulla est ita parva quantitas panis aut vini quae non possit consecrari. Ergo nulla est ita magna quae consecrari non possit.

RESPONDEO dicendum quod quidam dixerunt quod sacerdos non posset consecrare immensam quantitatem panis aut vini, puta totum panem qui venditur in foro, aut totum vinum quod est in dolio. Sed hoc non videtur esse verum. Quia in omnibus habentibus materiam, ratio determinationis materiae sumitur ex ordine ad finem, sicut materia serrae est ferrum, ut sit apta sectioni. Finis autem huius sacramenti est usus fidelium. Unde oportet quod quantitas materiae huius sacramenti determinetur per comparationem ad usum fidelium. Non autem potest esse quod determinetur per comparationem ad usum fidelium qui nunc occurrunt, alioquin sacerdos habens paucos parochianos, non posset consecrare multas hostias. Unde relinquitur quod materia huius sacramenti determinetur per comparationem ad usum fidelium absolute. Numerus autem fidelium est indeterminatus. Unde non potest dici quod quantitas materiae huius sacramenti sit determinata.

OBJECTION 1: It seems that a determinate quantity of bread and wine is required for the matter of this sacrament. Because the effects of grace are no less set in order than those of nature. But, *there is a limit set by nature upon all existing things, and a reckoning of size and development* (*De Anima* ii). Consequently, in this sacrament, which is called *Eucharist*, that is, *a good grace*, a determinate quantity of the bread and wine is required.

OBJ. 2: Further, Christ gave no power to the ministers of the Church regarding matters which involve derision of the faith and of His sacraments, according to 2 Cor. 10:8: *Of our power which the Lord hath given us unto edification, and not for your destruction.* But it would lead to mockery of this sacrament if the priest were to wish to consecrate all the bread which is sold in the market and all the wine in the cellar. Therefore he cannot do this.

OBJ. 3: Further, if anyone be baptized in the sea, the entire sea-water is not sanctified by the form of baptism, but only the water wherewith the body of the baptized is cleansed. Therefore, neither in this sacrament can a superfluous quantity of bread be consecrated.

ON THE CONTRARY, Much is opposed to little, and great to small. But there is no quantity, however small, of the bread and wine which cannot be consecrated. Therefore, neither is there any quantity, however great, which cannot be consecrated.

I ANSWER THAT, Some have maintained that the priest could not consecrate an immense quantity of bread and wine, for instance, all the bread in the market or all the wine in a cask. But this does not appear to be true, because in all things containing matter, the reason for the determination of the matter is drawn from its disposition to an end, just as the matter of a saw is iron, so as to adapt it for cutting. But the end of this sacrament is the use of the faithful. Consequently, the quantity of the matter of this sacrament must be determined by comparison with the use of the faithful. But this cannot be determined by comparison with the use of the faithful who are actually present; otherwise the parish priest having few parishioners could not consecrate many hosts. It remains, then, for the matter of this sacrament to be determined in reference to the number of the faithful absolutely. But the number of the faithful is not a determinate one. Hence it cannot be said that the quantity of the matter of this sacrament is restricted.

AD PRIMUM ergo dicendum quod cuiuslibet rei naturalis materia accipit determinatam quantitatem secundum comparationem ad formam determinatam. Sed numerus fidelium, ad quorum usum ordinatur hoc sacramentum, est indeterminatus. Unde non est simile.

AD SECUNDUM dicendum quod potestas ministrorum Ecclesiae ad duo ordinatur, primo quidem, ad effectum proprium; secundo, ad finem effectus. Secundum autem non tollit primum. Unde, si sacerdos intendat consecrare corpus Christi propter aliquem malum finem, puta ut irrideat vel veneficia faciat, propter intentionem mali finis peccat, nihilominus tamen, propter potestatem sibi datam, perficit sacramentum.

AD TERTIUM dicendum quod Baptismi sacramentum perficitur in usu materiae. Et ideo per formam Baptismi non plus de aqua sanctificatur quam quantum venit in usum. Sed hoc sacramentum perficitur in consecratione materiae. Et ideo non est simile.

REPLY OBJ. 1: The matter of every natural object has its determinate quantity by comparison with its determinate form. But the number of the faithful, for whose use this sacrament is ordained, is not a determinate one. Consequently there is no comparison.

REPLY OBJ. 2: The power of the Church's ministers is ordained for two purposes: first for the proper effect, and second for the end of the effect. But the second does not take away the first. Hence, if the priest intends to consecrate the body of Christ for an evil purpose, for instance, to make mockery of it, or to administer poison through it, he commits sin by his evil intention, nevertheless, on account of the power committed to him, he accomplishes the sacrament.

REPLY OBJ. 3: The sacrament of Baptism is perfected in the use of the matter: and therefore no more of the water is hallowed than what is used. But this sacrament is wrought in the consecration of the matter. Consequently there is no parallel.

Article 3

Whether Wheaten Bread Is Required for the Matter of This Sacrament?

AD TERTIUM SIC PROCEDITUR. Videtur quod non requiratur ad materiam huius sacramenti quod sit panis triticeus. Hoc enim sacramentum est rememorativum dominicae passionis. Sed magis videtur esse consonum dominicae passioni panis hordeaceus, qui est asperior, et de quo etiam turbas pavit in monte, ut dicitur Ioan. VI, quam panis triticeus. Ergo non est propria materia huius sacramenti panis triticeus.

PRAETEREA, figura est signum speciei in rebus naturalibus. Sed quaedam frumenta sunt quae habent similem figuram grano tritici, sicut far et spelta, de qua etiam in quibusdam locis panis conficitur ad usum huius sacramenti. Ergo panis triticeus non est propria materia huius sacramenti.

PRAETEREA, permixtio speciem solvit. Sed vix invenitur farina triticea quae alterius frumenti permixtionem non habeat, nisi forte electis granis studiose fiat. Non ergo videtur quod panis triticeus sit propria materia huius sacramenti.

PRAETEREA, illud quod est corruptum, videtur esse alterius speciei. Sed aliqui conficiunt ex pane corrupto, qui iam non videtur esse panis triticeus. Ergo videtur quod talis panis non sit propria materia huius sacramenti.

SED CONTRA est quod in hoc sacramento continetur Christus, qui se grano frumenti comparat, Ioan. XII, dicens, *nisi granum frumenti, cadens in terram, mortuum*

OBJECTION 1: It seems that wheaten bread is not requisite for the matter of this sacrament, because this sacrament is a reminder of our Lord's Passion. But barley bread seems to be more in keeping with the Passion than wheaten bread, as being more bitter, and because Christ used it to feed the multitudes upon the mountain, as narrated in John 6. Therefore wheaten bread is not the proper matter of this sacrament.

OBJ. 2: Further, in natural things the shape is a sign of species. But some cereals resemble wheat, such as spelt and maize, from which in some localities bread is made for the use of this sacrament. Therefore wheaten bread is not the proper matter of this sacrament.

OBJ. 3: Further, mixing dissolves species. But wheaten flour is hardly to be found unmixed with some other species of grain, except in the instance of specially selected grain. Therefore it does not seem that wheaten bread is the proper matter for this sacrament.

OBJ. 4: Further, what is corrupted appears to be of another species. But some make the sacrament from bread which is corrupted, and which no longer seems to be wheaten bread. Therefore, it seems that such bread is not the proper matter of this sacrament.

ON THE CONTRARY, Christ is contained in this sacrament, and He compares Himself to a grain of wheat, saying (John 12:24): *Unless the grain of wheat falling into the*

fuerit, ipsum solum manet. Ergo panis frumentinus, sive triticeus, est materia huius sacramenti.

RESPONDEO dicendum quod, sicut dictum est, ad usum sacramentorum assumitur talis materia quae communius apud homines in talem usum venit. Inter alios autem panes communius homines utuntur pane triticeo, nam alii panes videntur esse introducti in huius panis defectum. Et ideo Christus creditur in huius panis specie hoc sacramentum instituisse. Qui etiam panis confortat hominem, et ita convenientius significat effectum huius sacramenti. Et ideo propria materia huius sacramenti est panis triticeus.

AD PRIMUM ergo dicendum quod panis hordeaceus competit ad significandum duritiem veteris legis. Tum propter duritiem panis. Tum quia etiam, ut Augustinus dicit, in libro octogintatrium quaestionum, *hordei medulla, quae tenacissima palea tegitur, vel ipsam legem significat, quae ita data erat ut in ea vitale animae alimentum corporalibus sacramentis obtegeretur, vel ipsum populum, nondum exspoliatum carnali desiderio, quod tanquam palea cordi eius inhaerebat.* Hoc autem sacramentum pertinet ad suave iugum Christi, et ad veritatem iam manifestatam, et ad populum spiritualem. Unde non esset materia conveniens huius sacramenti panis hordeaceus.

AD SECUNDUM dicendum quod generans generat sibi simile in specie, fit tamen aliquando aliqua dissimilitudo generantis ad genitum quantum ad accidentia, vel propter materiam, vel propter debilitatem virtutis generativae. Et ideo, si qua frumenta sunt quae ex semine tritici generari possunt, sicut ex grano seminato in malis terris nascitur siligo, ex tali frumento panis confectus potest esse materia huius sacramenti. Quod tamen non videtur habere locum neque in hordeo, neque in spelta, neque etiam in farre, quod inter omnia est grano tritici similius. Similitudo autem figurae in talibus magis videtur significare propinquitatem quam identitatem speciei, sicut ex similitudine figurae manifestatur quod canis et lupus sunt propinquae speciei, non autem eiusdem. Unde ex talibus frumentis, quae nullo modo possunt ex semine grani generari, non potest confici panis qui sit debita materia huius sacramenti.

AD TERTIUM dicendum quod modica permixtio non solvit speciem, quia id quod est modicum, quodammodo absumitur a plurimo. Et ideo, si sit modica admixtio alterius frumenti ad multo maiorem quantitatem tritici, poterit exinde confici panis qui est materia huius sacramenti. Si vero sit magna permixtio, puta ex aequo vel quasi, talis commixtio speciem mutat. Unde panis inde confectus non erit materia debita huius sacramenti.

AD QUARTUM dicendum quod aliquando est tanta corruptio panis quod solvitur species panis, sicut cum continuitas solvitur, et sapor et color et alia accidentia

ground die, itself remaineth alone. Therefore bread from corn, i.e., wheaten bread, is the matter of this sacrament.

I ANSWER THAT, As stated above (A. 1), for the use of the sacraments such matter is adopted as is commonly made use of among men. Now among other breads wheaten bread is more commonly used by men; since other breads seem to be employed when this fails. And consequently Christ is believed to have instituted this sacrament under this species of bread. Moreover this bread strengthens man, and so it denotes more suitably the effect of this sacrament. Consequently, the proper matter for this sacrament is wheaten bread.

REPLY OBJ. 1: Barley bread serves to denote the hardness of the Old Law; both on account of the hardness of the bread, and because, as Augustine says (Q. 83): *The flour within the barley, wrapped up as it is within a most tenacious fibre, denotes either the Law itself, which was given in such manner as to be vested in bodily sacraments; or else it denotes the people themselves, who were not yet despoiled of carnal desires, which clung to their hearts like fibre.* But this sacrament belongs to Christ's *sweet yoke,* and to the truth already manifested, and to a spiritual people. Consequently barley bread would not be a suitable matter for this sacrament.

REPLY OBJ. 2: A begetter begets a thing like to itself in species, yet there is some unlikeness as to the accidents, owing either to the matter, or to weakness within the generative power. And therefore, if there be any cereals which can be grown from the seed of the wheat (as wild wheat from wheat seed grown in bad ground), the bread made from such grain can be the matter of this sacrament: and this does not obtain either in barley, or in spelt, or even in maize, which is of all grains the one most resembling the wheat grain. But the resemblance as to shape in such seems to denote closeness of species rather than identity; just as the resemblance in shape between the dog and the wolf goes to show that they are allied but not of the same species. Hence from such grains, which cannot in any way be generated from wheat grain, bread cannot be made such as to be the proper matter of this sacrament.

REPLY OBJ. 3: A moderate mixing does not alter the species, because that little is as it were absorbed by the greater. Consequently, then, if a small quantity of another grain be mixed with a much greater quantity of wheat, bread may be made therefrom so as to be the proper matter of this sacrament; but if the mixing be notable, for instance, half and half; or nearly so, then such mixing alters the species; consequently, bread made therefrom will not be the proper matter of this sacrament.

REPLY OBJ. 4: Sometimes there is such corruption of the bread that the species of bread is lost, as when the continuity of its parts is destroyed, and the taste, color, and other

mutantur. Unde ex tali materia non potest confici corpus Christi. Aliquando vero non est tanta corruptio quae speciem solvat, sed est aliqua dispositio ad corruptionem, quod declarat aliqualis immutatio saporis. Et ex tali pane potest confici corpus Christi, sed peccat conficiens, propter irreverentiam sacramenti. Et quia amidum est ex tritico corrupto, non videtur quod panis ex eo confectus possit fieri corpus Christi, quamvis quidam contrarium dicant.

accidents are changed; hence the body of Christ may not be made from such matter. But sometimes there is not such corruption as to alter the species, but merely disposition towards corruption, which a slight change in the savor betrays, and from such bread the body of Christ may be made: but he who does so, sins from irreverence towards the sacrament. And because starch comes of corrupted wheat, it does not seem as if the body of Christ could be made of the bread made therefrom, although some hold the contrary.

Article 4

Whether This Sacrament Ought to Be Made of Unleavened Bread?

AD QUARTUM SIC PROCEDITUR. Videtur quod hoc sacramentum non debeat confici ex pane azymo. Debemus enim in hoc sacramento imitari institutionem Christi. Sed Christus videtur hoc sacramentum instituisse in pane fermentato, quia, sicut legitur Exod. XII, Iudaei secundum legem incipiebant uti azymis in die Paschae, quod celebratur quartadecima luna; Christus autem instituit hoc sacramentum in cena, quam celebravit ante diem Paschae, ut habetur Ioan. XIII. Ergo et nos debemus hoc sacramentum celebrare in pane fermentato.

PRAETEREA, legalia non sunt observanda tempore gratiae. Sed uti azymis fuit quaedam legalis caeremonia, ut patet Exod. XII. Ergo in hoc sacramento gratiae non debemus azymis uti.

PRAETEREA, sicut supra dictum est, Eucharistia est sacramentum caritatis, sicut Baptismus fidei. Sed fervor caritatis significatur per fermentum, ut patet in Glossa, super illud Matth. XIII, *simile est regnum caelorum fermento* et cetera. Ergo hoc sacramentum debet confici de pane fermentato.

PRAETEREA, azymum et fermentatum sunt accidentia panis, non variantia eius speciem. Sed in materia Baptismi nulla discretio adhibetur circa differentiam accidentium aquae, puta si sit salsa vel dulcis, calida vel frigida. Ergo in hoc sacramento aliqua discretio adhiberi non debet utrum panis sit azymus vel fermentatus.

SED CONTRA est quod extra, de Celebrat. Missar., cap. litteras, punitur sacerdos qui *in pane fermentato et scypho ligneo Missarum solemnia celebrare praesumpsit.*

RESPONDEO dicendum quod circa materiam huius sacramenti duo possunt considerari, scilicet quid sit necessarium, et quid conveniens. Necessarium quidem est ut sit panis triticeus, sicut dictum est, sine quo non perficitur sacramentum. Non est autem de necessitate

OBJECTION 1: It seems that this sacrament ought not to be made of unleavened bread. Because in this sacrament we ought to imitate Christ's institution. But Christ appears to have instituted this sacrament in fermented bread, because, as we have read in Ex. 12, the Jews, according to the Law, began to use unleavened bread on the day of the Passover which is celebrated on the fourteenth day of the moon; and Christ instituted this sacrament at the supper which He celebrated *before the festival day of the Pasch* (John 13:1, 4). Therefore we ought likewise to celebrate this sacrament with fermented bread.

OBJ. 2: Further, legal observances ought not to be continued in the time of grace. But the use of unleavened bread was a ceremony of the Law, as is clear from Ex. 12. Therefore we ought not to use unfermented bread in this sacrament of grace.

OBJ. 3: Further, as stated above (Q. 65, A. 1; Q. 73, A. 3), the Eucharist is the sacrament of charity just as Baptism is the sacrament of faith. But the fervor of charity is signified by fermented bread, as is declared by the gloss on Matt. 13:33: *The kingdom of heaven is like unto leaven*, etc. Therefore this sacrament ought to be made of leavened bread.

OBJ. 4: Further, leavened or unleavened are mere accidents of bread, which do not vary the species. But in the matter for the sacrament of Baptism no difference is observed regarding the variation of the accidents, as to whether it be salt or fresh, warm or cold water. Therefore neither ought any distinction to be observed, as to whether the bread be unleavened or leavened.

ON THE CONTRARY, According to the *Decretals* (Extra, *De Celebr. Miss.*), a priest is punished *for presuming to celebrate, using fermented bread and a wooden cup.*

I ANSWER THAT, Two things may be considered touching the matter of this sacrament, namely, what is necessary, and what is suitable. It is necessary that the bread be wheaten, without which the sacrament is not valid, as stated above (A. 3). It is not, however, necessary for the sacrament

sacramenti quod sit azymus vel fermentatus, quia in utroque confici potest.

Conveniens autem est ut unusquisque servet ritum suae Ecclesiae in celebratione sacramenti. Super hoc autem sunt diversae Ecclesiarum consuetudines. Dicit enim beatus Gregorius, in registro, *Romana Ecclesia offert azymos panes, propterea quod dominus sine ulla commixtione suscepit carnem. Sed ceterae Ecclesiae offerunt fermentatum, pro eo quod verbum patris indutum est carne, sicut et fermentum miscetur farinae.* Unde, sicut peccat sacerdos in Ecclesia Latinorum celebrans de pane fermentato, ita peccaret presbyter Graecus in Ecclesia Graecorum celebrans de azymo pane, quasi pervertens Ecclesiae suae ritum. Et tamen consuetudo de pane azymo celebrandi rationabilior est. Primo quidem, propter institutionem Christi, qui hoc sacramentum instituit prima die azymorum, ut habetur Matth. XXVI, et Marc. XIV, et Luc. XXII, qua die nihil fermentatum in domibus Iudaeorum esse debebat, ut habetur Exod. XII. Secundo, quia panis est proprie sacramentum corporis Christi, quod sine corruptione conceptum est, magis quam divinitatis ipsius, ut infra patebit. Tertio, quia hoc magis competit sinceritati fidelium, quae requiritur ad usum huius sacramenti, secundum illud I Cor. V, *Pascha nostrum immolatus est Christus, itaque epulemur in azymis sinceritatis et veritatis.*

Habet tamen haec consuetudo Graecorum aliquam rationem, et propter significationem, quam tangit Gregorius; et in detestationem haeresis Nazaraeorum, qui legalia Evangelio miscebant.

AD PRIMUM ergo dicendum quod, sicut legitur Exod. XII, solemnitas paschalis incipiebat a vesperis quartae-decimae lunae. Et tunc Christus, post immolationem agni paschalis, hoc sacramentum instituit. Unde hic dies a Ioanne dicitur praecedere sequentem diem Paschae, et a tribus aliis Evangelistis dicitur prima dies azymorum, quando fermentatum in domibus Iudaeorum non inveniebatur, ut dictum est. Et de hoc supra notatum est plenius in tractatu dominicae passionis.

AD SECUNDUM dicendum quod conficientes ex azymo non intendunt caeremonias legis servare, sed conformare se institutioni Christi. Et ideo non iudaizant. Alioquin et celebrantes in pane fermentato iudaizarent, quia Iudaei panes primitiarum fermentatos offerebant.

AD TERTIUM dicendum quod fermentum significat caritatem propter aliquem effectum, quia scilicet panem facit sapidiorem et maiorem. Sed corruptionem significat ex ipsa ratione suae speciei.

AD QUARTUM dicendum quod, quia fermentum habet aliquid corruptionis, et ex pane corrupto non potest confici hoc sacramentum, ut dictum est; ideo magis attenditur circa panem differentia azymi et fermentati quam circa aquam Baptismi differentia calidi et frigidi.

that the bread be unleavened or leavened, since it can be celebrated in either.

But it is suitable that every priest observe the rite of his Church in the celebration of the sacrament. Now in this matter there are various customs of the Churches: for, Gregory says: *The Roman Church offers unleavened bread, because our Lord took flesh without union of sexes: but the Greek Churches offer leavened bread, because the Word of the Father was clothed with flesh; as leaven is mixed with the flour.* Hence, as a priest sins by celebrating with fermented bread in the Latin Church, so a Greek priest celebrating with unfermented bread in a church of the Greeks would also sin, as perverting the rite of his Church. Nevertheless the custom of celebrating with unleavened bread is more reasonable. First, on account of Christ's institution: for He instituted this sacrament *on the first day of the Azymes* (Matt 26:17; Mk. 14:12; Luke 22:7), on which day there ought to be nothing fermented in the houses of the Jews, as is stated in Ex. 12:15, 19. Second, because bread is properly the sacrament of Christ's body, which was conceived without corruption, rather than of His Godhead, as will be seen later (Q. 76, A. 1, ad 1). Third, because this is more in keeping with the sincerity of the faithful, which is required in the use of this sacrament, according to 1 Cor. 5:7: *Christ our Pasch is sacrificed: therefore let us feast . . . with the unleavened bread of sincerity and truth.*

However, this custom of the Greeks is not unreasonable both on account of its signification, to which Gregory refers, and in detestation of the heresy of the Nazarenes, who mixed up legal observances with the Gospel.

REPLY OBJ. 1: As we read in Ex. 12, the paschal solemnity began on the evening of the fourteenth day of the moon. So, then, after immolating the Paschal Lamb, Christ instituted this sacrament: hence this day is said by John to precede the day of the Pasch, while the other three Evangelists call it *the first day of the Azymes*, when fermented bread was not found in the houses of the Jews, as stated above. Fuller mention was made of this in the treatise on our Lord's Passion (Q. 46, A. 9, ad 1).

REPLY OBJ. 2: Those who celebrate the sacrament with unleavened bread do not intend to follow the ceremonial of the Law, but to conform to Christ's institution; so they are not Judaizing; otherwise those celebrating in fermented bread would be Judaizing, because the Jews offered up fermented bread for the first-fruits.

REPLY OBJ. 3: Leaven denotes charity on account of one single effect, because it makes the bread more savory and larger; but it also signifies corruption from its very nature.

REPLY OBJ. 4: Since whatever is fermented partakes of corruption, this sacrament may not be made from corrupt bread, as stated above (A. 3, ad 4); consequently, there is a wider difference between unleavened and leavened bread than between warm and cold baptismal water: because

Posset enim tanta esse corruptio fermenti quod ex eo non posset fieri sacramentum.

there might be such corruption of fermented bread that it could not be validly used for the sacrament.

Article 5

Whether Wine of the Grape Is the Proper Matter of This Sacrament?

AD QUINTUM SIC PROCEDITUR. Videtur quod non sit propria materia huius sacramenti vinum vitis. Sicut enim aqua est materia Baptismi, ita vinum est materia huius sacramenti. Sed in qualibet aqua potest fieri Baptismus. Ergo in quolibet vino, puta malorum granatorum vel mororum aut huiusmodi, potest confici hoc sacramentum, praesertim cum in quibusdam terris vites non crescant.

PRAETEREA, acetum est quaedam species vini quod de vite sumitur, ut Isidorus dicit. Sed de aceto non potest confici hoc sacramentum. Ergo videtur quod vinum vitis non sit propria materia huius sacramenti.

PRAETEREA, sicut de vite sumitur vinum depuratum, ita et agresta et mustum. Sed de his non videtur confici posse hoc sacramentum, secundum illud quod in sexta synodo legitur, *didicimus quod in quibusdam Ecclesiis sacerdotes sacrificio oblationis coniungunt uvas, et sic simul utrumque populo dispensant. Praecipimus igitur ut nullus sacerdos hoc ulterius faciat.* Et Iulius Papa reprehendit quosdam qui *expressum vinum in sacramento dominici calicis offerunt.* Ergo videtur quod vinum vitis non sit propria materia huius sacramenti.

SED CONTRA est quod, sicut dominus comparavit se grano frumenti, ita etiam se comparavit viti, dicens, Ioan. XV, *ego sum vitis vera.* Sed solus panis de frumento est materia huius sacramenti, ut dictum est. Ergo solum vinum de vite est propria materia huius sacramenti.

RESPONDEO dicendum quod de solo vino vitis potest confici hoc sacramentum. Primo quidem, propter institutionem Christi, qui in vino vitis hoc sacramentum instituit, ut patet ex eo quod ipse dicit, Luc. XXII, circa institutionem huius sacramenti, *amodo non bibam de hoc genimine vitis.* Secundo quia, sicut dictum est, ad materiam sacramentorum assumitur id quod proprie et communiter habet talem speciem. Proprie autem vinum dicitur quod de vite sumitur, alii autem liquores vinum dicuntur secundum quandam similitudinem ad vinum vitis. Tertio, quia vinum vitis magis competit ad effectum huius sacramenti, qui est spiritualis laetitia, quia scriptum est quod *vinum laetificat cor hominis.*

OBJECTION 1: It seems that wine of the grape is not the proper matter of this sacrament. Because, as water is the matter of Baptism, so is wine the matter of this sacrament. But Baptism can be conferred with any kind of water. Therefore this sacrament can be celebrated in any kind of wine, such as of pomegranates, or of mulberries; since vines do not grow in some countries.

OBJ. 2: Further, vinegar is a kind of wine drawn from the grape, as Isidore says (*Etym.* xx). But this sacrament cannot be celebrated with vinegar. Therefore, it seems that wine from the grape is not the proper matter of this sacrament.

OBJ. 3: Further, just as the clarified wine is drawn from grapes, so also are the juice of unripe grapes and must. But it does not appear that this sacrament may be made from such, according to what we read in the Sixth Council (*Trull.*, Can. 28): *We have learned that in some churches the priests add grapes to the sacrifice of the oblation; and so they dispense both together to the people. Consequently we give order that no priest shall do this in future.* And Pope Julius I rebukes some priests *who offer wine pressed from the grape in the sacrament of the Lord's chalice.* Consequently, it seems that wine from the grape is not the proper matter of this sacrament.

ON THE CONTRARY, As our Lord compared Himself to the grain of wheat, so also He compared Himself to the vine, saying (John 15:1): *I am the true vine.* But only bread from wheat is the matter of this sacrament, as stated above (A. 3). Therefore, only wine from the grape is the proper matter of this sacrament.

I ANSWER THAT, This sacrament can only be performed with wine from the grape. First of all on account of Christ's institution, since He instituted this sacrament in wine from the grape, as is evident from His own words, in instituting this sacrament (Matt 26:29): *I will not drink from henceforth of this fruit of the vine.* Second, because, as stated above (A. 3), that is adopted as the matter of the sacraments which is properly and universally considered as such. Now that is properly called wine, which is drawn from the grape, whereas other liquors are called wine from resemblance to the wine of the grape. Third, because the wine from the grape is more in keeping with the effect of this sacrament, which is spiritual; because it is written (Ps 103:15): *That wine may cheer the heart of man.*

AD PRIMUM ergo dicendum quod illi liquores non dicuntur proprie vinum, sed secundum similitudinem. Potest autem verum vinum ad terras illas deferri in quibus vites non crescunt, quantum sufficit ad hoc sacramentum.

AD SECUNDUM dicendum quod vinum fit acetum per corruptionem, unde non fit reditus de aceto in vinum, ut dicitur VIII Metaphys. Et ideo, sicut de pane totaliter corrupto non potest confici hoc sacramentum, ita nec de aceto potest confici. Potest tamen confici de vino acescenti, sicut de pane qui est in via ad corruptionem, licet peccet conficiens, ut prius dictum est.

AD TERTIUM dicendum quod agresta est in via generationis, et ideo nondum habet speciem vini. Et propter hoc de ea non potest confici hoc sacramentum. Mustum autem iam habet speciem vini, nam eius dulcedo attestatur digestioni, quae est *completio a naturali calore*, ut dicitur in IV Meteor. Et ideo de musto potest confici hoc sacramentum. Non tamen debent uvae integrae huic sacramento misceri, quia iam esset ibi aliquid praeter vinum. Prohibetur etiam ne mustum statim expressum de uva in calice offeratur, quia hoc est indecens, propter impuritatem musti. Potest tamen in necessitate fieri, dicitur enim ab eodem Iulio Papa, *si necesse fuerit, botrus in calicem prematur.*

REPLY OBJ. 1: Such liquors are called wine, not properly but only from their resemblance thereto. But genuine wine can be conveyed to such countries wherein the grapevine does not flourish, in a quantity sufficient for this sacrament.

REPLY OBJ. 2: Wine becomes vinegar by corruption; hence there is no returning from vinegar to wine, as is said in *Metaph.* viii. And consequently, just as this sacrament may not be made from bread which is utterly corrupt, so neither can it be made from vinegar. It can, however, be made from wine which is turning sour, just as from bread turning corrupt, although he who does so sins, as stated above (A. 3).

REPLY OBJ. 3: The juice of unripe grapes is at the stage of incomplete generation, and therefore it has not yet the species of wine: on which account it may not be used for this sacrament. Must, however, has already the species of wine, for its sweetness indicates fermentation which is *the result of its natural heat* (*Meteor.* iv); consequently this sacrament can be made from must. Nevertheless entire grapes ought not to be mixed with this sacrament, because then there would be something else besides wine. It is furthermore forbidden to offer must in the chalice, as soon as it has been squeezed from the grape, since this is unbecoming owing to the impurity of the must. But in case of necessity it may be done: for it is said by the same Pope Julius, in the passage quoted in the argument: *If necessary, let the grape be pressed into the chalice.*

Article 6

Whether Water Should Be Mixed with the Wine?

AD SEXTUM SIC PROCEDITUR. Videtur quod aqua non sit vino permiscenda. Sacrificium enim Christi figuratum fuit per oblationem Melchisedech, qui, Gen. XIV, non legitur obtulisse nisi panem et vinum. Ergo videtur quod in hoc sacramento non debeat adiungi aqua.

PRAETEREA, diversorum sacramentorum diversae sunt materiae. Sed aqua est materia Baptismi. Ergo non debet ad materiam assumi huius sacramenti.

PRAETEREA, panis et vinum sunt materia huius sacramenti. Sed pani nihil adiungitur. Ergo nec vino debet aliquid adiungi.

SED CONTRA est quod Alexander Papa scribit, *in sacramentorum oblationibus quae inter Missarum solemnia domino offeruntur, panis tantum et vinum aqua permixtum in sacrificium offerantur.*

RESPONDEO dicendum quod vino quod offertur in hoc sacramento debet aqua misceri. Primo quidem, propter institutionem. Probabiliter enim creditur quod

OBJECTION 1: It seems that water ought not to be mixed with the wine, since Christ's sacrifice was foreshadowed by that of Melchisedech, who (Gen 14:18) is related to have offered up bread and wine only. Consequently it seems that water should not be added in this sacrament.

OBJ. 2: Further, the various sacraments have their respective matters. But water is the matter of Baptism. Therefore it should not be employed as the matter of this sacrament.

OBJ. 3: Further, bread and wine are the matter of this sacrament. But nothing is added to the bread. Therefore neither should anything be added to the wine.

ON THE CONTRARY, Pope Alexander I writes (*Ep. 1 ad omnes orth.*): *In the sacramental oblations which in Mass are offered to the Lord, only bread and wine mixed with water are to be offered in sacrifice.*

I ANSWER THAT, Water ought to be mingled with the wine which is offered in this sacrament. First of all on account of its institution: for it is believed with probability

dominus hoc sacramentum instituerit in vino aqua permixto, secundum morem terrae illius, unde et Proverb. IX dicitur, *bibite vinum quod miscui vobis.* Secundo, quia hoc convenit repraesentationi dominicae passionis. Unde dicit Alexander Papa, *non debet in calice domini aut vinum solum, aut aqua sola offerri, sed utrumque permixtum, quia utrumque ex latere Christi in passione sua profluxisse legitur.* Tertio, quia hoc convenit ad significandum effectum huius sacramenti, qui est unio populi Christiani ad Christum, quia, ut Iulius Papa dicit, *videmus in aqua populum intelligi, in vino vero ostendi sanguinem Christi. Ergo, cum in calice vino aqua miscetur, Christo populus adunatur.* Quarto, quia hoc competit ad ultimum effectum huius sacramenti, qui est introitus ad vitam aeternam. Unde Ambrosius dicit, in libro de sacramentis, *redundat aqua in calicem, et salit in vitam aeternam.*

AD PRIMUM ergo dicendum quod, sicut Ambrosius dicit ibidem, sicut sacrificium Christi significatum est per oblationem Melchisedech, ita etiam significatum est per aquam quae in eremo fluxit de petra, secundum illud I Cor. X, *bibebant autem de spirituali consequente eos petra.*

AD SECUNDUM dicendum quod aqua sumitur in Baptismo ad usum ablutionis. In hoc autem sacramento assumitur ad usum refectionis, secundum illud Psalmi, *super aquam refectionis educavit me.*

AD TERTIUM dicendum quod panis ex aqua et farina conficitur. Et ideo, cum vino aqua miscetur, neutrum sine aqua existit.

that our Lord instituted this sacrament in wine tempered with water according to the custom of that country: hence it is written (Prov 9:5): *Drink the wine which I have mixed for you.* Second, because it harmonizes with the representation of our Lord's Passion: hence Pope Alexander I says (*Ep. 1 ad omnes orth.*): *In the Lord's chalice neither wine only nor water only ought to be offered, but both mixed because we read that both flowed from His side in the Passion.* Third, because this is adapted for signifying the effect of this sacrament, since as Pope Julius says (*Concil. Bracarens* iii, Can. 1): *We see that the people are signified by the water, but Christ's blood by the wine. Therefore when water is mixed with the wine in the chalice, the people is made one with Christ.* Fourth, because this is appropriate to the fourth effect of this sacrament, which is the entering into everlasting life: hence Ambrose says (*De Sacram. v*): *The water flows into the chalice, and springs forth unto everlasting life.*

REPLY OBJ. 1: As Ambrose says (*De Sacram. v*), just as Christ's sacrifice is denoted by the offering of Melchisedech, so likewise it is signified by the water which flowed from the rock in the desert, according to 1 Cor. 10:4: *But they drank of the spiritual rock which came after them.*

REPLY OBJ. 2: In Baptism water is used for the purpose of ablution: but in this sacrament it is used by way of refreshment, according to Ps. 22:3: *He hath brought me up on the water of refreshment.*

REPLY OBJ. 3: Bread is made of water and flour; and therefore, since water is mixed with the wine, neither is without water.

Article 7

Whether the Mixing with Water Is Essential to This Sacrament?

AD SEPTIMUM SIC PROCEDITUR. Videtur quod permixtio aquae sit de necessitate huius sacramenti. Dicit enim Cyprianus, ad Caecilium, *sic calix domini non est aqua sola et vinum solum, nisi utrumque misceatur, quomodo nec corpus domini potest esse farina sola, nisi utrumque, scilicet farina et aqua, fuerit adunatum.* Sed admixtio aquae ad farinam est de necessitate huius sacramenti ergo, pari ratione, admixtio aquae ad vinum.

PRAETEREA, in passione domini, cuius hoc sacramentum est memoriale, sicut, de latere eius exivit sanguis, ita et aqua. Sed vinum, quod est sacramentum sanguinis, est de necessitate huius sacramenti. Ergo, pari ratione, et aqua.

PRAETEREA, si aqua non esset de necessitate huius sacramenti, non referret quaecumque aqua huic sacramento apponeretur, et ita posset apponi aqua rosacea,

OBJECTION 1: It seems that the mixing with water is essential to this sacrament. Because Cyprian says to Cecilius (*Ep. lxiii*): *Thus the Lord's chalice is not water only and wine only, but both must be mixed together: in the same way as neither the Lord's body be of flour only, except both*, i.e., the flour and the water *be united as one.* But the admixture of water with the flour is necessary for this sacrament. Consequently, for the like reason, so is the mixing of water with the wine.

OBJ. 2: Further, at our Lord's Passion, of which this is the memorial, water as well as blood flowed from His side. But wine, which is the sacrament of the blood, is necessary for this sacrament. For the same reason, therefore, so is water.

OBJ. 3: Further, if water were not essential to this sacrament, it would not matter in the least what kind of water was used; and so water distilled from roses, or any other

vel quaecumque alia huiusmodi aqua. Quod non habet usus Ecclesiae. Aqua ergo est de necessitate huius sacramenti.

Sed contra est quod Cyprianus dicit, *si quis de antecessoribus nostris ignoranter vel simpliciter non observavit*, ut scilicet aquam vino misceret in sacramento, *potest simplicitati eius venia concedi*. Quod non esset si aqua esset de necessitate sacramenti, sicut est vinum vel panis. Non ergo aquae admixtio est de necessitate sacramenti.

Respondeo dicendum quod iudicium de signo sumendum est ex eo quod significatur. Appositio autem aquae ad vinum refertur ad significandum participationem huius sacramenti a fidelibus, quantum ad hoc quod per aquam mixtam vino significatur populus adunatus Christo, ut dictum est. Sed et hoc ipsum quod de latere Christi pendentis in cruce aqua profluxit, ad idem refertur, quia per aquam significabatur ablutio peccatorum, quae fiebat per passionem Christi. Dictum est autem supra quod hoc sacramentum perficitur in consecratione materiae, usus autem fidelium non est de necessitate sacramenti, sed est aliquid consequens ad sacramentum. Et ideo consequens est quod appositio aquae non sit de necessitate sacramenti.

Ad primum ergo dicendum quod verbum illud Cypriani est intelligendum secundum quod dicitur illud esse non posse quod convenienter esse non potest. Et sic similitudo illa attenditur quantum ad illud quod debet fieri, non autem quantum ad necessitatem, nam aqua est de essentia panis, non autem de essentia vini.

Ad secundum dicendum quod effusio sanguinis directe pertinebat ad ipsam Christi passionem, est enim naturale corpori humano vulnerato quod ex eo profluat sanguis. Sed effusio aquae non fuit de necessitate passionis, sed ad demonstrandum effectum, qui est ablutio a peccatis et refrigerium contra ardorem concupiscentiae. Et ideo aqua non seorsum offertur a vino in hoc sacramento, sicut vinum seorsum offertur a pane, sed aqua offertur vino permixta, ut ostendatur quod vinum per se pertinet ad hoc sacramentum, tanquam de eius necessitate existens, aqua autem secundum quod adiungitur vino.

Ad tertium dicendum quod, quia admixtio aquae ad vinum non est de necessitate sacramenti, non refert, quantum ad necessitatem sacramenti, quaecumque aqua misceatur vino, sive naturalis sive artificialis, ut rosacea. Quamvis, quantum ad convenientiam sacramenti, peccet qui aliam aquam miscet nisi naturalem et veram, quia de latere Christi pendentis in cruce vera aqua profluxit, non humor phlegmaticus, ut quidam dixerunt, ad ostendendum quod corpus Christi erat vere compositum ex quatuor elementis; sicut per sanguinem fluentem ostendebatur quod erat compositum ex quatuor humoribus; ut Innocentius III dicit in quadam decretali. Quia

kind might be employed; which is contrary to the usage of the Church. Consequently water is essential to this sacrament.

On the contrary, Cyprian says (*Ep. lxiii*): *If any of our predecessors, out of ignorance or simplicity, has not kept this usage,* i.e., of mixing water with the wine, *one may pardon his simplicity*; which would not be the case if water were essential to the sacrament, as the wine or the bread. Therefore the mingling of water with the wine is not essential to the sacrament.

I answer that, Judgment concerning a sign is to be drawn from the thing signified. Now the adding of water to the wine is for the purpose of signifying the sharing of this sacrament by the faithful, in this respect that by the mixing of the water with the wine is signified the union of the people with Christ, as stated (A. 6). Moreover, the flowing of water from the side of Christ hanging on the cross refers to the same, because by the water is denoted the cleansing from sins, which was the effect of Christ's Passion. Now it was observed above (Q. 73, A. 1, ad 3), that this sacrament is completed in the consecration of the matter: while the usage of the faithful is not essential to the sacrament, but only a consequence thereof. Consequently, then, the adding of water is not essential to the sacrament.

Reply Obj. 1: Cyprian's expression is to be taken in the same sense in which we say that a thing cannot be, which cannot be suitably. And so the comparison refers to what ought to be done, not to what is essential to be done; since water is of the essence of bread, but not of the essence of wine.

Reply Obj. 2: The shedding of the blood belonged directly to Christ's Passion: for it is natural for blood to flow from a wounded human body. But the flowing of the water was not necessary for the Passion; but merely to show its effect, which is to wash away sins, and to refresh us from the heat of concupiscence. And therefore the water is not offered apart from the wine in this sacrament, as the wine is offered apart from the bread; but the water is offered mixed with the wine to show that the wine belongs of itself to this sacrament, as of its very essence; but the water as something added to the wine.

Reply Obj. 3: Since the mixing of water with the wine is not necessary for the sacrament, it does not matter, as to the essence of the sacrament, what kind of water is added to the wine, whether natural water, or artificial, as rose-water, although, as to the propriety of the sacrament, he would sin who mixes any other than natural and true water, because true water flowed from the side of Christ hanging on the cross, and not phlegm, as some have said, in order to show that Christ's body was truly composed of the four elements; as by the flowing blood, it was shown to be composed of the four humors, as Pope Innocent III says in a certain Decree. But because the mixing of water with flour is essential

vero admixtio aquae ad farinam est de necessitate huius sacramenti, utpote constituens substantiam panis; si farinae admisceretur aqua rosacea, vel quicumque alius liquor quam vera aqua, non posset ex eo confici sacramentum, quia non est vere panis.

to this sacrament, as making the composition of bread, if rose-water, or any other liquor besides true water, be mixed with the flour, the sacrament would not be valid, because it would not be true bread.

Article 8

Whether Water Should Be Added in Great Quantity?

AD OCTAVUM SIC PROCEDITUR. Videtur quod debeat aqua in magna quantitate apponi. Sicut enim sanguis de latere Christi sensibiliter fluxit, ita et aqua, unde dicitur Ioan. XIX, *qui vidit, testimonium perhibuit.* Sed aqua non posset sensibiliter esse in hoc sacramento nisi in magna quantitate poneretur. Ergo videtur quod aqua debeat apponi in magna quantitate.

PRAETEREA, parva aqua multo vino admixta corrumpitur. Quod autem corruptum est, non est. Ergo idem est apponere parum de aqua in hoc sacramento, et nihil apponere. Sed non licet nihil apponere. Ergo non licet parum apponere.

PRAETEREA, si sufficeret parum apponere, per consequens esset sufficiens quod gutta aquae in totum dolium proiiceretur. Sed hoc videtur ridiculum. Ergo non sufficit quod parva quantitas ponatur.

SED CONTRA est quod extra, de Celebrat. Missar., dicitur, *perniciosus in tuis partibus inolevit abusus, videlicet quod in maiori quantitate de aqua ponitur in sacrificio quam de vino, cum, secundum rationabilem consuetudinem Ecclesiae generalis, plus in ipso sit de vino quam de aqua ponendum.*

RESPONDEO dicendum quod circa aquam adiunctam vino, ut Innocentius III dicit, in quadam decretali, triplex est opinio. Quidam enim dicunt quod aqua adiuncta vino per se manet, vino converso in sanguinem. Sed haec opinio omnino stare non potest. Quia in sacramento altaris, post consecrationem, nihil est nisi corpus et sanguis Christi, sicut Ambrosius dicit, in libro de officiis, *ante benedictionem alia species nominatur, post benedictionem corpus significatur.* Alioquin non adoraretur veneratione latriae. Et ideo alii dixerunt quod, sicut vinum convertitur in sanguinem, ita aqua convertitur in aquam quae de latere Christi fluxit. Sed hoc non rationabiliter dici potest. Quia secundum hoc, aqua seorsum consecraretur a vino, sicut vinum a pane.

Et ideo, sicut ipse dicit, aliorum opinio probabilior est, qui dicunt aquam converti in vinum, et vinum in sanguinem. Hoc autem fieri non posset nisi adeo modicum apponeretur de aqua quod converteretur in vinum. Et ideo semper tutius est parum de aqua apponere, et

OBJECTION 1: It seems that water ought to be added in great quantity, because as blood flowed sensibly from Christ's side, so did water: hence it is written (John 19:35): *He that saw it, hath given testimony.* But water could not be sensibly present in this sacrament except it were used in great quantity. Consequently it seems that water ought to be added in great quantity.

OBJ. 2: Further, a little water mixed with much wine is corrupted. But what is corrupted no longer exists. Therefore, it is the same thing to add a little water in this sacrament as to add none. But it is not lawful to add none. Therefore, neither is it lawful to add a little.

OBJ. 3: Further, if it sufficed to add a little, then as a consequence it would suffice to throw one drop of water into an entire cask. But this seems ridiculous. Therefore it does not suffice for a small quantity to be added.

ON THE CONTRARY, It is said in the *Decretals* (Extra, *De Celeb. Miss.*): *The pernicious abuse has prevailed in your country of adding water in greater quantity than the wine, in the sacrifice, where according to the reasonable custom of the entire Church more wine than water ought to be employed.*

I ANSWER THAT, There is a threefold opinion regarding the water added to the wine, as Pope Innocent III says in a certain *Decretal*. For some say that the water remains by itself when the wine is changed into blood: but such an opinion cannot stand, because in the sacrament of the altar after the consecration there is nothing else save the body and the blood of Christ. Because, as Ambrose says in *De Officiis* (*De Mysteriis* ix): *Before the blessing it is another species that is named, after the blessing the Body is signified; otherwise it would not be adored with adoration of latria.* And therefore others have said that as the wine is changed into blood, so the water is changed into the water which flowed from Christ's side. But this cannot be maintained reasonably, because according to this the water would be consecrated apart from the wine, as the wine is from the bread.

And therefore as he (Innocent III, *Decretals*, Extra, *De Celeb. Miss.*) says, the more probable opinion is that which holds that the water is changed into wine, and the wine into blood. Now, this could not be done unless so little water was used that it would be changed into wine. Consequently,

praecipue si vinum sit debile, quia, si tanta fieret appositio aquae quod solveretur species vini, non posset perfici sacramentum. Unde Iulius Papa reprehendit quosdam qui *pannum lineum musto intinctum per totum annum servant, et in tempore sacrificii aqua partem eius lavant, et sic offerunt.*

AD PRIMUM ergo dicendum quod sufficit ad significationem huius sacramenti quod sentiatur aqua dum apponitur vino, non autem oportet quod sit sensibilis post mixtionem.

AD SECUNDUM dicendum quod, si aqua omnino non apponeretur, totaliter excluderetur significatio, sed, cum aqua in vinum convertitur, significatur quod populus Christo incorporatur.

AD TERTIUM dicendum quod, si aqua apponeretur dolio, non sufficeret ad significationem huius sacramenti, sed oportet aquam vino apponi circa ipsam celebrationem sacramenti.

it is always safer to add little water, especially if the wine be weak, because the sacrament could not be celebrated if there were such addition of water as to destroy the species of the wine. Hence Pope Julius I reprehends some who *keep throughout the year a linen cloth steeped in must, and at the time of sacrifice wash a part of it with water, and so make the offering.*

REPLY OBJ. 1: For the signification of this sacrament it suffices for the water to be appreciable by sense when it is mixed with the wine: but it is not necessary for it to be sensible after the mingling.

REPLY OBJ. 2: If no water were added, the signification would be utterly excluded: but when the water is changed into wine, it is signified that the people is incorporated with Christ.

REPLY OBJ. 3: If water were added to a cask, it would not suffice for the signification of this sacrament, but the water must be added to the wine at the actual celebration of the sacrament.

QUESTION 75

THE CHANGE IN THE EUCHARIST

Deinde considerandum est de conversione panis et vini in corpus et sanguinem Christi. Et circa hoc quaeruntur octo.

Primo, utrum substantia panis et vini remaneat in hoc sacramento post consecrationem.

Secundo, utrum annihiletur.

Tertio, utrum convertatur in corpus et sanguinem Christi.

Quarto, utrum remaneant ibi accidentia post conversionem.

Quinto, utrum remaneat ibi forma substantialis.

Sexto, utrum conversio ista fiat subito.

Septimo, utrum sit miraculosior omni alia mutatione.

Octavo, quibus verbis convenienter exprimi possit.

We have to consider the change of the bread and wine into the body and blood of Christ; under which head there are eight points of inquiry:

(1) Whether the substance of bread and wine remain in this sacrament after the consecration?

(2) Whether it is annihilated?

(3) Whether it is changed into the body and blood of Christ?

(4) Whether the accidents remain after the change?

(5) Whether the substantial form remains there?

(6) Whether this change is instantaneous?

(7) Whether it is more miraculous than any other change?

(8) By what words it may be suitably expressed?

Article 1

Whether the Body of Christ Be in This Sacrament in Very Truth, or Merely As in a Figure or Sign?

AD PRIMUM SIC PROCEDITUR. Videtur quod in hoc sacramento non sit corpus Christi secundum veritatem, sed solum secundum figuram, vel sicut in signo. Dicitur enim Ioan. VI quod, cum dominus dixisset, *nisi manducaveritis carnem filii hominis et biberitis eius sanguinem, etc., multi ex discipulis eius audientes dixerunt, durus est hic sermo, quibus ipse, spiritus est qui vivificat, caro non prodest quidquam.* Quasi dicat, secundum expositionem Augustini, super quartum Psalmum, *spiritualiter intellige quae locutus sum. Non hoc corpus quod videtis manducaturi estis, et bibituri illum sanguinem quem fusuri sunt qui me crucifigent. Sacramentum aliquod vobis commendavi. Spiritualiter intellectum vivificabit vos, caro autem non prodest quidquam.*

PRAETEREA, dominus dicit, Matth. ult., *ecce, ego vobiscum sum omnibus diebus usque ad consummationem saeculi,* quod exponens Augustinus dicit, *donec saeculum finiatur, sursum est dominus, sed tamen et hic nobiscum est veritas dominus. Corpus enim in quo resurrexit, uno in loco esse oportet, veritas autem eius ubique diffusa est.* Non ergo secundum veritatem est corpus Christi in hoc sacramento, sed solum sicut in signo.

PRAETEREA, nullum corpus potest esse simul in pluribus locis, cum nec Angelo hoc conveniat, eadem enim ratione posset esse ubique. Sed corpus Christi est verum

OBJECTION 1: It seems that the body of Christ is not in this sacrament in very truth, but only as in a figure, or sign. For it is written (John 6:54) that when our Lord had uttered these words: *Except you eat the flesh of the Son of Man, and drink His blood,* etc., *Many of His disciples on hearing it said: 'this is a hard saying':* to whom He rejoined: *It is the spirit that quickeneth; the flesh profiteth nothing:* as if He were to say, according to Augustine's exposition on Ps. 4: *Give a spiritual meaning to what I have said. You are not to eat this body which you see, nor to drink the blood which they who crucify Me are to spill. It is a mystery that I put before you: in its spiritual sense it will quicken you; but the flesh profiteth nothing.*

OBJ. 2: Further, our Lord said (Matt 28:20): *Behold I am with you all days even to the consummation of the world.* Now in explaining this, Augustine makes this observation (*Tract. xxx in Joan.*): *The Lord is on high until the world be ended; nevertheless the truth of the Lord is here with us; for the body, in which He rose again, must be in one place; but His truth is spread abroad everywhere.* Therefore, the body of Christ is not in this sacrament in very truth, but only as in a sign.

OBJ. 3: Further, no body can be in several places at the same time. For this does not even belong to an angel; since for the same reason it could be everywhere. But Christ's is

corpus, et est in caelo. Ergo videtur quod non sit secundum veritatem in sacramento altaris, sed solum sicut in signo.

PRAETEREA, sacramenta Ecclesiae ad utilitatem fidelium ordinantur. Sed secundum Gregorium, in quadam homilia, regulus reprehenditur *quia quaerebat corporalem Christi praesentiam*. Apostoli etiam impediebantur recipere spiritum sanctum propter hoc quod affecti erant ad eius praesentiam corporalem, ut Augustinus dicit, super illud Ioan. XVI, *si non abiero, Paraclitus non veniet ad vos*. Non ergo Christus secundum praesentiam corporalem est in sacramento altaris.

SED CONTRA est quod Hilarius dicit, in VIII de Trin., *de veritate carnis et sanguinis Christi non est relictus ambigendi locus. Nunc et ipsius domini professione, et fide nostra, caro eius vere est cibus et sanguis eius vere est potus.* Et Ambrosius dicit, VI de sacramentis, *sicut verus est Dei filius dominus Iesus Christus, ita vera Christi caro est quam accipimus, et verus sanguis eius est potus.*

RESPONDEO dicendum quod verum corpus Christi et sanguinem esse in hoc sacramento, non sensu deprehendi potest, sed sola fide, quae auctoritati divinae innititur. Unde super illud Luc. XXII, *hoc est corpus meum quod pro vobis tradetur*, dicit Cyrillus, *non dubites an hoc verum sit, sed potius suscipe verba salvatoris in fide, cum enim sit veritas, non mentitur.*

Hoc autem conveniens est, primo quidem, perfectioni novae legis. Sacrificia enim veteris legis illud verum sacrificium passionis Christi continebant solum in figura, secundum illud Heb. X, *umbram habens lex futurorum bonorum, non ipsam rerum imaginem.* Et ideo oportuit ut aliquid plus haberet sacrificium novae legis a Christo institutum, ut scilicet contineret ipsum passum, non solum in significatione vel figura, sed etiam in rei veritate. Et ideo hoc sacramentum, quod ipsum Christum realiter continet, ut Dionysius dicit, III cap. Eccles. Hierar., est perfectivum omnium sacramentorum aliorum, in quibus virtus Christi participatur.

Secundo, hoc competit caritati Christi, ex qua pro salute nostra corpus verum nostrae naturae assumpsit. Et quia maxime proprium amicitiae est, convivere amicis, ut philosophus dicit, IX Ethic., sui praesentiam corporalem nobis repromittit in praemium, Matth. XXIV, *ubi fuerit corpus, illuc congregabuntur et aquilae.* Interim tamen nec sua praesentia corporali in hac peregrinatione destituit, sed per veritatem corporis et sanguinis sui nos sibi coniungit in hoc sacramento. Unde ipse dicit, Ioan. VI, *qui manducat meam carnem et bibit meum sanguinem, in me manet et ego in eo.* Unde hoc sacramentum est maximae caritatis signum, et nostrae spei sublevamentum, ex tam familiari coniunctione Christi ad nos.

Tertio, hoc competit perfectioni fidei, quae, sicut est de divinitate Christi, ita est de eius humanitate, secundum illud Ioan. XIV, *creditis in Deum, et in me credite.* Et

a true body, and it is in heaven. Consequently, it seems that it is not in very truth in the sacrament of the altar, but only as in a sign.

OBJ. 4: Further, the Church's sacraments are ordained for the profit of the faithful. But according to Gregory in a certain Homily (*xxviii in Evang.*), the ruler is rebuked *for demanding Christ's bodily presence.* Moreover the apostles were prevented from receiving the Holy Spirit because they were attached to His bodily presence, as Augustine says on John 16:7: *Except I go, the Paraclete will not come to you* (*Tract. xciv in Ioan.*). Therefore Christ is not in the sacrament of the altar according to His bodily presence.

ON THE CONTRARY, Hilary says (*De Trin.* viii): *There is no room for doubt regarding the truth of Christ's body and blood; for now by our Lord's own declaring and by our faith His flesh is truly food, and His blood is truly drink.* And Ambrose says (*De Sacram.* vi): *As the Lord Jesus Christ is God's true Son so is it Christ's true flesh which we take, and His true blood which we drink.*

I ANSWER THAT, The presence of Christ's true body and blood in this sacrament cannot be detected by sense, nor understanding, but by faith alone, which rests upon Divine authority. Hence, on Luke 22:19: *This is My body which shall be delivered up for you*, Cyril says: *Doubt not whether this be true; but take rather the Savior's words with faith; for since He is the Truth, He lieth not.*

Now this is suitable, first for the perfection of the New Law. For, the sacrifices of the Old Law contained only in figure that true sacrifice of Christ's Passion, according to Heb. 10:1: *For the law having a shadow of the good things to come, not the very image of the things.* And therefore it was necessary that the sacrifice of the New Law instituted by Christ should have something more, namely, that it should contain Christ Himself crucified, not merely in signification or figure, but also in very truth. And therefore this sacrament which contains Christ Himself, as Dionysius says (*Eccl. Hier.* iii), is perfective of all the other sacraments, in which Christ's virtue is participated.

Second, this belongs to Christ's love, out of which for our salvation He assumed a true body of our nature. And because it is the special feature of friendship to live together with friends, as the Philosopher says (*Ethic.* ix), He promises us His bodily presence as a reward, saying (Matt 24:28): *Where the body is, there shall the eagles be gathered together.* Yet meanwhile in our pilgrimage He does not deprive us of His bodily presence; but unites us with Himself in this sacrament through the truth of His body and blood. Hence (John 6:57) he says: *He that eateth My flesh, and drinketh My blood, abideth in Me, and I in him.* Hence this sacrament is the sign of supreme charity, and the uplifter of our hope, from such familiar union of Christ with us.

Third, it belongs to the perfection of faith, which concerns His humanity just as it does His Godhead, according to John 14:1: *You believe in God, believe also in Me.* And

quia fides est invisibilium, sicut divinitatem suam nobis exhibet Christus invisibiliter, ita et in hoc sacramento carnem suam nobis exhibet invisibili modo.

Quae quidam non attendentes, posuerunt corpus et sanguinem Christi non esse in hoc sacramento nisi sicut in signo. Quod est tanquam haereticum abiiciendum, utpote verbis Christi contrarium. Unde et Berengarius, qui primus inventor huius erroris fuerat, postea coactus est suum errorem revocare, et veritatem fidei confiteri.

AD PRIMUM ergo dicendum quod ex hac auctoritate praedicti haeretici occasionem errandi sumpserunt, male verba Augustini intelligentes. Cum enim Augustinus dicit, *non hoc corpus quod videtis manducaturi estis*, non intendit excludere veritatem corporis Christi, sed quod non erat manducandum in hac specie in qua ab eis videbatur. Per hoc autem quod subdit, *sacramentum vobis aliquod commendavi, spiritualiter intellectum vivificabit vos*, non intendit quod corpus Christi sit in hoc sacramento solum secundum mysticam significationem, sed spiritualiter dici, idest, invisibiliter et per virtutem spiritus. Unde, super Ioan., exponens illud quod dicitur, *caro non prodest quidquam*, dicit, *sed, quo modo illi intellexerunt. Carnem quippe sic intellexerunt manducandam, quo modo in cadavere dilaniatur aut in macello venditur, non quo modo spiritu vegetatur. Accedat spiritus ad carnem, et prodest plurimum, nam, si caro nihil prodesset, verbum caro non fieret, ut habitaret in nobis.*

AD SECUNDUM dicendum quod verbum illud Augustini, et omnia similia, sunt intelligenda de corpore Christi secundum quod videtur in propria specie, secundum quod etiam ipse dominus dixit, Matth. XXVI, *me autem non semper habebitis.* Invisibiliter tamen sub speciebus huius sacramenti est ubicumque hoc sacramentum perficitur.

AD TERTIUM dicendum quod corpus Christi non est eo modo in sacramento sicut corpus in loco, quod suis dimensionibus loco commensuratur, sed quodam speciali modo, qui est proprius huic sacramento. Unde dicimus quod corpus Christi est in diversis altaribus, non sicut in diversis locis, sed sicut in sacramento. Per quod non intelligimus quod Christus sit ibi solum sicut in signo, licet sacramentum sit in genere signi, sed intelligimus corpus Christi esse ibi, sicut dictum est, secundum modum proprium huic sacramento.

AD QUARTUM dicendum quod ratio illa procedit de praesentia corporis Christi prout est praesens per modum corporis, idest prout est in sua specie visibili, non autem prout spiritualiter, idest invisibiliter, modo et virtute spiritus. Unde Augustinus dicit, super Ioan., *si intellexisti spiritualiter verba Christi de carne sua, spiritus et vita tibi sunt, si intellexisti carnaliter, etiam spiritus et vita sunt, sed tibi non sunt.*

since faith is of things unseen, as Christ shows us His Godhead invisibly, so also in this sacrament He shows us His flesh in an invisible manner.

Some men accordingly, not paying heed to these things, have contended that Christ's body and blood are not in this sacrament except as in a sign, a thing to be rejected as heretical, since it is contrary to Christ's words. Hence Berengarius, who had been the first deviser of this heresy, was afterwards forced to withdraw his error, and to acknowledge the truth of the faith.

REPLY OBJ. 1: From this authority the aforesaid heretics have taken occasion to err from evilly understanding Augustine's words. For when Augustine says: *You are not to eat this body which you see*, he means not to exclude the truth of Christ's body, but that it was not to be eaten in this species in which it was seen by them. And by the words: *It is a mystery that I put before you; in its spiritual sense it will quicken you*, he intends not that the body of Christ is in this sacrament merely according to mystical signification, but *spiritually*, that is, invisibly, and by the power of the spirit. Hence (*Tract. xxvii*), expounding John 6:64: *the flesh profiteth nothing*, he says: *Yea, but as they understood it, for they understood that the flesh was to be eaten as it is divided piecemeal in a dead body, or as sold in the shambles, not as it is quickened by the spirit . . . Let the spirit draw nigh to the flesh . . . then the flesh profiteth very much: for if the flesh profiteth nothing, the Word had not been made flesh, that It might dwell among us.*

REPLY OBJ. 2: That saying of Augustine and all others like it are to be understood of Christ's body as it is beheld in its proper species; according as our Lord Himself says (Matt 26:11): *But Me you have not always.* Nevertheless He is invisibly under the species of this sacrament, wherever this sacrament is performed.

REPLY OBJ. 3: Christ's body is not in this sacrament in the same way as a body is in a place, which by its dimensions is commensurate with the place; but in a special manner which is proper to this sacrament. Hence we say that Christ's body is upon many altars, not as in different places, but *sacramentally*: and thereby we do not understand that Christ is there only as in a sign, although a sacrament is a kind of sign; but that Christ's body is here after a fashion proper to this sacrament, as stated above.

REPLY OBJ. 4: This argument holds good of Christ's bodily presence, as He is present after the manner of a body, that is, as it is in its visible appearance, but not as it is spiritually, that is, invisibly, after the manner and by the virtue of the spirit. Hence Augustine (*Tract. xxvii in Joan.*) says: *If thou hast understood Christ's words spiritually concerning His flesh, they are spirit and life to thee; if thou hast understood them carnally, they are also spirit and life, but not to thee.*

Article 2

Whether in This Sacrament the Substance of the Bread and Wine Remains After the Consecration?

Ad secundum sic proceditur. Videtur quod in hoc sacramento remaneat substantia panis et vini post consecrationem. Dicit enim Damascenus, in libro IV, *quia consuetudo est hominibus comedere panem et vinum, coniugavit eis deitatem, et fecit ea corpus et sanguinem suum*. Et infra, *panis communicationis non panis simplex est, sed unitus deitati*. Sed coniugatio est rerum actu existentium. Ergo panis et vinum simul sunt in hoc sacramento cum corpore et sanguine Christi.

Praeterea, inter Ecclesiae sacramenta debet esse conformitas. Sed in aliis sacramentis substantia materiae manet, sicut in Baptismo substantia aquae, et in confirmatione substantia chrismatis. Ergo et in hoc sacramento substantia panis et vini manet.

Praeterea, panis et vinum assumitur in hoc sacramento inquantum significat ecclesiasticam unitatem, prout *unus panis fit ex multis granis, et unum vinum ex multis racemis*, ut Augustinus dicit, in libro de symbolo. Sed hoc pertinet ad ipsam substantiam panis et vini. Ergo substantia panis et vini remanet in hoc sacramento.

Sed contra est quod Ambrosius dicit, in libro de sacramentis, *licet figura panis et vini videatur, nihil tamen aliud quam caro Christi et sanguis post consecrationem credenda sunt*.

Respondeo dicendum quod quidam posuerunt post consecrationem substantiam panis et vini in hoc sacramento remanere. Sed haec positio stare non potest. Primo quidem, quia per hanc positionem tollitur veritas huius sacramenti, ad quam pertinet ut verum corpus Christi in hoc sacramento existat. Quod quidem ibi non est ante consecrationem. Non autem aliquid potest esse alicubi ubi prius non erat, nisi per loci mutationem, vel per alterius conversionem in ipsum, sicut in domo aliqua de novo incipit esse ignis aut quod illuc defertur, aut quod ibi generatur. Manifestum est autem quod corpus Christi non incipit esse in hoc sacramento per motum localem. Primo quidem, quia sequeretur quod desineret esse in caelo, non enim quod localiter movetur, pervenit de novo ad aliquem locum, nisi deserat priorem. Secundo, quia omne corpus localiter motum pertransit omnia media, quod hic dici non potest. Tertio, quia impossibile est quod unus motus eiusdem corporis localiter moti terminetur simul ad diversa loca, cum tamen in pluribus locis corpus Christi sub hoc sacramento simul esse incipiat. Et propter hoc relinquitur quod non possit aliter corpus Christi incipere esse de novo in hoc sacramento nisi per conversionem substantiae panis in ipsum. Quod

Objection 1: It seems that the substance of the bread and wine does remain in this sacrament after the consecration: because Damascene says (*De Fide Orth.* iv): *Since it is customary for men to eat bread and drink wine, God has wedded his Godhead to them, and made them His body and blood*: and further on: *The bread of communication is not simple bread, but is united to the Godhead*. But wedding together belongs to things actually existing. Therefore the bread and wine are at the same time, in this sacrament, with the body and the blood of Christ.

Obj. 2: Further, there ought to be conformity between the sacraments. But in the other sacraments the substance of the matter remains, like the substance of water in Baptism, and the substance of chrism in Confirmation. Therefore the substance of the bread and wine remains also in this sacrament.

Obj. 3: Further, bread and wine are made use of in this sacrament, inasmuch as they denote ecclesiastical unity, as *one bread is made from many grains and wine from many grapes*, as Augustine says in his book on the Creed (*Tract. xxvi in Joan.*). But this belongs to the substance of bread and wine. Therefore, the substance of the bread and wine remains in this sacrament.

On the contrary, Ambrose says (*De Sacram.* iv): *Although the figure of the bread and wine be seen, still, after the Consecration, they are to be believed to be nothing else than the body and blood of Christ*.

I answer that, Some have held that the substance of the bread and wine remains in this sacrament after the consecration. But this opinion cannot stand: first of all, because by such an opinion the truth of this sacrament is destroyed, to which it belongs that Christ's true body exists in this sacrament; which indeed was not there before the consecration. Now a thing cannot be in any place, where it was not previously, except by change of place, or by the conversion of another thing into itself; just as fire begins anew to be in some house, either because it is carried thither, or because it is generated there. Now it is evident that Christ's body does not begin to be present in this sacrament by local motion. First of all, because it would follow that it would cease to be in heaven: for what is moved locally does not come anew to some place unless it quit the former one. Second, because every body moved locally passes through all intermediary spaces, which cannot be said here. Third, because it is not possible for one movement of the same body moved locally to be terminated in different places at the one time, whereas the body of Christ under this sacrament begins at the one time to be in several places. And consequently it remains that Christ's body cannot begin to be anew in this sacrament except by change of the substance of bread into itself.

autem convertitur in aliquid, facta conversione, non manet. Unde relinquitur quod, salva veritate huius sacramenti, substantia panis post consecrationem remanere non possit.

Secundo, quia haec positio contrariatur formae huius sacramenti, in qua dicitur, hoc est corpus meum. Quod non esset verum si substantia panis ibi remaneret, nunquam enim substantia panis est corpus Christi. Sed potius esset dicendum, hic est corpus meum.

Tertio, quia contrariaretur venerationi huius sacramenti, si aliqua substantia esset ibi quae non posset adorari adoratione latriae.

Quarto, quia contrariaretur ritui Ecclesiae, secundum quem post corporalem cibum non licet sumere corpus Christi, cum tamen post unam hostiam consecratam liceat sumere aliam. Unde haec positio vitanda est tanquam haeretica.

AD PRIMUM ergo dicendum quod Deus coniugavit divinitatem suam, idest divinam virtutem, pani et vino, non ut remaneant in hoc sacramento, sed ut faciat inde corpus et sanguinem suum.

AD SECUNDUM dicendum quod in aliis sacramentis non est ipse Christus realiter, sicut in hoc sacramento. Et ideo in sacramentis aliis manet substantia materiae, non autem in isto.

AD TERTIUM dicendum quod species quae remanent in hoc sacramento, ut infra dicetur, sufficiunt ad significationem huius sacramenti, nam per accidentia cognoscitur ratio substantiae.

But what is changed into another thing, no longer remains after such change. Hence the conclusion is that, saving the truth of this sacrament, the substance of the bread cannot remain after the consecration.

Second, because this position is contrary to the form of this sacrament, in which it is said: *This is My body*, which would not be true if the substance of the bread were to remain there; for the substance of bread never is the body of Christ. Rather should one say in that case: *Here is My body*.

Third, because it would be opposed to the veneration of this sacrament, if any substance were there, which could not be adored with adoration of latria.

Fourth, because it is contrary to the rite of the Church, according to which it is not lawful to take the body of Christ after bodily food, while it is nevertheless lawful to take one consecrated host after another. Hence this opinion is to be avoided as heretical.

REPLY OBJ. 1: God *wedded His Godhead*, i.e., His Divine power, to the bread and wine, not that these may remain in this sacrament, but in order that He may make from them His body and blood.

REPLY OBJ. 2: Christ is not really present in the other sacraments, as in this; and therefore the substance of the matter remains in the other sacraments, but not in this.

REPLY OBJ. 3: The species which remain in this sacrament, as shall be said later (A. 5), suffice for its signification; because the nature of the substance is known by its accidents.

Article 3

Whether the Substance of the Bread or Wine Is Annihilated After the Consecration of This Sacrament, or Dissolved into Their Original Matter?

AD TERTIUM SIC PROCEDITUR. Videtur quod substantia panis, post consecrationem huius sacramenti, annihiletur, aut in pristinam materiam resolvatur. Quod enim est aliquid corporale, oportet alicubi esse. Sed substantia panis, quae est quiddam corporale, non manet in hoc sacramento, ut dictum est, nec etiam est dare aliquem locum ubi sit. Ergo non est aliquid post consecrationem. Igitur aut est annihilata, aut in praeiacentem materiam resoluta.

PRAETEREA, illud quod est terminus a quo in qualibet mutatione, non remanet, nisi forte in potentia materiae, sicut, quando ex aere fit ignis, forma aeris non manet nisi in potentia materiae; et similiter quando ex albo fit nigrum. Sed in hoc sacramento substantia panis et vini se habet sicut terminus a quo corpus autem vel sanguis Christi sicut terminus ad quem, dicit enim Ambrosius, in libro de officiis, *ante benedictionem alia*

OBJECTION 1: It seems that the substance of the bread is annihilated after the consecration of this sacrament, or dissolved into its original matter. For whatever is corporeal must be somewhere. But the substance of bread, which is something corporeal, does not remain, in this sacrament, as stated above (A. 2); nor can we assign any place where it may be. Consequently it is nothing after the consecration. Therefore, it is either annihilated, or dissolved into its original matter.

OBJ. 2: Further, what is the term wherefrom in every change exists no longer, except in the potentiality of matter; e.g., when air is changed into fire, the form of the air remains only in the potentiality of matter; and in like fashion when what is white becomes black. But in this sacrament the substance of the bread or of the wine is the term wherefrom, while the body or the blood of Christ is the term *whereunto*: for Ambrose says in *De Officiis* (*De Myster*. ix): *Before the*

species nominatur, post benedictionem corpus significatur. Ergo, facta consecratione, substantia panis vel vini non manet, nisi forte resoluta in suam materiam.

Praeterea, oportet alterum contradictoriorum esse verum. Sed haec est falsa, facta consecratione, substantia panis vel vini est aliquid. Ergo haec est vera, substantia panis vel vini est nihil.

Sed contra est quod Augustinus dicit, in libro octogintatrium quaestionum, *Deus non est causa tendendi in non esse.* Sed hoc sacramentum divina virtute perficitur. Ergo in hoc sacramento non annihilatur substantia panis aut vini.

Respondeo dicendum quod, quia substantia panis vel vini non manet in hoc sacramento, quidam, impossibile reputantes quod substantia panis vel vini in corpus vel sanguinem Christi convertatur, posuerunt quod per consecrationem substantia panis vel vini vel resolvitur in praeiacentem materiam, vel quod annihiletur.

Praeiacens autem materia in quam corpora mixta resolvi possunt, sunt quatuor elementa, non enim potest fieri resolutio in materiam primam, ita quod sine forma existat, quia materia sine forma esse non potest. Cum autem post consecrationem nihil sub speciebus sacramenti remaneat nisi corpus et sanguis, oportebit dicere quod elementa in quae resoluta est substantia panis et vini, inde discedant per motum localem. Quod sensu perciperetur. Similiter etiam substantia panis vel vini manet usque ad ultimum instans consecrationis. In ultimo autem instanti consecrationis iam est ibi substantia vel corporis vel sanguinis Christi, sicut in ultimo instanti generationis iam inest forma. Unde non erit dare aliquod instans in quo sit ibi praeiacens materia. Non enim potest dici quod paulatim substantia panis vel vini resolvatur in praeiacentem materiam, vel successive egrediatur de loco specierum. Quia, si hoc inciperet fieri in ultimo instanti suae consecrationis, simul sub aliqua parte hostiae esset corpus Christi cum substantia panis, quod est contra praedicta. Si vero incipiat fieri ante consecrationem, erit dare aliquod tempus in quo sub aliqua parte hostiae neque erit substantia panis, neque erit corpus Christi, quod est inconveniens. Et hoc ipsimet perpendisse videntur. Unde posuerunt aliud sub disiunctione, scilicet quod annihiletur. Sed nec hoc potest esse. Quia non erit dare aliquem modum quo corpus Christi verum incipiat esse in hoc sacramento, nisi per conversionem substantiae panis in ipsum, quae quidem conversio tollitur, posita vel annihilatione panis, vel resolutione in praeiacentem materiam. Similiter etiam non est dare unde talis resolutio vel annihilatio in hoc sacramento causetur, cum effectus sacramenti significetur per formam; neutrum autem horum significatur per haec verba formae,

blessing it is called another species, after the blessing the body of Christ is signified. Therefore, when the consecration takes place, the substance of the bread or wine no longer remains, unless perchance dissolved into its (original) matter.

Obj. 3: Further, one of two contradictories must be true. But this proposition is false: *After the consecration the substance of the bread or wine is something.* Consequently, this is true: *The substance of the bread or wine is nothing.*

On the contrary, Augustine says (Q. 83): *God is not the cause of tending to nothing.* But this sacrament is wrought by Divine power. Therefore, in this sacrament the substance of the bread or wine is not annihilated.

I answer that, Because the substance of the bread and wine does not remain in this sacrament, some, deeming that it is impossible for the substance of the bread and wine to be changed into Christ's flesh and blood, have maintained that by the consecration, the substance of the bread and wine is either dissolved into the original matter, or that it is annihilated.

Now the original matter into which mixed bodies can be dissolved is the four elements. For dissolution cannot be made into primary matter, so that a subject can exist without a form, since matter cannot exist without a form. But since after the consecration nothing remains under the sacramental species except the body and the blood of Christ, it will be necessary to say that the elements into which the substance of the bread and wine is dissolved, depart from thence by local motion, which would be perceived by the senses. In like manner also the substance of the bread or wine remains until the last instant of the consecration; but in the last instant of the consecration there is already present there the substance of the body or blood of Christ, just as the form is already present in the last instant of generation. Hence no instant can be assigned in which the original matter can be there. For it cannot be said that the substance of the bread or wine is dissolved gradually into the original matter, or that it successively quits the species, for if this began to be done in the last instant of its consecration, then at the one time under part of the host there would be the body of Christ together with the substance of bread, which is contrary to what has been said above (A. 2). But if this begin to come to pass before the consecration, there will then be a time in which under one part of the host there will be neither the substance of bread nor the body of Christ, which is not fitting. They seem indeed to have taken this into careful consideration, wherefore they formulated their proposition with an alternative, viz. that (the substance) may be annihilated. But even this cannot stand, because no way can be assigned whereby Christ's true body can begin to be in this sacrament, except by the change of the substance of bread into it, which change is excluded the moment we admit either annihilation of the substance of the bread, or dissolution into the original

hoc est corpus meum. Unde patet praedictam positionem esse falsam.

AD PRIMUM ergo dicendum quod substantia panis vel vini, facta consecratione, neque sub speciebus sacramenti manet, neque alibi. Non tamen sequitur quod annihiletur, convertitur enim in corpus Christi. Sicut non sequitur, si aer ex quo generatus est ignis, non sit ibi vel alibi, quod sit annihilatus.

AD SECUNDUM dicendum quod forma quae est terminus a quo, non convertitur in aliam formam, sed una forma succedit alteri in subiecto, et ideo prima forma non remanet nisi in potentia materiae. Sed hic substantia panis convertitur in corpus Christi, ut supra dictum est. Unde ratio non sequitur.

AD TERTIUM dicendum quod, licet post consecrationem haec sit falsa substantia panis est aliquid; id tamen in quod substantia panis conversa est, est aliquid. Et ideo substantia panis non est annihilata.

matter. Likewise no cause can be assigned for such dissolution or annihilation, since the effect of the sacrament is signified by the form: *This is My body.* Hence it is clear that the aforesaid opinion is false.

REPLY OBJ. 1: The substance of the bread or wine, after the consecration, remains neither under the sacramental species, nor elsewhere; yet it does not follow that it is annihilated; for it is changed into the body of Christ; just as if the air, from which fire is generated, be not there or elsewhere, it does not follow that it is annihilated.

REPLY OBJ. 2: The form, which is the term wherefrom, is not changed into another form; but one form succeeds another in the subject; and therefore the first form remains only in the potentiality of matter. But here the substance of the bread is changed into the body of Christ, as stated above. Hence the conclusion does not follow.

REPLY OBJ. 3: Although after the consecration this proposition is false: *The substance of the bread is something*, still that into which the substance of the bread is changed, is something, and consequently the substance of the bread is not annihilated.

Article 4

Whether Bread Can Be Converted into the Body of Christ?

AD QUARTUM SIC PROCEDITUR. Videtur quod panis non possit converti in corpus Christi. Conversio enim quaedam mutatio est. Sed in omni mutatione oportet esse aliquod subiectum, quod prius est in potentia et postea est in actu, ut enim dicitur in III Physic., *motus est actus existentis in potentia.* Non est autem dare aliquod subiectum substantiae panis et corporis Christi, quia de ratione substantiae est quod non sit in subiecto, ut dicitur in praedicamentis. Non ergo potest esse quod tota substantia panis convertatur in corpus Christi.

PRAETEREA, forma illius in quod aliquid convertitur, de novo incipit esse in materia eius quod in ipsum convertitur, sicut, cum aer convertitur in ignem prius non existentem, forma ignis incipit de novo esse in materia aeris; et similiter, cum cibus convertitur in hominem prius non existentem, forma hominis incipit esse de novo in materia cibi. Si ergo panis convertitur in corpus Christi, necesse est quod forma corporis Christi de novo incipiat esse in materia panis, quod est falsum. Non ergo panis convertitur in substantiam corporis Christi.

PRAETEREA, quae sunt secundum se divisa, nunquam unum eorum fit alterum, sicut albedo nunquam fit nigredo, sed subiectum albedinis fit subiectum nigredinis, ut dicitur in I Physic. Sed, sicut duae formae

OBJECTION 1: It seems that bread cannot be converted into the body of Christ. For conversion is a kind of change. But in every change there must be some subject, which from being previously in potentiality is now in act. because as is said in *Phys.* iii: *motion is the act of a thing existing in potentiality*. But no subject can be assigned for the substance of the bread and of the body of Christ, because it is of the very nature of substance for it *not to be in a subject*, as it is said in Praedic. iii. Therefore it is not possible for the whole substance of the bread to be converted into the body of Christ.

OBJ. 2: Further, the form of the thing into which another is converted, begins anew to inhere in the matter of the thing converted into it: as when air is changed into fire not already existing, the form of fire begins anew to be in the matter of the air; and in like manner when food is converted into non-pre-existing man, the form of the man begins to be anew in the matter of the food. Therefore, if bread be changed into the body of Christ, the form of Christ's body must necessarily begin to be in the matter of the bread, which is false. Consequently, the bread is not changed into the substance of Christ's body.

OBJ. 3: Further, when two things are diverse, one never becomes the other, as whiteness never becomes blackness, as is stated in *Phys.* i. But since two contrary forms are of themselves diverse, as being the principles of formal

contrariae sunt secundum se divisae, utpote principia formalis differentiae existentes; ita duae materiae signatae sunt secundum se divisae, utpote existentes principium materialis divisionis. Ergo non potest esse quod haec materia panis fiat haec materia qua individuatur corpus Christi. Et ita non potest esse quod substantia huius panis convertatur in substantiam corporis Christi.

Sed contra est quod Eusebius Emesenus dicit, *novum tibi et impossibile esse non debet quod in Christi substantiam terrena et mortalia convertuntur.*

Respondeo dicendum quod, sicut supra dictum est, cum in hoc sacramento sit verum corpus Christi, nec incipiat ibi esse de novo per motum localem; cum etiam nec corpus Christi sit ibi sicut in loco, ut ex dictis patet, necesse est dicere quod ibi incipiat esse per conversionem substantiae panis in ipsum.

Haec tamen conversio non est similis conversionibus naturalibus, sed est omnino supernaturalis, sola Dei virtute effecta. Unde Ambrosius dicit, in libro de sacramentis, *liquet quod praeter naturae ordinem virgo generavit. Et hoc quod conficimus, corpus ex virgine est. Quid igitur quaeris naturae ordinem in Christi corpore, cum praeter naturam sit ipse dominus Iesus partus ex virgine?* Et super illud Ioan. VI, *verba quae ego locutus sum vobis,* scilicet de hoc sacramento, spiritus et vita sunt, dicit Chrysostomus, *idest, spiritualia sunt, nihil habentia carnale neque consequentiam naturalem, sed eruta sunt ab omni tali necessitate quae in terra, et a legibus quae hic positae sunt.*

Manifestum est enim quod omne agens agit inquantum est actu. Quodlibet autem agens creatum est determinatum in suo actu, cum sit determinati generis et speciei. Et ideo cuiuslibet agentis creati actio fertur super aliquem determinatum actum. Determinatio autem cuiuslibet rei in esse actuali est per eius formam. Unde nullum agens naturale vel creatum potest agere nisi ad immutationem formae. Et propter hoc omnis conversio quae fit secundum leges naturae, est formalis. Sed Deus est infinitus actus, ut in prima parte habitum est. Unde eius actio se extendit ad totam naturam entis. Non igitur solum potest perficere conversionem formalem, ut scilicet diversae formae sibi in eodem subiecto succedant, sed conversionem totius entis, ut scilicet tota substantia huius convertatur in totam substantiam illius. Et hoc agitur divina virtute in hoc sacramento. Nam tota substantia panis convertitur in totam substantiam corporis Christi, et tota substantia vini in totam substantiam sanguinis Christi. Unde haec conversio non est formalis, sed substantialis. Nec continetur inter species motus naturalis, sed proprio nomine potest dici transubstantiatio.

Ad primum ergo dicendum quod obiectio illa procedit de mutatione formali, quia formae proprium est in materia vel subiecto esse. Non autem habet locum in conversione totius substantiae. Unde, cum haec

difference, so two signate matters are of themselves diverse, as being the principles of material distinction. Consequently, it is not possible for this matter of bread to become this matter whereby Christ's body is individuated, and so it is not possible for this substance of bread to be changed into the substance of Christ's body.

On the contrary, Eusebius Emesenus says: *To thee it ought neither to be a novelty nor an impossibility that earthly and mortal things be changed into the substance of Christ.*

I answer that, As stated above (A. 2), since Christ's true body is in this sacrament, and since it does not begin to be there by local motion, nor is it contained therein as in a place, as is evident from what was stated above (A. 1, ad 2), it must be said then that it begins to be there by conversion of the substance of bread into itself.

Yet this change is not like natural changes, but is entirely supernatural, and effected by God's power alone. Hence Ambrose says (*De Myster.* iv): *It is clear that a Virgin begot beyond the order of nature: and what we make is the body from the Virgin. Why, then, do you look for nature's order in Christ's body, since the Lord Jesus was Himself brought forth of a Virgin beyond nature?* Chrysostom likewise (*Hom. xlvii*), commenting on John 6:64: *The words which I have spoken to you,* namely, of this sacrament, *are spirit and life,* says: i.e., *spiritual, having nothing carnal, nor natural consequence; but they are rent from all such necessity which exists upon earth, and from the laws here established.*

For it is evident that every agent acts according as it is in act. But every created agent is limited in its act, as being of a determinate genus and species: and consequently the action of every created agent bears upon some determinate act. Now the determination of every thing in actual existence comes from its form. Consequently, no natural or created agent can act except by changing the form in something; and on this account every change made according to nature's laws is a formal change. But God is infinite act, as stated in the First Part (Q. 7, A. 1; Q. 26, A. 2); hence His action extends to the whole nature of being. Therefore He can work not only formal conversion, so that diverse forms succeed each other in the same subject; but also the change of all being, so that, to wit, the whole substance of one thing be changed into the whole substance of another. And this is done by Divine power in this sacrament; for the whole substance of the bread is changed into the whole substance of Christ's body, and the whole substance of the wine into the whole substance of Christ's blood. Hence this is not a formal, but a substantial conversion; nor is it a kind of natural movement: but, with a name of its own, it can be called *transubstantiation.*

Reply Obj. 1: This objection holds good in respect of formal change, because it belongs to a form to be in matter or in a subject; but it does not hold good in respect of the change of the entire substance. Hence, since this substantial

conversio substantialis importet quendam ordinem substantiarum quarum una convertitur in alteram, est sicut in subiecto in utraque substantia, sicut ordo et numerus.

AD SECUNDUM dicendum quod etiam illa obiectio procedit de conversione formali, seu mutatione, quia oportet, sicut dictum est, formam esse in materia vel subiecto. Non autem habet locum in conversione totius substantiae, cuius non est accipere aliquod subiectum.

AD TERTIUM dicendum quod virtute agentis finiti non potest forma in formam mutari, nec materia in materiam. Sed virtute agentis infiniti, quod habet actionem in totum ens, potest talis conversio fieri, quia utrique formae et utrique materiae est communis natura entis; et id quod entitatis est in una, potest auctor entis convertere ad id quod est entitatis in altera, sublato eo per quod ab illa distinguebatur.

change implies a certain order of substances, one of which is changed into the other, it is in both substances as in a subject, just as order and number.

REPLY OBJ. 2: This argument also is true of formal conversion or change, because, as stated above (ad 1), a form must be in some matter or subject. But this is not so in a change of the entire substance; for in this case no subject is possible.

REPLY OBJ. 3: Form cannot be changed into form, nor matter into matter by the power of any finite agent. Such a change, however, can be made by the power of an infinite agent, which has control over all being, because the nature of being is common to both forms and to both matters; and whatever there is of being in the one, the author of being can change into whatever there is of being in the other, withdrawing that whereby it was distinguished from the other.

Article 5

Whether the Accidents of the Bread and Wine Remain in This Sacrament After the Change?

AD QUINTUM SIC PROCEDITUR. Videtur quod in hoc sacramento non remaneant accidentia panis et vini. Remoto enim priori, removetur posterius. Sed substantia est naturaliter prior accidente, ut probatur VII Metaphys. Cum ergo, facta consecratione, non remaneat substantia panis in hoc sacramento, videtur quod non possint remanere accidentia eius.

PRAETEREA, in sacramento veritatis non debet esse aliqua deceptio. Sed per accidentia iudicamus de substantia. Videtur ergo quod decipiatur humanum iudicium, si, remanentibus accidentibus, substantia panis non remaneat. Non ergo hoc est conveniens huic sacramento.

PRAETEREA, quamvis fides non sit subiecta rationi, non tamen est contra rationem, sed supra ipsam, ut in principio huius operis dictum est. Sed ratio nostra habet ortum a sensu. Ergo fides nostra non debet esse contra sensum, dum sensus noster iudicat esse panem, et fides nostra credit esse substantiam corporis Christi. Non ergo hoc est conveniens huic sacramento, quod accidentia panis subiecta sensibus maneant, et substantia panis non maneat.

PRAETEREA, illud quod manet, conversione facta, videtur esse subiectum mutationis. Si ergo accidentia panis manent conversione facta, videtur quod ipsa accidentia sint conversionis subiectum. Quod est impossibile, nam accidentis non est accidens. Non ergo in hoc sacramento debent remanere accidentia panis et vini.

OBJECTION 1: It seems that the accidents of the bread and wine do not remain in this sacrament. For when that which comes first is removed, that which follows is also taken away. But substance is naturally before accident, as is proved in *Metaph*. vii. Since, then, after consecration, the substance of the bread does not remain in this sacrament, it seems that its accidents cannot remain.

OBJ. 2: Further, there ought not to be any deception in a sacrament of truth. But we judge of substance by accidents. It seems, then, that human judgment is deceived, if, while the accidents remain, the substance of the bread does not. Consequently this is unbecoming to this sacrament.

OBJ. 3: Further, although our faith is not subject to reason, still it is not contrary to reason, but above it, as was said in the beginning of this work (I, Q. 1, A. 6, ad 2; A. 8). But our reason has its origin in the senses. Therefore our faith ought not to be contrary to the senses, as it is when sense judges that to be bread which faith believes to be the substance of Christ's body. Therefore it is not befitting this sacrament for the accidents of bread to remain subject to the senses, and for the substance of bread not to remain.

OBJ. 4: Further, what remains after the change has taken place seems to be the subject of change. If therefore the accidents of the bread remain after the change has been effected, it seems that the accidents are the subject of the change. But this is impossible; for *an accident cannot have an accident* (*Metaph*. iii). Therefore the accidents of the bread and wine ought not to remain in this sacrament.

SED CONTRA est quod Augustinus dicit, in libro sententiarum prosperi, *nos in specie panis et vini, quam videmus, res invisibiles, idest carnem et sanguinem, honoramus.*

RESPONDEO dicendum quod sensu apparet, facta consecratione, omnia accidentia panis et vini remanere. Quod quidem rationabiliter per divinam providentiam fit. Primo quidem, quia non est consuetum hominibus, sed horribile, carnem hominis comedere et sanguinem bibere, proponitur nobis caro et sanguis Christi sumenda sub speciebus illorum quae frequentius in usum hominis veniunt, scilicet panis et vini. Secundo, ne hoc sacramentum ab infidelibus irrideretur, si sub specie propria dominum nostrum manducemus. Tertio ut, dum invisibiliter corpus et sanguinem domini nostri sumimus, hoc proficiat ad meritum fidei.

AD PRIMUM ergo dicendum quod, sicut dicitur in libro de causis, effectus plus dependet a causa prima quam a causa secunda. Et ideo virtute Dei, qui est causa prima omnium, fieri potest ut remaneant posteriora, sublatis prioribus.

AD SECUNDUM dicendum quod in hoc sacramento nulla est deceptio, sunt enim secundum rei veritatem accidentia, quae sensibus diiudicantur. Intellectus autem, cuius est proprium obiectum substantia, ut dicitur in III de anima, per fidem a deceptione praeservatur.

ET SIC PATET responsio ad tertium. Nam fides non est contra sensum, sed est de eo ad quod sensus non attingit.

AD QUARTUM dicendum quod haec conversio non proprie habet subiectum, ut dictum est. Sed tamen accidentia, quae remanent, habent aliquam similitudinem subiecti.

ON THE CONTRARY, Augustine says in his book on the Sentences of Prosper (Lanfranc, *De Corp. et Sang. Dom.* xiii): *Under the species which we behold, of bread and wine, we honor invisible things, i.e., flesh and blood.*

I ANSWER THAT, It is evident to sense that all the accidents of the bread and wine remain after the consecration. And this is reasonably done by Divine Providence. First of all, because it is not customary, but horrible, for men to eat human flesh, and to drink blood. And therefore Christ's flesh and blood are set before us to be partaken of under the species of those things which are the more commonly used by men, namely, bread and wine. Second, lest this sacrament might be derided by unbelievers, if we were to eat our Lord under His own species. Third, that while we receive our Lord's body and blood invisibly, this may redound to the merit of faith.

REPLY OBJ. 1: As is said in the book De Causis, an effect depends more on the first cause than on the second. And therefore by God's power, which is the first cause of all things, it is possible for that which follows to remain, while that which is first is taken away.

REPLY OBJ. 2: There is no deception in this sacrament; for the accidents which are discerned by the senses are truly present. But the intellect, whose proper object is substance as is said in *De Anima* iii, is preserved by faith from deception.

AND THIS SERVES as answer to the third argument; because faith is not contrary to the senses, but concerns things to which sense does not reach.

REPLY OBJ. 4: This change has not properly a subject, as was stated above (A. 4, ad 1); nevertheless the accidents which remain have some resemblance of a subject.

Article 6

Whether the Substantial Form of the Bread Remains in This Sacrament After the Consecration?

AD SEXTUM SIC PROCEDITUR. Videtur quod, facta consecratione, remaneat in hoc sacramento forma substantialis panis. Dictum est enim quod, facta consecratione, remaneant accidentia. Sed, cum panis sit quiddam artificiale, etiam forma eius est accidens. Ergo remanet, facta consecratione.

PRAETEREA, forma corporis Christi est anima, dicitur enim in II de anima, quod *anima est actus corporis physici potentia vitam habentis.* Sed non potest dici quod forma substantialis panis convertatur in animam. Ergo videtur quod remaneat, facta consecratione.

PRAETEREA, propria operatio rei sequitur formam substantialem eius. Sed illud quod remanet in hoc sacramento, nutrit, et omnem operationem facit quam faceret

OBJECTION 1: It seems that the substantial form of the bread remains in this sacrament after the consecration. For it has been said (A. 5) that the accidents remain after the consecration. But since bread is an artificial thing, its form is an accident. Therefore it remains after the consecration.

OBJ. 2: Further, the form of Christ's body is His soul: for it is said in *De Anima* ii, that the soul *is the act of a physical body which has life in potentiality.* But it cannot be said that the substantial form of the bread is changed into the soul. Therefore it appears that it remains after the consecration.

OBJ. 3: Further, the proper operation of a things follows its substantial form. But what remains in this sacrament, nourishes, and performs every operation which bread

panis existens. Ergo forma substantialis panis remanet in hoc sacramento, facta consecratione.

SED CONTRA, forma substantialis panis est de substantia panis. Sed substantia panis convertitur in corpus Christi, sicut dictum est. Ergo forma substantialis panis non manet.

RESPONDEO dicendum quod quidam posuerunt quod, facta consecratione, non solum remanent accidentia panis, sed etiam forma substantialis eius. Sed hoc esse non potest. Primo quidem quia, si forma substantialis remaneret, nihil de pane converteretur in corpus Christi nisi sola materia. Et ita sequeretur quod non converteretur in corpus Christi totum, sed in eius materiam. Quod repugnat formae sacramenti, qua dicitur, *hoc est corpus meum.*

Secundo quia, si forma substantialis panis remaneret, aut remaneret in materia, aut a materia separata. Primum autem esse non potest. Quia, si remaneret in materia panis, tunc tota substantia panis remaneret, quod est contra praedicta. In alia autem materia remanere non posset, quia propria forma non est nisi in propria materia. Si autem remaneret a materia separata, iam esset forma intelligibilis actu, et etiam intellectus, nam omnes formae a materia separatae sunt tales.

Tertio, esset inconveniens huic sacramento. Nam accidentia panis in hoc sacramento remanent ut sub eis videatur corpus Christi, non autem sub propria specie, sicut supra dictum est.

Et ideo dicendum est quod forma substantialis panis non manet.

AD PRIMUM ergo dicendum quod nihil prohibet arte fieri aliquid cuius forma non est accidens, sed forma substantialis, sicut arte possunt produci ranae et serpentes. Talem enim formam non producit ars virtute propria, sed virtute naturalium principiorum. Et hoc modo producit formam substantialem panis, virtute ignis decoquentis materiam ex farina et aqua confectam.

AD SECUNDUM dicendum quod anima est forma corporis dans ei totum ordinem esse perfecti, scilicet esse, et esse corporeum, et esse animatum, et sic de aliis. Convertitur igitur forma panis in formam corporis Christi secundum quod dat esse corporeum, non autem secundum quod dat esse animatum tali anima.

AD TERTIUM dicendum quod operationum panis quaedam consequuntur ipsum ratione accidentium, sicut immutare sensum. Et tales operationes inveniuntur in speciebus panis post consecrationem, propter ipsa accidentia, quae remanent. Quaedam autem operationes consequuntur panem vel ratione materiae, sicut quod convertitur in aliquid; vel ratione formae substantialis, sicut est operatio consequens speciem eius, puta quod

would do were it present. Therefore the substantial form of the bread remains in this sacrament after the consecration.

ON THE CONTRARY, The substantial form of bread is of the substance of bread. But the substance of the bread is changed into the body of Christ, as stated above (AA. 2, 3, 4). Therefore the substantial form of the bread does not remain.

I ANSWER THAT, Some have contended that after the consecration not only do the accidents of the bread remain, but also its substantial form. But this cannot be. First of all, because if the substantial form of the bread were to remain, nothing of the bread would be changed into the body of Christ, excepting the matter; and so it would follow that it would be changed, not into the whole body of Christ, but into its matter, which is repugnant to the form of the sacrament, wherein it is said: *This is My body.*

Second, because if the substantial form of the bread were to remain, it would remain either in matter, or separated from matter. The first cannot be, for if it were to remain in the matter of the bread, then the whole substance of the bread would remain, which is against what was said above (A. 2). Nor could it remain in any other matter, because the proper form exists only in its proper matter. But if it were to remain separate from matter, it would then be an actually intelligible form, and also an intelligence; for all forms separated from matter are such.

Third, it would be unbefitting this sacrament: because the accidents of the bread remain in this sacrament, in order that the body of Christ may be seen under them, and not under its proper species, as stated above (A. 5).

And therefore it must be said that the substantial form of the bread does not remain.

REPLY OBJ. 1: There is nothing to prevent art from making a thing whose form is not an accident, but a substantial form; as frogs and serpents can be produced by art: for art produces such forms not by its own power, but by the power of natural energies. And in this way it produces the substantial forms of bread, by the power of fire baking the matter made up of flour and water.

REPLY OBJ. 2: The soul is the form of the body, giving it the whole order of perfect being, i.e., being, corporeal being, and animated being, and so on. Therefore the form of the bread is changed into the form of Christ's body, according as the latter gives corporeal being, but not according as it bestows animated being.

REPLY OBJ. 3: Some of the operations of bread follow it by reason of the accidents, such as to affect the senses, and such operations are found in the species of the bread after the consecration on account of the accidents which remain. But some other operations follow the bread either by reason of the matter, such as that it is changed into something else, or else by reason of the substantial form, such as an operation consequent upon its species, for instance, that it

confirmat cor hominis. Et tales operationes inveniuntur in hoc sacramento, non propter formam vel materiam quae remaneat, sed quia miraculose conferuntur ipsis accidentibus, ut infra dicetur.

strengthens man's heart (Ps 103:15); and such operations are found in this sacrament, not on account of the form or matter remaining, but because they are bestowed miraculously upon the accidents themselves, as will be said later (Q. 77, A. 3, ad 2, 3; AA. 5, 6).

Article 7

Whether This Change Is Wrought Instantaneously?

AD SEPTIMUM SIC PROCEDITUR. Videtur quod ista conversio non fiat in instanti, sed fiat successive. In hac enim conversione prius est substantia panis, et postea substantia corporis Christi. Non ergo utrumque est in eodem instanti, sed in duobus instantibus. Sed inter quaelibet duo instantia est tempus medium. Ergo oportet quod haec conversio fiat secundum successionem temporis quod est inter ultimum instans quo est ibi panis, et primum instans quo est ibi corpus Christi.

PRAETEREA, in omni conversione est fieri et factum esse. Sed haec duo non sunt simul, quia quod fit, non est; quod autem factum est, iam est. Ergo in hac conversione est prius et posterius. Et ita oportet quod non sit instantanea, sed successiva.

PRAETEREA, Ambrosius dicit, in libro de Sacram., quod istud sacramentum Christi sermone conficitur. Sed sermo Christi successive profertur. Ergo haec conversio fit successive.

SED CONTRA est quod haec conversio perficitur virtute infinita, cuius est subito operari.

RESPONDEO dicendum quod aliqua mutatio est instantanea triplici ratione. Uno quidem modo, ex parte formae, quae est terminus mutationis. Si enim sit aliqua forma quae recipiat magis aut minus, successive acquiritur subiecto, sicut sanitas. Et ideo, quia forma substantialis non recipit magis et minus, inde est quod subito fit eius introductio in materia.

Alio modo, ex parte subiecti, quod quandoque successive praeparatur ad susceptionem formae, et ideo aqua successive calefit. Quando vero ipsum subiectum est in ultima dispositione ad formam, subito recipit ipsam, sicut diaphanum subito illuminatur. Tertio, ex parte agentis, quod est infinitae virtutis, unde statim potest materiam ad formam disponere. Sicut dicitur Marc. VII, quod, cum Christus dixisset, *ephphetha, quod est adaperire, statim apertae sunt aures hominis, et solutum est vinculum linguae eius.*

Et his tribus rationibus haec conversio est instantanea. Primo quidem, quia substantia corporis Christi, ad quam terminatur ista conversio, non suscipit magis

OBJECTION 1: It seems that this change is not wrought instantaneously, but successively. For in this change there is first the substance of bread, and afterwards the substance of Christ's body. Neither, then, is in the same instant, but in two instants. But there is a mid-time between every two instants. Therefore this change must take place according to the succession of time, which is between the last instant in which the bread is there, and the first instant in which the body of Christ is present.

OBJ. 2: Further, in every change something is in becoming and something is in being. But these two things do not exist at the one time for, what is in becoming, is not yet, whereas what is in being, already is. Consequently, there is a before and an after in such change: and so necessarily the change cannot be instantaneous, but successive.

OBJ. 3: Further, Ambrose says (*De Sacram.* iv) that this sacrament *is made by the words of Christ*. But Christ's words are pronounced successively. Therefore the change takes place successively.

ON THE CONTRARY, This change is effected by a power which is infinite, to which it belongs to operate in an instant.

I ANSWER THAT, A change may be instantaneous from a threefold reason. First on the part of the form, which is the terminus of the change. For, if it be a form that receives more and less, it is acquired by its subject successively, such as health; and therefore because a substantial form does not receive more and less, it follows that its introduction into matter is instantaneous.

Second on the part of the subject, which sometimes is prepared successively for receiving the form; thus water is heated successively. When, however, the subject itself is in the ultimate disposition for receiving the form, it receives it suddenly, as a transparent body is illuminated suddenly. Third on the part of the agent, which possesses infinite power: wherefore it can instantly dispose the matter for the form. Thus it is written (Mark 7:34) that when Christ had said, '*Ephpheta*,' which is '*Be thou opened*,' *immediately his ears were opened, and the string of his tongue was loosed.*

For these three reasons this conversion is instantaneous. First, because the substance of Christ's body which is the term of this conversion, does not receive more or less.

neque minus. Secundo, quia in hac conversione non est aliquod subiectum, quod successive praeparetur. Tertio, quia agitur Dei virtute infinita.

AD PRIMUM ergo dicendum quod quidam non simpliciter concedunt quod inter quaelibet duo instantia sit tempus medium. Dicunt enim quod hoc habet locum in duobus instantibus quae referuntur ad eundem motum, non autem in duobus instantibus quae referuntur ad diversa. Unde inter instans quod mensurat finem quietis, et aliud instans quod mensurat principium motus, non est tempus medium. Sed in hoc decipiuntur. Quia unitas temporis et instantis, vel etiam pluralitas eorum, non accipitur secundum quoscumque motus, sed secundum primum motum caeli, qui est mensura omnis motus et quietis.

Et ideo alii hoc concedunt in tempore quod mensurat motum dependentem ex motu caeli. Sunt autem quidam motus ex motu caeli non dependentes, nec ab eo mensurati, sicut in prima parte dictum est de motibus Angelorum. Unde inter duo instantia illis motibus respondentia, non est tempus medium. Sed hoc non habet locum in proposito. Quia, quamvis ista conversio secundum se non habeat ordinem ad motum caeli, consequitur tamen prolationem verborum, quam necesse est motu caeli mensurari. Et ideo necesse est inter quaelibet duo instantia circa istam conversionem signata esse tempus medium.

Quidam ergo dicunt quod instans in quo ultimo est panis, et instans in quo primo est corpus Christi, sunt quidem duo per comparationem ad mensurata, sed sunt unum per comparationem ad tempus mensurans, sicut, cum duae lineae se contingunt, sunt duo puncta ex parte duarum linearum, unum autem punctum ex parte loci continentis. Sed hoc non est simile. Quia instans et tempus particularibus motibus non est mensura intrinseca, sicut linea et punctus corporibus, sed solum extrinseca, sicut corporibus locus.

Unde alii dicunt quod est idem instans re, sed aliud ratione. Sed secundum hoc sequeretur quod realiter opposita essent simul. Nam diversitas rationis non variat aliquid ex parte rei.

Et ideo dicendum est quod haec conversio, sicut dictum est, perficitur per verba Christi, quae a sacerdote proferuntur, ita quod ultimum instans prolationis verborum est primum instans in quo est in sacramento corpus Christi, in toto autem tempore praecedente est ibi substantia panis. Cuius temporis non est accipere aliquod instans proximo praecedens ultimum, quia tempus non componitur ex instantibus consequenter se habentibus, ut probatur in VI Physic. Et ideo est quidem dare instans in quo est corpus Christi, non est autem dare ultimum instans in quo sit substantia panis, sed est dare ultimum

Second, because in this conversion there is no subject to be disposed successively. Third, because it is effected by God's infinite power.

REPLY OBJ. 1: Some do not grant simply that there is a mid-time between every two instants. For they say that this is true of two instants referring to the same movement, but not if they refer to different things. Hence between the instant that marks the close of rest, and another which marks the beginning of movement, there is no mid-time. But in this they are mistaken, because the unity of time and of instant, or even their plurality, is not taken according to movements of any sort, but according to the first movement of the heavens, which is the measure of all movement and rest.

Accordingly others grant this of the time which measures movement depending on the movement of the heavens. But there are some movements which are not dependent on the movement of the heavens, nor measured by it, as was said in the First Part (Q. 53, A. 3) concerning the movements of the angels. Hence between two instants responding to those movements there is no mid-time. But this is not to the point, because although the change in question has no relation of itself to the movement of the heavens, still it follows the pronouncing of the words, which (pronouncing) must necessarily be measured by the movement of the heavens. And therefore there must of necessity be a mid-time between every two signate instants in connection with that change.

Some say therefore that the instant in which the bread was last, and the instant in which the body of Christ is first, are indeed two in comparison with the things measured, but are one comparatively to the time measuring; as when two lines touch, there are two points on the part of the two lines, but one point on the part of the place containing them. But here there is no likeness, because instant and time is not the intrinsic measure of particular movements, as a line and point are of a body, but only the extrinsic measure, as place is to bodies.

Hence others say that it is the same instant in fact, but another according to reason. But according to this it would follow that things really opposite would exist together; for diversity of reason does not change a thing objectively.

And therefore it must be said that this change, as stated above, is wrought by Christ's words which are spoken by the priest, so that the last instant of pronouncing the words is the first instant in which Christ's body is in the sacrament; and that the substance of the bread is there during the whole preceding time. Of this time no instant is to be taken as proximately preceding the last one, because time is not made up of successive instants, as is proved in *Phys.* vi. And therefore a first instant can be assigned in which Christ's body is present; but a last instant cannot be assigned in which the substance of bread is there, but a last

tempus. Et idem est in mutationibus naturalibus, ut patet per philosophum, in VIII physicorum.

AD SECUNDUM dicendum quod in mutationibus instantaneis simul est fieri et factum esse, sicut simul est illuminari et illuminatum esse. Dicitur enim in talibus factum esse secundum quod iam est, fieri autem, secundum quod ante non fuit.

AD TERTIUM dicendum quod ista conversio, sicut dictum est, fit in ultimo instanti prolationis verborum, tunc enim completur verborum significatio, quae est efficax in sacramentorum formis. Et ideo non sequitur quod ista conversio sit successiva.

time can be assigned. And the same holds good in natural changes, as is evident from the Philosopher (*Phys.* viii).

REPLY OBJ. 2: In instantaneous changes a thing is *in becoming*, and is *in being* simultaneously; just as becoming illuminated and to be actually illuminated are simultaneous: for in such, a thing is said to be *in being* according as it now is; but to be *in becoming*, according as it was not before.

REPLY OBJ. 3: As stated above (ad 1), this change comes about in the last instant of the pronouncing of the words. For then the meaning of the words is finished, which meaning is efficacious in the forms of the sacraments. And therefore it does not follow that this change is successive.

Article 8

Whether This Proposition Is False: The Body of Christ Is Made Out of Bread?

AD OCTAVUM SIC PROCEDITUR. Videtur quod haec sit falsa, ex pane fit corpus Christi. Omne enim id ex quo fit aliquid, est id quod fit illud, sed non convertitur, dicimus enim quod ex albo fit nigrum, et quod album fit nigrum; et licet dicamus quod homo fiat niger, non tamen dicimus quod ex homine fiat nigrum ut patet in I Physic. Si ergo verum est quod ex pane fiat corpus Christi, verum erit dicere quod panis fiat corpus Christi. Quod videtur esse falsum, quia panis non est subiectum factionis, sed magis est terminus. Ergo non vere dicitur quod ex pane fiat corpus Christi.

PRAETEREA, fieri terminatur ad esse, vel ad factum esse. Sed haec nunquam est vera, panis est corpus Christi, vel, panis est factus corpus Christi, vel etiam, panis erit corpus Christi. Ergo videtur quod nec haec sit vera, ex pane fit corpus Christi.

PRAETEREA, omne id ex quo fit aliquid, convertitur in id quod fit ex eo. Sed haec videtur esse falsa, panis convertitur in corpus Christi, quia haec conversio videtur esse miraculosior quam creatio; in qua tamen non dicitur quod non ens convertatur in ens. Ergo videtur quod etiam haec sit falsa, ex pane fit corpus Christi.

PRAETEREA, illud ex quo fit aliquid, potest esse illud. Sed haec est falsa, panis potest esse corpus Christi. Ergo etiam haec est falsa, ex pane fit corpus Christi.

SED CONTRA est quod Ambrosius dicit, in libro de sacramentis, *ubi accedit consecratio, de pane fit corpus Christi.*

RESPONDEO dicendum quod haec conversio panis in corpus Christi, quantum ad aliquid convenit cum

OBJECTION 1: It seems that this proposition is false: *The body of Christ is made out of bread.* For everything out of which another is made, is that which is made the other; but not conversely: for we say that a black thing is made out of a white thing, and that a white thing is made black: and although we may say that a man becomes black still we do not say that a black thing is made out of a man, as is shown in *Phys.* i. If it be true, then, that Christ's body is made out of bread, it will be true to say that bread is made the body of Christ. But this seems to be false, because the bread is not the subject of the making, but rather its term. Therefore, it is not said truly that Christ's body is made out of bread.

OBJ. 2: Further, the term of becoming is something that is, or something that is made. But this proposition is never true: *The bread is the body of Christ*; or *The bread is made the body of Christ*; or again, *The bread will be the body of Christ*. Therefore it seems that not even this is true: *The body of Christ is made out of bread.*

OBJ. 3: Further, everything out of which another is made is converted into that which is made from it. But this proposition seems to be false: *The bread is converted into the body of Christ*, because such conversion seems to be more miraculous than the creation of the world, in which it is not said that non-being is converted into being. Therefore it seems that this proposition likewise is false: *The body of Christ is made out of bread.*

OBJ. 4: Further, that out of which something is made, can be that thing. But this proposition is false: *Bread can be the body of Christ.* Therefore this is likewise false: *The body of Christ is made out of bread.*

ON THE CONTRARY, Ambrose says (*De Sacram.* iv): *When the consecration takes place, the body of Christ is made out of the bread.*

I ANSWER THAT, This conversion of bread into the body of Christ has something in common with creation,

creatione et cum transmutatione naturali, et quantum ad aliquid differt ab utroque. Est enim commune his tribus ordo terminorum, scilicet ut post hoc sit hoc, in creatione enim est esse post non esse, in hoc sacramento corpus Christi post substantiam panis, in transmutatione naturali album post nigrum vel ignis post aerem; et quod praedicti termini non sint simul.

Convenit autem conversio de qua nunc loquimur cum creatione, quia in neutra earum est aliquod commune subiectum utrique extremorum. Cuius contrarium apparet in omni transmutatione naturali.

Convenit vero haec conversio cum transmutatione naturali in duobus, licet non similiter. Primo quidem, quia in utraque unum extremorum transit in aliud, sicut panis in corpus Christi, et aer in ignem, non autem non ens convertitur in ens. Aliter tamen hoc accidit utrobique. Nam in hoc sacramento tota substantia panis transit in totum corpus Christi, sed in transmutatione naturali materia unius suscipit formam alterius, priori forma deposita. Secundo conveniunt in hoc, quod utrobique remanet aliquid idem, quod non accidit in creatione. Differenter tamen, nam in transmutatione naturali remanet eadem materia vel subiectum; in hoc autem sacramento remanent eadem accidentia.

Et ex his accipi potest qualiter differenter in talibus loqui debeamus. Quia enim in nullo praedictorum trium extrema sunt simul ideo in nullo eorum potest unum extremum de alio praedicari per verbum substantivum praesentis temporis, non enim dicimus, non ens est ens, vel, panis est corpus Christi, vel, aer est ignis aut album nigrum. Propter ordinem vero extremorum, possumus uti in omnibus hac praepositione ex, quae ordinem designat. Possumus enim vere et proprie dicere quod ex non ente fit ens, et ex pane corpus Christi, et ex aere ignis vel ex albo nigrum. Quia vero in creatione unum extremorum non transit in alterum, non possumus in creatione uti verbo conversionis, ut dicamus quod non ens convertitur in ens. Quo tamen verbo uti possumus in hoc sacramento, sicut et in transmutatione naturali. Sed quia in hoc sacramento tota substantia in totam mutatur, propter hoc haec conversio proprie transubstantiatio vocatur.

Rursus, quia huius conversionis non est accipere aliquod subiectum, ea quae verificantur in conversione naturali ratione subiecti, non sunt concedenda in hac conversione. Et primo quidem, manifestum est quod potentia ad oppositum consequitur subiectum, ratione cuius dicimus quod album potest esse nigrum, vel aer potest esse ignis. Licet haec non sit ita propria sicut prima, nam subiectum albi, in quo est potentia ad

and with natural transmutation, and in some respect differs from both. For the order of the terms is common to these three; that is, that after one thing there is another (for, in creation there is being after non-being; in this sacrament, Christ's body after the substance of bread; in natural transmutation white after black, or fire after air); and that the aforesaid terms are not coexistent.

Now the conversion, of which we are speaking, has this in common with creation, that in neither of them is there any common subject belonging to either of the extremes; the contrary of which appears in every natural transmutation.

Again, this conversion has something in common with natural transmutation in two respects, although not in the same fashion. First of all because in both, one of the extremes passes into the other, as bread into Christ's body, and air into fire; whereas non-being is not converted into being. But this comes to pass differently on the one side and on the other; for in this sacrament the whole substance of the bread passes into the whole body of Christ; whereas in natural transmutation the matter of the one receives the form of the other, the previous form being laid aside. Second, they have this in common, that on both sides something remains the same; whereas this does not happen in creation: yet differently; for the same matter or subject remains in natural transmutation; whereas in this sacrament the same accidents remain.

From these observations we can gather the various ways of speaking in such matters. For, because in no one of the aforesaid three things are the extremes coexistent, therefore in none of them can one extreme be predicated of the other by the substantive verb of the present tense: for we do not say, *Non-being is being* or, *Bread is the body of Christ*, or, *Air is fire*, or, *White is black*. Yet because of the relationship of the extremes in all of them we can use the preposition ex (out of), which denotes order; for we can truly and properly say that *being is made out of non-being*, and *out of bread, the body of Christ*, and *out of air, fire*, and *out of white, black*. But because in creation one of the extremes does not pass into the other, we cannot use the word *conversion* in creation, so as to say that *non-being is converted into being*: we can, however, use the word in this sacrament, just as in natural transmutation. But since in this sacrament the whole substance is converted into the whole substance, on that account this conversion is properly termed transubstantiation.

Again, since there is no subject of this conversion, the things which are true in natural conversion by reason of the subject, are not to be granted in this conversion. And in the first place indeed it is evident that potentiality to the opposite follows a subject, by reason whereof we say that *a white thing can be black*, or that *air can be fire*; although the latter is not so proper as the former: for the subject of whiteness, in which there is potentiality to blackness, is the

nigredinem, est tota substantia albi, non enim albedo est pars eius; subiectum autem formae aeris est pars eius; unde, cum dicitur, aer potest esse ignis, verificatur ratione partis per synecdochen. Sed in hac conversione et similiter in creatione, quia nullum est subiectum, non dicitur quod unum extremum possit esse aliud, sicut quod non ens possit esse ens, vel quod panis possit esse corpus Christi. Et eadem ratione non potest proprie dici quod de non ente fiat ens, vel quod de pane fiat corpus Christi, quia haec praepositio de designat causam consubstantialem; quae quidem consubstantialitas extremorum in transmutationibus naturalibus attenditur penes convenientiam in subiecto. Et simili ratione non conceditur quod panis erit corpus Christi, vel quod fiat corpus Christi, sicut neque conceditur in creatione quod non ens erit ens, vel quod non ens fiat ens, quia hic modus loquendi verificatur in transmutationibus naturalibus ratione subiecti, puta cum dicimus quod album fit nigrum, vel album erit nigrum.

Quia tamen in hoc sacramento, facta conversione, aliquid idem manet, scilicet accidentia panis, ut supra dictum est, secundum quandam similitudinem aliquae harum locutionum possunt concedi, scilicet quod panis sit corpus Christi, vel, panis erit corpus Christi, vel, de pane fit corpus Christi; ut nomine panis non intelligatur substantia panis, sed in universali hoc quod sub speciebus panis continetur, sub quibus prius continetur substantia panis, et postea corpus Christi.

AD PRIMUM ergo dicendum quod illud ex quo aliquid fit, quandoque quidem importat simul subiectum cum uno extremorum transmutationis, sicut cum dicitur, ex albo fit nigrum. Quandoque vero importat solum oppositum, vel extremum, sicut cum dicitur, ex mane fit dies. Et sic non conceditur quod hoc fiat illud, idest quod mane fiat dies. Et ita etiam in proposito, licet proprie dicatur quod ex pane fiat corpus Christi, non tamen proprie dicitur quod panis fiat corpus Christi, nisi secundum quandam similitudinem, ut dictum est.

AD SECUNDUM dicendum quod illud ex quo fit aliquid, quandoque erit illud, propter subiectum quod importatur. Et ideo, cum huius conversionis non sit aliquod subiectum, non est similis ratio.

AD TERTIUM dicendum quod in hac conversione sunt plura difficilia quam in creatione, in qua hoc solum difficile est, quod aliquid fit ex nihilo, quod tamen pertinet ad proprium modum productionis primae causae, quae nihil aliud praesupponit. Sed in hac conversione non solum est difficile quod hoc totum convertitur in illud totum, ita quod nihil prioris remaneat, quod non pertinet ad communem modum productionis alicuius causae, sed etiam habet hoc difficile, quod accidentia

whole substance of the white thing; since whiteness is not a part thereof; whereas the subject of the form of air is part thereof: hence when it is said, *Air can be fire*, it is verified by synecdoche by reason of the part. But in this conversion, and similarly in creation, because there is no subject, it is not said that one extreme can be the other, as that *non-being can be being*, or that *bread can be the body of Christ*: and for the same reason it cannot be properly said that *being is made of* (de) *non-being*, or that *the body of Christ is made of bread*, because this preposition *of* (de) denotes a consubstantial cause, which consubstantiality of the extremes in natural transmutations is considered according to something common in the subject. And for the same reason it is not granted that *bread will be the body of Christ*, or that it *may become the body of Christ*, just as it is not granted in creation that *non-being will be being*, or that *non-being may become being*, because this manner of speaking is verified in natural transmutations by reason of the subject: for instance, when we say that *a white thing becomes black*, or *a white thing will be black*.

Nevertheless, since in this sacrament, after the change, something remains the same, namely, the accidents of the bread, as stated above (A. 5), some of these expressions may be admitted by way of similitude, namely, that *bread is the body of Christ*, or, *bread will be the body of Christ*, or *the body of Christ is made of bread*; provided that by the word *bread* is not understood the substance of bread, but in general *that which is contained under the species of bread*, under which species there is first contained the substance of bread, and afterwards the body of Christ.

REPLY OBJ. 1: That out of which something else is made, sometimes implies together with the subject, one of the extremes of the transmutation, as when it is said *a black thing is made out of a white one*; but sometimes it implies only the opposite or the extreme, as when it is said—*out of morning comes the day*. And so it is not granted that the latter becomes the former, that is, *that morning becomes the day*. So likewise in the matter in hand, although it may be said properly that *the body of Christ is made out of bread*, yet it is not said properly that *bread becomes the body of Christ*, except by similitude, as was said above.

REPLY OBJ. 2: That out of which another is made, will sometimes be that other because of the subject which is implied. And therefore, since there is no subject of this change, the comparison does not hold.

REPLY OBJ. 3: In this change there are many more difficulties than in creation, in which there is but this one difficulty, that something is made out of nothing; yet this belongs to the proper mode of production of the first cause, which presupposes nothing else. But in this conversion not only is it difficult for this whole to be changed into that whole, so that nothing of the former may remain (which does not belong to the common mode of production of a cause), but furthermore it has this difficulty that the accidents remain

remanent corrupta substantia, et multa alia, de quibus in sequentibus agetur. Tamen verbum conversionis recipitur in hoc sacramento, non autem in creatione, sicut dictum est.

AD QUARTUM dicendum quod, sicut dictum est, potentia pertinet ad subiectum, quod non est accipere in hac conversione. Et ideo non conceditur quod panis possit esse corpus Christi, non enim haec conversio fit per potentiam passivam creaturae, sed per solam potentiam activam creatoris.

while the substance is destroyed, and many other difficulties of which we shall treat hereafter (Q. 77). Nevertheless the word *conversion* is admitted in this sacrament, but not in creation, as stated above.

REPLY OBJ. 4: As was observed above, potentiality belongs to the subject, whereas there is no subject in this conversion. And therefore it is not granted that bread can be the body of Christ: for this conversion does not come about by the passive potentiality of the creature, but solely by the active power of the Creator.

QUESTION 76

THE WAY IN WHICH CHRIST IS IN THIS SACRAMENT

Deinde considerandum est de modo quo Christus existit in hoc sacramento. Et circa hoc quaeruntur octo.

Primo, utrum totus Christus sit sub hoc sacramento.

Secundo, utrum totus Christus sit sub utraque specie sacramenti.

Tertio, utrum totus Christus sit sub qualibet parte specierum.

Quarto, utrum dimensiones corporis Christi totae sint in hoc sacramento.

Quinto, utrum corpus Christi sit in hoc sacramento localiter.

Sexto, utrum corpus Christi moveatur ad motum hostiae vel calicis post consecrationem.

Septimo, utrum corpus Christi sub hoc sacramento possit ab aliquo oculo videri.

Octavo, utrum verum corpus Christi remaneat in hoc sacramento quando miraculose apparet sub specie pueri vel carnis.

We have now to consider the manner in which Christ exists in this sacrament; and under this head there are eight points of inquiry:

(1) Whether the whole Christ is under this sacrament?

(2) Whether the entire Christ is under each species of the sacrament?

(3) Whether the entire Christ is under every part of the species?

(4) Whether all the dimensions of Christ's body are in this sacrament?

(5) Whether the body of Christ is in this sacrament locally?

(6) Whether after the consecration, the body of Christ is moved when the host or chalice is moved?

(7) Whether Christ's body, as it is in this sacrament, can be seen by the eye?

(8) Whether the true body of Christ remains in this sacrament when He is seen under the appearance of a child or of flesh?

Article 1

Whether the Whole Christ Is Contained Under This Sacrament?

AD PRIMUM SIC PROCEDITUR. Videtur quod non totus Christus contineatur sub hoc sacramento. Christus enim incipit esse in hoc sacramento per conversionem panis et vini. Sed manifestum est quod panis et vinum non possunt converti neque in divinitatem Christi, neque in eius animam. Cum ergo Christus existat ex tribus substantiis, scilicet divinitate, anima et corpore, ut supra habitum; videtur quod Christus totus non sit in hoc sacramento.

PRAETEREA, Christus est in hoc sacramento secundum quod competit refectioni fidelium, quae in cibo et potu consistit, sicut supra dictum est. Sed dominus dicit, Ioan. VI, *caro mea vere est cibus, et sanguis meus vere est potus.* Ergo solum caro et sanguis Christi continetur in hoc sacramento. Sunt autem multae aliae partes corporis Christi, puta nervi et ossa et alia huiusmodi. Non ergo totus Christus continetur sub hoc sacramento.

PRAETEREA, corpus maioris quantitatis non potest totum contineri sub minoris quantitatis mensura. Sed mensura panis et vini consecrati est multo minor quam

OBJECTION 1: It seems that the whole Christ is not contained under this sacrament, because Christ begins to be in this sacrament by conversion of the bread and wine. But it is evident that the bread and wine cannot be changed either into the Godhead or into the soul of Christ. Since therefore Christ exists in three substances, namely, the Godhead, soul and body, as shown above (Q. 2, A. 5; Q. 5, AA. 1, 3), it seems that the entire Christ is not under this sacrament.

OBJ. 2: Further, Christ is in this sacrament, forasmuch as it is ordained to the refection of the faithful, which consists in food and drink, as stated above (Q. 74, A. 1). But our Lord said (John 6:56): *My flesh is meat indeed, and My blood is drink indeed.* Therefore, only the flesh and blood of Christ are contained in this sacrament. But there are many other parts of Christ's body, for instance, the nerves, bones, and such like. Therefore the entire Christ is not contained under this sacrament.

OBJ. 3: Further, a body of greater quantity cannot be contained under the measure of a lesser. But the measure of the bread and wine is much smaller than the measure

propria mensura corporis Christi. Non potest ergo esse quod totus Christus sit sub hoc sacramento.

SED CONTRA est quod Ambrosius dicit, in libro de Offic., *in illo sacramento Christus est.*

RESPONDEO dicendum quod omnino necesse est confiteri secundum fidem Catholicam quod totus Christus sit in hoc sacramento. Sciendum tamen quod aliquid Christi est in hoc sacramento dupliciter, uno modo, quasi ex vi sacramenti; alio modo, ex naturali concomitantia. Ex vi quidem sacramenti, est sub speciebus huius sacramenti id in quod directe convertitur substantia panis et vini praeexistens, prout significatur per verba formae, quae sunt effectiva in hoc sacramento sicut et in ceteris, puta cum dicitur, *hoc est corpus meum, hic est sanguis meus.* Ex naturali autem concomitantia est in hoc sacramento illud quod realiter est coniunctum ei in quod praedicta conversio terminatur. Si enim aliqua duo sunt realiter coniuncta, ubicumque est unum realiter, oportet et aliud esse, sola enim operatione animae discernuntur quae realiter sunt coniuncta.

AD PRIMUM ergo dicendum quod, quia conversio panis et vini non terminatur ad divinitatem vel animam Christi, consequens est quod divinitas vel anima Christi non sit in hoc sacramento ex vi sacramenti, sed ex reali concomitantia. Quia enim divinitas corpus assumptum nunquam deposuit, ubicumque est corpus Christi, necesse est et eius divinitatem esse. Et ideo in hoc sacramento necesse est esse divinitatem Christi concomitantem eius corpus. Unde in symbolo Ephesino legitur, *participes efficimur corporis et sanguinis Christi, non ut communem carnem percipientes, nec viri sanctificati et verbo coniuncti secundum dignitatis unitatem, sed vere vivificatricem, et ipsius verbi propriam factam.*

Anima vero realiter separata fuit a corpore, ut supra dictum est. Et ideo, si in illo triduo mortis fuisset hoc sacramentum celebratum, non fuisset ibi anima, nec ex vi sacramenti nec ex reali concomitantia. Sed quia *Christus resurgens ex mortuis iam non moritur,* ut dicitur Rom. VI, anima eius semper est realiter corpori unita. Et ideo in hoc sacramento corpus quidem Christi est ex vi sacramenti, anima autem ex reali concomitantia.

AD SECUNDUM dicendum quod ex vi sacramenti sub hoc sacramento continetur, quantum ad species panis, non solum caro, sed totum corpus Christi, idest ossa et nervi et alia huiusmodi. Et hoc apparet ex forma huius sacramenti, in qua non dicitur, haec est caro mea, sed, *hoc est corpus meum.* Et ideo, cum dominus dixit, Ioan. VI, *caro mea vere est cibus,* caro ponitur ibi pro toto corpore, quia, secundum consuetudinem humanam, videtur esse magis manducationi accommodata, prout

of Christ's body. Therefore it is impossible that the entire Christ be contained under this sacrament.

ON THE CONTRARY, Ambrose says (*De Officiis*): *Christ is in this sacrament.*

I ANSWER THAT, It is absolutely necessary to confess according to Catholic faith that the entire Christ is in this sacrament. Yet we must know that there is something of Christ in this sacrament in a twofold manner: first, as it were, by the power of the sacrament; second, from natural concomitance. By the power of the sacrament, there is under the species of this sacrament that into which the pre-existing substance of the bread and wine is changed, as expressed by the words of the form, which are effective in this as in the other sacraments; for instance, by the words: *This is My body*, or, *This is My blood*. But from natural concomitance there is also in this sacrament that which is really united with that thing wherein the aforesaid conversion is terminated. For if any two things be really united, then wherever the one is really, there must the other also be: since things really united together are only distinguished by an operation of the mind.

REPLY OBJ. 1: Because the change of the bread and wine is not terminated at the Godhead or the soul of Christ, it follows as a consequence that the Godhead or the soul of Christ is in this sacrament not by the power of the sacrament, but from real concomitance. For since the Godhead never set aside the assumed body, wherever the body of Christ is, there, of necessity, must the Godhead be; and therefore it is necessary for the Godhead to be in this sacrament concomitantly with His body. Hence we read in the profession of faith at Ephesus (*P. I.*, chap. xxvi): *We are made partakers of the body and blood of Christ, not as taking common flesh, nor as of a holy man united to the Word in dignity, but the truly life-giving flesh of the Word Himself.*

On the other hand, His soul was truly separated from His body, as stated above (Q. 50, A. 5). And therefore had this sacrament been celebrated during those three days when He was dead, the soul of Christ would not have been there, neither by the power of the sacrament, nor from real concomitance. But since *Christ rising from the dead dieth now no more* (Rom 6:9), His soul is always really united with His body. And therefore in this sacrament the body indeed of Christ is present by the power of the sacrament, but His soul from real concomitance.

REPLY OBJ. 2: By the power of the sacrament there is contained under it, as to the species of the bread, not only the flesh, but the entire body of Christ, that is, the bones the nerves, and the like. And this is apparent from the form of this sacrament, wherein it is not said: *This is My flesh*, but *This is My body*. Accordingly, when our Lord said (John 6:56): *My flesh is meat indeed*, there the word flesh is put for the entire body, because according to human custom it seems to be more adapted for eating, as men

scilicet homines carnibus animalium vescuntur communiter, non ossibus vel aliis huiusmodi.

AD TERTIUM dicendum quod, sicut dictum est, facta conversione panis in corpus Christi vel vini in sanguinem, accidentia utriusque remanent. Ex quo patet quod dimensiones panis vel vini non convertuntur in dimensiones corporis Christi, sed substantia in substantiam. Et sic substantia corporis Christi vel sanguinis est in hoc sacramento ex vi sacramenti, non autem dimensiones corporis vel sanguinis Christi. Unde patet quod corpus Christi est in hoc sacramento per modum substantiae, et non per modum quantitatis. Propria autem totalitas substantiae continetur indifferenter in parva vel magna quantitate, sicut tota natura aeris in magno vel parvo aere, et tota natura hominis in magno vel parvo homine. Unde et tota substantia corporis Christi et sanguinis continetur in hoc sacramento post consecrationem, sicut ante consecrationem continebatur ibi substantia panis et vini.

commonly are fed on the flesh of animals, but not on the bones or the like.

REPLY OBJ. 3: As has been already stated (Q. 75, A. 5), after the consecration of the bread into the body of Christ, or of the wine into His blood, the accidents of both remain. From which it is evident that the dimensions of the bread or wine are not changed into the dimensions of the body of Christ, but substance into substance. And so the substance of Christ's body or blood is under this sacrament by the power of the sacrament, but not the dimensions of Christ's body or blood. Hence it is clear that the body of Christ is in this sacrament by way of substance, and not by way of quantity. But the proper totality of substance is contained indifferently in a small or large quantity; as the whole nature of air in a great or small amount of air, and the whole nature of a man in a big or small individual. Wherefore, after the consecration, the whole substance of Christ's body and blood is contained in this sacrament, just as the whole substance of the bread and wine was contained there before the consecration.

Article 2

Whether the Whole Christ Is Contained Under Each Species of This Sacrament?

AD SECUNDUM SIC PROCEDITUR. Videtur quod non sub utraque specie huius sacramenti totus Christus contineatur. Hoc enim sacramentum ad salutem fidelium ordinatur, non virtute specierum, sed virtute eius quod sub speciebus continetur, quia species erant etiam ante consecrationem, ex qua est virtus huius sacramenti. Si ergo nihil continetur sub una specie quod non contineatur sub alia, et totus Christus continetur sub utraque, videtur quod altera illarum superfluat in hoc sacramento.

PRAETEREA, dictum est quod sub nomine carnis omnes aliae partes corporis continentur, sicut ossa, nervi et alia huiusmodi. Sed sanguis est una partium humani corporis, sicut patet per Aristotelem, in libro animalium. Si ergo sanguis Christi continetur sub specie panis, sicut continentur ibi aliae partes corporis, non deberet seorsum sanguis consecrari, sicut neque seorsum consecratur alia pars corporis.

PRAETEREA, quod iam factum est, iterum fieri non potest. Sed corpus Christi iam incoepit esse in hoc sacramento per consecrationem panis. Ergo non potest esse quod denuo incipiat esse per consecrationem vini. Et ita sub specie vini non continebitur corpus Christi; et per consequens nec totus Christus. Non ergo sub utraque specie totus Christus continetur.

OBJECTION 1: It seems that the whole Christ is not contained under both species of this sacrament. For this sacrament is ordained for the salvation of the faithful, not by virtue of the species, but by virtue of what is contained under the species, because the species were there even before the consecration, from which comes the power of this sacrament. If nothing, then, be contained under one species, but what is contained under the other, and if the whole Christ be contained under both, it seems that one of them is superfluous in this sacrament.

OBJ. 2: Further, it was stated above (A. 1, ad 1) that all the other parts of the body, such as the bones, nerves, and the like, are comprised under the name of flesh. But the blood is one of the parts of the human body, as Aristotle proves (*De Anima Histor.* i). If, then, Christ's blood be contained under the species of bread, just as the other parts of the body are contained there, the blood ought not to be consecrated apart, just as no other part of the body is consecrated separately.

OBJ. 3: Further, what is once in being cannot be again in becoming. But Christ's body has already begun to be in this sacrament by the consecration of the bread. Therefore, it cannot begin again to be there by the consecration of the wine; and so Christ's body will not be contained under the species of the wine, and accordingly neither the entire Christ. Therefore the whole Christ is not contained under each species.

SED CONTRA est quod, I Cor. XI, super illud, calicem, dicit Glossa quod sub utraque specie, scilicet panis et vini, idem sumitur. Et ita videtur quod sub utraque specie totus Christus sit.

RESPONDEO dicendum certissime ex supra dictis tenendum esse quod sub utraque specie sacramenti totus est Christus, aliter tamen et aliter. Nam sub speciebus panis est quidem corpus Christi ex vi sacramenti, sanguis autem ex reali concomitantia, sicut supra dictum est de anima et divinitate Christi. Sub speciebus vero vini est quidem sanguis Christi ex vi sacramenti, corpus autem Christi ex reali concomitantia, sicut anima et divinitas, eo quod nunc sanguis Christi non est ab eius corpore separatus, sicut fuit tempore passionis et mortis. Unde, si tunc fuisset hoc sacramentum celebratum, sub speciebus panis fuisset corpus Christi sine sanguine, et sub specie vini sanguis sine corpore, sicut erat in rei veritate.

AD PRIMUM ergo dicendum quod, quamvis totus Christus sit sub utraque specie, non tamen frustra. Nam primo quidem, hoc valet ad repraesentandam passionem Christi, in qua seorsum sanguis fuit a corpore. Unde et in forma consecrationis sanguinis fit mentio de eius effusione. Secundo, hoc est conveniens usui huius sacramenti, ut seorsum exhibeatur fidelibus corpus Christi in cibum, et sanguis in potum. Tertio, quantum ad effectum, secundum quod supra dictum est quod *corpus exhibetur pro salute corporis, sanguis pro salute animae.*

AD SECUNDUM dicendum quod in passione Christi, cuius hoc sacramentum est memoriale, non fuerunt aliae partes corporis ab invicem separatae, sicut sanguis, sed corpus indissolutum permansit, secundum quod legitur Exod. XII, *os non comminuetis ex eo.* Et ideo in hoc sacramento seorsum consecratur sanguis a corpore, non autem alia pars ab alia.

AD TERTIUM dicendum quod, sicut dictum est, corpus Christi non est sub specie vini ex vi sacramenti, sed ex reali concomitantia. Et ideo per consecrationem vini non fit ibi corpus Christi per se, sed concomitanter.

ON THE CONTRARY, The gloss on 1 Cor. 11:25, commenting on the word *Chalice*, says that *under each species,* namely, of the bread and wine, *the same is received*; and thus it seems that Christ is entire under each species.

I ANSWER THAT, After what we have said above (A. 1), it must be held most certainly that the whole Christ is under each sacramental species yet not alike in each. For the body of Christ is indeed present under the species of bread by the power of the sacrament, while the blood is there from real concomitance, as stated above (A. 1, ad 1) in regard to the soul and Godhead of Christ; and under the species of wine the blood is present by the power of the sacrament, and His body by real concomitance, as is also His soul and Godhead: because now Christ's blood is not separated from His body, as it was at the time of His Passion and death. Hence if this sacrament had been celebrated then, the body of Christ would have been under the species of the bread, but without the blood; and, under the species of the wine, the blood would have been present without the body, as it was then, in fact.

REPLY OBJ. 1: Although the whole Christ is under each species, yet it is so not without purpose. For in the first place this serves to represent Christ's Passion, in which the blood was separated from the body; hence in the form for the consecration of the blood mention is made of its shedding. Second, it is in keeping with the use of this sacrament, that Christ's body be shown apart to the faithful as food, and the blood as drink. Third, it is in keeping with its effect, in which sense it was stated above (Q. 74, A. 1) that *the body is offered for the salvation of the body, and the blood for the salvation of the soul.*

REPLY OBJ. 2: In Christ's Passion, of which this is the memorial, the other parts of the body were not separated from one another, as the blood was, but the body remained entire, according to Ex. 12:46: *You shall not break a bone thereof.* And therefore in this sacrament the blood is consecrated apart from the body, but no other part is consecrated separately from the rest.

REPLY OBJ. 3: As stated above, the body of Christ is not under the species of wine by the power of the sacrament, but by real concomitance: and therefore by the consecration of the wine the body of Christ is not there of itself, but concomitantly.

Article 3

Whether Christ Is Entire Under Every Part of the Species of the Bread and Wine?

AD TERTIUM SIC PROCEDITUR. Videtur quod non sit totus Christus sub qualibet parte specierum panis vel vini. Species enim illae dividi possunt in infinitum. Si ergo Christus totus est sub qualibet parte specierum

OBJECTION 1: It seems that Christ is not entire under every part of the species of bread and wine. Because those species can be divided infinitely. If therefore Christ be entirely under every part of the said species, it would follow

praedictarum, sequeretur quod infinities esset in hoc sacramento. Quod est inconveniens, nam infinitum non solum repugnat naturae, sed etiam gratiae.

PRAETEREA, corpus Christi, cum sit organicum, habet partes determinate distantes, est enim de ratione organici corporis determinata distantia singularum partium ad invicem, sicut oculi ab oculo, et oculi ab aure. Sed hoc non posset esse si sub qualibet parte specierum esset totus Christus, oporteret enim quod sub qualibet parte esset quaelibet pars; et ita, ubi esset una pars, esset et alia. Non ergo potest esse quod totus Christus sit sub qualibet parte hostiae vel vini contenti in calice.

PRAETEREA, corpus Christi semper veram retinet corporis naturam, nec unquam mutatur in spiritum. Sed de ratione corporis est ut sit quantitas positionem habens, ut patet in praedicamentis. Sed ad rationem huius quantitatis pertinet quod diversae partes in diversis partibus loci existant. Non ergo potest esse, ut videtur, quod totus Christus sit sub qualibet parte specierum.

SED CONTRA est quod Augustinus dicit, in quodam sermone, *singuli accipiunt Christum dominum, et in singulis portionibus totus est, nec per singulas minuitur, sed integrum se praebet in singulis.*

RESPONDEO dicendum quod, sicut ex supra dictis patet, quia in hoc sacramento substantia corporis Christi est ex vi sacramenti, quantitas autem dimensiva ex vi realis concomitantiae, corpus Christi est in hoc sacramento per modum substantiae, idest, per modum quo substantia est sub dimensionibus, non autem per modum dimensionum, idest, non per illum modum quo quantitas dimensiva alicuius corporis est sub quantitate dimensiva loci.

Manifestum est autem quod natura substantiae tota est sub qualibet parte dimensionum sub quibus continetur, sicut sub qualibet parte aeris est tota natura aeris, et sub qualibet parte panis est tota natura panis. Et hoc indifferenter sive dimensiones sint actu divisae, sicut cum aer dividitur vel panis secatur, vel etiam sint actu indivisae, divisibiles vero potentia. Et ideo manifestum est quod Christus totus est sub qualibet parte specierum panis, etiam hostia integra manente, et non solum cum frangitur, sicut quidam dicunt, ponentes exemplum de imagine quae apparet in speculo, quae una apparet in speculo integro, infracto autem speculo apparent singulae in singulis partibus. Quod quidem non est omnino simile. Quia multiplicatio huiusmodi imaginum accidit in speculo fracto propter diversas reflexiones ad diversas partes speculi, hic autem non est nisi una consecratio propter quam corpus Christi est in sacramento.

AD PRIMUM ergo dicendum quod numerus sequitur divisionem. Et ideo, quandiu quantitas manet indivisa actu, neque substantia alicuius rei est pluries sub

that He is in this sacrament an infinite number of times: which is unreasonable; because the infinite is repugnant not only to nature, but likewise to grace.

OBJ. 2: Further, since Christ's is an organic body, it has parts determinately distant. For a determinate distance of the individual parts from each other is of the very nature of an organic body, as that of eye from eye, and eye from ear. But this could not be so, if Christ were entire under every part of the species; for every part would have to be under every other part, and so where one part would be, there another part would be. It cannot be then that the entire Christ is under every part of the host or of the wine contained in the chalice.

OBJ. 3: Further, Christ's body always retains the true nature of a body, nor is it ever changed into a spirit. Now it is the nature of a body for it to be *quantity having position* (*Predic.* iv). But it belongs to the nature of this quantity that the various parts exist in various parts of place. Therefore, apparently it is impossible for the entire Christ to be under every part of the species.

ON THE CONTRARY, Augustine says in a sermon (Gregory, *Sacramentarium*): *Each receives Christ the Lord, Who is entire under every morsel, nor is He less in each portion, but bestows Himself entire under each.*

I ANSWER THAT, As was observed above (A. 1, ad 3), because the substance of Christ's body is in this sacrament by the power of the sacrament, while dimensive quantity is there by reason of real concomitance, consequently Christ's body is in this sacrament substantively, that is, in the way in which substance is under dimensions, but not after the manner of dimensions, which means, not in the way in which the dimensive quantity of a body is under the dimensive quantity of place.

Now it is evident that the whole nature of a substance is under every part of the dimensions under which it is contained; just as the entire nature of air is under every part of air, and the entire nature of bread under every part of bread; and this indifferently, whether the dimensions be actually divided (as when the air is divided or the bread cut), or whether they be actually undivided, but potentially divisible. And therefore it is manifest that the entire Christ is under every part of the species of the bread, even while the host remains entire, and not merely when it is broken, as some say, giving the example of an image which appears in a mirror, which appears as one in the unbroken mirror, whereas when the mirror is broken, there is an image in each part of the broken mirror: for the comparison is not perfect, because the multiplying of such images results in the broken mirror on account of the various reflections in the various parts of the mirror; but here there is only one consecration, whereby Christ's body is in this sacrament.

REPLY OBJ. 1: Number follows division, and therefore so long as quantity remains actually undivided, neither is the substance of any thing several times under its proper

dimensionibus propriis, neque corpus Christi sub dimensionibus panis. Et per consequens neque infinities, sed toties in quot partes dividitur.

Ad secundum dicendum quod illa determinata distantia partium in corpore organico fundatur super quantitatem dimensivam ipsius, ipsa autem natura substantiae praecedit etiam quantitatem dimensivam. Et quia conversio substantiae panis directe terminatur ad substantiam corporis Christi, secundum cuius modum proprie et directe est in hoc sacramento corpus Christi, talis distantia partium est quidem in ipso corpore Christi vero, sed non secundum hanc distantiam comparatur ad hoc sacramentum, sed secundum modum suae substantiae, ut dictum est.

Ad tertium dicendum quod ratio illa procedit de natura corporis quam habet secundum quantitatem dimensivam. Dictum est autem quod corpus Christi non comparatur ad hoc sacramentum ratione quantitatis dimensivae, sed ratione substantiae, ut dictum est.

dimensions, nor is Christ's body several times under the dimensions of the bread; and consequently not an infinite number of times, but just as many times as it is divided into parts.

Reply Obj. 2: The determinate distance of parts in an organic body is based upon its dimensive quantity; but the nature of substance precedes even dimensive quantity. And since the conversion of the substance of the bread is terminated at the substance of the body of Christ, and since according to the manner of substance the body of Christ is properly and directly in this sacrament; such distance of parts is indeed in Christ's true body, which, however, is not compared to this sacrament according to such distance, but according to the manner of its substance, as stated above (A. 1, ad 3).

Reply Obj. 3: This argument is based on the nature of a body, arising from dimensive quantity. But it was said above (ad 2) that Christ's body is compared with this sacrament not by reason of dimensive quantity, but by reason of its substance, as already stated.

Article 4

Whether the Whole Dimensive Quantity of Christ's Body Is in This Sacrament?

Ad quartum sic proceditur. Videtur quod non tota quantitas dimensiva corporis Christi sit in hoc sacramento. Dictum est enim quod totum corpus Christi continetur sub qualibet parte hostiae consecratae. Sed nulla quantitas dimensiva tota continetur in aliquo toto et in qualibet parte eius. Est ergo impossibile quod tota quantitas dimensiva corporis Christi contineatur in hoc sacramento.

Praeterea, impossibile est duas quantitates dimensivas esse simul, etiam si una sit separata et alia in corpore naturali, ut patet per philosophum, in III Metaphys. Sed in hoc sacramento remanet quantitas dimensiva panis, ut sensu apparet. Non ergo est ibi quantitas dimensiva corporis Christi.

Praeterea, si duae quantitates dimensivae inaequales iuxta se ponantur, maior extenditur ultra minorem. Sed quantitas dimensiva corporis Christi est multo maior quam quantitas dimensiva hostiae eius consecratae, secundum omnem dimensionem. Si ergo in hoc sacramento sit quantitas dimensiva corporis Christi cum quantitate dimensiva hostiae, quantitas dimensiva corporis Christi extendetur ultra quantitatem hostiae. Quae tamen non est sine substantia corporis Christi. Ergo substantia corporis Christi erit in hoc sacramento etiam praeter species panis. Quod est inconveniens, cum substantia corporis Christi non sit in hoc sacramento nisi

Objection 1: It seems that the whole dimensive quantity of Christ's body is not in this sacrament. For it was said (A. 3) that Christ's entire body is contained under every part of the consecrated host. But no dimensive quantity is contained entirely in any whole, and in its every part. Therefore it is impossible for the entire dimensive quantity of Christ's body to be there.

Obj. 2: Further, it is impossible for two dimensive quantities to be together, even though one be separate from its subject, and the other in a natural body, as is clear from the Philosopher (*Metaph.* iii). But the dimensive quantity of the bread remains in this sacrament, as is evident to our senses. Consequently, the dimensive quantity of Christ's body is not there.

Obj. 3: Further, if two unequal dimensive quantities be set side by side, the greater will overlap the lesser. But the dimensive quantity of Christ's body is considerably larger than the dimensive quantity of the consecrated host according to every dimension. Therefore, if the dimensive quantity of Christ's body be in this sacrament together with the dimensive quantity of the host, the dimensive quantity of Christ's body is extended beyond the quantity of the host, which nevertheless is not without the substance of Christ's body. Therefore, the substance of Christ's body will be in this sacrament even outside the species of the bread, which is unreasonable, since the substance of Christ's body

per consecrationem panis, ut dictum est. Impossibile est ergo quod tota quantitas corporis Christi sit in hoc sacramento.

SED CONTRA est quod quantitas dimensiva corporis alicuius non separatur secundum esse a substantia eius. Sed in hoc sacramento est tota substantia corporis Christi, ut supra habitum est. Ergo tota quantitas dimensiva corporis Christi est in hoc sacramento.

RESPONDEO dicendum quod, sicut supra dictum est, dupliciter aliquid Christi est in hoc sacramento, uno modo, ex vi sacramenti; alio modo, ex naturali concomitantia. Ex vi quidem sacramenti quantitas dimensiva corporis Christi non est in hoc sacramento. Ex vi enim sacramenti est in hoc sacramento illud in quod directe conversio terminatur. Conversio autem quae fit in hoc sacramento, terminatur directe ad substantiam corporis Christi, non autem ad dimensiones eius. Quod patet ex hoc quod quantitas dimensiva remanet facta consecratione, sola substantia panis transeunte.

Quia tamen substantia corporis Christi realiter non denudatur a sua quantitate dimensiva et ab aliis accidentibus, inde est quod, ex vi realis concomitantiae, est in hoc sacramento tota quantitas dimensiva corporis Christi, et omnia alia accidentia eius.

AD PRIMUM ergo dicendum quod modus existendi cuiuslibet rei determinatur secundum illud quod est ei per se, non autem secundum illud quod est ei per accidens, sicut corpus est in visu secundum quod est album, non autem secundum quod est dulce, licet idem corpus sit album et dulce. Unde et dulcedo est in visu secundum modum albedinis, et non secundum modum dulcedinis. Quia igitur ex vi sacramenti huius est in altari substantia corporis Christi, quantitas autem dimensiva eius est ibi concomitanter et quasi per accidens, ideo quantitas dimensiva corporis Christi est in hoc sacramento, non secundum proprium modum, ut scilicet sit totum in toto et singulae partes in singulis partibus; sed per modum substantiae, cuius natura est tota in toto et tota in qualibet parte.

AD SECUNDUM dicendum quod duae quantitates dimensivae non possunt naturaliter simul esse in eodem ita quod utraque sit secundum proprium modum quantitatis dimensivae. In hoc autem sacramento quantitas dimensiva panis est secundum proprium modum, scilicet secundum commensurationem quandam, non autem quantitas dimensiva corporis Christi, sed est ibi per modum substantiae, ut dictum est.

AD TERTIUM dicendum quod quantitas dimensiva corporis Christi non est in hoc sacramento secundum modum commensurationis, qui est proprius quantitati,

is in this sacrament, only by the consecration of the bread, as stated above (A. 2). Consequently, it is impossible for the whole dimensive quantity of Christ's body to be in this sacrament.

ON THE CONTRARY, The existence of the dimensive quantity of any body cannot be separated from the existence of its substance. But in this sacrament the entire substance of Christ's body is present, as stated above (AA. 1, 3). Therefore the entire dimensive quantity of Christ's body is in this sacrament.

I ANSWER THAT, As stated above (A. 1), any part of Christ is in this sacrament in two ways: in one way, by the power of the sacrament; in another, from real concomitance. By the power of the sacrament the dimensive quantity of Christ's body is not in this sacrament; for, by the power of the sacrament that is present in this sacrament, whereat the conversion is terminated. But the conversion which takes place in this sacrament is terminated directly at the substance of Christ's body, and not at its dimensions; which is evident from the fact that the dimensive quantity of the bread remains after the consecration, while only the substance of the bread passes away.

Nevertheless, since the substance of Christ's body is not really deprived of its dimensive quantity and its other accidents, hence it comes that by reason of real concomitance the whole dimensive quantity of Christ's body and all its other accidents are in this sacrament.

REPLY OBJ. 1: The manner of being of every thing is determined by what belongs to it of itself, and not according to what is coupled accidentally with it: thus an object is present to the sight, according as it is white, and not according as it is sweet, although the same object may be both white and sweet; hence sweetness is in the sight after the manner of whiteness, and not after that of sweetness. Since, then, the substance of Christ's body is present on the altar by the power of this sacrament, while its dimensive quantity is there concomitantly and as it were accidentally, therefore the dimensive quantity of Christ's body is in this sacrament, not according to its proper manner (namely, that the whole is in the whole, and the individual parts in individual parts), but after the manner of substance, whose nature is for the whole to be in the whole, and the whole in every part.

REPLY OBJ. 2: Two dimensive quantities cannot naturally be in the same subject at the same time, so that each be there according to the proper manner of dimensive quantity. But in this sacrament the dimensive quantity of the bread is there after its proper manner, that is, according to commensuration: not so the dimensive quantity of Christ's body, for that is there after the manner of substance, as stated above (ad 1).

REPLY OBJ. 3: The dimensive quantity of Christ's body is in this sacrament not by way of commensuration, which is proper to quantity, and to which it belongs for the greater

ad quem pertinet quod maior quantitas extendatur ultra minorem, sed est ibi per modum iam dictum.

to be extended beyond the lesser; but in the way mentioned above (ad 1, 2).

Article 5

Whether Christ's Body Is in This Sacrament As in a Place?

AD QUINTUM SIC PROCEDITUR. Videtur quod corpus Christi sit in hoc sacramento sicut in loco. Esse enim in aliquo definitive vel circumscriptive est pars eius quod est esse in loco. Sed corpus Christi videtur esse definitive in hoc sacramento, quia ita est ubi sunt species panis vel vini, quod non est in alio loco altaris. Videtur etiam ibi esse circumscriptive, quia ita continetur superficie hostiae consecratae quod nec excedit nec exceditur. Ergo corpus Christi est in hoc sacramento sicut in loco.

PRAETEREA, locus specierum panis non est vacuus, natura enim non patitur vacuum. Nec est ibi substantia panis, ut supra habitum est, sed est ibi solum corpus Christi. Ergo corpus Christi replet locum illum. Sed omne quod replet locum aliquem, est in eo localiter. Ergo corpus Christi est in hoc sacramento localiter.

PRAETEREA, in hoc sacramento, sicut dictum est, corpus Christi est cum sua quantitate dimensiva et cum omnibus suis accidentibus. Sed esse in loco est accidens corporis, unde et ubi connumeratur inter novem genera accidentium. Ergo corpus Christi est in hoc sacramento localiter.

SED CONTRA est quod oportet locum et locatum esse aequalia, ut patet per philosophum, in IV Physic. Sed locus ubi est hoc sacramentum, est multo minor quam corpus Christi. Ergo corpus Christi non est in hoc sacramento sicut in loco.

RESPONDEO dicendum quod, sicut iam dictum est, corpus Christi non est in hoc sacramento secundum proprium modum quantitatis dimensivae, sed magis secundum modum substantiae. Omne autem corpus locatum est in loco secundum modum quantitatis dimensivae, inquantum scilicet commensuratur loco secundum suam quantitatem dimensivam. Unde relinquitur quod corpus Christi non est in hoc sacramento sicut in loco, sed per modum substantiae, eo scilicet modo quo substantia continetur a dimensionibus. Succedit enim substantia corporis Christi in hoc sacramento substantiae panis. Unde, sicut substantia panis non erat sub suis dimensionibus localiter, sed per modum substantiae, ita nec substantia corporis Christi. Non tamen substantia corporis Christi est subiectum illarum dimensionum, sicut erat substantia panis. Et ideo panis ratione suarum dimensionum localiter erat ibi, quia comparabatur ad

OBJECTION 1: It seems that Christ's body is in this sacrament as in a place. Because, to be in a place definitively or circumscriptively belongs to being in a place. But Christ's body seems to be definitively in this sacrament, because it is so present where the species of the bread and wine are, that it is nowhere else upon the altar: likewise it seems to be there circumscriptively, because it is so contained under the species of the consecrated host, that it neither exceeds it nor is exceeded by it. Therefore Christ's body is in this sacrament as in a place.

OBJ. 2: Further, the place of the bread and wine is not empty, because nature abhors a vacuum; nor is the substance of the bread there, as stated above (Q. 75, A. 2); but only the body of Christ is there. Consequently the body of Christ fills that place. But whatever fills a place is there locally. Therefore the body of Christ is in this sacrament locally.

OBJ. 3: Further, as stated above (A. 4), the body of Christ is in this sacrament with its dimensive quantity, and with all its accidents. But to be in a place is an accident of a body; hence *where* is numbered among the nine kinds of accidents. Therefore Christ's body is in this sacrament locally.

ON THE CONTRARY, The place and the object placed must be equal, as is clear from the Philosopher (*Phys.* iv). But the place, where this sacrament is, is much less than the body of Christ. Therefore Christ's body is not in this sacrament as in a place.

I ANSWER THAT, As stated above (A. 1, ad 3; A. 3), Christ's body is in this sacrament not after the proper manner of dimensive quantity, but rather after the manner of substance. But every body occupying a place is in the place according to the manner of dimensive quantity, namely, inasmuch as it is commensurate with the place according to its dimensive quantity. Hence it remains that Christ's body is not in this sacrament as in a place, but after the manner of substance, that is to say, in that way in which substance is contained by dimensions; because the substance of Christ's body succeeds the substance of bread in this sacrament: hence as the substance of bread was not locally under its dimensions, but after the manner of substance, so neither is the substance of Christ's body. Nevertheless the substance of Christ's body is not the subject of those dimensions, as was the substance of the bread: and therefore the substance of the bread was there locally by reason of its dimensions,

locum mediantibus propriis dimensionibus. Substantia autem corporis Christi comparatur ad locum illum mediantibus dimensionibus alienis, ita quod e converso dimensiones propriae corporis Christi comparantur ad locum illum mediante substantia. Quod est contra rationem corporis locati. Unde nullo modo corpus Christi est in hoc sacramento localiter.

AD PRIMUM ergo dicendum quod corpus Christi non est in hoc sacramento definitive, quia sic non esset alibi quam in hoc altari ubi conficitur hoc sacramentum; cum tamen sit et in caelo in propria specie, et in multis aliis altaribus sub specie sacramenti. Similiter etiam patet quod non est in hoc sacramento circumscriptive, quia non est ibi secundum commensurationem propriae quantitatis, ut dictum est. Quod autem non est extra superficiem sacramenti, nec est in alia parte altaris, non pertinet ad hoc quod sit ibi definitive vel circumscriptive, sed ad hoc quod incoepit ibi esse per consecrationem et conversionem panis et vini, ut supra dictum est.

AD SECUNDUM dicendum quod locus ille in quo est corpus Christi, non est vacuus. Neque tamen proprie est repletus substantia corporis Christi, quae non est ibi localiter, sicut dictum est. Sed est repletus speciebus sacramentorum, quae habent replere locum vel propter naturam dimensionum; vel saltem miraculose, sicut et miraculose subsistunt per modum substantiae.

AD TERTIUM dicendum quod accidentia corporis Christi sunt in hoc sacramento, sicut supra dictum est, secundum realem concomitantiam. Et ideo illa accidentia corporis Christi sunt in hoc sacramento quae sunt ei intrinseca. Esse autem in loco est accidens per comparationem ad extrinsecum continens. Et ideo non oportet quod Christus sit in hoc sacramento sicut in loco.

because it was compared with that place through the medium of its own dimensions; but the substance of Christ's body is compared with that place through the medium of foreign dimensions, so that, on the contrary, the proper dimensions of Christ's body are compared with that place through the medium of substance; which is contrary to the notion of a located body. Hence in no way is Christ's body locally in this sacrament.

REPLY OBJ. 1: Christ's body is not in this sacrament definitively, because then it would be only on the particular altar where this sacrament is performed: whereas it is in heaven under its own species, and on many other altars under the sacramental species. Likewise it is evident that it is not in this sacrament circumscriptively, because it is not there according to the commensuration of its own quantity, as stated above. But that it is not outside the superficies of the sacrament, nor on any other part of the altar, is due not to its being there definitively or circumscriptively, but to its being there by consecration and conversion of the bread and wine, as stated above (A. 1; Q. 15, A. 2, sqq.).

REPLY OBJ. 2: The place in which Christ's body is, is not empty; nor yet is it properly filled with the substance of Christ's body, which is not there locally, as stated above; but it is filled with the sacramental species, which have to fill the place either because of the nature of dimensions, or at least miraculously, as they also subsist miraculously after the fashion of substance.

REPLY OBJ. 3: As stated above (A. 4), the accidents of Christ's body are in this sacrament by real concomitance. And therefore those accidents of Christ's body which are intrinsic to it are in this sacrament. But to be in a place is an accident when compared with the extrinsic container. And therefore it is not necessary for Christ to be in this sacrament as in a place.

Article 6

Whether Christ's Body Is in This Sacrament Movably?

AD SEXTUM SIC PROCEDITUR. Videtur quod corpus Christi sit mobiliter in hoc sacramento. Dicit enim philosophus, in II Topic., quod, *moventibus nobis, moventur ea quae in nobis sunt.* Quod quidem verum est etiam de spirituali substantia animae. Sed Christus est in hoc sacramento, ut supra habitum est. Ergo movetur ad motum ipsius.

PRAETEREA, veritas debet respondere figurae. Sed de agno paschali, qui erat figura huius sacramenti, *non remanebat quidquam usque mane,* sicut praecipitur Exod. XII. Ergo neque etiam, si hoc sacramentum reservetur in

OBJECTION 1: It seems that Christ's body is movably in this sacrament, because the Philosopher says (*Topic.* ii) that *when we are moved, the things within us are moved*: and this is true even of the soul's spiritual substance. *But Christ is in this sacrament*, as shown above (Q. 74, A. 1). Therefore He is moved when it is moved.

OBJ. 2: Further, the truth ought to correspond with the figure. But, according to the commandment (Exod 12:10), concerning the Paschal Lamb, a figure of this sacrament, *there remained nothing until the morning.* Neither, therefore,

crastinum, erit ibi corpus Christi. Et ita non est immobiliter in hoc sacramento.

Praeterea, si corpus Christi remaneat sub hoc sacramento etiam in crastino, pari ratione remanebit et per totum sequens tempus, non enim potest dici quod desinat ibi esse cessantibus speciebus, quia esse corporis Christi non dependet a speciebus illis. Non autem remanet sub hoc sacramento Christus per totum tempus futurum. Videtur ergo quod statim in crastino, vel post modicum tempus, desinat esse sub hoc sacramento. Et ita videtur quod Christus mobiliter sit in hoc sacramento.

Sed contra, impossibile est idem esse motum et quietum, quia sic contradictoria verificarentur de eodem. Sed corpus Christi in caelo quietum residet. Non ergo est mobiliter in hoc sacramento.

Respondeo dicendum quod, cum aliquid est unum subiecto et multiplex secundum esse, nihil prohibet secundum aliquid moveri et secundum aliud immobile permanere, sicut corpori aliud est esse album, et aliud est esse magnum, unde potest moveri secundum albedinem, et permanere immobile secundum magnitudinem. Christo autem non est idem esse secundum se, et esse sub sacramento, quia per hoc ipsum quod dicimus ipsum esse sub sacramento, significatur quaedam habitudo eius ad hoc sacramentum. Secundum igitur hoc esse non movetur Christus per se secundum locum, sed solum per accidens. Quia Christus non est in hoc sacramento sicut in loco, sicut praedictum est, quod autem non est in loco, non movetur per se in loco, sed solum ad motum eius in quo est.

Similiter autem neque per se movetur, secundum esse quod habet in hoc sacramento, quacumque alia mutatione, puta quantum ad hoc quod desinat esse sub hoc sacramento. Quia illud quod de se habet esse indeficiens, non potest esse deficiendi principium, sed, alio deficiente, hoc desinit esse in eo; sicut Deus, cuius esse est indeficiens et immortale, desinit esse in aliqua creatura corruptibili per hoc quod creatura corruptibilis desinit esse. Et hoc modo, cum Christus habeat esse indeficiens et incorruptibile, non desinit esse sub sacramento neque per hoc quod ipsum desinat esse, neque etiam per motum localem sui, ut ex dictis patet, sed solum per hoc quod species huius sacramenti desinunt esse.

Unde patet quod Christus, per se loquendo, immobiliter est in hoc sacramento.

Ad primum ergo dicendum quod ratio illa procedit de motu per accidens, quo ad motum nostri moventur ea quae in nobis sunt. Aliter tamen ea quae per se possunt esse in loco, sicut corpora, et aliter ea quae per se non possunt esse in loco, sicut formae et spirituales substantiae. Ad quem modum potest reduci quod dicimus

if this sacrament be reserved until morning, will Christ's body be there; and so it is not immovably in this sacrament.

Obj. 3: Further, if Christ's body were to remain under this sacrament even until the morrow, for the same reason it will remain there during all coming time; for it cannot be said that it ceases to be there when the species pass, because the existence of Christ's body is not dependent on those species. Yet Christ does not remain in this sacrament for all coming time. It seems, then, that straightway on the morrow, or after a short time, He ceases to be under this sacrament. And so it seems that Christ is in this sacrament movably.

On the contrary, it is impossible for the same thing to be in motion and at rest, else contradictories would be verified of the same subject. But Christ's body is at rest in heaven. Therefore it is not movably in this sacrament.

I answer that, When any thing is one, as to subject, and manifold in being, there is nothing to hinder it from being moved in one respect, and yet to remain at rest in another just as it is one thing for a body to be white, and another thing, to be large; hence it can be moved as to its whiteness, and yet continue unmoved as to its magnitude. But in Christ, being in Himself and being under the sacrament are not the same thing, because when we say that He is under this sacrament, we express a kind of relationship to this sacrament. According to this being, then, Christ is not moved locally of Himself, but only accidentally, because Christ is not in this sacrament as in a place, as stated above (A. 5). But what is not in a place, is not moved of itself locally, but only according to the motion of the subject in which it is.

In the same way neither is it moved of itself according to the being which it has in this sacrament, by any other change whatever, as for instance, that it ceases to be under this sacrament: because whatever possesses unfailing existence of itself, cannot be the principle of failing; but when something else fails, then it ceases to be in it; just as God, Whose existence is unfailing and immortal, ceases to be in some corruptible creature because such corruptible creature ceases to exist. And in this way, since Christ has unfailing and incorruptible being, He ceases to be under this sacrament, not because He ceases to be, nor yet by local movement of His own, as is clear from what has been said, but only by the fact that the sacramental species cease to exist.

Hence it is clear that Christ, strictly speaking, is immovably in this sacrament.

Reply Obj. 1: This argument deals with accidental movement, whereby things within us are moved together with us. But with things which can of themselves be in a place, like bodies, it is otherwise than with things which cannot of themselves be in a place, such as forms and spiritual substances. And to this mode can be reduced what we say of Christ, being moved accidentally, according to the

Christum moveri per accidens secundum esse quod habet in hoc sacramento, in quo non est sicut in loco.

AD SECUNDUM dicendum quod hac ratione moti videntur fuisse quidam ponentes quod corpus Christi non remanet sub hoc sacramento si in crastinum reservetur. Contra quos Cyrillus dicit, *insaniunt quidam dicentes mysticam benedictionem a sanctificatione cessare si quae reliquiae remanserint eius in diem subsequentem. Non enim mutabitur sacrosanctum corpus Christi, sed virtus benedictionis et vivificativa gratia iugis in eo est.* Sicut et omnes aliae consecrationes immobiliter manent, permanentibus rebus consecratis, propter quod non iterantur. Veritas autem licet figurae respondeat, tamen figura non potest eam adaequare.

AD TERTIUM dicendum quod corpus Christi remanet in hoc sacramento non solum in crastinum, sed etiam in futurum, quousque species sacramentales manent. Quibus cessantibus, desinit esse corpus Christi sub eis, non quia ab eis dependeat, sed quia tollitur habitudo corporis Christi ad illas species. Per quem modum Deus desinit esse dominus creaturae desinentis.

existence which He has in this sacrament, in which He is not present as in a place.

REPLY OBJ. 2: It was this argument which seems to have convinced those who held that Christ's body does not remain under this sacrament if it be reserved until the morrow. It is against these that Cyril says (*Ep. lxxxiii*): *Some are so foolish as to say that the mystical blessing departs from the sacrament, if any of its fragments remain until the next day: for Christ's consecrated body is not changed, and the power of the blessing, and the life-giving grace is perpetually in it.* Thus are all other consecrations irremovable so long as the consecrated things endure; on which account they are not repeated. And although the truth corresponds with the figure, still the figure cannot equal it.

REPLY OBJ. 3: The body of Christ remains in this sacrament not only until the morrow, but also in the future, so long as the sacramental species remain: and when they cease, Christ's body ceases to be under them, not because it depends on them, but because the relationship of Christ's body to those species is taken away, in the same way as God ceases to be the Lord of a creature which ceases to exist.

Article 7

Whether the Body of Christ, As It Is in This Sacrament, Can Be Seen by Any Eye, at Least by a Glorified One?

AD SEPTIMUM SIC PROCEDITUR. Videtur quod corpus Christi prout est in hoc sacramento, possit videri ab aliquo oculo, saltem glorificato. Oculus enim noster impeditur a visione corporis Christi in hoc sacramento existentis, propter species sacramentales ipsum circumvelantes. Sed oculus glorificatus non potest ab aliquo impediri, quin corpora quaelibet videat prout sunt. Ergo oculus glorificatus potest videre corpus Christi prout est in hoc sacramento.

PRAETEREA, corpora gloriosa sanctorum erunt *configurata corpori claritatis Christi*, ut dicitur Philipp. III. Sed oculus Christi videt seipsum prout est in hoc sacramento. Ergo pari ratione quilibet alius oculus glorificatus potest ipsum videre.

PRAETEREA, sancti in resurrectione erunt aequales Angelis, ut dicitur Luc. XX. Sed Angeli vident corpus Christi prout est in hoc sacramento, quia etiam Daemones inveniuntur huic sacramento reverentiam exhibere, et ipsum timere. Ergo pari ratione oculus glorificatus potest ipsum videre prout est in hoc sacramento.

SED CONTRA, nihil idem existens potest simul ab eodem videri in diversis speciebus. Sed oculus glorificatus semper videt Christum prout est in sua specie, secundum illud Isaiae XXXIII, *regem in decore suo videbunt.*

OBJECTION 1: It seems that the body of Christ, as it is in this sacrament, can be seen by the eye, at least by a glorified one. For our eyes are hindered from beholding Christ's body in this sacrament, on account of the sacramental species veiling it. But the glorified eye cannot be hindered by anything from seeing bodies as they are. Therefore, the glorified eye can see Christ's body as it is in this sacrament.

OBJ. 2: Further, the glorified bodies of the saints will be *made like to the body* of Christ's *glory*, according to Phil. 3:21. But Christ's eye beholds Himself as He is in this sacrament. Therefore, for the same reason, every other glorified eye can see Him.

OBJ. 3: Further, in the resurrection the saints will be equal to the angels, according to Luke 20:36. But the angels see the body of Christ as it is in this sacrament, for even the devils are found to pay reverence thereto, and to fear it. Therefore, for like reason, the glorified eye can see Christ as He is in this sacrament.

ON THE CONTRARY, As long as a thing remains the same, it cannot at the same time be seen by the same eye under diverse species. But the glorified eye sees Christ always, as He is in His own species, according to Isa. 33:17:

Ergo videtur quod non videat Christum prout est sub specie huius sacramenti.

RESPONDEO dicendum quod duplex est oculus, scilicet corporalis, proprie dictus; et intellectualis, qui per similitudinem dicitur. A nullo autem oculo corporali corpus Christi potest videri prout est in hoc sacramento. Primo quidem, quia corpus visibile per sua accidentia immutat medium. Accidentia autem corporis Christi sunt in hoc sacramento mediante substantia, ita scilicet quod accidentia corporis Christi non habent immediatam habitudinem neque ad hoc sacramentum, neque ad corpora quae ipsum circumstant. Et ideo non possunt immutare medium, ut sic ab aliquo corporali oculo videri possint. Secundo quia, sicut supra dictum est, corpus Christi est in hoc sacramento per modum substantiae. Substantia autem, inquantum huiusmodi, non est visibilis oculo corporali, neque subiacet alicui sensui, neque imaginationi, sed soli intellectui, cuius obiectum est quod quid est, ut dicitur in III de anima. Et ideo, proprie loquendo, corpus Christi, secundum modum essendi quem habet in hoc sacramento, neque sensu neque imaginatione perceptibile est, sed solo intellectu, qui dicitur oculus spiritualis.

Percipitur autem diversimode a diversis intellectibus. Quia enim modus essendi quo Christus est in hoc sacramento, est penitus supernaturalis, a supernaturali intellectu, scilicet divino, secundum se visibilis est, et per consequens ab intellectu beato vel Angeli vel hominis, qui secundum participatam claritatem divini intellectus videt ea quae supernaturalia sunt, per visionem divinae essentiae. Ab intellectu autem hominis viatoris non potest conspici nisi per fidem, sicut et cetera supernaturalia. Sed nec etiam intellectus angelicus, secundum sua naturalia, sufficit ad hoc intuendum. Unde Daemones non possunt videre per intellectum Christum in hoc sacramento, nisi per fidem, cui non voluntate assentiunt, sed ad eam signorum evidentia convincuntur, prout dicitur, Iac. II, quod *Daemones credunt et contremiscunt.*

AD PRIMUM ergo dicendum quod oculus noster corporeus per species sacramentales impeditur a visione corporis Christi sub eis existentis, non solum per modum tegumenti, sicut impedimur videre id quod est velatum quocumque corporali velamine, sed quia corpus Christi non habet habitudinem ad medium quod circumstat hoc sacramentum mediantibus propriis accidentibus sed mediantibus speciebus sacramentalibus.

AD SECUNDUM dicendum quod oculus corporalis Christi videt seipsum sub sacramento existentem, non tamen potest videre ipsum modum essendi quo est sub sacramento, quod pertinet ad intellectum. Nec tamen est simile de alio oculo glorioso, quia et ipse oculus Christi est sub hoc sacramento; in quo non conformatur ei alius oculus gloriosus.

(His eyes) shall see the king in his beauty. It seems, then, that it does not see Christ, as He is under the species of this sacrament.

I ANSWER THAT, The eye is of two kinds, namely, the bodily eye properly so-called, and the intellectual eye, so-called by similitude. But Christ's body as it is in this sacrament cannot be seen by any bodily eye. First of all, because a body which is visible brings about an alteration in the medium, through its accidents. Now the accidents of Christ's body are in this sacrament by means of the substance; so that the accidents of Christ's body have no immediate relationship either to this sacrament or to adjacent bodies; consequently they do not act on the medium so as to be seen by any corporeal eye. Second, because, as stated above (A. 1, ad 3; A. 3), Christ's body is substantially present in this sacrament. But substance, as such, is not visible to the bodily eye, nor does it come under any one of the senses, nor under the imagination, but solely under the intellect, whose object is *what a thing is* (*De Anima* iii). And therefore, properly speaking, Christ's body, according to the mode of being which it has in this sacrament, is perceptible neither by the sense nor by the imagination, but only by the intellect, which is called the spiritual eye.

Moreover it is perceived differently by different intellects. For since the way in which Christ is in this sacrament is entirely supernatural, it is visible in itself to a supernatural, i.e., the Divine, intellect, and consequently to a beatified intellect, of angel or of man, which, through the participated glory of the Divine intellect, sees all supernatural things in the vision of the Divine Essence. But it can be seen by a wayfarer through faith alone, like other supernatural things. And not even the angelic intellect of its own natural power is capable of beholding it; consequently the devils cannot by their intellect perceive Christ in this sacrament, except through faith, to which they do not pay willing assent; yet they are convinced of it from the evidence of signs, according to James 2:19: *The devils believe, and tremble.*

REPLY OBJ. 1: Our bodily eye, on account of the sacramental species, is hindered from beholding the body of Christ underlying them, not merely as by way of veil (just as we are hindered from seeing what is covered with any corporeal veil), but also because Christ's body bears a relation to the medium surrounding this sacrament, not through its own accidents, but through the sacramental species.

REPLY OBJ. 2: Christ's own bodily eye sees Himself existing under the sacrament, yet it cannot see the way in which it exists under the sacrament, because that belongs to the intellect. But it is not the same with any other glorified eye, because Christ's eye is under this sacrament, in which no other glorified eye is conformed to it.

AD TERTIUM dicendum quod Angelus bonus vel malus non potest aliquid videre oculo corporeo, sed solum oculo intellectuali. Unde non est similis ratio, ut ex dictis patet.

REPLY OBJ. 3: No angel, good or bad, can see anything with a bodily eye, but only with the mental eye. Hence there is no parallel reason, as is evident from what was said above.

Article 8

Whether Christ's Body Is Truly There When Flesh or a Child Appears Miraculously in This Sacrament?

AD OCTAVUM SIC PROCEDITUR. Videtur quod, quando in hoc sacramento miraculose apparet vel caro vel puer, quod non sit ibi vere corpus Christi. Corpus enim Christi desinit esse sub hoc sacramento quando desinunt esse species sacramentales, ut dictum est. Sed quando apparet caro vel puer, desinunt esse species sacramentales. Ergo non est ibi vere corpus Christi.

PRAETEREA, ubicumque est corpus Christi, vel est ibi sub specie propria, vel sub specie sacramenti. Sed quando tales apparitiones fiunt, manifestum est quod non est ibi Christus sub specie propria, quia in hoc sacramento totus Christus continetur, qui permanet integer in forma qua ascendit in caelum; cum tamen id quod miraculose apparet in hoc sacramento, quandoque videatur ut quaedam parva caro, quandoque autem ut parvus puer. Manifestum est etiam quod non est ibi sub specie sacramenti, quae est species panis vel vini. Ergo videtur quod corpus Christi nullo modo sit ibi.

PRAETEREA, corpus Christi incipit esse in hoc sacramento per consecrationem et conversionem, ut supra dictum est. Sed caro aut sanguis miraculose apparens non sunt consecrata, nec conversa in verum corpus et sanguinem Christi. Non ergo sub his speciebus est corpus vel sanguis Christi.

SED CONTRA est quod, tali apparitione facta, eadem reverentia exhibetur ei quod apparet, quae et prius exhibebatur. Quod quidem non fieret si non vere esset ibi Christus, cui reverentiam latriae exhibemus. Ergo, etiam tali apparitione facta, Christus est sub hoc sacramento.

RESPONDEO dicendum quod dupliciter contingit talis apparitio, qua quandoque in hoc sacramento miraculose videtur caro aut sanguis, aut etiam aliquis puer. Quandoque enim hoc contingit ex parte videntium, quorum oculi immutantur tali immutatione ac si expresse viderent exterius carnem aut sanguinem vel puerum, nulla tamen immutatione facta ex parte sacramenti. Et hoc quidem videtur contingere quando uni videtur sub specie carnis vel pueri, aliis tamen videtur, sicut et prius, sub specie panis; vel quando eidem ad horam videtur sub specie carnis vel pueri, et postmodum sub specie panis. Nec tamen hoc pertinet ad aliquam deceptionem, sicut accidit in magorum praestigiis, quia talis species divinitus formatur in oculo ad aliquam veritatem figurandam,

OBJECTION 1: It seems that Christ's body is not truly there when flesh or a child appears miraculously in this sacrament. Because His body ceases to be under this sacrament when the sacramental species cease to be present, as stated above (A. 6). But when flesh or a child appears, the sacramental species cease to be present. Therefore Christ's body is not truly there.

OBJ. 2: Further, wherever Christ's body is, it is there either under its own species, or under those of the sacrament. But when such apparitions occur, it is evident that Christ is not present under His own species, because the entire Christ is contained in this sacrament, and He remains entire under the form in which He ascended to heaven: yet what appears miraculously in this sacrament is sometimes seen as a small particle of flesh, or at times as a small child. Now it is evident that He is not there under the sacramental species, which is that of bread or wine. Consequently, it seems that Christ's body is not there in any way.

OBJ. 3: Further, Christ's body begins to be in this sacrament by consecration and conversion, as was said above (Q. 75, AA. 2, 3, 4). But the flesh and blood which appear by miracle are not consecrated, nor are they converted into Christ's true body and blood. Therefore the body or the blood of Christ is not under those species.

ON THE CONTRARY, When such apparition takes place, the same reverence is shown to it as was shown at first, which would not be done if Christ were not truly there, to Whom we show reverence of latria. Therefore, when such apparition occurs, Christ is under the sacrament.

I ANSWER THAT, Such apparition comes about in two ways, when occasionally in this sacrament flesh, or blood, or a child, is seen. Sometimes it happens on the part of the beholders, whose eyes are so affected as if they outwardly saw flesh, or blood, or a child, while no change takes place in the sacrament. And this seems to happen when to one person it is seen under the species of flesh or of a child, while to others it is seen as before under the species of bread; or when to the same individual it appears for an hour under the appearance of flesh or a child, and afterwards under the appearance of bread. Nor is there any deception there, as occurs in the feats of magicians, because such species is divinely formed in the eye in order to represent some truth, namely, for the purpose of showing that Christ's

ad hoc scilicet quod manifestetur vere corpus Christi esse sub hoc sacramento; sicut etiam Christus absque deceptione apparuit discipulis euntibus in Emmaus. Dicit enim Augustinus, in libro de quaestionibus Evangelii, quod, *cum fictio nostra refertur ad aliquam significationem, non est mendacium, sed aliqua figura veritatis.* Et quia per hunc modum nulla immutatio fit ex parte sacramenti, manifestum est quod non desinit esse Christus sub hoc sacramento, tali apparitione facta.

Quandoque vero contingit talis apparitio non per solam immutationem videntium, sed specie quae videtur realiter exterius existente. Et hoc quidem videtur esse quando sub tali specie ab omnibus videtur; et non ad horam, sed per longum tempus ita permanet. Et in hoc casu quidam dicunt quod est propria species corporis Christi. Nec obstat quod quandoque non videtur ibi totus Christus, sed aliqua pars carnis; vel etiam videtur non in specie iuvenili, sed in effigie puerili, quia in potestate est corporis gloriosi, ut infra dicetur, quod videatur ab oculo non glorificato vel secundum totum vel secundum partem, et in effigie vel propria vel aliena, ut infra dicetur.

Sed hoc videtur esse inconveniens. Primo quidem, quia corpus Christi non potest in propria specie videri nisi in uno loco, in quo definitive continetur. Unde, cum videatur in propria specie et adoretur in caelo, sub propria specie non videtur in hoc sacramento. Secundo, quia corpus gloriosum, quod apparet ut vult, post apparitionem cum voluerit disparet, sicut dicitur, Luc. ult., quod *dominus ab oculis discipulorum evanuit.* Hoc autem quod sub specie carnis in hoc sacramento apparet, diu permanet, quinimmo quandoque legitur esse inclusum, et multorum episcoporum consilio in pixide reservatum; quod nefas est de Christo sentire secundum propriam speciem.

Et ideo dicendum quod, manentibus dimensionibus quae prius fuerunt, fit miraculose quaedam immutatio circa alia accidentia, puta figuram et colorem et alia huiusmodi, ut videatur caro vel sanguis, aut etiam puer. Et, sicut prius dictum est, hoc non est deceptio, quia fit in figuram cuiusdam veritatis, scilicet ad ostendendum per hanc miraculosam apparitionem quod in hoc sacramento est vere corpus Christi et sanguis. Et sic patet quod, remanentibus dimensionibus, quae sunt fundamenta aliorum accidentium, ut infra dicetur, remanet vere corpus Christi in hoc sacramento.

Ad primum ergo dicendum quod, facta tali apparitione, species sacramentales quandoque quidem totaliter manent in seipsis, quandoque autem secundum illud quod est principale in eis, ut dictum est.

Ad secundum dicendum quod in huiusmodi apparitionibus, sicut dictum est, non videtur propria species Christi, sed species miraculose formata vel in oculis

body is truly under this sacrament; just as Christ without deception appeared to the disciples who were going to Emmaus. For Augustine says (*De Qq. Evang.* ii) that *when our pretense is referred to some significance, it is not a lie, but a figure of the truth.* And since in this way no change is made in the sacrament, it is manifest that, when such apparition occurs, Christ does not cease to be under this sacrament.

But it sometimes happens that such apparition comes about not merely by a change wrought in the beholders, but by an appearance which really exists outwardly. And this indeed is seen to happen when it is beheld by everyone under such an appearance, and it remains so not for an hour, but for a considerable time; and, in this case some think that it is the proper species of Christ's body. Nor does it matter that sometimes Christ's entire body is not seen there, but part of His flesh, or else that it is not seen in youthful guise, but in the semblance of a child, because it lies within the power of a glorified body for it to be seen by a non-glorified eye either entirely or in part, and under its own semblance or in strange guise, as will be said later (Suppl., Q. 85, AA. 2, 3).

But this seems unlikely. First of all, because Christ's body under its proper species can be seen only in one place, wherein it is definitively contained. Hence since it is seen in its proper species, and is adored in heaven, it is not seen under its proper species in this sacrament. Second, because a glorified body, which appears at will, disappears when it wills after the apparition; thus it is related (Luke 24:31) that our Lord *vanished out of sight* of the disciples. But that which appears under the likeness of flesh in this sacrament, continues for a long time; indeed, one reads of its being sometimes enclosed, and, by order of many bishops, preserved in a pyx, which it would be wicked to think of Christ under His proper semblance.

Consequently, it remains to be said, that, while the dimensions remain the same as before, there is a miraculous change wrought in the other accidents, such as shape, color, and the rest, so that flesh, or blood, or a child, is seen. And, as was said already, this is not deception, because it is done *to represent the truth,* namely, to show by this miraculous apparition that Christ's body and blood are truly in this sacrament. And thus it is clear that as the dimensions remain, which are the foundation of the other accidents, as we shall see later on (Q. 77, A. 2), the body of Christ truly remains in this sacrament.

Reply Obj. 1: When such apparition takes place, the sacramental species sometimes continue entire in themselves; and sometimes only as to that which is principal, as was said above.

Reply Obj. 2: As stated above, during such apparitions Christ's proper semblance is not seen, but a species

intuentium, vel etiam in ipsis sacramentalibus dimensionibus, ut dictum est.

AD TERTIUM dicendum quod dimensiones panis et vini consecrati manent, immutatione circa eas miraculose facta quantum ad alia accidentia, ut dictum est.

miraculously formed either in the eyes of the beholders, or in the sacramental dimensions themselves, as was said above.

REPLY OBJ. 3: The dimensions of the consecrated bread and wine continue, while a miraculous change is wrought in the other accidents, as stated above.

QUESTION 77

THE ACCIDENTS WHICH REMAIN IN THIS SACRAMENT

Deinde considerandum est de accidentibus remanentibus in hoc sacramento. Et circa hoc quaeruntur octo.

Primo, utrum accidentia quae remanent, sint sine subiecto.

Secundo, utrum quantitas dimensiva sit subiectum aliorum accidentium.

Tertio, utrum huiusmodi accidentia possint immutare aliquod corpus extrinsecum.

Quarto, utrum possint corrumpi.

Quinto, utrum ex eis possit aliquid generari.

Sexto, utrum possint nutrire.

Septimo, de fractione panis consecrati.

Octavo, utrum vino consecrato possit aliquid admisceri.

We must now consider the accidents which remain in this sacrament; under which head there are eight points of inquiry:

(1) Whether the accidents which remain are without a subject?

(2) Whether dimensive quantity is the subject of the other accidents?

(3) Whether such accidents can affect an extrinsic body?

(4) Whether they can be corrupted?

(5) Whether anything can be generated from them?

(6) Whether they can nourish?

(7) Of the breaking of the consecrated bread?

(8) Whether anything can be mixed with the consecrated wine?

Article 1

Whether the Accidents Remain in This Sacrament Without a Subject?

AD PRIMUM SIC PROCEDITUR. Videtur quod accidentia non remaneant in hoc sacramento sine subiecto. Nihil enim inordinatum aut fallax debet esse in hoc sacramento veritatis. Sed accidentia esse sine subiecto est contra rerum ordinem, quem Deus naturae indidit. Videtur etiam ad quandam fallaciam pertinere, cum accidentia sint signa naturae subiecti. Ergo in hoc sacramento non sunt accidentia sine subiecto.

PRAETEREA, fieri non potest, etiam miraculose, quod definitio rei ab ea separetur; vel quod uni rei conveniat definitio alterius, puta quod homo, manens homo, sit animal irrationale. Ad hoc enim sequeretur contradictoria esse simul, *hoc enim quod significat nomen rei, est definitio,* ut dicitur in IV Metaphys. Sed ad definitionem accidentis pertinet quod sit in subiecto, ad definitionem vero substantiae, quod per se subsistat non in subiecto. Non potest ergo miraculose fieri quod in hoc sacramento sint accidentia sine subiecto.

PRAETEREA, accidens individuatur ex subiecto. Si ergo accidentia remanent in hoc sacramento sine subiecto, non erunt individua, sed universalia. Quod patet esse falsum, quia sic non essent sensibilia, sed intelligibilia tantum.

PRAETEREA, accidentia per consecrationem huius sacramenti non adipiscuntur aliquam compositionem.

OBJECTION 1: It seems that the accidents do not remain in this sacrament without a subject, because there ought not to be anything disorderly or deceitful in this sacrament of truth. But for accidents to be without a subject is contrary to the order which God established in nature; and furthermore it seems to savor of deceit, since accidents are naturally the signs of the nature of the subject. Therefore the accidents are not without a subject in this sacrament.

OBJ. 2: Further, not even by miracle can the definition of a thing be severed from it, or the definition of another thing be applied to it; for instance, that, while man remains a man, he can be an irrational animal. For it would follow that contradictories can exist at the one time: for the *definition of a thing is what its name expresses*, as is said in *Metaph.* iv. But it belongs to the definition of an accident for it to be in a subject, while the definition of substance is that it must subsist of itself, and not in another. Therefore it cannot come to pass, even by miracle, that the accidents exist without a subject in this sacrament.

OBJ. 3: Further, an accident is individuated by its subject. If therefore the accidents remain in this sacrament without a subject, they will not be individual, but general, which is clearly false, because thus they would not be sensible, but merely intelligible.

OBJ. 4: Further, the accidents after the consecration of this sacrament do not obtain any composition. But before

233

Sed ante consecrationem non erant composita neque ex materia et forma, neque ex quo est et quod est. Ergo etiam post consecrationem non sunt composita altero horum modorum. Quod est inconveniens, quia sic essent simpliciora quam Angeli; cum tamen haec accidentia sint sensibilia. Non ergo accidentia remanent in hoc sacramento sine subiecto.

Sed contra est quod Gregorius dicit, in homilia paschali, quod *species sacramentales sunt illarum rerum vocabula quae ante fuerunt, scilicet panis et vini.* Et ita, cum non remaneat substantia panis et vini, videtur quod huiusmodi species sint sine subiecto.

Respondeo dicendum quod accidentia panis et vini, quae sensu deprehenduntur in hoc sacramento remanere post consecrationem, non sunt sicut in subiecto in substantia panis et vini, quae non remanet, ut supra habitum est. Neque etiam in forma substantiali, quae non manet; et, si remaneret, subiectum esse non posset, ut patet per Boetium, in libro de Trin. Manifestum est etiam quod huiusmodi accidentia non sunt in substantia corporis et sanguinis Christi sicut in subiecto, quia substantia humani corporis nullo modo potest his accidentibus affici; neque etiam est possibile quod corpus Christi, gloriosum et impassibile existens, alteretur ad suscipiendas huiusmodi qualitates.

Dicunt autem quidam quod sunt, sicut in subiecto, in aere circumstante. Sed nec hoc esse potest. Primo quidem, quia aer non est huiusmodi accidentium susceptivus. Secundo, quia huiusmodi accidentia non sunt ubi est aer. Quinimmo ad motum harum specierum aer depellitur. Tertio, quia accidentia non transeunt de subiecto in subiectum, ut scilicet idem accidens numero quod primo fuit in uno subiecto, postmodum fiat in alio. Accidens enim numerum accipit a subiecto. Unde non potest esse quod, idem numero manens, sit quandoque in hoc, quandoque in alio subiecto. Quarto quia, cum aer non spolietur accidentibus propriis, simul haberet accidentia propria et aliena. Nec potest dici quod hoc fiat miraculose virtute consecrationis, quia verba consecrationis hoc non significant; quae tamen non efficiunt nisi significatum.

Et ideo relinquitur quod accidentia in hoc sacramento manent sine subiecto. Quod quidem virtute divina fieri potest. Cum enim effectus magis dependeat a causa prima quam a causa secunda, potest Deus, qui est prima causa substantiae et accidentis, per suam infinitam virtutem conservare in esse accidens subtracta substantia, per quam conservabatur in esse sicut per propriam causam, sicut etiam alios effectus naturalium causarum

the consecration they were not composed either of matter and form, nor of existence (*quo est*) and essence (*quod est*). Therefore, even after consecration they are not composite in either of these ways. But this is unreasonable, for thus they would be simpler than angels, whereas at the same time these accidents are perceptible to the senses. Therefore, in this sacrament the accidents do not remain without a subject.

On the contrary, Gregory says in an Easter Homily (Lanfranc, *De Corp. et Sang. Dom.* xx) that *the sacramental species are the names of those things which were there before, namely, of the bread and wine.* Therefore since the substance of the bread and the wine does not remain, it seems that these species remain without a subject.

I answer that, The species of the bread and wine, which are perceived by our senses to remain in this sacrament after consecration, are not subjected in the substance of the bread and wine, for that does not remain, as stated above (Q. 75, A. 2); nor in the substantial form, for that does not remain (Q. 75, A. 6), and if it did remain, *it could not be a subject*, as Boethius declares (*De Trin.* i). Furthermore it is manifest that these accidents are not subjected in the substance of Christ's body and blood, because the substance of the human body cannot in any way be affected by such accidents; nor is it possible for Christ's glorious and impassible body to be altered so as to receive these qualities.

Now there are some who say that they are in the surrounding atmosphere as in a subject. But even this cannot be: in the first place, because atmosphere is not susceptive of such accidents. Second, because these accidents are not where the atmosphere is, nay more, the atmosphere is displaced by the motion of these species. Third, because accidents do not pass from subject to subject, so that the same identical accident which was first in one subject be afterwards in another; because an accident is individuated by the subject; hence it cannot come to pass for an accident remaining identically the same to be at one time in one subject, and at another time in another. Fourth, since the atmosphere is not deprived of its own accidents, it would have at the one time its own accidents and others foreign to it. Nor can it be maintained that this is done miraculously in virtue of the consecration, because the words of consecration do not signify this, and they effect only what they signify.

Therefore it follows that the accidents continue in this sacrament without a subject. This can be done by Divine power: for since an effect depends more upon the first cause than on the second, God Who is the first cause both of substance and accident, can by His unlimited power preserve an accident in existence when the substance is withdrawn whereby it was preserved in existence as by its proper cause, just as without natural causes He can produce other effects of natural causes, even as He formed a human body in the

potest producere sine naturalibus causis; sicut corpus humanum formavit in utero virginis sine virili semine.

AD PRIMUM ergo dicendum quod nihil prohibet aliquid esse ordinatum secundum communem legem naturae, cuius tamen contrarium est ordinatum secundum speciale privilegium gratiae, ut patet in resuscitatione mortuorum, et in illuminatione caecorum, prout etiam in rebus humanis quaedam aliquibus conceduntur ex speciali privilegio praeter communem legem. Et ita, licet sit secundum communem naturae ordinem quod accidens sit in subiecto, ex speciali tamen ratione, secundum ordinem gratiae, accidentia sunt in hoc sacramento sine subiecto, propter rationes supra inductas.

AD SECUNDUM dicendum quod, cum ens non sit genus, hoc ipsum quod est esse, non potest esse essentia vel substantiae vel accidentis. Non ergo definitio substantiae est ens per se sine subiecto, nec definitio accidentis ens in subiecto sed quidditati seu essentiae substantiae competit habere esse non in subiecto; quidditati autem sive essentiae accidentis competit habere esse in subiecto. In hoc autem sacramento non datur accidentibus quod ex vi suae essentiae sint sine subiecto, sed ex divina virtute sustentante. Et ideo non desinunt esse accidentia, quia nec separatur ab eis definitio accidentis, nec competit eis definitio substantiae.

AD TERTIUM dicendum quod huiusmodi accidentia acquisierunt esse individuum in substantia panis et vini, qua conversa in corpus et sanguinem Christi, remanent virtute divina accidentia in illo esse individuato quod prius habebant. Unde sunt singularia et sensibilia.

AD QUARTUM dicendum quod accidentia huiusmodi, manente substantia panis et vini, non habebant ipsa esse nec alia accidentia, sed substantia eorum habebat huiusmodi esse per ea; sicut nix est alba per albedinem. Sed post consecrationem ipsa accidentia quae remanent, habent esse. Unde sunt composita ex esse et quod est, sicut in prima parte de Angelis dictum est. Et cum hoc, habent compositionem partium quantitativarum.

Virgin's womb, *without the seed of man* (Hymn for Christmas, First Vespers).

REPLY OBJ. 1: There is nothing to hinder the common law of nature from ordaining a thing, the contrary of which is nevertheless ordained by a special privilege of grace, as is evident in the raising of the dead, and in the restoring of sight to the blind: even thus in human affairs, to some individuals some things are granted by special privilege which are outside the common law. And so, even though it be according to the common law of nature for an accident to be in a subject, still for a special reason, according to the order of grace, the accidents exist in this sacrament without a subject, on account of the reasons given above (Q. 75, A. 5).

REPLY OBJ. 2: Since being is not a genus, then being cannot be of itself the essence of either substance or accident. Consequently, the definition of substance is not— *a being of itself without a subject*, nor is the definition of accident—*a being in a subject*; but it belongs to the quiddity or essence of substance *to have existence not in a subject*; while it belongs to the quiddity or essence of accident *to have existence in a subject*. But in this sacrament it is not in virtue of their essence that accidents are not in a subject, but through the Divine power sustaining them; and consequently they do not cease to be accidents, because neither is the definition of accident withdrawn from them, nor does the definition of substance apply to them.

REPLY OBJ. 3: These accidents acquired individual being in the substance of the bread and wine; and when this substance is changed into the body and blood of Christ, they remain in that individuated being which they possessed before, hence they are individual and sensible.

REPLY OBJ. 4: These accidents had no being of their own nor other accidents, so long as the substance of the bread and wine remained; but their subjects had such being through them, just as snow is white through whiteness. But after the consecration the accidents which remain have being; hence they are compounded of existence and essence, as was said of the angels, in the First Part (Q. 50, A. 2, ad 3); and besides they have composition of quantitative parts.

Article 2

Whether in This Sacrament the Dimensive Quantity of the Bread or Wine Is the Subject of the Other Accidents?

AD SECUNDUM SIC PROCEDITUR. Videtur quod in hoc sacramento quantitas dimensiva panis vel vini non sit aliorum accidentium subiectum. Accidentis enim non est accidens, nulla enim forma potest esse subiectum, cum subiici pertineat ad proprietatem materiae. Sed quantitas dimensiva est quoddam accidens. Ergo quantitas dimensiva non potest esse subiectum aliorum accidentium.

OBJECTION 1: It seems that in this sacrament the dimensive quantity of the bread or wine is not the subject of the other accidents. For accident is not the subject of accident; because no form can be a subject, since to be a subject is a property of matter. But dimensive quantity is an accident. Therefore dimensive quantity cannot be the subject of the other accidents.

PRAETEREA, sicut quantitas individuatur ex substantia, ita etiam et alia accidentia. Si ergo quantitas dimensiva panis aut vini remanet individuata secundum esse prius habitum, in quo conservatur, pari ratione et alia accidentia remanent individuata secundum esse quod prius habebant in substantia. Non ergo sunt in quantitate dimensiva sicut in subiecto, cum omne accidens individuetur per suum subiectum.

PRAETEREA, inter alia accidentia panis et vini quae remanent, deprehenduntur etiam sensu rarum et densum. Quae non possunt esse in quantitate dimensiva praeter materiam existente, quia rarum est quod habet parum de materia sub dimensionibus magnis; densum autem quod habet multum de materia sub dimensionibus parvis, ut dicitur in IV Physic. Ergo videtur quod quantitas dimensiva non possit esse subiectum accidentium quae remanent in hoc sacramento.

PRAETEREA, quantitas a subiecto separata videtur esse quantitas mathematica, quae non est subiectum qualitatum sensibilium. Cum ergo accidentia quae remanent in hoc sacramento sint sensibilia, videtur quod non possint esse in hoc sacramento sicut in subiecto in quantitate panis et vini remanente post consecrationem.

SED CONTRA est quod qualitates non sunt divisibiles nisi per accidens, scilicet ratione subiecti. Dividuntur autem qualitates remanentes in hoc sacramento per divisionem quantitatis dimensivae, sicut patet ad sensum. Ergo quantitas dimensiva est subiectum accidentium quae remanent in hoc sacramento.

RESPONDEO dicendum quod necesse est dicere accidentia alia quae remanent in hoc sacramento, esse sicut in subiecto in quantitate dimensiva panis vel vini remanente. Primo quidem, per hoc quod ad sensum apparet aliquod quantum esse ibi coloratum et aliis accidentibus affectum, nec in talibus sensus decipitur. Secundo, quia prima dispositio materiae est quantitas dimensiva, unde et Plato posuit primas differentias materiae magnum et parvum. Et quia primum subiectum est materia, consequens est quod omnia alia accidentia referantur ad subiectum mediante quantitate dimensiva, sicut et primum subiectum coloris dicitur superficies esse, ratione cuius quidam posuerunt dimensiones esse substantias corporum, ut dicitur in III Metaphys. Et quia, subtracto subiecto, remanent accidentia secundum esse quod prius habebant, consequens est quod omnia accidentia remanent fundata super quantitatem dimensivam.

Tertio quia, cum subiectum sit principium individuationis accidentium, oportet id quod ponitur aliquorum accidentium subiectum esse, aliquo modo esse individuationis principium. Est enim de ratione individui quod non possit in pluribus esse. Quod quidem contingit dupliciter. Uno modo, quia non est natum in aliquo esse, et hoc modo formae immateriales separatae, per

OBJ. 2: Further, just as quantity is individuated by substance, so also are the other accidents. If, then, the dimensive quantity of the bread or wine remains individuated according to the being it had before, in which it is preserved, for like reason the other accidents remain individuated according to the existence which they had before in the substance. Therefore they are not in dimensive quantity as in a subject, since every accident is individuated by its own subject.

OBJ. 3: Further, among the other accidents that remain, of the bread and wine, the senses perceive also rarity and density, which cannot be in dimensive quantity existing outside matter; because a thing is rare which has little matter under great dimensions, while a thing is dense which has much matter under small dimensions, as is said in *Phys.* iv. It does not seem, then, that dimensive quantity can be the subject of the accidents which remain in this sacrament.

OBJ. 4: Further, quantity abstract from matter seems to be mathematical quantity, which is not the subject of sensible qualities. Since, then, the remaining accidents in this sacrament are sensible, it seems that in this sacrament they cannot be subjected in the dimensive quantity of the bread and wine that remains after consecration.

ON THE CONTRARY, Qualities are divisible only accidentally, that is, by reason of the subject. But the qualities remaining in this sacrament are divided by the division of dimensive quantity, as is evident through our senses. Therefore, dimensive quantity is the subject of the accidents which remain in this sacrament.

I ANSWER THAT, It is necessary to say that the other accidents which remain in this sacrament are subjected in the dimensive quantity of the bread and wine that remains: first of all, because something having quantity and color and affected by other accidents is perceived by the senses; nor is sense deceived in such. Second, because the first disposition of matter is dimensive quantity, hence Plato also assigned *great* and *small* as the first differences of matter (*Aristotle, Metaph.* iv). And because the first subject is matter, the consequence is that all other accidents are related to their subject through the medium of dimensive quantity; just as the first subject of color is said to be the surface, on which account some have maintained that dimensions are the substances of bodies, as is said in *Metaph.* iii. And since, when the subject is withdrawn, the accidents remain according to the being which they had before, it follows that all accidents remain founded upon dimensive quantity.

Third, because, since the subject is the principle of individuation of the accidents, it is necessary for what is admitted as the subject of some accidents to be somehow the principle of individuation: for it is of the very notion of an individual that it cannot be in several; and this happens in two ways. First, because it is not natural to it to be in any one; and in this way immaterial separated forms, subsisting

se subsistentes, sunt etiam per seipsas individuae. Alio modo, ex eo quod forma substantialis vel accidentalis est quidem nata in aliquo esse, non tamen in pluribus, sicut haec albedo, quae est in hoc corpore. Quantum igitur ad primum, materia est individuationis principium omnibus formis inhaerentibus, quia, cum huiusmodi formae, quantum est de se, sint natae in aliquo esse sicut in subiecto, ex quo aliqua earum recipitur in materia, quae non est in alio, iam nec ipsa forma sic existens potest in alio esse. Quantum autem ad secundum, dicendum est quod individuationis principium est quantitas dimensiva. Ex hoc enim aliquid est natum esse in uno solo, quod illud est in se indivisum et divisum ab omnibus aliis. Divisio autem accidit substantiae ratione quantitatis, ut dicitur in I Physic. Et ideo ipsa quantitas dimensiva est quoddam individuationis principium huiusmodi formis, inquantum scilicet diversae formae numero sunt in diversis partibus materiae. Unde ipsa quantitas dimensiva secundum se habet quandam individuationem, ita quod possumus imaginari plures lineas eiusdem speciei differentes positione, quae cadit in ratione quantitatis huius; convenit enim dimensioni quod sit quantitas positionem habens. Et ideo potius quantitas dimensiva potest esse subiectum aliorum accidentium quam e converso.

AD PRIMUM ergo dicendum quod accidens per se non potest esse subiectum alterius accidentis, quia non per se est. Secundum vero quod est in alio, unum accidens dicitur esse subiectum alterius, inquantum unum accidens recipitur in subiecto alio mediante, sicut superficies dicitur esse subiectum coloris. Unde, quando accidenti datur divinitus ut per se sit, potest etiam per se alterius accidentis esse subiectum.

AD SECUNDUM dicendum quod alia accidentia, etiam secundum quod erant in substantia panis, individuabantur mediante quantitate dimensiva, sicut dictum est. Et ideo potius quantitas dimensiva est subiectum aliorum accidentium remanentium in hoc sacramento quam e converso.

AD TERTIUM dicendum quod rarum et densum sunt quaedam qualitates consequentes corpora ex hoc quod habent multum vel parum de materia sub dimensionibus, sicut etiam omnia alia accidentia consequuntur ex principiis substantiae. Et sicut, subtracta substantia, divina virtute conservantur alia accidentia; ita, subtracta materia, divina virtute conservantur qualitates materiam consequentes, sicut rarum et densum.

AD QUARTUM dicendum quod quantitas mathematica non abstrahit a materia intelligibili, sed a materia sensibili, ut dicitur VII Metaphys. Dicitur autem materia sensibilis ex hoc quod subiicitur sensibilibus qualitatibus. Et ideo manifestum est quod quantitas dimensiva quae remanet in hoc sacramento sine subiecto, non est quantitas mathematica.

of themselves, are also individuals of themselves. Second, because a form, be it substantial or accidental, is naturally in someone indeed, not in several, as this whiteness, which is in this body. As to the first, matter is the principle of individuation of all inherent forms, because, since these forms, considered in themselves, are naturally in something as in a subject, from the very fact that one of them is received in matter, which is not in another, it follows that neither can the form itself thus existing be in another. As to the second, it must be maintained that the principle of individuation is dimensive quantity. For that something is naturally in another one solely, is due to the fact that that other is undivided in itself, and distinct from all others. But it is on account of quantity that substance can be divided, as is said in *Phys.* i. And therefore dimensive quantity itself is a particular principle of individuation in forms of this kind, namely, inasmuch as forms numerically distinct are in different parts of the matter. Hence also dimensive quantity has of itself a kind of individuation, so that we can imagine several lines of the same species, differing in position, which is included in the notion of this quantity; for it belongs to dimension for it to be *quantity having position* (Aristotle, *Categor.* iv), and therefore dimensive quantity can be the subject of the other accidents, rather than the other way about.

REPLY OBJ. 1: One accident cannot of itself be the subject of another, because it does not exist of itself. But inasmuch as an accident is received in another thing, one is said to be the subject of the other, inasmuch as one is received in a subject through another, as the surface is said to be the subject of color. Hence when God makes an accident to exist of itself, it can also be of itself the subject of another.

REPLY OBJ. 2: The other accidents, even as they were in the substance of the bread, were individuated by means of dimensive quantity, as stated above. And therefore dimensive quantity is the subject of the other accidents remaining in this sacrament, rather than conversely.

REPLY OBJ. 3: Rarity and density are particular qualities accompanying bodies, by reason of their having much or little matter under dimensions; just as all other accidents likewise follow from the principles of substance. And consequently, as the accidents are preserved by Divine power when the substance is withdrawn, so, when matter is withdrawn, the qualities which go with matter, such as rarity and density, are preserved by Divine power.

REPLY OBJ. 4: Mathematical quantity abstracts not from intelligible matter, but from sensible matter, as is said in *Metaph.* vii. But matter is termed sensible because it underlies sensible qualities. And therefore it is manifest that the dimensive quantity, which remains in this sacrament without a subject, is not mathematical quantity.

Article 3

Whether the Species Remaining in This Sacrament Can Change External Objects?

AD TERTIUM SIC PROCEDITUR. Videtur quod species quae remanent in hoc sacramento, non possint immutare aliquod extrinsecum. Probatur enim in VII Metaphysic. quod formae quae sunt in materia, fiunt a formis quae sunt in materia, non autem a formis quae sunt sine materia, eo quod simile agit sibi simile. Sed species sacramentales sunt species sine materia, quia remanent sine subiecto, ut ex dictis patet. Non ergo possunt immutare materiam exteriorem, inducendo aliquam formam.

PRAETEREA, cessante actione primi agentis, necesse est quod cesset actio instrumenti, sicut, quiescente fabro, non movetur martellus. Sed omnes formae accidentales agunt instrumentaliter in virtute formae substantialis tanquam principalis agentis. Cum ergo in hoc sacramento non remaneat forma substantialis panis et vini, sicut supra habitum est, videtur quod formae accidentales remanentes agere non possunt ad immutationem exterioris materiae.

PRAETEREA, nihil agit extra suam speciem, quia effectus non potest esse potior causa. Sed species sacramentales omnes sunt accidentia. Non ergo possunt exteriorem materiam immutare, ad minus ad formam substantialem.

SED CONTRA est quod, si non possent immutare exteriora corpora, non possent sentiri, sentitur enim aliquid per hoc quod immutatur sensus a sensibili, ut dicitur II de anima.

RESPONDEO dicendum quod, quia unumquodque agit inquantum est ens actu, consequens est quod unumquodque, sicut se habet ad esse, ita se habet ad agere. Quia igitur, secundum praedicta, speciebus sacramentalibus datum est divina virtute ut remaneant in suo esse quod habebant substantia panis et vini existente, consequens est quod etiam remaneant in suo agere. Et ideo omnem actionem quam poterant agere substantia panis et vini existente, possunt etiam agere substantia panis et vini transeunte in corpus et sanguinem Christi. Unde non est dubium quod possunt immutare exteriora corpora.

AD PRIMUM ergo dicendum quod species sacramentales, licet sint formae sine materia existentes, retinent tamen idem esse quod habebant prius in materia. Et ideo secundum suum esse assimilantur formis quae sunt in materia.

AD SECUNDUM dicendum quod ita actio formae accidentalis dependet ab actione formae substantialis, sicut esse accidentis dependet ab esse substantiae. Et ideo, sicut divina virtute datur speciebus sacramentalibus ut possint esse sine substantia, ita datur eis ut possint agere

OBJECTION 1: It seems that the species which remain in this sacrament cannot affect external objects. For it is proved in *Phys.* vii, that forms which are in matter are produced by forms that are in matter, but not from forms which are without matter, because like makes like. But the sacramental species are species without matter, since they remain without a subject, as is evident from what was said above (A. 1). Therefore they cannot affect other matter by producing any form in it.

OBJ. 2: Further, when the action of the principal agent ceases, then the action of the instrument must cease, as when the carpenter rests, the hammer is moved no longer. But all accidental forms act instrumentally in virtue of the substantial form as the principal agent. Therefore, since the substantial form of the bread and wine does not remain in this sacrament, as was shown above (Q. 75, A. 6), it seems that the accidental forms which remain cannot act so as to change external matter.

OBJ. 3: Further, nothing acts outside its species, because an effect cannot surpass its cause. But all the sacramental species are accidents. Therefore they cannot change external matter, at least as to a substantial form.

ON THE CONTRARY, If they could not change external bodies, they could not be felt; for a thing is felt from the senses being changed by a sensible thing, as is said in *De Anima* ii.

I ANSWER THAT, Because everything acts in so far as it is an actual being, the consequence is that everything stands in the same relation to action as it does to being. Therefore, because, according to what was said above (A. 1), it is an effect of the Divine power that the sacramental species continue in the being which they had when the substance of the bread and wine was present, it follows that they continue in their action. Consequently they retain every action which they had while the substance of the bread and wine remained, now that the substance of the bread and wine has passed into the body and blood of Christ. Hence there is no doubt but that they can change external bodies.

REPLY OBJ. 1: The sacramental species, although they are forms existing without matter, still retain the same being which they had before in matter, and therefore as to their being they are like forms which are in matter.

REPLY OBJ. 2: The action of an accidental form depends upon the action of a substantial form in the same way as the being of accident depends upon the being of substance; and therefore, as it is an effect of Divine power that the sacramental species exist without substance, so is it an effect of

sine forma substantiali, virtute Dei, a quo sicut a primo agente dependet omnis actio formae et substantialis et accidentalis.

AD TERTIUM dicendum quod immutatio quae est ad formam substantialem, non fit a forma substantiali immediate, sed mediantibus qualitatibus activis et passivis, quae agunt in virtute formae substantialis. Haec autem virtus instrumentalis conservatur in speciebus sacramentalibus divina virtute sicut et prius erat. Et ideo possunt agere ad formam substantialem instrumentaliter, per quem modum aliquid potest agere ultra suam speciem, non quasi virtute propria, sed virtute principalis agentis.

Divine power that they can act without a substantial form, because every action of a substantial or accidental form depends upon God as the first agent.

REPLY OBJ. 3: The change which terminates in a substantial form is not effected by a substantial form directly, but by means of the active and passive qualities, which act in virtue of the substantial form. But by Divine power this instrumental energy is retained in the sacramental species, just as it was before: and consequently their action can be directed to a substantial form instrumentally, just in the same way as anything can act outside its species, not as by its own power, but by the power of the chief agent.

Article 4

Whether the Sacramental Species Can Be Corrupted?

AD QUARTUM SIC PROCEDITUR. Videtur quod species sacramentales corrumpi non possunt. Corruptio enim accidit per separationem formae a materia. Sed materia panis non remanet in hoc sacramento, ut ex supra dictis patet. Ergo huiusmodi species non possunt corrumpi.

PRAETEREA, nulla forma corrumpitur nisi per accidens, corrupto subiecto, unde formae per se subsistentes incorruptibiles sunt, sicut patet in substantiis spiritualibus. Sed species sacramentales sunt formae sine subiecto. Ergo corrumpi non possunt.

PRAETEREA, si corrumpuntur, aut hoc erit naturaliter, aut miraculose. Sed non naturaliter, quia non est ibi assignare aliquod corruptionis subiectum, quod maneat corruptione terminata. Similiter etiam nec miraculose, quia miracula quae sunt in hoc sacramento, fiunt virtute consecrationis, per quam species sacramentales conservantur; non est autem idem causa conservationis et corruptionis. Ergo nullo modo species sacramentales corrumpi possunt.

SED CONTRA est quod sensu deprehenditur hostias consecratas putrefieri et corrumpi.

RESPONDEO dicendum quod corruptio est motus ex esse in non esse. Dictum est autem supra quod species sacramentales retinent idem esse quod prius habebant substantia panis et vini existente. Et ideo, sicut esse horum accidentium poterat corrumpi substantia panis et vini existente, ita etiam potest corrumpi illa substantia abeunte.

Poterant autem huiusmodi accidentia primo corrumpi dupliciter, uno modo, per se; alio modo, per accidens. Per se quidem, sicut per alterationem qualitatum,

OBJECTION 1: It seems that the sacramental species cannot be corrupted, because corruption comes of the separation of the form from the matter. But the matter of the bread does not remain in this sacrament, as is clear from what was said above (Q. 75, A. 2). Therefore these species cannot be corrupted.

OBJ. 2: Further, no form is corrupted except accidentally, that is, when its subject is corrupted; hence self-subsisting forms are incorruptible, as is seen in spiritual substances. But the sacramental species are forms without a subject. Therefore they cannot be corrupted.

OBJ. 3: Further, if they be corrupted, it will either be naturally or miraculously. But they cannot be corrupted naturally, because no subject of corruption can be assigned as remaining after the corruption has taken place. Neither can they be corrupted miraculously, because the miracles which occur in this sacrament take place in virtue of the consecration, whereby the sacramental species are preserved: and the same thing is not the cause of preservation and of corruption. Therefore, in no way can the sacramental species be corrupted.

ON THE CONTRARY, We perceive by our senses that the consecrated hosts become putrefied and corrupted.

I ANSWER THAT, Corruption is *movement from being into non-being* (Aristotle, *Phys.* v). Now it has been stated (A. 3) that the sacramental species retain the same being as they had before when the substance of the bread was present. Consequently, as the being of those accidents could be corrupted while the substance of the bread and wine was present, so likewise they can be corrupted now that the substance has passed away.

But such accidents could have been previously corrupted in two ways: in one way, of themselves; in another way, accidentally. They could be corrupted of themselves,

et augmentum vel diminutionem quantitatis, non quidem per modum augmenti vel diminutionis, qui invenitur in solis corporibus animatis, qualia non sunt substantia panis et vini, sed per additionem vel divisionem; nam, sicut dicitur in III Metaphys., per divisionem una dimensio corrumpitur et fiunt duae, per additionem autem e converso ex duabus fit una. Et per hunc modum manifeste possunt corrumpi huiusmodi accidentia post consecrationem, quia et ipsa quantitas dimensiva remanens potest divisionem et additionem recipere; et, cum sit subiectum qualitatum sensibilium, sicut dictum est, potest etiam esse subiectum alterationis eorum, puta si alteretur color aut sapor panis aut vini.

Alio modo poterant corrumpi per accidens, per corruptionem subiecti. Et hoc modo possunt corrumpi etiam post consecrationem. Quamvis enim subiectum non remaneat, remanet tamen esse quod habebant huiusmodi accidentia in subiecto, quod quidem est proprium et conforme subiecto. Et ideo huiusmodi esse potest corrumpi a contrario agente, sicut corrumpebatur substantia panis vel vini, quae etiam non corrumpebatur nisi praecedente alteratione circa accidentia.

Distinguendum tamen est inter utramque praedictarum corruptionum. Quia, cum corpus Christi et sanguis succedant in hoc sacramento substantiae panis et vini, si fiat talis immutatio ex parte accidentium quae non suffecisset ad corruptionem panis et vini, propter talem immutationem non desinit corpus et sanguis Christi esse sub hoc sacramento, sive fiat immutatio ex parte qualitatis, puta cum modicum immutatur color aut sapor vini aut panis; sive ex parte quantitatis, sicut cum dividitur panis aut vinum in tales partes quod adhuc in eis possit salvari natura panis aut vini. Si vero fiat tanta immutatio quod fuisset corrupta substantia panis aut vini, non remanent corpus et sanguis Christi sub hoc sacramento. Et hoc tam ex parte qualitatum, sicut cum ita immutatur color et sapor et aliae qualitates panis aut vini quod nullo modo posset compati natura panis aut vini, sive etiam ex parte quantitatis, puta si pulverizetur panis, vel vinum in minimas partes dividatur, ut iam non remaneant species panis vel vini.

AD PRIMUM ergo dicendum quod, quia ad corruptionem per se pertinet quod auferatur esse rei inquantum esse alicuius formae est in materia, consequens est quod per corruptionem separetur forma a materia. Si vero huiusmodi esse non esset in materia, simile tamen ei quod est in materia, posset per corruptionem auferri etiam materia non existente, sicut accidit in hoc sacramento, ut ex dictis patet.

AD SECUNDUM dicendum quod species sacramentales, licet sint formae non in materia, habent tamen esse quod prius in materia habebant.

as by alteration of the qualities, and increase or decrease of the quantity, not in the way in which increase or decrease is found only in animated bodies, such as the substances of the bread and wine are not, but by addition or division; for, as is said in *Metaph.* iii, one dimension is dissolved by division, and two dimensions result; while on the contrary, by addition, two dimensions become one. And in this way such accidents can be corrupted manifestly after consecration, because the dimensive quantity which remains can receive division and addition; and since it is the subject of sensible qualities, as stated above (A. 1), it can likewise be the subject of their alteration, for instance, if the color or the savor of the bread or wine be altered.

An accident can be corrupted in another way, through the corruption of its subject, and in this way also they can be corrupted after consecration; for although the subject does not remain, still the being which they had in the subject does remain, which being is proper, and suited to the subject. And therefore such being can be corrupted by a contrary agent, as the substance of the bread or wine was subject to corruption, and, moreover, was not corrupted except by a preceding alteration regarding the accidents.

Nevertheless, a distinction must be made between each of the aforesaid corruptions; because, when the body and the blood of Christ succeed in this sacrament to the substance of the bread and wine, if there be such change on the part of the accidents as would not have sufficed for the corruption of the bread and wine, then the body and blood of Christ do not cease to be under this sacrament on account of such change, whether the change be on the part of the quality, as for instance, when the color or the savor of the bread or wine is slightly modified; or on the part of the quantity, as when the bread or the wine is divided into such parts as to keep in them the nature of bread or of wine. But if the change be so great that the substance of the bread or wine would have been corrupted, then Christ's body and blood do not remain under this sacrament; and this either on the part of the qualities, as when the color, savor, and other qualities of the bread and wine are so altered as to be incompatible with the nature of bread or of wine; or else on the part of the quantity, as, for instance, if the bread be reduced to fine particles, or the wine divided into such tiny drops that the species of bread or wine no longer remain.

REPLY OBJ. 1: Since it belongs essentially to corruption to take away the being of a thing, in so far as the being of some form is in matter, it results that by corruption the form is separated from the matter. But if such being were not in matter, yet like such being as is in matter, it could be taken away by corruption, even where there is no matter; as takes place in this sacrament, as is evident from what was said above.

REPLY OBJ. 2: Although the sacramental species are forms not in matter, yet they have the being which they had in matter.

AD TERTIUM dicendum quod corruptio illa specierum non est miraculosa, sed naturalis, praesupponit tamen miraculum quod est factum in consecratione, scilicet quod illae species sacramentales retineant esse sine subiecto quod prius habebant in subiecto; sicut et caecus miraculose illuminatus naturaliter videt.

REPLY OBJ. 3: This corruption of species is not miraculous, but natural; nevertheless, it presupposes the miracle which is wrought in the consecration, namely, that those sacramental species retain without a subject, the same being as they had in a subject; just as a blind man, to whom sight is given miraculously, sees naturally.

Article 5

Whether Anything Can Be Generated from the Sacramental Species?

AD QUINTUM SIC PROCEDITUR. Videtur quod ex speciebus sacramentalibus nihil possit generari. Omne enim quod generatur, ex aliqua materia generatur, ex nihilo enim nihil generatur, quamvis ex nihilo fiat aliquid per creationem. Sed speciebus sacramentalibus non subest aliqua materia nisi corporis Christi, quod est incorruptibile. Ergo videtur quod ex speciebus sacramentalibus nihil possit generari.

PRAETEREA, ea quae non sunt unius generis, non possunt ex invicem fieri, non enim ex albedine fit linea. Sed accidens et substantia differunt genere. Cum ergo species sacramentales sint accidentia, videtur quod ex eis non possit aliqua substantia generari.

PRAETEREA, si ex eis generatur aliqua substantia corporea, non erit sine accidente. Si ergo ex speciebus sacramentalibus generatur aliqua substantia corporea, oportet quod ex accidente generetur substantia et accidens, duo scilicet ex uno, quod est impossibile. Ergo impossibile est quod ex speciebus sacramentalibus aliqua substantia corporea generetur.

SED CONTRA est quod ad sensum videri potest ex speciebus sacramentalibus aliquid generari, vel cinerem, si comburantur; vel vermes, si putrefiant; vel pulverem, si conterantur.

RESPONDEO dicendum quod, *cum corruptio unius sit generatio alterius*, ut dicitur in I de Generat., necesse est quod ex speciebus sacramentalibus aliquid generetur, cum corrumpantur, ut dictum est. Non enim sic corrumpuntur ut omnino dispareant, quasi in nihilum redigantur, sed manifeste aliquid sensibile eis succedit.

Quomodo autem ex eis aliquid generari possit, difficile est videre. Manifestum est enim quod ex corpore et sanguine Christi, quae ibi veraciter sunt, non generatur aliquid, cum sint incorruptibilia. Si autem substantia panis aut vini remaneret in hoc sacramento, vel eorum materia, facile esset assignare quod ex eis generatur illud sensibile quod succedit, ut quidam posuerunt. Sed hoc est falsum, ut supra habitum est.

OBJECTION 1: It seems that nothing can be generated from the sacramental species: because, whatever is generated, is generated out of some matter: for nothing is generated out of nothing, although by creation something is made out of nothing. But there is no matter underlying the sacramental species except that of Christ's body, and that body is incorruptible. Therefore it seems that nothing can be generated from the sacramental species.

OBJ. 2: Further, things which are not of the same genus cannot spring from one another: thus a line is not made of whiteness. But accident and substance differ generically. Therefore, since the sacramental species are accidents, it seems that no substance can be generated from them.

OBJ. 3: Further, if any corporeal substance be generated from them, such substance will not be without accident. Therefore, if any corporeal substance be generated from the sacramental species, then substance and accident would be generated from accident, namely, two things from one, which is impossible. Consequently, it is impossible for any corporeal substance to be generated out of the sacramental species.

ON THE CONTRARY, The senses are witness that something is generated out of the sacramental species, either ashes, if they be burned, worms if they putrefy, or dust if they be crushed.

I ANSWER THAT, Since *the corruption of one thing is the generation of another* (De Gener. i), something must be generated necessarily from the sacramental species if they be corrupted, as stated above (A. 4); for they are not corrupted in such a way that they disappear altogether, as if reduced to nothing; on the contrary, something sensible manifestly succeeds to them.

Nevertheless, it is difficult to see how anything can be generated from them. For it is quite evident that nothing is generated out of the body and blood of Christ which are truly there, because these are incorruptible. But if the substance, or even the matter, of the bread and wine were to remain in this sacrament, then, as some have maintained, it would be easy to account for this sensible object which succeeds to them. But that supposition is false, as was stated above (Q. 75, AA. 2, 4, 8).

Et ideo quidam dixerunt quod ea quae generantur, non fiunt ex speciebus sacramentalibus, sed ex aere circumstante. Quod quidem multipliciter apparet esse impossibile. Primo quidem, quia ex eo generatur aliquid quod prius alteratum et corruptum apparet. Nulla autem alteratio et corruptio prius apparuit in aere circumstante. Unde ex eo vermes aut cineres non generantur. Secundo, quia natura aeris non est talis quod ex eo per tales alterationes talia generentur. Tertio, quia potest contingere in magna quantitate hostias consecratas comburi vel putrefieri, nec esset possibile tantum de corpore terreo ex aere generari, nisi magna et etiam valde sensibili inspissatione aeris facta. Quarto, quia idem potest accidere corporibus solidis circumstantibus, puta ferro aut lapidibus, quae integra remanent post praedictorum generationem. Unde haec positio stare non potest, quia contrariatur ei quod ad sensum apparet.

Et ideo alii dixerunt quod redit substantia panis et vini in ipsa corruptione specierum, et sic ex substantia panis et vini redeunte generantur cineres aut vermes aut aliquid huiusmodi. Sed haec positio non videtur esse possibilis. Primo quidem quia, si substantia panis et vini conversa est in corpus et sanguinem, ut supra habitum est, non potest substantia panis vel vini redire nisi corpore aut sanguine Christi iterum converso in substantiam panis et vini, quod est impossibile, sicut, si aer sit conversus in ignem, non potest aer redire nisi iterum ignis convertatur in aerem. Si vero substantia panis aut vini sit annihilata, non potest iterum redire, quia quod in nihilum decidit, non redit idem numero, nisi forte dicatur redire praedicta substantia, quia Deus de novo creat novam substantiam loco primae. Secundo videtur hoc esse impossibile, quia non est dare quando substantia panis redeat. Manifestum est enim ex supra dictis quod, manentibus speciebus panis et vini, manet corpus et sanguis Christi, quae non sunt simul cum substantia panis et vini in hoc sacramento, secundum praehabita. Unde substantia panis et vini non potest redire, speciebus sacramentalibus manentibus. Similiter etiam nec eis cessantibus, quia iam substantia panis et vini esset sine propriis accidentibus, quod est impossibile. Nisi forte dicatur quod in ipso ultimo instanti corruptionis specierum redit, non quidem substantia panis et vini, quia illud idem instans est in quo primo habent esse substantiae generatae ex speciebus, sed materia panis et vini magis quasi de novo creata diceretur quam rediens, proprie

Hence it is that others have said that the things generated have not sprung from the sacramental species, but from the surrounding atmosphere. But this can be shown in many ways to be impossible. In the first place, because when a thing is generated from another, the latter at first appears changed and corrupted; whereas no alteration or corruption appeared previously in the adjacent atmosphere; hence the worms or ashes are not generated therefrom. Second, because the nature of the atmosphere is not such as to permit of such things being generated by such alterations. Third, because it is possible for many consecrated hosts to be burned or putrefied; nor would it be possible for an earthen body, large enough to be generated from the atmosphere, unless a great and, in fact, exceedingly sensible condensation of the atmosphere took place. Fourth, because the same thing can happen to the solid bodies surrounding them, such as iron or stone, which remain entire after the generation of the aforesaid things. Hence this opinion cannot stand, because it is opposed to what is manifest to our senses.

And therefore others have said that the substance of the bread and wine returns during the corruption of the species, and so from the returning substance of the bread and wine, ashes or worms or something of the kind are generated. But this explanation seems an impossible one. First of all, because if the substance of the bread and wine be converted into the body and blood of Christ, as was shown above (Q. 75, AA. 2, 4), the substance of the bread and wine cannot return, except the body and blood of Christ be again changed back into the substance of bread and wine, which is impossible: thus if air be turned into fire, the air cannot return without the fire being again changed into air. But if the substance of bread or wine be annihilated, it cannot return again, because what lapses into nothing does not return numerically the same. Unless perchance it be said that the said substance returns, because God creates anew another new substance to replace the first. Second, this seems to be impossible, because no time can be assigned when the substance of the bread returns. For, from what was said above (A. 4; Q. 76, A. 6, ad 3), it is evident that while the species of the bread and wine remain, there remain also the body and blood of Christ, which are not present together with the substance of the bread and wine in this sacrament, according to what was stated above (Q. 75, A. 2). Hence the substance of the bread and wine cannot return while the sacramental species remain; nor, again, when these species pass away; because then the substance of the bread and wine would be without their proper accidents, which is impossible. Unless perchance it be said that in the last instant

loquendo. Et secundum hoc, posset sustineri praedicta positio.

Verum, quia non rationabiliter videtur dici quod miraculose aliquid accidit in hoc sacramento nisi ex ipsa consecratione, ex qua non est quod materia creetur vel redeat; melius videtur dicendum quod in ipsa consecratione miraculose datur quantitati dimensivae panis et vini quod sit primum subiectum subsequentium formarum. Hoc autem est proprium materiae. Et ideo ex consequenti datur praedictae quantitati dimensivae omne id quod ad materiam pertinet. Et ideo quidquid posset generari ex materia panis si esset, totum potest generari ex praedicta quantitate dimensiva panis vel vini, non quidem novo miraculo, sed ex vi miraculi prius facti.

AD PRIMUM ergo dicendum quod, quamvis non sit ibi materia ex qua aliquid generetur, quantitas tamen dimensiva supplet vicem materiae, ut dictum est.

AD SECUNDUM dicendum quod illae species sacramentales sunt quidem accidentia, habent tamen actum et vim substantiae, ut dictum est.

AD TERTIUM dicendum quod quantitas dimensiva panis et vini et retinet naturam propriam, et accipit miraculose vim et proprietatem substantiae. Et ideo potest transire in utrumque, idest in substantiam et dimensionem.

---

of the corruption of the species there returns (not, indeed, the substance of bread and wine, because it is in that very instant that they have the being of the substance generated from the species, but) the matter of the bread and wine; which, matter, properly speaking, would be more correctly described as created anew, than as returning. And in this sense the aforesaid position might be held.

However, since it does not seem reasonable to say that anything takes place miraculously in this sacrament, except in virtue of the consecration itself, which does not imply either creation or return of matter, it seems better to say that in the actual consecration it is miraculously bestowed on the dimensive quantity of the bread and wine to be the subject of subsequent forms. Now this is proper to matter; and therefore as a consequence everything which goes with matter is bestowed on dimensive quantity; and therefore everything which could be generated from the matter of bread or wine, if it were present, can be generated from the aforesaid dimensive quantity of the bread or wine, not, indeed, by a new miracle, but by virtue of the miracle which has already taken place.

REPLY OBJ. 1: Although no matter is there out of which a thing may be generated, nevertheless dimensive quantity supplies the place of matter, as stated above.

REPLY OBJ. 2: Those sacramental species are indeed accidents, yet they have the act and power of substance, as stated above (A. 3).

REPLY OBJ. 3: The dimensive quantity of the bread and wine retains its own nature, and receives miraculously the power and property of substance; and therefore it can pass to both, that is, into substance and dimension.

Article 6

Whether the Sacramental Species Can Nourish?

AD SEXTUM SIC PROCEDITUR. Videtur quod species sacramentales non possint nutrire. Dicit enim Ambrosius, in libro de sacramentis, *non iste panis est qui vadit in corpus, sed panis vitae aeternae, qui animae nostrae substantiam fulcit.* Sed omne quod nutrit, vadit in corpus. Ergo panis iste non nutrit. Et eadem ratio est de vino.

PRAETEREA, sicut dicitur in libro de Generat., *ex eisdem nutrimur ex quibus sumus.* Species autem sacramentales sunt accidentia, ex quibus homo non constat, non enim accidens est pars substantiae. Ergo videtur quod species sacramentales nutrire non possunt.

PRAETEREA, philosophus dicit, in II de anima, quod *alimentum nutrit prout est quaedam substantia, auget*

OBJECTION 1: It seems that the sacramental species cannot nourish, because, as Ambrose says (*De Sacram.* v), *it is not this bread that enters into our body, but the bread of everlasting life, which supports the substance of our soul.* But whatever nourishes enters into the body. Therefore this bread does not nourish: and the same reason holds good of the wine.

OBJ. 2: Further, as is said in *De Gener.* ii, *We are nourished by the very things of which we are made.* But the sacramental species are accidents, whereas man is not made of accidents, because accident is not a part of substance. Therefore it seems that the sacramental species cannot nourish.

OBJ. 3: Further, the Philosopher says (*De Anima* ii) that *food nourishes according as it is a substance, but it gives*

autem prout est aliquid quantum. Sed species sacramentales non sunt substantia. Ergo non possunt nutrire.

SED CONTRA est quod apostolus, I Cor. XI, loquens de hoc sacramento, dicit, *alius quidem esurit, alius autem ebrius est,* ubi dicit Glossa quod *notat illos qui, post celebrationem sacri mysterii et consecrationem panis et vini, suas oblationes vindicabant, et, aliis non communicantes, sibi solis sumebant, ita ut inde etiam inebriarentur.* Quod quidem non potest contingere si sacramentales species non nutrirent. Ergo species sacramentales nutriunt.

RESPONDEO dicendum quod haec quaestio difficultatem non habet, praecedenti quaestione soluta. Ex hoc enim, ut dicitur in II de anima, cibus nutrit, quod convertitur in substantiam nutriti. Dictum est autem quod species sacramentales possunt converti in substantiam aliquam quae ex eis generatur. Per eandem autem rationem possunt converti in corpus humanum, per quam possunt converti in cineres vel in vermes. Et ideo manifestum est quod nutriunt.

Quod autem quidam dicunt, quod non vere nutriunt, quasi in corpus humanum convertantur, sed reficiunt et confortant quadam sensuum immutatione, sicut homo confortatur ex odore cibi et inebriatur ex odore vini, ad sensum patet esse falsum. Talis enim refectio non diu sufficit homini, cuius corpus, propter continuam deperditionem, restauratione indiget. Et tamen homo diu sustentari posset, si hostias et vinum consecratum sumeret in magna quantitate.

Similiter etiam non potest stare quod quidam dicunt, quod species sacramentales nutriunt per formam substantialem panis et vini, quae remanet. Tum quia non remanet, ut supra habitum est. Tum quia non est actus formae nutrire, sed magis materiae, quae accipit formam nutriti, recedente forma nutrimenti. Unde dicitur in II de anima, quod nutrimentum in principio est dissimile, in fine autem simile.

AD PRIMUM ergo dicendum quod, facta consecratione, dupliciter potest dici panis in hoc sacramento. Uno modo, ipsae species panis, quae retinent nomen prioris substantiae, ut Gregorius dicit, in homilia paschali. Alio modo, potest dici panis ipsum corpus Christi, quod est panis mysticus de caelo descendens. Ambrosius ergo, cum dicit quod *iste panis non transit in corpus,* accipit panem secundo modo, quia scilicet corpus Christi non convertitur in corpus hominis, sed reficit mentem eius. Non autem loquitur de pane primo modo dicto.

AD SECUNDUM dicendum quod species sacramentales, etsi non sint ea ex quibus corpus hominis constat, tamen in ea convertuntur, sicut dictum est.

increase by reason of its quantity. But the sacramental species are not a substance. Consequently they cannot nourish.

ON THE CONTRARY, The Apostle speaking of this sacrament says (1 Cor 11:21): *One, indeed, is hungry, and another is drunk:* upon which the gloss observes that *he alludes to those who after the celebration of the sacred mystery, and after the consecration of the bread and wine, claimed their oblations, and not sharing them with others, took the whole, so as even to become intoxicated thereby.* But this could not happen if the sacramental species did not nourish. Therefore the sacramental species do nourish.

I ANSWER THAT, This question presents no difficulty, now that we have solved the preceding question. Because, as stated in *De Anima* ii, food nourishes by being converted into the substance of the individual nourished. Now it has been stated (A. 5) that the sacramental species can be converted into a substance generated from them. And they can be converted into the human body for the same reason as they can into ashes or worms. Consequently, it is evident that they nourish.

But the senses witness to the untruth of what some maintain; viz. that the species do not nourish as though they were changed into the human body, but merely refresh and hearten by acting upon the senses (as a man is heartened by the odor of meat, and intoxicated by the fumes of wine). Because such refreshment does not suffice long for a man, whose body needs repair owing to constant waste: and yet a man could be supported for long if he were to take hosts and consecrated wine in great quantity.

In like manner the statement advanced by others cannot stand, who hold that the sacramental species nourish owing to the remaining substantial form of the bread and wine: both because the form does not remain, as stated above (Q. 75, A. 6): and because to nourish is the act not of a form but rather of matter, which takes the form of the one nourished, while the form of the nourishment passes away: hence it is said in *De Anima* ii that nourishment is at first unlike, but at the end is like.

REPLY OBJ. 1: After the consecration bread can be said to be in this sacrament in two ways. First, as to the species, which retain the name of the previous substance, as Gregory says in an Easter Homily (Lanfranc, *De Corp. et Sang. Dom.* xx). Second, Christ's very body can be called bread, since it is the mystical bread *coming down from heaven.* Consequently, Ambrose uses the word *bread* in this second meaning, when he says that *this bread does not pass into the body,* because, to wit, Christ's body is not changed into man's body, but nourishes his soul. But he is not speaking of bread taken in the first acceptation.

REPLY OBJ. 2: Although the sacramental species are not those things out of which the human body is made, yet they are changed into those things stated above.

AD TERTIUM dicendum quod species sacramentales, quamvis non sint substantia, habent tamen virtutem substantiae, ut dictum est.

REPLY OBJ. 3: Although the sacramental species are not a substance, still they have the virtue of a substance, as stated above.

Article 7

Whether the Sacramental Species Are Broken in This Sacrament?

AD SEPTIMUM SIC PROCEDITUR. Videtur quod species sacramentales non frangantur in hoc sacramento. Dicit enim philosophus, in IV Meteor., quod corpora dicuntur frangibilia propter determinatam dispositionem pororum. Quod non potest attribui sacramentalibus speciebus. Ergo sacramentales species non possunt frangi.

PRAETEREA, fractionem sequitur sonus. Sed species sacramentales non sunt sonabiles, dicit enim philosophus, II de anima, quod sonabile est corpus durum habens superficiem levem. Ergo species sacramentales non franguntur.

PRAETEREA, eiusdem videtur esse frangi et masticari. Sed verum corpus Christi est quod manducatur, secundum illud Ioan. VI, *qui manducat meam carnem et bibit meum sanguinem*. Ergo corpus Christi est quod frangitur et masticatur. Unde et in confessione Berengarii dicitur, *consentio sanctae Romanae Ecclesiae, et corde et ore profiteor panem et vinum quae in altari ponuntur, post consecrationem verum corpus et sanguinem Christi esse, et in veritate manibus sacerdotum tractari, frangi et fidelium dentibus atteri*. Non ergo fractio debet attribui sacramentalibus speciebus.

SED CONTRA est quod fractio fit per divisionem quanti. Sed nullum quantum ibi dividitur nisi species sacramentales, quia neque corpus Christi, quod est incorruptibile; neque substantia panis, quae non manet. Ergo species sacramentales franguntur.

RESPONDEO dicendum quod apud antiquos circa hoc multiplex fuit opinio. Quidam enim dixerunt quod non erat in hoc sacramento fractio secundum rei veritatem, sed solum secundum aspectum intuentium. Sed hoc non potest stare. Quia in hoc sacramento veritatis sensus non decipitur circa ea quorum iudicium ad ipsum pertinet, inter quae est fractio, per quam ex uno fiunt multa, quae quidem sunt sensibilia communia, ut patet in libro de anima.

Unde alii dixerunt quod erat ibi vera fractio sine substantia existente. Sed hoc etiam sensui contradicit. Apparet enim in hoc sacramento aliquod quantum, prius

OBJECTION 1: It seems that the sacramental species are not broken in this sacrament, because the Philosopher says in Meteor. iv that bodies are breakable owing to a certain disposition of the pores; a thing which cannot be attributed to the sacramental species. Therefore the sacramental species cannot be broken.

OBJ. 2: Further, breaking is followed by sound. But the sacramental species emit no sound: because the Philosopher says (*De Anima* ii), that what emits sound is a hard body, having a smooth surface. Therefore the sacramental species are not broken.

OBJ. 3: Further, breaking and mastication are seemingly of the same object. But it is Christ's true body that is eaten, according to John 6:57: *He that eateth My flesh, and drinketh My blood*. Therefore it is Christ's body that is broken and masticated: and hence it is said in the confession of Berengarius: *I agree with the Holy Catholic Church, and with heart and lips I profess, that the bread and wine which are placed on the altar, are the true body and blood of Christ after consecration, and are truly handled and broken by the priest's hands, broken and crushed by the teeth of believers.* Consequently, the breaking ought not to be ascribed to the sacramental species.

ON THE CONTRARY, Breaking arises from the division of that which has quantity. But nothing having quantity except the sacramental species is broken here, because neither Christ's body is broken, as being incorruptible, nor is the substance of the bread, because it no longer remains. Therefore the sacramental species are broken.

I ANSWER THAT, Many opinions prevailed of old on this matter. Some held that in this sacrament there was no breaking at all in reality, but merely in the eyes of the beholders. But this contention cannot stand, because in this sacrament of truth the sense is not deceived with regard to its proper object of judgment, and one of these objects is breaking, whereby from one thing arise many: and these are common sensibles, as is stated in *De Anima* ii.

Others accordingly have said that there was indeed a genuine breaking, but without any subject. But this again contradicts our senses; because a quantitative body is seen

unum existens, postea in multa partitum, quod quidem oportet esse subiectum fractionis.

Non autem potest dici quod ipsum corpus Christi verum frangatur. Primo quidem, quia est incorruptibile et impassibile. Secundo, quia est totum sub qualibet parte, ut supra habitum est, quod est quidem contra rationem eius quod frangitur.

Unde relinquitur quod fractio sit sicut in subiecto in quantitate dimensiva panis, sicut et alia accidentia. Et sicut species sacramentales sunt sacramentum corporis Christi veri, ita fractio huiusmodi specierum est sacramentum dominicae passionis, quae fuit in corpore Christi vero.

AD PRIMUM ergo dicendum quod, sicut in speciebus sacramentalibus remanet rarum et densum, ut supra dictum est, ita etiam remanet ibi porositas, et per consequens frangibilitas.

AD SECUNDUM dicendum quod densitatem sequitur duritia. Et ideo, ex quo in speciebus sacramentalibus remanet densitas, consequens est quod remaneat ibi duritia, et per consequens sonabilitas.

AD TERTIUM dicendum quod illud quod manducatur in propria specie, ipsummet frangitur et masticatur in sua specie. Corpus autem Christi non manducatur in sua specie, sed in specie sacramentali. Unde super illud Ioannis VI, *caro non prodest quidquam*, dicit Augustinus, *hoc est intelligendum secundum illos qui carnaliter intelligebant carnem quippe sic intellexerunt quo modo in cadavere dilaniatur, aut in macello venditur*. Et ideo ipsum corpus Christi non frangitur, nisi secundum speciem sacramentalem. Et hoc modo intelligenda est confessio Berengarii, ut fractio et contritio dentium referatur ad speciem sacramentalem, sub qua vere est corpus Christi.

in this sacrament, which formerly was one, and is now divided into many, and this must be the subject of the breaking.

But it cannot be said that Christ's true body is broken. First of all, because it is incorruptible and impassible: second, because it is entire under every part, as was shown above (Q. 76, A. 3), which is contrary to the nature of a thing broken.

It remains, then, that the breaking is in the dimensive quantity of the bread, as in a subject, just as the other accidents. And as the sacramental species are the sacrament of Christ's true body, so is the breaking of these species the sacrament of our Lord's Passion, which was in Christ's true body.

REPLY OBJ. 1: As rarity and density remain under the sacramental species, as stated above (A. 2, ad 3), so likewise porousness remains, and in consequence breakableness.

REPLY OBJ. 2: Hardness results from density; therefore, as density remains under the sacramental species, hardness remains there too, and the capability of sound as a consequence.

REPLY OBJ. 3: What is eaten under its own species, is also broken and masticated under its own species; but Christ's body is eaten not under its proper, but under the sacramental species. Hence in explaining John 6:64, *The flesh profiteth nothing*, Augustine (*Tract. xxvii in Joan.*) says that this is to be taken as referring to those who understood carnally: *for they understood the flesh, thus, as it is divided piecemeal, in a dead body, or as sold in the shambles*. Consequently, Christ's very body is not broken, except according to its sacramental species. And the confession made by Berengarius is to be understood in this sense, that the breaking and the crushing with the teeth is to be referred to the sacramental species, under which the body of Christ truly is.

Article 8

Whether Any Liquid Can Be Mingled with the Consecrated Wine?

AD OCTAVUM SIC PROCEDITUR. Videtur quod vino consecrato non possit aliquis liquor misceri. Omne enim quod miscetur alicui, recipit qualitatem ipsius. Sed nullus liquor potest recipere qualitatem sacramentalium specierum, quia accidentia illa sunt sine subiecto, ut dictum est. Ergo videtur quod nullus liquor possit permisceri speciebus sacramentalibus vini.

PRAETEREA, si aliquis liquor permisceatur illis speciebus, oportet quod ex his fiat aliquod unum. Sed non potest fieri aliquod unum neque ex liquore, qui est substantia, et speciebus sacramentalibus, quae sunt

OBJECTION 1: It seems that no liquid can be mingled with the consecrated wine, because everything mingled with another partakes of its quality. But no liquid can share in the quality of the sacramental species, because those accidents are without a subject, as stated above (A. 1). Therefore it seems that no liquid can be mingled with the sacramental species of the wine.

OBJ. 2: Further, if any kind of liquid be mixed with those species, then some one thing must be the result. But no one thing can result from the liquid, which is a substance, and the sacramental species, which are accidents; nor from the

accidentia; neque ex liquore et sanguine Christi, qui, ratione suae incorruptibilitatis, neque additionem recipit neque diminutionem. Ergo nullus liquor potest admisceri vino consecrato.

PRAETEREA, si aliquis liquor admisceatur vino consecrato, videtur quod etiam ipsum efficiatur consecratum, sicut aqua quae admiscetur aquae benedictae, efficitur etiam benedicta. Sed vinum consecratum est vere sanguis Christi. Ergo etiam liquor permixtus esset sanguis Christi. Et ita aliquid fieret sanguis Christi aliter quam per consecrationem, quod est inconveniens. Non ergo vino consecrato potest aliquis liquor permisceri.

PRAETEREA, si duorum unum totaliter corrumpatur, non erit mixtio, ut dicitur in I de Generat. Sed ad permixtionem cuiuscumque liquoris videtur corrumpi species sacramentalis vini, ita quod sub ea desinat esse sanguis Christi. Tum quia magnum et parvum sunt differentiae quantitatis et diversificant ipsam, sicut album et nigrum colorem. Tum etiam quia liquor permixtus, cum non habeat obstaculum, videtur undique diffundi per totum, et ita desinit ibi esse sanguis Christi, qui non est ibi simul cum alia substantia. Non ergo aliquis liquor potest permisceri vino consecrato.

SED CONTRA est quod ad sensum patet alium liquorem vino permisceri posse post consecrationem, sicut et ante.

RESPONDEO dicendum quod istius quaestionis veritas manifesta est ex praemissis. Dictum est enim supra quod species in hoc sacramento permanentes, sicut adipiscuntur virtute consecrationis modum essendi substantiae, ita etiam adipiscuntur modum agendi et patiendi, ut scilicet agere et pati possint quidquid ageret vel pateretur substantia si ibi praesens existeret. Manifestum est autem quod, si esset ibi substantia vini, liquor aliquis posset ei permisceri.

Huius tamen permixtionis diversus esset effectus et secundum formam liquoris, et secundum quantitatem. Si enim permisceretur aliquis liquor in tanta quantitate quod posset diffundi per totum vinum, totum fieret permixtum. Quod autem est commixtum ex duobus, neutrum miscibilium est, sed utrumque transit in quoddam tertium ex his compositum. Unde sequeretur quod vinum prius existens non remaneret, si liquor permixtus esset alterius speciei. Si autem esset eiusdem speciei liquor adiunctus, puta si vinum permisceretur vino, remaneret quidem eadem species, sed non remaneret idem numero vinum. Quod declarat diversitas accidentium, puta si unum vinum esset album, et aliud rubeum.

Si vero liquor adiunctus esset tam parvae quantitatis quod non posset perfundi per totum, non fieret totum vinum permixtum, sed aliqua pars eius. Quae quidem

liquid and Christ's blood, which owing to its incorruptibility suffers neither increase nor decrease. Therefore no liquid can be mixed with the consecrated wine.

OBJ. 3: Further, if any liquid be mixed with the consecrated wine, then that also would appear to be consecrated; just as water added to holy-water becomes holy. But the consecrated wine is truly Christ's blood. Therefore the liquid added would likewise be Christ's blood otherwise than by consecration, which is unbecoming. Therefore no liquid can be mingled with the consecrated wine.

OBJ. 4: Further, if one of two things be entirely corrupted, there is no mixture (*De Gener.* i). But if we mix any liquid, it seems that the entire species of the sacramental wine is corrupted, so that the blood of Christ ceases to be beneath it; both because great and little are difference of quantity, and alter it, as white and black cause a difference of color; and because the liquid mixed, as having no obstacle, seems to permeate the whole, and so Christ's blood ceases to be there, since it is not there with any other substance. Consequently, no liquid can be mixed with the consecrated wine.

ON THE CONTRARY, It is evident to our senses that another liquid can be mixed with the wine after it is consecrated, just as before.

I ANSWER THAT, The truth of this question is evident from what has been said already. For it was said above (A. 3; A. 5, ad 2) that the species remaining in this sacrament, as they acquire the manner of being of substance in virtue of the consecration, so likewise do they obtain the mode of acting and of being acted upon, so that they can do or receive whatever their substance could do or receive, were it there present. But it is evident that if the substance of wine were there present, then some other liquid could be mingled with it.

Nevertheless there would be a different effect of such mixing both according to the form and according to the quantity of the liquid. For if sufficient liquid were mixed so as to spread itself all through the wine, then the whole would be a mixed substance. Now what is made up of things mixed is neither of them, but each passes into a third resulting from both: hence it would result that the former wine would remain no longer. But if the liquid added were of another species, for instance, if water were mixed, the species of the wine would be dissolved, and there would be a liquid of another species. But if liquid of the same species were added, of instance, wine with wine, the same species would remain, but the wine would not be the same numerically, as the diversity of the accidents shows: for instance, if one wine were white and the other red.

But if the liquid added were of such minute quantity that it could not permeate the whole, the entire wine would not be mixed, but only part of it, which would not remain

non remaneret eadem numero, propter permixtionem extraneae materiae. Remaneret tamen eadem specie, non solum si parvus liquor permixtus esset eiusdem speciei, sed etiam si esset alterius speciei, quia gutta aquae multo vino permixta transit in speciem vini, ut dicitur in I de generatione.

Manifestum est autem ex praedictis quod corpus et sanguis Christi remanent in hoc sacramento quandiu illae species manent eaedem in numero, consecratur enim hic panis et hoc vinum. Unde si fiat tanta permixtio liquoris cuiuscumque quod pertingat ad totum vinum consecratum et fiat permixtum, et erit aliud numero, et non remanebit ibi sanguis Christi. Si vero fiat tam parva alicuius liquoris adiunctio quod non possit diffundi per totum, sed usque ad aliquam partem specierum, desinet esse sanguis Christi sub illa parte vini consecrati, remanebit tamen sub alia.

AD PRIMUM ergo dicendum quod Innocentius III dicit, in quadam decretali, quod *ipsa accidentia vinum appositum videntur afficere, quia, si aqua fuerit apposita, vini saporem assumeret. Contingit igitur accidentia mutare subiectum, sicut et subiectum contingit accidentia permutare. Cedit quippe natura miraculo, et virtus supra consuetudinem operatur.* Hoc tamen non est sic intelligendum quasi idem numero accidens quod prius fuit in vino ante consecrationem, postmodum fiat in vino apposito, sed talis permutatio fit per actionem. Nam accidentia vini remanentia retinent actionem substantiae, secundum praedicta, et ita immutando afficiunt liquorem appositum.

AD SECUNDUM dicendum quod liquor appositus vino consecrato nullo modo miscetur substantiae sanguinis Christi. Miscetur tamen speciebus sacramentalibus, ita tamen quod, permixtione facta, corrumpuntur praedictae species, vel in toto vel in parte, secundum modum quo supra dictum est quod ex speciebus illis potest aliquid generari. Et si quidem corrumpantur in toto, nulla iam remanet quaestio, quia iam totum erit uniforme. Si autem corrumpantur in parte, erit quidem una dimensio secundum continuitatem quantitatis, non tamen una secundum modum essendi, quia una pars eius est sine subiecto, alia erit in subiecto; sicut, si aliquod corpus constituatur ex duobus metallis, erit unum corpus secundum rationem quantitatis, non tamen unum secundum speciem naturae.

AD TERTIUM dicendum quod, sicut Innocentius III dicit, in decretali praedicta, *si post calicis consecrationem aliud vinum mittatur in calicem, illud quidem non transit in sanguinem, neque sanguini commiscetur, sed, accidentibus prioris vini commixtum, corpori quod sub eis latet undique circumfunditur, non madidans circumfusum.* Quod quidem intelligendum est quando non fit tanta

the same numerically owing to the blending of extraneous matter: still it would remain the same specifically, not only if a little liquid of the same species were mixed with it, but even if it were of another species, since a drop of water blended with much wine passes into the species of wine (*De Gener*. i).

Now it is evident that the body and blood of Christ abide in this sacrament so long as the species remain numerically the same, as stated above (A. 4; Q. 76, A. 6, ad 3); because it is this bread and this wine which is consecrated. Hence, if the liquid of any kind whatsoever added be so much in quantity as to permeate the whole of the consecrated wine, and be mixed with it throughout, the result would be something numerically distinct, and the blood of Christ will remain there no longer. But if the quantity of the liquid added be so slight as not to permeate throughout, but to reach only a part of the species, Christ's blood will cease to be under that part of the consecrated wine, yet will remain under the rest.

REPLY OBJ. 1: Pope Innocent III in a *Decretal* writes thus: *The very accidents appear to affect the wine that is added, because, if water is added, it takes the savor of the wine. The result is, then, that the accidents change the subject, just as subject changes accidents; for nature yields to miracle, and power works beyond custom.* But this must not be understood as if the same identical accident, which was in the wine previous to consecration, is afterwards in the wine that is added; but such change is the result of action; because the remaining accidents of the wine retain the action of substance, as stated above, and so they act upon the liquid added, by changing it.

REPLY OBJ. 2: The liquid added to the consecrated wine is in no way mixed with the substance of Christ's blood. Nevertheless it is mixed with the sacramental species, yet so that after such mixing the aforesaid species are corrupted entirely or in part, after the way mentioned above (A. 5), whereby something can be generated from those species. And if they be entirely corrupted, there remains no further question, because the whole will be uniform. But if they be corrupted in part, there will be one dimension according to the continuity of quantity, but not one according to the mode of being, because one part thereof will be without a subject while the other is in a subject; as in a body that is made up of two metals, there will be one body quantitatively, but not one as to the species of the matter.

REPLY OBJ. 3: As Pope Innocent says in the aforesaid *Decretal, if after the consecration other wine be put in the chalice, it is not changed into the blood, nor is it mingled with the blood, but, mixed with the accidents of the previous wine, it is diffused throughout the body which underlies them, yet without wetting what surrounds it.* Now this is to be understood when there is not sufficient mixing of

permixtio liquoris extranei quod sanguis Christi desinat esse sub toto. Tunc enim undique dicitur circumfundi, non quia tangat sanguinem Christi secundum eius proprias dimensiones, sed secundum dimensiones sacramentales, sub quibus continetur. Nec est simile de aqua benedicta, quia illa benedictio nullam immutationem facit circa substantiam aquae, sicut facit consecratio vini.

AD QUARTUM dicendum quod quidam posuerunt quod, quantumcumque parva fiat extranei liquoris permixtio, substantia sanguinis Christi desinet esse sub toto. Et hoc ratione inducta. Quae tamen non cogit. Quia magnum et parvum diversificant quantitatem dimensivam non quantum ad eius essentiam, sed quantum ad determinationem mensurae. Similiter etiam liquor appositus adeo potest esse parvus quod sua parvitate impeditur ne diffundatur per totum, et non solum dimensionibus, quae, licet sint sine subiecto, tamen obstant alteri liquori sicut et substantia si ibi esset, secundum ea quae praemissa sunt.

extraneous liquid to cause the blood of Christ to cease to be under the whole; because a thing is said to be *diffused throughout*, not because it touches the body of Christ according to its proper dimensions, but according to the sacramental dimensions, under which it is contained. Now it is not the same with holy water, because the blessing works no change in the substance of the water, as the consecration of the wine does.

REPLY OBJ. 4: Some have held that however slight be the mixing of extraneous liquid, the substance of Christ's blood ceases to be under the whole, and for the reason given above (Obj. 4); which, however, is not a cogent one; because *more* or *less* diversify dimensive quantity, not as to its essence, but as to the determination of its measure. In like manner the liquid added can be so small as on that account to be hindered from permeating the whole, and not simply by the dimensions; which, although they are present without a subject, still they are opposed to another liquid, just as substance would be if it were present, according to what was said at the beginning of the article.

QUESTION 78

THE FORM OF THIS SACRAMENT

Deinde considerandum est de forma huius sacramenti. Et circa hoc quaeruntur sex.

Primo, quae sit forma huius sacramenti.

Secundo, utrum sit conveniens forma consecrationis panis.

Tertio, utrum sit conveniens forma consecrationis sanguinis.

Quarto, de virtute utriusque formae.

Quinto, de veritate locutionis.

Sexto, de comparatione unius formae ad aliam.

We must now consider the form of this sacrament; concerning which there are six points of inquiry:

(1) What is the form of this sacrament?

(2) Whether the form for the consecration of the bread is appropriate?

(3) Whether the form for the consecration of the blood is appropriate?

(4) Of the power of each form?

(5) Of the truth of the expression?

(6) Of the comparison of the one form with the other?

Article 1

Whether This Is the Form of This Sacrament: This Is My Body, and This Is the Chalice of My Blood?

AD PRIMUM SIC PROCEDITUR. Videtur quod haec non sit forma huius sacramenti, *hoc est corpus meum, et, hic est calix sanguinis mei.* Illa enim verba videntur pertinere ad formam sacramenti quibus Christus corpus suum et sanguinem consecravit. Sed Christus ante benedixit panem acceptum, et postea dixit, *accipite et comedite, hoc est corpus meum,* ut habetur Matth. XXVI; et similiter fecit de calice. Ergo praedicta verba non sunt forma huius sacramenti.

PRAETEREA, Eusebius Emesenus dicit quod *invisibilis sacerdos visibiles creaturas in suum corpus convertit, dicens, accipite et comedite, hoc est corpus meum.* Ergo totum hoc videtur pertinere ad formam sacramenti. Et eadem ratio est de verbis pertinentibus ad sanguinem.

PRAETEREA, in forma Baptismi exprimitur persona ministri et actus eius, cum dicitur, *ego te baptizo.* Sed in praemissis verbis nulla fit mentio de persona ministri, nec de actu eius. Ergo non est conveniens forma sacramenti.

PRAETEREA, forma sacramenti sufficit ad perfectionem sacramenti, unde sacramentum Baptismi quandoque perfici potest solis verbis formae prolatis, et omnibus aliis praetermissis. Si ergo praedicta verba sunt forma huius sacramenti, videtur quod aliquando possit hoc sacramentum perfici his solis verbis prolatis, et omnibus aliis praetermissis quae in Missa dicuntur. Quod tamen videtur esse falsum, quia, ubi verba alia praetermitterentur, praedicta verba acciperentur ex persona sacerdotis proferentis, in cuius corpus et sanguinem panis et vinum

OBJECTION 1: It seems that this is not the form of this sacrament: *This is My body*, and, *This is the chalice of My blood.* Because those words seem to belong to the form of this sacrament, wherewith Christ consecrated His body and blood. But Christ first blessed the bread which He took, and said afterwards: *Take ye and eat; this is My body* (Matt 26:26). Therefore the whole of this seems to belong to the form of this sacrament: and the same reason holds good of the words which go with the consecration of the blood.

OBJ. 2: Further, Eusebius Emissenus (Pseudo-Hieron: *Ep. xxix*; Pseudo-Isid.: *Hom. iv*) says: *The invisible Priest changes visible creatures into His own body, saying: 'Take ye and eat; this is My body.'* Therefore, the whole of this seems to belong to the form of this sacrament: and the same hold good of the works appertaining to the blood.

OBJ. 3: Further, in the form of Baptism both the minister and his act are expressed, when it is said, *I baptize thee.* But in the words set forth above there is no mention made either of the minister or of his act. Therefore the form of the sacrament is not a suitable one.

OBJ. 4: Further, the form of the sacrament suffices for its perfection; hence the sacrament of Baptism can be performed sometimes by pronouncing the words of the form only, omitting all the others. Therefore, if the aforesaid words be the form of this sacrament, it would seem as if this sacrament could be performed sometimes by uttering those words alone, while leaving out all the others which are said in the mass; yet this seems to be false, because, were the other words to be passed over, the said words would be taken as spoken in the person of the priest saying them, whereas the bread and wine are not changed into his body

non convertuntur. Non ergo praedicta verba sunt forma huius sacramenti.

SED CONTRA est quod Ambrosius dicit, in libro de sacramentis, *consecratio fit verbis et sermonibus domini Iesu. Nam per reliqua omnia quae dicuntur, laus Deo defertur, oratione petitur pro populo, pro regibus, pro ceteris. Ubi autem sacramentum conficitur, iam non suis sermonibus sacerdos utitur, sed utitur sermonibus Christi. Ergo sermo Christi hoc conficit sacramentum.*

RESPONDEO dicendum quod hoc sacramentum ab aliis sacramentis differt in duobus. Primo quidem quantum ad hoc, quod hoc sacramentum perficitur in consecratione materiae, alia vero sacramenta perficiuntur in usu materiae consecratae. Secundo, quia in aliis sacramentis consecratio materiae consistit solum in quadam benedictione, ex qua materia consecrata accipit instrumentaliter quandam spiritualem virtutem, quae per ministrum, qui est instrumentum animatum, potest ad instrumenta inanimata procedere. Sed in hoc sacramento consecratio materiae consistit in quadam miraculosa conversione substantiae, quae a solo Deo perfici potest. Unde minister in hoc sacramento perficiendo non habet alium actum nisi prolationem verborum. Et quia forma debet esse conveniens rei, ideo forma huius sacramenti differt a formis aliorum sacramentorum in duobus. Primo quidem, quia formae aliorum sacramentorum important usum materiae, puta baptizationem vel consignationem, sed forma huius sacramenti importat solam consecrationem materiae, quae in transubstantiatione consistit; puta cum dicitur, *hoc est corpus meum, vel, hic est calix sanguinis mei.* Secundo, quia formae aliorum sacramentorum proferuntur ex persona ministri, sive per modum exercentis actum, sicut cum dicitur, *ego te baptizo, vel, ego te confirmo;* sive per modum imperantis, sicut in sacramento ordinis dicitur, accipe potestatem, etc.; sive per modum deprecantis, sicut cum in sacramento extremae unctionis dicitur, *per istam unctionem et nostram intercessionem,* et cetera. Sed forma huius sacramenti profertur ex persona ipsius Christi loquentis, ut detur intelligi quod minister in perfectione huius sacramenti nihil agit nisi quod profert verba Christi.

AD PRIMUM ergo dicendum quod circa hoc est multiplex opinio. Quidam enim dixerunt quod Christus, qui habebat potestatem excellentiae in sacramentis, absque omni forma verborum hoc sacramentum perfecit; et postea verba protulit sub quibus alii postea consecrarent. Quod videntur sonare verba Innocentii III dicentis, *sane dici potest quod Christus virtute divina confecit, et postea formam expressit sub qua posteri benedicerent.* Sed contra hoc expresse sunt verba Evangelii, in quibus dicitur quod Christus benedixit, quae quidem benedictio

and blood. Consequently, the aforesaid words are not the form of this sacrament.

ON THE CONTRARY, Ambrose says (*De Sacram.* iv): *The consecration is accomplished by the words and expressions of the Lord Jesus. Because, by all the other words spoken, praise is rendered to God, prayer is put up for the people, for kings, and others; but when the time comes for perfecting the sacrament, the priest uses no longer his own words, but the words of Christ. Therefore, it is Christ's words that perfect this sacrament.*

I ANSWER THAT, This sacrament differs from the other sacraments in two respects. First of all, in this, that this sacrament is accomplished by the consecration of the matter, while the rest are perfected in the use of the consecrated matter. Second, because in the other sacraments the consecration of the matter consists only in a blessing, from which the matter consecrated derives instrumentally a spiritual power, which through the priest who is an animated instrument, can pass on to inanimate instruments. But in this sacrament the consecration of the matter consists in the miraculous change of the substance, which can only be done by God; hence the minister in performing this sacrament has no other act save the pronouncing of the words. And because the form should suit the thing, therefore the form of this sacrament differs from the forms of the other sacraments in two respects. First, because the form of the other sacraments implies the use of the matter, as for instance, baptizing, or signing; but the form of this sacrament implies merely the consecration of the matter, which consists in transubstantiation, as when it is said, *This is My body,* or, *This is the chalice of My blood.* Second, because the forms of the other sacraments are pronounced in the person of the minister, whether by way of exercising an act, as when it is said, *I baptize thee,* or *I confirm thee,* etc.; or by way of command, as when it is said in the sacrament of order, *Take the power,* etc.; or by way of entreaty, as when in the sacrament of Extreme Unction it is said, *By this anointing and our intercession,* etc. But the form of this sacrament is pronounced as if Christ were speaking in person, so that it is given to be understood that the minister does nothing in perfecting this sacrament, except to pronounce the words of Christ.

REPLY OBJ. 1: There are many opinions on this matter. Some have said that Christ, Who had power of excellence in the sacraments, performed this sacrament without using any form of words, and that afterwards He pronounced the words under which others were to consecrate thereafter. And the words of Pope Innocent III seem to convey the same sense (*De Sacr. Alt. Myst.* iv), where he says: *In good sooth it can be said that Christ accomplished this sacrament by His Divine power, and subsequently expressed the form under which those who came after were to consecrate. But*

aliquibus verbis facta est. Unde praedicta verba Innocentii sunt opinative magis dicta quam determinative.

Quidam autem dixerunt quod benedictio illa facta est quibusdam aliis verbis nobis ignotis. Sed nec hoc stare potest. Quia benedictio consecrationis nunc perficitur per recitationem eorum quae tunc acta sunt. Unde, si tunc per haec verba non est facta consecratio, nec modo fieret.

Et ideo alii dixerunt quod illa benedictio eisdem etiam verbis facta est quibus modo fit, sed Christus ea bis protulit, primo quidem secreto, ad consecrandum; secundo manifeste, ad instruendum. Sed nec hoc stare potest. Quia sacerdos consecrat proferens haec verba, non ut a Christo in occulta benedictione dicta, sed ut publice prolata. Unde, cum non habeant vim huiusmodi verba nisi ex Christi prolatione, videtur quod etiam Christus manifeste ea proferens consecraverit.

Et ideo alii dixerunt quod Evangelistae non semper eundem ordinem in recitando servaverunt quo res sunt gestae, ut patet per Augustinum, in libro de consensu Evangelistarum. Unde intelligendum est ordinem rei gestae sic exprimi posse, *accipiens panem, benedixit dicens, hoc est corpus meum, et deinde fregit et dedit discipulis suis.* Sed idem sensus potest esse in verbis Evangelii non mutatis. Nam hoc participium dicens concomitantiam quandam importat verborum prolatorum ad ea quae praecedunt. Non autem oportet quod haec concomitantia intelligatur solum respectu verbi ultimi prolati, quasi Christus tunc ista verba protulerit quando dedit discipulis suis, sed potest intelligi concomitantia respectu totius praecedentis, ut sit sensus, dum benediceret et frangeret et daret discipulis suis, haec verba dixit, accipite et cetera.

AD SECUNDUM dicendum quod in his verbis, accipite et comedite, intelligitur usus materiae consecratae, qui non est de necessitate huius sacramenti, ut supra habitum est. Et ideo nec haec verba sunt de substantia formae. Quia tamen ad quandam perfectionem sacramenti pertinet materiae consecratae usus, sicut operatio non est prima, sed secunda perfectio rei; ideo per omnia haec verba exprimitur tota perfectio huius sacramenti. Et hoc modo Eusebius intellexit his verbis confici sacramentum, quantum ad primam et secundam perfectionem ipsius.

AD TERTIUM dicendum quod in sacramento Baptismi minister aliquem actum exercet circa usum materiae, qui est de essentia sacramenti, quod non est in hoc sacramento. Et ideo non est similis ratio.

in opposition to this view are the words of the Gospel in which it is said that Christ *blessed*, and this blessing was effected by certain words. Accordingly those words of Innocent are to be considered as expressing an opinion, rather than determining the point.

Others, again, have said that the blessing was effected by other words not known to us. But this statement cannot stand, because the blessing of the consecration is now performed by reciting the things which were then accomplished; hence, if the consecration was not performed then by these words, neither would it be now.

Accordingly, others have maintained that this blessing was effected by the same words as are used now; but that Christ spoke them twice, at first secretly, in order to consecrate, and afterwards openly, to instruct others. But even this will not hold good, because the priest in consecrating uses these words, not as spoken in secret, but as openly pronounced. Accordingly, since these words have no power except from Christ pronouncing them, it seems that Christ also consecrated by pronouncing them openly.

And therefore others said that the Evangelists did not always follow the precise order in their narrative as that in which things actually happened, as is seen from Augustine (*De Consens. Evang.* ii). Hence it is to be understood that the order of what took place can be expressed thus: *Taking the bread He blessed it, saying: This is My body, and then He broke it, and gave it to His disciples.* But the same sense can be had even without changing the words of the Gospel; because the participle *saying* implies sequence of the words uttered with what goes before. And it is not necessary for the sequence to be understood only with respect to the last word spoken, as if Christ had just then pronounced those words, when He gave it to His disciples; but the sequence can be understood with regard to all that had gone before; so that the sense is: *While He was blessing, and breaking, and giving it to His disciples, He spoke the words, 'Take ye,'* etc.

REPLY OBJ. 2: In these words, *Take ye and eat*, the use of the consecrated, matter is indicated, which is not of the necessity of this sacrament, as stated above (Q. 74, A. 7). And therefore not even these words belong to the substance of the form. Nevertheless, because the use of the consecrated matter belongs to a certain perfection of the sacrament, in the same way as operation is not the first but the second perfection of a thing, consequently, the whole perfection of this sacrament is expressed by all those words: and it was in this way that Eusebius understood that the sacrament was accomplished by those words, as to its first and second perfection.

REPLY OBJ. 3: In the sacrament of Baptism the minister exercises an act regarding the use of the matter, which is of the essence of the sacrament: such is not the case in this sacrament; hence there is no parallel.

AD QUARTUM dicendum quod quidam dixerunt hoc sacramentum perfici non posse praedictis verbis prolatis et aliis praetermissis, praecipue quae sunt in canone Missae. Sed hoc patet esse falsum. Tum ex verbis Ambrosii supra inductis. Tum etiam quia canon Missae non est idem apud omnes, nec secundum omnia tempora, sed diversa sunt a diversis apposita.

Unde dicendum est quod, si sacerdos sola verba praedicta proferret cum intentione conficiendi hoc sacramentum, perficeretur hoc sacramentum, quia intentio faceret ut haec verba intelligerentur quasi ex persona Christi prolata, etiam si verbis praecedentibus hoc non recitaretur. Graviter tamen peccaret sacerdos sic conficiens hoc sacramentum, utpote ritum Ecclesiae non servans. Nec est simile de Baptismo, quod est sacramentum necessitatis, defectum autem huius sacramenti potest supplere spiritualis manducatio, ut Augustinus dicit.

REPLY OBJ. 4: Some have contended that this sacrament cannot be accomplished by uttering the aforesaid words, while leaving out the rest, especially the words in the Canon of the Mass. But that this is false can be seen both from Ambrose's words quoted above, as well as from the fact that the Canon of the Mass is not the same in all places or times, but various portions have been introduced by various people.

Accordingly it must be held that if the priest were to pronounce only the aforesaid words with the intention of consecrating this sacrament, this sacrament would be valid because the intention would cause these words to be understood as spoken in the person of Christ, even though the words were pronounced without those that precede. The priest, however, would sin gravely in consecrating the sacrament thus, as he would not be observing the rite of the Church. Nor does the comparison with Baptism prove anything; for it is a sacrament of necessity: whereas the lack of this sacrament can be supplied by the spiritual partaking thereof, as Augustine says (cf. Q. 73, A. 3, ad 1).

Article 2

Whether This Is the Proper Form for the Consecration of the Bread: This Is My Body?

AD SECUNDUM SIC PROCEDITUR. Videtur quod haec non sit conveniens forma consecrationis panis, *hoc est corpus meum*. Per formam enim sacramenti debet exprimi sacramenti effectus. Sed effectus qui fit in consecratione panis, est conversio substantiae panis in corpus Christi, quae magis exprimitur per hoc verbum fit, quam per hoc verbum est. Ergo in forma consecrationis deberet dici, hoc fit corpus meum.

PRAETEREA, Ambrosius dicit, in libro de sacramentis, *sermo Christi hoc conficit sacramentum. Quis sermo Christi? Hic quo facta sunt omnia, jussit dominus et facta sunt caeli et terra*. Ergo et forma huius sacramenti convenientior esset per verbum imperativum, ut diceretur, hoc sit corpus meum.

PRAETEREA, per subiectum huius locutionis importatur illud quod convertitur, sicut per praedicatum importatur conversionis terminus. Sed, sicut est determinatum id in quod fit conversio, non enim fit conversio nisi in corpus Christi; ita est determinatum id quod convertitur, non enim convertitur in corpus Christi nisi panis. Ergo, sicut ex parte praedicati ponitur nomen, ita ex parte subiecti debet poni nomen, ut dicatur, hic panis est corpus meum.

PRAETEREA, sicut id in quod terminatur conversio est determinatae naturae, quia est corpus; ita etiam est determinatae personae. Ergo, ad determinandam personam, debet dici, hoc est corpus Christi.

OBJECTION 1: It seems that this is not the proper form of this sacrament: *This is My body*. For the effect of a sacrament ought to be expressed in its form. But the effect of the consecration of the bread is the change of the substance of the bread into the body of Christ, and this is better expressed by the word *becomes* than by *is*. Therefore, in the form of the consecration we ought to say: *This becomes My body*.

OBJ. 2: Further, Ambrose says (*De Sacram.* iv), *Christ's words consecrate this sacrament. What word of Christ? This word, whereby all things are made. The Lord commanded, and the heavens and earth were made.* Therefore, it would be a more proper form of this sacrament if the imperative mood were employed, so as to say: *Be this My body*.

OBJ. 3: Further, that which is changed is implied in the subject of this phrase, just as the term of the change is implied in the predicate. But just as that into which the change is made is something determinate, for the change is into nothing else but the body of Christ, so also that which is converted is determinate, since only bread is converted into the body of Christ. Therefore, as a noun is inserted on the part of the predicate, so also should a noun be inserted in the subject, so that it be said: *This bread is My body*.

OBJ. 4: Further, just as the term of the change is determinate in nature, because it is a body, so also is it determinate in person. Consequently, in order to determine the person, it ought to be said: *This is the body of Christ*.

Praeterea, in verbis formae non debet poni aliquid quod non sit de substantia eius. Inconvenienter ergo additur in quibusdam libris haec coniunctio enim, quae non est de substantia formae.

Sed contra est quod dominus hac forma in consecrando est usus, ut patet Matth. XXVI.

Respondeo dicendum quod haec est conveniens forma consecrationis panis. Dictum est enim quod haec consecratio consistit in conversione substantiae panis in corpus Christi. Oportet autem formam sacramenti significare id quod in sacramento efficitur. Unde et forma consecrationis panis debet significare ipsam conversionem panis in corpus Christi. In qua tria considerantur, scilicet ipsa conversio, et terminus a quo, et terminus ad quem.

Conversio autem potest considerari dupliciter, uno modo, ut in fieri; alio modo, ut in facto esse. Non autem debuit significari conversio in hac forma ut in fieri, sed ut in facto esse. Primo quidem, quia haec conversio non est successiva, ut supra habitum est, sed instantanea, in huiusmodi autem mutationibus fieri non est nisi factum esse. Secundo, quia ita se habent formae sacramentales ad significandum effectum sacramenti, sicut se habent formae artificiales ad repraesentandum effectum artis. Forma autem artificialis est similitudo ultimi effectus in quem fertur intentio artificis, sicut forma artis in mente aedificatoris est forma domus aedificatae principaliter, aedificationis autem per consequens. Unde et in hac forma debet exprimi conversio ut in facto esse, ad quod fertur intentio.

Et quia ipsa conversio exprimitur in hac forma ut in facto esse, necesse est quod extrema conversionis significentur ut se habent in facto esse conversionis. Tunc autem terminus in quem habet propriam naturam suae substantiae, sed terminus a quo non manet secundum suam substantiam, sed solum secundum accidentia, quibus sensui subiacet, et ad sensum determinari potest. Unde convenienter terminus conversionis a quo exprimitur per pronomen demonstrativum relatum ad accidentia sensibilia, quae manent. Terminus autem ad quem exprimitur per nomen significans naturam eius in quod fit conversio, quod quidem est totum corpus Christi, et non sola caro eius, ut dictum est. Unde haec forma est convenientissima, *hoc est corpus meum*.

Ad primum ergo dicendum quod fieri non est ultimus effectus huius consecrationis, sed factum esse ut dictum est. Et ideo hoc potius exprimi debet in forma.

Ad secundum dicendum quod sermo Dei operatus est in creatione rerum, qui etiam operatur in hac consecratione, aliter tamen et aliter. Nam hic operatur sacramentaliter, idest secundum vim significationis. Et ideo oportet in hoc sermone significari ultimum effectum consecrationis per verbum substantivum indicativi

Obj. 5: Further, nothing ought to be inserted in the form except what is substantial to it. Consequently, the conjunction *for* is improperly added in some books, since it does not belong to the substance of the form.

On the contrary, our Lord used this form in consecrating, as is evident from Matt. 26:26.

I answer that, This is the proper form for the consecration of the bread. For it was said (A. 1) that this consecration consists in changing the substance of bread into the body of Christ. Now the form of a sacrament ought to denote what is done in the sacrament. Consequently the form for the consecration of the bread ought to signify the actual conversion of the bread into the body of Christ. And herein are three things to be considered: namely, the actual conversion, the term whence, and the term whereunto.

Now the conversion can be considered in two ways: first, in becoming, second, in being. But the conversion ought not to be signified in this form as in becoming, but as in being. First, because such conversion is not successive, as was said above (Q. 75, A. 7), but instantaneous; and in such changes the becoming is nothing else than the being. Second, because the sacramental forms bear the same relation to the signification of the sacramental effect as artificial forms to the representation of the effect of art. Now an artificial form is the likeness of the ultimate effect, on which the artist's intention is fixed; just as the art-form in the builder's mind is principally the form of the house constructed, and secondarily of the constructing. Accordingly, in this form also the conversion ought to be expressed as in being, to which the intention is referred.

And since the conversion is expressed in this form as in being, it is necessary for the extremes of the conversion to be signified as they exist in the fact of conversion. But then the term whereunto has the proper nature of its own substance; whereas the term whence does not remain in its own substance, but only as to the accidents whereby it comes under the senses, and can be determined in relation to the senses. Hence the term whence of the conversion is conveniently expressed by the demonstrative pronoun, relative to the sensible accidents which continue; but the term whereunto is expressed by the noun signifying the nature of the thing which terminates the conversion, and this is Christ's entire body, and not merely His flesh; as was said above (Q. 76, A. 1, ad 2). Hence this form is most appropriate: *This is My body*.

Reply Obj. 1: The ultimate effect of this conversion is not a becoming but a being, as stated above, and consequently prominence should be given to this in the form.

Reply Obj. 2: God's word operated in the creation of things, and it is the same which operates in this consecration, yet each in different fashion: because here it operates effectively and sacramentally, that is, in virtue of its signification. And consequently the last effect of the consecration must needs be signified in this sentence by a substantive

modi et praesentis temporis. Sed in creatione rerum operatus est solum effective, quae quidem efficientia est per imperium suae sapientiae. Et ideo in creatione rerum exprimitur sermo dominicus per verbum imperativi modi, secundum illud Gen. I, *fiat lux, et facta est lux.*

Ad tertium dicendum quod terminus a quo in ipso facto esse conversionis non retinet naturam suae substantiae, sicut terminus ad quem. Et ideo non est simile.

Ad quartum dicendum quod per hoc pronomen meum, quod includit demonstrationem primae personae, quae est persona loquentis, sufficienter exprimitur persona Christi, ex cuius persona haec proferuntur, ut dictum est.

Ad quintum dicendum quod haec coniunctio enim apponitur in hac forma secundum consuetudinem Romanae Ecclesiae a beato Petro apostolo derivatam. Et hoc propter continuationem ad verba praecedentia. Et ideo non est de forma, sicut nec praecedentia formam.

verb of the indicative mood and present time. But in the creation of things it worked merely effectively, and such efficiency is due to the command of His wisdom; and therefore in the creation of things the Lord's word is expressed by a verb in the imperative mood, as in Gen. 1:3: *Let there be light, and light was made.*

Reply Obj. 3: The term whence does not retain the nature of its substance in the being of the conversion, as the term whereunto does. Therefore there is no parallel.

Reply Obj. 4: The pronoun *My*, which implicitly points to the chief person, i.e., the person of the speaker, sufficiently indicates Christ's person, in Whose person these words are uttered, as stated above (A. 1).

Reply Obj. 5: The conjunction *for* is set in this form according to the custom of the Roman Church, who derived it from Peter the Apostle; and this on account of the sequence with the words preceding: and therefore it is not part of the form, just as the words preceding the form are not.

Article 3

Whether This Is the Proper Form for the Consecration of the Wine: This Is the Chalice of My Blood, Etc.?

Ad tertium sic proceditur. Videtur quod haec non sit conveniens forma consecrationis vini, *hic est calix sanguinis mei, novi et aeterni testamenti, mysterium fidei, qui pro vobis et pro multis effundetur in remissionem peccatorum.* Sicut enim panis convertitur in corpus Christi ex vi consecrationis, ita et vinum in sanguinem Christi, sicut ex praedictis patet. Sed in forma consecrationis panis ponitur in recto corpus Christi, nec aliquid aliud additur. Inconvenienter ergo in hac forma ponitur sanguis Christi in obliquo, et additur calix in recto, cum dicitur, *hic est calix sanguinis mei.*

Praeterea, non sunt maioris efficaciae verba quae proferuntur in consecratione panis quam ea quae proferuntur in consecratione vini, cum utraque sint verba Christi. Sed statim dicto, hoc est corpus meum, est perfecta consecratio panis. Ergo statim cum dictum est, hic est calix sanguinis mei, est perfecta consecratio sanguinis. Et ita ea quae consequuntur non videntur esse de substantia formae, praesertim cum pertineant ad proprietates huius sacramenti.

Praeterea, testamentum novum pertinere videtur ad internam inspirationem, ut patet ex hoc quod apostolus, ad Heb. VIII, introducit verba quae habentur in Ierem. XXXI, *consummabo super domum Israel testamentum novum, dando leges meas in mentibus eorum.*

Objection 1: It seems that this is not the proper form for the consecration of the wine. *This is the chalice of My blood, of the New and Eternal Testament, the Mystery of Faith, which shall be shed for you and for many unto the forgiveness of sins.* For as the bread is changed by the power of consecration into Christ's body, so is the wine changed into Christ's blood, as is clear from what was said above (Q. 76, AA. 1, 2, 3). But in the form of the consecration of the bread, the body of Christ is expressly mentioned, without any addition. Therefore in this form the blood of Christ is improperly expressed in the oblique case, and the chalice in the nominative, when it is said: *This is the chalice of My blood.*

Obj. 2: Further, the words spoken in the consecration of the bread are not more efficacious than those spoken in the consecration of the wine, since both are Christ's words. But directly the words are spoken—*This is My body,* there is perfect consecration of the bread. Therefore, directly these other words are uttered—*This is the chalice of My blood,* there is perfect consecration of the blood; and so the words which follow do not appeal to be of the substance of the form, especially since they refer to the properties of this sacrament.

Obj. 3: Further, the New Testament seems to be an internal inspiration, as is evident from the Apostle quoting the words of Jeremias (31:31): *I will perfect unto the house of Israel a New Testament . . . I will give My laws into their mind* (Heb 8:8). But a sacrament is an outward visible act.

Sacramentum autem exterius visibiliter agitur. Inconvenienter ergo in forma sacramenti dicitur, novi testamenti.

PRAETEREA, novum dicitur aliquid ex eo quod est prope principium sui esse. Aeternum autem non habet principium sui esse. Ergo inconvenienter dicitur novi et aeterni, quia videtur contradictionem implicare.

PRAETEREA, occasiones erroris sunt hominibus subtrahendae, secundum illud Isaiae LVII, *auferte offendicula de via populi mei*. Sed quidam erraverunt aestimantes mystice solum esse corpus et sanguinem Christi in hoc sacramento. Ergo in hac forma inconvenienter ponitur mysterium fidei.

PRAETEREA, supra dictum est quod, sicut Baptismus est sacramentum fidei, ita Eucharistia est sacramentum caritatis. Ergo in hac forma magis debuit poni caritas quam fides.

PRAETEREA, totum hoc sacramentum, et quantum ad corpus et quantum ad sanguinem, est memoriale dominicae passionis, secundum illud I Cor. XI, *quotiescumque manducabitis panem hunc et calicem bibetis, mortem domini annuntiabitis*. Non ergo magis debuit in forma consecrationis sanguinis fieri mentio de passione Christi et de eius fructu, quam in forma consecrationis corporis, praesertim cum, Luc. XXII, dominus dixerit, *hoc est corpus meum, quod pro vobis tradetur*.

PRAETEREA, passio Christi, ut supra habitum est, ad sufficientiam profuit omnibus, quantum vero ad efficaciam profuit multis. Debuit ergo dici quod effundetur pro omnibus, aut pro multis, sine hoc quod adderetur pro vobis.

PRAETEREA, verba quibus hoc sacramentum conficitur, efficaciam habent ex institutione Christi. Sed nullus Evangelista recitat Christum haec omnia verba dixisse. Ergo non est conveniens forma consecrationis vini.

SED CONTRA est quod Ecclesia, ab apostolis instructa, utitur hac forma in consecratione vini.

RESPONDEO dicendum quod circa hanc formam est duplex opinio. Quidam enim dixerunt quod de substantia formae huius est hoc solum quod dicitur, hic est calix sanguinis mei, non autem ea quae sequuntur. Sed hoc videtur inconveniens, quia ea quae sequuntur, sunt quaedam determinationes praedicati, idest sanguinis Christi; unde pertinent ad integritatem locutionis.

Et propter hoc sunt alii qui melius dicunt quod omnia sequentia sunt de substantia formae, usque ad hoc quod postea sequitur, hoc quotiescumque feceritis, quae pertinent ad usum huius sacramenti, unde non sunt de substantia formae. Et inde est quod sacerdos eodem ritu et modo, scilicet tenendo calicem in manibus, omnia haec verba profert. Lucae etiam XXII interponuntur

Therefore, in the form of the sacrament the words *of the New Testament* are improperly added.

OBJ. 4: Further, a thing is said to be new which is near the beginning of its existence. But what is eternal has no beginning of its existence. Therefore it is incorrect to say *of the New and Eternal*, because it seems to savor of a contradiction.

OBJ. 5: Further, occasions of error ought to be withheld from men, according to Isa. 57:14: *Take away the stumbling blocks out of the way of My people*. But some have fallen into error in thinking that Christ's body and blood are only mystically present in this sacrament. Therefore it is out of place to add *the mystery of faith*.

OBJ. 6: Further, it was said above (Q. 73, A. 3, ad 3), that as Baptism is the sacrament of faith, so is the Eucharist the sacrament of charity. Consequently, in this form the word *charity* ought rather to be used than *faith*.

OBJ. 7: Further, the whole of this sacrament, both as to body and blood, is a memorial of our Lord's Passion, according to 1 Cor. 11:26: *As often as you shall eat this bread and drink the chalice, you shall show the death of the Lord*. Consequently, mention ought to be made of Christ's Passion and its fruit rather in the form of the consecration of the blood, than in the form of the consecration of the body, especially since our Lord said: *This is My body, which shall be delivered up for you* (Luke 22:19).

OBJ. 8: Further, as was already observed (Q. 48, A. 2; Q. 49, A. 3), Christ's Passion sufficed for all; while as to its efficacy it was profitable for many. Therefore it ought to be said: *Which shall be shed for all*, or else *for many*, without adding, *for you*.

OBJ. 9: Further, the words whereby this sacrament is consecrated draw their efficacy from Christ's institution. But no Evangelist narrates that Christ spoke all these words. Therefore this is not an appropriate form for the consecration of the wine.

ON THE CONTRARY, The Church, instructed by the apostles, uses this form.

I ANSWER THAT, There is a twofold opinion regarding this form. Some have maintained that the words *This is the chalice of My blood* alone belong to the substance of this form, but not those words which follow. Now this seems incorrect, because the words which follow them are determinations of the predicate, that is, of Christ's blood. consequently they belong to the integrity of the expression.

And on this account others say more accurately that all the words which follow are of the substance of the form down to the words, *As often as ye shall do this*, which belong to the use of this sacrament, and consequently do not belong to the substance of the form. Hence it is that the priest pronounces all these words, under the same rite and manner, namely, holding the chalice in his hands. Moreover, in

verba sequentia verbis primis, cum dicitur, *hic calix novum testamentum est in sanguine meo.*

Dicendum est ergo quod omnia praedicta verba sunt de substantia formae, sed per prima verba, hic est calix sanguinis mei, significatur ipsa conversio vini in sanguinem, eo modo quo dictum est in forma consecrationis panis; per verba autem sequentia designatur virtus sanguinis effusi in passione, quae operatur in hoc sacramento. Quae quidem ad tria ordinatur. Primo quidem, et principaliter, ad adipiscendam aeternam hereditatem, secundum illud Heb. X, *habemus fiduciam in introitu sanctorum per sanguinem eius.* Et ad hoc designandum dicitur, novi testamenti et aeterni. Secundo, ad iustitiam gratiae, quae est per fidem, secundum illud Rom. III, *quem proposuit Deus propitiatorem per fidem in sanguine eius, ut sit ipse iustus, et iustificans eum qui ex fide est Iesu Christi.* Et quantum ad hoc subditur, *mysterium fidei.* Tertio autem, ad removendum impedimenta utriusque praedictorum, scilicet peccata, secundum illud Heb. IX, *sanguis Christi emundabit conscientias nostras ab operibus mortuis,* idest a peccatis. Et quantum ad hoc subditur, *qui pro vobis et pro multis aliis effundetur in remissionem peccatorum.*

AD PRIMUM ergo dicendum quod, cum dicitur, *hic est calix sanguinis mei,* est locutio figurativa, et potest dupliciter intelligi. Uno modo, secundum metonymiam, quia ponitur continens pro contento, ut sit sensus, hic est sanguis meus contentus in calice. De quo fit hic mentio, quia sanguis Christi in hoc sacramento consecratur inquantum est potus fidelium, quod non importatur in ratione sanguinis, et ideo oportuit hic designari per vas huic usui accommodatum.

Alio modo potest intelligi secundum metaphoram, prout per calicem similitudinarie intelligitur passio Christi, quae ad similitudinem calicis inebriat, secundum illud Thren. III, *replevit me amaritudinibus, inebriavit me absynthio,* unde et ipse dominus passionem suam calicem nominat, Matth. XXVI, dicens, *transeat a me calix iste;* ut sit sensus, hic est calix passionis meae. De qua fit mentio in sanguine seorsum a corpore consecrato, quia separatio sanguinis a corpore fuit per passionem.

AD SECUNDUM dicendum quod quia, ut dictum est, sanguis seorsum consecratus expresse passionem Christi repraesentat, ideo potius in consecratione sanguinis fit mentio de effectu passionis quam in consecratione corporis, quod est passionis subiectum. Quod etiam designatur in hoc quod dominus dicit, quod pro vobis tradetur, quasi dicat, quod pro vobis passioni subiicietur.

AD TERTIUM dicendum quod testamentum est dispositio hereditatis. Hereditatem autem caelestem Deus

Luke 22:20, the words that follow are interposed with the preceding words: *This is the chalice, the new testament in My blood.*

Consequently it must be said that all the aforesaid words belong to the substance of the form; but that by the first words, *This is the chalice of My blood,* the change of the wine into blood is denoted, as explained above (A. 2) in the form for the consecration of the bread; but by the words which come after is shown the power of the blood shed in the Passion, which power works in this sacrament, and is ordained for three purposes. First and principally for securing our eternal heritage, according to Heb. 10:19: *Having confidence in the entering into the holies by the blood of Christ;* and in order to denote this, we say, *of the New and Eternal Testament.* Second, for justifying by grace, which is by faith according to Rom. 3:25, 26: *Whom God hath proposed to be a propitiation, through faith in His blood . . . that He Himself may be just, and the justifier of him who is of the faith of Jesus Christ:* and on this account we add, *The Mystery of Faith.* Third, for removing sins which are the impediments to both of these things, according to Heb. 9:14: *The blood of Christ . . . shall cleanse our conscience from dead works,* that is, from sins; and on this account, we say, *which shall be shed for you and for many unto the forgiveness of sins.*

REPLY OBJ. 1: The expression *This is the chalice of My blood* is a figure of speech, which can be understood in two ways. First, as a figure of metonymy; because the container is put for the contained, so that the meaning is: *This is My blood contained in the chalice;* of which mention is now made, because Christ's blood is consecrated in this sacrament, inasmuch as it is the drink of the faithful, which is not implied under the notion of blood; consequently this had to be denoted by the vessel adapted for such usage.

Second, it can be taken by way of metaphor, so that Christ's Passion is understood by the chalice by way of comparison, because, like a cup, it inebriates, according to Lam. 3:15: *He hath filled me with bitterness, he hath inebriated me with wormwood:* hence our Lord Himself spoke of His Passion as a chalice, when He said (Matt 26:39): *Let this chalice pass away from Me:* so that the meaning is: *This is the chalice of My Passion.* This is denoted by the blood being consecrated apart from the body; because it was by the Passion that the blood was separated from the body.

REPLY OBJ. 2: As was said above (ad 1; Q. 76, A. 2, ad 1), the blood consecrated apart expressly represents Christ's Passion, and therefore mention is made of the fruits of the Passion in the consecration of the blood rather than in that of the body, since the body is the subject of the Passion. This is also pointed out in our Lord's saying, *which shall be delivered up for you,* as if to say, *which shall undergo the Passion for you.*

REPLY OBJ. 3: A testament is the disposal of a heritage. But God disposed of a heavenly heritage to men, to

disposuit hominibus dandam per virtutem sanguinis Iesu Christi, quia, ut dicitur Heb. IX, *ubi est testamentum, mors necesse est intercedat testatoris.* Sanguis autem Christi dupliciter est hominibus exhibitus. Primo quidem, in figura, quod pertinet ad vetus testamentum. Et ideo apostolus ibidem concludit, *unde nec primum testamentum sine sanguine dedicatum est,* quod patet ex hoc quod, sicut dicitur Exod. XXIV, *lecto omni mandato legis a Moyse, omnem populum aspersit, dicens, hic est sanguis testamenti quod mandavit ad vos Deus.*

Secundo autem est exhibitus in rei veritate, quod pertinet ad novum testamentum. Et hoc est quod apostolus ibidem praemittit, dicens, *ideo novi testamenti mediator est Christus, ut, morte intercedente, repromissionem accipiant qui vocati sunt aeternae hereditatis.* Dicitur ergo hic sanguis novi testamenti, quia iam non in figura, sed in veritate exhibetur. Unde subditur, qui pro vobis effundetur. Interna autem inspiratio ex sanguinis virtute procedit secundum quod passione Christi iustificamur.

AD QUARTUM dicendum quod hoc testamentum est novum ratione exhibitionis. Dicitur autem aeternum, tam ratione aeternae Dei praeordinationis; quam etiam ratione aeternae hereditatis, quae per hoc testamentum disponitur. Ipsa etiam persona Christi, cuius sanguine testamentum disponitur, est aeterna.

AD QUINTUM dicendum quod mysterium hic ponitur, non quidem ad excludendum rei veritatem, sed ad ostendendum occultationem. Quia et ipse sanguis Christi occulto modo est in hoc sacramento; et ipsa passio Christi occulte fuit figurata in veteri testamento.

AD SEXTUM dicendum quod dicitur sacramentum fidei, quasi fidei obiectum, quia quod sanguis Christi secundum rei veritatem sit in hoc sacramento, sola fide tenetur. Ipsa etiam passio Christi per fidem iustificat. Baptismus autem dicitur sacramentum fidei quia est quaedam fidei protestatio. Hoc autem est sacramentum caritatis quasi figurativum et effectivum.

AD SEPTIMUM dicendum quod, sicut dictum est, sanguis seorsum consecratus a corpore expressius repraesentat passionem Christi. Et ideo in consecratione sanguinis fit mentio de passione Christi et fructu ipsius, potius quam in consecratione corporis.

AD OCTAVUM dicendum quod sanguis passionis Christi non solum habet efficaciam in Iudaeis electis, quibus exhibitus est sanguis veteris testamenti, sed etiam in gentilibus; nec solum in sacerdotibus, qui hoc efficiunt sacramentum, vel aliis qui sumunt, sed etiam in illis pro quibus offertur. Et ideo signanter dicit, pro vobis Iudaeis, et pro multis, scilicet gentilibus, vel, pro vobis manducantibus, et pro multis pro quibus offertur.

AD NONUM dicendum quod Evangelistae non intendebant tradere formas sacramentorum, quas in primitiva

be bestowed through the virtue of the blood of Jesus Christ; because, according to Heb. 9:16: *Where there is a testament the death of the testator must of necessity come in.* Now Christ's blood was exhibited to men in two ways. First of all in figure, and this belongs to the Old Testament; consequently the Apostle concludes (Heb 9:16): *Whereupon neither was the first indeed dedicated without blood,* which is evident from this, that as related in Ex. 24:7, 8, *when every* commandment of the law *had been read* by Moses, *he sprinkled all the people* saying: *This is the blood of the testament which the Lord hath enjoined unto you.*

Second, it was shown in very truth; and this belongs to the New Testament. This is what the Apostle premises when he says (Rom 9:15): *Therefore He is the Mediator of the New Testament, that by means of His death . . . they that are called may receive the promise of eternal inheritance.* Consequently, we say here, *The blood of the New Testament,* because it is shown now not in figure but in truth; and therefore we add, *which shall be shed for you.* But the internal inspiration has its origin in the power of this blood, according as we are justified by Christ's Passion.

REPLY OBJ. 4: This Testament is a *new one* by reason of its showing forth: yet it is called *eternal* both on account of God's eternal pre-ordination, as well as on account of the eternal heritage which is prepared by this testament. Moreover, Christ's Person is eternal, in Whose blood this testament is appointed.

REPLY OBJ. 5: The word *mystery* is inserted, not in order to exclude reality, but to show that the reality is hidden, because Christ's blood is in this sacrament in a hidden manner, and His Passion was dimly foreshadowed in the Old Testament.

REPLY OBJ. 6: It is called the *Sacrament of Faith,* as being an object of faith: because by faith alone do we hold the presence of Christ's blood in this sacrament. Moreover Christ's Passion justifies by faith. Baptism is called the *Sacrament of Faith* because it is a profession of faith. This is called the *Sacrament of Charity,* as being figurative and effective thereof.

REPLY OBJ. 7: As stated above (ad 2), the blood consecrated apart represents Christ's blood more expressively; and therefore mention is made of Christ's Passion and its fruits, in the consecration of the blood rather than in that of the body.

REPLY OBJ. 8: The blood of Christ's Passion has its efficacy not merely in the elect among the Jews, to whom the blood of the Old Testament was exhibited, but also in the Gentiles; nor only in priests who consecrate this sacrament, and in those others who partake of it; but likewise in those for whom it is offered. And therefore He says expressly, *for you,* the Jews, *and for many,* namely the Gentiles; or, *for you* who eat of it, and *for many,* for whom it is offered.

REPLY OBJ. 9: The Evangelists did not intend to hand down the forms of the sacraments, which in the primitive

Ecclesia oportebat esse occultas, ut dicit Dionysius, in fine ecclesiasticae hierarchiae. Sed intenderunt historiam de Christo texere. Et tamen omnia haec verba fere ex diversis Scripturae locis accipi possunt. Nam quod dicitur, hic est calix, habetur Luc. XXII et I Cor. XI. Matthaei autem XXVI dicitur, *hic est sanguis meus novi testamenti, qui pro multis effundetur in remissionem peccatorum.* Quod autem additur, aeterni, et iterum, mysterium fidei, ex traditione domini habetur, quae ad Ecclesiam per apostolos pervenit, secundum illud I Cor. XI, *ego accepi a domino quod et tradidi vobis.*

Church had to be kept concealed, as Dionysius observes at the close of his book on the ecclesiastical hierarchy; their object was to write the story of Christ. Nevertheless nearly all these words can be culled from various passages of the Scriptures. Because the words, *This is the chalice,* are found in Luke 22:20, and 1 Cor. 11:25, while Matthew says in chapter 26:28: *This is My blood of the New Testament, which shall be shed for many unto the remission of sins.* The words added, namely, *eternal* and *mystery of faith,* were handed down to the Church by the apostles, who received them from our Lord, according to 1 Cor. 11:23: *I have received of the Lord that which also I delivered unto you.*

Article 4

Whether in the Aforesaid Words of the Forms There Be Any Created Power Which Causes the Consecration?

Ad quartum sic proceditur. Videtur quod praedictis verbis formarum non insit aliqua vis creata effectiva consecrationis. Dicit enim Damascenus, in IV libro, *sola virtute spiritus sancti fit conversio panis in corpus Christi.* Sed virtus spiritus sancti est virtus increata. Ergo nulla virtute creata horum verborum conficitur sacramentum hoc.

Praeterea, opera miraculosa non fiunt aliqua virtute creata, sed sola virtute divina, ut in prima parte habitum est. Sed conversio panis et vini in corpus et sanguinem Christi est opus non minus miraculosum quam creatio rerum, vel etiam formatio corporis Christi in utero virginali, quae quidem nulla virtute creata fieri potuerunt. Ergo neque hoc sacramentum consecratur virtute creata aliqua dictorum verborum.

Praeterea, praedicta verba non sunt simplicia, sed ex multis composita; nec simul, sed successive proferuntur. Conversio autem praedicta, ut supra dictum est, fit in instanti, unde oportet quod fiat per simplicem virtutem. Non ergo fit per virtutem horum verborum.

Sed contra est quod Ambrosius dicit, in libro de sacramentis, *si tanta est vis in sermone domini Iesu ut inciperet esse quod non erat, quanto magis operativus est ut sint quae erant, et in aliud commutentur? Et sic quod erat panis ante consecrationem, iam corpus Christi est post consecrationem, quia sermo Christi creaturam mutat.*

Respondeo dicendum quod quidam dixerunt nullam virtutem creatam esse nec in praedictis verbis ad transubstantiationem faciendam, nec etiam in aliis sacramentorum formis, vel etiam in ipsis sacramentis ad inducendos sacramentorum effectus. Quod, sicut supra dictum est, et dictis sanctorum repugnat, et derogat

Objection 1: It seems that in the aforesaid words of the forms there is no created power which causes the consecration. Because Damascene says (*De Fide Orth.* iv): *The change of the bread into Christ's body is caused solely by the power of the Holy Spirit.* But the power of the Holy Spirit is uncreated. Therefore this sacrament is not caused by any created power of those words.

Obj. 2: Further, miraculous works are wrought not by any created power, but solely by Divine power, as was stated in the First Part (Q. 110, A. 4). But the change of the bread and wine into Christ's body and blood is a work not less miraculous than the creation of things, or than the formation of Christ's body in the womb of a virgin: which things could not be done by any created power. Therefore, neither is this sacrament consecrated by any created power of the aforesaid words.

Obj. 3: Further, the aforesaid words are not simple, but composed of many; nor are they uttered simultaneously, but successively. But, as stated above (Q. 75, A. 7), this change is wrought instantaneously. Hence it must be done by a simple power. Therefore it is not effected by the power of those words.

On the contrary, Ambrose says (*De Sacram.* iv): *If there be such might in the word of the Lord Jesus that things non-existent came into being, how much more efficacious is it to make things existing to continue, and to be changed into something else? And so, what was bread before consecration is now the body of Christ after consecration, because Christ's word changes a creature into something different.*

I answer that, Some have maintained that neither in the above words is there any created power for causing the transubstantiation, nor in the other forms of the sacraments, or even in the sacraments themselves, for producing the sacramental effects. This, as was shown above (Q. 62, A. 1), is both contrary to the teachings of the saints,

dignitati sacramentorum novae legis. Unde, cum hoc sacramentum sit prae ceteris dignius, sicut supra dictum est, consequens est quod in verbis formalibus huius sacramenti sit quaedam virtus creata ad conversionem huius sacramenti faciendam, instrumentalis tamen, sicut et in aliis sacramentis, sicut supra dictum est. Cum enim haec verba ex persona Christi proferantur, ex eius mandato consequuntur virtutem instrumentalem a Christo, sicut et cetera eius facta vel dicta habent instrumentaliter salutiferam virtutem, ut supra habitum est.

AD PRIMUM ergo dicendum quod, cum dicitur sola virtute spiritus sancti panem in corpus Christi converti, non excluditur virtus instrumentalis quae est in forma huius sacramenti, sicut, cum dicitur quod solus faber facit cultellum, non excluditur virtus martelli.

AD SECUNDUM dicendum quod opera miraculosa nulla creatura potest facere quasi agens principale, potest tamen ea facere instrumentaliter, sicut ipse tactus manus Christi sanavit leprosum. Et per hunc modum verba eius convertunt panem in corpus Christi. Quod quidem non potuit in conceptione corporis Christi, qua corpus Christi formabatur, ut aliquid a corpore Christi procedens haberet instrumentalem virtutem ad ipsius corporis formationem. In creatione etiam non fuit aliquod extremum in quod instrumentalis actio creaturae posset terminari. Unde non est simile.

AD TERTIUM dicendum quod praedicta verba quibus fit consecratio, sacramentaliter operantur. Unde vis conversiva quae est in formis horum sacramentorum, sequitur significationem, quae in prolatione ultimae dictionis terminatur. Et ideo in ultimo instanti prolationis verborum praedicta verba consequuntur hanc virtutem, in ordine tamen ad praecedentia. Et haec virtus est simplex ratione significati, licet in ipsis verbis exterius prolatis fit quaedam compositio.

and detracts from the dignity of the sacraments of the New Law. Hence, since this sacrament is of greater worth than the others, as stated above (Q. 65, A. 3), the result is that there is in the words of the form of this sacrament a created power which causes the change to be wrought in it: instrumental, however, as in the other sacraments, as stated above (Q. 62, AA. 3, 4). For since these words are uttered in the person of Christ, it is from His command that they receive their instrumental power from Him, just as His other deeds and sayings derive their salutary power instrumentally, as was observed above (Q. 48, A. 6; Q. 56, A. 1, ad 3).

REPLY OBJ. 1: When the bread is said to be changed into Christ's body solely by the power of the Holy Spirit, the instrumental power which lies in the form of this sacrament is not excluded: just as when we say that the smith alone makes a knife we do not deny the power of the hammer.

REPLY OBJ. 2: No creature can work miracles as the chief agent. Yet it can do so instrumentally, just as the touch of Christ's hand healed the leper. And in this fashion Christ's words change the bread into His body. But in Christ's conception, whereby His body was fashioned, it was impossible for anything derived from His body to have the instrumental power of forming that very body. Likewise in creation there was no term wherein the instrumental action of a creature could be received. Consequently there is no comparison.

REPLY OBJ. 3: The aforesaid words, which work the consecration, operate sacramentally. Consequently, the converting power latent under the forms of these sacraments follows the meaning, which is terminated in the uttering of the last word. And therefore the aforesaid words have this power in the last instant of their being uttered, taken in conjunction with those uttered before. And this power is simple by reason of the thing signified, although there be composition in the words uttered outwardly.

Article 5

Whether the Aforesaid Expressions Are True?

AD QUINTUM SIC PROCEDITUR. Videtur quod praedictae locutiones non sunt verae. Cum enim dicitur, hoc est corpus meum, ly hoc est demonstrativum substantiae. Sed secundum praedicta, quando profertur hoc pronomen hoc, adhuc est substantia panis, quia transubstantiatio fit in ultimo prolationis verborum. Sed haec est falsa, panis est corpus Christi. Ergo etiam haec est falsa, hoc est corpus meum.

OBJECTION 1: It seems that the aforesaid expressions are not true. Because when we say: *This is My body*, the word *this* designates a substance. But according to what was said above (AA. 1, 4, ad 3; Q. 75, AA. 2, 7), when the pronoun *this* is spoken, the substance of the bread is still there, because the transubstantiation takes place in the last instant of pronouncing the words. But it is false to say: *Bread is Christ's body*. Consequently this expression, *This is My body*, is false.

PRAETEREA, hoc pronomen hoc facit demonstrationem ad sensum. Sed species sensibiles quae sunt in hoc sacramento neque sunt ipsum corpus Christi, neque sunt accidentia corporis Christi. Ergo haec locutio non potest esse vera, *hoc est corpus meum*.

PRAETEREA, haec verba, sicut supra dictum est, sua significatione efficiunt conversionem panis in corpus Christi. Sed causa effectiva praeintelligitur effectui. Ergo significatio horum verborum praeintelligitur conversioni panis in corpus Christi. Sed ante conversionem haec est falsa, hoc est corpus meum. Ergo simpliciter est iudicandum quod sit falsa. Et eadem ratio est de hac locutione, hic est calix sanguinis mei et cetera.

SED CONTRA est quod haec verba proferuntur ex persona Christi, qui de se dicit, Ioan. XIV, ego sum veritas.

RESPONDEO dicendum quod circa hoc multiplex fuit opinio. Quidam enim dixerunt quod in hac locutione, hoc est corpus meum, haec dictio hoc importat demonstrationem ut conceptam, non ut exercitam, quia tota ista locutio sumitur materialiter, cum recitative proferatur; recitat enim sacerdos Christum dixisse, hoc est corpus meum.

Sed hoc stare non potest. Quia secundum hoc, verba non applicarentur ad materiam corporalem praesentem, et ita non perficeretur sacramentum, dicit enim Augustinus, super Ioan., *accedit verbum ad elementum et fit sacramentum*. Et ex hoc totaliter non evitatur difficultas huius quaestionis, quia eaedem rationes manent circa primam prolationem qua Christus haec verba protulit; quia manifestum est quod non materialiter, sed significative sumebantur. Et ideo dicendum est quod etiam quando proferuntur a sacerdote, significative, et non tantum materialiter accipiuntur. Nec obstat quod sacerdos etiam recitative profert quasi a Christo dicta. Quia propter infinitam virtutem Christi, sicut ex contactu carnis suae vis regenerativa pervenit non solum ad illas aquas quae Christum tetigerunt, sed ad omnes ubique terrarum per omnia futura saecula; ita etiam ex prolatione ipsius Christi haec verba virtutem consecrativam sunt consecuta a quocumque sacerdote dicantur, ac si Christus ea praesentialiter proferret.

Et ideo alii dixerunt quod haec dictio hoc in hac locutione facit demonstrationem, non ad sensum, sed ad intellectum, ut sit sensus, hoc est corpus meum, idest, significatum per hoc est corpus meum. Sed nec hoc stare potest. Quia, cum in sacramentis hoc efficiatur quod significatur, non fieret per hanc formam ut corpus Christi sit in hoc sacramento secundum veritatem, sed solum sicut in signo. Quod est haereticum, ut supra dictum est.

OBJ. 2: Further, the pronoun *this* appeals to the senses. But the sensible species in this sacrament are neither Christ's body nor even its accidents. Therefore this expression, *This is My body*, cannot be true.

OBJ. 3: Further, as was observed above (A. 4, ad 3), these words, by their signification, effect the change of the bread into the body of Christ. But an effective cause is understood as preceding its effect. Therefore the meaning of these words is understood as preceding the change of the bread into the body of Christ. But previous to the change this expression, *This is My body*, is false. Therefore the expression is to be judged as false simply; and the same reason holds good of the other phrase: *This is the chalice of My blood*, etc.

ON THE CONTRARY, These words are pronounced in the person of Christ, Who says of Himself (John 14:6): *I am the truth*.

I ANSWER THAT, There have been many opinions on this point. Some have said that in this expression, *This is My body*, the word *this* implies demonstration as conceived, and not as exercised, because the whole phrase is taken materially, since it is uttered by a way of narration: for the priest relates that Christ said: *This is My body*.

But such a view cannot hold good, because then these words would not be applied to the corporeal matter present, and consequently the sacrament would not be valid: for Augustine says (*Tract. lxxx in Joan.*): *The word is added to the element, and this becomes a sacrament*. Moreover this solution ignores entirely the difficulty which this question presents: for there is still the objection in regard to the first uttering of these words by Christ; since it is evident that then they were employed, not materially, but significatively. And therefore it must be said that even when spoken by the priest they are taken significatively, and not merely materially. Nor does it matter that the priest pronounces them by way of recital, as though they were spoken by Christ, because owing to Christ's infinite power, just as through contact with His flesh the regenerative power entered not only into the waters which came into contact with Christ, but into all waters throughout the whole world and during all future ages, so likewise from Christ's uttering these words they derived their consecrating power, by whatever priest they be uttered, as if Christ present were saying them.

And therefore others have said that in this phrase the word *this* appeals, not to the senses, but to the intellect; so that the meaning is, *This is My body*—i.e., *The thing signified by 'this' is My body*. But neither can this stand, because, since in the sacraments the effect is that which is signified, from such a form it would not result that Christ's body was in very truth in this sacrament, but merely as in a sign, which is heretical, as stated above (Q. 85, A. 1).

Et ideo alii dixerunt quod haec dictio hoc facit demonstrationem ad sensum, sed intelligitur haec demonstratio non pro illo instanti locutionis quo profertur haec dictio, sed pro ultimo instanti locutionis, sicut, cum aliquis dicit, nunc taceo, hoc adverbium nunc facit demonstrationem pro instanti immediate sequenti locutionem; est enim sensus, statim dictis his verbis, taceo. Sed nec hoc stare potest. Quia secundum hoc, huius locutionis est sensus, corpus meum est corpus meum. Quod praedicta locutio non facit, quia hoc fuit etiam ante prolationem verborum. Unde neque hoc praedicta locutio significat.

Et ideo aliter dicendum est quod, sicut praedictum est, haec locutio habet virtutem factivam conversionis panis in corpus Christi. Et ideo comparatur ad alias locutiones, quae habent solum vim significativam et non factivam, sicut comparatur conceptio intellectus practici, quae est factiva rei, conceptioni intellectus nostri speculativi, quae est accepta a rebus, nam *voces sunt signa intellectuum*, secundum philosophum. Et ideo, sicut conceptio intellectus practici non praesupponit rem conceptam, sed facit eam, ita veritas huius locutionis non praesupponit rem significatam, sed facit eam, sic enim se habet verbum Dei ad res factas per verbum. Haec autem conversio non fit successive, sed in instanti, sicut dictum est. Et ideo oportet quidem intelligere praedictam locutionem secundum ultimum instans prolationis verborum, non tamen ita quod praesupponatur ex parte subiecti id quod est terminus conversionis, scilicet quod corpus Christi sit corpus Christi; neque etiam illud quod fuit ante conversionem, scilicet panis; sed id quod communiter se habet quantum ad utrumque, scilicet contentum in generali sub istis speciebus. Non enim faciunt haec verba quod corpus Christi sit corpus Christi; neque quod panis sit corpus Christi; sed quod contentum sub his speciebus, quod prius erat panis, sit corpus Christi. Et ideo signanter non dicit dominus, hic panis est corpus meum, quod esset secundum intellectum secundae opinionis; neque, hoc corpus meum est corpus meum, quod esset secundum intellectum tertiae; sed in generali, hoc est corpus meum, nullo nomine apposito ex parte subiecti, sed solo pronomine, quod significat substantiam in communi sine qualitate, idest forma determinata.

AD PRIMUM ergo dicendum quod haec dictio hoc demonstrat substantiam, sed absque determinatione propriae naturae, sicut dictum est.

AD SECUNDUM dicendum quod hoc pronomen hoc non demonstrat ipsa accidentia, sed substantiam sub accidentibus contentam, quae primo fuit panis, et postea

Consequently, others have said that the word *this* appeals to the senses; not at the precise instant of its being uttered, but merely at the last instant thereof; as when a man says, *Now I am silent*, this adverb *now* points to the instant immediately following the speech: because the sense is: *Directly these words are spoken I am silent*. But neither can this hold good, because in that case the meaning of the sentence would be: *My body is My body*, which the above phrase does not effect, because this was so even before the utterance of the words: hence neither does the aforesaid sentence mean this.

Consequently, then, it remains to be said, as stated above (A. 4), that this sentence possesses the power of effecting the conversion of the bread into the body of Christ. And therefore it is compared to other sentences, which have power only of signifying and not of producing, as the concept of the practical intellect, which is productive of the thing, is compared to the concept of our speculative intellect which is drawn from things, because *words are signs of concepts*, as the Philosopher says (*Peri Herm.* i). And therefore as the concept of the practical intellect does not presuppose the thing understood, but makes it, so the truth of this expression does not presuppose the thing signified, but makes it; for such is the relation of God's word to the things made by the Word. Now this change takes place not successively, but in an instant, as stated above (Q. 77, A. 7). Consequently one must understand the aforesaid expression with reference to the last instant of the words being spoken, yet not so that the subject may be understood to have stood for that which is the term of the conversion; viz. that the body of Christ is the body of Christ; nor again that the subject be understood to stand for that which it was before the conversion, namely, the bread, but for that which is commonly related to both, i.e., that which is contained in general under those species. For these words do not make the body of Christ to be the body of Christ, nor do they make the bread to be the body of Christ; but what was contained under those species, and was formerly bread, they make to be the body of Christ. And therefore expressly our Lord did not say: *This bread is My body*, which would be the meaning of the second opinion; nor *This My body is My body*, which would be the meaning of the third opinion: but in general: *This is My body*, assigning no noun on the part of the subject, but only a pronoun, which signifies substance in common, without quality, that is, without a determinate form.

REPLY OBJ. 1: The term *this* points to a substance, yet without determining its proper nature, as stated above.

REPLY OBJ. 2: The pronoun *this* does not indicate the accidents, but the substance underlying the accidents, which at first was bread, and is afterwards the body of

est corpus Christi, quod, licet non informetur his accidentibus, tamen sub eis continetur.

AD TERTIUM dicendum quod significatio huius locutionis praeintelligitur rei significatae ordine naturae, sicut causa naturaliter est prior effectu, non tamen ordine temporis, quia haec causa simul habet secum suum effectum. Et hoc sufficit ad veritatem locutionis.

REPLY OBJ. 3: The meaning of this expression is, in the order of nature, understood before the thing signified, just as a cause is naturally prior to the effect; but not in order of time, because this cause has its effect with it at the same time, and this suffices for the truth of the expression.

Article 6

Whether the Form of the Consecration of the Bread Accomplishes Its Effect
Before the Form of the Consecration of the Wine Be Completed?

AD SEXTUM SIC PROCEDITUR. Videtur quod forma consecrationis panis non consequatur effectum suum quousque perficiatur forma consecrationis vini. Sicut enim per consecrationem panis incipit esse corpus Christi sub hoc sacramento, ita per consecrationem vini incipit esse sanguis. Si ergo verba consecrationis panis haberent effectum suum ante consecrationem vini, sequeretur quod in hoc sacramento inciperet esse corpus Christi exsangue. Quod est inconveniens.

PRAETEREA, unum sacramentum unum habet complementum, unde, licet in Baptismo sint tres immersiones, non tamen prima immersio consequitur suum effectum quousque tertia fuerit terminata. Sed totum hoc sacramentum est unum, ut supra dictum est. Ergo verba quibus consecratur panis, non consequuntur suum effectum sine verbis sacramentalibus quibus consecratur vinum.

PRAETEREA, in ipsa forma consecrationis panis sunt plura verba, quorum prima non consequuntur effectum nisi prolato ultimo, sicut dictum est. Ergo, pari ratione, nec verba quibus consecratur corpus Christi habent effectum, nisi prolatis verbis quibus sanguis Christi consecratur.

SED CONTRA est quod, statim dictis verbis consecrationis panis, hostia consecrata proponitur populo adoranda. Quod non fieret si non esset ibi corpus Christi, quia hoc ad idololatriam pertineret. Ergo verba consecrationis suum effectum consequuntur antequam proferantur verba consecrationis vini.

RESPONDEO dicendum quod quidam antiqui doctores dixerunt quod hae duae formae, scilicet consecrationis panis et vini, se invicem expectant in agendo, ita scilicet quod prima non perficit suum effectum antequam secunda proferatur.

Sed hoc stare non potest. Quia, sicut dictum est, ad veritatem huius locutionis, hoc est corpus meum, requiritur, propter verbum praesentis temporis, quod res

OBJECTION 1: It seems that the form of the consecration of the bread does not accomplish its effect until the form for the consecration of the wine be completed. For, as Christ's body begins to be in this sacrament by the consecration of the bread, so does His blood come to be there by the consecration of the wine. If, then, the words for consecrating the bread were to produce their effect before the consecration of the wine, it would follow that Christ's body would be present in this sacrament without the blood, which is improper.

OBJ. 2: Further, one sacrament has one completion: hence although there be three immersions in Baptism, yet the first immersion does not produce its effect until the third be completed. But all this sacrament is one, as stated above (Q. 73, A. 2). Therefore the words whereby the bread is consecrated do not bring about their effect without the sacramental words whereby the wine is consecrated.

OBJ. 3: Further, there are several words in the form for consecrating the bread, the first of which do not secure their effect until the last be uttered, as stated above (A. 4, ad 3). Therefore, for the same reason, neither do the words for the consecration of Christ's body produce their effect, until the words for consecrating Christ's blood are spoken.

ON THE CONTRARY, Directly the words are uttered for consecrating the bread, the consecrated host is shown to the people to be adored, which would not be done if Christ's body were not there, for that would be an act of idolatry. Therefore the consecrating words of the bread produce their effect before the words are spoken for consecrating the wine.

I ANSWER THAT, Some of the earlier doctors said that these two forms, namely, for consecrating the bread and the wine, await each other's action, so that the first does not produce its effect until the second be uttered.

But this cannot stand, because, as stated above (A. 5, ad 3), for the truth of this phrase, *This is My body*, wherein the verb is in the present tense, it is required for

significata simul tempore sit cum ipsa significatione locutionis, alioquin, si in futurum expectaretur res significata, apponeretur verbum futuri temporis, non autem verbum praesentis; ita scilicet quod non diceretur, hoc est corpus meum, sed, hoc erit corpus meum. Significatio autem huius locutionis completur statim completa prolatione horum verborum. Et ideo oportet rem significatam statim adesse, quae quidem est effectus huius sacramenti, alioquin locutio non esset vera. Est etiam haec positio contra ritum Ecclesiae, quae statim post prolationem verborum corpus Christi adorat.

Unde dicendum est quod prima forma non expectat secundam in agendo, sed statim habet suum effectum.

AD PRIMUM ergo dicendum quod ex hac ratione videntur fuisse decepti illi qui praedictam positionem posuerunt. Unde intelligendum est quod, facta consecratione panis, est quidem corpus Christi ibi ex vi sacramenti, et sanguis ex reali concomitantia; sed postmodum, post consecrationem vini, fit ibi e converso sanguis Christi ex vi sacramenti, corpus autem Christi ex reali concomitantia; ita quod totus Christus est sub utraque specie, sicut supra dictum est.

AD SECUNDUM dicendum quod hoc sacramentum est unum perfectione, sicut supra dictum est, inquantum scilicet constituitur ex duobus, scilicet ex cibo et potu, quorum utrumque per se habet suam perfectionem. Sed tres immersiones Baptismi ordinantur ad unum simplicem effectum. Et ideo non est simile.

AD TERTIUM dicendum quod diversa verba quae sunt in forma consecrationis panis, constituunt veritatem unius locutionis, non autem verba diversarum formarum. Et ideo non est simile.

the thing signified to be present simultaneously in time with the signification of the expression used; otherwise, if the thing signified had to be awaited for afterwards, a verb of the future tense would be employed, and not one of the present tense, so that we should not say, *This is My body*, but *This will be My body*. But the signification of this speech is complete directly those words are spoken. And therefore the thing signified must be present instantaneously, and such is the effect of this sacrament; otherwise it would not be a true speech. Moreover, this opinion is against the rite of the Church, which forthwith adores the body of Christ after the words are uttered.

Hence it must be said that the first form does not await the second in its action, but has its effect on the instant.

REPLY OBJ. 1: It is on this account that they who maintained the above opinion seem to have erred. Hence it must be understood that directly the consecration of the bread is complete, the body of Christ is indeed present by the power of the sacrament, and the blood by real concomitance; but afterwards by the consecration of the wine, conversely, the blood of Christ is there by the power of the sacrament, and the body by real concomitance, so that the entire Christ is under either species, as stated above (Q. 76, A. 2).

REPLY OBJ. 2: This sacrament is one in perfection, as stated above (Q. 73, A. 2), namely, inasmuch as it is made up of two things, that is, of food and drink, each of which of itself has its own perfection; but the three immersions of Baptism are ordained to one simple effect, and therefore there is no resemblance.

REPLY OBJ. 3: The various words in the form for consecrating the bread constitute the truth of one speech, but the words of the different forms do not, and consequently there is no parallel.

QUESTION 79

THE EFFECTS OF THIS SACRAMENT

Deinde considerandum est de effectibus huius sacramenti. Et circa hoc quaeruntur octo.

Primo, utrum hoc sacramentum conferat gratiam.

Secundo, utrum effectus huius sacramenti sit adeptio gloriae.

Tertio, utrum effectus huius sacramenti sit remissio peccati mortalis.

Quarto, utrum per hoc sacramentum remittatur peccatum veniale.

Quinto, utrum per hoc sacramentum tota poena peccati remittatur.

Sexto, utrum hoc sacramentum hominem praeservet a peccatis futuris.

Septimo, utrum hoc sacramentum prosit aliis quam sumentibus.

Octavo, de impedimentis effectus huius sacramenti.

We must now consider the effects of this sacrament, and under this head there are eight points of inquiry:

(1) Whether this sacrament bestows grace?

(2) Whether the attaining of glory is an effect of this sacrament?

(3) Whether the forgiveness of mortal sin is an effect of this sacrament?

(4) Whether venial sin is forgiven by this sacrament?

(5) Whether the entire punishment due for sin is forgiven by this sacrament?

(6) Whether this sacrament preserves man from future sins?

(7) Whether this sacrament benefits others besides the recipients?

(8) Of the obstacles to the effect of this sacrament.

Article 1

Whether Grace Is Bestowed Through This Sacrament?

AD PRIMUM SIC PROCEDITUR. Videtur quod per hoc sacramentum non conferatur gratia. Hoc enim sacramentum est nutrimentum spirituale. Nutrimentum autem non datur nisi viventi. Cum ergo vita spiritualis sit per gratiam, non competit hoc sacramentum nisi iam habenti gratiam. Non ergo per hoc sacramentum confertur gratia ut primo habeatur. Similiter etiam nec ad hoc quod augeatur, quia augmentum spirituale pertinet ad sacramentum confirmationis, ut dictum est. Non ergo per hoc sacramentum gratia confertur.

PRAETEREA, hoc sacramentum assumitur ut quaedam spiritualis refectio. Sed refectio spiritualis magis videtur pertinere ad usum gratiae quam ad gratiae consecutionem. Ergo videtur quod per hoc sacramentum gratia non conferatur.

PRAETEREA, sicut supra dictum est, *in hoc sacramento corpus Christi offertur pro salute corporis, sanguis autem pro salute animae*. Sed corpus non est subiectum gratiae, sed anima, ut in secunda parte habitum est. Ergo ad minus quantum ad corpus per hoc sacramentum gratia non confertur.

SED CONTRA est quod dominus dicit, Ioan. VI, *panis quem ego dabo, caro mea est pro mundi vita*. Sed vita

OBJECTION 1: It seems that grace is not bestowed through this sacrament. For this sacrament is spiritual nourishment. But nourishment is only given to the living. Therefore since the spiritual life is the effect of grace, this sacrament belongs only to one in the state of grace. Therefore grace is not bestowed through this sacrament for it to be had in the first instance. In like manner neither is it given so as grace may be increased, because spiritual growth belongs to the sacrament of Confirmation, as stated above (Q. 72, A. 1). Consequently, grace is not bestowed through this sacrament.

OBJ. 2: Further, this sacrament is given as a spiritual refreshment. But spiritual refreshment seems to belong to the use of grace rather than to its bestowal. Therefore it seems that grace is not given through this sacrament.

OBJ. 3: Further, as was said above (Q. 74, A. 1), *Christ's body is offered up in this sacrament for the salvation of the body, and His blood for that of the soul*. Now it is not the body which is the subject of grace, but the soul, as was shown in the Second Part (I-II, Q. 110, A. 4). Therefore grace is not bestowed through this sacrament, at least so far as the body is concerned.

ON THE CONTRARY, Our Lord says (John 6:52): *The bread which I will give, is My flesh for the life of the world.*

spiritualis est per gratiam. Ergo per hoc sacramentum gratia confertur.

Respondeo dicendum quod effectus huius sacramenti debet considerari, primo quidem et principaliter, ex eo quod in hoc sacramento continetur, quod est Christus. Qui sicut, in mundum visibiliter veniens, contulit mundo vitam gratiae, secundum illud Ioan. I, *gratia et veritas per Iesum Christum facta est*; ita, in hominem sacramentaliter veniens, vitam gratiae operatur, secundum illud Ioan. VI, *qui manducat me, vivit propter me*. Unde et Cyrillus dicit, *vivificativum Dei verbum, uniens seipsum propriae carni, fecit ipsam vivificativam. Decebat ergo eum nostris quodammodo uniri corporibus per sacram eius carnem et pretiosum sanguinem, quae accipimus in benedictione vivificativa in pane et vino.*

Secundo consideratur ex eo quod per hoc sacramentum repraesentatur, quod est passio Christi, sicut supra dictum est. Et ideo effectum quem passio Christi fecit in mundo, hoc sacramentum facit in homine. Unde super illud Ioan. XIX, *continuo exivit sanguis et aqua*, dicit Chrysostomus, *quia hinc suscipiunt principium sacra mysteria, cum accesseris ad tremendum calicem, vel ab ipsa bibiturus Christi costa, ita accedas.* Unde et ipse dominus dicit, Matth. XXVI, *hic est sanguis meus, qui pro vobis effundetur in remissionem peccatorum.*

Tertio consideratur effectus huius sacramenti ex modo quo traditur hoc sacramentum, quod traditur per modum cibi et potus. Et ideo omnem effectum quem cibus et potus materialis facit quantum ad vitam corporalem, quod scilicet sustentat, auget, reparat et delectat, hoc totum facit hoc sacramentum quantum ad vitam spiritualem. Unde Ambrosius dicit, in libro de sacramentis, *iste panis est vitae aeternae, qui animae nostrae substantiam fulcit.* Et Chrysostomus dicit, supra Ioan., *praestat se nobis desiderantibus et palpare et comedere et amplecti.* Unde et ipse dominus dicit, Ioan. VI, *caro mea vere est cibus, et sanguis meus vere est potus.*

Quarto consideratur effectus huius sacramenti ex speciebus in quibus hoc traditur sacramentum. Unde et Augustinus, ibidem, dicit, *dominus noster corpus et sanguinem suum in eis rebus commendavit quae ad unum aliquod rediguntur ex multis, namque aliud, scilicet panis, ex multis granis in unum constat, aliud, scilicet vinum, ex multis racemis confluit.* Et ideo ipse alibi dicit, super Ioan., *o sacramentum pietatis, o signum unitatis, o vinculum caritatis.*

Et quia Christus et eius passio est causa gratiae, et spiritualis refectio et caritas sine gratia esse non potest, ex omnibus praemissis manifestum est quod hoc sacramentum gratiam confert.

Ad primum ergo dicendum quod hoc sacramentum ex seipso virtutem habet gratiam conferendi, nec aliquis habet gratiam ante susceptionem huius sacramenti

But the spiritual life is the effect of grace. Therefore grace is bestowed through this sacrament.

I answer that, The effect of this sacrament ought to be considered, first of all and principally, from what is contained in this sacrament, which is Christ; Who, just as by coming into the world, He visibly bestowed the life of grace upon the world, according to John 1:17: *Grace and truth came by Jesus Christ*, so also, by coming sacramentally into man causes the life of grace, according to John 6:58: *He that eateth Me, the same also shall live by Me.* Hence Cyril says on Luke 22:19: *God's life-giving Word by uniting Himself with His own flesh, made it to be productive of life. For it was becoming that He should be united somehow with bodies through His sacred flesh and precious blood, which we receive in a life-giving blessing in the bread and wine.*

Second, it is considered on the part of what is represented by this sacrament, which is Christ's Passion, as stated above (Q. 74, A. 1; Q. 76, A. 2, ad 1). And therefore this sacrament works in man the effect which Christ's Passion wrought in the world. Hence, Chrysostom says on the words, *Immediately there came out blood and water* (John 19:34): *Since the sacred mysteries derive their origin from thence, when you draw nigh to the awe-inspiring chalice, so approach as if you were going to drink from Christ's own side.* Hence our Lord Himself says (Matt 26:28): *This is My blood . . . which shall be shed for many unto the remission of sins.*

Third, the effect of this sacrament is considered from the way in which this sacrament is given; for it is given by way of food and drink. And therefore this sacrament does for the spiritual life all that material food does for the bodily life, namely, by sustaining, giving increase, restoring, and giving delight. Accordingly, Ambrose says (*De Sacram.* v): *This is the bread of everlasting life, which supports the substance of our soul.* And Chrysostom says (*Hom. xlvi in Joan.*): *When we desire it, He lets us feel Him, and eat Him, and embrace Him.* And hence our Lord says (John 6:56): *My flesh is meat indeed, and My blood is drink indeed.*

Fourth, the effect of this sacrament is considered from the species under which it is given. Hence Augustine says (*Tract. xxvi in Joan.*): *Our Lord betokened His body and blood in things which out of many units are made into some one whole: for out of many grains is one thing made,* viz. bread; *and many grapes flow into one thing,* viz. wine. And therefore he observes elsewhere (*Tract. xxvi in Joan.*): *O sacrament of piety, O sign of unity, O bond of charity!*

And since Christ and His Passion are the cause of grace, and since spiritual refreshment, and charity cannot be without grace, it is clear from all that has been set forth that this sacrament bestows grace.

Reply Obj. 1: This sacrament has of itself the power of bestowing grace; nor does anyone possess grace before receiving this sacrament except from some desire thereof;

nisi ex aliquali voto ipsius, vel per seipsum, sicut adulti, vel voto Ecclesiae, sicut parvuli, sicut supra dictum est. Unde ex efficacia virtutis ipsius est quod etiam ex voto ipsius aliquis gratiam consequatur, per quam spiritualiter vivificetur. Restat igitur ut, cum ipsum sacramentum realiter sumitur, gratia augeatur, et vita spiritualis perficiatur. Aliter tamen quam per sacramentum confirmationis, in quo augetur et perficitur gratia ad persistendum contra exteriores impugnationes inimicorum Christi. Per hoc autem sacramentum augetur gratia, et perficitur spiritualis vita, ad hoc quod homo in seipso perfectus existat per coniunctionem ad Deum.

AD SECUNDUM dicendum quod hoc sacramentum confert gratiam spiritualiter, cum virtute caritatis. Unde Damascenus comparat hoc sacramentum carboni quem Isaias vidit, Isaiae VI, *carbo enim lignum simplex non est, sed unitum igni, ita et panis communionis non simplex panis est, sed unitus divinitati.* Sicut autem Gregorius dicit, in homilia Pentecostes, *amor Dei non est otiosus, magna enim operatur, si est.* Et ideo per hoc sacramentum, quantum est ex sui virtute, non solum habitus gratiae et virtutis confertur, sed etiam excitatur in actum, secundum illud II Cor. V, *caritas Christi urget nos.* Et inde est quod ex virtute huius sacramenti anima spiritualiter reficitur, per hoc quod anima delectatur, et quodammodo inebriatur dulcedine bonitatis divinae, secundum illud Cant. V, *comedite, amici, et bibite; et inebriamini, carissimi.*

AD TERTIUM dicendum quod, quia sacramenta operantur secundum similitudinem per quam significant, ideo per quandam assimilationem dicitur quod in hoc sacramento *corpus offertur pro salute corporis, et sanguis pro salute animae,* quamvis utrumque ad salutem utriusque operetur, cum sub utroque totus sit Christus, ut supra dictum est. Et licet corpus non sit immediatum subiectum gratiae, ex anima tamen redundat effectus gratiae ad corpus, dum in praesenti *membra nostra exhibemus arma iustitiae Deo,* ut habetur Rom. VI; et in futuro corpus nostrum sortietur incorruptionem et gloriam animae.

from his own desire, as in the case of the adult, or from the Church's desire in the case of children, as stated above (Q. 73, A. 3). Hence it is due to the efficacy of its power, that even from desire thereof a man procures grace whereby he is enabled to lead the spiritual life. It remains, then, that when the sacrament itself is really received, grace is increased, and the spiritual life perfected: yet in different fashion from the sacrament of Confirmation, in which grace is increased and perfected for resisting the outward assaults of Christ's enemies. But by this sacrament grace receives increase, and the spiritual life is perfected, so that man may stand perfect in himself by union with God.

REPLY OBJ. 2: This sacrament confers grace spiritually together with the virtue of charity. Hence Damascene (*De Fide Orth.* iv) compares this sacrament to the burning coal which Isaias saw (Isa 6:6): *For a live ember is not simply wood, but wood united to fire; so also the bread of communion is not simple bread but bread united with the Godhead.* But as Gregory observes in a Homily for Pentecost, *God's love is never idle; for, wherever it is it does great works.* And consequently through this sacrament, as far as its power is concerned, not only is the habit of grace and of virtue bestowed, but it is furthermore aroused to act, according to 2 Cor. 5:14: *The charity of Christ presseth us.* Hence it is that the soul is spiritually nourished through the power of this sacrament, by being spiritually gladdened, and as it were inebriated with the sweetness of the Divine goodness, according to Cant 5:1: *Eat, O friends, and drink, and be inebriated, my dearly beloved.*

REPLY OBJ. 3: Because the sacraments operate according to the similitude by which they signify, therefore by way of assimilation it is said that in this sacrament *the body is offered for the salvation of the body, and the blood for the salvation of the soul,* although each works for the salvation of both, since the entire Christ is under each, as stated above (Q. 76, A. 2). And although the body is not the immediate subject of grace, still the effect of grace flows into the body while in the present life we present *our members as instruments of justice unto God* (Rom 6:13), and in the life to come our body will share in the incorruption and the glory of the soul.

Article 2

Whether the Attaining of Glory Is an Effect of This Sacrament?

AD SECUNDUM SIC PROCEDITUR. Videtur quod effectus huius sacramenti non sit adeptio gloriae. Effectus enim proportionatur suae causae. Sed hoc sacramentum competit viatoribus, unde et viaticum dicitur. Cum igitur viatores nondum sint capaces gloriae, videtur quod hoc sacramentum non causet adeptionem gloriae.

OBJECTION 1: It seems that the attaining of glory is not an effect of this sacrament. For an effect is proportioned to its cause. But this sacrament belongs to *wayfarers* (*viatoribus*), and hence it is termed *Viaticum*. Since, then, wayfarers are not yet capable of glory, it seems that this sacrament does not cause the attaining of glory.

Praeterea, posita causa sufficienti, ponitur effectus. Sed multi accipiunt hoc sacramentum qui nunquam pervenient ad gloriam, ut patet per Augustinum, XXI de Civ. Dei. Non ergo hoc sacramentum est causa adeptionis gloriae.

Praeterea, maius non efficitur a minori, quia nihil agit ultra suam speciem. Sed minus est percipere Christum sub specie aliena, quod fit in hoc sacramento, quam frui eo in specie propria, quod pertinet ad gloriam. Ergo hoc sacramentum non causat adeptionem gloriae.

Sed contra est quod dicitur Ioan. VI, *si quis manducaverit ex hoc pane, vivet in aeternum*. Sed vita aeterna est vita gloriae. Ergo effectus huius sacramenti est adeptio gloriae.

Respondeo dicendum quod in hoc sacramento potest considerari et id ex quo habet effectum, scilicet ipse Christus contentus, et passio eius repraesentata; et id per quod habet effectum, scilicet usus sacramenti et species eius.

Et quantum ad utrumque competit huic sacramento quod causet adeptionem vitae aeternae. Nam ipse Christus per suam passionem aperuit nobis aditum vitae aeternae, secundum illud Heb. IX, *novi testamenti mediator est, ut, morte intercedente, qui vocati sunt accipiant repromissionem aeternae hereditatis*. Unde et in forma huius sacramenti dicitur, *hic est calix sanguinis mei novi et aeterni testamenti*.

Similiter etiam refectio spiritualis cibi, et unitas significata per species panis et vini, habentur quidem in praesenti sed imperfecte, perfecte autem in statu gloriae. Unde Augustinus dicit, super illud Ioan. VI, *caro mea vere est cibus, cum cibo et potu id appetant homines ut non esuriant neque sitiant, hoc veraciter non praestat nisi iste cibus et potus, qui eos a quibus sumitur immortales et incorruptibiles facit in societate sanctorum, ubi pax erit et unitas plena atque perfecta*.

Ad primum ergo dicendum quod, sicut passio Christi, ex cuius virtute hoc sacramentum operatur, est quidem causa sufficiens gloriae, non tamen ita quod statim per ipsam introducamur in gloriam, sed oportet ut prius simul compatiamur, ut postea simul glorificemur, sicut dicitur Rom. VIII, ita hoc sacramentum non statim nos in gloriam introducit, sed dat nobis virtutem perveniendi ad gloriam. Et ideo viaticum dicitur. In cuius figuram, legitur III Reg. XIX, quod *Elias comedit et bibit, et ambulavit in fortitudine cibi illius quadraginta diebus et quadraginta noctibus, usque ad montem Dei Horeb*.

Ad secundum dicendum quod, sicut passio Christi non habet suum effectum in his qui se ad eam non habent ut debent, ita et per hoc sacramentum non adipiscuntur gloriam qui indecenter ipsum suscipiunt. Unde

Obj. 2: Further, given sufficient cause, the effect follows. But many take this sacrament who will never come to glory, as Augustine declares (*De Civ. Dei* xxi). Consequently, this sacrament is not the cause of attaining unto glory.

Obj. 3: Further, the greater is not brought about by the lesser, for nothing acts outside its species. But it is the lesser thing to receive Christ under a strange species, which happens in this sacrament, than to enjoy Him in His own species, which belongs to glory. Therefore this sacrament does not cause the attaining of glory.

On the contrary, It is written (John 6:52): *If any man eat of this bread, he shall live for ever*. But eternal life is the life of glory. Therefore the attaining of glory is an effect of this sacrament.

I answer that, In this sacrament we may consider both that from which it derives its effect, namely, Christ contained in it, as also His Passion represented by it; and that through which it works its effect, namely, the use of the sacrament, and its species.

Now as to both of these it belongs to this sacrament to cause the attaining of eternal life. Because it was by His Passion that Christ opened to us the approach to eternal life, according to Heb. 9:15: *He is the Mediator of the New Testament; that by means of His death . . . they that are called may receive the promise of eternal inheritance*. Accordingly in the form of this sacrament it is said: *This is the chalice of My blood, of the New and Eternal Testament*.

In like manner the refreshment of spiritual food and the unity denoted by the species of the bread and wine are to be had in the present life, although imperfectly, but perfectly in the state of glory. Hence Augustine says on the words, *My flesh is meat indeed* (John 6:56): *Seeing that in meat and drink, men aim at this, that they hunger not nor thirst, this verily naught doth afford save only this meat and drink which maketh them who partake thereof to be immortal and incorruptible, in the fellowship of the saints, where shall be peace, and unity, full and perfect*.

Reply Obj. 1: As Christ's Passion, in virtue whereof this sacrament is accomplished, is indeed the sufficient cause of glory, yet not so that we are thereby forthwith admitted to glory, but we must first *suffer with Him in order that we may also be glorified* afterwards *with Him* (Rom 8:17), so this sacrament does not at once admit us to glory, but bestows on us the power of coming unto glory. And therefore it is called *Viaticum*, a figure whereof we read in 3 Kings 19:8: *Elias ate and drank, and walked in the strength of that food forty days and forty nights unto the mount of God, Horeb*.

Reply Obj. 2: Just as Christ's Passion has not its effect in them who are not disposed towards it as they should be, so also they do not come to glory through this sacrament who receive it unworthily. Hence Augustine (*Tract. xxvi in*

Augustinus dicit, super Ioan., exponens illa verba, *aliud est sacramentum, aliud virtus sacramenti. Multi de altari accipiunt, et accipiendo moriuntur. Panem ergo caelestem spiritualiter manducate, innocentiam ad altare apportate.* Unde non est mirum si illi qui innocentiam non servant, effectum huius sacramenti non consequuntur.

AD TERTIUM dicendum quod hoc quod Christus sub aliena specie sumitur, pertinet ad rationem sacramenti, quod instrumentaliter agit. Nihil autem prohibet causam instrumentalem producere potiorem effectum, ut ex supra dictis patet.

Joan.), expounding the same passage, observes: *The sacrament is one thing, the power of the sacrament another. Many receive it from the altar . . . and by receiving . . . die . . . Eat, then, spiritually the heavenly bread, bring innocence to the altar.* It is no wonder, then, if those who do not keep innocence, do not secure the effect of this sacrament.

REPLY OBJ. 3: That Christ is received under another species belongs to the nature of a sacrament, which acts instrumentally. But there is nothing to prevent an instrumental cause from producing a more mighty effect, as is evident from what was said above (Q. 77, A. 3, ad 3).

Article 3

Whether the Forgiveness of Mortal Sin Is an Effect of This Sacrament?

AD TERTIUM SIC PROCEDITUR. Videtur quod effectus huius sacramenti sit remissio peccati mortalis. Dicitur enim in quadam collecta, *sit hoc sacramentum ablutio scelerum.* Sed scelera dicuntur peccata mortalia. Ergo per hoc sacramentum peccata mortalia abluuntur.

PRAETEREA, hoc sacramentum agit in virtute passionis Christi, sicut et Baptismus. Sed per Baptismum dimittuntur peccata mortalia, ut supra dictum est. Ergo et per hoc sacramentum, praesertim cum in forma huius sacramenti dicatur, *qui pro multis effundetur in remissionem peccatorum.*

PRAETEREA, per hoc sacramentum gratia confertur, ut dictum est. Sed per gratiam iustificatur homo a peccatis mortalibus, secundum illud Rom. III, *iustificati gratis per gratiam ipsius.* Ergo per hoc sacramentum remittuntur peccata mortalia.

SED CONTRA est quod dicitur I Cor. XI, *qui manducat et bibit indigne, iudicium sibi manducat et bibit.* Dicit autem Glossa ibidem quod *ille manducat et bibit indigne qui in crimine est, vel irreverenter tractat, et talis manducat et bibit sibi iudicium, idest damnationem.* Ergo ille qui est in peccato mortali, per hoc quod accipit hoc sacramentum, magis accumulat sibi peccatum, quam remissionem sui peccati consequatur.

RESPONDEO dicendum quod virtus huius sacramenti potest considerari dupliciter. Uno modo, secundum se. Et sic hoc sacramentum habet virtutem ad remittendum quaecumque peccata, ex passione Christi, quae est fons et causa remissionis peccatorum

alio modo potest considerari per comparationem ad eum qui recipit hoc sacramentum, prout in eo invenitur vel non invenitur impedimentum percipiendi hoc sacramentum. Quicumque autem habet conscientiam peccati mortalis, habet in se impedimentum percipiendi

OBJECTION 1: It seems that the forgiveness of mortal sin is an effect of this sacrament. For it is said in one of the Collects (Postcommunion, *Pro vivis et defunctis*): *May this sacrament be a cleansing from crimes.* But mortal sins are called crimes. Therefore mortal sins are blotted out by this sacrament.

OBJ. 2: Further, this sacrament, like Baptism, works by the power of Christ's Passion. But mortal sins are forgiven by Baptism, as stated above (Q. 69, A. 1). Therefore they are forgiven likewise by this sacrament, especially since in the form of this sacrament it is said: *Which shall be shed for many unto the forgiveness of sins.*

OBJ. 3: Further, grace is bestowed through this sacrament, as stated above (A. 1). But by grace a man is justified from mortal sins, according to Rom. 3:24: *Being justified freely by His grace.* Therefore mortal sins are forgiven by this sacrament.

ON THE CONTRARY, It is written (1 Cor 11:29): *He that eateth and drinketh unworthily, eateth and drinketh judgment to himself*: and a gloss of the same passage makes the following commentary: *He eats and drinks unworthily who is in the state of sin, or who handles (the sacrament) irreverently; and such a one eats and drinks judgment, i.e., damnation, unto himself.* Therefore, he that is in mortal sin, by taking the sacrament heaps sin upon sin, rather than obtains forgiveness of his sin.

I ANSWER THAT, The power of this sacrament can be considered in two ways. First of all, in itself: and thus this sacrament has from Christ's Passion the power of forgiving all sins, since the Passion is the fount and cause of the forgiveness of sins.

Second, it can be considered in comparison with the recipient of the sacrament, in so far as there is, or is not, found in him an obstacle to receiving the fruit of this sacrament. Now whoever is conscious of mortal sin, has within him an obstacle to receiving the effect of this sacrament;

effectum huius sacramenti, eo quod non est conveniens susceptor huius sacramenti, tum quia non vivit spiritualiter, et ita non debet spirituale nutrimentum suscipere, quod non est nisi viventis; tum quia non potest uniri Christo, quod fit per hoc sacramentum, dum est in affectu peccandi mortaliter. Et ideo, ut dicitur in libro de ecclesiasticis Dogmat., *si mens in affectu peccandi est, gravatur magis Eucharistiae perceptione quam purificetur.* Unde hoc sacramentum in eo qui ipsum percipit cum conscientia peccati mortalis, non operatur remissionem peccati.

Potest tamen hoc sacramentum operari remissionem peccati dupliciter. Uno modo, non perceptum actu, sed voto, sicut cum quis primo iustificatur a peccato. Alio modo, etiam perceptum ab eo qui est in peccato mortali, cuius conscientiam et affectum non habet. Forte enim primo non fuit sufficienter contritus, sed, devote et reverenter accedens, consequetur per hoc sacramentum gratiam caritatis, quae contritionem perficiet et remissionem peccati.

Ad primum ergo dicendum quod petimus quod illud sacramentum nobis sit ablutio scelerum, vel eorum quorum conscientiam non habemus, secundum illud Psalmi, *ab occultis meis munda me, domine*; vel ut contritio in nobis perficiatur ad scelerum remissionem; vel etiam ut robur nobis detur contra scelera vitanda.

Ad secundum dicendum quod Baptismus est spiritualis generatio, quae est mutatio de non esse spirituali in esse spirituale; et datur per modum ablutionis. Et ideo, quantum ad utrumque, non inconvenienter accedit ad Baptismum qui habet conscientiam peccati mortalis. Sed per hoc sacramentum homo sumit in se Christum per modum spiritualis nutrimenti, quod non competit mortuo in peccatis. Et ideo non est similis ratio.

Ad tertium dicendum quod gratia est sufficiens causa remissionis peccati mortalis, non tamen actu remittit peccatum mortale nisi cum primo datur peccatori. Sic autem non datur in hoc sacramento. Unde ratio non sequitur.

since he is not a proper recipient of this sacrament, both because he is not alive spiritually, and so he ought not to eat the spiritual nourishment, since nourishment is confined to the living; and because he cannot be united with Christ, which is the effect of this sacrament, as long as he retains an attachment towards mortal sin. Consequently, as is said in the book De Eccles. Dogm.: *If the soul leans towards sin, it is burdened rather than purified from partaking of the Eucharist.* Hence, in him who is conscious of mortal sin, this sacrament does not cause the forgiveness of sin.

Nevertheless this sacrament can effect the forgiveness of sin in two ways. First of all, by being received, not actually, but in desire; as when a man is first justified from sin. Second, when received by one in mortal sin of which he is not conscious, and for which he has no attachment; since possibly he was not sufficiently contrite at first, but by approaching this sacrament devoutly and reverently he obtains the grace of charity, which will perfect his contrition and bring forgiveness of sin.

Reply Obj. 1: We ask that this sacrament may be the *cleansing of crimes*, or of those sins of which we are unconscious, according to Ps. 18:13: *Lord, cleanse me from my hidden sins*; or that our contrition may be perfected for the forgiveness of our sins; or that strength be bestowed on us to avoid sin.

Reply Obj. 2: Baptism is spiritual generation, which is a transition from spiritual non-being into spiritual being, and is given by way of ablution. Consequently, in both respects he who is conscious of mortal sin does not improperly approach Baptism. But in this sacrament man receives Christ within himself by way of spiritual nourishment, which is unbecoming to one that lies dead in his sins. Therefore the comparison does not hold good.

Reply Obj. 3: Grace is the sufficient cause of the forgiveness of mortal sin; yet it does not forgive sin except when it is first bestowed on the sinner. But it is not given so in this sacrament. Hence the argument does not prove.

Article 4

Whether Venial Sins Are Forgiven Through This Sacrament?

Ad quartum sic proceditur. Videtur quod per hoc sacramentum non remittantur peccata venialia. Hoc enim sacramentum, ut Augustinus dicit, super Ioan., est sacramentum caritatis. Sed venialia peccata non contrariantur caritati, ut in secunda parte habitum est. Cum ergo contrarium tollatur per suum contrarium, videtur quod peccata venialia per hoc sacramentum non remittantur.

Objection 1: It seems that venial sins are not forgiven by this sacrament, because this is the *sacrament of charity*, as Augustine says (*Tract. xxvi in Joan.*). But venial sins are not contrary to charity, as was shown in the Second Part (I-II, Q. 88, AA. 1, 2; II-II, Q. 24, A. 10). Therefore, since contrary is taken away by its contrary, it seems that venial sins are not forgiven by this sacrament.

PRAETEREA, si peccata venialia per hoc sacramentum remittantur, qua ratione unum remittitur, et omnia remittentur. Sed non videtur quod omnia remittantur, quia sic frequenter aliquis esset absque omni peccato veniali, quod est contra id quod dicitur I Ioan. I, *si dixerimus quoniam peccatum non habemus, nos ipsos seducimus*. Non ergo per hoc sacramentum remittitur aliquod peccatum veniale.

PRAETEREA, contraria mutuo se expellunt. Sed peccata venialia non prohibent a perceptione huius sacramenti, dicit enim Augustinus, super illud Ioan. VI, *si quis ex ipso manducaverit, non morietur in aeternum, innocentiam, inquit, ad altare apportate, peccata, etsi sint quotidiana, non sint mortifera*. Ergo neque peccata venialia per hoc sacramentum tolluntur.

SED CONTRA est quod Innocentius III dicit, quod hoc sacramentum veniale delet et cavet mortalia.

RESPONDEO dicendum quod in hoc sacramento duo possunt considerari, scilicet ipsum sacramentum, et res sacramenti. Et ex utroque apparet quod hoc sacramentum habet virtutem ad remissionem venialium peccatorum. Nam hoc sacramentum sumitur sub specie cibi nutrientis. Nutrimentum autem cibi necessarium est corpori ad restaurandum id quod quotidie deperditur ex calore naturali. Spiritualiter autem quotidie in nobis aliquid deperditur ex calore concupiscentiae per peccata venialia, quae diminuunt fervorem caritatis, ut in secunda parte habitum est. Et ideo competit huic sacramento ut remittat peccata venialia. Unde et Ambrosius dicit, in libro de sacramentis, quod iste panis quotidianus sumitur in remedium quotidianae infirmitatis.

Res autem huius sacramenti est caritas, non solum quantum ad habitum, sed etiam quantum ad actum, qui excitatur in hoc sacramento, per quod peccata venialia solvuntur. Unde manifestum est quod virtute huius sacramenti remittuntur peccata venialia.

AD PRIMUM ergo dicendum quod peccata venialia, etsi non contrarientur caritati quantum ad habitum, contrariantur tamen ei quantum ad fervorem actus, qui excitatur per hoc sacramentum. Ratione cuius peccata venialia tolluntur.

AD SECUNDUM dicendum quod illud verbum non est intelligendum quin aliqua hora possit homo esse absque omni reatu peccati venialis, sed quia vitam istam sancti non ducunt sine peccatis venialibus.

AD TERTIUM dicendum quod maior est virtus caritatis, cuius est hoc sacramentum, quam venialium peccatorum, nam caritas tollit per suum actum peccata venialia, quae tamen non possunt totaliter impedire actum caritatis. Et eadem ratio est de hoc sacramento.

OBJ. 2: Further, if venial sins be forgiven by this sacrament, then all of them are forgiven for the same reason as one is. But it does not appear that all are forgiven, because thus one might frequently be without any venial sin, against what is said in 1 John 1:8: *If we say that we have no sin, we deceive ourselves.* Therefore no venial sin is forgiven by this sacrament.

OBJ. 3: Further, contraries mutually exclude each other. But venial sins do not forbid the receiving of this sacrament: because Augustine says on the words, *If any man eat of it he shall not die for ever* (John 6:50): *Bring innocence to the altar: your sins, though they be daily . . . let them not be deadly.* Therefore neither are venial sins taken away by this sacrament.

ON THE CONTRARY, Innocent III says (*De S. Alt. Myst.* iv) that this sacrament *blots out venial sins, and wards off mortal sins.*

I ANSWER THAT, Two things may be considered in this sacrament, to wit, the sacrament itself, and the reality of the sacrament: and it appears from both that this sacrament has the power of forgiving venial sins. For this sacrament is received under the form of nourishing food. Now nourishment from food is requisite for the body to make good the daily waste caused by the action of natural heat. But something is also lost daily of our spirituality from the heat of concupiscence through venial sins, which lessen the fervor of charity, as was shown in the Second Part (II-II, Q. 24, A. 10). And therefore it belongs to this sacrament to forgive venial sins. Hence Ambrose says (*De Sacram.* v) that this daily bread is taken *as a remedy against daily infirmity.*

The reality of this sacrament is charity, not only as to its habit, but also as to its act, which is kindled in this sacrament; and by this means venial sins are forgiven. Consequently, it is manifest that venial sins are forgiven by the power of this sacrament.

REPLY OBJ. 1: Venial sins, although not opposed to the habit of charity, are nevertheless opposed to the fervor of its act, which act is kindled by this sacrament; by reason of which act venial sins are blotted out.

REPLY OBJ. 1: The passage quoted is not to be understood as if a man could not at some time be without all guilt of venial sin: but that the just do not pass through this life without committing venial sins.

REPLY OBJ. 3: The power of charity, to which this sacrament belongs, is greater than that of venial sins: because charity by its act takes away venial sins, which nevertheless cannot entirely hinder the act of charity. And the same holds good of this sacrament.

Article 5

Whether the Entire Punishment Due to Sin Is Forgiven Through This Sacrament?

AD QUINTUM SIC PROCEDITUR. Videtur quod per hoc sacramentum tota poena peccati remittatur. Homo enim per hoc sacramentum suscipit in se effectum passionis Christi, ut dictum est, sicut et per Baptismum. Sed per Baptismum percipit homo remissionem omnis poenae virtute passionis Christi, quae sufficienter satisfecit pro omnibus peccatis, ut ex supra dictis patet. Ergo videtur quod per hoc sacramentum homini remittatur totus reatus poenae.

PRAETEREA, Alexander Papa dicit, *nihil in sacrificiis maius esse potest quam corpus et sanguis Christi.* Sed per sacrificia veteris legis homo satisfaciebat pro peccatis suis, dicitur enim Levit. IV et V, si peccaverit homo, offeret (hoc vel illud) pro peccato suo, et remittetur ei. Ergo multo magis hoc sacramentum valet ad remissionem omnis poenae.

PRAETEREA, constat quod per hoc sacramentum aliquid de reatu poenae dimittitur, unde et in satisfactione quibusdam iniungitur quod pro se faciant Missas celebrare. Sed qua ratione una pars poenae dimittitur, eadem ratione et alia, cum virtus Christi, quae in hoc sacramento continetur, sit infinita. Ergo videtur quod per hoc sacramentum tota poena tollatur.

SED CONTRA est quod, secundum hoc, non esset homini alia poena iniungenda, sicut nec baptizato iniungitur.

RESPONDEO dicendum quod hoc sacramentum simul est et sacrificium et sacramentum, sed rationem sacrificii habet inquantum offertur; rationem autem sacramenti inquantum sumitur. Et ideo effectum sacramenti habet in eo qui sumit, effectum autem sacrificii in eo qui offert, vel in his pro quibus offertur.

Si igitur consideretur ut sacramentum, habet dupliciter effectum, uno modo, directe ex vi sacramenti; alio modo, quasi ex quadam concomitantia; sicut et circa continentiam sacramenti dictum est. Ex vi quidem sacramenti, directe habet illum effectum ad quem est institutum. Non est autem institutum ad satisfaciendum, sed ad spiritualiter nutriendum per unionem ad Christum et ad membra eius, sicut et nutrimentum unitur nutrito. Sed quia haec unitas fit per caritatem, ex cuius fervore aliquis consequitur remissionem non solum culpae, sed etiam poenae; inde est quod ex consequenti, per quandam concomitantiam ad principalem effectum, homo consequitur remissionem poenae; non quidem totius, sed secundum modum suae devotionis et fervoris.

OBJECTION 1: It seems that the entire punishment due to sin is forgiven through this sacrament. For through this sacrament man receives the effect of Christ's Passion within himself as stated above (AA. 1, 2), just as he does through Baptism. But through Baptism man receives forgiveness of all punishment, through the virtue of Christ's Passion, which satisfied sufficiently for all sins, as was explained above (Q. 69, A. 2). Therefore it seems the whole debt of punishment is forgiven through this sacrament.

OBJ. 2: Further, Pope Alexander I says (*Ep. ad omnes orth.*): *No sacrifice can be greater than the body and the blood of Christ.* But man satisfied for his sins by the sacrifices of the old Law: for it is written (Lev 4, 5): *If a man shall sin, let him offer* (so and so) *for his sin, and it shall be forgiven him.* Therefore this sacrament avails much more for the forgiveness of all punishment.

OBJ. 3: Further, it is certain that some part of the debt of punishment is forgiven by this sacrament; for which reason it is sometimes enjoined upon a man, by way of satisfaction, to have masses said for himself. But if one part of the punishment is forgiven, for the same reason is the other forgiven: owing to Christ's infinite power contained in this sacrament. Consequently, it seems that the whole punishment can be taken away by this sacrament.

ON THE CONTRARY, In that case no other punishment would have to be enjoined; just as none is imposed upon the newly baptized.

I ANSWER THAT, This sacrament is both a sacrifice and a sacrament. it has the nature of a sacrifice inasmuch as it is offered up; and it has the nature of a sacrament inasmuch as it is received. And therefore it has the effect of a sacrament in the recipient, and the effect of a sacrifice in the offerer, or in them for whom it is offered.

If, then, it be considered as a sacrament, it produces its effect in two ways: first of all directly through the power of the sacrament; second as by a kind of concomitance, as was said above regarding what is contained in the sacrament (Q. 76, AA. 1, 2). Through the power of the sacrament it produces directly that effect for which it was instituted. Now it was instituted not for satisfaction, but for nourishing spiritually through union between Christ and His members, as nourishment is united with the person nourished. But because this union is the effect of charity, from the fervor of which man obtains forgiveness, not only of guilt but also of punishment, hence it is that as a consequence, and by concomitance with the chief effect, man obtains forgiveness of the punishment, not indeed of the entire punishment, but according to the measure of his devotion and fervor.

Inquantum vero est sacrificium, habet vim satisfactivam. Sed in satisfactione magis attenditur affectus offerentis quam quantitas oblationis, unde et dominus dixit, Luc. XXI, de vidua quae obtulit duo aera, quod plus omnibus misit. Quamvis igitur haec oblatio ex sui quantitate sufficiat ad satisfaciendum pro omni poena, tamen fit satisfactoria illis pro quibus offertur, vel etiam offerentibus, secundum quantitatem suae devotionis, et non pro tota poena.

AD PRIMUM ergo dicendum quod sacramentum Baptismi directe ordinatur ad remissionem culpae et poenae, non autem Eucharistia, quia Baptismus datur homini quasi commorienti Christo; Eucharistia autem quasi nutriendo et perficiendo per Christum. Unde non est similis ratio.

AD SECUNDUM dicendum quod alia sacrificia et oblationes non operabantur remissionem totius poenae, neque quantum ad quantitatem oblati, sicut hoc sacrificium; neque quantum ad devotionem hominis, ex qua contingit quod etiam hic non tollitur tota poena.

AD TERTIUM dicendum quod hoc quod tollitur pars poenae et non tota per hoc sacramentum, non contingit ex defectu virtutis Christi, sed ex defectu devotionis humanae.

But in so far as it is a sacrifice, it has a satisfactory power. Yet in satisfaction, the affection of the offerer is weighed rather than the quantity of the offering. Hence our Lord says (Mark 12:43: cf. Luke 21:4) of the widow who offered *two mites* that she *cast in more than all*. Therefore, although this offering suffices of its own quantity to satisfy for all punishment, yet it becomes satisfactory for them for whom it is offered, or even for the offerers, according to the measure of their devotion, and not for the whole punishment.

REPLY OBJ. 1: The sacrament of Baptism is directly ordained for the remission of punishment and guilt: not so the Eucharist, because Baptism is given to man as dying with Christ, whereas the Eucharist is given as by way of nourishing and perfecting him through Christ. Consequently there is no parallel.

REPLY OBJ. 2: Those other sacrifices and oblations did not effect the forgiveness of the whole punishment, neither as to the quantity of the thing offered, as this sacrament does, nor as to personal devotion; from which it comes to pass that even here the whole punishment is not taken away.

REPLY OBJ. 3: If part of the punishment and not the whole be taken away by this sacrament, it is due to a defect not on the part of Christ's power, but on the part of man's devotion.

Article 6

Whether Man Is Preserved by This Sacrament from Future Sins?

AD SEXTUM SIC PROCEDITUR. Videtur quod per hoc sacramentum non praeservetur homo a peccatis futuris. Multi enim digne sumentes hoc sacramentum postea in peccatum cadent. Quod non accideret si hoc sacramentum praeservaret a peccatis futuris. Non ergo effectus huius sacramenti est a peccatis futuris praeservare.

PRAETEREA, Eucharistia est sacramentum caritatis, ut supra dictum est. Sed caritas non videtur praeservare a peccatis futuris, quia semel habita potest amitti per peccatum, ut in secunda parte habitum est. Ergo videtur quod nec hoc sacramentum praeservet hominem a peccato.

PRAETEREA, origo peccati in nobis est *lex peccati, quae est in membris nostris,* ut patet per apostolum, Rom. VII. Sed mitigatio fomitis, qui est lex peccati, non ponitur effectus huius sacramenti, sed magis Baptismi. Ergo praeservare a peccatis futuris non est effectus huius sacramenti.

SED CONTRA est quod dominus dicit, Ioan. VI, *hic est panis de caelo descendens, ut, si quis ex eo manducaverit, non moriatur.* Quod quidem manifestum est non

OBJECTION 1: It seems that man is not preserved by this sacrament from future sins. For there are many that receive this sacrament worthily, who afterwards fall into sin. Now this would not happen if this sacrament were to preserve them from future sins. Consequently, it is not an effect of this sacrament to preserve from future sins.

OBJ. 2: Further, the Eucharist is the sacrament of charity, as stated above (A. 4). But charity does not seem to preserve from future sins, because it can be lost through sin after one has possessed it, as was stated in the Second Part (II-II, Q. 24, A. 11). Therefore it seems that this sacrament does not preserve man from sin.

OBJ. 3: Further, the origin of sin within us is *the law of sin, which is in our members,* as declared by the Apostle (Rom 7:23). But the lessening of the fomes, which is the law of sin, is set down as an effect not of this sacrament, but rather of Baptism. Therefore preservation from sin is not an effect of this sacrament.

ON THE CONTRARY, our Lord said (John 6:50): *This is the bread which cometh down from heaven; that if any man eat of it, he may not die*: which manifestly is not to

intelligi de morte corporali. Ergo intelligitur quod hoc sacramentum praeservet a morte spirituali, quae est per peccatum.

Respondeo dicendum quod peccatum est quaedam mors spiritualis animae. Unde hoc modo praeservatur aliquis a peccato futuro, quo praeservatur corpus a morte futura. Quod quidem fit dupliciter. Uno modo, inquantum natura hominis interius roboratur contra interiora corruptiva, et sic praeservatur a morte per cibum et medicinam. Alio modo, per hoc quod munitur contra exteriores impugnationes, et sic praeservatur per arma, quibus munitur corpus.

Utroque autem modo hoc sacramentum praeservat a peccato. Nam primo quidem, per hoc quod Christo coniungit per gratiam, roborat spiritualem vitam hominis, tanquam spiritualis cibus et spiritualis medicina, secundum illud Psalmi, *panis cor hominis confirmat*. Et Augustinus dicit, super Ioan., *securus accede, panis est, non venenum*. Alio modo, inquantum signum est passionis Christi, per quam victi sunt Daemones, repellit enim omnem Daemonum impugnationem. Unde Chrysostomus dicit, super Ioan., *ut leones flammam spirantes, sic ab illa mensa discedimus, terribiles effecti Diabolo*.

Ad primum ergo dicendum quod effectus huius sacramenti recipitur in homine secundum hominis conditionem, sicut contingit de qualibet causa activa quod eius effectus recipitur in materia secundum modum materiae. Homo autem in statu viae est huius conditionis quod liberum arbitrium eius potest flecti in bonum et in malum. Unde, licet hoc sacramentum, quantum est de se habeat virtutem praeservativam a peccato, non tamen aufert homini possibilitatem peccandi.

Ad secundum dicendum quod etiam caritas, quantum est de se, praeservat hominem a peccato, secundum illud Rom. XIII, *dilectio proximi malum non operatur*. Sed ex mutabilitate liberi arbitrii contingit quod aliquis post habitam caritatem peccat, sicut et post susceptionem huius sacramenti.

Ad tertium dicendum quod, licet hoc sacramentum non directe ordinetur ad diminutionem fomitis, diminuit tamen fomitem ex quadam consequentia, inquantum auget caritatem, quia, sicut Augustinus dicit, in libro octogintatrium quaestionum, *augmentum caritatis est diminutio cupiditatis*. Directe autem confirmat cor hominis in bono. Per quod etiam praeservatur homo a peccato.

be understood of the death of the body. Therefore it is to be understood that this sacrament preserves from spiritual death, which is through sin.

I answer that, Sin is the spiritual death of the soul. Hence man is preserved from future sin in the same way as the body is preserved from future death of the body: and this happens in two ways. First of all, in so far as man's nature is strengthened inwardly against inner decay, and so by means of food and medicine he is preserved from death. Second, by being guarded against outward assaults; and thus he is protected by means of arms by which he defends his body.

Now this sacrament preserves man from sin in both of these ways. For, first of all, by uniting man with Christ through grace, it strengthens his spiritual life, as spiritual food and spiritual medicine, according to Ps. 103:5: *(That) bread strengthens man's heart*. Augustine likewise says (*Tract. xxvi in Joan.*): *Approach without fear; it is bread, not poison*. Second, inasmuch as it is a sign of Christ's Passion, whereby the devils are conquered, it repels all the assaults of demons. Hence Chrysostom says (*Hom. xlvi in Joan.*): *Like lions breathing forth fire, thus do we depart from that table, being made terrible to the devil*.

Reply Obj. 1: The effect of this sacrament is received according to man's condition: such is the case with every active cause in that its effect is received in matter according to the condition of the matter. But such is the condition of man on earth that his free-will can be bent to good or evil. Hence, although this sacrament of itself has the power of preserving from sin, yet it does not take away from man the possibility of sinning.

Reply Obj. 2: Even charity of itself keeps man from sin, according to Rom. 13:10: *The love of our neighbor worketh no evil*: but it is due to the mutability of free-will that a man sins after possessing charity, just as after receiving this sacrament.

Reply Obj. 3: Although this sacrament is not ordained directly to lessen the fomes, yet it does lessen it as a consequence, inasmuch as it increases charity, because, as Augustine says (Q. 83), *the increase of charity is the lessening of concupiscence*. But it directly strengthens man's heart in good; whereby he is also preserved from sin.

Article 7

Whether This Sacrament Benefits Others Besides the Recipients?

AD SEPTIMUM SIC PROCEDITUR. Videtur quod hoc sacramentum non prosit nisi sumenti. Hoc enim sacramentum est unius generis cum aliis sacramentis, utpote aliis condivisum. Sed alia sacramenta non prosunt nisi sumentibus, sicut effectum Baptismi non suscipit nisi baptizatus. Ergo nec hoc sacramentum prodest aliis nisi sumenti.

PRAETEREA, effectus huius sacramenti est adeptio gratiae et gloriae, et remissio culpae, ad minus venialis. Si ergo hoc sacramentum haberet effectum in aliis quam in sumentibus, posset contingere quod aliquis adipisceretur gloriam et gratiam et remissionem culpae absque actione et passione propria, alio offerente vel sumente hoc sacramentum.

PRAETEREA, multiplicata causa, multiplicatur effectus. Si ergo hoc sacramentum prodest aliis quam sumentibus, sequeretur quod magis prodesset alicui si sumeret hoc sacramentum in multis hostiis in una Missa consecratis, quod non habet Ecclesiae consuetudo, ut scilicet multi communicent pro alicuius salute. Non ergo videtur quod hoc sacramentum prosit nisi sumenti.

SED CONTRA est quod in celebratione huius sacramenti fit pro multis aliis deprecatio. Quod frustra fieret nisi hoc sacramentum aliis prodesset. Ergo hoc sacramentum non solum sumentibus prodest.

RESPONDEO dicendum quod, sicut prius dictum est, hoc sacramentum non solum est sacramentum, sed etiam est sacrificium. Inquantum enim in hoc sacramento repraesentatur passio Christi, qua Christus obtulit se hostiam Deo, ut dicitur Ephes. V, habet rationem sacrificii, inquantum vero in hoc sacramento traditur invisibiliter gratia sub visibili specie, habet rationem sacramenti. Sic igitur hoc sacramentum sumentibus quidem prodest per modum sacramenti et per modum sacrificii, quia pro omnibus sumentibus offertur, dicitur enim in canone Missae, *quotquot ex hac altaris participatione sacrosanctum corpus et sanguinem filii tui sumpserimus, omni benedictione caelesti et gratia repleamur.*

Sed aliis, qui non sumunt, prodest per modum sacrificii, inquantum pro salute eorum offertur, unde et in canone Missae dicitur, *memento, domine, famulorum famularumque tuarum, pro quibus tibi offerimus, vel qui tibi offerunt, hoc sacrificium laudis, pro se suisque omnibus, pro redemptione animarum suarum, pro spe salutis et incolumitatis suae.* Et utrumque modum dominus exprimit, dicens, Matth. XXVI, qui pro vobis, scilicet

OBJECTION 1: It seems that this sacrament benefits only the recipients. For this sacrament is of the same genus as the other sacraments, being one of those into which that genus is divided. But the other sacraments only benefit the recipients; thus the baptized person alone receives effect of Baptism. Therefore, neither does this sacrament benefit others than the recipients.

OBJ. 2: Further, the effects of this sacrament are the attainment of grace and glory, and the forgiveness of sin, at least of venial sin. If therefore this sacrament were to produce its effects in others besides the recipients, a man might happen to acquire grace and glory and forgiveness of sin without doing or receiving anything himself, through another receiving or offering this sacrament.

OBJ. 3: Further, when the cause is multiplied, the effect is likewise multiplied. If therefore this sacrament benefit others besides the recipients, it would follow that it benefits a man more if he receive this sacrament through many hosts being consecrated in one Mass, whereas this is not the Church's custom: for instance, that many receive communion for the salvation of one individual. Consequently, it does not seem that this sacrament benefits anyone but the recipient.

ON THE CONTRARY, Prayer is made for many others during the celebration of this sacrament; which would serve no purpose were the sacrament not beneficial to others. Therefore, this sacrament is beneficial not merely to them who receive it.

I ANSWER THAT, As stated above (A. 3), this sacrament is not only a sacrament, but also a sacrifice. For, it has the nature of a sacrifice inasmuch as in this sacrament Christ's Passion is represented, whereby Christ *offered Himself a Victim to God* (Eph 5:2), and it has the nature of a sacrament inasmuch as invisible grace is bestowed in this sacrament under a visible species. So, then, this sacrament benefits recipients by way both of sacrament and of sacrifice, because it is offered for all who partake of it. For it is said in the Canon of the Mass: *May as many of us as, by participation at this Altar, shall receive the most sacred body and blood of Thy Son, be filled with all heavenly benediction and grace.*

But to others who do not receive it, it is beneficial by way of sacrifice, inasmuch as it is offered for their salvation. Hence it is said in the Canon of the Mass: *Be mindful, O Lord, of Thy servants, men and women . . . for whom we offer, or who offer up to Thee, this sacrifice of praise for themselves and for all their own, for the redemption of their souls, for the hope of their safety and salvation.* And our Lord expressed both ways, saying (Matt 26:28, with Luke 22:20):

sumentibus, et pro multis aliis, effundetur in remissionem peccatorum.

AD PRIMUM ergo dicendum quod hoc sacramentum prae aliis habet quod est sacrificium. Et ideo non est similis ratio.

AD SECUNDUM dicendum quod, sicut passio Christi prodest quidem omnibus ad remissionem culpae et adeptionem gratiae et gloriae, sed effectum non habet nisi in illis qui passioni Christi coniunguntur per fidem et caritatem; ita etiam hoc sacrificium, quod est memoriale dominicae passionis, non habet effectum nisi in illis qui coniunguntur huic sacramento per fidem et caritatem. Unde et Augustinus dicit, ad renatum, *quis offerat corpus Christi nisi pro his qui sunt membra Christi?* Unde et in canone Missae non oratur pro his qui sunt extra Ecclesiam. Illis tamen prodest plus vel minus, secundum modum devotionis eorum.

AD TERTIUM dicendum quod sumptio pertinet ad rationem sacramenti, sed oblatio pertinet ad rationem sacrificii. Et ideo ex hoc quod aliquis sumit corpus Christi, vel etiam plures, non accrescit aliis aliquod iuvamentum. Similiter etiam neque ex hoc quod sacerdos plures hostias consecrat in una Missa, non multiplicatur effectus huius sacramenti, quia non est nisi unum sacrificium, nihil enim virtutis plus est in multis hostiis consecratis quam in una, cum sub omnibus et sub una non sit nisi totus Christus. Unde nec si aliquis simul in una Missa multas hostias consecratas sumat, participabit maiorem effectum sacramenti. In pluribus vero Missis multiplicatur sacrificii oblatio. Et ideo multiplicatur effectus sacrificii et sacramenti.

Which for you, i.e., who receive it, *and for many*, i.e., others, *shall be shed unto remission of sins.*

REPLY OBJ. 1: This sacrament has this in addition to the others, that it is a sacrifice: and therefore the comparison fails.

REPLY OBJ. 2: As Christ's Passion benefits all, for the forgiveness of sin and the attaining of grace and glory, whereas it produces no effect except in those who are united with Christ's Passion through faith and charity, so likewise this sacrifice, which is the memorial of our Lord's Passion, has no effect except in those who are united with this sacrament through faith and charity. Hence Augustine says to Renatus (*De Anima et ejus origine* i): *Who may offer Christ's body except for them who are Christ's members?* Hence in the Canon of the Mass no prayer is made for them who are outside the pale of the Church. But it benefits them who are members, more or less, according to the measure of their devotion.

REPLY OBJ. 3: Receiving is of the very nature of the sacrament, but offering belongs to the nature of sacrifice: consequently, when one or even several receive the body of Christ, no help accrues to others. In like fashion even when the priest consecrates several hosts in one mass, the effect of this sacrament is not increased, since there is only one sacrifice; because there is no more power in several hosts than in one, since there is only one Christ present under all the hosts and under one. Hence, neither will any one receive greater effect from the sacrament by taking many consecrated hosts in one mass. But the oblation of the sacrifice is multiplied in several masses, and therefore the effect of the sacrifice and of the sacrament is multiplied.

Article 8

Whether the Effect of This Sacrament Is Hindered by Venial Sin?

AD OCTAVUM SIC PROCEDITUR. Videtur quod per veniale peccatum non impediatur effectus huius sacramenti. Dicit enim Augustinus, super illud Ioan. VI, *si quis ex ipso manducaverit etc., panem caelestem spiritualiter manducate; innocentiam ad altare portate; peccata, etsi sint quotidiana, non sint mortifera.* Ex quo patet quod quotidiana peccata, quae dicuntur venialia, spiritualem manducationem non impediunt. Sed spiritualiter manducantes effectum huius sacramenti percipiunt. Ergo peccata venialia non impediunt effectum huius sacramenti.

PRAETEREA, hoc sacramentum non est minoris virtutis quam Baptismus. Sed effectum Baptismi, sicut supra dictum est, impedit sola fictio, ad quam non pertinent peccata venialia, quia, sicut Sap. I dicitur, *Spiritus*

OBJECTION 1: It seems that the effect of this sacrament is not hindered by venial sin. For Augustine (*Tract. xxvi in Joan.*), commenting on John 6:52, *If any man eat of this bread*, etc., says: *Eat the heavenly bread spiritually; bring innocence to the altar; your sins, though they be daily, let them not be deadly.* From this it is evident that venial sins, which are called daily sins, do not prevent spiritual eating. But they who eat spiritually, receive the effect of this sacrament. Therefore, venial sins do not hinder the effect of this sacrament.

OBJ. 2: Further, this sacrament is not less powerful than Baptism. But, as stated above (Q. 69, AA. 9, 10), only pretense checks the effect of Baptism, and venial sins do not belong to pretense; because according to Wis. 1:5: *the Holy*

Sanctus disciplinae effugiet fictum, qui tamen per peccata venialia non fugatur. Ergo neque effectum huius sacramenti impediunt peccata venialia.

Praeterea, nihil quod removetur per actionem alicuius causae, potest impedire eius effectum. Sed peccata venialia tolluntur per hoc sacramentum. Ergo non impediunt eius effectum.

Sed contra est quod Damascenus dicit, in IV libro, *ignis eius quod in nobis est desiderii, assumens eam quae ex carbone, idest hoc sacramento, ignitionem, comburet nostra peccata, et illuminabit nostra corda, ut participatione divini ignis igniamur et deificemur.* Sed ignis nostri desiderii vel amoris impeditur per peccata venialia, quae impediunt fervorem caritatis, ut in secunda parte habitum est. Ergo peccata venialia impediunt effectum huius sacramenti.

Respondeo dicendum quod peccata venialia dupliciter accipi possunt, uno modo, prout sunt praeterita; alio modo, prout sunt actu exercita. Primo quidem modo, peccata venialia nullo modo impediunt effectum huius sacramenti. Potest enim contingere quod aliquis post multa peccata commissa venialia, devote accedat ad hoc sacramentum, et plenarie huius sacramenti consequetur effectum. Secundo autem modo, peccata venialia non ex toto impediunt effectum huius sacramenti, sed in parte. Dictum est enim quod effectus huius sacramenti non solum est adeptio habitualis gratiae vel caritatis, sed etiam quaedam actualis refectio spiritualis dulcedinis. Quae quidem impeditur si aliquis accedat ad hoc sacramentum mente distracta per peccata venialia. Non autem tollitur augmentum gratiae habitualis vel caritatis.

Ad primum ergo dicendum quod ille qui cum actu venialis peccati ad hoc sacramentum accedit, habitualiter quidem manducat spiritualiter, sed non actualiter. Et ideo habitualem effectum huius sacramenti percipit, non autem actualem.

Ad secundum dicendum quod Baptismus non ita ordinatur ad actualem effectum, idest ad fervorem caritatis, sicut hoc sacramentum. Nam Baptismus est spiritualis regeneratio, per quam acquiritur prima perfectio, quae est habitus vel forma, hoc autem sacramentum est spiritualis manducatio, quae habet actualem delectationem.

Ad tertium dicendum quod illa ratio procedit de venialibus praeteritis, quae per hoc sacramentum tolluntur.

Spirit of discipline will flee from the deceitful, yet He is not put to flight by venial sins. Therefore neither do venial sins hinder the effect of this sacrament.

Obj. 3: Further, nothing which is removed by the action of any cause, can hinder the effect of such cause. But venial sins are taken away by this sacrament. Therefore, they do not hinder its effect.

On the contrary, Damascene says (*De Fide Orth.* iv): *The fire of that desire which is within us, being kindled by the burning coal*, i.e., this sacrament, *will consume our sins, and enlighten our hearts, so that we shall be inflamed and made godlike.* But the fire of our desire or love is hindered by venial sins, which hinder the fervor of charity, as was shown in the Second Part (I-II, Q. 81, A. 4; II-II, Q. 24, A. 10). Therefore venial sins hinder the effect of this sacrament.

I answer that, Venial sins can be taken in two ways: first of all as past, second as in the act of being committed. Venial sins taken in the first way do not in any way hinder the effect of this sacrament. For it can come to pass that after many venial sins a man may approach devoutly to this sacrament and fully secure its effect. Considered in the second way venial sins do not utterly hinder the effect of this sacrament, but merely in part. For, it has been stated above (A. 1), that the effect of this sacrament is not only the obtaining of habitual grace or charity, but also a certain actual refreshment of spiritual sweetness: which is indeed hindered if anyone approach to this sacrament with mind distracted through venial sins; but the increase of habitual grace or of charity is not taken away.

Reply Obj. 1: He that approaches this sacrament with actual venial sin, eats spiritually indeed, in habit but not in act: and therefore he shares in the habitual effect of the sacrament, but not in its actual effect.

Reply Obj. 2: Baptism is not ordained, as this sacrament is, for the fervor of charity as its actual effect. Because Baptism is spiritual regeneration, through which the first perfection is acquired, which is a habit or form; but this sacrament is spiritual eating, which has actual delight.

Reply Obj. 3: This argument deals with past venial sins, which are taken away by this sacrament.

Question 80

The Use or Receiving of This Sacrament in General

Deinde considerandum est de usu sive sumptione huius sacramenti. Et primo, in communi; secundo, quomodo Christus est usus hoc sacramento.

Circa primum quaeruntur duodecim.

Primo, utrum sint duo modi manducandi hoc sacramentum, scilicet sacramentaliter et spiritualiter.

Secundo, utrum soli homini conveniat manducare spiritualiter.

Tertio, utrum solius hominis iusti sit manducare sacramentaliter.

Quarto, utrum peccator manducans sacramentaliter peccet.

Quinto, de quantitate huius peccati.

Sexto, utrum peccator accedens ad hoc sacramentum sit repellendus.

Septimo, utrum nocturna pollutio impediat hominem a sumptione huius sacramenti.

Octavo, utrum sit solum a ieiunis sumendum.

Nono, utrum sit exhibendum non habentibus usum rationis.

Decimo, utrum sit quotidie sumendum.

Undecimo, utrum liceat omnino abstinere.

Duodecimo, utrum liceat percipere corpus sine sanguine.

We have now to consider the use or receiving of this sacrament, first of all in general; second, how Christ used this sacrament.

Under the first heading there are twelve points of inquiry:

(1) Whether there are two ways of eating this sacrament, namely, sacramentally and spiritually?

(2) Whether it belongs to man alone to eat this sacrament spiritually?

(3) Whether it belongs to the just man only to eat it sacramentally?

(4) Whether the sinner sins in eating it sacramentally?

(5) Of the degree of this sin;

(6) Whether this sacrament should be refused to the sinner that approaches it?

(7) Whether nocturnal pollution prevents man from receiving this sacrament?

(8) Whether it is to be received only when one is fasting?

(9) Whether it is to be given to them who lack the use of reason?

(10) Whether it is to be received daily?

(11) Whether it is lawful to refrain from it altogether?

(12) Whether it is lawful to receive the body without the blood?

Article 1

Whether There Are Two Ways to Be Distinguished of Eating Christ's Body?

Ad primum sic proceditur. Videtur quod non debeant distingui duo modi manducandi corpus Christi, scilicet spiritualiter et sacramentaliter. Sicut enim Baptismus est spiritualis regeneratio, secundum illud Ioan. III, *nisi quis renatus fuerit ex aqua et spiritu sancto* etc., ita etiam hoc sacramentum est cibus spiritualis, unde dominus, loquens de hoc sacramento, dicit, Ioan. VI, *verba quae ego locutus sum vobis, spiritus et vita sunt.* Sed circa Baptismum non distinguitur duplex modus sumendi, scilicet sacramentalis et spiritualis. Ergo neque circa hoc sacramentum debet haec distinctio adhiberi.

Praeterea, ea quorum unum est propter alterum, non debent ad invicem dividi, quia unum ab alio speciem trahit. Sed sacramentalis manducatio ordinatur ad

Objection 1: It seems that two ways ought not to be distinguished of eating Christ's body, namely, sacramentally and spiritually. For, as Baptism is spiritual regeneration, according to John 3:5: *Unless a man be born again of water and the Holy Spirit,* etc., so also this sacrament is spiritual food: hence our Lord, speaking of this sacrament, says (John 6:64): *The words that I have spoken to you are spirit and life.* But there are no two distinct ways of receiving Baptism, namely, sacramentally and spiritually. Therefore neither ought this distinction to be made regarding this sacrament.

Obj. 2: Further, when two things are so related that one is on account of the other, they should not be put in contradistinction to one another, because the one derives its

spiritualem sicut ad finem. Non ergo debet sacramentalis manducatio contra spiritualem dividi.

PRAETEREA, ea quorum unum non potest esse sine altero, non debent contra se dividi. Sed videtur quod nullus possit manducare spiritualiter nisi etiam sacramentaliter manducet, alioquin antiqui patres hoc sacramentum spiritualiter manducassent. Frustra etiam esset sacramentalis manducatio, si sine ea spiritualis esse posset. Non ergo convenienter distinguitur duplex manducatio, scilicet sacramentalis et spiritualis.

SED CONTRA est quod, super illud I Cor. XI, *qui manducat et bibit indigne* etc., dicit Glossa, *duos dicimus esse modos manducandi, unum sacramentalem, et alium spiritualem.*

RESPONDEO dicendum quod in sumptione huius sacramenti duo sunt consideranda, scilicet ipsum sacramentum, et effectus ipsius, de quorum utroque supra iam dictum est. Perfectus igitur modus sumendi hoc sacramentum est quando aliquis ita hoc sacramentum suscipit quod percipit eius effectum. Contingit autem quandoque, sicut supra dictum est, quod aliquis impeditur a percipiendo effectum huius sacramenti, et talis sumptio huius sacramenti est imperfecta. Sicut igitur perfectum contra imperfectum dividitur, ita sacramentalis manducatio, per quam sumitur solum sacramentum sine effectu ipsius, dividitur contra spiritualem manducationem, per quam aliquis percipit effectum huius sacramenti quo spiritualiter homo Christo coniungitur per fidem et caritatem.

AD PRIMUM ergo dicendum quod etiam circa Baptismum, et alia huiusmodi sacramenta, similis distinctio adhibetur, nam quidam suscipiunt tantum sacramentum, quidam vero sacramentum et rem sacramenti. Hic tamen differt quia, cum alia sacramenta perficiantur in usu materiae, percipere sacramentum est ipsa perfectio sacramenti, hoc autem sacramentum perficitur in consecratione materiae, et ideo uterque usus est consequens hoc sacramentum. In Baptismo autem, et aliis sacramentis characterem imprimentibus, illi qui accipiunt sacramentum, recipiunt aliquem spiritualem effectum, scilicet characterem, quod non accidit in hoc sacramento. Et ideo magis in hoc sacramento distinguitur usus sacramentalis a spirituali quam in Baptismo.

AD SECUNDUM dicendum quod sacramentalis manducatio quae pertingit ad spiritualem, non dividitur contra spiritualem, sed includitur ab ea. Sed illa sacramentalis manducatio contra spiritualem dividitur quae effectum non consequitur, sicut imperfectum quod non pertingit ad perfectionem speciei, dividitur contra perfectum.

AD TERTIUM dicendum quod, sicut supra dictum est, effectus sacramenti potest ab aliquo percipi, si

species from the other. But sacramental eating is ordained for spiritual eating as its end. Therefore sacramental eating ought not to be divided in contrast with spiritual eating.

OBJ. 3: Further, things which cannot exist without one another ought not to be divided in contrast with each other. But it seems that no one can eat spiritually without eating sacramentally; otherwise the fathers of old would have eaten this sacrament spiritually. Moreover, sacramental eating would be to no purpose, if the spiritual eating could be had without it. Therefore it is not right to distinguish a twofold eating, namely, sacramental and spiritual.

ON THE CONTRARY, The gloss says on 1 Cor. 11:29: *He that eateth and drinketh unworthily*, etc.: *We hold that there are two ways of eating, the one sacramental, and the other spiritual.*

I ANSWER THAT, There are two things to be considered in the receiving of this sacrament, namely, the sacrament itself, and its fruits, and we have already spoken of both (QQ. 73, 79). The perfect way, then, of receiving this sacrament is when one takes it so as to partake of its effect. Now, as was stated above (Q. 79, AA. 3, 8), it sometimes happens that a man is hindered from receiving the effect of this sacrament; and such receiving of this sacrament is an imperfect one. Therefore, as the perfect is divided against the imperfect, so sacramental eating, whereby the sacrament only is received without its effect, is divided against spiritual eating, by which one receives the effect of this sacrament, whereby a man is spiritually united with Christ through faith and charity.

REPLY OBJ. 1: The same distinction is made regarding Baptism and the other sacraments: for, some receive the sacrament only, while others receive the sacrament and the reality of the sacrament. However, there is a difference, because, since the other sacraments are accomplished in the use of the matter, the receiving of the sacrament is the actual perfection of the sacrament; whereas this sacrament is accomplished in the consecration of the matter: and consequently both uses follow the sacrament. On the other hand, in Baptism and in the other sacraments that imprint a character, they who receive the sacrament receive some spiritual effect, that is, the character, which is not the case in this sacrament. And therefore, in this sacrament, rather than in Baptism, the sacramental use is distinguished from the spiritual use.

REPLY OBJ. 2: That sacramental eating which is also a spiritual eating is not divided in contrast with spiritual eating, but is included under it; but that sacramental eating which does not secure the effect, is divided in contrast with spiritual eating; just as the imperfect, which does not attain the perfection of its species, is divided in contrast with the perfect.

REPLY OBJ. 3: As stated above (Q. 73, A. 3), the effect of the sacrament can be secured by every man if he receive it

sacramentum habeatur in voto, quamvis non habeatur in re. Et ideo, sicut aliqui baptizantur Baptismo flaminis, propter desiderium Baptismi, antequam baptizentur Baptismo aquae; ita etiam aliqui manducant spiritualiter hoc sacramentum antequam sacramentaliter sumant. Sed hoc contingit dupliciter. Uno modo, propter desiderium sumendi ipsum sacramentum, et hoc modo dicuntur baptizari et manducare spiritualiter et non sacramentaliter, illi qui desiderant sumere haec sacramenta iam instituta. Alio modo, propter figuram, sicut dicit apostolus, I Cor. X, quod antiqui patres *baptizati sunt in nube et in mari, et quod spiritualem escam manducaverunt et spiritualem potum biberunt.* Nec tamen frustra adhibetur sacramentalis manducatio, quia plenius inducit sacramenti effectum ipsa sacramenti susceptio quam solum desiderium, sicut supra circa Baptismum dictum est.

in desire, though not in reality. Consequently, just as some are baptized with the Baptism of desire, through their desire of baptism, before being baptized in the Baptism of water; so likewise some eat this sacrament spiritually ere they receive it sacramentally. Now this happens in two ways. First of all, from desire of receiving the sacrament itself, and thus are said to be baptized, and to eat spiritually, and not sacramentally, they who desire to receive these sacraments since they have been instituted. Second, by a figure: thus the Apostle says (1 Cor 10:2), that the fathers of old were *baptized in the cloud and in the sea,* and that *they did eat . . . spiritual food, and . . . drank . . . spiritual drink.* Nevertheless sacramental eating is not without avail, because the actual receiving of the sacrament produces more fully the effect of the sacrament than does the desire thereof, as stated above of Baptism (Q. 69, A. 4, ad 2).

Article 2

Whether It Belongs to Man Alone to Eat This Sacrament Spiritually?

AD SECUNDUM SIC PROCEDITUR. Videtur quod non solius hominis sit hoc sacramentum sumere spiritualiter, sed etiam Angelorum. Quia super illud Psalmi, *panem Angelorum manducavit homo,* dicit Glossa, *idest, corpus Christi, qui est vere cibus Angelorum.* Sed hoc non esset si Angeli spiritualiter Christum non manducarent. Ergo Angeli spiritualiter Christum manducant.

PRAETEREA, Augustinus dicit, super Ioan., *hunc cibum et potum societatem vult intelligi corporis et membrorum suorum, quod est Ecclesia in praedestinatis.* Sed ad istam societatem non solum pertinent homines, sed etiam sancti Angeli. Ergo etiam sancti Angeli spiritualiter manducant.

PRAETEREA, Augustinus, in libro de verbis domini, dicit, *spiritualiter manducandus est Christus, quomodo ipse dicit, qui manducat meam carnem et bibit meum sanguinem, in me manet et ego in eo.* Sed hoc convenit non solum hominibus, sed etiam sanctis Angelis, in quibus per caritatem est Christus, et ipsi in eo. Ergo videtur quod spiritualiter manducare non solum sit hominum, sed etiam Angelorum.

SED CONTRA est quod Augustinus dicit, super Ioan., *panem de altari spiritualiter manducate, innocentiam ad altare portate.* Sed Angelorum non est accedere ad altare, tanquam aliquid inde sumpturi. Ergo Angelorum non est spiritualiter manducare.

RESPONDEO dicendum quod in hoc sacramento continetur ipse Christus, non quidem in specie propria, sed in specie sacramenti. Dupliciter ergo contingit manducare spiritualiter. Uno modo, ipsum Christum prout

OBJECTION 1: It seems that it does not belong to man alone to eat this sacrament spiritually, but likewise to angels. Because on Ps. 77:25: *Man ate the bread of angels,* the gloss says: *that is, the body of Christ, Who is truly the food of angels.* But it would not be so unless the angels were to eat Christ spiritually. Therefore the angels eat Christ spiritually.

OBJ. 2: Further, Augustine (*Tract. xxvi in Joan.*) says: By *this meat and drink, He would have us to understand the fellowship of His body and members, which is the Church in His predestined ones.* But not only men, but also the holy angels belong to that fellowship. Therefore the holy angels eat of it spiritually.

OBJ. 3: Further, Augustine in his book De Verbis Domini (*Serm. cxlii*) says: *Christ is to be eaten spiritually, as He Himself declares: 'He that eateth My flesh and drinketh My blood, abideth in Me, and I in him.'* But this belongs not only to men, but also to the holy angels, in whom Christ dwells by charity, and they in Him. Consequently, it seems that to eat Christ spiritually is not for men only, but also for the angels.

ON THE CONTRARY, Augustine (*Tract. xxvi in Joan.*) says: *Eat the bread* of the altar *spiritually; take innocence to the altar.* But angels do not approach the altar as for the purpose of taking something therefrom. Therefore the angels do not eat spiritually.

I ANSWER THAT, Christ Himself is contained in this sacrament, not under His proper species, but under the sacramental species. Consequently there are two ways of eating spiritually. First, as Christ Himself exists under His

in sua specie consistit. Et hoc modo Angeli spiritualiter manducant ipsum Christum, inquantum ei uniuntur fruitione caritatis perfectae et visione manifesta (quem panem expectamus in patria), non per fidem, sicut nos hic ei unimur.

Alio modo contingit spiritualiter manducare Christum prout est sub speciebus huius sacramenti, inquantum scilicet aliquis credit in Christum cum desiderio sumendi hoc sacramentum. Et hoc non solum est manducare Christum spiritualiter, sed etiam spiritualiter manducare hoc sacramentum. Quod non competit Angelis. Et ideo Angeli, etsi spiritualiter manducent Christum, non convenit tamen eis spiritualiter manducare hoc sacramentum.

AD PRIMUM ergo dicendum quod sumptio Christi sub hoc sacramento ordinatur, sicut ad finem, ad fruitionem patriae, qua Angeli eo fruuntur. Et quia ea quae sunt ad finem, derivantur a fine, inde est quod ista manducatio Christi qua eum sumimus sub hoc sacramento, quodammodo derivatur ab illa manducatione qua Angeli fruuntur Christo in patria. Et ideo dicitur homo manducare panem Angelorum, quia primo et principaliter est Angelorum, qui eo fruuntur in propria specie; secundario autem est hominum, qui Christum sub sacramento accipiunt.

AD SECUNDUM dicendum quod ad societatem corporis mystici pertinent quidem et homines per fidem, Angeli autem per manifestam visionem. Sacramenta autem proportionantur fidei, per quam veritas videtur in speculo et in aenigmate. Et ideo hic, proprie loquendo, non Angelis, sed hominibus proprie convenit manducare spiritualiter hoc sacramentum.

AD TERTIUM dicendum quod Christus manet in hominibus secundum praesentem statum per fidem, sed in Angelis beatis est per manifestam visionem. Et ideo non est simile, sicut dictum est.

proper species, and in this way the angels eat Christ spiritually inasmuch as they are united with Him in the enjoyment of perfect charity, and in clear vision (and this is the bread we hope for in heaven), and not by faith, as we are united with Him here.

In another way one may eat Christ spiritually, as He is under the sacramental species, inasmuch as a man believes in Christ, while desiring to receive this sacrament; and this is not merely to eat Christ spiritually, but likewise to eat this sacrament; which does not fall to the lot of the angels. And therefore although the angels feed on Christ spiritually, yet it does not belong to them to eat this sacrament spiritually.

REPLY OBJ. 1: The receiving of Christ under this sacrament is ordained to the enjoyment of heaven, as to its end, in the same way as the angels enjoy it; and since the means are gauged by the end, hence it is that such eating of Christ whereby we receive Him under this sacrament, is, as it were, derived from that eating whereby the angels enjoy Christ in heaven. Consequently, man is said to eat the *bread of angels*, because it belongs to the angels to do so first and principally, since they enjoy Him in his proper species; and second it belongs to men, who receive Christ under this sacrament.

REPLY OBJ. 2: Both men and angels belong to the fellowship of His mystical body; men by faith, and angels by manifest vision. But the sacraments are proportioned to faith, through which the truth is seen *through a glass* and *in a dark manner*. And therefore, properly speaking, it does not belong to angels, but to men, to eat this sacrament spiritually.

REPLY OBJ. 3: Christ dwells in men through faith, according to their present state, but He is in the blessed angels by manifest vision. Consequently the comparison does not hold, as stated above (ad 2).

Article 3

Whether the Just Man Alone May Eat Christ Sacramentally?

AD TERTIUM SIC PROCEDITUR. Videtur quod nullus possit manducare Christum sacramentaliter nisi homo iustus. Dicit enim Augustinus, in libro de remedio poenitentiae *ut quid paras dentem et ventrem? Crede, et manducasti. Credere enim in eum, hoc est panem vivum manducare.* Sed peccator non credit in eum, quia non habet fidem formatam, ad quam pertinet credere in Deum, ut in secunda parte habitum est. Ergo peccator non potest manducare hoc sacramentum, qui est panis vivus.

OBJECTION 1: It seems that none but the just man may eat Christ sacramentally. For Augustine says in his book De Remedio Penitentiae (*cf. Tract. in Joan.* xxv, n. 12; xxvi, n. 1): *Why make ready tooth and belly? Believe, and thou hast eaten . . . For to believe in Him, this it is, to eat the living bread.* But the sinner does not believe in Him; because he has not living faith, to which it belongs to believe *in God*, as stated above in the Second Part (II-II, Q. 2, A. 2; Q. 4, A. 5). Therefore the sinner cannot eat this sacrament, which is the living bread.

PRAETEREA, hoc sacramentum dicitur esse maxime sacramentum caritatis, ut supra dictum est. Sed, sicut infideles privantur fide, ita omnes peccatores sunt privati caritate. Infideles autem non videntur sacramentaliter posse sumere hoc sacramentum, cum in forma huius sacramenti dicatur, mysterium fidei. Ergo, pari ratione, nec aliquis peccatorum potest corpus Christi sacramentaliter manducare.

PRAETEREA, peccator magis est abominabilis Deo quam creatura irrationalis, dicitur enim in Psalmo de homine peccatore, *homo, cum in honore esset, non intellexit, comparatus est iumentis insipientibus, et similis factus est illis.* Sed animal brutum, puta mus aut canis, non potest sumere hoc sacramentum, sicut etiam non potest sumere sacramentum Baptismi. Ergo videtur quod, pari ratione, neque peccatores hoc sacramentum manducent.

SED CONTRA est quod super illud Ioan. VI, *ut si quis manducaverit non moriatur,* dicit Augustinus, *multi de altari accipiunt, et accipiendo moriuntur, unde dicit apostolus, iudicium sibi manducat et bibit.* Sed non moriuntur sumendo nisi peccatores. Ergo peccatores corpus Christi sacramentaliter manducant, et non solum iusti.

RESPONDEO dicendum quod circa hoc quidam antiqui erraverunt, dicentes quod corpus Christi nec etiam a peccatoribus sacramentaliter sumitur, sed, quam cito labiis peccatoris figitur, tam cito sub speciebus sacramentalibus desinit esse corpus Christi.

Sed hoc est erroneum. Derogat enim veritati huius sacramenti, ad quam pertinet, sicut supra dictum est, quod, manentibus speciebus corpus Christi sub eis esse non desinat. Species autem manent quandiu substantia panis maneret si ibi adesset, ut supra dictum est. Manifestum est autem quod substantia panis assumpta a peccatore non statim esse desinit, sed manet quandiu per calorem naturalem digeratur. Unde tandiu corpus Christi sub speciebus sacramentalibus manet a peccatoribus sumptis. Unde dicendum est quod peccator sacramentaliter corpus Christi manducare potest, et non solum iustus.

AD PRIMUM ergo dicendum quod verba illa, et similia, sunt intelligenda de spirituali manducatione, quae peccatoribus non convenit. Et ideo ex pravo intellectu horum verborum videtur praedictus error processisse, dum nescierunt distinguere inter corporalem et spiritualem manducationem.

AD SECUNDUM dicendum quod etiam si infidelis sumat species sacramentales, corpus Christi sub sacramento sumit. Unde manducat Christum sacramentaliter, si ly sacramentaliter determinat verbum ex parte manducati. Si autem ex parte manducantis, tunc, proprie loquendo, non manducat sacramentaliter, quia non utitur eo quod accipit ut sacramento, sed ut simplici cibo. Nisi forte infidelis intenderet recipere id quod Ecclesia confert, licet

OBJ. 2: Further, this sacrament is specially called *the sacrament of charity*, as stated above (Q. 78, A. 3, ad 6). But as unbelievers lack faith, so all sinners lack charity. Now unbelievers do not seem to be capable of eating this sacrament, since in the sacramental form it is called the *Mystery of Faith*. Therefore, for like reason, the sinner cannot eat Christ's body sacramentally.

OBJ. 3: Further, the sinner is more abominable before God than the irrational creature: for it is said of the sinner (Ps 48:21): *Man when he was in honor did not understand; he hath been compared to senseless beasts, and made like to them.* But an irrational animal, such as a mouse or a dog, cannot receive this sacrament, just as it cannot receive the sacrament of Baptism. Therefore it seems that for the like reason neither may sinners eat this sacrament.

ON THE CONTRARY, Augustine (*Tract. xxvi in Joan.*), commenting on the words, *that if any man eat of it he may not die*, says: *Many receive from the altar, and by receiving die: whence the Apostle saith, 'eateth and drinketh judgment to himself.'* But only sinners die by receiving. Therefore sinners eat the body of Christ sacramentally, and not the just only.

I ANSWER THAT, In the past, some have erred upon this point, saying that Christ's body is not received sacramentally by sinners; but that directly the body is touched by the lips of sinners, it ceases to be under the sacramental species.

But this is erroneous; because it detracts from the truth of this sacrament, to which truth it belongs that so long as the species last, Christ's body does not cease to be under them, as stated above (Q. 76, A. 6, ad 3; Q. 77, A. 8). But the species last so long as the substance of the bread would remain, if it were there, as was stated above (Q. 77, A. 4). Now it is clear that the substance of bread taken by a sinner does not at once cease to be, but it continues until digested by natural heat: hence Christ's body remains just as long under the sacramental species when taken by sinners. Hence it must be said that the sinner, and not merely the just, can eat Christ's body.

REPLY OBJ. 1: Such words and similar expressions are to be understood of spiritual eating, which does not belong to sinners. Consequently, it is from such expressions being misunderstood that the above error seems to have arisen, through ignorance of the distinction between corporeal and spiritual eating.

REPLY OBJ. 2: Should even an unbeliever receive the sacramental species, he would receive Christ's body under the sacrament: hence he would eat Christ sacramentally, if the word *sacramentally* qualify the verb on the part of the thing eaten. But if it qualify the verb on the part of the one eating, then, properly speaking, he does not eat sacramentally, because he uses what he takes, not as a sacrament, but as simple food. Unless perchance the unbeliever were to

non haberet fidem veram circa alios articulos, vel circa hoc sacramentum.

Ad tertium dicendum quod, etiam si mus aut canis hostiam consecratam manducet, substantia corporis Christi non desinet esse sub speciebus quandiu species illae manent, hoc est, quandiu substantia panis maneret, sicut etiam si proiiceretur in lutum. Nec hoc vergit in detrimentum dignitatis Christi, qui voluit a peccatoribus crucifigi absque diminutione suae dignitatis, praesertim cum mus aut canis non tangat ipsum corpus Christi secundum propriam speciem, sed solum secundum species sacramentales. Quidam autem dixerunt quod, statim cum sacramentum tangitur a mure vel cane, desinit ibi esse corpus Christi. Quod etiam derogat veritati sacramenti, sicut supra dictum est. Nec tamen dicendum est quod animal brutum sacramentaliter corpus Christi manducet, quia non est natum uti eo ut sacramento. Unde non sacramentaliter, sed per accidens corpus Christi manducat sicut manducaret ille qui sumeret hostiam consecratam quia nesciens eam esse consecratam. Et quia id quod est per accidens non cadit in divisione alicuius generis, ideo hic modus manducandi corpus Christi non ponitur tertius, praeter sacramentalem et spiritualem.

intend to receive what the Church bestows; without having proper faith regarding the other articles, or regarding this sacrament.

Reply Obj. 3: Even though a mouse or a dog were to eat the consecrated host, the substance of Christ's body would not cease to be under the species, so long as those species remain, and that is, so long as the substance of bread would have remained; just as if it were to be cast into the mire. Nor does this turn to any indignity regarding Christ's body, since He willed to be crucified by sinners without detracting from His dignity; especially since the mouse or dog does not touch Christ's body in its proper species, but only as to its sacramental species. Some, however, have said that Christ's body would cease to be there, directly it were touched by a mouse or a dog; but this again detracts from the truth of the sacrament, as stated above. None the less it must not be said that the irrational animal eats the body of Christ sacramentally; since it is incapable of using it as a sacrament. Hence it eats Christ's body accidentally, and not sacramentally, just as if anyone not knowing a host to be consecrated were to consume it. And since no genus is divided by an accidental difference, therefore this manner of eating Christ's body is not set down as a third way besides sacramental and spiritual eating.

Article 4

Whether the Sinner Sins in Receiving Christ's Body Sacramentally?

Ad quartum sic proceditur. Videtur quod peccator sumens corpus Christi sacramentaliter non peccet. Non enim est maioris dignitatis Christus sub specie sacramenti quam sub specie propria. Sed peccatores tangentes corpus Christi in substantia propria non peccabant, quin immo veniam peccatorum consequebantur, sicut legitur Luc. VII de muliere peccatrice; et Matth. XIV dicitur, *quicumque tetigerunt fimbriam vestimenti eius, salvi facti sunt.* Ergo non peccant, sed magis salutem consequuntur, sacramentum corporis Christi sumendo.

Praeterea, hoc sacramentum, sicut et alia, est quaedam spiritualis medicina. Sed medicina datur infirmis ad salutem, secundum illud Matth. IX, *non est opus valentibus medicus, sed male habentibus.* Infirmi autem vel male habentes spiritualiter sunt peccatores. Ergo hoc sacramentum sumi potest absque culpa.

Praeterea, hoc sacramentum, cum in se Christum contineat, est de maximis bonis. Maxima autem bona sunt, secundum Augustinum, in libro de Lib. Arbit., *quibus nullus male potest uti.* Nullus autem peccat nisi per abusum alicuius rei. Ergo nullus peccator sumens hoc sacramentum peccat.

Objection 1: It seems that the sinner does not sin in receiving Christ's body sacramentally, because Christ has no greater dignity under the sacramental species than under His own. But sinners did not sin when they touched Christ's body under its proper species; nay, rather they obtained forgiveness of their sins, as we read in Luke 7 of the woman who was a sinner; while it is written (Matt 14:36) that *as many as touched the hem of His garment were healed.* Therefore, they do not sin, but rather obtain salvation, by receiving the body of Christ.

Obj. 2: Further, this sacrament, like the others, is a spiritual medicine. But medicine is given to the sick for their recovery, according to Matt. 9:12: *They that are in health need not a physician.* Now they that are spiritually sick or infirm are sinners. Therefore this sacrament can be received by them without sin.

Obj. 3: Further, this sacrament is one of our greatest gifts, since it contains Christ. But according to Augustine (*De Lib. Arb.* ii), the greatest gifts are those *which no one can abuse.* Now no one sins except by abusing something. Therefore no sinner sins by receiving this sacrament.

PRAETEREA, sicut hoc sacramentum sentitur gustu et tactu, ita et visu. Si ergo peccator peccet ex eo quod sumit hoc sacramentum gustu et tactu, videtur quod etiam peccaret videndo. Quod patet esse falsum, cum Ecclesia omnibus hoc sacramentum videndum et adorandum proponat. Ergo peccator non peccat ex hoc quod manducat hoc sacramentum.

PRAETEREA, contingit quandoque quod aliquis peccator non habet conscientiam sui peccati. Nec tamen talis peccare videtur corpus Christi sumendo, quia, secundum hoc, omnes peccarent qui sumunt, quasi periculo se exponentes; cum apostolus dicit, I Cor. IV, *nihil mihi conscius sum, sed non in hoc iustificatus sum.* Non ergo videtur quod peccatori cedat in culpam si hoc sacramentum sumat.

SED CONTRA est quod apostolus dicit, I Cor. XI, *qui manducat et bibit indigne, iudicium sibi manducat et bibit.* Dicit autem Glossa ibidem, *indigne manducat et bibit qui in crimine est, vel irreverenter tractat.* Ergo qui est in peccato mortali, si hoc sacramentum accipiat, damnationem acquirit, mortaliter peccans.

RESPONDEO dicendum quod in hoc sacramento, sicut in aliis, id quod est sacramentum est signum eius quod est res sacramenti. Duplex autem est res huius sacramenti, sicut supra dictum est, una quidem quae est significata et contenta, scilicet ipse Christus; alia autem est significata et non contenta, scilicet corpus Christi mysticum, quod est societas sanctorum. Quicumque ergo hoc sacramentum sumit, ex hoc ipso significat se esse Christo unitum et membris eius incorporatum. Quod quidem fit per fidem formatam, quam nullus habet cum peccato mortali. Et ideo manifestum est quod quicumque cum peccato mortali hoc sacramentum sumit, falsitatem in hoc sacramento committit. Et ideo incurrit sacrilegium, tanquam sacramenti violator. Et propter hoc mortaliter peccat.

AD PRIMUM ergo dicendum quod Christus in propria specie apparens non exhibebat se tangendum hominibus in signum spiritualis unionis ad ipsum, sicut exhibetur sumendus in hoc sacramento. Et ideo peccatores eum in propria specie tangentes non incurrebant crimen falsitatis circa divina, sicut peccatores sumentes hoc sacramentum.

Et praeterea Christus adhuc gerebat similitudinem carnis peccati, et ideo convenienter se peccatoribus tangendum exhibebat. Sed, remota similitudine carnis peccati per gloriam resurrectionis se tangi prohibuit a muliere, quae defectum fidei circa ipsum patiebatur, secundum illud Ioan. XX, *noli me tangere, nondum enim ascendi ad patrem meum,* scilicet in corde tuo, ut Augustinus exponit. Et ideo peccatores, qui defectum fidei patiuntur formatae circa ipsum, repelluntur a contactu huius sacramenti.

OBJ. 4: Further, as this sacrament is perceived by taste and touch, so also is it by sight. Consequently, if the sinner sins by receiving the sacrament, it seems that he would sin by beholding it, which is manifestly untrue, since the Church exposes this sacrament to be seen and adored by all. Therefore the sinner does not sin by eating this sacrament.

OBJ. 5: Further, it happens sometimes that the sinner is unconscious of his sin. Yet such a one does not seem to sin by receiving the body of Christ, for according to this all who receive it would sin, as exposing themselves to danger, since the Apostle says (1 Cor 4:4): *I am not conscious to myself of anything, yet I am not hereby justified.* Therefore, the sinner, if he receive this sacrament, does not appear to be guilty of sin.

ON THE CONTRARY, The Apostle says (1 Cor 11:29): *He that eateth and drinketh unworthily, eateth and drinketh judgment to himself.* Now the gloss says on this passage: *He eats and drinks unworthily who is in sin, or who handles it irreverently.* Therefore, if anyone, while in mortal sin, receives this sacrament, he purchases damnation, by sinning mortally.

I ANSWER THAT, In this sacrament, as in the others, that which is a sacrament is a sign of the reality of the sacrament. Now there is a twofold reality of this sacrament, as stated above (Q. 73, A. 6): one which is signified and contained, namely, Christ Himself; while the other is signified but not contained, namely, Christ's mystical body, which is the fellowship of the saints. Therefore, whoever receives this sacrament, expresses thereby that he is made one with Christ, and incorporated in His members; and this is done by living faith, which no one has who is in mortal sin. And therefore it is manifest that whoever receives this sacrament while in mortal sin, is guilty of lying to this sacrament, and consequently of sacrilege, because he profanes the sacrament: and therefore he sins mortally.

REPLY OBJ. 1: When Christ appeared under His proper species, He did not give Himself to be touched by men as a sign of spiritual union with Himself, as He gives Himself to be received in this sacrament. And therefore sinners in touching Him under His proper species did not incur the sin of lying to Godlike things, as sinners do in receiving this sacrament.

Furthermore, Christ still bore the likeness of the body of sin; consequently He fittingly allowed Himself to be touched by sinners. But as soon as the body of sin was taken away by the glory of the Resurrection, he forbade the woman to touch Him, for her faith in Him was defective, according to John 20:17: *Do not touch Me, for I am not yet ascended to My Father,* i.e., *in your heart,* as Augustine explains (*Tract. cxxi in Joan.*). And therefore sinners, who lack living faith regarding Christ are not allowed to touch this sacrament.

AD SECUNDUM dicendum quod non quaelibet medicina competit secundum quemlibet statum. Nam medicina quae datur iam liberatis a febre ad confortationem, noceret si daretur adhuc febricitantibus. Ita etiam Baptismus et poenitentia sunt medicinae purgativae, quae dantur ad tollendam febrem peccati. Hoc autem sacramentum est medicina confortativa, quae non debet dari nisi liberatis a peccato.

AD TERTIUM dicendum quod maxima bona ibi intelligit Augustinus virtutes animae, quibus nullus male utitur quasi principiis mali usus. Utitur tamen eis aliquis male quasi obiectis mali usus, ut patet in his qui de virtutibus superbiunt. Ita et hoc sacramentum, quantum est ex se, non est principium mali usus, sed obiectum. Unde Augustinus dicit, *multi indigne accipiunt corpus domini, per quod docemur quam cavendum sit male accipere bonum. Ecce enim, factum est malum dum male accipitur bonum, sicut e contra apostolo factum est bonum cum bene accipitur malum, scilicet cum stimulus Satanae patienter portatur.*

AD QUARTUM dicendum quod per visum non accipitur ipsum corpus Christi, sed solum sacramentum eius, quia scilicet non pertingit visus ad substantiam corporis Christi, sed solum ad species sacramentales, ut supra dictum est. Sed ille qui manducat, non solum sumit species sacramentales, sed etiam Christum, qui est sub eis. Et ideo a visione corporis Christi nullus prohibetur qui sit sacramentum Christi consecutus, scilicet Baptismum, nonbaptizati autem non sunt admittendi etiam ad inspectionem huius sacramenti, ut patet per Dionysium, in libro Eccles. Hier. Sed ad manducationem non sunt admittendi nisi soli illi qui non solum sacramentaliter, sed etiam realiter sunt Christo coniuncti.

AD QUINTUM dicendum quod hoc quod non habet aliquis conscientiam sui peccati, potest contingere dupliciter. Uno modo, per culpam suam, vel quia per ignorantiam iuris, quae non excusat, reputat non esse peccatum quod est peccatum, puta si aliquis fornicator reputaret simplicem fornicationem non esse peccatum mortale; vel quia negligens est in examinatione sui ipsius, contra id quod apostolus dicit, I Cor. XI, *probet autem seipsum homo, et sic de pane illo edat et de calice bibat.* Et sic nihilominus peccat peccator sumens corpus Christi, licet non habeat conscientiam peccati, quia ipsa ignorantia est ei peccatum.

Alio modo potest contingere sine culpa ipsius, puta, cum doluit de peccato, sed non est sufficienter contritus. Et in tali casu non peccat sumendo corpus Christi, quia homo per certitudinem scire non potest utrum sit vere contritus. Sufficit tamen si in se signa contritionis inveniat, puta ut doleat de praeteritis et proponat cavere de

REPLY OBJ. 2: Every medicine does not suit every stage of sickness; because the tonic given to those who are recovering from fever would be hurtful to them if given while yet in their feverish condition. So likewise Baptism and Penance are as purgative medicines, given to take away the fever of sin; whereas this sacrament is a medicine given to strengthen, and it ought not to be given except to them who are quit of sin.

REPLY OBJ. 3: By the greatest gifts Augustine understands the soul's virtues, *which no one uses to evil purpose,* as though they were principles of evil. Nevertheless sometimes a man makes a bad use of them, as objects of an evil use, as is seen in those who are proud of their virtues. So likewise this sacrament, so far as the sacrament is concerned, is not the principle of an evil use, but the object thereof. Hence Augustine says (*Tract. lxii in Joan.*): *Many receive Christ's body unworthily; whence we are taught what need there is to beware of receiving a good thing evilly . . . For behold, of a good thing, received evilly, evil is wrought*: just as on the other hand, in the Apostle's case, *good was wrought through evil well received*, namely, by bearing patiently the sting of Satan.

REPLY OBJ. 4: Christ's body is not received by being seen, but only its sacrament, because sight does not penetrate to the substance of Christ's body, but only to the sacramental species, as stated above (Q. 76, A. 7). But he who eats, receives not only the sacramental species, but likewise Christ Himself Who is under them. Consequently, no one is forbidden to behold Christ's body, when once he has received Christ's sacrament, namely, Baptism: whereas the non-baptized are not to be allowed even to see this sacrament, as is clear from Dionysius (*Eccl. Hier.* vii). But only those are to be allowed to share in the eating who are united with Christ not merely sacramentally, but likewise really.

REPLY OBJ. 5: The fact of a man being unconscious of his sin can come about in two ways. First of all through his own fault, either because through ignorance of the law (which ignorance does not excuse him), he thinks something not to be sinful which is a sin, as for example if one guilty of fornication were to deem simple fornication not to be a mortal sin; or because he neglects to examine his conscience, which is opposed to what the Apostle says (1 Cor 11:28): *Let a man prove himself, and so let him eat of that bread, and drink of the chalice.* And in this way nevertheless the sinner who receives Christ's body commits sin, although unconscious thereof, because the very ignorance is a sin on his part.

Second, it may happen without fault on his part, as, for instance, when he has sorrowed over his sin, but is not sufficiently contrite: and in such a case he does not sin in receiving the body of Christ, because a man cannot know for certain whether he is truly contrite. It suffices, however, if he find in himself the marks of contrition, for instance, if

futuris. Si vero ignorat hoc quod fecit esse actum peccati propter ignorantiam facti, quae excusat, puta si accessit ad non suam quam credebat esse suam, non est ex hoc dicendus peccator. Similiter etiam, si totaliter est peccatum oblitus, sufficit ad eius deletionem generalis contritio, ut infra dicetur. Unde iam non est dicendus peccator.

he *grieve over past sins*, and *propose to avoid them in the future*. But if he be ignorant that what he did was a sinful act, through ignorance of the fact, which excuses, for instance, if a man approach a woman whom he believed to be his wife whereas she was not, he is not to be called a sinner on that account; in the same way if he has utterly forgotten his sin, general contrition suffices for blotting it out, as will be said hereafter (Suppl., Q. 2, A. 3, ad 2); hence he is no longer to be called a sinner.

Article 5

Whether to Approach This Sacrament with Consciousness of Sin Is the Gravest of All Sins?

AD QUINTUM SIC PROCEDITUR. Videtur quod accedere ad hoc sacramentum cum conscientia peccati sit gravissimum omnium peccatorum. Dicit enim apostolus, I Cor. XI, *quicumque manducaverit panem et biberit calicem domini indigne, reus erit corporis et sanguinis domini*, Glossa ibidem, *ac si Christum occiderit, punietur*. Sed peccatum Christum occidentium videtur fuisse gravissimum. Ergo et hoc peccatum, quo aliquis cum conscientia peccati ad mensam domini accedit, videtur esse gravissimum.

PRAETEREA, Hieronymus dicit, in quadam epistola, *quid tibi cum feminis, qui ad altare cum domino fabularis? Dic, sacerdos, dic, clerice, qualiter cum eisdem labiis filium Dei oscularis quibus osculatus es filiam meretricis. O Iuda, osculo filium hominis tradis.* Et sic videtur fornicator ad mensam Christi accedens peccare sicut Iudas peccavit, cuius peccatum fuit gravissimum. Sed multa alia peccata sunt graviora quam peccatum fornicationis, et praecipue peccatum infidelitatis. Ergo cuiuslibet peccatoris ad mensam Christi accedentis peccatum est gravissimum.

PRAETEREA, magis est abominabilis Deo immunditia spiritualis quam corporalis. Sed si quis proiiceret corpus Christi in lutum vel sterquilinium, gravissimum reputaretur esse peccatum. Ergo gravius peccat si ipsum sumat cum peccato, quod est immunditia spiritualis. Ergo hoc peccatum est gravissimum.

SED CONTRA est quod, super illud Ioan. XV, *si non venissem, et locutus eis non fuissem, peccatum non haberent*, dicit Augustinus hoc esse intelligendum de peccato infidelitatis, quo retinentur cuncta peccata. Et ita videtur hoc peccatum non esse gravissimum, sed magis peccatum infidelitatis.

RESPONDEO dicendum quod, sicut in secunda parte habitum est, dupliciter aliquod peccatum potest dici gravius alio, uno modo, per se; alio modo, per accidens. Per se quidem, secundum rationem suae speciei, quae attenditur ex parte obiecti. Et secundum hoc, quanto

OBJECTION 1: It seems that to approach this sacrament with consciousness of sin is the gravest of all sins; because the Apostle says (1 Cor 11:27): *Whosoever shall eat this bread, or drink the chalice of the Lord unworthily, shall be guilty of the body and of the blood of the Lord*: upon which the gloss observes: *He shall be punished as though he slew Christ.* But the sin of them who slew Christ seems to have been most grave. Therefore this sin, whereby a man approaches Christ's table with consciousness of sin, appears to be the gravest.

OBJ. 2: Further, Jerome says in an Epistle (xlix): *What hast thou to do with women, thou that speakest familiarly with God at the altar? Say, priest, say, cleric, how dost thou kiss the Son of God with the same lips wherewith thou hast kissed the daughter of a harlot? Judas, thou betrayest the Son of Man with a kiss!* And thus it appears that the fornicator approaching Christ's table sins as Judas did, whose sin was most grave. But there are many other sins which are graver than fornication, especially the sin of unbelief. Therefore the sin of every sinner approaching Christ's table is the gravest of all.

OBJ. 3: Further, spiritual uncleanness is more abominable to God than corporeal. But if anyone was to cast Christ's body into mud or a cess-pool, his sin would be reputed a most grave one. Therefore, he sins more deeply by receiving it with sin, which is spiritual uncleanness, upon his soul.

ON THE CONTRARY, Augustine says on the words, *If I had not come, and had not spoken to them, they would be without sin* (*Tract. lxxxix in Joan.*), that this is to be understood of the sin of unbelief, *in which all sins are comprised*, and so the greatest of all sins appears to be, not this, but rather the sin of unbelief.

I ANSWER THAT, As stated in the Second Part (I-II, Q. 73, AA. 3, 6; II-II, Q. 73, A. 3), one sin can be said to be graver than another in two ways: first of all essentially, second accidentally. Essentially, in regard to its species, which is taken from its object: and so a sin is greater according

id contra quod peccatur est maius, tanto peccatum est gravius. Et quia divinitas Christi est maior humanitate ipsius; et ipsa humanitas est potior quam sacramenta humanitatis, inde est quod gravissima peccata sunt quae committuntur in ipsam divinitatem, sicut est peccatum infidelitatis et blasphemiae. Secundario autem sunt gravia peccata quae committuntur in humanitatem Christi, unde Matth. XII dicitur, *qui dixerit verbum contra filium hominis, remittetur ei, qui autem dixerit verbum contra spiritum sanctum, non remittetur ei neque in hoc saeculo neque in futuro.* Tertio autem loco sunt peccata quae committuntur contra sacramenta, quae pertinent ad humanitatem Christi. Et post hoc sunt alia peccata, contra puras creaturas.

Per accidens autem unum peccatum est gravius alio ex parte peccantis, puta, peccatum quod est ex ignorantia vel infirmitate, est levius peccato quod est ex contemptu vel ex certa scientia; et eadem ratio est de aliis circumstantiis. Et secundum hoc, illud peccatum in quibusdam potest esse gravius, sicut in his qui ex actuali contemptu cum conscientia peccati ad hoc sacramentum accedunt; in quibusdam vero minus grave, puta in his qui ex quodam timore ne deprehendantur in peccato, cum conscientia peccati ad hoc sacramentum accedunt.

Sic igitur patet quod hoc peccatum est multis aliis gravius secundum suam speciem, non tamen omnium gravissimum.

Ad primum ergo dicendum quod peccatum indigne sumentium hoc sacramentum comparatur peccato occidentium Christum secundum similitudinem, quia utrumque committitur contra corpus Christi, non tamen secundum criminis quantitatem. Peccatum enim occidentium Christum fuit multo gravius. Primo quidem, quia illud peccatum fuit contra corpus Christi in sua specie propria, hoc autem est contra corpus Christi in specie sacramenti. Secundo, quia illud peccatum processit ex intentione nocendi Christo, non autem hoc peccatum.

Ad secundum dicendum quod fornicator accipiens corpus Christi comparatur Iudae Christum osculanti, quantum ad similitudinem criminis, quia uterque ex signo caritatis Christum offendit, non tamen quantum ad criminis quantitatem, sicut et prius dictum est. Haec tamen similitudo non minus competit aliis peccatoribus quam fornicatoribus, nam et per alia peccata mortalia agitur contra caritatem Christi, cuius signum est hoc sacramentum; et tanto magis quanto peccata sunt graviora. Secundum quid tamen peccatum fornicationis magis reddit hominem ineptum ad perceptionem huius sacramenti, inquantum scilicet per hoc peccatum spiritus maxime carni subiicitur, et ita impeditur fervor dilectionis, qui requiritur in hoc sacramento.

Plus tamen ponderat impedimentum ipsius caritatis quam fervoris eius. Unde etiam peccatum infidelitatis,

as that against which it is committed is greater. And since Christ's Godhead is greater than His humanity, and His humanity greater than the sacraments of His humanity, hence it is that those are the gravest sins which are committed against the Godhead, such as unbelief and blasphemy. The second degree of gravity is held by those sins which are committed against His humanity: hence it is written (Matt 12:32): *Whosoever shall speak a word against the Son of Man, it shall be forgiven him; but he that shall speak against the Holy Spirit, it shall not be forgiven him, neither in this world nor in the world to come.* In the third place come sins committed against the sacraments, which belong to Christ's humanity; and after these are the other sins committed against mere creatures.

Accidentally, one sin can be graver than another on the sinner's part. For example, the sin which is the result of ignorance or of weakness is lighter than one arising from contempt, or from sure knowledge; and the same reason holds good of other circumstances. And according to this, the above sin can be graver in some, as happens in them who from actual contempt and with consciousness of sin approach this sacrament: but in others it is less grave; for instance, in those who from fear of their sin being discovered, approach this sacrament with consciousness of sin.

So, then, it is evident that this sin is specifically graver than many others, yet it is not the greatest of all.

Reply Obj. 1: The sin of the unworthy recipient is compared to the sin of them who slew Christ, by way of similitude, because each is committed against Christ's body; but not according to the degree of the crime. Because the sin of Christ's slayers was much graver, first of all, because their sin was against Christ's body in its own species, while this sin is against it under sacramental species; second, because their sin came of the intent of injuring Christ, while this does not.

Reply Obj. 2: The sin of the fornicator receiving Christ's body is likened to Judas kissing Christ, as to the resemblance of the sin, because each outrages Christ with the sign of friendship. but not as to the extent of the sin, as was observed above (ad 1). And this resemblance in crime applies no less to other sinners than to fornicators: because by other mortal sins, sinners act against the charity of Christ, of which this sacrament is the sign, and all the more according as their sins are graver. But in a measure the sin of fornication makes one more unfit for receiving this sacrament, because thereby especially the spirit becomes enslaved by the flesh, which is a hindrance to the fervor of love required for this sacrament.

However, the hindrance to charity itself weighs more than the hindrance to its fervor. Hence the sin of unbelief,

quod funditus separat hominem ab Ecclesiae unitate, simpliciter loquendo, maxime hominem ineptum reddit ad susceptionem huius sacramenti, quod est sacramentum ecclesiasticae unitatis, ut dictum est. Unde et gravius peccat infidelis accipiens hoc sacramentum quam peccator fidelis; et magis contemnit Christum secundum quod est sub hoc sacramento, praesertim si non credat Christum vere sub hoc sacramento esse, quia, quantum est in se, diminuit sanctitatem huius sacramenti, et virtutem Christi operantis in hoc sacramento, quod est contemnere ipsum sacramentum in seipso. Fidelis autem qui cum conscientia peccati sumit, contemnit hoc sacramentum non in seipso, sed quantum ad usum, indigne accipiens. Unde et apostolus, I Cor. XI, assignans rationem huius peccati, dicit, *non diiudicans corpus domini*, idest, non discernens ipsum ab aliis cibis, quod maxime facit ille qui non credit Christum esse sub hoc sacramento.

Ad tertium dicendum quod ille qui proiiceret hoc sacramentum in lutum, gravius peccaret quam ille qui cum conscientia peccati mortalis ad hoc sacramentum accedit. Primo quidem, quia ille hoc faceret ex intentione iniuriam inferendi huic sacramento, quod non intendit peccator indigne corpus Christi accipiens. Secundo, quia homo peccator capax est gratiae, unde etiam magis est aptus ad suscipiendum hoc sacramentum quam quaecumque alia irrationalis creatura. Unde maxime inordinate uteretur hoc sacramento qui proiiceret ipsum canibus ad manducandum, vel qui proiiceret in lutum conculcandum.

which fundamentally severs a man from the unity of the Church, simply speaking, makes him to be utterly unfit for receiving this sacrament; because it is the sacrament of the Church's unity, as stated above (Q. 61, A. 2). Hence the unbeliever who receives this sacrament sins more grievously than the believer who is in sin; and shows greater contempt towards Christ Who is in the sacrament, especially if he does not believe Christ to be truly in this sacrament; because, so far as lies in him, he lessens the holiness of the sacrament, and the power of Christ acting in it, and this is to despise the sacrament in itself. But the believer who receives the sacrament with consciousness of sin, by receiving it unworthily despises the sacrament, not in itself, but in its use. Hence the Apostle (1 Cor 11:29) in assigning the cause of this sin, says, *not discerning the body of the Lord*, that is, not distinguishing it from other food: and this is what he does who disbelieves Christ's presence in this sacrament.

Reply Obj. 3: The man who would throw this sacrament into the mire would be guilty of more heinous sin than another approaching the sacrament fully conscious of mortal sin. First of all, because he would intend to outrage the sacrament, whereas the sinner receiving Christ's body unworthily has no such intent; second, because the sinner is capable of grace; hence he is more capable of receiving this sacrament than any irrational creature. Hence he would make a most revolting use of this sacrament who would throw it to dogs to eat, or fling it in the mire to be trodden upon.

Article 6

Whether the Priest Ought to Deny the Body of Christ to the Sinner Seeking It?

Ad sextum sic proceditur. Videtur quod sacerdos debeat denegare corpus Christi peccatori petenti. Non est enim faciendum contra Christi praeceptum propter vitandum scandalum, neque propter vitandum infamiam alicuius. Sed dominus praecepit, Matth. VII, *nolite sanctum dare canibus.* Maxime autem datur sanctum canibus cum hoc sacramentum peccatoribus exhibetur. Ergo neque propter vitandum scandalum, neque propter vitandam infamiam alicuius, debet hoc sacramentum peccatori petenti dari.

Praeterea, de duobus malis est minus malum eligendum. Sed minus malum esse videtur si peccator infametur, vel etiam si ei hostia non consecrata detur, quam si sumens corpus Christi mortaliter peccet. Ergo videtur hoc potius eligendum, quod vel infametur peccator petens corpus Christi, vel etiam detur ei hostia non consecrata.

Objection 1: It seems that the priest should deny the body of Christ to the sinner seeking it. For Christ's precept is not to be set aside for the sake of avoiding scandal or on account of infamy to anyone. But (Matt 7:6) our Lord gave this command: *Give not that which is holy to dogs.* Now it is especially casting holy things to dogs to give this sacrament to sinners. Therefore, neither on account of avoiding scandal or infamy should this sacrament be administered to the sinner who asks for it.

Obj. 2: Further, one must choose the lesser of two evils. But it seems to be the lesser evil if the sinner incur infamy; or if an unconsecrated host be given to him; than for him to sin mortally by receiving the body of Christ. Consequently, it seems that the course to be adopted is either that the sinner seeking the body of Christ be exposed to infamy, or that an unconsecrated host be given to him.

PRAETEREA, corpus Christi interdum datur suspectis de crimine ad eorum manifestationem, legitur enim in decretis, II, qu. IV, *saepe contingit ut in monasteriis monachorum furta perpetrentur. Idcirco statuimus ut, quando ipsi fratres de talibus expurgare se debent, Missa ab abbate celebretur vel ab aliquo ex praesentibus fratribus, et sic, expleta Missa, omnes communicent in haec verba, corpus Christi sit tibi hodie ad probationem.* Et infra, *si episcopo vel presbytero aliquod maleficium fuerit imputatum, in singulis Missa celebrari debet et communicari, et de singulis sibi imputatis innocentem se ostendere.* Sed peccatores occultos non oportet manifestari, quia, si frontem verecundiae abiecerint, liberius peccabunt, ut Augustinus dicit, in libro de verbis domini. Ergo peccatoribus occultis non est corpus Christi dandum, etiam si petant.

SED CONTRA est quod, super illud Psalmi, *manducaverunt et adoraverunt omnes pingues terrae,* dicit Augustinus, *non prohibeat dispensator pingues terrae,* idest peccatores, mensam domini manducare.

RESPONDEO dicendum quod circa peccatores distinguendum est. Quidam enim sunt occulti, quidam vero manifesti; scilicet per evidentiam facti, sicut publici usurarii aut publici raptores; vel etiam per aliquod iudicium ecclesiasticum vel saeculare. Manifestis ergo peccatoribus non debet, etiam petentibus, sacra communio dari. Unde Cyprianus scribit ad quendam, *pro dilectione tua consulendum me existimasti quid mihi videatur de histrionibus, et mago illo qui, apud vos constitutus, adhuc in artis suae dedecore perseverat, an talibus sacra communio cum ceteris Christianis debeat dari. Puto nec maiestati divinae, nec evangelicae disciplinae congruere ut pudor et honor Ecclesiae tam turpi et infami contagione foedetur.*

Si vero non sunt manifesti peccatores sed occulti, non potest eis petentibus sacra communio denegari. Cum enim quilibet Christianus, ex hoc ipso quod est baptizatus, sit admissus ad mensam dominicam, non potest eis ius suum tolli nisi pro aliqua causa manifesta. Unde super illud I Cor. V, *si is qui frater inter vos nominatur* etc., dicit Glossa Augustini, *nos a communione quemquam prohibere non possumus, nisi aut sponte confessum, aut in aliquo iudicio vel ecclesiastico vel saeculari nominatum atque convictum.* Potest tamen sacerdos qui est conscius criminis, occulte monere peccatorem occultum, vel etiam in publico generaliter omnes, ne ad mensam domini accedant antequam poeniteant et Ecclesiae reconcilientur. Nam post poenitentiam et reconciliationem, etiam publicis peccatoribus non est communio deneganda, praecipue in mortis articulo. Unde in Concilio Carthaginensi legitur, *scenicis atque histrionibus ceterisque huiusmodi personis, vel apostatis, conversis ad Deum reconciliatio non negetur.*

OBJ. 3: Further, the body of Christ is sometimes given to those suspected of crime in order to put them to proof. Because we read in the *Decretals*: *It often happens that thefts are perpetrated in monasteries of monks; wherefore we command that when the brethren have to exonerate themselves of such acts, that the abbot shall celebrate Mass, or someone else deputed by him, in the presence of the community; and so, when the Mass is over, all shall communicate under these words: 'May the body of Christ prove thee today.'* And further on: *If any evil deed be imputed to a bishop or priest, for each charge he must say Mass and communicate, and show that he is innocent of each act imputed.* But secret sinners must not be disclosed, for, once the blush of shame is set aside, they will indulge the more in sin, as Augustine says (*De Verbis. Dom.*; cf. *Serm. lxxxii*). Consequently, Christ's body is not to be given to occult sinners, even if they ask for it.

ON THE CONTRARY, on Ps. 21:30: *All the fat ones of the earth have eaten and have adored,* Augustine says: *Let not the dispenser hinder the fat ones of the earth,* i.e., sinners, *from eating at the table of the Lord.*

I ANSWER THAT, A distinction must be made among sinners: some are secret; others are notorious, either from evidence of the fact, as public usurers, or public robbers, or from being denounced as evil men by some ecclesiastical or civil tribunal. Therefore Holy Communion ought not to be given to open sinners when they ask for it. Hence Cyprian writes to someone (*Ep. lxi*): *You were so kind as to consider that I ought to be consulted regarding actors, and that magician who continues to practice his disgraceful arts among you; as to whether I thought that Holy Communion ought to be given to such with the other Christians. I think that it is beseeming neither the Divine majesty, nor Christian discipline, for the Church's modesty and honor to be defiled by such shameful and infamous contagion.*

But if they be not open sinners, but occult, the Holy Communion should not be denied them if they ask for it. For since every Christian, from the fact that he is baptized, is admitted to the Lord's table, he may not be robbed of his right, except from some open cause. Hence on 1 Cor. 5:11, *If he who is called a brother among you,* etc., Augustine's gloss remarks: *We cannot inhibit any person from Communion, except he has openly confessed, or has been named and convicted by some ecclesiastical or lay tribunal.* Nevertheless a priest who has knowledge of the crime can privately warn the secret sinner, or warn all openly in public, from approaching the Lord's table, until they have repented of their sins and have been reconciled to the Church; because after repentance and reconciliation, Communion must not be refused even to public sinners, especially in the hour of death. Hence in the (3rd) Council of Carthage (Can. xxxv) we read: *Reconciliation is not to be denied to stage-players or actors, or others of the sort, or to apostates, after their conversion to God.*

AD PRIMUM ergo dicendum quod sancta prohibentur dari canibus, idest peccatoribus manifestis. Sed occulta non possunt publice puniri, sed sunt divino iudicio reservanda.

AD SECUNDUM dicendum quod, licet peius sit peccatori occulto peccare mortaliter sumendo corpus Christi quam infamari, tamen sacerdoti ministranti corpus Christi peius est peccare mortaliter infamando iniuste peccatorem occultum, quam quod ille mortaliter peccet, quia nullus debet peccatum mortale committere ut alium liberet a peccato. Unde Augustinus dicit, in libro quaestionum super Gen., *periculosissime admittitur haec compensatio, ut nos faciamus aliquid mali, ne alius gravius malum faciat.* Peccator tamen occultus potius deberet eligere infamari quam indigne ad mensam Christi accedere.

Hostia tamen non consecrata nullo modo debet dari loco consecratae, quia sacerdos hoc faciens, quantum est in se, facit idololatrare illos qui credunt hostiam consecratam, sive alios praesentes, sive etiam ipsum sumentem; quia, ut Augustinus dicit, *nemo carnem Christi manducet nisi prius adoret.* Unde extra, de celebratione Missarum, cap. de homine, dicitur, *licet is qui pro sui criminis conscientia reputat se indignum, peccet graviter si se ingerat, tamen gravius videtur offendere qui fraudulenter illud praesumpserit simulare.*

AD TERTIUM dicendum quod decreta illa sunt abrogata per contraria documenta Romanorum pontificum. Dicit enim Stephanus Papa, *ferri candentis vel aquae ferventis examinatione confessionem extorqueri a quolibet sacri canones non concedunt. Spontanea enim confessione, vel testium approbatione publicata, delicta commissa sunt regimini nostro iudicare, occulta vero et incognita illi sunt relinquenda qui solus novit corda filiorum hominum.* Et idem habetur extra, de purgationibus, cap. ex tuarum. In omnibus enim talibus videtur Dei esse tentatio, unde sine peccato fieri non possunt. Et gravius videretur si in hoc sacramento, quod est institutum ad remedium salutis, aliquis incurreret iudicium mortis. Unde nullo modo corpus Christi debet dari alicui suspecto de crimine quasi ad examinationem.

REPLY OBJ. 1: Holy things are forbidden to be given to dogs, that is, to notorious sinners: whereas hidden deeds may not be published, but are to be left to the Divine judgment.

REPLY OBJ. 2: Although it is worse for the secret sinner to sin mortally in taking the body of Christ, rather than be defamed, nevertheless for the priest administering the body of Christ it is worse to commit mortal sin by unjustly defaming the hidden sinner than that the sinner should sin mortally; because no one ought to commit mortal sin in order to keep another out of mortal sin. Hence Augustine says (*Quaest. super Gen.* 42): *It is a most dangerous exchange, for us to do evil lest another perpetrate a greater evil.* But the secret sinner ought rather to prefer infamy than approach the Lord's table unworthily.

Yet by no means should an unconsecrated host be given in place of a consecrated one; because the priest by so doing, so far as he is concerned, makes others, either the bystanders or the communicant, commit idolatry by believing that it is a consecrated host; because, as Augustine says on Ps. 98:5: *Let no one eat Christ's flesh, except he first adore it.* Hence in the *Decretals* (Extra, *De Celeb. Miss.*, Ch. *De Homine*) it is said: *Although he who reputes himself unworthy of the Sacrament, through consciousness of his sin, sins gravely, if he receive; still he seems to offend more deeply who deceitfully has presumed to simulate it.*

REPLY OBJ. 3: Those decrees were abolished by contrary enactments of Roman Pontiffs: because Pope Stephen V writes as follows: *The Sacred Canons do not allow of a confession being extorted from any person by trial made by burning iron or boiling water; it belongs to our government to judge of public crimes committed, and that by means of confession made spontaneously, or by proof of witnesses: but private and unknown crimes are to be left to Him Who alone knows the hearts of the sons of men.* And the same is found in the *Decretals* (Extra, *De Purgationibus*, Ch. *Ex tuarum*). Because in all such practices there seems to be a tempting of God; hence such things cannot be done without sin. And it would seem graver still if anyone were to incur judgment of death through this sacrament, which was instituted as a means of salvation. Consequently, the body of Christ should never be given to anyone suspected of crime, as by way of examination.

Article 7

Whether the Seminal Loss That Occurs During Sleep Hinders Anyone from Receiving This Sacrament?

AD SEPTIMUM SIC PROCEDITUR. Videtur quod nocturna pollutio non impediat aliquem a sumptione corporis Christi. Nullus enim impeditur a sumptione

OBJECTION 1: It seems that seminal loss does not hinder anyone from receiving the body of Christ: because no one is prevented from receiving the body of Christ except

corporis Christi nisi propter peccatum. Sed nocturna pollutio accidit sine peccato, dicit enim Augustinus, XII super Gen. ad Litt., *ipsa phantasia quae fit in cogitatione sermocinantis, cum expressa fuerit in visione somniantis, ut inter illam et veram coniunctionem corporum non discernatur, continue movetur caro et sequitur quod eum motum sequi solet, cum hoc tam sine peccato fiat quam sine peccato a vigilantibus dicitur quod, ut diceretur, procul dubio cogitatum est.* Ergo nocturna pollutio non impedit hominem ab huius sacramenti perceptione.

PRAETEREA, Gregorius dicit, in epistola ad Augustinum episcopum Anglorum, *si quis sua coniuge, non cupidine voluptatis raptus, sed tantum creandorum liberorum gratia utitur, ille profecto, sive de ingressu Ecclesiae seu de sumendo corporis dominici mysterio, suo est iudicio relinquendus, quia prohiberi a nobis non debet accipere qui, in igne positus, nescit ardere.*

Ex quo patet quod carnalis pollutio etiam vigilantis, si sit sine peccato, non prohibet hominem a sumptione corporis Christi. Multo igitur minus prohibet nocturna pollutio dormientis.

PRAETEREA, nocturna pollutio videtur solam immunditiam corporalem habere. Sed aliae immunditiae corporales, quae secundum legem impediebant ab ingressu sanctorum, in nova lege non impediunt a sumptione corporis Christi, sicut de muliere pariente, vel menstruata, vel fluxum sanguinis patiente, scribit beatus Gregorius Augustino Anglorum episcopo. Ergo videtur quod neque etiam nocturna pollutio impediat hominem a sumptione huius sacramenti.

PRAETEREA, peccatum veniale non impedit hominem a sumptione huius sacramenti, sed nec etiam peccatum mortale post poenitentiam sed, dato quod nocturna pollutio provenerit ex aliquo peccato praecedenti sive crapulae sive turpium cogitationum, plerumque tale peccatum est veniale, et, si aliquando sit mortale, potest contingere quod de mane poenitet et peccatum suum confitetur. Ergo videtur quod non debeat impediri a sumptione huius sacramenti.

PRAETEREA, gravius peccatum est homicidii quam fornicationis. Sed si aliquis de nocte somniet homicidium perpetrare aut furtum, vel quodcumque aliud peccatum, non propter hoc impeditur a sumptione corporis Christi. Ergo videtur quod multo minus fornicatio somniata, cum pollutione subsequente, impediat a susceptione huius sacramenti.

SED CONTRA est quod Levit. XV dicitur, *vir a quocumque egreditur semen coitus, immundus erit usque ad vesperam.* Sed immundis non patet aditus ad sacramenta. Ergo videtur quod propter pollutionem nocturnam

on account of sin. But seminal loss happens without sin: for Augustine says (*Gen ad lit.* xii) that *the same image that comes into the mind of a speaker may present itself to the mind of the sleeper, so that the latter be unable to distinguish the image from the reality, and is moved carnally and with the result that usually follows such motions; and there is as little sin in this as there is in speaking and therefore thinking about such things.* Consequently these motions do not prevent one from receiving this sacrament.

OBJ. 2: Further, Gregory says in a Letter to Augustine, Bishop of the English (*Regist.* xi): *Those who pay the debt of marriage not from lust, but from desire to have children, should be left to their own judgment, as to whether they should enter the church and receive the mystery of our Lord's body, after such intercourse: because they ought not to be forbidden from receiving it, since they have passed through the fire unscorched.*

From this it is evident that seminal loss even of one awake, if it be without sin, is no hindrance to receiving the body of Christ. Consequently, much less is it in the case of one asleep.

OBJ. 3: Further, these movements of the flesh seem to bring with them only bodily uncleanness. But there are other bodily defilements which according to the Law forbade entrance into the holy places, yet which under the New Law do not prevent receiving this sacrament: as, for instance, in the case of a woman after child-birth, or in her periods, or suffering from issue of blood, as Gregory writes to Augustine, Bishop of the English (*Regist.* xi). Therefore it seems that neither do these movements of the flesh hinder a man from receiving this sacrament.

OBJ. 4: Further, venial sin is no hindrance to receiving the sacrament, nor is mortal sin after repentance. But even supposing that seminal loss arises from some foregoing sin, whether of intemperance, or of bad thoughts, for the most part such sin is venial; and if occasionally it be mortal, a man may repent of it by morning and confess it. Consequently, it seems that he ought not to be prevented from receiving this sacrament.

OBJ. 5: Further, a sin against the Fifth Commandment is greater than a sin against the Sixth. But if a man dream that he has broken the Fifth or Seventh or any other Commandment, he is not on that account debarred from receiving this sacrament. Therefore it seems that much less should he be debarred through defilement resulting from a dream against the Sixth Commandment.

ON THE CONTRARY, It is written (Lev 15:16): *The man from whom the seed of copulation goeth out . . . shall be unclean until evening.* But for the unclean there is no approaching to the sacraments. Therefore, it seems that owing

aliquis impeditur a sumptione huius sacramenti, quod est maximum sacramentum.

RESPONDEO dicendum quod circa pollutionem nocturnam duo possunt considerari, unum quidem ratione cuius ex necessitate impedit hominem a sumptione huius sacramenti; aliud autem ratione cuius non ex necessitate impedit hominem, sed ex quadam congruentia.

Ex necessitate quidem impedit hominem ab huius sacramenti perceptione solum mortale peccatum. Et quamvis ipsa nocturna pollutio, secundum se considerata, peccatum mortale esse non possit, nihilominus tamen, ratione suae causae, quandoque habet peccatum mortale annexum. Et ideo consideranda est causa pollutionis nocturnae. Quandoque enim provenit ex causa extrinseca spirituali, scilicet Daemonum illusione, qui, sicut in prima parte habitum est, phantasmata commovere possunt, ex quorum apparitione pollutio interdum subsequitur. Quandoque vero provenit pollutio ex causa intrinseca spirituali, scilicet ex praecedentibus cogitationibus. Aliquando autem ex causa intrinseca corporali, seu ex superfluitate sive debilitate naturae; seu etiam ex superfluitate cibi et potus. Quaelibet autem harum trium causarum potest et sine peccato, et cum peccato veniali vel mortali existere. Et si quidem sit sine peccato, vel cum peccato veniali, non ex necessitate impedit sumptionem huius sacramenti, ita scilicet quod homo sumendo sit reus corporis et sanguinis domini. Si vero sit cum peccato mortali impedit ex necessitate.

Illusio enim Daemonum quandoque provenit ex praecedenti negligentia praeparationis ad devotionem, quae potest esse vel mortale vel veniale peccatum. Quandoque vero provenit ex sola nequitia Daemonum volentium impedire hominem a sumptione huius sacramenti. Unde legitur in collationibus patrum quod, cum quidam pollutionem pateretur semper in festis in quibus erat communicandum, seniores, comperto quod nulla causa ab ipso praecesserat, decreverunt quod propter hoc a communione non cessaret, et ita cessavit illusio Daemonum.

Similiter etiam praecedentes cogitationes lascivae quandoque possunt esse omnino sine peccato, puta cum aliquis causa lectionis vel disputationis cogitur de talibus cogitare. Et si hoc sit sine concupiscentia et delectatione, non erunt cogitationes immundae, sed honestae, ex quibus tamen pollutio sequi potest, sicut patet ex auctoritate Augustini inducta. Quandoque vero praecedentes cogitationes sunt cum concupiscentia et delectatione et, si adsit consensus, peccatum mortale erit, sin autem, veniale.

Similiter etiam et causa corporalis quandoque est sine peccato, puta cum est ex infirmitate naturae, unde et quidam vigilando absque peccato fluxum seminis patiuntur; vel etiam si sit ex superfluitate naturae, sicut enim contingit sanguinem superfluere absque peccato,

to such defilement of the flesh a man is debarred from taking this which is the greatest of the sacraments.

I ANSWER THAT, There are two things to be weighed regarding the aforesaid movements: one on account of which they necessarily prevent a man from receiving this sacrament; the other, on account of which they do so, not of necessity, but from a sense of propriety.

Mortal sin alone necessarily prevents anyone from partaking of this sacrament: and although these movements during sleep, considered in themselves, cannot be a mortal sin, nevertheless, owing to their cause, they have mortal sin connected with them; which cause, therefore, must be investigated. Sometimes they are due to an external spiritual cause, viz. the deception of the demons, who can stir up phantasms, as was stated in the First Part (I, Q. 111, A. 3), through the apparition of which, these movements occasionally follow. Sometimes they are due to an internal spiritual cause, such as previous thoughts. At other times they arise from some internal corporeal cause, as from abundance or weakness of nature, or even from surfeit of meat or drink. Now every one of these three causes can be without sin at all, or else with venial sin, or with mortal sin. If it be without sin, or with venial sin, it does not necessarily prevent the receiving of this sacrament, so as to make a man guilty of the body and blood of the Lord: but should it be with mortal sin, it prevents it of necessity.

For such illusions on the part of demons sometimes come from one's not striving to receive fervently; and this can be either a mortal or a venial sin. At other times it is due to malice alone on the part of the demons who wish to keep men from receiving this sacrament. So we read in the Conferences of the Fathers (Cassian, *Collat.* xxii) that when a certain one always suffered thus on those feast-days on which he had to receive Communion, his superiors, discovering that there was no fault on his part, ruled that he was not to refrain from communicating on that account, and the demoniacal illusion ceased.

In like fashion previous evil thoughts can sometimes be without any sin whatever, as when one has to think of such things on account of lecturing or debating; and if it be done without concupiscence and delectation, the thoughts will not be unclean but honest; and yet defilement can come of such thoughts, as is clear from the authority of Augustine (Obj. 1). At other times such thoughts come of concupiscence and delectation, and should there be consent, it will be a mortal sin: otherwise it will be a venial sin.

In the same way too the corporeal cause can be without sin, as when it arises from bodily debility, and hence some individuals suffer seminal loss without sin even in their wakeful hours; or it can come from the abundance of nature: for, just as blood can flow without sin, so also can

ita et semen, quod est superfluitas sanguinis, secundum philosophum. Quandoque vero est cum peccato, puta cum provenit ex superfluitate cibi vel potus. Et hoc etiam potest esse peccatum veniale vel mortale, licet frequentius peccatum mortale accidat circa turpes cogitationes, propter facilitatem consensus, quam circa sumptionem cibi et potus. Unde Gregorius, scribens Augustino Anglorum episcopo, dicit cessandum esse a communione quando ex turpibus cogitationibus provenit, non autem quando provenit ex superfluitate cibi et potus, praesertim si necessitas adsit. Sic igitur ex causa pollutionis considerari potest utrum nocturna pollutio ex necessitate impediat sumptionem huius sacramenti.

Ex quadam vero congruentia impedit quantum ad duo. Quorum unum semper accidit, scilicet quaedam foeditas corporalis, cum qua, propter reverentiam sacramenti, non decet ad altare accedere, unde et volentes tangere aliquid sacrum manus lavant; nisi forte talis immunditia perpetua sit vel diuturna, sicut est lepra vel fluxus sanguinis vel aliquid huiusmodi. Aliud autem est evagatio mentis, quae sequitur pollutionem nocturnam, praecipue quando cum turpi imaginatione contingit. Hoc tamen impedimentum quod ex congruitate provenit, postponi debet propter aliquam necessitatem, puta, ut Gregorius dicit, *cum fortasse aut festus dies exigit, aut exhibere ministerium, pro eo quod sacerdos alius deest, ipsa necessitas compellit.*

AD PRIMUM ergo dicendum quod ex necessitate quidem non impeditur homo a sumptione huius sacramenti nisi propter peccatum mortale, sed ex quadam congruentia potest homo impediri propter alias causas, sicut dictum est.

AD SECUNDUM dicendum quod coitus coniugalis, si sit sine peccato, puta si fiat causa prolis generandae vel causa reddendi debitum, non alia ratione impedit sumptionem sacramenti nisi sicut dictum est de pollutione nocturna quae accidit sine peccato scilicet propter immunditiam corporalem et mentis distractionem. Ratione cuius Hieronymus dicit, super Matth., *si panes propositionis ab his qui uxores tetigerant comedi poterant, quanto magis panis qui de caelo descendit, non potest ab his qui coniugalibus paulo ante haesere amplexibus, violari atque contingi. Non quod nuptias condemnemus, sed quod, eo tempore quo carnes agni manducaturi sumus, vacare a carnalibus operibus debeamus.* Sed quia hoc secundum congruitatem, et non secundum necessitatem est intelligendum, Gregorius dicit quod talis *est suo iudicio relinquendus. Si vero non amor procreandae sobolis sed voluptas dominatur in opere,* ut ibidem Gregorius subdit, tunc prohiberi debet ne accedat ad hoc sacramentum.

the semen which is superfluity of the blood, according to the Philosopher (*De Gener. Animal.* i). But occasionally it is with sin, as when it is due to excess of food or drink. And this also can be either venial or mortal sin; although more frequently the sin is mortal in the case of evil thoughts on account of the proneness to consent, rather than in the case of consumption of food and drink. Hence Gregory, writing to Augustine, Bishop of the English (*Regist.* xi), says that one ought to refrain from Communion when this arises from evil thoughts, but not when it arises from excess of food or drink, especially if necessity call for Communion. So, then, one must judge from its cause whether such bodily defilement of necessity hinders the receiving of this sacrament.

At the same time a sense of decency forbids Communion on two accounts. The first of these is always verified, viz. the bodily defilement, with which, out of reverence for the sacrament, it is unbecoming to approach the altar (and hence those who wish to touch any sacred object, wash their hands): except perchance such uncleanness be perpetual or of long standing, such as leprosy or issue of blood, or anything else of the kind. The other reason is the mental distraction which follows after the aforesaid movements, especially when they take place with unclean imaginings. Now this obstacle, which arises from a sense of decency, can be set aside owing to any necessity, as Gregory says (*Regist.* xi): *As when perchance either a festival day calls for it, or necessity compels one to exercise the ministry because there is no other priest at hand.*

REPLY OBJ. 1: A person is hindered necessarily, only by mortal sin, from receiving this sacrament: but from a sense of decency one may be hindered through other causes, as stated above.

REPLY OBJ. 2: Conjugal intercourse, if it be without sin, (for instance, if it be done for the sake of begetting offspring, or of paying the marriage debt), does not prevent the receiving of this sacrament for any other reason than do those movements in question which happen without sin, as stated above; namely, on account of the defilement to the body and distraction to the mind. On this account Jerome expresses himself in the following terms in his commentary on Matthew (*Epist.* xxviii): *If the loaves of Proposition might not be eaten by them who had known their wives carnally, how much less may this bread which has come down from heaven be defiled and touched by them who shortly before have been in conjugal embraces? It is not that we condemn marriages, but that at the time when we are going to eat the flesh of the Lamb, we ought not to indulge in carnal acts.* But since this is to be understood in the sense of decency, and not of necessity, Gregory says that such a person *is to be left to his own judgment. But if,* as Gregory says (*Regist.* xi), *it be not desire of begetting offspring, but lust that prevails,* then such a one should be forbidden to approach this sacrament.

Ad tertium dicendum quod, sicut Gregorius dicit, in epistola supra dicta ad Augustinum Anglorum episcopum, in veteri testamento aliqui polluti dicebantur figuraliter, quod populus novae legis spiritualiter intelligit. Unde huiusmodi corporales immunditiae, si sint perpetuae vel diuturnae, non impediunt sumptionem huius sacramenti salutaris sicut impediebant accessum ad sacramenta figuralia. Si vero cito transeunt, sicut immunditia pollutionis nocturnae, ex quadam congruentia impedit sumptionem huius sacramenti per illum diem quo hoc accidit. Unde et Deut. XXIII dicitur, *si fuerit inter vos homo qui nocturno pollutus sit somnio, egredietur extra castra, et non revertetur priusquam ad vesperam lavetur aqua.*

Ad quartum dicendum quod, licet per contritionem et confessionem auferatur reatus culpae, non tamen aufertur corporalis immunditia et distractio mentis ex pollutione consecuta.

Ad quintum dicendum quod somnium homicidii non inducit corporalem immunditiam, nec etiam tantam distractionem mentis sicut fornicatio, propter intensionem delectationis. Si tamen somnium homicidii proveniat ex causa quae est peccatum, praesertim mortale, impedit a sumptione huius sacramenti ratione suae causae.

Reply Obj. 3: As Gregory says in his Letter quoted above to Augustine, Bishop of the English, in the Old Testament some persons were termed polluted figuratively, which the people of the New Law understand spiritually. Hence such bodily uncleannesses, if perpetual or of long standing, do not hinder the receiving of this saving sacrament, as they prevented approaching those figurative sacraments; but if they pass speedily, like the uncleanness of the aforesaid movements, then from a sense of fittingness they hinder the receiving of this sacrament during the day on which it happens. Hence it is written (Deut 23:10): *If there be among you any man, that is defiled in a dream by night, he shall go forth out of the camp; and he shall not return before he be washed with water in the evening.*

Reply Obj. 4: Although the stain of guilt be taken away by contrition and confession nevertheless the bodily defilement is not taken away, nor the mental distraction which follows therefrom.

Reply Obj. 5: To dream of homicide brings no bodily uncleanness, nor such distraction of mind as fornication, on account of its intense delectation; still if the dream of homicide comes of a cause sinful in itself, especially if it be mortal sin, then owing to its cause it hinders the receiving of this sacrament.

Article 8

Whether Food or Drink Taken Beforehand Hinders the Receiving of This Sacrament?

Ad octavum sic proceditur. Videtur quod cibus vel potus praeassumptus non impediat sumptionem huius sacramenti. Hoc enim sacramentum est a domino institutum in cena. Sed dominus, postquam cenavit, hoc sacramentum discipulis tradidit, sicut patet Luc. XXII et I Cor. XI. Ergo videtur quod etiam post alios cibos assumptos nos debeamus sumere hoc sacramentum.

Praeterea, I Cor. XI dicitur, *cum convenitis ad manducandum*, scilicet corpus domini, *invicem expectate, si quis autem esurit, domi manducet.* Et ita videtur quod, postquam aliquis domi manducavit, possit in Ecclesia corpus Christi manducare.

Praeterea, in Concilio Carthaginensi legitur, et habetur de Consecr., dist. I, *sacramenta altaris non nisi a ieiunis hominibus celebrentur, excepto uno die anniversario quo cena domini celebratur.* Ergo saltem illo die potest corpus Christi aliquis post alios cibos sumere.

Praeterea, sumptio aquae vel medicinae, vel alterius cibi vel potus in minima quantitate, vel etiam reliquiarum cibi in ore remanentium, neque ieiunium Ecclesiae solvit, neque sobrietatem tollit, quae exigitur

Objection 1: It seems that food or drink taken beforehand does not hinder the receiving of this sacrament. For this sacrament was instituted by our Lord at the supper. But when the supper was ended our Lord gave the sacrament to His disciples, as is evident from Luke 22:20, and from 1 Cor. 11:25. Therefore it seems that we ought to take this sacrament after receiving other food.

Obj. 2: Further, it is written (1 Cor 11:33): *When you come together to eat*, namely, the Lord's body, *wait for one another; if any man be hungry, let him eat at home*: and thus it seems that after eating at home a man may eat Christ's body in the Church.

Obj. 3: Further, we read in the (3rd) Council of Carthage (Can. xxix): *Let the sacraments of the altar be celebrated only by men who are fasting, with the exception of the anniversary day on which the Lord's Supper is celebrated.* Therefore, at least on that day, one may receive the body of Christ after partaking of other food.

Obj. 4: Further, the taking of water or medicine, or of any other food or drink in very slight quantity, or of the remains of food continuing in the mouth, neither breaks the Church's fast, nor takes away the sobriety required for

ad hoc quod aliquis reverenter hoc sacramentum sumat. Ergo per praedicta non impeditur aliquis a sumptione huius sacramenti.

PRAETEREA, quidam de nocte profunda comedunt aut bibunt, aut forte totam noctem insomnem ducentes, de mane percipiunt sacra mysteria, nondum plene digesti. Minus autem impediretur sobrietas hominis si in mane parum comederet, et postea circa nonam sumeret hoc sacramentum, cum etiam sit quandoque maior distantia temporis. Ergo videtur quod talis cibi praeassumptio non impediat hominem ab hoc sacramento.

PRAETEREA, non minor reverentia debetur huic sacramento iam sumpto quam ante sumptionem. Sed, sumpto sacramento, licet cibum aut potum sumere. Ergo et ante sumptionem.

SED CONTRA est quod Augustinus dicit, in libro responsionum ad Ianuarium, *placuit spiritui sancto ut, in honorem tanti sacramenti, prius in os Christiani dominicum corpus intraret quam ceteri cibi.*

RESPONDEO dicendum quod aliquid impedit sumptionem huius sacramenti dupliciter. Uno modo, secundum se, sicut peccatum mortale, quod habet repugnantiam ad significatum huius sacramenti, ut supra dictum est. Alio modo, propter prohibitionem Ecclesiae. Et sic impeditur aliquis a sumptione huius sacramenti post cibum vel potum assumptum, triplici ratione. Primo quidem, sicut Augustinus dicit, in honorem huius sacramenti, ut scilicet in os hominis intret nondum aliquo cibo vel potu infectum. Secundo, propter significationem, ut scilicet detur intelligi quod Christus, qui est res huius sacramenti, et caritas eius, debet primo fundari in cordibus nostris; secundum illud Matth. VI, *primo quaerite regnum Dei.* Tertio, propter periculum vomitus et ebrietatis, quae quandoque contingunt ex hoc quod homines inordinate cibis utuntur, sicut et apostolus dicit, I Cor. XI, *alius quidem esurit, alius vero ebrius est.*

Ab hac tamen generali regula excipiuntur infirmi, qui statim communicandi sunt, etiam post cibum, si de eorum periculo dubitetur ne sine communione decedant, quia necessitas legem non habet. Unde dicitur de Consecr., dist. II, *presbyter infirmum statim communicet, ne sine communione moriatur.*

AD PRIMUM ergo dicendum quod, sicut Augustinus in eodem libro dicit, *neque, quia post cibum dominus dedit, propterea pransi aut cenati fratres ad hoc sacramentum accipiendum convenire debeant, aut mensis suis miscere, sicut faciebant quos apostolus arguit et emendat. Namque salvator, quo vehementius commendaret mysterii illius altitudinem, ultimum hoc voluit infigere cordibus et memoriae discipulorum. Et ideo non praecepit ut deinceps*

reverently receiving this sacrament. Consequently, one is not prevented by the above things from receiving this sacrament.

OBJ. 5: Further, some eat and drink late at night, and possibly after passing a sleepless night receive the sacred mysteries in the morning when the food is not digested. But it would savor more of moderation if a man were to eat a little in the morning and afterwards receive this sacrament about the ninth hour, since also there is occasionally a longer interval of time. Consequently, it seems that such taking of food beforehand does not keep one from this sacrament.

OBJ. 6: Further, there is no less reverence due to this sacrament after receiving it, than before. But one may take food and drink after receiving the sacrament. Therefore one may do so before receiving it.

ON THE CONTRARY, Augustine says (*Resp. ad Januar., Ep. liv*): *It has pleased the Holy Spirit that, out of honor for this great sacrament, the Lord's body should enter the mouth of a Christian before other foods.*

I ANSWER THAT, A thing may prevent the receiving of this sacrament in two ways: first of all in itself, like mortal sin, which is repugnant to what is signified by this sacrament, as stated above (A. 4): second, on account of the Church's prohibition; and thus a man is prevented from taking this sacrament after receiving food or drink, for three reasons. First, as Augustine says (*Resp. ad Januar., Ep. liv*), *out of respect for this sacrament,* so that it may enter into a mouth not yet contaminated by any food or drink. Second, because of its signification, i.e., to give us to understand that Christ, Who is the reality of this sacrament, and His charity, ought to be first of all established in our hearts, according to Matt. 6:33: *Seek first the kingdom of God.* Third, on account of the danger of vomiting and intemperance, which sometimes arise from over-indulging in food, as the Apostle says (1 Cor 11:21): *One, indeed, is hungry, and another is drunk.*

Nevertheless the sick are exempted from this general rule, for they should be given Communion at once, even after food, should there be any doubt as to their danger, lest they die without Communion, because necessity has no law. Hence it is said in the Canon de Consecratione: *Let the priest at once take Communion to the sick person, lest he die without Communion.*

REPLY OBJ. 1: As Augustine says in the same book, *the fact that our Lord gave this sacrament after taking food is no reason why the brethren should assemble after dinner or supper in order to partake of it, or receive it at meal-time, as did those whom the Apostle reproves and corrects. For our Savior, in order the more strongly to commend the depth of this mystery, wished to fix it closely in the hearts and memories of the disciples; and on that account He gave no command for it to*

tali ordine sumeretur, ut apostolis, per quos Ecclesias dispositurus erat, servaret hunc locum.

AD SECUNDUM dicendum quod illud verbum in Glossa sic exponitur, *si quis esurit, et impatiens non vult expectare alios, manducet domi suos cibos, idest, pane terreno pascatur, nec post Eucharistiam sumat.*

AD TERTIUM dicendum quod capitulum illud loquitur secundum consuetudinem aliquando apud aliquos observatam, ut, in repraesentationem dominicae cenae, illo die a non ieiunis corpus Christi sumeretur. Sed nunc hoc est abrogatum. Nam, sicut Augustinus in libro praedicto dicit, *per universum orbem mos iste servatur,* ut scilicet corpus Christi a ieiunis sumatur.

AD QUARTUM dicendum quod, sicut in secunda parte habitum est, duplex est ieiunium. Primum est ieiunium naturae, quod importat privationem cuiuscumque praeassumpti per modum cibi vel potus. Et tale ieiunium requiritur ad hoc sacramentum, propter praedicta. Et ideo neque post assumptionem aquae vel alterius cibi aut potus vel etiam medicinae, in quantumcumque parva quantitate, licet accipere hoc sacramentum. Nec refert utrum aliquid huiusmodi nutriat vel non nutriat, aut per se aut cum aliis, dummodo sumatur per modum cibi vel potus. Reliquiae tamen cibi remanentes in ore, si casualiter transglutiantur, non impediunt sumptionem huius sacramenti, quia non traiiciuntur per modum cibi, sed per modum salivae. Et eadem ratio est de reliquiis aquae vel vini quibus os abluitur, dummodo traiiciantur non in magna quantitate, sed permixtae salivae, quod vitari non potest.

Aliud autem est ieiunium Ecclesiae, quod instituitur ad carnis macerationem. Et tale ieiunium per praedicta non impeditur, quia praedicta non multum nutriunt, sed magis ad alterandum sumuntur.

AD QUINTUM dicendum quod, cum dicitur, *hoc sacramentum prius quam alii cibi debet mitti in os Christiani,* non est intelligendum absolute respectu totius temporis, alioquin qui semel comedisset et bibisset, nunquam postea posset hoc sacramentum accipere. Sed est intelligendum quantum ad eundem diem. Et licet principium diei secundum diversos diversimode sumatur, nam quidam a meridie, quidam ab occasu, quidam a media nocte, quidam ab ortu solis diem incipiunt; Ecclesia tamen, secundum Romanos, diem a media nocte incipit. Et ideo, si post mediam noctem aliquis sumpserit aliquid per modum cibi vel potus, non potest eadem die hoc sumere sacramentum, potest vero si ante mediam noctem. Nec refert utrum post cibum vel potum dormierit, aut etiam digestus sit, quantum ad rationem praecepti. Refert autem quantum ad perturbationem mentis quam patiuntur homines propter insomnietatem vel indigestionem, ex quibus si mens multum perturbetur, homo redditur ineptus ad sumptionem huius sacramenti.

be received in that order, leaving this to the apostles, to whom He was about to entrust the government of the churches.

REPLY OBJ. 2: The text quoted is thus paraphrased by the gloss: *If any man be hungry and loath to await the rest, let him partake of his food at home, that is, let him fill himself with earthly bread, without partaking of the Eucharist afterwards.*

REPLY OBJ. 3: The wording of this decree is in accordance with the former custom observed by some of receiving the body of Christ on that day after breaking their fast, so as to represent the Lord's supper. But this is now abrogated, because as Augustine says (*Resp. ad Januar., Ep. liv*), it is customary throughout the whole world for Christ's body to be received before breaking the fast.

REPLY OBJ. 4: As stated in the Second Part (II-II, Q. 147, A. 6, ad 2), there are two kinds of fast. First, there is the natural fast, which implies privation of everything taken before-hand by way of food or drink: and such fast is required for this sacrament for the reasons given above. And therefore it is never lawful to take this sacrament after taking water, or other food or drink, or even medicine, no matter how small the quantity be. Nor does it matter whether it nourishes or not, whether it be taken by itself or with other things, provided it be taken by way of food or drink. But the remains of food left in the mouth, if swallowed accidentally, do not hinder receiving this sacrament, because they are swallowed not by way of food but by way of saliva. The same holds good of the unavoidable remains of the water or wine wherewith the mouth is rinsed, provided they be not swallowed in great quantity, but mixed with saliva.

Second, there is the fast of the Church, instituted for afflicting the body: and this fast is not hindered by the things mentioned (in the objection), because they do not give much nourishment, but are taken rather as an alterative.

REPLY OBJ. 5: That this sacrament ought to enter into the mouth of a Christian before any other food must not be understood absolutely of all time, otherwise he who had once eaten or drunk could never afterwards take this sacrament: but it must be understood of the same day; and although the beginning of the day varies according to different systems of reckoning (for some begin their day at noon, some at sunset, others at midnight, and others at sunrise), the Roman Church begins it at midnight. Consequently, if any person takes anything by way of food or drink after midnight, he may not receive this sacrament on that day; but he can do so if the food was taken before midnight. Nor does it matter, so far as the precept is concerned, whether he has slept after taking food or drink, or whether he has digested it; but it does matter as to the mental disturbance which one suffers from want of sleep or from indigestion, for, if the mind be much disturbed, one becomes unfit for receiving this sacrament.

AD SEXTUM dicendum quod maxima devotio requiritur in ipsa sumptione sacramenti, quia tunc percipitur sacramenti effectus. Quae quidem devotio magis impeditur per praecedentia quam per sequentia. Et ideo magis est institutum quod homines ieiunent ante sumptionem huius sacramenti quam post. Debet tamen esse aliqua mora inter sumptionem huius sacramenti et reliquos cibos. Unde et in Missa oratio gratiarum actionis post communionem dicitur; et communicantes etiam suas privatas orationes dicunt.

Secundum tamen antiquos canones statutum fuit a Papa Clemente, ut habetur de Consecr., dist. II, *si mane dominica portio editur, usque ad sextam ieiunent ministri qui eam sumpserunt, et si tertia vel quarta acceperint, ieiunent usque ad vesperum.* Antiquitus enim rarius Missarum solemnia celebrabantur, et cum maiori praeparatione. Nunc autem, quia oportet frequentius sacra mysteria celebrare, non posset de facili observari. Et ideo per contrariam consuetudinem est abrogatum.

REPLY OBJ. 6: The greatest devotion is called for at the moment of receiving this sacrament, because it is then that the effect of the sacrament is bestowed, and such devotion is hindered more by what goes before it than by what comes after it. And therefore it was ordained that men should fast before receiving the sacrament rather than after. Nevertheless there ought to be some interval between receiving this sacrament and taking other food. Consequently, both the Postcommunion prayer of thanksgiving is said in the Mass, and the communicants say their own private prayers.

However, according to the ancient Canons, the following ordination was made by Pope Clement I, (*Ep. ii*), *If the Lord's portion be eaten in the morning, the ministers who have taken it shall fast until the sixth hour, and if they take it at the third or fourth hour, they shall fast until evening.* For in olden times, the priest celebrated Mass less frequently, and with greater preparation: but now, because the sacred mysteries have to be celebrated oftener, the same could not be easily observed, and so it has been abrogated by contrary custom.

Article 9

Whether Those Who Have Not the Use of Reason Ought to Receive This Sacrament?

AD NONUM SIC PROCEDITUR. Videtur quod non habentes usum rationis non debeant hoc sacramentum accipere. Requiritur enim quod aliquis ad hoc sacramentum cum devotione et praecedenti sui examinatione accedat, secundum illud I Cor. XI, *probet autem seipsum homo, et sic de pane illo edat et de calice bibat.* Sed hoc non potest esse in his qui carent usu rationis. Ergo non debet eis hoc sacramentum dari.

PRAETEREA, inter alios qui carent usu rationis, sunt etiam arreptitii, qui energumeni dicuntur. Sed tales etiam ab inspectione huius sacramenti arcentur, secundum Dionysium, in libro Eccles. Hier. Ergo carentibus usu rationis hoc sacramentum dari non debet.

PRAETEREA, inter alios carentes usu rationis maxime pueri videntur esse innocentes. Sed pueris hoc sacramentum non exhibetur. Ergo multo minus aliis carentibus usu rationis.

SED CONTRA est quod legitur in Concilio Arausico, et habetur in decretis, XXVI, qu. VI, *amentibus quaecumque sunt pietatis, sunt conferenda.* Et ita est conferendum hoc sacramentum, quod est sacramentum pietatis.

RESPONDEO dicendum quod aliqui dicuntur non habere usum rationis dupliciter. Uno modo, quia habent debilem usum rationis, sicut dicitur non videns qui male videt. Et quia tales possunt aliquam devotionem

OBJECTION 1: It seems that those who have not the use of reason ought not to receive this sacrament. For it is required that man should approach this sacrament with devotion and previous self-examination, according to 1 Cor. 11:28: *Let a man prove himself, and so let him eat of that bread, and drink of the chalice.* But this is not possible for those who are devoid of reason. Therefore this sacrament should not be given to them.

OBJ. 2: Further, among those who have not the use of reason are the possessed, who are called energumens. But such persons are kept from even beholding this sacrament, according to Dionysius (*Eccl. Hier.* iii). Therefore this sacrament ought not to be given to those who have not the use of reason.

OBJ. 3: Further, among those that lack the use of reason are children, the most innocent of all. But this sacrament is not given to children. Therefore much less should it be given to others deprived of the use of reason.

ON THE CONTRARY, We read in the First Council of Orange, (Canon 13); and the same is to be found in the Decretals (xxvi, 6): *All things that pertain to piety are to be given to the insane*: and consequently, since this is the *sacrament of piety*, it must be given to them.

I ANSWER THAT, Men are said to be devoid of reason in two ways. First, when they are feeble-minded, as a man who sees dimly is said not to see: and since such persons

concipere huius sacramenti, non est eis hoc sacramentum denegandum.

Alio modo dicuntur aliqui non habere totaliter usum rationis. Aut igitur nunquam habuerunt usum rationis, sed sic a nativitate permanserunt, et sic talibus non est hoc sacramentum exhibendum, quia in eis nullo modo praecessit huius sacramenti devotio. Aut non semper caruerunt usu rationis. Et tunc, si prius, quando erant suae mentis compotes, apparuit in eis huius sacramenti devotio, debet eis in articulo mortis hoc sacramentum exhiberi, nisi forte timeatur periculum vomitus vel exspuitionis. Unde legitur in Concilio Carthaginensi IV, et habetur in decretis, XXVI, qu. VI, *is qui in infirmitate poenitentiam petit, si casu, dum ad eum invitatus sacerdos venit, oppressus infirmitate obmutuerit, vel in phrenesim conversus fuerit, dent testimonium qui eum audierunt, et accipiat poenitentiam, et, si continuo creditur moriturus, reconcilietur per manus impositionem et infundatur ori eius Eucharistia.*

AD PRIMUM ergo dicendum quod carentes usu rationis possunt devotionem ad sacramentum habere, quantum ad aliquos quidem praesentem, quantum ad alios autem praeteritam.

AD SECUNDUM dicendum quod Dionysius loquitur ibi de energumenis nondum baptizatis, in quibus scilicet nondum est vis Daemonis extincta, quae viget in eis per originale peccatum. Sed de baptizatis qui corporaliter ab immundis spiritibus vexantur, est eadem ratio et de aliis amentibus. Unde Cassianus dicit, eis, qui ab immundis vexantur spiritibus, *communionem sacrosanctam a senioribus nostris nunquam meminimus interdictam.*

AD TERTIUM dicendum quod eadem ratio est de pueris recenter natis et de amentibus qui nunquam habuerunt usum rationis. Unde talibus non sunt sacra mysteria danda, quamvis quidam Graeci contrarium faciant, propter hoc quod Dionysius, II cap. Eccles. Hier., dicit baptizatis esse sacram communionem dandam, non intelligentes quod Dionysius ibi loquitur de Baptismo adultorum. Nec tamen per hoc aliquod detrimentum vitae patiuntur, propter hoc quod dominus dicit, Ioan. VI, *nisi manducaveritis carnem filii hominis et biberitis eius sanguinem, non habebitis vitam in vobis,* quia, sicut Augustinus scribit Bonifacio, *tunc unusquisque fidelium corporis et sanguinis domini particeps fit, scilicet spiritualiter, quando in Baptismate membrum corporis Christi efficitur.* Sed quando iam pueri incipiunt aliqualem usum rationis habere, ut possint devotionem concipere huius sacramenti, tunc potest eis hoc sacramentum conferri.

can conceive some devotion towards this sacrament, it is not to be denied them.

In another way men are said not to possess fully the use of reason. Either, then, they never had the use of reason, and have remained so from birth; and in that case this sacrament is not to be given to them, because in no way has there been any preceding devotion towards the sacrament: or else, they were not always devoid of reason, and then, if when they formerly had their wits they showed devotion towards this sacrament, it ought to be given to them in the hour of death; unless danger be feared of vomiting or spitting it out. Hence we read in the acts of the Fourth Council of Carthage (Canon 76). and the same is to be found in the *Decretals* (xxvi, 6): *If a sick man ask to receive the sacrament of Penance; and if, when the priest who has been sent for comes to him, he be so weak as to be unable to speak, or becomes delirious, let them, who heard him ask, bear witness, and let him receive the sacrament of Penance. then if it be thought that he is going to die shortly, let him be reconciled by imposition of hands, and let the Eucharist be placed in his mouth.*

REPLY OBJ. 1: Those lacking the use of reason can have devotion towards the sacrament; actual devotion in some cases, and past in others.

REPLY OBJ. 2: Dionysius is speaking there of energumens who are not yet baptized, in whom the devil's power is not yet extinct, since it thrives in them through the presence of original sin. But as to baptized persons who are vexed in body by unclean spirits, the same reason holds good of them as of others who are demented. Hence Cassian says (*Collat.* vii): *We do not remember the most Holy Communion to have ever been denied by our elders to them who are vexed by unclean spirits.*

REPLY OBJ. 3: The same reason holds good of newly born children as of the insane who never have had the use of reason: consequently, the sacred mysteries are not to be given to them. Although certain Greeks do the contrary, because Dionysius says (*Eccl. Hier.* ii) that Holy Communion is to be given to them who are baptized; not understanding that Dionysius is speaking there of the Baptism of adults. Nor do they suffer any loss of life from the fact of our Lord saying (John 6:54), *Except you eat the flesh of the Son of Man, and drink His blood, you shall not have life in you;* because, as Augustine writes to Boniface (Pseudo-Beda, *Comment. in 1 Cor.* 10:17), *then every one of the faithful becomes a partaker,* i.e., spiritually, *of the body and blood of the Lord, when he is made a member of Christ's body in Baptism.* But when children once begin to have some use of reason so as to be able to conceive some devotion for the sacrament, then it can be given to them.

Article 10

Whether It Is Lawful to Receive This Sacrament Daily?

AD DECIMUM SIC PROCEDITUR. Videtur quod non liceat quotidie hoc sacramentum suscipere. Sicut enim Baptismus repraesentat dominicam passionem, ita et hoc sacramentum. Sed non licet pluries baptizari, sed semel tantum, quia Christus semel tantum pro peccatis nostris mortuus est, ut dicitur I Pet. III. Ergo videtur quod non liceat hoc sacramentum quotidie suscipere.

PRAETEREA, veritas debet respondere figurae. Sed agnus paschalis, qui fuit figura praecipua huius sacramenti, ut supra dictum est, non manducabatur nisi semel in anno. Sed Ecclesia semel in anno celebrat Christi passionem, cuius hoc sacramentum est memoriale. Ergo videtur quod non licet quotidie sumere hoc sacramentum, sed semel in anno.

PRAETEREA, huic sacramento, in quo totus Christus continetur, maxima reverentia debetur. Ad reverentiam autem pertinet quod aliquis ab hoc sacramento abstineat, unde et laudatur centurio, qui dixit, Matth. VIII, *domine, non sum dignus ut intres sub tectum meum*; et Petrus, qui dixit, Luc. V, *exi a me, domine, quia homo peccator ego sum*. Ergo non est laudabile quod homo quotidie hoc sacramentum suscipiat.

PRAETEREA, si laudabile esset frequenter hoc sacramentum suscipere quanto frequentius sumeretur, tanto esset laudabilius. Sed maior esset frequentia si homo pluries in die sumeret hoc sacramentum. Ergo esset laudabile quod homo pluries in die communicaret. Quod tamen non habet Ecclesiae consuetudo. Non ergo videtur esse laudabile quod aliquis quotidie hoc sacramentum accipiat.

PRAETEREA, Ecclesia intendit suis statutis fidelium utilitati providere. Sed ex statuto Ecclesiae fideles tenentur solum semel communicare in anno, unde dicitur extra, de Poenit. et Remiss., *omnis utriusque sexus fidelis suscipiat reverenter ad minus in Pascha Eucharistiae sacramentum, nisi forte, de proprii sacerdotis consilio, ob aliquam rationabilem causam, ad tempus ab eius perceptione duxerit abstinendum*. Non ergo est laudabile quod quotidie hoc sacramentum sumatur.

SED CONTRA est quod Augustinus dicit, in libro de verbis domini, *iste panis quotidianus est, accipe quotidie quod quotidie tibi prosit*.

RESPONDEO dicendum quod circa usum huius sacramenti duo possunt considerari. Unum quidem ex parte ipsius sacramenti, cuius virtus est hominibus salutaris. Et ideo utile est quotidie ipsum suscipere, ut homo quotidie eius fructum percipiat. Unde Ambrosius dicit, in libro de sacramentis, *si quoties effunditur sanguis Christi, in remissionem peccatorum effunditur, debeo semper accipere, qui semper pecco, debeo semper habere*

OBJECTION 1: It does not appear to be lawful to receive this sacrament daily, because, as Baptism shows forth our Lord's Passion, so also does this sacrament. Now one may not be baptized several times, but only once, because *Christ died once* only *for our sins*, according to 1 Pet. 3:18. Therefore, it seems unlawful to receive this sacrament daily.

OBJ. 2: Further, the reality ought to answer to the figure. But the Paschal Lamb, which was the chief figure of this sacrament, as was said above (Q. 73, A. 9) was eaten only once in the year; while the Church once a year commemorates Christ's Passion, of which this sacrament is the memorial. It seems, then, that it is lawful to receive this sacrament not daily, but only once in the year.

OBJ. 3: Further, the greatest reverence is due to this sacrament as containing Christ. But it is a token of reverence to refrain from receiving this sacrament; hence the Centurion is praised for saying (Matt 8:8), *Lord, I am not worthy that Thou shouldst enter under my roof*; also Peter, for saying (Luke 5:8), *Depart from me, for I am a sinful man, O Lord*. Therefore, it is not praiseworthy for a man to receive this sacrament daily.

OBJ. 4: Further, if it were a praiseworthy custom to receive this sacrament frequently, then the oftener it were taken the more praise-worthy it would be. But there would be greater frequency if one were to receive it several times daily; and yet this is not the custom of the Church. Consequently, it does not seem praiseworthy to receive it daily.

OBJ. 5: Further, the Church by her statutes intends to promote the welfare of the faithful. But the Church's statute only requires Communion once a year; hence it is enacted (*Extra, De Poenit. et Remiss.* xii): Let every person of either sex devoutly receive the sacrament of the Eucharist at least at Easter; unless by the advice of his parish priest, and for some reasonable cause, he considers he ought to refrain from receiving for a time. Consequently, it is not praiseworthy to receive this sacrament daily.

ON THE CONTRARY, Augustine says (*De Verb. Dom.*, Serm. xxviii): *This is our daily bread; take it daily, that it may profit thee daily*.

I ANSWER THAT, There are two things to be considered regarding the use of this sacrament. The first is on the part of the sacrament itself, the virtue of which gives health to men; and consequently it is profitable to receive it daily so as to receive its fruits daily. Hence Ambrose says (*De Sacram.* iv): If, whenever Christ's blood is shed, it is shed for the forgiveness of sins, I who sin often, should receive it often: I need a frequent remedy. The second thing

medicinam. Alio modo potest considerari ex parte sumentis, in quo requiritur quod cum magna devotione et reverentia ad hoc sacramentum accedat. Et ideo, si aliquis se quotidie ad hoc paratum inveniat, laudabile est quod quotidie sumat. Unde Augustinus, cum dixisset, *accipe quod quotidie tibi prosit*, subiungit, *sic vive ut quotidie merearis accipere*. Sed quia multoties in pluribus hominum multa impedimenta huius devotionis occurrunt, propter corporis indispositionem vel animae, non est utile omnibus hominibus quotidie ad hoc sacramentum accedere, sed quotiescumque se homo ad illud paratum invenerit. Unde in libro de ecclesiasticis Dogmat. dicitur, *quotidie Eucharistiae communionem accipere nec laudo nec vitupero*.

AD PRIMUM ergo dicendum quod per sacramentum Baptismi configuratur homo morti Christi, in se suscipiens eius characterem, et ideo, sicut Christus semel mortuus est, ita solum semel debet homo baptizari. Sed per hoc sacramentum non recipit homo Christi characterem, sed ipsum Christum, cuius virtus manet in aeternum, unde, ad Heb. X, *una oblatione consummavit sanctificatos in sempiternum*. Et ideo, quia quotidie homo indiget salutifera Christi virtute, quotidie potest laudabiliter hoc sacramentum percipere.

Et quia praecipue Baptismus est spiritualis regeneratio, ideo, sicut homo semel carnaliter nascitur, ita debet semel spiritualiter renasci per Baptismum, ut Augustinus dicit, super illud Ioan. III, *quomodo potest homo nasci cum sit senex?* Sed hoc sacramentum est cibus spiritualis, unde, sicut cibus corporalis quotidie sumitur, ita et hoc sacramentum quotidie sumere laudabile est. Unde dominus, Luc. XI, docet petere, *panem nostrum quotidianum da nobis hodie*, in cuius expositione Augustinus dicit, in libro de verbis domini, si quotidie acceperis, scilicet hoc sacramentum, *quotidie tibi est hodie, tibi Christus quotidie resurgit, hodie enim est quando Christus resurgit*.

AD SECUNDUM dicendum quod agnus paschalis praecipue fuit figura huius sacramenti quantum ad passionem Christi, quae repraesentatur per hoc sacramentum. Et ideo semel tantum in anno sumebatur, quia Christus semel mortuus est. Et propter hoc etiam Ecclesia semel in anno celebrat memoriam passionis Christi. Sed in hoc sacramento traditur nobis memoriale passionis Christi per modum cibi, qui quotidie sumitur. Et ideo quantum ad hoc significatur per manna, quod quotidie populo dabatur in deserto.

AD TERTIUM dicendum quod reverentia huius sacramenti habet timorem amori coniunctum, unde timor reverentiae ad Deum dicitur timor filialis, ut in secunda parte dictum est. Ex amore enim provocatur desiderium sumendi, ex timore autem consurgit humilitas reverendi. Et ideo utrumque pertinet ad reverentiam huius sacramenti, et quod quotidie sumatur, et quod aliquando

to be considered is on the part of the recipient, who is required to approach this sacrament with great reverence and devotion. Consequently, if anyone finds that he has these dispositions every day, he will do well to receive it daily. Hence, Augustine after saying, *Receive daily, that it may profit thee daily*, adds: *So live, as to deserve to receive it daily*. But because many persons are lacking in this devotion, on account of the many drawbacks both spiritual and corporal from which they suffer, it is not expedient for all to approach this sacrament every day; but they should do so as often as they find themselves properly disposed. Hence it is said in De Eccles. Dogmat. liii: *I neither praise nor blame daily reception of the Eucharist*.

REPLY OBJ. 1: In the sacrament of Baptism a man is conformed to Christ's death, by receiving His character within him. And therefore, as Christ died but once, so a man ought to be baptized but once. But a man does not receive Christ's character in this sacrament; He receives Christ Himself, Whose virtue endures for ever. Hence it is written (Heb 10:14): *By one oblation He hath perfected for ever them that are sanctified*. Consequently, since man has daily need of Christ's health-giving virtue, he may commendably receive this sacrament every day.

And since Baptism is above all a spiritual regeneration, therefore, as a man is born naturally but once, so ought he by Baptism to be reborn spiritually but once, as Augustine says (*Tract. xi in Joan.*), commenting on John 3:4, *How can a man be born again, when he is grown old?* But this sacrament is spiritual food; hence, just as bodily food is taken every day, so is it a good thing to receive this sacrament every day. Hence it is that our Lord (Luke 11:3), teaches us to pray, *Give us this day our daily bread*: in explaining which words Augustine observes (*De Verb. Dom.*, Serm. xxviii): *If you receive it*, i.e., this sacrament, every day, *every day is today for thee, and Christ rises again every day in thee, for when Christ riseth it is today*.

REPLY OBJ. 2: The Paschal Lamb was the figure of this sacrament chiefly as to Christ's Passion represented therein; and therefore it was partaken of once a year only, since Christ died but once. And on this account the Church celebrates once a year the remembrance of Christ's Passion. But in this sacrament the memorial of His Passion is given by way of food which is partaken of daily; and therefore in this respect it is represented by the manna which was given daily to the people in the desert.

REPLY OBJ. 3: Reverence for this sacrament consists in fear associated with love; consequently reverential fear of God is called filial fear, as was said in the Second Part (I-II, Q. 67, A. 4, ad 2; II-II, Q. 19, AA. 9, 11, 12); because the desire of receiving arises from love, while the humility of reverence springs from fear. Consequently, each of these belongs to the reverence due to this sacrament; both as to

abstineatur. Unde Augustinus dicit, *si dixerit quispiam non quotidie accipiendam Eucharistiam, alius affirmat quotidie, faciat unusquisque quod secundum fidem suam pie credit esse faciendum. Neque enim litigaverunt inter se Zacchaeus et ille centurio, cum alter eorum gaudens susceperit dominum, alter dixerit, non sum dignus ut intres sub tectum meum, ambo salvatorem honorificantes, quamvis non uno modo.* Amor tamen et spes, ad quae semper Scriptura nos provocat, praeferuntur timori, unde et, cum Petrus dixisset, *exi a me, domine, quia peccator homo ego sum,* respondit Iesus, *noli timere.*

A<small>D</small> <small>QUARTUM</small> dicendum quod, quia dominus dicit, *panem nostrum quotidianum da nobis hodie,* non est pluries in die communicandum, ut saltem per hoc quod aliquis semel in die communicat, repraesentetur unitas passionis Christi.

A<small>D</small> <small>QUINTUM</small> dicendum quod, secundum statum diversum Ecclesiae, diversa circa hoc statuta emanarunt. Nam in primitiva Ecclesia, quando magis vigebat devotio fidei Christianae, statutum fuit ut quotidie fideles communicarent. Unde Anacletus Papa dicit, *peracta consecratione, omnes communicent qui noluerint ecclesiasticis carere liminibus, sic enim et apostoli statuerunt, et sancta Romana tenet Ecclesia.* Postmodum vero, diminuto fidei fervore, Fabianus Papa indulsit *ut, si non frequentius, saltem ter in anno omnes communicent,* scilicet in Pascha, in Pentecoste et in nativitate domini. Soter etiam Papa in cena domini dicit esse communicandum, ut habetur in decretis, de Consecr., dist. II. *Postmodum vero, propter iniquitatis abundantiam refrigescente caritate multorum,* statuit Innocentius III ut saltem semel in anno, scilicet in Pascha, fideles communicent. Consulitur tamen in libro de ecclesiasticis Dogmat., *omnibus diebus dominicis communicandum.*

receiving it daily, and as to refraining from it sometimes. Hence Augustine says (*Ep. liv*): *If one says that the Eucharist should not be received daily, while another maintains the contrary, let each one do as according to his devotion he thinketh right; for Zaccheus and the Centurion did not contradict one another while the one received the Lord with joy, whereas the other said: 'Lord I am not worthy that Thou shouldst enter under my roof'; since both honored our Savior, though not in the same way.* But love and hope, whereunto the Scriptures constantly urge us, are preferable to fear. Hence, too, when Peter had said, *Depart from me, for I am a sinful man, O Lord,* Jesus answered: *Fear not.*

R<small>EPLY</small> O<small>BJ</small>. 4: Because our Lord said (Luke 11:3), *Give us this day our daily bread,* we are not on that account to communicate several times daily, for, by one daily communion the unity of Christ's Passion is set forth.

R<small>EPLY</small> O<small>BJ</small>. 5: Various statutes have emanated according to the various ages of the Church. In the primitive Church, when the devotion of the Christian faith was more flourishing, it was enacted that the faithful should communicate daily: hence Pope Anaclete says (*Ep. i*): *When the consecration is finished, let all communicate who do not wish to cut themselves off from the Church; for so the apostles have ordained, and the holy Roman Church holds.* Later on, when the fervor of faith relaxed, Pope Fabian (Third Council of Tours, Canon 1) gave permission *that all should communicate, if not more frequently, at least three times in the year,* namely, *at Easter, Pentecost, and Christmas.* Pope Soter likewise (Second Council of Chalon, Canon xlvii) declares that Communion should be received *on Holy Thursday,* as is set forth in the *Decretals* (*De Consecratione,* dist. 2). Later on, when *iniquity abounded and charity grew cold* (Matt 24:12), Pope Innocent III commanded that the faithful should communicate *at least once a year,* namely, *at Easter.* However, in De Eccles. Dogmat. xxiii, the faithful are counseled *to communicate on all Sundays.*

Article 11

Whether It Is Lawful to Abstain Altogether from Communion?

A<small>D</small> <small>UNDECIMUM</small> <small>SIC</small> <small>PROCEDITUR</small>. Videtur quod liceat cessare omnino a communione. Laudatur enim centurio de hoc quod dicit, Matth. VIII *domine, non sum dignus ut intres sub tectum meum.* Cui comparatur ille qui reputat sibi a communione esse abstinendum, ut dictum est. Cum ergo nunquam legatur Christum in eius domum venisse, videtur quod liceat alicui toto tempore vitae suae a communione abstinere.

O<small>BJECTION</small> 1: It seems to be lawful to abstain altogether from Communion. Because the Centurion is praised for saying (Matt 8:8): *Lord, I am not worthy that Thou shouldst enter under my roof;* and he who deems that he ought to refrain entirely from Communion can be compared to the Centurion, as stated above (A. 10, ad 3). Therefore, since we do not read of Christ entering his house, it seems to be lawful for any individual to abstain from Communion his whole life long.

PRAETEREA, cuilibet licet abstinere ab his quae non sunt de necessitate salutis. Sed hoc sacramentum non est de necessitate salutis, ut supra dictum est. Ergo licet a susceptione huius sacramenti omnino cessare.

PRAETEREA, peccatores non tenentur communicare, unde Fabianus Papa, cum dixisset, *ter in anno omnes communicent*, adiunxit *nisi forte quis maioribus criminibus impediatur*. Si ergo illi qui non sunt in peccato, tenentur communicare, videtur quod melioris conditionis sint peccatores quam iusti, quod est inconveniens. Ergo videtur quod etiam iustis liceat a communione cessare.

SED CONTRA est quod dominus dicit, Ioan. VI, *nisi manducaveritis carnem filii hominis et biberitis eius sanguinem, non habebitis vitam in vobis*.

RESPONDEO dicendum quod, sicut supra dictum est, duplex est modus percipiendi hoc sacramentum, spiritualis scilicet et sacramentalis. Manifestum est autem quod omnes tenentur saltem spiritualiter manducare, quia hoc est Christo incorporari, ut supra dictum est. Spiritualis autem manducatio includit votum seu desiderium percipiendi hoc sacramentum, ut supra dictum est. Et ideo sine voto percipiendi hoc sacramentum non potest homini esse salus.

Frustra autem esset votum nisi impleretur quando opportunitas adesset. Et ideo manifestum est quod homo tenetur hoc sacramentum sumere, non solum ex statuto Ecclesiae, sed etiam ex mandato domini, dicentis, Matth. XXVI, *hoc facite in meam commemorationem*. Ex statuto autem Ecclesiae sunt determinata tempora exequendi Christi praeceptum.

AD PRIMUM ergo dicendum quod, sicut Gregorius dicit, in pastorali, *illa est vera humilitas, cum ad respuendum hoc quod utiliter praecipitur, pertinax non est*. Et ideo non potest esse laudabilis humilitas si contra praeceptum Christi et Ecclesiae aliquis a communione abstineat. Neque enim centurioni praeceptum fuit ut Christum in sua domo reciperet.

AD SECUNDUM dicendum quod hoc sacramentum dicitur non esse necessitatis sicut Baptismus, quantum ad pueros, quibus potest esse salus sine hoc sacramento, non autem sine sacramento Baptismi. Quantum vero ad adultos, utrumque est necessitatis.

AD TERTIUM dicendum quod peccatores magnum detrimentum patiuntur ex hoc quod repelluntur a perceptione huius sacramenti, unde per hoc non sunt melioris conditionis. Et licet in peccatis permanentes non excusentur propter hoc a transgressione praecepti, poenitens tamen, qui, ut Innocentius dicit, secundum consilium sacerdotis abstinet, excusatur.

OBJ. 2: Further, it is lawful for anyone to refrain from what is not of necessity for salvation. But this sacrament is not of necessity for salvation, as was stated above (Q. 73, A. 3). Therefore it is permissible to abstain from Communion altogether.

OBJ. 3: Further, sinners are not bound to go to Communion: hence Pope Fabian (Third Council of Tours, Canon 1) after saying, *Let all communicate thrice each year*, adds: *Except those who are hindered by grievous crimes*. Consequently, if those who are not in the state of sin are bound to go to Communion, it seems that sinners are better off than good people, which is unfitting. Therefore, it seems lawful even for the godly to refrain from Communion.

ON THE CONTRARY, Our Lord said (John 6:54): *Except ye eat the flesh of the Son of Man, and drink His blood, you shall not have life in you.*

I ANSWER THAT, As stated above (A. 1), there are two ways of receiving this sacrament namely, spiritually and sacramentally. Now it is clear that all are bound to eat it at least spiritually, because this is to be incorporated in Christ, as was said above (Q. 73, A. 3, ad 1). Now spiritual eating comprises the desire or yearning for receiving this sacrament, as was said above (A. 1, ad 3, A. 2). Therefore, a man cannot be saved without desiring to receive this sacrament.

Now a desire would be vain except it were fulfilled when opportunity presented itself. Consequently, it is evident that a man is bound to receive this sacrament, not only by virtue of the Church's precept, but also by virtue of the Lord's command (Luke 22:19): *Do this in memory of Me.* But by the precept of the Church there are fixed times for fulfilling Christ's command.

REPLY OBJ. 1: As Gregory says: *He is truly humble, who is not obstinate in rejecting what is commanded for his good.* Consequently, humility is not praiseworthy if anyone abstains altogether from Communion against the precept of Christ and the Church. Again the Centurion was not commanded to receive Christ into his house.

REPLY OBJ. 2: This sacrament is said not to be as necessary as Baptism, with regard to children, who can be saved without the Eucharist, but not without the sacrament of Baptism: both, however, are of necessity with regard to adults.

REPLY OBJ. 3: Sinners suffer great loss in being kept back from receiving this sacrament, so that they are not better off on that account; and although while continuing in their sins they are not on that account excused from transgressing the precept, nevertheless, as Pope Innocent III says, penitents, *who refrain on the advice of their priest*, are excused.

Article 12

Whether It Is Lawful to Receive the Body of Christ Without the Blood?

AD DUODECIMUM SIC PROCEDITUR. Videtur quod non liceat sumere corpus domini sine sanguine. Dicit enim Gelasius Papa, et habetur de Consecrat., dist. II, *comperimus quod quidam, sumpta tantummodo corporis sacri portione, a calice sacrati cruoris abstinent. Qui procul dubio, quoniam nescio qua superstitione docentur adstringi, aut integra sacramenta percipiant, aut ab integris arceantur.* Non ergo licet corpus Christi sumere sine sanguine.

PRAETEREA, ad perfectionem huius sacramenti concurrit manducatio corporis et potatio sanguinis, ut supra habitum est. Si ergo sumatur corpus sine sanguine, erit sacramentum imperfectum. Quod ad sacrilegium pertinere videtur. Unde ibidem Gelasius subdit, *quia divisio unius eiusdemque mysterii sine grandi sacrilegio non potest provenire.*

PRAETEREA, hoc sacramentum celebratur in memoriam dominicae passionis, ut supra habitum est, et sumitur pro animae salute. Sed passio Christi magis exprimitur in sanguine quam in corpore, sanguis etiam pro salute animae offertur, ut supra habitum est. Ergo potius esset abstinendum a sumptione corporis quam a sumptione sanguinis. Non ergo accedentes ad hoc sacramentum debent sumere corpus sine eius sanguine.

SED CONTRA est multarum Ecclesiarum usus, in quibus populo communicanti datur corpus Christi sumendum, non autem sanguis.

RESPONDEO dicendum quod circa usum huius sacramenti duo possunt considerari, unum ex parte ipsius sacramenti; aliud ex parte sumentium. Ex parte ipsius sacramenti convenit quod utrumque sumatur, scilicet et corpus et sanguis, quia in utroque consistit perfectio sacramenti. Et ideo, quia ad sacerdotem pertinet hoc sacramentum consecrare et perficere, nullo modo debet corpus Christi sumere sine sanguine.

Ex parte autem sumentium requiritur summa reverentia, et cautela ne aliquid accidat quod vergat in iniuriam tanti mysterii. Quod praecipue posset accidere in sanguinis sumptione, qui quidem, si incaute sumeretur, de facili posset effundi. Et quia, crescente multitudine populi Christiani, in qua continentur senes et iuvenes et parvuli, quorum quidam non sunt tantae discretionis ut cautelam debitam circa usum huius sacramenti adhiberent, ideo provide in quibusdam Ecclesiis observatur ut populo sanguis sumendus non detur, sed solum a sacerdote sumatur.

AD PRIMUM ergo dicendum quod Gelasius Papa loquitur quantum ad sacerdotes, qui, sicut totum

OBJECTION 1: It seems unlawful to receive the body of Christ without the blood. For Pope Gelasius says (cf. *De Consecr.* ii): *We have learned that some persons after taking only a portion of the sacred body, abstain from the chalice of the sacred blood. I know not for what superstitious motive they do this: therefore let them either receive the entire sacrament, or let them be withheld from the sacrament altogether.* Therefore it is not lawful to receive the body of Christ without His blood.

OBJ. 2: Further, the eating of the body and the drinking of the blood are required for the perfection of this sacrament, as stated above (Q. 73, A. 2; Q. 76, A. 2, ad 1). Consequently, if the body be taken without the blood, it will be an imperfect sacrament, which seems to savor of sacrilege; hence Pope Gelasius adds (cf. *De Consecr.* ii), *because the dividing of one and the same mystery cannot happen without a great sacrilege.*

OBJ. 3: Further, this sacrament is celebrated in memory of our Lord's Passion, as stated above (Q. 73, AA. 4, 5; Q. 74, A. 1), and is received for the health of soul. But the Passion is expressed in the blood rather than in the body; moreover, as stated above (Q. 74, A. 1), the blood is offered for the health of the soul. Consequently, one ought to refrain from receiving the body rather than the blood. Therefore, such as approach this sacrament ought not to take Christ's body without His blood.

ON THE CONTRARY, It is the custom of many churches for the body of Christ to be given to the communicant without His blood.

I ANSWER THAT, Two points should be observed regarding the use of this sacrament, one on the part of the sacrament, the other on the part of the recipients; on the part of the sacrament it is proper for both the body and the blood to be received, since the perfection of the sacrament lies in both, and consequently, since it is the priest's duty both to consecrate and finish the sacrament, he ought on no account to receive Christ's body without the blood.

But on the part of the recipient the greatest reverence and caution are called for, lest anything happen which is unworthy of so great a mystery. Now this could especially happen in receiving the blood, for, if incautiously handled, it might easily be spilt. And because the multitude of the Christian people increased, in which there are old, young, and children, some of whom have not enough discretion to observe due caution in using this sacrament, on that account it is a prudent custom in some churches for the blood not to be offered to the reception of the people, but to be received by the priest alone.

REPLY OBJ. 1: Pope Gelasius is speaking of priests, who, as they consecrate the entire sacrament, ought to

consecrant sacramentum, ita etiam toti communicare debent. Ut enim legitur in Concilio Toletano, *quale erit sacrificium, ubi nec ipse sacrificans esse dignoscitur?*

AD SECUNDUM dicendum quod perfectio huius sacramenti non est in usu fidelium, sed in consecratione materiae. Et ideo nihil derogat perfectioni huius sacramenti si populus sumat corpus sine sanguine, dummodo sacerdos consecrans sumat utrumque.

AD TERTIUM dicendum quod repraesentatio dominicae passionis agitur in ipsa consecratione huius sacramenti, in qua non debet corpus sine sanguine consecrari. Potest autem a populo corpus sine sanguine sumi, nec exinde aliquod sequitur detrimentum. Quia sacerdos in persona omnium sanguinem offert et sumit, et sub utraque specie totus Christus continetur, ut supra habitum est.

communicate in the entire sacrament. For, as we read in the (Twelfth) Council of Toledo, *What kind of a sacrifice is that, wherein not even the sacrificer is known to have a share?*

REPLY OBJ. 2: The perfection of this sacrament does not lie in the use of the faithful, but in the consecration of the matter. And hence there is nothing derogatory to the perfection of this sacrament; if the people receive the body without the blood, provided that the priest who consecrates receive both.

REPLY OBJ. 3: Our Lord's Passion is represented in the very consecration of this sacrament, in which the body ought not to be consecrated without the blood. But the body can be received by the people without the blood: nor is this detrimental to the sacrament. Because the priest both offers and consumes the blood on behalf of all; and Christ is fully contained under either species, as was shown above (Q. 76, A. 2).

QUESTION 81

THE USE WHICH CHRIST MADE OF THIS SACRAMENT

Deinde considerandum est de usu huius sacramenti quo Christus usus est in prima sui institutione. Et circa hoc quaeruntur quatuor.

Primo, utrum ipse Christus sumpserit corpus et sanguinem suum.

Secundo, utrum Iudae dederit.

Tertio, quale corpus sumpserit aut dederit, scilicet passibile vel impassibile.

Quarto, quomodo se habuisset Christus sub hoc sacramento si fuisset in triduo mortis reservatum, aut etiam consecratum.

We have now to consider the use which Christ made of this sacrament at its institution; under which heading there are four points of inquiry:

(1) Whether Christ received His own body and blood?

(2) Whether He gave it to Judas?

(3) What kind of body did He receive or give, namely, was it passible or impassible?

(4) What would have been the condition of Christ's body under this sacrament, if it had been reserved or consecrated during the three days He lay dead?

Article 1

Whether Christ Received His Own Body and Blood?

AD PRIMUM SIC PROCEDITUR. Videtur quod Christus non sumpserit corpus suum et sanguinem. Non enim de factis Christi et dictis asseri debet quod auctoritate sacrae Scripturae non traditur. Sed in Evangeliis non habetur quod Christus corpus suum manducaverit aut sanguinem biberit. Non ergo est hoc asserendum.

PRAETEREA, nihil potest esse in seipso, nisi forte ratione partium, prout scilicet una pars eius est in alia, ut habetur in IV Physic. sed illud quod manducatur et bibitur, est in manducante et bibente. Cum ergo totus Christus sit in utraque specie sacramenti, videtur impossibile fuisse quod ipse sumpserit hoc sacramentum.

PRAETEREA, duplex est assumptio huius sacramenti, scilicet spiritualis et sacramentalis. Sed spiritualis non competebat Christo, quia nihil a sacramento accepit. Et per consequens nec sacramentalis, quae sine spirituali est imperfecta, ut supra habitum est. Ergo Christus nullo modo hoc sacramentum sumpsit.

SED CONTRA est quod Hieronymus dicit, ad Heldibiam, *dominus Iesus ipse conviva et convivium, ipse comedens et qui comeditur.*

RESPONDEO dicendum quod quidam dixerunt quod Christus in cena corpus et sanguinem suum discipulis tradidit, non tamen ipse sumpsit. Sed hoc non videtur convenienter dici. Quia Christus ea quae ab aliis observanda instituit, ipse primitus observavit, unde et ipse prius baptizari voluit quam aliis Baptismum imponeret, secundum illud Act. I, *coepit Iesus facere et docere.* Unde et ipse primo corpus suum et sanguinem sumpsit,

OBJECTION 1: It seems that Christ did not receive His own body and blood, because nothing ought to be asserted of either Christ's doings or sayings, which is not handed down by the authority of Sacred Scripture. But it is not narrated in the gospels that He ate His own body or drank His own blood. Therefore we must not assert this as a fact.

OBJ. 2: Further, nothing can be within itself except perchance by reason of its parts, for instance, as one part is in another, as is stated in *Phys.* iv. But what is eaten and drunk is in the eater and drinker. Therefore, since the entire Christ is under each species of the sacrament, it seems impossible for Him to have received this sacrament.

OBJ. 3: Further, the receiving of this sacrament is twofold, namely, spiritual and sacramental. But the spiritual was unsuitable for Christ, as He derived no benefit from the sacrament; and in consequence so was the sacramental, since it is imperfect without the spiritual, as was observed above (Q. 80, A. 1). Consequently, in no way did Christ partake of this sacrament.

ON THE CONTRARY, Jerome says (*Ad Hedib., Ep. xxx*), *The Lord Jesus Christ, Himself the guest and banquet, is both the partaker and what is eaten.*

I ANSWER THAT, Some have said that Christ during the supper gave His body and blood to His disciples, but did not partake of it Himself. But this seems improbable. Because Christ Himself was the first to fulfill what He required others to observe: hence He willed first to be baptized when imposing Baptism upon others: as we read in Acts 1:1: *Jesus began to do and to teach.* Hence He first of all took His own body and blood, and afterwards gave it to be

et postea discipulis suis tradidit sumendum. Et hoc est quod, Ruth III, super illud, *cumque comedisset et bibisset* etc., dicit Glossa, quod *Christus comedit et bibit in cena, cum corporis et sanguinis sui sacramentum discipulis tradidit. Unde, quia pueri communicaverunt carni et sanguini, et ipse participavit eisdem.*

AD PRIMUM ergo dicendum quod in Evangeliis legitur quod Christus accepit panem et calicem. Non est autem intelligendum quod acceperit solum in manibus, ut quidam dicunt, sed eo modo accepit quo aliis accipiendum tradidit. Unde, cum discipulis dixerit, accipite et comedite, et iterum, accipite et bibite, intelligendum est quod ipse dominus accipiens comederit et biberit. Unde et quidam metrice dixerunt, *rex sedet in cena, turba cinctus duodena, se tenet in manibus, se cibat ipse cibus.*

AD SECUNDUM dicendum quod, sicut supra dictum est, Christus, secundum quod est sub hoc sacramento, comparatur ad locum non secundum proprias dimensiones, sed secundum dimensiones specierum sacramentalium, ita quod in quocumque loco ubi sunt illae species, est ipse Christus. Et quia species illae potuerunt esse in manibus et in ore Christi, ipse totus Christus potuit esse in suis manibus et in suo ore. Non autem potuisset hoc esse secundum quod comparatur ad locum secundum proprias species.

AD TERTIUM dicendum quod, sicut supra dictum est, effectus huius sacramenti est non solum augmentum habitualis gratiae, sed etiam actualis delectatio spiritualis dulcedinis. Quamvis autem Christo gratia non fuerit augmentata ex susceptione huius sacramenti, habuit tamen quandam spiritualem delectationem in nova institutione huius sacramenti, unde ipse dicebat, Luc. XXII, *desiderio desideravi manducare hoc Pascha vobiscum,* quod Eusebius exponit de novo mysterio huius novi testamenti quod tradebat discipulis. Et ideo spiritualiter manducavit, et similiter sacramentaliter, inquantum corpus suum sub sacramento sumpsit, quod sacramentum sui corporis intellexit et disposuit. Aliter tamen quam ceteri sacramentaliter et spiritualiter sumant, qui augmentum gratiae suscipiunt, et sacramentalibus signis indigent ad veritatis perceptionem.

taken by the disciples. And hence the gloss upon Ruth 3:7, *When he had eaten and drunk,* says: *Christ ate and drank at the supper, when He gave to the disciples the sacrament of His body and blood.* Hence, 'because the children partook of His flesh and blood, He also hath been partaker in the same.'

REPLY OBJ. 1: We read in the Gospels how Christ *took the bread . . . and the chalice*; but it is not to be understood that He took them merely into His hands, as some say, but that He took them in the same way as He gave them to others to take. Hence when He said to the disciples, *Take ye and eat,* and again, *Take ye and drink,* it is to be understood that He Himself, in taking it, both ate and drank. Hence some have composed this rhyme: *The King at supper sits, The twelve as guests He greets, Clasping Himself in His hands, The food Himself now eats.*

REPLY OBJ. 2: As was said above (Q. 76, A. 5), Christ as contained under this sacrament stands in relation to place, not according to His own dimensions, but according to the dimensions of the sacramental species; so that Christ is Himself in every place where those species are. And because the species were able to be both in the hands and the mouth of Christ, the entire Christ could be in both His hands and mouth. Now this could not come to pass were His relation to place to be according to His proper dimensions.

REPLY OBJ. 3: As was stated above (Q. 79, A. 1, ad 2), the effect of this sacrament is not merely an increase of habitual grace, but furthermore a certain actual delectation of spiritual sweetness. But although grace was not increased in Christ through His receiving this sacrament, yet He had a certain spiritual delectation from the new institution of this sacrament. Hence He Himself said (Luke 22:15): *With desire I have desired to eat this Pasch with you,* which words Eusebius explains of the new mystery of the New Testament, which He gave to the disciples. And therefore He ate it both spiritually and sacramentally, inasmuch as He received His own body under the sacrament which sacrament of His own body He both understood and prepared; yet differently from others who partake of it both sacramentally and spiritually, for these receive an increase of grace, and they have need of the sacramental signs for perceiving its truth.

Article 2

Whether Christ Gave His Body to Judas?

AD SECUNDUM SIC PROCEDITUR. Videtur quod Christus Iudae non dederit corpus suum. Ut enim legitur Matth. XXVI, postquam dominus dederat corpus suum et sanguinem discipulis, dixit eis, *non bibam amodo de hoc genimine vitis usque in diem illum cum illud*

OBJECTION 1: It seems that Christ did not give His body to Judas. Because, as we read (Matt 26:29), our Lord, after giving His body and blood to the disciples, said to them: *I will not drink from henceforth of this fruit of the vine, until that day when I shall drink it with you new in the kingdom*

bibam vobiscum novum in regno patris mei. Ex quo videtur quod illi quibus corpus suum et sanguinem dederat, cum eo essent iterum bibituri. Sed Iudas postea cum ipso non bibit. Ergo non accepit cum aliis discipulis corpus Christi et sanguinem.

PRAETEREA, dominus implevit quod praecepit, secundum illud Act. I, *coepit Iesus facere et docere.* Sed ipse praecepit, Matth. VII, *nolite sanctum dare canibus.* Cum ergo ipse cognosceret Iudam peccatorem esse, videtur quod ei corpus suum et sanguinem non dederit.

PRAETEREA, Christus specialiter legitur Iudae panem intinctum porrexisse, Ioan. XIII. Si ergo corpus suum ei dederit, videtur quod sub buccella ei dederit, praecipue cum legatur ibidem, *et post buccellam introivit in eum Satanas*; ubi Augustinus dicit, *hinc nos docemur quam sit cavendum male accipere bonum. Si enim corripitur qui non diiudicat, idest, non discernit corpus domini a ceteris cibis, quomodo damnabitur qui ad eius mensam, fingens se amicum, accedit inimicus?* Sed cum buccella intincta non accepit corpus Christi, ut Augustinus dicit, super illud Ioan. XIII, *cum intinxisset panem, dedit Iudae Simonis Iscariotis, non, ut putant quidam negligenter legentes, tunc Iudas solus corpus Christi accepit.* Ergo videtur quod Iudas corpus Christi non acceperit.

SED CONTRA est quod Chrysostomus dicit, *Iudas, particeps existens mysteriorum, conversus non est. Unde fit scelus eius utrinque immanius, tum quia tali proposito imbutus adiit mysteria; tum quia adiens melior factus non fuit, nec metu nec beneficio nec honore.*

RESPONDEO dicendum quod Hilarius posuit, super Matth., quod Christus Iudae corpus suum et sanguinem non dedit. Et hoc quidem conveniens fuisset, considerata malitia Iudae. Sed quia Christus debuit nobis esse exemplum iustitiae, non conveniebat eius magisterio ut Iudam, occultum peccatorem, sine accusatore et evidenti probatione, ab aliorum communione separaret, ne per hoc daretur exemplum praelatis Ecclesiae similia faciendi; et ipse Iudas, inde exasperatus, sumeret occasionem peccandi. Et ideo dicendum est quod Iudas cum aliis discipulis corpus domini et sanguinem suscepit, ut dicit Dionysius in libro Eccles. Hier., et Augustinus, super Ioannem.

AD PRIMUM ergo dicendum quod illa est ratio Hilarii ad ostendendum quod Iudas corpus Christi non sumpsit. Non tamen cogit. Quia Christus loquitur discipulis, a quorum collegio Iudas se separavit, non autem Christus eum exclusit. Et ideo Christus, quantum est in se, etiam cum Iuda vinum in regno Dei bibit, sed hoc convivium ipse Iudas repudiavit.

of My Father. From this it appears that those to whom He had given His body and blood were to drink of it again with Him. But Judas did not drink of it afterwards with Him. Therefore he did not receive Christ's body and blood with the other disciples.

OBJ. 2: Further, what the Lord commanded, He Himself fulfilled, as is said in Acts 1:1: *Jesus began to do and to teach.* But He gave the command (Matt 7:6): *Give not that which is holy to dogs.* Therefore, knowing Judas to be a sinner, seemingly He did not give him His body and blood.

OBJ. 3: Further, it is distinctly related (John 13:26) that Christ gave dipped bread to Judas. Consequently, if He gave His body to him, it appears that He gave it him in the morsel, especially since we read (John 13:26) that *after the morsel, Satan entered into him.* And on this passage Augustine says (*Tract. lxii in Ioan.*): *From this we learn how we should beware of receiving a good thing in an evil way . . . For if he be 'chastised' who does 'not discern,' i.e., distinguish, the body of the Lord from other meats, how must he be 'condemned' who, feigning himself a friend, comes to His table a foe?* But (Judas) did not receive our Lord's body with the dipped morsel; thus Augustine commenting on John 13:26, *When He had dipped the bread, He gave it to Judas, the son of Simon the Iscariot,* says (*Tract. lxii in Ioan.*): *Judas did not receive Christ's body then, as some think who read carelessly.* Therefore it seems that Judas did not receive the body of Christ.

ON THE CONTRARY, Chrysostom says (*Hom. lxxxii in Matth.*): *Judas was not converted while partaking of the sacred mysteries: hence on both sides his crime becomes the more heinous, both because imbued with such a purpose he approached the mysteries, and because he became none the better for approaching, neither from fear, nor from the benefit received, nor from the honor conferred on him.*

I ANSWER THAT, Hilary, in commenting on Matt. 26:17, held that Christ did not give His body and blood to Judas. And this would have been quite proper, if the malice of Judas be considered. But since Christ was to serve us as a pattern of justice, it was not in keeping with His teaching authority to sever Judas, a hidden sinner, from Communion with the others without an accuser and evident proof; lest the Church's prelates might have an example for doing the like, and lest Judas himself being exasperated might take occasion of sinning. Therefore, it remains to be said that Judas received our Lord's body and blood with the other disciples, as Dionysius says (*Eccl. Hier.* iii), and Augustine (*Tract. lxii in Ioan.*).

REPLY OBJ. 1: This is Hilary's argument, to show that Judas did not receive Christ's body. But it is not cogent; because Christ is speaking to the disciples, from whose company Judas separated himself: and it was not Christ that excluded him. Therefore Christ for His part drinks the wine even with Judas in the kingdom of God; but Judas himself repudiated this banquet.

AD SECUNDUM dicendum quod Christo nota erat Iudae iniquitas sicut Deo, non autem erat sibi nota per modum quo hominibus innotescit. Et ideo Christus Iudam non repulit a communione, ut daret exemplum tales peccatores occultos non esse ab aliis sacerdotibus repellendos.

AD TERTIUM dicendum quod sine dubio Iudas sub pane intincto corpus Christi non sumpsit, sed simplicem panem. Significatur autem fortasis, ut Augustinus dicit ibidem, *per panis intinctionem fictio Iudae, ut enim inficiantur, nonnulla tinguntur. Si autem bonum aliquod hic significat tinctio,* scilicet dulcedinem bonitatis divinae, quia panis ex intinctione sapidior redditur, eidem bono ingratum non immerito secuta est damnatio. Et propter hanc ingratitudinem id quod est bonum, factum est ei malum, sicut accidit circa sumentes corpus Christi indigne.

Et, sicut Augustinus dicit ibidem, *intelligendum est quod dominus iam antea distribuerat omnibus discipulis suis sacramentum corporis et sanguinis sui, ubi et ipse Iudas erat, sicut Lucas narrat. Ac deinde ad hoc ventum est, ubi, secundum narrationem Ioannis, dominus per buccellam tinctam atque porrectam suum exprimit proditorem.*

REPLY OBJ. 2: The wickedness of Judas was known to Christ as God; but it was unknown to Him, after the manner in which men know it. Consequently, Christ did not repel Judas from Communion; so as to furnish an example that such secret sinners are not to be repelled by other priests.

REPLY OBJ. 3: Without any doubt Judas did not receive Christ's body in the dipped bread; he received mere bread. Yet as Augustine observes (*Tract. lxii in Joan.*), *perchance the feigning of Judas is denoted by the dipping of the bread; just as some things are dipped to be dyed. If, however, the dipping signifies here anything good* (for instance, the sweetness of the Divine goodness, since bread is rendered more savory by being dipped), *then, not undeservedly, did condemnation follow his ingratitude for that same good. And owing to that ingratitude, what is good became evil to him, as happens to them who receive Christ's body unworthily.*

And as Augustine says (*Tract. lxii in Joan.*), *it must be understood that our Lord had already distributed the sacrament of His body and blood to all His disciples, among whom was Judas also, as Luke narrates: and after that, we came to this, where, according to the relation of John, our Lord, by dipping and handing the morsel, does most openly declare His betrayer.*

Article 3

Whether Christ Received and Gave to the Disciples His Impassible Body?

AD TERTIUM SIC PROCEDITUR. Videtur quod Christus sumpserit et dederit corpus suum discipulis impassibile. Quia super illud Matth. XVII, *transfiguratus est ante illos,* dicit quaedam Glossa, *illud corpus quod habuit per naturam, dedit discipulis in cena, non mortale et passibile.* Et Levit. II, super illud, *si oblatio tua fuerit de sartagine,* dicit Glossa, *crux, super omnia fortis, carnem Christi, quae ante passionem non videbatur esui apta, post aptam fecit.* Sed Christus dedit corpus suum ut aptum ad manducandum. Ergo dedit tale quale habuit post passionem, scilicet impassibile et immortale.

PRAETEREA, omne corpus passibile per contactum et manducationem patitur. Si ergo corpus Christi erat passibile, per contactum et comestionem discipulorum passum fuisset.

PRAETEREA, verba sacramentalia non sunt modo maioris virtutis quando proferuntur a sacerdote in persona Christi, quam tunc quando fuerunt prolata ab ipso Christo. Sed nunc virtute verborum sacramentalium in altari consecratur corpus Christi impassibile et immortale. Ergo multo magis tunc.

SED CONTRA est quod, sicut Innocentius III dicit, *tale corpus tunc dedit discipulis quale habuit.* Habuit

OBJECTION 1: It seems that Christ both received and gave to the disciples His impassible body. Because on Matt. 17:2, *He was transfigured before them,* the gloss says: *He gave to the disciples at the supper that body which He had through nature, but neither mortal nor passible.* And again, on Lev. 2:5, *if thy oblation be from the frying-pan,* the gloss says: *The Cross mightier than all things made Christ's flesh fit for being eaten, which before the Passion did not seem so suited.* But Christ gave His body as suited for eating. Therefore He gave it just as it was after the Passion, that is, impassible and immortal.

OBJ. 2: Further, every passible body suffers by contact and by being eaten. Consequently, if Christ's body was passible, it would have suffered both from contact and from being eaten by the disciples.

OBJ. 3: Further, the sacramental words now spoken by the priest in the person of Christ are not more powerful than when uttered by Christ Himself. But now by virtue of the sacramental words it is Christ's impassible and immortal body which is consecrated upon the altar. Therefore, much more so was it then.

ON THE CONTRARY, As Innocent III says (*De Sacr. Alt. Myst.* iv), *He bestowed on the disciples His body such as it*

autem tunc corpus passibile et mortale. Ergo corpus passibile et mortale discipulis dedit.

RESPONDEO dicendum quod Hugo de sancto Victore posuit quod Christus ante passionem diversis temporibus quatuor dotes corporis glorificati assumpsit, scilicet subtilitatem in nativitate, quando exivit de clauso utero virginis; agilitatem, quando siccis pedibus super mare ambulavit; claritatem, in transfiguratione; impassibilitatem, in cena, quando corpus suum tradidit discipulis ad manducandum. Et secundum hoc, dedit discipulis suis corpus impassibile et immortale.

Sed, quidquid sit de aliis, de quibus supra dictum est quid sentiri debeat, circa impassibilitatem tamen impossibile est esse quod dicitur. Manifestum est enim quod idem verum corpus Christi erat quod a discipulis tunc in propria specie videbatur, et in specie sacramenti sumebatur. Non autem erat impassibile secundum quod in propria specie videbatur, quinimmo erat passioni paratum. Unde nec ipsum corpus quod in specie sacramenti dabatur, impassibile erat.

Impassibili tamen modo erat sub specie sacramenti quod in se erat passibile, sicut invisibiliter quod in se erat visibile. Sicut enim visio requirit contactum corporis quod videtur ad circumstans medium visionis, ita passio requirit contactum corporis quod patitur ad ea quae agunt. Corpus autem Christi, secundum quod est sub sacramento, ut supra dictum est, non comparatur ad ea quae circumstant mediantibus propriis dimensionibus, quibus corpora se tangunt, sed mediantibus dimensionibus specierum panis et vini. Et ideo species illae sunt quae patiuntur et videntur, non autem ipsum corpus Christi.

AD PRIMUM ergo dicendum quod Christus dicitur non dedisse in cena corpus suum mortale et passibile, quia non dedit corporali et passibili modo. Crux autem facit carnem Christi aptam manducationi, inquantum hoc sacramentum repraesentat passionem Christi.

AD SECUNDUM dicendum quod ratio illa procederet si corpus Christi sicut erat passibile, ita passibili modo fuisset sub sacramento.

AD TERTIUM dicendum quod, sicut supra dictum est, accidentia corporis Christi sunt in hoc sacramento ex reali concomitantia, non autem ex vi sacramenti, ex qua est ibi substantia corporis Christi. Et ideo virtus verborum sacramentalium ad hoc se extendit ut sit sub hoc sacramento corpus, Christi scilicet, quibuscumque accidentibus realiter in eo existentibus.

was. But then He had a passible and a mortal body. Therefore, He gave a passible and mortal body to the disciples.

I ANSWER THAT, Hugh of Saint Victor (Innocent III, *De Sacr. Alt. Myst.* iv), maintained, that before the Passion, Christ assumed at various times the four properties of a glorified body—namely, subtlety in His birth, when He came forth from the closed womb of the Virgin; agility, when He walked dryshod upon the sea; clarity, in the Transfiguration; and impassibility at the Last Supper, when He gave His body to the disciples to be eaten. And according to this He gave His body in an impassible and immortal condition to His disciples.

But whatever may be the case touching the other qualities, concerning which we have already stated what should be held (Q. 28, A. 2, ad 3; Q. 45, A. 2), nevertheless the above opinion regarding impassibility is inadmissible. For it is manifest that the same body of Christ which was then seen by the disciples in its own species, was received by them under the sacramental species. But as seen in its own species it was not impassible; nay more, it was ready for the Passion. Therefore, neither was Christ's body impassible when given under the sacramental species.

Yet there was present in the sacrament, in an impassible manner, that which was passible of itself; just as that was there invisibly which of itself was visible. For as sight requires that the body seen be in contact with the adjacent medium of sight, so does passion require contact of the suffering body with the active agents. But Christ's body, according as it is under the sacrament, as stated above (A. 1, ad 2; Q. 76, A. 5), is not compared with its surroundings through the intermediary of its own dimensions, whereby bodies touch each other, but through the dimensions of the bread and wine; consequently, it is those species which are acted upon and are seen, but not Christ's own body.

REPLY OBJ. 1: Christ is said not to have given His mortal and passible body at the supper, because He did not give it in mortal and passible fashion. But the Cross made His flesh adapted for eating, inasmuch as this sacrament represents Christ's Passion.

REPLY OBJ. 2: This argument would hold, if Christ's body, as it was passible, were also present in a passible manner in this sacrament.

REPLY OBJ. 3: As stated above (Q. 76, A. 4), the accidents of Christ's body are in this sacrament by real concomitance, but not by the power of the sacrament, whereby the substance of Christ's body comes to be there. And therefore the power of the sacramental words extends to this, that the body, i.e., Christ's, is under this sacrament, whatever accidents really exist in it.

Article 4

Whether, If This Sacrament Had Been Reserved in a Pyx, or Consecrated at the Moment of Christ's Death by One of the Apostles, Christ Himself Would Have Died There?

Ad quartum sic proceditur. Videtur quod, si hoc sacramentum tempore mortis Christi fuisset servatum in pyxide, vel ab aliquo apostolorum consecratum, non ibi moreretur. Mors enim Christi accidit per eius passionem. Sed Christus impassibili modo etiam tunc erat in hoc sacramento. Ergo non poterat mori in hoc sacramento.

Praeterea, in morte Christi separatus fuit sanguis eius a corpore. Sed in hoc sacramento simul est corpus Christi et sanguis. Ergo Christus in hoc sacramento non moreretur.

Praeterea, mors accidit per separationem animae a corpore. Sed in hoc sacramento continetur tam corpus Christi quam anima. Ergo in hoc sacramento non poterat Christus mori.

Sed contra est quod idem Christus qui erat in cruce, fuisset in sacramento. Sed in cruce moriebatur. Ergo et in sacramento conservato moreretur.

Respondeo dicendum quod corpus Christi idem in substantia est in hoc sacramento et in propria specie, sed non eodem modo, nam in propria specie contingit circumstantia corpora per proprias dimensiones, non autem prout est in hoc sacramento, ut supra dictum est. Et ideo quidquid pertinet ad Christum secundum quod est in se, potest attribui ei et in propria specie et in sacramento existenti, sicut vivere, mori, dolere, animatum vel inanimatum esse, et cetera huiusmodi. Quaecumque vero conveniunt ei per comparationem ad corpora extrinseca, possunt ei attribui in propria specie existenti, non autem prout est in sacramento, sicut irrideri, conspui, crucifigi, flagellari, et cetera huiusmodi. Unde quidam metrice dixerunt, *pyxide servato poteris sociare dolorem innatum, sed non illatus convenit illi.*

Ad primum ergo dicendum quod, sicut dictum est, passio convenit corpori passo per comparationem ad agens extrinsecum. Et ideo Christus, secundum quod est sub sacramento, pati non potest. Potest tamen mori.

Ad secundum dicendum quod, sicut supra dictum est, sub specie panis est corpus Christi ex vi consecrationis, sanguis autem sub specie vini. Sed nunc quidem, quando realiter sanguis Christi non est separatus ab eius corpore, ex reali concomitantia et sanguis Christi est sub specie panis simul cum corpore, et corpus sub specie vini simul cum sanguine. Sed, si in tempore passionis Christi, quando realiter sanguis fuit separatus a corpore, fuisset hoc sacramentum consecratum, sub specie panis

Objection 1: It seems that if this sacrament had been reserved in a pyx at the moment of Christ's death, or had then been consecrated by one of the apostles, that Christ would not have died there. For Christ's death happened through His Passion. But even then He was in this sacrament in an impassible manner. Therefore, He could not die in this sacrament.

Obj. 2: Further, on the death of Christ, His blood was separated from the body. But His flesh and blood are together in this sacrament. Therefore He could not die in this sacrament.

Obj. 3: Further, death ensues from the separation of the soul from the body. But both the body and the soul of Christ are contained in this sacrament. Therefore Christ could not die in this sacrament.

On the contrary, The same Christ Who was upon the cross would have been in this sacrament. But He died upon the cross. Therefore, if this sacrament had been reserved, He would have died therein.

I answer that, Christ's body is substantially the same in this sacrament, as in its proper species, but not after the same fashion; because in its proper species it comes in contact with surrounding bodies by its own dimensions: but it does not do so as it is in this sacrament, as stated above (A. 3). And therefore, all that belongs to Christ, as He is in Himself, can be attributed to Him both in His proper species, and as He exists in the sacrament; such as to live, to die, to grieve, to be animate or inanimate, and the like; while all that belongs to Him in relation to outward bodies, can be attributed to Him as He exists in His proper species, but not as He is in this sacrament; such as to be mocked, to be spat upon, to be crucified, to be scourged, and the rest. Hence some have composed this verse: *Our Lord can grieve beneath the sacramental veils, But cannot feel the piercing of the thorns and nails.*

Reply Obj. 1: As was stated above, suffering belongs to a body that suffers in respect of some extrinsic body. And therefore Christ, as in this sacrament, cannot suffer; yet He can die.

Reply Obj. 2: As was said above (Q. 76, A. 2), in virtue of the consecration, the body of Christ is under the species of bread, while His blood is under the species of wine. But now that His blood is not really separated from His body; by real concomitance, both His blood is present with the body under the species of the bread, and His body together with the blood under the species of the wine. But at the time when Christ suffered, when His blood was really separated from His body, if this sacrament had been

fuisset solum corpus, et sub specie vini fuisset solus sanguis.

AD TERTIUM dicendum quod, sicut supra dictum est, anima Christi est in hoc sacramento ex reali concomitantia, quia non est sine corpore, non autem ex vi consecrationis. Et ideo, si tunc fuisset hoc sacramentum consecratum vel servatum quando anima erat a corpore realiter separata, non fuisset anima Christi sub hoc sacramento, non propter defectum virtutis verborum sed propter aliam dispositionem rei.

consecrated, then the body only would have been present under the species of the bread, and the blood only under the species of the wine.

REPLY OBJ. 3: As was observed above (Q. 76, A. 1, ad 1), Christ's soul is in this sacrament by real concomitance; because it is not without the body: but it is not there in virtue of the consecration. And therefore, if this sacrament had been consecrated then, or reserved, when His soul was really separated from His body, Christ's soul would not have been under this sacrament, not from any defect in the form of the words, but owing to the different dispositions of the thing contained.

QUESTION 82

THE MINISTER OF THIS SACRAMENT

Deinde considerandum est de ministro huius sacramenti. Et circa hoc quaeruntur decem.

Primo, utrum consecrare hoc sacramentum sit proprium sacerdotis.

Secundo, utrum plures sacerdotes simul possent eandem hostiam consecrare.

Tertio, utrum dispensatio huius sacramenti pertineat ad solum sacerdotem.

Quarto, utrum liceat sacerdoti consecranti a communione abstinere.

Quinto, utrum liceat sacerdoti omnino a celebratione abstinere.

Sexto, utrum sacerdos peccator possit conficere hoc sacramentum.

Septimo, utrum Missa mali sacerdotis minus valeat quam boni.

Octavo, utrum haeretici, schismatici vel excommunicati possint conficere hoc sacramentum.

Nono, utrum degradati.

Decimo, utrum peccent a talibus communionem recipientes.

We now proceed to consider the minister of this sacrament: under which head there are ten points for our inquiry:

(1) Whether it belongs to a priest alone to consecrate this sacrament?

(2) Whether several priests can at the same time consecrate the same host?

(3) Whether it belongs to the priest alone to dispense this sacrament?

(4) Whether it is lawful for the priest consecrating to refrain from communicating?

(5) Whether a priest may lawfully refrain altogether from celebrating?

(6) Whether the Mass of a wicked priest is of less value than that of a good one?

(7) Whether those who are heretics, schismatics, or excommunicated, can perform this sacrament?

(8) Whether degraded priests can do so?

(9) Whether communicants receiving at their hands are guilty of sinning?

(10) Whether a priest in sin can perform this sacrament?

Article 1

Whether the Consecration of This Sacrament Belongs to a Priest Alone?

AD PRIMUM SIC PROCEDITUR. Videtur quod consecratio huius sacramenti non proprie sit sacerdotis. Dictum est enim supra quod hoc sacramentum consecratur virtute verborum quae sunt forma huius sacramenti. Sed illa verba non mutantur sive dicantur a sacerdote sive a quocumque alio. Ergo videtur quod non solus sacerdos, sed etiam quilibet alius possit hoc sacramentum consecrare.

PRAETEREA, sacerdos hoc sacramentum conficit in persona Christi. Sed laicus sanctus est unitus Christo per caritatem. Ergo videtur quod etiam laicus possit hoc sacramentum conficere. Unde et Chrysostomus dicit, super Matth., quod *omnis sanctus est sacerdos.*

PRAETEREA, sicut Baptismus ordinatur ad hominum salutem, ita et hoc sacramentum, ut ex supra dictis patet. Sed etiam laicus potest baptizare, ut supra

OBJECTION 1: It seems that the consecration of this sacrament does not belong exclusively to a priest. Because it was said above (Q. 78, A. 4) that this sacrament is consecrated in virtue of the words, which are the form of this sacrament. But those words are not changed, whether spoken by a priest or by anyone else. Therefore, it seems that not only a priest, but anyone else, can consecrate this sacrament.

OBJ. 2: Further, the priest performs this sacrament in the person of Christ. But a devout layman is united with Christ through charity. Therefore, it seems that even a layman can perform this sacrament. Hence Chrysostom (*Opus imperfectum in Matth., Hom. xliii*) says that *every holy man is a priest.*

OBJ. 3: Further, as Baptism is ordained for the salvation of mankind, so also is this sacrament, as is clear from what was said above (Q. 74, A. 1; Q. 79, A. 2). But a layman

317

habitum est. Ergo non est proprium sacerdotis conficere hoc sacramentum.

Praeterea, hoc sacramentum perficitur in consecratione materiae. Sed alias materias consecrare, scilicet chrisma et oleum sanctum et oleum benedictum, pertinet ad solum episcopum, quarum tamen consecratio non est tantae dignitatis sicut consecratio Eucharistiae, in qua est totus Christus. Ergo non est proprium sacerdotis, sed solius episcopi, hoc sacramentum conficere.

Sed contra est quod Isidorus dicit, in quadam epistola, et habetur in decretis, dist. XXV, *ad presbyterum pertinet sacramentum corporis et sanguinis domini in altari Dei conficere.*

Respondeo dicendum quod, sicut supra dictum est, hoc sacramentum tantae est dignitatis quod non conficitur nisi in persona Christi. Quicumque autem aliquid agit in persona alterius, oportet hoc fieri per potestatem ab illo concessam. Sicut autem baptizato conceditur a Christo potestas sumendi hoc sacramentum, ita sacerdoti, cum ordinatur, confertur potestas hoc sacramentum consecrandi in persona Christi, per hoc enim ponitur in gradu eorum quibus dictum est a domino, *hoc facite in meam commemorationem.* Et ideo dicendum est quod proprium est sacerdotum conficere hoc sacramentum.

Ad primum ergo dicendum quod virtus sacramentalis in pluribus consistit, et non in uno tantum, sicut virtus Baptismi consistit et in verbis et in aqua. Unde et virtus consecrativa non solum consistit in ipsis verbis, sed etiam in potestate sacerdoti tradita in sua consecratione vel ordinatione, cum ei dicitur ab episcopo, *accipe potestatem offerendi sacrificium in Ecclesia tam pro vivis quam pro mortuis.* Nam et virtus instrumentalis in pluribus instrumentis consistit, per quae agit principale agens.

Ad secundum dicendum quod laicus iustus unitus est Christo unione spirituali per fidem et caritatem, non autem per sacramentalem potestatem. Et ideo habet spirituale sacerdotium ad offerendum spirituales hostias, de quibus dicitur in Psalmo, *sacrificium Deo spiritus contribulatus,* et Rom. XII, *exhibeatis corpora vestra hostiam viventem.* Unde et I Petri II dicitur, *sacerdotium sanctum offerre spirituales hostias.*

Ad tertium dicendum quod perceptio huius sacramenti non est tantae necessitatis sicut perceptio Baptismi, ut ex supra dictis patet. Et ideo, licet in necessitatis articulo laicus possit baptizare, non tamen potest hoc sacramentum conficere.

Ad quartum dicendum quod episcopus accipit potestatem ut agat in persona Christi supra corpus eius mysticum, idest super Ecclesiam, quam quidem potestatem non accipit sacerdos in sua consecratione, licet

can also baptize, as was stated above (Q. 67, A. 3). Consequently, the consecration of this sacrament is not proper to a priest.

Obj. 4: Further, this sacrament is completed in the consecration of the matter. But the consecration of other matters such as the chrism, the holy oil, and blessed oil, belongs exclusively to a bishop; yet their consecration does not equal the dignity of the consecration of the Eucharist, in which the entire Christ is contained. Therefore it belongs, not to a priest, but only to a bishop, to perform this sacrament.

On the contrary, Isidore says in an Epistle to Ludifred (*Decretals*, dist. 25): *It belongs to a priest to consecrate this sacrament of the Lord's body and blood upon God's altar.*

I answer that, As stated above (Q. 78, AA. 1, 4), such is the dignity of this sacrament that it is performed only as in the person of Christ. Now whoever performs any act in another's stead, must do so by the power bestowed by such a one. But as the power of receiving this sacrament is conceded by Christ to the baptized person, so likewise the power of consecrating this sacrament on Christ's behalf is bestowed upon the priest at his ordination: for thereby he is put upon a level with them to whom the Lord said (Luke 22:19): *Do this for a commemoration of Me.* Therefore, it must be said that it belongs to priests to accomplish this sacrament.

Reply Obj. 1: The sacramental power is in several things, and not merely in one: thus the power of Baptism lies both in the words and in the water. Accordingly the consecrating power is not merely in the words, but likewise in the power delivered to the priest in his consecration and ordination, when the bishop says to him: *Receive the power of offering up the Sacrifice in the Church for the living as well as for the dead.* For instrumental power lies in several instruments through which the chief agent acts.

Reply Obj. 2: A devout layman is united with Christ by spiritual union through faith and charity, but not by sacramental power: consequently he has a spiritual priesthood for offering spiritual sacrifices, of which it is said (Ps 1:19): *A sacrifice to God is an afflicted spirit*; and (Rom 12:1): *Present your bodies a living sacrifice.* Hence, too, it is written (1 Pet 2:5): *A holy priesthood, to offer up spiritual sacrifices.*

Reply Obj. 3: The receiving of this sacrament is not of such necessity as the receiving of Baptism, as is evident from what was said above (Q. 65, AA. 3, 4; Q. 80, A. 11, ad 2). And therefore, although a layman can baptize in case of necessity, he cannot perform this sacrament.

Reply Obj. 4: The bishop receives power to act on Christ's behalf upon His mystical body, that is, upon the Church; but the priest receives no such power in his consecration, although he may have it by commission from the

possit eam habere ex episcopi commissione. Et ideo ea quae non pertinent ad dispositionem corporis mystici, non reservantur episcopo, sicut consecratio huius sacramenti. Ad episcopum vero pertinet non solum tradere populo, sed etiam sacerdotibus, ea ex quibus possunt propriis officiis uti. Et quia benedictio chrismatis et olei sancti et olei infirmorum, et aliorum quae consecrantur, puta altaris, Ecclesiae, vestium et vasorum, praestat quandam idoneitatem ad sacramenta perficienda quae pertinent ad officium sacerdotum, ideo tales consecrationes episcopo reservantur, tanquam principi totius ecclesiastici ordinis.

bishop. Consequently all such things as do not belong to the mystical body are not reserved to the bishop, such as the consecration of this sacrament. But it belongs to the bishop to deliver, not only to the people, but likewise to priests, such things as serve them in the fulfillment of their respective duties. And because the blessing of the chrism, and of the holy oil, and of the oil of the sick, and other consecrated things, such as altars, churches, vestments, and sacred vessels, makes such things fit for use in performing the sacraments which belong to the priestly duty, therefore such consecrations are reserved to the bishop as the head of the whole ecclesiastical order.

Article 2

Whether Several Priests Can Consecrate One and the Same Host?

AD SECUNDUM SIC PROCEDITUR. Videtur quod plures sacerdotes non possunt unam et eandem hostiam consecrare. Dictum est enim supra quod plures non possunt unum baptizare. Sed non minor vis est sacerdotis consecrantis quam hominis baptizantis. Ergo etiam non possunt simul plures unam hostiam consecrare.

PRAETEREA, quod potest fieri per unum, superflue fit per multos. In sacramentis autem Christi nihil debet esse superfluum. Cum igitur unus sufficiat ad consecrandum, videtur quod plures non possunt unam hostiam consecrare.

PRAETEREA, sicut Augustinus dicit, super Ioan., hoc sacramentum est sacramentum unitatis. Sed contrarium unitati videtur esse multitudo. Ergo non videtur conveniens esse huic sacramento quod plures sacerdotes eandem hostiam consecrent.

SED CONTRA est quod, secundum consuetudinem quarundam Ecclesiarum, sacerdotes, cum de novo ordinantur, concelebrant episcopo ordinanti.

RESPONDEO dicendum quod, sicut supra dictum est, sacerdos, cum ordinatur, constituitur in gradu eorum qui a domino acceperunt potestatem consecrandi in cena. Et ideo, secundum consuetudinem quarundam Ecclesiarum, sicut apostoli Christo cenanti concenaverunt, ita novi ordinati episcopo ordinanti concelebrant. Nec per hoc iteratur consecratio super eandem hostiam, quia, sicut Innocentius III dicit, omnium intentio debet ferri ad idem instans consecrationis.

AD PRIMUM ergo dicendum quod Christus non legitur simul baptizasse cum apostolis quando iniunxit eis officium baptizandi. Et ideo non est similis ratio.

AD SECUNDUM dicendum quod, si quilibet sacerdotum operaretur in virtute propria, superfluerent alii celebrantes, uno sufficienter celebrante. Sed quia sacerdos

OBJECTION 1: It seems that several priests cannot consecrate one and the same host. For it was said above (Q. 67, A. 6), that several cannot at the same time baptize one individual. But the power of a priest consecrating is not less than that of a man baptizing. Therefore, several priests cannot consecrate one host at the same time.

OBJ. 2: Further, what can be done by one, is superfluously done by several. But there ought to be nothing superfluous in the sacraments. Since, then, one is sufficient for consecrating, it seems that several cannot consecrate one host.

OBJ. 3: Further, as Augustine says (*Tract. xxvi in Joan.*), this is *the sacrament of unity*. But multitude seems to be opposed to unity. Therefore it seems inconsistent with the sacrament for several priests to consecrate the same host.

ON THE CONTRARY, It is the custom of some Churches for priests newly ordained to co-celebrate with the bishop ordaining them.

I ANSWER THAT, As stated above (A. 1), when a priest is ordained he is placed on a level with those who received consecrating power from our Lord at the Supper. And therefore, according to the custom of some Churches, as the apostles supped when Christ supped, so the newly ordained co-celebrate with the ordaining bishop. Nor is the consecration, on that account, repeated over the same host, because as Innocent III says (*De Sacr. Alt. Myst.* iv), the intention of all should be directed to the same instant of the consecration.

REPLY OBJ. 1: We do not read of Christ baptizing with the apostles when He committed to them the duty of baptizing; consequently there is no parallel.

REPLY OBJ. 2: If each individual priest were acting in his own power, then other celebrants would be superfluous, since one would be sufficient. But whereas the priest does

non consecrat nisi in persona Christi, multi autem sunt unum in Christo, ideo non refert utrum per unum vel per multos hoc sacramentum consecraretur, nisi quod oportet ritum Ecclesiae servari.

AD TERTIUM dicendum quod Eucharistia est sacramentum unitatis ecclesiasticae, quae attenditur secundum hoc quod multi sunt unum in Christo.

not consecrate except as in Christ's stead; and since many are *one in Christ* (Gal 3:28); consequently it does not matter whether this sacrament be consecrated by one or by many, except that the rite of the Church must be observed.

REPLY OBJ. 3: The Eucharist is the sacrament of ecclesiastical unity, which is brought about by many being *one in Christ*.

Article 3

Whether Dispensing of This Sacrament Belongs to a Priest Alone?

AD TERTIUM SIC PROCEDITUR. Videtur quod non pertineat solum ad sacerdotem dispensatio huius sacramenti. Sanguis enim Christi non minus pertinet ad hoc sacramentum quam corpus. Sed sanguis Christi dispensatur per diacones, unde et beatus Laurentius dixit beato Sixto, *experire utrum idoneum ministrum elegeris, cui commisisti dominici sanguinis dispensationem.* Ergo, pari ratione, dispensatio dominici corporis non pertinet ad solos sacerdotes.

PRAETEREA, sacerdotes constituuntur ministri sacramentorum. Sed hoc sacramentum perficitur in consecratione materiae, non in usu, ad quem pertinet dispensatio. Ergo videtur quod non pertineat ad sacerdotem corpus domini dispensare.

PRAETEREA, Dionysius dicit, in libro Eccles. Hier., quod hoc sacramentum habet perfectivam virtutem, sicut et chrisma. Sed signare chrismate baptizatos non pertinet ad sacerdotem, sed ad episcopum. Ergo etiam dispensare hoc sacramentum pertinet ad episcopum, non ad sacerdotem.

SED CONTRA est quod dicitur de Consecr., dist. II, *pervenit ad notitiam nostram quod quidam presbyteri laico aut feminae corpus domini tradunt ad deferendum infirmis. Ergo interdicit synodus ne talis praesumptio ulterius fiat, sed presbyter per semetipsum infirmos communicet.*

RESPONDEO dicendum quod ad sacerdotem pertinet dispensatio corporis Christi, propter tria. Primo quidem quia, sicut dictum est, ipse consecrat in persona Christi. Ipse autem Christus, sicut consecravit corpus suum in cena, ita et aliis sumendum dedit. Unde, sicut ad sacerdotem pertinet consecratio corporis Christi, ita ad eum pertinet dispensatio. Secundo, quia sacerdos constituitur medius inter Deum et populum. Unde, sicut ad eum pertinet dona populi Deo offerre, ita ad eum pertinet dona sanctificata divinitus populo tradere. Tertio quia, in reverentiam huius sacramenti, a nulla re contingitur nisi consecrata, unde et corporale et calix consecrantur, similiter et manus sacerdotis, ad tangendum hoc sacramentum. Unde nulli alii tangere licet, nisi in necessitate

OBJECTION 1: It seems that the dispensing of this sacrament does not belong to a priest alone. For Christ's blood belongs to this sacrament no less than His body. But Christ's blood is dispensed by deacons: hence the blessed Lawrence said to the blessed Sixtus (*Office of St. Lawrence*, Resp. at Matins): *Try whether you have chosen a fit minister, to whom you have entrusted the dispensing of the Lord's blood.* Therefore, with equal reason the dispensing of Christ's body does not belong to priests only.

OBJ. 2: Further, priests are the appointed ministers of the sacraments. But this sacrament is completed in the consecration of the matter, and not in the use, to which the dispensing belongs. Therefore it seems that it does not belong to a priest to dispense the Lord's body.

OBJ. 3: Further, Dionysius says (*Eccl. Hier.* iii, iv) that this sacrament, like chrism, has the power of perfecting. But it belongs, not to priests, but to bishops, to sign with the chrism. Therefore likewise, to dispense this sacrament belongs to the bishop and not to the priest.

ON THE CONTRARY, It is written (*De Consecr.*, dist. 12): *It has come to our knowledge that some priests deliver the Lord's body to a layman or to a woman to carry it to the sick: The synod therefore forbids such presumption to continue; and let the priest himself communicate the sick.*

I ANSWER THAT, The dispensing of Christ's body belongs to the priest for three reasons. First, because, as was said above (A. 1), he consecrates as in the person of Christ. But as Christ consecrated His body at the supper, so also He gave it to others to be partaken of by them. Accordingly, as the consecration of Christ's body belongs to the priest, so likewise does the dispensing belong to him. Second, because the priest is the appointed intermediary between God and the people; hence as it belongs to him to offer the people's gifts to God, so it belongs to him to deliver consecrated gifts to the people. Third, because out of reverence towards this sacrament, nothing touches it, but what is consecrated; hence the corporal and the chalice are consecrated, and likewise the priest's hands, for touching this

puta si caderet in terram, vel in aliquo alio necessitatis casu.

AD PRIMUM ergo dicendum quod diaconus, quasi propinquus ordini sacerdotali, aliquid participat de eius officio, ut scilicet dispenset sanguinem, non autem corpus, nisi in necessitate, iubente episcopo vel presbytero. Primo quidem, quia sanguis Christi continetur in vase. Unde non oportet quod tangatur a dispensante, sicut tangitur corpus Christi. Secundo, quia sanguis designat redemptionem a Christo in populum derivatam, unde et sanguini admiscetur aqua, quae significat populum. Et quia diaconi sunt inter sacerdotem et populum, magis convenit diaconibus dispensatio sanguinis quam dispensatio corporis.

AD SECUNDUM dicendum quod eiusdem est hoc sacramentum dispensare et consecrare, ratione iam dicta.

AD TERTIUM dicendum quod, sicut diaconus in aliquo participat illuminativam virtutem sacerdotis, inquantum dispensat sanguinem; ita sacerdos participat perfectivam dispensationem episcopi, inquantum dispensat hoc sacramentum, quo perficitur homo secundum se per coniunctionem ad Christum. Aliae autem perfectiones, quibus homo perficitur per comparationem ad alios, episcopo reservantur.

sacrament. Hence it is not lawful for anyone else to touch it except from necessity, for instance, if it were to fall upon the ground, or else in some other case of urgency.

REPLY OBJ. 1: The deacon, as being nigh to the priestly order, has a certain share in the latter's duties, so that he may dispense the blood; but not the body, except in case of necessity, at the bidding of a bishop or of a priest. First of all, because Christ's blood is contained in a vessel, hence there is no need for it to be touched by the dispenser, as Christ's body is touched. Second, because the blood denotes the redemption derived by the people from Christ; hence it is that water is mixed with the blood, which water denotes the people. And because deacons are between priest and people, the dispensing of the blood is in the competency of deacons, rather than the dispensing of the body.

REPLY OBJ. 2: For the reason given above, it belongs to the same person to dispense and to consecrate this sacrament.

REPLY OBJ. 3: As the deacon, in a measure, shares in the priest's *power of enlightening* (*Eccl. Hier.* v), inasmuch as he dispenses the blood, so the priest shares in the *perfective dispensing* (*Eccl. Hier.* v) of the bishop, inasmuch as he dispenses this sacrament whereby man is perfected in himself by union with Christ. But other perfections whereby a man is perfected in relation to others, are reserved to the bishop.

Article 4

Whether the Priest Who Consecrates Is Bound to Receive This Sacrament?

AD QUARTUM SIC PROCEDITUR. Videtur quod sacerdos consecrans non teneatur sumere hoc sacramentum. In aliis enim consecrationibus ille qui consecrat materiam, non utitur ea, sicut episcopus consecrans chrisma non linitur eodem. Sed hoc sacramentum consistit in consecratione materiae. Ergo sacerdos perficiens hoc sacramentum non necesse habet uti eodem, sed potest licite a sumptione eius abstinere.

PRAETEREA, in aliis sacramentis minister non praebet sacramentum sibi ipsi, nullus enim baptizare seipsum potest, ut supra habitum est. Sed, sicut Baptismus ordinate dispensatur, ita et hoc sacramentum. Ergo sacerdos perficiens hoc sacramentum non debet ipsum sumere a seipso.

PRAETEREA, contingit quandoque quod miraculose corpus Christi in altari apparet sub specie carnis, et sanguis sub specie sanguinis. Quae non sunt apta cibo vel potui, unde, sicut supra dictum est, propter hoc sub alia specie traduntur, ne sint horrori sumentibus. Ergo

OBJECTION 1: It seems that the priest who consecrates is not bound to receive this sacrament. Because, in the other consecrations, he who consecrates the matter does not use it, just as the bishop consecrating the chrism is not anointed therewith. But this sacrament consists in the consecration of the matter. Therefore, the priest performing this sacrament need not use the same, but may lawfully refrain from receiving it.

OBJ. 2: Further, in the other sacraments the minister does not give the sacrament to himself: for no one can baptize himself, as stated above (Q. 66, A. 5, ad 4). But as Baptism is dispensed in due order, so also is this sacrament. Therefore the priest who consecrates this sacrament ought not to receive it at his own hands.

OBJ. 3: Further, it sometimes happens that Christ's body appears upon the altar under the guise of flesh, and the blood under the guise of blood; which are unsuited for food and drink: hence, as was said above (Q. 75, A. 5), it is on that account that they are given under another species,

sacerdos consecrans non semper tenetur sumere hoc sacramentum.

SED CONTRA est quod in Concilio Toletano legitur, et habetur de Consecr., dist. II, cap. relatum, *modis omnibus tenendum est ut, quotiescumque sacrificans corpus et sanguinem domini nostri Iesu Christi in altario immolat, toties perceptione corporis et sanguinis participem se praebeat.*

RESPONDEO dicendum quod, sicut supra dictum est, Eucharistia non solum est sacramentum, sed etiam sacrificium. Quicumque autem sacrificium offert, debet fieri sacrificii particeps. Quia exterius sacrificium quod offert, signum est interioris sacrificii quo quis seipsum offert Deo, ut Augustinus dicit, X de Civ. Dei. Unde per hoc quod participat sacrificio, ostendit ad se sacrificium interius pertinere. Similiter etiam per hoc quod sacrificium populo dispensat, ostendit se esse dispensatorem divinorum populo. Quorum ipse primo debet esse particeps, sicut Dionysius dicit, in libro Eccles. Hier. Et ideo ipse ante sumere debet quam populo dispenset. Unde in praedicto capite legitur, *quale est sacrificium cui nec ipse sacrificans particeps esse dignoscitur?* Per hoc autem fit particeps quod de sacrificio sumit, secundum illud apostoli, I Cor. X, *nonne qui edunt hostias, participes sunt altaris?* Et ideo necesse est quod sacerdos, quotiescumque consecrat, sumat hoc sacramentum integre.

AD PRIMUM ergo dicendum quod consecratio chrismatis, vel cuiuscumque alterius materiae, non est sacrificium, sicut consecratio Eucharistiae. Et ideo non est similis ratio.

AD SECUNDUM dicendum quod sacramentum Baptismi perficitur in ipso usu materiae. Et ideo nullus potest baptizare seipsum, quia in sacramento non potest esse idem agens et patiens. Unde nec in hoc sacramento sacerdos consecrat seipsum, sed panem et vinum, in qua consecratione conficitur hoc sacramentum. Usus autem sacramenti est consequenter se habens ad hoc sacramentum. Et ideo non est simile.

AD TERTIUM dicendum quod, si miraculose corpus Christi in altari sub specie carnis appareat, aut sanguis sub specie sanguinis, non est sumendum. Dicit enim Hieronymus, super Levit., *de hac quidem hostia quae in Christi commemoratione mirabiliter fit, de illa vero quam Christus in ara crucis obtulit secundum se, nulli edere licet.* Nec propter hoc sacerdos transgressor efficitur, quia ea quae miraculose fiunt, legibus non subduntur. Consulendum tamen esset sacerdoti quod iterato corpus et sanguinem domini consecraret et sumeret.

lest they beget revulsion in the communicants. Therefore the priest who consecrates is not always bound to receive this sacrament.

ON THE CONTRARY, We read in the acts of the (Twelfth) Council of Toledo (Can. v), and again (*De Consecr.*, dist. 2): *It must be strictly observed that as often as the priest sacrifices the body and blood of our Lord Jesus Christ upon the altar, he must himself be a partaker of Christ's body and blood.*

I ANSWER THAT, As stated above (Q. 79, AA. 5, 7), the Eucharist is not only a sacrament, but also a sacrifice. Now whoever offers sacrifice must be a sharer in the sacrifice, because the outward sacrifice he offers is a sign of the inner sacrifice whereby he offers himself to God, as Augustine says (*De Civ. Dei* x). Hence by partaking of the sacrifice he shows that the inner one is likewise his. In the same way also, by dispensing the sacrifice to the people he shows that he is the dispenser of Divine gifts, of which he ought himself to be the first to partake, as Dionysius says (*Eccl. Hier.* iii). Consequently, he ought to receive before dispensing it to the people. Accordingly we read in the chapter mentioned above (Twelfth Council of Toledo, Can. v): *What kind of sacrifice is that wherein not even the sacrificer is known to have a share?* But it is by partaking of the sacrifice that he has a share in it, as the Apostle says (1 Cor 10:18): *Are not they that eat of the sacrifices, partakers of the altar?* Therefore it is necessary for the priest, as often as he consecrates, to receive this sacrament in its integrity.

REPLY OBJ. 1: The consecration of chrism or of anything else is not a sacrifice, as the consecration of the Eucharist is: consequently there is no parallel.

REPLY OBJ. 2: The sacrament of Baptism is accomplished in the use of the matter, and consequently no one can baptize himself, because the same person cannot be active and passive in a sacrament. Hence neither in this sacrament does the priest consecrate himself, but he consecrates the bread and wine, in which consecration the sacrament is completed. But the use thereof follows the sacrament, and therefore there is no parallel.

REPLY OBJ. 3: If Christ's body appears miraculously upon the altar under the guise of flesh, or the blood under the guise of blood, it is not to be received. For Jerome says upon Leviticus (cf. *De Consecr.*, dist. 2): *It is lawful to eat of this sacrifice which is wonderfully performed in memory of Christ: but it is not lawful for anyone to eat of that one which Christ offered on the altar of the cross.* Nor does the priest transgress on that account, because miraculous events are not subject to human laws. Nevertheless the priest would be well advised to consecrate again and receive the Lord's body and blood.

Article 5

Whether a Wicked Priest Can Consecrate the Eucharist?

AD QUINTUM SIC PROCEDITUR. Videtur quod malus sacerdos Eucharistiam consecrare non possit. Dicit enim Hieronymus, super Sophoniam, *sacerdotes, qui Eucharistiae serviunt et sanguinem domini dividunt, impie agunt in legem Christi, putantes Eucharistiam precantis facere verba, non vitam; et necessariam esse solemnem orationem, et non sacerdotis merita. De quibus dicitur, sacerdos, in quocumque fuerit macula, non accedat offerre oblationes domino.* Sed sacerdos peccator, cum sit maculosus, nec vitam habet nec merita huic convenientia sacramento. Ergo sacerdos peccator non potest consecrare Eucharistiam.

PRAETEREA, Damascenus dicit, in IV libro, quod *panis et vinum, per adventum sancti spiritus, supernaturaliter transit in corpus domini et sanguinem.* Sed Gelasius Papa dicit, et habetur in decretis, I, qu. I, cap. sacrosancta, *quomodo ad divini mysterii consecrationem caelestis spiritus invocatus adveniet, si sacerdos qui eum adesse deprecatur, criminosis plenus actionibus comprobetur?* Ergo per malum sacerdotem non potest Eucharistia consecrari.

PRAETEREA, hoc sacramentum sacerdotis benedictione consecratur. Sed benedictio sacerdotis peccatoris non est efficax ad consecrationem huius sacramenti, cum scriptum sit, *maledicam benedictionibus vestris.* Et Dionysius dicit, in epistola ad Demophilum monachum, *perfecte cecidit a sacerdotali ordine qui non est illuminatus, et audax quidem mihi videtur talis, sacerdotalibus manum apponens; et audet immundas infamias, non enim dicam orationes, super divina symbola Christiformiter enuntiare.*

SED CONTRA est quod Augustinus dicit, in libro de corpore domini, *intra Ecclesiam Catholicam, in mysterio corporis et sanguinis domini, nihil a bono maius, nihil a malo minus perficitur sacerdote, quia non in merito consecrantis, sed in verbo perficitur creatoris, et in virtute spiritus sancti.*

RESPONDEO dicendum quod, sicut supra dictum est, sacerdos consecrat hoc sacramentum non in virtute propria, sed sicut minister Christi, in cuius persona consecrat hoc sacramentum. Non autem ex hoc ipso desinit aliquis esse minister Christi quod est malus, habet enim dominus bonos et malos ministros seu servos. Unde, Matth. XXIV, dominus dicit, *quis, putas, est fidelis servus et prudens,* etc.; et postea subdit, *si autem dixerit malus ille servus in corde suo,* et cetera. Et apostolus dicit, I Cor. IV, *sic nos existimet homo ut ministros Christi,* et tamen postea subdit, *nihil mihi conscius sum, sed non in hoc iustificatus sum.* Erat ergo certus se esse ministrum

OBJECTION 1: It seems that a wicked priest cannot consecrate the Eucharist. For Jerome, commenting on Sophon. iii, 4, says: *The priests who perform the Eucharist, and who distribute our Lord's blood to the people, act wickedly against Christ's law, in deeming that the Eucharist is consecrated by a prayer rather than by a good life; and that only the solemn prayer is requisite, and not the priest's merits: of whom it is said: 'Let not the priest, in whatever defilement he may be, approach to offer oblations to the Lord'* (Lev 21:21, Septuagint). But the sinful priest, being defiled, has neither the life nor the merits befitting this sacrament. Therefore a sinful priest cannot consecrate the Eucharist.

OBJ. 2: Further, Damascene says (*De Fide Orth.* iv) that *the bread and wine are changed supernaturally into the body and blood of our Lord, by the coming of the Holy Spirit.* But Pope Gelasius I says (*Ep. ad Elphid.,* cf. *Decret.* i, q. 1): *How shall the Holy Spirit, when invoked, come for the consecration of the Divine Mystery, if the priest invoking him be proved full of guilty deeds?* Consequently, the Eucharist cannot be consecrated by a wicked priest.

OBJ. 3: Further, this sacrament is consecrated by the priest's blessing. But a sinful priest's blessing is not efficacious for consecrating this sacrament, since it is written (Mal 2:2): *I will curse your blessings.* Again, Dionysius says in his Epistle (viii) to the monk Demophilus: *He who is not enlightened has completely fallen away from the priestly order; and I wonder that such a man dare to employ his hands in priestly actions, and in the person of Christ to utter, over the Divine symbols, his unclean infamies, for I will not call them prayers.*

ON THE CONTRARY, Augustine (Paschasius) says (*De Corp. Dom.* xii): *Within the Catholic Church, in the mystery of the Lord's body and blood, nothing greater is done by a good priest, nothing less by an evil priest, because it is not by the merits of the consecrator that the sacrament is accomplished, but by the Creator's word, and by the power of the Holy Spirit.*

I ANSWER THAT, As was said above (AA. 1, 3), the priest consecrates this sacrament not by his own power, but as the minister of Christ, in Whose person he consecrates this sacrament. But from the fact of being wicked he does not cease to be Christ's minister; because our Lord has good and wicked ministers or servants. Hence (Matt 24:45) our Lord says: *Who, thinkest thou, is a faithful and wise servant?* and afterwards He adds: *But if that evil servant shall say in his heart,* etc. And the Apostle (1 Cor 4:1) says: *Let a man so account of us as of the ministers of Christ;* and afterwards he adds: *I am not conscious to myself of anything; yet am I not hereby justified.* He was therefore certain that

Christi, non tamen erat certus se esse iustum. Potest ergo aliquis esse minister Christi etiam si iustus non sit. Et hoc ad excellentiam Christi pertinet, cui, sicut vero Deo, serviunt non solum bona, sed etiam mala, quae per ipsius providentiam in eius gloriam ordinantur. Unde manifestum est quod sacerdotes, etiam si non sint iusti, sed peccatores, possunt Eucharistiam consecrare.

AD PRIMUM ergo dicendum quod Hieronymus per illa verba improbat errorem sacerdotum qui credebant se digne posse Eucharistiam consecrare ex hoc solo quod sunt sacerdotes, etiam si sint peccatores. Quod improbat Hieronymus per hoc quod maculosi ad altare accedere prohibentur. Non tamen removetur quin, si accesserint, sit verum sacrificium quod offerunt.

AD SECUNDUM dicendum quod ante illa verba Gelasius Papa praemittit, *sacrosancta religio, quae Catholicam continet disciplinam, tantam sibi reverentiam vindicat ut ad eam quilibet nisi pura conscientia non audeat pervenire.* Ex quo manifeste apparet eius intentionis esse quod peccator sacerdos non debet accedere ad hoc sacramentum. Unde per hoc quod subdit, *quomodo caelestis spiritus advocatus adveniet*, intelligi oportet quod non advenit ex merito sacerdotis, sed ex virtute Christi, cuius verba profert sacerdos.

AD TERTIUM dicendum quod, sicut eadem actio, inquantum fit ex prava intentione ministri, potest esse mala, bona autem inquantum fit ex bona intentione domini; ita benedictio sacerdotis peccatoris, inquantum ab ipso indigne fit, est maledictione digna, et quasi infamia seu blasphemia, et non oratio reputatur; inquantum autem profertur ex persona Christi, est sancta et efficax. Unde signanter dicitur, *maledicam benedictionibus vestris.*

he was Christ's minister; yet he was not certain that he was a just man. Consequently, a man can be Christ's minister even though he be not one of the just. And this belongs to Christ's excellence, Whom, as the true God, things both good and evil serve, since they are ordained by His providence for His glory. Hence it is evident that priests, even though they be not godly, but sinners, can consecrate the Eucharist.

REPLY OBJ. 1: In those words Jerome is condemning the error of priests who believed they could consecrate the Eucharist worthily, from the mere fact of being priests, even though they were sinners; and Jerome condemns this from the fact that persons defiled are forbidden to approach the altar; but this does not prevent the sacrifice, which they offer, from being a true sacrifice, if they do approach.

REPLY OBJ. 2: Previous to the words quoted, Pope Gelasius expresses himself as follows: *That most holy rite, which contains the Catholic discipline, claims for itself such reverence that no one may dare to approach it except with clean conscience.* From this it is evident that his meaning is that the priest who is a sinner ought not to approach this sacrament. Hence when he resumes, *How shall the Holy Spirit come when summoned*, it must be understood that He comes, not through the priest's merits, but through the power of Christ, Whose words the priest utters.

REPLY OBJ. 3: As the same action can be evil, inasmuch as it is done with a bad intention of the servant; and good from the good intention of the master; so the blessing of a sinful priest, inasmuch as he acts unworthily is deserving of a curse, and is reputed an infamy and a blasphemy, and not a prayer; whereas, inasmuch as it is pronounced in the person of Christ, it is holy and efficacious. Hence it is said with significance: *I will curse your blessings.*

Article 6

Whether the Mass of a Sinful Priest Is of Less Worth Than the Mass of a Good Priest?

AD SEXTUM SIC PROCEDITUR. Videtur quod Missa sacerdotis mali non minus valeat quam Missa sacerdotis boni. Dicit enim Gregorius, in registro, *heu, in quam magnum laqueum incidunt qui divina et occulta mysteria plus ab aliis sanctificata fieri posse credunt, cum unus idemque Spiritus Sanctus ea mysteria occulte atque invisibiliter operando sanctificet.* Sed haec occulta mysteria celebrantur in Missa. Ergo Missa mali sacerdotis non minus valet quam Missa boni.

PRAETEREA, sicut Baptismus traditur a ministro in virtute Christi, qui baptizat, ita et hoc sacramentum, quod in persona Christi consecratur. Sed non melior Baptismus datur a meliori ministro, ut supra habitum

OBJECTION 1: It seems that the mass of a sinful priest is not of less worth than that of a good priest. For Pope Gregory says in the Register: *Alas, into what a great snare they fall who believe that the Divine and hidden mysteries can be sanctified more by some than by others; since it is the one and the same Holy Spirit Who hallows those mysteries in a hidden and invisible manner.* But these hidden mysteries are celebrated in the mass. Therefore the mass of a sinful priest is not of less value than the mass of a good priest.

OBJ. 2: Further, as Baptism is conferred by a minister through the power of Christ Who baptizes, so likewise this sacrament is consecrated in the person of Christ. But Baptism is no better when conferred by a better priest, as was

est. Ergo neque etiam melior Missa est quae celebratur a meliori sacerdote.

PRAETEREA, sicut merita sacerdotum differunt per bonum et melius, ita etiam differunt per bonum et malum. Si ergo Missa melioris sacerdotis est melior, sequitur quod Missa mali sacerdotis sit mala. Quod est inconveniens, quia malitia ministrorum non potest redundare in Christi mysteria; sicut Augustinus dicit, in libro de Baptismo. Ergo neque Missa melioris sacerdotis est melior.

SED CONTRA est quod habetur I, qu. I, *quanto sacerdotes fuerint digniores, tanto facilius in necessitatibus pro quibus clamant, exaudiuntur.*

RESPONDEO dicendum quod in Missa duo est considerare; scilicet ipsum sacramentum, quod est principale; et orationes quae in Missa fiunt pro vivis et mortuis. Quantum ergo ad sacramentum, non minus valet Missa mali sacerdotis quam boni, quia utrobique idem conficitur sacramentum.

Oratio etiam quae fit in Missa, potest considerari dupliciter. Uno modo, inquantum habet efficaciam ex devotione sacerdotis orantis. Et sic non est dubium quod Missa melioris sacerdotis magis est fructuosa. Alio modo, inquantum oratio in Missa profertur a sacerdote in persona totius Ecclesiae, cuius sacerdos est minister. Quod quidem ministerium etiam in peccatoribus manet, sicut supra dictum est de ministerio Christi. Unde quantum ad hoc, est fructuosa non solum oratio sacerdotis peccatoris in Missa, sed etiam omnes aliae eius orationes quas facit in ecclesiasticis officiis, in quibus gerit personam Ecclesiae. Sed orationes eius privatae non sunt fructuosae, secundum illud Proverb. XXVIII, *qui declinat aurem suam ne audiat legem, oratio eius erit execrabilis.*

AD PRIMUM ergo dicendum quod Gregorius loquitur ibi quantum ad sanctitatem divini sacramenti.

AD SECUNDUM dicendum quod in sacramento Baptismi non fiunt solemnes orationes pro omnibus fidelibus, sicut in Missa. Et ideo quantum ad hoc non est simile. Est autem simile quantum ad effectum sacramenti.

AD TERTIUM dicendum quod propter virtutem spiritus sancti, qui per unitatem caritatis communicat invicem bona membrorum Christi, fit quod bonum privatum quod est in Missa sacerdotis boni, est fructuosum aliis. Malum autem privatum unius hominis non potest alteri nocere, nisi per aliqualem consensum, ut Augustinus dicit, in libro contra Parmenianum.

said above (Q. 64, A. 1, ad 2). Therefore neither is a mass the better, which is celebrated by a better priest.

OBJ. 3: Further, as the merits of priests differ in the point of being good and better, so they likewise differ in the point of being good and bad. Consequently, if the mass of a better priest be itself better, it follows that the mass of a bad priest must be bad. Now this is unreasonable, because the malice of the ministers cannot affect Christ's mysteries, as Augustine says in his work on Baptism (*Contra Donat.* xii). Therefore neither is the mass of a better priest the better.

ON THE CONTRARY, It is stated in *Decretal* i, q. 1: *The worthier the priest, the sooner is he heard in the needs for which he prays.*

I ANSWER THAT, There are two things to be considered in the mass, namely, the sacrament itself, which is the chief thing; and the prayers which are offered up in the mass for the quick and the dead. So far as the mass itself is concerned, the mass of a wicked priest is not of less value than that of a good priest, because the same sacrifice is offered by both.

Again, the prayer put up in the mass can be considered in two respects: first of all, in so far as it has its efficacy from the devotion of the priest interceding, and in this respect there is no doubt but that the mass of the better priest is the more fruitful. In another respect, inasmuch as the prayer is said by the priest in the mass in the place of the entire Church, of which the priest is the minister; and this ministry remains even in sinful men, as was said above (A. 5) in regard to Christ's ministry. Hence, in this respect the prayer even of the sinful priest is fruitful, not only that which he utters in the mass, but likewise all those he recites in the ecclesiastical offices, wherein he takes the place of the Church. On the other hand, his private prayers are not fruitful, according to Prov. 28:9: *He that turneth away his ears from hearing the law, his prayer shall be an abomination.*

REPLY OBJ. 1: Gregory is speaking there of the holiness of the Divine sacrament.

REPLY OBJ. 2: In the sacrament of Baptism solemn prayers are not made for all the faithful, as in the mass; therefore there is no parallel in this respect. There is, however, a resemblance as to the effect of the sacrament.

REPLY OBJ. 3: By reason of the power of the Holy Spirit, Who communicates to each one the blessings of Christ's members on account of their being united in charity, the private blessing in the mass of a good priest is fruitful to others. But the private evil of one man cannot hurt another, except the latter, in some way, consent, as Augustine says (*Contra Parmen.* ii).

Article 7

Whether Heretics, Schismatics, and Excommunicated Persons Can Consecrate?

AD SEPTIMUM SIC PROCEDITUR. Videtur quod haeretici et schismatici et excommunicati consecrare non possunt. Dicit enim Augustinus quod *extra Ecclesiam Catholicam non est locus veri sacrificii*. Et Leo Papa dicit, et habetur in decretis, I, qu. I, aliter, (scilicet quam in Ecclesia, quae corpus Christi est) *nec rata sunt sacerdotia, nec vera sacrificia*. Sed haeretici, schismatici et excommunicati sunt ab Ecclesia separati. Ergo non possunt verum sacrificium conficere.

PRAETEREA, sicut legitur ibidem, Innocentius Papa dicit, *Arianos, ceterasque huiusmodi pestes, quia laicos eorum sub imagine poenitentiae suscipimus, non videntur clerici eorum cum sacerdotii aut cuiuspiam mysterii suscipiendi dignitate esse, quibus solum Baptisma ratum esse permittimus*. Sed non potest aliquis consecrare Eucharistiam nisi sit cum sacerdotii dignitate. Ergo haeretici, et ceteri huiusmodi, non possunt Eucharistiam conficere.

PRAETEREA, ille qui est extra Ecclesiam, non videtur aliquid posse agere in persona totius Ecclesiae. Sed sacerdos consecrans Eucharistiam hoc agit in persona totius Ecclesiae, quod patet ex hoc quod omnes orationes proponit in persona Ecclesiae. Ergo videtur quod illi qui sunt extra Ecclesiam, scilicet haeretici et schismatici et excommunicati, non possunt consecrare Eucharistiam.

SED CONTRA est quod Augustinus dicit, in II contra Parmen., sicut Baptismus in eis, scilicet haereticis, schismaticis et excommunicatis, ita ordinatio mansit integra. Sed ex vi ordinationis sacerdos potest consecrare Eucharistiam. Ergo haeretici, schismatici et excommunicati, cum in eis maneat ordinatio integra, videtur quod possint consecrare Eucharistiam.

RESPONDEO dicendum quod quidam dixerunt quod haeretici, schismatici et excommunicati, quia sunt extra Ecclesiam, non possunt conficere hoc sacramentum. Sed in hoc decipiuntur. Quia, sicut Augustinus dicit, in II contra Parmen., *aliud est aliquid omnino non habere, aliud autem non recte habere, et similiter est etiam aliud non dare, et aliud non recte dare*. Illi igitur qui, intra Ecclesiam constituti, receperunt potestatem consecrandi in ordinatione sacerdotii, recte quidem habent potestatem, sed non recte ea utuntur, si postmodum per haeresim aut schisma vel excommunicationem ab Ecclesia separentur. Qui autem sic separati ordinantur, nec recte habent potestatem, nec recte utuntur. Quod tamen utrique potestatem habeant, per hoc patet quod, sicut Augustinus ibidem dicit, cum redeunt ad unitatem Ecclesiae, non reordinantur, sed recipiuntur in suis ordinibus. Et

OBJECTION 1: It seems that heretics, schismatics, and excommunicated persons are not able to consecrate the Eucharist. For Augustine says (*Liber sentent. Prosperi* xv) that *there is no such thing as a true sacrifice outside the Catholic Church*: and Pope Leo I says (*Ep. lxxx*; cf. *Decretal* i, q. 1): *Elsewhere (i.e., than in the Church which is Christ's body) there is neither valid priesthood nor true sacrifice*. But heretics, schismatics, and excommunicated persons are severed from the Church. Therefore they are unable to offer a true sacrifice.

OBJ. 2: Further (*Decretal*, caus. i, q. 1), Innocent I is quoted as saying: *Because we receive the laity of the Arians and other pestilential persons, if they seem to repent, it does not follow that their clergy have the dignity of the priesthood or of any other ministerial office, for we allow them to confer nothing save Baptism*. But none can consecrate the Eucharist, unless he have the dignity of the priesthood. Therefore heretics and the like cannot consecrate the Eucharist.

OBJ. 3: Further, it does not seem feasible for one outside the Church to act on behalf of the Church. But when the priest consecrates the Eucharist, he does so in the person of the entire Church, as is evident from the fact of his putting up all prayers in the person of the Church. Therefore, it seems that those who are outside the Church, such as those who are heretics, schismatics, and excommunicate, are not able to consecrate the Eucharist.

ON THE CONTRARY, Augustine says (*Contra Parmen.* ii): *Just as Baptism remains in them*, i.e., in heretics, schismatics, and those who are excommunicate, *so do their orders remain intact*. Now, by the power of his ordination, a priest can consecrate the Eucharist. Therefore, it seems that heretics, schismatics, and those who are excommunicate, can consecrate the Eucharist, since their orders remain entire.

I ANSWER THAT, Some have contended that heretics, schismatics, and the excommunicate, who are outside the pale of the Church, cannot perform this sacrament. But herein they are deceived, because, as Augustine says (*Contra Parmen.* ii), *it is one thing to lack something utterly, and another to have it improperly*; and in like fashion, *it is one thing not to bestow, and quite another to bestow, but not rightly*. Accordingly, such as, being within the Church, received the power of consecrating the Eucharist through being ordained to the priesthood, have such power rightly indeed; but they use it improperly if afterwards they be separated from the Church by heresy, schism, or excommunication. But such as are ordained while separated from the Church, have neither the power rightly, nor do they use it rightly. But that in both cases they have the power, is clear from what Augustine says (*Contra Parmen.* ii), that when they

quia consecratio Eucharistiae est actus consequens ordinis potestatem, illi qui sunt ab Ecclesia separati per haeresim aut schisma vel excommunicationem, possunt quidem consecrare Eucharistiam, quae ab eis consecrata verum corpus Christi et sanguinem continet, non tamen recte hoc faciunt, sed peccant facientes. Et ideo fructum sacrificii non percipiunt, quod est sacrificium spirituale.

AD PRIMUM ergo dicendum quod auctoritas illa et similes intelligendae sunt quantum ad hoc quod non recte extra Ecclesiam sacrificium offertur. Unde extra Ecclesiam non potest esse spirituale sacrificium, quod est verum veritate fructus, licet sit verum veritate sacramenti, sicut etiam supra dictum est quod peccator sumit corpus Christi sacramentaliter, sed non spiritualiter.

AD SECUNDUM dicendum quod solus Baptismus permittitur esse ratus haereticis et schismaticis, quia possunt licite baptizare in articulo necessitatis. In nullo autem casu licite possunt Eucharistiam consecrare, vel alia sacramenta conferre.

AD TERTIUM dicendum quod sacerdos in Missa in orationibus quidem loquitur in persona Ecclesiae, in cuius unitate consistit. Sed in consecratione sacramenti loquitur in persona Christi, cuius vicem in hoc gerit per ordinis potestatem. Et ideo, si sacerdos ab unitate Ecclesiae praecisus Missam celebret, quia potestatem ordinis non amittit, consecrat verum corpus et sanguinem Christi, sed quia est ab Ecclesiae unitate separatus, orationes eius efficaciam non habent.

return to the unity of the Church, they are not re-ordained, but are received in their orders. And since the consecration of the Eucharist is an act which follows the power of order, such persons as are separated from the Church by heresy, schism, or excommunication, can indeed consecrate the Eucharist, which on being consecrated by them contains Christ's true body and blood; but they act wrongly, and sin by doing so; and in consequence they do not receive the fruit of the sacrifice, which is a spiritual sacrifice.

REPLY OBJ. 1: Such and similar authorities are to be understood in this sense, that the sacrifice is offered wrongly outside the Church. Hence outside the Church there can be no spiritual sacrifice that is a true sacrifice with the truth of its fruit, although it be a true sacrifice with the truth of the sacrament; thus it was stated above (Q. 80, A. 3), that the sinner receives Christ's body sacramentally, but not spiritually.

REPLY OBJ. 2: Baptism alone is allowed to be conferred by heretics, and schismatics, because they can lawfully baptize in case of necessity; but in no case can they lawfully consecrate the Eucharist, or confer the other sacraments.

REPLY OBJ. 3: The priest, in reciting the prayers of the mass, speaks instead of the Church, in whose unity he remains; but in consecrating the sacrament he speaks as in the person of Christ, Whose place he holds by the power of his orders. Consequently, if a priest severed from the unity of the Church celebrates mass, not having lost the power of order, he consecrates Christ's true body and blood; but because he is severed from the unity of the Church, his prayers have no efficacy.

Article 8

Whether a Degraded Priest Can Consecrate This Sacrament?

AD OCTAVUM SIC PROCEDITUR. Videtur quod sacerdos degradatus non possit hoc sacramentum conficere. Nullus enim conficit hoc sacramentum nisi per potestatem consecrandi quam habet. *Sed degradatus non habet potestatem consecrandi, licet habeat potestatem baptizandi*, ut dicit canon. Ergo videtur quod presbyter degradatus non possit Eucharistiam consecrare.

PRAETEREA, ille qui aliquid dat, potest etiam auferre. Sed episcopus dat presbytero potestatem consecrandi ordinando ipsum. Ergo etiam potest ei auferre degradando ipsum.

PRAETEREA, sacerdos per degradationem aut amittit potestatem consecrandi, aut solam executionem. Sed non solam executionem, quia sic non plus amitteret degradatus quam excommunicatus, qui executione caret.

OBJECTION 1: It seems that a degraded priest cannot consecrate this sacrament. For no one can perform this sacrament except he have the power of consecrating. But the priest *who has been degraded has no power of consecrating, although he has the power of baptizing* (App. Gratiani). Therefore it seems that a degraded priest cannot consecrate the Eucharist.

OBJ. 2: Further, he who gives can take away. But the bishop in ordaining gives to the priest the power of consecrating. Therefore he can take it away by degrading him.

OBJ. 3: Further, the priest, by degradation, loses either the power of consecrating, or the use of such power. But he does not lose merely the use, for thus the degraded one would lose no more than one excommunicated, who also lacks the use. Therefore it seems that he loses the power to

Ergo videtur quod amittit potestatem consecrandi. Et ita videtur quod non possit conficere hoc sacramentum.

SED CONTRA est quod Augustinus, in II contra Parmen., probat quod apostatae a fide non carent Baptismate, per hoc quod *per poenitentiam redeuntibus non restituitur, et ideo non posse amitti iudicatur.* Sed similiter degradatus, si reconcilietur, non est iterum ordinandus. Ergo non amisit potestatem consecrandi. Et ita sacerdos degradatus potest conficere hoc sacramentum.

RESPONDEO dicendum quod potestas consecrandi Eucharistiam pertinet ad characterem sacerdotalis ordinis. Character autem quilibet, quia cum quadam consecratione datur, indelebilis est, ut supra dictum est, sicut et quarumcumque rerum consecrationes perpetuae sunt, nec amitti nec reiterari possunt. Unde manifestum est quod potestas consecrandi non amittitur per degradationem. Dicit enim Augustinus, in II contra Parmen., utrumque, scilicet Baptismus et ordo, sacramentum est, *et quadam consecratione utrumque homini datur, et illud cum baptizatur, et illud cum ordinatur. Ideo non licet a Catholicis utrumque iterari.* Et sic patet quod sacerdos degradatus potest conficere hoc sacramentum.

AD PRIMUM ergo dicendum quod canon ille non loquitur assertive, sed inquisitive, sicut ex circumstantia litterae haberi potest.

AD SECUNDUM dicendum quod episcopus non dat potestatem sacerdotalis ordinis propria virtute, sed instrumentaliter, sicut minister Dei, cuius effectus per hominem tolli non potest, secundum illud Matth. XIX, *quos Deus coniunxit, homo non separet.* Et ideo episcopus non potest hanc potestatem auferre, sicut nec ille qui baptizat potest auferre characterem baptismalem.

AD TERTIUM dicendum quod excommunicatio est medicinalis. Et ideo excommunicatis non aufertur executio sacerdotalis potestatis quasi in perpetuum, sed ad correctionem, usque ad tempus. Degradatis autem aufertur executio quasi in perpetuum condemnatis.

consecrate, and in consequence that he cannot perform this sacrament.

ON THE CONTRARY, Augustine (*Contra Parmen.* ii) proves that *apostates* from the faith *are not deprived of their Baptism*, from the fact that *it is not restored to them when they return repentant; and therefore it is deemed that it cannot be lost.* But in like fashion, if the degraded man be restored, he has not to be ordained over again. Consequently, he has not lost the power of consecrating, and so the degraded priest can perform this sacrament.

I ANSWER THAT, The power of consecrating the Eucharist belongs to the character of the priestly order. But every character is indelible, because it is given with a kind of consecration, as was said above (Q. 63, A. 5), just as the consecrations of all other things are perpetual, and cannot be lost or repeated. Hence it is clear that the power of consecrating is not lost by degradation. For, again, Augustine says (*Contra Parmen.* ii): *Both are sacraments*, namely Baptism and order, *and both are given to a man with a kind of consecration; the former, when he is baptized; the latter when he is ordained; and therefore it is not lawful for Catholics to repeat either of them.* And thus it is evident that the degraded priest can perform this sacrament.

REPLY OBJ. 1: That Canon is speaking, not as by way of assertion, but by way of inquiry, as can be gleaned from the context.

REPLY OBJ. 2: The bishop gives the priestly power of order, not as though coming from himself, but instrumentally, as God's minister, and its effect cannot be taken away by man, according to Matt. 19:6: *What God hath joined together, let no man put asunder.* And therefore the bishop cannot take this power away, just as neither can he who baptizes take away the baptismal character.

REPLY OBJ. 3: Excommunication is medicinal. And therefore the ministry of the priestly power is not taken away from the excommunicate, as it were, perpetually, but only for a time, that they may mend; but the exercise is withdrawn from the degraded, as though condemned perpetually.

Article 9

Whether It Is Permissible to Receive Communion from Heretical, Excommunicate, or Sinful Priests, and to Hear Mass Said by Them?

AD NONUM SIC PROCEDITUR. Videtur quod aliquis licite possit communionem recipere a sacerdotibus haereticis vel excommunicatis, vel etiam peccatoribus, et ab eis Missam audire. Sicut enim Augustinus, contra Petilianum, dicit, *neque in homine bono neque in homine malo aliquis Dei fugiat sacramenta.* Sed sacerdotes, quamvis sint peccatores et haeretici vel excommunicati,

OBJECTION 1: It seems that one may lawfully receive Communion from heretical, excommunicate, or even sinful priests, and to hear mass said by them. Because, as Augustine says (*Contra Petilian.* iii), *we should not avoid God's sacraments, whether they be given by a good man or by a wicked one.* But priests, even if they be sinful, or heretics, or excommunicate, perform a valid sacrament. Therefore

verum conficiunt sacramentum. Ergo videtur quod non sit vitandum ab eis communionem accipere vel eorum Missam audire.

PRAETEREA, corpus Christi verum figurativum est corporis mystici, sicut supra dictum est. Sed a praedictis sacerdotibus verum corpus Christi consecratur. Ergo videtur quod illi qui sunt de corpore mystico, possint eorum sacrificiis communicare.

PRAETEREA, multa peccata sunt graviora quam fornicatio. Sed non est prohibitum audire Missas sacerdotum aliter peccantium. Ergo etiam non debet esse prohibitum audire Missas sacerdotum fornicariorum.

SED CONTRA est quod canon dicit, XXXII dist., *nullus audiat Missam sacerdotis quem indubitanter concubinam novit habere. Et Gregorius dicit, in III Dialog., quod pater perfidus Arianum episcopum misit ad filium, ut ex eius manu sacrilegae consecrationis communionem acciperet, sed vir Deo devotus Ariano episcopo venienti exprobravit ut debuit.*

RESPONDEO dicendum quod, sicut supra dictum est, sacerdotes, si sint haeretici vel schismatici vel excommunicati, vel etiam peccatores, quamvis habeant potestatem consecrandi Eucharistiam, non tamen ea recte utuntur, sed peccant utentes. Quicumque autem communicat alicui in peccato, ipse particeps peccati efficitur, unde et in secunda canonica Ioannis legitur quod qui dixerit ei, ave, scilicet haeretico, *communicat operibus illius malignis.* Et ideo non licet a praedictis communionem accipere aut eorum Missam audire.

Differt tamen inter praedictas sectas. Nam haeretici et schismatici et excommunicati sunt per sententiam Ecclesiae executione consecrandi privati. Et ideo peccat quicumque eorum Missam audit vel ab eis accipit sacramenta. Sed non omnes peccatores sunt per sententiam Ecclesiae executione huius potestatis privati. Et sic, quamvis sint suspensi quantum est ex sententia divina, non tamen quantum ad alios ex sententia Ecclesiae. Et ideo, usque ad sententiam Ecclesiae, licet ab eis communionem accipere et eorum Missam audire. Unde super illud I Cor. V, *cum huiusmodi nec cibum sumere,* dicit Glossa Augustini, *hoc dicendo, noluit hominem ab homine iudicari ex arbitrio suspicionis, vel etiam extraordinario usurpato iudicio, sed potius ex lege Dei, secundum ordinem Ecclesiae, sive ultro confessum, vel accusatum et convictum.*

AD PRIMUM ergo dicendum quod in hoc quod refugimus audire talium sacerdotum Missam aut ab eis communionem recipere, non refugimus Dei sacramenta, sed potius ea veneramur, unde hostia a talibus sacerdotibus consecrata est adoranda, et, si reservetur, licite potest sumi a sacerdote legitimo. Sed refugimus culpam indigne ministrantium.

it seems that one ought not to refrain from receiving Communion at their hands, or from hearing their mass.

OBJ. 2: Further, Christ's true body is figurative of His mystical body, as was said above (Q. 67, A. 2). But Christ's true body is consecrated by the priests mentioned above. Therefore it seems that whoever belongs to His mystical body can communicate in their sacrifices.

OBJ. 3: Further, there are many sins graver than fornication. But it is not forbidden to hear the masses of priests who sin otherwise. Therefore, it ought not to be forbidden to hear the masses of priests guilty of this sin.

ON THE CONTRARY, The Canon says (Dist. 32): *Let no one hear the mass of a priest whom he knows without doubt to have a concubine.* Moreover, Gregory says (*Dial.* iii) that *the faithless father sent an Arian bishop to his son, for him to receive sacrilegiously the consecrated Communion at his hands. But, when the Arian bishop arrived, God's devoted servant rebuked him, as was right for him to do.*

I ANSWER THAT, As was said above (AA. 5, 7), heretical, schismatical, excommunicate, or even sinful priests, although they have the power to consecrate the Eucharist, yet they do not make a proper use of it; on the contrary, they sin by using it. But whoever communicates with another who is in sin, becomes a sharer in his sin. Hence we read in John's Second Canonical Epistle (11) that *He that saith unto him, God speed you, communicateth with his wicked works.* Consequently, it is not lawful to receive Communion from them, or to assist at their mass.

Still there is a difference among the above, because heretics, schismatics, and excommunicates, have been forbidden, by the Church's sentence, to perform the Eucharistic rite. And therefore whoever hears their mass or receives the sacraments from them, commits sin. But not all who are sinners are debarred by the Church's sentence from using this power: and so, although suspended by the Divine sentence, yet they are not suspended in regard to others by any ecclesiastical sentence: consequently, until the Church's sentence is pronounced, it is lawful to receive Communion at their hands, and to hear their mass. Hence on 1 Cor. 5:11, *with such a one not so much as to eat,* Augustine's gloss runs thus: *In saying this he was unwilling for a man to be judged by his fellow man on arbitrary suspicion, or even by usurped extraordinary judgment, but rather by God's law, according to the Church's ordering, whether he confess of his own accord, or whether he be accused and convicted.*

REPLY OBJ. 1: By refusing to hear the masses of such priests, or to receive Communion from them, we are not shunning God's sacraments; on the contrary, by so doing we are giving them honor (hence a host consecrated by such priests is to be adored, and if it be reserved, it can be consumed by a lawful priest): but what we shun is the sin of the unworthy ministers.

Ad secundum dicendum quod unitas corporis mystici est fructus corporis veri percepti. Illi autem qui indigne percipiunt vel ministrant, privantur fructu, ut supra dictum est. Et ideo non est sumendum ex eorum dispensatione sacramentum ab eis qui sunt in unitate Ecclesiae.

Ad tertium dicendum quod, licet fornicatio non sit gravior ceteris peccatis, tamen ad eam sunt homines proniores, propter carnis concupiscentiam. Et ideo specialiter hoc peccatum a sacerdotibus prohibitum est ab Ecclesia, ne aliquis audiat Missam concubinarii sacerdotis. Sed hoc intelligendum est de notorio, vel per sententiam quae fertur in convictum, vel confessionem in iure factam, vel quando non potest peccatum aliqua tergiversatione celari.

Reply Obj. 2: The unity of the mystical body is the fruit of the true body received. But those who receive or minister unworthily, are deprived of the fruit, as was said above (A. 7; Q. 80, A. 4). And therefore, those who belong to the unity of the Faith are not to receive the sacrament from their dispensing.

Reply Obj. 3: Although fornication is not graver than other sins, yet men are more prone to it, owing to fleshly concupiscence. Consequently, this sin is specially inhibited to priests by the Church, lest anyone hear the mass of one living in concubinage. However, this is to be understood of one who is notorious, either from being convicted and sentenced, or from having acknowledged his guilt in legal form, or from it being impossible to conceal his guilt by any subterfuge.

Article 10

Whether It Is Lawful for a Priest to Refrain Entirely from Consecrating the Eucharist?

Ad decimum sic proceditur. Videtur quod liceat sacerdoti omnino a consecratione Eucharistiae abstinere. Sicut enim ad officium sacerdotis pertinet Eucharistiam consecrare, ita etiam baptizare et in aliis sacramentis ministrare. Sed sacerdos non tenetur ministrare in aliis sacramentis, nisi propter curam animarum susceptam. Ergo videtur quod nec etiam teneatur Eucharistiam consecrare, si curam non habeat animarum.

Praeterea, nullus tenetur facere quod sibi non licet, alioquin esset perplexus. Sed sacerdoti peccatori, vel etiam excommunicato, non licet Eucharistiam consecrare, ut ex supra dictis patet. Ergo videtur quod tales non teneantur ad celebrandum. Et ita nec alii, alioquin ex sua culpa commodum reportarent.

Praeterea, dignitas sacerdotalis non perditur per subsequentem infirmitatem, dicit enim Gelasius Papa, et habetur in decretis, dist. LV, *praecepta canonum sicut non patiuntur venire ad sacerdotium debiles corpore, ita, si quis in eo fuerit constitutus ac tunc fuerit sauciatus, amittere non potest quod tempore suae sinceritatis accepit.* Contingit autem quandoque quod ordinati in sacerdotes incurrunt aliquos defectus ex quibus a celebratione impediuntur, sicut est lepra, vel morbus caducus, vel aliquid huiusmodi. Non ergo videtur quod sacerdotes ad celebrandum teneantur.

Sed contra est quod Ambrosius dicit, in quadam oratione, *grave est quod ad mensam tuam mundo corde et manibus innocentibus non venimus, sed gravius est si, dum peccata metuimus, etiam sacrificium non reddamus.*

Objection 1: It seems to be lawful for a priest to refrain entirely from consecrating the Eucharist. Because, as it is the priest's office to consecrate the Eucharist, so it is likewise to baptize and administer the other sacraments. But the priest is not bound to act as a minister of the other sacraments, unless he has undertaken the care of souls. Therefore, it seems that likewise he is not bound to consecrate the Eucharist except he be charged with the care of souls.

Obj. 2: Further, no one is bound to do what is unlawful for him to do; otherwise he would be in two minds. But it is not lawful for the priest who is in a state of sin, or excommunicate, to consecrate the Eucharist, as was said above (A. 7). Therefore it seems that such men are not bound to celebrate, and so neither are the others; otherwise they would be gainers by their fault.

Obj. 3: Further, the priestly dignity is not lost by subsequent weakness: because Pope Gelasius I says (cf. *Decretal*, Dist. 55): *As the canonical precepts do not permit them who are feeble in body to approach the priesthood, so if anyone be disabled when once in that state, he cannot lose that he received at the time he was well.* But it sometimes happens that those who are already ordained as priests incur defects whereby they are hindered from celebrating, such as leprosy or epilepsy, or the like. Consequently, it does not appear that priests are bound to celebrate.

On the contrary, Ambrose says in one of his Orations (xxxiii): *It is a grave matter if we do not approach Thy altar with clean heart and pure hands; but it is graver still if while shunning sins we also fail to offer our sacrifice.*

RESPONDEO dicendum quod quidam dixerunt quod sacerdos potest omnino licite a consecratione abstinere, nisi teneatur ex cura sibi commissa celebrare pro populo et sacramenta praebere.

Sed hoc irrationabiliter dicitur. Quia unusquisque tenetur uti gratia sibi data cum fuerit opportunum, secundum illud II Cor. VI, *hortamur vos ne in vacuum gratiam Dei recipiatis*. Opportunitas autem sacrificium offerendi non solum attenditur per comparationem ad fideles Christi, quibus oportet sacramenta ministrari, sed principaliter per comparationem ad Deum, cui in consecratione huius sacramenti sacrificium offertur. Unde sacerdoti, etiam si non habeat curam animarum, non licet omnino a celebratione cessare, sed saltem videtur quod celebrare tenetur in praecipuis festis, et maxime in illis diebus in quibus fideles communicare consueverunt. Et hinc est quod II Machab. IV dicitur contra quosdam sacerdotes quod *iam non circa altaris officia dediti erant, contempto templo et sacrificiis neglectis*.

AD PRIMUM ergo dicendum quod alia sacramenta perficiuntur in usu fidelium. Et ideo in illis ministrare non tenetur nisi ille qui super fideles suscipit curam. Sed hoc sacramentum perficitur in consecratione Eucharistiae, in qua sacrificium Deo offertur, ad quod sacerdos obligatur ex ordine iam suscepto.

AD SECUNDUM dicendum quod sacerdos peccator, si per sententiam Ecclesiae sit executione ordinis privatus vel simpliciter vel ad tempus, redditus est impotens ad sacrificium offerendum, et ideo obligatio tollitur. Hoc autem cedit sibi in detrimentum spiritualis fructus, magis quam in emolumentum. Si vero non sit privatus potestate celebrandi, non solvitur obligatio. Nec tamen est perplexus, quia potest de peccato poenitere et celebrare.

AD TERTIUM dicendum quod debilitas vel aegritudo superveniens ordini sacerdotali ordinem non tollit, executionem tamen ordinis impedit quantum ad consecrationem Eucharistiae. Quandoque quidem propter impossibilitatem executionis, sicut si privetur oculis aut digitis, aut usu linguae. Quandoque autem propter periculum, sicut patet de eo qui patitur morbum caducum, vel etiam quamcumque alienationem mentis. Quandoque propter abominationem, sicut patet de leproso, qui non debet publice celebrare. Potest tamen dicere Missam occulte, nisi lepra adeo invaluerit quod per corrosionem membrorum eum ad hoc reddiderit impotentem.

I ANSWER THAT, Some have said that a priest may lawfully refrain altogether from consecrating, except he be bound to do so, and to give the sacraments to the people, by reason of his being entrusted with the care of souls.

But this is said quite unreasonably, because everyone is bound to use the grace entrusted to him, when opportunity serves, according to 2 Cor. 6:1: *We exhort you that you receive not the grace of God in vain.* But the opportunity of offering sacrifice is considered not merely in relation to the faithful of Christ to whom the sacraments must be administered, but chiefly with regard to God to Whom the sacrifice of this sacrament is offered by consecrating. Hence, it is not lawful for the priest, even though he has not the care of souls, to refrain altogether from celebrating; and he seems to be bound to celebrate at least on the chief festivals, and especially on those days on which the faithful usually communicate. And hence it is that (2 Macc 4:14) it is said against some priests that they *were not now occupied about the offices of the altar . . . despising the temple and neglecting the sacrifices.*

REPLY OBJ. 1: The other sacraments are accomplished in being used by the faithful, and therefore he alone is bound to administer them who has undertaken the care of souls. But this sacrament is performed in the consecration of the Eucharist, whereby a sacrifice is offered to God, to which the priest is bound from the order he has received.

REPLY OBJ. 2: The sinful priest, if deprived by the Church's sentence from exercising his order, simply or for a time, is rendered incapable of offering sacrifice; consequently, the obligation lapses. But if not deprived of the power of celebrating, the obligation is not removed; nor is he in two minds, because he can repent of his sin and then celebrate.

REPLY OBJ. 3: Weakness or sickness contracted by a priest after his ordination does not deprive him of his orders; but hinders him from exercising them, as to the consecration of the Eucharist: sometimes by making it impossible to exercise them, as, for example, if he lose his sight, or his fingers, or the use of speech; and sometimes on account of danger, as in the case of one suffering from epilepsy, or indeed any disease of the mind; and sometimes, on account of loathsomeness, as is evident in the case of a leper, who ought not to celebrate in public: he can, however, say mass privately, unless the leprosy has gone so far that it has rendered him incapable owing to the wasting away of his limbs.

QUESTION 83

THE RITE OF THIS SACRAMENT

Deinde considerandum est de ritu huius sacramenti. Et circa hoc quaeruntur sex.

Primo, utrum in celebratione huius mysterii Christus immoletur.

Secundo, de tempore celebrationis.

Tertio, de loco, et aliis quae pertinent ad apparatum huius celebrationis.

Quarto, de his quae in celebratione huius mysterii dicuntur.

Quinto, de his quae circa celebrationem huius mysterii fiunt.

Sexto, de defectibus qui circa celebrationem huius sacramenti occurrunt.

We have now to consider the Rite of this sacrament, under which head there are six points of inquiry:

(1) Whether Christ is sacrificed in the celebration of this mystery?

(2) Of the time of celebrating;

(3) Of the place and other matters relating to the equipment for this celebration;

(4) Of the words uttered in celebrating this mystery;

(5) Of the actions performed in celebrating this mystery.

(6) Of the defects which occur in the celebration of this sacrament.

Article 1

Whether Christ Is Sacrificed in This Sacrament?

AD PRIMUM SIC PROCEDITUR. Videtur quod in celebratione huius sacramenti Christus non immoletur. Dicitur enim Hebr. X, quod *Christus una oblatione consummavit in sempiternum sanctificatos.* Sed illa oblatio fuit eius immolatio. Ergo Christus non immolatur in celebratione huius sacramenti.

PRAETEREA, immolatio Christi facta est in cruce, in qua *tradidit semetipsum oblationem et hostiam Deo in odorem suavitatis,* ut dicitur Ephes. V. Sed in celebratione huius mysterii Christus non crucifigitur. Ergo nec immolatur.

PRAETEREA, sicut Augustinus dicit, IV de Trin., in immolatione Christi idem est sacerdos et hostia. Sed in celebratione huius sacramenti non est idem sacerdos et hostia. Ergo celebratio huius sacramenti non est Christi immolatio.

SED CONTRA est quod Augustinus dicit, in libro sententiarum prosperi, *semel immolatus est in semetipso Christus, et tamen quotidie immolatur in sacramento.*

RESPONDEO dicendum quod duplici ratione celebratio huius sacramenti dicitur Christi immolatio. Primo quidem quia, sicut Augustinus dicit, ad Simplicianum, *solent imagines earum rerum nominibus appellari quarum imagines sunt, sicut cum, intuentes tabulam aut parietem pictum, dicimus, ille Cicero est, ille Sallustius.* Celebratio autem huius sacramenti, sicut supra dictum est, imago est quaedam repraesentativa passionis Christi, quae est vera immolatio. Unde Ambrosius dicit,

OBJECTION 1: It seems that Christ is not sacrificed in the celebration of this sacrament. For it is written (Heb 10:14) that *Christ by one oblation hath perfected for ever them that are sanctified.* But that oblation was His oblation. Therefore Christ is not sacrificed in the celebration of this sacrament.

OBJ. 2: Further, Christ's sacrifice was made upon the cross, whereon *He delivered Himself for us, an oblation and a sacrifice to God for an odor of sweetness,* as is said in Eph. 5:2. But Christ is not crucified in the celebration of this mystery. Therefore, neither is He sacrificed.

OBJ. 3: Further, as Augustine says (*De Trin.* iv), in Christ's sacrifice the priest and the victim are one and the same. But in the celebration of this sacrament the priest and the victim are not the same. Therefore, the celebration of this sacrament is not a sacrifice of Christ.

ON THE CONTRARY, Augustine says in the Liber Sentent. Prosp. (cf. *Ep.* xcviii): *Christ was sacrificed once in Himself, and yet He is sacrificed daily in the Sacrament.*

I ANSWER THAT, The celebration of this sacrament is called a sacrifice for two reasons. First, because, as Augustine says (*Ad Simplician.* ii), *the images of things are called by the names of the things whereof they are the images; as when we look upon a picture or a fresco, we say, 'This is Cicero and that is Sallust.'* But, as was said above (Q. 79, A. 1), the celebration of this sacrament is an image representing Christ's Passion, which is His true sacrifice. Accordingly the celebration of this sacrament is called Christ's sacrifice.

super epistolam ad Heb., *in Christo semel oblata est hostia ad salutem sempiternam potens. Quid ergo nos? Nonne per singulos dies offerimus ad recordationem mortis eius?* Alio modo, quantum ad effectum passionis, quia scilicet per hoc sacramentum participes efficimur fructus dominicae passionis. Unde et in quadam dominicali oratione secreta dicitur, *quoties huius hostiae commemoratio celebratur, opus nostrae redemptionis exercetur.* Quantum igitur ad primum modum, poterat Christus dici immolari etiam in figuris veteris testamenti, unde et in Apoc. XIII dicitur, *quorum nomina non sunt scripta in libro vitae agni, qui occisus est ab origine mundi.* Sed quantum ad modum secundum, proprium est huic sacramento quod in eius celebratione Christus immoletur.

AD PRIMUM ergo dicendum quod, sicut Ambrosius ibidem dicit, una est hostia, quam scilicet Christus obtulit et nos offerimus, *et non multae, quia semel oblatus est Christus, hoc autem sacrificium exemplum est illius. Sicut enim quod ubique offertur unum est corpus et non multa corpora, ita et unum sacrificium.*

AD SECUNDUM dicendum quod, sicut celebratio huius sacramenti est imago repraesentativa passionis Christi, ita altare est repraesentativum crucis ipsius, in qua Christus in propria specie immolatus est.

AD TERTIUM dicendum quod, per eandem rationem, etiam sacerdos gerit imaginem Christi, in cuius persona et virtute verba pronuntiat ad consecrandum, ut ex supra dictis patet. Et ita quodammodo idem est sacerdos et hostia.

Hence it is that Ambrose, in commenting on Heb. 10:1, says: *In Christ was offered up a sacrifice capable of giving eternal salvation; what then do we do? Do we not offer it up every day in memory of His death?* Second it is called a sacrifice, in respect of the effect of His Passion: because, to wit, by this sacrament, we are made partakers of the fruit of our Lord's Passion. Hence in one of the Sunday Secrets (Ninth Sunday after Pentecost) we say: *Whenever the commemoration of this sacrifice is celebrated, the work of our redemption is enacted.* Consequently, according to the first reason, it is true to say that Christ was sacrificed, even in the figures of the Old Testament: hence it is stated in the Apocalypse (13:8): *Whose names are not written in the Book of Life of the Lamb, which was slain from the beginning of the world.* But according to the second reason, it is proper to this sacrament for Christ to be sacrificed in its celebration.

REPLY OBJ. 1: As Ambrose says (commenting on Heb. 10:1), *there is but one victim*, namely that which Christ offered, and which we offer, *and not many victims, because Christ was offered but once: and this latter sacrifice is the pattern of the former. For, just as what is offered everywhere is one body, and not many bodies, so also is it but one sacrifice.*

REPLY OBJ. 2: As the celebration of this sacrament is an image representing Christ's Passion, so the altar is representative of the cross itself, upon which Christ was sacrificed in His proper species.

REPLY OBJ. 3: For the same reason (cf. Reply Obj. 2) the priest also bears Christ's image, in Whose person and by Whose power he pronounces the words of consecration, as is evident from what was said above (Q. 82, AA. 1, 3). And so, in a measure, the priest and victim are one and the same.

Article 2

Whether the Time for Celebrating This Mystery Has Been Properly Determined?

AD SECUNDUM SIC PROCEDITUR. Videtur quod inconvenienter sit determinatum tempus celebrationis huius mysterii. Hoc enim sacramentum est repraesentativum dominicae passionis, ut dictum est. Sed commemoratio dominicae passionis fit in Ecclesia semel in anno, dicit enim Augustinus, super Psalmos, *quoties Pascha celebratur, nunquid toties Christus occiditur? Sed tamen anniversaria recordatio repraesentat quod olim factum est, et sic nos facit moveri tanquam videamus dominum in cruce praesentem.* Ergo hoc sacramentum non debet celebrari nisi semel in anno.

PRAETEREA, passio Christi commemoratur in Ecclesia sexta feria ante Pascha, non autem in festo natalis. Cum ergo hoc sacramentum sit commemorativum

OBJECTION 1: It seems that the time for celebrating this mystery has not been properly determined. For as was observed above (A. 1), this sacrament is representative of our Lord's Passion. But the commemoration of our Lord's Passion takes place in the Church once in the year: because Augustine says (*Enarr. ii in Ps. 21*): *Is not Christ slain as often as the Pasch is celebrated? Nevertheless, the anniversary remembrance represents what took place in by-gone days; and so it does not cause us to be stirred as if we saw our Lord hanging upon the cross.* Therefore this sacrament ought to be celebrated but once a year.

OBJ. 2: Further, Christ's Passion is commemorated in the Church on the Friday before Easter, and not on Christmas Day. Consequently, since this sacrament is commemorative

dominicae passionis, videtur inconveniens quod in die natalis ter celebratur hoc sacramentum, in parasceve autem totaliter intermittitur.

PRAETEREA, in celebratione huius sacramenti Ecclesia debet imitari institutionem Christi. Sed Christus consecravit hoc sacramentum hora serotina. Ergo videtur quod tali hora debeat hoc sacramentum celebrari.

PRAETEREA, sicut habetur de Consecr., dist. I, Leo Papa scribit Dioscoro Alexandrino episcopo, quod in prima parte diei Missas celebrare licet. Sed dies incipit a media nocte, ut supra dictum est. Ergo videtur quod etiam post mediam noctem liceat celebrare.

PRAETEREA, in quadam dominicali oratione secreta dicitur, *concede nobis, domine, quaesumus, haec frequentare mysteria.* Sed maior erit frequentia si etiam pluribus horis in die sacerdos celebret. Ergo videtur quod non debeat prohiberi sacerdos pluries celebrare in die.

SED IN CONTRARIUM est consuetudo quam servat Ecclesia secundum canonum statuta.

RESPONDEO dicendum quod, sicut dictum est, in celebratione huius mysterii attenditur et repraesentatio dominicae passionis, et participatio fructus eius. Et secundum utrumque oportuit determinare tempus aptum celebrationi huius sacramenti. Quia enim fructu dominicae passionis quotidie indigemus propter quotidianos defectus, quotidie in Ecclesia regulariter hoc sacramentum offertur. Unde et dominus nos petere docet, Luc. XI, *panem nostrum quotidianum da nobis hodie,* quod exponens Augustinus, in libro de verbis domini, dicit, *si quotidianus est panis, cur post annum illum sumas, quemadmodum Graeci in oriente facere consueverunt? Accipe quotidie quod quotidie tibi prosit.*

Quia vero dominica passio celebrata est a tertia hora usque ad nonam, ideo regulariter in illa parte diei solemniter celebratur in Ecclesia hoc sacramentum.

AD PRIMUM ergo dicendum quod in hoc sacramento recolitur passio Christi secundum quod eius effectus ad fideles derivatur. Sed tempore passionis recolitur passio Christi solum secundum quod in ipso capite nostro fuit perfecta. Quod quidem factum est semel, quotidie autem fructum dominicae passionis fideles percipiunt. Et ideo sola commemoratio fit semel in anno, hoc autem quotidie, et propter fructum et propter iugem memoriam.

AD SECUNDUM dicendum quod, veniente veritate, cessat figura. Hoc autem sacramentum est figura quaedam et exemplum passionis dominicae, sicut dictum est. Et ideo in die quo ipsa passio domini recolitur prout realiter gesta est, non celebratur consecratio huius sacramenti. Ne tamen Ecclesia eo etiam die sit sine fructu

of our Lord's Passion, it seems unsuitable for this sacrament to be celebrated thrice on Christmas Day, and to be entirely omitted on Good Friday.

OBJ. 3: Further, in the celebration of this sacrament the Church ought to imitate Christ's institution. But it was in the evening that Christ consecrated this sacrament. Therefore it seems that this sacrament ought to be celebrated at that time of day.

OBJ. 4: Further, as is set down in the *Decretals* (*De Consecr.*, dist. i), Pope Leo I wrote to Dioscorus, Bishop of Alexandria, that *it is permissible to celebrate mass in the first part of the day.* But the day begins at midnight, as was said above (Q. 80, A. 8, ad 5). Therefore it seems that after midnight it is lawful to celebrate.

OBJ. 5: Further, in one of the Sunday Secrets (Ninth Sunday after Pentecost) we say: *Grant us, Lord, we beseech Thee, to frequent these mysteries.* But there will be greater frequency if the priest celebrates several times a day. Therefore it seems that the priest ought not to be hindered from celebrating several times daily.

ON THE CONTRARY is the custom which the Church observes according to the statutes of the Canons.

I ANSWER THAT, As stated above (A. 1), in the celebration of this mystery, we must take into consideration the representation of our Lord's Passion, and the participation of its fruits; and the time suitable for the celebration of this mystery ought to be determined by each of these considerations. Now since, owing to our daily defects, we stand in daily need of the fruits of our Lord's Passion, this sacrament is offered regularly every day in the Church. Hence our Lord teaches us to pray (Luke 11:3): *Give us this day our daily bread*: in explanation of which words Augustine says (*De Verb. Dom.* xxviii): *If it be a daily bread, why do you take it once a year, as the Greeks have the custom in the east? Receive it daily that it may benefit you every day.*

But since our Lord's Passion was celebrated from the third to the ninth hour, therefore this sacrament is solemnly celebrated by the Church in that part of the day.

REPLY OBJ. 1: Christ's Passion is recalled in this sacrament, inasmuch as its effect flows out to the faithful; but at Passion-tide Christ's Passion is recalled inasmuch as it was wrought in Him Who is our Head. This took place but once; whereas the faithful receive daily the fruits of His Passion: consequently, the former is commemorated but once in the year, whereas the latter takes place every day, both that we may partake of its fruit and in order that we may have a perpetual memorial.

REPLY OBJ. 2: The figure ceases on the advent of the reality. But this sacrament is a figure and a representation of our Lord's Passion, as stated above. And therefore on the day on which our Lord's Passion is recalled as it was really accomplished, this sacrament is not consecrated. Nevertheless, lest the Church be deprived on that day of

passionis per hoc sacramentum nobis exhibito, corpus Christi consecratum in die praecedenti reservatur sumendum in illa die. Non autem sanguis, propter periculum, et quia sanguis specialius est imago dominicae passionis, ut supra dictum est. Nec etiam verum est, quod quidam dicunt, quod per immissionem particulae corporis in vinum, convertatur vinum in sanguinem. Hoc enim aliter fieri non potest quam per consecrationem factam sub debita forma verborum.

In die autem nativitatis plures Missae celebrantur, propter triplicem Christi nativitatem. Quarum una est aeterna, quae, quantum ad nos, est occulta. Et ideo una Missa cantatur in nocte, in cuius introitu dicitur, *dominus dixit ad me, filius meus es tu, ego hodie genui te*. Alia autem est temporalis, sed spiritualis, qua scilicet Christus *oritur tanquam Lucifer in cordibus nostris*, ut dicitur II Pet. I. Et propter hoc cantatur Missa in aurora, in cuius introitu dicitur, *lux fulgebit super nos*. Tertia est Christi nativitas temporalis et corporalis, secundum quam visibilis nobis processit ex utero virginali carne indutus. Et ob hoc cantatur tertia Missa in plena luce, in cuius introitu dicitur, *puer natus est nobis*. Licet e converso posset dici quod nativitas aeterna, secundum se, est in plena luce, et ob hoc in Evangelio tertiae Missae fit mentio de nativitate aeterna. Secundum autem nativitatem corporalem, ad litteram, natus est de nocte, in signum quod veniebat ad tenebras infirmitatis nostrae, unde et in Missa nocturna dicitur Evangelium de corporali Christi nativitate.

Sicut etiam et in aliis diebus in quibus occurrunt plura Christi beneficia vel recolenda vel expetenda, plures Missae celebrantur in die, puta una pro festo, et alia pro ieiunio vel pro mortuis.

AD TERTIUM dicendum quod, sicut supra dictum est, Christus voluit ultimo hoc sacramentum discipulis tradere, ut fortius eorum cordibus imprimeretur. Et ideo post cenam et in fine diei hoc sacramentum consecravit et discipulis tradidit. A nobis autem celebratur hora dominicae passionis, scilicet vel in diebus festis in tertia, quando crucifixus est linguis Iudaeorum, ut dicitur Marc. XV, et quando Spiritus Sanctus descendit super discipulos; vel diebus profestis in sexta, quando crucifixus est manibus militum, ut habetur Ioan. XIX; vel diebus ieiuniorum in nona, quando *voce magna clamans emisit spiritum*, ut dicitur Matth. XXVII.

Potest tamen tardari, maxime quando sunt ordines faciendi, et praecipue in sabbato sancto; tum propter prolixitatem officii; tum etiam quia ordines pertinent ad diem dominicum, ut habetur in decretis, dist. LXXV, cap. quod a patribus.

the fruit of the Passion offered to us by this sacrament, the body of Christ consecrated the day before is reserved to be consumed on that day; but the blood is not reserved, on account of danger, and because the blood is more specially the image of our Lord's Passion, as stated above (Q. 78, A. 3, ad 2). Nor is it true, as some affirm, that the wine is changed into blood when the particle of Christ's body is dropped into it. Because this cannot be done otherwise than by consecration under the due form of words.

On Christmas Day, however, several masses are said on account of Christ's threefold nativity. Of these the first is His eternal birth, which is hidden in our regard, and therefore one mass is sung in the night, in the *Introit* of which we say: *The Lord said unto Me: Thou art My Son, this day have I begotten Thee*. The second is His nativity in time, and the spiritual birth, whereby Christ rises *as the day-star in our hearts* (2 Pet 1:19), and on this account the mass is sung at dawn, and in the *Introit* we say: *The light will shine on us today*. The third is Christ's temporal and bodily birth, according as He went forth from the virginal womb, becoming visible to us through being clothed with flesh: and on that account the third mass is sung in broad daylight, in the *Introit* of which we say: *A child is born to us*. Nevertheless, on the other hand, it can be said that His eternal generation, of itself, is in the full light, and on this account in the gospel of the third mass mention is made of His eternal birth. But regarding His birth in the body, He was literally born during the night, as a sign that He came to the darknesses of our infirmity; hence also in the midnight mass we say the gospel of Christ's nativity in the flesh.

Likewise on other days upon which many of God's benefits have to be recalled or besought, several masses are celebrated on one day, as for instance, one for the feast, and another for a fast or for the dead.

REPLY OBJ. 3: As already observed (Q. 73, A. 5), Christ wished to give this sacrament last of all, in order that it might make a deeper impression on the hearts of the disciples; and therefore it was after supper, at the close of day, that He consecrated this sacrament and gave it to His disciples. But we celebrate at the hour when our Lord suffered, i.e., either, as on feast-days, at the hour of Terce, when He was crucified by the tongues of the Jews (Mark 15:25), and when the Holy Spirit descended upon the disciples (Acts 2:15); or, as when no feast is kept, at the hour of Sext, when He was crucified at the hands of the soldiers (John 19:14), or, as on fasting days, at None, when crying out with a loud voice He gave up the ghost (Matt 27:46, 50).

Nevertheless the mass can be postponed, especially when Holy orders have to be conferred, and still more on Holy Saturday; both on account of the length of the office, and also because orders belong to the Sunday, as is set forth in the *Decretals* (dist. 75).

Possunt tamen etiam Missae celebrari in prima parte diei propter aliquam necessitatem, ut habetur de Consecr., dist. I, cap. necesse est et cetera.

AD QUARTUM dicendum quod regulariter Missa debet celebrari in die, et non in nocte, quia ipse Christus est praesens in hoc sacramento, qui dicit, Ioan. IX, *me oportet operari opera eius qui misit me, donec dies est. Venit nox, quando nemo potest operari. Quandiu in mundo sum, lux sum mundi.* Ita tamen quod principium diei sumatur non a media nocte; nec etiam ab ortu solis, idest quando substantia solis apparet super terram; sed quando incipit apparere aurora. Tunc enim quodammodo dicitur sol ortus, inquantum claritas radiorum eius apparet. Unde et Marc. XVI dicitur quod mulieres venerunt ad monumentum orto iam sole; cum tamen venerint, cum adhuc tenebrae essent, ad monumentum, ut dicitur Ioan. XX; sic enim hanc contrarietatem solvit Augustinus, in libro de consensu Evangelistarum.

Specialiter tamen in nocte natalis Missa celebratur, propter hoc quod dominus nocte natus est, ut habetur de Consecr., dist. I, cap. nocte et cetera. Et similiter etiam in sabbato sancto circa noctis principium, propter hoc quod dominus nocte surrexit, idest, cum adhuc tenebrae essent, ante manifestum solis ortum.

AD QUINTUM dicendum quod, sicut habetur de Consecr., dist. I, ex decreto Alexandri Papae, *sufficit sacerdoti in die unam Missam celebrare, quia Christus semel passus est et totum mundum redemit; et valde felix est qui unam digne celebrare potest. Quidam tamen pro defunctis unam faciunt et alteram diei, si necesse est. Qui vero pro pecunia aut adulationibus saecularium uno die praesumunt plures celebrare Missas, non aestimo evadere damnationem.* Et extra, de Celebr., dicit Innocentius III quod, *excepto die nativitatis dominicae, nisi causa necessitatis suaderet, sufficit sacerdoti semel in die unam Missam solummodo celebrare.*

Masses, however, can be celebrated *in the first part of the day*, owing to any necessity; as is stated *De Consecr.*, dist. 1.

REPLY OBJ. 4: As a rule mass ought to be said in the day and not in the night, because Christ is present in this sacrament, Who says (John 9:4, 5): *I must work the works of Him that sent Me, whilst it is day: because the night cometh when no man can work; as long as I am in the world, I am the light of the world.* Yet this should be done in such a manner that the beginning of the day is not to be taken from midnight; nor from sunrise, that is, when the substance of the sun appears above the earth; but when the dawn begins to show: because then the sun is said to be risen when the brightness of his beams appears. Accordingly it is written (Mark 16:1) that *the women came to the tomb, the sun being now risen;* though, as John relates (John 20:1), *while it was yet dark they came to the tomb.* It is in this way that Augustine explains this difference (*De Consens. Evang.* iii).

Exception is made on the night of Christmas eve, when mass is celebrated, because our Lord was born in the night (*De Consecr.*, dist. 1). And in like manner it is celebrated on Holy Saturday towards the beginning of the night, since our Lord rose in the night, that is, *when it was yet dark, before the sun's rising was manifest.*

REPLY OBJ. 5: As is set down in the decree (*De Consecr.*, dist. 1), in virtue of a decree of Pope Alexander II, *it is enough for a priest to celebrate one mass each day, because Christ suffered once and redeemed the whole world; and very happy is he who can worthily celebrate one mass. But there are some who say one mass for the dead, and another of the day, if need be. But I do not deem that those escape condemnation who presume to celebrate several masses daily, either for the sake of money, or to gain flattery from the laity.* And Pope Innocent III says (*Extra, De Celebr. Miss.,* chap. *Consuluisti*) that *except on the day of our Lord's birth, unless necessity urges, it suffices for a priest to celebrate only one mass each day.*

Article 3

Whether This Sacrament Ought to Be Celebrated in a House and with Sacred Vessels?

AD TERTIUM SIC PROCEDITUR. Videtur quod non oporteat hoc sacramentum celebrare in domo et vasis sacris. Hoc enim sacramentum est repraesentativum dominicae passionis. Sed Christus non est passus in domo, sed extra portam civitatis, secundum illud Heb. ult., *Iesus, ut per suum sanguinem sanctificaret populum, extra portam passus est.* Ergo videtur quod hoc sacramentum non debeat celebrari in domo, sed magis sub divo.

PRAETEREA, in celebratione huius sacramenti debet Ecclesia imitari morem Christi et apostolorum. Sed

OBJECTION 1: It seems that this sacrament ought not to be celebrated in a house and with sacred vessels. For this sacrament is a representation of our Lord's Passion. But Christ did not suffer in a house, but outside the city gate, according to Heb. 1:12: *Jesus, that He might sanctify the people by His own blood, suffered without the gate.* Therefore, it seems that this sacrament ought not to be celebrated in a house, but rather in the open air.

OBJ. 2: Further, in the celebration of this sacrament the Church ought to imitate the custom of Christ and the

domus in qua Christus primo hoc sacramentum confecit, non fuit consecrata, sed fuit quoddam commune cenaculum a quodam patrefamilias praeparatum, ut habetur Luc. XXII. Legitur etiam Act. II quod *apostoli erant perdurantes unanimiter in templo; et frangentes circa domos panem, sumebant cum exultatione.* Ergo nec modo oportet domos esse consecratas in quibus hoc sacramentum celebratur.

PRAETEREA, nihil fieri frustra in Ecclesia debet, quae spiritu sancto gubernatur. Sed frustra videtur adhiberi consecratio Ecclesiae vel altari, et huiusmodi rebus inanimatis, quae non sunt susceptiva gratiae vel spiritualis virtutis. Inconvenienter igitur huiusmodi consecrationes in Ecclesia fiunt.

PRAETEREA, solum divina opera debent recoli cum quadam solemnitate, secundum illud Psalmi, *in operibus manuum tuarum exultabo.* Sed Ecclesia vel altare opere humano consecratur, sicut et calix et ministri et alia huiusmodi. Sed horum consecrationes non recoluntur celebriter in Ecclesia. Ergo neque consecratio Ecclesiae vel altaris cum solemnitate recoli debet.

PRAETEREA, veritas debet respondere figurae. Sed in veteri testamento, quod gerebat figuram novi, non fiebat altare de lapidibus sectis, dicitur enim Exod. XX, *altare de terra facietis mihi. Quod si altare lapideum feceritis mihi, non aedificabitis illud de sectis lapidibus.* Exodi etiam XXVII mandatur fieri altare de lignis settim, vestitis aere; vel etiam auro, ut habetur Exod. XXV. Ergo videtur inconvenienter observari in Ecclesia quod altare fiat solum de lapidibus.

PRAETEREA, calix cum patena repraesentat sepulcrum Christi. Quod fuit excisum in petra, ut in Evangeliis habetur. Ergo calix debet de petra fieri, et non solum de argento vel auro, vel etiam de stanno.

PRAETEREA, sicut aurum pretiosius est inter materias vasorum, ita panni serici pretiosiores sunt inter alios pannos. Ergo, sicut calix fit de auro, ita pallae altaris debent fieri de serico, et non solum de panno lineo.

PRAETEREA, dispensatio sacramentorum et ordinatio eorum ad ministros Ecclesiae pertinet, sicut dispensatio rerum temporalium subiacet ordinationi principum saecularium, unde apostolus dicit, I Cor. IV, *sic nos existimet homo ut ministros Christi et dispensatores mysteriorum Dei.* Sed si circa dispensationem rerum temporalium aliquid fieret contra statuta principum, habetur irritum. Ergo, si haec quae dicta sunt, convenienter sunt statuta per praelatos Ecclesiae, videtur quod sine his confici non possit. Et sic videtur sequi quod verba Christi non sint sufficientia ad hoc sacramentum conficiendum, quod est inconveniens. Non ergo videtur

apostles. But the house wherein Christ first wrought this sacrament was not consecrated, but merely an ordinary supper-room prepared by the master of the house, as related in Luke 22:11, 12. Moreover, we read (Acts 2:46) that *the apostles were continuing daily with one accord in the temple; and, breaking bread from house to house, they took it with gladness.* Consequently, there is no need for houses, in which this sacrament is celebrated, to be consecrated.

OBJ. 3: Further, nothing that is to no purpose ought to be done in the Church, which is governed by the Holy Spirit. But it seems useless to consecrate a church, or an altar, or such like inanimate things, since they are not capable of receiving grace or spiritual virtue. Therefore it is unbecoming for such consecrations to be performed in the Church.

OBJ. 4: Further, only Divine works ought to be recalled with solemnity, according to Ps. 91:5: *I shall rejoice in the works of Thy hands.* Now the consecration of a church or altar, is the work of a man; as is also the consecration of the chalice, and of the ministers, and of other such things. But these latter consecrations are not commemorated in the Church. Therefore neither ought the consecration of a church or of an altar to be commemorated with solemnity.

OBJ. 5: Further, the truth ought to correspond with the figure. But in the Old Testament, which bore a figure of the New, the altar was not made of hewn stones: for, it is written (Exod 20:24): *You shall make an altar of earth unto Me . . . and if thou make an altar of stone unto Me, thou shalt not build it of hewn stones.* Again, the altar is commanded to be made of *setim-wood*, covered *with brass* (Exod 27:1, 2), or *with gold* (Exod 25). Consequently, it seems unfitting for the Church to make exclusive use of altars made of stone.

OBJ. 6: Further, the chalice with the paten represents Christ's tomb, which was *hewn in a rock*, as is narrated in the Gospels. Consequently, the chalice ought to be of stone, and not of gold or of silver or tin.

OBJ. 7: Further, just as gold is the most precious among the materials of the altar vessels, so are cloths of silk the most precious among other cloths. Consequently, since the chalice is of gold, the altar cloths ought to be made of silk and not of linen.

OBJ. 8: Further, the dispensing and ordering of the sacraments belong to the Church's ministers, just as the ordering of temporal affairs is subject to the ruling of secular princes; hence the Apostle says (1 Cor 4:1): *Let a man so esteem us as the ministers of Christ and the dispensers of the mysteries of God.* But if anything be done against the ordinances of princes it is deemed void. Therefore, if the various items mentioned above are suitably commanded by the Church's prelates, it seems that the body of Christ could not be consecrated unless they be observed; and so it appears to follow that Christ's words are not sufficient of themselves for consecrating this sacrament: which is contrary to the fact. Consequently, it does not seem fitting for

conveniens fuisse quod haec circa celebrationem sacramenti statuerentur.

SED CONTRA est quod ea quae per Ecclesiam statuuntur, ab ipso Christo ordinantur, qui dicit, Matth. XVIII, *ubicumque fuerint duo vel tres congregati in nomine meo, ibi sum in medio eorum.*

RESPONDEO dicendum quod in his quae circumstant hoc sacramentum, duo considerantur, quorum unum pertinet ad repraesentationem eorum quae circa dominicam passionem sunt acta; aliud autem pertinet ad reverentiam huius sacramenti, in quo Christus secundum veritatem continetur, et non solum sicut in figura.

Unde et consecrationes adhibentur his rebus quae veniunt in usum huius sacramenti, tum propter reverentiam sacramenti; tum ad repraesentandum effectum sanctitatis qui ex passione Christi provenit, secundum illud Heb. ult., *Iesus, ut sanctificaret per suum sanguinem populum,* et cetera.

AD PRIMUM ergo dicendum quod regulariter hoc sacramentum celebrari debet in domo, per quam significatur Ecclesia, secundum illud I Tim. III, *scias quomodo oporteat te in domo Dei conversari, quae est Ecclesia Dei vivi.* Extra Ecclesiam enim locus non est veri sacrificii, ut Augustinus dicit. Et quia Ecclesia non erat concludenda sub finibus gentis Iudaicae, sed erat in universo mundo fundanda, ideo passio Christi non est celebrata infra civitatem Iudaeorum, sed sub divo, ut sic totus mundus haberet se ad passionem Christi ut domus. Et tamen, ut dicitur de Consecr., dist. I, cap. concedimus, *in itinere positis, si Ecclesia defuerit, sub divo vel sub tentorio, si tabula consecrata ceteraque sacra mysteria ad id officium pertinentia ibi affuerint, Missarum solennia celebrari concedimus.*

AD SECUNDUM dicendum quod, quia domus in qua hoc sacramentum celebratur, Ecclesiam significat, sicut et Ecclesia nominatur, convenienter consecratur, tum ad repraesentandum sanctificationem quam Ecclesia consecuta est per passionem Christi; tum etiam ad significandum sanctitatem quae requiritur in his qui hoc sacramentum suscipere debent. Per altare autem significatur ipse Christus, de quo dicit apostolus, Heb. ult., *per ipsum offeramus hostiam laudis Deo.* Unde et consecratio altaris significat sanctitatem Christi, de qua dicitur Luc. I, *quod ex te nascetur sanctum, vocabitur filius Dei.* Unde de Consecr., dist. I, dicitur, *altaria placuit non solum unctione chrismatis, sed etiam sacerdotali benedictione sacrari.*

Et ideo regulariter non licet celebrare hoc sacramentum nisi in domibus consecratis. Unde sic habetur de Consecr., dist. I, *nullus presbyter Missam celebrare praesumat nisi in sacratis ab episcopo locis.* Propter quod etiam, quia Pagani non sunt de Ecclesia nec alii infideles, ideo eadem distinctione legitur, *Ecclesiam in qua cadavera*

such ordinances to be made touching the celebration of this sacrament.

ON THE CONTRARY, The Church's ordinances are Christ's own ordinances; since He said (Matt 18:20): *Wherever two or three are gathered together in My name, there am I in the midst of them.*

I ANSWER THAT, There are two things to be considered regarding the equipment of this sacrament: one of these belongs to the representation of the events connected with our Lord's Passion; while the other is connected with the reverence due to the sacrament, in which Christ is contained verily, and not in figure only.

Hence we consecrate those things which we make use of in this sacrament; both that we may show our reverence for the sacrament, and in order to represent the holiness which is the effect of the Passion of Christ, according to Heb. 13:12: *Jesus, that He might sanctify the people by His own blood,* etc.

REPLY OBJ. 1: This sacrament ought as a rule to be celebrated in a house, whereby the Church is signified, according to 1 Tim. 3:15: *That thou mayest know how thou oughtest to behave thyself in the house of God, which is the Church of the living God.* Because *outside the Church there is no place for the true sacrifice,* as Augustine says (*Liber Sentent. Prosp.* xv). And because the Church was not to be confined within the territories of the Jewish people, but was to be established throughout the whole world, therefore Christ's Passion was not celebrated within the city of the Jews, but in the open country, that so the whole world might serve as a house for Christ's Passion. Nevertheless, as is said in *De Consecr.,* dist. 1, *if a church be not to hand, we permit travelers to celebrate mass in the open air, or in a tent, if there be a consecrated altar-table to hand, and the other requisites belonging to the sacred function.*

REPLY OBJ. 2: The house in which this sacrament is celebrated denotes the Church, and is termed a church; and so it is fittingly consecrated, both to represent the holiness which the Church acquired from the Passion, as well as to denote the holiness required of them who have to receive this sacrament. By the altar Christ Himself is signified, of Whom the Apostle says (Heb 13:15): *Through Him we offer a sacrifice of praise to God.* Hence the consecration of the altar signifies Christ's holiness, of which it was said (Luke 1:35): *The Holy one born of thee shall be called the Son of God.* Hence we read in *De Consecr.,* dist. 1: *It has seemed pleasing for the altars to be consecrated not merely with the anointing of chrism, but likewise with the priestly blessing.*

And therefore, as a rule, it is not lawful to celebrate this sacrament except in a consecrated house. Hence it is enacted (*De Consecr.,* dist. 1): *Let no priest presume to say mass except in places consecrated by the bishop.* And furthermore because pagans and other unbelievers are not members of the Church, therefore we read (*De Consecr.,* dist. 1): *It is*

mortuorum infidelium sepeliuntur, sanctificare non licet, sed, si apta videtur ad consecrandum, inde evulsis corporibus, et rasis parietibus vel tignis eius loci, reaedificetur. Sed si haec consecrata prius fuerit, Missas in ea celebrare licet, tamen si fideles fuerunt qui in ea sepulti sunt. Propter necessitatem tamen potest hoc sacramentum peragi in domibus non consecratis, vel violatis, sed tamen de consensu episcopi. Unde in eadem distinctione legitur, *Missarum solennia non ubicumque, sed in locis ab episcopo consecratis, vel ubi ipse permiserit, celebranda censemus.* Non tamen sine altari portatili consecrato, unde in eadem distinctione legitur, *concedimus, si Ecclesiae fuerint incensae vel combustae, in capellis, cum tabula consecrata, Missas celebrare.* Quia enim sanctitas Christi fons est totius sanctitatis ecclesiasticae, ideo in necessitate sufficit ad peragendum hoc sacramentum altare sanctificatum. Propter quod etiam Ecclesia nunquam sine altari consecratur, tamen sine Ecclesia quandoque consecratur altare, cum reliquiis sanctorum, quorum *vita abscondita est cum Christo in Deo.* Unde in eadem distinctione legitur, *placuit ut altaria in quibus nullum corpus aut reliquiae martyris conditae comprobantur, ab episcopis qui eisdem locis praesunt, si fieri potest, evertantur.*

Ad tertium dicendum quod Ecclesia et altare et alia huiusmodi inanimata consecrantur, non quia sint gratiae susceptiva, sed quia ex consecratione adipiscuntur quandam spiritualem virtutem per quam apta redduntur divino cultui, ut scilicet homines devotionem quandam exinde percipiant, ut sint paratiores ad divina, nisi hoc propter irreverentiam impediatur. Unde et in II Machab. III dicitur, *vere Dei virtus quaedam est in loco, nam ipse qui habet in caelis habitationem, visitator et adiutor est loci illius.*

Et inde est quod huiusmodi ante consecrationem emundantur et exorcizantur, ut exinde virtus inimici pellatur. Et eadem ratione Ecclesiae *quae sanguinis effusione aut cuiuscumque semine pollutae fuerint,* reconciliantur, quia per peccatum ibi commissum apparet ibi aliqua operatio inimici. Propter quod etiam in eadem distinctione legitur, *Ecclesias Arianorum ubicumque inveneritis, Catholicas Ecclesias divinis precibus et operibus absque ulla mora consecrate.* Unde et quidam probabiliter dicunt quod per ingressum Ecclesiae consecratae homo consequitur remissionem peccatorum venialium, sicut et per aspersionem aquae benedictae, inducentes quod in Psalmo dicitur, *benedixisti, domine, terram tuam, remisisti iniquitatem plebis tuae.* Et ideo, propter virtutem quam ex consecratione acquirit, consecratio Ecclesiae non iteratur. Unde in eadem distinctione, ex Concilio Nicaeno, legitur, *Ecclesiis semel Deo consecratis non debet iterum consecratio adhiberi, nisi aut ab igne exustae, aut sanguinis effusione, aut cuiusquam semine*

not lawful to bless a church in which the bodies of unbelievers are buried, but if it seem suitable for consecration, then, after removing the corpses and tearing down the walls or beams, let it be rebuilt. If, however, it has been already consecrated, and the faithful lie in it, it is lawful to celebrate mass therein. Nevertheless in a case of necessity this sacrament can be performed in houses which have not been consecrated, or which have been profaned; but with the bishop's consent. Hence we read in the same distinction: *We deem that masses are not to be celebrated everywhere, but in places consecrated by the bishop, or where he gives permission.* But not without a portable altar consecrated by the bishop: hence in the same distinction we read: *We permit that, if the churches be devastated or burned, masses may be celebrated in chapels, with a consecrated altar.* For because Christ's holiness is the fount of all the Church's holiness, therefore in necessity a consecrated altar suffices for performing this sacrament. And on this account a church is never consecrated without consecrating the altar. Yet sometimes an altar is consecrated apart from the church, with the relics of the saints, *whose lives are hidden with Christ in God* (Col 3:3). Accordingly under the same distinction we read: *It is our pleasure that altars, in which no relics of saints are found enclosed, be thrown down, if possible, by the bishops presiding over such places.*

Reply Obj. 3: The church, altar, and other like inanimate things are consecrated, not because they are capable of receiving grace, but because they acquire special spiritual virtue from the consecration, whereby they are rendered fit for the Divine worship, so that man derives devotion therefrom, making him more fitted for Divine functions, unless this be hindered by want of reverence. Hence it is written (2 Macc 3:38): *There is undoubtedly in that place a certain power of God; for He that hath His dwelling in the heavens is the visitor, and the protector of that place.*

Hence it is that such places are cleansed and exorcised before being consecrated, that the enemy's power may be driven forth. And for the same reason churches defiled by shedding of blood or seed are reconciled: because some machination of the enemy is apparent on account of the sin committed there. And for this reason we read in the same distinction: *Wherever you find churches of the Arians, consecrate them as Catholic churches without delay by means of devout prayers and rites.* Hence, too, it is that some say with probability, that by entering a consecrated church one obtains forgiveness of venial sins, just as one does by the sprinkling of holy water; alleging the words of Ps. 84:2, 3: *Lord, Thou hast blessed Thy land . . . Thou hast forgiven the iniquity of Thy people.* And therefore, in consequence of the virtue acquired by a church's consecration, the consecration is never repeated. Accordingly we find in the same distinction the following words quoted from the Council of Nicaea: *Churches which have once been consecrated, must not be consecrated again, except they be devastated by fire, or*

pollutae fuerint, quia, sicut infans a qualicumque sacerdote in nomine patris et filii et spiritus sancti semel baptizatus, non debet iterum baptizari, ita nec locus Deo dedicatus est iterum consecrandus, nisi propter causas quas superius nominavimus; si tamen fidem sanctae Trinitatis tenuerunt qui consecraverunt. Alioquin, qui sunt extra Ecclesiam, consecrare non possunt. Sed, sicut in eadem distinctione legitur, *Ecclesiae vel altaria quae ambigua sunt de consecratione, consecrentur.*

Propter hoc etiam quod aliquam spiritualem virtutem adipiscuntur per consecrationem, in eadem distinctione legitur statutum, *ligna Ecclesiae dedicatae non debent ad aliud opus iungi, nisi ad aliam Ecclesiam, vel igni comburenda, vel ad profectum in monasterio fratribus, in laicorum autem opera non debent admitti.* Et ibidem legitur, *altaris palla, cathedra, candelabrum et velum, si fuerint vetustate consumpta, incendio dentur, cineres quoque eorum in baptisterio inferantur, aut in pariete aut in fossis pavimentorum iactentur, ne introeuntium pedibus inquinentur.*

AD QUARTUM dicendum quod, quia consecratio altaris repraesentat sanctitatem Christi, consecratio vero domus sanctitatem totius Ecclesiae, ideo convenientius recolitur cum solemnitate consecratio Ecclesiae vel altaris. Propter quod etiam octo diebus solemnitas dedicationis agitur, ad significandam beatam resurrectionem Christi et membrorum Ecclesiae. Nec est opus solius hominis consecratio Ecclesiae et altaris, cum habeat spiritualem virtutem. Unde de Consecr., distinctione eadem, dicitur, *solemnitates Ecclesiarum dedicationum per singulos annos solemniter sunt celebrandae. Quod autem octo diebus encaenia sint celebranda, III libro regum, perlecta dedicatione templi, reperies,* scilicet VIII.

AD QUINTUM dicendum quod, sicut legitur de Consecr., dist. I, *altaria, si non sint lapidea, chrismatis unctione non consecrentur.* Quod quidem competit et significationi huius sacramenti, tum quia altare significat Christum, dicitur autem I Cor. X, *petra autem erat Christus;* tum etiam quia corpus Christi in sepulcro lapideo fuit reconditum. Competit etiam quoad usum sacramenti, lapis enim et solidus est, et de facili potest inveniri ubique. Quod non erat necessarium in veteri lege, ubi fiebat in uno loco altare. Quod autem mandatur altare fieri de terra vel de lapidibus insectis, fuit ad idololatriam removendam.

AD SEXTUM dicendum quod, sicut in distinctione eadem dicitur, cap. vasa, *quondam sacerdotes non aureis, sed ligneis calicibus utebantur; Zephyrinus autem Papa patenis vitreis Missas celebrari instituit; deinde Urbanus omnia fecit argentea.* Postmodum autem statutum est *ut calix domini, cum patena, sive ex auro sive ex argento fiat, vel saltem stanneus calix habeatur. De aere autem aut ex aurichalco non fiat, quia hoc vini virtute aeruginem, pariter et vomitum provocat. Nullus autem in ligneo seu vitreo*

defiled by shedding of blood or of anyone's seed; because, just as a child once baptized in the name of the Father, and of the Son, and of the Holy Spirit, ought not to be baptized again, so neither ought a place, once dedicated to God, to be consecrated again, except owing to the causes mentioned above; provided that the consecrators held faith in the Holy Trinity: in fact, those outside the Church cannot consecrate. But, as we read in the same distinction: *Churches or altars of doubtful consecration are to be consecrated anew.*

And since they acquire special spiritual virtue from their consecration, we find it laid down in the same distinction that *the beams of a dedicated church ought not to be used for any other purpose, except it be for some other church, or else they are to be burned, or put to the use of brethren in some monastery: but on no account are they to be discarded for works of the laity.* We read there, too, that *the altar covering, chair, candlesticks, and veil, are to be burned when worn out; and their ashes are to be placed in the baptistery, or in the walls, or else cast into the trenches beneath the flag-stones, so as not to be defiled by the feet of those that enter.*

REPLY OBJ. 4: Since the consecration of the altar signifies Christ's holiness, and the consecration of a house the holiness of the entire Church, therefore the consecration of a church or of an altar is more fittingly commemorated. And on this account the solemnity of a church dedication is observed for eight days, in order to signify the happy resurrection of Christ and of the Church's members. Nor is the consecration of a church or altar man's doing only, since it has a spiritual virtue. Hence in the same distinction (*De Consecr.*) it is said: *The solemnities of the dedication of churches are to be solemnly celebrated each year: and that dedications are to be kept up for eight days, you will find in the third book of Kings* (8:66).

REPLY OBJ. 5: As we read in *De Consecr.*, dist. 1, *altars, if not of stone, are not to be consecrated with the anointing of chrism.* And this is in keeping with the signification of this sacrament; both because the altar signifies Christ, for in 1 Cor. 10:3, it is written, *But the rock was Christ*: and because Christ's body was laid in a stone sepulchre. This is also in keeping with the use of the sacrament. Because stone is solid, and may be found everywhere, which was not necessary in the old Law, when the altar was made in one place. As to the commandment to make the altar of earth, or of unhewn stones, this was given in order to remove idolatry.

REPLY OBJ. 6: As is laid down in the same distinction, *formerly the priests did not use golden but wooden chalices; but Pope Zephyrinus ordered the mass to be said with glass patens; and subsequently Pope Urban had everything made of silver.* Afterwards it was decided that *the Lord's chalice with the paten should be made entirely of gold, or of silver or at least of tin. But it is not to be made of brass, or copper, because the action of the wine thereon produces verdigris, and provokes vomiting.* But no one is to presume to sing

calice cantare praesumat Missam, quia scilicet lignum porosum est, et sanguis consecratus in eo remaneret; vitrum autem fragile est, et posset fractionis periculum imminere. Et eadem ratio est de lapide. Et ideo, propter reverentiam sacramenti, statutum est ut ex praedictis materiis calix fiat.

AD SEPTIMUM dicendum quod, ubi potuit sine periculo fieri, Ecclesia statuit circa hoc sacramentum id quod expressius repraesentat passionem Christi. Non autem erat tantum periculum circa corpus, quod ponitur in corporali, sicut circa sanguinem, qui continetur in calice. Et ideo, licet calix non fiat de petra, corporale tamen fit de panno lineo, quo corpus Christi fuit involutum. Unde in epistola Silvestri Papae, in eadem distinctione, legitur, *consulto omnium constituimus ut sacrificium altaris non in serico panno, aut intincto quisquam celebrare praesumat Missam, sed in puro lineo ab episcopo consecrato, sicut corpus Christi in sindone linea munda sepultum fuit.* Competit etiam pannus lineus, propter sui munditiam, ad significandum conscientiae puritatem; et, propter multiplicem laborem quo talis pannus praeparatur, ad significandam passionem Christi.

AD OCTAVUM dicendum quod dispensatio sacramentorum pertinet ad ministros Ecclesiae, sed consecratio eorum est ab ipso Deo. Et ideo ministri Ecclesiae non habent aliquid statuere circa formam consecrationis, sed circa usum sacramenti et modum celebrandi. Et ideo, si sacerdos verba consecrationis proferat super materia debita cum intentione consecrandi, absque omnibus praedictis, scilicet domo et altari, calice et corporali consecratis, et ceteris huiusmodi per Ecclesiam institutis, consecrat quidem in rei veritate corpus Christi, peccat tamen graviter, ritum Ecclesiae non servans.

mass with a chalice of wood or of glass, because as the wood is porous, the consecrated blood would remain in it; while glass is brittle and there might arise danger of breakage; and the same applies to stone. Consequently, out of reverence for the sacrament, it was enacted that the chalice should be made of the aforesaid materials.

REPLY OBJ. 7: Where it could be done without danger, the Church gave order for that thing to be used which more expressively represents Christ's Passion. But there was not so much danger regarding the body which is placed on the corporal, as there is with the blood contained in the chalice. And consequently, although the chalice is not made of stone, yet the corporal is made of linen, since Christ's body was wrapped therein. Hence we read in an Epistle of Pope Silvester, quoted in the same distinction: *By a unanimous decree we command that no one shall presume to celebrate the sacrifice of the altar upon a cloth of silk, or dyed material, but upon linen consecrated by the bishop; as Christ's body was buried in a clean linen winding-sheet.* Moreover, linen material is becoming, owing to its cleanness, to denote purity of conscience, and, owing to the manifold labor with which it is prepared, to denote Christ's Passion.

REPLY OBJ. 8: The dispensing of the sacraments belongs to the Church's ministers; but their consecration is from God Himself. Consequently, the Church's ministers can make no ordinances regarding the form of the consecration, but only concerning the use of the sacrament and the manner of celebrating. And therefore, if the priest pronounces the words of consecration over the proper matter with the intention of consecrating, then, without every one of the things mentioned above—namely, without house, and altar, consecrated chalice and corporal, and the other things instituted by the Church—he consecrates Christ's body in very truth; yet he is guilty of grave sin, in not following the rite of the Church.

Article 4

Whether the Words Spoken in This Sacrament Are Properly Framed?

AD QUARTUM SIC PROCEDITUR. Videtur quod inconvenienter ordinentur ea quae circa hoc sacramentum dicuntur. Hoc enim sacramentum verbis Christi consecratur, ut Ambrosius dicit, in libro de sacramentis. Non ergo debent aliqua alia in hoc sacramento dici quam verba Christi.

PRAETEREA, verba et facta Christi nobis per Evangelium innotescunt. Sed quaedam dicuntur circa consecrationem huius sacramenti quae in Evangeliis non ponuntur. Non enim legitur in Evangelio quod Christus in institutione huius sacramenti oculos ad caelum levaverit; similiter etiam in Evangeliis dicitur, accipite et

OBJECTION 1: It seems that the words spoken in this sacrament are not properly framed. For, as Ambrose says (*De Sacram.* iv), this sacrament is consecrated with Christ's own words. Therefore no other words besides Christ's should be spoken in this sacrament.

OBJ. 2: Further, Christ's words and deeds are made known to us through the Gospel. But in consecrating this sacrament words are used which are not set down in the Gospels: for we do not read in the Gospel, of Christ lifting up His eyes to heaven while consecrating this sacrament: and similarly it is said in the Gospel: *Take ye and eat*

comedite, nec ponitur omnes, cum in celebratione huius sacramenti dicatur, elevatis oculis in caelum, et iterum, accipite et manducate ex hoc omnes. Inconvenienter ergo huiusmodi verba dicuntur in celebratione huius sacramenti.

Praeterea, omnia alia sacramenta ordinantur ad salutem omnium fidelium. Sed in celebratione aliorum sacramentorum non fit communis oratio pro salute omnium fidelium et defunctorum. Ergo inconvenienter fit in hoc sacramento.

Praeterea, Baptismus dicitur specialiter fidei sacramentum. Ea ergo quae pertinent ad instructionem fidei, magis debent circa Baptismum tradi quam circa hoc sacramentum, sicut doctrina apostolica et evangelica.

Praeterea, in omni sacramento exigitur devotio fidelium. Non ergo magis in hoc sacramento quam in aliis deberet devotio fidelium excitari per laudes divinas et per admonitiones, puta cum dicitur, sursum corda.

Praeterea, minister huius sacramenti est sacerdos, ut dictum est. Omnia ergo quae in hoc sacramento dicuntur, a sacerdote dici deberent, et non quaedam a ministris, quaedam a choro.

Praeterea, hoc sacramentum per certitudinem operatur virtus divina. Superflue igitur sacerdos petit huius sacramenti perfectionem, cum dicit, *quam oblationem tu, Deus, in omnibus*, et cetera.

Praeterea, sacrificium novae legis multo est excellentius quam sacrificium antiquorum patrum. Inconvenienter ergo sacerdos petit quod hoc sacrificium habeatur sicut sacrificium Abel, Abrahae et Melchisedech.

Praeterea, corpus Christi, sicut non incoepit esse in hoc sacramento per loci mutationem, ut supra dictum est, ita etiam nec esse desinit. Inconvenienter ergo sacerdos petit, *iube haec perferri per manus sancti Angeli tui in sublime altare tuum*.

Sed contra est quod dicitur de Consecr., dist. I, *Iacobus frater domini secundum carnem, et Basilius Caesariensis episcopus, ediderunt Missae celebrationem*. Ex quorum auctoritate patet convenienter singula circa hoc dici.

Respondeo dicendum quod, quia in hoc sacramento totum mysterium nostrae salutis comprehenditur, ideo prae ceteris sacramentis cum maiori solemnitate agitur. Et quia scriptum est Eccle. IV, *custodi pedem tuum ingrediens domum domini*, et Eccli. XVIII, *ante orationem praepara animam tuam*, ideo ante celebrationem huius mysterii, primo quidem praemittitur praeparatio

(*comedite*) without the addition of the word *all*, whereas in celebrating this sacrament we say: *Lifting up His eyes to heaven*, and again, *Take ye and eat* (*manducate*) *of this*. Therefore such words as these are out of place when spoken in the celebration of this sacrament.

Obj. 3: Further, all the other sacraments are ordained for the salvation of all the faithful. But in the celebration of the other sacraments there is no common prayer put up for the salvation of all the faithful and of the departed. Consequently it is unbecoming in this sacrament.

Obj. 4: Further, Baptism especially is called the sacrament of faith. Consequently, the truths which belong to instruction in the faith ought rather to be given regarding Baptism than regarding this sacrament, such as the doctrine of the apostles and of the Gospels.

Obj. 5: Further, devotion on the part of the faithful is required in every sacrament. Consequently, the devotion of the faithful ought not to be stirred up in this sacrament more than in the others by Divine praises and by admonitions, such as, *Lift up your hearts*.

Obj. 6: Further, the minister of this sacrament is the priest, as stated above (Q. 82, A. 1). Consequently, all the words spoken in this sacrament ought to be uttered by the priest, and not some by the ministers, and some by the choir.

Obj. 7: Further, the Divine power works this sacrament unfailingly. Therefore it is to no purpose that the priest asks for the perfecting of this sacrament, saying: *Which oblation do thou, O God, in all*, etc.

Obj. 8: Further, the sacrifice of the New Law is much more excellent than the sacrifice of the fathers of old. Therefore, it is unfitting for the priest to pray that this sacrifice may be as acceptable as the sacrifice of Abel, Abraham, and Melchisedech.

Obj. 9: Further, just as Christ's body does not begin to be in this sacrament by change of place, as stated above (Q. 75, A. 2), so likewise neither does it cease to be there. Consequently, it is improper for the priest to ask: *Bid these things be borne by the hands of thy holy angel unto Thine altar on high*.

On the contrary, We find it stated in *De Consecr.*, dist. 1, that *James, the brother of the Lord according to the flesh, and Basil, bishop of Caesarea, edited the rite of celebrating the mass*: and from their authority it is manifest that whatever words are employed in this matter, are chosen becomingly.

I answer that, Since the whole mystery of our salvation is comprised in this sacrament, therefore is it performed with greater solemnity than the other sacraments. And since it is written (Eccl 4:17): *Keep thy foot when thou goest into the house of God*; and (Sir 18:23): *Before prayer prepare thy soul*, therefore the celebration of this mystery is preceded by a certain preparation in order that we may

quaedam ad digne agenda ea quae sequuntur. Cuius praeparationis prima pars est laus divina, quae fit in introitu, secundum illud Psalmi, *sacrificium laudis honorificabit me, et illic iter quo ostendam illi salutare Dei*. Et sumitur hoc, ut pluries, de Psalmis, vel saltem cum Psalmo cantatur, quia, ut Dionysius dicit, in III cap. Eccles. Hier., Psalmi comprehendunt per modum laudis quidquid in sacra Scriptura continetur.

Secunda pars continet commemorationem praesentis miseriae, dum misericordia petitur, dicendo kyrie eleison ter pro persona patris; ter pro persona filii, cum dicitur Christe eleison; et ter pro persona spiritus sancti, cum subditur kyrie eleison; contra triplicem miseriam ignorantiae, culpae et poenae; vel ad significandum quod omnes personae sunt in se invicem.

Tertia autem pars commemorat caelestem gloriam, ad quam tendimus post praesentem miseriam, dicendo, gloria in excelsis Deo. Quae cantatur in festis, in quibus commemoratur caelestis gloria, intermittitur autem in officiis luctuosis, quae ad commemorationem miseriae pertinent.

Quarta autem pars continet orationem, quam sacerdos pro populo facit, ut digni habeantur tantis mysteriis.

Secundo autem praemittitur instructio fidelis populi, quia hoc sacramentum est mysterium fidei, ut supra habitum est. Quae quidem instructio dispositive quidem fit per doctrinam prophetarum et apostolorum, quae in Ecclesia legitur per lectores et subdiacones. Post quam lectionem, cantatur a choro graduale, quod significat profectum vitae; et alleluia, quod significat spiritualem exultationem; vel tractus, in officiis luctuosis, qui significat spiritualem gemitum. Haec enim consequi debent in populo ex praedicta doctrina. Perfecte autem populus instruitur per doctrinam Christi in Evangelio contentam, quae a summis ministris legitur, scilicet a diaconibus. Et quia Christo credimus tanquam divinae veritati, secundum illud Ioan. VIII, *si veritatem dico vobis, quare vos non creditis mihi?*, Lecto Evangelio, symbolum fidei cantatur, in quo populus ostendit se per fidem doctrinae Christi assentire. Cantatur autem hoc symbolum in festis de quibus fit aliqua mentio in hoc symbolo, sicut in festis Christi et beatae virginis, et apostolorum, qui hanc fidem fundaverunt, et in aliis huiusmodi.

Sic igitur populo praeparato et instructo, acceditur ad celebrationem mysterii. Quod quidem et offertur ut sacrificium, et consecratur et sumitur ut sacramentum, primo enim peragitur oblatio; secundo, consecratio materiae oblatae; tertio, perceptio eiusdem.

Circa oblationem vero duo aguntur, scilicet laus populi, in cantu offertorii, per quod significatur laetitia offerentium; et oratio sacerdotis, qui petit ut oblatio populi

perform worthily that which follows after. The first part of this preparation is Divine praise, and consists in the *Introit*: according to Ps. 49:23: *The sacrifice of praise shall glorify me; and there is the way by which I will show him the salvation of God*: and this is taken for the most part from the Psalms, or, at least, is sung with a Psalm, because, as Dionysius says (*Eccl. Hier.* iii): *The Psalms comprise by way of praise whatever is contained in Sacred Scripture.*

The second part contains a commemoration of present misery, by reason of which we pray for mercy, saying: *Lord, have mercy on us*, thrice for the Person of the Father, and *Christ, have mercy on us*, thrice for the Person of the Son, and *Lord, have mercy on us*, thrice for the Person of the Holy Spirit; against the threefold misery of ignorance, sin, and punishment; or else to express the *circuminsession* of all the Divine Persons.

The third part commemorates the heavenly glory, to the possession of which, after this life of misery, we are tending, in the words, *Glory be to God on high*, which are sung on festival days, on which the heavenly glory is commemorated, but are omitted in those sorrowful offices which commemorate our unhappy state.

The fourth part contains the prayer which the priest makes for the people, that they may be made worthy of such great mysteries.

There precedes, in the second place, the instruction of the faithful, because this sacrament is *a mystery of faith*, as stated above (Q. 78, A. 3, ad 5). Now this instruction is given dispositively through the teachings of the prophets and apostles, which are read in the church by Lectors and Sub-deacons. After this *lesson*, the choir sing the *Gradual*, which signifies progress in life; then the *Alleluia* is intoned, and this denotes spiritual joy; or in mournful offices the *Tract*, expressive of spiritual sighing; for all these things ought to result from the aforesaid teaching. But the people are instructed perfectly by Christ's teaching contained in the Gospel, which is read by the higher ministers, that is, by the Deacons. And because we believe Christ as the Divine truth, according to John 8:46, *If I tell you the truth, why do you not believe Me?* after the Gospel has been read, the *Creed* is sung in which the people show that they assent by faith to Christ's doctrine. And it is sung on those festivals of which mention is made therein, as on the festivals of Christ, of the Blessed Virgin, and of the apostles, who laid the foundations of this faith, and on other such days.

So then, after the people have been prepared and instructed, the next step is to proceed to the celebration of the mystery, which is both offered as a sacrifice, and consecrated and received as a sacrament: since first we have the oblation; then the consecration of the matter offered; and third, its reception.

In regard to the oblation, two things are done, namely, the people's praise in singing the *offertory*, expressing the joy of the offerers, and the priest's prayer asking for the

sit Deo accepta. Unde, I Paralip., dixit David, *ego in simplicitate cordis mei obtuli universa haec, et populum tuum qui hic repertus est, vidi cum ingenti gaudio tibi offerre donaria*, et postea orat, dicens, *domine Deus, custodi hanc voluntatem.*

Deinde, circa consecrationem, quae supernaturali virtute agitur, primo excitatur populus ad devotionem in praefatione, unde et monetur sursum corda habere ad dominum. Et ideo, finita praefatione, populus cum devotione laudat divinitatem Christi cum Angelis, dicens, sanctus, sanctus, sanctus; et humanitatem cum pueris, dicens, benedictus qui venit. Deinde sacerdos secreto commemorat, primo quidem, illos pro quibus hoc sacrificium offertur, scilicet pro universali Ecclesia, et pro his qui in sublimitate sunt constituti, I Tim. II; et specialiter quosdam qui offerunt vel pro quibus offertur. Secundo, commemorat sanctos, quorum patrocinia implorat pro praedictis, cum dicit, communicantes et memoriam venerantes, et cetera. Tertio, petitionem concludit, cum dicit, hanc igitur oblationem etc. ut fiat oblatio pro quibus offertur salutaris.

Deinde accedit ad ipsam consecrationem. In qua primo petit consecrationis effectum, cum dicit, quam oblationem tu Deus. Secundo, consecrationem peragit per verba salvatoris, cum dicit, qui pridie, et cetera. Tertio, excusat praesumptionem per obedientiam ad mandatum Christi, cum dicit, unde et memores. Quarto, petit hoc sacrificium peractum esse Deo acceptum, cum dicit, supra quae propitio, et cetera. Quinto, petit huius sacrificii et sacramenti effectum, primo quidem, quantum ad ipsos sumentes, cum dicit, supplices te rogamus; secundo, quantum ad mortuos, qui iam sumere non possunt, cum dicit, memento etiam, domine, etc.; tertio, specialiter quantum ad ipsos sacerdotes offerentes, cum dicit, nobis quoque peccatoribus et cetera.

Deinde agitur de perceptione sacramenti. Et primo quidem, praeparatur populus ad percipiendum. Primo quidem, per orationem communem totius populi, quae est oratio dominica, in qua petimus panem nostrum quotidianum nobis dari; et etiam privatam, quam specialiter sacerdos pro populo offert, cum dicit, libera nos, quaesumus, domine. Secundo, praeparatur populus per pacem, quae datur dicendo, agnus Dei, est enim hoc sacramentum unitatis et pacis, ut supra dictum est. In Missis autem defunctorum, in quibus hoc sacrificium offertur non pro pace praesenti, sed pro requie mortuorum, pax intermittitur.

Deinde sequitur perceptio sacramenti, primo percipiente sacerdote, et postmodum aliis dante; quia, ut dicit Dionysius, III cap. Eccles. Hier., qui aliis divina tradit, primo debet ipse particeps esse.

people's oblation to be made acceptable to God. Hence David said (1 Chr 29:17): *In the simplicity of my heart, I have . . . offered all these things: and I have seen with great joy Thy people which are here present, offer Thee their offerings*: and then he makes the following prayer: *O Lord God . . . keep . . . this will* (1 Chr 29:18).

Then, regarding the consecration, performed by supernatural power, the people are first of all excited to devotion in the *Preface*, hence they are admonished *to lift up their hearts to the Lord*, and therefore when the *Preface* is ended the people devoutly praise Christ's Godhead, saying with the angels: *Holy, Holy, Holy*; and His humanity, saying with the children: *Blessed is he that cometh*. In the next place the priest makes a *commemoration*, first of those for whom this sacrifice is offered, namely, for the whole Church, and *for those set in high places* (1 Tim 2:2), and, in a special manner, of them *who offer, or for whom the mass is offered*. Second, he commemorates the saints, invoking their patronage for those mentioned above, when he says: *Communicating with, and honoring the memory*, etc. Third, he concludes the petition when he says: *Wherefore that this oblation*, etc., in order that the oblation may be salutary to them for whom it is offered.

Then he comes to the consecration itself. Here he asks first of all for the effect of the consecration, when he says: *Which oblation do Thou, O God*, etc. Second, he performs the consecration using our Savior's words, when he says: *Who the day before*, etc. Third, he makes excuse for his presumption in obeying Christ's command, saying: *Wherefore, calling to mind*, etc. Fourth, he asks that the sacrifice accomplished may find favor with God, when he says: *Look down upon them with a propitious*, etc. Fifth, he begs for the effect of this sacrifice and sacrament, first for the partakers, saying: *We humbly beseech Thee*; then for the dead, who can no longer receive it, saying: *Be mindful also, O Lord*, etc.; third, for the priests themselves who offer, saying: *And to us sinners*, etc.

Then follows the act of receiving the sacrament. First of all, the people are prepared for Communion; first, by the common prayer of the congregation, which is the Lord's Prayer, in which we ask for our daily bread to be given us; and also by private prayer, which the priest puts up specially for the people, when he says: *Deliver us, we beseech Thee, O Lord*, etc. Second, the people are prepared by the *Pax* which is given with the words, *Lamb of God*, etc., because this is the sacrament of unity and peace, as stated above (Q. 73, A. 4; Q. 79, A. 1). But in masses for the dead, in which the sacrifice is offered not for present peace, but for the repose of the dead, the *Pax* is omitted.

Then follows the reception of the sacrament, the priest receiving first, and afterwards giving it to others, because, as Dionysius says (*Eccl. Hier.* iii), he who gives Divine things to others, ought first to partake thereof himself.

Ultimo autem tota Missae celebratio in gratiarum actione terminatur, populo exultante pro sumptione mysterii, quod significat cantus post communionem; et sacerdote per orationem gratias offerente, sicut et Christus, celebrata cena cum discipulis, hymnum dixit, ut dicitur Matth. XXVI.

AD PRIMUM ergo dicendum quod consecratio solis verbis Christi conficitur. Alia vero necesse fuit addere ad praeparationem populi sumentis, ut dictum est.

AD SECUNDUM dicendum quod, sicut dicitur Ioan. ult., multa sunt a domino facta vel dicta quae Evangelistae non scripserunt. Inter quae fuit hoc quod dominus oculos levavit in caelum in cena, quod tamen Ecclesia ex traditione apostolorum habuit. Rationabile enim videtur ut qui in suscitatione Lazari, ut habetur Ioan. XI, et in oratione quam pro discipulis fecit, Ioan. XVII, oculos levavit ad patrem, in huius sacramenti institutione multo magis hoc fecerit, tanquam in re potiori.

Quod autem dicitur manducate, et non comedite, non differt quantum ad sensum. Nec multum refert quid dicatur, praesertim cum verba illa non sint de forma, ut supra dictum est.

Quod autem additur omnes, intelligitur in verbis Evangelii, licet non exprimatur, quia ipse dixerat, Ioan. VI, *nisi manducaveritis carnem filii hominis, non habebitis vitam in vobis.*

AD TERTIUM dicendum quod Eucharistia est sacramentum totius ecclesiasticae unitatis. Et ideo specialiter in hoc sacramento, magis quam in aliis, debet fieri mentio de omnibus quae pertinent ad salutem totius Ecclesiae.

AD QUARTUM dicendum quod duplex est instructio. Una, quae fit noviter imbuendis, scilicet catechumenis. Et talis instructio fit circa Baptismum. Alia autem est instructio in qua instruitur fidelis populus, qui communicat huic mysterio. Et talis instructio fit in hoc sacramento. Et tamen ab hac instructione non repelluntur etiam catechumeni et infideles. Unde dicitur de Consecr., dist. I, *episcopus nullum prohibeat Ecclesiam ingredi et audire verbum Dei, sive gentilem sive haereticum sive Iudaeum, usque ad Missam catechumenorum,* in qua scilicet continetur instructio fidei.

AD QUINTUM dicendum quod in hoc sacramento maior devotio requiritur quam in aliis sacramentis, propter hoc quod in hoc sacramento totus Christus continetur. Et etiam communior, quia in hoc sacramento requiritur devotio totius populi, pro quo sacrificium offertur, et non solum percipientium sacramentum, sicut in aliis sacramentis. Et ideo, sicut Cyprianus dicit, *sacerdos, praefatione praemissa, parat fratrum mentes, dicendo, sursum corda, ut, dum respondet plebs, habemus*

Finally, the whole celebration of mass ends with the thanksgiving, the people rejoicing for having received the mystery (and this is the meaning of the singing after the Communion); and the priest returning thanks by prayer, as Christ, at the close of the supper with His disciples, *said a hymn* (Matt 26:30).

REPLY OBJ. 1: The consecration is accomplished by Christ's words only; but the other words must be added to dispose the people for receiving it, as stated above.

REPLY OBJ. 2: As is stated in the last chapter of John (verse 25), our Lord said and did many things which are not written down by the Evangelists; and among them is the uplifting of His eyes to heaven at the supper; nevertheless the Roman Church had it by tradition from the apostles. For it seems reasonable that He Who lifted up His eyes to the Father in raising Lazarus to life, as related in John 11:41, and in the prayer which He made for the disciples (John 17:1), had more reason to do so in instituting this sacrament, as being of greater import.

The use of the word manducate instead of comedite makes no difference in the meaning, nor does the expression signify, especially since those words are no part of the form, as stated above (Q. 78, A. 1, ad 2, 4).

The additional word *all* is understood in the Gospels, although not expressed, because He had said (John 6:54): *Except you eat the flesh of the Son of Man . . . you shall not have life in you.*

REPLY OBJ. 3: The Eucharist is the sacrament of the unity of the whole Church: and therefore in this sacrament, more than in the others, mention ought to be made of all that belongs to the salvation of the entire Church.

REPLY OBJ. 4: There is a twofold instruction in the Faith: the first is for those receiving it for the first time, that is to say, for catechumens, and such instruction is given in connection with Baptism. The other is the instruction of the faithful who take part in this sacrament; and such instruction is given in connection with this sacrament. Nevertheless catechumens and unbelievers are not excluded therefrom. Hence in *De Consecr.*, dist. 1, it is laid down: *Let the bishop hinder no one from entering the church, and hearing the word of God, be they Gentiles, heretics, or Jews, as far as the mass of the Catechumens,* in which the instruction regarding the Faith is contained.

REPLY OBJ. 5: Greater devotion is required in this sacrament than in the others, for the reason that the entire Christ is contained therein. Moreover, this sacrament requires a more general devotion, i.e., on the part of the whole people, since for them it is offered; and not merely on the part of the recipients, as in the other sacraments. Hence Cyprian observes (*De Orat. Domin.* 31), *The priest, in saying the Preface, disposes the souls of the brethren by saying, 'Lift up your hearts,' and when the people answer—'We have*

ad dominum, admoneatur nihil aliud se cogitare quam Deum.

AD SEXTUM dicendum quod in hoc sacramento, sicut dictum est, tanguntur ea quae pertinent ad totam Ecclesiam. Et ideo quaedam dicuntur a choro, quae pertinent ad populum. Quorum quaedam chorus totaliter prosequitur, quae scilicet toti populo inspirantur. Quaedam vero populus prosequitur, sacerdote inchoante, qui personam Dei gerit, in signum quod talia pervenerunt ad populum ex revelatione divina, sicut fides et gloria caelestis. Et ideo sacerdos inchoat symbolum fidei et gloria in excelsis Deo. Quaedam vero dicuntur per ministros, sicut doctrina novi et veteris testamenti, in signum quod per ministros a Deo missos est haec doctrina populis nuntiata. Quaedam vero sacerdos solus prosequitur, quae scilicet ad proprium officium sacerdotis pertinent, ut scilicet dona et preces offerat pro populo, sicut dicitur Heb. V. In his tamen quaedam dicit publice, quae scilicet pertinent et ad sacerdotem et ad populum, sicut sunt orationes communes. Quaedam vero pertinent ad solum sacerdotem, sicut oblatio et consecratio. Et ideo quae circa haec sunt dicenda occulte a sacerdote dicuntur. In utrisque tamen excitat attentionem populi, dicendo, dominus vobiscum; et expectat assensum dicentium, amen. Et ideo in his quae secreto dicuntur, publice praemittit, dominus vobiscum, et subiungit, per omnia saecula saeculorum. Vel secrete aliqua sacerdos dicit in signum quod, circa Christi passionem, discipuli non nisi occulte Christum confitebantur.

AD SEPTIMUM dicendum quod efficacia verborum sacramentalium impediri potest per intentionem sacerdotis. Nec tamen est inconveniens quod a Deo petamus id quod certissime scimus ipsum facturum, sicut Christus, Ioan. XVII, petiit suam clarificationem.

Non tamen ibi videtur sacerdos orare ut consecratio impleatur, sed ut nobis fiat fructuosa, unde signanter dicit, ut nobis corpus et sanguis fiat. Et hoc significant verba quae praemittit dicens, hanc oblationem facere digneris benedictam, secundum Augustinum, idest, per quam benedicimur, scilicet per gratiam; adscriptam, idest, per quam in caelo adscribimur; ratam, idest, per quam visceribus Christi censeamur; rationabilem, idest, per quam a bestiali sensu exuamur; acceptabilem, idest, ut, qui nobis ipsis displicemus, per hanc acceptabiles eius unico filio simus.

AD OCTAVUM dicendum quod, licet hoc sacrificium ex seipso praeferatur omnibus antiquis sacrificiis, tamen sacrificia antiquorum fuerunt Deo acceptissima ex eorum devotione. Petit ergo sacerdos ut hoc sacrificium

lifted them up to the Lord,' let them remember that they are to think of nothing else but God.

REPLY OBJ. 6: As was said above (ad 3), those things are mentioned in this sacrament which belong to the entire Church; and consequently some things which refer to the people are sung by the choir, and some of these words are all sung by the choir, as though inspiring the entire people with them; and there are other words which the priest begins and the people take up, the priest then acting as in the person of God; to show that the things they denote have come to the people through Divine revelation, such as faith and heavenly glory; and therefore the priest intones the *Creed* and the *Gloria in excelsis Deo*. Other words are uttered by the ministers, such as the doctrine of the Old and New Testament, as a sign that this doctrine was announced to the peoples through ministers sent by God. And there are other words which the priest alone recites, namely, such as belong to his personal office, *that he may offer up gifts and prayers for the people* (Heb 5:1). Some of these, however, he says aloud, namely, such as are common to priest and people alike, such as the *common prayers*; other words, however, belong to the priest alone, such as the oblation and the consecration; consequently, the prayers that are said in connection with these have to be said by the priest in secret. Nevertheless, in both he calls the people to attention by saying: *The Lord be with you*, and he waits for them to assent by saying *Amen*. And therefore before the secret prayers he says aloud, *The Lord be with you*, and he concludes, *For ever and ever*. Or the priest secretly pronounces some of the words as a token that regarding Christ's Passion the disciples acknowledged Him only in secret.

REPLY OBJ. 7: The efficacy of the sacramental words can be hindered by the priest's intention. Nor is there anything unbecoming in our asking of God for what we know He will do, just as Christ (John 17:1, 5) asked for His glorification.

But the priest does not seem to pray there for the consecration to be fulfilled, but that it may be fruitful in our regard, hence he says expressively: *That it may become to us the body and the blood*. Again, the words preceding these have that meaning, when he says: *Vouchsafe to make this oblation blessed*, i.e., according to Augustine (Paschasius, *De Corp. et Sang. Dom.* xii), *that we may receive a blessing*, namely, through grace; 'enrolled,' i.e., *that we may be enrolled in heaven*; 'ratified,' i.e., *that we may be incorporated in Christ*; 'reasonable,' i.e., *that we may be stripped of our animal sense*; 'acceptable,' i.e., *that we who in ourselves are displeasing, may, by its means, be made acceptable to His only Son*.

REPLY OBJ. 8: Although this sacrament is of itself preferable to all ancient sacrifices, yet the sacrifices of the men of old were most acceptable to God on account of their devotion. Consequently the priest asks that this sacrifice may

accepetur Deo ex devotione offerentium, sicut illa accepta fuerunt Deo.

AD NONUM dicendum quod sacerdos non petit quod species sacramentales deferantur in caelum; neque corpus Christi verum, quod ibi esse non desinit. Sed petit hoc pro corpore mystico, quod scilicet in hoc sacramento significatur, ut scilicet orationes et populi et sacerdotis Angelus assistens divinis mysteriis Deo repraesentet; secundum illud Apoc. VIII, *ascendit fumus incensorum de oblationibus sanctorum de manu Angeli*. Sublime autem altare Dei dicitur vel ipsa Ecclesia triumphans, in quam transferri petimus, vel ipse Deus, cuius participationem petimus; de hoc enim altari dicitur Exod. XX, *non ascendes ad altare meum per gradus, idest, in Trinitate gradus non facies*. Vel per Angelum intelligitur ipse Christus, qui est magni consilii Angelus, qui corpus suum mysticum Deo patri coniungit et Ecclesiae triumphanti.

Et propter hoc etiam Missa nominatur. Quia per Angelum sacerdos preces ad Deum mittit, sicut populus per sacerdotem. Vel quia Christus est hostia nobis missa. Unde et in fine Missae diaconus in festis diebus populum licentiat, dicens, *ite, Missa est*, scilicet hostia ad Deum per Angelum, ut scilicet sit Deo accepta.

be accepted by God through the devotion of the offerers, just as the former sacrifices were accepted by Him.

REPLY OBJ. 9: The priest does not pray that the sacramental species may be borne up to heaven; nor that Christ's true body may be borne thither, for it does not cease to be there; but he offers this prayer for Christ's mystical body, which is signified in this sacrament, that the angel standing by at the Divine mysteries may present to God the prayers of both priest and people, according to Apoc. 8:4: *And the smoke of the incense of the prayers of the saints ascended up before God, from the hand of the angel*. But God's *altar on high* means either the Church triumphant, unto which we pray to be translated, or else God Himself, in Whom we ask to share; because it is said of this altar (Exod 20:26): *Thou shalt not go up by steps unto My altar*, i.e., *thou shalt make no steps towards the Trinity*. Or else by the angel we are to understand Christ Himself, Who is the *Angel of great counsel* (Isa 9:6: Septuagint), Who unites His mystical body with God the Father and the Church triumphant.

And from this the mass derives its name (*missa*); because the priest sends (*mittit*) his prayers up to God through the angel, as the people do through the priest, or else because Christ is the victim sent (*missa*) to us: accordingly the deacon on festival days *dismisses* the people at the end of the mass, by saying: *Ite, missa est*, that is, the victim has been sent (*missa est*) to God through the angel, so that it may be accepted by God.

Article 5

Whether the Actions Performed in Celebrating This Sacrament Are Becoming?

AD QUINTUM SIC PROCEDITUR. Videtur quod ea quae in celebratione huius sacramenti aguntur, non sunt convenientia. Hoc enim sacramentum ad novum testamentum pertinet, ut ex forma ipsius apparet. In novo autem testamento non sunt observandae caeremoniae veteris testamenti. Ad quas pertinebat quod sacerdos et ministri aqua lavabantur quando accedebant ad offerendum, legitur enim Exod. XXX, *lavabunt Aaron et filii eius manus suas ac pedes quando ingressuri sunt ad altare*. Non est ergo conveniens quod sacerdos lavet manus suas inter Missarum solemnia.

PRAETEREA, ibidem dominus mandavit quod sacerdos adoleret incensum suave fragrans super altare quod erat ante propitiatorium. Quod etiam pertinebat ad caeremoniam veteris testamenti. Inconvenienter ergo sacerdos in Missa thurificatione utitur.

PRAETEREA, ea quae in sacramentis Ecclesiae aguntur, non sunt iteranda. Inconvenienter ergo sacerdos iterat crucesignationes super hoc sacramentum.

OBJECTION 1: It seems that the actions performed in celebrating this mystery are not becoming. For, as is evident from its form, this sacrament belongs to the New Testament. But under the New Testament the ceremonies of the old are not to be observed, such as that the priests and ministers were purified with water when they drew nigh to offer up the sacrifice: for we read (Exod 30:19, 20): *Aaron and his sons shall wash their hands and feet . . . when they are going into the tabernacle of the testimony . . . and when they are to come to the altar*. Therefore it is not fitting that the priest should wash his hands when celebrating mass.

OBJ. 2: Further, (Exod 30:7), the Lord commanded Aaron to *burn sweet-smelling incense* upon the altar which was *before the propitiatory*: and the same action was part of the ceremonies of the Old Law. Therefore it is not fitting for the priest to use incense during mass.

OBJ. 3: Further, the ceremonies performed in the sacraments of the Church ought not to be repeated. Consequently it is not proper for the priest to repeat the sign of the cross many times over this sacrament.

PRAETEREA, apostolus dicit, Heb. VII, *sine ulla contradictione, quod minus est a maiori benedicitur.* Sed Christus, qui est in hoc sacramento post consecrationem, est multo maior sacerdote. Inconvenienter igitur sacerdos post consecrationem benedicit hoc sacramentum cruce signando.

PRAETEREA, in sacramento Ecclesiae nihil debet fieri quod ridiculosum videatur. Videtur autem ridiculosum gesticulationes facere, ad quas pertinere videtur quod sacerdos quandoque brachia extendit, manus iungit, digitos complicat, et seipsum incurvat. Ergo hoc non debet fieri in hoc sacramento.

PRAETEREA, ridiculosum etiam videtur quod sacerdos multoties se ad populum vertit, multoties etiam populum salutat. Non ergo debent haec fieri in celebratione huius sacramenti.

PRAETEREA, apostolus, I Cor. I, pro inconvenienti habet quod Christus sit divisus. Sed post consecrationem Christus est in hoc sacramento. Inconvenienter igitur hostia frangitur a sacerdote.

PRAETEREA, ea quae in hoc sacramento aguntur, passionem Christi repraesentant. Sed in passione Christi corpus fuit divisum in locis quinque vulnerum. Ergo corpus Christi in quinque partes frangi debet, magis quam in tres.

PRAETEREA, totum corpus Christi in hoc sacramento seorsum consecratur a sanguine. Inconvenienter igitur una pars eius sanguini miscetur.

PRAETEREA, sicut corpus Christi proponitur in hoc sacramento ut cibus, ita et sanguis Christi ut potus. Sed sumptioni corporis Christi non adiungitur in celebratione Missae alius corporalis cibus. Inconvenienter igitur sacerdos, post sumptionem sanguinis Christi, vinum non consecratum sumit.

PRAETEREA, veritas debet respondere figurae. Sed de agno paschali, qui fuit figura huius sacramenti, mandatur quod *non remaneret ex eo quidquam usque mane.* Inconvenienter ergo hostiae consecratae reservantur, et non statim sumuntur.

PRAETEREA, sacerdos pluraliter loquitur audientibus, puta cum dicit, dominus vobiscum, et, gratias agamus. Sed inconveniens videtur pluraliter loqui uni soli, et maxime minori. Ergo inconveniens videtur quod sacerdos, uno tantum ministro praesente, celebret Missam. Sic igitur videtur quod inconvenienter aliqua agantur in celebratione huius sacramenti.

SED IN CONTRARIUM est Ecclesiae consuetudo, quae errare non potest, utpote spiritu sancto instructa.

RESPONDEO dicendum quod, sicut supra dictum est, in sacramentis aliquid dupliciter significatur, scilicet

OBJ. 4: Further, the Apostle says (Heb 7:7): *And without all contradiction, that which is less, is blessed by the better.* But Christ, Who is in this sacrament after the consecration, is much greater than the priest. Therefore quite unseemingly the priest, after the consecration, blesses this sacrament, by signing it with the cross.

OBJ. 5: Further, nothing which appears ridiculous ought to be done in one of the Church's sacraments. But it seems ridiculous to perform gestures, e.g., for the priest to stretch out his arms at times, to join his hands, to join together his fingers, and to bow down. Consequently, such things ought not to be done in this sacrament.

OBJ. 6: Further, it seems ridiculous for the priest to turn round frequently towards the people, and often to greet the people. Consequently, such things ought not to be done in the celebration of this sacrament.

OBJ. 7: Further, the Apostle (1 Cor 13) deems it improper for Christ to be divided. But Christ is in this sacrament after the consecration. Therefore it is not proper for the priest to divide the host.

OBJ. 8: Further, the ceremonies performed in this sacrament represent Christ's Passion. But during the Passion Christ's body was divided in the places of the five wounds. Therefore Christ's body ought to be broken into five parts rather than into three.

OBJ. 9: Further, Christ's entire body is consecrated in this sacrament apart from the blood. Consequently, it is not proper for a particle of the body to be mixed with the blood.

OBJ. 10: Further, just as, in this sacrament, Christ's body is set before us as food, so is His blood, as drink. But in receiving Christ's body no other bodily food is added in the celebration of the mass. Therefore, it is out of place for the priest, after taking Christ's blood, to receive other wine which is not consecrated.

OBJ. 11: Further, the truth ought to be conformable with the figure. But regarding the Paschal Lamb, which was a figure of this sacrament, it was commanded that nothing of it should *remain until the morning.* It is improper therefore for consecrated hosts to be reserved, and not consumed at once.

OBJ. 12: Further, the priest addresses in the plural number those who are hearing mass, when he says, *The Lord be with you*: and, *Let us return thanks.* But it is out of keeping to address one individual in the plural number, especially an inferior. Consequently it seems unfitting for a priest to say mass with only a single server present. Therefore in the celebration of this sacrament it seems that some of the things done are out of place.

ON THE CONTRARY, The custom of the Church stands for these things: and the Church cannot err, since she is taught by the Holy Spirit.

I ANSWER THAT, As was said above (Q. 60, A. 6), there is a twofold manner of signification in the sacraments, by

verbis et factis, ad hoc quod sit perfectior significatio. Significantur autem verbis in celebratione huius sacramenti quaedam pertinentia ad passionem Christi, quae repraesentatur in hoc sacramento; vel etiam ad corpus mysticum, quod significatur in hoc sacramento; et quaedam pertinentia ad usum sacramenti, qui debet esse cum devotione et reverentia. Et ideo in celebratione huius mysterii quaedam aguntur ad repraesentandum passionem Christi; vel etiam dispositionem corporis mystici; et quaedam aguntur pertinentia ad devotionem et reverentiam usus huius sacramenti.

Ad primum ergo dicendum quod ablutio manuum fit in celebratione Missae propter reverentiam huius sacramenti. Et hoc dupliciter. Primo quidem, quia aliqua pretiosa tractare non consuevimus nisi manibus ablutis. Unde indecens videtur quod ad tantum sacramentum aliquis accedat manibus, etiam corporaliter, inquinatis. Secundo, propter significationem. Quia, ut Dionysius dicit, III cap. Eccles. Hier., extremitatum ablutio significat emundationem etiam a minimis peccatis, secundum illud Ioan. XIII, *qui lotus est, non indiget nisi ut pedes lavet*. Et talis emundatio requiritur ab eo qui accedit ad hoc sacramentum. Quod etiam significatur per confessionem quae fit ante introitum Missae. Et hoc idem significabat ablutio sacerdotum in veteri lege, ut ibidem Dionysius dicit. Nec tamen Ecclesia hoc servat tanquam caeremoniale veteris legis praeceptum, sed quasi ab Ecclesia institutum, sicut quiddam secundum se conveniens. Et ideo non eodem modo observatur sicut tunc. Praetermittitur enim pedum ablutio, et servatur ablutio manuum, quae potest fieri magis in promptu, et quae sufficit ad significandam perfectam munditiam. Cum enim manus sit organum organorum, ut dicitur in III de anima, omnia opera attribuuntur manibus. Unde et in Psalmo dicitur, *lavabo inter innocentes manus meas*.

Ad secundum dicendum quod thurificatione non utimur quasi caeremoniali praecepto legis, sed sicut Ecclesiae statuto. Unde non eodem modo utimur sicut in veteri lege erat statutum. Pertinet autem ad duo. Primo quidem, ad reverentiam huius sacramenti, ut scilicet per bonum odorem depellatur si quid corporaliter pravi odoris in loco fuerit, quod posset provocare horrorem. Secundo, pertinet ad repraesentandum effectum gratiae, qua, sicut bono odore, Christus plenus fuit, secundum illud Gen. XXVII, *ecce, odor filii mei sicut odor agri pleni*; et a Christo derivatur ad fideles officio ministrorum, secundum illud II Cor. II, *odorem notitiae suae spargit per nos in omni loco*. Et ideo, undique thurificato altari, per quod Christus designatur, thurificantur omnes per ordinem.

Ad tertium dicendum quod sacerdos in celebratione Missae utitur crucesignatione ad exprimendam passionem Christi, quae ad crucem est terminata. Est autem

words, and by actions, in order that the signification may thus be more perfect. Now, in the celebration of this sacrament words are used to signify things pertaining to Christ's Passion, which is represented in this sacrament; or again, pertaining to Christ's mystical body, which is signified therein; and again, things pertaining to the use of this sacrament, which use ought to be devout and reverent. Consequently, in the celebration of this mystery some things are done in order to represent Christ's Passion, or the disposing of His mystical body, and some others are done which pertain to the devotion and reverence due to this sacrament.

Reply Obj. 1: The washing of the hands is done in the celebration of mass out of reverence for this sacrament; and this for two reasons: first, because we are not wont to handle precious objects except the hands be washed; hence it seems indecent for anyone to approach so great a sacrament with hands that are, even literally, unclean. Second, on account of its signification, because, as Dionysius says (*Eccl. Hier.* iii), the washing of the extremities of the limbs denotes cleansing from even the smallest sins, according to John 13:10: *He that is washed needeth not but to wash his feet*. And such cleansing is required of him who approaches this sacrament; and this is denoted by the confession which is made before the *Introit* of the mass. Moreover, this was signified by the washing of the priests under the Old Law, as Dionysius says (*Eccl. Hier.* iii). However, the Church observes this ceremony, not because it was prescribed under the Old Law, but because it is becoming in itself, and therefore instituted by the Church. Hence it is not observed in the same way as it was then: because the washing of the feet is omitted, and the washing of the hands is observed; for this can be done more readily, and suffices for denoting perfect cleansing. For, since the hand is the *organ of organs* (*De Anima* iii), all works are attributed to the hands: hence it is said in Ps. 25:6: *I will wash my hands among the innocent*.

Reply Obj. 2: We use incense, not as commanded by a ceremonial precept of the Law, but as prescribed by the Church; accordingly we do not use it in the same fashion as it was ordered under the Old Law. It has reference to two things: first, to the reverence due to this sacrament, i.e., in order by its good odor, to remove any disagreeable smell that may be about the place; second, it serves to show the effect of grace, wherewith Christ was filled as with a good odor, according to Gen. 27:27: *Behold, the odor of my son is like the odor of a ripe field*; and from Christ it spreads to the faithful by the work of His ministers, according to 2 Cor. 2:14: *He manifesteth the odor of his knowledge by us in every place*; and therefore when the altar which represents Christ, has been incensed on every side, then all are incensed in their proper order.

Reply Obj. 3: The priest, in celebrating the mass, makes use of the sign of the cross to signify Christ's Passion which was ended upon the cross. Now, Christ's Passion was

passio Christi quibusdam quasi gradibus peracta. Nam primo fuit Christi traditio, quae facta est a Deo, a Iuda, et a Iudaeis. Quod significat trina crucesignatio super illa verba, *haec dona, haec munera, haec sancta sacrificia illibata.*

Secundo fuit Christi venditio. Est autem venditus sacerdotibus, Scribis et Pharisaeis. Ad quod significandum fit iterum trina crucesignatio super illa verba, *benedictam, adscriptam, ratam.* Vel ad ostendendum pretium venditionis, scilicet triginta denarios. Additur autem et duplex super illa verba, *ut nobis corpus et sanguis,* etc., ad designandam personam Iudae venditoris et Christi venditi.

Tertio autem fuit praesignatio passionis Christi facta in cena. Ad quod designandum, fiunt tertio duae cruces, una in consecratione corporis, alia in consecratione sanguinis, ubi utrobique dicitur benedixit.

Quarto autem fuit ipsa passio Christi. Unde, ad repraesentandum quinque plagas, fit quarto quintuplex crucesignatio super illa verba, *hostiam puram, hostiam sanctam, hostiam immaculatam, panem sanctum vitae aeternae, et calicem salutis perpetuae.*

Quinto, repraesentatur extensio corporis, et effusio sanguinis, et fructus passionis, per trinam crucesignationem quae fit super illis verbis, *corpus et sanguinem sumpserimus, omni benedictione* et cetera.

Sexto, repraesentatur triplex oratio quam fecit in cruce, unam pro persecutoribus, cum dixit, *pater, ignosce illis*; secundam pro liberatione a morte, cum dixit, *Deus, Deus meus, ut quid dereliquisti me?* Tertia pertinet ad adeptionem gloriae, cum dixit, *pater, in manus tuas commendo spiritum meum.* Et ad hoc significandum, fit trina crucesignatio super illa verba, *sanctificas, vivificas, benedicis,* et cetera.

Septimo, repraesentantur tres horae quibus pependit in cruce, scilicet a sexta hora usque ad nonam. Et ad hoc significandum, fit iterum trina crucesignatio ad illa verba, *per ipsum, et cum ipso, et in ipso.*

Octavo autem, repraesentatur separatio animae a corpore, per duas cruces subsequentes extra calicem factas.

Nono autem, repraesentatur resurrectio tertia die facta, per tres cruces quae fiunt ad illa verba, *pax domini sit semper vobiscum.*

Potest autem brevius dici quod consecratio huius sacramenti, et acceptio sacrificii, et fructus eius, procedit ex virtute crucis Christi. Et ideo, ubicumque fit mentio de aliquo horum, sacerdos crucesignatione utitur.

AD QUARTUM dicendum quod sacerdos post consecrationem non utitur crucesignatione ad benedicendum

accomplished in certain stages. First of all there was Christ's betrayal, which was the work of God, of Judas, and of the Jews; and this is signified by the triple sign of the cross at the words, *These gifts, these presents, these holy unspotted sacrifices.*

Second, there was the selling of Christ. Now he was sold to the Priests, to the Scribes, and to the Pharisees: and to signify this the threefold sign of the cross is repeated, at the words, *blessed, enrolled, ratified.* Or again, to signify the price for which He was sold, viz. thirty pence. And a double cross is added at the words—*that it may become to us the Body and the Blood,* etc., to signify the person of Judas the seller, and of Christ Who was sold.

Third, there was the foreshadowing of the Passion at the last supper. To denote this, in the third place, two crosses are made, one in consecrating the body, the other in consecrating the blood; each time while saying, *He blessed.*

Fourth, there was Christ's Passion itself. And so in order to represent His five wounds, in the fourth place, there is a fivefold signing of the cross at the words, *a pure Victim, a holy Victim, a spotless Victim, the holy bread of eternal life, and the cup of everlasting salvation.*

Fifth, the outstretching of Christ's body, and the shedding of the blood, and the fruits of the Passion, are signified by the triple signing of the cross at the words, *as many as shall receive the body and blood, may be filled with every blessing,* etc.

Sixth, Christ's threefold prayer upon the cross is represented; one for His persecutors when He said, *Father, forgive them*; the second for deliverance from death, when He cried, *My God, My God, why hast Thou forsaken Me?* the third referring to His entrance into glory, when He said, *Father, into Thy hands I commend My spirit*; and in order to denote these there is a triple signing with the cross made at the words, *Thou dost sanctify, quicken, bless.*

Seventh, the three hours during which He hung upon the cross, that is, from the sixth to the ninth hour, are represented; in signification of which we make once more a triple sign of the cross at the words, *Through Him, and with Him, and in Him.*

Eighth, the separation of His soul from the body is signified by the two subsequent crosses made over the chalice.

Ninth, the resurrection on the third day is represented by the three crosses made at the words—*May the peace of the Lord be ever with you.*

In short, we may say that the consecration of this sacrament, and the acceptance of this sacrifice, and its fruits, proceed from the virtue of the cross of Christ, and therefore wherever mention is made of these, the priest makes use of the sign of the cross.

REPLY OBJ. 4: After the consecration, the priest makes the sign of the cross, not for the purpose of blessing and

et consecrandum, sed solum ad commemorandum virtutem crucis et modum passionis Christi, ut ex dictis patet.

Ad quintum dicendum quod ea quae sacerdos in Missa facit, non sunt ridiculosae gesticulationes, fiunt enim ad aliquid repraesentandum. Quod enim sacerdos brachia extendit post consecrationem, significat extensionem brachiorum Christi in cruce. Levat etiam manus orando, ad designandum quod oratio eius pro populo dirigitur ad Deum, secundum illud Thren. III, *levemus corda nostra cum manibus ad Deum in caelum.* Et Exod. XVII dicitur quod, *cum levaret Moyses manus, vincebat Israel.* Quod autem manus interdum iungit, et inclinat se, suppliciter et humiliter orans, designat humilitatem et obedientiam Christi, ex qua passus est. Digitos autem iungit post consecrationem, scilicet pollicem cum indice, quibus corpus Christi consecratum tetigerat, ut, si qua particula digitis adhaeserat, non dispergatur. Quod pertinet ad reverentiam sacramenti.

Ad sextum dicendum quod quinquies se sacerdos vertit ad populum, ad designandum quod dominus die resurrectionis quinquies se manifestavit, ut supra dictum est in tractatu de resurrectione Christi. Salutat autem septies populum, scilicet quinque vicibus quando se convertit ad populum, et bis quando se non convertit, scilicet ante praefationem cum dicit, *dominus vobiscum,* et cum dicit, *pax domini sit semper vobiscum,* ad designandum septiformem gratiam spiritus sancti. Episcopus autem celebrans in festis in prima salutatione dicit, *pax vobis,* quod post resurrectionem dixit dominus, cuius personam repraesentat episcopus praecipue.

Ad septimum dicendum quod fractio hostiae tria significat, primo quidem, ipsam divisionem corporis Christi, quae facta est in passione; secundo, distinctionem corporis mystici secundum diversos status; tertio, distributionem gratiarum procedentium ex passione Christi, ut Dionysius dicit, III cap. Eccles. Hier. Unde talis fractio non inducit divisionem Christi.

Ad octavum dicendum quod, sicut Sergius Papa dicit, et habetur in decretis, de Consecr., dist. II, *triforme est corpus domini. Pars oblata in calicem Missa corpus Christi quod iam resurrexit, demonstrat,* scilicet ipsum Christum, et beatam virginem, vel si qui alii sancti cum corporibus sunt in gloria. *Pars comesta ambulans adhuc super terram,* quia scilicet viventes in terra sacramento uniuntur; et passionibus conteruntur, sicut panis comestus atteritur dentibus. *Pars in altari usque ad finem Missae remanens est corpus Christi in sepulcro remanens, quia usque in finem saeculi corpora sanctorum in sepulcris erunt,* quorum tamen animae sunt vel in Purgatorio vel in caelo. Hic tamen ritus non servatur modo, ut scilicet una pars servetur usque in finem Missae. Manet tamen eadem significatio partium. Quam quidam metrice

consecrating, but only for calling to mind the virtue of the cross, and the manner of Christ's suffering, as is evident from what has been said (ad 3).

Reply Obj. 5: The actions performed by the priest in mass are not ridiculous gestures, since they are done so as to represent something else. The priest in extending his arms signifies the outstretching of Christ's arms upon the cross. He also lifts up his hands as he prays, to point out that his prayer is directed to God for the people, according to Lam. 3:41: *Let us lift up our hearts with our hands to the Lord in the heavens*: and Ex. 17:11: *And when Moses lifted up his hands Israel overcame.* That at times he joins his hands, and bows down, praying earnestly and humbly, denotes the humility and obedience of Christ, out of which He suffered. He closes his fingers, i.e., the thumb and first finger, after the consecration, because, with them, he had touched the consecrated body of Christ; so that if any particle cling to the fingers, it may not be scattered: and this belongs to the reverence for this sacrament.

Reply Obj. 6: Five times does the priest turn round towards the people, to denote that our Lord manifested Himself five times on the day of His Resurrection, as stated above in the treatise on Christ's Resurrection (Q. 55, A. 3, Obj. 3). But the priest greets the people seven times, namely, five times, by turning round to the people, and twice without turning round, namely, when he says, *The Lord be with you* before the *Preface,* and again when he says, *May the peace of the Lord be ever with you*: and this is to denote the sevenfold grace of the Holy Spirit. But a bishop, when he celebrates on festival days, in his first greeting says, *Peace be to you,* which was our Lord's greeting after Resurrection, Whose person the bishop chiefly represents.

Reply Obj. 7: The breaking of the host denotes three things: first, the rending of Christ's body, which took place in the Passion; second, the distinction of His mystical body according to its various states; and third, the distribution of the graces which flow from Christ's Passion, as Dionysius observes (*Eccl. Hier.* iii). Hence this breaking does not imply severance in Christ.

Reply Obj. 8: As Pope Sergius says, and it is to be found in the *Decretals* (*De Consecr.,* dist. ii), *the Lord's body is threefold; the part offered and put into the chalice signifies Christ's risen body,* namely, Christ Himself, and the Blessed Virgin, and the other saints, if there be any, who are already in glory with their bodies. *The part consumed denotes those still walking upon earth,* because while living upon earth they are united together by this sacrament; and are bruised by the passions, just as the bread eaten is bruised by the teeth. *The part reserved on the altar till the close of the mass, is His body hidden in the sepulchre, because the bodies of the saints will be in their graves until the end of the world*: though their souls are either in purgatory, or in heaven. However, this rite of reserving one part on the altar till the close of the mass is no longer observed, on account of the

expresserunt, dicentes, *hostia dividitur in partes, tincta beatos plene, sicca notat vivos, servata sepultos.*

Quidam tamen dicunt quod pars in calicem Missa significat eos qui vivunt in hoc mundo; pars autem extra calicem servata significat plene beatos quantum ad animam et corpus; pars autem comesta significat ceteros.

AD NONUM dicendum quod per calicem duo possunt significari. Uno modo, ipsa passio, quae repraesentatur in hoc sacramento. Et secundum hoc, per partem in calicem missam significantur illi qui adhuc sunt participes passionum Christi. Alio modo, potest significari fruitio beata, quae etiam in hoc sacramento praefiguratur. Et ideo illi quorum corpora iam sunt in plena beatitudine, significantur per partem in calicem missam. Et est notandum quod pars in calicem missa non debet populo dari in supplementum communionis, quia panem intinctum non porrexit Christus nisi Iudae proditori.

AD DECIMUM dicendum quod vinum, ratione suae humiditatis, est ablutivum. Et ideo sumitur post perceptionem huius sacramenti, ad abluendum os, ne aliquae reliquiae remaneant, quod pertinet ad reverentiam sacramenti. Unde extra, de Celebrat. Miss., cap. ex parte, *sacerdos vino os perfundere debet postquam totum percepit sacramentum, nisi cum eodem die Missam aliam debuerit celebrare, ne, si forte vinum perfusionis acciperet, celebrationem aliam impediret.* Et eadem ratione perfundit vino digitos quibus corpus Christi tetigerat.

AD UNDECIMUM dicendum quod veritas quantum ad aliquid debet respondere figurae, quia scilicet non debet pars hostiae consecratae de qua sacerdos et ministri, vel etiam populus communicat, in crastinum reservari. Unde, ut habetur de Consecr., dist. II, Clemens Papa statuit, *tanta holocausta in altario offerantur, quanta populo sufficere debeant. Quod si remanserint, in crastinum non reserventur, sed cum timore et tremore clericorum diligentia consumantur.* Quia tamen hoc sacramentum quotidie sumendum est, non autem agnus paschalis quotidie sumebatur; ideo oportet alias hostias consecratas pro infirmis conservare. Unde in eadem distinctione legitur, *presbyter Eucharistiam semper habeat paratam, ut, quando quis infirmatus fuerit, statim eum communicet, ne sine communione moriatur.*

AD DUODECIMUM dicendum quod in solemni celebratione Missae plures debent adesse. Unde Soter Papa dicit, ut habetur de Consecr., dist. I, *hoc quoque statutum est, ut nullus presbyterorum Missarum solemnia celebrare praesumat, nisi, duobus praesentibus sibique respondentibus, ipse tertius habeatur, quia, cum pluraliter ab eo dicitur, dominus vobiscum, et illud in secretis, orate pro me, apertissime convenit ut ipsi respondeatur salutationi.*

danger; nevertheless, the same meaning of the parts continues, which some persons have expressed in verse, thus: *The host being rent— What is dipped, means the blest; What is dry, means the living; What is kept, those at rest.*

Others, however, say that the part put into the chalice denotes those still living in this world, while the part kept outside the chalice denotes those fully blessed both in soul and body; while the part consumed means the others.

REPLY OBJ. 9: Two things can be signified by the chalice: first, the Passion itself, which is represented in this sacrament, and according to this, by the part put into the chalice are denoted those who are still sharers of Christ's sufferings; second, the enjoyment of the Blessed can be signified, which is likewise foreshadowed in this sacrament; and therefore those whose bodies are already in full beatitude, are denoted by the part put into the chalice. And it is to be observed that the part put into the chalice ought not to be given to the people to supplement the communion, because Christ gave dipped bread only to Judas the betrayer.

REPLY OBJ. 10: Wine, by reason of its humidity, is capable of washing, consequently it is received in order to rinse the mouth after receiving this sacrament, lest any particles remain: and this belongs to reverence for the sacrament. Hence (*Extra, De Celebratione missae,* chap. *Ex parte*), it is said: *The priest should always cleanse his mouth with wine after receiving the entire sacrament of Eucharist: except when he has to celebrate another mass on the same day, lest from taking the ablution-wine he be prevented from celebrating again*; and it is for the same reason that wine is poured over the fingers with which he had touched the body of Christ.

REPLY OBJ. 11: The truth ought to be conformable with the figure, in some respect: namely, because a part of the host consecrated, of which the priest and ministers or even the people communicate, ought not to be reserved until the day following. Hence, as is laid down (*De Consecr.,* dist. ii), Pope Clement I ordered that *as many hosts are to be offered on the altar as shall suffice for the people; should any be left over, they are not to be reserved until the morrow, but let the clergy carefully consume them with fear and trembling.* Nevertheless, since this sacrament is to be received daily, whereas the Paschal Lamb was not, it is therefore necessary for other hosts to be reserved for the sick. Hence we read in the same distinction: *Let the priest always have the Eucharist ready, so that, when anyone fall sick, he may take Communion to him at once, lest he die without it.*

REPLY OBJ. 12: Several persons ought to be present at the solemn celebration of the mass. Hence Pope Soter says (*De Consecr.,* dist. 1): *It has also been ordained, that no priest is to presume to celebrate solemn mass, unless two others be present answering him, while he himself makes the third; because when he says in the plural, 'The Lord be with you,' and again in the Secrets, 'Pray ye for me,' it is most becoming that they should answer his greeting.* Hence it is for

Unde et, ad maiorem solemnitatem, ibidem statutum legitur quod episcopus cum pluribus Missarum solemnia peragat. In Missis tamen privatis sufficit unum habere ministrum, qui gerit personam totius populi Catholici, ex cuius persona sacerdoti pluraliter respondet.

the sake of greater solemnity that we find it decreed (*De Consecr.* dist. 1) that a bishop is to solemnize mass with several assistants. Nevertheless, in private masses it suffices to have one server, who takes the place of the whole Catholic people, on whose behalf he makes answer in the plural to the priest.

Article 6

Whether the Defects Occurring During the Celebration of This Sacrament
Can Be Sufficiently Met by Observing the Church's Statutes?

AD SEXTUM SIC PROCEDITUR. Videtur quod non possit sufficienter occurri defectibus qui circa celebrationem huius sacramenti occurrunt, statuta Ecclesiae observando. Contingit enim quandoque quod sacerdos, ante consecrationem vel post, moritur vel alienatur, vel aliqua alia infirmitate praepeditur ne sacramentum sumere possit et Missam perficere. Ergo videtur quod non possit impleri statutum Ecclesiae quo praecipitur quod sacerdos consecrans suo sacrificio communicet.

PRAETEREA, contingit quandoque quod sacerdos, ante consecrationem vel post, recolit se aliquid comedisse vel bibisse, vel alicui mortali peccato subiacere, vel etiam excommunicationi, cuius prius memoriam non habebat. Necesse est ergo quod ille qui est in tali articulo constitutus, peccet mortaliter contra statutum Ecclesiae faciens, sive sumat sive non sumat.

PRAETEREA, contingit quandoque quod in calicem musca aut aranea vel aliquod animal venenosum cadit post consecrationem; vel etiam cognoscit sacerdos calici venenum esse immissum ab aliquo malevolo causa occidendi ipsum. In quo casu, si sumat, videtur peccare mortaliter, se occidendo vel Deum tentando. Similiter, si non sumat, peccat, contra statutum Ecclesiae faciens. Ergo videtur esse perplexus et subiectus necessitati peccandi. Quod est inconveniens.

PRAETEREA, contingit quod per negligentiam ministri aut aqua non ponitur in calice, aut etiam nec vinum, et hoc sacerdos advertit. Ergo in hoc etiam casu videtur esse perplexus, sive sumat corpus sine sanguine, quasi imperfectum faciens sacrificium; sive non sumens nec corpus nec sanguinem.

PRAETEREA, contingit quod sacerdos non recolit se dixisse verba consecrationis, vel etiam alia quae in consecratione huius sacramenti dicuntur. Videtur ergo peccare in hoc casu, sive reiteret verba super eandem materiam, quae forte iam dixerat; sive utatur pane et vino non consecratis quasi consecratis.

OBJECTION 1: It seems that the defects occurring during the celebration of this sacrament cannot be sufficiently met by observing the statutes of the Church. For it sometimes happens that before or after the consecration the priest dies or goes mad, or is hindered by some other infirmity from receiving the sacrament and completing the mass. Consequently it seems impossible to observe the Church's statute, whereby the priest consecrating must communicate of his own sacrifice.

OBJ. 2: Further, it sometimes happens that, before the consecration, the priest remembers that he has eaten or drunk something, or that he is in mortal sin, or under excommunication, which he did not remember previously. Therefore, in such a dilemma a man must necessarily commit mortal sin by acting against the Church's statute, whether he receives or not.

OBJ. 3: Further, it sometimes happens that a fly or a spider, or some other poisonous creature falls into the chalice after the consecration. Or even that the priest comes to know that poison has been put in by some evilly disposed person in order to kill him. Now in this instance, if he takes it, he appears to sin by killing himself, or by tempting God: also in like manner if he does not take it, he sins by acting against the Church's statute. Consequently, he seems to be perplexed, and under necessity of sinning, which is not becoming.

OBJ. 4: Further, it sometimes happens from the server's want of heed that water is not added to the chalice, or even the wine overlooked, and that the priest discovers this. Therefore he seems to be perplexed likewise in this case, whether he receives the body without the blood, thus making the sacrifice to be incomplete, or whether he receives neither the body nor the blood.

OBJ. 5: Further, it sometimes happens that the priest cannot remember having said the words of consecration, or other words which are uttered in the celebration of this sacrament. In this case he seems to sin, whether he repeats the words over the same matter, which words possibly he has said before, or whether he uses bread and wine which are not consecrated, as if they were consecrated.

PRAETEREA, contingit quandoque, propter frigus, quod sacerdoti dilabitur hostia in calicem, sive ante fractionem sive post. In hoc ergo casu non poterit sacerdos implere ritum Ecclesiae vel de ipsa fractione, vel etiam de hoc quod sola tertia pars mittatur in calicem.

PRAETEREA, contingit quandoque quod per negligentiam sacerdotis sanguis Christi effunditur; vel etiam quod sacerdos sacramentum sumptum vomit; aut quod etiam hostiae consecratae tandiu conserventur quod putrefiant; vel etiam quod a muribus corrodantur; vel etiam qualitercumque perdantur. In quibus casibus non videtur posse huic sacramento debita reverentia exhiberi secundum Ecclesiae statuta. Non videtur ergo quod his defectibus seu periculis occurri possit, salvis Ecclesiae statutis.

SED CONTRA est quod, sicut Deus, sic Ecclesia non praecipit aliquid impossibile.

RESPONDEO dicendum quod periculis seu defectibus circa hoc sacramentum evenientibus dupliciter potest occurri. Uno modo, praeveniendo, ne scilicet periculum accidat. Alio modo, subsequendo, ut scilicet id quod accidit emendetur, vel adhibendo remedium, vel saltem per poenitentiam eius qui negligenter egit circa hoc sacramentum.

AD PRIMUM ergo dicendum quod, si sacerdos morte aut infirmitate gravi occupetur ante consecrationem corporis et sanguinis domini, non oportet ut per alium suppleatur. Si vero post incoeptam consecrationem hoc acciderit, puta consecrato corpore ante consecrationem sanguinis, vel etiam consecrato utroque, debet Missae celebritas per alium expleri. Unde, ut habetur in decretis, VII, qu. I, cap. *nihil*, in Toletano Concilio legitur, *censuimus convenire ut, cum a sacerdotibus Missarum tempore sacra mysteria consecrantur, si aegritudinis accidit cuiuslibet eventus quo coeptum nequeat expleri mysterium, sit liberum episcopo vel presbytero alteri consecrationem exequi incoepti officii. Non enim aliud competit ad supplementum initiatis mysteriis quam aut incipientis aut subsequentis benedictione sint completa sacerdotis, quia nec perfecta videri possunt nisi perfecto ordine compleantur. Cum enim omnes simus unum in Christo, nihil contrarium diversitas personarum format, ubi efficaciam prosperitatis unitas fidei repraesentat. Nec tamen quod naturae languoris causa consulitur, in praesumptionis perniciem convertatur. Nullus, absque patenti proventu molestiae, minister vel sacerdos, cum coeperit, imperfecta officia praesumat omnino relinquere. Si quis hoc temerarie praesumpserit, excommunicationis sententiam sustinebit.*

AD SECUNDUM dicendum quod, ubi difficultas occurrit, semper est accipiendum illud quod habet minus de periculo. Maxime autem periculosum circa hoc

OBJ. 6: Further, it sometimes comes to pass owing to the cold that the host will slip from the priest's hands into the chalice, either before or after the breaking. In this case then the priest will not be able to comply with the Church's rite, either as to the breaking, or else as to this, that only a third part is put into the chalice.

OBJ. 7: Further, sometimes, too, it happens, owing to the priest's want of care, that Christ's blood is spilled, or that he vomits the sacrament received, or that the consecrated hosts are kept so long that they become corrupt, or that they are nibbled by mice, or lost in any manner whatsoever; in which cases it does not seem possible for due reverence to be shown towards this sacrament, as the Church's ordinances require. It does not seem then that such defects or dangers can be met by keeping to the Church's statutes.

ON THE CONTRARY, Just as God does not command an impossibility, so neither does the Church.

I ANSWER THAT, Dangers or defects happening to this sacrament can be met in two ways: first, by preventing any such mishaps from occurring: second, by dealing with them in such a way, that what may have happened amiss is put right, either by employing a remedy, or at least by repentance on his part who has acted negligently regarding this sacrament.

REPLY OBJ. 1: If the priest be stricken by death or grave sickness before the consecration of our Lord's body and blood, there is no need for it to be completed by another. But if this happens after the consecration is begun, for instance, when the body has been consecrated and before the consecration of the blood, or even after both have been consecrated, then the celebration of the mass ought to be finished by someone else. Hence, as is laid down (*Decretal* vii, q. 1), we read the following decree of the (Seventh) Council of Toledo: *We consider it to be fitting that when the sacred mysteries are consecrated by priests during the time of mass, if any sickness supervenes, in consequence of which they cannot finish the mystery begun, let it be free for the bishop or another priest to finish the consecration of the office thus begun. For nothing else is suitable for completing the mysteries commenced, unless the consecration be completed either by the priest who began it, or by the one who follows him: because they cannot be completed except they be performed in perfect order. For since we are all one in Christ, the change of persons makes no difference, since unity of faith insures the happy issue of the mystery. Yet let not the course we propose for cases of natural debility, be presumptuously abused: and let no minister or priest presume ever to leave the Divine offices unfinished, unless he be absolutely prevented from continuing. If anyone shall have rashly presumed to do so, he will incur sentence of excommunication.*

REPLY OBJ. 2: Where difficulty arises, the less dangerous course should always be followed. But the greatest danger regarding this sacrament lies in whatever may

sacramentum est quod est contra perfectionem ipsius sacramenti, quia hoc est immane sacrilegium. Minus autem est illud quod pertinet ad qualitatem sumentis. Et ideo, si sacerdos, post consecrationem incoeptam, recordetur aliquid comedisse vel bibisse, nihilominus debet perficere sacrificium et sumere sacramentum. Similiter, si recordetur se peccatum aliquod commisisse, debet poenitere cum proposito confitendi et satisfaciendi, et sic non indigne, sed fructuose sumere sacramentum. Et eadem ratio est si se meminerit excommunicationi cuicumque subiacere. Debet enim assumere propositum absolutionem petendi, et sic per invisibilem pontificem, Iesum Christum, absolutionem consequitur quantum ad hunc actum, quod peragat divina mysteria.

Si vero ante consecrationem alicuius praedictorum sit memor, tutius reputarem, maxime in casu manducationis et excommunicationis, quod Missam incoeptam desereret, nisi grave scandalum timeretur.

AD TERTIUM dicendum quod, si musca vel aranea in calicem ante consecrationem ceciderit, aut etiam venenum deprehenderit esse immissum, debet effundi, et, abluto calice, denuo aliud vinum poni consecrandum. Si vero aliquid horum post consecrationem acciderit, debet animal caute capi, et diligenter lavari, et comburi, et ablutio, simul cum cineribus, in sacrarium mitti. Si vero venenum ibi adesse deprehenderit immissum, nullo modo debet sumere nec alii dare ne calix vitae vertatur in mortem, sed debet diligenter in aliquo vasculo ad hoc apto cum reliquiis conservari. Et, ne sacramentum remaneat imperfectum, debet vinum apponere in calice, et denuo resumere a consecratione sanguinis, et sacrificium perficere.

AD QUARTUM dicendum quod, si sacerdos, ante consecrationem sanguinis et post consecrationem corporis, percipiat aut vinum aut aquam non esse in calice, debet statim apponere et consecrare. Si vero hoc post consecrationis verba perceperit, quod aqua desit, debet nihilominus procedere, quia appositio aquae, ut supra dictum est, non est de necessitate sacramenti. Debet tamen puniri ille ex cuius negligentia hoc contingit. Nullo autem modo debet aqua vino iam consecrato misceri, quia sequeretur corruptio sacramenti pro aliqua parte, ut supra dictum est. Si vero percipiat post verba consecrationis quod vinum non fuerit positum in calice, si quidem hoc percipiat ante sumptionem corporis, debet, deposita aqua si ibi fuerit, imponere vinum cum aqua, et resumere a verbis consecrationis sanguinis. Si vero hoc perceperit post sumptionem corporis, debet apponere aliam hostiam iterum simul consecrandam cum sanguine. Quod ideo dico quia, si diceret sola verba consecrationis sanguinis, non servaretur debitus ordo consecrandi, et, sicut dicitur in praedicto capitulo Toletani

prevent its completion, because this is a heinous sacrilege; while that danger is of less account which regards the condition of the receiver. Consequently, if after the consecration has been begun the priest remembers that he has eaten or drunk anything, he ought nevertheless to complete the sacrifice and receive the sacrament. Likewise, if he recalls a sin committed, he ought to make an act of contrition, with the firm purpose of confessing and making satisfaction for it: and thus he will not receive the sacrament unworthily, but with profit. The same applies if he calls to mind that he is under some excommunication; for he ought to make the resolution of humbly seeking absolution; and so he will receive absolution from the invisible High Priest Jesus Christ for his act of completing the Divine mysteries.

But if he calls to mind any of the above facts previous to the consecration, I should deem it safer for him to interrupt the mass begun, especially if he has broken his fast, or is under excommunication, unless grave scandal were to be feared.

REPLY OBJ. 3: If a fly or a spider falls into the chalice before consecration, or if it be discovered that the wine is poisoned, it ought to be poured out, and after purifying the chalice, fresh wine should be served for consecration. But if anything of the sort happen after the consecration, the insect should be caught carefully and washed thoroughly, then burned, and the *ablution*, together with the ashes, thrown into the sacrarium. If it be discovered that the wine has been poisoned, the priest should neither receive it nor administer it to others on any account, lest the life-giving chalice become one of death, but it ought to be kept in a suitable vessel with the relics: and in order that the sacrament may not remain incomplete, he ought to put other wine into the chalice, resume the mass from the consecration of the blood, and complete the sacrifice.

REPLY OBJ. 4: If before the consecration of the blood, and after the consecration of the body the priest detect that either the wine or the water is absent, then he ought at once to add them and consecrate. But if after the words of consecration he discover that the water is absent, he ought notwithstanding to proceed straight on, because the addition of the water is not necessary for the sacrament, as stated above (Q. 74, A. 7): nevertheless the person responsible for the neglect ought to be punished. And on no account should water be mixed with the consecrated wine, because corruption of the sacrament would ensue in part, as was said above (Q. 77, A. 8). But if after the words of consecration the priest perceive that no wine has been put in the chalice, and if he detect it before receiving the body, then rejecting the water, he ought to pour in wine with water, and begin over again the consecrating words of the blood. But if he notice it after receiving the body, he ought to procure another host which must be consecrated together with the blood; and I say so for this reason, because if he were to say only the words of consecration of the blood, the proper

Concilii, *perfecta videri non possunt sacrificia nisi perfecto ordine compleantur.* Si vero inciperet a consecratione sanguinis et repeteret omnia verba consequentia, non competerent nisi adesset hostia consecrata, cum in verbis illis occurrant quaedam dicenda et fienda non solum circa sanguinem, sed etiam circa corpus. Et debet in fine sumere hostiam iterum consecratam et sanguinem, non obstante etiam si prius sumpserit aquam quae erat in calice, quia praeceptum de perfectione sacramenti maioris est ponderis quam praeceptum quod hoc sacramentum a ieiunis sumatur, ut supra dictum est.

AD QUINTUM dicendum quod, licet sacerdos non recolat se dixisse aliqua eorum quae dicere debuit, non tamen debet ex hoc mente perturbari. Non enim qui multa dicit, recolit omnium quae dixit, nisi forte in dicendo aliquid apprehenderit sub ratione iam dicti sic enim aliquid efficitur memorabile. Unde, si aliquis attente cogitet illud quod dicit, non tamen cogitet se dicere illud, non multum recolit postea se dixisse. Sic enim fit aliquid obiectum memoria, inquantum accipitur sub ratione praeteriti, sicut dicitur in libro de memoria.

Si tamen sacerdoti probabiliter constet se aliqua omisisse, si quidem non sunt de necessitate sacramenti, non aestimo quod propter hoc debeat resumere immutando ordinem sacrificii, sed debet ulterius procedere. Si vero certificetur se omisisse aliquid eorum quae sunt de necessitate sacramenti, scilicet formam consecrationis, cum forma sit de necessitate sacramenti sicut et materia, idem videtur faciendum quod dictum est in defectu materiae, ut scilicet resumatur a forma consecrationis, et cetera per ordinem reiterentur, ne mutetur ordo sacrificii.

AD SEXTUM dicendum quod fractio hostiae consecratae, et quod pars una sola mittatur in calicem, respicit corpus mysticum, sicut et admixtio aquae significat populum. Et ideo horum praetermissio non facit imperfectionem sacrificii, ut propter hoc sit necesse aliquid reiterare circa celebrationem huius sacramenti.

AD SEPTIMUM dicendum quod, sicut legitur de Consecr., dist. II, ex decreto pii Papae, *si per negligentiam aliquid stillaverit de sanguine in tabula quae terrae adhaeret, lingua lambetur et tabula radetur. Si vero non fuerit tabula, terra radetur, et igni comburetur, et cinis intra altare condetur. Et sacerdos quadraginta dies poeniteat. Si autem super altare stillaverit calix, sorbeat minister stillam. Et tribus diebus poeniteat. Si super linteum altaris, et ad aliud stilla pervenerit, quatuor diebus poeniteat. Si usque ad tertium, novem diebus poeniteat. Si usque ad*

order of consecrating would not be observed; and, as is laid down by the Council of Toledo, quoted above (ad 1), sacrifices cannot be perfect, except they be performed in perfect order. But if he were to begin from the consecration of the blood, and were to repeat all the words which follow, it would not suffice, unless there was a consecrated host present, since in those words there are things to be said and done not only regarding the blood, but also regarding the body; and at the close he ought once more to receive the consecrated host and blood, even if he had already taken the water which was in the chalice, because the precept of the completing this sacrament is of greater weight than the precept of receiving the sacrament while fasting, as stated above (Q. 80, A. 8).

REPLY OBJ. 5: Although the priest may not recollect having said some of the words he ought to say, he ought not to be disturbed mentally on that account; for a man who utters many words cannot recall to mind all that he has said; unless perchance in uttering them he adverts to something connected with the consecration; for so it is impressed on the memory. Hence, if a man pays attention to what he is saying, but without adverting to the fact that he is saying these particular words, he remembers soon after that he has said them; for, a thing is presented to the memory under the formality of the past (*De Mem. et Remin.* i).

But if it seem to the priest that he has probably omitted some of the words that are not necessary for the sacrament, I think that he ought not to repeat them on that account, changing the order of the sacrifice, but that he ought to proceed: but if he is certain that he has left out any of those that are necessary for the sacrament, namely, the form of the consecration, since the form of the consecration is necessary for the sacrament, just as the matter is, it seems that the same thing ought to be done as was stated above (ad 4) with regard to defect in the matter, namely, that he should begin again with the form of the consecration, and repeat the other things in order, lest the order of the sacrifice be altered.

REPLY OBJ. 6: The breaking of the consecrated host, and the putting of only one part into the chalice, regards the mystical body, just as the mixing with water signifies the people, and therefore the omission of either of them causes no such imperfection in the sacrifice, as calls for repetition regarding the celebration of this sacrament.

REPLY OBJ. 7: According to the decree, *De Consecr.*, dist. ii, quoting a decree of Pope Pius I, *If from neglect any of the blood falls upon a board which is fixed to the ground, let it be taken up with the tongue, and let the board be scraped. But if it be not a board, let the ground be scraped, and the scrapings burned, and the ashes buried inside the altar and let the priest do penance for forty days. But if a drop fall from the chalice on to the altar, let the minister suck up the drop, and do penance during three days; if it falls upon the altar cloth and penetrates to the second altar cloth, let him do*

quartum, viginti diebus poeniteat. Et linteamina quae stilla tetigit, tribus vicibus lavet minister, calice subtus posito, et aqua ablutionis sumatur et iuxta altare recondatur. Posset etiam sumi in potu a ministro, nisi propter abominationem dimitteretur. Quidam autem ulterius partem illam linteaminum incidunt et comburunt, et cinerem in altario vel sacrario reponunt. Subditur autem ibidem, ex poenitentiali Bedae presbyteri, *si quis per ebrietatem vel voracitatem Eucharistiam evomuerit, quadraginta diebus poeniteat; clerici vel monachi, seu diaconi vel presbyteri, sexaginta diebus; episcopus nonaginta. Si autem infirmitatis causa evomuerit, septem diebus poeniteat.* Et in eadem distinctione legitur, ex Concilio Aurelianensi, *qui non bene custodierit sacrificium, et mus vel aliquod aliud animal in Ecclesia comederit, quadraginta diebus poeniteat. Qui autem perdiderit illud in Ecclesia, aut pars eius ceciderit et non inventa fuerit, triginta diebus poeniteat.* Et eadem poenitentia videtur dignus sacerdos per cuius negligentiam hostiae consecratae putrefiunt. Praedictis autem diebus debet poenitens ieiunare et a communione cessare. Pensatis tamen conditionibus negotii et personae, potest minui vel addi ad poenitentiam praedictam. Hoc tamen observandum est, quod, ubicumque species integrae inveniuntur, sunt reverenter observandae, vel etiam sumendae, quia, manentibus speciebus, manet ibi corpus Christi, ut supra dictum est. Ea vero in quibus inveniuntur, comburenda sunt si commode fieri potest, cinere in sacrario recondito, sicut de rasura tabulae dictum est.

four days' penance; if it penetrates to the third, let him do nine days' penance; if to the fourth, let him do twenty days' penance; and let the altar linens which the drop touched be washed three times by the priest, holding the chalice below, then let the water be taken and put away nigh to the altar. It might even be drunk by the minister, unless it might be rejected from nausea. Some persons go further, and cut out that part of the linen, which they burn, putting the ashes in the altar or down the sacrarium. And the *Decretal* continues with a quotation from the Penitential of Bede the Priest: *If, owing to drunkenness or gluttony, anyone vomits up the Eucharist, let him do forty days' penance, if he be a layman; but let clerics or monks, deacons and priests, do seventy days' penance; and let a bishop do ninety days'.* But if they vomit from sickness, let them do penance for seven days. And in the same distinction, we read a decree of the (Fourth) Council of Arles: *They who do not keep proper custody over the sacrament, if a mouse or other animal consume it, must do forty days' penance: he who loses it in a church, or if a part fall and be not found, shall do thirty days' penance.* And the priest seems to deserve the same penance, who from neglect allows the hosts to putrefy. And on those days the one doing penance ought to fast, and abstain from Communion. However, after weighing the circumstances of the fact and of the person, the said penances may be lessened or increased. But it must be observed that wherever the species are found to be entire, they must be preserved reverently, or consumed; because Christ's body is there so long as the species last, as stated above (Q. 77, AA. 4, 5). But if it can be done conveniently, the things in which they are found are to be burned, and the ashes put in the sacrarium, as was said of the scrapings of the altar-table, here above.

QUESTION 84

THE SACRAMENT OF PENANCE

Consequenter considerandum est de sacramento poenitentiae. Circa quod primo considerandum est de ipsa poenitentia; secundo, de effectu ipsius; tertio, de partibus eius; quarto, de suscipientibus hoc sacramentum; quinto, de potestate ministrorum; sexto, de solemni ritu huius sacramenti.

Circa primum duo sunt consideranda, primo, de poenitentia secundum quod est sacramentum; secundo, de poenitentia secundum quod est virtus.

Circa primum quaeruntur decem.

Primo, utrum poenitentia sit sacramentum.

Secundo, de propria materia eius.

Tertio, de forma ipsius.

Quarto, utrum impositio manus requiratur ad hoc sacramentum.

Quinto, utrum hoc sacramentum sit de necessitate salutis.

Sexto, de ordine eius ad alia sacramenta.

Septimo, de institutione eius.

Octavo, de duratione ipsius.

Nono, de continuitate eius.

Decimo, utrum possit iterari.

We must now consider the Sacrament of Penance. We shall consider (1)Penance itself; (2) Its effect; (3) Its Parts; (4) The recipients of this sacrament; (5) The power of the ministers, which pertains to the keys; (6) The solemnization of this sacrament.

The first of these considerations will be twofold: (1) Penance as a sacrament; (2) Penance as a virtue.

Under the first head there are ten points of inquiry:
(1) Whether Penance is a sacrament?
(2) Of its proper matter;
(3) Of its form;
(4) Whether imposition of hands is necessary for this sacrament?
(5) Whether this sacrament is necessary for salvation?
(6) Of its relation to the other sacraments;
(7) Of its institution;
(8) Of its duration;
(9) Of its continuance;
(10) Whether it can be repeated?

Article 1

Whether Penance Is a Sacrament?

AD PRIMUM SIC PROCEDITUR. Videtur quod poenitentia non sit sacramentum. Gregorius enim dicit, et habetur in decretis, I, qu. I, *sacramenta sunt Baptisma, chrisma, corpus et sanguis Christi, quae ob id sacramenta dicuntur quia sub tegumento corporalium rerum divina virtus secretius operatur salutem.* Sed hoc non contingit in poenitentia, quia non adhibentur aliquae res corporales sub quibus divina virtus operetur salutem. Ergo poenitentia non est sacramentum.

PRAETEREA, sacramenta Ecclesiae a ministris Christi exhibentur, secundum illud I Cor. IV, *sic nos existimet homo ut ministros Christi et dispensatores mysteriorum Dei.* Sed poenitentia non exhibetur a ministris Christi, sed interius a Deo hominibus inspiratur, secundum illud Ierem. XXXI, *postquam convertisti me, egi poenitentiam.* Ergo videtur quod poenitentia non sit sacramentum.

PRAETEREA, in sacramentis de quibus supra diximus, est aliquid quod est sacramentum tantum, aliquid

OBJECTION 1: It would seem that Penance is not a sacrament. For Gregory says: *The sacraments are Baptism, Chrism, and the Body and Blood of Christ; which are called sacraments because under the veil of corporeal things the Divine power works out salvation in a hidden manner.* But this does not happen in Penance, because therein corporeal things are not employed that, under them, the power of God may work our salvation. Therefore Penance is not a sacrament.

OBJ. 2: Further, the sacraments of the Church are shown forth by the ministers of Christ, according to 1 Cor. 4:1: *Let a man so account of us as of the ministers of Christ, and the dispensers of the mysteries of God.* But Penance is not conferred by the ministers of Christ, but is inspired inwardly into man by God, according to Jer. 31:19: *After Thou didst convert me, I did penance.* Therefore it seems that Penance is not a sacrament.

OBJ. 3: Further, in the sacraments of which we have already spoken above, there is something that is sacrament

359

quod est res et sacramentum, aliquid vero quod est res tantum, ut ex praemissis patet. Sed hoc non invenitur in poenitentia. Ergo poenitentia non est sacramentum.

SED CONTRA est quod, sicut Baptismus adhibetur ad purificandum a peccato, ita et poenitentia, unde et Petrus dixit Simoni, Act. VIII, *poenitentiam age ab hac nequitia tua.* Sed Baptismus est sacramentum, ut supra dictum est. Ergo pari ratione et poenitentia.

RESPONDEO dicendum quod, sicut Gregorius dicit, in capite supra dicto, *sacramentum est in aliqua celebratione, cum res gesta ita fit ut aliquid significative accipiamus quod sancte accipiendum est.* Manifestum est autem quod in poenitentia ita res gesta fit quod aliquid sanctum significatur, tam ex parte peccatoris poenitentis, quam ex parte sacerdotis absolventis, nam peccator poenitens per ea quae agit et dicit, significat cor suum a peccato recessisse; similiter etiam sacerdos per ea quae agit et dicit circa poenitentem, significat opus Dei remittentis peccatum. Unde manifestum est quod poenitentia quae in Ecclesia agitur, est sacramentum.

AD PRIMUM ergo dicendum quod nomine corporalium rerum intelliguntur large etiam ipsi exteriores actus sensibiles, qui ita se habent in hoc sacramento sicut aqua in Baptismo vel chrisma in confirmatione. Est autem attendendum quod in illis sacramentis in quibus confertur excellens gratia, quae superabundat omnem facultatem humani actus, adhibetur aliqua corporalis materia exterius; sicut in Baptismo, ubi fit plena remissio peccatorum et quantum ad culpam et quantum ad poenam; et in confirmatione, ubi datur spiritus sancti plenitudo; et in extrema unctione, ubi confertur perfecta sanitas spiritualis; quae provenit ex virtute Christi quasi ex quodam extrinseco principio. Unde si qui actus humani sunt in talibus sacramentis, non sunt de essentia materiae sacramentorum, sed dispositive se habent ad sacramenta. In illis autem sacramentis quae habent effectum correspondentem humanis actibus, ipsi actus humani sensibiles sunt loco materiae, ut accidit in poenitentia et matrimonio. Sicut etiam in medicinis corporalibus quaedam sunt res exterius adhibitae, sicut emplastra et electuaria; quaedam vero sunt actus sanandorum, puta exercitationes quaedam.

AD SECUNDUM dicendum quod in sacramentis quae habent corporalem materiam, oportet quod illa materia adhibeatur a ministro Ecclesiae, qui gerit personam Christi, in signum quod excellentia virtutis in sacramento operantis est a Christo. In sacramento autem poenitentiae, sicut dictum est, sunt actus humani pro materia, qui proveniunt ex inspiratione interna. Unde materia non adhibetur a ministro, sed a Deo interius operante,

only, something that is both reality and sacrament, and something that is reality only, as is clear from what has been stated (Q. 66, A. 1). But this does not apply to Penance. Therefore Penance is not a sacrament.

ON THE CONTRARY, As Baptism is conferred that we may be cleansed from sin, so also is Penance: wherefore Peter said to Simon Magus (Acts 8:22): *Do penance . . . from this thy wickedness.* But Baptism is a sacrament as stated above (Q. 66, A. 1). Therefore for the same reason Penance is also a sacrament.

I ANSWER THAT, As Gregory says, *a sacrament consists in a solemn act, whereby something is so done that we understand it to signify the holiness which it confers.* Now it is evident that in Penance something is done so that something holy is signified both on the part of the penitent sinner, and on the part of the priest absolving, because the penitent sinner, by deed and word, shows his heart to have renounced sin, and in like manner the priest, by his deed and word with regard to the penitent, signifies the work of God Who forgives his sins. Therefore it is evident that Penance, as practiced in the Church, is a sacrament.

REPLY OBJ. 1: By corporeal things taken in a wide sense we may understand also external sensible actions, which are to this sacrament what water is to Baptism, or chrism to Confirmation. But it is to be observed that in those sacraments, whereby an exceptional grace surpassing altogether the proportion of a human act, is conferred, some corporeal matter is employed externally, e.g., in Baptism, which confers full remission of all sins, both as to guilt and as to punishment, and in Confirmation, wherein the fullness of the Holy Spirit is bestowed, and in Extreme Unction, which confers perfect spiritual health derived from the virtue of Christ as from an extrinsic principle. Wherefore, such human acts as are in these sacraments, are not the essential matter of the sacrament, but are dispositions thereto. On the other hand, in those sacraments whose effect corresponds to that of some human act, the sensible human act itself takes the place of matter, as in the case of Penance and Matrimony, even as in bodily medicines, some are applied externally, such as plasters and drugs, while others are acts of the person who seeks to be cured, such as certain exercises.

REPLY OBJ. 2: In those sacraments which have a corporeal matter, this matter needs to be applied by a minister of the Church, who stands in the place of Christ, which denotes that the excellence of the power which operates in the sacraments is from Christ. But in the sacrament of Penance, as stated above (ad 1), human actions take the place of matter, and these actions proceed from internal inspiration, wherefore the matter is not applied by the minister,

sed complementum sacramenti exhibet minister, dum poenitentem absolvit.

AD TERTIUM dicendum quod etiam in poenitentia est aliquid quod est sacramentum tantum, scilicet actus exercitus tam per peccatorem poenitentem, quam etiam per sacerdotem absolventem. Res autem et sacramentum est poenitentia interior peccatoris. Res autem tantum et non sacramentum est remissio peccati. Quorum primum totum simul sumptum est causa secundi; primum autem et secundum sunt causa tertii.

but by God working inwardly; while the minister furnishes the complement of the sacrament, when he absolves the penitent.

REPLY OBJ. 3: In Penance also, there is something which is sacrament only, viz. the acts performed outwardly both by the repentant sinner, and by the priest in giving absolution; that which is reality and sacrament is the sinner's inward repentance; while that which is reality, and not sacrament, is the forgiveness of sin. The first of these taken altogether is the cause of the second; and the first and second together are the cause of the third.

Article 2

Whether Sins Are the Proper Matter of This Sacrament?

AD SECUNDUM SIC PROCEDITUR. Videtur quod peccata non sint propria materia huius sacramenti. Materia enim in aliis sacramentis per aliqua verba sanctificatur, et sanctificata effectum sacramenti operatur. Peccata autem non possunt sanctificari, eo quod contrariantur effectui sacramenti, qui est gratia remittens peccata. Ergo peccata non sunt materia propria huius sacramenti.

PRAETEREA, Augustinus dicit, in libro de poenitentia, *nullus potest inchoare novam vitam nisi eum veteris vitae poeniteat.* Sed ad vetustatem vitae pertinent non solum peccata, sed etiam poenalitates praesentis vitae. Non ergo peccata sunt propria materia poenitentiae.

PRAETEREA, peccatorum quoddam est originale, quoddam mortale, quoddam veniale. Sed poenitentiae sacramentum non ordinatur contra originale peccatum, quod tollitur per Baptismum; neque etiam contra veniale, quod tollitur per tunsionem pectoris, et aquam benedictam, et alia huiusmodi. Ergo peccata non sunt propria materia poenitentiae.

SED CONTRA est quod apostolus dicit, II Cor. XII, *non egerunt poenitentiam super immunditia et fornicatione et impudicitia quam gesserunt.*

RESPONDEO dicendum quod duplex est materia, scilicet proxima et remota, sicut statuae proxima materia est metallum, remota vero aqua. Dictum est autem quod proxima materia huius sacramenti sunt actus poenitentis, cuius materia sunt peccata, de quibus dolet, et quae confitetur, et pro quibus satisfacit. Unde relinquitur quod remota materia poenitentiae sunt peccata, non attentanda, sed detestanda et destruenda.

AD PRIMUM ergo dicendum quod ratio illa procedit de proxima materia sacramenti.

AD SECUNDUM dicendum quod vetus et mortalis vita est obiectum poenitentiae, non ratione poenae, sed ratione culpae annexae.

OBJECTION 1: It would seem that sins are not the proper matter of this sacrament. Because, in the other sacraments, the matter is hallowed by the utterance of certain words, and being thus hallowed produces the sacramental effect. Now sins cannot be hallowed, for they are opposed to the effect of the sacrament, viz. grace which blots out sin. Therefore sins are not the proper matter of this sacrament.

OBJ. 2: Further, Augustine says in his book *De Poenitentia*: *No one can begin a new life, unless he repent of the old.* Now not only sins but also the penalties of the present life belong to the old life. Therefore sins are not the proper matter of Penance.

OBJ. 3: Further, sin is either original, mortal or venial. Now the sacrament of Penance is not ordained against original sin, for this is taken away by Baptism, nor against venial sin, which is taken away by the beating of the breast and the sprinkling of holy water and the like. Therefore sins are not the proper matter of Penance.

ON THE CONTRARY, The Apostle says (2 Cor 12:21): *(Who) have not done penance for the uncleanness and fornication and lasciviousness, that they have committed.*

I ANSWER THAT, Matter is twofold, viz. proximate and remote: thus the proximate matter of a statue is a metal, while the remote matter is water. Now it has been stated (A. 1, ad 1, ad 2), that the proximate matter of this sacrament consists in the acts of the penitent, the matter of which acts are the sins over which he grieves, which he confesses, and for which he satisfies. Hence it follows that sins are the remote matter of Penance, as a matter, not for approval, but for detestation, and destruction.

REPLY OBJ. 1: This argument considers the proximate matter of a sacrament.

REPLY OBJ. 2: The old life that was subject to death is the object of Penance, not as regards the punishment, but as regards the guilt connected with it.

Ad tertium dicendum quod poenitentia quodammodo est de quolibet peccatorum genere, non tamen eodem modo. Nam de peccato actuali mortali est poenitentia proprie et principaliter, proprie quidem, quia proprie dicimur poenitere de his quae nostra voluntate commisimus; principaliter autem, quia ad deletionem peccati mortalis hoc sacramentum est institutum. De peccatis autem venialibus est quaedam poenitentia proprie, inquantum sunt nostra voluntate facta, non tamen contra haec principaliter est hoc sacramentum institutum. De peccato vero originali poenitentia nec principaliter est, quia contra ipsum non ordinatur hoc sacramentum, sed magis Baptismus, nec etiam proprie, quia peccatum originale non est nostra voluntate peractum; nisi forte inquantum voluntas Adae reputatur nostra, secundum modum loquendi quo apostolus dicit, Rom. V, *in quo omnes peccaverunt.* Inquantum tamen accipitur poenitentia large pro quacumque detestatione rei praeteritae, potest dici poenitentia de peccato originali, sicut loquitur Augustinus in libro de poenitentia.

Reply Obj. 3: Penance regards every kind of sin in a way, but not each in the same way. Because Penance regards actual mortal sin properly and chiefly; properly, since, properly speaking, we are said to repent of what we have done of our own will; chiefly, since this sacrament was instituted chiefly for the blotting out of mortal sin. Penance regards venial sins, properly speaking indeed, in so far as they are committed of our own will, but this was not the chief purpose of its institution. But as to original sin, Penance regards it neither chiefly, since Baptism, and not Penance, is ordained against original sin, nor properly, because original sin is not done of our own will, except in so far as Adam's will is looked upon as ours, in which sense the Apostle says (Rom 5:12): *In whom all have sinned.* Nevertheless, Penance may be said to regard original sin, if we take it in a wide sense for any detestation of something past: in which sense Augustine uses the term in his book *De Poenitentia* (*Serm. cccli*).

Article 3

Whether the Form of This Sacrament Is: I Absolve Thee?

Ad tertium sic proceditur. Videtur quod haec non sit forma huius sacramenti, ego te absolvo. Formae enim sacramentorum ex institutione Christi et usu Ecclesiae habentur. Sed Christus non legitur hanc formam instituisse. Neque etiam in communi usu habetur, quinimmo in quibusdam absolutionibus quae in Ecclesia publice fiunt, sicut in prima et completorio et in cena domini, absolvens non utitur oratione indicativa, ut dicat, ego vos absolvo, sed oratione deprecativa, cum dicit, misereatur vestri omnipotens Deus, vel, absolutionem tribuat vobis omnipotens Deus. Ergo haec non est forma huius sacramenti, ego te absolvo.

Praeterea, Leo Papa dicit, *indulgentia Dei nisi supplicationibus sacerdotum nequit obtineri.* Loquitur autem de indulgentia Dei quae praestatur poenitentibus. Ergo forma huius sacramenti debet esse per modum deprecationis.

Praeterea, idem est absolvere a peccato quod peccatum remittere. Sed *solus Deus peccatum remittit, qui etiam solus interius a peccato mundat,* ut Augustinus dicit, super Ioan. Ergo videtur quod solus Deus a peccato absolvat. Non ergo debet dicere sacerdos, ego te absolvo, sicut non dicit, ego tibi peccata remitto.

Praeterea, sicut dominus dedit potestatem discipulis absolvendi a peccatis, ita etiam dedit eis potestatem curandi infirmitates, scilicet *ut Daemonia eiicerent et ut languores curarent,* ut habetur Matth. X et Luc. IX. Sed

Objection 1: It would seem that the form of this sacrament is not: *I absolve thee.* Because the forms of the sacraments are received from Christ's institution and the Church's custom. But we do not read that Christ instituted this form. Nor is it in common use; in fact in certain absolutions which are given publicly in church (e.g., at Prime and Compline and on Maundy Thursday), absolution is given not in the indicative form by saying: *I absolve thee,* but in the deprecatory form, by saying: *May Almighty God have mercy on you,* or: *May Almighty God grant you absolution and forgiveness.* Therefore the form of this sacrament is not: *I absolve thee.*

Obj. 2: Further, Pope Leo says (*Ep. cviii*) that God's forgiveness cannot be obtained without the priestly supplications: and he is speaking there of God's forgiveness granted to the penitent. Therefore the form of this sacrament should be deprecatory.

Obj. 3: Further, to absolve from sin is the same as to remit sin. But God alone remits sin, for He alone cleanses man inwardly from sin, as Augustine says (*Contra Donatist.* v, 21). Therefore it seems that God alone absolves from sin. Therefore the priest should say not: *I absolve thee,* as neither does he say: *I remit thy sins.*

Obj. 4: Further, just as our Lord gave His disciples the power to absolve from sins, so also did He give them the power *to heal infirmities, to cast out devils,* and *to cure diseases* (Matt 10:1; Luke 9:1). Now the apostles, in healing the

sanando infirmos apostoli non utebantur his verbis, ego te sano, sed, sanet te dominus Iesus Christus. Ergo videtur quod sacerdotes, habentes potestatem apostolis a Christo traditam, non debeant uti hac forma verborum, ego te absolvo, sed, absolutionem praebeat tibi Christus.

PRAETEREA, quidam hac forma utentes sic eam exponunt, *ego te absolvo, idest, absolutum ostendo.* Sed neque hoc sacerdos facere potest, nisi ei divinitus reveletur. Unde, ut legitur Matth. XVI, antequam Petro diceretur, *quodcumque solveris super terram, erit* etc., dictum est ei, *beatus es, Simon Bar Iona, quia caro et sanguis non revelavit tibi, sed pater meus, qui in caelis est.* Ergo videtur quod sacerdos cui non est facta revelatio, praesumptuose dicat, ego te absolvo, etiam si exponatur, idest, absolutum ostendo.

SED CONTRA est quod, sicut dominus dixit discipulis, Matth. ult., *euntes, docete omnes gentes, baptizantes eos,* ita dixit Petro, Matth. XVI, *quodcumque solveris.* Sed sacerdos, auctoritate illorum verborum Christi fretus, dicit, ego te baptizo. Ergo, eadem auctoritate, dicere debet in hoc sacramento, ego te absolvo.

RESPONDEO dicendum quod in qualibet re perfectio attribuitur formae. Dictum est autem supra quod hoc sacramentum perficitur per ea quae sunt ex parte sacerdotis. Unde oportet quod ea quae sunt ex parte poenitentis, sive sint verba sive facta, sint quaedam materia huius sacramenti, ea vero quae sunt ex parte sacerdotis, se habent per modum formae.

Cum autem sacramenta novae legis efficiant quod figurant, ut supra dictum est; oportet quod forma sacramenti significet id quod in sacramento agitur, proportionaliter materiae sacramenti. Unde forma Baptismi est, ego te baptizo, et forma confirmationis, *consigno te signo crucis et confirmo te chrismate salutis,* eo quod huiusmodi sacramenta perficiuntur in usu materiae. In sacramento autem Eucharistiae, quod consistit in ipsa consecratione materiae, exprimitur veritas consecrationis, cum dicitur, *hoc est corpus meum.*

Hoc autem sacramentum, scilicet poenitentiae, non consistit in consecratione alicuius materiae, nec in usu alicuius materiae sanctificatae, sed magis in remotione cuiusdam materiae, scilicet peccati, prout peccata dicuntur esse materia poenitentiae, ut ex supra dictis patet. Talis autem remotio significatur a sacerdote cum dicitur, ego te absolvo, nam peccata sunt quaedam vincula, secundum illud Proverb. V, *iniquitates suae capiunt impium, et funibus peccatorum suorum quisque constringitur.* Unde patet quod haec est convenientissima forma huius sacramenti, ego te absolvo.

AD PRIMUM ergo dicendum quod ista forma sumitur ex ipsis verbis Christi quibus Petro dixit, *quodcumque*

sick, did not use the words: *I heal thee,* but: *The Lord Jesus Christ heal thee,* as Peter said to the palsied man (Acts 9:34). Therefore since priests have the power which Christ gave His apostles, it seems that they should not use the form: *I absolve thee,* but: *May Christ absolve thee.*

OBJ. 5: Further, some explain this form by stating that when they say: *I absolve thee,* they mean *I declare you to be absolved.* But neither can this be done by a priest unless it be revealed to him by God, wherefore, as we read in Matt. 16:19 before it was said to Peter: *Whatsoever thou shalt bind upon earth,* etc., it was said to him (Matt 16:17): *Blessed art thou Simon Bar-Jona: because flesh and blood have not revealed it to thee, but My Father Who is in heaven.* Therefore it seems presumptuous for a priest, who has received no revelation on the matter, to say: *I absolve thee,* even if this be explained to mean: *I declare thee absolved.*

ON THE CONTRARY, As our Lord said to His disciples (Matt 28:19): *Going . . . teach ye all nations, baptizing them,* etc., so did He say to Peter (Matt 16:19): *Whatsoever thou shalt loose on earth,* etc. Now the priest, relying on the authority of those words of Christ, says: *I baptize thee.* Therefore on the same authority he should say in this sacrament: *I absolve thee.*

I ANSWER THAT, The perfection of a thing is ascribed to its form. Now it has been stated above (A. 1, ad 2) that this sacrament is perfected by that which is done by the priest. Wherefore the part taken by the penitent, whether it consist of words or deeds, must needs be the matter of this sacrament, while the part taken by the priest, takes the place of the form.

Now since the sacraments of the New Law accomplish what they signify, as stated above (Q. 62, A. 1, ad 1), it behooves the sacramental form to signify the sacramental effect in a manner that is in keeping with the matter. Hence the form of Baptism is: *I baptize thee,* and the form of Confirmation is: *I sign thee with the sign of the cross, and I confirm thee with the chrism of salvation,* because these sacraments are perfected in the use of their matter: while in the sacrament of the Eucharist, which consists in the very consecration of the matter, the reality of the consecration is expressed in the words: *This is My Body.*

Now this sacrament, namely the sacrament of Penance, consists not in the consecration of a matter, nor in the use of a hallowed matter, but rather in the removal of a certain matter, viz. sin, in so far as sins are said to be the matter of Penance, as explained above (A. 2). This removal is expressed by the priest saying: *I absolve thee:* because sins are fetters, according to Prov. 5:22. *His own iniquities catch the wicked, and he is fast bound with the ropes of his own sins.* Wherefore it is evident that this is the most fitting form of this sacrament: *I absolve thee.*

REPLY OBJ. 1: This form is taken from Christ's very words which He addressed to Peter (Matt 16:19):

solveris super terram, et cetera. Et tali forma utitur Ecclesia in sacramentali absolutione. Huiusmodi autem absolutiones in publico factae non sunt sacramentales, sed sunt orationes quaedam ordinatae ad remissionem venialium peccatorum. Unde in sacramentali absolutione non sufficeret dicere, misereatur tui omnipotens Deus, vel, absolutionem et remissionem tribuat tibi Deus, quia per haec verba sacerdos absolutionem non significat fieri, sed petit ut fiat. Praemittitur tamen etiam in sacramentali absolutione talis oratio, ne impediatur effectus sacramenti ex parte poenitentis, cuius actus materialiter se habent in hoc sacramento, non autem in Baptismo vel in confirmatione.

AD SECUNDUM dicendum quod verbum Leonis Papae est intelligendum quantum ad deprecationem quae praemittitur absolutioni. Non autem removet quin sacerdotes absolvant.

AD TERTIUM dicendum quod solus Deus per auctoritatem et a peccato absolvit et peccata remittit. Sacerdotes autem utrumque faciunt per ministerium, inquantum scilicet verba sacerdotis in hoc sacramento instrumentaliter operantur, sicut etiam in aliis sacramentis; nam virtus divina est quae interius operatur in omnibus sacramentalibus signis, sive sint res sive sint verba, sicut ex supra dictis patet. Unde et dominus utrumque expressit, nam Matth. XVI dixit Petro, *quodcumque solveris super terram*, etc.; et Ioan. XX dixit discipulis, *quorum remiseritis peccata, remittuntur eis*. Ideo tamen sacerdos potius dicit, ego te absolvo, quam, ego tibi peccata remitto, quia hoc magis congruit verbis quae dominus dixit virtutem clavium ostendens, per quas sacerdotes absolvunt. Quia tamen sacerdos sicut minister absolvit, convenienter apponitur aliquid quod pertineat ad primam auctoritatem Dei, scilicet ut dicatur, *ego te absolvo in nomine patris et filii et spiritus sancti*, vel, per virtutem passionis Christi, vel, auctoritate Dei, sicut Dionysius exponit, XIII cap. Caelest. Hier. Quia tamen hoc non est determinatum ex verbis Christi, sicut in Baptismo, talis appositio relinquitur arbitrio sacerdotis.

AD QUARTUM dicendum quod apostolis non est data potestas ut ipsi sanarent infirmos, sed ut ad eorum orationem infirmi sanarentur. Est autem eis collata potestas operandi instrumentaliter, sive ministerialiter, in sacramentis. Et ideo magis possunt in formis sacramentalibus exprimere actum suum quam in sanationibus infirmitatum. In quibus tamen non semper utebantur modo deprecativo, sed quandoque etiam modo indicativo et imperativo, sicut Act. III legitur quod Petrus dixit claudo, *quod habeo, hoc tibi do. In nomine Iesu Christi, surge et ambula.*

AD QUINTUM dicendum quod ista expositio, *ego te absolvo, idest, absolutum ostendo*, quantum ad aliquid quidem vera est, non tamen est perfecta. Sacramenta enim novae legis non solum significant, sed etiam

Whatsoever thou shalt loose on earth, etc., and such is the form employed by the Church in sacramental absolution. But such absolutions as are given in public are not sacramental, but are prayers for the remission of venial sins. Wherefore in giving sacramental absolution it would not suffice to say: *May Almighty God have mercy on thee*, or: *May God grant thee absolution and forgiveness*, because by such words the priest does not signify the giving of absolution, but prays that it may be given. Nevertheless the above prayer is said before the sacramental absolution is given, lest the sacramental effect be hindered on the part of the penitent, whose acts are as matter in this sacrament, but not in Baptism or Confirmation.

REPLY OBJ. 2: The words of Leo are to be understood of the prayer that precedes the absolution, and do not exclude the fact that the priest pronounces absolution.

REPLY OBJ. 3: God alone absolves from sin and forgives sins authoritatively; yet priests do both ministerially, because the words of the priest in this sacrament work as instruments of the Divine power, as in the other sacraments: because it is the Divine power that works inwardly in all the sacramental signs, be they things or words, as shown above (Q. 62, A. 4; Q. 64, AA. 1, 2). Wherefore our Lord expressed both: for He said to Peter (Matt 16:19): *Whatsoever thou shalt loose on earth*, etc., and to His disciples (John 20:23): *Whose sins you shall forgive, they are forgiven them*. Yet the priest says: *I absolve thee*, rather than: *I forgive thee thy sins*, because it is more in keeping with the words of our Lord, by expressing the power of the keys whereby priests absolve. Nevertheless, since the priest absolves ministerially, something is suitably added in reference to the supreme authority of God, by the priest saying: *I absolve thee in the name of the Father, and of the Son, and of the Holy Spirit*, or by the power of Christ's Passion, or by the authority of God. However, as this is not defined by the words of Christ, as it is for Baptism, this addition is left to the discretion of the priest.

REPLY OBJ. 4: Power was given to the apostles, not that they themselves might heal the sick, but that the sick might be healed at the prayer of the apostles: whereas power was given to them to work instrumentally or ministerially in the sacraments; wherefore they could express their own agency in the sacramental forms rather than in the healing of infirmities. Nevertheless in the latter case they did not always use the deprecatory form, but sometimes employed the indicative or imperative: thus we read (Acts 3:6) that Peter said to the lame man: *What I have, I give thee: In the name of Jesus Christ of Nazareth, arise and walk.*

REPLY OBJ. 5: It is true in a sense that the words, *I absolve thee* mean *I declare thee absolved*, but this explanation is incomplete. Because the sacraments of the New Law not only signify, but effect what they signify. Wherefore, just as

faciunt quod significant. Unde sicut sacerdos, baptizando aliquem, ostendit hominem interius ablutum per verba et facta, non solum significative, sed etiam effective; ita etiam cum dicit, ego te absolvo, ostendit hominem absolutum non solum significative, sed etiam effective. Nec tamen loquitur quasi de re incerta. Quia sicut alia sacramenta novae legis habent de se certum effectum ex virtute passionis Christi, licet possit impediri ex parte recipientis, ita etiam est et in hoc sacramento. Unde Augustinus dicit, in libro de Adult. Coniug., *non est turpis nec difficilis post patrata et purgata adulteria reconciliatio coniugii, ubi per claves regni caelorum non dubitatur fieri remissio peccatorum.* Unde nec sacerdos indiget speciali revelatione sibi facta, sed sufficit generalis revelatio fidei, per quam remittuntur peccata. Unde revelatio fidei dicitur Petro facta fuisse.

Esset autem perfectior expositio, ego te absolvo, idest, sacramentum absolutionis tibi impendo.

the priest in baptizing anyone, declares by deed and word that the person is washed inwardly, and this not only significatively but also effectively, so also when he says: *I absolve thee,* he declares the man to be absolved not only significatively but also effectively. And yet he does not speak as of something uncertain, because just as the other sacraments of the New Law have, of themselves, a sure effect through the power of Christ's Passion, which effect, nevertheless, may be impeded on the part of the recipient, so is it with this sacrament. Hence Augustine says (*De Adult. Conjug.* ii): *There is nothing disgraceful or onerous in the reconciliation of husband and wife, when adultery committed has been washed away, since there is no doubt that remission of sins is granted through the keys of the kingdom of heaven.* Consequently there is no need for a special revelation to be made to the priest, but the general revelation of faith suffices, through which sins are forgiven. Hence the revelation of faith is said to have been made to Peter.

It would be a more complete explanation to say that the words, *I absolve thee* mean: *I grant thee the sacrament of absolution.*

Article 4

Whether the Imposition of the Priest's Hands Is Necessary for This Sacrament?

AD QUARTUM SIC PROCEDITUR. Videtur quod impositio manuum sacerdotis requiratur ad hoc sacramentum. Dicitur enim Marc. ult., *super aegros manus imponent, et bene habebunt.* Aegri autem spiritualiter sunt peccatores, qui recipiunt bonam habitudinem per hoc sacramentum. Ergo in hoc sacramento est manus impositio facienda.

PRAETEREA, in sacramento poenitentiae recuperat homo spiritum sanctum amissum, unde ex persona poenitentis dicitur in Psalmo, *redde mihi laetitiam salutaris tui, et spiritu principali confirma me.* Sed Spiritus Sanctus datur per impositionem manuum, legitur enim Act. VIII, quod *apostoli imponebant manus super illos, et accipiebant spiritum sanctum*; et Matth. XIX dicitur quod *oblati sunt domino parvuli ut eis manus imponeret.* Ergo in hoc sacramento est manus impositio facienda.

PRAETEREA, verba sacerdotis in hoc sacramento non sunt maioris efficaciae quam in aliis sacramentis. Sed in aliis sacramentis non sufficiunt verba ministri, nisi aliquem actum exerceret, sicut in Baptismo, simul cum hoc quod dicit sacerdos, ego te baptizo, requiritur corporalis ablutio. Ergo etiam, simul cum hoc quod dicit sacerdos, ego te absolvo, oportet quod aliquem actum exerceat circa poenitentem, imponendo ei manus.

OBJECTION 1: It would seem that the imposition of the priest's hands is necessary for this sacrament. For it is written (Mark 16:18): *They shall lay hands upon the sick, and they shall recover.* Now sinners are sick spiritually, and obtain recovery through this sacrament. Therefore an imposition of hands should be made in this sacrament.

OBJ. 2: Further, in this sacrament man regains the Holy Spirit Whom he had lost, wherefore it is said in the person of the penitent (Ps 1:14): *Restore unto me the joy of Thy salvation, and strengthen me with a perfect spirit.* Now the Holy Spirit is given by the imposition of hands; for we read (Acts 8:17) that the apostles *laid their hands upon them, and they received the Holy Spirit*; and (Matt 19:13) that *little children were presented* to our Lord, *that He should impose hands upon them.* Therefore an imposition of hands should be made in this sacrament.

OBJ. 3: Further, the priest's words are not more efficacious in this than in the other sacraments. But in the other sacraments the words of the minister do not suffice, unless he perform some action: thus, in Baptism, the priest while saying: *I baptize thee,* has to perform a bodily washing. Therefore, also while saying: *I absolve thee,* the priest should perform some action in regard to the penitent, by laying hands on him.

SED CONTRA est quod dominus dixit Petro, *quodcumque solveris super terram, erit* etc., nullam mentionem de manus impositione faciens. Neque etiam cum omnibus apostolis simul dixit, *quorum remiseritis peccata, remittuntur eis*. Non ergo ad hoc sacramentum requiritur impositio manuum.

RESPONDEO dicendum quod impositio manuum in sacramentis Ecclesiae fit ad designandum aliquem copiosum effectum gratiae, quo illi quibus manus imponitur, quodammodo continuantur per quandam similitudinem ministris, in quibus copia esse debet. Et ideo manus impositio fit in sacramento confirmationis, in quo confertur plenitudo spiritus sancti; et in sacramento ordinis, in quo confertur quaedam excellentia potestatis in divinis ministeriis; unde et II Tim. I dicitur, *resuscites gratiam Dei quae est in te per impositionem manuum mearum*.

Sacramentum autem poenitentiae non ordinatur ad consequendum aliquam excellentiam gratiae, sed ad remissionem peccatorum. Et ideo ad hoc sacramentum non requiritur impositio, sicut etiam nec ad Baptismum, in quo tamen fit plenior remissio peccatorum.

AD PRIMUM ergo dicendum quod illa manus impositio non est sacramentalis, sed ordinatur ad miracula facienda, ut scilicet per contactum manus hominis sanctificati etiam corporalis infirmitas tollatur. Sicut etiam legitur de domino, Marci VI, quod *infirmos impositis manibus curavit*; et Matth. VIII legitur quod per contactum leprosum mundavit.

AD SECUNDUM dicendum quod non quaelibet acceptio spiritus sancti requirit manus impositionem, quia etiam in Baptismo accipit homo spiritum sanctum, nec tamen fit ibi manus impositio. Sed acceptio spiritus sancti cum plenitudine requirit manus impositionem, quod pertinet ad confirmationem.

AD TERTIUM dicendum quod in sacramentis quae perficiuntur in usu materiae, minister habet aliquem corporalem actum exercere circa eum qui suscipit sacramentum, sicut in Baptismo et confirmatione et extrema unctione. Sed hoc sacramentum non consistit in usu alicuius materiae exterius appositae, sed loco materiae se habent ea quae sunt ex parte poenitentis. Unde, sicut in Eucharistia sacerdos sola prolatione verborum super materiam perficit sacramentum, ita etiam sola verba sacerdotis absolventis super poenitentem perficiunt absolutionis sacramentum. Et si aliquis actus corporalis esset ex parte sacerdotis, non minus competeret crucesignatio, quae adhibetur in Eucharistia, quam manus impositio, in signum quod per sanguinem crucis Christi remittuntur peccata. Et tamen non est de necessitate sacramenti, sicut nec de necessitate Eucharistiae.

ON THE CONTRARY, When our Lord said to Peter (Matt 16:19): *Whatsoever thou shalt loose on earth*, etc., He made no mention of an imposition of hands; nor did He when He said to all the apostles (John 20:13): *Whose sins you shall forgive, they are forgiven them*. Therefore no imposition of hands is required for this sacrament.

I ANSWER THAT, In the sacraments of the Church the imposition of hands is made, to signify some abundant effect of grace, through those on whom the hands are laid being, as it were, united to the ministers in whom grace should be plentiful. Wherefore an imposition of hands is made in the sacrament of Confirmation, wherein the fullness of the Holy Spirit is conferred; and in the sacrament of order, wherein is bestowed a certain excellence of power over the Divine mysteries; hence it is written (2 Tim 1:6): *Stir up the grace of God which is in thee, by the imposition of my hands*.

Now the sacrament of Penance is ordained, not that man may receive some abundance of grace, but that his sins may be taken away; and therefore no imposition of hands is required for this sacrament, as neither is there for Baptism, wherein nevertheless a fuller remission of sins is bestowed.

REPLY OBJ. 1: That imposition of hands is not sacramental, but is intended for the working of miracles, namely, that by the contact of a sanctified man's hand, even bodily infirmity might be removed; even as we read of our Lord (Mark 6:5) that He cured the sick, *laying His hands upon them*, and (Matt 8:3) that He cleansed a leper by touching him.

REPLY OBJ. 2: It is not every reception of the Holy Spirit that requires an imposition of hands, since even in Baptism man receives the Holy Spirit, without any imposition of hands: it is at the reception of the fullness of the Holy Spirit which belongs to Confirmation that an imposition of hands is required.

REPLY OBJ. 3: In those sacraments which are perfected in the use of the matter, the minister has to perform some bodily action on the recipient of the sacrament, e.g., in Baptism, Confirmation, and Extreme Unction; whereas this sacrament does not consist in the use of matter employed outwardly, the matter being supplied by the part taken by the penitent: wherefore, just as in the Eucharist the priest perfects the sacrament by merely pronouncing the words over the matter, so the mere words which the priest while absolving pronounces over the penitent perfect the sacrament of absolution. If, indeed, any bodily act were necessary on the part of the priest, the sign of the cross, which is employed in the Eucharist, would not be less becoming than the imposition of hands, in token that sins are forgiven through the blood of Christ crucified; and yet this is not essential to this sacrament as neither is it to the Eucharist.

Article 5

Whether This Sacrament Is Necessary for Salvation?

Ad quintum sic proceditur. Videtur quod hoc sacramentum non sit de necessitate salutis. Quia super illud Psalmi, *qui seminant in lacrimis* etc., dicit Glossa, *noli esse tristis, si adsit tibi bona voluntas, unde metitur pax.* Sed tristitia est de ratione poenitentiae, secundum illud II Cor. VII, *quae secundum Deum est tristitia, poenitentiam in salutem stabilem operatur.* Ergo bona voluntas, sine poenitentia, sufficit ad salutem.

Praeterea, Proverb. X dicitur, *universa delicta operit caritas*; et infra, XV, *per misericordiam et fidem purgantur peccata.* Sed hoc sacramentum non est nisi ad purgandum peccata. Ergo, habendo caritatem et fidem et misericordiam, potest quisque salutem consequi, etiam sine poenitentiae sacramento.

Praeterea, sacramenta Ecclesiae initium habent ab institutione Christi. Sed, sicut legitur Ioan. VIII, Christus mulierem adulteram absolvit absque poenitentia. Ergo videtur quod poenitentia non sit de necessitate salutis.

Sed contra est quod dominus dicit, Luc. XIII, *si poenitentiam non egeritis, omnes simul peribitis.*

Respondeo dicendum quod aliquid est necessarium ad salutem dupliciter, uno modo, absolute; alio modo, ex suppositione. Absolute quidem necessarium est illud sine quo nullus salutem consequi potest, sicut gratia Christi, et sacramentum Baptismi, per quod aliquis in Christo renascitur. Ex suppositione autem est necessarium sacramentum poenitentiae, quod quidem necessarium non est omnibus, sed peccato subiacentibus; dicitur enim in II Paralip. ult., *et tu, domine iustorum, non posuisti poenitentiam iustis, Abraham, Isaac et Iacob, his qui tibi non peccaverunt. Peccatum autem, cum consummatum fuerit, generat mortem,* ut dicitur Iac. I. Et ideo necessarium est ad salutem peccatoris quod peccatum removeatur ab eo. Quod quidem fieri non potest sine poenitentiae sacramento, in quo operatur virtus passionis Christi per absolutionem sacerdotis simul cum opere poenitentis, qui cooperatur gratiae ad destructionem peccati, sicut enim dicit Augustinus, super Ioan., *qui creavit te sine te, non iustificabit te sine te.* Unde patet quod sacramentum poenitentiae est necessarium ad salutem post peccatum, sicut medicatio corporalis postquam homo in morbum periculosum inciderit.

Ad primum ergo dicendum quod Glossa illa videtur intelligenda de eo cui adest bona voluntas sine interpolatione quae fit per peccatum, tales autem non habent tristitiae causam. Sed ex quo bona voluntas tollitur per peccatum, non potest restitui sine tristitia, qua quis dolet de peccato praeterito, quod pertinet ad poenitentiam.

Objection 1: It would seem that this sacrament is not necessary for salvation. Because on Ps. 125:5, *They that sow in tears*, etc., the gloss says: *Be not sorrowful, if thou hast a good will, of which peace is the meed.* But sorrow is essential to Penance, according to 2 Cor. 7:10: *The sorrow that is according to God worketh penance steadfast unto salvation.* Therefore a good will without Penance suffices for salvation.

Obj. 2: Further, it is written (Prov 10:12): *Charity covereth all sins*, and further on (Prov 15:27): *By mercy and faith sins are purged away.* But this sacrament is for nothing else but the purging of sins. Therefore if one has charity, faith, and mercy, one can obtain salvation, without the sacrament of Penance.

Obj. 3: Further, the sacraments of the Church take their origin from the institution of Christ. But according to John 8 Christ absolved the adulterous woman without Penance. Therefore it seems that Penance is not necessary for salvation.

On the contrary, our Lord said (Luke 13:3): *Unless you shall do penance, you shall all likewise perish.*

I answer that, A thing is necessary for salvation in two ways: first, absolutely; second, on a supposition. A thing is absolutely necessary for salvation, if no one can obtain salvation without it, as, for example, the grace of Christ, and the sacrament of Baptism, whereby a man is born again in Christ. The sacrament of Penance is necessary on a supposition, for it is necessary, not for all, but for those who are in sin. For it is written (2 Chr 37), *Thou, Lord, God of the righteous, hast not appointed repentance to the righteous, to Abraham, Isaac and Jacob, nor to those who sinned not against Thee.* But *sin, when it is completed, begetteth death* (Jas 1:15). Consequently it is necessary for the sinner's salvation that sin be taken away from him; which cannot be done without the sacrament of Penance, wherein the power of Christ's Passion operates through the priest's absolution and the acts of the penitent, who co-operates with grace unto the destruction of his sin. For as Augustine says (*Tract. lxxii in Joan.*), *He Who created thee without thee, will not justify thee without thee.* Therefore it is evident that after sin the sacrament of Penance is necessary for salvation, even as bodily medicine after man has contracted a dangerous disease.

Reply Obj. 1: This gloss should apparently be understood as referring to the man who has a good will unimpaired by sin, for such a man has no cause for sorrow: but as soon as the good will is forfeited through sin, it cannot be restored without that sorrow whereby a man sorrows for his past sin, and which belongs to Penance.

AD SECUNDUM dicendum quod ex quo aliquis peccatum incurrit, caritas et fides et misericordia non liberant hominem a peccato sine poenitentia. Requirit enim caritas quod homo doleat de offensa in amicum commissa, et quod amico homo reconciliari studeat. Requirit etiam ipsa fides ut per virtutem passionis Christi, quae in sacramentis Ecclesiae operatur, quaerat iustificari a peccatis. Requirit etiam ipsa misericordia ordinata ut homo subveniat poenitendo suae miseriae, quam per peccatum incurrit, secundum illud Proverb. XIV, *miseros facit populos peccatum*, unde et Eccli. XXX dicitur, *miserere animae tuae placens Deo.*

AD TERTIUM dicendum quod ad potestatem excellentiae, quam solus Christus habuit, ut supra dictum est, pertinuit quod Christus effectum sacramenti poenitentiae, qui est remissio peccatorum, contulit mulieri adulterae sine poenitentiae sacramento, licet non sine interiori poenitentia, quam ipse in ea per gratiam est operatus.

REPLY OBJ. 2: As soon as a man falls into sin, charity, faith, and mercy do not deliver him from sin, without Penance. Because charity demands that a man should grieve for the offense committed against his friend, and that he should be anxious to make satisfaction to his friend; faith requires that he should seek to be justified from his sins through the power of Christ's Passion which operates in the sacraments of the Church; and well-ordered pity necessitates that man should succor himself by repenting of the pitiful condition into which sin has brought him, according to Prov. 14:34: *Sin maketh nations miserable*; wherefore it is written (Sir 30:24): *Have pity on thy own soul, pleasing God.*

REPLY OBJ. 3: It was due to His power of excellence, which He alone had, as stated above (Q. 64, A. 3), that Christ bestowed on the adulterous woman the effect of the sacrament of Penance, viz. the forgiveness of sins, without the sacrament of Penance, although not without internal repentance, which He operated in her by grace.

Article 6

Whether Penance Is a Second Plank After Shipwreck?

AD SEXTUM SIC PROCEDITUR. Videtur quod poenitentia non sit secunda tabula post naufragium. Quia super illud Isaiae III, *peccatum suum sicut Sodoma praedicaverunt*, dicit Glossa, *secunda tabula post naufragium est peccata abscondere*. Poenitentia autem non abscondit peccata, sed magis ea revelat. Ergo poenitentia non est secunda tabula.

PRAETEREA, fundamentum in aedificio non tenet secundum, sed primum locum. Poenitentia autem in spirituali aedificio est fundamentum, secundum illud Heb. VI, *non rursum iacientes fundamentum poenitentiae ab operibus mortuis*. Unde et praecedit ipsum Baptismum, secundum illud Act. II, *poenitentiam agite, et baptizetur unusquisque vestrum*. Ergo poenitentia non debet dici secunda tabula.

PRAETEREA, omnia sacramenta sunt quaedam tabulae, idest remedia contra peccatum. Sed poenitentia non tenet secundum locum inter sacramenta, sed magis quartum, ut ex supra dictis patet. Ergo poenitentia non debet dici secunda tabula post naufragium.

SED CONTRA est quod Hieronymus dicit quod *secunda tabula post naufragium est poenitentia.*

RESPONDEO dicendum quod id quod est per se, naturaliter prius est eo quod est per accidens, sicut et substantia prior est accidente. Sacramenta autem quaedam per se ordinantur ad salutem hominis, sicut Baptismus, qui est spiritualis generatio, et confirmatio, quae est spirituale augmentum, et Eucharistia, quae est spirituale

OBJECTION 1: It would seem that Penance is not a second plank after shipwreck. Because on Isa. 3:9, *They have proclaimed abroad their sin as Sodom*, a gloss says: *The second plank after shipwreck is to hide one's sins*. Now Penance does not hide sins, but reveals them. Therefore Penance is not a second plank.

OBJ. 2: Further, in a building the foundation takes the first, not the second place. Now in the spiritual edifice, Penance is the foundation, according to Heb. 6:1: *Not laying again the foundation of Penance from dead works*; wherefore it precedes even Baptism, according to Acts 2:38: *Do penance, and be baptized every one of you*. Therefore Penance should not be called a second plank.

OBJ. 3: Further, all the sacraments are planks, i.e., helps against sin. Now Penance holds, not the second but the fourth, place among the sacraments, as is clear from what has been said above (Q. 65, AA. 1, 2). Therefore Penance should not be called a second plank after shipwreck.

ON THE CONTRARY, Jerome says (*Ep. cxxx*) that *Penance is a second plank after shipwreck.*

I ANSWER THAT, That which is of itself precedes naturally that which is accidental, as substance precedes accident. Now some sacraments are, of themselves, ordained to man's salvation, e.g., Baptism, which is the spiritual birth, Confirmation which is the spiritual growth, the Eucharist which is the spiritual food; whereas Penance is ordained to

nutrimentum. Poenitentia autem ordinatur ad salutem hominis quasi per accidens, supposito quodam, scilicet ex suppositione peccati. Nisi enim homo peccaret actualiter, poenitentia non indigeret, indigeret tamen Baptismo et confirmatione et Eucharistia, sicut et in vita corporali non indigeret homo medicatione nisi infirmaretur, indiget autem homo per se ad vitam generatione, augmento et nutrimento.

Et ideo poenitentia tenet secundum locum respectu status integritatis, qui confertur et conservatur per sacramenta praedicta. Unde metaphorice dicitur secunda tabula post naufragium. Nam primum remedium mare transeuntibus est ut conserventur in navi integra, secundum autem remedium est, post navim fractam, ut aliquis tabulae adhaereat. Ita etiam primum remedium in mari huius vitae est quod homo integritatem servet, secundum autem remedium est, si per peccatum integritatem perdiderit, quod per poenitentiam redeat.

AD PRIMUM ergo dicendum quod abscondere peccata contingit dupliciter. Uno modo, dum ipsa peccata fiunt. Est autem peius peccare publice quam occulte, tum quia peccator publicus videtur ex contemptu maiori peccare; tum etiam quia peccat cum scandalo aliorum. Et ideo est quoddam remedium in peccatis quod aliquis in occulto peccet. Et secundum hoc dicit Glossa quod *secunda tabula post naufragium est peccata abscondere*, non quod per hoc tollatur peccatum, sicut per poenitentiam; sed quia per hoc peccatum fit minus. Alio modo, aliquis abscondit peccatum prius factum per negligentiam confessionis. Et hoc contrariatur poenitentiae. Et sic abscondere peccatum non est secunda tabula, sed magis contrarium tabulae, dicitur enim Proverb. XXVIII, *qui abscondit scelera sua, non dirigetur*.

AD SECUNDUM dicendum quod poenitentia non potest dici fundamentum spiritualis aedificii simpliciter, idest in prima aedificatione, sed est fundamentum in secunda reaedificatione, quae fit post destructionem peccati; nam primo redeuntibus ad Deum occurrit poenitentia. Apostolus tamen ibi loquitur de fundamento spiritualis doctrinae. Poenitentia autem quae Baptismum praecedit, non est poenitentiae sacramentum.

AD TERTIUM dicendum quod tria praecedentia sacramenta pertinent ad navem integram, idest ad statum integritatis, respectu cuius poenitentia dicitur secunda tabula.

man's salvation accidentally as it were, and on something being supposed, viz. sin: for unless man were to sin actually, he would not stand in need of Penance and yet he would need Baptism, Confirmation, and the Eucharist; even as in the life of the body, man would need no medical treatment, unless he were ill, and yet life, birth, growth, and food are, of themselves, necessary to man.

Consequently Penance holds the second place with regard to the state of integrity which is bestowed and safeguarded by the aforesaid sacraments, so that it is called metaphorically *a second plank after shipwreck*. For just as the first help for those who cross the sea is to be safeguarded in a whole ship, while the second help when the ship is wrecked, is to cling to a plank; so too the first help in this life's ocean is that man safeguard his integrity, while the second help is, if he lose his integrity through sin, that he regain it by means of Penance.

REPLY OBJ. 1: To hide one's sins may happen in two ways: first, in the very act of sinning. Now it is worse to sin in public than in private, both because a public sinner seems to sin more from contempt, and because by sinning he gives scandal to others. Consequently in sin it is a kind of remedy to sin secretly, and it is in this sense that the gloss says that *to hide one's sins is a second plank after shipwreck*; not that it takes away sin, as Penance does, but because it makes the sin less grievous. Second, one hides one's sin previously committed, by neglecting to confess it: this is opposed to Penance, and to hide one's sins thus is not a second plank, but is the reverse, since it is written (Prov 28:13): *He that hideth his sins shall not prosper*.

REPLY OBJ. 2: Penance cannot be called the foundation of the spiritual edifice simply, i.e., in the first building thereof; but it is the foundation in the second building which is accomplished by destroying sin, because man, on his return to God, needs Penance first. However, the Apostle is speaking there of the foundation of spiritual doctrine. Moreover, the penance which precedes Baptism is not the sacrament of Penance.

REPLY OBJ. 3: The three sacraments which precede Penance refer to the ship in its integrity, i.e., to man's state of integrity, with regard to which Penance is called a second plank.

Article 7

Whether This Sacrament Was Suitably Instituted in the New Law?

AD SEPTIMUM SIC PROCEDITUR. Videtur quod hoc sacramentum non fuerit convenienter institutum in nova lege. Ea enim quae sunt de iure naturali, institutione non indigent. Sed poenitere de malis quae quis gessit, est de iure naturali, non enim potest aliquis bonum diligere quin de contrario doleat. Ergo non est poenitentia convenienter instituta in nova lege.

PRAETEREA, illud quod fuit in veteri lege, instituendum non fuit. Sed etiam in veteri lege fuit poenitentia, unde et dominus conqueritur, Ierem. VIII, dicens, *nullus est qui agat poenitentiam super peccato suo, dicens, quid feci?* Ergo poenitentia non debuit institui in nova lege.

PRAETEREA, poenitentia consequenter se habet ad Baptismum, cum sit secunda tabula, ut supra dictum est. Sed poenitentia videtur a domino instituta ante Baptismum, nam in principio praedicationis suae legitur dominus dixisse, Matth. IV, *poenitentiam agite, appropinquabit enim regnum caelorum.* Ergo hoc sacramentum non fuit convenienter institutum in nova lege.

PRAETEREA, sacramenta novae legis institutionem habent a Christo, ex cuius virtute operantur, ut supra dictum est. Sed Christus non videtur instituisse hoc sacramentum, cum ipse non sit usus eo, sicut aliis sacramentis quae ipse instituit. Ergo hoc sacramentum non fuit convenienter institutum in nova lege.

SED CONTRA est quod dominus dicit, Luc. ult., *oportebat Christum pati, et resurgere a mortuis die tertia, et praedicari in nomine eius poenitentiam et remissionem peccatorum in omnes gentes.*

RESPONDEO dicendum quod, sicut dictum est, in hoc sacramento actus poenitentis se habet sicut materia; id autem quod est ex parte sacerdotis, qui operatur ut minister Christi, se habet ut formale et completivum sacramenti. Materia vero, etiam in aliis sacramentis, praeexistit a natura, ut aqua, vel ab aliqua arte, ut panis, sed quod talis materia ad sacramentum assumatur, indiget institutione hoc determinante. Sed forma sacramenti, et virtus ipsius, totaliter est ex institutione Christi, ex cuius passione procedit virtus sacramentorum.

Sic igitur materia praeexistit a natura, ex naturali enim ratione homo movetur ad poenitendum de malis quae fecit, sed quod hoc vel illo modo homo poenitentiam agat, est ex institutione divina. Unde et dominus, in principio praedicationis suae, indixit hominibus ut non solum poeniterent, sed etiam poenitentiam agerent, significans determinatos modos actuum qui requiruntur ad hoc sacramentum. Sed id quod pertinet ad officium ministrorum, determinavit Matth. XVI, ubi dixit

OBJECTION 1: It would seem that this sacrament was unsuitably instituted in the New Law. Because those things which belong to the natural law need not to be instituted. Now it belongs to the natural law that one should repent of the evil one has done: for it is impossible to love good without grieving for its contrary. Therefore Penance was unsuitably instituted in the New Law.

OBJ. 2: Further, that which existed in the Old Law had not to be instituted in the New. Now there was Penance in the old Law wherefore the Lord complains (Jer 8:6) saying: *There is none that doth penance for his sin, saying: What have I done?* Therefore Penance should not have been instituted in the New Law.

OBJ. 3: Further, Penance comes after Baptism, since it is a second plank, as stated above (A. 6). Now it seems that our Lord instituted Penance before Baptism, because we read that at the beginning of His preaching He said (Matt 4:17): *Do penance, for the kingdom of heaven is at hand.* Therefore this sacrament was not suitably instituted in the New Law.

OBJ. 4: Further, the sacraments of the New Law were instituted by Christ, by Whose power they work, as stated above (Q. 62, A. 5; Q. 64, A. 1). But Christ does not seem to have instituted this sacrament, since He made no use of it, as of the other sacraments which He instituted. Therefore this sacrament was unsuitably instituted in the New Law.

ON THE CONTRARY, our Lord said (Luke 24:46, 47): *It behooved Christ to suffer, and to rise again from the dead the third day: and that penance and remission of sins should be preached in His name unto all nations.*

I ANSWER THAT, As stated above (A. 1, ad 1, ad 2), in this sacrament the acts of the penitent are as matter, while the part taken by the priest, who works as Christ's minister, is the formal and completive element of the sacrament. Now in the other sacraments the matter pre-exists, being provided by nature, as water, or by art, as bread: but that such and such a matter be employed for a sacrament requires to be decided by the institution; while the sacrament derives its form and power entirely from the institution of Christ, from Whose Passion the power of the sacraments proceeds.

Accordingly the matter of this sacrament pre-exists, being provided by nature; since it is by a natural principle of reason that man is moved to repent of the evil he has done: yet it is due to Divine institution that man does penance in this or that way. Wherefore at the outset of His preaching, our Lord admonished men, not only to repent, but also to *do penance*, thus pointing to the particular manner of actions required for this sacrament. As to the part to be taken by the ministers, this was fixed by our Lord when He

Petro, *tibi dabo claves regni caelorum*, et cetera. Efficaciam autem huius sacramenti, et originem virtutis eius, manifestavit post resurrectionem, Luc. ult., ubi dixit quod *oportebat praedicari in nomine eius poenitentiam et remissionem peccatorum in omnes gentes*, praemisso de passione et resurrectione, virtute enim nominis Iesu Christi patientis et resurgentis hoc sacramentum efficaciam habet ad remissionem peccatorum.

Et sic patet convenienter hoc sacramentum in nova lege fuisse institutum.

AD PRIMUM ergo dicendum quod de iure naturali est quod aliquis poeniteat de malis quae fecit, quantum ad hoc quod doleat se fecisse, et doloris remedium quaerat per aliquem modum, et quod etiam aliqua signa doloris ostendat, sicut Ninivitae fecerunt, ut legitur Ionae III. In quibus tamen aliquid fuit adiunctum fidei quam ceperant ex praedicatione Ionae, ut scilicet hoc agerent sub spe veniae consequendae a Deo, secundum illud quod legitur ibi, *quis scit si convertatur et ignoscat Deus, et revertatur a furore irae suae, et non peribimus?* Sed, sicut alia quae sunt de iure naturali determinationem acceperunt ex institutione legis divinae, ut in secunda parte dictum est, ita etiam et poenitentia.

AD SECUNDUM dicendum quod ea quae sunt iuris naturalis diversimode determinationem accipiunt in veteri et nova lege, secundum quod congruit imperfectioni veteris legis et perfectioni novae. Unde et poenitentia in veteri lege aliquam determinationem habuit. Quantum quidem ad dolorem, ut esset magis in corde quam in exterioribus signis, secundum illud Ioel II, *scindite corda vestra, et non vestimenta vestra.* Quantum autem ad remedium doloris quaerendum, ut aliquo modo ministris Dei peccata sua confiterentur, ad minus in generali, unde dominus, Levit. V, dicit, *anima quae peccaverit per ignorantiam, offeret arietem immaculatum de gregibus sacerdoti, iuxta mensuram aestimationemque peccati, qui orabit pro eo quod nesciens fecerit, et dimittetur ei*; in hoc enim ipso quod oblationem faciebat aliquis pro peccato suo, quodammodo peccatum suum sacerdoti confitebatur; et secundum hoc dicitur Proverb. XXVIII, *qui abscondit scelera sua, non dirigetur, qui autem confessus fuerit et reliquerit ea, misericordiam consequetur.* Nondum autem instituta erat potestas clavium, quae a passione Christi derivatur. Et per consequens nondum erat institutum quod aliquis doleret de peccato cum proposito subiiciendi se per confessionem et satisfactionem clavibus Ecclesiae, sub spe consequendae veniae virtute passionis Christi.

AD TERTIUM dicendum quod, si quis recte consideret ea quae dominus dixit de necessitate Baptismi, Ioan. III, tempore praecesserunt ea quae dixit, Matth. IV, de

said to Peter (Matt 16:19): *To thee will I give the keys of the kingdom of heaven*, etc.; but it was after His resurrection that He made known the efficacy of this sacrament and the source of its power, when He said (Luke 24:47) that *penance and remission of sins should be preached in His name unto all nations*, after speaking of His Passion and resurrection. Because it is from the power of the name of Jesus Christ suffering and rising again that this sacrament is efficacious unto the remission of sins.

It is therefore evident that this sacrament was suitably instituted in the New Law.

REPLY OBJ. 1: It is a natural law that one should repent of the evil one has done, by grieving for having done it, and by seeking a remedy for one's grief in some way or other, and also that one should show some signs of grief, even as the Ninevites did, as we read in John 3. And yet even in their case there was also something of faith which they had received through Jonas' preaching, inasmuch as they did these things in the hope that they would receive pardon from God, according as we read (John 3:9): *Who can tell if God will turn and forgive, and will turn away from His fierce anger, and we shall not perish?* But just as other matters which are of the natural law were fixed in detail by the institution of the Divine law, as we have stated in the Second Part (I-II, Q. 91, A. 4; I-II, Q. 95, A. 2; Q. 99), so was it with Penance.

REPLY OBJ. 2: Things which are of the natural law were determined in various ways in the Old and in the New Law, in keeping with the imperfection of the Old, and the perfection of the New. Wherefore Penance was fixed in a certain way in the Old Law—with regard to sorrow, that it should be in the heart rather than in external signs, according to Joel 2:13: *Rend your hearts and not your garments*; and with regard to seeking a remedy for sorrow, that they should in some way confess their sins, at least in general, to God's ministers. Wherefore the Lord said (Lev 5:17, 18): *If anyone sin through ignorance . . . he shall offer of the flocks a ram without blemish to the priest, according to the measure and estimation of the sin, and the priest shall pray for him, because he did it ignorantly, and it shall be forgiven him*; since by the very fact of making an offering for his sin, a man, in a fashion, confessed his sin to the priest. And accordingly it is written (Prov 28:13): *He that hideth his sins, shall not prosper: but he that shall confess, and forsake them, shall obtain mercy.* Not yet, however, was the power of the keys instituted, which is derived from Christ's Passion, and consequently it was not yet ordained that a man should grieve for his sin, with the purpose of submitting himself by confession and satisfaction to the keys of the Church, in the hope of receiving forgiveness through the power of Christ's Passion.

REPLY OBJ. 3: If we note carefully what our Lord said about the necessity of Baptism (John 3:3, seqq.), we shall see that this was said before His words about the necessity

necessitate poenitentiae. Nam id quod dixit Nicodemo de Baptismo, fuit ante incarcerationem Ioannis, de quo postea subditur quod baptizabat, illud vero quod de poenitentia dixit, Matth. IV, fuit post incarcerationem Ioannis.

Si tamen prius ad poenitentiam induxisset quam ad Baptismum, hoc ideo esset quia ante Baptismum etiam requiritur quaedam poenitentia, sicut et Petrus dixit, Act. II, *poenitentiam agite, et baptizetur unusquisque vestrum.*

Ad quartum dicendum quod Christus non est usus Baptismo quem ipse instituit, sed est baptizatus Baptismo Ioannis, ut supra dictum est. Sed nec active usus est suo ministerio, quia ipse non baptizabat communiter, sed discipuli eius, ut dicitur Ioan. IV; quamvis credendum videtur quod discipulos baptizaverit, ut Augustinus dicit, ad Seleucianum. Usus autem huius sacramenti, ab eo instituti, nullo modo competebat, neque quantum ad hoc quod ipse poeniteret, in quo peccatum non fuit; neque quantum ad hoc quod hoc sacramentum aliis praeberet, quia, ad ostendendum misericordiam et virtutem suam, effectum huius sacramenti sine sacramento praebebat, ut supra dictum est. Sacramentum autem Eucharistiae et ipse sumpsit, et aliis dedit. Tum ad commendandam excellentiam huius sacramenti. Tum quia hoc sacramentum est memoriale suae passionis, inquantum Christus est sacerdos et hostia.

of Penance (Matt 4:17); because He spoke to Nicodemus about Baptism before the imprisonment of John, of whom it is related afterwards (John 3:23, 24) that he baptized, whereas His words about Penance were said after John was cast into prison.

If, however, He had admonished men to do penance before admonishing them to be baptized, this would be because also before Baptism some kind of penance is required, according to the words of Peter (Acts 2:38): *Do penance, and be baptized, every one of you.*

Reply Obj. 4: Christ did not use the Baptism which He instituted, but was baptized with the baptism of John, as stated above (Q. 39, AA. 1, 2). Nor did He use it actively by administering it Himself, because He *did not baptize* as a rule, *but His disciples* did, as related in John 4:2, although it is to be believed that He baptized His disciples, as Augustine asserts (*Ep. cclxv, ad Seleuc.*). But with regard to His institution of this sacrament it was nowise fitting that He should use it, neither by repenting Himself, in Whom there was no sin, nor by administering the sacrament to others, since, in order to show His mercy and power, He was wont to confer the effect of this sacrament without the sacrament itself, as stated above (A. 5, ad 3). On the other hand, He both received and gave to others the sacrament of the Eucharist, both in order to commend the excellence of that sacrament, and because that sacrament is a memorial of His Passion, in which Christ is both priest and victim.

Article 8

Whether Penance Should Last Till the End of Life?

Ad octavum sic proceditur. Videtur quod poenitentia non debeat durare usque ad finem vitae. Poenitentia enim ordinatur ad deletionem peccati. Sed poenitens statim consequitur remissionem peccatorum, secundum illud Ezech. XVIII, *si poenitentiam egerit impius ab omnibus peccatis suis quae operatus est, vita vivet et non morietur.* Ergo non oportet ulterius poenitentiam protendi.

Praeterea, agere poenitentiam pertinet ad statum incipientium. Sed homo de hoc statu debet procedere ad statum proficientium, et ulterius ad statum perfectorum. Ergo non debet homo poenitentiam agere usque ad finem vitae.

Praeterea, sicut in aliis sacramentis homo debet conservare statuta Ecclesiae, ita et in hoc sacramento. Sed secundum canones determinata sunt tempora poenitendi, ut scilicet ille qui hoc vel illud peccatum commiserit, tot annis poeniteat. Ergo videtur quod non sit poenitentia extendenda usque ad finem vitae.

Objection 1: It would seem that Penance should not last till the end of life. Because Penance is ordained for the blotting out of sin. Now the penitent receives forgiveness of his sins at once, according to Ezech. 18:21: *If the wicked do penance for all his sins which he hath committed . . . he shall live and shall not die.* Therefore there is no need for Penance to be further prolonged.

Obj. 2: Further, Penance belongs to the state of beginners. But man ought to advance from that state to the state of the proficient, and, from this, on to the state of the perfect. Therefore man need not do Penance till the end of his life.

Obj. 3: Further, man is bound to observe the laws of the Church in this as in the other sacraments. But the duration of repentance is fixed by the canons, so that, to wit, for such and such a sin one is bound to do penance for so many years. Therefore it seems that Penance should not be prolonged till the end of life.

SED CONTRA est quod dicit Augustinus, in libro de poenitentia, *quid restat nobis nisi dolere in vita? Ubi enim dolor finitur, deficit poenitentia. Si vero poenitentia finitur, quid derelinquitur de venia?*

RESPONDEO dicendum quod duplex est poenitentia, scilicet interior, et exterior. Interior quidem poenitentia est qua quis dolet de peccato commisso. Et talis poenitentia debet durare usque ad finem vitae. Semper enim debet homini displicere quod peccavit, si enim ei placeret peccasse, iam ex hoc ipso peccatum incurreret, et fructus veniae perderet. Displicentia autem dolorem causat in eo qui est susceptivus doloris, qualis est homo in hac vita. Post hanc vitam autem sancti non sunt susceptivi doloris. Unde displicebunt eis peccata praeterita sine omni tristitia, secundum illud Isaiae LXV, *oblivioni traditae sunt angustiae priores.*

Poenitentia vero exterior est qua quis exteriora signa doloris ostendit, et verbotenus confitetur peccata sua sacerdoti absolventi, et iuxta eius arbitrium satisfacit. Et talis poenitentia non oportet quod duret usque ad finem vitae, sed usque ad determinatum tempus, secundum mensuram peccati.

AD PRIMUM ergo dicendum quod vera poenitentia non solum removet peccata praeterita, sed etiam praeservat eum a peccatis futuris. Quamvis igitur homo in primo instanti verae poenitentiae remissionem consequatur praeteritorum peccatorum, oportet tamen in homine perseverare poenitentiam, ne iterum incidat in peccatum.

AD SECUNDUM dicendum quod agere poenitentiam interiorem simul et exteriorem pertinet ad statum incipientium, qui scilicet de novo redeunt a peccato. Sed poenitentia interior habet locum etiam in proficientibus et perfectis, secundum illud Psalmi, *ascensiones in corde suo disposuit in valle lacrimarum.* Unde et ipse Paulus dicebat, I Cor. XV, *non sum dignus vocari apostolus, quoniam persecutus sum Ecclesiam Dei.*

AD TERTIUM dicendum quod illa tempora praefiguntur poenitentibus quantum ad actionem exterioris poenitentiae.

ON THE CONTRARY, Augustine says in his book, *De Poenitentia: What remains for us to do, save to sorrow ever in this life? For when sorrow ceases, repentance fails; and if repentance fails, what becomes of pardon?*

I ANSWER THAT, Penance is twofold, internal and external. Internal penance is that whereby one grieves for a sin one has committed, and this penance should last until the end of life. Because man should always be displeased at having sinned, for if he were to be pleased thereat, he would for this very reason fall into sin and lose the fruit of pardon. Now displeasure causes sorrow in one who is susceptible to sorrow, as man is in this life; but after this life the saints are not susceptible to sorrow, wherefore they will be displeased at, without sorrowing for, their past sins, according to Isa. 65:16. *The former distresses are forgotten.*

External penance is that whereby a man shows external signs of sorrow, confesses his sins verbally to the priest who absolves him, and makes satisfaction for his sins according to the judgment of the priest. Such penance need not last until the end of life, but only for a fixed time according to the measure of the sin.

REPLY OBJ. 1: True penance not only removes past sins, but also preserves man from future sins. Consequently, although a man receives forgiveness of past sins in the first instant of his true penance, nevertheless he must persevere in his penance, lest he fall again into sin.

REPLY OBJ. 2: To do penance both internal and external belongs to the state of beginners, of those, to wit, who are making a fresh start from the state of sin. But there is room for internal penance even in the proficient and the perfect, according to Ps. 83:7: *In his heart he hath disposed to ascend by steps, in the vale of tears.* Wherefore Paul says (1 Cor 15:9): *I . . . am not worthy to be called an apostle because I persecuted the Church of God.*

REPLY OBJ. 3: These durations of time are fixed for penitents as regards the exercise of external penance.

Article 9

Whether Penance Can Be Continuous?

AD NONUM SIC PROCEDITUR. Videtur quod poenitentia non possit esse continua. Dicitur enim Ierem. XXXI, *quiescat vox tua a ploratu, et oculi tui a lacrimis.* Sed hoc esse non posset si poenitentia continuaretur, quae consistit in ploratu et lacrimis. Ergo poenitentia non potest continuari.

OBJECTION 1: It would seem that penance cannot be continuous. For it is written (Jer 31:16): *Let thy voice cease from weeping, and thy eyes from tears.* But this would be impossible if penance were continuous, for it consists in weeping and tears. Therefore penance cannot be continuous.

PRAETEREA, de quolibet bono opere debet homo gaudere, secundum illud Psalmi, *servite domino in laetitia.* Sed agere poenitentiam est bonum opus. Ergo de hoc ipso debet homo gaudere. Sed *non potest homo simul tristari et gaudere,* ut patet per philosophum, IX Ethic. Ergo non potest esse quod poenitens simul tristetur de peccatis praeteritis, quod pertinet ad rationem poenitentiae.

PRAETEREA, II ad Cor. II, apostolus dicit, *consolemini,* scilicet poenitentem, *ne forte abundantiori tristitia absorbeatur qui est huiusmodi.* Sed consolatio depellit tristitiam, quae pertinet ad rationem poenitentiae. Ergo poenitentia non debet esse continua.

SED CONTRA est quod Augustinus dicit, in libro de poenitentia, *dolor in poenitentia continue custodiatur.*

RESPONDEO dicendum quod poenitere dicitur dupliciter, scilicet secundum actum, et secundum habitum. Actu quidem impossibile est quod homo continue poeniteat, quia necesse est quod actus poenitentis, sive interior sive exterior, interpoletur, ad minus somno et aliis quae ad necessitatem corporis pertinent. Alio modo dicitur poenitere secundum habitum. Et sic oportet quod homo continue poeniteat, et quantum ad hoc quod homo nunquam aliquid contrarium faciat poenitentiae, per quod habitualis dispositio poenitentis tollatur; et quantum ad hoc quod debet in proposito gerere quod semper sibi peccata praeterita displiceant.

AD PRIMUM ergo dicendum quod ploratus et lacrimae ad actum exterioris poenitentiae pertinent, qui non solum non debet esse continuus, sed nec etiam oportet quod duret usque ad finem vitae, ut dictum est. Unde et signanter ibi subditur quod est merces operi tuo. Est autem merces operis poenitentis plena remissio peccati et quantum ad culpam et quantum ad poenam, post cuius consecutionem non est necesse quod homo ulterius exteriorem poenitentiam agat. Per hoc tamen non excluditur continuitas poenitentiae qualis dicta est.

AD SECUNDUM dicendum quod de dolore et gaudio dupliciter loqui possumus. Uno modo, secundum quod sunt passiones appetitus sensitivi. Et sic nullo modo possunt esse simul, eo quod sunt omnino contrariae, vel ex parte obiecti, puta cum sunt de eodem; vel saltem ex parte motus cordis, nam gaudium est cum dilatatione cordis, tristitia vero cum constrictione. Et hoc modo loquitur philosophus in IX Ethicorum. Alio modo loqui possumus de gaudio et tristitia secundum quod consistunt in simplici actu voluntatis, cui aliquid placet vel displicet. Et secundum hoc, non possunt habere contrarietatem nisi ex parte obiecti, puta cum sunt de eodem et secundum idem. Et sic non possunt simul esse gaudium et tristitia, quia non potest simul idem secundum idem placere et displicere. Si vero gaudium et tristitia sic accepta non sint de eodem et secundum idem, sed vel de diversis vel de eodem secundum diversa, sic non

OBJ. 2: Further, man ought to rejoice at every good work, according to Ps. 99:1: *Serve ye the Lord with gladness.* Now to do penance is a good work. Therefore man should rejoice at it. But man cannot rejoice and grieve at the same time, as the Philosopher declares (*Ethic.* ix, 4). Therefore a penitent cannot grieve continually for his past sins, which is essential to penance. Therefore penance cannot be continuous.

OBJ. 3: Further, the Apostle says (2 Cor 2:7): *Comfort him,* viz. the penitent, *lest perhaps such an one be swallowed up with overmuch sorrow.* But comfort dispels grief, which is essential to penance. Therefore penance need not be continuous.

ON THE CONTRARY, Augustine says in his book *De Poenitentia: In doing penance grief should be continual.*

I ANSWER THAT, One is said to repent in two ways, actually and habitually. It is impossible for a man continually to repent actually, for the acts, whether internal or external, of a penitent must needs be interrupted by sleep and other things which the body needs. Second, a man is said to repent habitually. And thus he should repent continually, both by never doing anything contrary to penance, so as to destroy the habitual disposition of the penitent, and by being resolved that his past sins should always be displeasing to him.

REPLY OBJ. 1: Weeping and tears belong to the act of external penance, and this act needs neither to be continuous, nor to last until the end of life, as stated above (A. 8): wherefore it is significantly added: *For there is a reward for thy work.* Now the reward of the penitent's work is the full remission of sin both as to guilt and as to punishment; and after receiving this reward there is no need for man to proceed to acts of external penance. This, however, does not prevent penance being continual, as explained above.

REPLY OBJ. 2: Of sorrow and joy we may speak in two ways: first, as being passions of the sensitive appetite; and thus they can nowise be together, since they are altogether contrary to one another, either on the part of the object (as when they have the same object), or at least on the part of the movement, for joy is with expansion of the heart, whereas sorrow is with contraction; and it is in this sense that the Philosopher speaks in *Ethic.* ix. Second, we may speak of joy and sorrow as being simple acts of the will, to which something is pleasing or displeasing. Accordingly, they cannot be contrary to one another, except on the part of the object, as when they concern the same object in the same respect, in which way joy and sorrow cannot be simultaneous, because the same thing in the same respect cannot be pleasing and displeasing. If, on the other hand, joy and sorrow, understood thus, be not of the same object in the same respect, but either of different objects,

est contrarietas gaudii et tristitiae. Unde nihil prohibet hominem simul gaudere et tristari, puta, si videamus iustum affligi, simul placet nobis eius iustitia, et displicet afflictio. Et hoc modo potest alicui displicere quod peccavit, et placere quod hoc ei displicet cum spe veniae, ita quod ipsa tristitia sit materia gaudii. Unde et Augustinus dicit, in libro de poenitentia, *semper doleat poenitens, et de dolore gaudeat.*

Si tamen tristitia nullo modo compateretur sibi gaudium, per hoc non tolleretur habitualis continuitas poenitentiae, sed actualis.

AD TERTIUM dicendum quod, secundum philosophum, in II Ethic., ad virtutem pertinet tenere medium in passionibus. Tristitia autem quae in appetitu poenitentis sensitivo consequitur ex displicentia voluntatis, passio quaedam est. Unde moderanda est secundum virtutem, et eius superfluitas est vitiosa, quia inducit in desperationem. Quod significat apostolus ibidem dicens, *ne maiori tristitia absorbeatur qui eiusmodi est.* Et sic consolatio de qua ibi apostolus loquitur, est moderativa tristitiae, non autem totaliter ablativa.

or of the same object in different respects, in that case joy and sorrow are not contrary to one another, so that nothing hinders a man from being joyful and sorrowful at the same time—for instance, if we see a good man suffer, we both rejoice at his goodness and at the same time grieve for his suffering. In this way a man may be displeased at having sinned, and be pleased at his displeasure together with his hope for pardon, so that his very sorrow is a matter of joy. Hence Augustine says: *The penitent should ever grieve and rejoice at his grief.*

If, however, sorrow were altogether incompatible with joy, this would prevent the continuance, not of habitual penance, but only of actual penance.

REPLY OBJ. 3: According to the Philosopher (*Ethic.* ii, 3, 6, 7, 9) it belongs to virtue to establish the mean in the passions. Now the sorrow which, in the sensitive appetite of the penitent, arises from the displeasure of his will, is a passion; wherefore it should be moderated according to virtue, and if it be excessive it is sinful, because it leads to despair, as the Apostle teaches (2 Cor 2:7), saying: *Lest such an one be swallowed up with overmuch sorrow.* Accordingly comfort, of which the Apostle speaks, moderates sorrow but does not destroy it altogether.

Article 10

Whether the Sacrament of Penance May Be Repeated?

AD DECIMUM SIC PROCEDITUR. Videtur quod sacramentum poenitentiae non debeat iterari. Dicit enim apostolus, Heb. VI, *impossibile est eos qui semel illuminati sunt, et gustaverunt donum caeleste, et participes facti sunt spiritus sancti, et prolapsi sunt, rursus renovari ad poenitentiam.* Sed quicumque poenituerunt, sunt illuminati, et acceperunt donum spiritus sancti. Ergo quicumque peccat post poenitentiam, non potest iterato poenitere.

PRAETEREA, Ambrosius dicit, in libro de poenitentia, *reperiuntur qui saepius agendam poenitentiam putant. Qui luxuriantur in Christo. Nam, si vere poenitentiam agerent, iterandam postea non putarent, quia, sicut unum est Baptisma, ita una poenitentia.* Sed Baptismus non iteratur. Ergo nec poenitentia.

PRAETEREA, miracula quibus dominus infirmitates corporales sanavit, significant sanationes spiritualium infirmitatum, quibus scilicet homines liberantur a peccatis. Sed non legitur quod dominus aliquem caecum bis illuminaverit, vel aliquem leprosum bis mundaverit, aut aliquem mortuum bis suscitaverit. Ergo videtur quod nec alicui peccatori bis per poenitentiam veniam largiatur.

OBJECTION 1: It would seem that the sacrament of Penance should not be repeated. For the Apostle says (Heb 6:4, seqq.): *It is impossible for those, who were once illuminated, have tasted also the heavenly gift, and were made partakers of the Holy Spirit . . . and are fallen away, to be renewed again to penance.* Now whosoever have done penance, have been illuminated, and have received the gift of the Holy Spirit. Therefore whosoever sin after doing penance, cannot do penance again.

OBJ. 2: Further, Ambrose says (*De Poenit.* ii): *Some are to be found who think they ought often to do penance, who take liberties with Christ: for if they were truly penitent, they would not think of doing penance over again, since there is but one Penance even as there is but one Baptism.* Now Baptism is not repeated. Neither, therefore, is Penance to be repeated.

OBJ. 3: Further, the miracles whereby our Lord healed bodily diseases, signify the healing of spiritual diseases, whereby men are delivered from sins. Now we do not read that our Lord restored the sight to any blind man twice, or that He cleansed any leper twice, or twice raised any dead man to life. Therefore it seems that He does not twice grant pardon to any sinner.

PRAETEREA, Gregorius dicit, in homilia Quadragesimae, *poenitentia est anteacta peccata deflere, et flenda iterum non committere*. Et Isidorus dicit, in libro de summo bono, *irrisor est, et non poenitens, qui adhuc agit quod poenitet*. Si ergo aliquis vere poeniteat, iterum non peccabit. Ergo non potest quod poenitentia iteretur.

PRAETEREA, sicut Baptismus habet efficaciam ex passione Christi, ita et poenitentia. Sed Baptismus non iteratur, propter unitatem passionis et mortis Christi. Ergo pari ratione et poenitentia non iteratur.

PRAETEREA, Gregorius dicit, *facilitas veniae incentivum praebet delinquendi*. Si ergo Deus frequenter veniam praebet per poenitentiam, videtur quod ipse incentivum praebeat hominibus delinquendi, et sic videtur delectari in peccatis. Quod eius bonitati non congruit. Non ergo potest poenitentia iterari.

SED CONTRA est quod homo inducitur ad misericordiam exemplo divinae misericordiae, secundum illud Luc. VI, *estote misericordes, sicut et pater vester misericors est*. Sed dominus hanc misericordiam discipulis imponit, ut saepius remittant fratribus contra se peccantibus, unde, sicut dicitur Matth. XVIII, Petro quaerenti, *quoties peccaverit in me frater meus, dimittam ei usque septies?* Respondit Iesus, *non dico tibi usque septies, sed usque septuagesies septies*. Ergo etiam Deus saepius per poenitentiam veniam peccantibus praebet, praesertim cum doceat nos petere, *dimitte nobis debita nostra sicut et nos dimittimus debitoribus nostris*.

RESPONDEO dicendum quod circa poenitentiam erraverunt quidam dicentes non posse hominem per poenitentiam secundo consequi veniam peccatorum. Quorum quidam, scilicet Novatiani, hoc in tantum extenderunt quod dixerunt post primam poenitentiam quae agitur in Baptismo, peccantes non posse per poenitentiam iterato restitui. Alii vero fuerunt haeretici, ut Augustinus dicit, in libro de poenitentia, qui post Baptismum dicebant quidem esse utilem poenitentiam, non tamen pluries, sed semel tantum.

Videntur autem huiusmodi errores ex duobus processisse. Primo quidem, ex eo quod errabant circa rationem verae poenitentiae. Cum enim ad veram poenitentiam caritas requiratur, sine qua non delentur peccata, credebant quod caritas semel habita non possit amitti, et per consequens quod poenitentia, si sit vera, nunquam per peccatum tollatur, ut sit necesse eam iterari. Sed hoc improbatum est in secunda parte, ubi ostensum est quod caritas semel habita, propter libertatem arbitrii, potest amitti; et per consequens post veram poenitentiam potest aliquis peccare mortaliter. Secundo, ex eo quod errabant circa aestimationem gravitatis peccati. Putabant enim adeo grave esse peccatum quod aliquis committit post veniam impetratam, quod non sit possibile ipsum remitti. In quo quidem errabant et ex parte peccati,

OBJ. 4: Further, Gregory says (*Hom. xxxiv in Evang.*): *Penance consists in deploring past sins, and in not committing again those we have deplored*: and Isidore says (*De Summo Bono* ii): *He is a mocker and no penitent who still does what he has repented of*. If, therefore, a man is truly penitent, he will not sin again. Therefore Penance cannot be repeated.

OBJ. 5: Further, just as Baptism derives its efficacy from the Passion of Christ, so does Penance. Now Baptism is not repeated, on account of the unity of Christ's Passion and death. Therefore in like manner Penance is not repeated.

OBJ. 6: Further, Ambrose says on Ps. 118:58, *I entreated Thy face*, etc., that *facility of obtaining pardon is an incentive to sin*. If, therefore, God frequently grants pardon through Penance, it seems that He affords man an incentive to sin, and thus He seems to take pleasure in sin, which is contrary to His goodness. Therefore Penance cannot be repeated.

ON THE CONTRARY, Man is induced to be merciful by the example of Divine mercy, according to Luke 6:36: *Be ye . . . merciful, as your Father also is merciful*. Now our Lord commanded His disciples to be merciful by frequently pardoning their brethren who had sinned against them; wherefore, as related in Matt. 18:21, when Peter asked: *How often shall my brother offend against me, and I forgive him? till seven times?* Jesus answered: *I say not to thee, till seven times, but till seventy times seven times*. Therefore also God over and over again, through Penance, grants pardon to sinners, especially as He teaches us to pray (Matt 6:12): *Forgive us our trespasses, as we forgive them that trespass against us*.

I ANSWER THAT, As regards Penance, some have erred, saying that a man cannot obtain pardon of his sins through Penance a second time. Some of these, viz. the Novatians, went so far as to say that he who sins after the first Penance which is done in Baptism, cannot be restored again through Penance. There were also other heretics who, as Augustine relates in *De Poenitentia*, said that, after Baptism, Penance is useful, not many times, but only once.

These errors seem to have arisen from a twofold source: first from not knowing the nature of true Penance. For since true Penance requires charity, without which sins are not taken away, they thought that charity once possessed could not be lost, and that, consequently, Penance, if true, could never be removed by sin, so that it should be necessary to repeat it. But this was refuted in the Second Part (II, Q. 24, A. 11), where it was shown that on account of free-will charity, once possessed, can be lost, and that, consequently, after true Penance, a man can sin mortally.—Second, they erred in their estimation of the gravity of sin. For they deemed a sin committed by a man after he had received pardon, to be so grave that it could not be forgiven. In this they erred not only with regard to sin which, even after a sin has been forgiven, can be either more or less grievous than the first,

quod, etiam post remissionem consecutam, potest esse et gravius et levius etiam quam fuerit ipsum primum peccatum remissum, et multo magis contra infinitatem divinae misericordiae, quae est super omnem numerum et magnitudinem peccatorum, secundum illud Psalmi, *miserere mei, Deus, secundum magnam misericordiam tuam, et secundum multitudinem miserationum tuarum, dele iniquitatem meam.* Unde reprobatur verbum Caini dicentis, Genes. IV, *maior est iniquitas mea quam ut veniam merear.* Et ideo misericordia Dei peccantibus per poenitentiam veniam praebet absque ullo termino. Unde dicitur II Paralip. ult., *immensa et investigabilis misericordia promissionis tuae super malitias hominum.* Unde manifestum est quod poenitentia est pluries iterabilis.

AD PRIMUM ergo dicendum quod, quia apud Iudaeos erant secundum legem quaedam lavacra instituta, quibus pluries se ab immunditiis purgabant, credebant aliqui Iudaeorum quod etiam per lavacrum Baptismi aliquis pluries purificari possit. Ad quod excludendum, apostolus scribit Hebraeis quod impossibile est eos qui semel sunt illuminati, scilicet per Baptismum, rursum renovari ad poenitentiam, scilicet per Baptismum, qui est *lavacrum regenerationis et renovationis spiritus sancti,* ut dicitur ad Tit. III. Et rationem assignat ex hoc quod per Baptismum homo Christo commoritur, unde sequitur, *rursum crucifigentes in semetipsis filium Dei.*

AD SECUNDUM dicendum quod Ambrosius loquitur de poenitentia solemni, quae in Ecclesia non iteratur, ut infra dicetur.

AD TERTIUM dicendum quod, sicut Augustinus dicit, in libro de poenitentia, *multos caecos in diverso tempore dominus illuminavit, et multos debiles confortavit, ostendens in diversis illis eadem saepe peccata dimitti, ut quem prius sanavit leprosum, alio tempore illuminat caecum. Ideo enim tot sanavit caecos, claudos et aridos, ne desperet saepe peccator. Ideo non scribitur aliquem nisi semel sanasse, ut quisque timeat se iungi peccato. Medicum se vocat, et non sanis, sed male habentibus opportunum, sed qualis hic medicus qui malum iteratum nesciret curare? Medicorum enim est centies infirmum centies curare. Qui ceteris minor esset, si alii possibilia ignoraret.*

AD QUARTUM dicendum quod poenitere est anteacta peccata deflere et flenda non committere simul dum flet, vel actu vel proposito. Ille enim est irrisor et non poenitens qui, simul dum poenitet, agit quod poenitet, proponit enim iterum se facturum quod gessit, vel etiam actualiter peccat eodem vel alio genere peccati. Quod autem aliquis postea peccat, vel actu vel proposito, non excludit quin prima poenitentia vera fuerit. Nunquam enim veritas prioris actus excluditur per actum

which was forgiven, but much more did they err against the infinity of Divine mercy, which surpasses any number and magnitude of sins, according to Ps. 50:1, 2: *Have mercy on me, O God, according to Thy great mercy: and according to the multitude of Thy tender mercies, blot out my iniquity.* Wherefore the words of Cain were reprehensible, when he said (Gen 4:13): *My iniquity is greater than that I may deserve pardon.* And so God's mercy, through Penance, grants pardon to sinners without any end, wherefore it is written (2 Chr 37): *Thy merciful promise is unmeasurable and unsearchable . . . (and Thou repentest) for the evil brought upon man.* It is therefore evident that Penance can be repeated many times.

REPLY OBJ. 1: Some of the Jews thought that a man could be washed several times in the laver of Baptism, because among them the Law prescribed certain washing-places where they were wont to cleanse themselves repeatedly from their uncleannesses. In order to disprove this the Apostle wrote to the Hebrews that *it is impossible for those who were once illuminated,* viz. through Baptism, *to be renewed again to penance,* viz. through Baptism, which is *the laver of regeneration, and renovation of the Holy Spirit,* as stated in Titus 3:5: and he declares the reason to be that by Baptism man dies with Christ, wherefore he adds (Heb 6:6): *Crucifying again to themselves the Son of God.*

REPLY OBJ. 2: Ambrose is speaking of solemn Penance, which is not repeated in the Church, as we shall state further on (Suppl., Q. 28, A. 2).

REPLY OBJ. 3: As Augustine says, *Our Lord gave sight to many blind men at various times, and strength to many infirm, thereby showing, in these different men, that the same sins are repeatedly forgiven, at one time healing a man from leprosy and afterwards from blindness. For this reason He healed so many stricken with fever, so many feeble in body, so many lame, blind, and withered, that the sinner might not despair; for this reason He is not described as healing anyone but once, that every one might fear to link himself with sin; for this reason He declares Himself to be the physician welcomed not of the hale, but of the unhealthy. What sort of a physician is he who knows not how to heal a recurring disease? For if a man ail a hundred times it is for the physician to heal him a hundred times: and if he failed where others succeed, he would be a poor physician in comparison with them.*

REPLY OBJ. 4: Penance is to deplore past sins, and, while deploring them, not to commit again, either by act or by intention, those which we have to deplore. Because a man is a mocker and not a penitent, who, while doing penance, does what he repents having done, or intends to do again what he did before, or even commits actually the same or another kind of sin. But if a man sin afterwards either by act or intention, this does not destroy the fact that his former penance was real, because the reality of a

contrarium subsequentem, sicut enim vere cucurrit qui postea sedet, ita vere poenituit qui postea peccat.

AD QUINTUM dicendum quod Baptismus habet virtutem ex passione Christi sicut quaedam spiritualis regeneratio, cum spirituali morte praecedentis vitae. Statutum est autem hominibus semel mori, et semel nasci. Et ideo semel tantum debet homo baptizari. Sed poenitentia habet virtutem ex passione Christi sicut spiritualis medicatio, quae frequenter iterari potest.

AD SEXTUM dicendum quod Augustinus, in libro de poenitentia, dicit quod *constat Deo multum displicere peccata, qui semper praesto est ea destruere, ne solvatur quod creavit, ne corrumpatur quod amavit*, scilicet per desperationem.

former act is never destroyed by a subsequent contrary act: for even as he truly ran who afterwards sits, so he truly repented who subsequently sins.

REPLY OBJ. 5: Baptism derives its power from Christ's Passion, as a spiritual regeneration, with a spiritual death, of a previous life. Now *it is appointed unto man once to die* (Heb 9:27), and to be born once, wherefore man should be baptized but once. On the other hand, Penance derives its power from Christ's Passion, as a spiritual medicine, which can be repeated frequently.

REPLY OBJ. 6: According to Augustine (*De vera et falsa Poenitentia*, the authorship of which is unknown), *it is evident that sins displease God exceedingly, for He is always ready to destroy them, lest what He created should perish, and what He loved be lost*, viz. by despair.

QUESTION 85

PENANCE AS A VIRTURE

Deinde considerandum est de poenitentia secundum quod est virtus. Et circa hoc quaeruntur sex.

Primo, utrum poenitentia sit virtus.

Secundo, utrum sit virtus specialis.

Tertio, sub qua specie virtutis contineatur.

Quarto, de subiecto eius.

Quinto, de causa ipsius.

Sexto, de ordine eius ad alias virtutes.

We must now consider penance as a virtue, under which head there are six points of inquiry:

(1) Whether penance is a virtue?

(2) Whether it is a special virtue?

(3) To what species of virtue does it belong?

(4) Of its subject;

(5) Of its cause;

(6) Of its relation to the other virtues.

Article 1

Whether Penance Is a Virtue?

Ad primum sic proceditur. Videtur quod poenitentia non sit virtus. Poenitentia enim est quoddam sacramentum aliis sacramentis connumeratum, ut ex supra dictis patet. Sed nullum aliud sacramentorum est virtus. Ergo neque poenitentia est virtus.

Praeterea, secundum philosophum, in IV Ethic., verecundia non est virtus, tum quia est passio habens corporalem immutationem; tum etiam quia non est dispositio perfecti, cum sit de turpi acto, quod non habet locum in homine virtuoso. Sed similiter poenitentia est quaedam passio habens corporalem immutationem, scilicet ploratum, sicut Gregorius dicit quod *poenitere est peccata praeterita plangere*. Est etiam de turpibus factis, scilicet de peccatis, quae non habent locum in homine virtuoso. Ergo poenitentia non est virtus.

Praeterea, secundum philosophum, in IV Ethic., *nullus est stultus eorum qui sunt secundum virtutem*. Sed stultum videtur dolere de commisso praeterito, quod non potest non esse, quod tamen pertinet ad poenitentiam. Ergo poenitentia non est virtus.

Sed contra est quod praecepta legis dantur de actibus virtutum, quia legislator intendit cives facere virtuosos, ut dicitur in II Ethic. Sed praeceptum divinae legis est de poenitentia, secundum illud Matth. III, poenitentiam agite, et cetera. Ergo poenitentia est virtus.

Respondeo dicendum quod, sicut ex dictis patet, poenitere est de aliquo a se prius facto dolere. Dictum est autem supra quod dolor vel tristitia dupliciter dicitur. Uno modo, secundum quod est passio quaedam appetitus sensitivi. Et quantum ad hoc, poenitentia non est virtus, sed passio alio modo, secundum quod consistit in voluntate. Et hoc modo est cum quadam electione. Quae quidem si sit recta, necesse est quod sit actus virtutis,

Objection 1: It would seem that penance is not a virtue. For penance is a sacrament numbered among the other sacraments, as was shown above (Q. 84, A. 1; Q. 65, A. 1). Now no other sacrament is a virtue. Therefore neither is penance a virtue.

Obj. 2: Further, according to the Philosopher (*Ethic.* iv, 9), *shame is not a virtue*, both because it is a passion accompanied by a bodily alteration, and because it is not the disposition of a perfect thing, since it is about an evil act, so that it has no place in a virtuous man. Now, in like manner, penance is a passion accompanied by a bodily alteration, viz. tears, according to Gregory, who says (*Hom. xxxiv in Evang.*) that *penance consists in deploring past sins*: moreover it is about evil deeds, viz. sins, which have no place in a virtuous man. Therefore penance is not a virtue.

Obj. 3: Further, according to the Philosopher (*Ethic.* iv, 3), *no virtuous man is foolish*. But it seems foolish to deplore what has been done in the past, since it cannot be otherwise, and yet this is what we understand by penance. Therefore penance is not a virtue.

On the contrary, The precepts of the Law are about acts of virtue, because *a lawgiver intends to make the citizens virtuous* (*Ethic.* ii, 1). But there is a precept about penance in the Divine law, according to Matt. 4:17: *Do penance*, etc. Therefore penance is a virtue.

I answer that, As stated above (Obj. 2; Q. 84, A. 10, ad 4), to repent is to deplore something one has done. Now it has been stated above (Q. 84, A. 9) that sorrow or sadness is twofold. First, it denotes a passion of the sensitive appetite, and in this sense penance is not a virtue, but a passion. Second, it denotes an act of the will, and in this way it implies choice, and if this be right, it must, of necessity, be an act of virtue. For it is stated in *Ethic.* ii, 6 that virtue is a

dicitur enim in II Ethic. quod *virtus est habitus electivus secundum rationem rectam*. Pertinet autem ad rationem rectam quod aliquis doleat de quo dolendum est. Quod quidem observatur in poenitentia de qua nunc loquimur, nam poenitens assumit moderatum dolorem de peccatis praeteritis, cum intentione removendi ea. Unde manifestum est quod poenitentia de qua nunc loquimur, vel est virtus, vel actus virtutis.

AD PRIMUM ergo dicendum quod, sicut dictum est, in sacramento poenitentiae materialiter se habent actus humani, quod non contingit in Baptismo vel confirmatione. Et ideo, cum virtus sit principium alicuius actus, potius poenitentia est virtus, vel cum virtute, quam Baptismus vel confirmatio.

AD SECUNDUM dicendum quod poenitentia, secundum quod est passio, non est virtus, ut dictum est. Sic autem habet corporalem transmutationem adiunctam. Est autem virtus secundum quod habet ex parte voluntatis electionem rectam. Quod tamen magis potest dici de poenitentia quam de verecundia. Nam verecundia respicit turpe factum ut praesens, poenitentia vero respicit turpe factum ut praeteritum. Est autem contra perfectionem virtutis quod aliquis in praesenti habeat turpe factum, de quo oporteat eum verecundari. Non autem est contra perfectionem virtutis quod aliquis prius commiserit turpia facta, de quibus oporteat eum poenitere, cum ex vitioso fiat aliquis virtuosus.

AD TERTIUM dicendum quod dolere de eo quod prius factum est cum hac intentione conandi ad hoc quod factum non fuerit, esset stultum. Hoc autem non intendit poenitens, sed dolor eius est displicentia seu reprobatio facti praeteriti cum intentione removendi sequelam ipsius, scilicet offensam Dei et reatum poenae. Et hoc non est stultum.

habit of choosing according to right reason. Now it belongs to right reason than one should grieve for a proper object of grief as one ought to grieve, and for an end for which one ought to grieve. And this is observed in the penance of which we are speaking now; since the penitent assumes a moderated grief for his past sins, with the intention of removing them. Hence it is evident that the penance of which we are speaking now, is either a virtue or the act of a virtue.

REPLY OBJ. 1: As stated above (Q. 84, A. 1, ad 1; AA. 2, 3), in the sacrament of Penance, human acts take the place of matter, which is not the case in Baptism and Confirmation. Wherefore, since virtue is a principle of an act, penance is either a virtue or accompanies a virtue, rather than Baptism or Confirmation.

REPLY OBJ. 2: Penance, considered as a passion, is not a virtue, as stated above, and it is thus that it is accompanied by a bodily alteration. On the other hand, it is a virtue, according as it includes a right choice on the part of the will; which, however, applies to penance rather than to shame. Because shame regards the evil deed as present, whereas penance regards the evil deed as past. Now it is contrary to the perfection of virtue that one should have an evil deed actually present, of which one ought to be ashamed; whereas it is not contrary to the perfection of virtue that we should have previously committed evil deeds, of which it behooves us to repent, since a man from being wicked becomes virtuous.

REPLY OBJ. 3: It would indeed be foolish to grieve for what has already been done, with the intention of trying to make it not done. But the penitent does not intend this: for his sorrow is displeasure or disapproval with regard to the past deed, with the intention of removing its result, viz. the anger of God and the debt of punishment: and this is not foolish.

Article 2

Whether Penance Is a Special Virtue?

AD SECUNDUM SIC PROCEDITUR. Videtur quod poenitentia non sit specialis virtus. Eiusdem enim rationis videtur esse gaudere de bonis prius actis, et dolere de malis perpetratis. Sed gaudium de bono prius facto non est specialis virtus, sed est quidam affectus laudabilis ex caritate proveniens, ut patet per Augustinum, XIV de Civ. Dei, unde et apostolus, I Cor. XIII, dicit quod *caritas non gaudet super iniquitate, congaudet autem veritati*. Ergo pari ratione poenitentia, quae est dolor de peccatis praeteritis, non est specialis virtus, sed est quidam affectus ex caritate proveniens.

PRAETEREA, quaelibet virtus specialis habet materiam specialem, quia habitus distinguuntur per actus, et

OBJECTION 1: It would seem that penance is not a special virtue. For it seems that to rejoice at the good one has done, and to grieve for the evil one has done are acts of the same nature. But joy for the good one has done is not a special virtue, but is a praiseworthy emotion proceeding from charity, as Augustine states (*De Civ. Dei* xiv, 7, 8, 9): wherefore the Apostle says (1 Cor 13:6) that charity *rejoiceth not at iniquity, but rejoiceth with the truth*. Therefore, in like manner, neither is penance, which is sorrow for past sins, a special virtue, but an emotion resulting from charity.

OBJ. 2: Further, every special virtue has its special matter, because habits are distinguished by their acts, and acts

actus per obiecta. Sed poenitentia non habet materiam specialem, sunt enim eius materia peccata praeterita circa quamcumque materiam. Ergo poenitentia non est specialis virtus.

Praeterea, nihil expellitur nisi a suo contrario. Sed poenitentia expellit omnia peccata. Ergo contrariatur omnibus peccatis. Non est ergo specialis virtus.

Sed contra est quod de ea datur speciale legis praeceptum, ut supra habitum est.

Respondeo dicendum quod, sicut in secunda parte habitum est, species habituum distinguuntur secundum species actuum, et ideo ubi occurrit specialis actus laudabilis, ibi necesse est ponere specialem habitum virtutis. Manifestum est autem quod in poenitentia invenitur specialis ratio actus laudabilis, scilicet operari ad destructionem peccati praeteriti inquantum est Dei offensa, quod non pertinet ad rationem alterius virtutis. Unde necesse est ponere quod poenitentia sit specialis virtus.

Ad primum ergo dicendum quod a caritate derivatur aliquis actus dupliciter. Uno modo, sicut ab ea elicitus. Et talis actus virtuosus non requirit aliam virtutem praeter caritatem, sicut diligere bonum et gaudere de eo, et tristari de opposito. Alio modo aliquis actus a caritate procedit quasi a caritate imperatus. Et sic, quia ipsa imperat omnibus virtutibus, utpote ordinans eas ad finem suum, actus a caritate procedens potest etiam ad aliam virtutem specialem pertinere. Si ergo in actu poenitentis consideretur sola displicentia peccati praeteriti, hoc immediate ad caritatem pertinet, sicut et gaudere de bonis praeteritis. Sed intentio operandi ad deletionem peccati praeteriti requirit specialem virtutem sub caritate.

Ad secundum dicendum quod poenitentia habet quidem realiter generalem materiam, inquantum respicit omnia peccata, sed tamen sub ratione speciali, inquantum sunt emendabilia per actum hominis cooperantis Deo ad suam iustificationem.

Ad tertium dicendum quod quaelibet virtus specialis expellit habitum vitii oppositi, sicut albedo expellit nigredinem ab eodem subiecto. Sed poenitentia expellit omne peccatum effective, inquantum operatur ad destructionem peccati, prout est remissibile ex divina gratia homine cooperante. Unde non sequitur quod sit virtus generalis.

by their objects. But penance has no special matter, because its matter is past sins in any matter whatever. Therefore penance is not a special virtue.

Obj. 3: Further, nothing is removed except by its contrary. But penance removes all sins. Therefore it is contrary to all sins, and consequently is not a special virtue.

On the contrary, The Law has a special precept about penance, as stated above (Q. 84, AA. 5, 7).

I answer that, As stated in the Second Part (I-II, Q. 54, A. 1, ad 1, A. 2), habits are specifically distinguished according to the species of their acts, so that whenever an act has a special reason for being praiseworthy, there must needs be a special habit. Now it is evident that there is a special reason for praising the act of penance, because it aims at the destruction of past sin, considered as an offense against God, which does not apply to any other virtue. We must therefore conclude that penance is a special virtue.

Reply Obj. 1: An act springs from charity in two ways: first as being elicited by charity, and a like virtuous act requires no other virtue than charity, e.g., to love the good, to rejoice therein, and to grieve for what is opposed to it. Second, an act springs from charity, being, so to speak, commanded by charity; and thus, since charity commands all the virtues, inasmuch as it directs them to its own end, an act springing from charity may belong even to another special virtue. Accordingly, if in the act of the penitent we consider the mere displeasure in the past sin, it belongs to charity immediately, in the same way as joy for past good acts; but the intention to aim at the destruction of past sin requires a special virtue subordinate to charity.

Reply Obj. 2: In point of fact, penance has indeed a general matter, inasmuch as it regards all sins; but it does so under a special aspect, inasmuch as they can be remedied by an act of man in co-operating with God for his justification.

Reply Obj. 3: Every special virtue removes formally the habit of the opposite vice, just as whiteness removes blackness from the same subject: but penance removes every sin effectively, inasmuch as it works for the destruction of sins, according as they are pardonable through the grace of God if man co-operate therewith. Wherefore it does not follow that it is a general virtue.

Article 3

Whether the Virtue of Penance Is a Species of Justice?

Ad tertium sic proceditur. Videtur quod virtus poenitentiae non sit species iustitiae. Iustitia enim non est virtus theologica sed moralis, ut in secunda parte patet. Poenitentia autem videtur virtus esse theologica,

Objection 1: It would seem that the virtue of penance is not a species of justice. For justice is not a theological but a moral virtue, as was shown in the Second Part (II-II, Q. 62, A. 3). But penance seems to be a theological virtue,

quia habet Deum pro obiecto, satisfacit enim Deo, cui etiam reconciliat peccatorem. Ergo videtur quod poenitentia non sit pars iustitiae.

Praeterea, iustitia, cum sit virtus moralis, consistit in medio. Sed poenitentia non consistit in medio, sed in quodam excessu, secundum illud Ierem. VI, *luctum unigeniti fac tibi, planctum amarum*. Ergo poenitentia non est species iustitiae.

Praeterea, duae sunt species iustitiae, ut dicitur in V Ethic., scilicet distributiva et commutativa. Sed sub neutra videtur poenitentia contineri. Ergo videtur quod poenitentia non sit species iustitiae.

Praeterea, super illud Luc. VI, *beati qui nunc fletis*, dicit Glossa, *ecce prudentia, per quam ostenditur quam haec terrena sint misera, et quam beata caelestia*. Sed flere est actus poenitentiae. Ergo poenitentia magis est prudentiae quam iustitiae.

Sed contra est quod Augustinus dicit, in libro de poenitentia, *poenitentia est quaedam dolentis vindicta, semper puniens in se quod dolet se commisisse*. Sed facere vindictam pertinet ad iustitiam, unde Tullius, in sua rhetorica, ponit vindicativam unam speciem iustitiae. Ergo videtur quod poenitentia sit species iustitiae.

Respondeo dicendum quod, sicut supra dictum est, poenitentia non habet quod sit virtus specialis ex hoc solo quod dolet de malo perpetrato, ad hoc enim sufficeret caritas, sed ex eo quod poenitens dolet de peccato commisso inquantum est offensa Dei, cum emendationis proposito. Emendatio autem offensae contra aliquem commissae fit non per solam cessationem offensae, sed exigitur ulterius quaedam recompensatio, quae habet locum in offensis in alterum commissis sicut et retributio, nisi quod recompensatio est ex parte eius qui offendit, ut puta cum satisfactione; retributio autem est ex parte eius in quem fuit offensa commissa. Utrumque autem ad materiam iustitiae pertinet, quia utrumque est commutatio quaedam. Unde manifestum est quod poenitentia, secundum quod est virtus, est pars iustitiae.

Sciendum tamen quod, secundum philosophum, in V Ethic., dupliciter dicitur iustum, scilicet simpliciter, et secundum quid. Simpliciter quidem iustum est inter aequales, eo quod iustitia est aequalitas quaedam. Quod ipse vocat iustum politicum vel civile, eo quod omnes cives aequales sunt, quantum ad hoc quod immediate sunt sub principe, sicut liberi existentes. Iustum autem secundum quid dicitur quod est inter illos quorum unus est sub potestate alterius, sicut servus sub domino, filius sub patre, uxor sub viro. Et tale iustum consideratur in poenitentia. Unde poenitens recurrit ad Deum, cum emendationis proposito, sicut servus ad dominum, secundum illud Psalmi, *sicut oculi servorum in manibus dominorum suorum, ita oculi nostri ad dominum Deum nostrum, donec misereatur nostri*; et sicut filius ad patrem, secundum illud Luc. XV, *pater, peccavi in caelum et*

since God is its object, for it makes satisfaction to God, to Whom, moreover, it reconciles the sinner. Therefore it seems that penance is not a species of justice.

Obj. 2: Further, since justice is a moral virtue it observes the mean. Now penance does not observe the mean, but rather goes to the extreme, according to Jer. 6:26: *Make thee mourning as for an only son, a bitter lamentation*. Therefore penance is not a species of justice.

Obj. 3: Further, there are two species of justice, as stated in *Ethic.* v, 4, viz. *distributive* and *commutative*. But penance does not seem to be contained under either of them. Therefore it seems that penance is not a species of justice.

Obj. 4: Further, a gloss on Luke 6:21, *Blessed are ye that weep now*, says: *It is prudence that teaches us the unhappiness of earthly things and the happiness of heavenly things*. But weeping is an act of penance. Therefore penance is a species of prudence rather than of justice.

On the contrary, Augustine says in *De Poenitentia*: *Penance is the vengeance of the sorrowful, ever punishing in them what they are sorry for having done*. But to take vengeance is an act of justice, wherefore Tully says (*De Inv. Rhet.* ii) that one kind of justice is called vindictive. Therefore it seems that penance is a species of justice.

I answer that, As stated above (A. 1, ad 2) penance is a special virtue not merely because it sorrows for evil done (since charity would suffice for that), but also because the penitent grieves for the sin he has committed, inasmuch as it is an offense against God, and purposes to amend. Now amendment for an offense committed against anyone is not made by merely ceasing to offend, but it is necessary to make some kind of compensation, which obtains in offenses committed against another, just as retribution does, only that compensation is on the part of the offender, as when he makes satisfaction, whereas retribution is on the part of the person offended against. Each of these belongs to the matter of justice, because each is a kind of commutation. Wherefore it is evident that penance, as a virtue, is a part of justice.

It must be observed, however, that according to the Philosopher (*Ethic.* v, 6) a thing is said to be just in two ways, simply and relatively. A thing is just simply when it is between equals, since justice is a kind of equality, and he calls this the politic or civil just, because all citizens are equal, in the point of being immediately under the ruler, retaining their freedom. But a thing is just relatively when it is between parties of whom one is subject to the other, as a servant under his master, a son under his father, a wife under her husband. It is this kind of just that we consider in penance. Wherefore the penitent has recourse to God with a purpose of amendment, as a servant to his master, according to Ps. 122:2: *Behold, as the eyes of servants are on the hands of their masters . . . so are our eyes unto the Lord our God, until He have mercy on us*; and as a son to his father, according to Luke 15:21: *Father, I have sinned against*

coram te; et sicut uxor ad virum, secundum illud Ierem. III, *fornicata es cum amatoribus multis, tamen revertere ad me, dicit dominus.*

AD PRIMUM ergo dicendum quod, sicut in V Ethic. dicitur, iustitia est ad alterum. Ille autem ad quem est iustitia, non dicitur esse materia iustitiae, sed magis res quae distribuuntur vel commutantur. Unde et materia poenitentiae non est Deus, sed actus humani quibus Deus offenditur vel placatur, sed Deus se habet sicut ille ad quem est iustitia. Ex quo patet quod poenitentia non est virtus theologica, quia non habet Deum pro materia vel pro obiecto.

AD SECUNDUM dicendum quod medium iustitiae est aequalitas quae constituitur inter illos inter quos est iustitia, ut dicitur in V Ethic. In quibusdam autem non potest perfecta aequalitas constitui, propter alterius excellentiam, sicut inter filium et patrem, inter hominem et Deum, ut philosophus dicit, in VIII Ethic. Unde in talibus ille qui est deficiens, debet facere quidquid potest, nec tamen hoc erit sufficiens, sed solum secundum acceptationem superioris. Et hoc significatur per excessum qui attribuitur poenitentiae.

AD TERTIUM dicendum quod, sicut est commutatio quaedam in beneficiis, cum scilicet aliquis pro beneficio recepto gratiam rependit, ita etiam est commutatio in offensis, cum aliquis pro offensa in alterum commissa vel invitus punitur, quod pertinet ad vindicativam iustitiam; vel voluntarie recompensat emendam, quod pertinet ad poenitentiam, quae respicit personam peccatoris sicut iustitia vindicativa personam iudicis. Unde manifestum est quod utraque sub iustitia commutativa continetur.

AD QUARTUM dicendum quod poenitentia, licet directe sit species iustitiae, comprehendit tamen quodammodo ea quae pertinent ad omnes virtutes. Inquantum enim est iustitia quaedam hominis ad Deum, oportet quod participet ea quae sunt virtutum theologicarum, quae habent Deum pro obiecto. Unde poenitentia est cum fide passionis Christi, per quam iustificamur a peccatis; et cum spe veniae; et cum odio vitiorum, quod pertinet ad caritatem inquantum vero est virtus moralis, participat aliquid prudentiae, quae est directiva omnium virtutum moralium. Sed ex ipsa ratione iustitiae non solum habet id quod iustitiae est, sed etiam ea quae sunt temperantiae et fortitudinis, inquantum scilicet ea quae delectationem causant ad temperantiam pertinentem, vel terrorem incutiunt, quem fortitudo moderatur, in commutationem iustitiae veniunt. Et secundum hoc ad iustitiam pertinet et abstinere a delectabilibus, quod pertinet ad temperantiam; et sustinere dura, quod pertinet ad fortitudinem.

heaven and before thee; and as a wife to her husband, according to Jer. 3:1: *Thou hast prostituted thyself to many lovers; nevertheless return to Me, saith the Lord.*

REPLY OBJ. 1: As stated in *Ethic.* v, 1, justice is a virtue towards another person, and the matter of justice is not so much the person to whom justice is due as the thing which is the subject of distribution or commutation. Hence the matter of penance is not God, but human acts, whereby God is offended or appeased; whereas God is as one to whom justice is due. Wherefore it is evident that penance is not a theological virtue, because God is not its matter or object.

REPLY OBJ. 2: The mean of justice is the equality that is established between those between whom justice is, as stated in *Ethic.* v. But in certain cases perfect equality cannot be established, on account of the excellence of one, as between father and son, God and man, as the Philosopher states (*Ethic.* viii, 14), wherefore in such cases, he that falls short of the other must do whatever he can. Yet this will not be sufficient simply, but only according to the acceptance of the higher one; and this is what is meant by ascribing excess to penance.

REPLY OBJ. 3: As there is a kind of commutation in favors, when, to wit, a man gives thanks for a favor received, so also is there commutation in the matter of offenses, when, on account of an offense committed against another, a man is either punished against his will, which pertains to vindictive justice, or makes amends of his own accord, which belongs to penance, which regards the person of the sinner, just as vindictive justice regards the person of the judge. Therefore it is evident that both are comprised under commutative justice.

REPLY OBJ. 4: Although penance is directly a species of justice, yet, in a fashion, it comprises things pertaining to all the virtues; for inasmuch as there is a justice of man towards God, it must have a share in matter pertaining to the theological virtues, the object of which is God. Consequently penance comprises faith in Christ's Passion, whereby we are cleansed of our sins, hope for pardon, and hatred of vice, which pertains to charity. Inasmuch as it is a moral virtue, it has a share of prudence, which directs all the moral virtues: but from the very nature of justice, it has not only something belonging to justice, but also something belonging to temperance and fortitude, inasmuch as those things which cause pleasure, and which pertain to temperance, and those which cause terror, which fortitude moderates, are objects of commutative justice. Accordingly it belongs to justice both to abstain from pleasure, which belongs to temperance, and to bear with hardships, which belongs to fortitude.

Article 4

Whether the Will Is Properly the Subject of Penance?

AD QUARTUM SIC PROCEDITUR. Videtur quod subiectum poenitentiae non sit proprie voluntas. Poenitentia enim est tristitiae species. Sed tristitia est in concupiscibili, sicut et gaudium. Ergo poenitentia est in concupiscibili.

PRAETEREA, poenitentia est vindicta quaedam, ut Augustinus dicit, in libro de poenitentia. Sed vindicta videtur ad irascibilem pertinere, quia ira est appetitus vindictae. Ergo videtur quod poenitentia sit in irascibili.

PRAETEREA, praeteritum est proprium obiectum memoriae, secundum philosophum, in libro de memoria. Sed poenitentia est de praeterito, ut dictum est. Ergo poenitentia est in memoria sicuti in subiecto.

PRAETEREA, nihil agit ubi non est. Sed poenitentia excludit peccata ab omnibus viribus animae. Ergo poenitentia est in qualibet vi animae, et non in voluntate tantum.

SED CONTRA, poenitentia est sacrificium quoddam, secundum illud Psalmi, *sacrificium Deo spiritus contribulatus*. Sed offerre sacrificium est actus voluntatis, secundum illud Psalmi, *voluntarie sacrificabo tibi*. Ergo poenitentia est in voluntate.

RESPONDEO dicendum quod de poenitentia dupliciter loqui possumus. Uno modo, secundum quod est passio quaedam. Et sic, cum sit species tristitiae, est in concupiscibili sicut in subiecto. Alio modo, secundum quod est virtus. Et sic, sicut dictum est, est species iustitiae. Iustitia autem, ut in secunda parte dictum est, habet pro subiecto appetitum rationis, qui est voluntas. Unde manifestum est quod poenitentia, secundum quod est virtus, est in voluntate sicut in subiecto. Et proprius eius actus est propositum emendandi Deo quod contra eum commissum est.

AD PRIMUM ergo dicendum quod ratio illa procedit de poenitentia secundum quod est passio.

AD SECUNDUM dicendum quod vindictam expetere ex passione de alio pertinet ad irascibilem. Sed appetere vel facere vindictam ex ratione de se vel de alio, pertinet ad voluntatem.

AD TERTIUM dicendum quod memoria est vis apprehensiva praeteriti. Poenitentia autem non pertinet ad vim apprehensivam, sed ad appetitivam, quae praesupponit actum apprehensivae. Unde poenitentia non est in memoria, sed supponit eam.

AD QUARTUM dicendum quod voluntas, sicut in prima parte habitum est, movet omnes alias potentias

OBJECTION 1: It would seem that the subject of penance is not properly the will. For penance is a species of sorrow. But sorrow is in the concupiscible part, even as joy is. Therefore penance is in the concupiscible faculty.

OBJ. 2: Further, penance is a kind of vengeance, as Augustine states in *De Poenitentia*. But vengeance seems to regard the irascible faculty, since anger is the desire for vengeance. Therefore it seems that penance is in the irascible part.

OBJ. 3: Further, the past is the proper object of the memory, according to the Philosopher (*De Memoria* i). Now penance regards the past, as stated above (A. 1, ad 2, ad 3). Therefore penance is subjected in the memory.

OBJ. 4: Further, nothing acts where it is not. Now penance removes sin from all the powers of the soul. Therefore penance is in every power of the soul, and not only in the will.

ON THE CONTRARY, Penance is a kind of sacrifice, according to Ps. 50:19: *A sacrifice to God is an afflicted spirit*. But to offer a sacrifice is an act of the will, according to Ps. 53:8: *I will freely sacrifice to Thee*. Therefore penance is in the will.

I ANSWER THAT, We can speak of penance in two ways: first, in so far as it is a passion, and thus, since it is a kind of sorrow, it is in the concupiscible part as its subject; second, in so far as it is a virtue, and thus, as stated above (A. 3), it is a species of justice. Now justice, as stated in the Second Part (I-II, Q. 56, A. 6), is subjected in the rational appetite which is the will. Therefore it is evident that penance, in so far as it is a virtue, is subjected in the will, and its proper act is the purpose of amending what was committed against God.

REPLY OBJ. 1: This argument considers penance as a passion.

REPLY OBJ. 2: To desire vengeance on another, through passion, belongs to the irascible appetite, but to desire or take vengeance on oneself or on another, through reason, belongs to the will.

REPLY OBJ. 3: The memory is a power that apprehends the past. But penance belongs not to the apprehensive but to the appetitive power, which presupposes an act of the apprehension. Wherefore penance is not in the memory, but presupposes it.

REPLY OBJ. 4: The will, as stated above (I, Q. 82, A. 4; I-II, Q. 9, A. 1), moves all the other powers of the soul; so

animae. Et ideo non est inconveniens si poenitentia, in voluntate existens, aliquid in singulis potentiis animae operatur.

that it is not unreasonable for penance to be subjected in the will, and to produce an effect in each power of the soul.

Article 5

Whether Penance Originates from Fear?

AD QUINTUM SIC PROCEDITUR. Videtur quod principium poenitentiae non sit ex timore. Poenitentia enim incipit in displicentia peccatorum. Sed hoc pertinet ad caritatem, ut supra dictum est. Ergo poenitentia magis oritur ex amore quam ex timore.

PRAETEREA, ad poenitentiam homines provocantur per expectationem regni caelestis, secundum illud Matth. IV, *poenitentiam agite, appropinquabit enim regnum caelorum.* Sed regnum caelorum est obiectum spei. Ergo poenitentia magis procedit ex spe quam ex timore.

PRAETEREA, timor est interior actus hominis. Poenitentia autem non videtur esse ex opere hominis, sed ex opere Dei, secundum illud Ierem. XXXI, *postquam convertisti me, egi poenitentiam.* Ergo poenitentia non procedit ex timore.

SED CONTRA est quod Isaiae XXVI dicitur, *sicut quae concipit, cum appropinquaverit ad partum, dolens clamat in doloribus suis, sic facti sumus,* scilicet per poenitentiam, et postea subditur, secundum aliam litteram, *a timore tuo, domine, concepimus, et parturivimus, et peperimus spiritum salutis,* idest poenitentiae salutaris, ut per praemissa patet. Ergo poenitentia procedit ex timore.

RESPONDEO dicendum quod de poenitentia loqui possumus dupliciter. Uno modo, quantum ad habitum. Et sic immediate a Deo infunditur, sine nobis principaliter operantibus, non tamen sine nobis dispositive cooperantibus per aliquos actus. Alio modo possumus loqui de poenitentia quantum ad actus quibus Deo operanti in poenitentia cooperamur. Quorum actuum primum principium est Dei operatio convertentis cor, secundum illud Thren. ult., *converte nos, domine, ad te, et convertemur.* Secundus actus est motus fidei. Tertius actus est motus timoris servilis, quo quis timore suppliciorum a peccatis retrahitur. Quartus actus est motus spei, quo quis, sub spe veniae consequendae, assumit propositum emendandi. Quintus actus est motus caritatis, quo alicui peccatum displicet secundum seipsum, et non iam propter supplicia. Sextus actus est motus timoris filialis, quo, propter reverentiam Dei, aliquis emendam Deo voluntarius offert.

Sic igitur patet quod actus poenitentiae a timore servili procedit sicut a primo motu affectus ad hoc

OBJECTION 1: It would seem that penance does not originate from fear. For penance originates in displeasure at sin. But this belongs to charity, as stated above (A. 3). Therefore penance originates from love rather than fear.

OBJ. 2: Further, men are induced to do penance, through the expectation of the heavenly kingdom, according to Matt. 3:2 and Matt. 4:17: *Do penance, for the kingdom of heaven is at hand.* Now the kingdom of heaven is the object of hope. Therefore penance results from hope rather than from fear.

OBJ. 3: Further, fear is an internal act of man. But penance does not seem to arise in us through any work of man, but through the operation of God, according to Jer. 31:19: *After Thou didst convert me I did penance.* Therefore penance does not result from fear.

ON THE CONTRARY, It is written (Isa 26:17): *As a woman with child, when she draweth near the time of her delivery, is in pain, and crieth out in her pangs, so ere we become,* by penance, to wit; and according to another version the text continues: *Through fear of Thee, O Lord, we have conceived, and been as it were in labor, and have brought forth the spirit of salvation,* i.e., of salutary penance, as is clear from what precedes. Therefore penance results from fear.

I ANSWER THAT, We may speak of penance in two ways: first, as to the habit, and then it is infused by God immediately without our operating as principal agents, but not without our co-operating dispositively by certain acts. Second, we may speak of penance, with regard to the acts whereby in penance we co-operate with God operating, the first principle of which acts is the operation of God in turning the heart, according to Lam. 5:21: *Convert us, O Lord, to Thee, and we shall be converted;* the second, an act of faith; the third, a movement of servile fear, whereby a man is withdrawn from sin through fear of punishment; the fourth, a movement of hope, whereby a man makes a purpose of amendment, in the hope of obtaining pardon; the fifth, a movement of charity, whereby sin is displeasing to man for its own sake and no longer for the sake of the punishment; the sixth, a movement of filial fear whereby a man, of his own accord, offers to make amends to God through fear of Him.

Accordingly it is evident that the act of penance results from servile fear as from the first movement of the appetite

ordinante, a timore autem filiali sicut ab immediato et proximo principio.

AD PRIMUM ergo dicendum quod peccatum prius incipit homini displicere, maxime peccatori, propter supplicia, quae respicit timor servilis, quam propter Dei offensam vel peccati turpitudinem, quod pertinet ad caritatem.

AD SECUNDUM dicendum quod in regno caelorum appropinquante intelligitur adventus regis non solum praemiantis, sed etiam punientis. Unde et, Matth. III, Ioannes Baptista dicebat, *progenies viperarum, quis demonstravit vobis fugere a ventura ira?*

AD TERTIUM dicendum quod etiam ipse motus timoris procedit ex actu Dei convertentis cor, unde dicitur Deuteron. V, *quis det eos talem habere mentem ut timeant me?* Et ideo per hoc quod poenitentia a timore procedit, non excluditur quin procedat ex actu Dei convertentis cor.

in this direction and from filial fear as from its immediate and proper principle.

REPLY OBJ. 1: Sin begins to displease a man, especially a sinner, on account of the punishments which servile fear regards, before it displeases him on account of its being an offense against God, or on account of its wickedness, which pertains to charity.

REPLY OBJ. 2: When the kingdom of heaven is said to be at hand, we are to understand that the king is on his way, not only to reward but also to punish. Wherefore John the Baptist said (Matt 3:7): *Ye brood of vipers, who hath showed you to flee from the wrath to come?*

REPLY OBJ. 3: Even the movement of fear proceeds from God's act in turning the heart; wherefore it is written (Deut 5:29): *Who shall give them to have such a mind, to fear Me?* And so the fact that penance results from fear does not hinder its resulting from the act of God in turning the heart.

Article 6

Whether Penance Is the First of the Virtues?

AD SEXTUM SIC PROCEDITUR. Videtur quod poenitentia sit prima virtutum. Quia super illud Matth. III, *poenitentiam agite*, dicit Glossa, *prima virtus est per poenitentiam punire veterem hominem et vitia odire.*

PRAETEREA, recedere a termino prius esse videtur quam accedere ad terminum. Sed omnes aliae virtutes pertinere videntur ad accessum ad terminum, quia per omnes homo ordinatur ad bonum agendum. Poenitentia autem videtur ordinari ad recessum a malo. Ergo poenitentia videtur prior esse omnibus aliis virtutibus.

PRAETEREA, ante poenitentiam est peccatum in anima. Sed simul cum peccato nulla virtus animae inest. Ergo nulla virtus est ante poenitentiam, sed ipsa videtur esse prima, quae aliis aditum aperit excludendo peccatum.

SED CONTRA est quod poenitentia procedit ex fide, spe et caritate, sicut iam dictum est. Non ergo poenitentia est prima virtutum.

RESPONDEO dicendum quod in virtutibus non attenditur ordo temporis quantum ad habitus, quia, cum virtutes sint connexae, ut in secunda parte habitum est, omnes simul incipiunt esse in anima. Sed dicitur una earum esse prior altera ordine naturae, qui consideratur ex ordine actuum, secundum scilicet quod actus unius virtutis praesupponit actum alterius virtutis. Secundum hoc ergo dicendum est quod actus quidam laudabiles etiam tempore praecedere possunt actum et habitum poenitentiae, sicut actus fidei et spei informium, et actus timoris servilis. Actus autem et habitus caritatis simul

OBJECTION 1: It would seem that penance is the first of the virtues. Because, on Matt. 3:2, *Do penance*, etc., a gloss says: *The first virtue is to destroy the old man, and hate sin by means of penance.*

OBJ. 2: Further, withdrawal from one extreme seems to precede approach to the other. Now all the other virtues seem to regard approach to a term, because they all direct man to do good; whereas penance seems to direct him to withdraw from evil. Therefore it seems that penance precedes all the other virtues.

OBJ. 3: Further, before penance, there is sin in the soul. Now no virtue is compatible with sin in the soul. Therefore no virtue precedes penance, which is itself the first of all and opens the door to the others by expelling sin.

ON THE CONTRARY, Penance results from faith, hope, and charity, as already stated (AA. 2, 5). Therefore penance is not the first of the virtues.

I ANSWER THAT, In speaking of the virtues, we do not consider the order of time with regard to the habits, because, since the virtues are connected with one another, as stated in the Second Part (I-II, Q. 65, A. 1), they all begin at the same time to be in the soul; but one is said to precede the other in the order of nature, which order depends on the order of their acts, in so far as the act of one virtue presupposes the act of another. Accordingly, then, one must say that, even in the order of time, certain praiseworthy acts can precede the act and the habit of penance, e.g., acts of dead faith and hope, and an act of servile fear; while the

sunt tempore cum actu et habitu poenitentiae, et cum habitibus aliarum virtutum, nam, sicut in secunda parte habitum est, in iustificatione impii simul est motus liberi arbitrii in Deum, qui est actus fidei per caritatem formatus, et motus liberi arbitrii in peccatum, qui est actus poenitentiae. Horum tamen duorum actuum primus naturaliter praecedit secundum, nam actus poenitentiae virtutis est contra peccatum ex amore Dei, unde primus actus est ratio et causa secundi.

Sic igitur poenitentia non est simpliciter prima virtutum, nec ordine temporis nec ordine naturae, quia ordine naturae simpliciter praecedunt ipsam virtutes theologicae. Sed quantum ad aliquid est prima inter ceteras virtutes ordine temporis, quantum ad actum eius qui primus occurrit in iustificatione impii. Sed ordine naturae videntur esse aliae virtutes priores, sicut quod est per se prius est eo quod est per accidens, nam aliae virtutes per se videntur esse necessariae ad bonum hominis, poenitentia autem supposito quodam, scilicet peccato praeexistenti; sicut etiam dictum est circa ordinem sacramenti poenitentiae ad alia sacramenta praedicta.

AD PRIMUM ergo dicendum quod Glossa illa loquitur quantum ad hoc quod actus poenitentiae primus est tempore inter actus aliarum virtutum.

AD SECUNDUM dicendum quod in motibus successivis recedere a termino est prius tempore quam pervenire ad terminum; et prius natura quantum est ex parte subiecti, sive secundum ordinem causae materialis. Sed secundum ordinem causae agentis et finalis, prius est pervenire ad terminum, hoc enim est quod primo agens intendit. Et hic ordo praecipue attenditur in actibus animae, ut dicitur in II physicorum.

AD TERTIUM dicendum quod poenitentia aperit aditum virtutibus expellendo peccatum per virtutem fidei et caritatis, quae sunt naturaliter priores. Ita tamen aperit eis aditum quod ipsae simul intrant cum ipsa, nam in iustificatione impii simul cum motu liberi arbitrii in Deum et in peccatum, est remissio culpae et infusio gratiae, cum qua simul infunduntur omnes virtutes, ut in secunda parte habitum est.

act and habit of charity are, in point of time, simultaneous with the act and habit of penance, and with the habits of the other virtues. For, as was stated in the Second Part (I-II, Q. 113, AA. 7, 8), in the justification of the ungodly, the movement of the free-will towards God, which is an act of faith quickened by charity, and the movement of the free-will towards sin, which is the act of penance, are simultaneous. Yet of these two acts, the former naturally precedes the latter, because the act of the virtue of penance is directed against sin, through love of God; where the first-mentioned act is the reason and cause of the second.

Consequently penance is not simply the first of the virtues, either in the order of time, or in the order of nature, because, in the order of nature, the theological virtues precede it simply. Nevertheless, in a certain respect, it is the first of the other virtues in the order of time, as regards its act, because this act is the first in the justification of the ungodly; whereas in the order of nature, the other virtues seem to precede, as that which is natural precedes that which is accidental; because the other virtues seem to be necessary for man's good, by reason of their very nature, whereas penance is only necessary if something, viz. sin, be presupposed, as stated above (Q. 55, A. 2), when we spoke of the relation of the sacrament of penance to the other sacraments aforesaid.

REPLY OBJ. 1: This gloss is to be taken as meaning that the act of penance is the first in point of time, in comparison with the acts of the other virtues.

REPLY OBJ. 2: In successive movements withdrawal from one extreme precedes approach to the other, in point of time; and also in the order of nature, if we consider the subject, i.e., the order of the material cause; but if we consider the order of the efficient and final causes, approach to the end is first, for it is this that the efficient cause intends first of all: and it is this order which we consider chiefly in the acts of the soul, as stated in *Phys.* ii.

REPLY OBJ. 3: Penance opens the door to the other virtues, because it expels sin by the virtues of faith, hope and charity, which precede it in the order of nature; yet it so opens the door to them that they enter at the same time as it: because, in the justification of the ungodly, at the same time as the free-will is moved towards God and against sin, the sin is pardoned and grace infused, and with grace all the virtues, as stated in the I-II, Q. 65, AA. 3, 5.

QUESTION 86

THE EFFECT OF PENANCE, AS REGARDS THE PARDON OF MORTAL SIN

Deinde considerandum est de effectu poenitentiae. Et primo, quantum ad remissionem peccatorum mortalium; secundo, quantum ad remissionem peccatorum venialium; tertio, quantum ad reditum peccatorum dimissorum; quarto, quantum ad restitutionem virtutum.

Circa primum quaeruntur sex.

Primo, utrum peccata mortalia per poenitentiam auferantur.

Secundo, utrum possint sine poenitentia tolli.

Tertio, utrum possit remitti unum sine alio.

Quarto, utrum poenitentia auferat culpam remanente reatu.

Quinto, utrum remaneant reliquiae peccatorum.

Sexto, utrum auferre peccatum sit effectus poenitentiae inquantum est virtus, vel inquantum est sacramentum.

We must now consider the effect of Penance; and (1) as regards the pardon of mortal sins; (2) as regards the pardon of venial sins; (3) as regards the return of sins which have been pardoned; (4) as regards the recovery of the virtues.

Under the first head there are six points of inquiry:
(1) Whether all mortal sins are taken away by Penance?

(2) Whether they can be taken away without Penance?
(3) Whether one can be taken away without the other?
(4) Whether Penance takes away the guilt while the debt remains?
(5) Whether any remnants of sin remain?
(6) Whether the removal of sin is the effect of Penance as a virtue, or as a sacrament?

Article 1

Whether All Sins Are Taken Away by Penance?

AD PRIMUM SIC PROCEDITUR. Videtur quod per poenitentiam non removeantur omnia peccata. Dicit enim apostolus, Heb. XII, quod *Esau non invenit locum poenitentiae, quamvis cum lacrimis inquisisset eam,* Glossa, *idest, non invenit locum veniae et benedictionis per poenitentiam.* Et II Machab. IX dicitur de Antiocho, *orabat scelestus ille dominum, a quo non erat misericordiam consecuturus.* Non ergo videtur quod per poenitentiam omnia peccata tollantur.

PRAETEREA, dicit Augustinus, in libro de sermone Dom. in monte, quod *tanta est labes illius peccati (scilicet, cum post agnitionem Dei per gratiam Christi, oppugnat aliquis fraternitatem, et adversus ipsam gratiam invidiae facibus agitatur), ut deprecandi humilitatem subire non possit, etiam si peccatum suum mala conscientia agnoscere et annuntiare cogatur.* Non ergo omne peccatum potest per poenitentiam tolli.

PRAETEREA, dominus dicit, Matth. XII, *qui dixerit contra spiritum sanctum verbum, non remittetur ei neque in hoc saeculo neque in futuro.* Non ergo omne peccatum remitti potest per poenitentiam.

SED CONTRA est quod dicitur Ezech. XVIII, *omnium iniquitatum eius quas operatus est, non recordabor amplius.*

OBJECTION 1: It would seem that not all sins are taken away by Penance. For the Apostle says (Heb 12:17) that Esau *found no place of repentance, although with tears he had sought it,* which a gloss explains as meaning that *he found no place of pardon and blessing through Penance:* and it is related (2 Macc 9:13) of Antiochus, that *this wicked man prayed to the Lord, of Whom he was not to obtain mercy.* Therefore it does not seem that all sins are taken away by Penance.

OBJ. 2: Further, Augustine says (*De Serm. Dom. in Monte* i) that *so great is the stain of that sin (namely, when a man, after coming to the knowledge of God through the grace of Christ, resists fraternal charity, and by the brands of envy combats grace itself) that he is unable to humble himself in prayer, although he is forced by his wicked conscience to acknowledge and confess his sin.* Therefore not every sin can be taken away by Penance.

OBJ. 3: Further, our Lord said (Matt 12:32): *He that shall speak against the Holy Spirit, it shall not be forgiven him, neither in this world nor in the world to come.* Therefore not every sin can be pardoned through Penance.

ON THE CONTRARY, It is written (Ezek 18:22): *I will not remember* any more *all his iniquities that he hath done.*

RESPONDEO dicendum quod hoc quod aliquod peccatum per poenitentiam tolli non possit, posset contingere dupliciter, uno modo, quia aliquis de peccato poenitere non posset; alio modo, quia poenitentia non posset delere peccatum. Et primo quidem modo, non possunt deleri peccata Daemonum, et etiam hominum damnatorum, quia affectus eorum sunt in malo confirmati, ita quod non potest eis displicere peccatum inquantum est culpa, sed solum displicet eis inquantum est poena quam patiuntur; ratione cuius aliquam poenitentiam, sed infructuosam habent, secundum illud Sap. V, *poenitentiam agentes, et prae angustia spiritus gementes.* Unde talis poenitentia non est cum spe veniae, sed cum desperatione. Tale autem non potest esse peccatum aliquod hominis viatoris, cuius liberum arbitrium flexibile est ad bonum et ad malum. Unde dicere quod aliquod peccatum sit in hac vita de quo aliquis poenitere non possit, est erroneum. Primo quidem, quia per hoc tolleretur libertas arbitrii. Secundo, quia derogaretur virtuti gratiae, per quam moveri potest cor cuiuscumque peccatoris ad poenitendum, secundum illud Proverb. XXI *cor regis in manu Dei, et quocumque voluerit vertet illud.*

Quod autem secundo modo non possit per veram poenitentiam aliquod peccatum remitti, est etiam erroneum. Primo quidem, quia repugnat divinae misericordiae, de qua dicitur, Ioel II, quod *benignus et misericors est, et multae misericordiae, et praestabilis super malitia.* Vinceretur quodammodo enim Deus ab homine, si homo peccatum vellet deleri, quod Deus delere non vellet. Secundo, quia hoc derogaret virtuti passionis Christi, per quam poenitentia operatur, sicut et cetera sacramenta, cum scriptum sit, I Ioan. II, *ipse est propitiatio pro peccatis nostris, non solum nostris, sed etiam totius mundi.*

Unde simpliciter dicendum est quod omne peccatum in hac vita per poenitentiam deleri potest.

AD PRIMUM ergo dicendum quod Esau non vere poenituit. Quod patet ex hoc quod dixit, *venient dies luctus patris mei, et occidam Iacob fratrem meum.* Similiter etiam nec Antiochus vere poenituit. Dolebat enim de culpa praeterita non propter offensam Dei, sed propter infirmitatem corporalem quam patiebatur.

AD SECUNDUM dicendum quod illud verbum Augustini sic est intelligendum, tanta est labes illius peccati ut deprecandi humilitatem subire non possit, scilicet, de facili, secundum quod dicitur ille non posse sanari qui non potest de facili sanari. Potest tamen hoc fieri per virtutem divinae gratiae, quae etiam interdum in profundum maris convertit, ut dicitur in Psalmo.

AD TERTIUM dicendum quod illud verbum vel blasphemia contra spiritum sanctum est finalis impoenitentia, ut Augustinus dicit, in libro de verbis domini, quae penitus irremissibilis est, quia post finem huius

I ANSWER THAT, The fact that a sin cannot be taken away by Penance may happen in two ways: first, because of the impossibility of repenting of sin; second, because of Penance being unable to blot out a sin. In the first way the sins of the demons and of men who are lost, cannot be blotted out by Penance, because their will is confirmed in evil, so that sin cannot displease them as to its guilt, but only as to the punishment which they suffer, by reason of which they have a kind of repentance, which yet is fruitless, according to Wis. 5:3: *Repenting, and groaning for anguish of spirit.* Consequently such Penance brings no hope of pardon, but only despair. Nevertheless no sin of a wayfarer can be such as that, because his will is flexible to good and evil. Wherefore to say that in this life there is any sin of which one cannot repent, is erroneous, first, because this would destroy free-will, second, because this would be derogatory to the power of grace, whereby the heart of any sinner whatsoever can be moved to repent, according to Prov. 21:1: *The heart of the king is in the hand of the Lord: whithersoever He will He shall turn it.*

It is also erroneous to say that any sin cannot be pardoned through true Penance. First, because this is contrary to Divine mercy, of which it is written (Joel 2:13) that God is *gracious and merciful, patient, and rich in mercy, and ready to repent of the evil*; for, in a manner, God would be overcome by man, if man wished a sin to be blotted out, which God were unwilling to blot out. Second, because this would be derogatory to the power of Christ's Passion, through which Penance produces its effect, as do the other sacraments, since it is written (1 John 2:2): *He is the propitiation for our sins, and not for ours only, but also for those of the whole world.*

Therefore we must say simply that, in this life, every sin can be blotted out by true Penance.

REPLY OBJ. 1: Esau did not truly repent. This is evident from his saying (Gen 27:41): *The days will come of the mourning of my father, and I will kill my brother Jacob.* Likewise neither did Antiochus repent truly; since he grieved for his past sin, not because he had offended God thereby, but on account of the sickness which he suffered in his body.

REPLY OBJ. 2: These words of Augustine should be understood thus: *So great is the stain of that sin, that man is unable to humble himself in prayer*, i.e., it is not easy for him to do so; in which sense we say that a man cannot be healed, when it is difficult to heal him. Yet this is possible by the power of God's grace, which sometimes turns men even *into the depths of the sea* (Ps 67:23).

REPLY OBJ. 3: The word or blasphemy spoken against the Holy Spirit is final impenitence, as Augustine states (*De Verb. Dom.* xi), which is altogether unpardonable, because after this life is ended, there is no pardon of sins. Or, if by

vitae non est remissio peccatorum. Vel, si intelligatur per blasphemiam spiritus sancti peccatum quod fit ex certa malitia, vel etiam ipsa blasphemia spiritus sancti, dicitur non remitti, scilicet de facili, quia tale non habet in se causam excusationis; vel quia pro tali peccato punitur aliquis et in hoc saeculo et in futuro; ut in secunda parte expositum est.

the blasphemy against the Holy Spirit, we understand sin committed through certain malice, this means either that the blasphemy itself against the Holy Spirit is unpardonable, i.e., not easily pardonable, or that such a sin does not contain in itself any motive for pardon, or that for such a sin a man is punished both in this and in the next world, as we explained in the Second Part (III, Q. 14, A. 3).

Article 2

Whether Sin Can Be Pardoned Without Penance?

AD SECUNDUM SIC PROCEDITUR. Videtur quod sine poenitentia peccatum remitti possit. Non enim est minor virtus Dei circa adultos quam circa pueros. Sed pueris peccata dimittit sine poenitentia. Ergo etiam et adultis.

PRAETEREA, Deus virtutem suam sacramentis non alligavit. Sed poenitentia est quoddam sacramentum. Ergo virtute divina possunt peccata sine poenitentia dimitti.

PRAETEREA, maior est misericordia Dei quam misericordia hominis. Sed homo interdum remittit offensam suam homini etiam non poenitenti, unde et ipse dominus mandat, Matth. V, *diligite inimicos vestros, benefacite his qui oderunt vos.* Ergo multo magis Deus dimittit offensam suam hominibus non poenitentibus.

SED CONTRA est quod dominus dicit, Ierem. XVIII, *si poenitentiam egerit gens illa a malo quod fecit, agam et ego poenitentiam a malo quod cogitavi ut facerem ei.* Et sic e converso videtur quod, si homo poenitentiam non agat, quod Deus ei non remittat offensam.

RESPONDEO dicendum quod impossibile est peccatum actuale mortale sine poenitentia remitti, loquendo de poenitentia quae est virtus. Cum enim peccatum sit Dei offensa, eo modo Deus peccatum remittit quo remittit offensam in se commissam. Offensa autem directe opponitur gratiae, ex hoc enim dicitur aliquis alteri esse offensus, quod repellit eum a gratia sua. Sicut autem habitum est in secunda parte, hoc interest inter gratiam Dei et gratiam hominis, quod gratia hominis non causat, sed praesupponit bonitatem, veram vel apparentem, in homine grato, sed gratia Dei causat bonitatem in homine grato, eo quod bona voluntas Dei, quae in nomine gratiae intelligitur, est causa boni creati. Unde potest contingere quod homo remittat offensam qua offensus est alicui, absque aliqua immutatione voluntatis eius, non autem potest contingere quod Deus remittat offensam alicui absque immutatione voluntatis eius. Offensa autem peccati mortalis procedit ex hoc quod voluntas hominis est aversa a Deo per conversionem ad aliquod bonum commutabile. Unde requiritur ad remissionem

OBJECTION 1: It would seem that sin can be pardoned without Penance. For the power of God is no less with regard to adults than with regard to children. But He pardons the sins of children without Penance. Therefore He also pardons adults without penance.

OBJ. 2: Further, God did not bind His power to the sacraments. But Penance is a sacrament. Therefore by God's power sin can be pardoned without Penance.

OBJ. 3: Further, God's mercy is greater than man's. Now man sometimes forgives another for offending him, without his repenting: wherefore our Lord commanded us (Matt 5:44): *Love your enemies, do good to them that hate you.* Much more, therefore, does God pardon men for offending him, without their repenting.

ON THE CONTRARY, The Lord said (Jer 18:8): *If that nation . . . shall repent of their evil* which they have done, *I also will repent of the evil that I have thought to do them,* so that, on the other hand, if man *do not penance,* it seems that God will not pardon him his sin.

I ANSWER THAT, It is impossible for a mortal actual sin to be pardoned without penance, if we speak of penance as a virtue. For, as sin is an offense against God, He pardons sin in the same way as he pardons an offense committed against Him. Now an offense is directly opposed to grace, since one man is said to be offended with another, because he excludes him from his grace. Now, as stated in the Second Part (I-II, Q. 110, A. 1), the difference between the grace of God and the grace of man, is that the latter does not cause, but presupposes true or apparent goodness in him who is graced, whereas the grace of God causes goodness in the man who is graced, because the good-will of God, which is denoted by the word *grace*, is the cause of all created good. Hence it is possible for a man to pardon an offense, for which he is offended with someone, without any change in the latter's will; but it is impossible that God pardon a man for an offense, without his will being changed. Now the offense of mortal sin is due to man's will being turned away from God, through being turned to some mutable good. Consequently, for the pardon of this

divinae offensae quod voluntas hominis sic immutetur quod convertatur ad Deum, cum detestatione praedictae conversionis et proposito emendae. Quod pertinet ad rationem poenitentiae secundum quod est virtus. Et ideo impossibile est quod peccatum alicui remittatur sine poenitentia secundum quod est virtus.

Sacramentum autem poenitentiae, sicut supra dictum est, perficitur per officium sacerdotis ligantis et solventis. Sine quo potest Deus peccatum remittere, sicut remisit Christus mulieri adulterae, ut legitur Ioan. VIII, et peccatrici, ut legitur Luc. VII. Quibus tamen non remisit peccata sine virtute poenitentiae; nam, sicut Gregorius dicit, in homilia, per gratiam traxit intus, scilicet ad poenitentiam, *quam per misericordiam suscepit foris.*

AD PRIMUM ergo dicendum quod in pueris non est nisi peccatum originale, quod non consistit in actuali deordinatione voluntatis, sed in quadam habituali deordinatione naturae, ut in secunda parte habitum est. Et ideo remittitur eis peccatum cum habituali immutatione per infusionem gratiae et virtutum, non autem cum actuali. Sed adulto in quo sunt actualia peccata, quae consistunt in deordinatione actuali voluntatis, non remittuntur peccata, etiam in Baptismo, sine actuali immutatione voluntatis, quod fit per poenitentiam.

AD SECUNDUM dicendum quod ratio illa procedit de poenitentia secundum quod est sacramentum.

AD TERTIUM dicendum quod misericordia Dei est maioris virtutis quam misericordia hominis in hoc, quod immutat voluntatem hominis ad poenitendum, quod misericordia hominis facere non potest.

offense against God, it is necessary for man's will to be so changed as to turn to God and to renounce having turned to something else in the aforesaid manner, together with a purpose of amendment; all of which belongs to the nature of penance as a virtue. Therefore it is impossible for a sin to be pardoned anyone without penance as a virtue.

But the sacrament of Penance, as stated above (Q. 88, A. 3), is perfected by the priestly office of binding and loosing, without which God can forgive sins, even as Christ pardoned the adulterous woman, as related in John 8, and the woman that was a sinner, as related in Luke vii, whose sins, however, He did not forgive without the virtue of penance: for as Gregory states (*Hom. xxxiii in Evang.*), *He drew inwardly by grace*, i.e., by penance, *her whom He received outwardly by His mercy.*

REPLY OBJ. 1: In children there is none but original sin, which consists, not in an actual disorder of the will, but in a habitual disorder of nature, as explained in the Second Part (I-II, Q. 82, A. 1), and so in them the forgiveness of sin is accompanied by a habitual change resulting from the infusion of grace and virtues, but not by an actual change. On the other hand, in the case of an adult, in whom there are actual sins, which consist in an actual disorder of the will, there is no remission of sins, even in Baptism, without an actual change of the will, which is the effect of Penance.

REPLY OBJ. 2: This argument takes Penance as a sacrament.

REPLY OBJ. 3: God's mercy is more powerful than man's, in that it moves man's will to repent, which man's mercy cannot do.

Article 3

Whether by Penance One Sin Can Be Pardoned Without Another?

AD TERTIUM SIC PROCEDITUR. Videtur quod possit per poenitentiam unum peccatum sine alio remitti. Dicitur enim Amos IV, *plui super unam civitatem, et super alteram non plui, pars una compluta est, et pars super quam non plui, aruit.* Quod exponens Gregorius, super Ezech., dicit, *cum ille qui proximum odit ab aliis vitiis se corrigit, una et eadem civitas ex parte compluitur, et ex parte arida manet, quia sunt qui, cum quaedam vitia resecant, in aliis graviter perdurant.* Ergo potest unum peccatum per poenitentiam remitti sine alio.

PRAETEREA, Ambrosius dicit, super beati immaculati, *prima consolatio est, quia non obliviscitur misereri Deus, secunda per punitionem, ubi, et si fides desit, poena*

OBJECTION 1: It would seem that by Penance one sin can be pardoned without another. For it is written (Amos 4:7): *I caused it to rain upon one city, and caused it not to rain upon another city; one piece was rained upon: and the piece whereupon I rained not, withered.* These words are expounded by Gregory, who says (*Hom. x super Ezech.*): *When a man who hates his neighbor, breaks himself of other vices, rain falls on one part of the city, leaving the other part withered, for there are some men who, when they prune some vices, become much more rooted in others.* Therefore one sin can be forgiven by Penance, without another.

OBJ. 2: Further, Ambrose in commenting on Ps. 118, *Blessed are the undefiled in the way*, after expounding verse 136 (*My eyes have sent forth springs of water*), says that *the*

satisfacit et relevat. Potest ergo aliquis relevari ab aliquo peccato manente peccato infidelitatis.

PRAETEREA, eorum quae non necesse est esse simul, unum potest auferri sine alio. Sed peccata, ut in secunda parte habitum est, non sunt connexa, et ita unum eorum potest esse sine alio. Ergo unum eorum potest remitti sine alio per poenitentiam.

PRAETEREA, peccata sunt debita quae nobis relaxari petimus cum dicimus in oratione dominica, dimitte nobis debita nostra. Sed homo quandoque dimittit debitum unum sine alio. Ergo etiam Deus per poenitentiam dimittit unum peccatum sine alio.

PRAETEREA, per dilectionem Dei relaxantur hominibus peccata, secundum illud Ierem. XXXI, *in caritate perpetua dilexi te, ideo attraxi te miserans.* Sed nihil prohibet quin Deus diligat hominem quantum ad unum, et sit ei offensus quantum ad aliud, sicut peccatorem diligit quantum ad naturam, odit autem quantum ad culpam. Ergo videtur possibile quod Deus per poenitentiam remittat unum peccatum sine alio.

SED CONTRA est quod Augustinus dicit, in libro de poenitentia, *sunt plures quos poenitet peccasse, sed non omnino, reservantes sibi quaedam in quibus delectentur, non animadvertentes dominum simul mutum et surdum a Daemonio liberasse, per hoc docens nos nunquam nisi de omnibus sanari.*

RESPONDEO dicendum quod impossibile est per poenitentiam unum peccatum sine alio remitti. Primo quidem, quia peccatum remittitur inquantum tollitur Dei offensa per gratiam, unde in secunda parte habitum est quod nullum peccatum potest remitti sine gratia. Omne autem peccatum mortale contrariatur gratiae, et excludit eam. Unde impossibile est quod unum peccatum sine alio remittatur. Secundo quia, sicut ostensum est, peccatum mortale non potest sine vera poenitentia remitti, ad quam pertinet deserere peccatum inquantum est contra Deum. Quod quidem est commune omnibus peccatis mortalibus. Ubi autem eadem ratio est et idem effectus. Unde non potest esse vere poenitens qui de uno peccato poenitet et non de alio. Si enim displiceret ei illud peccatum quia est contra Deum super omnia dilectum, quod requiritur ad rationem verae poenitentiae, sequeretur quod de omnibus peccatis poeniteret. Unde sequitur quod impossibile sit unum peccatum remitti sine alio. Tertio, quia hoc esset contra perfectionem misericordiae Dei, cuius perfecta sunt opera, ut dicitur Deut. XXXII. Unde cuius miseretur, totaliter miseretur. Et hoc est quod Augustinus dicit, in libro de poenitentia, *quaedam impietas infidelitatis est ab illo qui iustus et iustitia est, dimidiam sperare veniam.*

first consolation is that God is mindful to have mercy; and the second, that He punishes, for although faith be wanting, punishment makes satisfaction and raises us up. Therefore a man can be raised up from one sin, while the sin of unbelief remains.

OBJ. 3: Further, when several things are not necessarily together, one can be removed without the other. Now it was stated in the Second Part (I-II, Q. 73, A. 1) that sins are not connected together, so that one sin can be without another. Therefore also one sin can be taken away by Penance without another being taken away.

OBJ. 4: Further, sins are the debts, for which we pray for pardon when we say in the Lord's Prayer: *Forgive us our trespasses*, etc. Now man sometimes forgives one debt without forgiving another. Therefore God also, by Penance, forgives one sin without another.

OBJ. 5: Further, man's sins are forgiven him through the love of God, according to Jer. 31:3: *I have loved thee with an everlasting love, therefore have I drawn thee, taking pity on thee.* Now there is nothing to hinder God from loving a man in one respect, while being offended with him in another, even as He loves the sinner as regards his nature, while hating him for his sin. Therefore it seems possible for God, by Penance, to pardon one sin without another.

ON THE CONTRARY, Augustine says in *De Poenitentia*: *There are many who repent having sinned, but not completely; for they except certain things which give them pleasure, forgetting that our Lord delivered from the devil the man who was both dumb and deaf, whereby He shows us that we are never healed unless it be from all sins.*

I ANSWER THAT, It is impossible for Penance to take one sin away without another. First because sin is taken away by grace removing the offense against God. Wherefore it was stated in the Second Part (I-II, Q. 109, A. 7; Q. 113, A. 2) that without grace no sin can be forgiven. Now every mortal sin is opposed to grace and excludes it. Therefore it is impossible for one sin to be pardoned without another. Second, because, as shown above (A. 2) mortal sin cannot be forgiven without true Penance, to which it belongs to renounce sin, by reason of its being against God, which is common to all mortal sins: and where the same reason applies, the result will be the same. Consequently a man cannot be truly penitent, if he repent of one sin and not of another. For if one particular sin were displeasing to him, because it is against the love of God above all things (which motive is necessary for true repentance), it follows that he would repent of all. Whence it follows that it is impossible for one sin to be pardoned through Penance, without another. Third, because this would be contrary to the perfection of God's mercy, since His works are perfect, as stated in Deut. 32:4; wherefore whomsoever He pardons, He pardons altogether. Hence Augustine says, that *it is irreverent and heretical to expect half a pardon from Him Who is just and justice itself.*

AD PRIMUM ergo dicendum quod verbum illud Gregorii non est intelligendum quantum ad remissionem culpae, sed quantum ad cessationem ab actu, quia interdum ille qui plura peccata consuevit committere, deserit unum, non tamen aliud. Quod quidem fit auxilio divino, quod tamen non pertingit usque ad remissionem culpae.

AD SECUNDUM dicendum quod in verbo illo Ambrosii fides non potest accipi qua creditur in Christum, quia, ut Augustinus dicit, super illud Ioan. XV, *si non venissem et locutus eis non fuissem, peccatum non haberent,* scilicet infidelitatis, *hoc enim est peccatum quo tenentur cuncta peccata.* Sed accipitur fides pro conscientia, quia interdum per poenas quas quis patienter sustinet, consequitur remissionem peccati cuius conscientiam non habet.

AD TERTIUM dicendum quod peccata, quamvis non sint connexa quantum ad conversionem ad bonum commutabile, sunt tamen connexa quantum ad aversionem a bono incommutabili, in qua conveniunt omnia peccata mortalia. Et ex hac parte habent rationem offensae, quam oportet per poenitentiam tolli.

AD QUARTUM dicendum quod debitum exterioris rei, puta pecuniae, non contrariatur amicitiae, ex qua debitum remittitur. Et ideo potest unum dimitti sine alio. Sed debitum culpae contrariatur amicitiae. Et ideo una culpa vel offensa non remittitur sine altera. Ridiculum etiam videretur quod aliquis ab homine veniam peteret de una offensa et non de alia.

AD QUINTUM dicendum quod dilectio qua Deus diligit hominis naturam, non ordinatur ad bonum gloriae, a qua impeditur homo per quodlibet mortale peccatum. Sed dilectio gratiae, per quam fit remissio peccati mortalis, ordinat hominem ad vitam aeternam, secundum illud Rom. VI, *gratia Dei vita aeterna.* Unde non est similis ratio.

REPLY OBJ. 1: These words of Gregory do not refer to the forgiveness of the guilt, but to the cessation from act, because sometimes a man who has been wont to commit several kinds of sin, renounces one and not the other; which is indeed due to God's assistance, but does not reach to the pardon of the sin.

REPLY OBJ. 2: In this saying of Ambrose *faith* cannot denote the faith whereby we believe in Christ, because, as Augustine says on John 15:22, *If I had not come, and spoken to them, they would not have sin* (viz. unbelief): *for this is the sin which contains all others*: but it stands for consciousness, because sometimes a man receives pardon for a sin of which he is not conscious, through the punishment which he bears patiently.

REPLY OBJ. 3: Although sins are not connected in so far as they turn towards a mutable good, yet they are connected in so far as they turn away from the immutable Good, which applies to all mortal sins in common; and it is thus that they have the character of an offense which needs to be removed by Penance.

REPLY OBJ. 4: Debt as regards external things, e.g., money, is not opposed to friendship through which the debt is pardoned; hence one debt can be condoned without another. On the other hand, the debt of sin is opposed to friendship, and so one sin or offense is not pardoned without another; for it would seem absurd for anyone to ask even a man to forgive him one offense and not another.

REPLY OBJ. 5: The love whereby God loves man's nature, does not ordain man to the good of glory from which man is excluded by any mortal sin; but the love of grace, whereby mortal sin is forgiven, ordains man to eternal life, according to Rom. 6:23: *The grace of God (is) life everlasting.* Hence there is no comparison.

Article 4

Whether the Debt of Punishment Remains After the Guilt Has Been Forgiven Through Penance?

AD QUARTUM SIC PROCEDITUR. Videtur quod, remissa culpa per poenitentiam, non remaneat reatus poenae. Remota enim causa, removetur effectus. Sed culpa est causa reatus poenae, ideo enim est aliquis dignus poena quia culpam commisit. Ergo, remissa culpa, non potest remanere reatus poenae.

PRAETEREA, sicut apostolus dicit, Rom. V, donum Christi est efficacius quam peccatum. Sed peccando homo simul incurrit culpam et poenae reatum. Ergo

OBJECTION 1: It would seem that no debt of punishment remains after the guilt has been forgiven through Penance. For when the cause is removed, the effect is removed. But the guilt is the cause of the debt of punishment: since a man deserves to be punished because he has been guilty of a sin. Therefore when the sin has been forgiven, no debt of punishment can remain.

OBJ. 2: Further, according to the Apostle (Rom 5) the gift of Christ is more effective than the sin of Adam. Now, by sinning, man incurs at the same time guilt and the debt

multo magis per donum gratiae simul remittitur culpa et tollitur poenae reatus.

PRAETEREA, remissio peccatorum fit in poenitentia per virtutem passionis Christi, secundum illud Rom. III, *quem proposuit Deus propitiatorem per fidem in sanguine ipsius, propter remissionem praecedentium delictorum.* Sed passio Christi sufficienter est satisfactoria pro omnibus peccatis, ut supra habitum est. Non ergo post remissionem culpae remanet aliquis reatus poenae.

SED CONTRA est quod, II Reg. XII, dicitur quod, cum David poenitens dixisset ad Nathan, peccavi domino, dixit Nathan ad illum, *dominus quoque transtulit peccatum tuum, non morieris. Veruntamen filius qui natus est tibi, morte morietur*, quod fuit in poenam praecedentis peccati, ut ibidem dicitur. Ergo, remissa culpa, remanet reatus alicuius poenae.

RESPONDEO dicendum quod, sicut in secunda parte habitum est, in peccato mortali sunt duo, scilicet aversio ab incommutabili bono, et conversio ad commutabile bonum inordinata. Ex parte igitur aversionis ab incommutabili bono, consequitur peccatum mortale reatus poenae aeternae, ut qui contra aeternum bonum peccavit, in aeternum puniatur. Ex parte etiam conversionis ad bonum commutabile, inquantum est inordinata, consequitur peccatum mortale reatus alicuius poenae, quia inordinatio culpae non reducitur ad ordinem iustitiae nisi per poenam; iustum est enim ut qui voluntati suae plus indulsit quam debuit, contra voluntatem suam aliquid patiatur, sic enim erit aequalitas; unde et Apoc. XVIII dicitur, *quantum glorificavit se et in deliciis fuit, tantum date illi tormentum et luctum.*

Quia tamen conversio ad bonum commutabile finita est, non habet ex hac parte peccatum mortale quod debeatur ei poena aeterna. Unde, si sit inordinata conversio ad bonum commutabile sine aversione a Deo, sicut est in peccatis venialibus, non debetur peccato poena aeterna, sed temporalis. Quando igitur per gratiam remittitur culpa, tollitur aversio animae a Deo, inquantum per gratiam anima Deo coniungitur. Unde et per consequens simul tollitur reatus poenae aeternae. Potest tamen remanere reatus alicuius poenae temporalis.

AD PRIMUM ergo dicendum quod culpa mortalis utrumque habet, et aversionem a Deo et conversionem ad bonum creatum, sed, sicut in secunda parte habitum est, aversio a Deo est ibi sicut formale, conversio autem ad bonum creatum est ibi sicut materiale. Remoto autem formali cuiuscumque rei, tollitur species, sicut, remoto rationali, tollitur species humana. Et ideo ex hoc ipso dicitur culpa mortalis remitti, quod per gratiam tollitur aversio mentis a Deo, simul cum reatu poenae aeternae. Remanet tamen id quod est materiale, scilicet inordinata

of punishment. Much more therefore, by the gift of grace, is the guilt forgiven and at the same time the debt of punishment remitted.

OBJ. 3: Further, the forgiveness of sins is effected in Penance through the power of Christ's Passion, according to Rom. 3:25: *Whom God hath proposed to be a propitiation, through faith in His Blood . . . for the remission of former sins.* Now Christ's Passion made satisfaction sufficient for all sins, as stated above (QQ. 48, 49, 79, A. 5). Therefore after the guilt has been pardoned, no debt of punishment remains.

ON THE CONTRARY, It is related (2 Kgs 12:13) that when David penitent had said to Nathan: *I have sinned against the Lord*, Nathan said to him: *The Lord also hath taken away thy sin, thou shalt not die. Nevertheless . . . the child that is born to thee shall surely die*, which was to punish him for the sin he had committed, as stated in the same place. Therefore a debt of some punishment remains after the guilt has been forgiven.

I ANSWER THAT, As stated in the Second Part (I-II, Q. 87, A. 4), in mortal sin there are two things, namely, a turning from the immutable Good, and an inordinate turning to mutable good. Accordingly, in so far as mortal sin turns away from the immutable Good, it induces a debt of eternal punishment, so that whosoever sins against the eternal Good should be punished eternally. Again, in so far as mortal sin turns inordinately to a mutable good, it gives rise to a debt of some punishment, because the disorder of guilt is not brought back to the order of justice, except by punishment: since it is just that he who has been too indulgent to his will, should suffer something against his will, for thus will equality be restored. Hence it is written (Rev 18:7): *As much as she hath glorified herself, and lived in delicacies, so much torment and sorrow give ye to her.*

Since, however, the turning to mutable good is finite, sin does not, in this respect, induce a debt of eternal punishment. Wherefore, if man turns inordinately to a mutable good, without turning from God, as happens in venial sins, he incurs a debt, not of eternal but of temporal punishment. Consequently when guilt is pardoned through grace, the soul ceases to be turned away from God, through being united to God by grace: so that at the same time, the debt of punishment is taken away, albeit a debt of some temporal punishment may yet remain.

REPLY OBJ. 1: Mortal sin both turns away from God and turns to a created good. But, as stated in the Second Part (I-II, Q. 71, A. 6), the turning away from God is as its form while the turning to created good is as its matter. Now if the formal element of anything be removed, the species is taken away: thus, if you take away rational, you take away the human species. Consequently mortal sin is said to be pardoned from the very fact that, by means of grace, the aversion of the mind from God is taken away together with the debt of eternal punishment: and yet the material

conversio ad bonum creatum. Pro qua debetur reatus poenae temporalis.

AD SECUNDUM dicendum quod, sicut in secunda parte habitum est, ad gratiam pertinet operari in homine iustificando a peccato, et cooperari homini ad recte operandum. Remissio igitur culpae et reatus poenae aeternae pertinet ad gratiam operantem, sed remissio reatus poenae temporalis pertinet ad gratiam cooperantem, inquantum scilicet homo, cum auxilio divinae gratiae, patienter poenas tolerando, absolvitur etiam a reatu poenae temporalis. Sicut igitur prius est effectus gratiae operantis quam cooperantis, ita etiam prius est remissio culpae et poenae aeternae quam plena absolutio a poena temporali, utrumque enim est a gratia, sed primum a gratia sola, secundum ex gratia et ex libero arbitrio.

AD TERTIUM dicendum est quod passio Christi de se sufficiens est ad tollendum omnem reatum poenae non solum aeternae, sed etiam temporalis, et secundum modum quo homo participat virtutem passionis Christi, percipit etiam absolutionem a reatu poenae. In Baptismo autem homo participat totaliter virtutem passionis Christi, utpote per aquam et spiritum Christo commortuus peccato et in eo regeneratus ad novam vitam. Et ideo in Baptismo homo consequitur remissionem reatus totius poenae. In poenitentia vero consequitur virtutem passionis Christi secundum modum propriorum actuum, qui sunt materia poenitentiae, sicut aqua Baptismi, ut supra dictum est. Et ideo non statim per primum actum poenitentiae, quo remittitur culpa, solvitur reatus totius poenae, sed completis omnibus poenitentiae actibus.

element remains, viz. the inordinate turning to a created good, for which a debt of temporal punishment is due.

REPLY OBJ. 2: As stated in the Second Part (I-II, Q. 109, AA. 7, 8; Q. 111, A. 2), it belongs to grace to operate in man by justifying him from sin, and to co-operate with man that his work may be rightly done. Consequently the forgiveness of guilt and of the debt of eternal punishment belongs to operating grace, while the remission of the debt of temporal punishment belongs to co-operating grace, in so far as man, by bearing punishment patiently with the help of Divine grace, is released also from the debt of temporal punishment. Consequently just as the effect of operating grace precedes the effect of co-operating grace, so too, the remission of guilt and of eternal punishment precedes the complete release from temporal punishment, since both are from grace, but the former, from grace alone, the latter, from grace and free-will.

REPLY OBJ. 3: Christ's Passion is of itself sufficient to remove all debt of punishment, not only eternal, but also temporal; and man is released from the debt of punishment according to the measure of his share in the power of Christ's Passion. Now in Baptism man shares the Power of Christ's Passion fully, since by water and the Spirit of Christ, he dies with Him to sin, and is born again in Him to a new life, so that, in Baptism, man receives the remission of all debt of punishment. In Penance, on the other hand, man shares in the power of Christ's Passion according to the measure of his own acts, which are the matter of Penance, as water is of Baptism, as stated above (Q. 84, AA. 1, 3). Wherefore the entire debt of punishment is not remitted at once after the first act of Penance, by which act the guilt is remitted, but only when all the acts of Penance have been completed.

Article 5

Whether the Remnants of Sin Are Removed When a Mortal Sin Is Forgiven?

AD QUINTUM SIC PROCEDITUR. Videtur quod, remissa culpa mortali, tollantur omnes reliquiae peccati. Dicit enim Augustinus, in libro de poenitentia, *nunquam dominus aliquem sanavit quem omnino non liberavit, totum enim hominem sanavit in sabbato, quia corpus ab omni infirmitate, et animam ab omni contagione.* Sed reliquiae peccati pertinent ad infirmitatem peccati. Ergo non videtur possibile quod, remissa culpa, remaneant reliquiae peccati.

PRAETEREA, secundum Dionysium, IV cap. de Div. Nom., bonum est efficacius quam malum, quia malum non agit nisi in virtute boni. Sed homo peccando simul totam infectionem peccati contrahit. Ergo multo magis poenitendo liberatur etiam ab omnibus peccati reliquiis.

OBJECTION 1: It would seem that all the remnants of sin are removed when a mortal sin is forgiven. For Augustine says in *De Poenitentia*: *Our Lord never healed anyone without delivering him wholly; for He wholly healed the man on the Sabbath, since He delivered his body from all disease, and his soul from all taint.* Now the remnants of sin belong to the disease of sin. Therefore it does not seem possible for any remnants of sin to remain when the guilt has been pardoned.

OBJ. 2: Further, according to Dionysius (*Div. Nom.* iv), *good is more efficacious than evil, since evil does not act save in virtue of some good.* Now, by sinning, man incurs the taint of sin all at once. Much more, therefore, by repenting, is he delivered also from all remnants of sin.

PRAETEREA, opus Dei est efficacius quam opus hominis. Sed per exercitium humanorum operum ad bonum tolluntur reliquiae peccati contrarii. Ergo multo magis tolluntur per remissionem culpae, quae est opus Dei.

SED CONTRA est quod Marci VIII legitur quod caecus illuminatus a domino, primo restitutus est ad imperfectum visum, unde ait, *video homines velut arbores ambulare*; deinde restitutus est perfecte, ita ut videret clare omnia. Illuminatio autem caeci significat liberationem peccatoris. Post primam ergo remissionem culpae, qua peccator restituitur ad visum spiritualem, adhuc remanent in eo reliquiae aliquae peccati praeteriti.

RESPONDEO dicendum quod peccatum mortale ex parte conversionis inordinatae ad bonum commutabile quandam dispositionem causat in anima; vel etiam habitum, si actus frequenter iteretur. Sicut autem dictum est, culpa mortalis peccati remittitur inquantum tollitur per gratiam aversio mentis a Deo. Sublato autem eo quod est ex parte aversionis, nihilominus remanere potest id quod est ex parte conversionis inordinatae, cum hanc contingat esse sine illa, sicut prius dictum est. Et ideo nihil prohibet quin remissa culpa, remaneant dispositiones ex praecedentibus actibus causatae, quae dicuntur peccati reliquiae. Remanent tamen debilitatae et diminutae, ita quod homini non dominentur. Et hoc magis per modum dispositionum quam per modum habituum, sicut etiam remanet fomes post Baptismum.

AD PRIMUM ergo dicendum quod Deus totum hominem perfecte curat, sed quandoque subito, sicut socrum Petri statim restituit perfectae sanitati, ita ut surgens ministraret ei, ut legitur Luc. IV; quandoque autem successive, sicut dictum est de caeco illuminato, Marci VIII. Et ita etiam spiritualiter quandoque tanta commotione convertit cor hominis ut subito perfecte consequatur sanitatem spiritualem, non solum remissa culpa, sed sublatis omnibus peccati reliquiis, ut patet de Magdalena, Luc. VII. Quandoque autem prius remittit culpam per gratiam operantem, et postea per gratiam cooperantem successive tollit peccati reliquias.

AD SECUNDUM dicendum quod peccatum etiam quandoque statim inducit debilem dispositionem, utpote per unum actum causatam, quandoque autem fortiorem, causatam per multos actus.

AD TERTIUM dicendum quod uno actu humano non tolluntur omnes reliquiae peccati, quia, ut dicitur in praedicamentis, *pravus, ad meliores exercitationes deductus, ad modicum aliquid proficiet, ut melior sit*, multiplicato autem exercitio, ad hoc pervenit ut sit bonus virtute acquisita. Hoc autem multo efficacius facit divina gratia, sive uno sive pluribus actibus.

OBJ. 3: Further, God's work is more efficacious than man's. Now by the exercise of good human works the remnants of contrary sins are removed. Much more, therefore, are they taken away by the remission of guilt, which is a work of God.

ON THE CONTRARY, We read (Mark 8) that the blind man whom our Lord enlightened, was restored first of all to imperfect sight, wherefore he said (Mark 8:24): *I see men, as it were trees, walking*; and afterwards he was restored perfectly, *so that he saw all things clearly*. Now the enlightenment of the blind man signifies the delivery of the sinner. Therefore after the first remission of sin, whereby the sinner is restored to spiritual sight, there still remain in him some remnants of his past sin.

I ANSWER THAT, Mortal sin, in so far as it turns inordinately to a mutable good, produces in the soul a certain disposition, or even a habit, if the acts be repeated frequently. Now it has been said above (A. 4) that the guilt of mortal sin is pardoned through grace removing the aversion of the mind from God. Nevertheless when that which is on the part of the aversion has been taken away by grace, that which is on the part of the inordinate turning to a mutable good can remain, since this may happen to be without the other, as stated above (A. 4). Consequently, there is no reason why, after the guilt has been forgiven, the dispositions caused by preceding acts should not remain, which are called the remnants of sin. Yet they remain weakened and diminished, so as not to domineer over man, and they are after the manner of dispositions rather than of habits, like the fomes which remains after Baptism.

REPLY OBJ. 1: God heals the whole man perfectly; but sometimes suddenly, as Peter's mother-in-law was restored at once to perfect health, so that *rising she ministered to them* (Luke 4:39), and sometimes by degrees, as we said above (Q. 44, A. 3, ad 2) about the blind man who was restored to sight (Matt 8). And so too, He sometimes turns the heart of man with such power, that it receives at once perfect spiritual health, not only the guilt being pardoned, but all remnants of sin being removed as was the case with Magdalen (Luke 7); whereas at other times He sometimes first pardons the guilt by operating grace, and afterwards, by co-operating grace, removes the remnants of sin by degrees.

REPLY OBJ. 2: Sin too, sometimes induces at once a weak disposition, such as is the result of one act, and sometimes a stronger disposition, the result of many acts.

REPLY OBJ. 3: One human act does not remove all the remnants of sin, because, as stated in the *Predicaments* (Categor. viii) *a vicious man by doing good works will make but little progress so as to be any better, but if he continue in good practice, he will end in being good as to acquired virtue*. But God's grace does this much more effectively, whether by one or by several acts.

Article 6

Whether the Forgiveness of Guilt Is an Effect of Penance?

AD SEXTUM SIC PROCEDITUR. Videtur quod remissio culpae non sit effectus poenitentiae secundum quod est virtus. Dicitur enim poenitentia virtus secundum quod est principium humani actus. Sed humani actus non operantur ad remissionem culpae, quae est effectus gratiae operantis. Ergo remissio culpae non est effectus poenitentiae secundum quod est virtus.

PRAETEREA, quaedam aliae virtutes sunt excellentiores poenitentia. Sed remissio culpae non dicitur effectus alicuius alterius virtutis. Ergo etiam non est effectus poenitentiae secundum quod est virtus.

PRAETEREA, remissio culpae non est nisi ex virtute passionis Christi, secundum illud Heb. IX, *sine sanguinis effusione non fit remissio.* Sed poenitentia inquantum est sacramentum, operatur in virtute passionis Christi, sicut et cetera sacramenta, ut ex supra dictis patet. Ergo remissio culpae non est effectus poenitentiae inquantum est virtus, sed inquantum est sacramentum.

SED CONTRA, illud est proprie causa alicuius sine quo esse non potest, omnis enim effectus dependet a sua causa. Sed remissio culpae potest esse a Deo sine poenitentiae sacramento, non autem sine poenitentia secundum quod est virtus, ut supra dictum est. Unde et ante sacramenta novae legis poenitentibus Deus peccata remittebat. Ergo remissio culpae est effectus poenitentiae secundum quod est virtus.

RESPONDEO dicendum quod poenitentia est virtus secundum quod est principium quorundam actuum humanorum. Actus autem humani qui sunt ex parte peccatoris, materialiter se habent in sacramento poenitentiae. Omne autem sacramentum producit effectum suum non solum virtute formae, sed etiam virtute materiae, ex utroque enim est unum sacramentum, ut supra habitum est. Unde, sicut remissio culpae fit in Baptismo non solum virtute formae, ex qua et ipsa aqua virtutem recipit; ita etiam remissio culpae est effectus poenitentiae, principalius quidem ex virtute clavium, quam habent ministri, ex quorum parte accipitur id quod est formale in hoc sacramento, ut supra dictum est; secundario autem ex vi actuum poenitentis pertinentium ad virtutem poenitentiae, tamen prout hi actus aliqualiter ordinantur ad claves Ecclesiae. Et sic patet quod remissio culpae est effectus poenitentiae secundum quod est virtus, principalius tamen secundum quod est sacramentum.

AD PRIMUM ergo dicendum quod effectus gratiae operantis est iustificatio impii, ut in secunda parte dictum est. In qua, ut ibidem dictum est, non solum est gratiae infusio et remissio culpae, sed etiam motus liberi

OBJECTION 1: It would seem that the forgiveness of guilt is not an effect of penance as a virtue. For penance is said to be a virtue, in so far as it is a principle of a human action. But human action does nothing towards the remission of guilt, since this is an effect of operating grace. Therefore the forgiveness of guilt is not an effect of penance as a virtue.

OBJ. 2: Further, certain other virtues are more excellent than penance. But the forgiveness of sin is not said to be the effect of any other virtue. Neither, therefore, is it the effect of penance as a virtue.

OBJ. 3: Further, there is no forgiveness of sin except through the power of Christ's Passion, according to Heb. 9:22: *Without shedding of blood there is no remission.* Now Penance, as a sacrament, produces its effect through the power of Christ's Passion, even as the other sacraments do, as was shown above (Q. 62, AA. 4, 5). Therefore the forgiveness of sin is the effect of Penance, not as a virtue, but as a sacrament.

ON THE CONTRARY, Properly speaking, the cause of a thing is that without which it cannot be, since every defect depends on its cause. Now forgiveness of sin can come from God without the sacrament of Penance, but not without the virtue of penance, as stated above (Q. 84, A. 5, ad 3; Q. 85, A. 2); so that, even before the sacraments of the New Law were instituted, God pardoned the sins of the penitent. Therefore the forgiveness of sin is chiefly the effect of penance as a virtue.

I ANSWER THAT, Penance is a virtue in so far as it is a principle of certain human acts. Now the human acts, which are performed by the sinner, are the material element in the sacrament of Penance. Moreover every sacrament produces its effect, in virtue not only of its form, but also of its matter; because both these together make the one sacrament, as stated above (Q. 60, A. 6, ad 2, A. 7). Hence in Baptism forgiveness of sin is effected, in virtue not only of the form, from which the water receives its power—and, similarly, the forgiveness of sin is the effect of Penance, chiefly by the power of the keys, which is vested in the ministers, who furnish the formal part of the sacrament, as stated above (Q. 84, A. 3), and secondarily by the instrumentality of those acts of the penitent which pertain to the virtue of penance, but only in so far as such acts are, in some way, subordinate to the keys of the Church. Accordingly it is evident that the forgiveness of sin is the effect of penance as a virtue, but still more of Penance as a sacrament.

REPLY OBJ. 1: The effect of operating grace is the justification of the ungodly (as stated in the Second Part, I-II, Q. 113), wherein there is, as was there stated (AA. 1, 2, 3), not only infusion of grace and forgiveness of sin, but also a

arbitrii in Deum, qui est actus fidei formatae, et motus liberi arbitrii in peccatum, qui est actus poenitentiae. Hi tamen actus humani sunt ibi ut effectus gratiae operantis simul producti cum remissione culpae. Unde remissio culpae non fit sine actu poenitentiae virtutis, licet sit effectus gratiae operantis.

Ad secundum dicendum quod in iustificatione impii non solum est actus poenitentiae, sed etiam actus fidei, ut dictum est. Et ideo remissio culpae non ponitur effectus solum poenitentiae virtutis, sed principalius fidei et caritatis.

Ad tertium dicendum quod ad passionem Christi ordinatur actus poenitentiae virtutis et per fidem et per ordinem ad claves Ecclesiae. Et ideo utroque modo causat remissionem culpae virtute passionis Christi.

Ad id autem quod in contrarium obiicitur, dicendum est quod actus poenitentiae virtutis habet quod sine eo non possit fieri remissio culpae, inquantum est inseparabilis effectus gratiae, per quam principaliter culpa remittitur, quae etiam operatur in omnibus sacramentis. Et ideo per hoc non potest concludi nisi quod gratia est principalior causa remissionis culpae quam poenitentiae sacramentum. Sciendum tamen quod etiam in veteri lege et in lege naturae erat aliqualiter sacramentum poenitentiae, ut supra dictum est.

movement of the free-will towards God, which is an act of faith quickened by charity, and a movement of the free-will against sin, which is the act of penance. Yet these human acts are there as the effects of operating grace, and are produced at the same time as the forgiveness of sin. Consequently the forgiveness of sin does not take place without an act of the virtue of penance, although it is the effect of operating grace.

Reply Obj. 2: In the justification of the ungodly there is not only an act of penance, but also an act of faith, as stated above (ad 1: I-II, Q. 113, A. 4). Wherefore the forgiveness of sin is accounted the effect not only of the virtue of penance, but also, and that chiefly, of faith and charity.

Reply Obj. 3: The act of the virtue of penance is subordinate to Christ's Passion both by faith, and by its relation to the keys of the Church; and so, in both ways, it causes the forgiveness of sin, by the power of Christ's Passion.

To the argument advanced in the contrary sense we reply that the act of the virtue of penance is necessary for the forgiveness of sin, through being an inseparable effect of grace, whereby chiefly is sin pardoned, and which produces its effect in all the sacraments. Consequently it only follows that grace is a higher cause of the forgiveness of sin than the sacrament of Penance. Moreover, it must be observed that, under the Old Law and the law of nature, there was a sacrament of Penance after a fashion, as stated above (Q. 84, A. 7, ad 2).

QUESTION 87

THE REMISSION OF VENIAL SIN

Deinde considerandum est de remissione venialium peccatorum. Et circa hoc quaeruntur quatuor.

Primo, utrum sine poenitentia peccatum veniale possit dimitti.

Secundo, utrum possit dimitti sine gratiae infusione.

Tertio, utrum peccata venialia remittantur per aspersionem aquae benedictae, et tunsionem pectoris, et orationem dominicam, et alia huiusmodi.

Quarto, utrum veniale possit dimitti sine mortali.

We must now consider the forgiveness of venial sins, under which head there are four points of inquiry:

(1) Whether venial sin can be forgiven without Penance?

(2) Whether it can be forgiven without the infusion of grace?

(3) Whether venial sins are forgiven by the sprinkling of holy water, a bishop's blessing, the beating of the breast, the Lord's Prayer, and the like?

(4) Whether a venial sin can be taken away without a mortal sin?

Article 1

Whether Venial Sin Can Be Forgiven Without Penance?

AD PRIMUM SIC PROCEDITUR. Videtur quod veniale peccatum possit remitti sine poenitentia. Pertinet enim, ut supra dictum est, ad rationem verae poenitentiae quod non solum homo doleat de peccato praeterito, sed etiam proponat cavere de futuro. Sed sine tali proposito peccata venialia dimittuntur, cum certum sit homini quod sine peccatis venialibus praesentem vitam ducere non possit. Ergo peccata venialia possunt remitti sine poenitentia.

PRAETEREA, poenitentia non est sine actuali displicentia peccatorum. Sed peccata venialia possunt dimitti sine displicentia eorum, sicut patet in eo qui dormiens occideretur propter Christum; statim enim evolaret, quod non contingit manentibus peccatis venialibus. Ergo peccata venialia possunt remitti sine poenitentia.

PRAETEREA, peccata venialia opponuntur fervori caritatis, ut in secunda parte dictum est. Sed unum oppositorum tollitur per aliud. Ergo per fervorem caritatis, quem contingit esse sine actuali displicentia peccati venialis, fit remissio peccatorum venialium.

SED CONTRA est quod Augustinus dicit, in libro de poenitentia, quod *est quaedam poenitentia quae quotidie agitur in Ecclesia pro peccatis venialibus.* Quae frustra esset si sine poenitentia peccata venialia possunt dimitti.

RESPONDEO dicendum quod remissio culpae, sicut dictum est, fit per coniunctionem ad Deum, a quo aliqualiter separat culpa. Sed haec separatio perfecte quidem fit per peccatum mortale, imperfecte autem per

OBJECTION 1: It would seem that venial sin can be forgiven without penance. For, as stated above (Q. 84, A. 10, ad 4), it is essential to true penance that man should not only sorrow for his past sins, but also that he should purpose to avoid them for the future. Now venial sins are forgiven without any such purpose, for it is certain that man cannot lead the present life without committing venial sins. Therefore venial sins can be forgiven without penance.

OBJ. 2: Further, there is no penance without actual displeasure at one's sins. But venial sins can be taken away without any actual displeasure at them, as would be the case if a man were to be killed in his sleep, for Christ's sake, since he would go to heaven at once, which would not happen if his venial sins remained. Therefore venial sins can be forgiven without penance.

OBJ. 3: Further, venial sins are contrary to the fervor of charity, as stated in the Second Part (II-II, Q. 24, A. 10). Now one contrary is removed by another. Therefore forgiveness of venial sins is caused by the fervor of charity, which may be without actual displeasure at venial sin.

ON THE CONTRARY, Augustine says in *De Poenitentia,* that *there is a penance which is done for venial sins in the Church every day* which would be useless if venial sins could be forgiven without Penance.

I ANSWER THAT, Forgiveness of sin, as stated above (Q. 86, A. 2), is effected by man being united to God from Whom sin separates him in some way. Now this separation is made complete by mortal sin, and incomplete by venial

peccatum veniale, nam per peccatum mortale mens omnino a Deo avertitur, utpote contra caritatem agens; per peccatum autem veniale retardatur affectus hominis ne prompte in Deum feratur. Et ideo utrumque peccatum per poenitentiam quidem remittitur, quia per utrumque deordinatur voluntas hominis per immoderatam conversionem ad bonum creatum, sicut enim peccatum mortale remitti non potest quandiu voluntas peccato adhaeret, ita etiam nec peccatum veniale, quia, manente causa, manet effectus.

Exigitur autem ad remissionem peccati mortalis perfectior poenitentia, ut scilicet homo actualiter peccatum mortale commissum detestetur quantum in ipso est, ut scilicet diligentiam adhibeat ad rememorandum singula peccata mortalia, ut singula detestetur. Sed hoc non requiritur ad remissionem venialium peccatorum. Non tamen sufficit habitualis displicentia, quae habetur per habitum caritatis vel poenitentiae virtutis, quia sic caritas non compateretur peccatum veniale, quod patet esse falsum. Unde sequitur quod requiratur quaedam virtualis displicentia, puta cum aliquis fertur hoc modo secundum affectum in Deum et res divinas ut quidquid ei occurrat quod eum ab hoc motu retardaret, displiceret ei, et doleret se hoc commisisse, etiam si actu de illo non cogitaret. Quod tamen non sufficit ad remissionem peccati mortalis, nisi quantum ad peccata oblita post diligentem inquisitionem.

AD PRIMUM ergo dicendum quod homo in gratia constitutus potest vitare omnia peccata mortalia et singula; potest etiam vitare singula peccata venialia, sed non omnia; ut patet ex his quae in secunda parte dicta sunt. Et ideo poenitentia de peccatis mortalibus requirit quod homo proponat abstinere ab omnibus et singulis peccatis mortalibus. Sed ad poenitentiam peccatorum venialium requiritur quod proponat abstinere a singulis, non tamen ab omnibus, quia hoc infirmitas huius vitae non patitur. Debet tamen habere propositum se praeparandi ad peccata venialia minuenda, alioquin esset ei periculum deficiendi, cum desereret appetitum proficiendi, seu tollendi impedimenta spiritualis profectus, quae sunt peccata venialia.

AD SECUNDUM dicendum quod passio pro Christo suscepta, sicut supra dictum est, obtinet vim Baptismi. Et ideo purgat ab omni culpa et mortali et veniali, nisi actualiter voluntatem peccato invenerit inhaerentem.

AD TERTIUM dicendum quod fervor caritatis virtualiter implicat displicentiam venialium peccatorum, ut supra dictum est.

sin: because, by mortal sin, the mind through acting against charity is altogether turned away from God; whereas by venial sin man's affections are clogged, so that they are slow in tending towards God. Consequently both kinds of sin are taken away by penance, because by both of them man's will is disordered through turning inordinately to a created good; for just as mortal sin cannot be forgiven so long as the will is attached to sin, so neither can venial sin, because while the cause remains, the effect remains.

Yet a more perfect penance is requisite for the forgiveness of mortal sin, namely that man should detest actually the mortal sin which he committed, so far as lies in his power, that is to say, he should endeavor to remember each single mortal sin, in order to detest each one. But this is, not required for the forgiveness of venial sins; although it does not suffice to have habitual displeasure, which is included in the habit of charity or of penance as a virtue, since then venial sin would be incompatible with charity, which is evidently untrue. Consequently it is necessary to have a certain virtual displeasure, so that, for instance, a man's affections so tend to God and Divine things, that whatever might happen to him to hamper that tendency would be displeasing to him, and would grieve him, were he to commit it, even though he were not to think of it actually: and this is not sufficient for the remission of mortal sin, except as regards those sins which he fails to remember after a careful examination.

REPLY OBJ. 1: When man is in a state of grace, he can avoid all mortal sins, and each single one; and he can avoid each single venial sin, but not all, as was explained in the Second Part (I-II, Q. 74, A. 8, ad 2; Q. 109, A. 8). Consequently penance for mortal sins requires man to purpose abstaining from mortal sins, all and each; whereas penance for venial sins requires man to purpose abstaining from each, but not from all, because the weakness of this life does not allow of this. Nevertheless he needs to have the purpose of taking steps to commit fewer venial sins, else he would be in danger of falling back, if he gave up the desire of going forward, or of removing the obstacles to spiritual progress, such as venial sins are.

REPLY OBJ. 2: Death for Christ's sake, as stated above (Q. 66, A. 11), obtains the power of Baptism, wherefore it washes away all sin, both venial and mortal, unless it find the will attached to sin.

REPLY OBJ. 3: The fervor of charity implies virtual displeasure at venial sins, as stated above (Q. 79, A. 4).

Article 2

Whether Infusion of Grace Is Necessary for the Remission of Venial Sins?

AD SECUNDUM SIC PROCEDITUR. Videtur quod ad remissionem venialium peccatorum requiratur gratiae infusio. Effectus enim non est sine propria causa. Sed propria causa remissionis peccatorum est gratia, non enim ex meritis propriis hominis peccata propria remittuntur; unde dicitur Ephes. II, *Deus, qui dives est in misericordia, propter nimiam caritatem qua dilexit nos, cum essemus mortui peccatis, convivificavit nos in Christo, cuius gratia salvati estis.* Ergo peccata venialia non remittuntur sine gratiae infusione.

PRAETEREA, peccata venialia non remittuntur sine poenitentia. Sed in poenitentia infunditur gratia, sicut et in aliis sacramentis novae legis. Ergo peccata venialia non remittuntur sine gratiae infusione.

PRAETEREA, peccatum veniale maculam quandam animae infert. Sed macula non aufertur nisi per gratiam, quae est spiritualis animae decor. Ergo videtur quod peccata venialia non remittantur sine gratiae infusione.

SED CONTRA est quod peccatum veniale adveniens non tollit gratiam, neque etiam diminuit eam, ut in secunda parte habitum est. Ergo, pari ratione, ad hoc quod peccatum veniale remittatur, non requiritur novae gratiae infusio.

RESPONDEO dicendum quod unumquodque tollitur per suum oppositum. Peccatum autem veniale non contrariatur habituali gratiae vel caritati, sed retardat actum eius, inquantum nimis haeret homo bono creato, licet non contra Deum, ut in secunda parte habitum est. Et ideo ad hoc quod peccatum tollatur, non requiritur aliqua habitualis gratia, sed sufficit aliquis motus gratiae vel caritatis ad eius remissionem.

Quia tamen in habentibus usum liberi arbitrii, in quibus solum possunt esse peccata venialia, non contingit esse infusionem gratiae sine actuali motu liberi arbitrii in Deum et in peccatum; ideo, quandocumque de novo gratia infunditur, peccata venialia remittuntur.

AD PRIMUM ergo dicendum quod etiam remissio peccatorum venialium est effectus gratiae, per actum scilicet quem de novo elicit, non autem per aliquid habituale de novo animae infusum.

AD SECUNDUM dicendum quod veniale peccatum nunquam remittitur sine aliquali actu poenitentiae virtutis, explicito scilicet vel implicito, ut supra dictum est. Potest tamen remitti veniale peccatum sine poenitentiae sacramento, quod in absolutione sacerdotis formaliter perficitur, ut supra dictum est. Et ideo non sequitur quod ad remissionem venialis requiratur gratiae infusio, quae licet sit in quolibet sacramento, non tamen in quolibet actu virtutis.

OBJECTION 1: It would seem that infusion of grace is necessary for the remission of venial sins. Because an effect is not produced without its proper cause. Now the proper cause of the remission of sins is grace; for man's sins are not forgiven through his own merits; wherefore it is written (Eph 2:4, 5): *God, Who is rich in mercy, for His exceeding charity, wherewith He loved us, even when we were dead in sins, hath quickened us together in Christ, by Whose grace you are saved.* Therefore venial sins are not forgiven without infusion of grace.

OBJ. 2: Further, venial sins are not forgiven without Penance. Now grace is infused, in Penance as in the other sacraments of the New Law. Therefore venial sins are not forgiven without infusion of grace.

OBJ. 3: Further, venial sin produces a stain on the soul. Now a stain is not removed save by grace which is the spiritual beauty of the soul. Therefore it seems that venial sins are not forgiven without infusion of grace.

ON THE CONTRARY, The advent of venial sin neither destroys nor diminishes grace, as stated in the Second Part (II-II, Q. 24, A. 10). Therefore, in like manner, an infusion of grace is not necessary in order to remove venial sin.

I ANSWER THAT, Each thing is removed by its contrary. But venial sin is not contrary to habitual grace or charity, but hampers its act, through man being too much attached to a created good, albeit not in opposition to God, as stated in the Second Part (I-II, Q. 88, A. 1; II-II, Q. 24, A. 10). Therefore, in order that venial sin be removed, it is not necessary that habitual grace be infused, but a movement of grace or charity suffices for its forgiveness.

Nevertheless, since in those who have the use of free-will (in whom alone can there be venial sins), there can be no infusion of grace without an actual movement of the free-will towards God and against sin, consequently whenever grace is infused anew, venial sins are forgiven.

REPLY OBJ. 1: Even the forgiveness of venial sins is an effect of grace, in virtue of the act which grace produces anew, but not through any habit infused anew into the soul.

REPLY OBJ. 2: Venial sin is never forgiven without some act, explicit or implicit, of the virtue of penance, as stated above (A. 1): it can, however, be forgiven without the sacrament of Penance, which is formally perfected by the priestly absolution, as stated above (Q. 87, A. 2). Hence it does not follow that infusion of grace is required for the forgiveness of venial sin, for although this infusion takes place in every sacrament, it does not occur in every act of virtue.

AD TERTIUM dicendum quod, sicut in corpore contingit esse maculam dupliciter, uno modo per privationem eius quod requiritur ad decorem, puta debiti coloris aut debitae proportionis membrorum, alio modo per superinductionem alicuius impedientis decorem, puta luti aut pulveris; ita etiam in anima inducitur macula uno modo per privationem decoris gratiae per peccatum mortale, alio modo per inclinationem inordinatam affectus ad aliquid temporale; et hoc fit per peccatum veniale. Et ideo ad tollendam maculam mortalis peccati requiritur infusio gratiae, sed ad tollendam maculam peccati venialis, requiritur aliquis actus procedens a gratia per quem removeatur inordinata adhaesio ad rem temporalem.

REPLY OBJ. 3: Just as there are two kinds of bodily stain, one consisting in the privation of something required for beauty, e.g., the right color or the due proportion of members, and another by the introduction of some hindrance to beauty, e.g., mud or dust; so too, a stain is put on the soul, in one way, by the privation of the beauty of grace through mortal sin, in another, by the inordinate inclination of the affections to some temporal thing, and this is the result of venial sin. Consequently, an infusion of grace is necessary for the removal of mortal sin, but in order to remove venial sin, it is necessary to have a movement proceeding from grace, removing the inordinate attachment to the temporal thing.

Article 3

Whether Venial Sins Are Removed by the Sprinkling of Holy Water and the Like?

AD TERTIUM SIC PROCEDITUR. Videtur quod peccata venialia non remittantur per aspersionem aquae benedictae, et episcopalem benedictionem, et alia huiusmodi. Peccata enim venialia non remittuntur sine poenitentia, ut dictum est. Sed poenitentia per se sufficit ad remissionem venialium peccatorum. Ergo ista nihil operantur ad huiusmodi remissionem.

PRAETEREA, quodlibet istorum relationem habet ad unum peccatum veniale, et ad omnia. Si ergo per aliquod istorum remittitur peccatum veniale, sequetur quod pari ratione remittantur omnia. Et ita per unam tunsionem pectoris, vel per unam aspersionem aquae benedictae, redderetur homo immunis ab omnibus peccatis venialibus. Quod videtur inconveniens.

PRAETEREA, peccata venialia inducunt reatum alicuius poenae, licet temporalis, dicitur enim, I Cor. III, de eo qui *superaedificat lignum, faenum et stipulam, quod salvus erit, sic tamen quasi per ignem.* Sed huiusmodi per quae dicitur peccatum veniale remitti, vel nullam vel minimam poenam in se habent. Ergo non sufficiunt ad plenam remissionem venialium peccatorum.

SED CONTRA est quod Augustinus dicit, in libro de poenitentia, quod pro levibus peccatis pectora nostra tundimus, *et dicimus, dimitte nobis debita nostra.* Et ita videtur quod tunsio pectoris et oratio dominica causent remissionem peccatorum. Et eadem ratio videtur esse de aliis.

RESPONDEO dicendum quod, sicut dictum est, ad remissionem venialis peccati non requiritur novae gratiae infusio, sed sufficit aliquis actus procedens ex gratia quo homo detestetur peccatum vel explicite, vel saltem implicite, sicut cum aliquis ferventer movetur in Deum. Et ideo triplici ratione aliqua causant remissionem

OBJECTION 1: It would seem that venial sins are not removed by the sprinkling of holy water, a bishop's blessing, and the like. For venial sins are not forgiven without Penance, as stated above (A. 1). But Penance suffices by itself for the remission of venial sins. Therefore the above have nothing to do with the remission of venial sins.

OBJ. 2: Further, each of the above bears the same relation to one venial sin as to all. If therefore, by means of one of them, some venial sin is remitted, it follows that in like manner all are remitted, so that by beating his breast once, or by being sprinkled once with holy water, a man would be delivered from all his venial sins, which seems unreasonable.

OBJ. 3: Further, venial sins occasion a debt of some punishment, albeit temporal; for it is written (1 Cor 3:12, 15) of him that builds up *wood, hay, stubble* that *he shall be saved, yet so as by fire.* Now the above things whereby venial sins are said to be taken away, contain either no punishment at all, or very little. Therefore they do not suffice for the full remission of venial sins.

ON THE CONTRARY, Augustine says in *De Poenitentia* that *for our slight sins we strike our breasts, and say: Forgive us our trespasses*, and so it seems that striking one's breast, and the Lord's Prayer cause the remission of venial sins: and the same seems to apply to the other things.

I ANSWER THAT, As stated above (A. 2), no infusion of fresh grace is required for the forgiveness of a venial sin, but it is enough to have an act proceeding from grace, in detestation of that venial sin, either explicit or at least implicit, as when one is moved fervently to God. Hence, for three reasons, certain things cause the remission of venial sins:

venialium peccatorum. Uno modo, inquantum in eis infunditur gratia, quia per infusionem gratiae tolluntur peccata venialia, ut supra dictum est. Et hoc modo per Eucharistiam et extremam unctionem, et universaliter per omnia sacramenta novae legis, in quibus confertur gratia, peccata venialia remittuntur. Secundo, inquantum sunt cum aliquo motu detestationis peccatorum. Et hoc modo confessio generalis, tunsio pectoris, et oratio dominica operantur ad remissionem venialium peccatorum, nam in oratione dominica petimus, dimitte nobis debita nostra. Tertio, inquantum sunt cum aliquo motu reverentiae in Deum et ad res divinas. Et hoc modo benedictio episcopalis, aspersio aquae benedictae, quaelibet sacramentalis unctio, oratio in Ecclesia dedicata, et si qua alia sunt huiusmodi, operantur ad remissionem peccatorum.

Ad primum ergo dicendum quod omnia ista causant remissionem peccatorum venialium inquantum inclinant animam ad motum poenitentiae, qui est detestatio peccatorum, vel implicite vel explicite.

Ad secundum dicendum quod omnia ista, quantum est de se, operantur ad remissionem omnium venialium peccatorum. Potest tamen impediri remissio quantum ad aliqua peccata venialia, quibus mens actualiter inhaeret, sicut etiam per fictionem impeditur aliquando effectus Baptismi.

Ad tertium dicendum quod per praedicta tolluntur quidem peccata venialia quantum ad culpam, tum virtute alicuius sanctificationis, tum etiam virtute caritatis, cuius motus per praedicta excitatur.

Non autem per quodlibet praedictorum semper tollitur totus reatus poenae, quia sic qui esset omnino immunis a peccato mortali, aspersus aqua benedicta statim evolaret. Sed reatus poenae remittitur per praedicta secundum motum fervoris in Deum, qui per praedicta excitatur quandoque magis, quandoque minus.

first, because they imply the infusion of grace, since the infusion of grace removes venial sins, as stated above (A. 2); and so, by the Eucharist, Extreme Unction, and by all the sacraments of the New Law without exception, wherein grace is conferred, venial sins are remitted. Second, because they imply a movement of detestation for sin, and in this way the general confession, the beating of one's breast, and the Lord's Prayer conduce to the remission of venial sins, for we ask in the Lord's Prayer: *Forgive us our trespasses.* Third, because they include a movement of reverence for God and Divine things; and in this way a bishop's blessing, the sprinkling of holy water, any sacramental anointing, a prayer said in a dedicated church, and anything else of the kind, conduce to the remission of venial sins.

Reply Obj. 1: All these things cause the remission of venial sins, in so far as they incline the soul to the movement of penance, viz., the implicit or explicit detestation of one's sins.

Reply Obj. 2: All these things, so far as they are concerned, conduce to the remission of all venial sins: but the remission may be hindered as regards certain venial sins, to which the mind is still actually attached, even as insincerity sometimes impedes the effect of Baptism.

Reply Obj. 3: By the above things, venial sins are indeed taken away as regards the guilt, both because those things are a kind of satisfaction, and through the virtue of charity whose movement is aroused by such things.

Yet it does not always happen that, by means of each one, the whole guilt of punishment is taken away, because, in that case, whoever was entirely free from mortal sin, would go straight to heaven if sprinkled with holy water: but the debt of punishment is remitted by means of the above, according to the movement of fervor towards God, which fervor is aroused by such things, sometimes more, sometimes less.

Article 4

Whether Venial Sin Can Be Taken Away Without Mortal Sin?

Ad quartum sic proceditur. Videtur quod veniale peccatum possit remitti sine mortali. Quia super illud Ioan. VIII, *qui sine peccato est vestrum, primus in illam lapidem mittat*, dicit quaedam Glossa quod *omnes illi erant in peccato mortali, venialia enim eis dimittebantur per caeremonias.* Ergo veniale peccatum potest remitti sine mortali.

Praeterea, ad remissionem peccati venialis non requiritur gratiae infusio. Requiritur autem ad

Objection 1: It would seem that venial sin can be taken away without mortal sin. For, on John 8:7: *He that is without sin among you, let him first cast a stone at her*, a gloss says that *all those men were in a state of mortal sin: for venial offenses were forgiven them through the legal ceremonies.* Therefore venial sin can be taken away without mortal sin.

Obj. 2: Further, no infusion of grace is required for the remission of venial sin, but it is required for the forgiveness

remissionem mortalis. Ergo veniale peccatum potest remitti sine mortali.

Praeterea, plus distat veniale peccatum a mortali quam ab alio veniali. Sed unum veniale potest dimitti sine alio, ut dictum est. Ergo veniale potest dimitti sine mortali.

Sed contra est quod dicitur Matth. V, non exibis inde, scilicet de carcere, in quem introducitur homo pro peccato mortali, donec reddas novissimum quadrantem, per quem significatur veniale peccatum. Ergo veniale peccatum non remittitur sine mortali.

Respondeo dicendum quod, sicut supra dictum est, remissio culpae cuiuscumque nunquam fit nisi per virtutem gratiae, quia, ut apostolus dicit, Rom. IV, ad gratiam Dei pertinet quod Deus alicui non imputat peccatum, quod Glossa ibi exponit de veniali. Ille autem qui est in peccato mortali, caret gratia Dei. Unde nullum peccatum veniale sibi remittitur.

Ad primum ergo dicendum quod venialia ibi dicuntur irregularitates sive immunditiae quas contrahebant secundum legem.

Ad secundum dicendum quod, licet ad remissionem peccati venialis non requiratur nova infusio habitualis gratiae, requiritur tamen aliquis gratiae actus. Qui non potest esse in eo qui subiacet peccato mortali.

Ad tertium dicendum quod peccatum veniale non excludit omnem actum gratiae, per quem possunt omnia peccata venialia dimitti. Sed peccatum mortale excludit totaliter habitum gratiae, sine quo nullum peccatum mortale vel veniale remittitur. Et ideo non est similis ratio.

of mortal sin. Therefore venial sin can be taken away without mortal sin.

Obj. 3: Further, a venial sin differs from a mortal sin more than from another venial sin. But one venial sin can be pardoned without another, as stated above (A. 3, ad 2; Q. 87, A. 3). Therefore a venial sin can be taken away without a mortal sin.

On the contrary, It is written (Matt 5:26): *Amen I say to thee, thou shalt not go out from thence*, viz., from the prison, into which a man is cast for mortal sin, *till thou repay the last farthing*, by which venial sin is denoted. Therefore a venial sin is not forgiven without mortal sin.

I answer that, As stated above (Q. 87, A. 3), there is no remission of any sin whatever except by the power of grace, because, as the Apostle declares (Rom 4:8), it is owing to God's grace that He does not impute sin to a man, which a gloss on that passage expounds as referring to venial sin. Now he that is in a state of mortal sin is without the grace of God. Therefore no venial sin is forgiven him.

Reply Obj. 1: Venial offenses, in the passage quoted, denote the irregularities or uncleannesses which men contracted in accordance with the Law.

Reply Obj. 2: Although no new infusion of habitual grace is requisite for the remission of venial sin, yet it is necessary to exercise some act of grace, which cannot be in one who is a subject of mortal sin.

Reply Obj. 3: Venial sin does not preclude every act of grace whereby all venial sins can be removed; whereas mortal sin excludes altogether the habit of grace, without which no sin, either mortal or venial, is remitted. Hence the comparison fails.

QUESTION 88

THE RETURN OF SINS WHICH HAVE BEEN TAKEN AWAY BY PENANCE

Deinde considerandum est de reditu peccatorum post poenitentiam dimissorum. Et circa hoc quaeruntur quatuor.

Primo, utrum peccata per poenitentiam dimissa redeant simpliciter per sequens peccatum.

Secundo, utrum aliquo modo per ingratitudinem redeant specialius secundum quaedam peccata.

Tertio, utrum redeant in aequali reatu.

Quarto, utrum illa ingratitudo per quam redeunt, sit speciale peccatum.

We must now consider the return of sins which have been taken away by Penance: under which head there are four points of inquiry:

(1) Whether sins which have been taken away by Penance return simply through a subsequent sin?

(2) Whether more specially as regards certain sins they return, in a way, on account of ingratitude?

(3) Whether the debt of punishment remains the same for sins thus returned?

(4) Whether this ingratitude, on account of which sins return, is a special sin?

Article 1

Whether Sins Once Forgiven Return Through a Subsequent Sin?

AD PRIMUM SIC PROCEDITUR. Videtur quod peccata dimissa redeant per sequens peccatum. Dicit enim Augustinus, in libro I de Baptismo, *redire dimissa peccata ubi fraterna caritas non est, apertissime dominus in Evangelio docet in illo servo a quo dimissum debitum dominus petiit eo quod ille conservo suo debitum nollet dimittere.* Sed fraterna caritas tollitur per quodlibet peccatum mortale. Ergo per quodlibet sequens mortale peccatum redeunt peccata prius per poenitentiam dimissa.

PRAETEREA, super illud Luc. XI, *revertar in domum meam unde exivi,* dicit Beda, *timendus est ille versiculus, non exponendus, ne culpa quam in nobis extinctam credebamus, per incuriam nos vacantes opprimat.* Hoc autem non esset nisi rediret. Ergo culpa per poenitentiam dimissa redit.

PRAETEREA, Ezech. XVIII dominus dicit, *si averterit se iustus a iustitia sua et fecerit iniquitatem, omnes iustitiae eius quas fecerat, non recordabuntur amplius.* Sed inter alias iustitias quas fecit, etiam praecedens poenitentia concurrit, cum supra dictum sit poenitentiam esse partem iustitiae. Ergo, postquam poenitens peccat, non imputatur ei praecedens poenitentia, per quam consecutus est veniam peccatorum. Redeunt ergo illa peccata.

PRAETEREA, peccata praeterita per gratiam teguntur, ut patet per apostolum, Rom. IV, inducentem illud Psalmi, *beati quorum remissae sunt iniquitates et quorum tecta sunt peccata.* Sed per peccatum mortale sequens

OBJECTION 1: It would seem that sins once forgiven return through a subsequent sin. For Augustine says (*De Bapt. contra Donat.* i, 12): *Our Lord teaches most explicitly in the Gospel that sins which have been forgiven return, when fraternal charity ceases, in the example of the servant from whom his master exacted the payment of the debt already forgiven, because he had refused to forgive the debt of his fellow-servant.* Now fraternal charity is destroyed through each mortal sin. Therefore sins already taken away through Penance, return through each subsequent mortal sin.

OBJ. 2: Further, on Luke 11:24, *I will return into my house, whence I came out,* Bede says: *This verse should make us tremble, we should not endeavor to explain it away lest through carelessness we give place to the sin which we thought to have been taken away, and become its slave once more.* Now this would not be so unless it returned. Therefore a sin returns after once being taken away by Penance.

OBJ. 3: Further, the Lord said (Ezek 18:24): *If the just man turn himself away from his justice, and do iniquity . . . all his justices which he hath done, shall not be remembered.* Now among the other *justices* which he had done, is also his previous penance, since it was said above (Q. 85, A. 3) that penance is a part of justice. Therefore when one who has done penance, sins, his previous penance, whereby he received forgiveness of his sins, is not imputed to him. Therefore his sins return.

OBJ. 4: Further, past sins are covered by grace, as the Apostle declares (Rom 4:7) where he quotes Ps. 31:1: *Blessed are they whose iniquities are forgiven, and whose sins are covered.* But a subsequent mortal sin takes away grace.

gratia tollitur. Ergo peccata quae fuerant prius commissa, remanent detecta. Et ita videtur quod redeant.

SED CONTRA est quod apostolus dicit, Rom. XI, *sine poenitentia sunt dona Dei, et vocatio.* Sed peccata poenitentis sunt remissa per donum Dei. Ergo per peccatum sequens non redeunt dimissa peccata, quasi Deus de dono remissionis poeniteat.

Praeterea, Augustinus dicit, in libro responsionum prosperi, *qui recedit a Christo et alienatus a gratia finit hanc vitam, quid nisi in perditionem vadit? Sed non in id quod dimissum est recidit, nec pro originali peccato damnabitur.*

RESPONDEO dicendum quod, sicut supra dictum est, in peccato mortali sunt duo, scilicet aversio a Deo, et conversio ad bonum creatum. Quidquid autem est aversionis in peccato mortali secundum se consideratum, est commune omnibus peccatis mortalibus, quia per quodlibet peccatum mortale homo avertitur a Deo. Unde et per consequens macula, quae est per privationem gratiae, et reatus poenae aeternae, communia sunt omnibus peccatis mortalibus. Et secundum hoc intelligitur id quod dicitur Iac. II, *qui offendit in uno, factus est omnium reus.* Sed ex parte conversionis, peccata mortalia sunt diversa, et interdum contraria. Unde manifestum est quod ex parte conversionis peccatum mortale sequens non facit redire peccata mortalia prius abolita. Alioquin sequeretur quod homo per peccatum prodigalitatis reduceretur in habitum vel dispositionem avaritiae prius abolitae et sic contrarium esset causa sui contrarii, quod est impossibile. Sed considerando in peccatis mortalibus id quod est ex parte aversionis absolute, per peccatum mortale sequens homo privatur gratia et fit reus poenae aeternae, sicut et prius erat. Verum, quia aversio in peccato mortali ex conversione quodammodo diversitatem induit per comparationem ad diversas conversiones sicut ad diversas causas, ita quod sit alia aversio et alia macula et alius reatus prout consurgit ex alio actu peccati mortalis, hoc ergo in quaestionem vertitur, utrum macula et reatus poenae aeternae, secundum quod causabantur ex actibus peccatorum prius dimissorum, redeant per peccatum mortale sequens.

Quibusdam igitur visum est quod simpliciter hoc modo redeant. Sed hoc non potest esse. Quia opus Dei per opus hominis irritari non potest. Remissio autem priorum peccatorum est opus divinae misericordiae. Unde non potest irritari per sequens peccatum hominis, secundum illud Rom. III, *nunquid incredulitas illorum fidem Dei evacuavit?*

Et ideo alii, ponentes peccata redire, dixerunt quod Deus non remittit peccata poenitenti postmodum peccaturo secundum praescientiam, sed solum secundum praesentem iustitiam. Praescit enim eum pro his peccatis aeternaliter puniendum, et tamen per gratiam facit eum

Therefore the sins committed previously, become uncovered: and so, seemingly, they return.

ON THE CONTRARY, The Apostle says (Rom 11:29): *The gifts and the calling of God are without repentance.* Now the penitent's sins are taken away by a gift of God. Therefore the sins which have been taken away do not return through a subsequent sin, as though God repented His gift of forgiveness.

Moreover, Augustine says (*Lib. Resp. Prosperi* i): *When he that turns away from Christ, comes to the end of this life a stranger to grace, whither does he go, except to perdition? Yet he does not fall back into that which had been forgiven, nor will he be condemned for original sin.*

I ANSWER THAT, As stated above (Q. 86, A. 4), mortal sin contains two things, aversion from God and adherence to a created good. Now, in mortal sin, whatever attaches to the aversion, is, considered in itself, common to all mortal sins, since man turns away from God by every mortal sin, so that, in consequence, the stain resulting from the privation of grace, and the debt of everlasting punishment are common to all mortal sins. This is what is meant by what is written (Jas 2:10): *Whosoever . . . shall offend in one point, is become guilty of all.* On the other hand, as regards their adherence they are different from, and sometimes contrary to one another. Hence it is evident, that on the part of the adherence, a subsequent mortal sin does not cause the return of mortal sins previously dispelled, else it would follow that by a sin of wastefulness a man would be brought back to the habit or disposition of avarice previously dispelled, so that one contrary would be the cause of another, which is impossible. But if in mortal sins we consider that which attaches to the aversion absolutely, then a subsequent mortal sin deprives man of grace, and makes him deserving of everlasting punishment, just as he was before. Nevertheless, since the aversion of mortal sin is diversified somewhat in relation to various adherences, as it were to various causes, so that there will be a different aversion, a different stain, a different debt of punishment, according to the different acts of mortal sin from which they arise; hence the question is moved whether the stain and the debt of eternal punishment, as caused by acts of sins previously pardoned, return through a subsequent mortal sin.

Accordingly some have maintained that they return simply even in this way. But this is impossible, because what God has done cannot be undone by the work of man. Now the pardon of the previous sins was a work of Divine mercy, so that it cannot be undone by man's subsequent sin, according to Rom. 3:3: *Shall their unbelief make the faith of God without effect?*

Wherefore others who maintained the possibility of sins returning, said that God pardons the sins of a penitent who will afterwards sin again, not according to His foreknowledge, but only according to His present justice: since He foresees that He will punish such a man eternally for his

praesentialiter iustum. Sed nec hoc stare potest. Quia, si causa absolute ponatur, et effectus ponitur absolute. Si ergo absolute non fieret peccatorum remissio, sed cum quadam conditione in futurum dependente, per gratiam et gratiae sacramenta, sequeretur quod gratia et gratiae sacramenta non essent sufficiens causa remissionis peccatorum. Quod est erroneum, utpote derogans gratiae Dei.

Et ideo nullo modo potest esse quod macula et reatus praecedentium peccatorum redeant secundum quod ex talibus actibus causabantur. Contingit autem quod sequens actus peccati virtualiter continet reatum prioris peccati, inquantum scilicet aliquis secundo peccans ex hoc ipso videtur gravius peccare quam prius peccaverat; secundum illud Rom. II, *secundum duritiam tuam et cor impoenitens thesaurizas tibi iram in die irae,* ex hoc solo scilicet quod contemnitur Dei bonitas, quae ad poenitentiam expectat; multo autem magis contemnitur Dei bonitas si, post remissionem prioris peccati, secundo peccatum iteretur; quanto maius est beneficium peccatum remittere quam sustinere peccatorem.

Sic igitur per peccatum sequens poenitentiam redit quodammodo reatus peccatorum prius dimissorum, non inquantum causabatur ex illis peccatis prius dimissis, sed inquantum causatur ex peccato ultimo perpetrato, quod aggravatur ex peccatis prioribus. Et hoc non est peccata dimissa redire simpliciter, sed secundum quid, inquantum scilicet virtualiter in peccato sequenti continentur.

AD PRIMUM ergo dicendum quod illud verbum Augustini videtur esse intelligendum de reditu peccatorum quantum ad reatum poenae aeternae in se consideratum, quia scilicet post poenitentiam peccans incurrit reatum poenae aeternae sicut et prius; non tamen omnino propter eandem rationem. Unde Augustinus, in libro de responsionibus prosperi, cum dixisset quod *non in id quod remissum est recidit, nec pro originali peccato damnabitur,* subdit, *qui tamen ea morte afficitur quae ei propter peccata dimissa debebatur,* quia scilicet incurrit mortem aeternam, quam meruerat per peccata praeterita.

AD SECUNDUM dicendum quod in illis verbis non intendit Beda dicere quod culpa prius dimissa hominem opprimat per reditum praeteriti reatus, sed per iterationem actus.

AD TERTIUM dicendum quod per sequens peccatum iustitiae priores oblivioni traduntur inquantum erant meritoriae vitae aeternae, non tamen inquantum erant impeditivae peccati. Unde, si aliquis peccet mortaliter postquam restituit debitum, non efficitur reus quasi debitum non reddidisset. Et multo minus traditur oblivioni poenitentia prius acta quantum ad remissionem culpae, cum remissio culpae magis sit opus Dei quam hominis.

sins, and yet, by His grace, He makes him righteous for the present. But this cannot stand: because if a cause be placed absolutely, its effect is placed absolutely; so that if the remission of sins were effected by grace and the sacraments of grace, not absolutely but under some condition dependent on some future event, it would follow that grace and the sacraments of grace are not the sufficient causes of the remission of sins, which is erroneous, as being derogatory to God's grace.

Consequently it is in no way possible for the stain of past sins and the debt of punishment incurred thereby, to return, as caused by those acts. Yet it may happen that a subsequent sinful act virtually contains the debt of punishment due to the previous sin, in so far as when a man sins a second time, for this very reason he seems to sin more grievously than before, as stated in Rom. 2:5: *According to thy hardness and impenitent heart, thou treasurest up to thyself wrath against the day of wrath,* from the mere fact, namely, that God's goodness, which waits for us to repent, is despised. And so much the more is God's goodness despised, if the first sin is committed a second time after having been forgiven, as it is a greater favor for the sin to be forgiven than for the sinner to be endured.

Accordingly the sin which follows repentance brings back, in a sense, the debt of punishment due to the sins previously forgiven, not as caused by those sins already forgiven but as caused by this last sin being committed, on account of its being aggravated in view of those previous sins. This means that those sins return, not simply, but in a restricted sense, viz., in so far as they are virtually contained in the subsequent sin.

REPLY OBJ. 1: This saying of Augustine seems to refer to the return of sins as to the debt of eternal punishment considered in itself, namely, that he who sins after doing penance incurs a debt of eternal punishment, just as before, but not altogether for the same reason. Wherefore Augustine, after saying (*Lib. Resp. Prosperi* i) that *he does not fall back into that which was forgiven, nor will he be condemned for original sin,* adds: *Nevertheless, for these last sins he will be condemned to the same death, which he deserved to suffer for the former,* because he incurs the punishment of eternal death which he deserved for his previous sins.

REPLY OBJ. 2: By these words Bede means that the guilt already forgiven enslaves man, not by the return of his former debt of punishment, but by the repetition of his act.

REPLY OBJ. 3: The effect of a subsequent sin is that the former *justices* are not remembered, in so far as they were deserving of eternal life, but not in so far as they were a hindrance to sin. Consequently if a man sins mortally after making restitution, he does not become guilty as though he had not paid back what he owed; and much less is penance previously done forgotten as to the pardon of the guilt, since this is the work of God rather than of man.

AD QUARTUM dicendum quod gratia simpliciter tollit maculam et reatum poenae aeternae, tegit autem actus peccati praeteritos, ne scilicet propter eos Deus hominem gratia privet et reum habeat poenae aeternae. Et quod gratia semel facit, perpetuo manet.

REPLY OBJ. 4: Grace removes the stain and the debt of eternal punishment simply; but it covers the past sinful acts, lest, on their account, God deprive man of grace, and judge him deserving of eternal punishment; and what grace has once done, endures for ever.

Article 2

Whether Sins That Have Been Forgiven, Return Through Ingratitude Which Is Shown Especially in Four Kinds of Sin?

AD SECUNDUM SIC PROCEDITUR. Videtur quod peccata dimissa non redeant per ingratitudinem quae specialiter est secundum quatuor genera peccatorum, scilicet secundum odium fraternum, apostasiam a fide, contemptum confessionis, et dolorem de poenitentia habita, secundum quod quidam metrice dixerunt, *fratres odit, apostata fit, spernitque fateri, poenituisse piget, pristina culpa redit.*

Tanto enim est maior ingratitudo quanto gravius est peccatum quod quis contra Deum committit post beneficium remissionis peccatorum. Sed quaedam alia peccata sunt his graviora, sicut blasphemia contra Deum, et peccatum in spiritum sanctum. Ergo videtur quod peccata dimissa non redeant magis secundum ingratitudinem commissam secundum haec peccata, quam secundum alia.

PRAETEREA, Rabanus dicit, *nequam servum tradidit Deus tortoribus quoadusque redderet universum debitum, quia non solum peccata quae post Baptismum homo egit reputabuntur ei ad poenam, sed originalia, quae ei sunt dimissa in Baptismo.* Sed etiam inter debita peccata venialia computantur, pro quibus dicimus, dimitte nobis debita nostra. Ergo ipsa etiam redeunt per ingratitudinem. Et pari ratione videtur quod per peccata venialia redeant peccata prius dimissa, et non solum per praedicta peccata.

PRAETEREA, tanto est maior ingratitudo quanto post maius beneficium acceptum aliquis peccat. Sed beneficium Dei est etiam ipsa innocentia, qua peccatum vitamus, dicit enim Augustinus, in II Confess., *gratiae tuae deputo quaecumque peccata non feci.* Maius autem donum est innocentia quam etiam remissio omnium peccatorum. Ergo non minus est ingratus Deo qui primo peccat post innocentiam, quam qui peccat post poenitentiam. Et ita videtur quod per ingratitudinem quae fit secundum peccata praedicta, non maxime redeant peccata dimissa.

SED CONTRA est quod Gregorius dicit, XVIII Moral., *ex dictis evangelicis constat quia, si quod in nos delinquitur ex corde non dimittimus, et illud rursus exigetur quod nobis iam per poenitentiam dimissum fuisse gaudebamus.*

OBJECTION 1: It would seem that sins do not return through ingratitude, which is shown especially in four kinds of sin, viz., hatred of one's neighbor, apostasy from faith, contempt of confession and regret for past repentance, and which have been expressed in the following verse: *whoever hates his brothers, becomes apostate, scorns confession, regrets repentance: his former sin returns.*

For the more grievous the sin committed against God after one has received the grace of pardon, the greater the ingratitude. But there are sins more grievous than these, such as blasphemy against God, and the sin against the Holy Spirit. Therefore it seems that sins already pardoned do not return through ingratitude as manifested in these sins, any more than as shown in other sins.

OBJ. 2: Further, Rabanus says: *God delivered the wicked servant to the torturers, until he should pay the whole debt, because a man will be deemed punishable not only for the sins he commits after Baptism, but also for original sin which was taken away when he was baptized.* Now venial sins are reckoned among our debts, since we pray in their regard: *Forgive us our trespasses (debita).* Therefore they too return through ingratitude; and, in like manner seemingly, sins already pardoned return through venial sins, and not only through those sins mentioned above.

OBJ. 3: Further, ingratitude is all the greater, according as one sins after receiving a greater favor. Now innocence whereby one avoids sin is a Divine favor, for Augustine says (*Confess.* ii): *Whatever sins I have avoided committing, I owe it to Thy grace.* Now innocence is a greater gift, than even the forgiveness of all sins. Therefore the first sin committed after innocence is no less an ingratitude to God, than a sin committed after repentance, so that seemingly ingratitude in respect of the aforesaid sins is not the chief cause of sins returning.

ON THE CONTRARY, Gregory says (*Moral.* xviii): *It is evident from the words of the Gospel that if we do not forgive from our hearts the offenses committed against us, we become once more accountable for what we rejoiced in as*

Et ita propter odium fraternum specialiter peccata dimissa redeunt per ingratitudinem. Et eadem ratio videtur de aliis.

Respondeo dicendum quod, sicut supra dictum est, peccata dimissa per poenitentiam redire dicuntur inquantum reatus eorum, ratione ingratitudinis, virtualiter continetur in peccato sequenti. Ingratitudo autem potest committi dupliciter. Uno modo, ex eo quod aliquid fit contra beneficium. Et hoc modo per omne peccatum mortale quo Deum offendit, redditur homo ingratus Deo, qui peccata remisit. Et sic per quodlibet peccatum mortale sequens redeunt peccata prius dimissa, ratione ingratitudinis. Alio modo committitur ingratitudo non solum faciendo contra ipsum beneficium, sed etiam faciendo contra formam beneficii praestiti. Quae quidem forma, si attendatur ex parte benefactoris, est remissio debitorum. Unde contra hanc formam facit qui fratri petenti veniam non remittit, sed odium tenet. Si autem attendatur ex parte poenitentis, qui recipit hoc beneficium, invenitur duplex motus liberi arbitrii. Quorum primus est motus liberi arbitrii in Deum, qui est actus fidei formatae, et contra hoc facit homo apostatando a fide, secundus autem, motus liberi arbitrii in peccatum, qui est actus poenitentiae. Ad quam primo pertinet, ut supra dictum est, quod homo detestetur peccata praeterita, et contra hoc facit ille qui dolet se poenituisse. Secundo pertinet ad actum poenitentiae ut poenitens proponat se subiicere clavibus Ecclesiae per confessionem, secundum illud Psalmi, *dixi, confitebor adversum me iniustitiam meam domino, et ut remisisti impietatem peccati mei.* Et contra hoc facit ille qui contemnit confiteri, secundum quod proposuerat.

Et ideo dicitur quod specialiter ingratitudo horum peccatorum facit redire peccata prius dimissa.

Ad primum ergo dicendum quod hoc non dicitur specialiter de istis peccatis quia sint ceteris graviora, sed quia directius opponuntur beneficio remissionis peccatorum.

Ad secundum dicendum quod etiam peccata venialia et peccatum originale redeunt modo praedicto, sicut et peccata mortalia, inquantum contemnitur Dei beneficium quo haec peccata sunt remissa. Non tamen per peccatum veniale aliquis incurrit ingratitudinem, quia homo, peccando venialiter, non facit contra Deum, sed praeter ipsum. Et ideo per peccata venialia nullo modo peccata dimissa redeunt.

Ad tertium dicendum quod beneficium aliquod habet pensari dupliciter. Uno modo, ex quantitate ipsius beneficii. Et secundum hoc, innocentia est maius Dei beneficium quam poenitentia, quae dicitur secunda tabula post naufragium. Alio modo potest pensari beneficium ex parte recipientis, qui minus est dignus, et sic magis sibi fit gratia. Unde et ipse magis est ingratus

forgiven through Penance: so that ingratitude implied in the hatred of one's brother is a special cause of the return of sins already forgiven: and the same seems to apply to the others.

I answer that, As stated above (A. 1), sins pardoned through Penance are said to return, in so far as their debt of punishment, by reason of ingratitude, is virtually contained in the subsequent sin. Now one may be guilty of ingratitude in two ways: first by doing something against the favor received, and, in this way, man is ungrateful to God in every mortal sin whereby he offends God Who forgave his sins, so that by every subsequent mortal sin, the sins previously pardoned return, on account of the ingratitude. Second, one is guilty of ingratitude, by doing something not only against the favor itself, but also against the form of the favor received. If this form be considered on the part of the benefactor, it is the remission of something due to him; wherefore he who does not forgive his brother when he asks pardon, and persists in his hatred, acts against this form. If, however, this form be taken in regard to the penitent who receives this favor, we find on his part a twofold movement of the free-will. The first is the movement of the free-will towards God, and is an act of faith quickened by charity; and against this a man acts by apostatizing from the faith. The second is a movement of the free-will against sin, and is the act of penance. This act consists first, as we have stated above (Q. 85, AA. 2, 5) in man's detestation of his past sins; and against this a man acts when he regrets having done penance. Second, the act of penance consists in the penitent purposing to subject himself to the keys of the Church by confession, according to Ps. 31:5: *I said: I will confess against myself my injustice to the Lord: and Thou hast forgiven the wickedness of my sin*: and against this a man acts when he scorns to confess as he had purposed to do.

Accordingly it is said that the ingratitude of sinners is a special cause of the return of sins previously forgiven.

Reply Obj. 1: This is not said of these sins as though they were more grievous than others, but because they are more directly opposed to the favor of the forgiveness of sin.

Reply Obj. 2: Even venial sins and original sin return in the way explained above, just as mortal sins do, in so far as the favor conferred by God in forgiving those sins is despised. A man does not, however, incur ingratitude by committing a venial sin, because by sinning venially man does not act against God, but apart from Him, wherefore venial sins nowise cause the return of sins already forgiven.

Reply Obj. 3: A favor can be weighed in two ways. First by the quantity of the favor itself, and in this way innocence is a greater favor from God than penance, which is called the second plank after shipwreck (cf. Q. 84, A. 6). Second, a favor may be weighed with regard to the recipient, who is less worthy, wherefore a greater favor is bestowed on him, so that he is the more ungrateful if he scorns it. In this way

si contemnat. Et hoc modo beneficium remissionis culpae est maius, inquantum praestatur totaliter indigno. Et ideo ex hoc sequitur maior ingratitudo.

the favor of the pardon of sins is greater when bestowed on one who is altogether unworthy, so that the ingratitude which follows is all the greater.

Article 3

Whether the Debt of Punishment That Arises Through Ingratitude in Respect of a Subsequent Sin Is As Great As That of the Sins Previously Pardoned?

AD TERTIUM SIC PROCEDITUR. Videtur quod per ingratitudinem peccati sequentis consurgat tantus reatus quantus fuerat peccatorum prius dimissorum. Quia secundum magnitudinem peccati est magnitudo beneficii quo peccatum remittitur; et per consequens magnitudo ingratitudinis qua hoc beneficium contemnitur. Sed secundum quantitatem ingratitudinis est quantitas reatus consequentis. Ergo tantus reatus surgit ex ingratitudine sequentis peccati quantus fuit reatus omnium praecedentium peccatorum.

PRAETEREA, magis peccat qui offendit Deum quam qui offendit hominem. Sed servus manumissus ab aliquo domino reducitur in eandem servitutem a qua prius fuerat liberatus, vel etiam in graviorem. Ergo multo magis ille qui contra Deum peccat post liberationem a peccato, reducitur in tantum reatum poenae quantum primo habuerat.

PRAETEREA, Matth. XVIII dicitur quod iratus dominus tradidit eum, cui replicantur peccata dimissa propter ingratitudinem, tortoribus, quoadusque redderet universum debitum. Sed hoc non esset nisi consurgeret ex ingratitudine tantus reatus quantus fuit omnium praeteritorum peccatorum. Ergo aequalis reatus per ingratitudinem redit.

SED CONTRA est quod dicitur Deuteron. XXV, *pro mensura peccati erit et plagarum modus.* Ex quo patet quod ex parvo peccato non consurgit magnus reatus. Sed quandoque mortale peccatum sequens est multo minus quolibet peccatorum prius dimissorum. Non ergo ex peccato sequenti redit tantus reatus quantus fuit peccatorum prius dimissorum.

RESPONDEO dicendum quod quidam dixerunt quod ex peccato sequenti, propter ingratitudinem, consurgit tantus reatus quantus fuit reatus omnium peccatorum prius dimissorum, supra reatum proprium huius peccati. Sed hoc non est necesse. Quia supra dictum est quod reatus praecedentium peccatorum non redit per peccatum sequens inquantum sequebatur ex actibus praecedentium peccatorum, sed inquantum consequitur actum sequentis peccati. Et ita oportet quod quantitas reatus redeuntis sit secundum gravitatem peccati subsequentis.

OBJECTION 1: It would seem that the debt of punishment arising through ingratitude in respect of a subsequent sin is as great as that of the sins previously pardoned. Because the greatness of the favor of the pardon of sins is according to the greatness of the sin pardoned, and so too, in consequence, is the greatness of the ingratitude whereby this favor is scorned. But the greatness of the consequent debt of punishment is in accord with the greatness of the ingratitude. Therefore the debt of punishment arising through ingratitude in respect of a subsequent sin is as great as the debt of punishment due for all the previous sins.

OBJ. 2: Further, it is a greater sin to offend God than to offend man. But a slave who is freed by his master returns to the same state of slavery from which he was freed, or even to a worse state. Much more therefore he that sins against God after being freed from sin, returns to the debt of as great a punishment as he had incurred before.

OBJ. 3: Further, it is written (Matt 18:34) that *his lord being angry, delivered him* (whose sins returned to him on account of his ingratitude) *to the torturers, until he paid all the debt.* But this would not be so unless the debt of punishment incurred through ingratitude were as great as that incurred through all previous sins. Therefore an equal debt of punishment returns through ingratitude.

ON THE CONTRARY, It is written (Deut 25:2): *According to the measure of the sin shall the measure also of the stripes be,* whence it is evident that a great debt of punishment does not arise from a slight sin. But sometimes a subsequent mortal sin is much less grievous than any one of those previously pardoned. Therefore the debt of punishment incurred through subsequent sins is not equal to that of sins previously forgiven.

I ANSWER THAT, Some have maintained that the debt of punishment incurred through ingratitude in respect of a subsequent sin is equal to that of the sins previously pardoned, in addition to the debt proper to this subsequent sin. But there is no need for this, because, as stated above (A. 1), the debt of punishment incurred by previous sins does not return on account of a subsequent sin, as resulting from the acts of the subsequent sin. Wherefore the amount of the debt that returns must be according to the gravity of the subsequent sin.

Potest autem contingere quod gravitas peccati subsequentis adaequat gravitatem omnium praecedentium peccatorum, sed hoc non semper est necesse, sive loquamur de gravitate eius quam habet ex sua specie, cum quandoque peccatum sequens sit simplex fornicatio, peccata vero praeterita fuerunt homicidia vel adulteria seu sacrilegia; sive etiam loquamur de gravitate quam habet ex ingratitudine annexa. Non enim oportet quod quantitas ingratitudinis sit absolute aequalis quantitati beneficii suscepti, cuius quantitas attenditur secundum quantitatem peccatorum prius dimissorum. Contingit enim quod contra idem beneficium unus est multum ingratus, vel secundum intensionem contemptus beneficii, vel secundum gravitatem culpae contra benefactorem commissae; alius autem parum, vel quia minus contemnit, vel quia minus contra benefactorem agit. Sed proportionaliter quantitas ingratitudinis adaequatur quantitati beneficii, supposito enim aequali contemptu beneficii, vel offensa benefactoris, tanto erit gravior ingratitudo quanto beneficium fuit maius.

Unde manifestum est quod non est necesse quod propter ingratitudinem semper per peccatum sequens redeat tantus reatus quantus fuit praecedentium peccatorum, sed necesse est quod proportionaliter, quanto peccata prius dimissa fuerunt plura et maiora, tanto redeat maior reatus per qualecumque sequens peccatum mortale.

AD PRIMUM ergo dicendum quod beneficium remissionis culpae recipit quantitatem absolutam secundum quantitatem peccatorum dimissorum. Sed peccatum ingratitudinis non recipit quantitatem absolutam secundum quantitatem beneficii, sed secundum quantitatem contemptus vel offensae, ut dictum est. Et ideo ratio non sequitur.

AD SECUNDUM dicendum quod servus manumissus non reducitur in pristinam servitutem pro qualicumque ingratitudine, sed pro aliqua gravi.

AD TERTIUM dicendum quod illi cui peccata dimissa replicantur propter subsequentem ingratitudinem, redit universum debitum, inquantum quantitas peccatorum praecedentium proportionaliter invenitur in ingratitudine subsequenti, non autem absolute, ut dictum est.

It is possible, however, for the gravity of the subsequent sin to equal the gravity of all previous sins. But it need not always be so, whether we speak of the gravity which a sin has from its species (since the subsequent sin may be one of simple fornication, while the previous sins were adulteries, murders, or sacrileges); or of the gravity which it incurs through the ingratitude connected with it. For it is not necessary that the measure of ingratitude should be exactly equal to the measure of the favor received, which latter is measured according to the greatness of the sins previously pardoned. Because it may happen that in respect of the same favor, one man is very ungrateful, either on account of the intensity of his scorn for the favor received, or on account of the gravity of the offense committed against the benefactor, while another man is slightly ungrateful, either because his scorn is less intense, or because his offense against the benefactor is less grave. But the measure of ingratitude is proportionately equal to the measure of the favor received: for supposing an equal contempt of the favor, or an equal offense against the benefactor, the ingratitude will be so much the greater, as the favor received is greater.

Hence it is evident that the debt of punishment incurred by a subsequent sin need not always be equal to that of previous sins; but it must be in proportion thereto, so that the more numerous or the greater the sins previously pardoned, the greater must be the debt of punishment incurred by any subsequent mortal sin whatever.

REPLY OBJ. 1: The favor of the pardon of sins takes its absolute quantity from the quantity of the sins previously pardoned: but the sin of ingratitude does not take its absolute quantity from the measure of the favor bestowed, but from the measure of the contempt or of the offense, as stated above: and so the objection does not prove.

REPLY OBJ. 2: A slave who has been given his freedom is not brought back to his previous state of slavery for any kind of ingratitude, but only when this is grave.

REPLY OBJ. 3: He whose forgiven sins return to him on account of subsequent ingratitude, incurs the debt for all, in so far as the measure of his previous sins is contained proportionally in his subsequent ingratitude, but not absolutely, as stated above.

Article 4

Whether the Ingratitude Whereby a Subsequent Sin Causes the Return of Previous Sins, Is a Special Sin?

AD QUARTUM SIC PROCEDITUR. Videtur quod ingratitudo ratione cuius sequens peccatum facit redire peccata prius dimissa, sit speciale peccatum. Retributio enim gratiarum pertinet ad contrapassum, quod

OBJECTION 1: It would seem that the ingratitude, whereby a subsequent sin causes the return of sins previously forgiven, is a special sin. For the giving of thanks belongs to counterpassion which is a necessary condition of

requiritur in iustitia, ut patet per philosophum, in V Ethic. Sed iustitia est specialis virtus. Ergo ingratitudo est speciale peccatum.

PRAETEREA, Tullius, in II Rhetoric., ponit quod gratia est specialis virtus. Sed ingratitudo opponitur gratiae. Ergo ingratitudo est speciale peccatum.

PRAETEREA, specialis effectus a speciali causa procedit. Sed ingratitudo habet specialem effectum, scilicet quod facit aliqualiter redire peccata prius dimissa. Ergo ingratitudo est speciale peccatum.

SED CONTRA est. Id quod sequitur omnia peccata, non est speciale peccatum. Sed per quodcumque peccatum mortale aliquis efficitur Deo ingratus, ut ex praemissis patet. Ergo ingratitudo non est speciale peccatum.

RESPONDEO dicendum quod ingratitudo peccantis quandoque est speciale peccatum; quandoque non, sed est circumstantia generaliter consequens omne peccatum mortale quod contra Deum committitur. Peccatum enim speciem recipit ex intentione peccantis, unde, ut philosophus dicit, in V Ethic., *ille qui moechatur ut furetur, magis est fur quam moechus.*

Si igitur aliquis peccator in contemptum Dei et suscepti beneficii aliquod peccatum committit, illud peccatum trahitur ad speciem ingratitudinis, et haec ingratitudo peccantis est speciale peccatum. Si vero aliquis intendens aliquod peccatum committere, puta homicidium aut adulterium, non retrahatur ab hoc propter hoc quod pertinet ad Dei contemptum, ingratitudo non erit speciale peccatum, sed traheretur ad speciem alterius peccati sicut circumstantia quaedam. Ut autem Augustinus dicit, in libro de natura et gratia, non omne peccatum est ex contemptu, et tamen in omni peccato Deus contemnitur in suis praeceptis. Unde manifestum est quod ingratitudo peccantis quandoque est speciale peccatum, sed non semper.

ET PER HOC patet responsio ad obiecta. Nam primae rationes concludunt quod ingratitudo secundum se sit quaedam species peccati. Ultima autem ratio concludit quod ingratitudo secundum quod invenitur in omni peccato, non sit speciale peccatum.

justice, as the Philosopher shows (*Ethic.* v, 5). But justice is a special virtue. Therefore this ingratitude is a special sin.

OBJ. 2: Further, Tully says (*De Inv. Rhet.* ii) that thanksgiving is a special virtue. But ingratitude is opposed to thanksgiving. Therefore ingratitude is a special sin.

OBJ. 3: Further, a special effect proceeds from a special cause. Now ingratitude has a special effect, viz. the return, after a fashion, of sins already forgiven. Therefore ingratitude is a special sin.

ON THE CONTRARY, That which is a sequel to every sin is not a special sin. Now by any mortal sin whatever, a man becomes ungrateful to God, as evidenced from what has been said (A. 1). Therefore ingratitude is not a special sin.

I ANSWER THAT, The ingratitude of the sinner is sometimes a special sin; and sometimes it is not, but a circumstance arising from all mortal sins in common committed against God. For a sin takes its species according to the sinner's intention, wherefore the Philosopher says (*Ethic.* v, 2) that *he who commits adultery in order to steal is a thief rather than an adulterer.*

If, therefore, a sinner commits a sin in contempt of God and of the favor received from Him, that sin is drawn to the species of ingratitude, and in this way a sinner's ingratitude is a special sin. If, however, a man, while intending to commit a sin, e.g., murder or adultery, is not withheld from it on account of its implying contempt of God, his ingratitude will not be a special sin, but will be drawn to the species of the other sin, as a circumstance thereof. And, as Augustine observes (*De Nat. et Grat.* xxix), not every sin implies contempt of God in His commandments. Therefore it is evident that the sinner's ingratitude is sometimes a special sin, sometimes not.

THIS SUFFICES for the Replies to the Objections: for the first objections prove that ingratitude is in itself a special sin; while the last objection proves that ingratitude, as included in every sin, is not a special sin.

QUESTION 89

THE RECOVERY OF VIRTUE BY MEANS OF PENANCE

Deinde considerandum est de recuperatione virtutum per poenitentiam. Et circa hoc quaeruntur sex.

Primo, utrum per poenitentiam restituantur virtutes.

Secundo, utrum restituantur in aequali quantitate.

Tertio, utrum restituatur poenitenti aequalis dignitas.

Quarto, utrum opera virtutum per peccatum mortificentur.

Quinto, utrum opera mortificata per peccatum per poenitentiam reviviscant.

Sexto, utrum opera mortua, idest absque caritate facta, per poenitentiam vivificentur.

We must now consider the recovery of virtues by means of Penance, under which head there are six points of inquiry:

(1) Whether virtues are restored through Penance?

(2) Whether they are restored in equal measure?

(3) Whether equal dignity is restored to the penitent?

(4) Whether works of virtue are deadened by subsequent sin?

(5) Whether works deadened by sin revive through Penance?

(6) Whether dead works, i.e., works that are done without charity, are quickened by Penance?

Article 1

Whether the Virtues Are Restored Through Penance?

AD PRIMUM SIC PROCEDITUR. Videtur quod per poenitentiam virtutes non restituantur. Non enim possent virtutes amissae per poenitentiam restitui nisi poenitentia virtutes causaret. Sed poenitentia, cum sit virtus, non potest esse causa omnium virtutum, praesertim cum quaedam virtutes sint naturaliter priores poenitentia, ut supra dictum est. Ergo per poenitentiam non restituuntur.

PRAETEREA, poenitentia in quibusdam actibus poenitentis consistit. Sed virtutes gratuitae non causantur ex actibus nostris, dicit enim Augustinus, in libro de Lib. Arbit., quod virtutes Deus in nobis sine nobis operatur. Ergo videtur quod per poenitentiam non restituuntur virtutes.

PRAETEREA, habens virtutem sine difficultate et delectabiliter actus virtutum operatur, unde philosophus dicit, in I Ethic., quod *non est iustus qui non gaudet iusta operatione*. Sed multi poenitentes adhuc difficultatem patiuntur in operando actus virtutum. Non ergo per poenitentiam restituuntur virtutes.

SED CONTRA est quod, Luc. XV, pater mandavit quod filius poenitens indueretur stola prima, quae, secundum Ambrosium, est amictus sapientiae, quam simul consequuntur omnes virtutes, secundum illud Sap. VIII, *sobrietatem et iustitiam docet, prudentiam et virtutem,*

OBJECTION 1: It would seem that the virtues are not restored through penance. Because lost virtue cannot be restored by penance, unless penance be the cause of virtue. But, since penance is itself a virtue, it cannot be the cause of all the virtues, and all the more, since some virtues naturally precede penance, viz., faith, hope, and charity, as stated above (Q. 85, A. 6). Therefore the virtues are not restored through penance.

OBJ. 2: Further, Penance consists in certain acts of the penitent. But the gratuitous virtues are not caused through any act of ours: for Augustine says (*De Lib. Arb.* ii, 18: In Ps. 118) that *God forms the virtues in us without us*. Therefore it seems that the virtues are not restored through Penance.

OBJ. 3: Further, he that has virtue performs works of virtue with ease and pleasure: wherefore the Philosopher says (*Ethic.* i, 8) that *a man is not just if he does not rejoice in just deeds*. Now many penitents find difficulty in performing deeds of virtue. Therefore the virtues are not restored through Penance.

ON THE CONTRARY, We read (Luke 15:22) that the father commanded his penitent son to be clothed in *the first robe*, which, according to Ambrose (*Expos. in Luc.* vii), is the *mantle of wisdom*, from which all the virtues flow together, according to Wis. 8:7: *She teacheth temperance, and*

quibus in vita nihil est utilius hominibus. Ergo per poenitentiam omnes virtutes restituuntur.

RESPONDEO dicendum quod per poenitentiam, sicut dictum est supra, remittuntur peccata. Remissio autem peccatorum non potest esse nisi per infusionem gratiae. Unde relinquitur quod per poenitentiam gratia homini infundatur. Ex gratia autem consequuntur omnes virtutes gratuitae, sicut ex essentia animae fluunt omnes potentiae, ut in secunda parte habitum est. Unde relinquitur quod per poenitentiam omnes virtutes restituantur.

AD PRIMUM ergo dicendum quod eodem modo poenitentia restituit virtutes per quem modum est causa gratiae, ut iam dictum est. Est autem causa gratiae inquantum est sacramentum, nam inquantum est virtus, est magis gratiae effectus. Et ideo non oportet quod poenitentia, secundum quod est virtus, sit causa omnium aliarum virtutum, sed quod habitus poenitentiae simul cum habitibus aliarum virtutum per sacramentum causetur.

AD SECUNDUM dicendum quod in sacramento poenitentiae actus humani se habent materialiter, sed formalis vis huius sacramenti dependet ex virtute clavium. Et ideo virtus clavium effective causat gratiam et virtutes, instrumentaliter tamen. Sed actus primus poenitentis se habet ut ultima dispositio ad gratiam consequendam, scilicet contritio, alii vero sequentes actus poenitentiae procedunt iam ex gratia et virtutibus.

AD TERTIUM dicendum quod, sicut supra dictum est, quandoque post primum actum poenitentiae, qui est contritio, remanent quaedam reliquiae peccatorum, scilicet dispositiones ex prioribus actibus peccatorum causatae, ex quibus praestatur difficultas quaedam poenitenti ad operandum opera virtutum, sed quantum est ex ipsa inclinatione caritatis et aliarum virtutum, poenitens opera virtutum delectabiliter et sine difficultate operatur; sicut si virtuosus per accidens difficultatem pateretur in executione actus virtutis propter somnum aut aliquam corporis dispositionem.

prudence, and justice, and fortitude, which are such things as men can have nothing more profitable in life. Therefore all the virtues are restored through Penance.

I ANSWER THAT, Sins are pardoned through Penance, as stated above (Q. 86, A. 1). But there can be no remission of sins except through the infusion of grace. Wherefore it follows that grace is infused into man through Penance. Now all the gratuitous virtues flow from grace, even as all the powers result from the essence of the soul; as stated in the Second Part (I-II, Q. 110, A. 4, ad 1). Therefore all the virtues are restored through Penance.

REPLY OBJ. 1: Penance restores the virtues in the same way as it causes grace, as stated above (Q. 86, A. 1). Now it is a cause of grace, in so far as it is a sacrament, because, in so far as it is a virtue, it is rather an effect of grace. Consequently it does not follow that penance, as a virtue, needs to be the cause of all the other virtues, but that the habit of penance together with the habits of the other virtues is caused through the sacrament of Penance.

REPLY OBJ. 2: In the sacrament of Penance human acts stand as matter, while the formal power of this sacrament is derived from the power of the keys. Consequently the power of the keys causes grace and virtue effectively indeed, but instrumentally; and the first act of the penitent, viz., contrition, stands as ultimate disposition to the reception of grace, while the subsequent acts of Penance proceed from the grace and virtues which are already there.

REPLY OBJ. 3: As stated above (Q. 86, A. 5), sometimes after the first act of Penance, which is contrition, certain remnants of sin remain, viz. dispositions caused by previous acts, the result being that the penitent finds difficulty in doing deeds of virtue. Nevertheless, so far as the inclination itself of charity and of the other virtues is concerned, the penitent performs works of virtue with pleasure and ease, even as a virtuous man may accidentally find it hard to do an act of virtue, on account of sleepiness or some indisposition of the body.

Article 2

Whether, After Penance, Man Rises Again to Equal Virtue?

AD SECUNDUM SIC PROCEDITUR. Videtur quod post poenitentiam resurgat homo in aequali virtute. Dicit enim apostolus, Rom. VIII, *diligentibus Deum omnia cooperantur in bonum,* ubi dicit Glossa Augustini quod hoc adeo verum est *ut, si qui horum devient et exorbitent,*

OBJECTION 1: It would seem that, after Penance, man rises again to equal virtue. For the Apostle says (Rom 8:28): *To them that love God all things work together unto good,* whereupon a gloss of Augustine says that *this is so true that, if any such man goes astray and wanders from the path, God*

hoc ipsum Deus faciat eis in bonum proficere. Sed hoc non esset si homo resurgeret in minori virtute.

PRAETEREA, Ambrosius dicit quod *poenitentia optima res est, quae omnes defectus revocat ad perfectum.* Sed hoc non esset nisi virtutes in aequali quantitate recuperarentur. Ergo per poenitentiam semper recuperatur aequalis virtus.

PRAETEREA, super illud Genes. I, *factum est vespere et mane dies unus,* dicit Glossa, *vespertina lux est a qua quis cecidit, matutina in qua resurgit.* Sed lux matutina est maior quam vespertina. Ergo aliquis resurgit in maiori gratia vel caritate quam prius habuerat. Quod etiam videtur per id quod apostolus dicit, Rom. V, *ubi abundavit delictum, superabundavit et gratia.*

SED CONTRA, caritas proficiens vel perfecta maior est quam caritas incipiens. Sed quandoque aliquis cadit a caritate proficiente, resurgit autem in caritate incipiente. Ergo semper resurgit homo in minori etiam virtute.

RESPONDEO dicendum quod, sicut dictum est, motus liberi arbitrii qui est in iustificatione impii, est ultima dispositio ad gratiam, unde in eodem instanti est gratiae infusio cum praedicto motu liberi arbitrii, ut in secunda parte habitum est. In quo quidem motu comprehenditur actus poenitentiae, ut supra dictum est. Manifestum est autem quod formae quae possunt recipere magis et minus, intenduntur et remittuntur secundum diversam dispositionem subiecti, ut in secunda parte habitum est. Et inde est quod, secundum quod motus liberi arbitrii in poenitentia est intensior vel remissior, secundum hoc poenitens consequitur maiorem vel minorem gratiam. Contingit autem intensionem motus poenitentis quandoque proportionatam esse maiori gratiae quam illa a qua cecidit per peccatum; quandoque vero aequali; quandoque vero minori. Et ideo poenitens quandoque resurgit in maiori gratia quam prius habuerat; quandoque autem in aequali; quandoque etiam in minori. Et eadem ratio est de virtutibus, quae ex gratia consequuntur.

AD PRIMUM ergo dicendum quod non omnibus diligentibus Deum cooperatur in bonum hoc ipsum quod per peccatum a Dei amore cadunt, quod patet in his qui cadunt et nunquam resurgunt, vel qui resurgunt iterum casuri, sed in *his qui secundum propositum vocati sunt sancti,* scilicet praedestinatis, qui, quotiescumque cadunt, finaliter tamen resurgunt. Cedit igitur eis in bonum hoc quod cadunt, non quia semper in maiori gratia resurgant, sed quia resurgunt in permanentiori gratia, non quidem ex parte ipsius gratiae, quia, quanto gratia est maior, tanto de se est permanentior; sed ex parte hominis, qui tanto stabilius in gratia permanet quanto est

makes even this conduce to his good. But this would not be true if he rose again to lesser virtue. Therefore it seems that a penitent never rises again to lesser virtue.

OBJ. 2: Further, Ambrose says that *Penance is a very good thing, for it restores every defect to a state of perfection.* But this would not be true unless virtues were recovered in equal measure. Therefore equal virtue is always recovered through Penance.

OBJ. 3: Further, on Gen. 1:5: *There was evening and morning, one day,* a gloss says: *The evening light is that from which we fall; the morning light is that to which we rise again.* Now the morning light is greater than the evening light. Therefore a man rises to greater grace or charity than that which he had before; which is confirmed by the Apostle's words (Rom 5:20): *Where sin abounded, grace did more abound.*

ON THE CONTRARY, Charity whether proficient or perfect is greater than incipient charity. But sometimes a man falls from proficient charity, and rises again to incipient charity. Therefore man always rises again to less virtue.

I ANSWER THAT, As stated above (Q. 86, A. 6, ad 3; Q. 89, A. 1, ad 2), the movement of the free-will, in the justification of the ungodly, is the ultimate disposition to grace; so that in the same instant there is infusion of grace together with the aforesaid movement of the free-will, as stated in the Second Part (I-II, Q. 113, AA. 5, 7), which movement includes an act of penance, as stated above (Q. 86, A. 2). But it is evident that forms which admit of being more or less, become intense or remiss, according to the different dispositions of the subject, as stated in the Second Part (I-II, Q. 52, AA. 1, 2; Q. 66, A. 1). Hence it is that, in Penance, according to the degree of intensity or remissness in the movement of the free-will, the penitent receives greater or lesser grace. Now the intensity of the penitent's movement may be proportionate sometimes to a greater grace than that from which man fell by sinning, sometimes to an equal grace, sometimes to a lesser. Wherefore the penitent sometimes arises to a greater grace than that which he had before, sometimes to an equal, sometimes to a lesser grace: and the same applies to the virtues, which flow from grace.

REPLY OBJ. 1: The very fact of falling away from the love of God by sin, does not work unto the good of all those who love God, which is evident in the case of those who fall and never rise again, or who rise and fall yet again; but only to the good of *such as according to His purpose are called to be saints,* viz. the predestined, who, however often they may fall, yet rise again finally. Consequently good comes of their falling, not that they always rise again to greater grace, but that they rise to more abiding grace, not indeed on the part of grace itself, because the greater the grace, the more abiding it is, but on the part of man, who, the more careful and humble he is, abides the more steadfastly in grace. Hence

cautior et humilior. Unde et Glossa ibidem subdit quod ideo proficit eis in bonum quod cadunt, quia humiliores redeunt, et quia doctiores fiunt.

AD SECUNDUM dicendum quod poenitentia, quantum est de se, habet virtutem reparandi omnes defectus ad perfectum, et etiam promovendi in ulteriorem statum, sed hoc quandoque impeditur ex parte hominis, qui remissius movetur in Deum et in detestationem peccati. Sicut etiam in Baptismo aliqui adulti consequuntur maiorem vel minorem gratiam, secundum quod diversimode se disponunt.

AD TERTIUM dicendum quod illa assimilatio utriusque gratiae ad lucem vespertinam et matutinam fit propter similitudinem ordinis, quia post lucem vespertinam sequuntur tenebrae noctis, post lucem autem matutinam sequitur lux diei, non autem propter maiorem vel minorem similitudinem quantitatis. Illud etiam verbum apostoli intelligitur de gratia, quae exsuperat omnem abundantiam humanorum peccatorum. Non autem hoc est verum in omnibus, quod quanto abundantius peccavit, tanto abundantiorem gratiam consequatur, pensata quantitate habitualis gratiae. Est tamen superabundans gratia quantum ad ipsam gratiae rationem, quia magis gratis beneficium remissionis magis peccatori confertur. Quamvis quandoque abundanter peccantes abundanter dolent, et sic abundantiorem habitum gratiae et virtutum consequuntur, sicut patet in Magdalena.

AD ID VERO quod in contrarium obiicitur, dicendum quod una et eadem gratia maior est proficiens quam incipiens, sed in diversis hoc non est necesse. Unus enim incipit a maiori gratia quam alius habeat in statu profectus, sicut Gregorius dicit, in II Dialog., *praesentes et secuturi omnes cognoscant, Benedictus puer a quanta perfectione conversionis gratiam incoepisset.*

the same gloss adds that *their fall conduces to their good, because they rise more humble and more enlightened.*

REPLY OBJ. 2: Penance, considered in itself, has the power to bring all defects back to perfection, and even to advance man to a higher state; but this is sometimes hindered on the part of man, whose movement towards God and in detestation of sin is too remiss, just as in Baptism adults receive a greater or a lesser grace, according to the various ways in which they prepare themselves.

REPLY OBJ. 3: This comparison of the two graces to the evening and morning light is made on account of a likeness of order, since the darkness of night follows after the evening light, and the light of day after the light of morning, but not on account of a likeness of greater or lesser quantity. Again, this saying of the Apostle refers to the grace of Christ, which abounds more than any number of man's sins. Nor is it true of all, that the more their sins abound, the more abundant grace they receive, if we measure habitual grace by the quantity. Grace is, however, more abundant, as regards the very notion of grace, because to him who sins more a more gratuitous favor is vouchsafed by his pardon; although sometimes those whose sins abound, abound also in sorrow, so that they receive a more abundant habit of grace and virtue, as was the case with Magdalen.

TO THE ARGUMENT advanced in the contrary sense it must be replied that in one and the same man proficient grace is greater than incipient grace, but this is not necessarily the case in different men, for one begins with a greater grace than another has in the state of proficiency: thus Gregory says (*Dial.* ii, 1): *Let all, both now and hereafter, acknowledge how perfectly the boy Benedict turned to the life of grace from the very beginning.*

Article 3

Whether, by Penance, Man Is Restored to His Former Dignity?

AD TERTIUM SIC PROCEDITUR. Videtur quod per poenitentiam non restituatur homo in pristinam dignitatem. Quia super illud Amos V, *virgo Israel cecidit,* dicit Glossa, *non negat ut resurgat, sed ut resurgere virgo possit, quia semel oberrans ovis, etsi reportetur in humeris pastoris, non habet tantam gloriam quantam quae nunquam erravit.* Ergo per poenitentiam non recuperat homo pristinam dignitatem.

PRAETEREA, Hieronymus dicit, *quicumque dignitatem divini gradus non custodiunt, contenti fiant animam salvare, reverti enim in pristinum gradum difficile est. Et Innocentius Papa dicit quod apud Nicaeam constituti*

OBJECTION 1: It would seem that man is not restored by Penance to his former dignity: because a gloss on Amos 5:2, *The virgin of Israel is cast down,* observes: *It is not said that she cannot rise up, but that the virgin of Israel shall not rise; because the sheep that has once strayed, although the shepherd bring it back on his shoulder, has not the same glory as if it had never strayed.* Therefore man does not, through Penance, recover his former dignity.

OBJ. 2: Further, Jerome says: *Whoever fail to preserve the dignity of the sacred order, must be content with saving their souls; for it is a difficult thing to return to their former degree.* Again, Pope Innocent I says (*Ep. vi ad Agapit.*) that

canones poenitentes etiam ab infimis clericorum officiis excludunt. Non ergo per poenitentiam homo recuperat pristinam dignitatem.

PRAETEREA, ante peccatum potest aliquis ad maiorem gradum ascendere. Non autem hoc post peccatum conceditur poenitenti, dicitur enim Ezech. XLIV, *Levitae qui recesserunt a me, nunquam appropinquabunt mihi, ut sacerdotio fungantur.* Et, sicut habetur in decretis, dist. l, in Hilerdensi Concilio legitur, *hi qui sancto altario deserviunt, si subito flenda debilitate carnis corruerint, et, domino respiciente, poenituerint, officiorum suorum loca recipiant, nec possint ad altiora officia ulterius promoveri.* Non ergo poenitentia restituit hominem in pristinam dignitatem.

SED CONTRA est quod, sicut in eadem distinctione legitur, Gregorius, scribens Secundino, dixit, *post dignam satisfactionem, credimus hominem posse redire ad suum honorem.* Et in Concilio Agathensi legitur, *contumaces clerici, prout dignitatis ordo permiserit, ab episcopis corrigantur, ita ut, cum eos poenitentia correxerit, gradum suum dignitatemque recipiant.*

RESPONDEO dicendum quod homo per peccatum duplicem dignitatem amittit, unam quantum ad Deum, aliam vero quantum ad Ecclesiam. Quantum autem ad Deum, amittit duplicem dignitatem. Unam principalem, qua scilicet computatus erat inter filios Dei per gratiam. Et hanc dignitatem recuperat per poenitentiam. Quod significatur Luc. XV de filio prodigo, cui pater poenitenti iussit restitui stolam primam et anulum et calceamenta. Aliam vero dignitatem amittit secundariam, scilicet innocentiam, de qua, sicut ibidem legitur, gloriabatur filius senior, dicens, *ecce, tot annis servio tibi, et nunquam mandatum tuum praeterivi.* Et hanc dignitatem poenitens recuperare non potest. Recuperat tamen quandoque aliquid maius. Quia, ut Gregorius dicit, in homilia de centum ovibus, *qui errasse a Deo se considerant, damna praecedentia lucris sequentibus recompensant. Maius ergo gaudium de eis fit in caelo, quia et dux in praelio plus eum militem diligit qui post fugam reversus hostem fortiter premit, quam illum qui nunquam terga praebuit et nunquam aliquid fortiter fecit.*

Dignitatem autem ecclesiasticam homo per peccatum perdit, qui indignum se reddit ad ea quae competunt dignitati ecclesiasticae exercenda. Quam quidem recuperare prohibentur, uno modo, quia non poenitent. Unde Isidorus ad Misianum episcopum scribit, sicut in eadem distinctione legitur, cap. domino, *illos ad pristinos gradus canones redire praecipiunt quos poenitentiae praecessit satisfactio, vel condigna peccatorum confessio.*

the canons framed at the council of Nicaea exclude penitents from even the lowest orders of clerics. Therefore man does not, through Penance, recover his former dignity.

OBJ. 3: Further, before sinning a man can advance to a higher sacred order. But this is not permitted to a penitent after his sin, for it is written (Ezek 44:10, 13): *The Levites that went away . . . from Me . . . shall never come near to Me, to do the office of priest*: and as laid down in the *Decretals* (Dist. 1, ch. 52), and taken from the council of Lerida: *If those who serve at the Holy Altar fall suddenly into some deplorable weakness of the flesh, and by God's mercy do proper penance, let them return to their duties, yet so as not to receive further promotion.* Therefore Penance does not restore man to his former dignity.

ON THE CONTRARY, As we read in the same Distinction, Gregory writing to Secundinus (*Regist.* vii) says: *We consider that when a man has made proper satisfaction, he may return to his honorable position*: and moreover we read in the acts of the council of Agde: *Contumacious clerics, so far as their position allows, should be corrected by their bishops, so that when Penance has reformed them, they may recover their degree and dignity.*

I ANSWER THAT, By sin, man loses a twofold dignity, one in respect of God, the other in respect of the Church. In respect of God he again loses a twofold dignity. One is his principal dignity, whereby he was counted among the children of God, and this he recovers by Penance, which is signified (Luke 15) in the prodigal son, for when he repented, his father commanded that the first garment should be restored to him, together with a ring and shoes. The other is his secondary dignity, viz. innocence, of which, as we read in the same chapter, the elder son boasted saying (Luke 15:29): *Behold, for so many years do I serve thee, and I have never transgressed thy commandments*: and this dignity the penitent cannot recover. Nevertheless he recovers something greater sometimes; because as Gregory says (*Hom. de centum Ovibus,* 34 in Evang.), *those who acknowledge themselves to have strayed away from God, make up for their past losses, by subsequent gains: so that there is more joy in heaven on their account, even as in battle, the commanding officer thinks more of the soldier who, after running away, returns and bravely attacks the foe, than of one who has never turned his back, but has done nothing brave.*

By sin man loses his ecclesiastical dignity, because thereby he becomes unworthy of those things which appertain to the exercise of the ecclesiastical dignity. This he is debarred from recovering: first, because he fails to repent; wherefore Isidore wrote to the bishop Masso, and as we read in the Distinction quoted above (Obj. 3): *The canons order those to be restored to their former degree, who by repentance have made satisfaction for their sins, or have*

At contra hi qui a vitio corruptionis non emendantur, nec gradum honoris, nec gratiam recipiunt communionis.

Secundo, quia poenitentiam negligenter agunt. Unde in eadem distinctione, cap. si quis diaconus, dicitur, *cum in aliquibus nec compunctio humilitatis, nec instantia orandi appareat, nec ieiuniis vel lectionibus eos vacare videamus, possumus agnoscere, si ad pristinos honores redirent, cum quanta negligentia permanerent.*

Tertio, si commisit aliquod peccatum habens irregularitatem aliquam admixtam. Unde in eadem distinctione, ex Concilio Martini Papae, dicitur, *si quis viduam, vel ab alio relictam duxerit, non admittatur ad clerum. Quod si irrepserit, deiiciatur. Similiter si homicidii aut facto aut praecepto aut consilio aut defensione, post Baptismum, conscius fuerit.* Sed hoc non est ratione peccati, sed ratione irregularitatis.

Quarto, propter scandalum. Unde in eadem distinctione legitur, cap. de his vero, *Rabanus dicit, hi qui deprehensi vel capti fuerint publice in periurio, furto aut fornicatione, et ceteris criminibus, secundum canonum sacrorum instituta a proprio gradu decidant, quia scandalum est populo Dei tales personas superpositas habere. Qui autem de praedictis peccatis absconse a se commissis sacerdoti confitentur, si se per ieiunia et eleemosynas vigiliasque et sacras orationes purgaverint, his etiam, gradu proprio servato, spes veniae de misericordia Dei promittenda est.* Et hoc etiam dicitur extra, de qualitate Ordinand., cap. quaesitum, *si crimina ordine iudiciario comprobata, vel alias notoria non fuerint, praeter reos homicidii, post poenitentiam in susceptis vel iam suscipiendis ordinibus impedire non possunt.*

AD PRIMUM ergo dicendum quod eadem ratio est de recuperatione virginitatis et de recuperatione innocentiae, quae pertinet ad secundariam dignitatem quoad Deum.

AD SECUNDUM dicendum quod Hieronymus in verbis illis non dicit esse impossibile, sed dicit esse difficile hominem recuperare post peccatum pristinum gradum, quia hoc non conceditur nisi perfecte poenitenti, ut dictum est. Ad statuta autem canonum qui hoc prohibere videntur, respondet Augustinus, Bonifacio scribens, *ut constitueretur in Ecclesia ne quisquam post alicuius criminis poenitentiam clericatum accipiat, vel ad clericatum redeat, vel in clericatu maneat, non desperatione indulgentiae, sed rigore factum est disciplinae. Alioquin contra claves datas Ecclesiae disputabitur, de quibus dictum est, quaecumque solveritis super terram, erunt soluta et in caelo.* Et postea subdit, *nam et sanctus David de criminibus egit poenitentiam, et tamen in honore suo perstitit.*

made worthy confession of them. On the other hand, those who do not mend their corrupt and wicked ways are neither allowed to exercise their order, nor received to the grace of communion.

Second, because he does penance negligently, wherefore it is written in the same Distinction (Obj. 3): *We can be sure that those who show no signs of humble compunction, or of earnest prayer, who avoid fasting or study, would exercise their former duties with great negligence if they were restored to them.*

Third, if he has committed a sin to which an irregularity is attached; wherefore it is said in the same Distinction (Obj. 3), quoting the council of Pope Martin: *If a man marry a widow or the relict of another, he must not be admitted to the ranks of the clergy: and if he has succeeded in creeping in, he must be turned out. In like manner, if anyone after Baptism be guilty of homicide, whether by deed, or by command, or by counsel, or in self-defense.* But this is in consequence not of sin, but of irregularity.

Fourth, on account of scandal, wherefore it is said in the same Distinction (Obj. 3): *Those who have been publicly convicted or caught in the act of perjury, robbery, fornication, and of such like crimes, according to the prescription of the sacred canons must be deprived of the exercise of their respective orders, because it is a scandal to God's people that such persons should be placed over them. But those who commit such sins occultly and confess them secretly to a priest, may be retained in the exercise of their respective orders, with the assurance of God's merciful forgiveness, provided they be careful to expiate their sins by fasts and alms, vigils and holy deeds.* The same is expressed (*Extra, De Qual. Ordinand.*): *If the aforesaid crimes are not proved by a judicial process, or in some other way made notorious, those who are guilty of them must not be hindered, after they have done penance, from exercising the orders they have received, or from receiving further orders, except in cases of homicide.*

REPLY OBJ. 1: The same is to be said of the recovery of virginity as of the recovery of innocence which belongs to man's secondary dignity in the sight of God.

REPLY OBJ. 2: In these words Jerome does not say that it is impossible, but that it is difficult, for man to recover his former dignity after having sinned, because this is allowed to none but those who repent perfectly, as stated above. To those canonical statutes, which seem to forbid this, Augustine replies in his letter to Boniface (*Ep. clxxxv*): *If the law of the Church forbids anyone, after doing penance for a crime, to become a cleric, or to return to his clerical duties, or to retain them, the intention was not to deprive him of the hope of pardon, but to preserve the rigor of discipline; else we should have to deny the keys given to the Church, of which it was said: 'Whatsoever you shall loose on earth shall be loosed in heaven.'* And further on he adds: *For holy David did penance for his deadly crimes, and yet he retained his dignity;*

Et beatum Petrum, quando amarissimas lacrimas fudit, utique dominum negasse poenituit, et tamen apostolus permansit. Sed non ideo putanda est supervacua posteriorum diligentia, qui, ubi saluti nihil detrahebatur, humilitati aliquid addiderunt, experti, ut credo, aliquorum fictas poenitentias per affectatas honorum potentias.

Ad tertium dicendum quod illud statutum intelligitur de illis qui publicam poenitentiam agunt, qui postmodum non possunt ad maiorem provehi gradum. Nam et Petrus post negationem pastor ovium Christi constitutus est, ut patet Ioan. ult. Ubi dicit Chrysostomus quod *Petrus post negationem et poenitentiam ostendit se habere maiorem fiduciam ad Christum. Qui enim in cena non audebat interrogare, sed Ioanni interrogationem commisit, huic postea et praepositura fratrum credita est, et non solum non committit alteri interrogare quae ad ipsum pertinent, sed de reliquo ipse pro Ioanne magistrum interrogat.*

and Blessed Peter by shedding most bitter tears did indeed repent him of having denied his Lord, and yet he remained an apostle. Nevertheless we must not deem the care of later teachers excessive, who without endangering a man's salvation, exacted more from his humility, having, in my opinion, found by experience, that some assumed a pretended repentance through hankering after honors and power.

Reply Obj. 3: This statute is to be understood as applying to those who do public penance, for these cannot be promoted to a higher order. For Peter, after his denial, was made shepherd of Christ's sheep, as appears from John 21:21, where Chrysostom comments as follows: *After his denial and repentance Peter gives proof of greater confidence in Christ: for whereas, at the supper, he durst not ask Him, but deputed John to ask in his stead, afterwards he was placed at the head of his brethren, and not only did not depute another to ask for him, what concerned him, but henceforth asks the Master instead of John.*

Article 4

Whether Virtuous Deeds Done in Charity Can Be Deadened?

Ad quartum sic proceditur. Videtur quod opera virtutum in caritate facta mortificari non possunt. Quod enim non est, immutari non potest. Sed mortificatio est quaedam mutatio de vita in mortem. Cum ergo opera virtutum, postquam facta sunt, iam non sint, videtur quod ulterius mortificari non possunt.

Praeterea, per opera virtutis in caritate facta homo meretur vitam aeternam. Sed subtrahere mercedem merenti est iniustitia, quae non cadit in Deum. Ergo non potest esse quod opera virtutum in caritate facta per peccatum sequens mortificentur.

Praeterea, fortius non corrumpitur a debiliori. Sed opera caritatis sunt fortiora quibuslibet peccatis, quia, ut dicitur Proverb. X, *universa delicta operit caritas.* Ergo videtur quod opera in caritate facta per sequens mortale peccatum mortificari non possunt.

Sed contra est quod dicitur Ezech. XVIII, *si averterit se iustus a iustitia sua, omnes iustitiae eius quas fecerat, non recordabuntur.*

Respondeo dicendum quod res viva per mortem perdit operationem vitae, unde per quandam similitudinem dicuntur res mortificari quando impediuntur a proprio suo effectu vel operatione.

Effectus autem operum virtuosorum quae in caritate fiunt, est perducere ad vitam aeternam. Quod quidem impeditur per peccatum mortale sequens, quod gratiam tollit. Et secundum hoc, opera in caritate facta dicuntur mortificari per sequens peccatum mortale.

Objection 1: It would seem that virtuous deeds done in charity cannot be deadened. For that which is not cannot be changed. But to be deadened is to be changed from life to death. Since therefore virtuous deeds, after being done, are no more, it seems that they cannot afterwards be deadened.

Obj. 2: Further, by virtuous deeds done in charity, man merits eternal life. But to take away the reward from one who has merited it is an injustice, which cannot be ascribed to God. Therefore it is not possible for virtuous deeds done in charity to be deadened by a subsequent sin.

Obj. 3: Further, the strong is not corrupted by the weak. Now works of charity are stronger than any sins, because, as it is written (Prov 10:12), *charity covereth all sins.* Therefore it seems that deeds done in charity cannot be deadened by a subsequent mortal sin.

On the contrary, It is written (Ezek 18:24): *If the just man turn himself away from his justice . . . all his justices which he hath done shall not be remembered.*

I answer that, A living thing, by dying, ceases to have vital operations: for which reason, by a kind of metaphor, a thing is said to be deadened when it is hindered from producing its proper effect or operation.

Now the effect of virtuous works, which are done in charity, is to bring man to eternal life; and this is hindered by a subsequent mortal sin, inasmuch as it takes away grace. Wherefore deeds done in charity are said to be deadened by a subsequent mortal sin.

AD PRIMUM ergo dicendum quod, sicut opera peccatorum transeunt actu et manent reatu, ita opera in caritate facta, postquam transeunt actu, manent merito in Dei acceptatione. Et secundum hoc mortificantur, inquantum impeditur homo ne consequatur suam mercedem.

AD SECUNDUM dicendum quod sine iniustitia potest subtrahi merces merenti quando ipse reddiderit se indignum mercede per culpam sequentem. Nam et ea quae homo iam accepit, quandoque iuste propter culpam perdit.

AD TERTIUM dicendum quod non est propter fortitudinem operum peccati quod mortificantur opera prius in caritate facta, sed est propter libertatem voluntatis, quae potest a bono in malum deflecti.

REPLY OBJ. 1: Just as sinful deeds pass as to the act but remain as to guilt, so deeds done in charity, after passing, as to the act, remain as to merit, in so far as they are acceptable to God. It is in this respect that they are deadened, inasmuch as man is hindered from receiving his reward.

REPLY OBJ. 2: There is no injustice in withdrawing the reward from him who has deserved it, if he has made himself unworthy by his subsequent fault, since at times a man justly forfeits through his own fault, even that which he has already received.

REPLY OBJ. 3: It is not on account of the strength of sinful deeds that deeds, previously done in charity, are deadened, but on account of the freedom of the will which can be turned away from good to evil.

Article 5

Whether Deeds Deadened by Sin, Are Revived by Penance?

AD QUINTUM SIC PROCEDITUR. Videtur quod opera mortificata per peccatum per poenitentiam non reviviscant. Sicut enim per poenitentiam subsequentem remittuntur peccata praeterita, ita etiam per peccatum sequens mortificantur opera prius in caritate facta. Sed peccata dimissa per poenitentiam non redeunt, ut supra dictum est. Ergo videtur quod etiam opera mortificata per caritatem non reviviscant.

PRAETEREA, opera dicuntur mortificari ad similitudinem animalium quae moriuntur, ut dictum est. Sed animal mortuum non potest iterum vivificari. Ergo nec opera mortificata possunt iterum per poenitentiam reviviscere.

PRAETEREA, opera in caritate facta merentur gloriam secundum quantitatem gratiae vel caritatis. Sed quandoque per poenitentiam homo resurgit in minori gratia vel caritate. Ergo non consequetur gloriam secundum merita priorum operum. Et ita videtur quod opera mortificata per peccatum non reviviscant.

SED CONTRA est quod, super illud Ioel II, *reddam vobis annos quos comedit locusta*, dicit Glossa, *non patiar perire ubertatem quam cum perturbatione animi amisistis*. Sed illa ubertas est meritum bonorum operum, quod fuit perditum per peccatum. Ergo per poenitentiam reviviscunt opera meritoria prius facta.

RESPONDEO dicendum quod quidam dixerunt quod opera meritoria per peccatum sequens mortificata non reviviscunt per poenitentiam sequentem, considerantes quod opera illa non remanent, ut iterum vivificari possent. Sed hoc impedire non potest quin vivificentur. Non enim habent vim perducendi in vitam aeternam, quod pertinet ad eorum vitam, solum secundum quod actu

OBJECTION 1: It would seem that deeds deadened by sin are not revived by Penance. Because just as past sins are remitted by subsequent Penance, so are deeds previously done in charity, deadened by subsequent sin. But sins remitted by Penance do not return, as stated above (Q. 88, AA. 1, 2). Therefore it seems that neither are dead deeds revived by charity.

OBJ. 2: Further, deeds are said to be deadened by comparison with animals who die, as stated above (A. 4). But a dead animal cannot be revived. Therefore neither can dead works be revived by Penance.

OBJ. 3: Further, deeds done in charity are deserving of glory according to the quantity of grace or charity. But sometimes man arises through Penance to lesser grace or charity. Therefore he does not receive glory according to the merit of his previous works; so that it seems that deeds deadened by sin are not revived.

ON THE CONTRARY, on Joel 2:25, *I will restore to you the years, which the locust . . . hath eaten*, a gloss says: *I will not suffer to perish the fruit which you lost when your soul was disturbed*. But this fruit is the merit of good works which was lost through sin. Therefore meritorious deeds done before are revived by Penance.

I ANSWER THAT, Some have said that meritorious works deadened by subsequent sin are not revived by the ensuing Penance, because they deemed such works to have passed away, so that they could not be revived. But that is no reason why they should not be revived: because they are conducive to eternal life (wherein their life consists) not only as actually existing, but also after they cease to exist

existunt, sed etiam postquam actu esse desinunt secundum quod remanent in acceptatione divina. Sic autem remanent, quantum est de se, etiam postquam per peccatum mortificantur, quia semper Deus illa opera, prout facta fuerunt, acceptabit, et sancti de eis gaudebunt, secundum illud Apoc. III, *tene quod habes, ne alius accipiat coronam tuam.* Sed quod isti qui ea fecit non sint efficacia ad ducendum ad vitam aeternam, provenit ex impedimento peccati supervenientis, per quod ipse redditur indignus vita aeterna. Hoc autem impedimentum tollitur per poenitentiam, inquantum per eam remittuntur peccata. Unde restat quod opera prius mortificata per poenitentiam recuperant efficaciam perducendi eum qui fecit ea in vitam aeternam, quod est ea reviviscere. Et ita patet quod opera mortificata per poenitentiam reviviscunt.

AD PRIMUM ergo dicendum quod opera peccati per poenitentiam abolentur secundum se, ita scilicet quod ex eis ulterius, Deo indulgente, nec macula nec reatus inducitur. Sed opera ex caritate facta non abolentur a Deo, in cuius acceptatione remanent, sed impedimentum accipiunt ex parte hominis operantis. Et ideo, remoto impedimento quod est ex parte hominis, Deus implet ex parte sua illud quod opera merebantur.

AD SECUNDUM dicendum quod opera in caritate facta non mortificantur secundum se, sicut dictum est, sed solum per impedimentum superveniens ex parte operantis. Animalia autem moriuntur secundum se, inquantum privantur principio vitae. Et ideo non est simile.

AD TERTIUM dicendum quod ille qui per poenitentiam resurgit in minori caritate, consequetur quidem praemium essentiale secundum quantitatem caritatis in qua invenitur, habebit tamen gaudium maius de operibus in prima caritate factis quam de operibus quae in secunda fecit. Quod pertinet ad praemium accidentale.

actually, and as abiding in the Divine acceptance. Now, they abide thus, so far as they are concerned, even after they have been deadened by sin, because those works, according as they were done, will ever be acceptable to God and give joy to the saints, according to Apoc. 3:11: *Hold fast that which thou hast, that no man take thy crown.* That they fail in their efficacy to bring the man, who did them, to eternal life, is due to the impediment of the supervening sin whereby he is become unworthy of eternal life. But this impediment is removed by Penance, inasmuch as sins are taken away thereby. Hence it follows that deeds previously deadened, recover, through Penance, their efficacy in bringing him, who did them, to eternal life, and, in other words, they are revived. It is therefore evident that deadened works are revived by Penance.

REPLY OBJ. 1: The very works themselves of sin are removed by Penance, so that, by God's mercy, no further stain or debt of punishment is incurred on their account: on the other hand, works done in charity are not removed by God, since they abide in His acceptance, but they are hindered on the part of the man who does them; wherefore if this hindrance, on the part of the man who does those works, be removed, God on His side fulfills what those works deserved.

REPLY OBJ. 2: Deeds done in charity are not in themselves deadened, as explained above, but only with regard to a supervening impediment on the part of the man who does them. On the other hand, an animal dies in itself, through being deprived of the principle of life: so that the comparison fails.

REPLY OBJ. 3: He who, through Penance, arises to lesser charity, will receive the essential reward according to the degree of charity in which he is found. Yet he will have greater joy for the works he had done in his former charity, than for those which he did in his subsequent charity: and this joy belongs to the accidental reward.

Article 6

Whether the Effect of Subsequent Penance Is to Quicken Even Dead Works?

AD SEXTUM SIC PROCEDITUR. Videtur quod per poenitentiam subsequentem etiam opera mortua, quae scilicet non sunt in caritate facta, vivificentur. Difficilius enim videtur quod ad vitam perveniat illud quod fuit mortificatum, quod nunquam fit secundum naturam, quam illud quod nunquam fuit vivum, vivificetur, quia ex non vivis secundum naturam viva aliqua generantur. Sed opera mortificata per poenitentiam vivificantur, ut dictum est. Ergo multo magis opera mortua vivificantur.

OBJECTION 1: It would seem that the effect of subsequent Penance is to quicken even dead works, those, namely, that were not done in charity. For it seems more difficult to bring to life that which has been deadened, since this is never done naturally, than to quicken that which never had life, since certain living things are engendered naturally from things without life. Now deadened works are revived by Penance, as stated above (A. 5). Much more, therefore, are dead works revived.

PRAETEREA, remota causa, removetur effectus. Sed causa quare opera de genere bonorum sine caritate facta non fuerunt viva, fuit defectus caritatis et gratiae. Sed iste defectus tollitur per poenitentiam. Ergo per poenitentiam opera mortua vivificantur.

PRAETEREA, Hieronymus dicit, *si quando videris inter multa opera peccatorum facere quemquam aliqua quae iusta sunt, non est tam iniustus Deus ut propter multa mala obliviscatur paucorum bonorum*. Sed hoc videtur maxime quando mala praeterita per poenitentiam tolluntur. Ergo videtur quod post poenitentiam Deus remuneret priora bona in statu peccati facta, quod est ea vivificari.

SED CONTRA est quod apostolus dicit, I Cor. XIII, *si distribuero in cibos pauperum omnes facultates meas, et si tradidero corpus meum ita ut ardeam, caritatem autem non habuero, nihil mihi prodest*. Hoc autem non esset si saltem per poenitentiam subsequentem vivificarentur. Non ergo poenitentia vivificat opera prius mortua.

RESPONDEO dicendum quod opus aliquod dicitur mortuum dupliciter. Uno modo, effective, quia scilicet est causa mortis. Et secundum hoc, opera peccati dicuntur opera mortua, secundum illud Heb. IX, *sanguis Christi emundabit conscientias nostras ab operibus mortuis*. Haec igitur opera mortua non vivificantur per poenitentiam, sed magis abolentur, secundum illud Heb. VI, *non rursus iacientes fundamentum poenitentiae ab operibus mortuis*. Alio modo dicuntur opera mortua privative, scilicet quia carent vita spirituali, quae est ex caritate, per quam anima Deo coniungitur, ex quo vivit sicut corpus per animam. Et per hunc modum etiam fides quae est sine caritate, dicitur mortua, secundum illud Iac. II, *fides sine operibus mortua est*. Et per hunc etiam modum omnia opera quae sunt bona ex genere, si sine caritate fiant, dicuntur mortua, inquantum scilicet non procedunt ex principio vitae; sicut si dicamus sonum citharae vocem mortuam dare. Sic igitur differentia mortis et vitae in operibus est secundum comparationem ad principium a quo procedunt. Opera autem non possunt iterum a principio procedere, quia transeunt, et iterum eadem numero assumi non possunt. Unde impossibile est quod opera mortua iterum fiant viva per poenitentiam.

AD PRIMUM ergo dicendum quod in rebus naturalibus tam mortua quam mortificata carent principio vitae. Sed opera dicuntur mortificata non ex parte principii a quo processerunt, sed ex parte impedimenti extrinseci. Mortua autem dicuntur ex parte principii. Et ideo non est similis ratio.

AD SECUNDUM dicendum quod opera de genere bonorum sine caritate facta dicuntur mortua propter defectum caritatis et gratiae sicut principii. Hoc autem non praestatur eis per poenitentiam subsequentem, ut ex tali principio procedant. Unde ratio non sequitur.

OBJ. 2: Further, if the cause be removed, the effect is removed. But the cause of the lack of life in works generically good done without charity, was the lack of charity and grace, which lack is removed by Penance. Therefore dead works are quickened by charity.

OBJ. 3: Further, Jerome says: *If at any time you find a sinner, among his many evil deeds, doing that which is right, God is not so unjust as to forget the few good deeds on account of his many evil deeds*. Now this seems to be the case chiefly when past evil deeds are removed by Penance. Therefore it seems that through Penance, God rewards the former deeds done in the state of sin, which implies that they are quickened.

ON THE CONTRARY, The Apostle says (1 Cor 13:3): *If I should distribute all my goods to feed the poor, and if I should deliver my body to be burned, and have not charity, it profiteth me nothing*. But this would not be true, if, at least by subsequent Penance, they were quickened. Therefore Penance does not quicken works which before were dead.

I ANSWER THAT, A work is said to be dead in two ways: first, effectively, because, to wit, it is a cause of death, in which sense sinful works are said to be dead, according to Heb. 9:14: *The blood of Christ . . . shall cleanse our conscience from dead works*. These dead works are not quickened but removed by Penance, according to Heb. 6:1: *Not laying again the foundation of Penance from dead works*. Second, works are said to be dead privatively, because, to wit, they lack spiritual life, which is founded on charity, whereby the soul is united to God, the result being that it is quickened as the body by the soul: in which sense too, faith, if it lack charity, is said to be dead, according to James 2:20: *Faith without works is dead*. In this way also, all works that are generically good, are said to be dead, if they be done without charity, inasmuch as they fail to proceed from the principle of life; even as we might call the sound of a harp, a dead voice. Accordingly, the difference of life and death in works is in relation to the principle from which they proceed. But works cannot proceed a second time from a principle, because they are transitory, and the same identical deed cannot be resumed. Therefore it is impossible for dead works to be quickened by Penance.

REPLY OBJ. 1: In the physical order things whether dead or deadened lack the principle of life. But works are said to be deadened, not in relation to the principle whence they proceeded, but in relation to an extrinsic impediment; while they are said to be dead in relation to a principle. Consequently there is no comparison.

REPLY OBJ. 2: Works generically good done without charity are said to be dead on account of the lack of grace and charity, as principles. Now the subsequent Penance does not supply that want, so as to make them proceed from such a principle. Hence the argument does not prove.

Ad tertium dicendum quod Deus recordatur bonorum quae quis facit in statu peccati, non ut remuneret ea in vita aeterna, quod debetur solis operibus vivis, idest ex caritate factis, sed remunerat temporali remuneratione. Sicut Gregorius dicit, in homilia de divite et Lazaro, quod, *nisi dives ille aliquod bonum egisset et in praesenti saeculo remunerationem accepisset, nequaquam ei Abraham diceret, recepisti bona in vita tua.* Vel hoc etiam potest referri ad hoc quod patietur tolerabilius iudicium. Unde dicit Augustinus, in libro de patientia, *non possumus dicere schismatico melius fuisse ei ut, Christum negando, nihil eorum pateretur quae passus est confitendo, ut illud quod ait apostolus, si tradidero corpus meum ita ut ardeam, caritatem autem non habuero, nihil mihi prodest, intelligatur ad regnum caelorum obtinendum, non ad extremi iudicii supplicium tolerabilius subeundum.*

Reply Obj. 3: God remembers the good deeds a man does when in a state of sin, not by rewarding them in eternal life, which is due only to living works, i.e., those done from charity, but by a temporal reward: thus Gregory declares (*Hom. de Divite et Lazaro, 41 in Evang.*) that *unless that rich man had done some good deed, and had received his reward in this world, Abraham would certainly not have said to him: 'Thou didst receive good things in thy lifetime.'* Or again, this may mean that he will be judged less severely: wherefore Augustine says (*De Patientia* xxvi): *We cannot say that it would be better for the schismatic that by denying Christ he should suffer none of those things which he suffered by confessing Him; but we must believe that he will be judged with less severity, than if by denying Christ, he had suffered none of those things. Thus the words of the Apostle, 'If I should deliver my body to be burned and have not charity, it profiteth me nothing,' refer to the obtaining of the kingdom of heaven, and do not exclude the possibility of being sentenced with less severity at the last judgment.*

QUESTION 90

THE PARTS OF PENANCE, IN GENERAL

Deinde considerandum est de partibus poenitentiae. Et primo, in generali; secundo, in speciali de singulis.

Circa primum quaeruntur quatuor.

Primo, utrum poenitentia habeat partes.

Secundo, de numero partium.

Tertio, quales partes sint.

Quarto, de divisione eius in partes subiectivas.

We must now consider the parts of Penance: (1) in general; (2) each one in particular.

Under the first head there are four points of inquiry:

(1) Whether Penance has any parts?

(2) Of the number of its parts;

(3) What kind of parts are they?

(4) Of its division into subjective parts.

Article 1

Whether Penance Should Be Assigned Any Parts?

AD PRIMUM SIC PROCEDITUR. Videtur quod poenitentiae non debent partes assignari. Sacramenta enim sunt in quibus divina virtus secretius operatur salutem. Sed virtus divina est una et simplex. Non ergo poenitentiae, cum sit sacramentum, debent partes assignari.

PRAETEREA, poenitentia est virtus, et est sacramentum. Sed ei inquantum est virtus, non assignantur partes, cum virtus sit habitus quidam, qui est simplex qualitas mentis. Similiter etiam ei poenitentiae inquantum est sacramentum, non videtur quod partes sint assignandae, quia Baptismo et aliis sacramentis non assignantur partes. Ergo poenitentiae nullae debent partes assignari.

PRAETEREA, poenitentiae materia est peccatum, ut supra dictum est. Sed peccato non assignantur partes. Ergo etiam nec poenitentiae sunt partes assignandae.

SED CONTRA est quod partes sunt ex quibus perfectio alicuius integratur. Sed poenitentiae perfectio integratur ex pluribus, scilicet ex contritione, confessione et satisfactione. Ergo poenitentia habet partes.

RESPONDEO dicendum quod partes rei sunt in quas materialiter totum dividitur, habent enim se partes ad totum sicut materia ad formam; unde in II Physic. partes ponuntur in genere causae materialis, totum autem in genere causae formalis. Ubicumque igitur ex parte materiae invenitur aliqua pluralitas, ibi est invenire partium rationem.

Dictum est autem supra quod in sacramento poenitentiae actus humani se habent per modum materiae. Et ideo, cum plures actus humani requirantur ad perfectionem poenitentiae, scilicet contritio, confessio et satisfactio, ut infra patebit, consequens est quod sacramentum poenitentiae habeat partes.

AD PRIMUM ergo dicendum quod quodlibet sacramentum habet simplicitatem ratione virtutis divinae,

OBJECTION 1: It would seem that parts should not be assigned to Penance. For it is the Divine power that works our salvation most secretly in the sacraments. Now the Divine power is one and simple. Therefore Penance, being a sacrament, should have no parts assigned to it.

OBJ. 2: Further, Penance is both a virtue and a sacrament. Now no parts are assigned to it as a virtue, since virtue is a habit, which is a simple quality of the mind. In like manner, it seems that parts should not be assigned to Penance as a sacrament, because no parts are assigned to Baptism and the other sacraments. Therefore no parts at all should be assigned to Penance.

OBJ. 3: Further, the matter of Penance is sin, as stated above (Q. 84, A. 2). But no parts are assigned to sin. Neither, therefore, should parts be assigned to Penance.

ON THE CONTRARY, The parts of a thing are those out of which the whole is composed. Now the perfection of Penance is composed of several things, viz. contrition, confession, and satisfaction. Therefore Penance has parts.

I ANSWER THAT, The parts of a thing are those into which the whole is divided materially, for the parts of a thing are to the whole, what matter is to the form; wherefore the parts are reckoned as a kind of material cause, and the whole as a kind of formal cause (*Phys.* ii). Accordingly wherever, on the part of matter, we find a kind of plurality, there we shall find a reason for assigning parts.

Now it has been stated above (Q. 84, AA. 2, 3), that, in the sacrament of Penance, human actions stand as matter: and so, since several actions are requisite for the perfection of Penance, viz., contrition, confession, and satisfaction, as we shall show further on (A. 2), it follows that the sacrament of Penance has parts.

REPLY OBJ. 1: Every sacrament is something simple by reason of the Divine power, which operates therein: but the

quae in eo operatur. Sed virtus divina, propter sui magnitudinem, operari potest et per unum et per multa, ratione quorum alicui sacramento possunt partes assignari.

AD SECUNDUM dicendum quod poenitentiae secundum quod est virtus, non assignantur partes, actus enim humani, qui multiplicantur in poenitentia, non comparantur ad habitum virtutis sicut partes, sed sicut effectus. Unde relinquitur quod partes assignentur poenitentiae inquantum est sacramentum, ad quod actus humani comparantur ut materia. In aliis autem sacramentis materia non sunt actus humani, sed aliqua res exterior, una quidem simplex, ut aqua vel oleum; sive composita, ut chrisma. Et ideo aliis sacramentis non assignantur partes.

AD TERTIUM dicendum quod peccata sunt materia remota poenitentiae, inquantum scilicet sunt ut materia vel obiectum humanorum actuum, qui sunt propria materia poenitentiae prout est sacramentum.

Divine power is so great that it can operate both through one and through many, and by reason of these many, parts may be assigned to a particular sacrament.

REPLY OBJ. 2: Parts are not assigned to penance as a virtue: because the human acts of which there are several in penance, are related to the habit of virtue, not as its parts, but as its effects. It follows, therefore, that parts are assigned to Penance as a sacrament, to which the human acts are related as matter: whereas in the other sacraments the matter does not consist of human acts, but of some one external thing, either simple, as water or oil, or compound, as chrism, and so parts are not assigned to the other sacraments.

REPLY OBJ. 3: Sins are the remote matter of Penance, inasmuch, to wit, as they are the matter or object of the human acts, which are the proper matter of Penance as a sacrament.

Article 2

Whether Contrition, Confession, and Satisfaction Are Fittingly Assigned As Parts of Penance?

AD SECUNDUM SIC PROCEDITUR. Videtur quod inconvenienter assignentur partes poenitentiae contritio, confessio et satisfactio. Contritio enim est in corde, et sic pertinet ad interiorem poenitentiam. Confessio autem est in ore, et satisfactio in opere, et sic duo ultima pertinent ad poenitentiam exteriorem. Poenitentia autem interior non est sacramentum, sed sola poenitentia exterior, quae sensui subiacet. Non ergo convenienter assignantur hae partes sacramento poenitentiae.

PRAETEREA, in sacramento novae legis confertur gratia, ut supra habitum est. Sed in satisfactione non confertur aliqua gratia. Ergo satisfactio non est pars sacramenti.

PRAETEREA, non est idem fructus rei et pars. Sed satisfactio est fructus poenitentiae, secundum illud Luc. III, *facite vobis dignos fructus poenitentiae.* Ergo non est pars poenitentiae.

PRAETEREA, poenitentia ordinatur contra peccatum. Sed peccatum potest perfici solum in corde per consensum, ut in secunda parte habitum est. Ergo et poenitentia. Non ergo debent poenitentiae partes poni confessio oris et satisfactio operis.

SED CONTRA, videtur quod debeant poni plures partes poenitentiae. Pars enim hominis ponitur non solum corpus, quasi materia, sed etiam anima, quae est forma. Sed tria praedicta, cum sint actus poenitentis, se habent sicut materia, absolutio autem sacerdotis se habet per

OBJECTION 1: It would seem that contrition, confession, and satisfaction are not fittingly assigned as parts of Penance. For contrition is in the heart, and so belongs to interior penance; while confession consists of words, and satisfaction in deeds; so that the two latter belong to interior penance. Now interior penance is not a sacrament, but only exterior penance which is perceptible by the senses. Therefore these three parts are not fittingly assigned to the sacrament of Penance.

OBJ. 2: Further, grace is conferred in the sacraments of the New Law, as stated above (Q. 62, AA. 1, 3). But no grace is conferred in satisfaction. Therefore satisfaction is not part of a sacrament.

OBJ. 3: Further, the fruit of a thing is not the same as its part. But satisfaction is a fruit of penance, according to Luke 3:8: *Bring forth . . . fruits worthy of penance.* Therefore it is not a part of Penance.

OBJ. 4: Further, Penance is ordained against sin. But sin can be completed merely in the thought by consent, as stated in the Second Part (I-II, Q. 72, A. 7): therefore Penance can also. Therefore confession in word and satisfaction in deed should not be reckoned as parts of Penance.

ON THE CONTRARY, It seems that yet more parts should be assigned to Penance. For not only is the body assigned as a part of man, as being the matter, but also the soul, which is his form. But the aforesaid three, being the acts of the penitent, stand as matter, while the priestly absolution

modum formae. Ergo absolutio sacerdotis debet poni quarta pars poenitentiae.

RESPONDEO dicendum quod duplex est pars, ut dicitur in V Metaphys. scilicet pars essentiae, et pars quantitatis. Partes quidem essentiae sunt, naturaliter quidem, forma et materia, logice autem, genus et differentia. Hoc autem modo quodlibet sacramentum distinguitur in materiam et formam sicut in partes essentiae, unde et supra dictum est quod sacramenta consistunt in rebus et verbis. Sed quia quantitas se tenet ex parte materiae, partes quantitatis sunt partes materiae. Et hoc modo sacramento poenitentiae specialiter assignantur partes, ut supra dictum est, quantum ad actus poenitentis, qui sunt materia huius sacramenti.

Dictum est autem supra quod alio modo fit recompensatio offensae in poenitentia, et in vindicativa iustitia. Nam in vindicativa iustitia fit recompensatio secundum arbitrium iudicis, non secundum voluntatem offendentis vel offensi, sed in poenitentia fit recompensatio offensae secundum voluntatem peccantis, et secundum arbitrium Dei, in quem peccatur; quia hic non quaeritur sola reintegratio aequalitatis iustitiae, sicut in iustitia vindicativa, sed magis reconciliatio amicitiae, quod fit dum offendens recompensat secundum voluntatem eius quem offendit. Sic igitur requiritur ex parte poenitentis, primo quidem, voluntas recompensandi, quod fit per contritionem; secundo, quod se subiiciat arbitrio sacerdotis loco Dei, quod fit in confessione; tertio, quod recompenset secundum arbitrium ministri Dei, quod fit in satisfactione. Et ideo contritio, confessio et satisfactio ponuntur partes poenitentiae.

AD PRIMUM ergo dicendum quod contritio secundum essentiam quidem est in corde, et pertinet ad interiorem poenitentiam, virtualiter autem pertinet ad poenitentiam exteriorem, inquantum scilicet implicat propositum confitendi et satisfaciendi.

AD SECUNDUM dicendum quod satisfactio confert gratiam prout est in proposito, et auget eam prout est in executione, sicut Baptismus in adultis, ut supra dictum est.

AD TERTIUM dicendum quod satisfactio est pars poenitentiae sacramenti; fructus autem poenitentiae virtutis.

AD QUARTUM dicendum quod plura requiruntur ad bonum, quod procedit ex integra causa, quam ad malum, quod procedit ex singularibus defectibus, secundum Dionysium, IV cap. de Div. Nom. Et ideo, licet peccatum perficiatur in consensu cordis, ad perfectionem tamen poenitentiae requiritur et contritio cordis, et confessio oris, et satisfactio operis.

stands as form. Therefore the priestly absolution should be assigned as a fourth part of Penance.

I ANSWER THAT, A part is twofold, essential and quantitative. The essential parts are naturally the form and the matter, and logically the genus and the difference. In this way, each sacrament is divided into matter and form as its essential parts. Hence it has been said above (Q. 60, AA. 5, 6) that sacraments consist of things and words. But since quantity is on the part of matter, quantitative parts are parts of matter: and, in this way, as stated above (A. 1), parts are assigned specially to the sacrament of Penance, as regards the acts of the penitent, which are the matter of this sacrament.

Now it has been said above (Q. 85, A. 3, ad 3) that an offense is atoned otherwise in Penance than in vindictive justice. Because, in vindictive justice the atonement is made according to the judge's decision, and not according to the discretion of the offender or of the person offended; whereas, in Penance, the offense is atoned according to the will of the sinner, and the judgment of God against Whom the sin was committed, because in the latter case we seek not only the restoration of the equality of justice, as in vindictive justice, but also and still more the reconciliation of friendship, which is accomplished by the offender making atonement according to the will of the person offended. Accordingly the first requisite on the part of the penitent is the will to atone, and this is done by contrition; the second is that he submit to the judgment of the priest standing in God's place, and this is done in confession; and the third is that he atone according to the decision of God's minister, and this is done in satisfaction: and so contrition, confession, and satisfaction are assigned as parts of Penance.

REPLY OBJ. 1: Contrition, as to its essence, is in the heart, and belongs to interior penance; yet, virtually, it belongs to exterior penance, inasmuch as it implies the purpose of confessing and making satisfaction.

REPLY OBJ. 2: Satisfaction confers grace, in so far as it is in man's purpose, and it increases grace, according as it is accomplished, just as Baptism does in adults, as stated above (Q. 68, A. 2; Q. 69, A. 8).

REPLY OBJ. 3: Satisfaction is a part of Penance as a sacrament, and a fruit of penance as a virtue.

REPLY OBJ. 4: More things are required for good, *which proceeds from a cause that is entire,* than for evil, *which results from each single defect,* as Dionysius states (*Div. Nom.* iv). And thus, although sin is completed in the consent of the heart, yet the perfection of Penance requires contrition of the heart, together with confession in word and satisfaction in deed.

AD CONTRARIUM patet solutio per ea quae dicta sunt.

THE REPLY to the Fifth Objection is clear from what has been said.

Article 3

Whether These Three Are Integral Parts of Penance?

AD TERTIUM SIC PROCEDITUR. Videtur quod praedicta tria non sint partes integrales poenitentiae. Poenitentia enim, ut dictum est, contra peccatum ordinatur. Sed peccatum cordis, oris et operis sunt partes subiectivae peccati, et non partes integrales, quia peccatum de quolibet horum praedicatur. Ergo etiam in poenitentia contritio cordis et confessio oris et satisfactio operis non sunt partes integrales.

PRAETEREA, nulla pars integralis in se continet aliam sibi condivisam. Sed contritio continet in se confessionem et satisfactionem in proposito. Ergo non sunt partes integrales.

PRAETEREA, ex partibus integralibus simul et aequaliter constituitur totum, sicut linea ex suis partibus. Sed hoc non contingit hic. Ergo praedicta non sunt partes integrales poenitentiae.

SED CONTRA, illae dicuntur partes integrales ex quibus integratur perfectio totius. Sed ex tribus praedictis integratur perfectio poenitentiae. Ergo sunt partes integrales poenitentiae.

RESPONDEO dicendum quod quidam dixerunt haec tria esse partes subiectivas poenitentiae. Sed hoc non potest esse. Quia partibus subiectivis singulis adest tota virtus totius, et simul, et aequaliter, sicut tota virtus animalis, inquantum est animal, salvatur in qualibet specie animalis, quae simul et aequaliter dividunt animal. Sed hoc non est in proposito. Et ideo alii dixerunt quod sunt partes potentiales. Sed nec hoc iterum esse potest. Quia singulis partibus potentialibus adest totum secundum totam essentiam, sicut tota essentia animae adest cuilibet eius potentiae. Sed hoc non est in proposito. Unde relinquitur quod praedicta tria sint partes integrales poenitentiae, ad quarum rationem exigitur ut totum non adsit singulis partibus neque secundum totam virtutem eius, neque secundum totam essentiam, sed omnibus simul.

AD PRIMUM ergo dicendum quod peccatum, quia rationem mali habet, potest in uno tantum perfici, ut dictum est. Et ideo peccatum quod in solo corde perficitur, est una species peccati. Alia vero species est peccatum quod perficitur in corde et ore. Tertia vero species est peccatum quod perficitur in corde et opere. Et huius peccati partes quasi integrales sunt quod est in corde, et quod est in ore, et quod est in opere. Et ideo

OBJECTION 1: It would seem that these three are not integral parts of Penance. For, as stated above (Q. 84, A. 3), Penance is ordained against sin. But sins of thought, word, and deed are the subjective and not integral parts of sin, because sin is predicated of each one of them. Therefore in Penance also, contrition in thought, confession in word, and satisfaction in deed are not integral parts.

OBJ. 2: Further, no integral part includes within itself another that is condivided with it. But contrition includes both confession and satisfaction in the purpose of amendment. Therefore they are not integral parts.

OBJ. 3: Further, a whole is composed of its integral parts, taken at the same time and equally, just as a line is made up of its parts. But such is not the case here. Therefore these are not integral parts of Penance.

ON THE CONTRARY, Integral parts are those by which the perfection of the whole is integrated. But the perfection of Penance is integrated by these three. Therefore they are integral parts of Penance.

I ANSWER THAT, Some have said that these three are subjective parts of Penance. But this is impossible, because the entire power of the whole is present in each subjective part at the same time and equally, just as the entire power of an animal, as such, is assured to each animal species, all of which species divide the animal genus at the same time and equally: which does not apply to the point in question. Wherefore others have said that these are potential parts: yet neither can this be true, since the whole is present, as to the entire essence, in each potential part, just as the entire essence of the soul is present in each of its powers: which does not apply to the case in point. Therefore it follows that these three are integral parts of Penance, the nature of which is that the whole is not present in each of the parts, either as to its entire power, or as to its entire essence, but that it is present to all of them together at the same time.

REPLY OBJ. 1: Sin forasmuch as it is an evil, can be completed in one single point, as stated above (A. 2, ad 4); and so the sin which is completed in thought alone, is a special kind of sin. Another species is the sin that is completed in thought and word: and yet a third species is the sin that is completed in thought, word, and deed; and the quasi-integral parts of this last sin, are that which is in thought, that which is in word, and that which is in deed. Wherefore

poenitentiae, quae in his tribus perficitur, haec tria sunt partes integrales.

AD SECUNDUM dicendum quod una pars integralis potest continere totum, licet non secundum essentiam, fundamentum enim quodammodo virtute continet totum aedificium. Et hoc modo contritio continet virtute totam poenitentiam.

AD TERTIUM dicendum quod omnes partes integrales habent ordinem quendam ad invicem. Sed quaedam habent ordinem tantum in situ, sive consequenter se habeant, sicut partes exercitus; sive se tangant, sicut partes acervi; sive etiam colligentur, sicut partes domus; sive etiam continuentur, sicut partes lineae. Quaedam vero habent insuper ordinem virtutis, sicut partes animalis, quarum prima virtute est cor, et aliae quodam ordine virtutis dependent ab invicem. Tertio modo ordinantur ordine temporis, sicut partes temporis et motus. Partes igitur poenitentiae habent ad invicem ordinem virtutis et temporis, quia sunt actus; non autem ordinem situs, quia non habent positionem.

these three are the integral parts of Penance, which is completed in them.

REPLY OBJ. 2: One integral part can include the whole, though not as to its essence: because the foundation, in a way, contains virtually the whole building. In this way contrition includes virtually the whole of Penance.

REPLY OBJ. 3: All integral parts have a certain relation of order to one another: but some are only related as to position, whether in sequence as the parts of an army, or by contact, as the parts of a heap, or by being fitted together, as the parts of a house, or by continuation, as the parts of a line; while some are related, in addition, as to power, as the parts of an animal, the first of which is the heart, the others in a certain order being dependent on one another: and third, some are related in the order of time: as the parts of time and movement. Accordingly the parts of Penance are related to one another in the order of power and time, since they are actions, but not in the order of position, since they do not occupy a place.

Article 4

Whether Penance Is Fittingly Divided into Penance Before Baptism, Penance for Mortal Sins, and Penance for Venial Sins?

AD QUARTUM SIC PROCEDITUR. Videtur quod inconvenienter dividatur poenitentia in poenitentiam ante Baptismum, et poenitentiam mortalium, et poenitentiam venialium. Poenitentia enim est secunda tabula post naufragium, ut supra dictum est, Baptismus autem prima. Illud ergo quod est ante Baptismum, non debet poni species poenitentiae.

PRAETEREA, quod potest destruere maius, potest etiam destruere minus. Sed mortale est maius peccatum quam veniale. Illa vero poenitentia quae est de mortalibus, eadem etiam est de venialibus. Non ergo debent poni diversae species poenitentiae.

PRAETEREA, sicut post Baptismum peccatur venialiter et mortaliter, ita etiam ante Baptismum. Si ergo post Baptismum distinguitur poenitentia venialium et mortalium, pari ratione debet distingui ante Baptismum. Non ergo convenienter distinguitur poenitentia per has species.

SED CONTRA est quod Augustinus, in libro de poenitentia, ponit praedictas tres species poenitentiae.

RESPONDEO dicendum quod haec divisio est poenitentiae secundum quod est virtus. Est autem considerandum quod quaelibet virtus operatur secundum congruentiam temporis, sicut et secundum alias debitas circumstantias. Unde et virtus poenitentiae actum suum habet in hoc tempore secundum quod convenit novae

OBJECTION 1: It would seem that penance is unfittingly divided into penance before Baptism, penance for mortal, and penance for venial sins. For Penance is the second plank after shipwreck, as stated above (Q. 84, A. 6), while Baptism is the first. Therefore that which precedes Baptism should not be called a species of penance.

OBJ. 2: Further, that which can destroy the greater, can destroy the lesser. Now mortal sin is greater than venial; and penance which regards mortal sins regards also venial sins. Therefore they should not be considered as different species of penance.

OBJ. 3: Further, just as after Baptism man commits venial and mortal sins, so does he before Baptism. If therefore penance for venial sins is distinct from penance for mortal sins after Baptism, in like manner they should be distinguished before Baptism. Therefore penance is not fittingly divided into these species.

ON THE CONTRARY, Augustine says in *De Poenitentia* that these three are species of Penance.

I ANSWER THAT, This is a division of penance as a virtue. Now it must be observed that every virtue acts in accordance with the time being, as also in keeping with other due circumstances, wherefore the virtue of penance has its act at this time, according to the requirements of the New Law. Now it belongs to penance to detest one's past sins,

legi pertinet autem ad poenitentiam ut detestetur peccata praeterita, cum proposito immutandi vitam in melius, quod est quasi poenitentiae finis.

Et quia moralia recipiunt speciem secundum finem, ut in secunda parte habitum est; consequens est quod diversae species poenitentiae accipiantur secundum diversas immutationes quas poenitens intendit.

Est autem triplex immutatio a poenitente intenta. Prima quidem per regenerationem in novam vitam. Et haec pertinet ad poenitentiam quae est ante Baptismum. Secunda autem immutatio est per reformationem vitae praeteritae iam corruptae. Et haec pertinet ad poenitentiam mortalium post Baptismum. Tertia autem immutatio est in perfectiorem operationem vitae. Et haec pertinet ad poenitentiam venialium, quae remittuntur per aliquem ferventem actum caritatis, ut supra dictum est.

AD PRIMUM ergo dicendum quod poenitentia quae est ante Baptismum, non est sacramentum, sed est actus virtutis disponens ad sacramentum Baptismi.

AD SECUNDUM dicendum quod poenitentia quae delet peccata mortalia delet etiam venialia, sed non convertitur. Et ideo hae duae poenitentiae se habent sicut perfectum et imperfectum.

AD TERTIUM dicendum quod ante Baptismum non sunt peccata venialia sine mortalibus. Et quia veniale sine mortali dimitti non potest, ut supra dictum est; ideo ante Baptismum non distinguitur poenitentia mortalium et venialium.

and to purpose, at the same time, to change one's life for the better, which is the end, so to speak, of penance.

And since moral matters take their species from the end, as stated in the Second Part (I-II, Q. 1, A. 3; Q. 18, AA. 4, 6), it is reasonable to distinguish various species of penance, according to the various changes intended by the penitent.

Accordingly there is a threefold change intended by the penitent. The first is by regeneration unto a new life, and this belongs to that penance which precedes Baptism. The second is by reforming one's past life after it has been already destroyed, and this belongs to penance for mortal sins committed after Baptism. The third is by changing to a more perfect operation of life, and this belongs to penance for venial sins, which are remitted through a fervent act of charity, as stated above (Q. 87, AA. 2, 3).

REPLY OBJ. 1: The penance which precedes Baptism is not a sacrament, but an act of virtue disposing one to that sacrament.

REPLY OBJ. 2: The penance which washes away mortal sins, washes away venial sins also, but the converse does not hold. Wherefore these two species of penance are related to one another as perfect and imperfect.

REPLY OBJ. 3: Before Baptism there are no venial sins without mortal sins. And since a venial sin cannot be remitted without mortal sin, as stated above (Q. 87, A. 4), before Baptism, penance for mortal sins is not distinct from penance for venial sins.